THE
SOURCE BOOK
OF
FRANCHISE
OPPORTUNITIES
1993

Robert E. Bond
Jeffrey M. Bond

BUSINESS ONE IRWIN
Homewood, Illinois 60430

DISCLAIMER

The information provided in the listings that follow has been submitted by the franchisors themselves. Although the authors and Business One Irwin feel confident that the information provided is accurate and reliable, we have not attempted to independently verify or corroborate the data submitted. Therefore, we cannot guarantee the accuracy of the information displayed, nor do we in any way endorse any of the franchisors listed. Any subsequent agreements that might be made as a result of information provided herein shall be the sole responsibility of the reader.

While every effort has been made to insure that the listing of franchisors is both current and complete, some active franchisors may not be included. Others who have been included may have subsequently decided to terminate franchising operations.

The inherent advantage of having an annual publication is that new franchisors can be added and those no longer franchising can be deleted. Accordingly, we would encourage franchisors to keep us apprised of any change in their status or address. Those included in the *1993 Source Book of Franchise Opportunities* will be contacted again in July, 1993 to update the data currently presented. Please address all correspondence to:

> **SOURCE BOOK**
> P.O. Box 12488
> Oakland, California 94604
> FAX: (510) 547-3245

This publication is designed to provide accurate and authoritative information in regard to the subject matter covered. It is sold with the understanding that the publisher is not engaged in rendering legal, accounting, or other professional service. If legal advice or other expert assistance is required, the services of a competent professional person should be sought.

From a Declaration of Principles jointly adopted by a Committee of the American Bar Association and a Committee of Publishers.

Sponsoring Editor: Amy Hollands
Production Manager: Irene H. Sotiroff
Printer: Malloy Lithographing, Inc.

ISBN 1-55623-899-1

Library of Congress Catalog Card No. 88 - 649161 (Annual Paperback)
ISSN 1056 - 8654

Printed in the United States of America
1 2 3 4 5 6 7 8 9 0 ML 0 9 8 7 6 5 4 3

To My Wife Leslie -

For Hanging In There

PREFACE

The seed for the first edition of this book began in 1979 as I was writing business plans for two companies I was trying to develop. Although I had no direct experience in franchising, I felt intuitively that franchising would be the logical business format for each of these pro forma businesses.

In researching the industry to determine how successful franchisors developed their products, services and support systems for their franchisees, I found that the available literature fell into one of two categories:

1. The first group was made up of publications written in a sophomoric manner and intended for the potential franchisee who had only a modest business background. Basically, these were "how-to" books that started with the premise that the reader had no applied business experience and which, accordingly, provided little insight into the intricacies of what is a very complex and demanding industry.

2. The second group was made up of "knock-offs" of the U.S. Department of Commerce publication *Franchise Opportunities Handbook*. Without exaggeration, there were at least four publications that copied word for word the information in this publication. Most clearly left the impression that it was original research on the part of the author(s).

While the Government data was very informational, it was nevertheless incomplete in terms of providing data on a number of key areas of critical importance in the initial evaluation process, as well as being unwieldy in comparing similar franchising opportunities. In addition, it provided data on less than half of the firms in the franchising universe (including only a modest listing of Canadian franchises).

Realizing that there was a market need for a value-added publication that acted as a <u>source book for the sophisticated potential franchisee</u>, I initiated the due diligence phase of this book. Like most "reinvent-the-wheel" efforts, there were numerous false starts and several faulty assumptions about 1) what information was most helpful and 2) what information the franchisors themselves were actually willing to provide. Ultimately, the book assumed its current form, and, while there is less instructional material than originally intended, the end result is a great deal of in-depth information on both domestic and Canadian franchisors. Most importantly, the data is directly comparable, thus allowing the reader to evaluate numerous franchising opportunities in the same industry and to feel comfortable that he has enough data to go to the next logical step. Basically, the book allows the potential franchisee to narrow his options - to focus only on those franchising opportunities that most closely meet his needs, experience and financial position.

For those who have read earlier editions of the book, you will notice several changes in format and content. Of real significance, however, is a change in emphasis from "more (franchisor listings) is better" to "accuracy is of greater importance than sheer volume." In previous editions, I mistakenly felt it was important to list all companies purported to franchise - even though I couldn't get any direct confirmation or acknowledgment that they were still (or ever) franchising. This edition has eliminated some 1,000 companies that I couldn't confirm as active franchisors, as well as various distributors that had listed themselves as franchisors in my annual franchisor survey. My hope is that this reduction in the number of listings will save you much unnecessary time and effort in trying to correspond with firms that won't respond to your inquiry.

The book is admittedly only the first step in the long and tedious process of selecting a franchise that combines operating independence on the part of the franchisee with a successful marketing and management system that has already proven itself in the field. To those who follow the process to its final conclusion, I can only hope that the book has been of value in introducing you to an industry that has an incredibly successful track record, and in helping you to efficiently evaluate the vast number of franchising opportunities that are open to you. If you are rigorous in your analysis and evaluation, realistic about your capabilities and shortcomings, willing to take full advantage of the franchising formula that you have chosen, and have the fortitude to "put in the hours," you will find the franchise that is right for you. I wish you every success in this time-consuming and often frustrating process.

Be advised at the outset, however, that your ultimate **success** is a function of two key variables: *first, the thoroughness with which you evaluate the industry and ultimately select a single franchisor; second, the hard work and dedication you are willing to devote to making the system work as designed.* Because this book is not intended to be inspirational or motivational, we can be of no help in the latter area. We can, however, expedite the evaluation process - insuring that the potential franchisee is exposed to the full universe of options open to him and that he goes about the selection process in a logical and thorough manner.

Some 2,900 franchising opportunities are listed on the following pages. An in-depth franchisor format is available on roughly 1,060 franchisors. This is the result of the detailed 3-page questionnaire noted in Appendix A. The names, addresses and industry segment are available on over 1,800 additional active franchisors. No doubt you will have either heard of or be familiar with a large number of the listings. Pick out the ones that interest you. Request additional information on each of these. Carefully analyze the information that is sent. Develop a thorough knowledge of the business/services that you are considering. Seek the advice of professionals, even if you are experienced in various areas of the evaluation process. **DO YOUR HOMEWORK!**

REMEMBER, the hours that you spend in the short-term can save you the embarrassment and potential financial loss that accompany a poor decision that was not well thought out.

TABLE OF CONTENTS

RENT OUR CUSTOM FRANCHISOR MAILING LIST

♦

- **GUARANTEED ACCURACY** - $1.00 REFUND FOR ANY RETURNED MAILING

- **CONTINUOUSLY UPDATED** FOR ADDRESS CHANGES/NEW ADDITIONS

- SORTED BY ZIP CODE/BUSINESS CATEGORY/MARKET AREAS

- **QUICK TURN-AROUND TIME**

- ALSO, **CUSTOM SORTING** AND CUSTOM LABELS

- APPROXIMATELY **2,800 LISTINGS:**   ~2,450 U. S., ~ 350 CANADIAN

♦

3 OPTIONS:

1) **Standard Pressure-Sensitive Labels**:

> Mr. Warren Berest, Fran. Dev. Mgr.
> AAMCO TRANSMISSIONS
> One Presidential Blvd.
> Bala Cynwyd, PA 19004

Cost: $275.00

2) **Data Disk** (PC) for Personalized Correspondence, Custom Sorting, Multiple Mailings:

Mr. Warren Berest, Fran. Dev. Mgr.		
AAMCO TRANSMISSIONS		
One Presidential Blvd.	Industry Category:	1
Bala Cynwyd, PA 19004	Franchised Units:	650
TEL: (800) 523-0402 (215) 668-2900	Total Units:	650
FAX: (215) 664-4570	Associations:	IFA

Cost: $500.00   ($75.00 For Subsequent Quarterly Updates)

3) **Standard Pressure-Sensitive Labels with Print-Out** of Additional Data in 2) Above:

Cost: $375.00

♦

Contact: **Source Book Publications**
P. O. Box 12488
Oakland, CA 94604
(510) 839-5471
FAX (510) 547-3245

CHAPTER 1

30 MINUTE OVERVIEW

The reason for writing this book is to provide the maximum amount of in-depth data on the maximum number of companies currently franchising. In short, the intent was to be a *source book* for the sophisticated businessperson seriously interested in franchising. Three basic assumptions have been made. The first is that the reader is interested in the data provided, not in what I might say about how he should go about his selection process. The second is that the reader has a basic understanding of business and franchising. Little space, therefore, will be devoted to detailing the advantages, disadvantages, pitfalls, etc. associated with franchising. As with any investment, it goes without saying that the reader must vigorously evaluate and investigate the various companies under consideration, their promises vs. their historical performance, the industry, the proposed territory and the franchise agreement. The last assumption presupposes that the potential franchisee knows himself - his strengths and weaknesses, whether he has the drive to make the system work and whether he is willing, over the long term, to work within the system, without trying to modify or improve on it.

To the extent that the reader requires background information on the franchising industry, he should pursue some of the books noted in Chapter 3 - Bibliography. While a strong working knowledge of the industry is critical in the evaluation process, good business sense, access to trusted professional guidance and dedication to hard work are equally essential.

Having dispensed with these critical assumptions in a very cavalier manner, let me provide a brief overview of the industry and how to initiate the selection process.

FRANCHISING DEFINED

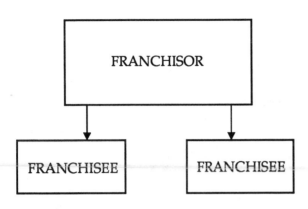

CLASSIC BUSINESS FORMAT MODEL

In its most basic form, shown above, franchising is a marketing technique, or method of doing business, whereby a parent company (the franchisor) grants (via a franchise agreement) an individual outlet owner (the franchisee) the right to market its products and services while using the parent's proven name, reputation and marketing techniques. This is known as business format franchising. Following a lengthy and mutually rigorous selection process, the franchisor assists the new franchisee in selecting a site, negotiating a lease (if necessary), hiring and training staff, outfitting the site, establishing supply lines and generally setting the franchisee up in business. In return for this, the franchisee pays the franchisor a front-end franchise fee, generally in the neighborhood of $15,000 - $35,000. In addition to this initial hand-holding, business format franchising is characterized by an on-going relationship that includes not only the product, service and trademark, but also the entire business format itself - a marketing strategy and plan, operating manuals and standards, quality control and continuing two-way communications. In return, the franchisee is obligated to pay an on-going royalty fee to the franchisor. Although the formula varies considerably among industries and franchisors, the standard royalty fee is usually 4 - 8 % of gross sales. In order to effectively mount a national or regional advertising campaign, the franchisor generally requires the franchisee to pay for his pro rata share of the costs incurred. This takes the form an advertising fee.

The end result is a pre-packaged, or "paint by the numbers," business that allows 1) the franchisor to expand his distribution more rapidly than he could on his own and 2) the franchisee to substantially reduce his risk and exposure by riding on the coat-tails of the franchisor's success. To work, the relationship must be continuing and symbiotic - both parties must be better off together than apart. Generally speaking, what is good for one is good for the other.

FRANCHISING IN THE ECONOMY

The size and importance of the franchising industry should be put into perspective. For an industry that didn't exist thirty years ago, franchising has certainly come of age. It has grown at a rate substantially higher than the GNP and this trend is expected to continue into the foreseeable future. When one includes automotive and truck dealers, soft drink bottlers and gasoline service stations in the statistics, franchising accounted for over $750 billion of retail sales in 1991, or approximately one third of all retail sales. Backing out automotive and truck dealers, soft drink bottlers and gasoline service stations, which are not considered as true business format franchisors for the purposes of this book, franchise sales of goods and services totaled roughly $250 billion in 1991. Put into context, this means that for every $100 the average consumer spends at the retail level, over $10 is spent in franchised establishments. Employment in franchising, both at the part-time and full-time level, totals 7 million.

Exhibits 1-6 on the following pages break these gross numbers for the years 1989, 1990 and 1991 down into meaningful industry groupings by type of service/product provided. The reader should spend a few minutes trying to digest this general data, then go to the chapter that relates to his specific level(s) of interest for a detailed analysis of the trends and relationships within that area of the franchising industry. An analysis of these exhibits may be helpful in determining which areas of the franchising industry can be expected to grow the most rapidly and where there may already some overcapacity. To the extent that you wish to approach the selection process from a market need standpoint, you should purchase a copy of *Franchising In The Economy 1991*, published by the International Franchise Association and Horwath

Exhibit 1

BUSINESS FORMAT FRANCHISING IN THE USA
1991

NUMBER OF ESTABLISHMENTS

	Company-Owned	Franchisee-Owned	Total
Restaurants – All Types	30,533	72,780	103,313
Hotels, Motels & Campgrounds	1,307	10,091	11,398
Recreation, Entertainment & Travel	705	10,849	11,554
Automotive Products & Services	5,618	36,604	42,222
Business Aids & Services	8,205	61,330	69,535
Accounting, Credit, Collection Agencies & General Business Systems	31	1,904	1,935
Employment Services	3,227	5,038	8,265
Printing & Copying Services	231	7,191	7,422
Tax Preparation	3,456	5,000	8,456
Real Estate	130	18,039	18,169
Miscellaneous Business Systems	1,130	24,158	25,288
Construction, Home Improvements, Maintenance & Cleaning Services	680	29,899	30,579
Educational Products & Services	1,106	12,744	13,850
Laundry & Dry Cleaning Services	154	3,338	3,492
Rental Services (Auto–Truck)	804	2,094	2,898
Rental Services (Equipment)	2,570	8,543	11,113
Retail (Non–Food)	14,621	42,414	57,035
Retail Food (Non–Convenience)	3,546	21,832	25,378
Convenience Stores	10,325	6,940	17,265
Miscellaneous	631	7,954	8,585
TOTAL ESTABLISHMENTS	89,010	388,742	477,752

SALES ($000)

	Company-Owned	Franchisee-Owned	Total
Restaurants – All Types	30,498,783	54,998,628	85,497,411
Hotels, Motels & Campgrounds	7,073,476	18,912,699	25,986,175
Recreation, Entertainment & Travel	1,105,216	3,704,017	4,809,233
Automotive Products & Services	5,145,326	10,315,339	15,460,665
Business Aids & Services	4,913,762	15,862,805	20,776,567
Accounting, Credit, Collection Agencies & General Business Systems	9,667	211,394	221,061
Employment Services	3,166,047	3,240,350	6,406,397
Printing & Copying Services	59,293	1,910,530	1,969,823
Tax Preparation	386,542	325,190	711,732
Real Estate	820,296	6,859,969	7,680,265
Miscellaneous Business Systems	471,917	3,315,372	3,787,289
Construction, Home Improvements, Maintenance & Cleaning Services	1,742,907	5,349,763	7,092,670
Educational Products & Services	677,272	1,577,733	2,255,005
Laundry & Dry Cleaning Services	45,720	406,320	452,040
Rental Services (Auto–Truck)	257,095	514,093	771,188
Rental Services (Equipment)	4,354,066	3,683,319	8,037,385
Retail (Non–Food)	10,505,085	20,879,902	31,384,987
Retail Food (Non–Convenience)	1,646,039	10,529,297	12,175,336
Convenience Stores	9,607,303	5,385,425	14,992,728
Miscellaneous	528,394	2,023,582	2,551,976
TOTAL SALES	83,014,206	170,005,727	253,019,933

Source: Franchising In The Economy 1991, IFA Educational Foundation & Horwath International.

Exhibit 2

BUSINESS FORMAT FRANCHISING IN THE USA
1991

RATIO OF TOTAL ESTABLISHMENTS

	Company-Owned	Franchisee-Owned	Total
Restaurants – All Types	29.6%	70.4%	100.0%
Hotels, Motels & Campgrounds	11.5%	88.5%	100.0%
Recreation, Entertainment & Travel	6.1%	93.9%	100.0%
Automotive Products & Services	13.3%	86.7%	100.0%
Business Aids & Services	11.8%	88.2%	100.0%
Accounting, Credit, Collection Agencies & General Business Systems	1.6%	98.4%	100.0%
Employment Services	39.0%	61.0%	100.0%
Printing & Copying Services	3.1%	96.9%	100.0%
Tax Preparation	40.9%	59.1%	100.0%
Real Estate	0.7%	99.3%	100.0%
Miscellaneous Business Systems	4.5%	95.5%	100.0%
Construction, Home Improvements, Maintenance & Cleaning Services	2.2%	97.8%	100.0%
Educational Products & Services	8.0%	92.0%	100.0%
Laundry & Dry Cleaning Services	4.4%	95.6%	100.0%
Rental Services (Auto–Truck)	27.7%	72.3%	100.0%
Rental Services (Equipment)	23.1%	76.9%	100.0%
Retail (Non–Food)	25.6%	74.4%	100.0%
Retail Food (Non–Convenience)	14.0%	86.0%	100.0%
Convenience Stores	59.8%	40.2%	100.0%
Miscellaneous	7.4%	92.6%	100.0%

AVERAGE SALES PER UNIT ($000)

	Company-Owned	Franchisee-Owned	Industry Average
Restaurants – All Types	$999	$756	$828
Hotels, Motels & Campgrounds	$5,412	$1,874	$2,280
Recreation, Entertainment & Travel	$1,568	$341	$416
Automotive Products & Services	$916	$282	$366
Business Aids & Services	$599	$259	$299
Accounting, Credit, Collection Agencies & General Business Systems	$312	$111	$114
Employment Services	$981	$643	$775
Printing & Copying Services	$257	$266	$265
Tax Preparation	$112	$65	$84
Real Estate	$6,310	$380	$423
Miscellaneous Business Systems	$418	$137	$150
Construction, Home Improvements, Maintenance & Cleaning Services	$2,563	$179	$232
Educational Products & Services	$612	$124	$163
Laundry & Dry Cleaning Services	$297	$122	$129
Rental Services (Auto–Truck)	$320	$246	$266
Rental Services (Equipment)	$1,694	$431	$723
Retail (Non–Food)	$718	$492	$550
Retail Food (Non–Convenience)	$464	$482	$480
Convenience Stores	$930	$776	$868
Miscellaneous	$837	$254	$297
INDUSTRY AVERAGE	$933	$437	$530

Source: Franchising In The Economy 1991, IFA Educational Foundation & Horwath International.

Exhibit 3

BUSINESS FORMAT FRANCHISING IN THE USA
1990

NUMBER OF ESTABLISHMENTS

	Company-Owned	Franchisee-Owned	Total
Restaurants – All Types	29,152	70,188	99,340
Hotels, Motels & Campgrounds	1,261	9,785	11,046
Recreation, Entertainment & Travel	587	10,300	10,887
Automotive Products & Services	5,128	34,121	39,249
Business Aids & Services	7,541	56,866	64,407
Accounting, Credit, Collection Agencies & General Business Systems	28	1,730	1,758
Employment Services	2,939	4,569	7,508
Printing & Copying Services	204	6,641	6,845
Tax Preparation	3,425	4,870	8,295
Real Estate	118	16,322	16,440
Miscellaneous Business Systems	827	22,734	23,561
Construction, Home Improvements, Maintenance & Cleaning Services	615	26,800	27,415
Educational Products & Services	1,081	11,458	12,539
Laundry & Dry Cleaning Services	142	3,054	3,196
Rental Services (Auto–Truck)	784	1,962	2,746
Rental Services (Equipment)	2,485	8,255	10,740
Retail (Non–Food)	14,151	40,277	54,428
Retail Food (Non–Convenience)	3,389	21,122	24,511
Convenience Stores	10,295	6,913	17,208
Miscellaneous	606	7,800	8,406
TOTAL ESTABLISHMENTS	**84,758**	**365,767**	**450,525**

SALES ($000)

	Company-Owned	Franchisee-Owned	Total
Restaurants – All Types	27,901,355	49,954,288	77,855,643
Hotels, Motels & Campgrounds	6,459,292	18,356,349	24,815,641
Recreation, Entertainment & Travel	978,791	3,253,133	4,231,924
Automotive Products & Services	4,685,210	9,181,184	13,866,394
Business Aids & Services	4,408,570	14,231,924	18,640,494
Accounting, Credit, Collection Agencies & General Business Systems	8,519	187,208	195,727
Employment Services	2,825,088	2,906,728	5,731,816
Printing & Copying Services	50,937	1,708,039	1,758,976
Tax Preparation	368,696	304,846	673,542
Real Estate	726,416	6,060,247	6,786,663
Miscellaneous Business Systems	428,914	3,064,856	3,493,770
Construction, Home Improvements, Maintenance & Cleaning Services	1,609,740	4,844,625	6,454,365
Educational Products & Services	620,020	1,411,379	2,031,399
Laundry & Dry Cleaning Services	41,000	360,077	401,077
Rental Services (Auto–Truck)	243,001	488,682	731,683
Rental Services (Equipment)	4,115,169	3,422,743	7,537,912
Retail (Non–Food)	9,831,140	19,433,781	29,264,921
Retail Food (Non–Convenience)	1,504,322	10,201,502	11,705,824
Convenience Stores	9,179,116	5,142,135	14,321,251
Miscellaneous	484,761	1,815,697	2,300,458
TOTAL SALES	**76,470,057**	**156,329,423**	**232,799,480**

Source: Franchising In The Economy 1991, IFA Educational Foundation & Horwath International.

Exhibit 4

BUSINESS FORMAT FRANCHISING IN THE USA
1990

RATIO OF TOTAL ESTABLISHMENTS

	Company-Owned	Franchisee-Owned	Total
Restaurants – All Types	29.3%	70.7%	100.0%
Hotels, Motels & Campgrounds	11.4%	88.6%	100.0%
Recreation, Entertainment & Travel	5.4%	94.6%	100.0%
Automotive Products & Services	13.1%	86.9%	100.0%
Business Aids & Services	11.7%	88.3%	100.0%
Accounting, Credit, Collection			
Agencies & General Business Systems	1.6%	98.4%	100.0%
Employment Services	39.1%	60.9%	100.0%
Printing & Copying Services	3.0%	97.0%	100.0%
Tax Preparation	41.3%	58.7%	100.0%
Real Estate	0.7%	99.3%	100.0%
Miscellaneous Business Systems	3.5%	96.5%	100.0%
Construction, Home Improvements,			
Maintenance & Cleaning Services	2.2%	97.8%	100.0%
Educational Products & Services	8.6%	91.4%	100.0%
Laundry & Dry Cleaning Services	4.4%	95.6%	100.0%
Rental Services (Auto–Truck)	28.6%	71.4%	100.0%
Rental Services (Equipment)	23.1%	76.9%	100.0%
Retail (Non–Food)	26.0%	74.0%	100.0%
Retail Food (Non–Convenience)	13.8%	86.2%	100.0%
Convenience Stores	59.8%	40.2%	100.0%
Miscellaneous	7.2%	92.8%	100.0%

AVERAGE SALES PER UNIT ($000):

	Company-Owned	Franchisee-Owned	Industry Average
Restaurants – All Types	$957	$712	$784
Hotels, Motels & Campgrounds	$5,122	$1,876	$2,247
Recreation, Entertainment & Travel	$1,667	$316	$389
Automotive Products & Services	$914	$269	$353
Business Aids & Services	$585	$250	$289
Accounting, Credit, Collection			
Agencies & General Business Systems	$304	$108	$111
Employment Services	$961	$636	$763
Printing & Copying Services	$250	$257	$257
Tax Preparation	$108	$63	$81
Real Estate	$6,156	$371	$413
Miscellaneous Business Systems	$519	$135	$148
Construction, Home Improvements,			
Maintenance & Cleaning Services	$2,617	$181	$235
Educational Products & Services	$574	$123	$162
Laundry & Dry Cleaning Services	$289	$118	$125
Rental Services (Auto–Truck)	$310	$249	$266
Rental Services (Equipment)	$1,656	$415	$702
Retail (Non–Food)	$695	$483	$538
Retail Food (Non–Convenience)	$444	$483	$478
Convenience Stores	$892	$744	$832
Miscellaneous	$800	$233	$274
INDUSTRY AVERAGE	$902	$427	$517

Source: Franchising In The Economy 1991, IFA Educational Foundation & Horwath International.

Exhibit 5

BUSINESS FORMAT FRANCHISING IN THE USA
1989

NUMBER OF ESTABLISHMENTS

	Company-Owned	Franchisee-Owned	Total
Restaurants – All Types	27,596	64,359	91,955
Hotels, Motels & Campgrounds	1,232	8,880	10,112
Recreation, Entertainment & Travel	480	9,322	9,802
Automotive Products & Services	4,741	31,483	36,224
Business Aids & Services	7,075	51,115	58,190
Accounting, Credit, Collection Agencies & General Business Systems	27	1,706	1,733
Employment Services	2,654	3,969	6,623
Printing & Copying Services	195	6,133	6,328
Tax Preparation	3,359	4,850	8,209
Real Estate	118	15,688	15,806
Miscellaneous Business Systems	722	18,805	19,527
Construction, Home Improvements, Maintenance & Cleaning Services	620	23,468	24,088
Educational Products & Services	841	10,236	11,077
Laundry & Dry Cleaning Services	131	2,862	2,993
Rental Services (Auto–Truck)	731	1,885	2,616
Rental Services (Equipment)	2,451	7,432	9,883
Retail (Non–Food)	13,497	36,582	50,079
Retail Food (Non–Convenience)	3,210	17,854	21,064
Convenience Stores	10,864	6,703	17,567
Miscellaneous	569	6,998	7,567
TOTAL ESTABLISHMENTS	81,113	330,330	411,443

SALES ($000)

	Company-Owned	Franchisee-Owned	Total
Restaurants – All Types	25,490,936	44,622,772	70,113,708
Hotels, Motels & Campgrounds	6,233,245	15,337,833	21,571,078
Recreation, Entertainment & Travel	818,929	2,708,687	3,527,616
Automotive Products & Services	4,285,689	8,225,488	12,511,177
Business Aids & Services	4,007,304	12,936,539	16,943,843
Accounting, Credit, Collection Agencies & General Business Systems	8,014	178,368	186,382
Employment Services	2,515,652	2,465,837	4,981,489
Printing & Copying Services	47,782	1,544,940	1,592,722
Tax Preparation	349,619	294,247	643,866
Real Estate	680,295	5,504,207	6,184,502
Miscellaneous Business Systems	405,941	2,948,940	3,354,881
Construction, Home Improvements, Maintenance & Cleaning Services	1,487,066	4,272,756	5,759,822
Educational Products & Services	540,803	1,113,527	1,654,330
Laundry & Dry Cleaning Services	36,327	323,045	359,372
Rental Services (Auto–Truck)	229,901	457,139	687,040
Rental Services (Equipment)	3,860,136	3,042,014	6,902,150
Retail (Non–Food)	9,061,059	17,608,429	26,669,488
Retail Food (Non–Convenience)	1,389,493	8,611,630	10,001,123
Convenience Stores	9,363,335	4,932,657	14,295,992
Miscellaneous	424,127	1,532,878	1,957,005
TOTAL SALES	71,235,653	138,661,933	209,897,586

Source: Franchising In The Economy 1991, IFA Educational Foundation & Horwath International.

Exhibit 6

BUSINESS FORMAT FRANCHISING IN THE USA
1989

RATIO OF TOTAL ESTABLISHMENTS

	Company-Owned	Franchisee-Owned	Total
Restaurants – All Types	30.0%	70.0%	100.0%
Hotels, Motels & Campgrounds	12.2%	87.8%	100.0%
Recreation, Entertainment & Travel	4.9%	95.1%	100.0%
Automotive Products & Services	13.1%	86.9%	100.0%
Business Aids & Services	12.2%	87.8%	100.0%
Accounting, Credit, Collection Agencies & General Business Systems	1.6%	98.4%	100.0%
Employment Services	40.1%	59.9%	100.0%
Printing & Copying Services	3.1%	96.9%	100.0%
Tax Preparation	40.9%	59.1%	100.0%
Real Estate	0.7%	99.3%	100.0%
Miscellaneous Business Systems	3.7%	96.3%	100.0%
Construction, Home Improvements, Maintenance & Cleaning Services	2.6%	97.4%	100.0%
Educational Products & Services	7.6%	92.4%	100.0%
Laundry & Dry Cleaning Services	4.4%	95.6%	100.0%
Rental Services (Auto–Truck)	27.9%	72.1%	100.0%
Rental Services (Equipment)	24.8%	75.2%	100.0%
Retail (Non–Food)	27.0%	73.0%	100.0%
Retail Food (Non–Convenience)	15.2%	84.8%	100.0%
Convenience Stores	61.8%	38.2%	100.0%
Miscellaneous	7.5%	92.5%	100.0%

AVERAGE SALES PER UNIT ($000)

	Company-Owned	Franchisee-Owned	Industry Average
Restaurants – All Types	$924	$693	$762
Hotels, Motels & Campgrounds	$5,059	$1,727	$2,133
Recreation, Entertainment & Travel	$1,706	$291	$360
Automotive Products & Services	$904	$261	$345
Business Aids & Services	$566	$253	$291
Accounting, Credit, Collection Agencies & General Business Systems	$297	$105	$108
Employment Services	$948	$621	$752
Printing & Copying Services	$245	$252	$252
Tax Preparation	$104	$61	$78
Real Estate	$5,765	$351	$391
Miscellaneous Business Systems	$562	$157	$172
Construction, Home Improvements, Maintenance & Cleaning Services	$2,398	$182	$239
Educational Products & Services	$643	$109	$149
Laundry & Dry Cleaning Services	$277	$113	$120
Rental Services (Auto–Truck)	$315	$243	$263
Rental Services (Equipment)	$1,575	$409	$698
Retail (Non–Food)	$671	$481	$533
Retail Food (Non–Convenience)	$433	$482	$475
Convenience Stores	$862	$736	$814
Miscellaneous	$745	$219	$259
INDUSTRY AVERAGE	$878	$420	$510

Source: Franchising In The Economy 1991, IFA Educational Foundation & Horwath International.

Exhibit 7

FRANCHISING IN NORTH AMERICA
ACTIVE FRANCHISORS BY STATE/PROVINCE
(ALPHABETIC RANKING)

UNITED STATES	UNITS	%		UNITS	%
Alabama	14	0.6%	New York	150	6.1%
Alaska	1	0.0%	Ohio	123	5.0%
Arkansas	13	0.5%	Oklahoma	19	0.8%
Arizona	58	2.3%	Oregon	23	0.9%
California	331	13.4%	Pennsylvania	101	4.1%
Colorado	60	2.4%	Rhode Island	19	0.8%
Connecticut	54	2.2%	South Carolina	15	0.6%
Delaware	9	0.4%	South Dakota	6	0.2%
District of Columbia	6	0.2%	Tennessee	64	2.6%
Florida	189	7.6%	Texas	164	6.6%
Georgia	85	3.4%	Utah	17	0.7%
Hawaii	8	0.3%	Vermont	3	0.1%
Idaho	7	0.3%	Virginia	36	1.5%
Illinois	121	4.9%	Washington	31	1.3%
Indiana	30	1.2%	West Virginia	8	0.3%
Iowa	22	0.9%	Wisconsin	32	1.3%
Kansas	21	0.8%	Wyoming	4	0.2%
Kentucky	29	1.2%			
Louisiana	29	1.2%	Sub-Total US	2,473	100.0%
Maine	10	0.4%			
Maryland	50	2.0%	CANADA		
Massachusetts	86	3.5%			
Michigan	88	3.6%	Alberta	24	6.6%
Minnesota	78	3.2%	British Columbia	43	11.8%
Mississippi	10	0.4%	Manitoba	12	3.3%
Missouri	40	1.6%	New Brunswick	3	0.8%
Montana	5	0.2%	Newfoundland	4	1.1%
North Carolina	46	1.9%	Nova Scotia	2	0.5%
North Dakota	7	0.3%	Ontario	248	67.9%
Nebraska	24	1.0%	Quebec	25	6.8%
Nevada	12	0.5%	Saskatchewan	4	1.1%
New Hampshire	7	0.3%			
New Jersey	105	4.2%	Sub-Total Canada	365	100.0%
New Mexico	3	0.1%			
			Grand Total	2,838	

Exhibit 8

FRANCHISING IN NORTH AMERICA
ACTIVE FRANCHISORS BY STATE/PROVINCE
(RANKING BY # OF UNITS)

UNITED STATES	UNITS	%		UNITS	%
California	331	13.4%	Arkansas	13	0.5%
Florida	189	7.6%	Nevada	12	0.5%
Texas	164	6.6%	Maine	10	0.4%
New York	150	6.1%	Mississippi	10	0.4%
Ohio	123	5.0%	Delaware	9	0.4%
Illinois	121	4.9%	West Virginia	8	0.3%
New Jersey	105	4.2%	Hawaii	8	0.3%
Pennsylvania	101	4.1%	Idaho	7	0.3%
Michigan	88	3.6%	New Hampshire	7	0.3%
Massachusetts	86	3.5%	North Dakota	7	0.3%
Georgia	85	3.4%	District of Columbia	6	0.2%
Minnesota	78	3.2%	South Dakota	6	0.2%
Tennessee	64	2.6%	Montana	5	0.2%
Colorado	60	2.4%	Wyoming	4	0.2%
Arizona	58	2.3%	New Mexico	3	0.1%
Connecticut	54	2.2%	Vermont	3	0.1%
Maryland	50	2.0%	Alaska	1	0.0%
North Carolina	46	1.9%			
Missouri	40	1.6%	Sub-Total US	2,473	100.0%
Virginia	36	1.5%			
Wisconsin	32	1.3%	CANADA		
Washington	31	1.3%			
Indiana	30	1.2%	Ontario	248	67.9%
Kentucky	29	1.2%	British Columbia	43	11.8%
Louisiana	29	1.2%	Quebec	25	6.8%
Nebraska	24	1.0%	Alberta	24	6.6%
Oregon	23	0.9%	Manitoba	12	3.3%
Iowa	22	0.9%	Newfoundland	4	1.1%
Kansas	21	0.8%	Saskatchewan	4	1.1%
Oklahoma	19	0.8%	New Brunswick	3	0.8%
Rhode Island	19	0.8%	Nova Scotia	2	0.5%
Utah	17	0.7%			
South Carolina	15	0.6%	Sub-Total Canada	365	100.0%
Alabama	14	0.6%			
			Grand Total	2,838	

International. (See Chapter 3 - Bibliography).

FRANCHISING IN NORTH AMERICA

As a point of interest, I have included Exhibits 7 and 8. These show the composition, by headquarters state and province, of the 2,838 franchisors noted in this book.

SURVIVAL/FAILURE RATE

According to the U.S. Department of Commerce, a staggering 38% of new, independent businesses fail within the first year of operation and 77% fail within the first 5 years. While everyone would agree that the comparable failure figure for franchised businesses is substantially lower than the failure rate for independent businesses, there are no reliable statistics available.

The only meaningful statistics that are available suggest that 4.4% of franchisees leave their franchise systems annually. In this study, FranData, a Washington DC-based company specializing in franchise research, analysis and document retrieval, conducted a comprehensive study of the registered franchise offering circulars from 584 of the nation's leading franchise systems, representing a total of approximately 213,000 franchise operations. Franchise departures, which cover only terminations and non-renewals, were categorized as follows:

1.2% of franchise contracts were canceled, terminated or were not renewed for unspecified reasons.

1.0% left for specified reasons (e.g. abandonment, bankruptcy, health reasons, etc.).

.8% were terminated by mutual agreement between franchisee and franchisor, or voluntarily by the franchisee.

.7% were terminated for failure to pay royalties, for quality control reasons or for failure to meet other contractual obligations.

.7% were reacquired by purchase or by other means.

(Copies of the full FranData Franchise Termination and Relationship Report area available from FranData, 1155 Connecticut Ave., NW, # 275, Washington, DC 20036. (202) 659-8640; FAX (202) 457-0618).

Although these statistics are helpful, the real issue here is not in assessing terminations and non-renewals, but in how one defines failure. I would maintain that failure is the inability of a franchisee to "make a living" as a franchisee. If he sells his business to someone else, and suffers a loss on his investment in the process, I would suggest that the business, as far as that particular franchisee is concerned, has been a failure. The fact that he may have found a "bigger fool" to take over the operation should not be interpreted to mean that the operation should be considered a "success" simply because the operation is still in business. Sales to third parties are not considered as part of the 4.4% departure rate noted above.

Based on the feedback I get each year as a result of my on-going correspondence with the franchising community, my sense is that the annual failure rate is in excess of 5%. Not only is a significant amount of mail returned as undeliverable (suggesting that the franchisor itself is no longer in business), but a surprising number of franchisors report sizable reductions in the number of franchised units from year to year and significant shifts in the distribution of those remaining operating units. If a franchisor had a total of 50 units at the end of 1990 and has 47 by the end of 1992, generally speaking, 3 units have failed. On the other hand, if 25 of the 50 units were company-owned at the end of 1990 and 29 of 47 are company-owned at the end of 1991, my guess is that those 4 units that went from franchisee-owned to company-owned probably failed and that the franchisor bought out the failed franchisee at a bargain price.

The failure rate of franchisees is a critical factor in determining which franchisor to join. Unfortunately, the system currently allows franchisors to mask the fact that a large number of franchisees may have been unsuccessful, for whatever reason, in running a profitable franchise operation. As far as the general public is concerned, by looking only at the historical growth of total operating units, the franchisees and the franchisor are assumed to have been successful. The franchisor is not obligated to provided the potential franchisee with the names of owners who have been out of the system for over 12 months. The ability to talk with previous, unsuccessful owners would clearly be an invaluable resource to potential franchisees. Potential franchisees could determine on their own whether the departed franchisee was unsuccessful because of his own inadequacies or because of some fault on the part of the franchisor. I would strongly recommend that the UFOC be amended to somehow compel franchisors to provide information on the turn-over of units among franchisees and the underlying reasons. Such data could and should be made available through an exit interview with the franchisee leaving the system. While I can understand the reluctance of franchisors to make the information available to the public, it is hard to imagine that a responsible franchisor would not demand that the reasons for the change in ownership be clearly determined.

In general, however, I would agree that the success rate of franchisees is far greater than the success rate of independent business owners. The magnitude of the differential, however, is probably less than the franchising lobby would have us believe.

THE 4 R'S

As in school, where we learned that the 3 R's of reading, 'riting, and 'rithmatic were critical to scholastic success, franchising success is also largely dependent on what I will refer to as the 4 R's. In this case, however, the 4 R's refer to 1) *realism* about your personal strengths and weaknesses, 2) *research* into the industry and the careful selection of a specific franchisor and 3) *resources* to insure that you have the financial wherewithal to survive the initial stages of developing your business. A fourth R that should not be overlooked is *resolve* - the willingness to continue to work within the system as it has been designed *after you have achieved personal success.* Each of these attributes will be discussed very briefly below.

REALISM

Realism is essential for one to maximize his happi-

ness in life in general. It is possible to avoid reality in one's day-to-day life, however, and still survive. This is equally true when you work for someone else. It clearly in not true when you are in business for yourself. In this case, the realities of the marketplace are swift and unforgiving. To the extent that this interpretation is true, you, as a potential franchisee, should be realistic about all variables effecting your choice of and operation of a franchise.

This should start with a clear understanding of your personal strengths and weaknesses. Do you have the ability to deal with financial insecurity? Know at the outset that there will be plenty of this, at least during the initial start-up period. Do you have the strong support of your spouse? Absolutely essential is there is any deviation from your business plan! Can you manage people effectively? Can you smile when you know that the customer is wrong? There are literally hundreds of similar introspective questions that should be addressed truthfully and in a straightforward manner. Some of the books noted in the bibliography are especially helpful in this regard, as are various books that specialize in personal growth and career path choices. I would strongly recommend that anyone wishing to invest his life's savings in a franchise take the time necessary to do a personal audit of his personal strengths and weaknesses - possibly with the help of outside professionals.

Having passed muster in your personal audit, then be equally realistic about the advantages and disadvantages of the products/services offered by the franchisor, the unique demographics of your particular maket area, the trends in the marketplace, pro forma financials, etc. Although these latter points will be determined in large part by exhaustive research, be objective and open-minded in interpreting the results.

RESEARCH

The sole lasting value of this book is to assist the reader in researching the franchising industry and in narrowing down the myriad of choices that are open to him. Some 1,060 franchises are listed in a great deal of detail. Another 1,800 are listed by type of business. This effectively represents the universe that is out there for you to investigate. Given the universe, request information from all those that may potentially be of interest to you. Don't necessarily limit yourself to a particular type of service or product. Explore the options. Even if you think that you already know what the best franchise would be through personal experience, it is still important that you evaluate other firms that provide a similar product and/or service to convince yourself that you have made the optimal choice. Don't find out after the fact that there is a competing franchise with a nearly identical product/service, but which charges a royalty fee of 5% vs. the 7% of gross sales that you are locked into. The incremental cost of fully researching all of the franchisors within a chosen industry is negligible compared to the cost of making a sub-optimal choice. Once you have been able to narrow the field of potential franchisors down to a manageable size, say 5 to 9 companies, be equally aggressive in the manner in which you research each firm. I have found that the most meaningful and persuasive research results from talking with actual franchisees, preferably at their site. For the most part, they tend to be completely open in discussing their level of satisfaction with the franchisor and the industry they have chosen. Before making a final commitment, I would make every effort to talk with as many franchisees as I could. Within reason, I would disregard the minor costs of visiting actual franchisee sites and the amount of time off from my current employment.

RESOURCES

Lack of adequate working capital is the single most common reason for business failure. Make sure that you have adequate financial resources before committing to a business that has an uncertain source of cash inflows but which has required fixed operating costs that must be paid regardless of profitability. Whether these resources are obtained from savings, relatives, bank loans, etc. make sure that they are available when and if you need them. Again, be realistic about the potential need for additional funds. Don't underestimate the period needed before you achieve break-even and find out that you have run out of cash 6 months before revenues cover costs. There will be great temptation to assume, because of your raw talents, drive, dedication, etc. that you can achieve a break-even operating position faster than the period recom-

mended by the franchisor. Don't bet the ranch on it. Literally! If anything, the franchisor will have an incentive to underestimate the break-even period himself. To be safe, assume that you will need an additional 3 - 6 months of working capital on top of the period recommended by the franchisor.

RESOLVE

After you have gotten to the point of a positive cash flow, you now need resolve to insure that you are going to succeed in franchising over the long-term. Recall the compelling reasons why you chose franchising in the first place - to take advantage of someone else's proven formula for success, the desire to beat the odds of business failure, etc. Keep in mind the symbiotic basis upon which franchising is built - franchisor and all franchisees working within the system for the common good. Unfortunately, two problems invariably come up.

The first is the difficulty in writing a monthly royalty check to the franchisor. It is easy to forget the fact that they brought you into the business in the first place, that they taught you everything you now know about the business, that they provide on-going product improvements and refinements, an 800-telephone number to resolve problems as they come up, and the entire panorama of services that good franchisors provide on a continuing basis. Conversely, it is hard not to notice the check that goes out monthly in increasing amounts, and that is expected to increase over the length of the franchise relationship. Although this is a difficult intellectual process, keep in mind that royalty fees are simply another cost of doing business. It is a legal obligation that you incurred when you entered franchising and a cost you knowingly agreed to pay in return for being part of a successful team. Now that you have achieved that objective, don't begrudge the franchisor the chance to share in that success. Keep in mind that, if the franchisor isn't successful and profitable, your franchise will flounder and you will no longer receive the centralized support that you have come to count on.

Similarly, you need resolve in your willingness to live within the system. The franchise is successful in large part because of the establishment of a common format for doing business, consistent quality control, routinized operating procedures, rigorous market research on new products and services, etc. Now is not the time to become an entrepreneur and unilaterally test the market with modifications you feel will streamline the business or increase profits in your particular market. These ideas should instead be submitted as recommendations to the franchisor for evaluation. You will have to trust his wisdom in what he does with the idea from that point on. If you find that you cannot accept the role of a good and loyal soldier in the field over the long term, you will probably not make a good franchisee.

THE CHOICE IS YOURS

Choosing the optimal franchise for your personal needs requires many times the hard work and energy that goes into buying a home. The prudent man would not buy into a new area without first considering all the important variables (schools, taxes, condition of the house, zoning, etc.) before making his offer. Unlike homebuying, however, where the penalty for poor research is a maximum 10-20% loss in original investment, a flawed choice of franchisors can result in a 100% loss of your savings, the equity in your house, your marriage (to the extent that your spouse was not equally committed to franchising and the inherent risks involved), and, possibly most importantly, your self-esteem. The risks are high. There are no guarantees. To think that you can automatically pay a franchise fee and step into a guaranteed money machine is naive at best and calamitous to your financial well-being at worst. There is no sub-

stitute for the attributes noted above. The burden is on you to do your homework and to insure that the choice is researched to the fullest extent possible. Only then can you maximize the chances of success and minimize the chances of failure or unfulfilled expectations.

My strong recommendation is that you plan on taking 8 - 12 months before deciding on a specific franchising company. Establish an orderly and well-thought out business plan for going through the evaluation process (including a realistic self-appraisal and lining up the necessary financial resources). Although there will be a great deal of pressure on you to speed up the process, especially if you are working with an aggressive marketing or brokerage firm, don't be browbeaten into making a premature decision. Try to stick with your business plan. You will most likely spend the majority of your business life working with the company you ultimately choose. Another few months spent in insuring you have made the right choice is a small price to pay.

Enough narrative! You are now on your own to select those franchises that best meet your needs and experience. Without being tedious, I can only repeat the recommendation of every writer on franchising. That recommendation - **Investigate! Investigate! Investigate!**

CHAPTER 2

HOW TO USE THE DATA

The 38 questions noted on the 3-page questionnaire in Appendix A have been condensed into the format shown on the following pages. Each piece of data provided is felt to be of value in helping the reader in his decision-making process. In addition to consolidating a great deal of data into a small space, the consistent layout of the data results in direct comparability and efficient evaluation of alternative franchising opportunities. Rather than bypass this section, you should take 30 minutes to familiarize yourself with the format and what the data provided really means. Where relevant, I have attempted to add any observations I felt would be helpful in interpreting the franchisor's response.

Again, I would like to emphasize that neither Business One Irwin nor the author assumes any responsibility for the accuracy of the information provided. All of the data displayed has been submitted by the franchisors themselves (including numerous follow-up phone calls). No effort has been made to independently corroborate or verify their accuracy or completeness. You should feel comfortable, however, in knowing that any intentionally misleading information submitted by the franchisor would be self-defeating from the franchisor's standpoint. Any half-truths or "puffery" would undoubtedly be uncovered by the potential franchisee upon any subsequent rigorous examination of the franchisor. To the extent that the deception were of a serious nature, it would most likely terminate the relationship, meaning an unnecessary loss of time and effort on everyone's part. Given this, there is no incentive for the franchisor to play games or to intentionally mislead the reader.

WORLD CLASS ATHLETE, a San Francisco Bay Area franchising company that has enjoyed considerable success over the past 16 years, has been

WORLD CLASS ATHLETE

1814 Franklin St., # 820
Oakland, CA 94612
TEL: (800) SURF-RAT (510) 839-5471 C
FAX: (510) 547-3245
Mr. Jeff McKee, President

WORLD CLASS ATHLETE offers a unique, specialty sporting goods concept. Product mix concentrates on athletic footwear, running, tennis and swimwear. Emphasis on race sponsorship, training programs and custom fitting. All major lines of footwear, accessories, warm-up suits and bags. Custom re-soling at Company-owned distribution centers.

HISTORY: . . . . IFA, CFA	**FINANCIAL:** Earnings Claim: . Yes	**FRANCHISOR TRAINING/SUPPORT:**
Established in 1976; . . 1st Franchised in 1977	Cash Investment: $75K	Financial Assistance Provided: . . .Yes(D)
Company-Owned Units (As of 8/31/1992): . 15	Total Investment: $120-225K	Site Selection Assistance: . . . . . . .Yes
Franchised Units (As of 8/31/1992): **66**	Fees: Franchise - $18K	Lease Negotiation Assistance: . . . . .Yes
Total Units (As of 8/31/1992): 81	Royalty: 6%, Advert: 2%	Co-operative Advertising: . . . . .Yes
Projected New Units for 1993: 12	Contract Periods (Yrs.): 15/15	Training: . . . . 3 Wks. Headquarters,
Distribution: US-74;Can-7;Overseas-0	Area Development Agreement: Yes/15	. . . . 2 Wks. On-Site, On-Going
North America: . . . . 15 States, 2 Provinces	Sub-Franchise Contract: . . . . . Yes	On-Going Support: a,B,C,D,E,f,G,H,I/ . 24
Concentration: . . 25 in CA, 8 in WA, 5 in KY	Expand in Territory: . . . . .No	**EXPANSION PLANS:**
Registered: . . . CA,FL,HI,IL,MN,MI,NY,OR	Passive Ownership: . . . Not Allowed	US: . . . . .All US
. . . . WA,WI,AB	Encourage Conversions: . . . . . Yes	Canada: . . . . .All Canada
Type Space: FS, SF, SC, RM;~1,800-2,200 SF	Average # Employees: . . 2 FT, 4 PT	Overseas: . . . .EUR, UK, AU, NZ

chosen as a sample company for illustrative purposes. Please refer to the sample format when reading the description that follows.

GENERAL INFORMATION

1. The name and address are self-explanatory.

2. **(800) SURF-RAT (510) 839-5417 C.**

A "C" following the telephone number listed means that the company will accept a collect call, usually from in-state callers. Initial calls should be made using the (800) number. Where in-state (800) numbers are available, the abbreviation for the state is noted in parentheses.

> **Observation:** Keep in mind that maintaining an (800) telephone number is a significant additional expense. It is, nevertheless, an indication of management priorities - in this case the need to attract potential franchisees as efficiently as possible, as well as to respond to problems encountered by existing franchisees. My sense is that it is a very positive indication. Those companies that require the caller to foot the bill are unnecessarily restricting the number of potential franchisees.

3. Whether calling or writing, all initial correspondence should be directed to the individual noted.

> **Observation:** Although it is unfair in many cases, one could draw some general conclusions from the

position of the company contact. Where the contact is identified as the Vice President or Director of Franchising (or the equivalent), the Company is obviously large enough and successful enough to delegate marketing and franchisee selection responsibilities to a second-tier manager. Where all incoming correspondence is directed to the attention of the Chairman or President, however, it may be that there is only a very modest staff. One would think that there would be an upper limit on the number of franchised units and the ability of the President/CEO to effectively respond directly with potential franchisees. To the extent that he is answering the phone on a routine basis, he is not attending to other, possibly more pressing, business.

DESCRIPTION OF BUSINESS

4. Franchisors were given complete latitude and discretion in describing their business. The only constraint was that they had to limit their comments to 6 lines of text. To the extent that they over-indulged or gave a boiler-plate description from another write-up of the business, some editing may have been required.

> **Observation:** In a surprising number of cases, the franchisors merely noted that they were in the "fast food - chicken" business (or some equally unimaginative description). While it may be premature to judge a company on the basis of the answer provided by a single employee, a disinterested response may be indicative of the enthusiasm, involvement and attention to detail on the part of the

company's management. I personally find it hard to believe that a respondent would not take the minimal time required to distinguish his company from the competition. Basically, the description of the company provides free exposure to the 25,000 - 40,000 potential franchisees who will ultimately purchase and/or read this book. And yet, these same companies may be willing to spend thousands of dollars and hours of time to develop a short ad in the *Wall Street Journal* that may be read by only 1,000 potential franchisees.

HISTORY

5. IFA , CFA. This means that the franchisor is an active member in either the International Franchise Association (IFA) or the Canadian Franchise Association (CFA).

The **International Franchise Association (IFA)** is a non-profit trade association representing more than 520 franchising companies in the U.S. and around the world. It is recognized as the leading spokesperson for responsible franchising. The IFA has historically supported the principle of full disclosure of all pertinent information to potential franchisees, as well as being a strong advocate of reasonable legislation to assure greater protection of potential investors. The IFA was founded in 1960 by a group of franchising executives who saw the need for an organization that would 1) speak on behalf of franchising, 2) provide services to member companies as well as those interested in franchising, 3) set standards of business practice, serve as a medium for the exchange of experience and expertise and 5) offer educational programs for top industry executives and managers. Membership is purported to be highly selective and must be approved by the Association's Executive Committee. A *Full* Member must 1) have a satisfactory financial statement, 2) have been in business for at least 2 years, 3) have complied with all applicable state and federal disclosure requirements and 4) have satisfactory business and personal references. *Associate* Membership is reserved for those companies who are either new in franchising, considering franchising or who cannot meet all of the requirements of Full Membership. Further information of the IFA's array of services and membership requirements may be obtained from the Association's offices at 1350 New York Avenue,

NW, Suite 900, Washington, DC 20005. (202) 628-8000; FAX (202) 628-0812.

The **Canadian Franchise Association (CFA)** is similar in function to the IFA, but is specifically focused on franchising in Canada. It is a trade association of franchisors and companies providing products and services to franchisors. As a condition of membership, all members must agree to adhere to the CFA Code of Ethics. Founded in 1967 as the Association of Canadian Franchisors, the CFA currently has some 250+ members. There are three types of membership; 1) a *Regular* Member - who has been in business in Canada at least 2 years, has a minimum of 4 units in operation and has the right to sell franchises, 2) an *Associate* Member, who is engaged in the business of franchising or can demonstrate the intent to become a franchisor and 3) an *Affiliate* Member, who provides products and/or services to franchisors. The CFA's address is 88 University Avenue, Suite 607, Toronto ON M5J 1T6 Canada. (416) 595-5005; FAX (416) 595-9519.

6. Established in 1976 represents the year the Company was founded. To the extent the Company has been around for 5 or more years, this lends some credibility to its ability to be around for 5 more.

7. 1st Franchised in 1977 represents the year the Company first became a franchisor of franchised unit(s). Again, the longer the Company has been around, the better staying power it has to weather times of uncertainty in the future.

> **Observation:** From the perspective of the franchisee, it is important that the franchisor have actual franchising experience in house, and that he not be forced to rely on outside consultants to make the system work. This is a form of business that requires specific skills and experience - skills and experience that are markedly different from those required to manage a non-franchised business. To the extent that you are thinking about establishing a long-term relationship with a firm just starting out in franchising, I would not feel remotely awkward about insisting that the franchisor prove that he has the team on board and in place that will insure its and, more importantly, your success.

8. Company-Owned Units: . . . . 15 are basically

franchised units that, as of 8/31/1992, are owned by the franchisor, rather than by franchisees.

Observation: The mix of Company-owned units vs. franchised units is indicative of the willingness of the franchisor to "put his money where his mouth is" to some extent. One important thing to find out from the franchisor, however, is the trend in Company-owned units, i.e. is the Company increasing its ownership of outlets or not, and why? My own feeling is that the acquisition of existing units or opening of new units would generally be a favorable trend, as the franchisor is obviously convinced of the long-term profitability of the business and of its ability to compete successfully. (Hopefully, the franchisor is not buying units from franchisees to preclude litigation from unhappy franchisees. To the extent that the franchisor is buying out existing units, I would most certainly call each franchisees that is selling his unit and determine the real reason.)

9. Franchised Units: . . . . 66 are outlets owned and operated by franchisees as of 8/31/1992.

10. Projected New Units for 1993 . . . . 12 is based on the Company's forecast that it will open 12 new units during 1993.

Observation: In your discussions with franchisors, most will be extremely optimistic about Company growth in the near-term. It should be noted that an extremely ambitious growth program is very expensive to achieve and maintain. Unless the franchisor has direct access to the working capital necessary to support both its projected growth and to provide the necessary on-going support for its existing franchisees, it is possible that neither of these objectives can be satisfactorily maintained. I would want some strong assurances from the franchisor that I would receive the start-up training and assistance and on-going support I had been promised. Without this required corporate support (especially if your success is largely tied to a national advertising campaign), you will be left largely to your own devices. A second problem associated with rapid growth is that talented and experienced management can only cover so many bases before it becomes ineffective. It will take sufficient time and on-the-job experience before new management can perform as well as the original management team. To the extent that the original management is devot-

ing its limited time and energies to expansion and opening new franchised outlets, the new franchisee may well be forced to work with a less experienced staff that doesn't yet fully understand the system. Again, I would want to know that any transition to new personnel would be smooth and well thought out.

To reiterate, system expansion is an extremely important area to cover with the franchisor before you commit yourself to his program. Other things being equal, controlled growth is preferred to rampant growth. The fact that management is convinced that its franchise is the hottest franchise in the country in terms of growth may sound very attractive to the new franchisee who has the opportunity to "get in on the ground floor." Keep in mind, however, that someone has to make it all work as designed, and this takes the same people who have made the system what it is today. Management can only do so many things well before the system gets overloaded.

11. Distribution: . . . . US : 74; Can : 7; Overseas : 0 means that, of the 81 units operating as of 8/31/1992, 74 were in the US, 7 were in Canada and none (0) were Overseas.

12. Distribution: North America: . . . . 15 States, 2 Provinces means that the Company had units in 15 States and 2 Provinces in Canada.

Observation: If the Company has wide geographic representation and has been able to maintain it for several years, this is an exceptionally strong indication of its ability to develop, market and support a sustainable national or regional program. It has been able to overcome one of the most serious obstacles to franchise success - the ability to grow on its own merits without the overriding influence of its developers.

13. Distribution: Concentration: . . . . 25 in CA, 8 in WA, 5 in KY means that the franchisor has 25 units in California, 8 in Washington and 5 in Kentucky. (The franchisor was asked to note which 3 states and/or provinces had the highest concentration of operating units, whether Company-owned or franchisee-owned).

Observation: Unless there were offsetting benefits

in terms of a "special deal" or guaranteed support, I would be hesitant to be the pioneer in a new area. For instance, if the franchisor has 25 units operating on the West Coast, and none east of the Rockies, and I were considering opening a unit in Florida, I would tend to be very skeptical about verbal assurances of "don't worry, we'll support you." On the other hand, if the franchisor has a successful franchised operation and has the financial wherewithal to initiate and support an expansion 3,000 miles away, it may be a great opportunity to get in on the ground floor. This is especially true if you have an option to open new outlets within your territory after you have proven yourself. Keep in mind the incremental risks associated with being a missionary in a new area.

14. Registered refers to specific states that require registration before the franchisor may offer franchises in that state. Disclosure to the Federal Trade Commission and State registration are separate issues and are discussed briefly below:

Federal Trade Commission Rule 436

After 7 years of effort, Federal Trade Commission Rule 436 was enacted in 1979, thereby requiring the submission of certain specific information and disclosure requirements about companies wishing to franchise. Franchises may not be sold without this disclosure.

Basically, the Rule requires the following information:

1. Identifying Information As To Franchisor.

2. Business Experience Of Franchisor's Directors And Executive Officers.

3. Business Experience Of The Franchisor.

4. Litigation History.

5. Bankruptcy History.

6. Description Of Franchise.

7. Initial Funds Required To Be Paid By A Franchisee.

8. Recurring Funds Required To Be Paid By A Franchisee.

9. Affiliated Persons The Franchisee Is Required To Do Business With By The Franchisor.

10. Obligations To Purchase.

11. Revenues Received By The Franchisor In Consideration Of Purchases By A Franchisee.

12. Financing Arrangements.

13. Restriction Of Sales.

14. Personal Participation Required Of The Franchisee In The Operation Of The Franchise.

15. Termination, Cancellation, and Renewal Of The Franchise.

16. Statistical Information Concerning The Number Of Franchises (And Company-Owned Outlets).

17. Site Selection.

18. Training Programs.

19. Public Figure Involvement In The Franchise.

20. Financial Information Concerning The Franchisor.

As a potential franchisee, it is imperative that you review and fully understand the disclosure statement before making any commitment. As noted earlier, this should be thoroughly reviewed by a lawyer who is familiar with the intricacies of franchising. You should also be aware of the requirements placed on the franchisor by the FTC to provide you with this information on a timely basis. It must be made available to you upon your first face-to-face meeting with the franchisor and at least 10 days *before* either 1) any money changes hands or 2) a franchise agreement is signed. The end result of these disclosure regulations is that you are infinitely better protected and informed than you would have been before the legislation was enacted. It is up to you to take full advantage of all of the information at your disposal.

State Registration

Whereas FTC Rule 436 is a national disclosure statement, several states have taken it upon themselves to add a further element of protection for their residents. Before a franchise may be offered in these states, additional information (not necessarily the same as that required by the FTC) must be submitted and approved by the relevant state regulatory agencies. The states requiring this additional registration are: California, Florida, Hawaii, Illinois, Indiana, Maryland, Michigan, Minnesota, New York, North Dakota, Oregon, Rhode Island, South Dakota, Virginia, Washington and Wisconsin. The province of Alberta also requires separate registration. Some states, such as California and Illinois, have especially demanding requirements for registration. The more states in which the franchisor has "passed muster," the more confidence you should have that every rock has already been overturned in evaluating past and current operations.

Unfortunately, separate registration in multiple states is expensive, time-consuming and generally an unnecessary duplication of effort of the part of franchisors. It would appear to be much more efficient if the FTC or some other national body could act on behalf of the states in protecting the franchisees, and maybe this will come about in the near-term. In the interim, however, if you happen to live in a state that requires separate registration, you cannot become a franchisee until the franchisor has gone through the registration process. Keeping in mind that this process may serve to weed out some potentially fraudulent franchisors, it may also mean that you cannot take advantage of a particular franchising opportunity until the franchisor can afford the time and funds to register in your state.

States that do not require a separate registration allow the franchisor to supply the potential franchisee with a Uniform Franchise Offering Circular (U.F.O.C.). This is a standardized, uniform disclosure document that details information about the Company similar to that required by the FTC.

15. Type Space: FS,SF,SC,RM; ~ 1,800-2,200 SF.
This question was designed to give the franchisee some idea of the type of space he will have to rent,

the average square footage requirements and the ability to estimate monthly rental expense. In this case, the Company suggests that its retail locations are equally suitable for a Free-Standing (FS) building, a Storefront (SF) location, a Strip Center (SC) or a Regional Mall (RM). In addition, square footage requirements may vary between 1,800 and 2,200 square feet *on average*. Other abbreviations used were (OB) Office Building, (HB) Home Based, (WH) Warehouse, (KI) Kiosk, (PC) Power Center, (IP) Industrial Park and (ES) Executive Suite.

FINANCIAL

16. Earnings Claim: . . . . Yes. Some franchisors are willing to provide potential franchisees with actual operating results for their Company-owned and/or franchised units. While this information can be exceedingly helpful to the potential franchisee in considering a franchise, there is considerable inherent risk to the franchisor if the published results can be interpreted in any way as a sales or income projection applicable to new units. Given today's highly litigious society, and the propensity of courts to award large settlements to the "little guy," I am surprised that franchisors still provide the information.

> **Observation:** The potential franchisee's inability to obtain reliable pro formas is a major shortcoming of the system. While I can well empathize with franchisors who are increasingly being sued (or losing sleep over the prospect) by their franchisees, there is no reason why a non-binding projection cannot be provided to the franchisee before he invests his life's savings in a venture. Clearly the franchisor has a better idea than anyone else as to how much business a good operator could realistically expect to generate in a specific location. Most prospective franchisees do not have the financial sophistication to make these projections without considerable help from the franchisor. Because of the threat of being sued, as well as the fact that the franchisee's projections may well be more optimistic than those of the franchisor who truly knows the business, far too little valuable information changes hands. Everyone knows that success is largely a function of location, the degree of service provided, reliability, consistency, hard work, luck etc. These caveats notwithstanding, the franchisor can and

should provide more data, clearly identified as an educated guess on their part and accepted as such by the prospective franchisee. At a very minimum, actual gross sales per location should be provided, as this represents verifiable data, not affected by proprietary operating costs. Once accepted and signed for by the franchisee, the franchisor should be free of the threat of being sued unless there is a clear case of intent to mislead or defraud.

17. Cash Investment: . . . . $75K means that, *on average*, the franchisee will be required to make a *cash investment of approximately* $75,000 by the time he opens his franchise.

> **Observation:** Although franchisors may interpret the question differently (i.e. does it include X months working capital until the outlet reaches break-even, etc.), it nevertheless suggests the level of financial commitment expected of the franchisee. If you can't raise this amount of cash without unnecessarily stretching yourself, you would probably do better finding a franchise that is less financially demanding. The last thing that any new franchisee needs is the additional stress created by unforeseen financial requirements. Accordingly, be completely candid with the franchisor in discussing your current financial position. Bluffing on your part could ultimately be disastrous. If you are prepared to trust the franchisor in every other facet of your business, don't let financial counseling by the sole exception. Remember that the franchisor has no motive to disqualify you on financial grounds other than to protect both himself and you from potential future problems.

18. Total Investment: . . . . $120 - 225K means that, *on average*, your total investment, including both cash and debt, will total approximately $120,000 - 225,000.

> **Observation:** Again, there may be room for interpreting this question, especially if the building/facilities/equipment may be purchased or leased. What is important, however, is the relative magnitude of the investment, and your understanding that you may well be liable for paying this amount off if things don't work out as planned. Keep in mind that a single-purpose building in a sub-optimal location or highly specialized equipment on the auction block may be worth only 35 -

50% of its original value. In your discussions with the franchisor, insure that these totals include adequate working capital for the initial start-up period, which in most cases is in excess of 6 months.

19. Fees: Franchise . . . . $18K means that the franchisor will require a front-end payment (generally cash) of $18,000 before you can become a franchisee. This amount is considered a franchise fee and is a non-recurring expense to reimburse the franchisor for his costs in locating, selecting, qualifying and training new franchisees. In many cases, the franchisor will assist the franchisee by deferring part of the fee.

> **Observation:** Keep in mind that the franchise fee is generally considered a break-even proposition as far as the franchisor is concerned. When one considers the expense of running ads in the *Wall Street Journal*, of meeting with and selecting potential franchisees (only some small percentage of whom actually become franchisees), of the initial training and hand-holding, etc., the fees may not be unreasonable at all. Most franchisors try to keep the franchise fee in the $15,000 - 35,000 range. It would be a good idea to determine what that average franchise fee is within a given industry and compare that with the fee charged by the firms you are interested in joining. If their fees are significantly above the average, there should be some reasonable explanation.

20. Fees: Royalty: . . . . 6% means that 6% of gross sales (or other measure as defined in the Franchise Agreement) are paid directly to the franchisor in the form of royalties. These payments represent your on-going cost of doing business as a part of the franchise organization - i.e. of funding your share of the costs of running a centralized national organization that is working on your behalf. In some cases the Royalty Fee is fixed at a certain amount per period.

> **Observation:** A basic tenet of franchising is that the franchisor should make no profit on the franchise fee. His rewards instead come in future years as the franchisee's sales grow and the royalty proceeds grow. As the system grows from 6 units to 80 units, and as sales per outlet increase from $250,000 to $400,000, royalty fees (at 6%) would increase from $90,000 to $1,920,000 per year. Again, this may

seem like a lot of money, but consider the franchisor's overhead in supporting 80 separate businesses before you condemn his "excessive profits."

What you, as a potential franchisee, have to resolve before you commit to franchising is whether the support you get in setting up and managing the business is worth the annual royalty fee, both in the short-term and long-term. If you make the decision that it is, keep in mind that the royalty fee is going to grow as you grow. Begrudging the franchisor his profits in the future, after he has helped make your business a success, is counter- productive and useless.

By the same token, however, a 1% difference is royalty fees charged by 2 otherwise equal franchisors can amount to a great deal of money over the 15 - 20 years of a relationship. It pays to choose carefully, but never make the royalty % the over-riding consideration in your decision.

21. Fees: Advertising: . . . . 2% means that 2% of gross sales (or other measure as defined in the Franchise Agreement) will go toward corporate advertising. In most cases, the % is given and is a function of sales volume. In some cases, the fee is fixed.

> **Observation:** Since the percentage for advertising varies significantly throughout this book, there are no hard and fast rules. To the extent that your business is dependent upon name association by the general public, expenditures for advertising, if well done, should be justified. Rigorous market research, both before and after any major advertising campaign, should be able to determine the effectiveness of the campaign. Of all the functions provided by the franchisor, advertising has the greatest economy of scale. Consider the time, effort and expense it would take each franchisee to independently advertise his products and/or services. It is doubtful that a single franchisee could do this at twice the cost of the advertising fee paid to the franchisor.

22. Contract Period(Yrs.) : . . . . 15 / 15 refers to the term of the original franchise agreement and to the term of the first renewal period. In most cases, the longer the term of the contract, the better. At a very minimum, the Contract Term should exceed the term of any property that is leased.

> **Observation:** It is critical to fully understand and to document in writing under what circumstances the Franchise Contract cannot be renewed and/or may be canceled. You would hate to spend years developing a business, only to find out that a poorly worded Franchise Agreement allows the franchisor the unilateral right to cancel the relationship. This requires specific legal expertise that few franchisees possess.

MULTI-LEVEL FRANCHISING

In recent years, the classic business format model shown in Chapter 1 has been modified to provide the franchisor with additional options to grow more rapidly and at less cost than might otherwise be the case. Generically, these options are known as multi-level franchising. Although there are numerous variations on the classic franchising theme, there are three primary methods that are generally employed. These are: 1) Master (or regional) Franchising, 2) Sub-franchising and 3) Area Development Franchising. In each case, the franchisee still receives all of the benefits normally associated with franchising - the full use of the franchisor's trademarks and logos, the use of the business format system, initial training, site selection, on-going support, etc. The primary difference lies in 1) the on-going relationship between the franchisee and the franchisor, 2) to whom the franchisee should look for this support and 3) to whom he pays the required fees. Each of these methods will be described briefly.

With **Master Franchising**, the franchisor chooses to expand in a particular geographic area, which may be metropolitan, state, or national in scope. Realizing that he may not have the financial wherewithal or staff to expand on his own as rapidly as he might wish, he enlists the support of a Master Franchisee. The Master Franchisee has the responsibility to not only sign up new franchisees within his geographic area, but also to provide these new franchisees with the initial training and support that are normally provided directly by the franchisor. Once established, on-going support of the franchisee is generally provided directly and totally by the franchisor. The Master Franchisee is nevertheless

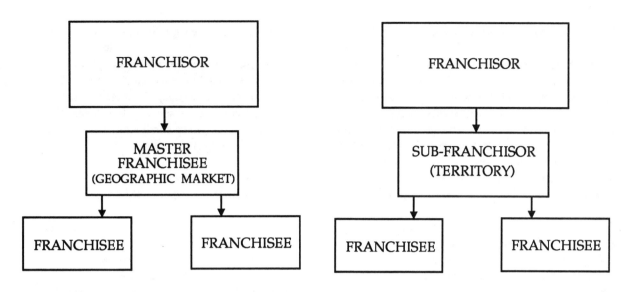

MASTER FRANCHISING MODEL   SUB-FRANCHISING MODEL

involved in the on-going sharing of future royalty fees (and frequently the advertising fees). Again, the franchisee still receives all the benefits normally associated with franchising for which he pays an on-going percentage royalty fee and (usually) advertising fee directly to the franchisor. The contract between the franchisor and the Master Franchisee clearly spells out what is expected of each party and sets a specific period within which the Master Franchisee must meet certain objectives. In return for the front-end fee paid to the franchisor for his exclusive geographic market, the Master Franchisee receives a future stream of royalty payments from the franchisor based strictly on the performance (usually gross sales) of the franchisees that he brings into the system. Unlike other methods of sub-contracting out the development of new franchisees, this method is successful for all parties concerned because the Master Franchisor has to be selective at the outset and supportive throughout the relationship in order to personally profit.

In **Sub-franchising,** the Sub-franchisor also develops a specific territory and provides the initial training, site selection, etc. noted above to those franchisees he signs up. What differs, however, is that the franchisee deals directly with the Sub-franchisor on an on-going basis and has only limited direct involvement with the franchisor. He pays the royalty and advertising fees directly to the Sub-franchisor, who in turn pays a portion to the

franchisor. Basically, the Sub-franchisor becomes the franchisor for his territory, and the franchisee is dependent upon him for his on-going support. To the extent that the Sub-franchisor lacks the necessary financial, managerial or marketing skills normally expected of the franchisor, the franchisee will suffer. Accordingly, the potential franchisee should be extremely franchisor as well as the franchisor.

In an **Area Development Agreement,** the

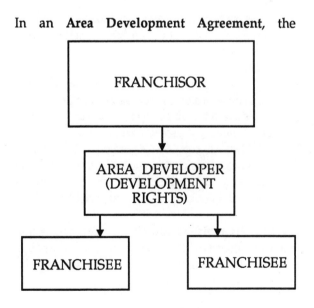

AREA DEVELOPMENT MODEL

franchisor grants exclusive development rights to a group of investors for a particular geographic area. The investors in turn either develop individual franchise units within their territory which they own directly or find franchisees to develop units within their territory. In the latter case, the Area Developer has a residual ownership position. In return for the rights to develop this exclusive territory, the Area Developer pays the franchisor a front-end fee and is required to develop a certain number of units within a specified time period. Once established, the individual franchisees within the territory pay all royalty and advertising fees directly to the franchisor. The Area Developer shares in neither the franchise fee nor in on-going royalties or advertising fees. Instead, he shares only in the profitability of the individual franchises that he has established.

Note: For a more detailed explanation of multi-level franchising, and the benefits see "Multi-Level Franchising: How Far? How Fast?" by John Campbell in *Franchising World*, February, 1988, pp. 36 - 39 published by the IFA.

23. Area Development Agreement: .... Yes/15 indicates that the franchisor permits Area Development Agreements and that the term of the agreement is 15 years.

> **Observation:** This may be an attractive option for an investor who has considerable experience with franchising and who has the financial backing to commit to opening multiple units over a specified period. If you are convinced that the franchisor has come up with a unique service and can provide the necessary continuing support, you may want to tie up an entire geographic area in order to preserve future growth potential for yourself. It most certainly in not an option that should be explored by an individual who has limited or no previous franchising experience and/or limited financial strength.

24. Sub-Franchise Contract: .... Yes means that the franchisor will consider using a Sub-Franchising Agreement in order to expand more rapidly than he could otherwise.

> **Observation:** Reiterating the point made above, it is imperative that the Sub-franchisor have the strength to support the franchisee throughout the long-term relationship of the franchise agreement.

If he should be unable to follow through as expected, your ability to work directly with the franchisor may be severely constrained because of the terms of the Sub-franchise Agreement. Be sure that you know everything about the Sub-franchisor that you should know about the franchisor. Also, be fully versed about the conditions spelled out in the Sub-franchising Agreement.

25. Expand In Territory: .... No refers to the right of the franchisee to establish additional units within his franchised territory or area. This right is frequently granted to an individual franchisee in place of the Area Development Agreement noted above. If the franchise should prove successful and the franchisee is convinced that he could effectively manage additional units, it would certainly be desirable to have the right to expand. Usually this right would be granted without the requirement to pay an additional franchise fee.

26. Passive Ownership: .... Not Allowed means that the franchisor will not allow the franchisee/investor to hire an on-site manager to manage the business on a day-to-day basis. Instead, the franchisee himself must be the owner/operator. Other franchisors either discourage or allow the practice within certain guidelines.

> **Observation:** My own feeling is that active, "hands-on" management of the unit is necessary in most cases, at least until the franchisee has built up the experience and know-how to properly monitor the management of others.

27. Encourage Conversions: .... Yes means that the franchisor actively encourages existing businesses that are operating independently to become a member of the franchise team, enjoy the benefits of franchising and prosper to a greater extent that by continuing to run as a "mom and pop" operation. Other franchisors may feel that it is preferable to start afresh with a franchisee who has no preconceived notions as to how the business ought to be run and who will follow the dictates of the franchisor to the letter.

28. Average # of Employees : .... 2 FT, 4 PT means that the *average* franchised unit is recommended to have 2 full-time employees and 4 part-time employees. Where relevant, these totals *include* the services of the owner/operator.

Observation: As a franchisee, once the number of employees reaches a certain level, the bulk of your time will be spent in managing them and their daily problems, and not in managing the business. Be sure that you feel comfortable with being a people manager and that you have the temperament to do it well. Working with part-time, minimum wage employees can be particularly vexing. If you are not people-oriented, and this requires some close introspection, you should opt for a franchise that draws on other strengths that you possess.

FRANCHISOR TRAINING / SUPPORT

29. Financial Assistance Provided: . . . . Yes(D) means that the franchisor is *directly* involved in helping the franchisee secure the investment necessary to start and finance a franchise. Generally this would be in the form of leases or loans made by the franchisor. Other franchisors are *indirectly* involved, meaning that they may assist by introducing the franchisee to their financial contacts and standing behind him, possibly as a co-guarantor of a loan or lease

Observation: There is an increasing trend within the industry to let potential franchisees secure their own financing without any assistance from the franchisor. The objective, presumably, is to let the franchisee stand on his own two feet - to see if he is enough of a businessman to deal directly with lending institutions. It may turn out that the prospect is unable to secure the necessary funding. If so, the franchisor's attitude would be that he may not have been a strong team member in the long-run and the franchisor is better off from having learned this at the outset.

30. Site Selection Assistance: . . . . Yes means that the franchisor will assist in determining the site location for the franchise. Site selection is an especially critical variable in the long-term profitability of many types of franchises, especially those with a strong retail orientation. Determining the optimal location within a franchised territory requires a thorough knowledge of the area and the type of business and should be left to experienced professionals.

Observation: Assuming that site selection were essential, I would be very reluctant to involve myself with a company that was not actively involved in the site selection process, either directly or through a consulting firm. No amount of hard work or business savvy can overcome a poor choice of location. In many cases, the franchise agreement will not allow the franchisee to move from one location to another - so make certain that your first choice is your best shot.

31. Lease Negotiation Assistance: . . . . Yes means that the franchisor will assist in negotiating the original lease on the franchise site. Again, negotiating a lease is not something that someone inexperienced in real estate can jump into. There are a number of trade-offs that must be considered and negotiated before signing a contract. This also is an area best left to the professionals - hopefully with the active involvement of the franchisor.

32. Co-operative Advertising: . . . Yes refers to the franchisor's willingness to pick up part of the franchisee's costs incurred in promoting (usually on a local level) the products and/or services each has a vested interest in selling. The most common media include direct mail, newspaper, radio, billboards, etc. Even where the franchisor will not pick up at least a portion of the out-of-pocket expenses, it should at least provide samples of effective advertising and promotional campaigns to the franchisee. Co-op advertising is especially important during the pre-opening and grand-opening period when the franchisee is making his debut.

33. Training is critical to the success of the franchise. To the extent that the franchisor cannot successfully impart to the franchisee his knowledge, formulae , short-cuts and methods of doing business (those reasons why he has been successful where others have failed), then the franchisee is only marginally better off than the entrepreneur starting from scratch. Consequently, the duration and depth of initial training is of paramount importance in most cases. Although space limitations preclude any elaboration of the training provided, one should nevertheless be able to derive an overall impression about the franchisor's emphasis on training.

34. On-Going Support. Like initial training, the on-going support services provided by the franchisor are of paramount importance. Having a solid and responsive team behind you can certainly make your life much easier and allow you to concentrate your energies on other areas. As is noted below, franchisors were asked to indicate their support for 9 separate on-going services:

SERVICE PROVIDED	Incl. In Fees	At Add'l Cost	NA
Central Data Processing	A	a	NA
Central Purchasing	B	b	NA
Field Operations Evaluation	C	c	NA
Field Training	D	d	NA
Initial Store Opening	E	e	NA
Inventory Control	F	f	NA
Newsletter	G	g	NA
Regional/National Meetings	H	h	NA
Telephone Hotline	I	i	NA

If the franchisor provides the service (as indicated by letters A-I) at no additional cost to the franchisee, a Capital letter was used to indicate this. If the service is provided, but only at an additional cost, then a Lower Case letter was used. If the franchisor responded N. A. or failed to note an answer for a particular service, the corresponding letter was omitted from the data sheet.

The / . . . . 24 means that the franchisor has 24 full-time employees on his staff.

> **Observation:** The intent was to establish the level of on-going support a franchisee could expect from the franchisor. For example, a staff of 3 to service 47 units would not provide a very high comfort level for the franchisee who needs questions answered right away or who needs on-site support to resolve a major problem. Even though there is ample room for the franchisor to be very creative in answering the question, it is assumed that the franchisee will find out about the actual support capability before signing on. While the question could be improved, one nevertheless gets an impression of relative support potential.

EXPANSION PLANS

35. US: . . . . All US tells you that the franchisor is actively seeking to franchise his business throughout the entire United States. Alternatively, the franchisor could have listed particular states or regions into which he wished to expand.

36. Canada: . . . . All Canada indicates that the franchisor is interested in adding units throughout Canada. To the extent that the franchisor is only interested in expanding into certain provinces or markets, he was given the option to be as specific as he wished.

37) Overseas: . . . . EUR, UK, AU, NZ notes the franchisor's desire to expand overseas into the specific markets of Europe, Britain, Australia and New Zealand. Other countries noted with an abbreviation are Germany (GR), Japan (JA), France (FR), Italy (IT), China (CH), Hong Kong (HK), Korea (KO), Mexico (MX) and Spain (SP). All other countries are spelled out.

> **Observation:** As noted above, rapid expansion of a franchise, or any business for that matter, is fine at the conceptual level. Unfortunately, it is extremely difficult to put into practice where it counts - in the market. My sense is that it is unrealistic to think that a fledgling franchise with less than 10 or so operating units in a specific geographic area can concurrently expand throughout the US, Canada and Overseas. You will note, however, that many of the firms listed suggest that this is their objective. Be properly skeptical. Make them prove to your satisfaction that they have the necessary management and financial wherewithal to make it work.

Note: Keep in mind that the questionnaires were answered by one employee of the company and may not have been reviewed by the president or senior management. If the information supplied by a particular company is of interest to you, but you are concerned about a few answers, give the franchisor the benefit of the doubt and assume that the answer may have been mistakenly answered or interpreted.

STATISTICAL DATA

In many cases, I have included the most current statistical data on various segments of the franchising industry. This data is extracted from *Franchising In The Economy 1991* published by the IFA Educational Foundation and Horwath International. A careful review of the data is particularly useful in determining expected average sales per unit within a particular industry. The data is also helpful in arriving at a better understanding of the dynamics of a segment of franchising - average employees per outlet, the split between company-owned units and franchised units, recent and expected trends, etc. Unfortunately, the industries broken out by the study do not coincide in all cases with the segments outlined in this book. Therefore, extrapolation of the statistical data to the industry groupings outlined below may not be appropriate.

SUPPLEMENTAL LISTING OF FRANCHISORS

In addition to staying abreast of the franchising industry through various general business publications, I have used various sources to update the lists of franchisors noted throughout the book

1) **Canadian Franchise Association (CFA) National Membership Directory, 1992**. 88 University Ave., # 607, Toronto, ON M5J 1T6 Canada. (416) 595-5005. 88 pp. $10.00.

2) **Entrepreneur Magazine**, "Annual Franchise 500," January, 1992. $4.50.

3) **The Franchise Handbook**, Enterprise Magazine, 1020 North Broadway, # 111, Milwaukee, WI 53202. 200 pp. Published quarterly. $4.95.

4) **Franchising World**, International Franchise Association, 1350 New York Avenue, N.W., Suite 900, Washington, D.C. 20005. $12.00 per year.

5) **The IFA Franchise Opportunities Guide**, IFA. Published semi-annually. $10.00.

6) **Wall Street Journal**, Thursday Section on "New Business Offerings."

Note: Having been through the process of sending questionnaires and mailings to all known franchisors on several occasions, my experience is that, over a 12 month period, roughly 15% of the mailings are returned as "undeliverable" for various reasons. As all of the addresses noted below were felt to be current as of August, 1992 the return rate should be well under 10%. If, however, you wish to get in touch with a franchisor and you cannot find his current address, please send us the name of the company in question, enclose a self-addressed, stamped envelope and we will let you know the most recent address we have in our files. Similarly, if you are a new franchisor, or an existing franchisor who has inadvertently been left out of this publication, please let us know. You will be sent a questionnaire in July, 1993 for the 1994 update. Our mailing address is:

Source Book

P.O. Box 12488

Oakland, CA 94604

FAX: (510) 547-3245

CHAPTER 3

BIBLIOGRAPHY

For an industry that has had such a dramatic impact on the national economy, and which represents a vast and ready market for true value-added publications, the paucity of sophisticated and current literature on franchising is disconcerting. There are, however, several publications that provide an adequate starting point for the potential franchisee's due diligence process.

As you will note, most of the publications cited focus on the franchisor rather than the franchisee. Anyone interested in learning the fundamentals of the industry, however, and this should include every serious potential franchisee, should become well acquainted with the dynamics of the industry before he commits to franchising or a particular franchising company.

There are four publications that I would heartily recommend to anyone wanting a sound overview of the industry. These are:

1) **FRANCHISES: DOLLARS & SENSE**, Warren L. Lewis, Kendall/Hunt Publishing Co., Dubuque, IA, 1991. 544 pp. $49.95.

This book discloses never-before-published information about the sales, costs and profits of franchisees in 70 different types of businesses. It is the only book of its kind, and is an invaluable resource for prospective franchisees and their advisors, franchise consultants, lawyers and accountants, and even franchisors themselves. In addition to revealing franchisees' earnings, the book provides good basic information and advice for prospective franchisees. Features include: worksheets for estimating initial investment, income and cash flow; questions to ask franchisors; checklists of typical franchise agreement provisions; and typical disclosures in franchisors' offering circulars.

2) FRANCHISE UPDATE PUBLICATIONS, P. O. Box 20547, San Jose, CA 95160; (408) 997-7795; FAX (408) 997-9377.

Franchise UPDATE Publications is a leading publisher of franchise information, serving both the existing franchisor marketplace and those considering the business of franchising. Its specialized publications include:

Franchise UPDATE Magazine. Franchise UPDATE focuses on the issues, research and data that are critical to franchise professionals.

The Directory of Franchise Attorneys. This directory is a source of franchise legal professionals and is referenced both alphabetically and geographically. Each firm offers on overview of experience, education and areas of specialization.

The Executives' Guide to Franchise Opportunities. This publication is designed for individuals thinking about going into business for themselves. Over 100 franchise companies actively seeking qualified franchise candidates are included. It is also complete with franchise statistics, franchise evaluation tips and financing options.

Franchisor News UPDATE. This is a bi-monthly newsletter designed to update those who want to be in the know about the latest happenings in the franchise community as reported by franchisors.

State of the States. This newsletter is written in layman's terminology and is an update on specific federal and state legislation and judicial decisions that affect franchising.

International Franchise Newsletter. This newsletter features articles relating to international franchising.

3) THE CONTINENTAL FRANCHISE REVIEW, by Sparks Publishing Co., Inc., P. O. Box 3283, Englewood, CO 80155; (303) 649-1044; FAX (303) 649-1059. Subscription fees: $155 per year US, $175 per year Outside US. 26 issues annually, plus four special reports. (Sample copies are provided).

This 8-page, bi-weekly analytical newsletter has provided franchising decision-makers with timely, accurate information for 25 years. CFR is well written and highly informative. Given the constantly changing registration and disclosure requirements of franchising, it is especially helpful in keeping the reader abreast of this tricky aspect of the franchise system. It keeps readers updated on franchising, state legislation, FTC investigations, court decisions, tax issues, operations and environmental issues. The format is broken down into: Bulletins, Trends, Finance, Legal and Editorial. All subjects covered are indexed annually.

4) THE FRANCHISE OPTION, EXPANDING YOUR BUSINESS THROUGH FRANCHISING, DeBanks M. Henward, III and William Ginalski, Franchise Group Publishers, International Franchise Association (IFA), 1350 New York Avenue, NW, Suite 900, Washington, D.C. 20005; (202) 628-8000; FAX (202) 628-0812. 1985. $25.95.

Although the revised edition of this classic is written primarily for potential franchisors, it is nevertheless an excellent overview of the interworkings of the industry from the franchisee's standpoint. Basically, the book offers a do-it-yourself approach to successful franchise development and in so doing discusses what franchising is, how it works, what it takes to be a successful franchisor and how to undertake the development of a franchise system. There is an in-depth discussion of planning for a franchise system, test-marketing the franchise concept, system implementation, prohibitions and liabilities and when and how to terminate a franchise relationship. The Appendix contains the Federal Trade Commission's Franchising Rule 436 and a useful glossary of franchising terms. Unlike most other books available on franchising, this book is addressed to the sophisticated potential franchisee/franchisor.

Although there are well in excess of 200 books, periodicals, directories, etc. that relate to the franchising industry, I have attempted to use some discretion in listing those that I feel best cover the industry. The following listing is alphabetic:

A) BLUEPRINT FOR FRANCHISING A BUSINESS, Steven S. Raab with Gregory Matusky, John Wiley & Sons, New York, NY. 1987. 244 pp. $24.95.

One of the few books on franchising written by someone who actually has years of industry experience. Raab discusses how franchising works, its advantages and disadvantages (including legal, business, marketing and sales issues) and the crucial steps required to launch a successful franchise program. The book is interspersed with "nuggets" - insightful summaries of the author's experience in various facets of franchising. The appeal is for potential and actual franchisors rather than franchisees. Understanding the mechanics, however, better prepares the franchisee for a knowledgeable investment decision.

B) THE FRANCHISE ADVANTAGE, Donald and Patrick Boroian, Francorp, 20200 Governors Dr., Olympia Fields, IL 60461. 1987. 235 pp. $30.00.

Although clearly a marketing effort to solicit potential clients for their consulting business, the authors nevertheless do a good job of explaining the steps from franchise concept to successful franchisor, as well as a look at the costs of getting there. Don't accept the precept, however, that any reasonable idea has franchise potential or that the average person can convert a great idea into a successful franchise operation. Both the concept and the entrepreneur have to be exceptional to successfully launch a new franchise.

C) FRANCHISE BIBLE: A COMPREHENSIVE GUIDE, Erwin J. Keup, Oasis Press/PSI Research, 300 N. Valley Dr., Grants Pass, OR 97526. 1991. 311 pp. $19.95.

This recent publication is equally useful to prospective franchisees and franchisors alike. The comprehensive guide and workbook explain in detail what the franchise system entails and the precise benefits it offers. The book contains an actual offering circular to familiarize the reader with its terms and conditions and what must be included in the circular if you are a franchisor. Of particular interest are the checklists and forms provided to assist the prospective franchisee in rating a potential franchisor. Also noted are the franchisor's contractual obligations to the franchisee and what the franchisee should expect from the franchisor in the way of services and support.

D) A FRANCHISE CONTRACT, Jerrold G. Van Cise, IFA. $4.95.

A legal examination of the proper elements of a contract to protect both franchisor and franchisee.

E) THE FRANCHISE GAME, (RULES AND PLAYERS), Harold Nedell, Olempco, Dept. C, P. O. Box 27963, Houston, TX 77027. $8.00
Deals with the potential emotional, physical and mental traumas experienced by franchisees and provides insight from the point of view of both franchisors and franchisees.

F) THE FRANCHISE MANUAL, Dr. Alfred J. Modica and Dr. Anthony F. Libertella, National/International Institute for Franchise Research and Development, 3 Barker Avenue, White Plains, NY 10601. 1986. 2 volumes, 450 pp. $85.00.

This weighty manual provides step-by-step direction on how to franchise your business from concept to design, proving out your program before selling a franchise, making the go or no-go decision, projecting pro forma cash flow, legal ramifications and marketing techniques. Examples of case studies, legal franchise agreements and how to capitalize your franchise program from blueprint to opening your pilot operation.

G) FRANCHISE RESTAURANTS, The National Restaurant Association, 311 1st Street, NW, Washington, D.C. 20001. 1987. $5.00

Statistical appendix highlighting franchise restaurant growth between 1973 and 1986. Includes sales and establishment data, employment, international franchising and minority ownership.

H) FRANCHISE SELECTION: SEPARATING FACT FROM FICTION, Raymond Munna, Granite Publishers, 80 Granada Dr., Kenner, LA 70065. 1986. 215 pp. $19.95.

A valuable source of checklists for the franchisee who is unaware of the potential pitfalls that clearly exist. Especially helpful are the sections on analyzing the franchise contract, laws affecting franchising and the critical, but hard to find, information on a franchisor and how to get it.

I) FRANCHISING: A PLANNING AND SALES COMPLIANCE GUIDE, Norman D. Axelrod and Lewis G. Rudnick, IFA. $35.00

A realistic discussion of the industry and the legal and procedural considerations of a franchise program. Divided into two sections, this guide addresses the major business decisions and typical management problems, as well as state and federal regulations of franchise and business opportunity sales.

J) FRANCHISING AND LICENSING: TWO WAYS TO BUILD YOUR BUSINESS, Andrew J. Sherman, Amacom Press, 135 W. 50th St., New York, NY 10020. 1991. 250 pp. $27.95.

Franchising a business can be a low-cost path to tremendous growth for small- to mid-sized businesses. It can also be a journey through the valley of despair. Although the financial potential is exciting, a franchise program requires extremely careful planning, development and carry-through. This book covers the how to's of creating a franchise program. In simple language, it covers all the management, legal and operational issues that must be faced. With checklists, case studies and sample contracts, this guidebook makes illusive concepts easy to grasp. The author notes how 1) to raise capital, 2) create and test a prototype, 3)structure franchise agreements, 4) develop operations manuals and 5) market the franchise.

K) FRANCHISING FOR FREE, OWNING YOUR OWN BUSINESS WITHOUT INVESTING YOUR OWN CASH, Dennis L. Foster, John Wiley & Sons, New York, NY. 1988. 229 pp. $12.95.

This book concentrates on the two primary reasons that businesses, including franchises, fail - inadequate financing and poor planning. In addition to a methodology for financing a franchise investment with little or no cash, the book also covers tips on packaging and circulating a loan application, names and addresses of financial sources, comparative advantages and disadvantages of various sources and a partial listing of those franchisors

that offer financial assistance.

L) FRANCHISING: THE HOW-TO BOOK, Lloyd T. Tarbutton, Prentice-Hall, Englewood Cliffs, NJ. 1986. 226 pp. $17.95.

A practical guide presented by an acknowledged industry expert, providing a soup-to-nuts action plan for building and expanding a successful franchising operation. In addition to valuable checklists, the book answers critical questions on franchise marketing and sales, fee structures, franchise agreements, franchisee training programs and various assistance programs. Worthwhile reading for franchisor and franchisee alike.

M) FRANCHISING: THE INSIDE STORY, John Kinch, Trimark Publishing, P. O. Box 10530, Wilmington, DE 19850. $17.95.

This book will lead you through the basic and essential steps in exploring the opportunities in franchising. A comprehensive overview of the how's and why's of buying a franchise.

N) FRANCHISING IN THE ECONOMY 1991, IFA Educational Foundation, Inc. and Horwath International, IFA. 113 pp. $75.00.

For the past 16 years, this detailed and highly reliable statistical analysis of franchising in the US has been published by the US Department of Commerce. With the Government's decision to discontinue its publication, the IFA and Horwath International have very capably filled the void and come out with a slicker, more readable, version. In so doing, they provide the industry with a very valuable service. This statistical analysis covers virtually all facets of the industry and documents the growth and success that the industry has enjoyed over the past 2 decades. Not only is the industry as a whole covered, but key product/service categories within the industry are covered in great detail. An excellent source book for potential franchisees, who can ask prospective franchisors hard questions as to how their franchise compares with other franchisors in terms of average sales per unit, average employees per unit, averages sales of company-owned vs. franchised units, etc. This is clearly the most authoritative source of any statistics regarding the industry.

Excerpts from *Franchising In The Economy 1991* are used throughout this book to demonstrate the overall sales, number of establishments, break-out of company-owned vs. franchised units, average sales per outlet, etc. by major industry category.

O) FTC FRANCHISING RULE: THE IFA COMPLIANCE KIT, IFA. $100.00.

A newly revised edition contains a comprehensive overview of the Federal Trade Commission rule on franchising. It also includes an analysis of the rule, an outline of compliance steps and requirements, considerations in selecting a format, comparisons with state laws, bibliographies and more.

P) FRANCHISING WORLD, IFA. $12.00 per year. This glossy trade magazine is published 6 times per year by the International Franchising Association and gives the most current news on what's happening in franchising in a news magazine format. The key elements covered are franchise operations, franchisee relationships, legislative information, marketing and industry developments. While intended for franchisors, the publication is of interest to prospective franchisees in terms of staying abreast of the industry. Keep in mind, however, that its primary focus is in the promotion of its own membership, thus severely limiting the scope for potential franchisees who would like information on the universe of franchisors.

Q) HOW TO BE A FRANCHISOR, Robert E. Kushell and Carl E. Zwisler, III, IFA. $5.00.

This booklet describes step-by-step details about how to launch a franchise program. Written from both the operational and legal perspectives, this is necessary reading for all potential franchisors.

R) HOW TO SELECT A FRANCHISE, Robert McIntosh, IFA. $10.00.

A workbook and cassette tape, designed to help individuals decide whether and how to become a franchisee.

S) IS FRANCHISING FOR YOU?, Robert K. McIntosh, IFA. $3.95.

Basic primer for prospective franchisees with emphasis on self-evaluation to determine whether the opportunities and challenges offered by a franchise system meet the ambitions and abilities of a prospective franchisee.

T) ROADSIDE EMPIRES - HOW THE CHAINS FRANCHISED AMERICA, Stan Luxenberg, Viking Penguin Press, New York, NY. 1985. $17.95.

A readable history of how franchising has transformed the American landscape, diet and economy. Includes folklore on advertising and marketing techniques, the fanatic attention to detail displayed by certain franchisors and profiles on franchising legends Ray Kroc, Colonel Sanders, Howard Johnson and others. Most informative, however, is the critical look that Luxenberg takes at the real effect of franchising on the economy. This includes the diversion of capital from real factories to fast-food factories, mass standardization, get-rich-quick schemes, and, sadly, the transition of the American workforce from skill-intensive jobs to often dead-end, stultifying, minimum wage jobs.

U) U.F.O.C. GUIDELINES, IFA. $30.

Instructions for completing the Uniform Franchise Offering Circular. Prepared by the Midwest Securities Commissioners Association for use by franchisors in meeting state and Federal disclosure requirements.

Note: For authors whose books are not noted above, I would encourage you to send copies for evaluation to: SOURCE BOOK, P. O. BOX 12488, OAKLAND, CA 94604.

CHAPTER 4

AUTOMOTIVE PRODUCTS AND SERVICES

AAMCO TRANSMISSIONS

One Presidential Blvd.
Bala Cynwyd, PA 19004
TEL: (800) 523-0402 (215) 668-2900 C
FAX: (215) 664-4570
Mr. Warren Berest, Fran. Dev. Mgr.

AAMCO, the world's largest chain of transmission specialists, makes in-house resources available to help you build a customer-satisfying, successful business. Among these: extensive training programs, effective advertising and marketing and solid operational assistance. AAMCO CENTERS' warranties are honored throughout the US and Canada.

HISTORY: . . . . IFA
Established in 1963;   . . 1st Franchised in 1963
Company-Owned Units (As of 8/31/1992):   . .0
Franchised Units (As of 8/31/1992):   650
Total Units (As of 8/31/1992):   650
Projected New Units for 1993: 15
Distribution: US-630;Can-20;Overseas-0
  North America: . . . . 48 States, 3 Provinces
  Concentration: . 94 in CA, 60 in FL, 43 in NY
Registered: . . . . .All
. . . .
Type Space: . . . . FS;~4,000 SF

FINANCIAL: Earnings Claim: . Yes
Cash Investment: $48K
Total Investment: $125K
Fees: Franchise - $30K
  Royalty: 7%, Advert: . . . . Varies
Contract Periods (Yrs.): 15/15
Area Development Agreement: . .No
Sub-Franchise Contract: . . . . .No
Expand in Territory: . . . . Yes
Passive Ownership: . . . Not Allowed
Encourage Conversions: . . . . .No
Average # Employees: . . . . . .5 FT

FRANCHISOR TRAINING/SUPPORT:
Financial Assistance Provided: . . . Yes(I)
Site Selection Assistance: . . . . .Yes
Lease Negotiation Assistance: . . . . .Yes
Co-operative Advertising: . . . . .No
Training: . . . . 5 Wks. Headquarters
. . . .
On-Going Support: G,I/ 160
EXPANSION PLANS:
  US: . . . . .All US
  Canada: . . . . .All Canada
  Overseas: . . . . No

AUTOMOTIVE PRODUCTS AND SERVICES

	1989	1990	1991	Percentage Change 90/89	Percentage Change 91/90
Total Number of Establishments:					
Company-Owned	4,741	5,128	5,618	8.16%	9.56%
Franchisee-Owned	31,483	34,121	36,604	8.38%	7.28%
Total	36,224	39,249	42,222	8.35%	7.57%
Ratio of Total Establishments:					
Company-Owned	13.1%	13.1%	13.3%		
Franchisee-Owned	86.9%	86.9%	86.7%		
Total	100.0%	100.0%	100.0%		
Total Sales ($000):					
Company-Owned	4,285,689	4,685,210	5,145,326	9.32%	9.82%
Franchisee-Owned	8,225,488	9,181,184	10,315,339	11.62%	12.35%
Total	12,511,177	13,866,394	15,460,665	10.83%	11.50%
Ratio of Total Sales:					
Company-Owned	34.3%	33.8%	33.3%		
Franchisee-Owned	65.7%	66.2%	66.7%		
Total	100.0%	100.0%	100.0%		
Average Sales Per Unit ($000):					
Company-Owned	904	914	916	1.07%	0.24%
Franchisee-Owned	261	269	282	2.99%	4.73%
Total	345	353	366	2.29%	3.65%
Relative Average Sales Ratio:	346.0%	339.6%	325.0%		

	Number Of Employees	Employees Per Unit	Avg. Sales Per Employee
Total 1989 Employment:			
Company-Owned	40,608	8.6	$105,538
Franchisee-Owned	131,765	4.2	$62,425
Total	172,373	4.8	$72,582
Relative Employee Performance Ratios:		204.7%	169.1%

	1st Quartile	Median	4th Quartile
Average 1989 Total Investment:			
Company-Owned	$75,000	$125,000	$275,000
Franchisee-Owned	$75,000	$100,000	$150,000
Single Unit Franchise Fee	$15,000	$22,500	$27,500
Mult. Unit Franchise Fee	$17,500	$22,500	$30,000
Franchise Start-Up Cost	$25,000	$42,500	$75,000

Source: Franchising In The Economy 1991, IFA Educational Foundation & Horwath International.

ACC-U-TUNE & BRAKE

2510 Old Middlefield Way
Mountain View, CA 94043
TEL: (415) 968-8863
FAX: (415) 968-1869
Mr. John Johnson, Dir. Fran. Dev.

We have successfully packaged the most profitable auto services: drive-thru oil change, tune-up, state inspections, coupled with While-U-Wait brake and manufacturer's 15/30,000 mile service packages. A one-stop, well-lighted, modern, clean place, where customers can have all their vehicle preventative maintenance needs taken care of.

HISTORY: . . . . IFA	FINANCIAL: Earnings Claim: . .No	FRANCHISOR TRAINING/SUPPORT:
Established in 1975; . . 1st Franchised in 1979	Cash Investment: $70K	Financial Assistance Provided: . . . Yes(I)
Company-Owned Units (As of 8/31/1992): . .4	Total Investment: $113-240K	Site Selection Assistance: . . . . . . .Yes
Franchised Units (As of 8/31/1992): 15	Fees: Franchise - $27.5K	Lease Negotiation Assistance: . . . .Yes
Total Units (As of 8/31/1992): 19	Royalty: 7.5%, Advert: . $750/Wk.	Co-operative Advertising: . . . . . . .Yes
Projected New Units for 1993: 5	Contract Periods (Yrs.): . . 10/30/10	Training: . . . . 3 Wks. Headquarters
Distribution: US-19;Can-0;Overseas-0	Area Development Agreement: Yes/10	. . . .
North America: . . . . .1 State	Sub-Franchise Contract: . . . . . Yes	On-Going Support: a,B,C,D,e,F,G,H/ . . 10
Concentration: . . . . 19 in CA	Expand in Territory: . . . . Yes	EXPANSION PLANS:
Registered: . . . . CA	Passive Ownership: . . . Not Allowed	US: . . . . .CA Only
. . . .	Encourage Conversions: . . . . . .No	Canada: . . . . .No
Type Space: . . . FS/Auto Centers;~3,500 SF	Average # Employees: . . 5 FT, 2 PT	Overseas: . . . . No

AID AUTO STORES

275 Grand Blvd., P. O. Box 281
Westbury, NY 11590
TEL: (516) 338-7889
FAX: (516) 338-7803
Mr. Philip L. Stephen, President

Retail sales of automotive parts, accessories, tools, chemicals and equipment.

HISTORY:	FINANCIAL: Earnings Claim: . .No	FRANCHISOR TRAINING/SUPPORT:
Established in 1954; . . 1st Franchised in 1966	Cash Investment: $175K	Financial Assistance Provided: . . . . .No
Company-Owned Units (As of 8/31/1992): . .3	Total Investment: $175K	Site Selection Assistance: . . . . . . .Yes
Franchised Units (As of 8/31/1992): 88	Fees: Franchise - $20K	Lease Negotiation Assistance: . . . .Yes
Total Units (As of 8/31/1992): 91	Royalty: $400, Advert: $775	Co-operative Advertising: . . . . . . .Yes
Projected New Units for 1993: 9	Contract Periods (Yrs.): 10/10	Training: . . . . . Minimum 30 Days Train-
Distribution: US-91;Can-0;Overseas-0	Area Development Agreement: . .No	. . . . ing at Headquarters/Stores
North America: . . . . 2 States	Sub-Franchise Contract: . . . . . .No	On-Going Support: A,B,C,D,E,F,G,H,I/ 35
Concentration: . . . . 82 in NY, 9 in NJ	Expand in Territory: . . . . Yes	EXPANSION PLANS:
Registered:	Passive Ownership: . . . Discouraged	US: . . . . . . New York and New Jersey
. . . .	Encourage Conversions: . . . . . Yes	Canada: . . . . .No
Type Space: . . FS, SC, RM;~4,000-5,000 SF	Average # Employees: . . 3 FT, 3 PT	Overseas: . . . . No

AIRCHEK

6600 SW 62 Ave.
Miami, FL 33143
TEL: (800) 288-6247 (305) 661-8963
FAX: (305) 667-4568
Franchise Marketing Director

Automotive air conditioning repair and parts replacement center for domestic and foreign-make motor vehicles.

HISTORY:	FINANCIAL: Earnings Claim: . Yes	FRANCHISOR TRAINING/SUPPORT:
Established in 1992; . . 1st Franchised in 1992	Cash Investment: $33K	Financial Assistance Provided: . . .Yes(D)
Company-Owned Units (As of 8/31/1992): . .2	Total Investment: $90.3K	Site Selection Assistance: . . . . . . .Yes
Franchised Units (As of 8/31/1992): 2	Fees: Franchise - $25K	Lease Negotiation Assistance: . . . .Yes
Total Units (As of 8/31/1992): 4	Royalty: 5%, Advert: 4%	Co-operative Advertising: . . . . . . .Yes
Projected New Units for 1993: 10	Contract Periods (Yrs.): 15/5	Training: . . . . . 80 Hours Classroom and
Distribution: US-4;Can-0;Overseas-0	Area Development Agreement: Yes/25	. . . . .Hands-on at Headquarters
North America: . . . . .1 State	Sub-Franchise Contract: . . . . Yes	On-Going Support: a,B,C,d,E,F,G,H,I/ . 12
Concentration: . . . . 4 in FL	Expand in Territory: . . . . Yes	EXPANSION PLANS:
Registered: . . . . .FL	Passive Ownership: . . . Discouraged	US: . . . . South
. . . .	Encourage Conversions: . . . . Yes	Canada: . . . . .No
Type Space: . . . Min. 2 Workbays;~2,000 SF	Average # Employees: . . 3 FT, 2 PT	Overseas: . . . . No

AMERICAN BRAKE SERVICE

935 Brighton Ave., # 3
Portland, ME 04102
TEL: (800) 227-7285 (207) 774-7285
FAX: (207) 774-3961
Mr. Jay Apsey, Dir. Fran.

ABS CENTERS provide expert automotive brake and undercar services. A complete equipment and inventory package, as well as up to 5 weeks of training, make the franchise a very attractive investment even for those without automotive experience. Complete advertising, management assistance and technical support. Franchisees also purchase parts at significant savings. 40 years of experience in the auto service industry.

HISTORY: . . . . IFA
Established in 1991; . . 1st Franchised in 1991
Company-Owned Units (As of 8/31/1992): . .0
Franchised Units (As of 8/31/1992): 3
Total Units (As of 8/31/1992): 3
Projected New Units for 1993: 15
Distribution: US-3;Can-0;Overseas-0
  North America: . . . . 2 States
  Concentration: . . . . .2 in MA, 1 in ME
Registered: . . . . . CA,IL,MD,NY,RI,VA,DC
. . . .
Type Space: . . . . RM;~2,000 SF

FINANCIAL: Earnings Claim: . . Yes
Cash Investment: $20-40K
Total Investment: $89-134K
Fees: Franchise - $19.5K
  Royalty: 6%, Advert: 6%
Contract Periods (Yrs.): . . . 15/10
Area Development Agreement: . Yes
Sub-Franchise Contract: . . . . . .No
Expand in Territory: . . . . Yes
Passive Ownership: . . . . .Allowed
Encourage Conversions: . . . . . Yes
Average # Employees: . . 2 FT, 1 PT

FRANCHISOR TRAINING/SUPPORT:
Financial Assistance Provided: . . .Yes(D)
Site Selection Assistance: . . . . . . .Yes
Lease Negotiation Assistance: . . . .Yes
Co-operative Advertising: . . . . . . .Yes
Training: . . . . 2 Wks. Headquarters,
. . . . .2 Wks. Franchisee Location
On-Going Support: A,B,C,D,E,F,G,H,I/ . 5
EXPANSION PLANS:
US: . . . . Northeast
Canada: . . . . .No
Overseas: . . . . No

AMERICAN DISCOUNT TIRE & AUTO CENTERS

4517 NW 31st Ave.
Ft. Lauderdale, FL 33309
TEL: (800) 275-2066 (305) 730-8464
FAX: (305) 730-7550
Mr. Jamie Hundley, Fran. Consultant

The concept behind the company is to provide the consumer with an up-scale tire and auto repair center, using the latest state-of-the-art equipment and services. ADT mechanics are highly trained in all aspects of the "after-market" auto repair and service business. Your customer can feel confident of "Better Quality at Affordable Prices."

HISTORY: . . . .
Established in 1990; . . 1st Franchised in 1992
Company-Owned Units (As of 8/31/1992): . .2
Franchised Units (As of 8/31/1992): 3
Total Units (As of 8/31/1992): 5
Projected New Units for 1993: 15
Distribution: US-5;Can-0;Overseas-0
  North America: . . . . .1 State
  Concentration: . . . . 5 in FL
Registered: . . . . .FL
. . . .
Type Space: . . . . .FS, SC;~4,500 SF

FINANCIAL: Earnings Claim: . .No
Cash Investment: $61K
Total Investment: $106K
Fees: Franchise - $27.5K
  Royalty: 2-5%, Advert: 1%
Contract Periods (Yrs.): 10/10
Area Development Agreement: Yes/10
Sub-Franchise Contract: . . . . . .No
Expand in Territory: . . . . Yes
Passive Ownership: . . . Discouraged
Encourage Conversions: . . . . . .No
Average # Employees: . . 4 FT, 1 PT

FRANCHISOR TRAINING/SUPPORT:
Financial Assistance Provided: . . .Yes(D)
Site Selection Assistance: . . . . . . .Yes
Lease Negotiation Assistance: . . . .Yes
Co-operative Advertising: . . . . . . .Yes
Training: . . . . 2 Wks. On-Site,
. . . . 1 Wk. Headquarters
On-Going Support: a,B,C,D,E,F,G,H,I/ . 30
EXPANSION PLANS:
US: . . . . All US
Canada: . . . . .No
Overseas: . . . . No

AMERICAN FLUID TECHNOLOGY

9 Fletcher St.
Chelmsford, MA 01824
TEL: (800) 344-4AFT (508) 256-9013
FAX:
Mr. Ed Rosamilio, Sales Coord.

AFT mobile on-site recycling services are wanted and needed by industry to turn environmental expenses into profitable solutions. With exclusive Prestone recycling formulas and patented Prestone technology, the AFT service is like a factory on wheels - totally self-contained and van powered. GM and Prestone approved. AFT comes to the workplace and minimizes waste 99%.

HISTORY: . . . .
Established in 1990; . . 1st Franchised in 1991
Company-Owned Units (As of 8/31/1992): . .1
Franchised Units (As of 8/31/1992): 9
Total Units (As of 8/31/1992): 10
Projected New Units for 1993: 25
Distribution: US-10;Can-0;Overseas-0
  North America: . . . . 13 States
  Concentration: . . . 3 in CA, 2 in NJ, 2 in MD
Registered: . . . . .All
. . . .
Type Space: . . . . NA;~NA SF

FINANCIAL: Earnings Claim: . .No
Cash Investment: $65K
Total Investment: $185K
Fees: Franchise - $25K
  Royalty: 10%, Advert: 2%
Contract Periods (Yrs.): . . . 10/10
Area Development Agreement: Yes/3
Sub-Franchise Contract: . . . . . .No
Expand in Territory: . . . . Yes
Passive Ownership: . . . . . .Allowed
Encourage Conversions: . . . . NA
Average # Employees: . . . . . .2 FT

FRANCHISOR TRAINING/SUPPORT:
Financial Assistance Provided: . . . Yes(I)
Site Selection Assistance: . . . . . . .NA
Lease Negotiation Assistance: . . . .NA
Co-operative Advertising: . . . . . . .NA
Training: . . . .2 Days HQ, 1 Day Prestone
. . . . Labs, 5 Days Manufacturer
On-Going Support: B,c,D,F,G,h,I/ 6
EXPANSION PLANS:
US: . . . . All US
Canada: . . . . .All Canada
Overseas: . . . . No

AMERICAN TURBO WASH

4517 NW 31st Ave.
Ft. Lauderdale, FL 33309
TEL: (800) 275-2067 (305) 730-9025
FAX: (305) 730-7550
Mr. Jamie Hundley, Fran. Consultant

AMERICAN TURBO WASH offers its customers the advantage of caring for their cars with the finest state-of-the-art car cleaning technology. All the water used is demineralized to prevent spotting. Most locations are 6-bay, self-service and coin-operated. Open 7 days/24 hours, creating an absentee ownership, all cash business. It's efficient and cost effective. What's more, it's simple and easy to maintain.

HISTORY:
Established in 1987; . . 1st Franchised in 1992
Company-Owned Units (As of 8/31/1992): . .6
Franchised Units (As of 8/31/1992): 2
Total Units (As of 8/31/1992): 8
Projected New Units for 1993: 24
Distribution: US-8;Can-0;Overseas-0
North America: . . . . .1 State
Concentration: . . . . 8 in FL
Registered: . . . . .FL
. . . .
Type Space: . . . . FS;~20,000 SF

FINANCIAL: Earnings Claim: . Yes
Cash Investment: $21K
Total Investment: $116-200K
Fees: Franchise - $17.5K
Royalty: $300/Mo., Advert: . . 0%
Contract Periods (Yrs.): 20/5
Area Development Agreement: Yes/20
Sub-Franchise Contract: . . . . .No
Expand in Territory: . . . . . . Yes
Passive Ownership: . . . . .Allowed
Encourage Conversions: . . . . Yes
Average # Employees: . . . .

FRANCHISOR TRAINING/SUPPORT:
Financial Assistance Provided: . . .Yes(D)
Site Selection Assistance: . . . . . . .Yes
Lease Negotiation Assistance: . . . . .Yes
Co-operative Advertising: . . . . . . .NA
Training: . . . . .1 Wk. Headquarters,
. . . . 1 Wk. On-Site
On-Going Support: C,D,E,G,I/ 20
EXPANSION PLANS:
US: . . . . All US
Canada: . . . . .Yes
Overseas: . . . . No

ATLAS TRANSMISSION

10303 Northwest Freeway, # 201
Houston, TX 77092
TEL: (800) 852-8286 (713) 683-7999
FAX: (713) 956-9220
Mr. Paul R. Segreto, President

Transmission repair facilities. "The Strongest Name in the Business" provides service and repairs to retail, fleet and wholesale customers. Since ATLAS' extensive training program covers all aspects of operating a transmission repair facility, no prior automotive experience is required - only the desire to succeed.

HISTORY:
Established in 1964; . . 1st Franchised in 1982
Company-Owned Units (As of 8/31/1992): . .1
Franchised Units (As of 8/31/1992): 30
Total Units (As of 8/31/1992): 31
Projected New Units for 1993: 10
Distribution: US-31;Can-0;Overseas-0
North America: . . . . .1 State
Concentration: . . . . 31 in TX
Registered: . . . .
. . . .
Type Space: . . . . . . .FS, SC;~4,000 SF

FINANCIAL: Earnings Claim: . .No
Cash Investment: $30-50K
Total Investment: $80-95K
Fees: Franchise - $17.5K
Royalty: 6.5%, Advert: 5%
Contract Periods (Yrs.): . . . 10/10
Area Development Agreement: .No
Sub-Franchise Contract: . . . . .No
Expand in Territory: . . . . . . Yes
Passive Ownership: . . . . .Allowed
Encourage Conversions: . . . . Yes
Average # Employees: . . 4 FT, 1 PT

FRANCHISOR TRAINING/SUPPORT:
Financial Assistance Provided: . . .Yes(D)
Site Selection Assistance: . . . . . . .Yes
Lease Negotiation Assistance: . . . . .Yes
Co-operative Advertising: . . . . . . .Yes
Training: . . . . 1 Wk. Headquarters, 1 Wk.
. . . . Corp. Training Facility, 1 Wk. Site
On-Going Support: b,C,D,E,G,H,I/ 6
EXPANSION PLANS:
US: . . . . .TX, Southwest US
Canada: . . . . .No
Overseas: . . . . No

AUTO AMERICA

2107 Grand Ave.
Kansas City, MO 64108
TEL: (800) 274-6733 (816) 346-4609
FAX: (816) 346-4188
Mr. Chuck Hutchens, VP Fran. Dev.

Discount automotive superstore featuring tires, batteries, parts, accessories and service - all under one roof. Most popular name brands include Diehard, Michelin, Craftsman, AC/Delco and many more. Franchisees are supported by more than 80 years of experience. Billion-dollar buying power and a proven retail business plan.

HISTORY:
Established in 1909; . . 1st Franchised in 1935
Company-Owned Units (As of 8/31/1992): 375
Franchised Units (As of 8/31/1992): 972
Total Units (As of 8/31/1992): 1347
Projected New Units for 1993: 35
Distribution: US-1347;Can-0;Overseas-0
North America: . . . . 47 States
Concentration: . . 127 in TX, 71 in MS, 67 NC
Registered: . . . . IN,MI,NY,VA
. . . .
Type Space: . . . . FS;~9,000 SF

FINANCIAL: Earnings Claim: . .No
Cash Investment: $130-170K
Total Investment: $390-510K
Fees: Franchise - $25K
Royalty: 5%, Advert: . . Up to 2%
Contract Periods (Yrs.): . . . 10/10
Area Development Agreement: .No
Sub-Franchise Contract: . . . . .No
Expand in Territory: . . . . . . Yes
Passive Ownership: . . . Discouraged
Encourage Conversions: . . . . .No
Average # Employees: . 10 FT, 10 PT

FRANCHISOR TRAINING/SUPPORT:
Financial Assistance Provided: . . . Yes(I)
Site Selection Assistance: . . . . . . .Yes
Lease Negotiation Assistance: . . . . .NA
Co-operative Advertising: . . . . . . .Yes
Training: . . . . . . 4 Wks. Company Store,
. . . . 1 Wk. HQ, 1 Wk. Franchisee Store
On-Going Support: A,B,C,D,E,F,G,h/ . . .
EXPANSION PLANS:
US: . . . . . . Midwest, Mid-Atlantic, NE
Canada: . . . . .No
Overseas: . . . . No

AUTO LABS DIAGNOSTIC/TUNE-UP CENTER
15919 W. 10 Mile Rd., # 201
Southfield, MI 48075
TEL: (313) 559-1415
FAX: (313) 557-7931
Mr. Geoffrey Stebbins, President

Automotive diagnostic and tune-up center, specializing in engine performance and computer, engine, electrical and fuel system, service and repair, EPA, air conditioning. Reclaiming and recycling available. All types of underhood repair, complete automotive electrical service and engine repair.

HISTORY:	FINANCIAL: Earnings Claim: . .No	FRANCHISOR TRAINING/SUPPORT:
Established in 1984; . . 1st Franchised in 1989	Cash Investment: $30-60K	Financial Assistance Provided: . . . Yes(I)
Company-Owned Units (As of 8/31/1992): . .0	Total Investment: $105-135K	Site Selection Assistance: . . . . . . .Yes
Franchised Units (As of 8/31/1992): 15	Fees: Franchise - $15K	Lease Negotiation Assistance: . . . .Yes
Total Units (As of 8/31/1992): 15	Royalty: 7%, Advert: 3%	Co-operative Advertising: . . . . . . .Yes
Projected New Units for 1993: 10	Contract Periods (Yrs.): . . . 10/10	Training: . . . . 4 Wks. Headquarters,
Distribution: US-15;Can-0;Overseas	Area Development Agreement: Yes/10	. . . . .1 Wk. In-Store
North America: . . . . .1 State	Sub-Franchise Contract: . . . . Yes	On-Going Support: B,C,D,E,F,G,H/ . . 10
Concentration: . . . . .15 in MI	Expand in Territory: . . . . . . Yes	EXPANSION PLANS:
Registered: . . . . .MI	Passive Ownership: . . . Not Allowed	US: . . . . Midwest
. . . .	Encourage Conversions: . . . . . Yes	Canada: . . . . .No
Type Space: .FS, Auto Malls;~2,500-3,500 SF	Average # Employees: . . . 4-5 FT	Overseas: . . . . No

AUTO ONE
2301 E. Michigan Ave., # 203
Jackson, MI 49202
TEL: (800) 922-8861 (517) 783-6442
FAX: (517) 783-6782
Mr. Hank Weber, President

Installed products and services which enhance the value of automotive vehicles. Strong retail merchandizing programs for auto glass, automotive security systems, cellular phones, car and truck accessories, and protection from the environment with paint sealants, fabric protection and rust proofing.

HISTORY:	FINANCIAL: Earnings Claim: . .No	FRANCHISOR TRAINING/SUPPORT:
Established in 1984; . . 1st Franchised in 1984	Cash Investment: $30-50K	Financial Assistance Provided: . . . Yes(I)
Company-Owned Units (As of 8/31/1992): . .0	Total Investment: $75-95K	Site Selection Assistance: . . . . . . .Yes
Franchised Units (As of 8/31/1992): 40	Fees: Franchise - $20K	Lease Negotiation Assistance: . . . .Yes
Total Units (As of 8/31/1992): 40	Royalty: 5%, Advert: 2.5%	Co-operative Advertising: . . . . .No
Projected New Units for 1993: 12	Contract Periods (Yrs.): . . . 10/10	Training: . . . . 2 Wks. Headquarters
Distribution: US-40;Can-0;Overseas-0	Area Development Agreement: . .No	. . . .
North America: . . . . 2 States	Sub-Franchise Contract: . . . . .No	On-Going Support: C,D,E,F,G,H,I/ 6
Concentration: . . . . 35 in MI, 5 in IN	Expand in Territory: . . . . . . .No	EXPANSION PLANS:
Registered: . . . . IN,MI	Passive Ownership: . . . Discouraged	US: . . . . .Indiana
. . . .	Encourage Conversions: . . . . . Yes	Canada: . . . . .No
Type Space: . . . . . FS, SC, RM;~2,500 SF	Average # Employees: . . 4 FT, 2 PT	Overseas: . . . . No

AUTOLIST CORPORATIONS
1101 Gulf Breeze Pkwy., # 227
Gulf Breeze, FL 32561
TEL: (800) 967-6432 (904) 932-4431 C
FAX: (904) 934-3198
Mr. Robert W. Smith, President

AUTOLIST CORP. utilizes the latest telemarketing software to send vehicles to its member dealers for consignment. Each member dealer enjoys "Free Inventory" and the tools and training to effectively engage in the "Private Owner Car Business," which last year accounted for over 54% of all used car sales in the US.

HISTORY:	FINANCIAL: Earnings Claim: . .No	FRANCHISOR TRAINING/SUPPORT:
Established in 1988; . . 1st Franchised in 1988	Cash Investment: $12.5K	Financial Assistance Provided: . . . Yes(I)
Company-Owned Units (As of 8/31/1992): . .0	Total Investment: $12.5K	Site Selection Assistance: . . . . . . .Yes
Franchised Units (As of 8/31/1992): 12	Fees: Franchise - $12.5K	Lease Negotiation Assistance: . . . .Yes
Total Units (As of 8/31/1992): 12	Royalty: Varies, Advert: . . Varies	Co-operative Advertising: . . . . .Yes
Projected New Units for 1993: 6	Contract Periods (Yrs.): 3/3	Training: . . . . 4 Days Headquarters,
Distribution: US-12;Can-0;Overseas-0	Area Development Agreement: . .No	. . . . 4 Days Franchisee Site
North America: . . . . 4 States	Sub-Franchise Contract: . . . . .No	On-Going Support: A,C,D,E,F,G,H,I/ . .8
Concentration: . . . .4 in FL, 4 in AL, 4 in GA	Expand in Territory: . . . . . . Yes	EXPANSION PLANS:
Registered:	Passive Ownership: . . . Discouraged	US: . . . . . Only Non-Registration States
. . . .	Encourage Conversions: . . . . . Yes	Canada: . . . . .No
Type Space: Auto Dealership;~~50 Vehicles SF	Average # Employees: . . 3 FT, 1 PT	Overseas: . . . . No

AUTOPRO

7025 Ontario St. E.
Montreal, PQ H1N 2B3 CAN
TEL: (514) 256-5031
FAX: (514) 256-6984
Mr. Pierre Vocelle, Director

AUTOPRO is the perfect add-on program for a regular station or independent repair shop wishing to compete with the market's big names. AUTOPRO offers marketing and advertising assistance, along with lifetime warranties in 5 specialties: brakes, mufflers, suspensions, front-end and FWD parts.

HISTORY:	FINANCIAL: Earnings Claim: . .No	FRANCHISOR TRAINING/SUPPORT:
Established in 1926; . . 1st Franchised in 1983	Cash Investment: $10-12K	Financial Assistance Provided: . . . . .No
Company-Owned Units (As of 8/31/1992): . .0	Total Investment: $10-12K	Site Selection Assistance: . . . . .No
Franchised Units (As of 8/31/1992): 570	Fees: Franchise - $4K	Lease Negotiation Assistance: . . . . . .No
Total Units (As of 8/31/1992): 570	Royalty: 0%, Advert: 3%	Co-operative Advertising: . . . . .Yes
Projected New Units for 1993: 75	Contract Periods (Yrs.): 1/1	Training: . . . . .On-Going Manufacturer's
Distribution: US-0;Can-570;Overseas-0	Area Development Agreement: . .No	. . . . Training
North America: . . . . 8 Provinces	Sub-Franchise Contract: . . . . .No	On-Going Support: A,D,H/ 7
Concentration: . 340 in PQ, 142 in ON, 22 BC	Expand in Territory: . . . . . . Yes	EXPANSION PLANS:
Registered: . . . . AB	Passive Ownership: . . . . .Allowed	US: .No
. . . .	Encourage Conversions: . . . . Yes	Canada: . . . . .All Canada
Type Space: . . . . FS;~2,000+ SF	Average # Employees: . . . . . .4 FT	Overseas: . . . . No

BATTERIES PLUS

2830 N. Grandview Blvd.
Pewaukee, WI 53072
TEL: (800) 274-9155 (414) 548-9155
FAX: (414) 548-9175
Mr. Curt Mauer, Fran. Sales

BATTERIES PLUS is "America's Battery Store," providing 1,000's of batteries for 1,000's of items, serving both retail and commercial customers. The $7 billion battery market, growing 5% annually, is driven by technology and lifestyles. BATTERIES PLUS is a unique opportunity in this growth industry not yet saturated with competitors. Our turn-key program includes a unique store design, graphics, signage and product brands and proven operating methods.

HISTORY: . . . . IFA	FINANCIAL: Earnings Claim: . .No	FRANCHISOR TRAINING/SUPPORT:
Established in 1988; . . 1st Franchised in 1992	Cash Investment: $85-150K	Financial Assistance Provided: . . . Yes(I)
Company-Owned Units (As of 8/31/1992): . .5	Total Investment: $126-350K	Site Selection Assistance: . . . . . . .Yes
Franchised Units (As of 8/31/1992): 0	Fees: Franchise - $17.5K	Lease Negotiation Assistance: . . . .Yes
Total Units (As of 8/31/1992): 5	Royalty: 2-3%, Advert: 1%	Co-operative Advertising: . . . . .No
Projected New Units for 1993: 25	Contract Periods (Yrs.): 10/10	Training: . . . . 3 Wks. Headquarters,
Distribution: US-5;Can-0;Overseas-0	Area Development Agreement: Yes/3	. . . . .7 Days Franchisee Location
North America: . . . . .1 State	Sub-Franchise Contract: . . . . .No	On-Going Support: C,D,E,G,h,I/ 5
Concentration: . . . . 5 in WI	Expand in Territory: . . . . . . .No	EXPANSION PLANS:
Registered: . . . . .All	Passive Ownership: . . . . .Allowed	US: . . . . .All US
. . . .	Encourage Conversions: . . . . Yes	Canada: . . . . .No
Type Space: . . . . . . FS;~1,200-1,800 SF	Average # Employees: . . . . 2-3 FT	Overseas: . . . . No

BRAKE SHOP, THE

44899 Centre Court, # 104
Mount Clemens, MI 48044
TEL: (800) 866-2725 (313) 228-9010
FAX: (313) 228-2111
Mr. Ken Rempel, Dir. Fran. Dev.

THE BRAKE SHOP experts handle all automotive brake system repair needs. THE BRAKE SHOP, typically 1,500-4,000 SF, is located in strip malls, auto malls or free-standing units. Prior automotive experience is not required. Benefits of THE BRAKE SHOP name is focus on a single aspect of the automotive repair - brakes. The company slogan is "Our Name Says It All."

HISTORY: . . . . IFA	FINANCIAL: Earnings Claim: . .No	FRANCHISOR TRAINING/SUPPORT:
Established in 1987; . . 1st Franchised in 1989	Cash Investment: $50-60K	Financial Assistance Provided: . . . Yes(I)
Company-Owned Units (As of 8/31/1992): . .5	Total Investment: $50-80K	Site Selection Assistance: . . . . . . .Yes
Franchised Units (As of 8/31/1992): 45	Fees: Franchise - $19.5K	Lease Negotiation Assistance: . . . .Yes
Total Units (As of 8/31/1992): 50	Royalty: 8%, Advert: 4%	Co-operative Advertising: . . . . .No
Projected New Units for 1993: 100	Contract Periods (Yrs.): 10/10	Training: . . . . . 2 Wks. Corporate Office
Distribution: US-50;Can-0;Overseas-0	Area Development Agreement: . .No	. . . . Training Center, 2 Wks. On-Site
North America: . . . . 7 States	Sub-Franchise Contract: . . . . .No	On-Going Support: B,C,D,E,F,G,H,I/ . . 15
Concentration: . . .22 in MI, 12 in NJ, 8 in PA	Expand in Territory: . . . . Yes	EXPANSION PLANS:
Registered: . . . . FL,MD,MI	Passive Ownership: . . . Discouraged	US: . . . . All US
. . . .	Encourage Conversions: . . . . Yes	Canada: . . . . .Ontario
Type Space: FS, SC, Auto Mall;~1,500-4,000 SF	Average # Employees: . . . . . .3 FT	Overseas: . . . . No

CAR CHECKERS OF AMERICA

1011 Route 22 West
Bridgewater, NJ 08807
TEL: (800) 242-CHEX (908) 704-1221
FAX: (908) 704-1224
Mr. Lee Geller, VP Devel.

CAR CHECKERS OF AMERICA is a worldwide, high-tech automotive evaluation resource center. With our expertise, we are changing the gamble of dealing with a used car into an educated decision by providing these services to individuals and corporations: computerized diagnostic inspections, easy to understand reports, appraised values, limited warranties and extended service programs and on-site service through mobile evaluation centers.

HISTORY: . . . .
Established in 1986; . . 1st Franchised in 1989
Company-Owned Units (As of 8/31/1992): . .1
Franchised Units (As of 8/31/1992): 124
Total Units (As of 8/31/1992): 125
Projected New Units for 1993: 150
Distribution: US-124;Can-1;Overseas-0
 North America: . . . . . 17 States, 1 Province
 Concentration: . . . .
Registered: . . . .
 . . . .
Type Space: . . . . Home Based;~ SF

FINANCIAL: Earnings Claim: . .No
Cash Investment: $5.5K
Total Investment: $20K
Fees: Franchise - $495
 Royalty: As Used, Advert: . . . 0%
Contract Periods (Yrs.): 1
Area Development Agreement: .No
Sub-Franchise Contract: . . . . .No
Expand in Territory: . . . . . . Yes
Passive Ownership: . . . . . .Allowed
Encourage Conversions: . . . . NA
Average # Employees: . . 2 FT, 1 PT

FRANCHISOR TRAINING/SUPPORT:
Financial Assistance Provided: . . .Yes(D)
Site Selection Assistance: . . . . . . .NA
Lease Negotiation Assistance: . . . . .Yes
Co-operative Advertising: . . . . . . .NA
Training: . . . . . 2 Wks. Corporate Offices

On-Going Support: a,b,c,d,G,h,i/ 18
EXPANSION PLANS:
 US: .All US
 Canada: . . . . .All Canada
 Overseas: MX, EUR, Southeast Asia

CAR-X MUFFLER & BRAKE

8430 W. Bryn Mawr, # 400
Chicago, IL 60631
TEL: (800) 736-6733 (312) 693-1000
FAX: (312) 693-0309
Mr. Bill Olsen, Dir. Fran. Dev.

CAR-X MUFFLER and BRAKE is a retail automotive service chain, specializing in undercar services, such as exhaust systems, brakes, ride control and front-end repair.

HISTORY: . . . .
Established in 1971; . . 1st Franchised in 1973
Company-Owned Units (As of 8/31/1992): . 54
Franchised Units (As of 8/31/1992): 92
Total Units (As of 8/31/1992): 146
Projected New Units for 1993: 10
Distribution: US-146;Can-0;Overseas-0
 North America: . . . . 10 States
 Concentration: . .51 in IL, 17 in MO, 16 in WI
Registered: . . . . . . IL,IN,MN,ND,SD,WI
 . . . .
Type Space: . . . . . . Auto Malls;~4,000 SF

FINANCIAL: Earnings Claim: . .No
Cash Investment: $80-90K
Total Investment: $200K
Fees: Franchise - $18.5K
 Royalty: 5%, Advert: . . . 5-10%
Contract Periods (Yrs.): 10/5
Area Development Agreement: .No
Sub-Franchise Contract: . . . . .No
Expand in Territory: . . . . . . Yes
Passive Ownership: . . . Discouraged
Encourage Conversions: . . . . Yes
Average # Employees: . . . . .4 FT

FRANCHISOR TRAINING/SUPPORT:
Financial Assistance Provided: . . . Yes(I)
Site Selection Assistance: . . . . . . .Yes
Lease Negotiation Assistance: . . . . .Yes
Co-operative Advertising: . . . . No
Training: . . . . . . 3 Wks. Ann Arbor, MI,
 . .1 Wk. OJT, 1 Wk. HQ, 1 Wk. Opening
On-Going Support: B,C,D,E,F,G,H,I/ . . 25
EXPANSION PLANS:
 US: . . . . Midwest
 Canada: . . . . .No
 Overseas: . . . . No

CARTEX LIMITED

42816 Mound Rd.
Sterling Heights, MI 48314
TEL: (313) 739-4330
FAX: (313) 739-4331
Mr. Larry Klukowski, President

Franchisor of Fabrion fabric repair system used to repair burns, cuts and tears in automobile cloth and velour interiors. Mobile service to auto dealers and rental car agencies.

HISTORY: . . . . IFA
Established in 1988; . . 1st Franchised in 1988
Company-Owned Units (As of 8/31/1992): . .2
Franchised Units (As of 8/31/1992): 70
Total Units (As of 8/31/1992): 72
Projected New Units for 1993: 20
Distribution: US-72;Can-0;Overseas-0
 North America: . . . . 24 States
 Concentration: . . . 12 in FL, 5 in OH, 5 in TX
Registered: . . . CA,FL,IL,IN,MD,MI,MN,NY
 . . . . VA
Type Space: . . . .;~ SF

FINANCIAL: Earnings Claim: . .No
Cash Investment: $18.5K
Total Investment: $19.5K
Fees: Franchise - $18.5K
 Royalty: $240/Mo., Advert: . . 0%
Contract Periods (Yrs.): 5/5
Area Development Agreement: .No
Sub-Franchise Contract: . . . . .No
Expand in Territory: . . . . . . Yes
Passive Ownership: . . . Discouraged
Encourage Conversions: . . . . NA
Average # Employees: . . 6 FT, 1 PT

FRANCHISOR TRAINING/SUPPORT:
Financial Assistance Provided: . . . . .Yes
Site Selection Assistance: . . . . . . .NA
Lease Negotiation Assistance: . . . .NA
Co-operative Advertising: . . . . . . .NA
Training: . . . . 1 Wk. on Location in
 . . . . the Field
On-Going Support: B,C,D,G,H,I/ 5
EXPANSION PLANS:
 US: . . . . .All US
 Canada: . . . . .Yes
 Overseas: . . . . No

CERTIGARD / PETRO-CANADA

111 - 5th Ave. SW
Calgary, AB T2P 3E3 CAN
TEL: (403) 296-4259
FAX: (403) 296-3649
Mr. Steven Keith

CERTIGARD is a one-stop convenience automotive service concept, built on the belief that financial success results from trust and professionalism. It consists of a nationwide network of service bay outlets offering a sophisticated and comprehensive response system to provide customers with dependable service.

HISTORY:	FINANCIAL: Earnings Claim: . Yes	FRANCHISOR TRAINING/SUPPORT:
Established in 1973; . . 1st Franchised in 1987	Cash Investment: $80K	Financial Assistance Provided: . . . . . No
Company-Owned Units (As of 8/31/1992): . 13	Total Investment: $250K	Site Selection Assistance: . . . . . . .Yes
Franchised Units (As of 8/31/1992): 151	Fees: Franchise - $10.5K	Lease Negotiation Assistance: . . . .Yes
Total Units (As of 8/31/1992): 164	Royalty: 5%, Advert: 2%	Co-operative Advertising: . . . . . . .Yes
Projected New Units for 1993: 41	Contract Periods (Yrs.): 5/5	Training: . . . . . 5-10 Days Headquarters,
Distribution: . . . US-0;Can-164;Overseas-0	Area Development Agreement: . .No	. . . On-Going At Site Toronto/Montreal
North America: . . . . 7 Provinces	Sub-Franchise Contract: . . . . .No	On-Going Support: C,D,E,F,G,H/ 40
Concentration: . 53 in ON, 23 in BC, 23 in AB	Expand in Territory: . . . . Yes	EXPANSION PLANS:
Registered: . . . . AB	Passive Ownership: . . . Not Allowed	US: . . . . .No
. . . .	Encourage Conversions: . . . . . Yes	Canada: . . . . .All Canada
Type Space: . . Gas Sales Facil.;~500-750 SF	Average # Employees: . . 6 FT, 1 PT	Overseas: . . . . No

CHAMPION AUTO STORES

5520 N. Highway 169
New Hope, MN 55428
TEL: (800) 279-9377 (612) 535-5984
FAX:
Mr. Earl Farr, Dir. Fran.

CHAMPION AUTO STORES are retailers, selling auto parts and accessories to the "do-it-yourself" segment of the auto aftermarket, providing the right parts, right prices and the right answers. Extensive support is provided during development and operation of a new location.

HISTORY: . . . . IFA	FINANCIAL: Earnings Claim: . Yes	FRANCHISOR TRAINING/SUPPORT:
Established in 1956; . . 1st Franchised in 1961	Cash Investment: $90-130K	Financial Assistance Provided: . . . Yes(I)
Company-Owned Units (As of 8/31/1992): . 42	Total Investment: $180-260K	Site Selection Assistance: . . . . . . .Yes
Franchised Units (As of 8/31/1992): 138	Fees: Franchise - $20K	Lease Negotiation Assistance: . . . . .Yes
Total Units (As of 8/31/1992): 180	Royalty: 5%, Advert: 4%	Co-operative Advertising: . . . . . . .Yes
Projected New Units for 1993: 20	Contract Periods (Yrs.): 10/10	Training: . . . . 6 Days HQ, 175 Hrs. Min.
Distribution: . . . US-180;Can-0;Overseas-0	Area Development Agreement: . .No	. . . . Corp. Store, 5 Days Post-Opening
North America: . . . . 9 States	Sub-Franchise Contract: . . . . .No	On-Going Support: A,B,C,D,E,F,G,H,I/ 99
Concentration: . 66 in MN, 16 in CO, 16 in NE	Expand in Territory: . . . . . . .No	EXPANSION PLANS:
Registered: . . . . IL,IN,MI,MN,ND,SD,WI	Passive Ownership: . . . Discouraged	US: . . . . .Midwest, N. Central, Rockies
. . . .	Encourage Conversions: . . . . .No	Canada: . . . . .No
Type Space: . . . . SF;~4,000 SF	Average # Employees: . . 3 FT, 4 PT	Overseas: . . . . No

COTTMAN TRANSMISSION SYSTEMS

240 New York Dr.
Fort Washington, PA 19034
TEL: (800) 233-5515 (215) 643-5885 C
FAX: (215) 643-2519
Mr. Joe Sanfellipo, Dir. Fran. Dev.

Automotive transmission service centers with national network. As the second largest chain in the industry, we are a market leader with many new opportunities in major markets as a result of our new expansion plan developed to capitalize on the changes in the industry.

HISTORY: . . . . IFA	FINANCIAL: Earnings Claim: . .No	FRANCHISOR TRAINING/SUPPORT:
Established in 1962; . . 1st Franchised in 1964	Cash Investment: $35-40K	Financial Assistance Provided: . . . Yes(I)
Company-Owned Units (As of 8/31/1992): . .4	Total Investment: $97.5K	Site Selection Assistance: . . . . . . .Yes
Franchised Units (As of 8/31/1992): 142	Fees: Franchise - $22.5K	Lease Negotiation Assistance: . . . . .Yes
Total Units (As of 8/31/1992): 146	Royalty: 7.5%, Advert: . . . Varies	Co-operative Advertising: . . . . . . .Yes
Projected New Units for 1993: 13	Contract Periods (Yrs.): 15/15	Training: . . . . 3 Wks. Headquarters,
Distribution: . . . US-145;Can-1;Overseas-0	Area Development Agreement: Yes/5	. . . . .1 Wk. On-Site
North America: . . . . . 19 States, 1 Province	Sub-Franchise Contract: . . . . .No	On-Going Support: C,D,E,G,H,I/ 36
Concentration: . . 30 in PA, 28 in MI, 19 in NJ	Expand in Territory: . . . . . . Yes	EXPANSION PLANS:
Registered: . . . CA,FL,IL,IN,MD,MI,MN,NY	Passive Ownership: . . . Discouraged	US: . . . . All US
. . . . ND,RI,VA,DC	Encourage Conversions: . . . . . Yes	Canada: . . . . .No
Type Space: . . FS, SC, Auto Mall;~3,000 SF	Average # Employees: . . . . . .4 FT	Overseas: . . . . No

DENT DOCTOR

7708 Cantrell Rd.
Little Rock, AR 72207
TEL: (800) 946-3368 (501) 224-0500
FAX: (501) 224-0507
Mr. Tom Harris, Fran. Sales Dir.

Professional, paintless, minor dent removal service on a mobile basis for automobile dealerships. Minor dents, door dings and hail damage removed with No Painting. Successful system proven in the marketplace since 1986. DENT DOCTOR is the industry leader, committed to franchisee success.

HISTORY:	IFA
Established in 1986;	1st Franchised in 1990
Company-Owned Units (As of 8/31/1992):	7
Franchised Units (As of 8/31/1992):	35
Total Units (As of 8/31/1992):	42
Projected New Units for 1993:	6
Distribution:	US-42;Can-0;Overseas-0
North America:	12 States
Concentration:	6 in TX, 3 in AR, 3 in CO
Registered:	
Type Space:	;~ SF

FINANCIAL: Earnings Claim:	No
Cash Investment:	$29K
Total Investment:	$49K
Fees: Franchise -	$29.5K
Royalty: 6%, Advert:	0%
Contract Periods (Yrs.):	10/10
Area Development Agreement:	No
Sub-Franchise Contract:	No
Expand in Territory:	Yes
Passive Ownership:	Allowed
Encourage Conversions:	NA
Average # Employees:	1 FT

FRANCHISOR TRAINING/SUPPORT:	
Financial Assistance Provided:	No
Site Selection Assistance:	Yes
Lease Negotiation Assistance:	Yes
Co-operative Advertising:	Yes
Training:	8 Wks. Headquarters
On-Going Support: a,b,C,D,E,F,G,H,I/	9
EXPANSION PLANS:	
US:	All US
Canada:	No
Overseas:	No

DETAIL PLUS CAR APPEARANCE CENTERS

P. O. Box 591
Clackamas, OR 97015
TEL: (800) 284-0123 (503) 656-8286
FAX: (503) 656-8553
Mr. Bud Abraham, President

DETAIL PLUS CAR APPEARANCE CENTERS offers a high-tech, professional facility that provides a wide selection of auto detail services, including automatic car washing, engine cleaning, interior shampoo, buff and wax, etc. The company provides everything - equipment, accessories, chemicals, training and management systems.

HISTORY:	
Established in 1982;	1st Franchised in 1982
Company-Owned Units (As of 8/31/1992):	2
Franchised Units (As of 8/31/1992):	200
Total Units (As of 8/31/1992):	202
Projected New Units for 1993:	25
Distribution:	US-125;Can-6;Overseas-19
North America:	15 States, 5 Provinces
Concentration:	10 in CA, 5 in PA, 3 in ON
Registered:	AB
Type Space:	FS, SC;~2,500 SF

FINANCIAL: Earnings Claim:	No
Cash Investment:	$25-100K
Total Investment:	$75K-1.0MM
Fees: Franchise -	$0
Royalty: 0%, Advert:	0%
Contract Periods (Yrs.):	Varies
Area Development Agreement:	Yes/Var
Sub-Franchise Contract:	Yes
Expand in Territory:	Yes
Passive Ownership:	Discouraged
Encourage Conversions:	Yes
Average # Employees:	3 FT, 3 PT

FRANCHISOR TRAINING/SUPPORT:	
Financial Assistance Provided:	Yes(I)
Site Selection Assistance:	Yes
Lease Negotiation Assistance:	NA
Co-operative Advertising:	NA
Training:	1-2 Wks. On-Site
On-Going Support: b,C,D,E,F,h,I/	15
EXPANSION PLANS:	
US:	All US
Canada:	All Canada
Overseas:	All Exc. Saudi Arabia

DORAN'S TIRE & ALIGNMENT

P. O. Box 83009
Baton Rouge, LA 70884
TEL: (504) 928-8989
FAX: (504) 344-4848
Mr. Ronnie Doran, President

DORAN'S TIRE AND ALIGNMENT is a retail automotive repair center, specializing in tires, alignments, front-end repairs, brakes, shocks and minor mechanical repairs, such as oil changes, fluids, belts, hoses, tune-ups and batteries. We offer our customers convenient one-day service and 90 days interest-free financing on all products and services.

HISTORY:	
Established in 1974;	1st Franchised in 1991
Company-Owned Units (As of 8/31/1992):	0
Franchised Units (As of 8/31/1992):	3
Total Units (As of 8/31/1992):	3
Projected New Units for 1993:	3
Distribution:	US-3;Can-0;Overseas-0
North America:	1 State
Concentration:	3 in LA
Registered:	FL
Type Space:	FS, SC, RM;~3,500 SF

FINANCIAL: Earnings Claim:	No
Cash Investment:	$25-40K
Total Investment:	$95-275K
Fees: Franchise -	$10K
Royalty: 5%, Advert:	2.5%
Contract Periods (Yrs.):	10/5
Area Development Agreement:	No
Sub-Franchise Contract:	No
Expand in Territory:	Yes
Passive Ownership:	Discouraged
Encourage Conversions:	Yes
Average # Employees:	5 FT

FRANCHISOR TRAINING/SUPPORT:	
Financial Assistance Provided:	Yes(I)
Site Selection Assistance:	Yes
Lease Negotiation Assistance:	Yes
Co-operative Advertising:	Yes
Training:	1 Wk. Franchisee Location
On-Going Support: C,D,E,F/	1
EXPANSION PLANS:	
US:	Southeast
Canada:	No
Overseas:	No

DR. NICK'S TRANSMISSIONS

64 Enter Ln.
Hauppauge, NY 11788
TEL: (516) 232-1919
FAX:
Mr. Nicholas Costa, Sales Director

Transmission service centers, providing quality repairs to all types of auto and light-duty commercial vehicles in both the retail and wholesale trade.

HISTORY:	FINANCIAL: Earnings Claim: . .No	FRANCHISOR TRAINING/SUPPORT:
Established in 1971; . . 1st Franchised in 1977	Cash Investment: $35-45K	Financial Assistance Provided: . . . Yes(I)
Company-Owned Units (As of 8/31/1992): . .1	Total Investment: $75-85K	Site Selection Assistance: . . . . . . .Yes
Franchised Units (As of 8/31/1992): 36	Fees: Franchise - $21.5K	Lease Negotiation Assistance: . . . . .Yes
Total Units (As of 8/31/1992): 37	Royalty: 7%, Advert: . . . . Flat	Co-operative Advertising: . . . . . . .Yes
Projected New Units for 1993: 3	Contract Periods (Yrs.): 15/15	Training: . . . . 2 Wks. Headquarters,
Distribution: US-37;Can-0;Overseas-0	Area Development Agreement: . .No	. . . . 2 Wks. On-Site, On-Going
North America: . . . . 5 States	Sub-Franchise Contract: . . . . .No	On-Going Support: A,C,D,E,F,G,H,I/ . .6
Concentration: . . .18 in NY, 5 in MA, 4 in NJ	Expand in Territory: . . . . Yes	EXPANSION PLANS:
Registered: . . . . .FL,NY,RI	Passive Ownership: . . . Not Allowed	US: . . . . Northeast
. . . .	Encourage Conversions: . . . . . Yes	Canada: . . . . .No
Type Space: . . . . FS;~3,000 SF	Average # Employees: . . . . . .4 FT	Overseas: . . . . No

ECONO LUBE N' TUNE

2402 Michelson Dr., # 200
Irvine, CA 92715
TEL: (800) 628-0253CA (800) 327-4802
FAX: (714) 852-6688
Mr. David Wisok, dir. Fran. Sales

Turn-key franchise opportunity, specializing in automotive aftermarket services. We feature Multi-Service menu including: lube/oil, tune-up, brakes, emission control and minor repairs. Custom, free-standing 5- or 6-bay buildings in high-traffic/growth areas.

HISTORY:	FINANCIAL: Earnings Claim: . .No	FRANCHISOR TRAINING/SUPPORT:
Established in 1973; . . 1st Franchised in 1978	Cash Investment: $85-115K	Financial Assistance Provided: . . .Yes(D)
Company-Owned Units (As of 8/31/1992): . 51	Total Investment: $190-210K	Site Selection Assistance: . . . . . . .Yes
Franchised Units (As of 8/31/1992): 132	Fees: Franchise - $79.5K	Lease Negotiation Assistance: . . . . .Yes
Total Units (As of 8/31/1992): 183	Royalty: 6%, Advert: . . . . 3+5%	Co-operative Advertising: . . . . . . .Yes
Projected New Units for 1993: 20	Contract Periods (Yrs.): 15/5	Training: . . . . 2 Wks. Headquarters,
Distribution: US-183;Can-0;Overseas-0	Area Development Agreement: . .No	. . . . 2 Wks. On-Site
North America: . . . . 11 States	Sub-Franchise Contract: . . . . .No	On-Going Support: B,C,D,E,F/ 60
Concentration: . . . . .118 in CA	Expand in Territory: . . . . . . .No	EXPANSION PLANS:
Registered: . . . . CA,MD,VA,WA	Passive Ownership: . . . Not Allowed	US: . . . . .All US
. . . .	Encourage Conversions: . . . . . .No	Canada: . . . . .No
Type Space: . . . . FS;~ SF	Average # Employees: . . . . 4-5 FT	Overseas: . . . . No

EXPRESS OIL CHANGE

P. O. Box 19968
Birmingham, AL 35219
TEL: (205) 945-1771
FAX: (205) 940-6025
Mr. Robert T. Daniel, EVP

A fast automobile maintenance store, designed to provide 4 quality services: 1) 10 Minute Express Oil Change; 2) 20 Minute Express Transmission Service; 3) 30 Minute Express Tune-Up; 4) 60 Minute Express Brake Service.

HISTORY:	FINANCIAL: Earnings Claim: . .No	FRANCHISOR TRAINING/SUPPORT:
Established in 1979; . . 1st Franchised in 1983	Cash Investment: $80.5-147.5K	Financial Assistance Provided: . . . . .No
Company-Owned Units (As of 8/31/1992): . 10	Total Investment: $135-385K	Site Selection Assistance: . . . . . . No
Franchised Units (As of 8/31/1992): 22	Fees: Franchise - $10K	Lease Negotiation Assistance: . . . . . No
Total Units (As of 8/31/1992): 32	Royalty: 5%, Advert: 3%	Co-operative Advertising: . . . . . . .Yes
Projected New Units for 1993: 6	Contract Periods (Yrs.): 10/10	Training: . . . . 2 Wks. Headquarters,
Distribution: US-32;Can-0;Overseas-0	Area Development Agreement: . Yes	. . . . .1 Wk. On-Site
North America: . . . . 2 States	Sub-Franchise Contract: . . . . .No	On-Going Support: B,C,D,E,G,H/ . . .99
Concentration: . . . . 30 in AL, 2 in SC	Expand in Territory: . . . . . . .No	EXPANSION PLANS:
Registered: . . . . .FL	Passive Ownership: . . . Discouraged	US: . . . . Southeast
. . . .	Encourage Conversions: . . . . Yes	Canada: . . . . No
Type Space: . . . . . . FS;~3,000-4,000 SF	Average # Employees: . . . . . .6 FT	Overseas: . . . . No

GAS TANK RENU-USA

12727 Greenfield
Detroit, MI 48227
TEL: (800) 932-2766 (313) 837-6122
FAX: (313) 273-4759
Mr. Dan Sullivan, Managing Partner

A patented process for the repair of all fuel tanks.

HISTORY:	FINANCIAL: Earnings Claim: . .No	FRANCHISOR TRAINING/SUPPORT:
Established in 1987; . . 1st Franchised in 1987	Cash Investment: $10-15K	Financial Assistance Provided: . . . Yes(I)
Company-Owned Units (As of 8/31/1992): . .0	Total Investment: $20-50K	Site Selection Assistance: . . . . . . .Yes
Franchised Units (As of 8/31/1992): 67	Fees: Franchise - $9-25K	Lease Negotiation Assistance: . . . . .NA
Total Units (As of 8/31/1992): 67	Royalty: 0%, Advert: 0%	Co-operative Advertising: . . . . . . .Yes
Projected New Units for 1993: 6	Contract Periods (Yrs.): 10/10	Training: . . . . .Franchisee Location
Distribution: US-34;Can-33;Overseas-0	Area Development Agreement: . .No	. . . .
North America: . . . . 11 States, 9 Provinces	Sub-Franchise Contract: . . . . . Yes	On-Going Support: C,D,E,G,H,I/ 5
Concentration: . .11 in MI, 10 in ON, 10 in PQ	Expand in Territory: . . . . Yes	EXPANSION PLANS:
Registered: . . . . . . .IL,IN,MI,MN,NY,WI	Passive Ownership: . . . Discouraged	US: . . . . Midwest, Northeast
. . . .	Encourage Conversions: . . . . . NA	Canada: . . . . .All Canada
Type Space: . . . . FS;~1,500 SF	Average # Employees: . . 2 FT, 1 PT	Overseas: . . . .S. America, Israel, Others

GREASE MONKEY INTERNATIONAL

216 16th St. Mall, # 1100
Denver, CO 80202
TEL: (800) 822-7706 (303) 534-1660
FAX: (303) 534-2906
Mr. Roger D. Auker, Dir. Fran. Dev.

Currently ranked fourth in size in the overall quick-lube industry, GREASE MONKEY INTERNATIONAL is the largest quick lube franchise organization not owned by a major oil company. With our vision focused solely on becoming the most successful franchised quick-lube company in the business, GREASE MONKEY is targeting to expand its number of centers by 20% in 1992-1993.

HISTORY:	FINANCIAL: Earnings Claim: . . .	FRANCHISOR TRAINING/SUPPORT:
Established in 1978; . . 1st Franchised in 1979	Cash Investment: $80K	Financial Assistance Provided: . . . Yes(I)
Company-Owned Units (As of 8/31/1992): . 31	Total Investment: $100-125K	Site Selection Assistance: . . . . . . .Yes
Franchised Units (As of 8/31/1992): 160	Fees: Franchise - $28K	Lease Negotiation Assistance: . . . . .Yes
Total Units (As of 8/31/1992): 191	Royalty: 5%, Advert: 1%	Co-operative Advertising: . . . . . . .Yes
Projected New Units for 1993: 34	Contract Periods (Yrs.): 15/15	Training: . . . . 1 Wk. Headquarters
Distribution: US-191;Can-0;Overseas-0	Area Development Agreement: Yes/4	. . . .
North America: . . . . 33 States	Sub-Franchise Contract: . . . . .No	On-Going Support: B,C,D,E,F,G,H,I/ . . 46
Concentration: . 42 in CO, 13 in OH, 12 in CA	Expand in Territory: . . . . Yes	EXPANSION PLANS:
Registered: . . . . .All	Passive Ownership: . . . Discouraged	US: . . . . All US
. . . .	Encourage Conversions: . . . . . Yes	Canada: . . . . .No
Type Space: . . . . FS;~10,000 SF	Average # Employees: . . . . . .6 FT	Overseas: . . . . .MX

GUARANTEED TUNE UP

101 Eisenhower Pkwy.
Roseland, NJ 07068
TEL: (800) 543-5829 (201) 403-1996 C
FAX: (201) 226-3096
Mr.Thomas J. Michaels, Dir. Mktg.

Although we specialize in automotive tune-ups for $59.88, with a 6 month/6,000 mile guarantee, we allow our franchisees to perform all automotive repairs, such as brakes, engine repairs, etc., thereby increasing their cash flow and sales volume.

HISTORY: . . . . IFA	FINANCIAL: Earnings Claim: . .No	FRANCHISOR TRAINING/SUPPORT:
Established in 1983; . . 1st Franchised in 1984	Cash Investment: $35K	Financial Assistance Provided: . . . Yes(I)
Company-Owned Units (As of 8/31/1992): . .1	Total Investment: $85-115K	Site Selection Assistance: . . . . . . .Yes
Franchised Units (As of 8/31/1992): 18	Fees: Franchise - $15K	Lease Negotiation Assistance: . . . . .Yes
Total Units (As of 8/31/1992): 19	Royalty: 6%, Advert: 3%	Co-operative Advertising: . . . . . . .Yes
Projected New Units for 1993: 30	Contract Periods (Yrs.): 10/10	Training: . . . . 1 Wk. New Jersey,
Distribution: US-19;Can-0;Overseas-0	Area Development Agreement: Yes/10	. . . . 1 Wk. Local Franchisor
North America: . . . . 6 States	Sub-Franchise Contract: . . . . . Yes	On-Going Support: B,C,D,E,F,H/ 5
Concentration: . . . 10 in NJ, 2 in NC, 1 in NY	Expand in Territory: . . . . Yes	EXPANSION PLANS:
Registered: . . . . CA,FL,MN,NY,RI,VA	Passive Ownership: . . . . . .Allowed	US: . . . . All US
. . . .	Encourage Conversions: . . . . . Yes	Canada: . . . . .All Canada
Type Space: . . . . FS;~2,400 SF	Average # Employees: . . . . . .5 FT	Overseas: EUR, Pacific Rim, C & S Amer

INDY LUBE 10-MINUTE OIL CHANGE

6505 East 82nd St., # 209
Indianapolis, IN 46250
TEL: (800) 326-LUBE (317) 845-9444
FAX: (317) 577-3169
Mr. Jim R. Sapp, President

INDY LUBE 10-MINUTE OIL CHANGE specializes in fluid maintenance of both passenger and light industrial vehicles. Each INDY LUBE facility is up-scale, with a spacious reception room with television, wallpaper and courtesy telephone. The INDY LUBE full-service oil change includes a 15-point safety and fluid check. Each center also has a point-of-sale computer system, which was the first in Indiana.

HISTORY: . . . .
Established in 1986; . . 1st Franchised in 1989
Company-Owned Units (As of 8/31/1992): . .9
Franchised Units (As of 8/31/1992): 5
Total Units (As of 8/31/1992): 14
Projected New Units for 1993: 6
Distribution: US-14;Can-0;Overseas-0
  North America: . . . . .1 State
  Concentration: . . . . 14 in IN
Registered: . . . . IN
. . . .
Type Space: . . . . FS;~2,100 SF

FINANCIAL: Earnings Claim: . .No
Cash Investment: $100K
Total Investment: $350K
Fees: Franchise - $18K
  Royalty: 5%, Advert: 2%
Contract Periods (Yrs.): 20/5
Area Development Agreement: . Yes
Sub-Franchise Contract: . . . . .No
Expand in Territory: . . . . . . Yes
Passive Ownership: . . . Discouraged
Encourage Conversions: . . . . .No
Average # Employees: . . 6 FT, 2 PT

FRANCHISOR TRAINING/SUPPORT:
Financial Assistance Provided: . . . Yes(I)
Site Selection Assistance: . . . . . . .Yes
Lease Negotiation Assistance: . . . . .Yes
Co-operative Advertising: . . . . . . .Yes
Training: . . . . . . 2-3 Wks. Headquarters
. . . .
On-Going Support: B,C,D,E,F,G,H,I/ . . . 7
EXPANSION PLANS:
US: . . . . Midwest and East
Canada: . . . . No
Overseas: . . . . No

INTERNATIONAL FLYING COLORS

10696 Haddington Dr., # 130
Houston, TX 77043
TEL: (800) 232-1244 (713) 683-9900 C
FAX: (713) 932-1898
Mr. Benjamin Litalien, President

Premier provider of mobile automotive touch-up painting, featuring the patented FLYING COLORS Process. Franchise support includes complete mobile unit built-out, 800 Hotline, newsletters and technical bulletins, annual convention, proprietary chemicals and formal reports.

HISTORY: . . . . IFA
Established in 1985; . . 1st Franchised in 1986
Company-Owned Units (As of 8/31/1992): . .3
Franchised Units (As of 8/31/1992): 63
Total Units (As of 8/31/1992): 66
Projected New Units for 1993: 15
Distribution: US-65;Can-1;Overseas-0
  North America: . . . . 15 States, 1 Province
  Concentration: . . .23 in TX, 8 in GA, 5 in CO
Registered: . . . . WA
. . . .
Type Space: . . . . . . .Home Based;~NA SF

FINANCIAL: Earnings Claim: . .No
Cash Investment: $5-10K
Total Investment: $26-30K
Fees: Franchise - $7.5K
  Royalty: 6%, Advert: 0%
Contract Periods (Yrs.): 4/4
Area Development Agreement: . .No
Sub-Franchise Contract: . . . . .No
Expand in Territory: . . . . . . Yes
Passive Ownership: . . . . . .Allowed
Encourage Conversions: . . . . .No
Average # Employees: . . . . 1-2 FT

FRANCHISOR TRAINING/SUPPORT:
Financial Assistance Provided: . . . Yes(I)
Site Selection Assistance: . . . . . . .Yes
Lease Negotiation Assistance: . . . .NA
Co-operative Advertising: . . . . . . .Yes
Training: . . . . .1 Wk. Headquarters,
. . . . . . 10-14 Days Franchisee Area
On-Going Support: b,C,D,E,G,h,I/ 8
EXPANSION PLANS:
US: . . . .NW, W, Central and Midwest
Canada: . . . . All Exc. Alberta
Overseas: . . . . Yes

J. D. BYRIDER SYSTEMS

1640 W. Factory Ave.
Marion, IN 46952
TEL: (317) 668-4643 C
FAX: (317) 668-1546
Mr. Steve Sobalvarro, Fran. Dev. Mgr.

We are the only franchisor in an $80 billion retail market (used cars). We are in the "Dealer Carried Finance" business. Our franchisees finance marginal credit customers to provide them with dependable transportation at affordable terms. By doing this, we help them establish/reestablish their credit by reporting to the major credit bureaus.

HISTORY: . . . . IFA
Established in 1978; . . 1st Franchised in 1989
Company-Owned Units (As of 8/31/1992): . .1
Franchised Units (As of 8/31/1992): 41
Total Units (As of 8/31/1992): 42
Projected New Units for 1993: 72
Distribution: US-41;Can-1;Overseas-0
  North America: . . . . . 19 States, 1 Province
  Concentration: . . . .6 in IN, 5 in OH, 4 in TN
Registered: . . . . .All
. . . .
Type Space: . . . . FS;~2,000 SF

FINANCIAL: Earnings Claim: . Yes
Cash Investment: $29-500K
Total Investment: . . .$29K-1.0MM
Fees: Franchise - $29K
  Royalty: 3%, Advert: 2%
Contract Periods (Yrs.): 7/7
Area Development Agreement: . Yes
Sub-Franchise Contract: . . . . Yes
Expand in Territory: . . . . . . Yes
Passive Ownership: . . . Discouraged
Encourage Conversions: . . . . Yes
Average # Employees: . 3 FT, 1-2 PT

FRANCHISOR TRAINING/SUPPORT:
Financial Assistance Provided: . . . Yes(I)
Site Selection Assistance: . . . . . . .Yes
Lease Negotiation Assistance: . . . . .Yes
Co-operative Advertising: . . . . . . .Yes
Training: . . . .7 Courses HQ, Up to 2 Wks
. . . . . On-Site, Every 45 Days at Site
On-Going Support: B,E,G,H,I/ 42
EXPANSION PLANS:
US: . . . . IN, OH, IL, MI and KY
Canada: . . . . .All Canada
Overseas: . . . . No

JIFFY LUBE INTERNATIONAL

P. O. Box 2967
Houston, TX 77252
TEL: (800) 327-9532 (713) 546-4100
FAX: (713) 546-8484
Ms. Carolyn Foster, Dir. Public Affairs

Automotive fluid specialists, providing preventive maintenance for your car's vital fluids. We offer the consumer quality and convenience at a competitive price.

HISTORY: . . . . IFA	FINANCIAL: Earnings Claim: . .No	FRANCHISOR TRAINING/SUPPORT:
Established in 1979; . . 1st Franchised in 1979	Cash Investment: $100K	Financial Assistance Provided: . . . Yes(I)
Company-Owned Units (As of 8/31/1992): 367	Total Investment: $158-164K	Site Selection Assistance: . . . . . . .Yes
Franchised Units (As of 8/31/1992): 678	Fees: Franchise - $35K	Lease Negotiation Assistance: . . . . .Yes
Total Units (As of 8/31/1992): 1045	Royalty: 5%, Advert: 5%	Co-operative Advertising: . . . . . . .Yes
Projected New Units for 1993: 50	Contract Periods (Yrs.): 20	Training: . . . . .1 Wk. Class, 2 Wks.
Distribution: US-1045;Can-0;Overseas-0	Area Development Agreement: . .No	. . . . in a Unit
North America: . . . . 48 States	Sub-Franchise Contract: . . . . .No	On-Going Support: B,C,D,E,G,H,I/ . . . . .
Concentration: . . .108 in CA, 97 in TX, 70 IL	Expand in Territory: . . . . . . Yes	EXPANSION PLANS:
Registered: . . . . All States	Passive Ownership: . . . Discouraged	US: . . . . All US
. . . .	Encourage Conversions: . . . . Yes	Canada: . . . . .No
Type Space: . . . . . . FS;~9,000-15,000 SF	Average # Employees: . . 7 FT, 3 PT	Overseas: . . . . .Yes

KENNEDY TRANSMISSION

410 Gateway Blvd.
Burnsville, MN 55337
TEL: (612) 894-7020
FAX: (612) 894-1849
Mr. Andrew Hammond, President

KENNEDY TRANSMISSION is a 30-year old company, providing service and repair of automobile and light truck transmissions and drive line components. We practice a "low pressure" sales technique that permits the customer to trust us while we help them. Low entry cost. Technical experience very helpful.

HISTORY:	FINANCIAL: Earnings Claim: . .No	FRANCHISOR TRAINING/SUPPORT:
Established in 1962; . . 1st Franchised in 1975	Cash Investment: $40-50K	Financial Assistance Provided: . . . Yes(I)
Company-Owned Units (As of 8/31/1992): . .1	Total Investment: $90-125K	Site Selection Assistance: . . . . . . .Yes
Franchised Units (As of 8/31/1992): 15	Fees: Franchise - $17.5K	Lease Negotiation Assistance: . . . .Yes
Total Units (As of 8/31/1992): 16	Royalty: 6%, Advert: . . . . Varies	Co-operative Advertising: . . . . . . .Yes
Projected New Units for 1993: 4	Contract Periods (Yrs.): . . . 15/10	Training: . . . . 2 Wks. Headquarters
Distribution: US-16;Can-0;Overseas-0	Area Development Agreement: Yes/15	. . . .
North America: . . . . 3 States	Sub-Franchise Contract: . . . . . .No	On-Going Support: C,D,E,G,H/ 4
Concentration: . . 14 in MN, 1 in ND, 1 in WI	Expand in Territory: . . . . . . Yes	EXPANSION PLANS:
Registered: . . . . MN,ND,WI	Passive Ownership: . . . Discouraged	US: . . . . Upper Midwest
. . . .	Encourage Conversions: . . . . . Yes	Canada: . . . . .No
Type Space: .FS, Auto Malls;~2,600-3,000 SF	Average # Employees: . . . . . .3 FT	Overseas: . . . . No

KING BEAR AUTO SERVICE CENTERS

1390 Jerusalem Ave.
North Merrick, NY 11566
TEL: (516) 483-3500
FAX: (516) 483-0615
Mr. Frank Garton, Dir. Fran./RE

KING BEAR AUTO SERVICE CENTERS, specializing in automotive repairs and sales, general auto repairs. All work performed by our specially-trained mechanics. Franchisees are not required to have any automotive backgrounds, but must have some sales or managerial experience.

HISTORY: . . . . IFA	FINANCIAL: Earnings Claim: . .No	FRANCHISOR TRAINING/SUPPORT:
Established in 1973; . . . 1st Franchised in 1974	Cash Investment: $30-45K	Financial Assistance Provided: . . . Yes(I)
Company-Owned Units (As of 8/31/1992): . .0	Total Investment: $135K	Site Selection Assistance: . . . . . . .Yes
Franchised Units (As of 8/31/1992): 62	Fees: Franchise - $25K	Lease Negotiation Assistance: . . . .Yes
Total Units (As of 8/31/1992): 62	Royalty: 5%, Advert: 7%	Co-operative Advertising: . . . . .No
Projected New Units for 1993: 4	Contract Periods (Yrs.): . . 15/10/10	Training: . . . . 2 Wks. Headquarters
Distribution: US-62;Can-0;Overseas-0	Area Development Agreement: Yes/15	. . . .
North America: . . . . 2 States	Sub-Franchise Contract: . . . . . Yes	On-Going Support: C,D,E,F,H/ 5
Concentration: . . . . . . .39 in NY, 23 in CA	Expand in Territory: . . . . . . Yes	EXPANSION PLANS:
Registered: . . . . CA,NY	Passive Ownership: . . . . . .Allowed	US: . . . . Northeast
. . . .	Encourage Conversions: . . . . Yes	Canada: . . . . .No
Type Space: . . . . FS;~3,000 SF	Average # Employees: . . 4 FT, 1 PT	Overseas: . . . . . . Eastern Europe

LEE MYLES TRANSMISSIONS

25 E. Spring Valley Ave.
Maywood, NJ 07607
TEL: (800) LEE-MYLE (201) 843-3200
FAX: (201) 843-7706
Ms. Sandi Greenberg, Fran. Sales

LEE MYLES automotive transmission service and repair. Operational, administrative and sales support systems. Lowest weekly franchise fees - 6%. Amongst the lowest license fee - $20,000. Business format franchisor. Automotive after-market repair business.

HISTORY: . . . . IFA	FINANCIAL: Earnings Claim: . .No	FRANCHISOR TRAINING/SUPPORT:
Established in 1947; . . 1st Franchised in 1964	Cash Investment: $106K	Financial Assistance Provided: . . . Yes(I)
Company-Owned Units (As of 8/31/1992): . .1	Total Investment: $106K	Site Selection Assistance: . . . . . . .Yes
Franchised Units (As of 8/31/1992): 101	Fees: Franchise - $20K	Lease Negotiation Assistance: . . . . .Yes
Total Units (As of 8/31/1992): 102	Royalty: 6%, Advert: . . . . Varies	Co-operative Advertising: . . . . . . .Yes
Projected New Units for 1993:	Contract Periods (Yrs.): 15/15	Training: . . . . 2 Wks. Headquarters
Distribution: US-102;Can-0;Overseas-0	Area Development Agreement: Yes/15	. . . .
North America: . . . . 5 States	Sub-Franchise Contract: . . . . . Yes	On-Going Support: A,C,D,E,F,G,H,I/ . 28
Concentration: . . 48 in NY, 28 in NE, 7 in AZ	Expand in Territory: . . . . Yes	EXPANSION PLANS:
Registered: . . . . .FL,NY,RI	Passive Ownership: . . . Discouraged	US: . . . . East Coast, Arizona
. . . .	Encourage Conversions: . . . . Yes	Canada: . . . . .No
Type Space: . . . . ;~ SF	Average # Employees: . . 1 FT, 3 PT	Overseas: . . . . No

LENTZ U.S.A. SERVICE CENTER

1001 Riverview Dr.
Kalamazoo, MI 49001
TEL: (800) 354-2131 (616) 342-2200
FAX: (616) 342-9461
Mr. Gordon Lentz, President

Automotive services - specializing in exhaust systems, braking systems, suspension systems and front-end work.

HISTORY: . . . . IFA	FINANCIAL: Earnings Claim: . .No	FRANCHISOR TRAINING/SUPPORT:
Established in 1983; . . 1st Franchised in 1986	Cash Investment: $35-50K	Financial Assistance Provided: . . . Yes(I)
Company-Owned Units (As of 8/31/1992): . 11	Total Investment: . . . . $60-80K+RE	Site Selection Assistance: . . . . . . .Yes
Franchised Units (As of 8/31/1992): 9	Fees: Franchise - $18.5K	Lease Negotiation Assistance: . . . . .Yes
Total Units (As of 8/31/1992): 20	Royalty: Varies, Advert: 5%	Co-operative Advertising: . . . . . . .Yes
Projected New Units for 1993: 10	Contract Periods (Yrs.): 15/15	Training: . . . . 2 Wks. Headquarters
Distribution: US-20;Can-0;Overseas-0	Area Development Agreement: . Yes	. . . .
North America: . . . . 3 States	Sub-Franchise Contract: . . . . . .No	On-Going Support: C,D,E,F,H,I/ 53
Concentration: . . . . 17 in MI, 2 in IL, 1 in IN	Expand in Territory: . . . . Yes	EXPANSION PLANS:
Registered: . . . . .MI	Passive Ownership: . . . Discouraged	US: . . . . .Northwest
. . . .	Encourage Conversions: . . . . Yes	Canada: . . . . .No
Type Space: . . . . .FS, SC;~3,200 SF	Average # Employees: . . 4 FT, 1 PT	Overseas: . . . . No

LUBE FACTORY, THE

1180 Stellar, # 10
Newmarket, ON L3Y 7B9 CAN
TEL: (416) 898-3590
FAX: (416) 853-3590
Mr. Jack Petrie, VP Corp. Dev.

Automobile and light truck lubrication centres.

HISTORY:	FINANCIAL: Earnings Claim: . Yes	FRANCHISOR TRAINING/SUPPORT:
Established in 1980; . . 1st Franchised in 1983	Cash Investment: $80K	Financial Assistance Provided: . . . Yes(I)
Company-Owned Units (As of 8/31/1992): . .2	Total Investment: $140K	Site Selection Assistance: . . . . . . .Yes
Franchised Units (As of 8/31/1992): 16	Fees: Franchise - $20K	Lease Negotiation Assistance: . . . . .Yes
Total Units (As of 8/31/1992): 18	Royalty: 7%, Advert: 2%	Co-operative Advertising: . . . . . . .Yes
Projected New Units for 1993: 34	Contract Periods (Yrs.): 10/5	Training: . . . . . . .1 Wk. Headquarters,
Distribution: US-0;Can-18;Overseas-0	Area Development Agreement: Yes/20	. . .1-2 Wks. On-Site, On-Going Support
North America: . . . . .1 Province	Sub-Franchise Contract: . . . . . Yes	On-Going Support: a,B,C,D,E,F,H/ 2
Concentration: . . . . 18 in ON	Expand in Territory: . . . . Yes	EXPANSION PLANS:
Registered:	Passive Ownership: . . . Discouraged	US: . . . . .No
. . . .	Encourage Conversions: . . . . .No	Canada: . . . . .Ontario
Type Space: . . . . .FS;~1,530 SF	Average # Employees: . . 3 FT, 3 PT	Overseas: . . . . No

LUBE ON WHEELS INTERNATIONAL

3165 23rd Ave. N.
St. Petersburg, FL 33713
TEL: (800) 234-LUBE (813) 327-1400 C
FAX: (813) 323-7747
Mr. Michael L. Fisher, President

On-site oil and lube service done at customer's location. Specializing in commercial vehicles and equipment.

HISTORY:	FINANCIAL: Earnings Claim: . .No	FRANCHISOR TRAINING/SUPPORT:
Established in 1988; . . 1st Franchised in 1989	Cash Investment: $15-25K	Financial Assistance Provided: . . .Yes(D)
Company-Owned Units (As of 8/31/1992): . .0	Total Investment: $55K	Site Selection Assistance: . . . . . . .NA
Franchised Units (As of 8/31/1992): 25	Fees: Franchise - $15K	Lease Negotiation Assistance: . . . .Yes
Total Units (As of 8/31/1992): 25	Royalty: $275/Mo., Advert: . . 2%	Co-operative Advertising: . . . . . . .NA
Projected New Units for 1993: 36	Contract Periods (Yrs.): . . . 20/20	Training: . . . . 1 Wk. Headquarters
Distribution: US-25;Can-0;Overseas-0	Area Development Agreement: . .No	
North America: . . . . 11 States	Sub-Franchise Contract: . . . . .No	On-Going Support: A,C,D,E,F,G,H,I/ . .6
Concentration: . . . .4 in FL, 4 in GA, 2 in TN	Expand in Territory: . . . . . . Yes	EXPANSION PLANS:
Registered: . . . . FL,HI,MD,VA	Passive Ownership: . . . . .Allowed	US: . . . . .All US
	Encourage Conversions: . . . . NA	Canada: . . . . .All Canada
Type Space: . . . . NA;~NA SF	Average # Employees: . . . . .1 FT	Overseas: . . .English Speaking Countries

LUBE WAGON, THE

9430 Mission Blvd.
Riverside, CA 92509
TEL: (909) 685-8570
FAX:
Mr. Ray Teagarden, President

Portable quick-lube service business on wheels. Low overhead lube service that goes to the customer's home or business. Can be operated from your home phone.

HISTORY:	FINANCIAL: Earnings Claim: . .No	FRANCHISOR TRAINING/SUPPORT:
Established in 1974; . . 1st Franchised in 1977	Cash Investment: $12K	Financial Assistance Provided: . . . . .No
Company-Owned Units (As of 8/31/1992): . .0	Total Investment: $12K	Site Selection Assistance: . . . . . . .NA
Franchised Units (As of 8/31/1992): 34	Fees: Franchise - $0	Lease Negotiation Assistance: . . . . .NA
Total Units (As of 8/31/1992): 34	Royalty: 0%, Advert: 0%	Co-operative Advertising: . . . . . . .No
Projected New Units for 1993: 3	Contract Periods (Yrs.): . . . Infinite	Training: . . . . Not Required
Distribution: US-34;Can-0;Overseas-0	Area Development Agreement: . .No	
North America: . . . . 29 States	Sub-Franchise Contract: . . . . .No	On-Going Support: / 2
Concentration: . . . . 4 in CA	Expand in Territory: . . . . . . Yes	EXPANSION PLANS:
Registered:	Passive Ownership: . . . . .Allowed	US: . . . . .All US
	Encourage Conversions: . . . . Yes	Canada: . . . . .Yes
Type Space: . . . . Home Based;~ SF	Average # Employees: . . . . .1 FT	Overseas: . . . . No

LUBEPRO'S INTERNATIONAL

1630 Colonial Pkwy.
Inverness, IL 60067
TEL: (800) 654-5823 (708) 776-2500
FAX: (708) 776-2542
Mr. Phil Robinson

Automotive quick-oil change and lubrication service. Site evaluation, 10 days of training. Multiple Unit Development available.

HISTORY: . . . . .IFA	FINANCIAL: Earnings Claim: . .No	FRANCHISOR TRAINING/SUPPORT:
Established in 1978; . . 1st Franchised in 1985	Cash Investment: $100-160K	Financial Assistance Provided: . . . . .No
Company-Owned Units (As of 8/31/1992): . .7	Total Investment: $160-660K	Site Selection Assistance: . . . . . . .Yes
Franchised Units (As of 8/31/1992): 25	Fees: Franchise - $25K	Lease Negotiation Assistance: . . . .Yes
Total Units (As of 8/31/1992): 32	Royalty: 5%, Advert: 5%	Co-operative Advertising: . . . . . . .No
Projected New Units for 1993: 5	Contract Periods (Yrs.): . . . 20/10	Training: . . . . . . .10 Days Headquarters
Distribution: US-32;Can-0;Overseas-0	Area Development Agreement: . .No	
North America: . . . . 6 States	Sub-Franchise Contract: . . . . .No	On-Going Support: B,C,D,E,G,I/ 7
Concentration: . . . 15 in IL, 6 in WI, 1 in TN	Expand in Territory: . . . . . . Yes	EXPANSION PLANS:
Registered: . . . . IL,IN,MI	Passive Ownership: . . . . .Allowed	US: . . . . NE, SE and Midwest
	Encourage Conversions: . . . . Yes	Canada: . . . . .No
Type Space: . . . . FS;~1,800 SF	Average # Employees: . . . . .5 FT	Overseas: . . . . No

MAACO AUTO PAINTING AND BODYWORKS
381 Brooks Rd.
King of Prussia, PA 19406
TEL: (800) 521-6282 (215) 265-6606
FAX: (215) 337-6113
Ms. Linda Kemp, Fran. Mgr.

MAACO has developed a system relating to the establishment and operation of centers specializing in auto painting and body repair. The system includes market analysis, research and development, sales and merchandising methods, training, record keeping, advertising and business management, all of which are constantly being improved, updated and further developed by a fully staffed and knowledgeable corporate structure to service its owners.

HISTORY:	. . . . IFA
Established in 1972;	. . 1st Franchised in 1972
Company-Owned Units (As of 8/31/1992):	. .0
Franchised Units (As of 8/31/1992):	 428
Total Units (As of 8/31/1992):	 428
Projected New Units for 1993:	 60
Distribution:	. . . . US-407;Can-21;Overseas-0
North America:	. . . . 43 States, 5 Provinces
Concentration:	. .29 in CA, 26 in PA, 23 in NJ
Registered:	. . . . .All
Type Space:	. . . . . . FS;~7,500-10,000 SF

FINANCIAL: Earnings Claim: . .No
Cash Investment: $55K
Total Investment: $170K
Fees: Franchise - $25K
  Royalty: 8%, Advert: . . $500/Wk.
Contract Periods (Yrs.): 15/5
Area Development Agreement: . .No
Sub-Franchise Contract: . . . . .No
Expand in Territory: . . . . . . Yes
Passive Ownership: . . . Not Allowed
Encourage Conversions: . . . . .No
Average # Employees: . . . . 11 FT

FRANCHISOR TRAINING/SUPPORT:
Financial Assistance Provided: . . . Yes(I)
Site Selection Assistance: . . . . . . .Yes
Lease Negotiation Assistance: . . . . .Yes
Co-operative Advertising: . . . . . . .Yes
Training: . . . . 4 Wks. Headquarters,
. . . . 3 Wks. On-Site
On-Going Support: A,B,C,D,E,F,G,h,I/ .150
EXPANSION PLANS:
US: . . . . .All US
Canada: . . . . .All Canada
Overseas: . . . . No

MASTER MECHANIC, THE
1981 Dundas St. E.
Mississauga, ON L4X 1M1 CAN
TEL: (416) 629-1222
FAX: (416) 629-3864
Mr. Andrew Wanie, President

General automotive repair. The franchisor appeals to potential owner/operators who require modest initial capital outlay, considerable individual freedom to utilize special talents, low cost royalties and services from franchisor, on-going technical and business management training and assistance.

HISTORY:	. . . .
Established in 1979;	. . 1st Franchised in 1985
Company-Owned Units (As of 8/31/1992):	. .2
Franchised Units (As of 8/31/1992):	 15
Total Units (As of 8/31/1992):	 17
Projected New Units for 1993:	3
Distribution:	. . . . . US-0;Can-17;Overseas-0
North America:	. . . . .1 Province
Concentration:	. . . . 17 in ON
Registered:	. . . .
Type Space:	. . . . .SC, RM;~2,500-3,000 SF

FINANCIAL: Earnings Claim: . Yes
Cash Investment: $60-75K
Total Investment: $90-125K
Fees: Franchise - $20K
  Royalty: 6%, Advert: 3%
Contract Periods (Yrs.): . . 10-20/10
Area Development Agreement: Yes/20
Sub-Franchise Contract: . . . . Yes
Expand in Territory: . . . . . . Yes
Passive Ownership: . . . Discouraged
Encourage Conversions: . . . . Yes
Average # Employees: . . 4 FT, 1 PT

FRANCHISOR TRAINING/SUPPORT:
Financial Assistance Provided: . . . Yes(I)
Site Selection Assistance: . . . . . . .Yes
Lease Negotiation Assistance: . . . .Yes
Co-operative Advertising: . . . . . . .Yes
Training: . . . . 2 Days Classroom HQ,
. . 2-4 Wks. On-Site, Min. 1 Day/Month
On-Going Support: a,B,C,D,E,F,G,H/ . . 8
EXPANSION PLANS:
US: . . . . No
Canada: . . . . .Ontario
Overseas: . . . . No

MCQUIK'S OILUBE
P. O. Box 46
Muncie, IN 47308
TEL: (800) 445-6393 (317) 282-2183
FAX: (317) 747-8127
Mr. Alan Jackson, Dir. Fran. Ops.

MCQUIK'S OILUBE provides to the general public high-quality, reasonably-priced, fast-service oil change, lubrication and related automotive services through its centers. The services at the centers are provided by trained personnel who follow a detailed vehicle service system.

HISTORY:	. . . .
Established in 1980;	. . 1st Franchised in 1985
Company-Owned Units (As of 8/31/1992):	. 34
Franchised Units (As of 8/31/1992):	 52
Total Units (As of 8/31/1992):	 86
Projected New Units for 1993:	6
Distribution:	. . . . . US-86;Can-0;Overseas-0
North America:	. . . . 8 States
Concentration:	. . 52 in IN, 17 in OH, 4 in FL
Registered:	. . . . FL,IL,IN,MI
Type Space:	. . . . FS (1,800 SF);~13,000 SF

FINANCIAL: Earnings Claim: . .No
Cash Investment: $100-225K
Total Investment: $300-650K
Fees: Franchise - $15K
  Royalty: 4%, Advert: 6%
Contract Periods (Yrs.): 15/15
Area Development Agreement: . .No
Sub-Franchise Contract: . . . . .No
Expand in Territory: . . . . . . Yes
Passive Ownership: . . . Discouraged
Encourage Conversions: . . . . Yes
Average # Employees: . . 6 FT, 2 PT

FRANCHISOR TRAINING/SUPPORT:
Financial Assistance Provided: . . . Yes(I)
Site Selection Assistance: . . . . . . .Yes
Lease Negotiation Assistance: . . . .Yes
Co-operative Advertising: . . . . . . .Yes
Training: . . . . . 2 Wks. Indianapolis, IN,
. . . . .2 Wks. Franchisee Location
On-Going Support: B,C,D,E,F,G,H,I/ . . 12
EXPANSION PLANS:
US: . . . IN, OH, MI, SC, FL,TN and KY
Canada: . . . . No
Overseas: . . . . No

MEINEKE DISCOUNT MUFFLER SHOPS

128 S. Tryon St., # 900
Charlotte, NC 28202
TEL: (800) MEINEKE (704) 377-8855
FAX: (704) 358-4706
Ms. Amy Daniel, Fran. Sales Admin.

MEINEKE DISCOUNT MUFFLER SHOPS offer fast, courteous service in the merchandising of automotive exhaust systems, shock absorbers, struts and brakes. Unique inventory control and group purchasing power enable MEINEKE dealers to support a Discount Concept and deliver quality service. No mechanical skills required.

HISTORY: . . . . IFA	FINANCIAL: Earnings Claim: . .No	FRANCHISOR TRAINING/SUPPORT:
Established in 1972; . . 1st Franchised in 1972	Cash Investment: $83K	Financial Assistance Provided: . . . Yes(I)
Company-Owned Units (As of 8/31/1992): . .7	Total Investment: $120K	Site Selection Assistance: . . . . . . .Yes
Franchised Units (As of 8/31/1992): 886	Fees: Franchise - $22.5K	Lease Negotiation Assistance: . . . . .No
Total Units (As of 8/31/1992): 893	Royalty: 7%, Advert: 10%	Co-operative Advertising: . . . .
Projected New Units for 1993: 26	Contract Periods (Yrs.): 15/15	Training: . . . . 4 Wks. Headquarters
Distribution: US-877;Can-16;Overseas-0	Area Development Agreement: . .No	. . . .
North America: . . . . 45 States, 3 Provinces	Sub-Franchise Contract: . . . . .No	On-Going Support: C,D,E,F,G,H,I/ . . 88
Concentration: . 84 in NY, 76 in PA, 62 in TX	Expand in Territory: . . . . . . Yes	EXPANSION PLANS:
Registered: . . . . .All	Passive Ownership: . . . Discouraged	US: .All US
. . . .	Encourage Conversions:	Canada: . . . . .All Canada
Type Space: . . . . FS;~2,700 SF	Average # Employees:	Overseas: . . . . No

MERLIN'S MUFFLER & BRAKE

33 W. Higgins, # 2050
South Barrington, IL 60010
TEL: (800) 652-9900 (312) 428-5000
FAX: (708) 428-8259
Mr. Mark Hameister, Dir. Fran. Dev.

Central to MERLIN'S retail concept is an up-scale, 6-bay building, designed and developed as an important result of MERLIN'S complete real estate program. MERLIN'S typical franchise business plan and working cash requirement facilitates first year cash flows appropriate to owner operation, as well as semi-absentee management.

HISTORY: . . . . IFA	FINANCIAL: Earnings Claim: . .No	FRANCHISOR TRAINING/SUPPORT:
Established in 1975; . . 1st Franchised in 1975	Cash Investment: $45-50K	Financial Assistance Provided: . . . Yes(I)
Company-Owned Units (As of 8/31/1992): . .5	Total Investment: $155-170K	Site Selection Assistance: . . . . . . .Yes
Franchised Units (As of 8/31/1992): 39	Fees: Franchise - $26-30K	Lease Negotiation Assistance: . . . .Yes
Total Units (As of 8/31/1992): 44	Royalty: 4.9%, Advert: 5%	Co-operative Advertising: . . . . . . .Yes
Projected New Units for 1993: 10	Contract Periods (Yrs.): . . . 20/20	Training: . . . . 4 Wks. Headquarters/Shop,
Distribution: US-44;Can-0;Overseas-0	Area Development Agreement: . .No	. . . . .1 Wk. Technical School
North America: . . . . 5 States	Sub-Franchise Contract: . . . . .No	On-Going Support: B,C,D,E,H,I/ 11
Concentration: . . . 36 in IL, 3 in GA, 2 in MI	Expand in Territory: . . . . . . .No	EXPANSION PLANS:
Registered: . . . . IL,MI,WI	Passive Ownership: . . . . .Allowed	US: . . . . . Chicago, Atlanta, Detroit,TX
. . . .	Encourage Conversions: . . . . . Yes	Canada: . . . . .No
Type Space: . . .FS, SC, RM, Mall;~3,600 SF	Average # Employees: . . 2 FT, 1 PT	Overseas: . . . . No

MERMAID CAR WASH

526 Grand Canyon Dr.
Madison, WI 53719
TEL: (608) 833-9274
FAX:
Mr. Peter Aspinwall, President

Own a MERMAID franchise. MERMAID CAR WASH was designed with the feeling that our customers have a love affair with their vehicle. It is our desire to have customers visit an enjoyable, attractive business run by friendly, helpful, well-groomed, well-trained employees and leave MERMAID with a pleasant experience and a professionally-cleaned vehicle.

HISTORY:	FINANCIAL: Earnings Claim: . . .	FRANCHISOR TRAINING/SUPPORT:
Established in 1984; . . 1st Franchised in 1986	Cash Investment: $50-300K	Financial Assistance Provided: . . . . No
Company-Owned Units (As of 8/31/1992): . .2	Total Investment: $1.6-1.8MM	Site Selection Assistance: . . . . . . .Yes
Franchised Units (As of 8/31/1992): 4	Fees: Franchise - $50K	Lease Negotiation Assistance: . . . .Yes
Total Units (As of 8/31/1992): 6	Royalty: 2%, Advert: 0%	Co-operative Advertising: . . . . No
Projected New Units for 1993: 0	Contract Periods (Yrs.): 20/20	Training: . . . . 3 Wks. Minimum at Head-
Distribution: US-6;Can-0;Overseas-0	Area Development Agreement: . .No	. . . . quarters, As Needed Site Location
North America: . . . . 3 States	Sub-Franchise Contract: . . . . .No	On-Going Support: C,D,E,F,h,I/ 4
Concentration: . . . .3 in MN, 2 in WI, 1 in IL	Expand in Territory: . . . . . . Yes	EXPANSION PLANS:
Registered:	Passive Ownership: . . . . . .Allowed	US: . . . . .All US
. . . .	Encourage Conversions: . . . . Yes	Canada: . . . . .No
Type Space: . . . . ;~ SF	Average # Employees: . . . 30-60 FT	Overseas: . . . . No

MIDAS

225 N. Michigan Ave.
Chicago, IL 60601
TEL: (800) 621-0144 (312) 565-7500
FAX: (312) 565-7881
Mr. Richard C. Pope, Dir. Fran. Dev.

MIDAS MUFFLER AND BRAKE SHOPS engage in the retail sale and installation of automotive exhaust systems, brake components, suspension and alignment and other related automotive parts and services.

HISTORY: . . . . IFA	FINANCIAL: Earnings Claim: . .No	FRANCHISOR TRAINING/SUPPORT:
Established in 1956; . . 1st Franchised in 1956	Cash Investment: $75-100K	Financial Assistance Provided: . . . Yes(I)
Company-Owned Units (As of 8/31/1992): 298	Total Investment: $250-300K	Site Selection Assistance: . . . . . . .Yes
Franchised Units (As of 8/31/1992): . . .2174	Fees: Franchise - $10K	Lease Negotiation Assistance: . . . . .Yes
Total Units (As of 8/31/1992): 2472	Royalty: 10%, Advert: 0%	Co-operative Advertising: . . . . . . .Yes
Projected New Units for 1993: 100	Contract Periods (Yrs.): 20/20	Training: . . . . 4 Wks. Palatine, IL
Distribution: . US-1808;Can-245;Overseas-419	Area Development Agreement: . .No	. . . .
North America:	Sub-Franchise Contract: . . . . .No	On-Going Support: A,B,C,D,E,F,G,H,I/ . .
Concentration: . . . . CA, NY, OH	Expand in Territory: . . . . Yes	EXPANSION PLANS:
Registered: . . . . .All	Passive Ownership: . . . Discouraged	US: . . . . All US, Selected Markets
. . . .	Encourage Conversions: . . . . . Yes	Canada: . . . . .All Canada
Type Space: . . . . FS;~4,100+ SF	Average # Employees: . . 6 FT, 4 PT	Overseas: . . . . . EUR, AU, NZ

MINIT-TUNE & BRAKE AUTO CENTRES

398 W. Fifth Ave.
Vancouver, BC V5Y 1J5 CAN
TEL: (604) 873-5551
FAX: (604) 873-5553
Mr. Roy Shand, President

We utilize computerized scopes to provide tune-ups and diagnostic service for our customers. We also provide oil changes and brake service and other minor repairs.

HISTORY:	FINANCIAL: Earnings Claim: . Yes	FRANCHISOR TRAINING/SUPPORT:
Established in 1976; . . 1st Franchised in 1976	Cash Investment: $50-60K	Financial Assistance Provided: . . . Yes(I)
Company-Owned Units (As of 8/31/1992): . .2	Total Investment: $95-120K	Site Selection Assistance: . . . . . . .Yes
Franchised Units (As of 8/31/1992): 4	Fees: Franchise - $20K	Lease Negotiation Assistance: . . . .Yes
Total Units (As of 8/31/1992): 6	Royalty: 5%, Advert: 5%	Co-operative Advertising: . . . . . . .Yes
Projected New Units for 1993: 0	Contract Periods (Yrs.): . . 10/10/10	Training: . . . . 2 Wks. Headquarters,
Distribution: US-0;Can-59;Overseas-0	Area Development Agreement: Yes/10	. . . . . 2 Wks. Calgary, 2 Wks. Totonto
North America: . . . . 4 Provinces	Sub-Franchise Contract: . . . . . Yes	On-Going Support: C,D,E,G/ 3
Concentration: . . 22 in BC, 17 in AB, 17 in ON	Expand in Territory: . . . . Yes	EXPANSION PLANS:
Registered: . . . . AB	Passive Ownership: . . . Not Allowed	US: . . . . No
. . . .	Encourage Conversions: . . . . . Yes	Canada: . . . . BC, AB, SK & ON
Type Space: . . . . FS;~2,250 SF	Average # Employees: . . 3 FT, 1 PT	Overseas: . . . . No

MISTER TRANSMISSION

30 Wertheim Ct., # 5
Richmond Hill, ON L4B 1B9 CAN
TEL: (416) 886-1511
FAX: (416) 886-1545
Mr. Kevin Brillinger, VP Corp. Dev.

MISTER TRANSMISSION is Canada's largest automatic transmission repair specialist, serving Canadian motorists since 1963. MISTER TRANSMISSION offers first-rate advertising support, a nationwide warranty program and a national network of dealers.

HISTORY: . . . . .CFA	FINANCIAL: Earnings Claim: . .No	FRANCHISOR TRAINING/SUPPORT:
Established in 1963; . . 1st Franchised in 1969	Cash Investment: $30-60K	Financial Assistance Provided: . . . Yes(I)
Company-Owned Units (As of 8/31/1992): . .0	Total Investment: $60-90K	Site Selection Assistance: . . . . . . .Yes
Franchised Units (As of 8/31/1992): 95	Fees: Franchise - $25K	Lease Negotiation Assistance: . . . .Yes
Total Units (As of 8/31/1992): 95	Royalty: 7%, Advert: 4-7%	Co-operative Advertising: . . . . . . .Yes
Projected New Units for 1993: 5	Contract Periods (Yrs.): . . . 10/10	Training: . . . . .1 Wk. Headquarters,
Distribution: US-0;Can-95;Overseas-0	Area Development Agreement: . .No	. . . . .1 Wk. In Shop
North America: . . . . 8 Provinces	Sub-Franchise Contract: . . . . .No	On-Going Support: A,C,D,E,G,H/ . . . 10
Concentration: . . 70 in ON, 10 in BC, 4 in PQ	Expand in Territory: . . . . . . Yes	EXPANSION PLANS:
Registered: . . . . AB	Passive Ownership: . . . Not Allowed	US: . . . . .No
. . . .	Encourage Conversions: . . . . Yes	Canada: . . . . .All Canada
Type Space: . . . . SC, Auto Malls;~2,400 SF	Average # Employees: . . 4 FT, 1 PT	Overseas: . . . . No

MR. TRANSMISSION

4444 W. 147th St.
Midlothian, IL 60445
TEL: (800) 377-9247 (708) 389-5922
FAX: (708) 389-9882
Mr. Mel Patterson, Dir. Mktg.

Transmission repair service centers with the support of a central factory to supply hard-to-service or difficult-to-find transmissions. Complete driveline service center.

HISTORY: . . . .
Established in 1969; . . 1st Franchised in 1975
Company-Owned Units (As of 8/31/1992): . .2
Franchised Units (As of 8/31/1992): 121
Total Units (As of 8/31/1992): 123
Projected New Units for 1993: 30
Distribution: US-123;Can-0;Overseas-0
North America: . . . . 20 States
Concentration: . . 20 in IL, 18 in GA, 14 in TN
Registered: . . . CA,FL,IL,IN,MD,MI,MN,ND
. . . . RI,SD,VA,WA,WI
Type Space: . . . . . . FS, SC, RM;~4,000 SF

FINANCIAL: Earnings Claim: . Yes
Cash Investment: $35K
Total Investment: $100-120K
Fees: Franchise - $29.5K
Royalty: 7%, Advert: 1-3%
Contract Periods (Yrs.): . . . 20/20
Area Development Agreement: Yes/5
Sub-Franchise Contract: . . . . . Yes
Expand in Territory: . . . . . . Yes
Passive Ownership: . . . Not Allowed
Encourage Conversions: . . . . . Yes
Average # Employees: . . 4 FT, 1 PT

FRANCHISOR TRAINING/SUPPORT:
Financial Assistance Provided: . . . .Yes
Site Selection Assistance: . . . . . . .Yes
Lease Negotiation Assistance: . . . .Yes
Co-operative Advertising: . . . . . . .Yes
Training: . . . . 3 Wks. Headquarters,
. . . . On-Going (Management)
On-Going Support: B,C,E,F,G,H,I/ . . . 33
EXPANSION PLANS:
US: . . . . All US
Canada: . . . . No
Overseas: . . . . No

OIL CAN HENRY'S INTERNATIONAL

1200 NW Front Ave., # 690
Portland, OR 97209
TEL: (503) 243-6311
FAX: (503) 228-5227
Mr. Chris Stepanek, Dir. Fran. Dev.

Automotive lubrication and filter specialist. Our concept blends old-fashioned American service values with some high technology. Staff wear striped shirts, bow ties and gatsby caps. Customers remain in the car and watch service on the monitors. We offer a high-profile building design and impeccably clean facilities and state-of- the-art point-of-sale computers.

HISTORY: . . . .
Established in 1978; . . 1st Franchised in 1987
Company-Owned Units (As of 8/31/1992): . .1
Franchised Units (As of 8/31/1992): 21
Total Units (As of 8/31/1992): 22
Projected New Units for 1993: 12
Distribution: US-22;Can-0;Overseas-0
North America: . . . . 5 States
Concentration: . . . .9 in FL, 5 in CA, 4 in OR
Registered: . . . . CA,FL,OR,WA
. . . .
Type Space: . . . . . . FS;~10,000-15,000 SF

FINANCIAL: Earnings Claim: . .No
Cash Investment: $75K
Total Investment: $300-750K
Fees: Franchise - $25K
Royalty: 5.5%, Advert: 8%
Contract Periods (Yrs.): . . . 10/10
Area Development Agreement: Yes/Var
Sub-Franchise Contract: . . . . . .No
Expand in Territory: . . . . . . Yes
Passive Ownership: . . . Discouraged
Encourage Conversions: . . . . Yes
Average # Employees: . 4-8 FT, 2 PT

FRANCHISOR TRAINING/SUPPORT:
Financial Assistance Provided: . . . Yes(I)
Site Selection Assistance: . . . . . . .Yes
Lease Negotiation Assistance: . . . .Yes
Co-operative Advertising: . . . . . . .NA
Training: . . . . 5 Wks. Headquarters
. . . .
On-Going Support: C,D,E,G,H,I/ 8
EXPANSION PLANS:
US: . . . . . . Northwest, CA, AZ and FL
Canada: . . . . .All Canada
Overseas: . . . . No

OIL EXPRESS FAST LUBE SYSTEMS

15 Spinning Wheel Rd., # 428
Hinsdale, IL 60521
TEL: (708) 325-8666
FAX: (708) 325-8683
Mr. Daniel R. Barnas, EVP

OIL EXPRESS began in 1980. 38 centralized locations and growing. All brand new buildings, with drive-thrus and full basements. Extensive management development school (classroom) and on-the-job training. No failures and very high average store volume. All owner-operated franchises.

HISTORY: . . . .
Established in 1980; . . 1st Franchised in 1981
Company-Owned Units (As of 8/31/1992): . 18
Franchised Units (As of 8/31/1992): 32
Total Units (As of 8/31/1992): 50
Projected New Units for 1993: 5
Distribution: US-50;Can-0;Overseas-0
North America: . . . . 4 States
Concentration: . . . . 34 in IL, 6 in MI, 3 in IN
Registered: . . . . IL,IN
. . . .
Type Space: . . . . FS;~12,000 SF

FINANCIAL: Earnings Claim: . .No
Cash Investment: $75-100K
Total Investment: $425-500K
Fees: Franchise - $25K
Royalty: 6%, Advert: 4.5%
Contract Periods (Yrs.): 20
Area Development Agreement: Yes/Var
Sub-Franchise Contract: . . . . Yes
Expand in Territory: . . . . . . Yes
Passive Ownership: . . . Not Allowed
Encourage Conversions: . . . . .No
Average # Employees: . . . . 6-9 FT

FRANCHISOR TRAINING/SUPPORT:
Financial Assistance Provided: . . . Yes(I)
Site Selection Assistance: . . . . . . .Yes
Lease Negotiation Assistance: . . . .Yes
Co-operative Advertising: . . . . . . .Yes
Training: . . . . . .9 Wks. (27 Hr. Total) at
. . Headquarters, Min. 10 Days OJT Site
On-Going Support: B,C,D,E,G,H,I/ 8
EXPANSION PLANS:
US: . . . . Midwest
Canada: . . . . No
Overseas: . . . . No

PREVENT-A-CRACK

3116 E. Shea Blvd., # 247
Phoenix, AZ 85028
TEL: (602) 996-4450
FAX: (602) 996-4450
Mr. Gerd-D. Linke, President

A company which sells franchises for the operation of windshield and glass repairs, known as PREVENT-A-CRACK Mobile Services. Vehicles which experience cracks to their windshields can be repaired. The repair will permanently stop cracks.

HISTORY:	FINANCIAL: Earnings Claim: . .No	FRANCHISOR TRAINING/SUPPORT:
Established in 1985; . . 1st Franchised in 1987	Cash Investment: $2.2K	Financial Assistance Provided: . . . . . No
Company-Owned Units (As of 8/31/1992): . .0	Total Investment: $2.5-5K	Site Selection Assistance: . . . . . . .Yes
Franchised Units (As of 8/31/1992): 19	Fees: Franchise - $1.5K	Lease Negotiation Assistance: . . . . .Yes
Total Units (As of 8/31/1992): 19	Royalty: $50, Advert: 2%	Co-operative Advertising: . . . . . . .Yes
Projected New Units for 1993: 10	Contract Periods (Yrs.): 10/10	Training: . . . . 1 Day On-Site
Distribution: US-10;Can-1;Overseas-8	Area Development Agreement: . .No	. . . .
North America: . . . . 3 States	Sub-Franchise Contract: . . . . .No	On-Going Support: b,D,G/ 2
Concentration: . . . 3 in AZ, 3 in CA, 3 in WA	Expand in Territory: . . . . . . Yes	EXPANSION PLANS:
Registered:	Passive Ownership: . . . . . .Allowed	US: . . . . .All US
. . . .	Encourage Conversions: . . . . .No	Canada: . . . . .Yes
Type Space: . . . . NA;~NA SF	Average # Employees: . . . . .1 FT	Overseas: . . . . . . EUR, Far East

PRO-AUTOFINDERS

132 2nd St. E., #304, P.O. Box 1916
Cornwall, ON K6H 1Y4 CAN
TEL: (613) 932-1007
FAX: (613) 932-2856
Mr. Ron Chenier, President

Fact: $42 billion of used car transactions take place per year between private individuals, not car dealers! Why? Dealers offer them wholesale! Answer: We sell automobiles like a real estate company sells homes! Test marketed since 1985, profits average over $800 per car! Available to the emerging auto salesperson by consultant or franchise agreement.

HISTORY:	FINANCIAL: Earnings Claim: . .No	FRANCHISOR TRAINING/SUPPORT:
Established in 1985; . . 1st Franchised in 1986	Cash Investment: $10-30K	Financial Assistance Provided: . . . . . No
Company-Owned Units (As of 8/31/1992): . .0	Total Investment: $10-30K	Site Selection Assistance: . . . . . . .Yes
Franchised Units (As of 8/31/1992): 1	Fees: Franchise - $10K	Lease Negotiation Assistance: . . . .Yes
Total Units (As of 8/31/1992): 1	Royalty: 1%, Advert: 1/4%	Co-operative Advertising: . . . . . . .Yes
Projected New Units for 1993:	Contract Periods (Yrs.): 5/5	Training: . . . . 2 Days On-Site,
Distribution: US-0;Can-1;Overseas-0	Area Development Agreement: Yes/5	. . . . 2 Days Headquarters
North America: . . . . .1 Province	Sub-Franchise Contract: . . . . .No	On-Going Support: A,B,C,D,E,F,G,H,I/ . 3
Concentration: . . . . 1 in ON	Expand in Territory: . . . . . . Yes	EXPANSION PLANS:
Registered:	Passive Ownership: . . . Discouraged	US: . . . . .No
. . . .	Encourage Conversions: . . . . . Yes	Canada: . . . . .Yes
Type Space: . . . . FS;~ SF	Average # Employees: . . 2 FT, 1 PT	Overseas: . . . . No

PROLUBE

625 E. Merritt Ave.
Merritt Island, FL 32953
TEL: (407) 784-9737
FAX: (407) 453-6309
Mr. Joe Haggard, President

Drive-thru lubrication, fluid and inspection service. 34 items performed. Marketing emphasis on convenience, confidence and ego gratification. Solid state fluid dispensing system with no pumps or reels. Unique percentage control system and compensation system. Precise, methodical, sequenced method of performance service.

HISTORY:	FINANCIAL: Earnings Claim: . .No	FRANCHISOR TRAINING/SUPPORT:
Established in 1975; . . 1st Franchised in 1986	Cash Investment: $90-140K	Financial Assistance Provided: . . . . .No
Company-Owned Units (As of 8/31/1992): . .5	Total Investment: $240-350K	Site Selection Assistance: . . . . . . .Yes
Franchised Units (As of 8/31/1992): 3	Fees: Franchise - $10K	Lease Negotiation Assistance: . . . . .Yes
Total Units (As of 8/31/1992): 8	Royalty: 6%, Advert: 0%	Co-operative Advertising: . . . . . . .Yes
Projected New Units for 1993:	Contract Periods (Yrs.): 5/5	Training: . . . . 2 Wks. Headquarters
Distribution: US-8;Can-0;Overseas-0	Area Development Agreement: Yes/5	. . . .
North America: . . . . 2 States	Sub-Franchise Contract: . . . . .No	On-Going Support: E,F,G,H,I/ 6
Concentration: . . . . 7 in FL, 1 in IA	Expand in Territory: . . . . . . Yes	EXPANSION PLANS:
Registered: . . . . .FL	Passive Ownership: . . . . . .Allowed	US: . . . . .All US
. . . .	Encourage Conversions: . . . . Yes	Canada: . . . . .No
Type Space: . . . . FS;~1,500 SF	Average # Employees: . . . . . .6 FT	Overseas: . . . . No

RUST CHECK CENTER

1285 Britannia Rd. E.
Mississauga, ON L4W 1C7 CAN
TEL: (800) 465-9262 (416) 670-7878
FAX: (416) 670-7539
Mr. Lloyd MacEachern, VP/GM

RUST CHECK CENTERS provide top-quality automotive rust protection. Unique preventive maintenance system is guaranteed forever on new and qualified used vehicles treated annually. Product proven effective over 20 years with no warranty claims for product failure.

HISTORY:	FINANCIAL: Earnings Claim: . .No	FRANCHISOR TRAINING/SUPPORT:
Established in 1972; . . 1st Franchised in 1981	Cash Investment: $10K	Financial Assistance Provided: . . . . .NA
Company-Owned Units (As of 8/31/1992): . .1	Total Investment: $12K	Site Selection Assistance: . . . . . . .NA
Franchised Units (As of 8/31/1992): 301	Fees: Franchise - . . . . $Varies	Lease Negotiation Assistance: . . . .NA
Total Units (As of 8/31/1992): 302	Royalty: 0%, Advert: 0%	Co-operative Advertising: . . . . . . .Yes
Projected New Units for 1993: 6	Contract Periods (Yrs.): . . . .Varies	Training: . . . . . . 5 Days Franchisee Site
Distribution: . . . US-12;Can-230;Overseas-60	Area Development Agreement: . .No	. . . .
North America: . . . . 3 States, 11 Provinces	Sub-Franchise Contract: . . . . .No	On-Going Support: A,B,C,D,G,H,I/ . . 11
Concentration: . 75 in ON, 45 in PQ, 30 in NS	Expand in Territory: . . . . . . .No	EXPANSION PLANS:
Registered:	Passive Ownership: . . . Not Allowed	US: . . . . . . New York and Michigan
. . . .	Encourage Conversions: . . . . . .No	Canada: . . . . .All Canada
Type Space: . . . Add-on To Exist.;~1,200 SF	Average # Employees: . . . . . .2 FT	Overseas: . . . . .Yes

SAF-T AUTO CENTERS

121 N. Plains Industrial Rd., Unit H
Wallingford, CT 06492
TEL: (800) 382-7238 (203) 269-2532
FAX: (203) 269-2532
Mr. Richard Bilodeau, President

SAF-T AUTO CENTERS is an owner-operated auto repair shop, offering steering, suspension, brake, muffler, lubrication and minor repair. Our main effort is to put good mechanics in a business opportunity where they can capitalize on their trade.

HISTORY:	FINANCIAL: Earnings Claim: . .No	FRANCHISOR TRAINING/SUPPORT:
Established in 1978; . . 1st Franchised in 1985	Cash Investment: $15K	Financial Assistance Provided: . . . Yes(I)
Company-Owned Units (As of 8/31/1992): . .0	Total Investment: $32.5-65K	Site Selection Assistance: . . . . . . .Yes
Franchised Units (As of 8/31/1992): 13	Fees: Franchise - $15K	Lease Negotiation Assistance: . . . . .Yes
Total Units (As of 8/31/1992): 13	Royalty: $400/Mo., Advert: . . 1%	Co-operative Advertising: . . . . . . .Yes
Projected New Units for 1993: 3	Contract Periods (Yrs.): . . . 5/5/5	Training: . . . . 1 Wk. On-Location,
Distribution: US-13;Can-0;Overseas-0	Area Development Agreement: Yes/50	. . . . On-Going
North America: . . . . 2 States	Sub-Franchise Contract: . . . . . Yes	On-Going Support: A,C,D,E,F,H,I/ 5
Concentration: . . . . 12 in CT, 1 in FL	Expand in Territory: . . . . . . Yes	EXPANSION PLANS:
Registered: . . . . .FL	Passive Ownership: . . . Not Allowed	US: . . . . .CT, FL and RI
. . . .	Encourage Conversions: . . . . . .No	Canada: . . . . No
Type Space: . . . . . . FS, SC, RM;~1,500 SF	Average # Employees: . . 1 FT, 1 PT	Overseas: . . . . No

SHINE FACTORY, THE

3519 14th St., SW, 2nd Fl.
Calgary, AB T2T 3W2 CAN
TEL: (403) 243-3030
FAX: (403) 243-8137
Mr. Bruce Cousens, President

A solid, proven program to put individuals into the automotive protection and detail business.

HISTORY:	FINANCIAL: Earnings Claim: . .No	FRANCHISOR TRAINING/SUPPORT:
Established in 1979; . . 1st Franchised in 1979	Cash Investment: $50K	Financial Assistance Provided: . . . . .No
Company-Owned Units (As of 8/31/1992): . .0	Total Investment: $100K	Site Selection Assistance: . . . . . . .Yes
Franchised Units (As of 8/31/1992): 28	Fees: Franchise - $25K	Lease Negotiation Assistance: . . . . .Yes
Total Units (As of 8/31/1992): 28	Royalty: 8%, Advert: 5%	Co-operative Advertising: . . . . .No
Projected New Units for 1993: 5	Contract Periods (Yrs.): 5/5	Training: . . . . . .2 Wks. Training Center,
Distribution: US-0;Can-28;Overseas-0	Area Development Agreement: Yes/5	. . 1st Wk. On-Site, Monthly Follow-Up
North America: . . . . 6 Provinces	Sub-Franchise Contract: . . . . . Yes	On-Going Support: B,C,d,E,G,H/ 3
Concentration: . . .12 in NS, 9 in AB, 3 in BC	Expand in Territory: . . . . . . Yes	EXPANSION PLANS:
Registered: . . . . AB	Passive Ownership: . . . Discouraged	US: . . . . .No
. . . .	Encourage Conversions: . . . . . Yes	Canada: . . . . .All Canada
Type Space: . . . . .FS, SC;~4,000 SF	Average # Employees: . . 4 FT, 2 PT	Overseas: . . . . .No

SPEEDY AUTO GLASS

9675 SE 36th St.
Mercer Island, WA 98053
TEL: (800) 87-GLASS (206) 232-9500
FAX: (206) 232-6405
Mr. Thomas L. Reid, Fran. Sales

Auto glass replacement specialist, along with commercial and residential glass replacement, sunroofs, sliding doors, mirrors, table tops and screen doors.

HISTORY: . . . . IFA
Established in 1946; . . 1st Franchised in 1980
Company-Owned Units (As of 8/31/1992): 372
Franchised Units (As of 8/31/1992): 270
Total Units (As of 8/31/1992): 642
Projected New Units for 1993: 25
Distribution: . . . US-45;Can-283;Overseas-61
  North America: . . . . 3 States
  Concentration: . 35 in WA, 12 in NH, 12 in UT
Registered: . . . . All States
. . . .
Type Space: . . . .FS, SF, SC, RM;~2,500 SF

FINANCIAL: Earnings Claim: . .No
Cash Investment: $40-75K
Total Investment: $130-145K
Fees: Franchise - $10-30K
  Royalty: 6%, Advert: 7%
Contract Periods (Yrs.): 10/10
Area Development Agreement: Yes/10
Sub-Franchise Contract: . . . . .No
Expand in Territory: . . . . . . Yes
Passive Ownership: . . . Discouraged
Encourage Conversions: . . . . Yes
Average # Employees: . . 3 FT, 1 PT

FRANCHISOR TRAINING/SUPPORT:
Financial Assistance Provided: . . . . . No
Site Selection Assistance: . . . . . . .Yes
Lease Negotiation Assistance: . . . . .Yes
Co-operative Advertising: . . . . . . .Yes
Training: . . . . 2 Wks. Seattle, WA
. . . .
On-Going Support: A,B,C,D,E,F,G,h,I/ . 38
EXPANSION PLANS:
US: . . . . .All US
Canada: . . . . .No
Overseas: . . . . No

SPEEDY MUFFLER KING

8430 W. Bryn Mawr Ave., # 400
Chicago, IL 60631
TEL: (800) 736-6733 (312) 693-1000
FAX: (312) 693-0309
Mr. Bill Olsen, Dir. Fran. Dev.

SPEEDY MUFFLER KING is a retail automotive service chain, specializing in the undercar services of: exhaust systems, brakes, ride control and front-end repair.

HISTORY: . . . . IFA
Established in 1956; . . 1st Franchised in 1986
Company-Owned Units (As of 8/31/1992): . 22
Franchised Units (As of 8/31/1992): 662
Total Units (As of 8/31/1992): 684
Projected New Units for 1993: 15
Distribution: . . US-216;Can-155;Overseas-313
  North America: . . . . 12 States
  Concentration: . 38 in OH, 33 in MA, 32 in PA
Registered: . . . . MD,MI,NY,RI,VA
. . . .
Type Space: . . . . FS, Auto Malls;~4,000 SF

FINANCIAL: Earnings Claim: . .No
Cash Investment: $80-90K
Total Investment: $220K
Fees: Franchise - $18.5K
  Royalty: 5%, Advert: 5-10%
Contract Periods (Yrs.): 10/5
Area Development Agreement: . .No
Sub-Franchise Contract: . . . . .No
Expand in Territory: . . . . . . Yes
Passive Ownership: . . . Discouraged
Encourage Conversions: . . . . Yes
Average # Employees: . . . . . .4 FT

FRANCHISOR TRAINING/SUPPORT:
Financial Assistance Provided: . . . Yes(I)
Site Selection Assistance: . . . . . . .Yes
Lease Negotiation Assistance: . . . .Yes
Co-operative Advertising: . . . . No
Training: . . . . 3 Wks. Ann Arbor, MI,
  . .1 Wk. OJT, 1 Wk. HQ, 1 Wk. Opening
On-Going Support: B,C,D,E,F,G,H,I/ . . 25
EXPANSION PLANS:
US: . . . . .Eastern US
Canada: . . . . .All Canada
Overseas: . . . . No

SPOT-NOT CAR WASHES

2011 W. 4th St.
Joplin, MO 64801
TEL: (800) 682-7629 (417) 781-2140
FAX: (417) 781-3906
Mr. Forrest Uppendahl, VP Fran.

Coin-operated, self-service and brushless automatic car wash. Equipment, including the NO-SPOT Rinses feature, is exclusively available to SPOT-NOT franchisees. Parent company is the oldest continuous manufacturer of high-pressure, no-touch systems. Business is simple to operate with few employees. Low inventory. No receivables. Little direct competition in a stable industry.

HISTORY: . . . . IFA
Established in 1967; . . 1st Franchised in 1985
Company-Owned Units (As of 8/31/1992): . .0
Franchised Units (As of 8/31/1992): 23
Total Units (As of 8/31/1992): 23
Projected New Units for 1993: 6
Distribution: US-23;Can-0;Overseas-0
  North America: . . . . 4 States
  Concentration: . . . . 9 in IL, 8 in IN, 5 in MO
Registered: . . . . IL,IN,MI,WI
. . . .
Type Space: . . . . FS;~40,000 Site SF

FINANCIAL: Earnings Claim: . .No
Cash Investment: $200-300K
Total Investment: $546-940K
Fees: Franchise - $25K
  Royalty: 5%, Advert: 1%
Contract Periods (Yrs.): 10/5
Area Development Agreement: Yes/10
Sub-Franchise Contract: . . . . .No
Expand in Territory: . . . . . . Yes
Passive Ownership: . . . . . .Allowed
Encourage Conversions: . . . . Yes
Average # Employees: . . 1 FT, 3 PT

FRANCHISOR TRAINING/SUPPORT:
Financial Assistance Provided: . . . Yes(I)
Site Selection Assistance: . . . . . . .Yes
Lease Negotiation Assistance: . . . .NA
Co-operative Advertising: . . . . . . .Yes
Training: . . . . 4 Days HQ - Management,
  . . 4 Days HQ Technical, 5 Days On-Site
On-Going Support: B,C,D,E,F,G,H,I/ . . . 6
EXPANSION PLANS:
US: . . . . Midwest, Middle Atlantic, SE
Canada: . . . . .No
Overseas: . . . . No

STAR TECHNOLOGY WINDSHIELD REPAIR
6350-F McDonough Dr.
Norcross, GA 30093
TEL: (404) 263-0660
FAX:
Mr. David A. Casey, President

Mobile and fixed location windshield repair of rock-damaged and cracked windshields. Primary market is commercial fleets, auto dealerships and insurance industry. All training, equipment, clothing, literature and marketing assistance in franchise territory is included in franchise package.

HISTORY: . . . .
Established in 1983; . . 1st Franchised in 1984
Company-Owned Units (As of 8/31/1992): . .1
Franchised Units (As of 8/31/1992): 163
Total Units (As of 8/31/1992): 164
Projected New Units for 1993: 25
Distribution: US-161;Can-0;Overseas-3
  North America: . . . . 38 States
  Concentration: . . .12 in CO, 7 in OH, 6 in AR
Registered: . . . .
. . . .
Type Space: . . . . .Mobile;~NA SF

FINANCIAL: Earnings Claim: . .No
Cash Investment: . . . .$
Total Investment: $10K
Fees: Franchise - $4.5K
  Royalty: 3%, Advert: 0%
Contract Periods (Yrs.): 10/10
Area Development Agreement: Yes/20
Sub-Franchise Contract: . . . . . Yes
Expand in Territory: . . . . Yes
Passive Ownership: . . . Discouraged
Encourage Conversions: . . . . . .No
Average # Employees: . . . . .2 FT

FRANCHISOR TRAINING/SUPPORT:
Financial Assistance Provided: . . .Yes(D)
Site Selection Assistance: . . . . . . .Yes
Lease Negotiation Assistance: . . . . .NA
Co-operative Advertising: . . . . . . .Yes
Training: . . . . .1 Wk. Headquarters,
. . . . 1 Wk. Franchisee Location
On-Going Support: B,C,D,E,G,H/ 6
EXPANSION PLANS:
US: . . . . All US
Canada: . . . . .All Canada
Overseas: . . . . .Yes

STOP BRAKE SHOPS
3300 Irvine Blvd., # 300
Newport Beach, CA 92660
TEL: (800) 955-1415 (714) 863-9444
FAX: (714) 863-0140
Mr. Don St. Ours, President

STOP BRAKE SHOPS offers a high-tech service for brakes, tune-up and smog check, with emphasis on service while you wait. We use only the latest in equipment and on-going service bulletins. With our high volume and low overhead, we maintain the highest in gross profit margins.

HISTORY: . . . .
Established in 1980; . . 1st Franchised in 1981
Company-Owned Units (As of 8/31/1992): . .1
Franchised Units (As of 8/31/1992): 23
Total Units (As of 8/31/1992): 24
Projected New Units for 1993: 8
Distribution: US-24;Can-0;Overseas-0
  North America: . . . . .1 State
  Concentration: . . . . 24 in CA
Registered: . . . . CA
. . . .
Type Space: . . . . .FS, SC;~3,000 SF

FINANCIAL: Earnings Claim: . .No
Cash Investment: $50K
Total Investment: $135K
Fees: Franchise - $25K
  Royalty: 6%, Advert: 3%
Contract Periods (Yrs.): 10/10
Area Development Agreement: Yes/10
Sub-Franchise Contract: . . . . . Yes
Expand in Territory: . . . . Yes
Passive Ownership: . . . Discouraged
Encourage Conversions: . . . . . Yes
Average # Employees: . . 3 FT, 1 PT

FRANCHISOR TRAINING/SUPPORT:
Financial Assistance Provided: . . . Yes(I)
Site Selection Assistance: . . . . . . .Yes
Lease Negotiation Assistance: . . . .Yes
Co-operative Advertising: . . . . . . .Yes
Training: . . . .~ 2 Wks. Covina, CA,
. . . . . .~ 2 Wks. Rowland Heights, CA
On-Going Support: B,C,D,E,F,G,H,I/ . . .6
EXPANSION PLANS:
US: . . . . All US
Canada: . . . . .All Canada
Overseas: . . . . No

THREE STAR MUFFLER
7691 McHenry Circle N.
Germantown, TN 38138
TEL: (901) 755-2179
FAX:
Mr. Ray Zedlitz, Dir. Fran.

Complete under-car service: exhaust, brakes, chassis, alignment, drive line, C-V joints and oil change and lube.

HISTORY: . . . .
Established in 1971; . . 1st Franchised in 1980
Company-Owned Units (As of 8/31/1992): . .2
Franchised Units (As of 8/31/1992): 11
Total Units (As of 8/31/1992): 13
Projected New Units for 1993: 2
Distribution: US-13;Can-0;Overseas-0
  North America: . . . . 2 States
  Concentration: . . . . 12 in TN, 1 in MS
Registered: . . . . .All
. . . .
Type Space: . . . . FS;~2,050 SF

FINANCIAL: Earnings Claim: . .No
Cash Investment: $40K
Total Investment: $90K
Fees: Franchise - $15K
  Royalty: 5%, Advert: 2%
Contract Periods (Yrs.): . . . 10/10
Area Development Agreement: Yes/10
Sub-Franchise Contract: . . . . . Yes
Expand in Territory: . . . . Yes
Passive Ownership: . . . Not Allowed
Encourage Conversions: . . . . Yes
Average # Employees: . . 3 FT, 1 PT

FRANCHISOR TRAINING/SUPPORT:
Financial Assistance Provided: . . . Yes(I)
Site Selection Assistance: . . . . . . .Yes
Lease Negotiation Assistance: . . . . .Yes
Co-operative Advertising: . . . . . . .Yes
Training: . . . . 2 Wks. Headquarters,
. . . . 1 Wk. On-Site (More if Required)
On-Going Support: A,B,C,D,E,F,g,h,I/ . .4
EXPANSION PLANS:
US: . . . . All US
Canada: . . . . No
Overseas: . . . . No

TUNEX AUTOMOTIVE SPECIALISTS

556 East 2100 S.
Salt Lake City, UT 84106
TEL: (800) HI-TUNEX (801) 486-8133
FAX: (801) 484-4740
Franchise Sales Dept.

Diagnostic and environmentally correct tune-up services and repairs of engine-related systems (i.e. ignition, carburetion, fuel injection, emission, computer controls, cooling, air conditioning). For maximum customer satisfaction, we analyze all systems for problems so that the customer can make service and repair decision.

HISTORY: . . . . IFA	FINANCIAL: Earnings Claim: . .No	FRANCHISOR TRAINING/SUPPORT:
Established in 1974; . . 1st Franchised in 1975	Cash Investment: $65K	Financial Assistance Provided: . . . . . No
Company-Owned Units (As of 8/31/1992): . .5	Total Investment: $105-120K	Site Selection Assistance: . . . . .Yes
Franchised Units (As of 8/31/1992): 14	Fees: Franchise - $19K	Lease Negotiation Assistance: . . . . .Yes
Total Units (As of 8/31/1992): 19	Royalty: 5%, Advert: . . $500/Mo.	Co-operative Advertising: . . . . . . .Yes
Projected New Units for 1993: 6	Contract Periods (Yrs.): 10/10	Training: . . . . . 1-2 Wks. HQ, 1 Wk. Site
Distribution: US-19;Can-0;Overseas-0	Area Development Agreement: . .No	. . . . for Grand Opening, 2-3 Days Site
North America: . . . . 6 States	Sub-Franchise Contract: . . . . .No	On-Going Support: C,d,E,F,G,I/ 6
Concentration: . . .11 in UT, 3 in CO, 2 in NV	Expand in Territory: . . . . Yes	EXPANSION PLANS:
Registered:	Passive Ownership: . . . Discouraged	US: . . . . .Mountain States, Southwest
. . . .	Encourage Conversions: . . . . .No	Canada: . . . . No
Type Space: . . . . FS, Auto Malls;~2,500 SF	Average # Employees: . . . . .4 FT	Overseas: . . . . .MX

US-1 AUTO PARTS

5 Dakota Dr., # 210
Lake Success, NY 11042
TEL: (516) 358-5100
FAX: (516) 358-2717
Mr. Reuben Alcalay, President

Auto parts and accessories. Retail stores.

HISTORY:	FINANCIAL: Earnings Claim: . . .	FRANCHISOR TRAINING/SUPPORT:
Established in 1983; . . 1st Franchised in 1991	Cash Investment: $150K	Financial Assistance Provided: . . . . . No
Company-Owned Units (As of 8/31/1992): . .1	Total Investment: $250K	Site Selection Assistance: . . . . .Yes
Franchised Units (As of 8/31/1992): 19	Fees: Franchise - $25K	Lease Negotiation Assistance: . . . . .Yes
Total Units (As of 8/31/1992): 20	Royalty: 6%, Advert: . . 3.5%	Co-operative Advertising: . . . . . . .Yes
Projected New Units for 1993: 20	Contract Periods (Yrs.): 20	Training: . . . . . . .1 Month Headquarters
Distribution: US-20;Can-0;Overseas-0	Area Development Agreement: Yes/1	. . . .
North America: . . . . .1 State	Sub-Franchise Contract: . . . . Yes	On-Going Support: C,D,e,f,G,H/ 3
Concentration: . . . . 20 in NY	Expand in Territory: . . . . . . Yes	EXPANSION PLANS:
Registered: . . . . NY	Passive Ownership: . . . Discouraged	US: . . . . . New York and New Jersey
. . . .	Encourage Conversions:	Canada: . . . . No
Type Space: . . . . FS;~5,000 SF	Average # Employees: . . 2 FT, 1 PT	Overseas: . . . . EUR, Middle East

VALVOLINE INSTANT OIL CHANGE

301 E. Main St., # 1200
Lexington, KY 40507
TEL: (800) 622-6846 (606) 264-7070
FAX: (606) 264-7049
Mr. Jeff Malicote, Sales

The licensor offers licenses and development agreements for the establishment and operation of a business which provides a quick oil change, chassis lubrication and routine maintenance checks on automobiles. The licensor and/or its affiliates will offer (to qualified prospects) leasing programs for land, building, equipment, signage and POS system.

HISTORY: . . . . IFA	FINANCIAL: Earnings Claim: . Yes	FRANCHISOR TRAINING/SUPPORT:
Established in 1988; . . 1st Franchised in 1988	Cash Investment: $83-133K	Financial Assistance Provided: . . . Yes(I)
Company-Owned Units (As of 8/31/1992): 304	Total Investment: $85-135K	Site Selection Assistance: . . . . .Yes
Franchised Units (As of 8/31/1992): 33	Fees: Franchise - $25K	Lease Negotiation Assistance: . . . . .Yes
Total Units (As of 8/31/1992): 337	Royalty: 4-6%, Advert: 8%	Co-operative Advertising: . . . . No
Projected New Units for 1993: 30	Contract Periods (Yrs.): 15/5/5	Training: . . . . . . 1 Wk. HQ, 3 Wks. HQ,
Distribution: US-337;Can-0;Overseas-0	Area Development Agreement: Yes/Var	. . . . 1 Wk. On-Site
North America: . . . . 34 States	Sub-Franchise Contract: . . . . .No	On-Going Support: a,B,C,D,E,F,G,H,I/ . . 6
Concentration: . 65 in OH, 63 in MI, 41 in MN	Expand in Territory: . . . . . . Yes	EXPANSION PLANS:
Registered: . . . . .All	Passive Ownership: . . . Discouraged	US: . . . . NW, SE, SW, Middle Atlantic
. . . .	Encourage Conversions: . . . . . Yes	Canada: . . . . No
Type Space: . . . . FS;~15,000 SF	Average # Employees: . . 4 FT, 2 PT	Overseas: . . . . No

WASH ON WHEELS / WOW

5401 S. Bryant Ave.
Sanford, FL 32773
TEL: (800) 345-1969 (407) 321-4010
FAX: (407) 321-3409
Mr. Jim Good, President

WOW is a general purpose mobile wash cleaning service addressing all surface dirt: indoor and outdoor, directed at the residential, commercial and industrial marketplace. Our chemicals, training, customized software and continuing franchise development program support growth and success.

HISTORY:	FINANCIAL: Earnings Claim: . .No	FRANCHISOR TRAINING/SUPPORT:
Established in 1964; . . 1st Franchised in 1987	Cash Investment: $10-65K	Financial Assistance Provided: . . . Yes(I)
Company-Owned Units (As of 8/31/1992): . .0	Total Investment: $10-65K	Site Selection Assistance: . . . . .NA
Franchised Units (As of 8/31/1992): 55	Fees: Franchise - $7.5K	Lease Negotiation Assistance: . . . . .NA
Total Units (As of 8/31/1992): 55	Royalty: $250/Mo., Advert: . . 0%	Co-operative Advertising: . . . . . . .NA
Projected New Units for 1993: 25	Contract Periods (Yrs.): 5/5	Training: . . . . 2 Wks. Headquarters
Distribution: US-55;Can-0;Overseas-0	Area Development Agreement: Yes/5	. . . .
North America: . . . . 21 States	Sub-Franchise Contract: . . . . .No	On-Going Support: B,C,D,F,G,H,I/ 8
Concentration: . . . 8 in CA, 8 in FL, 6 in OH	Expand in Territory: . . . . Yes	EXPANSION PLANS:
Registered: . . . . .All	Passive Ownership: . . . Discouraged	US: . . . . .All US
. . . .	Encourage Conversions: . . . . . NA	Canada: . . . . .All Canada
Type Space: . . . . NA;~NA SF	Average # Employees:	Overseas: . . . . EUR

WESTERN AUTO SUPPLY COMPANY

2107 Grand Ave.
Kansas City, MO 64108
TEL: (800) 274-6733 (816) 346-4397
FAX: (816) 346-4188
Mr. Chuck Hutchens, VP Fran. Dev.

Auto America: discount automotive superstore, featuring dominant assortments (tires, batteries, parts, accessories and maintenance products) and automotive service - under one roof.

HISTORY: . . . . IFA	FINANCIAL: Earnings Claim: . .No	FRANCHISOR TRAINING/SUPPORT:
Established in 1909; . . 1st Franchised in 1935	Cash Investment: $130-175K	Financial Assistance Provided: . . . . .No
Company-Owned Units (As of 8/31/1992): 373	Total Investment: $390-515K	Site Selection Assistance: . . . . .Yes
Franchised Units (As of 8/31/1992): 1113	Fees: Franchise - $25K	Lease Negotiation Assistance: . . . . .NA
Total Units (As of 8/31/1992): 1486	Royalty: 5%, Advert: 2%	Co-operative Advertising: . . . . . . .Yes
Projected New Units for 1993: 30	Contract Periods (Yrs.): 10/10	Training: . . . . 5 Wks. Company Store,
Distribution: US-1486;Can-0;Overseas-0	Area Development Agreement: . .No	. . . . .2 Wks. Franchisee Store
North America: . . . . 47 States	Sub-Franchise Contract: . . . . .No	On-Going Support: A,B,C,D,E,F,h/ . . . 99
Concentration: . 193 in TX, 109 in NC, 85 LA	Expand in Territory: . . . . Yes	EXPANSION PLANS:
Registered: . . . . .FL,IN,MI,NY	Passive Ownership: . . . Discouraged	US: . . . . Midwest and Northeast
. . . .	Encourage Conversions: . . . . .No	Canada: . . . . .No
Type Space: . . . . .FS;~9,000 SF	Average # Employees:6-10 FT, 6-10 PT	Overseas: . . . . No

ZIEBART TIDY CAR

1290 E. Maple Rd., P. O. Box 1290
Troy, MI 48007
TEL: (800) 877-1312 (313) 588-4100
FAX: (313) 588-1444
Mr. Greg Longe, Mgr. Fran. Dev.

Business format consists of detailing, accessories and protection services. Ultra-modern showrooms maximize the exposure for the services offered by the franchisee. The customer base consists of retail, wholesale and fleet - making ZIEBART TIDY CAR #1 in the world.

HISTORY: . . . . IFA	FINANCIAL: Earnings Claim: . .No	FRANCHISOR TRAINING/SUPPORT:
Established in 1954; . . 1st Franchised in 1962	Cash Investment: $90-150K	Financial Assistance Provided: . . . . .Yes
Company-Owned Units (As of 8/31/1992): . 22	Total Investment: $90-150K	Site Selection Assistance: . . . . .Yes
Franchised Units (As of 8/31/1992): 628	Fees: Franchise - $60K	Lease Negotiation Assistance: . . . . .Yes
Total Units (As of 8/31/1992): 650	Royalty: 5-8%, Advert: 5%	Co-operative Advertising: . . . . . . .Yes
Projected New Units for 1993: 54	Contract Periods (Yrs.): . . . 10/10	Training: . . . . 5 Wks. Headquarters
Distribution: . . . US-355;Can-0;Overseas-295	Area Development Agreement: . .No	. . . .
North America: . . . . 39 States	Sub-Franchise Contract: . . . . .No	On-Going Support: B,C,D,E,G,H/ . . . 99
Concentration:	Expand in Territory: . . . . Yes	EXPANSION PLANS:
Registered: . . . . .All	Passive Ownership: . . . Not Allowed	US: . . . . .All US
. . . .	Encourage Conversions: . . . . . Yes	Canada: . . . . .All Canada
Type Space: . . . . .FS;~2,750 SF	Average # Employees: . . . . .4 FT	Overseas: . . . . .Yes

SUPPLEMENTAL LISTING OF FRANCHISORS

AAUTO MOTOR EXCHANGE . . . . 204 Auburn St., Pittsburgh, PA 15206
Contact: Mr. Mark R. Lando, Sales Consultant; Tel: (412) 687-3725
ABT SERVICE CENTERS . . . . .2339 South 2700 West, Salt Lake City, UT 84119
Contact: Mr. Edward A. Vigil; Tel: (801) 972-1702
ACE QUICK OIL CHANGE . . . . 1775 Acushnet Ave., New Bedford, MA 02745
Contact: Mr. Dave Lima, VP Ops.; Tel: (508) 636-3968
ACTION AUTO STORES . . . . 2128 S. Dort Hwy., Flint, MI 48507
Contact: Mr. Richard Sabo, President; Tel: (313) 235-5600
ACTIVE TIRE & AUTO CENTRE . . . . .580 Evans Ave., Etobicoke, ON M8W 2W1   CAN
Contact: Mr. Douglas Moody, GM; Tel: (416) 255-5581
ADA SYSTEMS INTERNATIONAL . . . . .752 Caledonia Ave., Victoria, BC V4T 1E5   CAN
Contact: Mr. Jack Lidstone, Mana. Dir.; Tel: (604) 388-5612
AIRVAC BRAKE, LIMITED . . . . 5920 35th St., SE, Calgary, AB T2C 2G3   CAN
Contact: President; Tel: (402) 279-3377
ALL TUNE AND LUBE SYSTEM . . . . 407 Headquarters Dr., # 7, Millersville, MD 21108
Contact: Mr. Bruce Frazier, Franchise Sales; Tel: (800) 333-9263 (301) 987-1011
ALLSTAR SERVICE PLUS . . . . .2955 Main St., 3rd Fl., Irvine, CA 92714
Contact: Mr. Chuck Sasse; Tel: (714) 757-1278
APPEARANCE RECONDITIONING CO. . . . . . 12833 Industrial Park Blvd., Minneapolis, MN 55441
Contact: Mr. Daniel Aumen, President; Tel: (800) 255-8537 (612) 559-3292
APPLE POLISHING SYSTEMS . . . . 6103 Johns Rd., # 2, Tampa, FL 33634
Contact: Mr. Makr Chapin, President; Tel: (813) 882-0077
AUTO ACCENTS . . . . 6215 Pearl, Cleveland, OH 44130
Contact: Mr. Amid A. Yousef, President; Tel: (216) 888-8886
AUTO CRITIC OF AMERICA . . . . 13720 Midway Rd., # 105, Dallas, TX 75244
Contact: Mr. Patrick Ludwick, President; Tel: (800) 765-1857 (214) 404-8033
AUTO GENICS TOTAL AUTO SERVICE . . . . 820 Nipissing Rd., # 4, Milton, ON M9T 4Z9   CAN
Contact: Mr. Douglas Williams, President; Tel: (416) 876-0166
AUTO-LIFE . . . . 1430 South Cherokee St., Denver, CO 80223
Contact: Mr. Nigel Reed, President; Tel: (303) 722-5320
AUTOFAIR . . . . 1501 W. 15th St., Houston, TX 77008
Contact: Mr. Pat Henerling; Tel: (713) 862-6060
AUTOINSPECT MASTER OF AMERICA . . . . 305 Linden St., Mahwah, NJ 07430
Contact: Mr. Robert E. Farrell, President; Tel: (800) 288-6467
AUTOMASTERS . . . . 3200 SW 34th St., Gainesville, FL 32608
Contact: President; Tel: (904) 374-4933
AUTOMOTIVE LUBE SHOP LIMITED . . . . 130 Dearborn Place, Waterloo, ON N2J 4N5   CAN
Contact: President; Tel: (519) 886-0561
AUTOSTOCK/G. LEBEAU/MONSIEUR MUFFLER . . . . . 8288 boul. PIE IX, Montreal, PQ H1Z 3T6   CAN
Contact: M. Claude Dutil; Tel: (514) 593-7000
AVIS LUBE FAST OIL CHANGE . . . . 900 Old Country Rd., Garden City, NY 11530
Contact: Mr. Jay Sanderson, Dir. Bus. Dev.; Tel: (516) 222-3400
BATTERY BANK, THE . . . . 2053 Johns Drive, Glenview, IL 60025
Contact: Mr. Alan Schulman; Tel: (708) BAT-TERY (312) 998-0445
BIG O TIRES . . . . 11755 E. Peakview Ave., Englewood, CO 80111
Contact: Ms. Maureen Hoffman, Compliance; Tel: (800) 622-2446 (303) 790-2800
BP PROCARE . . . . 200 Public Square, Cleveland, OH 44114
Contact: Mr. Chet Bowling, Fran. Mgr.; Tel: (216) 586-2446
BRAHMA PLUS . . . . Centre Point III, 600 Six Flags Dr., Arlington, TX 76011
Contact: Mr. Harris N. Hollin, CEO; Tel: (800) BRAHMAS (817) 640-2158
BRAKE WORLD . . . . 7700 NW 27th Ave., Miami, FL 33147
Contact: Mr. Gerald D. Hopkins; Tel: (305) 836-4434
BUDGET BRAKE & MUFFLER . . . . # 422 - 4940 Canada Way, Burnaby, BC V5G 4K7   CAN
Contact: Mr. Warren Swanson, President; Tel: (604) 294-6114
CAP-A-RADIATOR SHOPS OF AMERICA . . . . 2879 Long Beach Rd., Oceanside, NY 11572
Contact: Mr. Joseph Fels, President; Tel: (516) 536-5145
CARRIAGE TRADE PERSONAL AUTO. LIAISON . . . . . 2242 E. 45th Ave., Vancouver, BC V5P 1N8   CAN
Contact: Mr. Neal R. McRae, President; Tel: (604) 321-5058
CERTIFIED POWER TRAIN SPECIALISTS . . . . 2441 26th Ave., S., Minneapolis, MN 55406
Contact: President; Tel: (612) 721-2418

CHEM-GLASS WINDSHIELD REPAIR . . . . 7111 Ohms Ln., Minneapolis, MN 55439
    Contact: Mr. Scott L. Smith, VP; Tel: (800) 333-8523 (612) 835-1338
CITYWIDE AUTO GLASS . . . . 787 S. Main St., Brockton, MA 02401
    Contact: Mr. Bud Owens; Tel: (617) 588-8068
CLASSIC CAR WASH . . . . 871 E. Hamilton Ave, Ste. C, Campbell, CA 95008
    Contact: Mr. Barney Dallas, VP; Tel: (800) 538-7836 (408) 371-2414
CLASSIC SHINE AUTO FITNESS CENTER . . . . 249 Railroad Ave., Greenwich, CT 06830
    Contact: Mr. Stephen Grisanti, President; Tel: (800) 72-SHINE (203) 629-2109 C
CONTINENTAL TRANSMISSION . . . . 2328 Fort St., Lincoln Park, MI 48146
    Contact: President; Tel: (313) 388-8906
CRESTLINE VENTURES CORP. . . . . 802 57th St. E., Saskatoon, SK S7K 5Z1   CAN
    Contact: Mr. Ken Sawatsky, President; Tel: (306) 934-5875
DER WAGEN HAUS . . . . 5316 W. Market St., P.O. Box 18421, Greensboro, NC 27419
    Contact: Mr. Randy Beeninga; Tel: (919) 292-6640
DIAMOND QUALITY TRANSMISSION CENTERS . . . . . . P.O. Box 6147, Philadelphia, PA 19115
    Contact: President; Tel: (215) 742-8333
DRIVE LINE SERVICE . . . . 7307 Roseville Rd., # 9, Sacramento, CA 95842
    Contact: Mr. L. D. Wilson, President; Tel: (916) 371-8117
DURA-BUILT TRANSMISSIONS . . . . 455 University Ave., # 100, Sacramento, CA 95825
    Contact: Mr. Jay Byers; Tel: (916) 920-2243
ENGINE XPRESS INSTALLATION & SALES . . . West 10th St. Extension, Roanoke Rapids, NC 27870
    Contact: Mr. Chuck McGill; Tel: (800) 334-1931
EXPRESS 10 MINUTE LUBE CENTER . . . . 66 Rte. 125, Unit 5, Kingston, NH 03848
    Contact: Mr. Gary Krause, Dir. Fran. Ops.; Tel: (603) 642-8893 C
FANTASY COACHWORKS . . . . 6034 S. Lindbergh Blvd., St. Louis, MO 63123
    Contact: Mr. James Smoot, President; Tel: (314) 487-0054
FIRESTONE TIRE & AUTOMOTIVE CENTRES . . . . . 120 King St., # 750, Hamilton, ON L8N 4C6   CAN
    Contact: Mr. Timothy Tibbs, Sales Dir.; Tel: (416) 545-4711
FIRESTONE TIRE & RUBBER COMPANY . . . . 50 Century Blvd., Nashville, TN 37214
    Contact: Franchise Department; Tel: (615) 391-0088
FLY-N-HI OFFROAD CENTER . . . . 701 S. 7th St., Phoenix, AZ 85034
    Contact: Mr. Paul Harris; Tel: (602) 263-1936
FLYING COLORS . . . . 10696 Haddington Dr., # 130, Houston, TX 77043
    Contact: Mr. Ben Litalien, President; Tel: (800) 232-1244 (713) 683-9900
GE CAPITAL AUTO RESALE SERVICE . . . . 1000 Hart Rd., # 300, Barrington, IL 60010
    Contact: Mr. Stephen A. McNeely, President; Tel: (708) 304-3001
GKN-PARTS INDUSTRIES . . . . 601 S. Dudley St., Memphis, TN 38104
    Contact: Mr. John A. Christiansen EVP/CFO; Tel: (901) 523-7711
GLAS-WELD SYSTEMS . . . . 20578 Empire Blvd., P. O. Box 5755, Bend, OR 97701
    Contact: Mr. Robert Beveridge, GM; Tel: (800) 321-2597 (503) 388-1156
GOODEAL DISCOUNT TRANSMISSIONS . . . . P. O. Box 50, National Park, NJ 08063
    Contact: Mr. John Mikulski, President; Tel: (800) 626-8695 (609) 488-4455
GOODYEAR CERTIFIED AUTO SERVICE . . . . . . 10 Four Seasons Place, Etobicoke, ON M9B 6G2   CAN
    Contact: Mr. Mario Ricci, Mgr. of Finance; Tel: (416) 626-4611
GOODYEAR TIRE CENTERS . . . . 1144 E. Market St., Akron, OH 44316
    Contact: Mr. H. M. Harding, Manager; Tel: (216) 796-3467
GRACELAINE SERVICE CENTERS . . . . 3001 Ashley Ave., Montgomery, AL 36109
    Contact: Mr. B. A. Dickman, President; Tel: (205) 272-6138
GREASE 'N GO . . . . P. O. Box 12339, # 232, Scottsdale, AZ 85267
    Contact: Mr. Richard Lindstrom; Tel: (602) 497-4710
GREASE N' GO ATLANTIC . . . . 6720 Curran St., McLean, VA 22101
    Contact: Mr. James W. Reid, President; Tel: (703) 556-6166
GREAT BEAR AUTOMOTIVE CENTERS . . . . 325 Great Neck Rd., Great Neck, NY 11021
    Contact: Mr. Steven Kunen, President; Tel: (800) US-BEARS (516) 764-6700
HAMILTON RADIATOR . . . . 624 Parkdale Ave. N., P. O. Box 3760, Hamilton, ON L8H 7N1   CAN
    Contact: Mr. Paul Jeffrey; Tel: (416) 549-4181
HANNA CAR WASH SYSTEMS . . . . 2001 Hanna Dr., Portland, OR 97222
    Contact: Mr. Ron Garrison; Tel: (503) 659-0361
HOMETOWN AUTO SERVICE . . . . 2062 W. Main St., Jeffersonville, PA 19403
    Contact: Mr. Dan Rhode, President; Tel: (800) 231-2254 (215) 539-1400
HOUSE OF MUFFLERS . . . . 8504 L St., Omaha, NE 68127
    Contact: President; Tel: (402) 571-3389
IN SHEEP'S CLOTHING . . . . P.O. Box 12374, Fort Worth, TX 76116
    Contact: President; Tel: (817) 244-2856
JIFFIWASH . . . . P. O. Box 5307, 520 Rawhide Dr., Tahoe City, CA 95730
    Contact: Mr. Merle Akers, President; Tel: (800) 543-3483

JOHNNY RUTHERFORD TUNE/LUBE . . . . . 95 Madison Ave., P. O. Box 2088, Morristown, NJ 07960
    Contact: Mr. Terry Nelson, Dir. Fran. Sales; Tel: (201) 539-1039
KALE'S COLLISION . . . . 3250 W. Big Beaver Rd., # 116, Troy, MI 48084
    Contact: Mr. Kale Roscoe, President; Tel: (313) 649-4449
LEAVERTON AUTO . . . . 827 S. 9th, St. Joseph, MO 64501
    Contact: Mr. Ronald J. Martin, President; Tel: (816) 279-7483
LEMONBUSTERS . . . . .1802 W. 6th, # 2B, Austin, TX 78703
    Contact: Mr. A. Bary Sprague, President; Tel: (800) 74L-EMON (512) 477-2299
LUBE & TUNE USA . . . . .4195 S. Tamiami Tr., # 118, Venice, FL 43293
    Contact: President; Tel:
LUBE RANGER, THE . . . . P. O. Box 27884, Houston, TX 77227
    Contact: President; Tel: (713) 622-7545
LUBE SHOP, THE . . . . P. O. Box 4204, Mesa, AZ 85211
    Contact: Mr. J. H. McKinney, President; Tel: (602) 962-4851
MAACO AUTO PAINTING/BODYWORKS (CANADA) . 5915 Airport Rd., # 330, Mississauga, ON L4V 1T1   CAN
    Contact: Mr. HermanN Delisle; Tel: (416) 678-7104
MAD HATTER CAR CARE CENTERS . . . . 4012 Park Rd., # 101, Charlotte, NC 28209
    Contact: Mr. Joe Kotow, President; Tel: (800) 523-1023 (704) 523-1023
MALCO PRODUCTS . . . . 361 Fairview Ave., Barberton, OH 44203
    Contact: President; Tel: (216) 753-0361
MARK I AUTO SERVICE CENTERS . . . . 10825 Old Halls Ferry Rd., St. Louis, MO 63136
    Contact: President; Tel: (314) 993-6636
MARK-2 COLLISION CENTERS . . . . P. O. Box 327, Edmonds, WA 98020
    Contact: President; Tel:
MASTER-KLEEN . . . . 12350 S. Belcher Rd., Largo, FL 33545
    Contact: President; Tel:
METRO 25 TIRE CENTERS . . . . 6031 Joy Rd., Detroit, MI 48204
    Contact: Mr. Duane T. Rao; Tel: (313) 895-1200
MIDAS CANADA . . . . .105 Commander Blvd., Agincourt, ON M1S 3X8   CAN
    Contact: Mr. Michael Claener, Dir. Ret. Dev.; Tel: (416) 291-4261
MILEX TUNE UP & BRAKE CENTERS . . . . 4914 N. Lincoln Ave., Chicago, IL 60625
    Contact: Mr. Werner E. Ament, CEO; Tel: (800) 288-6030 (312) 561-1214
MINOR DETAILS . . . . .P. O. Box 30802, Santa Barbara, CA 93130
    Contact: President; Tel: (805) 962-1819
MINUTE MUFFLER . . . . 1600 3rd Ave. S., Lethbridge, AB T1S 0L2   CAN
    Contact: Mr. Robb Sloan; Tel: (403) 329-1020
MIRACLE AUTO PAINTING & BODY REPAIR . . . . . . .3157 Corporate Pl., Hayward, CA 94545
    Contact: Mr. Jim Jordan, Mktg. Dir.; Tel: (510) 887-2211
MISTER FRONT-END . . . . 192 N. Queen St., Etobicoke, ON M9C 1A8   CAN
    Contact: Mr. Gerry R. Jones; Tel: (416) 622-9999
MOBILE AUTO SYSTEMS . . . . 2133 Las Positas Ct., # B, Livermore, CA 94550
    Contact: Mr. Mark Trujillo, President; Tel: (415) 828-2131
MOBILE MECHANIC . . . . 4189 Willowview Ave., # 1219, Memphis, TN 38111
    Contact: Mr. Phil Meyers; Tel: (901) 743-5084
MOBILE OIL BUTLER INTERNATIONAL . . . . 1599 Rte. 22 West, Union, NJ 07083
    Contact: Mr. Robert DelVecchio, Dir. Fran. Dev.; Tel: (301) 790-0097 (908) 687-3283
MOTORWORKS . . . . .4210 Salem St., Philadelphia, PA 19124
    Contact: Mr. Richard L. Robinson, VP Ops.; Tel: (800) 327-9905 (215) 533-4112
MR. LUBE CANADA . . . . 111 Brunel Rd., # 210, Mississauga, ON L4Z 1X3   CAN
    Contact: Ms. J'Neene Horth; Tel: (416) 8890-5500
MUFFLER XPRESS & BRAKE CENTERS . . . . . W. 10th St. Extension, Roanoke Rapids, NC 27870
    Contact: Mr. Chuck McGill; Tel: (800) 334-1931 (919) 537-2460
MULTI-TUNE AND TIRE . . . . 2461 Covington Park Way, Memphis, TN 38128
    Contact: Mr. Glen Whiteman, Owner; Tel: (901) 386-9600
MULTISTATE TRANSMISSIONS . . . . .4645 147th St., Midlothian, IL 60445
    Contact: Mr. Aaron Reavis, VP; Tel: (313) 478-9206 C
NATIONAL AUTO SERVICE CENTERS . . . . 1605 S. Missouri Ave., Clearwater, FL 33516
    Contact: President; Tel: (813) 581-4061
NATIONAL CAR CARE CENTERS . . . . 2470 Windy Hill Rd., # 451, Marietta, GA 30067
    Contact: Mr. Donald Zachman; Tel: (404) 955-4506
NOVUS WINDSHIELD REPAIR . . . . 10425 Hampshire Ave. S., Minneapolis, MN 55438
    Contact: Mr. Gerald Keinath, President; Tel: (800) 328-1117 (612) 944-8000 C
NTW (NATIONAL TIRE WHOLESALE) . . . . . . .13871 Telegraph Rd., Woodbridge, VA 22192
    Contact: President; Tel:
NU-GLOW AUTO DETAILING . . . . 1285 Britannia Rd. East, Mississauga, ON L4W 2J5   CAN
    Contact: President; Tel: (416) 677-7878

PERMA-SHINE CAR CARE CENTRES . . . . 1380 Speers Rd., # 4, Oakville, ON L6L 5Y3   CAN
    Contact: Mr. Don C. Smith; Tel: (416) 827-7266
PIT STOP . . . . 300 Summit Street, P. O. Box 40, Hartford, CT 06106
    Contact: Mr. Christo Hoser; Tel: (502) 839-5471
PRECISION TUNE . . . . 748 Miller Dr., SE, P.O. Box 5000, Leesburg, VA 22075
    Contact: Mr. David Groce, General Counsel; Tel: (800) 231-0588 (703) 777-9095
PROMPTO 10 MINUTE OIL, FILTER & LUBE . . . . 13 Scott Dr., Westbrook, ME 04092
    Contact: Mr. Kevin A. King; Tel: (207) 775-4016
QUAL-TECH IMPORT CENTER . . . . 4000 Atlanta Rd., Smyrna, GA 30080
    Contact: Mr. Barry Rosenberg, President; Tel: (404) 432-8293
RADIATOR WORKS . . . . 2702 West Ave., # 102, San Antonio, TX 78201
    Contact: Mr. Al Heizer, VP Fran. Devel.; Tel: (512) 340-1918
ROADWAY MUFFLER & BRAKE CENTERS . . . 23193A Sandalfoot Plaza Dr., Boca Raton, FL 33428
    Contact: President; Tel: (305) 492-9988
SHINE FACTORY . . . . .116 Monument Pl., SE, Calgary, AB T2A 1X3   CAN
    Contact: Mr. B. Cousens, President; Tel: (403) 273-3525
SHIP SHAPE CAR WASHES . . . . 2004 Highland Ave., Eau Claire, WI 54701
    Contact: Mr. Kevin Koehn, President; Tel: (715) 836-9274 C
SPARKS TUNE UP CENTERS . . . . . 1400 Opus Pl., # 800, Opus West III, Downers Grove, IL 60515
    Contact: Mr. Joseph J. Marley, Dir. Fran. Dev.; Tel: (800) 458-9289 (312) 515-5134
SPEEDEE OIL CHANGE & TUNE-UP . . . . .6660 Riverside Dr., # 101, Metairie, LA 70003
    Contact: Mr. Gary Copp, President; Tel: (800) 451-7461 (504) 454-3783
SPEEDY TRANSMISSION CENTERS . . . 1239 E. Newport Center Dr., # 115, Deerfield Beach, FL 33442
    Contact: Mr. D'Arcy J. Williams, President; Tel: (800) 326-0310 (305) 428-0077
SUPERFORMANCE FRANCHISING . . . . 2950 Airway Ave., # A5, Costa Mesa, CA 92626
    Contact: Mr. Harry Schader; Tel: (714) 966-0999 (714) 662-1911
T. S. T. VEHICLE APPEARANCE CENTER . . . . .65 Terence Dr., Pittsburgh, PA 15236
    Contact: President; Tel: (800) 245-4828
TINT KING MOTORING ACCESSORIES . . . . 1950 Hwy. # 7, Unit 10, Toronto, ON L4K 3B2   CAN
    Contact: Mr. Allan Starkman; Tel: (416) 646-TINT
TINT KING OF CALIFORNIA . . . . 264 Eddystone Ave., Downsview, ON M3N 1H7   CAN
    Contact: President; Tel: (416) 743-5511
TUFFY AUTO SERVICE CENTER . . . . 1414 Baronial Plaza Dr., Toledo, OH 43615
    Contact: Mr. Keenan Moran, President; Tel: (800) 228-8339 (419) 865-6900
TUNE-UP CLINIC . . . . 1165 N. Chase Parkway, # 450, Marietta, GA 30067
    Contact: President; Tel: (404) 953-4454
U. S. AUTO BODY NETWORKS . . . . . . P.O. Box 310, 1915 East 7th St., Grand Island, NE 68802
    Contact: President; Tel: (308) 381-2169
USA MUFFLER SHOPS . . . . . . 2624 W. Lincoln Hwy. Marshall Sq., Merrillville, IN 46410
    Contact: Mr. Evangelos Proimos, CEO; Tel: (219) 769-9441
VEHICARE . . . . 295 Woodcliff Dr., Fairport, NY 14450
    Contact: Mr. Ron Armstrong; Tel: (716) 248-0270
VICTORY LANE QUICK OIL CHANGE . . . . . . 2610 W. Liberty St., # C, Ann Arbor, MI 48103
    Contact: Mr. Tom Stegeman, Dir. Fran. Dev.; Tel: (800) 541-0491 (313) 996-1199 C
WASH ON WHEELS / WOW . . . . .5401 S. Bryant Ave., Sanford, FL 32773
    Contact: Mr. Jim Good, President; Tel: (800) 345-1969 (407) 321-4010
WHEEL TO WHEEL DISCOUNT PARTS/SERVICE . . . . . 19885 57-A Ave., Langley, BC V3A 7J4   CAN
    Contact: Mr. Harmel S. Rayat; Tel: (604) 533-9222
WINDOW WELDER . . . . 6367 E. Cub River Rd., Preston, ID 83263
    Contact: Mr. Jerry Murdock, President; Tel: (800) 737-9353 (208) 852-2124
WIPER HUT SYSTEMS . . . . 1191 E. Newport Ctr. Dr., # 102, Deerfield Beach, FL 33442
    Contact: Mr. Robert Roch, COO; Tel: (305) 426-2233
YIPES STRIPES . . . . 907 S. Governors Ave., Dover, DE 19901
    Contact: Mr. Robert DelVecchio; Tel: (800) 828-7874 (302) 736-1735
ZIEBART RUSTPROOFING (CANADA) . . . . .150 Oakdale Rd., Downsview, ON M3N 1W1   CAN
    Contact: Mr. W. Doug Johnston, VP/GM; Tel: (416) 742-6613

CHAPTER 5

AUTO / TRUCK / TRAILER RENTAL

BUDGET CAR AND TRUCK

4225 Naperville Rd.
Lisle, IL 60532
TEL: (708) 955-1900
FAX: (708) 955-7799
Mr. Larry Lanham, Dir. Fran. Dev.

Car and truck rental. Benefits include: exclusive concessionaire for Sears Roebuck & Co., reservation system, one-way car and truck rental, corporate account sales staff, regional licensee support and system, plus many more.

HISTORY: . . . . IFA
Established in 1958; . . 1st Franchised in 1960
Company-Owned Units (As of 8/31/1992):   558
Franchised Units (As of 8/31/1992): 2819
Total Units (As of 8/31/1992): 3377
Projected New Units for 1993: . . . .
Distribution: US-1129;Can-379;Overseas-1869
  North America: . . . . 50 States,10 Provinces
  Concentration: . .126 in FL, 120 in CA, 64 TX
Registered: . . . . .All
. . . .
Type Space: . . . .;~Varies SF

FINANCIAL: Earnings Claim: . .No
Cash Investment: . . . . $40K+
Total Investment: . . . .$500K+
Fees: Franchise - . . . . . $15K Min.
  Royalty: 5%, Advert: 2.5%
Contract Periods (Yrs.): 5/5
Area Development Agreement: . .No
Sub-Franchise Contract: . . . . . Yes
Expand in Territory: . . . . Yes
Passive Ownership: . . . Discouraged
Encourage Conversions: . . . . . Yes
Average # Employees: . . . . .Varies

FRANCHISOR TRAINING/SUPPORT:
Financial Assistance Provided: . . . . .No
Site Selection Assistance: . . . . .Yes
Lease Negotiation Assistance: . . . . .Yes
Co-operative Advertising: . . . . .Yes
Training: . . . . .1 Wk. Headquarters,
 . . . . .On-Going On-Site
On-Going Support: b,C,D,E,G,H/ . . . . . .
EXPANSION PLANS:
  US: . . . . .All US
  Canada: . . . . .Yes
  Overseas: . . . . .Yes

RENTAL SERVICES: AUTO AND TRUCK

	1989	1990	1991	Percentage Change 90/89	91/90
Total Number of Establishments:					
Company–Owned	2,451	2,485	2,570	1.39%	3.42%
Franchisee–Owned	7,432	8,255	8,543	11.07%	3.49%
Total	9,883	10,740	11,113	8.67%	3.47%
Ratio of Total Establishments:					
Company–Owned	24.8%	23.1%	23.1%		
Franchisee–Owned	75.2%	76.9%	76.9%		
Total	100.0%	100.0%	100.0%		
Total Sales ($000):					
Company–Owned	3,860,136	4,115,169	4,354,066	6.61%	5.81%
Franchisee–Owned	3,042,014	3,422,743	3,683,319	12.52%	7.61%
Total	6,902,150	7,537,912	8,037,385	9.21%	6.63%
Ratio of Total Sales:					
Company–Owned	55.9%	54.6%	54.2%		
Franchisee–Owned	44.1%	45.4%	45.8%		
Total	100.0%	100.0%	100.0%		
Average Sales Per Unit ($000):					
Company–Owned	1,575	1,656	1,694	5.15%	2.31%
Franchisee–Owned	409	415	431	1.30%	3.99%
Total	698	702	723	0.50%	3.05%
Relative Average Sales Ratio:	384.8%	399.4%	392.9%		

	Number Of Employees	Employees Per Unit	Avg. Sales Per Employee
Total 1989 Employment:			
Company–Owned	31,084	12.7	$124,184
Franchisee–Owned	43,499	5.9	$69,933
Total	74,583	7.5	$92,543
Relative Employee Performance Ratios:		216.7%	177.6%

	1st Quartile	Median	4th Quartile
Average 1989 Total Investment:			
Company–Owned	NA	$150,000	NA
Franchisee–Owned	$75,000	$150,000	$255,000
Single Unit Franchise Fee	$7,500	$25,000	$27,500
Mult. Unit Franchise Fee	NA	NA	NA
Franchise Start–Up Cost	$25,000	$30,000	$75,000

Source: Franchising In The Economy 1991, IFA Educational Foundation & Horwath International.

DISCOUNT CAR AND TRUCK RENTALS

3000 Langstaff Rd., # 16
Concord, ON L4K 4R7 CAN
TEL: (416) 738-0123
FAX: (416) 738-8297
Mr. John Stanaitis, Dir. Fran. Ops.

DISCOUNT CAR AND TRUCK RENTALS offers a unique approach to the rental business. We specialize in the replacement car market, with a flair for leisure business. Our emphasis is on service and value to the rental customer.

HISTORY: . . . .
Established in 1980; . . . 1st Franchised in 1984
Company-Owned Units (As of 8/31/1992): . 33
Franchised Units (As of 8/31/1992): 77
Total Units (As of 8/31/1992): 110
Projected New Units for 1993: 10
Distribution: US-2;Can-108;Overseas-0
  North America: . . . . . 1 State, 10 Provinces
  Concentration: . . 64 in ON, 16 in PQ, 8 in AB
Registered: . . . . FL,NY,AB
. . . .
Type Space: . . . . .FS, SF, SC, RM;~800 SF

FINANCIAL: Earnings Claim: . .No
Cash Investment: . . . .$
Total Investment: . . . .$
Fees: Franchise - . . . .$
  Royalty: 6%, Advert: 2%
Contract Periods (Yrs.): 10/10
Area Development Agreement: Yes/10
Sub-Franchise Contract: . . . . Yes
Expand in Territory: . . . . . . Yes
Passive Ownership: . . . Not Allowed
Encourage Conversions: . . . . Yes
Average # Employees: . . 3 FT, 1 PT

FRANCHISOR TRAINING/SUPPORT:
Financial Assistance Provided: . . . Yes(I)
Site Selection Assistance: . . . . . . .Yes
Lease Negotiation Assistance: . . . . .Yes
Co-operative Advertising: . . . . . . .Yes
Training: . . . . 1 Wk. Classroom,
  . . . . 1-3 Months Field, 1 Wk. On-Site
On-Going Support: a,B,C,D,E,F,G,h/ . . 25
EXPANSION PLANS:
  US: . . . . All US
  Canada: . . . . .All Canada
  Overseas: . . . . EUR

DOLLAR RENT A CAR

6141 W. Century Blvd.
Los Angeles, CA 90045
TEL: (213) 776-8100
FAX: (310) 641-0410
Mr. Mario E. Nargi, VP Fran. Dev.

DOLLAR RENT A CAR operates a worldwide network of full-service and in-city locations. As a subsidiary of Chrysler Corporation, DOLLAR attracts renters by offering low rates, outstanding customer services and a complete range of new automobiles.

HISTORY: . . . .
Established in 1966; . . 1st Franchised in 1967
Company-Owned Units (As of 8/31/1992): . 35
Franchised Units (As of 8/31/1992): 1050
Total Units (As of 8/31/1992): 1085
Projected New Units for 1993: 50
Distribution: . . US-290;Can-10;Overseas-750
  North America: . . . . 50 States, 4 Provinces
  Concentration: . .43 in CA, 28 in NY, 21 in HI
Registered: . . . . .All
. . . .
Type Space: . . . . FS;~Varies SF

FINANCIAL: Earnings Claim: . .No
Cash Investment: . . . . . $50K Min.
Total Investment: . . . . . $50K Min.
Fees: Franchise - . . . . . $Min. 7.5K
  Royalty: 8%, Advert: 0%
Contract Periods (Yrs.): 10/10
Area Development Agreement: . .No
Sub-Franchise Contract: . . . . . Yes
Expand in Territory: . . . . . . Yes
Passive Ownership: . . . Discouraged
Encourage Conversions: . . . . Yes
Average # Employees: Varies By Location

FRANCHISOR TRAINING/SUPPORT:
Financial Assistance Provided: . . .Yes(D)
Site Selection Assistance: . . . . . . .Yes
Lease Negotiation Assistance: . . . .Yes
Co-operative Advertising: . . . . . . .Yes
Training: . . . . . . Varies at Site, Based on
  . . Location Size & Licensee Experience
On-Going Support: a,b,C,D,E,f,G,H,I/ . 99
EXPANSION PLANS:
  US: . . . . .All US
  Canada: . . . . No
  Overseas: . . . . .Yes

DOLLAR RENT A CAR (CANADA)

2235 Sheppard Ave., E., # 909
North York, ON M2J 5B5 CAN
TEL: (416) 756-4444 C
FAX: (416) 756-7805
Mr. Richard Pett, Dir. Fran./Mktg.

Join the fastest-growing fleet in the rent-a-car business. DOLLAR-RENT-A-CAR is now in Canada with a world-wide fleet of 80,000 cars and over 2,000 locations in six continents. You'll be joining a world class team.

HISTORY: . . . . .CFA
Established in 1989; . . 1st Franchised in 1990
Company-Owned Units (As of 8/31/1992): . .4
Franchised Units (As of 8/31/1992): 26
Total Units (As of 8/31/1992): 30
Projected New Units for 1993: 25
Distribution: US-0;Can-30;Overseas-0
  North America: . . . . 6 Provinces
  Concentration: . . . .
Registered: . . . . AB
. . . .
Type Space: . . . . .FS, SF;~600 SF

FINANCIAL: Earnings Claim: . . Yes
Cash Investment: . . . . . $50K Min.
Total Investment: . . . . . $50K Min.
Fees: Franchise - . . . . . $25K Min.
  Royalty: 7%, Advert: 2%
Contract Periods (Yrs.): 5/5/5
Area Development Agreement: . Yes
Sub-Franchise Contract: . . . . . Yes
Expand in Territory: . . . . . . Yes
Passive Ownership: . . . . . .Allowed
Encourage Conversions: . . . . Yes
Average # Employees: . . 3 FT, 1 PT

FRANCHISOR TRAINING/SUPPORT:
Financial Assistance Provided: . . . Yes(I)
Site Selection Assistance: . . . . . . .Yes
Lease Negotiation Assistance: . . . . .Yes
Co-operative Advertising: . . . . . . .Yes
Training: . . . . . . .On-Site and Classroom,
  . . . Duration Varies w/ Location/Exper.
On-Going Support: A,B,C,D,E,F,G,H,I/ 12
EXPANSION PLANS:
  US: . . . . No
  Canada: . . . . .All Canada
  Overseas: . . . . No

PAYLESS CAR RENTAL SYSTEM

2350 34th St., N.
St. Petersburg, FL 33713
TEL: (800) 729-5255 (813) 321-6352
FAX: (813) 323-3529
Mr. Chuck Pratt, VP Fran. Sales

Now is the moment for PAYLESS. We are poised to take advantage of the booming business and leisure travel industry and the new markets opening up all over the world. We have the financial resource, thanks to our billion dollar owner/investor, The Sampo Group, to move quickly and to do whatever needs to be done to generate and handle new business. Your business. Our new headquarters, reservation system and 800 #s make us second to none.

HISTORY: IFA	FINANCIAL: Earnings Claim: .No	FRANCHISOR TRAINING/SUPPORT:
Established in 1971; . . 1st Franchised in 1971	Cash Investment: $15-400K	Financial Assistance Provided: . . . . .No
Company-Owned Units (As of 8/31/1992): . .0	Total Investment: $60-500K	Site Selection Assistance: . . . . . . .Yes
Franchised Units (As of 8/31/1992): 134	Fees: Franchise - $6-250K	Lease Negotiation Assistance: . . . . . .Yes
Total Units (As of 8/31/1992): 134	Royalty: 3-5%, Advert: 1-3%	Co-operative Advertising: . . . . .Yes
Projected New Units for 1993: 60	Contract Periods (Yrs.): 5/5	Training: . . . . .1 Wk. Headquarters,
Distribution: US-86;Can-0;Overseas-48	Area Development Agreement: Yes/5	. . . . 1 Wk. Franchisee Location
North America: . . . . 30 States	Sub-Franchise Contract: . . . . .No	On-Going Support: a,B,C,D,E,F,G,H,I/ . 58
Concentration: . . .14 in FL, 8 in CA, 7 in MT	Expand in Territory: . . . . Yes	EXPANSION PLANS:
Registered: . . . CA,FL,HI,IL,IN,MD,MI,MN	Passive Ownership: . . . Discouraged	US: . . . . All US
. . . . NY,OR,RI,VA,WI,DC,AB	Encourage Conversions: . . . . . Yes	Canada: . . . . .All Canada
Type Space: . . .FS, SF, Hotel;~900-1,500 SF	Average # Employees: . . 8 FT, 9 PT	Overseas: . . . . .Yes

PRACTICAL RENT A CAR

705-B Yucca St.
Boulder City, NV 89005
TEL: (800) 424-7722 (702) 293-1663
FAX: (702) 294-1075
Mr. Bert Frost, GM

Recruit, train and develop operators in the car rental business as independently-owned operations in local markets.

HISTORY:	FINANCIAL: Earnings Claim: .No	FRANCHISOR TRAINING/SUPPORT:
Established in 1989; . . 1st Franchised in 1989	Cash Investment: $10-25K	Financial Assistance Provided: . . . . .No
Company-Owned Units (As of 8/31/1992): . .0	Total Investment: $75K	Site Selection Assistance: . . . . . . .Yes
Franchised Units (As of 8/31/1992): 110	Fees: Franchise - $3.5K	Lease Negotiation Assistance: . . . .Yes
Total Units (As of 8/31/1992): 110	Royalty: Flat Fee, Advert: . . . 0%	Co-operative Advertising: . . . . .No
Projected New Units for 1993: 24	Contract Periods (Yrs.): 10/5	Training: . . . . 1 Wk. Headquarters
Distribution: US-110;Can-0;Overseas-0	Area Development Agreement: . .No	
North America: . . . . 36 States	Sub-Franchise Contract: . . . . . .No	On-Going Support: B,C,D,E,G,H,I/ 4
Concentration:	Expand in Territory: . . . . Yes	EXPANSION PLANS:
Registered: . . . . All States	Passive Ownership: . . . Discouraged	US: . . . . All US
. . . .	Encourage Conversions: . . . . . Yes	Canada: . . . . .No
Type Space: . . . . ;~Varies SF	Average # Employees: . . 1 FT, 1 PT	Overseas: . . . . No

RENT A WRECK

6053 W. Century Blvd., # 550
Los Angeles, CA 90045
TEL: (800) 421-7253 (310) 641-4000
FAX: (310) 641-4086
Mr. Henry Gross, VP Sales

A proven, world-wide auto rental system, offering franchises for exclusive territories, automobile leasing and financing programs, A+15-rated liability insurance for any age vehicle, national and co-op advertising, training, on-going operational support, newsletters, meetings and more.

HISTORY:	FINANCIAL: Earnings Claim: .No	FRANCHISOR TRAINING/SUPPORT:
Established in 1973; . . . 1st Franchised in 1978	Cash Investment: $15-45K	Financial Assistance Provided: . . . Yes(I)
Company-Owned Units (As of 8/31/1992): . .1	Total Investment: $26.5-179K	Site Selection Assistance: . . . . . . .Yes
Franchised Units (As of 8/31/1992): 387	Fees: Franchise - $4-38K	Lease Negotiation Assistance: . . . .Yes
Total Units (As of 8/31/1992): 388	Royalty: 6%, Advert: 2%	Co-operative Advertising: . . . . .Yes
Projected New Units for 1993: 84	Contract Periods (Yrs.): . . . 10/10	Training: . . . . 5 Days Headquarters,
Distribution: US-370;Can-0;Overseas-18	Area Development Agreement: . .No	. . . . .3 Days Brunswick, NJ
North America: . . . . 48 States	Sub-Franchise Contract: . . . . . .No	On-Going Support: a,B,C,D,e,G,h,I/ . . 21
Concentration: . .42 in CA, 38 in NJ, 27 in NY	Expand in Territory: . . . . Yes	EXPANSION PLANS:
Registered: . . . . .All	Passive Ownership: . . . Discouraged	US: . . . . All US
. . . .	Encourage Conversions: . . . . . Yes	Canada: . . . . .No
Type Space: . . . . SF;~500 SF	Average # Employees: . . 2 FT, 1 PT	Overseas: . EUR, Asia, S. America

THRIFTY RENT-A-CAR SYSTEM

5330 E. 31st, # 900
Tulsa, OK 74135
TEL: (918) 669-2219
FAX: (918) 669-2640
Mr. Brett Thomas, Dir. Fran. Sales

Our licensees can take advantage of company-sponsored fleet leasing programs, insurance programs, training, volume purchasing power, national corporate accounts. Licensees benefit from being affiliated with Inter-network.

HISTORY: . . . . IFA
Established in 1950; . . 1st Franchised in 1962
Company-Owned Units (As of 8/31/1992): . 20
Franchised Units (As of 8/31/1992): 790
Total Units (As of 8/31/1992): 810
Projected New Units for 1993: 25
Distribution: . . US-434;Can-151;Overseas-225
 North America: . . . .
 Concentration: . . . .
Registered: . . .CA,HI,IL,MD,MN,ND,SD,VA
 . . . . WA,WI
Type Space: . . . . FS;~1,500 SF

FINANCIAL: Earnings Claim: . .No
Cash Investment: $80-100K
Total Investment: . . . .$70-80K Min.
Fees: Franchise - $8.5K
 Royalty: 3%, Advert: 5%
Contract Periods (Yrs.): 10/5
Area Development Agreement: Yes/1-2
Sub-Franchise Contract: . . . . . .No
Expand in Territory: . . . . . . Yes
Passive Ownership: . . . .
Encourage Conversions: . . . . Yes
Average # Employees: . . . .

FRANCHISOR TRAINING/SUPPORT:
Financial Assistance Provided: . . . . .Yes
Site Selection Assistance: . . . . . . .Yes
Lease Negotiation Assistance: . . . . No
Co-operative Advertising: . . . . No
Training: . . . . .5 Days Licensee
 . . . . Orientation
On-Going Support: a,b,C,D,E,G,h,I/ . . . .
EXPANSION PLANS:
US: . . . . .All US
Canada: . . . . .All Canada
Overseas: . . . . Yes

UGLY DUCKLING RENT-A-CAR

2425 E. Camelback Rd., # 650
Phoenix, AZ 85016
TEL: (800) 843-3825 (602) 381-8459
FAX: (602) 553-7070
Mr. Bob Holt, SVP

Premier used car rentals. "America's Second Car." We offer the most economical, reliable and practical alternative to the Big Guys in the industry. We provide continuing support and training and the best profit-oriented programs for our licensees. Our success comes from your success.

HISTORY: . . . .
Established in 1977; . . 1st Franchised in 1977
Company-Owned Units (As of 8/31/1992): . .1
Franchised Units (As of 8/31/1992): 125
Total Units (As of 8/31/1992): 126
Projected New Units for 1993: 50
Distribution: US-126;Can-0;Overseas-0
 North America: . . . . 36 States
 Concentration: . . 22 in CT, 12 in CA, 8 in FL
Registered: . . . .CA,FL,HI,IN,MI,ND,OR,RI
 . . . . .SD,VA,WA,DC
Type Space: . . . . NA;~NA SF

FINANCIAL: Earnings Claim: . .No
Cash Investment: $25-50K
Total Investment: $100-125K
Fees: Franchise - $25-255K
 Royalty:$6/Car/M, Advert: $2/Car/M
Contract Periods (Yrs.): . . 10/10/10
Area Development Agreement: Yes/10
Sub-Franchise Contract: . . . . . .No
Expand in Territory: . . . . . . Yes
Passive Ownership: . . . Discouraged
Encourage Conversions: . . . . .No
Average # Employees: . . 3 FT, 1 PT

FRANCHISOR TRAINING/SUPPORT:
Financial Assistance Provided: . . . . .NA
Site Selection Assistance: . . . . . . .Yes
Lease Negotiation Assistance: . . . .NA
Co-operative Advertising: . . . . . . .Yes
Training: . . . . 5 Days Headquarters
 . . . .
On-Going Support: b,C,D,G,H,i/ 4
EXPANSION PLANS:
US: . . . . .All US
Canada: . . . . .All Canada
Overseas: . . . . Yes

SUPPLEMENTAL LISTING OF FRANCHISORS

ADA RENT A USED CAR/CANA RENT A CAR . . . . . 3035 Keparo Rd., RR2, Mill Bay, BC V0R 2P0 CAN
 Contact: Mr. Peter Schoch; Tel: (604) 743-3631
AFFORDABLE USED CAR RENTAL SYSTEM . . . . 96 Freneau Ave., # 2, Matawan, NJ 07747
 Contact: Mr. Charles A. Vitale, GM; Tel: (800) 631-2290 (908) 290-8300
AIRWAYS RENT-A-CAR . . . . 4025 N. Mannheim Rd., Schiller Park, IL 60176
 Contact: Mr. Michael Zaransky, President; Tel: (708) 678-2300
ALLSTAR RENT-A-CAR . . . . 705-B Yucca St., Boulder City, NV 89005
 Contact: Mr. Bert Forcheskie, GM; Tel: (800) 424-7722 (702) 293-1663
ALTMANS AMERICA NATIONWIDE MOTOR HOME . 1155 Baldwin Park Blvd., Baldwin Park, CA 91706
 Contact: President; Tel: (800) ALT-MANS
AMERICAN INTERNATIONAL RENT A CAR . . . . One Harborside Dr., Boston, MA 02128
 Contact: Mr. Bob Cunha, VP Fran. Sales; Tel: (800) 247-1272 (617) 561-1000
AVON RENT-A-CAR . . . . 8459 Sunset Blvd., Hollywood, CA 90069
 Contact: President; Tel: (213) 654-5533
BUDGET RENT A CAR OF CANADA . . . . . . .185 The West Mall, # 900, Etobicoke, ON M9C 5L5 CAN
 Contact: Mr. David Gooderham; Tel: (416) 622-3366
CREDIT AUTO MART . . . . 8855 Atlanta, # 156, Huntington Beach, CA 92646
 Contact: Mr. Terry Lewis; Tel: (714) 635-6501

EMPIRE AUTO LEASING . . . . 7040 W. Palmetto Pk., Rd., # 2, Boca Raton, FL 33069
    Contact: President; Tel: (305) 971-6000
FAMILY RENT A CAR . . . . 2438 N. Broadwell, Grand Island, NB 68801
    Contact: Ms. Gale Mettenbrink, VP; Tel: (308) 381-7676
FREEDOM RENT-A-CAR SYSTEM . . . . 705-B Yucca St., Boulder City, NV 89005
    Contact: Mr. Bert Forcheskie, GM; Tel: (800) 424-7722 (702) 293-1663
HANDY RENT A CAR SYSTEMS . . . . 1405 Stevenson Dr., Springfield, IL 62703
    Contact: President; Tel: (217) 529-3377
HERTZ SYSTEM . . . . 225 Brae Blvd., Park Ridge, NJ 07656
    Contact: Mr. Richard Hollenbeck; Tel: (201) 307-2000
MR. RENT A CAR/MR. LEASE A CAR . . . . 45 Haverhill St., Andover, MA 01810
    Contact: Mr. Henry Bronson, Vice President; Tel: (617) 475-0915
NATIONAL CAR RENTAL SYSTEM . . . . 7700 France Ave. S., Minneapolis, MN 55435
    Contact: President; Tel: (612) 830-2121
RENT-RITE TRUCK/CAR RENTALS & LEASING . . . . . 404 Meridian Rd., NE, Calgary, AB T2A 2N6 CAN
    Contact: Mr. Fintan A. Mealia; Tel: (403) 273-7300
SENSIBLE CAR RENTAL . . . . 96 Freneau Ave., # 2, Matawan, NJ 07747
    Contact: Mr. Charles A. Vitale, President; Tel: (800) 367-5159 (908) 583-8500
THRIFTY CAR RENTAL . . . . 6050 Indian Line, Mississauga, ON L4V 1G5 CAN
    Contact: Mr. Robert Swanborough; Tel: (416) 612-1881
U-SAVE AUTO RENTAL OF AMERICA . . . . 7525 Connelley Dr., # A, Hanover, MD 21076
    Contact: Mr. William Edwards; Tel: (800) 438-2300 (301) 760-8727
WHEELCHAIR GETAWAYS . . . . 9 Cambridge Ln., P. O. Box 819, Newtown, PA 18940
    Contact: Mr. Ed Van Artsdalen, President; Tel: (800) 642-2042 (215) 579-9120
WHEELRIGHT CAR RENTAL . . . . 760 S. Country Club Rd., Mesa, AZ 85210
    Contact: President; Tel: (602) 833-0995

For Information On Renting Our Custom Franchisor Mailing List Or Franchisor Data Base, Please Refer To Page IX

CHAPTER 6

BUILDING AND REMODELING

AMERICAN CONCRETE RAISING

918 Fairway Dr.
Bensenville, IL 60106
TEL: (708) 595-5225
FAX: (708) 595-5366
Mr. John G. Meyers, President

The franchisee has the right to operate an AMERICAN CONCRETE RAISING SERVICE CENTER, which engages in the business of inspecting, evaluating and raising settled concrete by a method of pressure injection and providing such services to businesses, homes, commercial shopping centers, apartment complexes, municipalities, hotels and other related entities following a detailed service plan.

HISTORY: . . . .
Established in 1983; . . 1st Franchised in 1989
Company-Owned Units (As of 8/31/1992): . .1
Franchised Units (As of 8/31/1992): 1
Total Units (As of 8/31/1992): 2
Projected New Units for 1993: 6
Distribution: US-2;Can-0;Overseas-0
  North America: . . . . .1 State
  Concentration: . . . . .2 in IL
Registered: . . . . IL,IN
. . . .
Type Space: . . . . NA;~ SF

FINANCIAL: Earnings Claim: . .No
Cash Investment: $20-30K
Total Investment: $42-66K
Fees: Franchise - $15K
  Royalty: 8%, Advert: 2%
Contract Periods (Yrs.): 10/10
Area Development Agreement: . .No
Sub-Franchise Contract: . . . . . .No
Expand in Territory: . . . . . . .No
Passive Ownership: . . . Not Allowed
Encourage Conversions: . . . . . NA
Average # Employees: . . 5 FT, 4 PT

FRANCHISOR TRAINING/SUPPORT:
Financial Assistance Provided: . . . . . No
Site Selection Assistance: . . . . . . .NA
Lease Negotiation Assistance: . . . . .NA
Co-operative Advertising: . . . . .No
Training: . . . . 2 Wks. Chicago Area
. . . .
On-Going Support: C,D,H,i/ 3
EXPANSION PLANS:
US: . . . . Midwest
Canada: . . . . No
Overseas: . . . . No

CONSTRUCTION, HOME IMPROVEMENT, MAINTENANCE AND CLEANING SERVICES

	1989	1990	1991	Percentage Change 90/89	Percentage Change 91/90
Total Number of Establishments:					
Company–Owned	620	615	680	–0.81%	10.57%
Franchisee–Owned	23,468	26,800	29,899	14.20%	11.56%
Total	24,088	27,415	30,579	13.81%	11.54%
Ratio of Total Establishments:					
Company–Owned	2.6%	2.2%	2.2%		
Franchisee–Owned	97.4%	97.8%	97.8%		
Total	100.0%	100.0%	100.0%		
Total Sales ($000):					
Company–Owned	1,487,066	1,609,740	1,742,907	8.25%	8.27%
Franchisee–Owned	4,272,756	4,844,625	5,349,763	13.38%	10.43%
Total	5,759,822	6,454,365	7,092,670	12.06%	9.89%
Ratio of Total Sales:					
Company–Owned	25.8%	24.9%	24.6%		
Franchisee–Owned	74.2%	75.1%	75.4%		
Total	100.0%	100.0%	100.0%		
Average Sales Per Unit ($000):					
Company–Owned	2,398	2,617	2,563	9.13%	–2.08%
Franchisee–Owned	182	181	179	–0.71%	–1.02%
Total	239	235	232	–1.54%	–1.48%
Relative Average Sales Ratio:	1317.4%	1448.0%	1432.5%		

	Number Of Employees	Employees Per Unit	Avg. Sales Per Employee
Total 1989 Employment:			
Company–Owned	16,232	26.2	$91,613
Franchisee–Owned	120,478	5.1	$35,465
Total	136,710	5.7	$42,132
Relative Employee Performance Ratios:		510.0%	258.3%

	1st Quartile	Median	4th Quartile
Average 1989 Total Investment:			
Company–Owned	$25,000	$45,000	$240,000
Franchisee–Owned	$25,000	$40,000	$75,000
Single Unit Franchise Fee	$10,000	$15,000	$25,000
Mult. Unit Franchise Fee	$10,500	$20,000	$75,000
Franchise Start–Up Cost	$15,000	$25,000	$50,000

Source: Franchising In The Economy 1991, IFA Educational Foundation & Horwath International.

AMERICAN ROOF-BRITE

3398 Sanford Dr.
Marietta, GA 30066
TEL: (404) 429-0232
FAX:
Mr. Larry Stevens, President

Clean ugly, stained asphalt, roofing shingles. Work performed for roofing manufacturers and home owners.

HISTORY:	FINANCIAL: Earnings Claim: . .No	FRANCHISOR TRAINING/SUPPORT:
Established in 1973; . . 1st Franchised in 1990	Cash Investment: . . . .$	Financial Assistance Provided: . . . . .Yes
Company-Owned Units (As of 8/31/1992): . .1	Total Investment: $5K	Site Selection Assistance: . . . . . . .No
Franchised Units (As of 8/31/1992): 10	Fees: Franchise - $0	Lease Negotiation Assistance: . . . . .NA
Total Units (As of 8/31/1992): 11	Royalty: 20% Chem, Advert: . . 5%	Co-operative Advertising: . . . . . . .Yes
Projected New Units for 1993: 20	Contract Periods (Yrs.):	Training: . . . . . . .Either at Headquarters
Distribution: US-11;Can-0;Overseas-0	Area Development Agreement: . .No	. . . . or Cleaners' Location
North America: . . . . 6 States	Sub-Franchise Contract: . . . . . Yes	On-Going Support: B,C,D,G,I/ 3
Concentration: . . . 6 in FL, 2 in GA, 1 in NY	Expand in Territory: . . . . . . .No	EXPANSION PLANS:
Registered:	Passive Ownership: . . . Discouraged	US: . . . . .All US
. . . .	Encourage Conversions: . . . . . Yes	Canada: . . . . .All Canada
Type Space: . . . . NA;~ SF	Average # Employees: . . . . . .2 FT	Overseas: . . . . Yes

ARCHADECK

2112 W. Laburnum Ave., # 109
Richmond, VA 23227
TEL: (800) 722-4668 (804) 353-6999 C
FAX: (804) 358-1878
Mr. Stan Adams, Fran. Dev.

Direct in-home sales of construction services, primarily patio decks, screened porches and gazebos. Does not require major investment in leasehold improvements and inventory. Average sale is very large, with good income potential. No organized competition.

HISTORY: . . . . IFA	FINANCIAL: Earnings Claim: . .No	FRANCHISOR TRAINING/SUPPORT:
Established in 1980; . . 1st Franchised in 1985	Cash Investment: $50-80K	Financial Assistance Provided: . . . . .Yes
Company-Owned Units (As of 8/31/1992): . .0	Total Investment: $50-80K	Site Selection Assistance: . . . . .No
Franchised Units (As of 8/31/1992): 77	Fees: Franchise - $16-32.5K	Lease Negotiation Assistance: . . . .NA
Total Units (As of 8/31/1992): 77	Royalty: 7%, Advert: 1%	Co-operative Advertising: . . . . . . .Yes
Projected New Units for 1993: 40	Contract Periods (Yrs.): 10/10	Training: . . . . Currently 3 Wks. HQ
Distribution: US-77;Can-0;Overseas-0	Area Development Agreement: . . .	
North America: . . . . 18 States	Sub-Franchise Contract: . . . . . .No	On-Going Support: C,D,G,H,I/ 24
Concentration: . . . . . . East of Mississippi	Expand in Territory: . . . . Yes	EXPANSION PLANS:
Registered: . . . .IL,IN,MD,MI,NY,RI,VA,WI	Passive Ownership: . . . Discouraged	US: . . . . . . .East Coast, Midwest
. . . .	Encourage Conversions: . . . . NA	Canada: . . . . .Yes
Type Space: . . . . ;~ SF	Average # Employees:	Overseas: . . . . .Yes

B-DRY SYSTEM

1341 Copley Rd.
Akron, OH 44320
TEL: (800) 321-0985 (216) 867-2567 C
FAX: (216) 867-7693
Mr. Joe Garfinkel, VP

Basement waterproofing system. Low cash investment - high return on investment. Intensive and continuous training. No high-cost site expenditure. High gross profit. No previous experience necessary. Unique patented system. Full customer warranty for the life of the structure.

HISTORY: . . . . IFA	FINANCIAL: Earnings Claim: . .No	FRANCHISOR TRAINING/SUPPORT:
Established in 1958; . . 1st Franchised in 1978	Cash Investment: $15K	Financial Assistance Provided: . . .Yes(D)
Company-Owned Units (As of 8/31/1992): . .1	Total Investment: $40-74K	Site Selection Assistance: . . . . . . .NA
Franchised Units (As of 8/31/1992): 70	Fees: Franchise - $15-30K	Lease Negotiation Assistance: . . . . No
Total Units (As of 8/31/1992): 71	Royalty: 6%, Advert: 0%	Co-operative Advertising: . . . . . . .Yes
Projected New Units for 1993: 6	Contract Periods (Yrs.): 5/5	Training: . . . . 2 Wks. Headquarters
Distribution: US-70;Can-1;Overseas-0	Area Development Agreement: Yes/5	. . . .
North America:	Sub-Franchise Contract: . . . . . .No	On-Going Support: B,C,D,G,H,I/ 6
Concentration: . . . 8 in OH, 8 in PA, 7 in NY	Expand in Territory: . . . . Yes	EXPANSION PLANS:
Registered: . . . IL,IN,MD,MI,MN,NY,RI,VA	Passive Ownership: . . . Discouraged	US: . . . . . . .Northwest and Midwest
. . . . WA,WI,DC	Encourage Conversions: . . . . .No	Canada: . . . . .All Canada
Type Space: . . . . FS;~4,000 SF	Average # Employees: . . 6 FT, 1 PT	Overseas: . . . . .UK and GR

CHISHOLM TRAIL BUILDERS

P. O. Box 335
San Marcos, TX 78667
TEL: (512) 629-1400
FAX: (512) 353-5333
Mr. Floyd MacKenzie, Treasurer

Construction of pre-designed residential houses for the suburban family. Houses are modestly priced and may be constructed completely or partially. Customer preference.

HISTORY:	FINANCIAL: Earnings Claim: . . .	FRANCHISOR TRAINING/SUPPORT:
Established in 1983; . . 1st Franchised in 1986	Cash Investment: $15-20K	Financial Assistance Provided: . . . . .No
Company-Owned Units (As of 8/31/1992): . .1	Total Investment: $30-50K	Site Selection Assistance: . . . . . . .NA
Franchised Units (As of 8/31/1992): 0	Fees: Franchise - $0	Lease Negotiation Assistance: . . . .NA
Total Units (As of 8/31/1992): 1	Royalty: Flat, Advert: 0%	Co-operative Advertising: . . . . . . .Yes
Projected New Units for 1993:	Contract Periods (Yrs.): 5/5	Training: . . . . . . Continuous at Territory
Distribution: US-1;Can-0;Overseas-0	Area Development Agreement: . .No	. . . .
North America: . . . . .1 State	Sub-Franchise Contract: . . . . . .No	On-Going Support: a,B,C,D,F,G,h,I/ . . . 3
Concentration: . . . . 1 in TX	Expand in Territory: . . . . Yes	EXPANSION PLANS:
Registered:	Passive Ownership: . . . Discouraged	US: . . . . .All US
. . . .	Encourage Conversions: . . . . .No	Canada: . . . . .Yes
Type Space: . . . . ;~ SF	Average # Employees: . .2 FT, 10 PT	Overseas: . . . . .Yes

ELDORADO STONE

P.O. Box 27X
Carnation, WA 98014
TEL: (206) 883-1991 C
FAX: (206) 333-4755
Mr. Phil Pearlman, VP Fran. Growth

ELDORADO STONE franchisees manufacture and sell ELDORADO STONE, simulated stone, brick veneer building products and concrete landscape pavers. ELDORADO STONE is made of durable, lightweight concrete. It is hard to distinguish from natural stone, yet is much easier to install and much less expensive than natural stone.

HISTORY:	FINANCIAL: Earnings Claim: . .No	FRANCHISOR TRAINING/SUPPORT:
Established in 1969; . . 1st Franchised in 1969	Cash Investment: $49-150K	Financial Assistance Provided: . . . . .No
Company-Owned Units (As of 8/31/1992): . .0	Total Investment: $50-150K	Site Selection Assistance: . . . . . . .Yes
Franchised Units (As of 8/31/1992): 33	Fees: Franchise - $5-6K	Lease Negotiation Assistance: . . . . .No
Total Units (As of 8/31/1992): 33	Royalty: 4%, Advert: 0%	Co-operative Advertising: . . . . . . .Yes
Projected New Units for 1993: 4	Contract Periods (Yrs.): 10/10	Training: . . . . 1 Wk. Existing Plant,
Distribution: US-24;Can-4;Overseas-5	Area Development Agreement: . .No	. . . . 1 Wk. New Site Plant
North America: . . . . 19 States	Sub-Franchise Contract: . . . . . .No	On-Going Support: B,D,E,G,H/ 3
Concentration: . . . . 2 in PA	Expand in Territory: . . . . Yes	EXPANSION PLANS:
Registered: . . . . .All	Passive Ownership: . . . . . .Allowed	US: . . . . .All US
. . . .	Encourage Conversions: . . . . . Yes	Canada: . . . . .All Canada
Type Space: . . . . FS;~5,000-8,000 SF	Average # Employees: . . . . . .6 FT	Overseas: . . .S. Arabia, Turkey, Fin., UK

EVERDRY WATERPROOFING

365 E. Highland Rd.
Macedonia, OH 44056
TEL: (800) 365-7295 (216) 467-1055
FAX: (216) 468-3231
Mr. Jack M. Jones, VP

Patented residential basement waterproofing system. Training in lead generation, advertising, sales, payroll, production installation and overall management.

HISTORY:	FINANCIAL: Earnings Claim: . .No	FRANCHISOR TRAINING/SUPPORT:
Established in 1978; . . 1st Franchised in 1984	Cash Investment: $110K	Financial Assistance Provided: . . . . .No
Company-Owned Units (As of 8/31/1992): . .3	Total Investment: $110K	Site Selection Assistance: . . . . . . .Yes
Franchised Units (As of 8/31/1992): 18	Fees: Franchise - $50K	Lease Negotiation Assistance: . . . . .Yes
Total Units (As of 8/31/1992): 21	Royalty: 6%, Advert: 1%	Co-operative Advertising: . . . . . . .Yes
Projected New Units for 1993: 4	Contract Periods (Yrs.): 10/10	Training: . . . .6 Wks. HQ, 6 Wks. On-Site
Distribution: US-21;Can-0;Overseas-0	Area Development Agreement: . .No	. . . . .Min. 1 Visit/Yr., 10 Seminars/Yr.
North America: . . . . 10 States	Sub-Franchise Contract: . . . . . .No	On-Going Support: b,c,,D,E,G,H,I/ . . . 40
Concentration: . . . 5 in OH, 2 in MI, 2 in NY	Expand in Territory: . . . . .No	EXPANSION PLANS:
Registered: . . . . .IL,IN,MD,MI,NY,WI	Passive Ownership: . . . Not Allowed	US: . . . . Midwest, East and Some South
. . . .	Encourage Conversions: . . . . .No	Canada: . . . . .All Canada
Type Space: . . . . FS;~5,000 SF	Average # Employees: . 20 FT, 15 PT	Overseas: . . . . No

HOLIDAY-PACIFIC HOMES

4 Snowshoe Millway
Willowdale, ON M2L 1T5 CAN
TEL: (416) 445-1590
FAX: (416) 445-7597
Mr. Merv Archall, President

Custom-engineered shell home packages.

HISTORY: . . . .
Established in 1980; . . 1st Franchised in 1991
Company-Owned Units (As of 8/31/1992): . .0
Franchised Units (As of 8/31/1992): 8
Total Units (As of 8/31/1992): 8
Projected New Units for 1993: . . . .
Distribution: US-0;Can-8;Overseas-0
 North America: . . . . 3 Provinces
 Concentration: . . . 6 in ON, 1 in PQ, 1 in NB
Registered: . . . .
 . . . .
Type Space: . . . . .Display Home;~ SF

FINANCIAL: Earnings Claim: . .No
Cash Investment: . . . .$
Total Investment: $15-20K
Fees: Franchise - $0
 Royalty: 3%, Advert: 1%
Contract Periods (Yrs.): 5/5
Area Development Agreement: . .No
Sub-Franchise Contract: . . . . Yes
Expand in Territory: . . . . . . Yes
Passive Ownership: . . . . . .Allowed
Encourage Conversions: . . . . NA
Average # Employees: . . . . .6 FT

FRANCHISOR TRAINING/SUPPORT:
Financial Assistance Provided: . . . . .No
Site Selection Assistance: . . . . . . .Yes
Lease Negotiation Assistance: . . . .No
Co-operative Advertising: . . . . . . .Yes
Training: . . . . .1 Wk. Headquarters
 . . . .
On-Going Support: A,B,C,D,E,F,H/ . . . .
EXPANSION PLANS:
 US: . . . . . . All US - Each State Master
 Canada: . . . . .All Exc. Ontario
 Overseas: . . . . . .JA and Korea

KITCHEN SAVER OF CANADA

13 Main St. W.
Lambeth, ON N0L 1S0 CAN
TEL: (519) 652-6390
FAX: (519) 652-0590
Mr. Craig Jones, President

KITCHEN SAVER specializes in affordable kitchen remodeling by offering cabinet front replacement (commonly known as refacing) and a line of high-quality, low-cost cabinets. The remodelling service is completed with the addition of custom countertops, sinks, islands and storage options.

HISTORY: . . . .
Established in 1986; . . 1st Franchised in 1986
Company-Owned Units (As of 8/31/1992): . .0
Franchised Units (As of 8/31/1992): 17
Total Units (As of 8/31/1992): 17
Projected New Units for 1993: 4
Distribution: US-0;Can-17;Overseas-0
 North America: . . . . .1 Province
 Concentration: . . . . 16 in ON
Registered: . . . .
 . . . .
Type Space: . . . Indust. Mall;~500-1,000 SF

FINANCIAL: Earnings Claim: . Yes
Cash Investment: $20K
Total Investment: $25-30K
Fees: Franchise - $10-20K
 Royalty: 0%, Advert: 0%
Contract Periods (Yrs.): . . . 5/5/5
Area Development Agreement: . .No
Sub-Franchise Contract: . . . . .No
Expand in Territory: . . . . . . Yes
Passive Ownership: . . . Discouraged
Encourage Conversions: . . . . NA
Average # Employees: . . . . . .1 FT

FRANCHISOR TRAINING/SUPPORT:
Financial Assistance Provided: . . . Yes(I)
Site Selection Assistance: . . . . . . .Yes
Lease Negotiation Assistance: . . . .Yes
Co-operative Advertising: . . . . . . .Yes
Training: . . . . . 2 Wks. Headquarters and
 . . . . Existing Dealer Location
On-Going Support: B,c,d,E,G,H,I/ 8
EXPANSION PLANS:
 US: . . . . .No
 Canada: . . . . .All Canada
 Overseas: . . . . No

KITCHEN SOLVERS

401 Jay St.
La Crosse, WI 54601
TEL: (800) 845-6779 (608) 784-2855
FAX: (608) 784-2917
Mr. Dave Woggon, Dir. Fran.

KITCHEN SOLVERS transforms old, worn-out, dingy cabinets into elegant "new" cabinets by installing new doors and drawer fronts and covering existing framework with 1/8" 3-ply wood panel. This saves the customer up to 50% of replacement cost.

HISTORY: . . . .
Established in 1982; . . 1st Franchised in 1984
Company-Owned Units (As of 8/31/1992): . .1
Franchised Units (As of 8/31/1992): 25
Total Units (As of 8/31/1992): 26
Projected New Units for 1993: 12
Distribution: US-26;Can-0;Overseas-0
 North America: . . . . 6 States
 Concentration: . . . 13 in WI, 5 in IA, 3 in MN
Registered: . . . . FL,IL,MI,ND,WI
 . . . .
Type Space: . . . . . . .Home Based;~NA SF

FINANCIAL: Earnings Claim: . .No
Cash Investment: $10K
Total Investment: $15-30K
Fees: Franchise - $10K
 Royalty: 5%, Advert: 0%
Contract Periods (Yrs.): . . . 10/10
Area Development Agreement: . .No
Sub-Franchise Contract: . . . . .No
Expand in Territory: . . . . . . .No
Passive Ownership: . . . Not Allowed
Encourage Conversions: . . . . Yes
Average # Employees: . . . 1-2 FT

FRANCHISOR TRAINING/SUPPORT:
Financial Assistance Provided: . . . . .No
Site Selection Assistance: . . . . . . .NA
Lease Negotiation Assistance: . . . .NA
Co-operative Advertising: . . . . . . .NA
Training: . . . . 5 Days Headquarters
 . . . .
On-Going Support: G,H,I/ . . . .
EXPANSION PLANS:
 US: . . . . .All US
 Canada: . . . . .No
 Overseas: . . . . No

KITCHEN TUNE-UP

131 N. Roosevelt
Aberdeen, SD 57401
TEL: (800) 333-6385 (605) 225-4049 C
FAX: (605) 225-1371
Mr. Tony Haglund, Fran. Dir.

KITCHEN TUNE-UP offers a unique cabinet and wood restoration and treatment service. We are America's #1 Wood Care Specialists. This franchise is a home-based business with no inventory requirements.

HISTORY:	FINANCIAL: Earnings Claim: . .No	FRANCHISOR TRAINING/SUPPORT:
Established in 1988; . . 1st Franchised in 1989	Cash Investment: $14-30K	Financial Assistance Provided: . . . .NA
Company-Owned Units (As of 8/31/1992): . .0	Total Investment: $14-30K	Site Selection Assistance: . . . . . . .NA
Franchised Units (As of 8/31/1992): 182	Fees: Franchise - $10K	Lease Negotiation Assistance: . . . . .NA
Total Units (As of 8/31/1992): 182	Royalty: 7%, Advert: 0%	Co-operative Advertising: . . . . . . .NA
Projected New Units for 1993: 60	Contract Periods (Yrs.): 8/32	Training: . . . . 5 Days Headquarters
Distribution: . . . US-173;Can-9;Overseas-0	Area Development Agreement: . .No	. . . .
North America: . . . . 36 States	Sub-Franchise Contract: . . . . .No	On-Going Support: B,C,D,G,h,I/ 6
Concentration: . . . 13 in MN, 5 in IL, 5 in OH	Expand in Territory: . . . . Yes	EXPANSION PLANS:
Registered: . . .CA,FL,IL,IN,MD,MI,MN,ND	Passive Ownership: . . . Discouraged	US: . . . . All US
. . . . OR,SD,WA,WI	Encourage Conversions: . . . . NA	Canada: . . . . .Yes
Type Space: . . . .;~ SF	Average # Employees: . . 1 FT, 1 PT	Overseas: . . . . Yes

MAGNUM PIERING

13230 Ferguson Ln.
Bridgeton, MO 63044
TEL: (800) 822-7437 (314) 291-7437
FAX: (314) 291-1115
Mr. Gregg A. Roby, VP/GM

MAGNUM PIERING is a complete, multi-patented system designed to raise, level and stabilize building foundations. Steel columns are hydraulically driven to bedrock for ultimate stability. A second system, Slab-Jack, performs the same function on concrete flatwork which has settled or drifted.

HISTORY:	FINANCIAL: Earnings Claim: . .No	FRANCHISOR TRAINING/SUPPORT:
Established in 1985; . . 1st Franchised in 1985	Cash Investment: $50-100K	Financial Assistance Provided: . . . . .No
Company-Owned Units (As of 8/31/1992): . .0	Total Investment: $100-150K	Site Selection Assistance: . . . . . . .NA
Franchised Units (As of 8/31/1992): 9	Fees: Franchise - $20K	Lease Negotiation Assistance: . . . .NA
Total Units (As of 8/31/1992): 9	Royalty: 6%, Advert: 6%	Co-operative Advertising: . . . . . . .Yes
Projected New Units for 1993: 5	Contract Periods (Yrs.): 5/5	Training: . . . . . .7 Days - 2 Wks. Kansas
Distribution: US-9;Can-0;Overseas-0	Area Development Agreement: . .No	. . . City, MO, 7 Days - 2 Wks. St. Louis
North America: . . . . 6 States	Sub-Franchise Contract: . . . . .No	On-Going Support: B,c,d,G,I/ 4
Concentration: . . . . 3 in MO, 2 in FL	Expand in Territory: . . . . Yes	EXPANSION PLANS:
Registered: . . . . .FL	Passive Ownership: . . . . .Allowed	US: . . . . . . All US Exc. Existing Area
. . . .	Encourage Conversions: . . . . NA	Canada: . . . . .All Canada
Type Space: . . . . .FS, SF;~2,500 SF	Average # Employees: . . . .5-10 FT	Overseas: . . . . No

PERMA-JACK COMPANY

9066 Watson Rd.
St. Louis, MO 63126
TEL: (800) 843-1888 (314) 843-1957
FAX: (314) 843-7898
Ms. Joan L. Robinson, President

The PERMA-JACK SYSTEM is a patented Foundation Stabilizing System, using hydraulic pressure to force steel tubing through the Perma-Jack support bracket down to bedrock or equal load-bearing strata. We stabilize your building's foundation and, in many cases, raise it back to near-original position.

HISTORY:	FINANCIAL: Earnings Claim: . .No	FRANCHISOR TRAINING/SUPPORT:
Established in 1974; . . . 1st Franchised in 1975	Cash Investment: $7.5-20K	Financial Assistance Provided: . . . . .No
Company-Owned Units (As of 8/31/1992): . .0	Total Investment: $24-68K	Site Selection Assistance: . . . . . . .No
Franchised Units (As of 8/31/1992): 22	Fees: Franchise - $7-20K	Lease Negotiation Assistance: . . . . .No
Total Units (As of 8/31/1992): 22	Royalty: 10%, Advert: 0%	Co-operative Advertising: . . . . . . .No
Projected New Units for 1993: 2	Contract Periods (Yrs.): 2/4	Training: . . . . As Needed at Headquarters
Distribution: US-22;Can-0;Overseas-0	Area Development Agreement: . .No	. . . . or Job Site(s)
North America: . . . . 14 States	Sub-Franchise Contract: . . . . .No	On-Going Support: B,C,D,E,F,H,I/ 5
Concentration: . . . 4 in TX, 2 in CA, 2 in MO	Expand in Territory: . . . . Yes	EXPANSION PLANS:
Registered: . . .CA,FL,IL,IN,MD,OR,VA,WA	Passive Ownership: . . . Not Allowed	US: . . . . All US
. . . .	Encourage Conversions:	Canada: . . . . .No
Type Space: . . . .;~ SF	Average # Employees: . . . . . .5 FT	Overseas: . . . . No

RE-SSIDE AMERICA

11002 Park Rd.
Fairfax, VA 22030
TEL: (703) 691-3991
FAX: (703) 591-3993
Mr. Richard G. Ressa, President

Siding and windows make up more that 25% of an annual $85 billion market. Quick, simple installation, no inventory, no receivables, low overhead, equals great profits. We have a complete system for building a business on a professional level which will set you apart from the competition.

HISTORY:	FINANCIAL: Earnings Claim: . .No	FRANCHISOR TRAINING/SUPPORT:
Established in 1976; . . 1st Franchised in 1990	Cash Investment: $25K	Financial Assistance Provided: . . . Yes(I)
Company-Owned Units (As of 8/31/1992): . .1	Total Investment: $50K	Site Selection Assistance: . . . . . . .Yes
Franchised Units (As of 8/31/1992): 0	Fees: Franchise - $25K	Lease Negotiation Assistance: . . . . .NA
Total Units (As of 8/31/1992): 1	Royalty: 7%, Advert: 1%	Co-operative Advertising: . . . . . . .Yes
Projected New Units for 1993: 10	Contract Periods (Yrs.): 15/10	Training: . . . . 2 Wks. Headquarters
Distribution: US-1;Can-0;Overseas-0	Area Development Agreement: . .No	. . . .
North America: . . . . .1 State	Sub-Franchise Contract: . . . . .No	On-Going Support: B,C,D,G,H/ 2
Concentration: . . . . 1 in VA	Expand in Territory: . . . . . . .No	EXPANSION PLANS:
Registered: . . . . .MD,VA	Passive Ownership: . . . . .Allowed	US: . . . . East Coast
. . . .	Encourage Conversions: . . . . .No	Canada: . . . . No
Type Space: . . . . . . FS, SF, SC;~500 SF	Average # Employees: . . 3 FT, 1 PT	Overseas: . . . . No

SCREEN MACHINE, THE

19636 8th St. E.
Sonoma, CA 95476
TEL: (707) 996-5551
FAX: (707) 996-0139
Mr. Wayne T. Wirick, President

THE SCREEN MACHINE is a mobile service business, specializing in custom fabrication, replacement and repair of windows and door screens, as well as other related services.

HISTORY:	FINANCIAL: Earnings Claim: . .No	FRANCHISOR TRAINING/SUPPORT:
Established in 1986; . . 1st Franchised in 1988	Cash Investment: $32.6-53K	Financial Assistance Provided: . . . . .NA
Company-Owned Units (As of 8/31/1992): . .1	Total Investment: $32.6-53K	Site Selection Assistance: . . . . . . .Yes
Franchised Units (As of 8/31/1992): 7	Fees: Franchise - $15K	Lease Negotiation Assistance: . . . .NA
Total Units (As of 8/31/1992): 8	Royalty: 5%, Advert: 3%	Co-operative Advertising: . . . . . . .Yes
Projected New Units for 1993: 2	Contract Periods (Yrs.): 10/10	Training: . . . . . . 6-7 Days Headquarters
Distribution: US-8;Can-0;Overseas-0	Area Development Agreement: . Yes	. . . .
North America: . . . . .1 State	Sub-Franchise Contract: . . . . .No	On-Going Support: C,D,G,H/ 2
Concentration: . . . . 8 in CA	Expand in Territory: . . . . . . Yes	EXPANSION PLANS:
Registered: . . . . CA	Passive Ownership: . . . Not Allowed	US: . . . . .West
. . . .	Encourage Conversions:	Canada: . . . . No
Type Space: . . . . NA;~ SF	Average # Employees: . . . . . .1 FT	Overseas: . . . . No

SMI KITCHEN & BATH IDEA CENTERS

600 E. 48th St. N.
Sioux Falls, SD 57104
TEL: (605) 336-5590
FAX: (605) 336-5566
Mr. Randall Pooley, Natl. Fran. Mgr.

A unique kitchen and bath cabinetry business, which markets to the remodeling retail homeowner and to the custom home builder through a professionally-designed showroom. The franchisor, a division of a national cabinet manufacturer, offers complete product, design, sales and business systems training to individuals with sales and management backgrounds.

HISTORY:	FINANCIAL: Earnings Claim: . . .	FRANCHISOR TRAINING/SUPPORT:
Established in 1979; . . 1st Franchised in 1992	Cash Investment: $75K	Financial Assistance Provided: . . . Yes(I)
Company-Owned Units (As of 8/31/1992): . .3	Total Investment: $150-200K	Site Selection Assistance: . . . . . . .Yes
Franchised Units (As of 8/31/1992): 0	Fees: Franchise - $25K	Lease Negotiation Assistance: . . . . .No
Total Units (As of 8/31/1992): 3	Royalty: 3%, Advert: 1%	Co-operative Advertising: . . . . . . .Yes
Projected New Units for 1993: 5	Contract Periods (Yrs.): 5/20	Training: . . . . 6 Wks. Headquarters,
Distribution: US-3;Can-0;Overseas-0	Area Development Agreement: . .No	. . . . 2 Wks. Business Site
North America: . . . . 3 States	Sub-Franchise Contract: . . . . .No	On-Going Support: a,C,D,E,G,H,I/ 4
Concentration: . . . 1 in SD, 1 in CO, 1 in VA	Expand in Territory: . . . . . . Yes	EXPANSION PLANS:
Registered: . . . . All States Exc. DC	Passive Ownership: . . . Discouraged	US: . . . . Upper Midwest Region
. . . .	Encourage Conversions: . . . . Yes	Canada: . . . . No
Type Space: . . . . .FS, SC;~2,500 SF	Average # Employees: . . . . . .6 FT	Overseas: . . . . No

STAR-VALLEY INSTALLATIONS

2253 Linda St.
Saginaw, MI 48603
TEL: (517) 793-4484
FAX:
Mr. Monty Cazier, President

Each franchisee will be provided with the training and the products to professionally install: closet and garage organizers, mailboxes, flag poles, landscape lighting, wood playgrounds and much more. No other company offers such a complete product line as does STAR-VALLEY INSTALLATIONS.

HISTORY:	FINANCIAL: Earnings Claim: . .No	FRANCHISOR TRAINING/SUPPORT:
Established in 1987; . . . 1st Franchised in 1992	Cash Investment: $10-12K	Financial Assistance Provided: . . . . .NA
Company-Owned Units (As of 8/31/1992): . .1	Total Investment: $10-12K	Site Selection Assistance: . . . . . . .NA
Franchised Units (As of 8/31/1992): 0	Fees: Franchise - $7K	Lease Negotiation Assistance: . . . .NA
Total Units (As of 8/31/1992): 1	Royalty: 8%, Advert: 0%	Co-operative Advertising: . . . . .No
Projected New Units for 1993: 10	Contract Periods (Yrs.): 5/5	Training: . . . . 3 Days Headquarters
Distribution: US-1;Can-0;Overseas-0	Area Development Agreement: . .No	. . . .
North America: . . . . .1 State	Sub-Franchise Contract: . . . . .No	On-Going Support: B,C,D,E,G,H/ 1
Concentration: . . . . 1 in MI	Expand in Territory: . . . . . . .No	EXPANSION PLANS:
Registered: . . . . .MI	Passive Ownership: . . . Discouraged	US: . . . . .All US
. . . .	Encourage Conversions: . . . . . NA	Canada: . . . . .No
Type Space: . . . . . Garage/Storage;~600 SF	Average # Employees: . . . . . .1 FT	Overseas: . . . . No

SUPER SEAMLESS STEEL SIDING

560 Henderson Dr.
Regina, SK S4N 5X2 CAN
TEL: (800) 565-4334 (306) 721-8000 C
FAX:
Ms. Marilyn Myrglod, Dir. Fran.

On-site manufacturing of seamless steel siding from 1" to 100' in one length. 24 profiles, wide variety of colors. Also soffits, fascia, capping and other exterior products.

HISTORY:	FINANCIAL: Earnings Claim: . .No	FRANCHISOR TRAINING/SUPPORT:
Established in 1978; . . 1st Franchised in 1985	Cash Investment: $20-30K	Financial Assistance Provided: . . . . .No
Company-Owned Units (As of 8/31/1992): . .2	Total Investment: $70-100K	Site Selection Assistance: . . . . . . .Yes
Franchised Units (As of 8/31/1992): 16	Fees: Franchise - $9.8K	Lease Negotiation Assistance: . . . .NA
Total Units (As of 8/31/1992): 18	Royalty: $1.2K/Yr, Advert: . . 1.5%	Co-operative Advertising: . . . . .NA
Projected New Units for 1993: 5	Contract Periods (Yrs.): 10/10	Training: . . . . .1 Wk. Headquarters,
Distribution: US-0;Can-18;Overseas-0	Area Development Agreement: . .No	. . . . 1 Wk. On-Site
North America: . . . . 8 Provinces, 2 Territ.	Sub-Franchise Contract: . . . . .No	On-Going Support: C,D,E,G,H,I/ 6
Concentration: . . . 4 in SK, 2 in MB, 2 in NB	Expand in Territory: . . . . Yes	EXPANSION PLANS:
Registered: . . . . AB	Passive Ownership: . . . Discouraged	US: . . . . No
. . . .	Encourage Conversions: . . . . . Yes	Canada: . . . . .All Canada
Type Space: . . . . FS, SF, SC;~ SF	Average # Employees: . . . . . .4 FT	Overseas: . . . . No

WIMBERLEY HOMES

P.O. Box 8
San Marcos, TX 78667
TEL: (512) 629-1400
FAX: (512) 353-5333
Mr. Floyd MacKenzie, Treasurer

Construction and remodeling of residential houses in suburban areas. Factory-designed country houses for the discriminating buyer at a modest price level.

HISTORY:	FINANCIAL: Earnings Claim: . Yes	FRANCHISOR TRAINING/SUPPORT:
Established in 1985; . . 1st Franchised in 1987	Cash Investment: $1-25K	Financial Assistance Provided: . . . . .No
Company-Owned Units (As of 8/31/1992): . .1	Total Investment: $35K	Site Selection Assistance: . . . . . . .NA
Franchised Units (As of 8/31/1992): 0	Fees: Franchise - $0	Lease Negotiation Assistance: . . . .NA
Total Units (As of 8/31/1992): 1	Royalty: Flat, Advert: 0%	Co-operative Advertising: . . . . .Yes
Projected New Units for 1993: 1	Contract Periods (Yrs.): 5/5	Training: . . . . Continuous in
Distribution: US-1;Can-0;Overseas-0	Area Development Agreement: . .No	. . . . Field & Territory
North America: . . . . .1 State	Sub-Franchise Contract: . . . . .No	On-Going Support: a,B,C,D,F,G,h,I/ . . . 1
Concentration: . . . . 1 in TX	Expand in Territory: . . . . Yes	EXPANSION PLANS:
Registered:	Passive Ownership: . . . Discouraged	US: . . . . .All US
. . . .	Encourage Conversions: . . . . . .No	Canada: . . . . .All Canada
Type Space: . . . . . . Home Based;~100 SF	Average # Employees: . . . . . .2 FT	Overseas: . . . . No

SUPPLEMENTAL LISTING OF FRANCHISORS

ABC SEAMLESS . . . . 3001 Fiechtner Dr., SW, Fargo, ND 58103
    Contact: Mr. Lee Wagner, Fran. Sales; Tel: (800) 732-6577 (701) 293-5952 C
ADD-VENTURES OF AMERICA . . . . 38 Park St. Station, Medfield, MA 02052
    Contact: Mr. Thomas Sullivan, President; Tel: (508) 359-9603
ALLEN PROCESS . . . . P. O. Box 10041, Napa, CA 94581
    Contact: President; Tel: (800) 533-3965
AMERICAN RESTORATION SERVICES . . . . 2061 Monongahela Ave., Pittsburgh, PA 15218
    Contact: Mr. Russell Case, President; Tel: (800) 245-1617 (412) 351-7100
AMERLINK . . . . .P. O. Box 669, Battleboro, NC 27809
    Contact: Mr. Thomas Slocum, EVP; Tel: (800) 872-4254 (919) 977-2545
ARTECH WINDOW TINTING . . . . 1600 Airport Fwy., # 342, Bedford, TX 76022
    Contact: Mr. Chris Doskocil; Tel: (817) 540-4949 C
BARN YARD, THE . . . . 345 Ella Grasso Tnpk., Rte. 75, Windsor Locks, CT 06096
    Contact: Mr. Everett W. Skinner, III; Tel: (203) 623-4644
BASEMENT DE-WATERING / SAFE-AIRE . . . . P. O. Box 160, 162 E. Chestnut St., Canton, IL 61520
    Contact: Mr. Robert Beckner, Natl. Director; Tel: (800) 331-2943 (309) 647-0331
BELLET COMPANY . . . . 3160 Webster Ave., Bronx, NY 10467
    Contact: President; Tel: (212) 798-9000
CABINET CONNECTION, THE . . . . .2636 United Ln., Elk Grove Village, IL 60007
    Contact: Mr. Dave Arlasky, President; Tel: (708) 616-1181 C
CALIFORNIA POOLS . . . . 4600 Santa Anita Ave., El Monte, CA 91731
    Contact: President; Tel: (213) 443-1243
CLASSIC STORAGE . . . . 12 Sterling Ln., Scotts Valley, CA 95066
    Contact: Mr. Bart L. Ross, Chairman; Tel: (800) 852-7435 (408) 438-2959
COUNTRY SQUIRE CONSTRUCTION . . . . 11002 Park Rd., Fairfax, VA 22030
    Contact: President; Tel: (703) 591-3991
DAY CONSTRUCTION . . . . 8100 San Gabriel Rd., Atascadero, CA 93422
    Contact: President; Tel: (805) 466-4479
DECK DIRECTORS . . . . .1810 W. Price St., Tucson, AZ 85705
    Contact: Ms. Carole Rychtarik, Fran. Mgr.; Tel: (800) 999-1393 (602) 292-1393
DORACO . . . . 20 E. Herman St., Philadelphia, PA 19144
    Contact: Mr. Dan Puleio, President; Tel: (800) 338-5330 (215) 843-5300
EASI-SET INDUSTRIES . . . . P.O. Box 300, Midland, VA 22728
    Contact: Mr. John F. Bradfield, CEO; Tel: (703) 439-8911
ENERGY MISER WINDOWS . . . . 340 West 4th St., Conshohocken, PA 19428
    Contact: Mr. Jerry Freid; Tel: (215) 834-7283
EUREKA LOG HOMES . . . . P. O. Box 348, Shell Knob, MO 65747
    Contact: Mr. Shannon Smith, President; Tel: (417) 858-6108
EXOTIC DECKS . . . . 5005 Veterans Memorial Hwy., Holbrook, NY 11741
    Contact: Mr. Don Staib, Dir. Natl. Accounts; Tel: (800) 521-0179 (516) 563-4000
FLEX-SHIELD INTERNATIONAL . . . . .P.O. Box 1790, Gilbert, AZ 85234
    Contact: Mr. Charles Carroll; Tel: (602) 892-3030
FOUR SEASONS DESIGN & REMODELING CTRS. . 5005 Veterans Memorial Hwy., Holbrook, NY 11741
    Contact: Mr. Chris Esposito, President; Tel: (800) 521-0179 (516) 563-3381
GOURMET GARAGES . . . . 2139 63rd Ave., E., Bradenton, FL 34203
    Contact: Mr. John P. Hacker, Dir. Fran. Ops.; Tel: (813) 758-9121
H2 OULTON . . . . 750 E. Sample Rd., P. O. Box 1060, Pompano Beach, FL 33061
    Contact: Mr. Robert F. Oulton, President; Tel: (305) 783-0225
HORIZON PLAN CORP. . . . . 215 N. Marengo Ave., # 115, Pasadena, CA 91101
    Contact: President; Tel: (818) 906-8331
JOHN THE ROOFER . . . . 91 Sumner St., Woonsocket, RI 02895
    Contact: President; Tel: (401) 769-8145
KITCHEN SOLVERS . . . . 401 Jay St., La Crosse, WI 54601
    Contact: Mr. Dave Woggon, Dir. Fran.; Tel: (800) 845-6779 (608) 784-2855
LINC CORPORATION, THE . . . . 4 Northshore Center, 106 Isabella, Pittsburgh, PA 15212
    Contact: President; Tel: (412) 359-2197
LUMADOME . . . . 10360 72nd St., N, # 808, Largo, FL 34647
    Contact: Mr. Richard Desforges, President; Tel: (800) 782-1244 (813) 545-0232
MR. BUILD . . . . .276 Turnpike Rd., Westboro, MA 10581
    Contact: Mr. Paul Carlson, Mgr. Fran.; Tel: (800) 242-8453 (203) 657-3607

MR. CABINET CARE . . . . 101 Pacifica, # 250, Irvine, CA 92718
    Contact: Mr. Vince Paglia, EVP; Tel: (800) 843-6222 (714) 727-9600
NATURAL LOG HOMES . . . . Rt. 2, Box 164, South Kings Hwy., Noel, MO 64854
    Contact: Mr. Monte Jones; Tel: (417) 475-3183
NORTHERN PRODUCTS LOG HOMES . . . . . . P.O. Box 616, 25 Bomarc Rd., Bangor, ME 04402
    Contact: Mr. David Caliendo, President; Tel: (800) 447-4050 (207) 945-6413
PACIFIC GULL INTERNATIONAL . . . . 1416 N. Cleve-Mass Rd., Akron, OH 44313
    Contact: President; Tel: (216) 666-7855
PAUL DAVIS SYSTEMS (CANADA) . . . . 3025 Kennedy Rd., # 2, Scarborough, ON M1V 1S3   CAN
    Contact: Mr. William F. Robinson; Tel: (416) 299-8890
PAVEMENT MEDICS . . . . 820 McKay Rd., Pickering, ON L1W 2Y4   CAN
    Contact: Mr. Gordon W. Edminston; Tel: (416) 686-1261
PERFECT SURFACE . . . . 1625 Oak Meadow, Irving, TX 75061
    Contact: Ms. Shirley Perkins, President; Tel: (800) 444-8925 (214) 251-1634
PERMAFLU CHIMNEY LINING SYSTEM . . .105 W. Merrimack St., Box #4035, Manchester, NH 03108
    Contact: Mr. Ed Frankavitz, Natl. Sales Manager; Tel: (603) 668-5195
PERMAR WINDOWS . . . . 10 Dunlop Dr., St. Catharines, ON L2R 1A2   CAN
    Contact: Mr. Gordon Fraser, VP Fran.; Tel: (416) 641-2927
PROS PRODUCTIONS, THE . . . . 2449 Golf Rd., Philadelphia, PA 19131
    Contact: Mr. Herbert Cohen, President; Tel: (215) 877-7777
RE-MODELERS UNLIMITED . . . . 254 Hinman Rd., Watertown, CT 06795
    Contact: President; Tel: (203) 888-8921
RYAN HOMES . . . . 100 Ryan Court, Pittsburgh, PA 15205
    Contact: President; Tel: (412) 276-8000
SCREENMOBILE . . . . .457 W. Allen Ave., # 107, San Dimas, CA 91773
    Contact: Mr. Monte M. Walker, President; Tel: (818) 335-8813
SERVICE AMERICA . . . . P. O. Box 768822, Atlanta, GA 30076
    Contact: Mr. Ronald L. Smith; Tel: (404) 392-0020
SMOKEY MOUNTAIN LOG CABINS . . . . P.O. Box 549, Maggie Valley, NC 28751
    Contact: President; Tel: (704) 926-0886
SOLID / FLUE CHIMNEY SYSTEMS . . . . .370 100th St. SW, Byron Center, MI 49315
    Contact: Mr. Doug La Fleur, President; Tel: (800) 444-FLUE (616) 877-4900 C
SPEED FAB-CRETE . . . . 1150 E. Mansfield Hwy., Fort Worth, TX 76119
    Contact: Mr. David Bloxom, President; Tel: (817) 478-1137
SUPERIOR WALLS OF AMERICA . . . . .P. O. Box 427, Ephrata, PA 17522
    Contact: Mr. Bruce A. Senft, GM; Tel: (800) 452-9255 (717) 626-9255
THERMOCRETE CHIMNEY LININGS . . . . 7111 Ohms Lane, Minneapolis, MN 53435
    Contact: President; Tel: (612) 835-1386
TIMBERMILL STORAGE BARNS . . . . One Wolf Run, Glen Ellen, CA 95442
    Contact: Mr. A. G. Phillips, President; Tel: (707) 996-BARN
WALL-FILL WORLDWIDE . . . . 649 Childs St., Wheaton, IL 60187
    Contact: Mr. Ed Lowrie, President; Tel: (708) 668-3400
WAYNE'S SCREEN MACHINES . . . . 446 Claudia Dr., Sonoma, CA 95476
    Contact: President; Tel: (707) 996-5551
WINDOW MAN, THE/WINDOWS OF OPPORTUNITY . . . . . 711 Rigsbee Ave., Durham, NC 27701
    Contact: Mr. Conrad Harris, President; Tel: (800) 458-5858 (919) 682-5515

For a full explanation of the data provided in

the Franchisor Format, please refer to Chapter 2,

"How To Use The Data."

CHAPTER 7

BUSINESS: ACCOUNTING / CREDIT / COLLECTION

ACCOUNTAX SERVICES (CANADA)

951 Wilson Ave., # 4
North York, ON M3K 2A7 CAN
TEL: (416) 638-1303
FAX: (416) 638-1443
Mr. Vijay Kapur, Marketing Director

Accounting, bookkeeping, taxation and financial consulting.

HISTORY: . . . .
Established in 1980; . . 1st Franchised in 1981
Company-Owned Units (As of 8/31/1992): . .2
Franchised Units (As of 8/31/1992): 7
Total Units (As of 8/31/1992): 9
Projected New Units for 1993: 6
Distribution: US-0;Can-9;Overseas-0
  North America: . . . . .3 Provinces
  Concentration: . . . .
Registered: . . . . CA,FL,NY
. . . .
Type Space: . . .SF, SC, RM;~800 and Up SF

FINANCIAL: Earnings Claim: . .No
Cash Investment: . . . . . . $10K+
Total Investment: $10-25K
Fees: Franchise - $10K
  Royalty: 4%, Advert: 2%
Contract Periods (Yrs.): 5/5
Area Development Agreement: Yes/5
Sub-Franchise Contract: . . . . . .No
Expand in Territory: . . . . Yes
Passive Ownership: . . . . . .Allowed
Encourage Conversions: . . . . . NA
Average # Employees: . .2 FT, 1+ PT

FRANCHISOR TRAINING/SUPPORT:
Financial Assistance Provided: . . . Yes(I)
Site Selection Assistance: . . . . .Yes
Lease Negotiation Assistance: . . . . .Yes
Co-operative Advertising: . . . . .Yes
Training: . . . . 1-6 Months
. . . .
On-Going Support: b,c,d,f,G,h/ 10
EXPANSION PLANS:
US: . . . . All US
Canada: . . . . .All Canada
Overseas: . . . . .MX

ACCOUNTING, CREDIT, COLLECTION AGENCIES AND GENERAL BUSINESS SYSTEMS

	1989	1990	1991	Percentage Change 90/89	Percentage Change 91/90
Total Number of Establishments:					
Company–Owned	27	28	31	3.70%	10.71%
Franchisee–Owned	1,706	1,730	1,904	1.41%	10.06%
Total	1,733	1,758	1,935	1.44%	10.07%
Ratio of Total Establishments:					
Company–Owned	1.6%	1.6%	1.6%		
Franchisee–Owned	98.4%	98.4%	98.4%		
Total	100.0%	100.0%	100.0%		
Total Sales ($000):					
Company–Owned	8,014	8,519	9,667	6.30%	13.48%
Franchisee–Owned	178,368	187,208	211,394	4.96%	12.92%
Total	186,382	195,727	221,061	5.01%	12.94%
Ratio of Total Sales:					
Company–Owned	4.3%	4.4%	4.4%		
Franchisee–Owned	95.7%	95.6%	95.6%		
Total	100.0%	100.0%	100.0%		
Average Sales Per Unit ($000):					
Company–Owned	297	304	312	2.50%	2.49%
Franchisee–Owned	105	108	111	3.50%	2.60%
Total	108	111	114	3.52%	2.61%
Relative Average Sales Ratio:	283.9%	281.2%	280.9%		

	Number Of Employees	Employees Per Unit	Avg. Sales Per Employee
Total 1989 Employment:			
Company–Owned	175	6.5	$45,794
Franchisee–Owned	4,969	2.9	$35,896
Total	5,144	3.0	$36,233
Relative Employee Performance Ratios:		222.5%	127.6%

	1st Quartile	Median	4th Quartile
Average 1989 Total Investment:			
Company–Owned	NA	NA	NA
Franchisee–Owned	$22,500	$40,000	$55,000
Single Unit Franchise Fee	$15,000	$20,000	$27,500
Mult. Unit Franchise Fee	NA	NA	NA
Franchise Start–Up Cost	NA	$27,500	NA

Source: Franchising In The Economy 1991, IFA Educational Foundation & Horwath International.

ADVANTAGE PAYROLL SERVICES

800 Center St., P.O. Box 1330
Auburn, ME 04210
TEL: (800) 876-0178 (207) 783-2068
FAX: (207) 786-0490
Mr. David Friedrich, President

The unique ADVANTAGE franchise relationship allows a proven salesperson with no computer or payroll experience to become self-employed in the computer services industry.ADVANTAGE franchisees provide local personalized service, while using the company's large mainframe computer processing power, sophisticated software and proven payroll tax filing service.

HISTORY: . . . . IFA	FINANCIAL: Earnings Claim: . .No	FRANCHISOR TRAINING/SUPPORT:
Established in 1967; . . 1st Franchised in 1983	Cash Investment: $15-20K	Financial Assistance Provided: . . .Yes(D)
Company-Owned Units (As of 8/31/1992): . .1	Total Investment: $20-40K	Site Selection Assistance: . . . . . . .NA
Franchised Units (As of 8/31/1992): 30	Fees: Franchise - $14.5K	Lease Negotiation Assistance: . . . . .NA
Total Units (As of 8/31/1992): 31	Royalty: 0%, Advert: 0%	Co-operative Advertising: . . . . . . .Yes
Projected New Units for 1993: 12	Contract Periods (Yrs.): 10/10	Training: . . . . 2 Wks. Headquarters,
Distribution: US-31;Can-0;Overseas-0	Area Development Agreement: . .No	. . . . 10 Days Franchisee Territory
North America: . . . . 12 States	Sub-Franchise Contract: . . . . .No	On-Going Support: a,B,C,D,G,H,I/ . . . 60
Concentration: . . .6 in ME, 2 in NH, 2 in MA	Expand in Territory: . . . . . . .No	EXPANSION PLANS:
Registered: . . . . All States	Passive Ownership: . . . Not Allowed	US: . . . . .All US
. . . .	Encourage Conversions: . . . . . Yes	Canada: . . . . .No
Type Space: . . . . ;~ SF	Average # Employees: . . 1 FT, 1 PT	Overseas: . . . . No

COMPREHENSIVE BUSINESS SERVICES

1925 Palomar Oaks Way, # 105
Carlsbad, CA 92008
TEL: (800) 323-9000 (619) 431-2150
FAX: (619) 431-2156
Mr. Peter Nelson, Sales Admn.

A true accounting franchise, servicing the nation's small and medium-sized businesses. Bookkeeping, taxes, double entry systems provide monthly service to clients. Input/output terminal and processing via central mainframe computer. Must have accounting degree or equivalent. Extensive client services, including loan packages and consulting.

HISTORY: . . . . IFA	FINANCIAL: Earnings Claim: . .No	FRANCHISOR TRAINING/SUPPORT:
Established in 1949; . . 1st Franchised in 1965	Cash Investment: $39K	Financial Assistance Provided: . . . Yes(I)
Company-Owned Units (As of 8/31/1992): . .0	Total Investment: $45-60K	Site Selection Assistance: . . . . . . .Yes
Franchised Units (As of 8/31/1992): 210	Fees: Franchise - $17.5K	Lease Negotiation Assistance: . . . . .Yes
Total Units (As of 8/31/1992): 210	Royalty: 6%, Advert: 2%	Co-operative Advertising: . . . . . . .NA
Projected New Units for 1993: 36	Contract Periods (Yrs.): 20	Training: . . . . . . 14 Days Headquarters,
Distribution: US-210;Can-0;Overseas-0	Area Development Agreement: . .No	. . 7-10 Days Regional Center, On-Going
North America:	Sub-Franchise Contract: . . . . .No	On-Going Support: a,b,c,d,e,f,g,h,i/ . . . 20
Concentration: . . 21 in IL, 18 in PA, 14 in TX	Expand in Territory: . . . . . . Yes	EXPANSION PLANS:
Registered: . . . . .All	Passive Ownership: . . . Not Allowed	US: . . . . .All US
. . . .	Encourage Conversions: . . . . . Yes	Canada: . . . . .All Canada
Type Space: . . . . FS;~ SF	Average # Employees: . . . . 1-5 FT	Overseas: . . . . Yes

EDWIN K. WILLIAMS & CO.

8774 Yates Dr., # 210
Westminster, CO 80030
TEL: (800) 255-2359 (303) 427-4989
FAX: (303) 650-7286
Mr. David Hinze, Dir. Field Support

EKW is a business management business, specializing in the "how-to" of maximizing small business profits through a network of franchised offices. This network of local offices provides the most up-to-date accounting, tax and business counseling services plus a wide range of computer services. EKW has developed and markets record keeping systems for small businesses.

HISTORY: . . . . IFA	FINANCIAL: Earnings Claim: . .No	FRANCHISOR TRAINING/SUPPORT:
Established in 1935; . . 1st Franchised in 1947	Cash Investment: $50-75K	Financial Assistance Provided: . . . . .No
Company-Owned Units (As of 8/31/1992): . .1	Total Investment: $50-75K	Site Selection Assistance: . . . . . . .NA
Franchised Units (As of 8/31/1992): 379	Fees: Franchise - $25K	Lease Negotiation Assistance: . . . . .No
Total Units (As of 8/31/1992): 380	Royalty: 8-6-4%, Advert: 0%	Co-operative Advertising: . . . . . . .No
Projected New Units for 1993: 10	Contract Periods (Yrs.): 10/10	Training: . . . . 2 Wks. Headquarters,
Distribution: . . . US-300;Can-30;Overseas-50	Area Development Agreement: . .No	. . . . 1 Wk. Existing Office
North America: . . . . 48 States	Sub-Franchise Contract: . . . . .No	On-Going Support: C,D,E,G,H,I/ 35
Concentration: . .57 in CA, 22 in FL, 14 in TX	Expand in Territory: . . . . Yes	EXPANSION PLANS:
Registered: . . . . All States	Passive Ownership: . . . Not Allowed	US: . . . . .All US
. . . .	Encourage Conversions: . . . . . Yes	Canada: . . . . .Yes
Type Space: . . . . FS;~600 SF	Average # Employees: . . 2 FT, 2 PT	Overseas: . . . . Yes

FINANCIAL EXPRESS

4100 Alpha Rd., # 111
Dallas, TX 75244
TEL: (800) 242-1065 (214) 991-9255 C
FAX: (214) 991-8117
Mr. Bill Pike, Dir. Fran. Dev.

Financial management centers designed for servicing professionals and small businesses by providing payroll administration, bookkeeping, tax preparation, consulting, accounting, hardware/software installation and support. Cash collected when finished - no A/R's. Sales oriented. Our marketing system includes selection, training and supervision of full-time marketing staff.

HISTORY:	FINANCIAL: Earnings Claim: . .No	FRANCHISOR TRAINING/SUPPORT:
Established in 1986; . . 1st Franchised in 1986	Cash Investment: $35K	Financial Assistance Provided: . . .Yes(D)
Company-Owned Units (As of 8/31/1992): . .0	Total Investment: $60K	Site Selection Assistance: . . . . . . .Yes
Franchised Units (As of 8/31/1992): 48	Fees: Franchise - $25K	Lease Negotiation Assistance: . . . . .Yes
Total Units (As of 8/31/1992): 48	Royalty: 8%, Advert: . . . . . . NA	Co-operative Advertising: . . . . .Yes
Projected New Units for 1993: 60	Contract Periods (Yrs.): 5/5	Training: . . . 3 Wks. HQ Sales/Ops.,
Distribution: US-48;Can-0;Overseas-0	Area Development Agreement: Yes/3	. . . . 1 Wk. on Location Sales
North America: . . . . 6 States	Sub-Franchise Contract: . . . . . .No	On-Going Support: b,C,D,E,G,h,I/ . . . 14
Concentration: . . .20 in TX, 5 in OH, 5 in GA	Expand in Territory: . . . . Yes	EXPANSION PLANS:
Registered: . . . . .CA,FL,IN,MI,VA	Passive Ownership: . . . . . .Allowed	US: . . . . All US
. . . .	Encourage Conversions: . . . . . Yes	Canada: . . . . .All Exc. Alberta
Type Space: . . . . .SC, Off. Bldg.;~1,500 SF	Average # Employees: . . 3 FT, 1 PT	Overseas: AU, UK, Other Commonwealth

PADGETT BUSINESS SERVICES

160 Hawthorne Park
Athens, GA 30606
TEL: (800) 323-7292 (706) 548-1040
FAX: (706) 543-8537
Mr. Greg Williams, VP Mktg.

PBS grants licenses to individuals who desire to operate their own accounting, income tax and business consulting practice, utilizing the unique forms and successful systems of operation developed by the franchisor. The franchisee markets to small owner-operated businesses located in his own territory.

HISTORY: . . . . IFA	FINANCIAL: Earnings Claim: . .No	FRANCHISOR TRAINING/SUPPORT:
Established in 1966; . . 1st Franchised in 1977	Cash Investment: $35-75K	Financial Assistance Provided: . . .Yes(D)
Company-Owned Units (As of 8/31/1992): . .0	Total Investment: $35-75K	Site Selection Assistance: . . . . . . .Yes
Franchised Units (As of 8/31/1992): 195	Fees: Franchise - $29.5K	Lease Negotiation Assistance: . . . . .Yes
Total Units (As of 8/31/1992): 195	Royalty: 9%, Advert: 0%	Co-operative Advertising: . . . . .No
Projected New Units for 1993: 50	Contract Periods (Yrs.): . . . 20/20	Training: . . . . 2 Wks. Headquarters,
Distribution: US-150;Can-45;Overseas-0	Area Development Agreement: . .No	. . . . . .1 Wk. Field, 1 Wk. New Office
North America: . . . . 35 States, 2 Provinces	Sub-Franchise Contract: . . . . . .No	On-Going Support: C,D,G,H,I/ 20
Concentration: . 40 in ON, 25 in GA, 16 in FL	Expand in Territory: . . . . Yes	EXPANSION PLANS:
Registered: . . . .CA,FL,HI,IL,MD,NY,OR,RI	Passive Ownership: . . . Discouraged	US: . . . . All US
. . . . SD,VA,WA	Encourage Conversions: . . . . . Yes	Canada: . . . . .All Canada
Type Space: . . . . Varies;~800 SF	Average # Employees: . . . . . .1 FT	Overseas: . . . . No

PAYX

4102 42 Ave. S.
Minneapolis, MN 55406
TEL: (800) 999-6633 (612) 729-8361
FAX:
Mr. C. J. Howard, Trainer

Payroll preparation for smaller businesses. Payroll and other business software for sale and installation, including point-of-sale, inventory, job costing, video store and tool rental. Only PAYX software can be easily modified to do exactly what the business owner wants and needs. Can be operated from home.

HISTORY:	FINANCIAL: Earnings Claim: . .No	FRANCHISOR TRAINING/SUPPORT:
Established in 1990; . . 1st Franchised in 1992	Cash Investment: . . . .$	Financial Assistance Provided: . . . . .Yes
Company-Owned Units (As of 8/31/1992): . .1	Total Investment: . . . .$	Site Selection Assistance: . . . . . . .NA
Franchised Units (As of 8/31/1992): 0	Fees: Franchise - $2K	Lease Negotiation Assistance: . . . . .NA
Total Units (As of 8/31/1992): 1	Royalty: 3%, Advert: 5%	Co-operative Advertising: . . . . .Yes
Projected New Units for 1993: 18	Contract Periods (Yrs.): 10/10	Training: . . . . 2 Days Headquarters
Distribution: US-1;Can-0;Overseas-0	Area Development Agreement: . .No	. . . .
North America: . . . . .1 State	Sub-Franchise Contract: . . . . . .No	On-Going Support: A,B,C,D,G,I/ 5
Concentration: . . . . .1 in MN	Expand in Territory: . . . . Yes	EXPANSION PLANS:
Registered: . . . . . .Applications in Process	Passive Ownership: . . . Not Allowed	US: . . . . All US
. . . .	Encourage Conversions: . . . . . NA	Canada: . . . . .No
Type Space: . . . . . Home Based;~300 SF	Average # Employees: . . 1 FT, 1 PT	Overseas: . . . . No

SUPPLEMENTAL LISTING OF FRANCHISORS

ACCOUNTANT'S CHOICE, THE . . . . 401 St. Francis St., Tallahassee, FL 32301
    Contact: President; Tel:
ACCOUNTANTS, INC. . . . . 111 Anza Blvd., # 400, Burlingame, CA 94010
    Contact: Ms. Dianne Burr, President; Tel: (415) 579-1111
BINEX AUTOMATED BUSINESS SYSTEMS . . . . . 4441 Auburn Blvd., E., Sacramento, CA 95841
    Contact: Mr. Walter Heidig, President; Tel: (916) 483-8080 C
COMCHEQ SERVICES LIMITED . . . . 298 Garry St., Winnipeg, MB R3C 1H3   CAN
    Contact: Mr. Jerry Butler, Licensee Coord.; Tel: (204) 947-9400
COMPREHENSIVE ACCOUNTING SERVICES . . . . . . .2111 Comprehensive Dr., Aurora, IL 60507
    Contact: Mr. John Kean, VP; Tel: (800) 323-9000 (312) 898-1234
COMPREHENSIVE BUSINESS SERVICES (CAN) . . . . . 2851 John St., # 200, Markham, ON L3R 5R7   CAN
    Contact: Mr. Leo G. Lauzen; Tel: (416) 946-0399
CORRECT CREDIT COMPANY . . . . 721 Auth Ave., Oakhurst, NJ 07755
    Contact: Mr. Joe Caribia, Project Mgr.; Tel: (800) 848-3464 (908) 517-0077
M. G. C. SERVICE . . . . .P.O. Box 345, Blair, NE 68008
    Contact: Mr. Charlie Randone; Tel: (402) 572-7065

CHAPTER 8

BUSINESS: ADVERTISING AND PROMOTION

BRIDE'S CLUB, THE

P. O. Box 654
Nesconset, NY 11767
TEL: (800) 562-7433 (516) 361-9108
FAX: (516) 361-7326
Mr. Josh Frankel, President

This award-winning program allows a franchisee to provide a complete target marketing and advertising plan to thousands of local wedding-related companies as brides-to-be "Join the Club." Sales include full-color display advertising, direct mail services, incentive programs and more. Complete training and support is provided for this low capital investment within the $33 billion wedding industry.

HISTORY: . . . .
Established in 1987;   . . 1st Franchised in 1991
Company-Owned Units (As of 8/31/1992):   . .8
Franchised Units (As of 8/31/1992): 4
Total Units (As of 8/31/1992): 12
Projected New Units for 1993: 10
Distribution: US-12;Can-0;Overseas-0
   North America: . . . . 3 States
   Concentration: . . . .2 in NJ, 1 in NY, 1 in PA
Registered: . . . . NY
. . . .
Type Space: . . . . NA;~ SF

FINANCIAL: Earnings Claim: . .No
Cash Investment: $2-5K
Total Investment: $13-35K
Fees: Franchise - $15K
   Royalty: 10%, Advert: 0%
Contract Periods (Yrs.): 5/5
Area Development Agreement: . .No
Sub-Franchise Contract: . . . . . .No
Expand in Territory: . . . . Yes
Passive Ownership: . . . Discouraged
Encourage Conversions: . . . . . NA
Average # Employees: . . 1 FT, 1 PT

FRANCHISOR TRAINING/SUPPORT:
Financial Assistance Provided: . . . Yes(I)
Site Selection Assistance: . . . . . . .Yes
Lease Negotiation Assistance: . . . . .NA
Co-operative Advertising: . . . . .NA
Training: . . . . 1 Wk. Headquarters
. . . .
On-Going Support: A,b,C,D,E,F,G,H,I/   . 5
EXPANSION PLANS:
US: . . . . All US
Canada: . . . . No
Overseas: . . . . No

COUPON MADNESS

64 Wall St.
Norwalk, CT 06850
TEL: (203) 866-0299 C
FAX: (203) 831-8023
Mr. Guy F. Darter, President

COUPON MADNESS offers a unique opportunity in the hot business services segment. Direct mail coupon magazine, targeted towards a huge range of customers in retail and service professions. Special format offers clients a low-cost method of reaching the maximum audience with longer than average exposure to the target market. Magazine sent bi-monthly to minimum of 50,000 households. Small business must advertise to survive.

HISTORY: . . . . IFA	FINANCIAL: Earnings Claim: . .No	FRANCHISOR TRAINING/SUPPORT:
Established in 1990; . . 1st Franchised in 1991	Cash Investment: $12K	Financial Assistance Provided: . . .Yes(D)
Company-Owned Units (As of 8/31/1992): . .0	Total Investment: $12-22K	Site Selection Assistance: . . . . . . .NA
Franchised Units (As of 8/31/1992): 5	Fees: Franchise - $19.5K	Lease Negotiation Assistance: . . . . .NA
Total Units (As of 8/31/1992): 5	Royalty: 6%, Advert: 2%	Co-operative Advertising: . . . . . . .NA
Projected New Units for 1993: 5	Contract Periods (Yrs.): . . . . Life	Training: . . . . . . 1-2 Wks. Home Office,
Distribution: US-5;Can-0;Overseas-0	Area Development Agreement: . .No	. . . . .On-Going In-Field Training
North America: . . . . .1 State	Sub-Franchise Contract: . . . . .No	On-Going Support: D,H/ 2
Concentration: . . . . 5 in CT	Expand in Territory: . . . . . . .No	EXPANSION PLANS:
Registered: . . . . .NY,RI	Passive Ownership: . . . Not Allowed	US: . . . . Northeast
. . . .	Encourage Conversions: . . . . . Yes	Canada: . . . . .No
Type Space: . . . . NA;~ SF	Average # Employees: . . . . . .1 FT	Overseas: . . . . No

COUPON-CASH SAVER

925 N. Milwaukee Ave.
Wheeling, IL 60090
TEL: (708) 537-6420
FAX: (708) 537-6499
Ms. Myrna O'Reilly, President

COUPON-CASH SAVER offers a unique direct mail advertising concept. Everyone needs to advertise - our industry is booming! We can put you into business - quickly, easily and affordably. A little coupon could be your ticket to something big.

HISTORY: . . . . IFA	FINANCIAL: Earnings Claim: . Yes	FRANCHISOR TRAINING/SUPPORT:
Established in 1984; . . 1st Franchised in 1990	Cash Investment: $26K	Financial Assistance Provided: . . . . .Yes
Company-Owned Units (As of 8/31/1992): . .4	Total Investment: $26K	Site Selection Assistance: . . . . . . .Yes
Franchised Units (As of 8/31/1992): 8	Fees: Franchise - $18.5K	Lease Negotiation Assistance: . . . .NA
Total Units (As of 8/31/1992): 12	Royalty: 8%, Advert: . . Up To 1%	Co-operative Advertising: . . . . . . .NA
Projected New Units for 1993:	Contract Periods (Yrs.): 5/15	Training: . . . . .1 Wk. Headquarters,
Distribution: US-12;Can-0;Overseas-0	Area Development Agreement: . . .	. . . . .2 Wks. Franchisee Location
North America: . . . . .1 State	Sub-Franchise Contract: . . . . .No	On-Going Support: b,C,D,H/ 2
Concentration: . . . . .6 in IL	Expand in Territory: . . . . Yes	EXPANSION PLANS:
Registered: . . . . IL,IN,WI	Passive Ownership: . . . Not Allowed	US: . . . . .IL, IN and WI
. . . .	Encourage Conversions: . . . . .No	Canada: . . . . .No
Type Space: . . . . Home Based;~ SF	Average # Employees: . . . . . .1 FT	Overseas: . . . . No

GOOD NEWS ADVERTISING

36 C Stoffel Dr.
Rexdale, ON M9W 1A8 CAN
TEL: (416) 248-5555 C
FAX: (416) 248-5558
Mr. Thom Tyson, President

GOOD NEWS ADVERTISING provides a cost-effective and professional advertising service through a network of independent direct mail associates. We train, protect exclusivity and provide on-going, hands-on help to our DMA's. Coupon College, manuals, workshops, audio and video make high, secure earnings possible from the first week of activity.

HISTORY:	FINANCIAL: Earnings Claim: . .No	FRANCHISOR TRAINING/SUPPORT:
Established in 1984; . . 1st Franchised in 1989	Cash Investment: $0	Financial Assistance Provided: . . . . .No
Company-Owned Units (As of 8/31/1992): . .2	Total Investment: $5-25K	Site Selection Assistance: . . . . . . .NA
Franchised Units (As of 8/31/1992): 42	Fees: Franchise - $5-25K	Lease Negotiation Assistance: . . . . .NA
Total Units (As of 8/31/1992): 44	Royalty: 0%, Advert: 0%	Co-operative Advertising: . . . . . . .NA
Projected New Units for 1993: 24	Contract Periods (Yrs.): 1/1	Training: . . . . . 3 Days Coupon College,
Distribution: US-0;Can-44;Overseas-0	Area Development Agreement: . .No	. . . 2 Days Local Centre, 5-10 Days Site
North America: . . . . 7 Provinces	Sub-Franchise Contract: . . . . .No	On-Going Support: B,C,D,E,G,H,I/ 9
Concentration: . . .35 in ON, 3 in BC, 2 in NB	Expand in Territory: . . . . . . .No	EXPANSION PLANS:
Registered:	Passive Ownership: . . . Not Allowed	US: . . . . Northeast, Midwest
. . . .	Encourage Conversions: . . . . . NA	Canada: . . . . .All Canada
Type Space: . . . . . . .Home Based;~NA SF	Average # Employees: . . . . 2-3 FT	Overseas: . . . . No

GREETINGS

P. O. Box 25623
Lexington, KY 40524
TEL: (606) 272-5624
FAX: (606) 273-2636
Mr. Larry Kargel, President

Target market advertising, addressing new homeowners, apartment residences, colleges and universities.

HISTORY:	FINANCIAL: Earnings Claim: . .No	FRANCHISOR TRAINING/SUPPORT:
Established in 1984; . . 1st Franchised in 1990	Cash Investment: $20-25K	Financial Assistance Provided: . . . Yes(I)
Company-Owned Units (As of 8/31/1992): . .4	Total Investment: $20-30K	Site Selection Assistance: . . . . .Yes
Franchised Units (As of 8/31/1992): 4	Fees: Franchise - $15K	Lease Negotiation Assistance: . . . .Yes
Total Units (As of 8/31/1992): 8	Royalty: 5%, Advert: 0%	Co-operative Advertising: . . . . . . .NA
Projected New Units for 1993:	Contract Periods (Yrs.): 10/5	Training: . . . . .1 Wk. Headquarters,
Distribution: US-8;Can-0;Overseas-0	Area Development Agreement: Yes/10	. . . . 1 Wk. Franchisee Location
North America: . . . . 4 States	Sub-Franchise Contract: . . . . . .No	On-Going Support: C,D,F/ 2
Concentration: . . . 4 in KY, 2 in OH, 1 in TN	Expand in Territory: . . . . Yes	EXPANSION PLANS:
Registered:	Passive Ownership: . . . Discouraged	US: . . . . .Southeast, Ohio
. . . .	Encourage Conversions: . . . . . NA	Canada: . . . . .No
Type Space: . . . . Home Based;~200-500 SF	Average # Employees: . . . . 6-8 PT	Overseas: . . . . No

INFORMATION DISPLAYS

3276 Kitchen Dr.
Carson City, NV 89701
TEL: (800) 782-5000
FAX:
Ms. Arlene Stankus, Dir. Fran.

INFORMATION DISPLAYS offers a highly focused, proven program of selling advertising space on unique, trademarked outdoor displays and related paper maps. Our system provides for initial development and creative opportunity, while presenting the enhanced market awareness available through the nation's largest Mini Billboard Display producer.

HISTORY:	FINANCIAL: Earnings Claim: . Yes	FRANCHISOR TRAINING/SUPPORT:
Established in 1978; . . . 1st Franchised in 1991	Cash Investment: . . . $17.5-37.5K	Financial Assistance Provided: . . . Yes(I)
Company-Owned Units (As of 8/31/1992): . .0	Total Investment: $40.5-42.1K	Site Selection Assistance: . . . . .NA
Franchised Units (As of 8/31/1992): 1	Fees: Franchise - $25K	Lease Negotiation Assistance: . . . .NA
Total Units (As of 8/31/1992): 1	Royalty: 0%, Advert: 0%	Co-operative Advertising: . . . . . . .NA
Projected New Units for 1993: 6	Contract Periods (Yrs.): 10/10	Training: . . . . 5 Days Headquarters
Distribution: US-1;Can-0;Overseas-0	Area Development Agreement: . .No	. . . .
North America: . . . . .1 State	Sub-Franchise Contract: . . . . . .No	On-Going Support: B,C,d,F,G,h,I/ 2
Concentration: . . . . 1 in CA	Expand in Territory: . . . . . . .No	EXPANSION PLANS:
Registered: . . . . CA,WA	Passive Ownership: . . . . . .Allowed	US: . . . . All US
. . . .	Encourage Conversions: . . . . . NA	Canada: . . . . .Yes
Type Space: . . . . Home Based;~ SF	Average # Employees: . . . . . .1 FT	Overseas: . . . . Yes

MERCHANT ADVERTISING SYSTEMS

4115 Tiverton Rd.
Randallstown, MD 21133
TEL: (410) 655-3201 C
FAX:
Mr. Donald A. Goldvarg, President

Local merchant display centers for supermarkets and malls. Utilize as customer information center. Co-op advertising with local merchants. Large custom-made sign and literature dispensers sold to merchants for 1-year term. Unique, high visibility, cost-effective and professional advertising display. High profitability and cash flow.

HISTORY:	FINANCIAL: Earnings Claim: . .No	FRANCHISOR TRAINING/SUPPORT:
Established in 1987; . . 1st Franchised in 1987	Cash Investment: $20-25K	Financial Assistance Provided: . . .Yes(D)
Company-Owned Units (As of 8/31/1992): . .0	Total Investment: . . . $27.5-33.5K	Site Selection Assistance: . . . . .NA
Franchised Units (As of 8/31/1992): 3	Fees: Franchise - $23.5-29.5K	Lease Negotiation Assistance: . . . .NA
Total Units (As of 8/31/1992): 3	Royalty: 8%, Advert: 0%	Co-operative Advertising: . . . . . . .Yes
Projected New Units for 1993: 6	Contract Periods (Yrs.): 10/10	Training: . . . . .1 Wk. Headquarters,
Distribution: US-3;Can-0;Overseas-0	Area Development Agreement: . .No	. . . . 1 Wk. Franchisee Territory
North America: . . . . 2 States	Sub-Franchise Contract: . . . . . Yes	On-Going Support: B,C,D,E,F,G,H/ . . . 4
Concentration: . . . . 2 in MD, 1 in PA	Expand in Territory: . . . . Yes	EXPANSION PLANS:
Registered: . . . . . .FL,MD,MI,OR,VA,DC	Passive Ownership: . . . Discouraged	US: . . . . All US
. . . .	Encourage Conversions: . . . . .No	Canada: . . . . .No
Type Space: . . . . NA;~NA SF	Average # Employees: . . 2 FT, 2 PT	Overseas: . . . . No

MONEY MAILER

14271 Corporate Dr.
Garden Grove, CA 92643
TEL: (800) MAILER-1 (714) 265-4100
FAX: (714) 265-4091
Franchise Sales Dept.

MONEY MAILER, co-operative direct mail advertising, is the sales professional's franchise opportunity. With low receivables, no inventory and no store front requirements, sales pros can concentrate on what they do best - selling. Our franchisees offer cost-effective advertising services for local business services/merchants. MONEY MAILER provides comprehensive training in sales, management & communication techniques, as well as continuing training.

HISTORY: . . . . IFA	FINANCIAL: Earnings Claim: . . .	FRANCHISOR TRAINING/SUPPORT:
Established in 1979; . . 1st Franchised in 1980	Cash Investment: $5-15K	Financial Assistance Provided: . . .Yes(D)
Company-Owned Units (As of 8/31/1992): . .0	Total Investment: $22-80K	Site Selection Assistance: . . . . .NA
Franchised Units (As of 8/31/1992): 389	Fees: Franchise - $20K	Lease Negotiation Assistance: . . . . .NA
Total Units (As of 8/31/1992): 389	Royalty: 10%, Advert: 0%	Co-operative Advertising: . . . . . . .Yes
Projected New Units for 1993: 160	Contract Periods (Yrs.): 5/5	Training: . . . . 3 Wks. Headquarters,
Distribution: . . . US-380;Can-9;Overseas-0	Area Development Agreement: . .No	. . . 1 Wk. Regional Office, 1 Wk. Field
North America: . . . . . 30 States, 1 Province	Sub-Franchise Contract: . . . . . Yes	On-Going Support: C,D,G,H,I/ 205
Concentration: . . 56 in CA, 45 in NJ. 37 in IL	Expand in Territory: . . . . Yes	EXPANSION PLANS:
Registered: . . . . .All	Passive Ownership: . . . Not Allowed	US: . . . . All US
. . . .	Encourage Conversions: . . . . . .No	Canada: . . . . .All Canada
Type Space: . . . . NA;~NA SF	Average # Employees: . . . . . .1 FT	Overseas: . . . . UK

POINTS FOR PROFIT

P. O. Box 81023
San Diego, CA 92138
TEL: (619) 588-0664 (916) 588-0664
FAX: (619) 588-0664
Ms. Rosilyn D. Nesler, President

Proof of purchase advertising and marketing package sold to broadcast stations. Attracts major advertisers. Sold as an exclusive to one broadcast station in each market area. Franchisee, besides receiving a cash guarantee from stations, also receives commercial air time for own use or sales. Currently franchising in California only. Also available to broadcast stations, as well as individuals.

HISTORY:	FINANCIAL: Earnings Claim: . Yes	FRANCHISOR TRAINING/SUPPORT:
Established in 1970; . . 1st Franchised in 1975	Cash Investment: $12K	Financial Assistance Provided: . . . . . No
Company-Owned Units (As of 8/31/1992): . .2	Total Investment: $12K	Site Selection Assistance: . . . . .NA
Franchised Units (As of 8/31/1992): 11	Fees: Franchise - $12K	Lease Negotiation Assistance: . . . .NA
Total Units (As of 8/31/1992): 13	Royalty: 0%, Advert: 0%	Co-operative Advertising: . . . . . . .NA
Projected New Units for 1993: 3	Contract Periods (Yrs.): 5/5	Training: . . . . . . 1 Wk.+ at Franchisee's
Distribution: US-13;Can-0;Overseas-0	Area Development Agreement: Yes/5	. . . . Area
North America: . . . . .1 State	Sub-Franchise Contract: . . . . .No	On-Going Support: C,D,G/ 1
Concentration: . . . . 13 in CA	Expand in Territory: . . . . Yes	EXPANSION PLANS:
Registered: . . . . CA	Passive Ownership: . . . Discouraged	US: . . . . .All US
. . . .	Encourage Conversions: . . . . .No	Canada: . . . . .No
Type Space: . . . . Home Based;~ SF	Average # Employees: . . 4 FT, 1 PT	Overseas: . . . .~ No

SUPER COUPS

180 Bodwell St.
Avon, MA 02322
TEL: (800) 626-2620 (508) 580-4340
FAX: (508) 588-2000
Mr. David Siersdale, Fran. Dir.

Co-operative direct mail advertising company, servicing the needs of small, local merchants and large national advertisers.

HISTORY:	FINANCIAL: Earnings Claim: . .No	FRANCHISOR TRAINING/SUPPORT:
Established in 1983; . . 1st Franchised in 1983	Cash Investment: $12-24K	Financial Assistance Provided: . . .Yes(D)
Company-Owned Units (As of 8/31/1992): . .0	Total Investment: $24K	Site Selection Assistance: . . . . .Yes
Franchised Units (As of 8/31/1992): 105	Fees: Franchise - $23K	Lease Negotiation Assistance: . . . .NA
Total Units (As of 8/31/1992): 105	Royalty: Flat, Advert: 0%	Co-operative Advertising: . . . . . . .Yes
Projected New Units for 1993: 30	Contract Periods (Yrs.): 10/10	Training: . . . . 5 Days Headquarters,
Distribution: US-105;Can-0;Overseas-0	Area Development Agreement: . .No	. . . . .5 Days Franchisee Location
North America: . . . . 23 States	Sub-Franchise Contract: . . . . . .No	On-Going Support: A,B,C,D,E,G,H,I/ . 45
Concentration: . 25 in MA, 18 in NJ, 15 in NY	Expand in Territory: . . . . Yes	EXPANSION PLANS:
Registered: . . . . FL,NY,RI,VA,WA	Passive Ownership: . . . . . .Allowed	US: . . . . .All US
. . . .	Encourage Conversions: . . . . . Yes	Canada: . . . . .All Canada
Type Space: . . . . . . .Home Based;~NA SF	Average # Employees: . . 2 FT, 1 PT	Overseas: . . . . No

TRIMARK

184 Quigley Blvd., P. O. Box 10530
Wilmington, DE 19850
TEL: (800) TRI-MARK (302) 322-2143
FAX: (302) 322-2163
Mr. Gilbert L. Kinch, VP Sales/Mktg.

Co-op direct mail advertising and marketing franchise. Master and single franchises. Franchisee is responsible for retail sales and marketing for TRIMARK with local and national merchants, including professionals, in their exclusive territory. Franchisor provides the printing and mailing of the advertising packets from the publishing company.

HISTORY: . . . . IFA	FINANCIAL: Earnings Claim: . .No	FRANCHISOR TRAINING/SUPPORT:
Established in 1977; . . 1st Franchised in 1978	Cash Investment: $9.5-35K	Financial Assistance Provided: . . . . .Yes
Company-Owned Units (As of 8/31/1992): . .2	Total Investment: $9.5-35K	Site Selection Assistance: . . . . . . .NA
Franchised Units (As of 8/31/1992): 35	Fees: Franchise - $7-29K	Lease Negotiation Assistance: . . . .NA
Total Units (As of 8/31/1992): 37	Royalty: , Advert: $15/Ad	Co-operative Advertising: . . . . . . .NA
Projected New Units for 1993: 10	Contract Periods (Yrs.): 10	Training: . . . . .1 Wk. Headquarters,
Distribution: US-37;Can-0;Overseas-0	Area Development Agreement: . .No	. . . . 1 Wk. Franchisee Location
North America: . . . . 19 States	Sub-Franchise Contract: . . . . . Yes	On-Going Support: D,G,H,I/ 39
Concentration: . . . 4 in PA, 4 in ME, 3 in MI	Expand in Territory: . . . . Yes	EXPANSION PLANS:
Registered: . . . . .FL,MI,OR	Passive Ownership: . . . Discouraged	US: . . . . .All US
. . . .	Encourage Conversions: . . . . Yes	Canada: . . . . .All Canada
Type Space: . . . . NA;~ SF	Average # Employees:	Overseas: . . . . No

UNITED COUPON CORPORATION

8380 Alban Rd.
Springfield, VA 22150
TEL: (800) 368-3501 (703) 644-0200 C
FAX: (703) 569-1465
Mr. Robert F. Pulliza, EVP

UNITED is a full-service advertising agency, specializing in providing co-operative direct mail advertising services to small business owners and professionals through a network of franchisees. The company provides initial training, a comprehensive operations manual and on-going training and support in all phases of operating the business.

HISTORY: . . . . IFA	FINANCIAL: Earnings Claim: . .No	FRANCHISOR TRAINING/SUPPORT:
Established in 1982; . . . 1st Franchised in 1982	Cash Investment: $16-28K	Financial Assistance Provided: . . . Yes(I)
Company-Owned Units (As of 8/31/1992): . .0	Total Investment: $16-28K	Site Selection Assistance: . . . . .No
Franchised Units (As of 8/31/1992): 94	Fees: Franchise - $8.9-29.9K	Lease Negotiation Assistance: . . . .NA
Total Units (As of 8/31/1992): 94	Royalty: 0%, Advert: 0%	Co-operative Advertising: . . . . . . .Yes
Projected New Units for 1993: 20	Contract Periods (Yrs.): 10/10	Training: . . . . 2 Wks. Headquarters
Distribution: US-94;Can-0;Overseas-0	Area Development Agreement: . .No	. . . .
North America: . . . . 28 States	Sub-Franchise Contract: . . . . . .No	On-Going Support: C,D,G,H,i/ 100
Concentration: . . .11 in NY, 9 in NJ, 9 in MA	Expand in Territory: . . . . . . .No	EXPANSION PLANS:
Registered: . . . CA,FL,IL,IN,MD,MI,MN,NY	Passive Ownership: . . . Not Allowed	US: . . . . .All US
. . . . .OR,RI,SD,VA,WA,WI,DC	Encourage Conversions: . . . . . Yes	Canada: . . . . No
Type Space: . . . . NA;~NA SF	Average # Employees: . . 2 FT, 1 PT	Overseas: . . . . No

VAL-PAK DIRECT MARKETING

8605 Largo Lakes Dr.
Largo, FL 33708
TEL: (800) 237-6266 (813) 393-1270
FAX: (813) 397-4968
Mr. Joseph H. Bourdow, VP

North America's oldest and largest local co-operative direct mail advertising franchisor, with distribution of over 225 million coupon envelopes annually to over 43 million unduplicated homes. Subsidiary of Cox Enterprises, Inc. VAL-PAK of Canada is Canadian franchisor.

HISTORY: . . . . IFA	FINANCIAL: Earnings Claim: . Yes	FRANCHISOR TRAINING/SUPPORT:
Established in 1968; . . 1st Franchised in 1989	Cash Investment: . . . . $Varies	Financial Assistance Provided: . . . Yes(I)
Company-Owned Units (As of 8/31/1992): . .1	Total Investment: . . . . $Varies	Site Selection Assistance: . . . . . . .NA
Franchised Units (As of 8/31/1992): 209	Fees: Franchise - $500	Lease Negotiation Assistance: . . . . .NA
Total Units (As of 8/31/1992): 210	Royalty: 0%, Advert: 0%	Co-operative Advertising: . . . . . . .Yes
Projected New Units for 1993: 10	Contract Periods (Yrs.): 10/5	Training: . . . . . 5 Days Home Study, 4-5
Distribution: US-158;Can-52;Overseas-0	Area Development Agreement: . .No	. . . .Days Headquarters, Varies On-Site
North America: . . . . 50 States, 9 Provinces	Sub-Franchise Contract: . . . . . .No	On-Going Support: a,C,D,G,h,I/ 750
Concentration:	Expand in Territory: . . . . Yes	EXPANSION PLANS:
Registered: . . . . .All	Passive Ownership: . . . Discouraged	US: . . . . All US, Limited Areas Remain
. . . .	Encourage Conversions: . . . NA	Canada: . . . . .Yes
Type Space: . . . . NA;~NA SF	Average # Employees: . . . . .Varies	Overseas: . . . . No

**YELLOW JACKET DIRECT MAIL
ADVERTISING**
101 Pacifica, # 250
Irvine, CA 92718
TEL: (714) 753-9700
FAX: (714) 727-4455
Mr. David Haney, President

Co-op direct mail advertising. Protected territories and Area Development rights available. Franchisee provided substantial initial training and on-going support, management of co-op system fund, management of the network of authorized suppliers to the franchisees, sponsorship of regional and system-wide conferences of the franchise system.

HISTORY: . . . .
Established in 19; . . . 1st Franchised in 1990
Company-Owned Units (As of 8/31/1992): . .0
Franchised Units (As of 8/31/1992): 10
Total Units (As of 8/31/1992): 10
Projected New Units for 1993: 6
Distribution: US-10;Can-0;Overseas-0
 North America: . . . .
 Concentration: . . . . .CA, NC
Registered: . . . . CA
. . . .
Type Space: . . . . NA;~ SF

FINANCIAL: Earnings Claim: . .No
Cash Investment: $10-19K
Total Investment: $14-26K
Fees: Franchise - $9-18K
 Royalty: 5%, Advert: 1%
Contract Periods (Yrs.): 15/15
Area Development Agreement: Yes/Var
Sub-Franchise Contract: . . . . .No
Expand in Territory: . . . . . . .No
Passive Ownership: . . . Discouraged
Encourage Conversions: . . . . .No
Average # Employees: . . . . . .2 FT

FRANCHISOR TRAINING/SUPPORT:
Financial Assistance Provided: . . . Yes(I)
Site Selection Assistance: . . . . . . .Yes
Lease Negotiation Assistance: . . . . .NA
Co-operative Advertising: . . . . . . .Yes
Training: . . . . 3 Wks. Headquarters
. . . .
On-Going Support: A,B,D,H/ 4
EXPANSION PLANS:
 US: . . . . .All US
 Canada: . . . . .No
 Overseas: . . . . No

SUPPLEMENTAL LISTING OF FRANCHISORS

AMERICAN ADVERTISING DISTRIBUTORS . . . . P. O. Box 16964, Mesa, AZ 85201
 Contact: Ms. Tracey Campbell, Fran. Sales Coord.; Tel: (800) 528-8249 (602) 964-9393
AMERICAN PARKING METER ADVERTISING . . . . 1625 St. Paul St., Baltimore, MD 21202
 Contact: President; Tel: (301) 467-9008
BREAD BOX, THE . . . . 1010 South Taylor St., Little Rock, AR 72204
 Contact: Mr. John Reynolds, President; Tel: (501) 666-6742
HEADLINES USA . . . . 9219 Katy Freeway, # 157, Houston, TX 77024
 Contact: Mr. Gary Gates, VP; Tel: (713) 781-2102 C
IDEAL PAK . . . . 32 Andrea Rd., Ajax, ON L1S 3V7 CAN
 Contact: Ms. Ingrid Kivi, President; Tel: (416) 427-2685
INNOVATIVE PROMOTIONS & GAMES . . . . . . 800 N. Magnolia Ave., # 1400, Orlando, FL 32801
 Contact: Mr. Tim Hewitt, Acct. Exec.; Tel: (407) 425-GAME
MARSHALL ADVERTISING & SIGN . . . . Salina Rd., Seneca, PA 16346
 Contact: Mr. Tom Marshall, Owner; Tel: (814) 676-8971
ROBERT ELEN & ASSOCIATES . . . . .6430 Sunset Blvd., Los Angeles, CA 90028
 Contact: President; Tel: (213) 464-3536
VIDEO IMPACT . . . . 5828 Ridgebrook SE, Grand Rapids, MI 49508
 Contact: President; Tel: (616) 281-1591
WEDDING INFORMATION NETWORK . . . . 11128 John Galt Blvd., Omaha, NE 68137
 Contact: President; Tel: (800) 843-4983
XPO MOBILE ADVERTISING . . . . 1274 49th Street, Brooklyn, NY 11219
 Contact: President; Tel: (718) 436-4692
YELLOW PAGE COUPON ADVERTISING . . . . 101 Pacifica, # 250, Irvine, CA 92718
 Contact: Mr. David Haney, President; Tel: (714) 753-0800
ZOOM MOBILE ADVERTISING . . . . 528 N. 26th St., Allentown, PA 18104
 Contact: Mr. Ken Wnek; Tel: (215) 434-8740

CHAPTER 9

BUSINESS: OFFICE SERVICES AND TELECOMMUNICATIONS

COMMWORLD

6025 S. Quebec St., # 300
Englewood, CO 80111
TEL: (800) 525-3200 (303) 721-8200
FAX: (303) 721-8299
Mr. Tony Hildebrand, VP Fran.

Looking for existing interconnect/telecommunications businesses to convert to COMMAND program. Offer top brand-name products with excellent discounts, advertising and marketing support, training, national service, national identity. Royalties are based on purchases, not on sales. Few restrictions - great benefits.

HISTORY:		
HISTORY: . . . . IFA	FINANCIAL: Earnings Claim: . .No	FRANCHISOR TRAINING/SUPPORT:
Established in 1979; . . 1st Franchised in 1982	Cash Investment: $10-135K	Financial Assistance Provided: . . . . . No
Company-Owned Units (As of 8/31/1992): . .1	Total Investment: $12.7-136K	Site Selection Assistance: . . . . .NA
Franchised Units (As of 8/31/1992): 39	Fees: Franchise - $10K	Lease Negotiation Assistance: . . . .
Total Units (As of 8/31/1992): 40	Royalty: 2-20%, Advert: 0%	Co-operative Advertising: . . . . .Yes
Projected New Units for 1993: 50	Contract Periods (Yrs.): 10/10	Training: . . . . . . 4-5 Days Headquarters
Distribution: US-40;Can-0;Overseas-0	Area Development Agreement: . .No	
North America: . . . . 14 States	Sub-Franchise Contract: . . . . . .No	On-Going Support: B,C,d,E,F,h,I/ . . . 15
Concentration: . . . 8 in CA, 5 in CO, 5 in AZ	Expand in Territory: . . . . .No	EXPANSION PLANS:
Registered: . . . . .All	Passive Ownership: . . . Discouraged	US: . . . . .All US
. . . .	Encourage Conversions: . . . . . Yes	Canada: . . . . .No
Type Space: . . . . .FS, SC;~1,500 SF	Average # Employees: . . . .3-10 FT	Overseas: . . . . No

CONTROL-O-FAX SYSTEMS

P. O. Box 5800, 3022 Airport Blvd.
Waterloo, IA 50704
TEL: (800) 553-0011 (319) 234-4896
FAX: (319) 236-7350
Ms. Sandy Halvorson, Fran. Dir.

Franchisor of office automation systems sold to the medical and dental industries.

HISTORY: . . . . IFA	FINANCIAL: Earnings Claim: . .No	FRANCHISOR TRAINING/SUPPORT:
Established in 1969; . . 1st Franchised in 1971	Cash Investment: $3K	Financial Assistance Provided: . . . . .Yes
Company-Owned Units (As of 8/31/1992): . .0	Total Investment: $20-50K	Site Selection Assistance: . . . . .NA
Franchised Units (As of 8/31/1992): 63	Fees: Franchise - $2K	Lease Negotiation Assistance: . . . . .NA
Total Units (As of 8/31/1992): 63	Royalty: 0%, Advert: 0%	Co-operative Advertising: . . . . .Yes
Projected New Units for 1993: 12	Contract Periods (Yrs.): . . . Infinite	Training: . . . . 3 Wks. Sales Seminar HQ,
Distribution: US-63;Can-0;Overseas-0	Area Development Agreement: . .No	.3 Wks. Customer Support HQ,On-Going
North America: . . . . 49 States	Sub-Franchise Contract: . . . . .No	On-Going Support: A,B,C,D,E,G,H,I/ . 14
Concentration: . . . 8 in TX, 7 in PA, 4 in MA	Expand in Territory: . . . . Yes	EXPANSION PLANS:
Registered: . . . CA,IL,IN,MD,MI,NY,OR,RI	Passive Ownership: . . . Not Allowed	US: . . . . .All US
. . . . VA,WA	Encourage Conversions: . . . . . NA	Canada: . . . . .No
Type Space: . . . . Home or Office;~450 SF	Average # Employees: . . . . .3 FT	Overseas: . . . . No

FAX-9

1609 S. Murray Blvd.
Colorado Springs, CO 80916
TEL: (800) 727-3299 (719) 380-1133
FAX: (719) 380-1143
Mr. Michael Jones, VP Sales

FAX-9, a nation-wide network of franchises offering fax machines for public use. Individuals or businesses can send or receive fax transmissions worldwide at any FAX-9 location. FAX-9 will locate and install the service in an existing retail store, which then operates the fax service for the individual. Expert technical, advertising and marketing assistance is on-going.

HISTORY:	FINANCIAL: Earnings Claim: . .No	FRANCHISOR TRAINING/SUPPORT:
Established in 1988; . . 1st Franchised in 1988	Cash Investment: $1.5K	Financial Assistance Provided: . . .Yes(D)
Company-Owned Units (As of 8/31/1992): . .9	Total Investment: $3.5K	Site Selection Assistance: . . . . .Yes
Franchised Units (As of 8/31/1992): 421	Fees: Franchise - $3.5K	Lease Negotiation Assistance: . . . . .NA
Total Units (As of 8/31/1992): 430	Royalty: $25/Mo., Advert: . . . 0%	Co-operative Advertising: . . . . .Yes
Projected New Units for 1993: 140	Contract Periods (Yrs.): 1/1	Training: . . . . . 1-2 Days During Install-
Distribution: US-401;Can-29;Overseas-0	Area Development Agreement: . .No	. . . . ation at Site
North America: . . . . 42 States, 2 Provinces	Sub-Franchise Contract: . . . . . .No	On-Going Support: B,C,D,G,I/ 14
Concentration: . .34 in CA, 24 in CO, 13 in IL	Expand in Territory: . . . . Yes	EXPANSION PLANS:
Registered: . . CA,FL,IL,MD,MI,MN,NY,WA	Passive Ownership: . . . . . .Allowed	US: . . . . All US
. . . .	Encourage Conversions: . . . . Yes	Canada: . . . . .All Canada
Type Space: . . . . SF;~ SF	Average # Employees: . . . . . NA	Overseas: . . . . EUR

FAX-IT CORPORATION

P. O. Box 1359
Mount Laurel, NJ 08054
TEL: (800) 228-7363 (609) 866-9559
FAX: (609) 866-2920
Mr. Keith Fenton, GM

Sale and placement of public fax machines.

HISTORY:	FINANCIAL: Earnings Claim: . .No	FRANCHISOR TRAINING/SUPPORT:
Established in 1987; . . 1st Franchised in 1989	Cash Investment: $15K	Financial Assistance Provided: . . .Yes(D)
Company-Owned Units (As of 8/31/1992): 850	Total Investment: $25K	Site Selection Assistance: . . . . .Yes
Franchised Units (As of 8/31/1992): 200	Fees: Franchise - $10K	Lease Negotiation Assistance: . . . .Yes
Total Units (As of 8/31/1992): 1050	Royalty: 0%, Advert: 0%	Co-operative Advertising: . . . . .Yes
Projected New Units for 1993: 800	Contract Periods (Yrs.): 3/3	Training: . . . . 3 Days Headquarters
Distribution: . . US-1050;Can-50;Overseas-200	Area Development Agreement: . .No	. . . .
North America: . . . . 13 States	Sub-Franchise Contract: . . . . . Yes	On-Going Support: a,b,c,d,e,i/ 22
Concentration: . 300 in CA, 300 in FL, 200 NY	Expand in Territory: . . . . Yes	EXPANSION PLANS:
Registered: . . . . .All	Passive Ownership: . . . . . .Allowed	US: . . . . All US
. . . .	Encourage Conversions: . . . . NA	Canada: . . . . .Yes
Type Space: . . . . NA;~NA SF	Average # Employees: . . . . . .1 PT	Overseas: . . . . .Yes

ILPS

1350 East 4th Ave.
Vancouver, BC V5N 1J5 CAN
TEL: (604) 255-5000
FAX: (604) 254-2575
Mr. Ian Abramson, President

An alternative to coin-op payphones - a coilless, cordless payphone brought to customer at restaurants, lounges, clubs, etc. The dealer shares in the revenue.

HISTORY:	FINANCIAL: Earnings Claim: . .No	FRANCHISOR TRAINING/SUPPORT:
Established in 1987; . . 1st Franchised in 1987	Cash Investment: $5K	Financial Assistance Provided: . . . . . No
Company-Owned Units (As of 8/31/1992): . .0	Total Investment: $5K	Site Selection Assistance: . . . . No
Franchised Units (As of 8/31/1992): 12	Fees: Franchise - $0	Lease Negotiation Assistance: . . . . .No
Total Units (As of 8/31/1992): 12	Royalty: 5%, Advert: 1%	Co-operative Advertising: . . . . .Yes
Projected New Units for 1993: 8	Contract Periods (Yrs.): 3/3	Training: . . . . 2 Days Headquarters
Distribution: US-0;Can-12;Overseas-0	Area Development Agreement: . .No	
North America: . . . . 10 Provinces	Sub-Franchise Contract: . . . . .No	On-Going Support: A,B,C,D,G,h,I/ 8
Concentration:	Expand in Territory: . . . . Yes	EXPANSION PLANS:
Registered: . . . . AB	Passive Ownership: . . . Discouraged	US: . . . . All US
. . . .	Encourage Conversions: . . . . .No	Canada: . . . . .BC, ON,SK,Marit.
Type Space: . . . . Home Based;~ SF	Average # Employees: . . . . . .4 FT	Overseas: . . . . .EUR, S. America

---

OFFICE ANSWER

520 W. Hwy. 436, # 1180
Altamonte Springs, FL 32714
TEL: (407) 774-5800 C
FAX: (407) 774-8103
Mr. K. J. Wari

Personalized telephone answering service by company name. Other services include word processing, fax, copies.

HISTORY:	FINANCIAL: Earnings Claim: . .No	FRANCHISOR TRAINING/SUPPORT:
Established in 1983; . . 1st Franchised in 1983	Cash Investment: $8.5K	Financial Assistance Provided: . . . Yes(I)
Company-Owned Units (As of 8/31/1992): . .1	Total Investment: $15K	Site Selection Assistance: . . . . . . .Yes
Franchised Units (As of 8/31/1992): 5	Fees: Franchise - $8.5K	Lease Negotiation Assistance: . . . . .Yes
Total Units (As of 8/31/1992): 6	Royalty: 3%, Advert: 2%	Co-operative Advertising: . . . . . .Yes
Projected New Units for 1993: 12	Contract Periods (Yrs.): 10/10	Training: . . . . 2 Wks. On-Site
Distribution: US-6;Can-0;Overseas-0	Area Development Agreement: Yes/5	. . . .
North America: . . . . 4 States	Sub-Franchise Contract: . . . . .No	On-Going Support: C,D,E,G,H,I/ 4
Concentration:	Expand in Territory: . . . . Yes	EXPANSION PLANS:
Registered: . . . . .All	Passive Ownership: . . . Not Allowed	US: . . . . All US
. . . .	Encourage Conversions: . . . . . NA	Canada: . . . . .All Canada
Type Space: . . Comm. Office Bldg;~1,000 SF	Average # Employees: . . 2 FT, 1 PT	Overseas: . . . . No

---

VOICE-TEL ENTERPRISES

23200 Chagrin Blvd., # 800
Cleveland, OH 44122
TEL: (800) 247-4237 (216) 360-4400
FAX: (216) 360-4410
Mr. William H. Stephens, VP Fran. Dev.

VOICE-TEL is the leading provider of interactive voice messaging - a service that enables people to communicate without delay. Independent, locally-owned and managed service centers are strategically linked to form a superior nationwide network. This network enables messages to be sent and received cost-effectively locally or long distance, through all domestic locations.

HISTORY: . . . . IFA	FINANCIAL: Earnings Claim: . .No	FRANCHISOR TRAINING/SUPPORT:
Established in 1986; . . 1st Franchised in 1986	Cash Investment: $100-150K	Financial Assistance Provided: . . . Yes(I)
Company-Owned Units (As of 8/31/1992): . 20	Total Investment: $85-240K	Site Selection Assistance: . . . . No
Franchised Units (As of 8/31/1992): 97	Fees: Franchise - $27.5-97.5K	Lease Negotiation Assistance: . . . . .Yes
Total Units (As of 8/31/1992): 117	Royalty: 6-10%, Advert: . . . 2%	Co-operative Advertising: . . . . .Yes
Projected New Units for 1993: 30	Contract Periods (Yrs.): 20/10	Training: . . . . . . 10 Days Headquarters,
Distribution: US-115;Can-1;Overseas-1	Area Development Agreement: . .No	. . . . .3 Days Regional
North America: . . . . . 36 States, 1 Province	Sub-Franchise Contract: . . . . .No	On-Going Support: b,C,D,F,G,h,I/ . . . 60
Concentration: . . 25 in CA, 11 in OH, 7 in NC	Expand in Territory: . . . . Yes	EXPANSION PLANS:
Registered: . . . CA,FL,HI,IL,IN,MD,MI,MN	Passive Ownership: . . . Discouraged	US: . . . . .All US
. . . . .NY,OR,RI,VA,WA,WI	Encourage Conversions: . . . . .No	Canada: . . . . .All Canada
Type Space: . . . . . Office Building;~600 SF	Average # Employees: . . . . .2 FT	Overseas: . . . . .UK, JA

SUPPLEMENTAL LISTING OF FRANCHISORS

ACI TELETEC . . . . 6250 Judy Ln., Beaumont, TX 77708
    Contact: Ms. Francis Fuentes; Tel: (800) 256-8273 (409) 892-2836
ANSWERING SPECIALISTS . . . . 119 W. Doty Ave., Summerville, SC 29483
    Contact: Mr. Bud Doty, President; Tel: (803) 724-6300
BELL MOBILITY CELLULAR . . . . 20 Carlson Court, Etobicoke, ON M9W 6V4   CAN
    Contact: Mr. Carl Maynard; Tel: (416) 674-2220
CELLULAR PHONE RENTAL . . . . 280 Lincoln St., Boston, MA 02134
    Contact: Ms. Susan Albert Athas; Tel: (617) 254-8020
COMMUNICATIONS RESEARCH GROUP . . . . . . 5615 Corporation Blvd., Baton Rouge, LA 70808
    Contact: President; Tel: (504) 923-0988
COMMUNICATIONS WORLD INTERNATIONAL . . . . . 14828 W. 6th Ave., # 13B, Golden, CO 80401
    Contact: Ms. Aletha Zens, VP; Tel: (800) 525-3200 (303) 279-8200
EXECUTIVE BUSINESS CENTERS / EBC . . . 1080 Holcomb Bridge Rd., #100-310, Roswell, GA 30076
    Contact: Mr. Thomas Dye, President; Tel: (800) 635-6641 (404) 992-1119
FAXTODAY . . . . 1200 Network Centre Dr., Box 1107, Effingham, Il 62401
    Contact: Mr. James M. Schultz; Tel: (217) 342-5400
GOFAX 190 Commerce Dr., Warwick, RI 02886 . . . .
    Contact: Mr. George Strouthopoulos, President; Tel: (401) 737-3250
MARTING RADIO DIAGNOSTIC SERVICES . . . . 504 S. Egbert St., Monona, IA 52159
    Contact: Mr. Elmer L. Marting; Tel: (319) 539-2670
NATIONAL CAR PHONES . . . . 999 Bethel Rd., Columbus, OH 43214
    Contact: President; Tel: (614) 451-0204
NATIONAL TELE-CONSULTANTS . . . . 500 DeMott Ln., Box 5597, Somerset, NJ 08875
    Contact: Mr. Ronald Patetta, Natl. Fran. Sales; Tel: (800) NTL-OPPT
PYRAVISION . . . . 11956 bERNARDO pLAZA, # 401, San Diego, CA 92128
    Contact: Mr. Peter Bellanova; Tel: (619) 592-9250
SNC TELECOM PROBLEM SOLVERS . . . . 101 W. Waukau Ave., Oshkosh, WI 54901
    Contact: Mr. Wally Petersen, Mktg. Dir.; Tel: (800) 558-3325 (414) 231-7370
TELE BROADCASTING SYSTEMS . . . . P.O. Box D Sunny Lane, Beach Lake, PA 18405
    Contact: President; Tel: (717) 729-8205
TELEPHONE AMERICAN CORP. . . . . 4685 North Shore, Orono, MN 55364
    Contact: President; Tel: (612) 472-1202
TELEVOICE . . . . 400 Interstate N. Pkwy., # 790, Atlanta, GA 30339
    Contact: Mr. Jeff Smalley, President; Tel: (800) 288-5882 (404) 618-5888
U. S. CENTRAL . . . . Lehigh Tower, East Rock Rd., Allentown, PA 18103
    Contact: President; Tel: (215) 797-4530
UNITERRA . . . . 4179 W. Irving Park Rd., Chicago, IL 60641
    Contact: Mr. Dante Montaverde, President; Tel: (312) 725-0222

CHAPTER 10

BUSINESS: PRINTING /
MAIL SERVICES / PACKAGING

AIM MAIL CENTERS

20381 Lake Forest Dr., # B-2
Lake Forest, CA 92630
TEL: (714) 837-4151
FAX: (714) 837-4537
Mr. Michael Sawitz, Franchise Dir.

AIM MAIL CENTERS take care of all your business service needs. From renting mailboxes, buying stamps, sending faxes and making copies to gift wrapping, greeting cards and passport photos, AIM MAIL CENTERS offer it all, quickly and efficiently, without all the run-around. It's like having a post office, office supply store, gift shop and print shop all rolled into one!

HISTORY: . . . .
Established in 1985; . . 1st Franchised in 1989
Company-Owned Units (As of 8/31/1992): . .1
Franchised Units (As of 8/31/1992): 15
Total Units (As of 8/31/1992): 16
Projected New Units for 1993: 10
Distribution: US-16;Can-0;Overseas-0
 North America: . . . . 3 States
 Concentration: . . 14 in CA, 1 in NM, 1 in NV
Registered: . . . . CA
. . . .
Type Space: . . .100,000+ SF Ctrs.;~1,200 SF

FINANCIAL: Earnings Claim: . .No
Cash Investment: $45-65K
Total Investment: $55-85K
Fees: Franchise - $15.5K
 Royalty: 1-5%, Advert: 1.5%
Contract Periods (Yrs.): 10/5/5
Area Development Agreement: . .No
Sub-Franchise Contract: . . . . .No
Expand in Territory: . . . . . . .Yes
Passive Ownership: . . . Discouraged
Encourage Conversions: . . . . .No
Average # Employees: . . . . . .1 FT

FRANCHISOR TRAINING/SUPPORT:
Financial Assistance Provided: . . . Yes(I)
Site Selection Assistance: . . . . .Yes
Lease Negotiation Assistance: . . . . .Yes
Co-operative Advertising: . . . . .Yes
Training: . . . . . . 1 Wk. Class Room HQ,
 . . . . 3 Days In-Store
On-Going Support: B,C,D,E,H,I/ 3
EXPANSION PLANS:
 US: . . . . .West and Southwest
 Canada: . . . . No
 Overseas: . . . . No

PRINTING AND COPYING SERVICES

	1989	1990	1991	Percentage Change 90/89	Percentage Change 91/90
Total Number of Establishments:					
Company–Owned	195	204	231	4.62%	13.24%
Franchisee–Owned	6,133	6,641	7,191	8.28%	8.28%
Total	6,328	6,845	7,422	8.17%	8.43%
Ratio of Total Establishments:					
Company–Owned	3.1%	3.0%	3.1%		
Franchisee–Owned	96.9%	97.0%	96.9%		
Total	100.0%	100.0%	100.0%		
Total Sales ($000):					
Company–Owned	47,782	50,937	59,293	6.60%	16.40%
Franchisee–Owned	1,544,940	1,708,039	1,910,530	10.56%	11.86%
Total	1,592,722	1,758,976	1,969,823	10.44%	11.99%
Ratio of Total Sales:					
Company–Owned	3.0%	2.9%	3.0%		
Franchisee–Owned	97.0%	97.1%	97.0%		
Total	100.0%	100.0%	100.0%		
Average Sales Per Unit ($000):					
Company–Owned	245	250	257	1.90%	2.80%
Franchisee–Owned	252	257	266	2.10%	3.30%
Total	252	257	265	2.10%	3.28%
Relative Average Sales Ratio:	97.3%	97.1%	96.6%		

	Number Of Employees	Employees Per Unit	Avg. Sales Per Employee
Total 1989 Employment:			
Company–Owned	814	4.2	$58,700
Franchisee–Owned	25,389	4.1	$60,851
Total	26,203	4.1	$60,784
Relative Employee Performance Ratios:		100.8%	96.5%

	1st Quartile	Median	4th Quartile
Average 1989 Total Investment:			
Company–Owned	$67,500	$132,500	$220,000
Franchisee–Owned	$91,250	$115,500	$150,000
Single Unit Franchise Fee	$20,000	$22,500	$35,000
Mult. Unit Franchise Fee	$7,500	$17,500	$30,000
Franchise Start–Up Cost	$32,500	$47,500	$80,000

Source: Franchising In The Economy 1991, IFA Educational Foundation & Horwath International.

AMERICAN SPEEDY PRINTING CENTERS
2555 S. Telegraph Rd., # 450
Bloomfield Hills, MI 48302
TEL: (800) 726-9050 (313) 335-6200
FAX: (313) 335-0267
Mr. Joey Farah, Mktg. Coord.

High-quality offset printing centers, which also offer high-speed copying, desktop publishing, color copying, facsimile, design services, pick-up and delivery.

HISTORY: . . . . IFA	FINANCIAL: Earnings Claim: . .No	FRANCHISOR TRAINING/SUPPORT:
Established in 1976; . . 1st Franchised in 1977	Cash Investment: $40K	Financial Assistance Provided: . . . Yes(I)
Company-Owned Units (As of 8/31/1992): . .0	Total Investment: $160K	Site Selection Assistance: . . . . . . .Yes
Franchised Units (As of 8/31/1992): 609	Fees: Franchise - $42.5K	Lease Negotiation Assistance: . . . .Yes
Total Units (As of 8/31/1992): 609	Royalty: 6%, Advert: 2%	Co-operative Advertising: . . . . . . .Yes
Projected New Units for 1993:	Contract Periods (Yrs.): . . . 20/20	Training: . . . . 2 Wks. Headquarters,
Distribution: US-575;Can-30;Overseas-4	Area Development Agreement: Yes/10	. . . . 1 Wk. On-Site Training
North America: . . . . 43 States, 3 Provinces	Sub-Franchise Contract: . . . . Yes	On-Going Support: B,C,D,E,G,H,I/ . . . 39
Concentration: . . 106 in MI, 90 in CA, 44 FL	Expand in Territory:	EXPANSION PLANS:
Registered:	Passive Ownership: . . . Discouraged	US: . . . . No
. . . .	Encourage Conversions: . . . . Yes	Canada: . . . . .All Canada
Type Space: . . . . .SC;~1,200 SF	Average # Employees: . . 4 FT, 1 PT	Overseas: . . . JA, UK, Phillipines

AMERICAN WHOLESALE THERMOGRAPHERS / AWT
One Kwik Kopy Ln., P. O. Box 777
Cypress, TX 77429
TEL: (800) 942-9526 (713) 373-3535
FAX: (713) 373-4450
Mr. Kevin Camp, President

AMERICAN WHOLESALE THERMOGRAPHERS is a member of the International Center for Entrepreneurial Development, the world's largest alliance of printing franchises. AWT offers a specialized niche in the printing industry, training and on-going support for a limited number of franchises.

HISTORY: . . . . IFA	FINANCIAL: Earnings Claim: . .No	FRANCHISOR TRAINING/SUPPORT:
Established in 1981; . . 1st Franchised in 1981	Cash Investment: . . . . . $65K Min.	Financial Assistance Provided: . . .Yes(D)
Company-Owned Units (As of 8/31/1992): . .0	Total Investment: $137-147K	Site Selection Assistance: . . . . . . .Yes
Franchised Units (As of 8/31/1992): 20	Fees: Franchise - $38.5K	Lease Negotiation Assistance: . . . .Yes
Total Units (As of 8/31/1992): 20	Royalty: 5%, Advert: 0%	Co-operative Advertising: . . . . No
Projected New Units for 1993: 2	Contract Periods (Yrs.): . . . 25/25	Training: . . 2 Wks. HQ, 2 Wks. an AWT
Distribution: US-17;Can-3;Overseas-0	Area Development Agreement: . .No	. . . . Center, 1 Wk. Initial On-Site
North America: . . . . . 14 States, 1 Province	Sub-Franchise Contract: . . . . .No	On-Going Support: C,D,E,G,h,I/ 3
Concentration: . . . 3 in ON, 2 in TX, 2 in OK	Expand in Territory: . . . . . . .No	EXPANSION PLANS:
Registered: . . . CA,FL,IL,IN,MD,MI,MN,NY	Passive Ownership: . . . Not Allowed	US: . . . . All US
. . . . OR,RI,VA,WA,WI,DC	Encourage Conversions:	Canada: . . . . .All Canada
Type Space: . Business Park;~2,500-3,500 SF	Average # Employees: . . 9 FT, 4 PT	Overseas: . . . . No

ASSOCIATED AIR FREIGHT

3333 New Hyde Park Rd.
New Hyde Park, NY 11042
TEL: (800) 666-8387 (516) 627-8910
FAX: (516) 627-6051
Mr. Walter G. Mahland, VP Devel.

ASSOCIATED AIR FREIGHT is the premier opportunity for experienced transportation and business-to-business sales professionals. ASSOCIATED is one of the oldest and largest air freight forwarders, offering a complete menu of transportation services. ASSOCIATED provides on-going assistance and special attention to the support of newly-opened offices. No initial fee for sales/operations agents.

HISTORY:	FINANCIAL: Earnings Claim: . .No	FRANCHISOR TRAINING/SUPPORT:
Established in 1958; . . 1st Franchised in 1985	Cash Investment: $10-65K	Financial Assistance Provided: . . . . .Yes
Company-Owned Units (As of 8/31/1992): . 19	Total Investment: $10-65K	Site Selection Assistance: . . . . . . .Yes
Franchised Units (As of 8/31/1992): 49	Fees: Franchise - $5-25K	Lease Negotiation Assistance: . . . .Yes
Total Units (As of 8/31/1992): 68	Royalty: 15%, Advert: 1.5%	Co-operative Advertising: . . . . .Yes
Projected New Units for 1993: 9	Contract Periods (Yrs.): 10/10	Training: . . . . . . 1-2 Wks. Regional HQ,
Distribution: US-67;Can-0;Overseas-1	Area Development Agreement: . .No	. . . 1 Wk. Headquarters, 2 Days On-Site
North America: . . . . 29 States	Sub-Franchise Contract: . . . . . .No	On-Going Support: A,B,C,D,E,F,G,H,I/ 92
Concentration: . . . 6 in CA, 3 in PA, 3 in NY	Expand in Territory: . . . . . . .No	EXPANSION PLANS:
Registered: . . . . .FL,HI,NY	Passive Ownership: . . . Not Allowed	US: . . . . All US
. . . .	Encourage Conversions: . . . . . Yes	Canada: . . . . .Yes
Type Space: . . . . . . Warehouse;~2,500 SF	Average # Employees: . . 3 FT, 2 PT	Overseas: . . . . No

COPIES NOW, A FRANCHISE OF SIR SPEEDY
23131 Verdugo Dr.
Laguna Hills, CA 92653
TEL: (800) 854-3321 (714) 472-0330
FAX: (714) 458-1297
Mr. Dave Collins, VP Fran.

COPIES NOW is a high-speed duplicating, desktop publishing, presentation graphics and other business communication center.

HISTORY: . . . .
Established in 1983; . . 1st Franchised in 1984
Company-Owned Units (As of 8/31/1992): . .0
Franchised Units (As of 8/31/1992): 75
Total Units (As of 8/31/1992): . . . 75
Projected New Units for 1993: 15
Distribution: US-73;Can-2;Overseas-0
North America: . . . . . 10 States, 1 Province
Concentration: . . . .
Registered: . . . . .All
. . . .
Type Space: . . . . SF;~800-1,000 SF

FINANCIAL: Earnings Claim: . .No
Cash Investment: $30K
Total Investment: $105K
Fees: Franchise - $30K
Royalty: 4-6%, Advert: 2%
Contract Periods (Yrs.): . . . 20/20
Area Development Agreement: Yes/20
Sub-Franchise Contract: . . . . .No
Expand in Territory: . . . . . . Yes
Passive Ownership: . . . Discouraged
Encourage Conversions: . . . . Yes
Average # Employees: . . . . .2 FT

FRANCHISOR TRAINING/SUPPORT:
Financial Assistance Provided: . . . Yes(I)
Site Selection Assistance: . . . . . . .Yes
Lease Negotiation Assistance: . . . .Yes
Co-operative Advertising: . . . . . . .Yes
Training: . . . . . . 2 Wks. Headquarters,
. . . . 1-2 Wks. On-Site
On-Going Support: B,C,D,E,G,H,I/ . . . 65
EXPANSION PLANS:
US: . . . . .All US
Canada: . . . . .All Canada
Overseas: . . . . .Yes

FRANKLIN'S PRINTING & COPY SERVICE
135 International Blvd. NW
Atlanta, GA 30303
TEL: (800) 554-5699 (404) 522-7100
FAX: (404) 522-0492
Mr. David Lent, VP Ops.

Commercial quick printing, hi-speed/hi-tech copying, desktop publishing, laser graphics, color laser copies, convenience office supplies. Proprietary computerized estimating, pricing, accounts receivable, management and marketing system.

HISTORY: . . . . IFA
Established in 1971; . . 1st Franchised in 1977
Company-Owned Units (As of 8/31/1992): . .0
Franchised Units (As of 8/31/1992): 74
Total Units (As of 8/31/1992): 74
Projected New Units for 1993: 15
Distribution: US-70;Can-4;Overseas-0
North America: . . . . 14 States, 1 Province
Concentration: . . 27 in GA, 15 in FL, 5 in TN
Registered: . . . FL,IL,MD,MI,MN,NY,RI,VA
. . . . WI,DC
Type Space: . . . . .FS, SC;~1,800 SF

FINANCIAL: Earnings Claim: . .No
Cash Investment: . . . . . . $55K+
Total Investment: $190K
Fees: Franchise - $25K
Royalty: 5%, Advert: 1.5%
Contract Periods (Yrs.): . . . 15/15
Area Development Agreement: . .No
Sub-Franchise Contract: . . . . .No
Expand in Territory: . . . . . . Yes
Passive Ownership: . . . Discouraged
Encourage Conversions: . . . . .No
Average # Employees: . . 3 FT, 1 PT

FRANCHISOR TRAINING/SUPPORT:
Financial Assistance Provided: . . . Yes(I)
Site Selection Assistance: . . . . . . .Yes
Lease Negotiation Assistance: . . . .Yes
Co-operative Advertising: . . . . No
Training: . . . . 2 Wks. Headquarters,
. . . . 2 Wks. On-Site
On-Going Support: B,C,D,E,F,G,h,I/ . . 12
EXPANSION PLANS:
US: . . . . . NE, SE, Central, S. Central
Canada: . . . . .All Canada
Overseas: . . . . . C. & S. America

GNOMON COPY
119 University Ave.
Lowell, MA 01854
TEL: (508) 934-9212 C
FAX: (508) 934-9211
Mr. James A. Sutherland, President

GNOMON COPY offers a unique "franchise to sole ownership" program. Franchisees can own their business after 10 years. No royalty fees after 10 years. Franchise prospects benefit before signing: franchise agreement signed at time of lease signing. No pre-closing, pre-signing fees or deposits. Understanding and patience instead of franchisor imposed pressure.

HISTORY: . . . . IFA
Established in 1966; . . 1st Franchised in 1980
Company-Owned Units (As of 8/31/1992): . .1
Franchised Units (As of 8/31/1992): 17
Total Units (As of 8/31/1992): 18
Projected New Units for 1993: 3
Distribution: US-18;Can-0;Overseas-0
North America: . . . . 6 States
Concentration: . . .10 in MA, 2 in NH, 2 in NJ
Registered: . . . .
. . . .
Type Space: . . . . SF;~1,000 SF

FINANCIAL: Earnings Claim: . Yes
Cash Investment: . . . $45.4-72.3K
Total Investment: . . . $102.3-150.8K
Fees: Franchise - $25K
Royalty: 7%, Advert: 1%
Contract Periods (Yrs.): 10
Area Development Agreement: . .No
Sub-Franchise Contract: . . . . .No
Expand in Territory: . . . . . . Yes
Passive Ownership: . . . Discouraged
Encourage Conversions: . . . . Yes
Average # Employees: 1-2 FT, 2-3 PT

FRANCHISOR TRAINING/SUPPORT:
Financial Assistance Provided: . . . . .Yes
Site Selection Assistance: . . . . . . .Yes
Lease Negotiation Assistance: . . . .Yes
Co-operative Advertising: . . . . No
Training: . . . . . . 2-3 Wks. Headquarters,
. . . . 2-3 Wks. On-Site
On-Going Support: B,C,D,E,F/ 2
EXPANSION PLANS:
US: . . Northeast-VT,ME,MA,CT,PA,NJ
Canada: . . . . No
Overseas: . . . . No

HANDLE WITH CARE PACKAGING STORE

5675 DTC Blvd., # 280
Englewood, CO 80111
TEL: (800) 525-6309 (303) 741-6626
FAX: (303) 741-6653
Mr. Richard T. Godwin, President

HANDLE WITH CARE PACKAGING STORES specialize in FLAV, those items that are fragile, large, awkward or valuable - from 1 - 1,000 pounds. Known as the packaging and shipping experts, HANDLE WITH CARE PACKAGING STORES often receive referrals from other postal service centers to package and ship items like artwork, antiques, furniture and electronics. They have the skill, the equipment and the knowledge to get such jobs done right.

HISTORY:	FINANCIAL: Earnings Claim: . .No	FRANCHISOR TRAINING/SUPPORT:
Established in 1980; . . 1st Franchised in 1984	Cash Investment: $40K	Financial Assistance Provided: . . . . .No
Company-Owned Units (As of 8/31/1992): . .0	Total Investment: $30-60K	Site Selection Assistance: . . . . . . .Yes
Franchised Units (As of 8/31/1992): 362	Fees: Franchise - $17.5K	Lease Negotiation Assistance: . . . No
Total Units (As of 8/31/1992): 362	Royalty: 5%, Advert: 1%	Co-operative Advertising: . . . . . . .Yes
Projected New Units for 1993: 100	Contract Periods (Yrs.):	Training: . . . . . . .10 Days Headquarters
Distribution: US-362;Can-0;Overseas-0	Area Development Agreement: . Yes	. . . .
North America: . . . . 40 States	Sub-Franchise Contract: . . . . .No	On-Going Support: C,D,E,G,H,I/ 11
Concentration: . 69 in CA, 29 in FL, 27 in VA	Expand in Territory: . . . . . . Yes	EXPANSION PLANS:
Registered: . . . . .All	Passive Ownership: . . . Discouraged	US: . . . . .All US
. . . .	Encourage Conversions: . . . . . Yes	Canada: . . . . .Yes
Type Space: . . . . SC;~800-1,200 SF	Average # Employees: 2 FT (Seasonal)	Overseas: . . . . Yes

INK WELL, THE

540 Officenter Pl., # 250
Gahanna, OH 43230
TEL: (800) 235-2221 (614) 337-9937
FAX: (614) 337-3636
Mr. Ronald L. Strahler, President

THE INK WELL sells franchises that offer full-service printing capabilities to a wide variety of customers whose needs must be satisfied in a prompt manner. INK WELL franchises specialize in high quality, multi-color printing, design and consultation.

HISTORY: . . . . .IFA	FINANCIAL: Earnings Claim: . .No	FRANCHISOR TRAINING/SUPPORT:
Established in 1972; . . 1st Franchised in 1981	Cash Investment: $40-60K	Financial Assistance Provided: . . . . .Yes
Company-Owned Units (As of 8/31/1992): . .1	Total Investment: $180-200K	Site Selection Assistance: . . . . . . .Yes
Franchised Units (As of 8/31/1992): 66	Fees: Franchise - $29.5K	Lease Negotiation Assistance: . . . . .Yes
Total Units (As of 8/31/1992): 67	Royalty: 4-6%, Advert: 2.5%	Co-operative Advertising: . . . . No
Projected New Units for 1993: 7	Contract Periods (Yrs.): 25/25	Training: . . . . .3 Wks. Houston, TX
Distribution: US-67;Can-0;Overseas-0	Area Development Agreement: . .No	. . . . 1 Wk. Columbus, OH
North America: . . . . 10 States	Sub-Franchise Contract: . . . . . Yes	On-Going Support: C,D,E,G,h,I/ 9
Concentration: . . .39 in OH, 6 in NC, 6 in MI	Expand in Territory: . . . . Yes	EXPANSION PLANS:
Registered: . . . FL,IL,IN,MD,MI.MN,ND,OR	Passive Ownership: . . . Discouraged	US: . . . . .All US
. . . . RI,SD,VA,WA,WI,DC	Encourage Conversions: . . . . . Yes	Canada: . . . . No
Type Space: . . .SC, Office Center;~2,000 SF	Average # Employees: . 3 FT, 1-2 PT	Overseas: . . . . No

INSTY-PRINTS

1010 S. Seventh St., # 450
Minneapolis, MN 55415
TEL: (800) 779-1000 (612) 337-9800
FAX: (800) 369-1234
Mr. Gene O'Neil, VP Sales/Mktg.

Provides high-quality printing and copying services, as well as a wide range of pre-printing and finishing services. Emphasis on fast, convenient service in a friendly, professional manner.

HISTORY: . . . . .IFA	FINANCIAL: Earnings Claim: . .No	FRANCHISOR TRAINING/SUPPORT:
Established in 1965; . . 1st Franchised in 1967	Cash Investment: $60-87.5K	Financial Assistance Provided: . . . . .No
Company-Owned Units (As of 8/31/1992): . .1	Total Investment: $144-203.5K	Site Selection Assistance: . . . . . . .Yes
Franchised Units (As of 8/31/1992): 298	Fees: Franchise - $24.5K	Lease Negotiation Assistance: . . . . .Yes
Total Units (As of 8/31/1992): 299	Royalty: 4.5%, Advert: 2%	Co-operative Advertising: . . . . . . .Yes
Projected New Units for 1993: 10	Contract Periods (Yrs.): 15/15	Training: . . . . 3 Wks. Headquarters
Distribution: US-297;Can-2;Overseas-0	Area Development Agreement: . .No	
North America: . . . . . 40 States, 1 Province	Sub-Franchise Contract: . . . . .No	On-Going Support: C,D,E,G,H,I/ 27
Concentration: . . 34 in IL, 33 in MN, 22 in FL	Expand in Territory: . . . . . . Yes	EXPANSION PLANS:
Registered: . . . . .All	Passive Ownership: . . . Not Allowed	US: . . . . .All US
. . . .	Encourage Conversions: . . . . . Yes	Canada: . . . . No
Type Space: . . . . .SF, SC;~1,800 SF	Average # Employees: . . . . .4 FT	Overseas: . . . . No

KWIK-KOPY PRINTING

One Kwik-Kopy Ln.
Cypress, TX 77429
TEL: (800) 231-1304 (713) 373-3535
FAX: (713) 373-4450
Ms. LaDonna Meadow, VP

KWIK-KOPY PRINTING Centers offer complete printing and related services to the business community, from graphic design to the finished product. KWIK-KOPY PRINTING is a member of the International Center for Entrepreneurial Development, the largest alliance of printing franchises in the world. Benefit from support from an industry leader with over 25 years' experience. Centers available worldwide.

HISTORY: . . . . IFA
Established in 1967; . . . 1st Franchised in 1967
Company-Owned Units (As of 8/31/1992): . .2
Franchised Units (As of 8/31/1992): 961
Total Units (As of 8/31/1992): 963
Projected New Units for 1993: 12
Distribution: . . US-556;Can-94;Overseas-313
  North America: . . . . 38 States
  Concentration: . . .152 in TX, 43 in CA, 39 IL
Registered: . . . . All Except SD
. . . .
Type Space: . . . . . . SC;~1,200-1,500 SF

FINANCIAL: Earnings Claim: . Yes
Cash Investment: $47.5-76.5K
Total Investment: . . . $115.8-122.8K
Fees: Franchise - $25K
  Royalty: 4,6,8%, Advert: 0%
Contract Periods (Yrs.): 25/25
Area Development Agreement: . .No
Sub-Franchise Contract: . . . . .No
Expand in Territory: . . . . . . Yes
Passive Ownership: . . . Not Allowed
Encourage Conversions: . . . . .No
Average # Employees: . 4-6 FT, 1 PT

FRANCHISOR TRAINING/SUPPORT:
Financial Assistance Provided: . . .Yes(D)
Site Selection Assistance: . . . . . . .Yes
Lease Negotiation Assistance: . . . . .Yes
Co-operative Advertising: . . . . .No
Training: . . . . . . .3 Wks. Corp. Training
  . . . . .Center, 6 Days Field, 5 Days Site
On-Going Support: B,C,d,E,G,h,I/ . . .125
EXPANSION PLANS:
  US: . . . . .All US, Exc. SD
  Canada: . . . . .All Canada
  Overseas: UK,AU,MX,BZ,ISR,IRE,S. Afr.

KWIK-KOPY PRINTING (CANADA)

15900 Yonge St.
Aurora, ON L4G 3G8 CAN
TEL: (800) 387-9725 (416) 798-7007
FAX: (416) 727-1952
Mr. John Johnson, VP Mktg.

KWIK-KOPY PRINTING CANADA offers complete printing and photo-copying services. We are the largest printing franchisor in Canada, providing coast-to-coast support service. The integrity of the franchisee is key, the service they provide is the difference. If you want your own business, join us at the top.

HISTORY: . . . . .IFA, CFA
Established in 1978; . . 1st Franchised in 1978
Company-Owned Units (As of 8/31/1992): . .0
Franchised Units (As of 8/31/1992): 110
Total Units (As of 8/31/1992): 110
Projected New Units for 1993: 6
Distribution: US-0;Can-110;Overseas-0
  North America: . . . . 9 Provinces
  Concentration: . . . . . . .61 in ON, 7 in PQ
Registered: . . . . AB
. . . .
Type Space: . . . . ;~1,800 SF

FINANCIAL: Earnings Claim: . Yes
Cash Investment: $80K
Total Investment: $170K
Fees: Franchise - $25K
  Royalty: 6%, Advert: 3%
Contract Periods (Yrs.): 25
Area Development Agreement: . .No
Sub-Franchise Contract: . . . . .No
Expand in Territory: . . . . . . Yes
Passive Ownership: . . . Not Allowed
Encourage Conversions: . . . . Yes
Average # Employees: . . 6 FT, 1 PT

FRANCHISOR TRAINING/SUPPORT:
Financial Assistance Provided: . . .Yes(D)
Site Selection Assistance: . . . . . . .Yes
Lease Negotiation Assistance: . . . . .Yes
Co-operative Advertising: . . . . . . .Yes
Training: . . . . . . .3 Wks. Houston, TX

On-Going Support: A,B,C,D,E,F,G,H,I/ 20
EXPANSION PLANS:
  US: . . . . .No
  Canada: . . . . .All Canada
  Overseas: . . . EUR, SE Asia, S. America

LAZERQUICK COPIES

27375 SW Parkway Ave.
Wilsonville, OR 97070
TEL: (800) 477-COPY (503) 682-1322
FAX: (503) 682-1670
Mr. Michael Hart, Dir. Fran.

LAZERQUICK COPIES is a full-service printing and copying business. As the pioneer in desktop publishing in the industry, we have combined technology and a customer service approach into a winning formula. Our large base of company-owned centers keeps fees and royalties low and franchisee value high.

HISTORY: . . . .
Established in 1968; . . 1st Franchised in 1990
Company-Owned Units (As of 8/31/1992): . 34
Franchised Units (As of 8/31/1992): 6
Total Units (As of 8/31/1992): 40
Projected New Units for 1993: 5
Distribution: US-40;Can-0;Overseas-0
  North America: . . . . 3 States
  Concentration: . . . . OR, WA, CA
Registered: . . . . CA,FL,OR,WA
. . . .
Type Space: FS, SF, SC, OB;~1,000-1,500 SF

FINANCIAL: Earnings Claim: . Yes
Cash Investment: $27-52.5K
Total Investment: $135-175K
Fees: Franchise - $20K
  Royalty: 5%, Advert: 0%
Contract Periods (Yrs.): . . . 5/5/5/5
Area Development Agreement: . .No
Sub-Franchise Contract: . . . . .No
Expand in Territory: . . . . . . Yes
Passive Ownership: . . . Not Allowed
Encourage Conversions: . . . . Yes
Average # Employees: . . . . . .2 FT

FRANCHISOR TRAINING/SUPPORT:
Financial Assistance Provided: . . .Yes(I)
Site Selection Assistance: . . . . . . .Yes
Lease Negotiation Assistance: . . . .Yes
Co-operative Advertising: . . . . . . .NA
Training: . . . . 5 Wks. Headquarters

On-Going Support: B,C,D,E,G,I/ 36
EXPANSION PLANS:
  US: . . . . . . All US, Start-ups - West
  Canada: . . . . No
  Overseas: . . . . No

MAIL BOXES ETC.

6060 Cornerstone Court West
San Diego, CA 92121
TEL: (800) 456-0414 (619) 455-8800
FAX: (619) 546-7488
Mr. Ken Sully, VP Fran. Dev.

MAIL BOXES ETC. is the largest national franchisor of postal, business and communications services, with over 1,400 centers. Its unique marketing niche provides 30 services, offering convenience for customers and support for small businesses. MBE is international, with centers currently in Canada, Mexico and Japan.

HISTORY: . . . . IFA	FINANCIAL: Earnings Claim: . .No	FRANCHISOR TRAINING/SUPPORT:
Established in 1980; . . 1st Franchised in 1980	Cash Investment: $55K	Financial Assistance Provided: . . .Yes(D)
Company-Owned Units (As of 8/31/1992): . .1	Total Investment: $60-75K	Site Selection Assistance: . . . . . . .Yes
Franchised Units (As of 8/31/1992): 1870	Fees: Franchise - $23K	Lease Negotiation Assistance: . . . . .Yes
Total Units (As of 8/31/1992): 1871	Royalty: 5%, Advert: 2%	Co-operative Advertising: . . . . . . .Yes
Projected New Units for 1993: 350	Contract Periods (Yrs.): . . . 10/10	Training: . . . . . . 2 Wks. Headquarters,
Distribution: US-1861;Can-8;Overseas-1	Area Development Agreement: Yes/10	. . . . 1 Wk. Franchisee Site
North America: . . . . 48 States	Sub-Franchise Contract: . . . . .No	On-Going Support: A,B,C,d,E,F,G,H,I/ . 99
Concentration: . . 434 in CA, 139 FL, 112 NY	Expand in Territory: . . . . . . Yes	EXPANSION PLANS:
Registered: . . . . .All	Passive Ownership: . . . Discouraged	US: . . . . .All US
. . . .	Encourage Conversions: . . . . Yes	Canada: . . . . .All Canada
Type Space: Anchored Center;~1,000-1,400 SF	Average # Employees: . . 1 FT, 2 PT	Overseas: . . . . .Yes

MINUTEMAN PRESS INTERNATIONAL

Full-service printing center.

1640 New Highway
Farmingdale, NY 11735
TEL: (800) 645-3006 (516) 249-1370
FAX: (516) 249-5618
Mr. Roy Titus, VP

HISTORY: . . . . IFA	FINANCIAL: Earnings Claim: . .No	FRANCHISOR TRAINING/SUPPORT:
Established in 1973; . . 1st Franchised in 1975	Cash Investment: $30-40K	Financial Assistance Provided: . . . Yes(I)
Company-Owned Units (As of 8/31/1992): . .0	Total Investment: $90-100K	Site Selection Assistance: . . . . . . .Yes
Franchised Units (As of 8/31/1992): 900	Fees: Franchise - $32.5K	Lease Negotiation Assistance: . . . . .Yes
Total Units (As of 8/31/1992): 900	Royalty: 6%, Advert: 0%	Co-operative Advertising: . . . . .NA
Projected New Units for 1993:	Contract Periods (Yrs.): . . . 35/35	Training: . . . . 2 Wks. Headquarters
Distribution: US-850;Can-50;Overseas-0	Area Development Agreement: . .No	. . . .
North America: . . . . 40 States, 3 Provinces	Sub-Franchise Contract: . . . . .No	On-Going Support: b,C,D,E,F,G,H,I/ . . 75
Concentration: . . . . CA, NY, TX	Expand in Territory: . . . . . . Yes	EXPANSION PLANS:
Registered: . . . . All States	Passive Ownership: . . . Discouraged	US: . . . . Prime Areas Available
. . . .	Encourage Conversions: . . . . .No	Canada: . . . . BC and ON
Type Space: . . . . .SF, SC;~1,000 SF	Avg. # Employees: 3 PT For Start-Up	Overseas: . . . . .Throughout EUR

P.K.G.'s

5400 Cornell Rd.
Cincinnati, OH 45242
TEL: (800) 543-7547 (513) 489-7547 C
FAX: (513) 489-3874
Mr. Thomas R. Sizer, President

P.K.G.'S is a packaging and shipping franchise. P.K.G.'S is the "leader of the pack" who pack and ship anything, anywhere!

HISTORY: . . . . IFA	FINANCIAL: Earnings Claim: . .No	FRANCHISOR TRAINING/SUPPORT:
Established in 1983; . . 1st Franchised in 1984	Cash Investment: . . . .$	Financial Assistance Provided: . . . . .No
Company-Owned Units (As of 8/31/1992): . 10	Total Investment: $43K	Site Selection Assistance: . . . . . . .Yes
Franchised Units (As of 8/31/1992): 35	Fees: Franchise - $15.5K	Lease Negotiation Assistance: . . . . .Yes
Total Units (As of 8/31/1992): 45	Royalty: 5%, Advert: 1%	Co-operative Advertising: . . . . .No
Projected New Units for 1993: 12	Contract Periods (Yrs.): . . . 10/10	Training: . . . . . . .1 Wk. Headquarters,
Distribution: US-45;Can-0;Overseas-0	Area Development Agreement: Yes/5	. . . . 1 Wk. On-Site
North America: . . . . 45 States	Sub-Franchise Contract: . . . . .No	On-Going Support: b,C,D,E,F,G,H,I/ . . .7
Concentration: . . .14 in OH, 7 in FL, 4 in GA	Expand in Territory: . . . . . . Yes	EXPANSION PLANS:
Registered: . . . . FL,IL,IN,MD,MI	Passive Ownership: . . . Discouraged	US: . . . . .All US
. . . .	Encourage Conversions: . . . . Yes	Canada: . . . . .No
Type Space: . . . . .SC;~1,200 SF	Average # Employees: . 1 FT, 1/2 PT	Overseas: . . . . .No

PACK 'N' MAIL MAILING CENTER

5701 Slide Rd., # C
Lubbock, TX 79414
TEL: (800) 877-8884 (806) 797-3400
FAX: (806) 797-8142
Mr. Mike Gallagher, President

We are a complete mailing and shipping center (UPS, US Mail, overnight services, fax, copier, Western Union, furniture shipping and box rental). We ship anything anywhere. Complete training, site location, lease negotiations. No royalties and, of course, on-going assistance.

HISTORY: . . . .
Established in 1981; . . 1st Franchised in 1987
Company-Owned Units (As of 8/31/1992): . .6
Franchised Units (As of 8/31/1992): 191
Total Units (As of 8/31/1992): 197
Projected New Units for 1993: 125
Distribution: US-195;Can-1;Overseas-1
  North America: . . . . 36 States
  Concentration: . . . 50 in TX, 12 in IL, 8 in NJ
Registered: . . . . .All
. . . .
Type Space: . . SF, SC, RM;~1,000-1,500 SF

FINANCIAL: Earnings Claim: . Yes
Cash Investment: $24K
Total Investment: $40-65K
Fees: Franchise - $17.5K
  Royalty: 0%, Advert: 0%
Contract Periods (Yrs.): 5/5
Area Development Agreement: Yes/5
Sub-Franchise Contract: . . . . Yes
Expand in Territory: . . . . . . Yes
Passive Ownership: . . . . .Allowed
Encourage Conversions: . . . . Yes
Average # Employees: . . 1 FT, 1 PT

FRANCHISOR TRAINING/SUPPORT:
Financial Assistance Provided: . . .Yes(D)
Site Selection Assistance: . . . . . . .Yes
Lease Negotiation Assistance: . . . . .Yes
Co-operative Advertising: . . . . . . .Yes
Training: . . . . .5-10 Days HQ, 5-10 Days
  . . . Newport News, 5-10 Days Portland
On-Going Support: A,B,C,D,E,F,G,H,I/ 25
EXPANSION PLANS:
  US: . . . . .All US
  Canada: . . . . .All Canada
  Overseas: . . . . All Possible

PACKAGING PLUS SERVICES

20 S. Terminal Dr.
Plainview, NY 11803
TEL: (800) 922-7225 (516) 349-1300
FAX: (516) 349-8036
Mr. Richard A. Altomare, President

PACKAGING PLUS SERVICES is engaged in franchising service centers which offer convenient packaging, shipping, mailing and communication services to business, retailers, professionals and residential customers. PPS offers all convenient services, plus a full-service corporate mail room.

HISTORY: . . . .
Established in 1985; . . 1st Franchised in 1986
Company-Owned Units (As of 8/31/1992): . .0
Franchised Units (As of 8/31/1992): 81
Total Units (As of 8/31/1992): 81
Projected New Units for 1993: 25
Distribution: US-81;Can-0;Overseas-0
  North America: . . . . 15 States
  Concentration: . . 34 in NY, 14 in NJ, 5 in CT
Registered: . . . . . . FL,MD,MI,NY,RI,VA
. . . .
Type Space: . . . . SC, RM;~1,000 SF

FINANCIAL: Earnings Claim: . .No
Cash Investment: $15-30K
Total Investment: $35-50K
Fees: Franchise - $19.5K
  Royalty: 2.5%, Advert: 1%
Contract Periods (Yrs.): 10/5
Area Development Agreement: Yes/10
Sub-Franchise Contract: . . . . Yes
Expand in Territory: . . . . . . Yes
Passive Ownership: . . . Discouraged
Encourage Conversions: . . . . Yes
Average # Employees: . . 1 FT, 1 PT

FRANCHISOR TRAINING/SUPPORT:
Financial Assistance Provided: . . .Yes(D)
Site Selection Assistance: . . . . . . .Yes
Lease Negotiation Assistance: . . . .Yes
Co-operative Advertising: . . . . . . .Yes
Training: . . . . . . .7-21 Days Convenient
  . . . . .On-Site Locations
On-Going Support: B,C,D,E,G,H,I/ 6
EXPANSION PLANS:
  US: . . . . .All US
  Canada: . . . . .All Canada
  Overseas: . . . . EUR, Asia

PARCEL PLUS

2666 Riva Rd., # 120
Annapolis, MD 21401
TEL: (800) 662-5553 (410) 266-3200
FAX: (410) 266-3266
Mr. David G. Campbell, President

Complete mail and business support services for consumer and commercial markets. Services include: packaging, shipping, mailbox rentals, secretarial, computer services, high-speed copying, fax, data base management and shipping room management programs. Our slogan "We Do Everything First Class" reflects our commitment to excellence in people, site selection, lease negotiation, training and on-going franchisee support. Excellent locations available.

HISTORY: . . . . IFA
Established in 1986; . . 1st Franchised in 1988
Company-Owned Units (As of 8/31/1992): . .0
Franchised Units (As of 8/31/1992): 62
Total Units (As of 8/31/1992): 62
Projected New Units for 1993: 20
Distribution: US-62;Can-0;Overseas-0
  North America: . . . . 7 States
  Concentration: . . . . . . 19 in VA, 17 in MD
Registered: . . . . CA,FL,NY,VA,WI
. . . .
Type Space:.SC,Grocery Anchor;~1,000-1,200 SF

FINANCIAL: Earnings Claim: . Yes
Cash Investment: $50-60K
Total Investment: $50-60K
Fees: Franchise - $15.5K
  Royalty: 4%, Advert: 1%
Contract Periods (Yrs.): . . . 5/5/5/5
Area Development Agreement: . .No
Sub-Franchise Contract: . . . . .No
Expand in Territory: . . . . . . Yes
Passive Ownership: . . . . .Allowed
Encourage Conversions: . . . . Yes
Average # Employees: . . 1 FT, 1 PT

FRANCHISOR TRAINING/SUPPORT:
Financial Assistance Provided: . . . Yes(I)
Site Selection Assistance: . . . . . . .Yes
Lease Negotiation Assistance: . . . . .Yes
Co-operative Advertising: . . . . . . .Yes
Training: . . . . . .5 Days Corporate Store,
  . . . . 5 Days On-Site
On-Going Support: B,C,D,E,F,G,H,I/ . . . 5
EXPANSION PLANS:
  US: . . . . .All US
  Canada: . . . . .All Canada
  Overseas: . . . . No

PARCELWAY COURIER SYSTEMS

3122 N. Third Ave.
Phoenix, AZ 85013
TEL: (800) 343-0200 (602) 263-4900
FAX: (602) 263-7404
Mr. George Siegel, President

PARCELWAY is the leader in service and computer technology in messenger services. Same day delivery of documents, packages and parts locally and nationally. Rapid growth through company-owned and franchised market. State-of-the-art systems backed by the industry's most knowledgeable support team.

HISTORY:	FINANCIAL: Earnings Claim: . .No	FRANCHISOR TRAINING/SUPPORT:
Established in 1990; . . 1st Franchised in 1991	Cash Investment: $30-40K	Financial Assistance Provided: . . . Yes(I)
Company-Owned Units (As of 8/31/1992): . .1	Total Investment: $68.4-114K	Site Selection Assistance: . . . . . . .Yes
Franchised Units (As of 8/31/1992): 0	Fees: Franchise - $15K	Lease Negotiation Assistance: . . . .NA
Total Units (As of 8/31/1992): 1	Royalty: 5%, Advert: 2%	Co-operative Advertising: . . . . . . .NA
Projected New Units for 1993: 12	Contract Periods (Yrs.): 10/10	Training: . . . . . . 1-3 Wks. Headquarters
Distribution: US-1;Can-0;Overseas-0	Area Development Agreement: . .No	
North America: . . . . .1 State	Sub-Franchise Contract: . . . . . .No	On-Going Support: A,C,D,E,G,h,I/ 5
Concentration: . . . . 1 in AZ	Expand in Territory: . . . . Yes	EXPANSION PLANS:
Registered: . . . . .CA,FL,IL,MI,OR	Passive Ownership: . . . . .Allowed	US: . . . . All US
	Encourage Conversions: . . . . Yes	Canada: . . . . .All Canada
Type Space: . . . . . . Office Space;~600 SF	Average # Employees: . 10 FT, 10 PT	Overseas: . . EUR, AU, S. America

PONY MAIL BOX & BUSINESS CENTER

13110 NE 177th Place
Woodinville, WA 98072
TEL: (800) 767-7668 (206) 483-0360
FAX: (206) 486-6495
Mr. R. E. Howell, President

Commercial mail receiving, packaging, mail boxes, fax, Western Union, office supplies, word processing, UPS, all freight carriers.

HISTORY:	FINANCIAL: Earnings Claim: . .No	FRANCHISOR TRAINING/SUPPORT:
Established in 1982; . . 1st Franchised in 1986	Cash Investment: $50K	Financial Assistance Provided: . . . . .No
Company-Owned Units (As of 8/31/1992): . .1	Total Investment: $50-70K	Site Selection Assistance: . . . . . . .Yes
Franchised Units (As of 8/31/1992): 18	Fees: Franchise - $13K	Lease Negotiation Assistance: . . . .Yes
Total Units (As of 8/31/1992): 19	Royalty: $1K/Yr., Advert: . . . 0%	Co-operative Advertising: . . . . . . .NA
Projected New Units for 1993: 4	Contract Periods (Yrs.): 6/5	Training: . . . . 3-4 Days Minimum Head-
Distribution: US-19;Can-0;Overseas-0	Area Development Agreement: Yes/5	. . . . quarters, Longer If Needed
North America: . . . . 10 States	Sub-Franchise Contract: . . . . . .No	On-Going Support: C,D,G,I/ 5
Concentration:	Expand in Territory: . . . . Yes	EXPANSION PLANS:
Registered: . . . . All States Exc. CA	Passive Ownership: . . . Not Allowed	US: . . . . .All US
	Encourage Conversions: . . . . NA	Canada: . . . . No
Type Space: . . . . . FS, SC, RM;~1,000 SF	Average # Employees: 1 FT, Varies PT	Overseas: . . . . No

POSTAL PLUS SERVICES

70 E. Beaver Creek Rd., # 29
Richmond Hill, ON L4B 1J6 CAN
TEL: (800) 833-2821 (416) 731-9733 C
FAX: (416) 886-7745
Ms. Shelly Basser, Sales & Mktg.

Full-service Canada Post post office, plus courier, keys, money order, wire service, fax, photography, stationery, cards, mailbox, printing and great service.

HISTORY:	FINANCIAL: Earnings Claim: . .No	FRANCHISOR TRAINING/SUPPORT:
Established in 1991; . . 1st Franchised in 1991	Cash Investment: $50K	Financial Assistance Provided: . . . Yes(D)
Company-Owned Units (As of 8/31/1992): . .1	Total Investment: $50K	Site Selection Assistance: . . . . . . .Yes
Franchised Units (As of 8/31/1992): 10	Fees: Franchise - $27.5K	Lease Negotiation Assistance: . . . . .Yes
Total Units (As of 8/31/1992): 11	Royalty: 5%, Advert: 2%	Co-operative Advertising: . . . . . . .Yes
Projected New Units for 1993: 50	Contract Periods (Yrs.): . . 10/Varies	Training: . . . . 1 Wk. Headquarters
Distribution: US-0;Can-11;Overseas-0	Area Development Agreement: . .No	
North America: . . . . .1 Province	Sub-Franchise Contract: . . . . . .No	On-Going Support: B,C,D,E,F,G,H,I/ . . .3
Concentration: . . . . 11 in ON	Expand in Territory: . . . . Yes	EXPANSION PLANS:
Registered:	Passive Ownership: . . . . .Allowed	US: . . . . .Yes
	Encourage Conversions: . . . . Yes	Canada: . . . . .All Canada
Type Space: . . . . .SC;~500 SF	Average # Employees: . . 2 FT, 2 PT	Overseas: . . . . UK, GR

POSTALANNEX+

9050 Friars Rd., # 400
San Diego, CA 92108
TEL: (800) 456-1525 (619) 563-4800 C
FAX: (619) 563-9850
Mr. Dan. Crotta, VP Fran. Dev.

POSTALANNEX+ offers the most comprehensive mix of products and services in the postal services industry. Our franchisees say it all. The support and achievement they enjoy as business owners in the booming postal, parcel and business service industry can also be yours. Three franchises in one: copying, packaging and shipping, business services (faxing, telephone answering, office supplies and more).

HISTORY: . . . . IFA	FINANCIAL: Earnings Claim: . .No	FRANCHISOR TRAINING/SUPPORT:
Established in 1985; . . 1st Franchised in 1986	Cash Investment: $55-72K	Financial Assistance Provided: . . . Yes(I)
Company-Owned Units (As of 8/31/1992): . .1	Total Investment: $60-90K	Site Selection Assistance: . . . . . . .Yes
Franchised Units (As of 8/31/1992): 145	Fees: Franchise - $19.5K	Lease Negotiation Assistance: . . . . .Yes
Total Units (As of 8/31/1992): 146	Royalty: 5%, Advert: 2%	Co-operative Advertising: . . . . . . .Yes
Projected New Units for 1993: 98	Contract Periods (Yrs.): 10/10	Training: . . . . 2 Wks. Classroom,
Distribution: US-146;Can-0;Overseas-0	Area Development Agreement: Yes/10	. . . . . . 1 Wk. Training Center (Store)
North America: . . . . 16 States	Sub-Franchise Contract: . . . . Yes	On-Going Support: A,B,C,D,E,F,G,H,I/ 25
Concentration: . . 110 in CA, 5 in OR, 4 in TX	Expand in Territory: . . . . . . Yes	EXPANSION PLANS:
Registered: . . . . All States	Passive Ownership: . . . Discouraged	US: . . . . .All US
. . . .	Encourage Conversions: . . . . Yes	Canada: . . . . .All Canada
Type Space: . . . . RM;~1,200 SF	Average # Employees: . . 1 FT, 2 PT	Overseas: . EUR, Asia, S. America

PRINTHOUSE EXPRESS, THE

222 Catoctin Circle, SE
Leesburg, VA 22075
TEL: (800) 779-0029 (703) 777-0020
FAX: (703) 777-3551
Mr. Tom Galloway, President

THE PRINTHOUSE EXPRESS is a regional franchise system. Because of this, the company can offer unmatched service to its franchisees. The system includes desktop publishing, point-of-sale computer invoicing and estimating, a complete computerized management system, including work in process reports and accounting, plus a unique commercial print brokering system.

HISTORY: . . . . IFA	FINANCIAL: Earnings Claim: . Yes	FRANCHISOR TRAINING/SUPPORT:
Established in 1982; . . 1st Franchised in 1984	Cash Investment: $65K	Financial Assistance Provided: . . .Yes(D)
Company-Owned Units (As of 8/31/1992): . .1	Total Investment: $165K	Site Selection Assistance: . . . . . . .Yes
Franchised Units (As of 8/31/1992): 16	Fees: Franchise - $42K	Lease Negotiation Assistance: . . . . .Yes
Total Units (As of 8/31/1992): 17	Royalty: 3.5%, Advert: 0%	Co-operative Advertising: . . . . . . .Yes
Projected New Units for 1993:	Contract Periods (Yrs.): 20/10	Training: . . . . ~40 Hour Course at Home,
Distribution: US-17;Can-0;Overseas-0	Area Development Agreement: . Yes	. . . . . . 10 Days HQ, 10 Days On-Site
North America: . . . . 3 States	Sub-Franchise Contract: . . . . Yes	On-Going Support: B,C,D,E,F,G,H,I/ . . .5
Concentration: . . 14 in VA, 2 in MD, 1 in DC	Expand in Territory: . . . . . . Yes	EXPANSION PLANS:
Registered: . . . . .MD,VA,DC	Passive Ownership: . . . Not Allowed	US: . . . . . New York to North Carolina
. . . .	Encourage Conversions: . . . . Yes	Canada: . . . . .No
Type Space: . . . . SC;~1,300 SF	Average # Employees: . . . . .4 FT	Overseas: . . . . No

PROFORMA

4705 Van Epps Rd.
Cleveland, OH 44131
TEL: (800) 825-1525 (216) 741-0400
FAX: (216) 741-8887
Mr. John H. Campbell, VP Fran. Mktg.

Distributor of business forms and commercial printing. Not a retail business. Seeking owner/operator with strong marketing and management background to develop this business. $42,000-48,000 minimum investment.

HISTORY: . . . . IFA	FINANCIAL: Earnings Claim: . .No	FRANCHISOR TRAINING/SUPPORT:
Established in 1978; . . 1st Franchised in 1985	Cash Investment: $42-48K	Financial Assistance Provided: . . . . .Yes
Company-Owned Units (As of 8/31/1992): . .2	Total Investment: . . . .$	Site Selection Assistance: . . . . . . .NA
Franchised Units (As of 8/31/1992): 98	Fees: Franchise - $39.5K	Lease Negotiation Assistance: . . . .NA
Total Units (As of 8/31/1992): 100	Royalty: 7%, Advert: 1%	Co-operative Advertising: . . . . . . .NA
Projected New Units for 1993: 20	Contract Periods (Yrs.): . . 10/Varies	Training: . . . . 1 Wk. Headquarters
Distribution: US-100;Can-0;Overseas-0	Area Development Agreement: . .No	. . . .
North America: . . . . 28 States	Sub-Franchise Contract: . . . . .No	On-Going Support: A,C,D,G,H,I/ 60
Concentration: . . . .7 in NC, 7 in OH, 6 in NJ	Expand in Territory: . . . . . . Yes	EXPANSION PLANS:
Registered: . . . CA,FL,IL,IN,MD,MI,MN,NY	Passive Ownership: . . . Not Allowed	US: . . . . .All US
. . . . OR,RI,VA,WA,WI	Encourage Conversions: . . . . Yes	Canada: . . . . .All Canada
Type Space: . . . . FS;~200 SF	Average # Employees: . . . . . .1 FT	Overseas: . . . . No

QUIK PRINT

3445 N. Webb Rd.
Wichita, KS 67226
TEL: (800) 825-COPY (316) 636-5666
FAX: (316) 636-5678
Mr. Johnny Tarrant, Sr. VP

Nation-wide fast offset printing and copying network; est. 1963; expanding to offer additional related services (typesetting, facsimile, thermography, etc.). Complete professional training and support program (site selection, advertising, bookkeeping, improvements, etc.) both at home office and on-site continues beyond initial opening as needed.

HISTORY:	FINANCIAL: Earnings Claim: . .No	FRANCHISOR TRAINING/SUPPORT:
Established in 1963; . . 1st Franchised in 1967	Cash Investment: $50K	Financial Assistance Provided: . . .Yes(D)
Company-Owned Units (As of 8/31/1992): . 69	Total Investment: $150K	Site Selection Assistance: . . . . . . .Yes
Franchised Units (As of 8/31/1992): 141	Fees: Franchise - $15K	Lease Negotiation Assistance: . . . . . . .Yes
Total Units (As of 8/31/1992): 210	Royalty: 5%, Advert: 0%	Co-operative Advertising: . . . . .No
Projected New Units for 1993:	Contract Periods (Yrs.): 25/25	Training: . . . . 4 Wks. Headquarters,
Distribution: US-210;Can-0;Overseas-0	Area Development Agreement: Yes/25	. . . . 2 Wks. On-Site
North America: . . . . 28 States	Sub-Franchise Contract: . . . . .No	On-Going Support: B,C,D,E,F,G,H,I/ . . 35
Concentration: . 45 in TX, 26 in CA, 20 in CO	Expand in Territory: . . . . Yes	EXPANSION PLANS:
Registered: . . . . CA,FL,IL,MN,VA	Passive Ownership: . . . Discouraged	US: . . . . .All US
. . . .	Encourage Conversions: . . . . .No	Canada: . . . . .No
Type Space: . . . . .SC;~1,200 SF	Average # Employees: . . . . 3-5 FT	Overseas: . . . . No

SCREEN PRINTING USA

534 W. Shawnee Ave.
Plymouth, PA 18651
TEL: (717) 779-5175
FAX:
Mr. Russell Owens, President

Unique, computer-aided silk screen printing operation. Printing on t-shirts, hats, jackets, decals, signs, wood, metal, glass and 100 more items.

HISTORY:	FINANCIAL: Earnings Claim: . .No	FRANCHISOR TRAINING/SUPPORT:
Established in 1988; . . 1st Franchised in 1988	Cash Investment: $25K	Financial Assistance Provided: . . . Yes(I)
Company-Owned Units (As of 8/31/1992): . .2	Total Investment: $60K	Site Selection Assistance: . . . . . . .Yes
Franchised Units (As of 8/31/1992): 26	Fees: Franchise - $25K	Lease Negotiation Assistance: . . . . .Yes
Total Units (As of 8/31/1992): 28	Royalty: 6%, Advert: 2%	Co-operative Advertising: . . . . .Yes
Projected New Units for 1993: 40	Contract Periods (Yrs.): 10/5	Training: . . . . 2 Wks. Headquarters
Distribution: US-28;Can-0;Overseas-0	Area Development Agreement: Yes/10	
North America: . . . . 4 States	Sub-Franchise Contract: . . . . . Yes	On-Going Support: B,C,D,E,G,H,I/ 2
Concentration: . . . . NY	Expand in Territory: . . . . Yes	EXPANSION PLANS:
Registered:	Passive Ownership: . . . . . .Allowed	US: . . . . .All US
. . . .	Encourage Conversions: . . . . .No	Canada: . . . . .Yes
Type Space: . . . . . FS, SF, SC;~1,000 SF	Average # Employees: . . . . . .1 FT	Overseas: . . . . No

SHIPPING CONNECTION

7220 W. Jefferson Ave., # 305
Denver, CO 80235
TEL: (800) 727-6720 (303) 980-9595
FAX: (303) 985-1982
Ms. Betty Russotti, President

Specializing in packing and shipping for retail and business customers. Our proprietary, custom-designed computer system, extensive training and successful track record provide you with the key to your personal success in this proven and profitable business. Company founded by ex-UPS management personnel.

HISTORY:	FINANCIAL: Earnings Claim: . .No	FRANCHISOR TRAINING/SUPPORT:
Established in 1982; . . 1st Franchised in 1987	Cash Investment: $30-40K	Financial Assistance Provided: . . . . .No
Company-Owned Units (As of 8/31/1992): . .1	Total Investment: $30-43K	Site Selection Assistance: . . . . . . .Yes
Franchised Units (As of 8/31/1992): 20	Fees: Franchise - $15.5K	Lease Negotiation Assistance: . . . . .Yes
Total Units (As of 8/31/1992): 21	Royalty: 5%, Advert: 2%	Co-operative Advertising: . . . . .Yes
Projected New Units for 1993: 20	Contract Periods (Yrs.): 10/5	Training: . . . . 2 Wks. Headquarters,
Distribution: US-21;Can-0;Overseas-0	Area Development Agreement: . .No	. . . . 1 Wk. Store Site
North America: . . . . 7 States	Sub-Franchise Contract: . . . . .No	On-Going Support: B,C,D,E,G,H/ 5
Concentration: . . . 6 in CO, 5 in OH, 3 in NC	Expand in Territory: . . . . Yes	EXPANSION PLANS:
Registered: . . . . . . .FL,IL,IN,MI,MN,NY	Passive Ownership: . . . . . .Allowed	US: . . . IL,IN,NY,MN, Non-Reg. States
. . . .	Encourage Conversions: . . . . Yes	Canada: . . . . .No
Type Space: . . . . .SC;~1,200 SF	Average # Employees: . . . . . .1 FT	Overseas: . . . . No

SHIPPING DEPARTMENT, THE

5880 Siegen Ln., # G
Baton Rouge, LA 70809
TEL: (504) 295-1085
FAX: (504) 295-1085
Mr. Robert Hafele, President

Packing and shipping experts, specializing in household and industrial shipments under 2,100 pounds (filling the market void between UPS and major moving lines). We provide the means to move a small household at the most affordable price.

HISTORY: . . . .
Established in 1985;   . . 1st Franchised in 1989
Company-Owned Units (As of 8/31/1992):   . .2
Franchised Units (As of 8/31/1992): 1
Total Units (As of 8/31/1992): 3
Projected New Units for 1993: 2
Distribution: US-3;Can-0;Overseas-0
  North America: . . . . 3 States
  Concentration: . . . . 1 in LA
Registered: . . . .
. . . .
Type Space: . . . . . Warehouse;~3,000 SF

FINANCIAL: Earnings Claim: . Yes
Cash Investment: $20-24K
Total Investment: $24K
Fees: Franchise - $12K
  Royalty: 5%, Advert: 1%
Contract Periods (Yrs.): 5/5
Area Development Agreement: . .No
Sub-Franchise Contract: . . . . .No
Expand in Territory: . . . . . . Yes
Passive Ownership: . . . Discouraged
Encourage Conversions: . . . . Yes
Average # Employees: . . 2 FT, 1 PT

FRANCHISOR TRAINING/SUPPORT:
Financial Assistance Provided: . . . . . No
Site Selection Assistance: . . . . Yes
Lease Negotiation Assistance: . . . . .Yes
Co-operative Advertising: . . . . .Yes
Training: . . . . . . 1-2 Wks. Headquarters
. . . .
On-Going Support: C,D,E,F,I/ 1
EXPANSION PLANS:
  US: . . . . All US
  Canada: . . . . .No
  Overseas: . . . . No

SIGNAL GRAPHICS PRINTING

848 Broadway
Denver, CO 80203
TEL: (800) 852-6336 (303) 837-9998
FAX: (303) 837-0256
Mr. Bob Mitchell, Dir. Fran. Sales

A full range of services places SIGNAL GRAPHICS PRINTING ahead of the competition. Our franchising program will enable the owner having no previous printing experience to market quick printing, copying, typesetting and high-quality commercial printing to a wide range of customers in the business community.

HISTORY: . . . . IFA
Established in 1974;   . . 1st Franchised in 1982
Company-Owned Units (As of 8/31/1992):   . .0
Franchised Units (As of 8/31/1992): 33
Total Units (As of 8/31/1992): 33
Projected New Units for 1993: 12
Distribution: US-33;Can-0;Overseas-0
  North America: . . . . 10 States
  Concentration: . . .15 in CO, 7 in CA, 3 in TX
Registered: . . . . . .All States Exc. ND & SD
. . . .
Type Space: . . . . .SC;~1,400 SF

FINANCIAL: Earnings Claim: . .No
Cash Investment: $53-60K
Total Investment: $168-195K
Fees: Franchise - $29.5K
  Royalty: 5-0%, Advert: 1%
Contract Periods (Yrs.):   . . . 25/25
Area Development Agreement: . .No
Sub-Franchise Contract: . . . . .No
Expand in Territory: . . . . . . Yes
Passive Ownership: . . . Discouraged
Encourage Conversions: . . . . Yes
Average # Employees: . . 4 FT, 1 PT

FRANCHISOR TRAINING/SUPPORT:
Financial Assistance Provided: . . . Yes(I)
Site Selection Assistance: . . . . .Yes
Lease Negotiation Assistance: . . . . .Yes
Co-operative Advertising: . . . . .Yes
Training: . . . . 3 Wks. Headquarters,
. . . . 1 Wk. On-Site
On-Going Support: B,C,d,E,G,H,I/   6
EXPANSION PLANS:
  US: . . . . All US
  Canada: . . . . No
  Overseas: . . . . No

SIR SPEEDY

23131 Verdugo Dr.
Laguna Hills, CA 92653
TEL: (800) 854-3321 (714) 472-0330
FAX: (714) 472-3444
Mr. Dave Collins, VP

SIR SPEEDY is the business printer. Provide digital and traditional typeset and pre-press. Black and white printwork, color printwork, high-speed copying and finishing to small businesses. Highest system-wide sales in industry for 4 years in a row. Full training and support. Financing available with $60,000 minimum cash investment.

HISTORY: . . . . IFA
Established in 1968;   . . 1st Franchised in 1968
Company-Owned Units (As of 8/31/1992):   . .0
Franchised Units (As of 8/31/1992):   885
Total Units (As of 8/31/1992):   885
Projected New Units for 1993: 60
Distribution: . . . US-838;Can-16;Overseas-31
  North America: . . . . 45 States, 4 Provinces
  Concentration: . . . 168 in CA, 92 in FL, 55 IL
Registered: . . . . .All
. . . .
Type Space: . . . SF, SC, Ind. Park;~1,600 SF

FINANCIAL: Earnings Claim: . .No
Cash Investment: $60K
Total Investment: $197.K
Fees: Franchise - $17.5K
  Royalty: 4-6%, Advert: 2%
Contract Periods (Yrs.):   . . . 20/20
Area Development Agreement: Yes/20
Sub-Franchise Contract: . . . . Yes
Expand in Territory: . . . . . . Yes
Passive Ownership: . . . Discouraged
Encourage Conversions: . . . . Yes
Average # Employees: . . 4 FT, 1 PT

FRANCHISOR TRAINING/SUPPORT:
Financial Assistance Provided: . . . Yes(I)
Site Selection Assistance: . . . . . . .Yes
Lease Negotiation Assistance: . . . . .Yes
Co-operative Advertising: . . . . .Yes
Training: . . . . . . 2 Wks. HQ, 2 Wks. On
  . . . Location, 1 Wk. On-Site Consultant
On-Going Support: B,C,D,E,F,G,H,I/   . . 68
EXPANSION PLANS:
  US: . . . . All US
  Canada: . . . . Mainly BC and ON
  Overseas: . S. America, Pacific Rim, EUR

SPEEDY PRINTING CENTERS

7100 Woodbine Ave., # 310
Markham, ON L3R 5J2 CAN
TEL: (800) 668-0119 (416) 940-3151 C
FAX: (416) 940-8141
Mr. Tom Davidson, President

Full-service printing/copying centers, offering allied services and an unconditional printing guarantee.

HISTORY: . . . . .CFA
Established in 1986; . . 1st Franchised in 1987
Company-Owned Units (As of 8/31/1992): . .0
Franchised Units (As of 8/31/1992): 32
Total Units (As of 8/31/1992): 32
Projected New Units for 1993: 4
Distribution: US-0;Can-32;Overseas-0
  North America: . . . . 3 Provinces
  Concentration: . . 19 in ON, 12 in BC, 1 in NF
Registered: . . . .
. . . .
Type Space: . . . . .SC;~1,300 SF

FINANCIAL: Earnings Claim: . Yes
Cash Investment: $70-100K
Total Investment: $150-200K
Fees: Franchise - $19.5K
  Royalty: 6%, Advert: 2%
Contract Periods (Yrs.): . . 20/20
Area Development Agreement: Yes/20
Sub-Franchise Contract: . . . . . Yes
Expand in Territory: . . . . . . Yes
Passive Ownership: . . . Discouraged
Encourage Conversions: . . . . Yes
Average # Employees: . . . . .4 FT

FRANCHISOR TRAINING/SUPPORT:
Financial Assistance Provided: . . .Yes(D)
Site Selection Assistance: . . . . . . .Yes
Lease Negotiation Assistance: . . . . .Yes
Co-operative Advertising: . . . . . . .Yes
Training: . . . . 2 Wks. Headquarters,
  . . . .1 Wk. Existing Ctr., 1 Wk. On-Site
On-Going Support: C,D,E,G,H,I/ 8
EXPANSION PLANS:
US: . . . . No
Canada: . . . . All Exc. Alberta
Overseas: . . . . No

UNITED PRINTING UNLIMITED

P.O. Box 616249
Orlando, FL 32861
TEL: (407) 246-0207 C
FAX:
Mr. Jack Swat, GM

Training, support, support after opening. 90% financing available.

HISTORY: . . . .
Established in 1984; . . 1st Franchised in 1984
Company-Owned Units (As of 8/31/1992): . .1
Franchised Units (As of 8/31/1992): 12
Total Units (As of 8/31/1992): 13
Projected New Units for 1993: 12
Distribution: US-13;Can-0;Overseas-0
  North America: . . . . 3 States
  Concentration: . . . 11 in FL, 1 in IL, 1 in GA
Registered: . . . . .All
. . . .
Type Space: . . . . .FS, SF;~1,000 SF

FINANCIAL: Earnings Claim: . .No
Cash Investment: $7.5K
Total Investment: $95K
Fees: Franchise - $25K
  Royalty: 5%, Advert: . . . .
Contract Periods (Yrs.): . . . 20/20
Area Development Agreement: Yes/3
Sub-Franchise Contract: . . . . . Yes
Expand in Territory: . . . . . . Yes
Passive Ownership: . . . Discouraged
Encourage Conversions: . . . . Yes
Average # Employees: . . . . .2 FT

FRANCHISOR TRAINING/SUPPORT:
Financial Assistance Provided: . . . . .Yes
Site Selection Assistance: . . . . . . .Yes
Lease Negotiation Assistance: . . . . .Yes
Co-operative Advertising: . . . . . . .Yes
Training: . . . . 3 Wks. Headquarters
. . . .
On-Going Support: B,C,D,E,F,H/ 5
EXPANSION PLANS:
US: . . . . .All US
Canada: . . . . .Yes
Overseas: . . . . .Yes

ZIPPY PRINT

5800 Ambler Dr., # 114
Mississauga, ON L4W 4J4 CAN
TEL: (416) 629-4300
FAX: (416) 629-2753
Ms. Sandra B. Edwards, Dir. Fran. Dev.

Full-service quick print and fast copy, including all related services, such as bindery, fax, desktop publishing, etc.

HISTORY: . . . .
Established in 1979; . . 1st Franchised in 1981
Company-Owned Units (As of 8/31/1992): . .0
Franchised Units (As of 8/31/1992): 65
Total Units (As of 8/31/1992): 65
Projected New Units for 1993: 6
Distribution: US-0;Can-65;Overseas-0
  North America: . . . . 7 Provinces
  Concentration: . . 45 in On, 13 in BC, 2 in SK
Registered: . . . . AB
. . . .
Type Space: . . . . .FS, SC;~1,800 SF

FINANCIAL: Earnings Claim: . .No
Cash Investment: $80K
Total Investment: $150K
Fees: Franchise - $40K
  Royalty: 5%, Advert: 5%
Contract Periods (Yrs.): . . . 10/10
Area Development Agreement: . .No
Sub-Franchise Contract: . . . . .No
Expand in Territory: . . . . . . Yes
Passive Ownership: . . . Not Allowed
Encourage Conversions: . . . . NA
Average # Employees: . . . . .3 FT

FRANCHISOR TRAINING/SUPPORT:
Financial Assistance Provided: . . . . .Yes
Site Selection Assistance: . . . . . . .Yes
Lease Negotiation Assistance: . . . . .Yes
Co-operative Advertising: . . . . . . .Yes
Training: . . . . 3 Wks. Headquarters
On-Going Support: B,c,D,E,H/ 12
EXPANSION PLANS:
US: . . . . No
Canada: . . . . .All Canada
Overseas: . . . . No

SUPPLEMENTAL LISTING OF FRANCHISORS

AIR SOURCE EXPRESS . . . . 3357 Hollenberg Dr., Bridgeton, MO 63044
    Contact: Mr. Richard Baum, VP-Finance; Tel: (800) 325-4727 (314) 739-0077
ALPHAGRAPHICS PRINTSHOPS (CANADA) . . . . . . 10 Cheshire Pl., Richmond Hill, ON L4C 6G5   CAN
    Contact: Mr. Richard Sadowski; Tel: (416) 886-6126
ALPHAGRAPHICS PRINTSHOPS OF THE FUTURE . . . . . 3760 N. Commerce Dr., Tucson, AZ 85705
    Contact: Ms. Helen Franklin, Dir. of Sales; Tel: (800) 528-4885 (602) 293-9200
AMERICAN POST 'N PARCEL . . . . 315 W. Pondera St., # F, Lancaster, CA 93534
    Contact: Mr. Fred Mauldin, President; Tel: (800) 2PARCEL (805) 949-3990 C
BCX PRINTING CENTERS . . . . 613 E. Indian School Rd., Phoenix, AZ 85012
    Contact: Mr. Gene Cufone, Pres.; Tel: (602) 241-1231 C
BEKINS BOXSTORE . . . . 777 Flower St., Glendale, CA 91201
    Contact: Mr. Robert Wheaton, President; Tel: (800) 777-7269 (818) 507-1200
BOX BROS. . . . . 7050 Owensmouth Ave., # 200, Canoga Park, CA 91303
    Contact: Mr. Robert Goodman, CEO; Tel: (818) 713-8530
BOX SHOPPE, THE . . . . .7165 E. 87th St., Indianapolis, IN 46220
    Contact: Mr. Duke Smith; Tel: (317) 842-4120
BOX STOP, THE . . . . 812 East Main St., Wytheville, VA 24382
    Contact: President; Tel: (703) 228-8594
BUDGET COPIES . . . . 600 5th Ave. Plaza, Des Moines, IA 50309
    Contact: Ms. Phyllis Tasler; Tel: (515) 245-4206
BUDGET PRINTING CENTERS . . . . 4133 Presidential, # 1, Lafayette Hill, PA 19444
    Contact: Mr. Leonard Stevens, President; Tel: (800) 955-5215 (215) 836-5215
BUSINESS CARDS TOMORROW / BCT . . . . . 3000 NE 30th Place, 5th Fl., Ft. Lauderdale, FL 33306
    Contact: Mr. Chuck Barlow, VP; Tel: (800) 627-9998 (305) 563-1224
CANADA POST CORPORATION . . . . . . Sir Alex. Campbell Bldg., # C-319, Ottawa, ON K1A OB1   CAN
    Contact: Mr. Dick Dinelle; Tel: (613) 734-6574
COPYRITE . . . . 231 King St., Charleston, SC 29401
    Contact: Mr. Monty Kohli, President; Tel: (803) 577-6375
DELUXE CHECK PRINTERS . . . . 2199 N. Pascal, St. Paul, MN 55113
    Contact: President; Tel: (612) 631-2924
DYNAMIC AIR FREIGHT . . . . P. O. Box 167848, Irving, TX 75016
    Contact: Mr. Bob Harrah, EVP; Tel: (800) 433-7931 (214) 751-0011
EXPRESS POSTAL CENTERS . . . . .6475 28th St., SE, Grand Rapids, MI 49546
    Contact: Mr. John VanDellen, President; Tel: (800) 968-6870 (616) 530-9605
FAX MAIL INTERNATIONAL . . . . . . 8170 Corporate Park Dr., Cincinnati, OH 45242
    Contact: President; Tel: (513) 489-3830
INSTANT COPY PRINTING/COPYING/COMM. . . . . . 232 W. Wayne St., Fort Wayne, IN 46802
    Contact: Mr. John Thistlewaite, Dir. Fran.; Tel: (219) 422-1585
LASERMASTER . . . . 7156-7160 Shady Oak Rd., Eden Prairie, MN 55344
    Contact: President; Tel: (612) 944-6069
LITERATURE CONTROL SERVICE . . . . . 3400 Robards Ct., PO Box 34470, Louisville, KY 40232
    Contact: President; Tel: (502) 454-6600
MADE 'N-A-MINUTE PRINTERS . . . . 2050 Rosser Ave., Burnaby, BC V5C 5Y1   CAN
    Contact: Mr. Paul McCrea; Tel: (604) 291-7266
MAIL BOXES ETC. (CANADA) . . . . 505 Iroquois Shore Rd., # 4, Oakville, ON L6H 3R3   CAN
    Contact: Mr. Michael J. Martino; Tel: (416) 338-9754
MAIL CENTER USA . . . . .5807 Babcock Rd., San Antonio, TX 78240
    Contact: Mr. Brian G. Bearden, Dir. Fran.; Tel: (800) 969-MAIL (512) 699-3933
MOVING EXPRESS . . . . .3379 Coleman Rd., Memphis, TN 38128
    Contact: President; Tel: (901) 377-8989
PACKAGE & WRAP . . . . .17 Linwood Ave., Newton, NJ 07860
    Contact: President; Tel:
PACKAGE EXPRESS . . . . 4959 W. Tuscarawas St., Canton, OH 44708
    Contact: Mr. Dave Staudt, Owner; Tel: (800) 458-8698 (800) ILUVMYT
PACKAGE SHIPPERS . . . . P.O. Box 82184, Tampa, FL 33682
    Contact: Licensing Department; Tel: (813) 960-2267
PACKY THE SHIPPER/PACK 'N SHIP/PNS . . . . . . 409 Main St., Racine, WI 53403
    Contact: Mr. James Hill; Tel: (414) 633-9540
PAK MAIL CENTERS OF AMERICA . . . . .3033 S. Parker Rd., # 1200, Aurora, CO 80014
    Contact: Mr. John E. Kelly, President; Tel: (800) 833-2821 (303) 752-3500

PILOT AIR FREIGHT CORPORATION . . . . Rte. 352, P. O. Box 97, Lima, PA 19037
    Contact: Mr. Chet Spencer; Tel: (215) 891-8100
POST ALL . . . . 1151 Aquidneck Ave., Middletown, RI 02840
    Contact: Mr. Timothy Harnett, President; Tel: (401) 847-7930
POSTAL OPTIONS . . . . .520 N. State Rd. 135, # M, Greenwood, IN 46142
    Contact: Mr. John Werner; Tel: (317) 881-4226
POSTAL, BUSINESS & COMMUN. CENTERS . . . . . 2225 E. Flamingo, # 310, Las Vegas, NV 89119
    Contact: Mr. Brian Spindel; Tel: (800) 338-7401 (702) 792-7100
PRINT THREE . . . . 184 Shorting Rd., Scarborough, ON M1S 3S7   CAN
    Contact: Mr. Joe Osiel, President; Tel: (800) 268-4177 (416) 754-8700
PRINTING NETWORK . . . . .156 Willowdale Ave., North York, ON M2N 4Y6   CAN
    Contact: Mr. Joe Osiel, President; Tel: (416) 250-0241 C
PRINTMASTERS . . . . 370 S. Crenshaw Blvd., # E-100, Torrance, CA 90503
    Contact: Mr. Thomas P. Vitacco, President; Tel: (800) 221-8945 (310) 328-0303
PRINTSOURCE . . . . 969 Park Ave., Cranston, RI 02910
    Contact: Mr. Donald Shortman, President; Tel: (800) 341-6300 (401) 943-6601
PROFESSOR PRINT COPY CENTRES . . . . 36 C Stoffel Dr., Rexdale, ON M9W 1A8   CAN
    Contact: Ms. Valerie Tyson; Tel: (416) 248-5558
SQP COPY CENTERS . . . . 1525 E. Park Place Blvd., Stone Mountain, GA 30087
    Contact: Mr. G. David Binniv; Tel: (404) 469-0452
SURE GRAPHICS . . . . 1704 - 12 St. NW, Calgary, AB T2M 3M7   CAN
    Contact: Mr. Par Almani; Tel: (403) 282-2131 (604) 584-8313
TRANSAMERICA PRINTING . . . . 1286-F Citizens Pkwy., # F, Morrow, GA 30260
    Contact: Mr. Patrick Koehler, President; Tel: (800) 628-5522 (404) 968-5800
UNISHIPPERS ASSOCIATION . . . . .P. O. Box 17397, Salt Lake City, UT 84117
    Contact: Mr. Steve Nelson, VP; Tel: (800) 999-8721 (801) 262-3300
WHOLESALE PRINTING SPECIALISTS . . . . 28 Hemlock St., Rochester, NH 03867
    Contact: Mr. James E. McGlinchey; Tel: (800) 235-6328

For a full explanation of the data provided in
the Franchisor Format, please refer to Chapter 2,

"How To Use The Data."

CHAPTER 11

BUSINESS: TAX PREPARATION

ABS SYSTEMS

1355 Orange Ave., # 5
Winter Park, FL 32789
TEL: (407) 644-5400 C
FAX: (407) 628-4160
Mr. Mark Silberberg, President

Complete small business accounting and tax franchise. Multi-client, user-friendly software, operational forms and practice procedures. Complete training, including innovative client marketing. Suited for home or office. No percentage royalties. On-going support. The affordable alternative.

HISTORY:	
Established in 1987; . . 1st Franchised in 1989	
Company-Owned Units (As of 8/31/1992): . .0	
Franchised Units (As of 8/31/1992): . . . . . <u>30</u>	
Total Units (As of 8/31/1992): 30	
Projected New Units for 1993: 18	
Distribution: US-30;Can-0;Overseas-0	
North America: . . . . 8 States	
Concentration: . . . . .14 in FL	
Registered: . . . . .FL	
Type Space: . . . . NA;~NA SF	

FINANCIAL: Earnings Claim: . .No	
Cash Investment: $6.5-9K	
Total Investment: $10-12.5K	
Fees: Franchise - $9.5K	
Royalty: $125+/Mo, Advert: . . 0%	
Contract Periods (Yrs.): 10/10	
Area Development Agreement: .No	
Sub-Franchise Contract: . . . . .No	
Expand in Territory: . . . . Yes	
Passive Ownership: . . . . . .Allowed	
Encourage Conversions: . . . . NA	
Average # Employees:	

FRANCHISOR TRAINING/SUPPORT:	
Financial Assistance Provided: . . .Yes(D)	
Site Selection Assistance: . . . . .NA	
Lease Negotiation Assistance: . . . . .No	
Co-operative Advertising: . . . . .NA	
Training: . . . . 4-5 Days Orlando, FL	
On-Going Support: G,H/ 5	
EXPANSION PLANS:	
US: . . . . .All US	
Canada: . . . . .All Canada	
Overseas: . . . . .Yes	

TAX PREPARATION SERVICES

	1989	1990	1991	Percentage Change 90/89	Percentage Change 91/90
Total Number of Establishments:					
Company–Owned	3,359	3,425	3,456	1.96%	0.91%
Franchisee–Owned	4,850	4,870	5,000	0.41%	2.67%
Total	8,209	8,295	8,456	1.05%	1.94%
Ratio of Total Establishments:					
Company–Owned	40.9%	41.3%	40.9%		
Franchisee–Owned	59.1%	58.7%	59.1%		
Total	100.0%	100.0%	100.0%		
Total Sales ($000):					
Company–Owned	349,619	368,696	386,542	5.46%	4.84%
Franchisee–Owned	294,247	304,846	325,190	3.60%	6.67%
Total	643,866	673,542	711,732	4.61%	5.67%
Ratio of Total Sales:					
Company–Owned	54.3%	54.7%	54.3%		
Franchisee–Owned	45.7%	45.3%	45.7%		
Total	100.0%	100.0%	100.0%		
Average Sales Per Unit ($000):					
Company–Owned	104	108	112	3.42%	3.90%
Franchisee–Owned	61	63	65	3.18%	3.90%
Total	78	81	84	3.52%	3.66%
Relative Average Sales Ratio:	171.6%	172.0%	172.0%		

	Number Of Employees	Employees Per Unit	Avg. Sales Per Employee
Total 1989 Employment:			
Company–Owned	46,238	13.8	$7,561
Franchisee–Owned	39,685	8.2	$7,415
Total	85,923	10.5	$7,494
Relative Employee Performance Ratios:		168.2%	102.0%

	1st Quartile	Median	4th Quartile
Average 1989 Total Investment:			
Company–Owned	NA	$10,000	NA
Franchisee–Owned	NA	$10,000	NA
Single Unit Franchise Fee	$27,500	$5,000	$10,000
Mult. Unit Franchise Fee	NA	$11,250	NA
Franchise Start–Up Cost	NA	NA	NA

Source: Franchising In The Economy 1991, IFA Educational Foundation & Horwath International.

AFTE BUSINESS ANALYSTS

2180 N. Loop W., # 300
Houston, TX 77018
TEL: (713) 957-1592
FAX: (713) 957-0935
Mr. Don Willmoth, President

Computerized bookkeeping and tax service. Unique method of obtaining clients.

HISTORY:	FINANCIAL: Earnings Claim: . .No	FRANCHISOR TRAINING/SUPPORT:
Established in 1979; . . 1st Franchised in 1986	Cash Investment: $6.3K	Financial Assistance Provided: . . . . . No
Company-Owned Units (As of 8/31/1992): . .0	Total Investment: $6.3K	Site Selection Assistance: . . . . . . .Yes
Franchised Units (As of 8/31/1992): 16	Fees: Franchise - $4K	Lease Negotiation Assistance: . . . . .Yes
Total Units (As of 8/31/1992): 16	Royalty: 7%, Advert: 0%	Co-operative Advertising: . . . . . . .Yes
Projected New Units for 1993: 10	Contract Periods (Yrs.): 15/15	Training: . . . . 2 Wks. Headquarters
Distribution: US-16;Can-0;Overseas-0	Area Development Agreement: . .No	. . . .
North America: . . . . 6 States	Sub-Franchise Contract: . . . . .No	On-Going Support: b,g,h/ 3
Concentration: . . . . 6 in TX	Expand in Territory: . . . . . . Yes	EXPANSION PLANS:
Registered:	Passive Ownership: . . . . .Allowed	US: . . . . All US
. . . .	Encourage Conversions: . . . . NA	Canada: . . . . .No
Type Space: . . . . FS;~500 SF	Average # Employees: . . . . . .2 FT	Overseas: . . . . No

ECONOTAX

P. O. Box 13829
Jackson, MS 39236
TEL: (800) 748-9106 (601) 956-0500
FAX: (601) 956-0583
Mr. James T. Marsh, President

ECONOTAX provides the public with a full range of tax services, including tax preparation, electronic tax filing, refund loans, tax planning and audit representation. Franchisees receive training and support in all aspects of the tax business, including marketing, technical support for computer operations, tax research and training and management planning.

HISTORY:	FINANCIAL: Earnings Claim: . .No	FRANCHISOR TRAINING/SUPPORT:
Established in 1965; . . 1st Franchised in 1968	Cash Investment: $2.5-7.5K	Financial Assistance Provided: . . . . .NA
Company-Owned Units (As of 8/31/1992): . 14	Total Investment: $2.5-10K	Site Selection Assistance: . . . . . . .Yes
Franchised Units (As of 8/31/1992): 58	Fees: Franchise - $2.5K	Lease Negotiation Assistance: . . . .NA
Total Units (As of 8/31/1992): 72	Royalty: 15%, Advert: . $10/RAL	Co-operative Advertising: . . . . . . .Yes
Projected New Units for 1993: 20	Contract Periods (Yrs.): 5/1	Training: . . . . 1 Wk. Headquarters
Distribution: US-72;Can-0;Overseas-0	Area Development Agreement: Yes/2	. . . .
North America: . . . . 7 States	Sub-Franchise Contract: . . . . .No	On-Going Support: b,G,H,I/ 7
Concentration: . . . 48 in MI, 9 in AL, 4 in LA	Expand in Territory: . . . . . . Yes	EXPANSION PLANS:
Registered: . . . . .FL	Passive Ownership: . . . Not Allowed	US: . . . . All US
. . . .	Encourage Conversions: . . . . . Yes	Canada: . . . . .No
Type Space: . . . . SC;~600-1,000 SF	Average # Employees: 3 FT (Seasonal)	Overseas: . . . . No

JACKSON HEWITT TAX SERVICE

224 Groveland Rd.
Virginia Beach, VA 23452
TEL: (800) 277-3278 (804) 463-0548
FAX: (804) 463-8612
Mr. John T. Hewitt, President

Computerized income tax preparation, electronic filing and refund anticipation loans. Franchisees are provided with proprietary software and annual updates at no charge. The company is the fastest-growing income tax service in the country, and supports franchisees through home office and field support staff.

HISTORY: . . . . IFA	FINANCIAL: Earnings Claim: . .No	FRANCHISOR TRAINING/SUPPORT:
Established in 1960; . . 1st Franchised in 1986	Cash Investment: $16.7K	Financial Assistance Provided: . . . . .NA
Company-Owned Units (As of 8/31/1992): . 34	Total Investment: $25-30K	Site Selection Assistance: . . . . . . .Yes
Franchised Units (As of 8/31/1992): 481	Fees: Franchise - $12K	Lease Negotiation Assistance: . . . .Yes
Total Units (As of 8/31/1992): 515	Royalty: 12%, Advert: 6%	Co-operative Advertising: . . . . No
Projected New Units for 1993: 200	Contract Periods (Yrs.): 5/5	Training: . . . . 5 Days Headquarters,
Distribution: US-515;Can-0;Overseas-0	Area Development Agreement: . .No	. . . . 2 Days Headquarters
North America: . . . . 29 States	Sub-Franchise Contract: . . . . .No	On-Going Support: A,B,C,D,G,H,I/ . . 70
Concentration: . . 60 in IL, 55 in VA, 50 in CA	Expand in Territory: . . . . . . Yes	EXPANSION PLANS:
Registered: . . . CA,FL,IL,IN,MD,MI,MN,NY	Passive Ownership: . . . Discouraged	US: . . . . . Current Operating States,WI
. . . . OR,VA,DC	Encourage Conversions: . . . . . Yes	Canada: . . . . .No
Type Space: . FS, SF, SC, RM;~700-1,000 SF	Average # Employees: . 1-3 FT, 8 PT	Overseas: . . . . No

LEADLEY, GUNNING & CULP INTERNATIONAL
7134 Columbia Gateway Dr.
Columbus, MD 21046
TEL: (800) 638-7940 (410) 290-1040
FAX: (410) 290-1233
Mr. L. Magee, VP Fran. Licensing

Advisors to small business owners and professionals in business, financial and tax management.

HISTORY:	FINANCIAL: Earnings Claim: . .No	FRANCHISOR TRAINING/SUPPORT:
Established in 1978; . . 1st Franchised in 1991	Cash Investment: $10-60K	Financial Assistance Provided: . . . . .No
Company-Owned Units (As of 8/31/1992): . .0	Total Investment: $40-60K	Site Selection Assistance: . . . . . . .Yes
Franchised Units (As of 8/31/1992): . . . . _179_	Fees: Franchise - $25-40K	Lease Negotiation Assistance: . . . . .No
Total Units (As of 8/31/1992): 179	Royalty: 10%, Advert: 0%	Co-operative Advertising: . . . . .No
Projected New Units for 1993: 200	Contract Periods (Yrs.): 10/10	Training: . . . . 2 Wks. Headquarters,
Distribution: US-66;Can-113;Overseas-0	Area Development Agreement: . .No	. . . . .2 Days Field
North America: . . . . 15 States, 6 Provinces	Sub-Franchise Contract: . . . . .No	On-Going Support: B,C,D,E,G,H,I/ . . . 30
Concentration: . 79 in ON, 20 in AB, 18 in OH	Expand in Territory: . . . . . . .No	EXPANSION PLANS:
Registered: . . . CA,FL,IL,IN,MI,NY,WA,WI	Passive Ownership: . . . Not Allowed	US: . . . . All US
. . . . AB	Encourage Conversions: . . . . . Yes	Canada: . . . . BC,AB,SK,MB,ON
Type Space: . . . . SF, General Off.;~300 SF	Average # Employees: . . . . . .1 FT	Overseas: . . . . No

NATIONWIDE INCOME TAX SERVICE

14507 W. Warren
Dearborn, MI 48126
TEL: (313) 584-7640
FAX: (313) 584-6829
Mr. Carl K. Gilbert, President

Preparation of federal, state and local tax returns. Electronic filing and refund anticipation loans (RALS).

HISTORY:	FINANCIAL: Earnings Claim: . .No	FRANCHISOR TRAINING/SUPPORT:
Established in 1964; . . 1st Franchised in 1966	Cash Investment: $10-15K	Financial Assistance Provided: . . . . .No
Company-Owned Units (As of 8/31/1992): . .8	Total Investment: $10-30K	Site Selection Assistance: . . . . . . .Yes
Franchised Units (As of 8/31/1992): . . . . _32_	Fees: Franchise - $10K	Lease Negotiation Assistance: . . . . .Yes
Total Units (As of 8/31/1992): 40	Royalty: 7-10%, Advert: . . 5-10%	Co-operative Advertising: . . . . . . .Yes
Projected New Units for 1993: 40	Contract Periods (Yrs.): 10/10	Training: . . . . . . 1-2 Wks. Headquarters
Distribution: US-40;Can-0;Overseas-0	Area Development Agreement: . Yes	. . . .
North America: . . . . .1 State	Sub-Franchise Contract: . . . . .No	On-Going Support: B,C,d,E,G,H,I/ 5
Concentration: . . . . .40 in MI	Expand in Territory: . . . . . . Yes	EXPANSION PLANS:
Registered: . . . . .MI	Passive Ownership: . . . Discouraged	US: . . . . .All US
. . . .	Encourage Conversions: . . . . . Yes	Canada: . . . . .No
Type Space: . . . . FS, SF, SC;~600-1,000 SF	Average # Employees: . 6 FT, 2-6 PT	Overseas: . . . . No

PEYRON TAX SERVICE

3212 Preston St.
Louisville, KY 40213
TEL: (800) 821-4965 (502) 637-7483
FAX:
Mr. Dan Peyron, President

License opportunities to provide tax return preparation service in stores and malls, using PEYRON SYSTEM and warranties. Also, offer electronic filing and refund loans.

HISTORY:	FINANCIAL: Earnings Claim: . .No	FRANCHISOR TRAINING/SUPPORT:
Established in 1960; . . 1st Franchised in 1965	Cash Investment: $5K	Financial Assistance Provided: . . . . .NA
Company-Owned Units (As of 8/31/1992): . .2	Total Investment: $5K	Site Selection Assistance: . . . . . . .Yes
Franchised Units (As of 8/31/1992): . . . . _450_	Fees: Franchise - $3K	Lease Negotiation Assistance: . . . . .Yes
Total Units (As of 8/31/1992): 452	Royalty: 5%, Advert:	Co-operative Advertising: . . . . .No
Projected New Units for 1993:	Contract Periods (Yrs.): . . . . Indef.	Training: . . . . 1 Day Seminar Local Area
Distribution: US-452;Can-0;Overseas-0	Area Development Agreement: Yes/Var	. . . .
North America: . . . . 40 States	Sub-Franchise Contract: . . . . . Yes	On-Going Support: G,H,I/ . . . .
Concentration:	Expand in Territory: . . . . . Yes	EXPANSION PLANS:
Registered: . . . . .All	Passive Ownership: . . . . . .Allowed	US: . . . . .All US
. . . .	Encourage Conversions: . . . . . Yes	Canada: . . . . .No
Type Space: . . FS, SF, SC, RM;~35 Min. SF	Average # Employees: . . . . . .3 FT	Overseas: . . . . No

**TRIPLE CHECK INCOME
TAX SERVICE**
727 S. Main St.
Burbank, CA 91506
TEL: (800) 283-1040 (818) 840-9077
FAX: (818) 840-9309
Mr. David Lieberman, President

Franchisor offers full range of support services to independent tax practitioners, including training, technical (hotline), marketing (including group referral programs), proprietary worksheet schedule system and reduced computer costs. Through a sister company (Triple Check Financial Services), franchisees have an opportunity to engage in financial and investment planning services.

HISTORY:	. . . . IFA
Established in 1941;	. . 1st Franchised in 1979
Company-Owned Units (As of 8/31/1992):	. .0
Franchised Units (As of 8/31/1992):	 348
Total Units (As of 8/31/1992):	 348
Projected New Units for 1993:	 75
Distribution:	. . . . US-347;Can-0;Overseas-1
North America:	. . . . 42 States
Concentration:	. . 122 in CA, 25 in FL, 13 NY
Registered:	. . . . . .All States Exc. ND & SD
. . . .	
Type Space:	. . SF, SC, Off. Park;~Varies SF

FINANCIAL: Earnings Claim:	. .No
Cash Investment:	. . . . $.5-8K
Total Investment:	. . . .$3-8K
Fees: Franchise -	. . . .$0
Royalty: Varies, Advert:	. . Varies
Contract Periods (Yrs.):	. . . . . 5/5
Area Development Agreement:	. .No
Sub-Franchise Contract:	. . . . .No
Expand in Territory:	. . . . . . Yes
Passive Ownership:	. . . Discouraged
Encourage Conversions:	. . . . Yes
Average # Employees:	. . . . .Varies

FRANCHISOR TRAINING/SUPPORT:	
Financial Assistance Provided:	. . . Yes(I)
Site Selection Assistance:	. . . . No
Lease Negotiation Assistance:	. . . . . No
Co-operative Advertising:	. . . . No
Training:	. . . . 80 Hours on Tape
. . . .	
On-Going Support: a,b,C,G,h,I/	 25
EXPANSION PLANS:	
US:	. . . . .All US
Canada:	. . . . .No
Overseas:	. . . . No

U & R TAX SERVICES

#201 - 1345 Pembina Hwy.
Winnipeg, MB R3T 2B6 CAN
TEL: (204) 949-3636
FAX: (204) 284-8954
Mr. Donald G. Jacks, Director

Income tax preparation. Income tax discounting (refund purchasing). Income tax in-class and correspondence courses.

HISTORY:	. . . .
Established in 1972;	. . 1st Franchised in 1973
Company-Owned Units (As of 8/31/1992):	. 30
Franchised Units (As of 8/31/1992):	 45
Total Units (As of 8/31/1992):	 75
Projected New Units for 1993:	 15
Distribution:	. . . . . US-0;Can-75;Overseas-0
North America:	. . . . 7 Provinces
Concentration:	. 35 in MB, 12 in SK, 10 in BC
Registered:	. . . . AB
. . . .	
Type Space:	. FS, SF, SC, RM;~800-1,500 SF

FINANCIAL: Earnings Claim:	. .No
Cash Investment:	. . . . $5-15K
Total Investment:	. . . . $5-15K
Fees: Franchise -	. . . . . .$3.5-7.5K
Royalty: 3%, Advert:	. . . . . . 0%
Contract Periods (Yrs.):	. . . . . 5/5
Area Development Agreement:	. Yes
Sub-Franchise Contract:	. . . . Yes
Expand in Territory:	. . . . . . Yes
Passive Ownership:	. . . . . .Allowed
Encourage Conversions:	. . . . NA
Average # Employees:	. . . Seasonal

FRANCHISOR TRAINING/SUPPORT:	
Financial Assistance Provided:	. . . Yes(I)
Site Selection Assistance:	. . . . . . .Yes
Lease Negotiation Assistance:	. . . . .Yes
Co-operative Advertising:	. . . . . . .Yes
Training:	. . . . .2-3 Days Training Course
. . . On-Site, Headquarters If Convenient	
On-Going Support: A,C,D,E,G,H,I/	. . . 12
EXPANSION PLANS:	
US:	. . . . .No
Canada:	. . . . .All Canada
Overseas:	. . . . No

SUPPLEMENTAL LISTING OF FRANCHISORS

ELECTRONIC TAX FILERS . . . . 1143-D Executive Circle, Cary, NC 27511
    Contact: Mr. Robert L. Wishon, Fran. Dev.; Tel: (800) 348-5852 (919) 469-0651
H & R BLOCK . . . . 4410 Main St., Kansas City, MO 64111
    Contact: Mr. Jerome Grossman, EVP; Tel: (816) 932-8481
H & R BLOCK CANADA . . . . 3440 Pharmacy Ave., # 3, Scarborough, ON M1W 2P8   CAN
    Contact: Mr. Irving Bonar, VP; Tel: (416) 493-2244
INCOTAX SYSTEMS . . . . 809 Lucerne Ave., Lake Worth, FL 33460
    Contact: President; Tel: (305) 588-6717
PINNACLE 1 INTERNATIONAL . . . . 3350 Lenape St., N. Charleston, SC 29405
    Contact: Mr. Bob Roe, CEO; Tel: (803) 744-5861
RELIABLE BUSINESS SYSTEMS . . . . 19 Ransom Rd., Newton Square, MA 02159
    Contact: Mr. Michael Licker, President; Tel: (617) 244-4166
SOLUTION 2000 . . . . 1895 est, rue Beaubien, Montreal, PQ H2G 1L8   CAN
    Contact: Mr. Francois Poirier, GM; Tel: (514) 722-4284
TAX MAN . . . . 678 Massachusetts Ave., Cambridge, MA 02139
    Contact: Mr. Gerald S. Garon; Tel: (617) 868-1374
TAX OFFICES OF AMERICA/HEALTH CLUBS . . . . Box 4098, Waterbury, CT 06704
    Contact: Mr. Gregg Nolan, Fran. Dir.; Tel: (203) 879-4675

TAXRUSH REFUND SERVICES . . . . 1345 Pembina Highway, Winnipeg, MB R3T 2B6   CAN
Contact: President; Tel: (204) 284-1806

CHAPTER 12

BUSINESS: MISCELLANEOUS

ADVANCED BUSINESS CONCEPTS

145 N. Second Ave., # 5
Oakdale, CA 95361
TEL: (800) 543-3976 (209) 848-9000
FAX: (209) 848-9009
Mr. Norman H. Cole, President

Aggressive and effective sales management will earn you an exclusive territory as large as your abilities and desires. We need top notch sales professionals to offer our program to business owners. Our sales systems and products have been proven over the past 7 years. Call today for more information.

HISTORY: . . . .
Established in 1986; . . 1st Franchised in 1991
Company-Owned Units (As of 8/31/1992): . .0
Franchised Units (As of 8/31/1992): 6
Total Units (As of 8/31/1992): 6
Projected New Units for 1993: 12
Distribution: US-6;Can-0;Overseas-0
North America: . . . . 4 States
Concentration: . . . 2 in CA, 1 in WA, 1 in UT
Registered: . . . . .CA,NY,WA
. . . .
Type Space: . . . . Executive Office;~750 SF

FINANCIAL: Earnings Claim: . .No
Cash Investment: $35-50K
Total Investment: $50-65K
Fees: Franchise - $15K
 Royalty: 0%, Advert: 0%
Contract Periods (Yrs.): 10/10
Area Development Agreement: . .No
Sub-Franchise Contract: . . . . .No
Expand in Territory: . . . . . . Yes
Passive Ownership: . . . . .Allowed
Encourage Conversions: . . . . NA
Average # Employees: . . 4 FT, 4 PT

FRANCHISOR TRAINING/SUPPORT:
Financial Assistance Provided: . . . . .No
Site Selection Assistance: . . . . .NA
Lease Negotiation Assistance: . . . . .No
Co-operative Advertising: . . . . .No
Training: . . . . . Home Stuty Plus 3 Days,
 . . . . 6 Days and 3 Days for Franchisee
On-Going Support: A,B,C,D,E,I/ 5
EXPANSION PLANS:
US: . . . . .All US
Canada: . . . . .No
Overseas: . . . . No

MISCELLANEOUS BUSINESS SYSTEMS

	1989	1990	1991	Percentage Change 90/89	91/90
Total Number of Establishments:					
Company-Owned	722	827	1,130	14.54%	36.64%
Franchisee-Owned	18,805	22,734	24,158	20.89%	6.26%
Total	19,527	23,561	25,288	20.66%	7.33%
Ratio of Total Establishments:					
Company-Owned	3.7%	3.5%	4.5%		
Franchisee-Owned	96.3%	96.5%	95.5%		
Total	100.0%	100.0%	100.0%		
Total Sales ($000):					
Company-Owned	405,941	428,914	471,917	5.66%	10.03%
Franchisee-Owned	2,948,940	3,064,856	3,315,372	3.93%	8.17%
Total	3,354,881	3,493,770	3,787,289	4.14%	8.40%
Ratio of Total Sales:					
Company-Owned	12.1%	12.3%	12.5%		
Franchisee-Owned	87.9%	87.7%	87.5%		
Total	100.0%	100.0%	100.0%		
Average Sales Per Unit ($000):					
Company-Owned	562	519	418	-7.76%	-19.48%
Franchisee-Owned	157	135	137	-14.03%	1.80%
Total	172	148	150	-13.69%	1.00%
Relative Average Sales Ratio:	358.5%	384.7%	304.3%		

	Number Of Employees		Employees Per Unit		Avg. Sales Per Employee
Total 1989 Employment:					
Company-Owned	15,420		21.4		$26,326
Franchisee-Owned	49,247		2.6		$59,881
Total	64,667		3.3		$51,879
Relative Employee Performance Ratios:			815.5%		44.0%

	1st Quartile		Median		4th Quartile
Average 1989 Total Investment:					
Company-Owned	$25,000		$60,000		$150,000
Franchisee-Owned	$22,500		$51,000		$100,000
Single Unit Franchise Fee	$10,000		$17,000		$25,000
Mult. Unit Franchise Fee	$10,500		$15,500		$30,000
Franchise Start-Up Cost	$15,000		$25,000		$50,000

Source: Franchising In The Economy 1991, IFA Educational Foundation & Horwath International.

AMERICAN BUSINESS CENTERS INTERNATIONAL

520 W. Hwy. 436, # 1180
Altamonte Springs, FL 32714
TEL: (407) 682-8660 C
FAX: (407) 774-8103
Ms. Kelli M. Yardley, VP Fran. Support

Mini-suite and conference room rental, with all the office support services required to support small- to medium-size businesses and professional business people.

HISTORY:	FINANCIAL: Earnings Claim: . .No	FRANCHISOR TRAINING/SUPPORT:
Established in 1992; . . 1st Franchised in 1992	Cash Investment: . . . . . . $~50K	Financial Assistance Provided: . . . Yes(I)
Company-Owned Units (As of 8/31/1992): . .1	Total Investment: . . . . . . $~75K	Site Selection Assistance: . . . . . . .Yes
Franchised Units (As of 8/31/1992): 1	Fees: Franchise - $25K	Lease Negotiation Assistance: . . . . .Yes
Total Units (As of 8/31/1992): 2	Royalty: $3.00, Advert: $2.00	Co-operative Advertising: . . . . . . .NA
Projected New Units for 1993: 10	Contract Periods (Yrs.): 10/10	Training: . . . . 1 Wk. Headquarters, 1 Wk.
Distribution: US-1;Can-0;Overseas-1	Area Development Agreement: Yes/5	. . On-Site Both Before & After Opening
North America: . . . . .1 State	Sub-Franchise Contract: . . . . .No	On-Going Support: C,D,E,G,H,I/ 5
Concentration: . . . . 1 in FL	Expand in Territory: . . . . . . Yes	EXPANSION PLANS:
Registered: . . . . .FL	Passive Ownership: . . . Discouraged	US: . . . . All US
. . . .	Encourage Conversions: . . . . . Yes	Canada: . . . . .All Canada
Type Space: . . . . . .FS, SF, SC;~~3,000 SF	Average # Employees: . . . . . .2 FT	Overseas: . . .S. America and EUR

AMERICAN INSTITUTE OF SMALL BUSINESS

7515 Wayzata Blvd., # 201
Minneapolis, MN 55426
TEL: (800) 328-2906 (612) 545-7001
FAX: (612) 545-7020
Mr. Max Fallek, President

THE AMERICAN INSTITUTE OF SMALL BUSINESS provides educational materials, including books, on Small Business and Entrepreneurship. It also provides a seminar for training people on how to set up and operate their own small business. THE INSTITUTE also supplies business software sold by franchisees.

HISTORY:	FINANCIAL: Earnings Claim: . . .	FRANCHISOR TRAINING/SUPPORT:
Established in 1985; . . 1st Franchised in 1988	Cash Investment: $5K	Financial Assistance Provided: . . . . .No
Company-Owned Units (As of 8/31/1992): . .1	Total Investment: $10K	Site Selection Assistance: . . . . . . .Yes
Franchised Units (As of 8/31/1992): 5	Fees: Franchise - $5K	Lease Negotiation Assistance: . . . .NA
Total Units (As of 8/31/1992): 6	Royalty: 0%, Advert: 0%	Co-operative Advertising: . . . . . . .NA
Projected New Units for 1993:	Contract Periods (Yrs.): . . .2/Varies	Training: . . . . 2 Days Headquarters
Distribution: US-6;Can-0;Overseas-0	Area Development Agreement: .No	. . . .
North America: . . . . 4 States	Sub-Franchise Contract: . . . . .No	On-Going Support: D,E,I/ 8
Concentration: . . . .1 in MN, 1 in CO, 1 in IL	Expand in Territory: . . . . . . Yes	EXPANSION PLANS:
Registered: . . . . MN	Passive Ownership: . . . . . .Allowed	US: . . . . All US
. . . .	Encourage Conversions: . . . . . NA	Canada: . . . . .All Canada
Type Space: . . . . ;~ SF	Average # Employees: . . . . . .1 PT	Overseas: . . . . .Yes

AMERICAN LENDERS SERVICE CO.

P.O. Box 7238
Odessa, TX 79760
TEL: (915) 332-0361
FAX: (915) 332-1065
Mr. Jim Golden, President

AMERICAN LENDERS SERVICE CO. is a national network of professional collateral recovery agencies, supplying repossession, investigation and collateral liquidation services to commercial lenders.

HISTORY:	FINANCIAL: Earnings Claim: . .No	FRANCHISOR TRAINING/SUPPORT:
Established in 1979; . . 1st Franchised in 1979	Cash Investment: $35-199K	Financial Assistance Provided: . . .Yes(D)
Company-Owned Units (As of 8/31/1992): . .2	Total Investment: $35-199K	Site Selection Assistance: . . . . . . .Yes
Franchised Units (As of 8/31/1992): 123	Fees: Franchise - $2K	Lease Negotiation Assistance: . . . . . No
Total Units (As of 8/31/1992): 125	Royalty: 5%, Advert: 0%	Co-operative Advertising: . . . . . . .NA
Projected New Units for 1993: 26	Contract Periods (Yrs.): 10/10	Training: . . . . . .2-12 Wks. Headquarters
Distribution: US-125;Can-0;Overseas-0	Area Development Agreement: .No	. . . .
North America: . . . . 46 States	Sub-Franchise Contract: . . . . .No	On-Going Support: b,d,E,G,h/ 46
Concentration: . . . 10 in FL, 9 in TX, 7 in CA	Expand in Territory: . . . . . . .No	EXPANSION PLANS:
Registered: . . . CA,FL,IL,IN,MD,MI,MN,NY	Passive Ownership: . . . Discouraged	US: . . . . All US
. . . . OR,RI,VA,WA,WI	Encourage Conversions: . . . . . Yes	Canada: . . . . No
Type Space: . . . . . . Office + Storage;~ SF	Average # Employees: . . 3 FT, 1 PT	Overseas: . . . . No

AMERICAN NATIONAL FIDELITY GROUP

300 Continental Blvd., # 195
El Segundo, CA 90245
TEL: (310) 416-9000
FAX: (310) 416-9643
Mr. Barry Lastinger. EVP

Mobile (on-site) payroll check cashing service.

HISTORY:	FINANCIAL: Earnings Claim: . .No	FRANCHISOR TRAINING/SUPPORT:
Established in 1990; . . . 1st Franchised in 1990	Cash Investment: $45K	Financial Assistance Provided: . . . Yes(I)
Company-Owned Units (As of 8/31/1992): . .3	Total Investment: $110-135K	Site Selection Assistance: . . . . . . .NA
Franchised Units (As of 8/31/1992): 28	Fees: Franchise - $29.5K	Lease Negotiation Assistance: . . . . .NA
Total Units (As of 8/31/1992): 31	Royalty: 5%, Advert: 0%	Co-operative Advertising: . . . . . . .NA
Projected New Units for 1993: 24	Contract Periods (Yrs.): . . . 5/5/5/5	Training: . . . . .1 Wk. Headquarters,
Distribution: US-31;Can-0;Overseas-0	Area Development Agreement: Yes/5	. . . . .2 Wks. Franchisee Area
North America: . . . . 23 States	Sub-Franchise Contract: . . . . . Yes	On-Going Support: B,C,D,F,G,H,I/ 7
Concentration: . . . 5 in CA, 3 in FL, 3 in OH	Expand in Territory: . . . . . . Yes	EXPANSION PLANS:
Registered: . . .CA,FL,IN,MD,MI,MN,OR,RI	Passive Ownership: . . . . . .Allowed	US: . . . . All US
. . . . VA,WI,DC	Encourage Conversions: . . . . NA	Canada: . . . . .No
Type Space: . . . . NA;~ SF	Average # Employees: . . 1 FT, 1 PT	Overseas: . . . . No

BUSINESS AMERICA

250 Mt. Lebanon Blvd.
Pittsburgh, PA 15234
TEL: (800) 451-5723 (412) 276-7701
FAX: (412) 276-7702
Mr. Thomas D. Atkins, President

Confidential listing and selling of businesses - also sells various start-up franchises and business opportunities.

HISTORY:	FINANCIAL: Earnings Claim: . .No	FRANCHISOR TRAINING/SUPPORT:
Established in 1984; . . 1st Franchised in 1985	Cash Investment: $10K	Financial Assistance Provided: . . . . .NA
Company-Owned Units (As of 8/31/1992): . .0	Total Investment: $15K	Site Selection Assistance: . . . . . . .NA
Franchised Units (As of 8/31/1992): 4	Fees: Franchise - $5K	Lease Negotiation Assistance: . . . . .NA
Total Units (As of 8/31/1992): 4	Royalty: 0%, Advert: 0%	Co-operative Advertising: . . . . . . .NA
Projected New Units for 1993: 5	Contract Periods (Yrs.): 5/5	Training: . . . . 2 Days Headquarters
Distribution: US-4;Can-0;Overseas-0	Area Development Agreement: . .No	. . . .
North America: . . . . 2 States	Sub-Franchise Contract: . . . . .No	On-Going Support: c,d,e/ 2
Concentration: . . . . 3 in PA, 1 in CO	Expand in Territory: . . . . . . Yes	EXPANSION PLANS:
Registered:	Passive Ownership: . . . Not Allowed	US: . . . . All US
. . . .	Encourage Conversions: . . . . NA	Canada: . . . . .Yes
Type Space: . . . . Office;~500 SF	Average # Employees: . . . . .2 PT	Overseas: . . . . No

BUSINESS CONNECTION, THE

1873 S. Bellaire St., # 600
Denver, CO 80222
TEL: (800) 275-9000 (303) 782-1865
FAX: (303) 756-4299
Mr. Johnny Wilson, President

A data base matching service for business/franchise buyers and sellers. A media-based electronic computer matching of qualified business prospects.

HISTORY:	FINANCIAL: Earnings Claim: . .No	FRANCHISOR TRAINING/SUPPORT:
Established in 1990; . . . 1st Franchised in 1992	Cash Investment: $50K	Financial Assistance Provided: . . . . .No
Company-Owned Units (As of 8/31/1992): . .1	Total Investment: $75-100K	Site Selection Assistance: . . . . . . .Yes
Franchised Units (As of 8/31/1992): 0	Fees: Franchise - $25K	Lease Negotiation Assistance: . . . .Yes
Total Units (As of 8/31/1992): 1	Royalty: 7%, Advert: 2%	Co-operative Advertising: . . . . . . .Yes
Projected New Units for 1993: 5	Contract Periods (Yrs.): 10/10	Training: . . . . .1 Wk. Headquarters,
Distribution: US-1;Can-0;Overseas-0	Area Development Agreement: . .No	. . . . 2 Wks. On-Site
North America: . . . . .1 State	Sub-Franchise Contract: . . . . .No	On-Going Support: A,C,D,E,G,H,I/ 4
Concentration: . . . . 1 in CO	Expand in Territory: . . . . . . Yes	EXPANSION PLANS:
Registered:	Passive Ownership: . . . . . .Allowed	US: . . . . All US
. . . .	Encourage Conversions: . . . . Yes	Canada: . . . . .All Canada
Type Space: . Office Building;~900-1,400 SF	Average # Employees: . . . . . .4 FT	Overseas: . . . . No

CA$H PLUS

4020 Chicago Ave.
Riverside, CA 92507
TEL: (800) 729-3142 (714) 682-2274 C
FAX: (714) 752-9316
Mr. John Collins, Int'l. Dev. Dir.

For those of you looking for the ideal business, look no further!. With a CA$H PLUS check cashing franchise, there are no accounts receivable, no returns, no spoilage, no inventory, low overhead and high returns.

HISTORY:	FINANCIAL: Earnings Claim: . .No	FRANCHISOR TRAINING/SUPPORT:
Established in 1984; . . 1st Franchised in 1988	Cash Investment: $35-45K	Financial Assistance Provided: . . . . . No
Company-Owned Units (As of 8/31/1992): . .1	Total Investment: $40-60K	Site Selection Assistance: . . . . . . .Yes
Franchised Units (As of 8/31/1992): 16	Fees: Franchise - $14.5K	Lease Negotiation Assistance: . . . . .Yes
Total Units (As of 8/31/1992): 17	Royalty: 6%, Advert: 0%	Co-operative Advertising: . . . . No
Projected New Units for 1993: 10	Contract Periods (Yrs.): 5/5	Training: . . . . Period Varies at
Distribution: US-17;Can-0;Overseas-0	Area Development Agreement: Yes/5	. . . . Headquarters
North America: . . . . 4 States	Sub-Franchise Contract: . . . . Yes	On-Going Support: B,C,D,E,F,G,H,I/ . . . 4
Concentration: . . . . CA, NV, KY	Expand in Territory: . . . . Yes	EXPANSION PLANS:
Registered: . . . . All States	Passive Ownership: . . . Discouraged	US: . . . . All US Exc. NY
. . . .	Encourage Conversions: . . . . . Yes	Canada: . . . . No
Type Space: . . . . . . SC;~1,000-1,400 SF	Average # Employees: . . 2 FT, 1 PT	Overseas: . . . . No

CANADIAN PROCESS SERVING

25 Hughson St. S., # 502
Hamilton, ON L8N 2A5 CAN
TEL: (800) 465-7378 (416) 529-2770
FAX: (416) 529-2770
Ms. Sandra Muys, Office Mgr.

Our company is privately owned and run, providing the serving of legal papers to individuals, businesses, etc. This is a home-based business, with flexible hours, and an excellent earning potential. As a franchise owner, you can expect immediate revenue in our fast-growing company.

HISTORY:	FINANCIAL: Earnings Claim: . .No	FRANCHISOR TRAINING/SUPPORT:
Established in 1986; . . 1st Franchised in 1991	Cash Investment: $5K	Financial Assistance Provided: . . .Yes(D)
Company-Owned Units (As of 8/31/1992): . .1	Total Investment: . . . . . . $Varies	Site Selection Assistance: . . . . . . .Yes
Franchised Units (As of 8/31/1992): 7	Fees: Franchise - $5K	Lease Negotiation Assistance: . . . . .NA
Total Units (As of 8/31/1992): 8	Royalty: 7%, Advert: 1%	Co-operative Advertising: . . . . .Yes
Projected New Units for 1993: 20	Contract Periods (Yrs.): 5/5	Training: . . . . 1-2 Wks. Headquarters and
Distribution: US-0;Can-8;Overseas-0	Area Development Agreement: Yes/5	. . . . Location of Franchisee
North America: . . . . .1 Province	Sub-Franchise Contract: . . . . . Yes	On-Going Support: A,B,C,D,E,G,H,I/ . . 4
Concentration: . . . . 8 in ON	Expand in Territory: . . . . Yes	EXPANSION PLANS:
Registered:	Passive Ownership: . . . . . .Allowed	US: . . . . No
. . . .	Encourage Conversions:	Canada: . . . . .All Exc. PQ, AB
Type Space: . . . . Home Based;~ SF	Average # Employees: . . 1 FT, 1 PT	Overseas: . . . . No

CHECK EXPRESS USA

5201 W. Kennedy Blvd., # 750
Tampa, FL 33609
TEL: (800) 521-8211 (813) 289-2888
FAX: (813) 289-2999
Mr. Michael Riordon, Dir. Fran. Sales

Complete computerized check cashing service. All types of checks: payroll, government, personal, out of town, money orders, insurance drafts. Other services include postal boxes, Western Union wire transfers, money orders, income tax electronic filing and tax advance loan program. Proprietary computer system.

HISTORY: . . . . IFA	FINANCIAL: Earnings Claim: . .No	FRANCHISOR TRAINING/SUPPORT:
Established in 1982; . . 1st Franchised in 1988	Cash Investment: $50-100K	Financial Assistance Provided: . . . Yes(I)
Company-Owned Units (As of 8/31/1992): . 17	Total Investment: $115-130K	Site Selection Assistance: . . . . . . .Yes
Franchised Units (As of 8/31/1992): 39	Fees: Franchise - $24.5K	Lease Negotiation Assistance: . . . . .Yes
Total Units (As of 8/31/1992): 56	Royalty: 5%/$750, Advert: . . . 3%	Co-operative Advertising: . . . . .Yes
Projected New Units for 1993: 25	Contract Periods (Yrs.): 15/5	Training: . . . . 2 Wks. Headquarters
Distribution: US-56;Can-0;Overseas-0	Area Development Agreement: Yes/15	. . . .
North America: . . . . 14 States	Sub-Franchise Contract: . . . . . No	On-Going Support: B,C,D,E,F,G,H,I/ . . . 7
Concentration: . . .16 in FL, 4 in WA, 3 in CA	Expand in Territory: . . . . Yes	EXPANSION PLANS:
Registered: . . .CA,FL,HI,IN,MD,MI,MN,ND	Passive Ownership: . . . . . .Allowed	US: . . . . All US
. . . . .OR,RI,SD,VA,WA,WI,DC	Encourage Conversions: . . . . Yes	Canada: . . . . .Ontario
Type Space: . . . . . FS, SF, SC;~1,000 SF	Average # Employees: . . . . . .4 FT	Overseas: . . . . No

CHECKCARE SYSTEMS

3907 Macon Rd., P. O. Box 9636
Columbus, GA 31908
TEL: (706) 563-3660
FAX: (706) 563-3713
Mr. Mike Stalnaker, VP Fran. Dev.

CHECKCARE SYSTEMS is the fastest-growing check guarantee and verification company in the US. Proprietary software and hardware configuration included in total investment. Our national account base makes this opportunity a "must investigate."

HISTORY:	FINANCIAL: Earnings Claim: . Yes	FRANCHISOR TRAINING/SUPPORT:
Established in 1982; . . 1st Franchised in 1984	Cash Investment: $62-98K	Financial Assistance Provided: . . . Yes(I)
Company-Owned Units (As of 8/31/1992): . .0	Total Investment: $70-120K	Site Selection Assistance: . . . . . . .Yes
Franchised Units (As of 8/31/1992): 49	Fees: Franchise - $15-45K	Lease Negotiation Assistance: . . . . .Yes
Total Units (As of 8/31/1992): 49	Royalty: 5%, Advert: 1/2%	Co-operative Advertising: . . . . .NA
Projected New Units for 1993: 8	Contract Periods (Yrs.): 7/7	Training: . . . . 2 Wks. Headquarters
Distribution: US-49;Can-0;Overseas-0	Area Development Agreement: Yes/1.5	. . . .
North America: . . . . 20 States	Sub-Franchise Contract: . . . . .No	On-Going Support: c,d,G,h/ 9
Concentration: . . . .7 in FL, 6 in GA, 4 in AL	Expand in Territory: . . . . .No	EXPANSION PLANS:
Registered: . . . FL,IL,IN,MD,MI,MN,VA,DC	Passive Ownership: . . . Discouraged	US: . . . .Northwest, Southwest,Midwest
. . . .	Encourage Conversions: . . . . . Yes	Canada: . . . . No
Type Space: . . . . FS;~2,000 SF	Average # Employees: . .10 FT, 3 PT	Overseas: . . . . No

CORPORATE FINANCE ASSOCIATES

1801 Broadway, # 1200
Denver, CO 80202
TEL: (303) 296-6300
FAX: (303) 296-2838
Mr. James Baker, Natl. VP Mktg.

We assist mid-sized businesses with strategic decisions, sell-merge-finance decisions and help to improve profit. We do acquisition search work for companies seeking expansion. We prepare companies for sale or merger.

HISTORY:	FINANCIAL: Earnings Claim: . .No	FRANCHISOR TRAINING/SUPPORT:
Established in 1956; . . 1st Franchised in 1960	Cash Investment: $15-100K	Financial Assistance Provided: . . . . .No
Company-Owned Units (As of 8/31/1992): . .1	Total Investment: $15-100K	Site Selection Assistance: . . . . .No
Franchised Units (As of 8/31/1992): 41	Fees: Franchise - $15K	Lease Negotiation Assistance: . . . . . .No
Total Units (As of 8/31/1992): 42	Royalty: 7%, Advert: 0%	Co-operative Advertising: . . . . .No
Projected New Units for 1993: 10	Contract Periods (Yrs.): 1/1	Training: . . . . 3 Days Headquarters,
Distribution: US-32;Can-1;Overseas-9	Area Development Agreement: . .No	. . . 3 Days/Yr. Region. 3 Days/Yr. Natl.
North America: . . . . 20 States	Sub-Franchise Contract: . . . . . .No	On-Going Support: G,h/ 5
Concentration: . . . 5 in CA, 4 in OH, 2 in CO	Expand in Territory: . . . . .No	EXPANSION PLANS:
Registered:	Passive Ownership: . . . Not Allowed	US: . . . . All US
. . . .	Encourage Conversions: . . . . . . Yes	Canada: . . . . .All Canada
Type Space: . . . . NA;~NA SF	Average # Employees: . . 3 FT, 1 PT	Overseas: . . . . Yes

CREATIVE ASSET MANAGEMENT

120 Wood Ave. S., # 300
Iselin, NJ 08830
TEL: (800) 245-0530 (908) 549-1011
FAX: (908) 603-7705
Mr. Rich Rodman, President

CREATIVE ASSET MANAGEMENT is the nation's first investment advisory franchise. Income is not dependent on commission, as it is fee-based. Complete training and on-going support are provided for this unique program.

HISTORY:	FINANCIAL: Earnings Claim: . .No	FRANCHISOR TRAINING/SUPPORT:
Established in 1988; . . 1st Franchised in 1988	Cash Investment: $15-20K	Financial Assistance Provided: . . . Yes(I)
Company-Owned Units (As of 8/31/1992): . .0	Total Investment: $15-20K	Site Selection Assistance: . . . . .No
Franchised Units (As of 8/31/1992): 35	Fees: Franchise - $12.5-17.5K	Lease Negotiation Assistance: . . . . .No
Total Units (As of 8/31/1992): 35	Royalty: $300/Mo., Advert: . . 0%	Co-operative Advertising: . . . . .No
Projected New Units for 1993: 40	Contract Periods (Yrs.): 15/15	Training: . . . . 3 Days Headquarters
Distribution: US-35;Can-0;Overseas-0	Area Development Agreement: . .No	
North America: . . . . 12 States	Sub-Franchise Contract: . . . . .No	On-Going Support: g,H,I/ 4
Concentration: . . . .8 in NJ, 4 in NY, 3 in CT	Expand in Territory: . . . . Yes	EXPANSION PLANS:
Registered: . . . . FL,IL,MD,MN,NY	Passive Ownership: . . . . .Allowed	US: . . . . All US
. . . .	Encourage Conversions: . . . . . Yes	Canada: . . . . No
Type Space: . . . . . Co-op Office;~250 SF	Average # Employees: . . . . . .1 FT	Overseas: . . . . No

EMPIRE BUSINESS BROKERS

3465 Broadway
Buffalo, NY 14227
TEL: (716) 681-3088
FAX: (716) 681-6483
Mr. Nicholas R. Gugliuzza, President

On a local and national sales level, we sell existing businesses and business opportunities. We assist buyers, seller and others seeking to raise capital as financial brokers on a fee basis.

HISTORY: . . . .
Established in 1981; . . 1st Franchised in 1989
Company-Owned Units (As of 8/31/1992): . .2
Franchised Units (As of 8/31/1992): 13
Total Units (As of 8/31/1992): 15
Projected New Units for 1993: 5
Distribution: US-14;Can-1;Overseas-0
North America: . . . . . .7 States, 1 Province
Concentration: . . . 3 in NY, 2 in NC, 1 in OH
Registered: . . . . .All
. . . .
Type Space: . . . . Office;~400 SF

FINANCIAL: Earnings Claim: . .No
Cash Investment: $10-29K
Total Investment: $10-29K
Fees: Franchise - $15K
Royalty: 0%, Advert: 0%
Contract Periods (Yrs.): . . . .
Area Development Agreement: . .No
Sub-Franchise Contract: . . . . .No
Expand in Territory: . . . . . . Yes
Passive Ownership: . . . . . .Allowed
Encourage Conversions: . . . . Yes
Average # Employees: . . 2 FT, 1 PT

FRANCHISOR TRAINING/SUPPORT:
Financial Assistance Provided: . . .Yes(D)
Site Selection Assistance: . . . . . . .Yes
Lease Negotiation Assistance: . . . .Yes
Co-operative Advertising: . . . . . . .Yes
Training: . . . . .1 Wk. Home Office,
. . . . .3 Days Local Office
On-Going Support: c,d,E,h/ 4
EXPANSION PLANS:
US: . . . . .All US
Canada: . . . . .All Canada
Overseas: . . . . No

HQ BUSINESS CENTERS

120 Montgomery St., # 1040
San Francisco, CA 94104
TEL: (800) 950-3004 (415) 781-7811
FAX: (415) 781-8034
Ms. Kitty McEntee, Mgr. of Devel.

Office space, full- or part-time; business support services; and telecommunications in a shared office environment, with over 80 business centers throughout the US and Europe.

HISTORY: . . . . IFA
Established in 1967; . . 1st Franchised in 1977
Company-Owned Units (As of 8/31/1992): . .0
Franchised Units (As of 8/31/1992): 111
Total Units (As of 8/31/1992): 111
Projected New Units for 1993: 10
Distribution: US-98;Can-3;Overseas-10
North America: . . . . . 23 States, 1 Province
Concentration: . . . 25 in CA, 9 in FL, 9 in IL
Registered: . . . CA,FL,IL,IN,MD,MI,MN,NY
. . . . .OR,RI,VA,WA,WI,DC
Type Space: Class A Off. Bldg;~6,000-26,000 SF

FINANCIAL: Earnings Claim: . .No
Cash Investment: $70-250K
Total Investment: $1MM
Fees: Franchise - $30-50K
Royalty: 1%, Advert: 1/2%
Contract Periods (Yrs.): . . . .
Area Development Agreement: . Yes
Sub-Franchise Contract: . . . . .No
Expand in Territory: . . . . . . Yes
Passive Ownership: . . . Discouraged
Encourage Conversions: . . . . Yes
Average # Employees: . . 8 FT, 2 PT

FRANCHISOR TRAINING/SUPPORT:
Financial Assistance Provided: . . . . . No
Site Selection Assistance: . . . . No
Lease Negotiation Assistance: . . . . . No
Co-operative Advertising: . . . . . . .Yes
Training: . . . .
. . . .
On-Going Support: A,B,C,D,E,F,G,H,I/ 15
EXPANSION PLANS:
US: . . . . .All US
Canada: . . . . All
Overseas: . . . . .Yes

INTERNATIONAL MERGERS & ACQUISITIONS

4300 N. Miller Rd., # 220
Scottsdale, AZ 85251
TEL: (602) 990-3899
FAX: (602) 990-7480
Mr. Neil D. Lewis, President

International affiliation of members engaged in the profession of serving M & A-minded companies, offering consulting services, financing, M & A and other services of a distinctive nature.

HISTORY: . . . .
Established in 1969; . . 1st Franchised in 1979
Company-Owned Units (As of 8/31/1992): . .1
Franchised Units (As of 8/31/1992): 44
Total Units (As of 8/31/1992): 45
Projected New Units for 1993: 30
Distribution: US-43;Can-0;Overseas-2
North America: . . . . 18 States
Concentration: . . . 6 in AZ, 5 in SD, 3 in CO
Registered: . . . . .All
. . . .
Type Space: . . . . ;~NA SF

FINANCIAL: Earnings Claim: . .No
Cash Investment: $5K
Total Investment: . . . . . . $Varies
Fees: Franchise - $5K
Royalty: $375/Qtr, Advert: . . . . .
Contract Periods (Yrs.): 5/5
Area Development Agreement: . .No
Sub-Franchise Contract: . . . . .No
Expand in Territory: . . . . . . .No
Passive Ownership: . . . Not Allowed
Encourage Conversions: . . . . . NA
Average # Employees: . . . . . .1 PT

FRANCHISOR TRAINING/SUPPORT:
Financial Assistance Provided: . . . . . No
Site Selection Assistance: . . . . . . .NA
Lease Negotiation Assistance: . . . . .NA
Co-operative Advertising: . . . . No
Training: . . . . . As Needed Headquarters,
. . . . . As Needed Member's Location
On-Going Support: a,C,d,G,H/ 2
EXPANSION PLANS:
US: . . . . .All US
Canada: . . . . .All Canada
Overseas: . . . . .Yes

JAY ROBERTS & ASSOCIATES

81 N. Chicago St., # 105
Joliet, IL 60431
TEL: (312) 236-6640 (815) 722-0683
FAX: (815) 741-0148
Mr. John S. Meers, President

Consultants to turn-around or Chapter 11 clients. Loan brokers. Packagers of Government loans and grants.

HISTORY:	FINANCIAL: Earnings Claim: . .No	FRANCHISOR TRAINING/SUPPORT:
Established in 1965; . . 1st Franchised in 1970	Cash Investment: $1K	Financial Assistance Provided: . . . . .No
Company-Owned Units (As of 8/31/1992): . .2	Total Investment: $5K	Site Selection Assistance: . . . . . . .NA
Franchised Units (As of 8/31/1992): 20	Fees: Franchise - $1K	Lease Negotiation Assistance: . . . .NA
Total Units (As of 8/31/1992): 22	Royalty: 10%, Advert: 0%	Co-operative Advertising: . . . . . .NA
Projected New Units for 1993: 12	Contract Periods (Yrs.): 20/10	Training: . . . . .1 Day Headquarters
Distribution: US-22;Can-0;Overseas-0	Area Development Agreement: . .No	. . . .
North America: . . . . 16 States	Sub-Franchise Contract: . . . . .No	On-Going Support: G,H/ 6
Concentration: . . . . 3 in IL, 2 in PA, 2 in CA	Expand in Territory: . . . . Yes	EXPANSION PLANS:
Registered: IL	Passive Ownership: . . . Not Allowed	US: . . . . All US
. . . .	Encourage Conversions: . . . . . NA	Canada: . . . . .No
Type Space: . . . . NA;~NA SF	Average # Employees: . . 1 FT, 1 PT	Overseas: . . . . No

MANUFACTURING MANAGEMENT ASSOCIATES

1301 W. 22nd St., # 516
Oak Brook, IL 60521
TEL: (708) 575-8700
FAX: (708) 574-0309
Mr. Alan D. Anderson, President

MMA was started in 1982 and has grown to over $2.5 million by providing highly-skilled manufacturing consulting services to the small/medium-sized manufacturers. Its staff of 25 full-time consultants, plus formal agreements with other consulting firms (100 consultants) provide many of the skills and benefits found only with large firms, yet lower overhead translates into much lower rates than the big firms charge.

HISTORY:	FINANCIAL: Earnings Claim: . .No	FRANCHISOR TRAINING/SUPPORT:
Established in 1982; . . 1st Franchised in 1990	Cash Investment: $15-80K	Financial Assistance Provided: . . . . .No
Company-Owned Units (As of 8/31/1992): . .2	Total Investment: $15-80K	Site Selection Assistance: . . . . . . .Yes
Franchised Units (As of 8/31/1992): 0	Fees: Franchise - $5-50K	Lease Negotiation Assistance: . . . .No
Total Units (As of 8/31/1992): 2	Royalty: 5-9%, Advert: 0-1%	Co-operative Advertising: . . . . . . .Yes
Projected New Units for 1993: 2	Contract Periods (Yrs.): 10/5	Training: . . . . . .5 Days HQ, 3 Months at
Distribution: US-2;Can-0;Overseas-0	Area Development Agreement: . .No	. . Franchisee Location, ~4 Wks./Yr. HQ
North America: . . . . 2 States	Sub-Franchise Contract: . . . . .No	On-Going Support: C,D,E,H/ 25
Concentration: . . . . 1 in IL, 1 in IN	Expand in Territory: . . . . . . .No	EXPANSION PLANS:
Registered: . . . . .IL,IN,MI,MN,WI	Passive Ownership: . . . Discouraged	US: . . . . Middle 1/3 of US
. . . .	Encourage Conversions: . . . . . Yes	Canada: . . . . .No
Type Space: . . . . . . Office Building;~ SF	Average # Employees: . Initially 3 FT	Overseas: . . . . No

MONEY BROKER ONE

1097-C Irongate Ln.
Columbus, OH 43213
TEL: (614) 684-1440
FAX:
Mr. Raymond A. Strohl, President

Money broker, offering loans and financing to individuals, businesses and churches for financing almost any worthwhile project. We offer real estate loans and business loans and equipment leases. There is no upper limit on the size of the loans. We also act as a business broker regarding sales of businesses.

HISTORY:	FINANCIAL: Earnings Claim: . .No	FRANCHISOR TRAINING/SUPPORT:
Established in 1983; . . 1st Franchised in 1989	Cash Investment: . . . .$Varies	Financial Assistance Provided: . . . . .NA
Company-Owned Units (As of 8/31/1992): . .1	Total Investment: . . . .$Varies	Site Selection Assistance: . . . . . . .Yes
Franchised Units (As of 8/31/1992): 5	Fees: Franchise - . . . .$Varies	Lease Negotiation Assistance: . . . . .No
Total Units (As of 8/31/1992): 6	Royalty: Varies, Advert: 0%	Co-operative Advertising: . . . . . . .No
Projected New Units for 1993: 3	Contract Periods (Yrs.): 1/1	Training: . . . .
Distribution: US-6;Can-0;Overseas-0	Area Development Agreement: . .No	. . . .
North America: . . . . 5 States	Sub-Franchise Contract: . . . . .No	On-Going Support: / 1
Concentration: . . . 2 in OH, 1 in CA, 1 in FL	Expand in Territory: . . . . Yes	EXPANSION PLANS:
Registered: . . . . .CA,FL	Passive Ownership: . . . . . .Allowed	US: . . . . All US
. . . .	Encourage Conversions: . . . . . NA	Canada: . . . . .No
Type Space: . . . . .Leased Space;~Varies SF	Average # Employees: . . . . 1-2 FT	Overseas: . . . . No

NATIONAL FINANCIAL COMPANY

7332 Caverna Dr.
Hollywood, CA 90068
TEL: (800) 245-4627 (213) 969-0100
FAX: (213) 850-6406
Mr. Leonard vander Bie, President

Computer matches client's capital needs with sources of capital. Data base contains over 15,000 variable sources of capital. Consultants licensed by company have access to data base for their own clients, who are in need of capital. Consultants earn both retainer and finder's fees.

HISTORY:	FINANCIAL: Earnings Claim: . .No	FRANCHISOR TRAINING/SUPPORT:
Established in 1957; . . 1st Franchised in 1957	Cash Investment: $18K	Financial Assistance Provided: . . . . . No
Company-Owned Units (As of 8/31/1992): . .1	Total Investment: $18K	Site Selection Assistance: . . . . . . .Yes
Franchised Units (As of 8/31/1992): 608	Fees: Franchise - $18K	Lease Negotiation Assistance: . . . . .Yes
Total Units (As of 8/31/1992): 609	Royalty: 0%, Advert: 0%	Co-operative Advertising: . . . . No
Projected New Units for 1993: 50	Contract Periods (Yrs.): 4/4	Training: . . . . 3 Days On-Site
Distribution: US-564;Can-0;Overseas-45	Area Development Agreement: . .No	. . . .
North America: . . . . 50 States	Sub-Franchise Contract: . . . . .No	On-Going Support: A,F,G,I/ 14
Concentration:	Expand in Territory: . . . . Yes	EXPANSION PLANS:
Registered:	Passive Ownership: . . . Not Allowed	US: . . . . .All US
. . . .	Encourage Conversions: . . . . .No	Canada: . . . . .All Canada
Type Space: . . . . Home Based, OB;~600 SF	Average # Employees: . . . . 14 FT	Overseas: . . . . Anywhere

PARA-LEGAL-OFFICE

3116 E. Shea Blvd., # 247
Phoenix, AZ 85028
TEL: (602) 996-4450
FAX: (602) 996-4450
Mr. Gerd-D. Linke, VP

Computerized document preparation service in the following areas: bankruptcy, divorces, wills, trust, corporations, real estate transfer, homesteads, insurance forms, credit counseling, small claims court, worker's compensation, personal injury, SBA loans, etc.

HISTORY:	FINANCIAL: Earnings Claim: . .No	FRANCHISOR TRAINING/SUPPORT:
Established in 1991; . . 1st Franchised in 1991	Cash Investment: $20K	Financial Assistance Provided: . . . . .No
Company-Owned Units (As of 8/31/1992): . .0	Total Investment: $20K	Site Selection Assistance: . . . . . . .Yes
Franchised Units (As of 8/31/1992): 3	Fees: Franchise - $10K	Lease Negotiation Assistance: . . . .Yes
Total Units (As of 8/31/1992): 3	Royalty: 8%, Advert: 2%	Co-operative Advertising: . . . . . . .Yes
Projected New Units for 1993: 2	Contract Periods (Yrs.): 10/10	Training: . . . . 3 Days On-Site
Distribution: US-3;Can-0;Overseas-0	Area Development Agreement: . .No	. . . .
North America: . . . . .1 State	Sub-Franchise Contract: . . . . .No	On-Going Support: b,C,D,E,G,H/ 2
Concentration: . . . . 3 in AZ	Expand in Territory: . . . . Yes	EXPANSION PLANS:
Registered:	Passive Ownership: . . . . . .Allowed	US: . . . . All US
. . . .	Encourage Conversions: . . . . .No	Canada: . . . . No
Type Space: . . . . . . .Office Suite;~40 SF	Average # Employees: . . 1 FT, 1 PT	Overseas: . . . . No

PARSON-BISHOP SERVICES

7870 Camargo Rd.
Cincinnati, OH 45243
TEL: (800) 543-0468 (513) 561-5560
FAX: (513) 527-8910
Mr. Lou Bishop, President

Creative plans and systems to collect and control slow accounts receivable. PB plans solve this perennial problem for an average cost of 6% vs. 25% from the typical competition. Long-term repeat business. Perfect for the sales-oriented, professional person.

HISTORY: . . . . IFA	FINANCIAL: Earnings Claim: . .No	FRANCHISOR TRAINING/SUPPORT:
Established in 1973; . . 1st Franchised in 1986	Cash Investment: $16-39.5K	Financial Assistance Provided: . . . . .No
Company-Owned Units (As of 8/31/1992): . .0	Total Investment: $20-46K	Site Selection Assistance: . . . . . . .NA
Franchised Units (As of 8/31/1992): 59	Fees: Franchise - $16-39.5K	Lease Negotiation Assistance: . . . . .NA
Total Units (As of 8/31/1992): 59	Royalty: 0%, Advert: 0%	Co-operative Advertising: . . . . . . .Yes
Projected New Units for 1993: 10	Contract Periods (Yrs.): 5/5	Training: . . . . 1 Wk. Class Headquarters,
Distribution: US-59;Can-0;Overseas-0	Area Development Agreement: Yes/5	. . . . 3 Days On-Site, 3 Days On-Site
North America: . . . . 23 States	Sub-Franchise Contract: . . . . Yes	On-Going Support: a,b,C,D,,G,H/ 35
Concentration: . . . 6 in OH, 4 in NY, 4 in CA	Expand in Territory: . . . . Yes	EXPANSION PLANS:
Registered: . . . CA,FL,IL,IN,MI,MN,NY,VA	Passive Ownership: . . . Not Allowed	US: . . . . .All US
. . . . WA,WI	Encourage Conversions: . . . . .No	Canada: . . . . No
Type Space: . . . . NA;~NA SF	Average # Employees: . . . . 1-2 PT	Overseas: . . . . No

PEOPLE HELPING PEOPLE

3101 N. Central Ave., # 920
Bellevue, WA 85012
TEL: (602) 420-1490
FAX: (602) 266-0495
Mr. John Hananay, President

To be the leader in networking business leads, people, and ideas for the purpose of increasing business and development friendships.

HISTORY:	FINANCIAL: Earnings Claim: . .No	FRANCHISOR TRAINING/SUPPORT:
Established in 1992; . . 1st Franchised in 1992	Cash Investment: $2.5K	Financial Assistance Provided: . . . . . No
Company-Owned Units (As of 8/31/1992): . .0	Total Investment: $2.5-5K	Site Selection Assistance: . . . . .Yes
Franchised Units (As of 8/31/1992): 1	Fees: Franchise - $2K	Lease Negotiation Assistance: . . . .Yes
Total Units (As of 8/31/1992): 1	Royalty: 7%, Advert: 2%	Co-operative Advertising: . . . . . . .Yes
Projected New Units for 1993: 5	Contract Periods (Yrs.): 10/10	Training: . . . . . . 1 Day Franchisee Area
Distribution: US-1;Can-0;Overseas-0	Area Development Agreement: . .No	. . . .
North America: . . . . .1 State	Sub-Franchise Contract: . . . . . Yes	On-Going Support: B,D,G,H/ 1
Concentration: . . . . 1 in AZ	Expand in Territory: . . . . Yes	EXPANSION PLANS:
Registered:	Passive Ownership: . . . Discouraged	US: . . . . .All US
. . . .	Encourage Conversions: . . . . .No	Canada: . . . . .Yes
Type Space: . . . . NA;~NA SF	Average # Employees: . . 1 FT, 4 PT	Overseas: . . . . .Yes

PROVENTURE BUSINESS GROUP

79 Parkingway
Quincy, MA 02169
TEL: (617) 773-0530
FAX: (617) 444-8278
Mr. William J. Tedoldi, President

PROVENTURE is an all-inclusive, New England-based business brokerage, consulting and management company. The Group lists and sells going businesses, franchises (up to $25 million in value) and other business opportunities on a fee basis. Also offered is a moderately-priced consulting service for new franchise start-ups.

HISTORY:	FINANCIAL: Earnings Claim: . .No	FRANCHISOR TRAINING/SUPPORT:
Established in 1979; . . 1st Franchised in 1981	Cash Investment: $35K	Financial Assistance Provided: . . . . . No
Company-Owned Units (As of 8/31/1992): . .4	Total Investment: $35K	Site Selection Assistance: . . . . .Yes
Franchised Units (As of 8/31/1992): 5	Fees: Franchise - $10K	Lease Negotiation Assistance: . . . .Yes
Total Units (As of 8/31/1992): 9	Royalty: 6%, Advert: 0%	Co-operative Advertising: . . . . .No
Projected New Units for 1993: 2	Contract Periods (Yrs.): 10/10	Training: . . . . 1 Wk. Headquarters
Distribution: US-9;Can-0;Overseas-0	Area Development Agreement: . .No	. . . .
North America: . . . . 2 States	Sub-Franchise Contract: . . . . . .No	On-Going Support: C,D,E,H/ 2
Concentration: . . . . 8 in MA, 1 in NH	Expand in Territory: . . . . Yes	EXPANSION PLANS:
Registered:	Passive Ownership: . . . Discouraged	US: . . . . New England
. . . .	Encourage Conversions: . . . . . Yes	Canada: . . . . .Ontario & Quebec
Type Space: . . . . Office;~500 SF	Average # Employees: . . 2 FT, 5 PT	Overseas: . . . . . MX, EUR, Asia

SERVING BY IRVING

233 Broadway, # 1036
New York, NY 10279
TEL: (800) 233-3343 (212) 233-3346
FAX: (212) 349-0338
Mr. Irving Botwinick, President

Expert quality service of legal papers. We work for attorneys who depend on us to get the job done correctly.

HISTORY:	FINANCIAL: Earnings Claim: . .No	FRANCHISOR TRAINING/SUPPORT:
Established in 1990; . . 1st Franchised in 1991	Cash Investment: $100K	Financial Assistance Provided: . . .Yes(D)
Company-Owned Units (As of 8/31/1992): . .1	Total Investment: $100K	Site Selection Assistance: . . . . .Yes
Franchised Units (As of 8/31/1992): 3	Fees: Franchise - $85K	Lease Negotiation Assistance: . . . .Yes
Total Units (As of 8/31/1992): 4	Royalty: 7%, Advert: 2%	Co-operative Advertising: . . . . .Yes
Projected New Units for 1993: 4	Contract Periods (Yrs.): 10/10	Training: . . . . 2 Wks. Headquarters,
Distribution: US-4;Can-0;Overseas-0	Area Development Agreement: Yes/Var	. . . . 1 Wk. In Field, Varies at Location
North America:	Sub-Franchise Contract: . . . . . Yes	On-Going Support: B,C,D,G,H,I/ 8
Concentration:	Expand in Territory: . . . . Yes	EXPANSION PLANS:
Registered: . . . . .All	Passive Ownership: . . . . . .Allowed	US: . . . . .All US
. . . .	Encourage Conversions: . . . . Yes	Canada: . . . . .No
Type Space: . . . . ;~Varies SF	Average # Employees: . . . . .1 FT	Overseas: . . . . .No

TYPING TIGERS

P. O. Box 8
San Marcos, TX 78667
TEL: (512) 629-1400
FAX: (512) 353-5333
Mr. Floyd MacKenzie

Computer, typesetting services to the small business.

HISTORY:	FINANCIAL: Earnings Claim: . Yes	FRANCHISOR TRAINING/SUPPORT:
Established in 1985; . . 1st Franchised in 1987	Cash Investment: $15K	Financial Assistance Provided: . . . . .No
Company-Owned Units (As of 8/31/1992): . .1	Total Investment: $15K	Site Selection Assistance: . . . . . . .NA
Franchised Units (As of 8/31/1992): 0	Fees: Franchise - $0	Lease Negotiation Assistance: . . . . .Yes
Total Units (As of 8/31/1992): 1	Royalty: $300/Mo., Advert: . . 0%	Co-operative Advertising: . . . . . . .Yes
Projected New Units for 1993: 1	Contract Periods (Yrs.): 5/5	Training: . . . . As Required On-Site
Distribution: US-1;Can-0;Overseas-0	Area Development Agreement: . .No	. . . .
North America: . . . . .1 State	Sub-Franchise Contract: . . . . . .No	On-Going Support: a,C,D,e,f,G,h,i/ . . . 11
Concentration: . . . . 1 in TX	Expand in Territory: . . . . . . Yes	EXPANSION PLANS:
Registered:	Passive Ownership: . . . Not Allowed	US: . . . . All US
. . . .	Encourage Conversions: . . . . . NA	Canada: . . . . .All Canada
Type Space: . . . . ;~300 SF	Avg. # Employees: .2 FT, As Req. PT	Overseas: . . . . No

UNITED CHECK CASHING COMPANY

325 Chestnut St., # 1005
Philadelphia, PA 19106
TEL: (800) 626-0787 (215) 336-5070
FAX: (215) 755-5031
Mr. Ron London, Fran. Sales

Check cashing, money orders, Western Union wire transfer, credit card cash advances, fax service, notary, photo ID's. P. O. Box rental, sale of fine jewelry, tax service and related financial services.

HISTORY:	FINANCIAL: Earnings Claim: . Yes	FRANCHISOR TRAINING/SUPPORT:
Established in 1977; . . 1st Franchised in 1991	Cash Investment: $60K	Financial Assistance Provided: . . .Yes(D)
Company-Owned Units (As of 8/31/1992): . .2	Total Investment: $60-90K	Site Selection Assistance: . . . . . . .Yes
Franchised Units (As of 8/31/1992): 10	Fees: Franchise - $17.5K	Lease Negotiation Assistance: . . . . .Yes
Total Units (As of 8/31/1992): 12	Royalty: .3%, Advert:	Co-operative Advertising: . . . . .NA
Projected New Units for 1993: 4	Contract Periods (Yrs.): 15/15	Training: . . . . 2 Wks. Headquarters
Distribution: US-12;Can-0;Overseas-0	Area Development Agreement: . .No	. . . .
North America: . . . . .1 State	Sub-Franchise Contract: . . . . . .No	On-Going Support: B,C,D,E,F,I/ 10
Concentration: . . . . .12 in PA	Expand in Territory: . . . . . . Yes	EXPANSION PLANS:
Registered: . . . . .All	Passive Ownership: . . . . . .Allowed	US: . . . . All US
. . . .	Encourage Conversions: . . . . . Yes	Canada: . . . . No
Type Space: . . . FS, SF, SC, RM;~800+ SF	Average # Employees: . . . . . .2 FT	Overseas: . . . . No

WORLDWIDE CANADIAN MANAGE-MENT CONSULTANTS

4 Hufton Court
Ajax, ON L1T 2R3 CAN
TEL: (416) 686-1152
FAX: (416) 686-0469
Mr. Kelly Rogers, Admin. Dir.

Excellent opportunities for entrepreneurial women and men of all ages and backgrounds. High profit. Low cost and extensive on-the-job training program. Worldwide network. Total support system.

HISTORY:	FINANCIAL: Earnings Claim: . .No	FRANCHISOR TRAINING/SUPPORT:
Established in 1976; . . 1st Franchised in 1980	Cash Investment: $50-120K	Financial Assistance Provided: . . .Yes(D)
Company-Owned Units (As of 8/31/1992): . .2	Total Investment: $50-120K	Site Selection Assistance: . . . . . . .No
Franchised Units (As of 8/31/1992): 35	Fees: Franchise - $20K	Lease Negotiation Assistance: . . . . .No
Total Units (As of 8/31/1992): 37	Royalty: 8%, Advert: 5%	Co-operative Advertising: . . . . . . .Yes
Projected New Units for 1993: 2	Contract Periods (Yrs.): 3-10/5	Training: . . . . .Toronto, ON
Distribution: US-0;Can-2;Overseas-35	Area Development Agreement: . .No	. . . .
North America:	Sub-Franchise Contract: . . . . . .No	On-Going Support: b,D,H/ 5
Concentration:	Expand in Territory: . . . . . . Yes	EXPANSION PLANS:
Registered:	Passive Ownership: . . . Not Allowed	US: . . . . All US
. . . .	Encourage Conversions: . . . . . .No	Canada: . . . . .All Canada
Type Space: . . . . Office Building;~ SF	Average # Employees: . . 1 FT, 2 PT	Overseas: . . Middle/Far East, S. America

SUPPLEMENTAL LISTING OF FRANCHISORS

!SOLUTIONS! . . . . 8016 Plainfield Rd., Cincinnati, OH 45236
    Contact: Ms. Dana C. Ewell, President; Tel: (513) 891-6145
AAA ADJUSTERS . . . . 1018 E. Tennessee St., Tucson, AZ 85714
    Contact: President; Tel: (602) 747-7019
AD COM EXPRESS . . . . 7424 W. 78th St., Edina, MN 55439
    Contact: Mr. Robert F. Friedman; Tel: (612) 829-7990
ADAGE PRODUCTS CORP. . . . . 1200 N. Las Brisas, Anaheim, CA 92806
    Contact: President; Tel: (714) 632-8966
ALLIED CORPORATE INVESTMENTS . . . . .500 S. Sepulveda, # 415, Los Angeles, CA 90049
    Contact: Mr. Alex Parsinia; Tel: (818) 907-0666
AMERICA ONE . . . . 2214 University Park Dr., Okemos, MI 48864
    Contact: Ms. Joanne Dillman, VP Operations; Tel: (517) 394-3880 (517) 349-1988
AMERICAN INVENTORY SERVICE . . . . P. O. Box 9045, Jackson, TN 38314
    Contact: Mr. Murray Ragan; Tel: (901) 664-6283
ASSET ONE . . . . 1097 Irongate Ln., # C, Columbus, OH 43213
    Contact: Mr. Raymond A. Strohl, President; Tel: (614) 684-1440
BARTER EXCHANGE . . . . 1120 S. Capital of Texas Hwy., # 300, Austin, TX 78746
    Contact: Mr. Mike Odom, GM; Tel: (800) 44-TRADE (512) 329-7250
BUSINESS BROKERS, HAWAII . . . . 2395 S. Kihei Rd., # 206, Kihei, HI 96753
    Contact: Mr. Milton Docktor, President; Tel: (808) 879-8833
BUSINESS MATCHUPS . . . . 35 Kinmont Dr., Rochester, NY 14612
    Contact: President; Tel: (716) 247-8044
CENTRIX GROUP, THE . . . . 79 Parkingway, P. O. Box 7169, Quincy, MA 02169
    Contact: Mr. Leo Meady, President; Tel: (617) 984-0405
CHECK-X-CHANGE . . . . 111 SW Columbia, # 1080, Portland, OR 97201
    Contact: Mr. Dennis Steinman, VP Mktg.; Tel: (800) 423-3371 (503) 241-1800
CREATIVE BUSINESS CONNECTIONS . . . . 10 Claremont Park, Boston, MA 02118
    Contact: President; Tel: (617) 437-1132
CUNA MUTUAL INSURANCE SOCIETY . . . . P. O. Box 391, Madison, WI 53701
    Contact: Mr. Steve Donovan, Dir.; Tel: (608) 231-7297
DATA MANAGEMENT . . . . P. O. Box 789, Farmington, CT 06032
    Contact: President; Tel: (203) 677-8586
DAVIS ANTENNA . . . . Box 335, Hwy. 925 North, Waldorf, MD 20601
    Contact: President; Tel: (301) 843-1166
DIAGRAMIX . . . . 60 S. Michillinda Ave., Sierra Madre, CA 91024
    Contact: President; Tel: (818) 355-0974
DP SOLUTIONS . . . . 207-M South Westgate Dr., Greensboro, NC 27407
    Contact: President; Tel: (919) 854-7700
FINANCIAL MARKETING CORP. . . . . 216 S. Michigan St., Prairie du Chien, WI 53821
    Contact: President; Tel: (608) 326-4444
FLEET PRO . . . . 4617 Benson Ave., Baltimore, MD 21227
    Contact: President; Tel: (301) 621-4750
FRANKLIN TRAFFIC SERVICE . . . . . . 9521 Shawnee Rd., P. O. Box 100, Ransomville, NY 14131
    Contact: Mr. G. S. Homokay, Acct. Mgr.; Tel: (716) 731-3131
GENERAL BUSINESS SERVICES . . . . 7134 Columbia Gateway Dr., Columbia, MD 21046
    Contact: Mr. Robert Pirtle, President; Tel: (800) 638-7940 (301) 290-1040
GREAT WESTERN BUSINESS SERVICES . . . . . . 4975 Preston Park Blvd., # 210, Plano, TX 75093
    Contact: Mr. David L. Oliver, Dir. Fran.; Tel: (214) 612-0072
HOSPITALIZATION ASSISTANCE . . . . 3409 Liberty, P. O. Box 73, Vermillion, OH 44089
    Contact: Ms. Linda Fritos, President; Tel: (216) 967-0946
INFOPLAN INTERNATIONAL . . . . .5741 N. Placita de; Trueno, Tucson, AZ 85718
    Contact: Mr. Michael Wing, President; Tel: (800) 367-0222 (602) 721-7405
INFORM 1562 First Ave., # 246, New York, NY 10028 . . . .
    Contact: Mr. John G. Barrett; Tel: (212) 831-7337
INSURANCE CONSULTING ASSOCIATES . . . . P. O. Box 600, Fair Lawn, NJ 07410
    Contact: President; Tel:
INSURANCE NETWORK USA . . . . P. O. Box 1778, Sarasota, FL 33578
    Contact: President; Tel: (800) 722-3360
INTERNATIONAL BUSINESS OPPORTUNITIES . . . . P. O. Box 639, Pickering, ON L1V 3T3   CAN
    Contact: Mr. Kelly Rogers; Tel: (416) 686-1152

INTERNATIONAL CONFERENCE MANAGEMENT . . . . . 7152 Southwest 47th St., Miami, FL 33155
    Contact: President; Tel: (305) 661-5115
INTERNATIONAL INSURANCE BROKERS . . . . 3524 16th St., # B, Metairie, LA 70002
    Contact: Mr. Otto Mehrgut, CEO; Tel: (800) 875-4754 (504)885-7133
INVENTION SUBMISSION CORP. . . . . 903 Liberty Ave., Pittsburgh, PA 15222
    Contact: President; Tel: (412) 288-1300
ISU/INSURORS GROUP . . . . 100 Pine St., # 1700, San Francisco, CA 94111
    Contact: Ms. Susan Mead; Tel: (415) 788-9810
K. K. NIHON LCA . . . . 200 E. 61st St., # 22E, New York, NY 10021
    Contact: Mr. Emi Hayashi, President; Tel: (212) 953-3434
KARANA'S SECRETARY SERVICE . . . . 1509 Westheimer, Houston, TX 77006
    Contact: President; Tel: (800) 527-2627 (713) 528-2088
LEASE MART SYSTEMS . . . . 3350 Merrittville Hwy., # 7, Thorold, ON L2V 4Y6   CAN
    Contact: Mr. Douglas McNaughton, President; Tel: (416) 682-4648
LETTER WRITER, THE . . . . 9357 Haggerty Rd., Plymouth, MI 48170
    Contact: Ms. Ginny Eades; Tel: (313) 455-8892
LOAN SOURCE, THE . . . . 3840 Rosin Ct., Sacramento, CA 95834
    Contact: Mr. Rick Bauman; Tel: (916) 648-7100
MARKETING SOLUTION . . . . P. O. Box 348, Reynoldsburg, OH 43068
    Contact: President; Tel: (614) 866-9400
MARTIN-ROCHE ASSOCIATES . . . . 64 Division Ave., # 217, Levittown, NY 11756
    Contact: Mr. John E. Roche, President; Tel: (516) 579-3140
MOBILE BANKERS . . . . 300 Continental Blvd., # 195, El Segundo, CA 90245
    Contact: Mr. Barry Lastinger, EVP; Tel: (310) 416-9000
NATIONWIDE INSURANCE COMPANIES . . 1 Nationwide Insurance Pl., OBA-28T, Columbus, OH 43216
    Contact: President; Tel:
NEIGHBORHOOD CHECK CASHERS . . . . 2825 Wilcrest, # 360, Houston, TX 77042
    Contact: Mr. Joe Broadhurst, Sr. VP; Tel: (800) 829-02-1 (713) 789-1060
NIX CHECK CASHING . . . . 17019 Kingsview Ave., Carson, CA 90746
    Contact: Mr. Mark Perry; Tel: (213) 538-2242
OFFICE ALTERNATIVE, THE . . . . One SeaGate, # 1001, Toledo, OH 43604
    Contact: Mr. William W. Clow, President; Tel: (800) 262-4181 (419) 247-5400 C
OWNER/MANAGER SYSTEMS . . . . 4102 42nd Ave. South, Minneapolis, MN 55406
    Contact: Mr. C. J. Howard, Manager; Tel: (800) 999-6633 (612) 729-8361
PACIFIC INFORMATION SYSTEMS . . . . 421 Karen Way, Tiburon, CA 94920
    Contact: President; Tel:
PAUL W. DAVIS SYSTEMS . . . . 8933 Western Way, # 12, Jacksonville, FL 32256
    Contact: Mr. Mark Mullins, President; Tel: (800) 722-1818 (904) 363-1029
PERSONAL INJURY NETWORK . . . . P.O. Box 150, San Rafael, CA 94915
    Contact: President; Tel:
PRICECHECK . . . . 11 Pylon Pl., Etobicoke, ON M9W 293   CAN
    Contact: Mr. Bob Miller, GM; Tel: (416) 740-6764
PROFESSIONAL MORTGAGE BANKER . . . . . . 3810 Wilshire Blvd., 1102, Los Angeles, CA 90010
    Contact: Mr. Charlie Chi, President; Tel: (213) 738-9956
RESUME CORNER . . . . 1851 W. Eringhaus St., Box 253, Elizabeth City, NC 04112
    Contact: Ms. Debbie Krueger; Tel: (919) 426-8369
SAMPLER OF AMERICA . . . . 84 Hawley St., P. O. Box 502, Binghamton, NY 13902
    Contact: Mr. Joel Levy, CEO; Tel: (607) 722-7929
SERVICE LIGHTING ASSOCIATES . . . . . 73 E. Hanover Ave., P. O. Box 1518, Morristown, NJ 07962
    Contact: Mr. William Belgard, President; Tel: (201) 267-4172
SOFT INDUSTRIES CORP. . . . . 92 N. Summit St., Southington, CT 06489
    Contact: President; Tel: (207) 621-7308
STRATEGIC LIVING INTERNATIONAL . . . . 10411 Stevenson Rd., Stevenson, MD 21153
    Contact: Mr. Bruce Seidman, President; Tel: (800) 727-4754 (301) 653-1993
STRATEGIC OVERSEAS RESEARCH & DEV. . . . . 1281 Madison Ave., New York, NY 10128
    Contact: Mr. Bruce Pettibone, President; Tel: (212) 369-1616
STUDDARD MCMORDIE INTERNATIONAL . . . . . . 1201 Louisiana, # 3400, Houston, TX 77002
    Contact: Mr. Ken Studdart, Co-Chairman; Tel: (713) 650-3344
SUCCESS CENTERS INTERNATIONAL . . . . 681 Marshall Rd., Rochester, NY 14624
    Contact: Mr. H. B. Vought, Mktg. Dir.; Tel: (716) 247-4485
TBC BUSINESS BROKERS . . . . 61 Dewey Ave., Warwick, RI 02886
    Contact: Mr. Stephen A. Bressard; Tel: (401) 738-4206
TELECHECK SERVICES . . . . P. O. Box 17370, Denver, CO 80217
    Contact: Ms. Sylvia Little; Tel: (800) 525-8999 (303) 752-5200
TOWERS FRANCHISE CORP. . . . . 400 W. Cummings Park, Wobury, MA 01801
    Contact: Mr. Mitchell Bester, President; Tel: (800) 553-3322 (617) 935-7558

TRADE LABOR . . . . P. O. Box 70661, Nashville, TN 37207
Contact: Mr. G. J. Shafer; Tel: (800) 321-2825 (615) 824-2825
UNITED NEIGHBORS OF AMERICA . . . . 727 S. Range Line Rd., Carmel, IN 46032
Contact: President; Tel: (317) 844-8622
VERTIS GROUP . . . . P. O. Box 1030, Coraopolis, PA 15101
Contact: Ms. Joyce Hallas, President; Tel: (412) 264-7008
VR BUSINESS BROKERS . . . . 230 Western Ave., Boston, MA 02134
Contact: Ms. Laura Bueermann, Dir. Services; Tel: (800) 343-4416 (617) 254-4100

CHAPTER 13

CONVENIENCE STORES / SUPER-MARKETS / DRUGS

6-TWELVE CONVENIENT MART

Up-scale convenience store chain.

77 S. Washington St., # 207
Rockville, MD 20850
TEL: (301) 294-5300
FAX: (301) 294-5306
Mr. Lee Meizlesh, Dir. Fran.

HISTORY: . . . . IFA
Established in 1986; . . 1st Franchised in 1987
Company-Owned Units (As of 8/31/1992): . .2
Franchised Units (As of 8/31/1992): . . . . . <u>23</u>
Total Units (As of 8/31/1992): 25
Projected New Units for 1993: 5
Distribution: US-25;Can-0;Overseas-0
North America: . . . . 3 States
Concentration: . . . . MD, VA, PA
Registered: . . . . .FL,MD,VA,DC
. . . .
Type Space: . . . . .FS, SC;~2,500 SF

FINANCIAL: Earnings Claim: . .No
Cash Investment: $75K
Total Investment: $225K
Fees: Franchise - $30K
 Royalty: 6%, Advert: 2%
Contract Periods (Yrs.): 10/10
Area Development Agreement: Yes/10
Sub-Franchise Contract: . . . . .No
Expand in Territory: . . . . . . Yes
Passive Ownership: . . . Not Allowed
Encourage Conversions: . . . . . Yes
Average # Employees: . . 2 FT, 2 PT

FRANCHISOR TRAINING/SUPPORT:
Financial Assistance Provided: . . . Yes(I)
Site Selection Assistance: . . . . . . .Yes
Lease Negotiation Assistance: . . . . .Yes
Co-operative Advertising: . . . . .No
Training: . . . . 3 Wks. Headquarters,
 . . . . 1 Wk. Franchisee Site
On-Going Support: C,D,E,F/ 15
EXPANSION PLANS:
US: . . . . Northwest
Canada: . . . . .No
Overseas: . . . . No

CONVENIENCE STORES

	1989	1990	1991	Percentage Change 90/89	91/90
Total Number of Establishments:					
Company–Owned	10,864	10,295	10,325	–5.24%	0.29%
Franchisee–Owned	6,703	6,913	6,940	3.13%	0.39%
Total	17,567	17,208	17,265	–2.04%	0.33%
Ratio of Total Establishments:					
Company–Owned	61.8%	59.8%	59.8%		
Franchisee–Owned	38.2%	40.2%	40.2%		
Total	100.0%	100.0%	100.0%		
Total Sales ($000):					
Company–Owned	9,363,335	9,179,116	9,607,303	–1.97%	4.66%
Franchisee–Owned	4,932,657	5,142,135	5,385,425	4.25%	4.73%
Total	14,295,992	14,321,251	14,992,728	0.18%	4.69%
Ratio of Total Sales:					
Company–Owned	65.5%	64.1%	64.1%		
Franchisee–Owned	34.5%	35.9%	35.9%		
Total	100.0%	100.0%	100.0%		
Average Sales Per Unit ($000):					
Company–Owned	862	892	930	3.45%	4.36%
Franchisee–Owned	736	744	776	1.08%	4.32%
Total	814	832	868	2.27%	4.34%
Relative Average Sales Ratio:	117.1%	119.9%	119.9%		

	Number Of Employees	Employees Per Unit	Avg. Sales Per Employee
Total 1989 Employment:			
Company–Owned	116,589	10.7	$80,311
Franchisee–Owned	53,017	7.9	$93,039
Total	169,606	9.7	$84,289
Relative Employee Performance Ratios:		135.7%	86.3%

	1st Quartile	Median	4th Quartile
Average 1989 Total Investment:			
Company–Owned	$90,000	$250,000	$750,000
Franchisee–Owned	$100,000	$190,000	$470,000
Single Unit Franchise Fee	$7,200	$7,500	$41,000
Mult. Unit Franchise Fee	NA	NA	NA
Franchise Start–Up Cost	$29,500	$47,500	$94,700

Source: Franchising In The Economy 1991, IFA Educational Foundation & Horwath International.

7-ELEVEN FOOD STORES

2711 N. Haskell Ave.
Dallas, TX 75204
TEL: (800) 255-0711 (214) 828-7764
FAX:
Franchise Department

7-ELEVEN offers an extended hour retail convenience store, providing groceries, take-out foods and beverages, dairy products, non-food merchandise, specialty items and selected services which emphasize convenience to the customer.

HISTORY: . . . . IFA	FINANCIAL: Earnings Claim: . .No	FRANCHISOR TRAINING/SUPPORT:
Established in 1927; . . 1st Franchised in 1964	Cash Investment: $13-161K	Financial Assistance Provided: . . .Yes(D)
Company-Owned Units (As of 8/31/1992): 3238	Total Investment: $13-161K	Site Selection Assistance: . . . . .NA
Franchised Units (As of 8/31/1992): 9845	Fees: Franchise - $0-98K	Lease Negotiation Assistance: . . . . .NA
Total Units (As of 8/31/1992): 13083	Royalty: NA, Advert: . . . . . . NA	Co-operative Advertising: . . . . .NA
Projected New Units for 1993: 0	Contract Periods (Yrs.): . . 10/Lease	Training: . . . . 5 Days San Diego, 5 Days
Distribution: US-3645;Can-502;Overseas-6200	Area Development Agreement: . .No	. . Bethlehem, PA, 10 Days On Location
North America: . . . . 36 States, 5 Provinces	Sub-Franchise Contract: . . . . .No	On-Going Support: A,B,C,D,E,F,G,H,I/ 90
Concentration: 1300 in CA, 700 in TX,680 VA	Expand in Territory: . . . . . . Yes	EXPANSION PLANS:
Registered: . . . CA,IL,IN,MD,NY,OR,RI,VA	Passive Ownership: . . . Not Allowed	US: . . . NW, CA, NV, AZ, Midwest, NE
. . . . WA	Encourage Conversions: . . . . . NA	Canada: . . . . No
Type Space: . . . . .FS;~2,400 SF	Average # Employees: . . 4 FT, 4 PT	Overseas: . . . . License Countries

AM/PM INTERNATIONAL

1055 W. Seventh St., P. O. Box 2570
Los Angeles, CA 90051
TEL: (213) 486-3452
FAX: (213) 486-0770
Ms. April Z. Peterson, Mgr. Mktg.

AM/PM is currently one of the largest convenience store chains on the West Coast. AM/PM INTERNATIONAL is now expanding the AM/PM mini-market program outside the US to pursue the opportunities presented by worldwide economic growth and changing lifestyles.

HISTORY:	FINANCIAL: Earnings Claim: . . .	FRANCHISOR TRAINING/SUPPORT:
Established in 1988; . . 1st Franchised in 1988	Cash Investment: . . . .$	Financial Assistance Provided: . . . .
Company-Owned Units (As of 8/31/1992): . .0	Total Investment: . . . .$	Site Selection Assistance: . . . .
Franchised Units (As of 8/31/1992): 113	Fees: Franchise - . . . .$	Lease Negotiation Assistance: . . . .
Total Units (As of 8/31/1992): 113	Royalty: , Advert:	Co-operative Advertising: . . . .
Projected New Units for 1993: 167	Contract Periods (Yrs.):	Training: . . . .
Distribution: US-0;Can-3;Overseas-113	Area Development Agreement:	
North America: . . . . .1 Province	Sub-Franchise Contract:	On-Going Support: / . . . .
Concentration:	Expand in Territory:	EXPANSION PLANS:
Registered:	Passive Ownership:	US: . . . . No
. . . .	Encourage Conversions:	Canada: . . . . .All Canada
Type Space: . . . . ;~ SF	Average # Employees:	Overseas: EUR, Pacific Rim, S & C Amer

CONVENIENT FOOD MART

929 N. Plum Grove Rd.
Schaumburg, IL 60173
TEL: (708) 995-1124
FAX: (708) 995-9334
Director of Franchising

CONVENIENT FOOD MART has restructured itself to be a high-level organization. The new stores represent a fresh approach to convenience and have a focused niche in the market place. We have a corporate staff, as well as a regional staff, which is there to aid the franchise owner. Our unique concept offers the ability to build equity while benefiting from a strong franchise system of operating and a mildly recognized trademark.

HISTORY:	FINANCIAL: Earnings Claim: . .No	FRANCHISOR TRAINING/SUPPORT:
Established in 1958; . . 1st Franchised in 1961	Cash Investment: . . . . . $30K Min.	Financial Assistance Provided: . . . . .No
Company-Owned Units (As of 8/31/1992): . 12	Total Investment: $100K	Site Selection Assistance: . . . . . . .Yes
Franchised Units (As of 8/31/1992): 408	Fees: Franchise - $18-22K	Lease Negotiation Assistance: . . . .Yes
Total Units (As of 8/31/1992): 420	Royalty: 1.5%, Advert: . . Included	Co-operative Advertising: . . . . . . .Yes
Projected New Units for 1993: 7	Contract Periods (Yrs.): . . 10/Varies	Training: . . . . .3 Wks.
Distribution: US-420;Can-0;Overseas-0	Area Development Agreement: Yes/5	
North America: . . . . 14 States	Sub-Franchise Contract: . . . . .No	On-Going Support: A,C,D,E,f,G,I/ . . . 72
Concentration: . . 130 in OH, 80 in NY, 74 IL	Expand in Territory: . . . . . . Yes	EXPANSION PLANS:
Registered: . . . . FL,IL,IN,NY	Passive Ownership: . . . Discouraged	US: . . . . IL, NY and OH
. . . .	Encourage Conversions: . . . . NA	Canada: . . . . .No
Type Space: . . . . .SC;~3,000 SF	Average # Employees: . . 2 FT, 5 PT	Overseas: . . . . No

CRUISERS SHOP AROUND

619 Divesadero St.
Fresno, CA 93701
TEL: (209) 237-3345
FAX:
Mr. George A. Prath, Founder

Walkin' or Rollin', shopping is AUTO-matic with the ultimate in convenience. The drive-thru with everything. Our food store is the future of this mobile society. Join our team of stores on the cutting edge of technology. It's here at C.S.A. drive-thru food stores.

HISTORY:	FINANCIAL: Earnings Claim: . .No	FRANCHISOR TRAINING/SUPPORT:
Established in 1986; . . 1st Franchised in 1988	Cash Investment: $40K	Financial Assistance Provided: . . . Yes(I)
Company-Owned Units (As of 8/31/1992): . .1	Total Investment: $40-200K	Site Selection Assistance: . . . . . . .Yes
Franchised Units (As of 8/31/1992): 1	Fees: Franchise - $10K	Lease Negotiation Assistance: . . . . .Yes
Total Units (As of 8/31/1992): 2	Royalty: 3%, Advert: 2.5%	Co-operative Advertising: . . . . . . .Yes
Projected New Units for 1993:	Contract Periods (Yrs.): 10	Training: . . . . 2 Wks. Headquarters
Distribution: US-2;Can-0;Overseas-0	Area Development Agreement: Yes/10	. . . .
North America: . . . . .1 State	Sub-Franchise Contract: . . . . .No	On-Going Support: C,D,E,F,G,H/ . . . . . .
Concentration: . . . . 2 in CA	Expand in Territory: . . . . . . Yes	EXPANSION PLANS:
Registered:	Passive Ownership: . . . . . .Allowed	US: . . . . .All US
. . . .	Encourage Conversions: . . . . Yes	Canada: . . . . .All Canada
Type Space: . . . .FS, SF, SC, RM;~1,700 SF	Average # Employees: . . . . .2 FT	Overseas: . . . . .Yes

EXPRESS MART

6567 Kinne Rd.
Dewitt, NY 13214
TEL: (315) 446-0125
FAX: (315) 446-1355
Mr. Mark E. Maher, Dir. Fran.

Convenience store, with strong emphasis on fast-food operations. Company will design store specifically to the demographics of each site selected.

HISTORY: . . . . IFA	FINANCIAL: Earnings Claim: . .No	FRANCHISOR TRAINING/SUPPORT:
Established in 1975; . . 1st Franchised in 1990	Cash Investment: $35-110K	Financial Assistance Provided: . . . Yes(I)
Company-Owned Units (As of 8/31/1992): . 35	Total Investment: $135-650K	Site Selection Assistance: . . . . . . .Yes
Franchised Units (As of 8/31/1992): 16	Fees: Franchise - $15K	Lease Negotiation Assistance: . . . .Yes
Total Units (As of 8/31/1992): 51	Royalty: 3%, Advert: 1%	Co-operative Advertising: . . . . . . .Yes
Projected New Units for 1993: 10	Contract Periods (Yrs.): 5/5	Training: . . . . 1 Wk. Classroom,
Distribution: US-51;Can-0;Overseas-0	Area Development Agreement: .No	. . . . 1 Wk. Corporate Store
North America: . . . . .1 State	Sub-Franchise Contract: . . . . .No	On-Going Support: A,B,C,D,E,F,G,h/ . .7
Concentration: . . . . 51 in NY	Expand in Territory: . . . . . . Yes	EXPANSION PLANS:
Registered: . . . . NY	Passive Ownership: . . . Discouraged	US: . . . . .Northeast
. . . .	Encourage Conversions: . . . . Yes	Canada: . . . . .All Canada
Type Space: . . . . . FS, SF, SC;~2,000 SF	Average # Employees: . . 6 FT, 4 PT	Overseas: . . Saudi Arabia, Taiwan

GATEWAY NEWSTANDS

30 E. Beaver Creek Rd., # 206
Richmond Hill, ON L4B 1J2 CAN
TEL: (416) 886-8900
FAX: (416) 886-8904
Mr. David Goldman, President

GATEWAY NEWSTANDS operate newsstand/lottery/limited food service locations in high-rise office towers and shopping centers throughout Canada and the US. Our stores sell nationally-advertised, pre-sold, pre-packaged goods to a captive customer base. The business is recession proof and inflation proof.

HISTORY:	FINANCIAL: Earnings Claim: . .No	FRANCHISOR TRAINING/SUPPORT:
Established in 1983; . . 1st Franchised in 1983	Cash Investment: $30-100K	Financial Assistance Provided: . . .Yes(D)
Company-Owned Units (As of 8/31/1992): . .0	Total Investment: $40-150K	Site Selection Assistance: . . . . . . .Yes
Franchised Units (As of 8/31/1992): 80	Fees: Franchise - $15-75K	Lease Negotiation Assistance: . . . . .Yes
Total Units (As of 8/31/1992): 80	Royalty: 3%, Advert: 0%	Co-operative Advertising: . . . . .No
Projected New Units for 1993: 20	Contract Periods (Yrs.): 5/5	Training: . . . . As Needed at Other
Distribution: US-11;Can-69;Overseas-0	Area Development Agreement: .No	. . .Company Stores, As Needed On-Site
North America: . . . . . . 6 States, 4 Provinces	Sub-Franchise Contract: . . . . .No	On-Going Support: C,D,E,I/ 7
Concentration: . . 55 in ON, 6 in IL, 5 in PQ	Expand in Territory: . . . . . . Yes	EXPANSION PLANS:
Registered: . . . . CA,FL,IL,MI,MN	Passive Ownership: . . . Discouraged	US: . . . . .All US
. . . .	Encourage Conversions: . . . . .No	Canada: . . . . .All Canada
Type Space: . . . RM, Office Tower;~350 SF	Average # Employees: . . 1 FT, 1 PT	Overseas: . . . . .No

JR. FOOD MART

P. O. Box 3500
Jackson, MS 39207
TEL: (601) 944-0873
FAX: (601) 354-3543
Mr. Joe Fisher, VP RE/Fran. Sales

Convenience store, fast-food restaurant (creole fried chicken) and self-serve gasoline operation.

HISTORY:	FINANCIAL: Earnings Claim: . .No	FRANCHISOR TRAINING/SUPPORT:
Established in 1919; . . 1st Franchised in 1920	Cash Investment: $100-200K	Financial Assistance Provided: . . . Yes(I)
Company-Owned Units (As of 8/31/1992): 104	Total Investment: $350K	Site Selection Assistance: . . . . . . .Yes
Franchised Units (As of 8/31/1992): . . . 306	Fees: Franchise - $35K	Lease Negotiation Assistance: . . . .Yes
Total Units (As of 8/31/1992): 410	Royalty: 1.5%, Advert: 0%	Co-operative Advertising: . . . . . . .Yes
Projected New Units for 1993: 15	Contract Periods (Yrs.): 15/15	Training: . . . . 2 Wks. Headquarters,
Distribution: . . . US-410;Can-0;Overseas-0	Area Development Agreement: Yes/15	. . . . 2-3 Wks. First Store Site
North America: . . . . 21 States	Sub-Franchise Contract: . . . . .No	On-Going Support: B,C,D,E,F,G,H/ . . 65
Concentration: . . . . .MI, AR, AL	Expand in Territory: . . . . . . Yes	EXPANSION PLANS:
Registered: . . . . FL,IL,IN,MI	Passive Ownership: . . . Not Allowed	US: . . . . Southeast and West
. . . .	Encourage Conversions: . . . . . Yes	Canada: . . . . .No
Type Space: . . . . .FS;~2,800 SF	Average # Employees: . . 8 FT, 5 PT	Overseas: . . . . No

LI'L PEACH

101 Billerica Ave.
N. Billerica, MA 01862
TEL: (617) 721-0000
FAX: (508) 663-9622
Mr. Robert Chapman, Dir. Fran.

LI'L PEACH CONVENIENCE FOOD STORES offer individuals the opportunity to operate their own business with the support of an established business format. Our full-service franchise program includes initial and on-going training, continued operational and sales assistance, as well as accounting, taxes and payroll services.

HISTORY:	FINANCIAL: Earnings Claim: . .No	FRANCHISOR TRAINING/SUPPORT:
Established in 1971; . . 1st Franchised in 1974	Cash Investment: $50-60K	Financial Assistance Provided: . . . . .No
Company-Owned Units (As of 8/31/1992): . .2	Total Investment: $50-60K	Site Selection Assistance: . . . . . . .Yes
Franchised Units (As of 8/31/1992): 61	Fees: Franchise - $15K	Lease Negotiation Assistance: . . . . .Yes
Total Units (As of 8/31/1992): 63	Royalty: 15.5%, Advert: 0%	Co-operative Advertising: . . . . . . .Yes
Projected New Units for 1993: 5	Contract Periods (Yrs.): 5/0	Training: . . . . . .3 Wks. OJT Orientation
Distribution: US-63;Can-0;Overseas-0	Area Development Agreement: .No	. . . . .Store, 4 Wks. Follow-Up On-Site
North America: . . . . .1 State	Sub-Franchise Contract: . . . . .No	On-Going Support: A,C,D,E,G,H/ . . . 17
Concentration: . . . . 63 in MA	Expand in Territory: . . . . . . .No	EXPANSION PLANS:
Registered:	Passive Ownership: . . . Not Allowed	US: . . . . .Massachusetts Only
. . . .	Encourage Conversions: . . . . . Yes	Canada: . . . . .No
Type Space: . . . . . FS, SF, SC;~2,400 SF	Average # Employees: . . 2 FT, 5 PT	Overseas: . . . . No

MEDICAP PHARMACY

4700 Westown Pkwy, # 300, Regency W4
West Des Moines, IA 50265
TEL: (800) 445-2244 (515) 224-8400
FAX: (515) 224-8415
Mr. Calvin C. James, VP Fran. Dev.

MEDICAP PHARMACIES are convenient and low-cost professional pharmacies. They typically operate in an 800-1,000 SF location with 90% of the business being the filling of prescriptions. Providing over-the-counter, medically-oriented products is 10% of the business. New store start-up as well as conversion of full-line drug stores and independent pharmacies to the MEDICAP concept.

HISTORY: . . . . .IFA	FINANCIAL: Earnings Claim: . .No	FRANCHISOR TRAINING/SUPPORT:
Established in 1971; . . 1st Franchised in 1974	Cash Investment: $25-35K	Financial Assistance Provided: . . . Yes(I)
Company-Owned Units (As of 8/31/1992): . .0	Total Investment: $120-145K	Site Selection Assistance: . . . . . . .Yes
Franchised Units (As of 8/31/1992): 83	Fees: Franchise - $8.5-15K	Lease Negotiation Assistance: . . . . .Yes
Total Units (As of 8/31/1992): 83	Royalty: 4/2%, Advert: 1%	Co-operative Advertising: . . . . .NA
Projected New Units for 1993: 21	Contract Periods (Yrs.): 20/20	Training: . . . . 3 Days Headquarters,
Distribution: US-83;Can-0;Overseas-0	Area Development Agreement: .No	. . . . 3 Days On-Site, 3 Days Computer
North America: . . . . 19 States	Sub-Franchise Contract: . . . . .No	On-Going Support: C,D,E,F,G,H,I/ . . . 20
Concentration: . . . 50 in IA, 7 in IL, 6 in MO	Expand in Territory: . . . . . . Yes	EXPANSION PLANS:
Registered: . . . CA,FL,IL,IN,MD,MN,ND,SD	Passive Ownership: . . . . . .Allowed	US: . . . . . Midwest, S, SE, E and NW
. . . . .WI	Encourage Conversions: . . . . . Yes	Canada: . . . . .No
Type Space: . . . . . . FS, SC;~800-1,000 SF	Average # Employees: . . . . . .2 FT	Overseas: . . . . No

MEDICINE SHOPPE, THE

1100 N. Lindgbergh Blvd.
St. Louis, MO 63132
TEL: (800) 325-1397 (314) 993-6000
FAX: (314) 569-9780
Mr. Mike Eicher, VP Fran. Dev.

MEDICINE SHOPPE is the largest and fastest-growing chain of franchised pharmacies in the US. Our stores are apothecary-style, 1,000 SF stores owned and operated by pharmacists. We have over 150 stores waiting to open in the US.

HISTORY: . . . . IFA	FINANCIAL: Earnings Claim: . Yes	FRANCHISOR TRAINING/SUPPORT:
Established in 1970; . . 1st Franchised in 1971	Cash Investment: $18-29K	Financial Assistance Provided: . . . Yes(D)
Company-Owned Units (As of 8/31/1992): . .0	Total Investment: $78-88K	Site Selection Assistance: . . . . .Yes
Franchised Units (As of 8/31/1992): 925	Fees: Franchise - $18K	Lease Negotiation Assistance: . . . . .Yes
Total Units (As of 8/31/1992): 925	Royalty: 5.5%, Advert: . . . 1.5%	Co-operative Advertising: . . . . . . .Yes
Projected New Units for 1993: 100	Contract Periods (Yrs.): 20/10	Training: . . . . 1 Wk. Headquarters, 5-7
Distribution: US-919;Can-3;Overseas-3	Area Development Agreement: . .No	. . . . Days/Yr. Natl./Regional Meetings
North America: . . . . 48 States	Sub-Franchise Contract: . . . . .No	On-Going Support: A,B,C,D,E,F,G,H,I/ 99
Concentration: . . 84 in PA, 80 in CA, 43 in IL	Expand in Territory: . . . . . . Yes	EXPANSION PLANS:
Registered: . . . . All States	Passive Ownership: . . . . . .Allowed	US: . . . . .All US
. . . .	Encourage Conversions: . . . . Yes	Canada: . . . . .All Canada
Type Space: . . . . . FS, SF, SC;~1,000 SF	Average # Employees: . . 1 FT, 2 PT	Overseas: . . MX, Far East, KO, Thailand

SUNSHINE FAST MARTS

P.O. Box 1467
Thousand Oaks, CA 91358
TEL: (805) 497-3576
FAX:
Mr. Geoffrey C. Prouse, VP

Franchisor of convenience stores and mini-marts.

HISTORY:	FINANCIAL: Earnings Claim: . . .	FRANCHISOR TRAINING/SUPPORT:
Established in 1983; . . 1st Franchised in 1983	Cash Investment: $70K	Financial Assistance Provided: . . . Yes(I)
Company-Owned Units (As of 8/31/1992): . .0	Total Investment: $145K	Site Selection Assistance: . . . . .Yes
Franchised Units (As of 8/31/1992): 6	Fees: Franchise - $15K	Lease Negotiation Assistance: . . . . .Yes
Total Units (As of 8/31/1992): 6	Royalty: 4%, Advert: 0%	Co-operative Advertising: . . . . . . .Yes
Projected New Units for 1993:	Contract Periods (Yrs.): 10/10	Training: . . . . 4 Wks. Headquarters
Distribution: US-6;Can-0;Overseas-0	Area Development Agreement: . .No	. . . .
North America: . . . . .1 State	Sub-Franchise Contract: . . . . .No	On-Going Support: A,B,C,D,E,f/ 10
Concentration: . . . . 6 in CA	Expand in Territory: . . . . . . .No	EXPANSION PLANS:
Registered: . . . . CA	Passive Ownership: . . . . . .Allowed	US: . . . . California Only
. . . .	Encourage Conversions: . . . . Yes	Canada: . . . . .No
Type Space: . . . . ;~ SF	Average # Employees: . . 4 FT, 4 PT	Overseas: . . . . No

WHITE HEN PANTRY

660 Industrial Dr.
Elmhurst, IL 60126
TEL: (800) 833-8544 (708) 833-3100
FAX: (708) 833-0292
Mr. James O. Williams, Fran. Mgr.

WHITE HEN PANTRY is a neighborhood convenience food store, emphasizing freshness and quality. Includes full-service deli, fresh sandwiches, private label dairy and gourmet coffee, fresh produce and bakery. Training concentrates on service, food handling and preparation, and operating skills. Franchise package includes ready to operate store, regular business counseling, as well as accounting, merchandising, advertising, payroll and insurance.

HISTORY: . . . . IFA	FINANCIAL: Earnings Claim: . .No	FRANCHISOR TRAINING/SUPPORT:
Established in 1965; . . 1st Franchised in 1965	Cash Investment: $20-30K	Financial Assistance Provided: . . .Yes(D)
Company-Owned Units (As of 8/31/1992): . .3	Total Investment: $60-65K	Site Selection Assistance: . . . . .NA
Franchised Units (As of 8/31/1992): 340	Fees: Franchise - $20K	Lease Negotiation Assistance: . . . . .NA
Total Units (As of 8/31/1992): 343	Royalty: 13-16%, Advert: . . . 0%	Co-operative Advertising: . . . . . . .Yes
Projected New Units for 1993: 15	Contract Periods (Yrs.): 10/10	Training: . . . . 2 Wks. Headquarters
Distribution: US-343;Can-0;Overseas-0	Area Development Agreement: . .No	. . . .
North America: . . . . 5 States	Sub-Franchise Contract: . . . . .No	On-Going Support: A,C,D,E,F,G,H,I/ .195
Concentration: . . .259 in IL, 63 in MA, 12 IN	Expand in Territory: . . . . . . .No	EXPANSION PLANS:
Registered: . . . . .IL,IN,RI,WI	Passive Ownership: . . . Not Allowed	US: . . . . . . IL, IN, NH and MA Only
. . . .	Encourage Conversions: . . . . NA	Canada: . . . . .No
Type Space: . . . .FS, SC, Hi-Rise;~2,500 SF	Average # Employees: .2 FT, 7-15 PT	Overseas: . . . . No

SUPPLEMENTAL LISTING OF FRANCHISORS

A & M FOOD STORES . . . . 19578 Trails End Terrace, Juniper, FL 33458
    Contact: Mr. Asjok G. Patel, VP; Tel: (305) 747-4384
AM/PM MINI-MARKET . . . . 1055 W. Seventh St., P. O. Box 2570, Los Angeles, CA 90051
    Contact: Mr. Joseph J. Tebo, President; Tel: (213) 486-2228
AMPRIDE . . . . P. O. Box 7305, Dept. 13, Kansas City, MO 64116
    Contact: Mr. David Hoppe; Tel: (816) 459-5551 (816) 459-5564
ARROW PRESCRIPTION CENTERS . . . . 40 East St., P. O. Box 600, Plainville, CT 06062
    Contact: Mr. Edgardo Mercadante, President; Tel: (203) 747-4538 C
BECKER MILK COMPANY . . . . .671 Warden Ave., Scarborough, ON M1L 3Z7   CAN
    Contact: Mr. Geoffrey Pottow; Tel: (416) 698-2591
DAIRY MART CONVENIENCE STORES . . . . .240 South Rd., Enfield, CT 06082
    Contact: Mr. Mitchell Kupperman, VP; Tel: (203) 741-3611 (216) 923-0421
DRUG CASTLE FRANCHISES . . . . 810 East High St., Springfield, OH 45505
    Contact: Mr. Todd A. Holmes, VP; Tel: (513) 323-4436
DRUG EMPORIUM . . . . 155 Hidden Ravines Dr., Powell, OH 43065
    Contact: Mr. Terry Ruh, Dir. Fran.; Tel: (800) 688-3784 (614) 548-7080
FLYING J TRAVEL PLAZA . . . . .P. O. Box 678, Brigham City, UT 84302
    Contact: Mr. J. Phillip Adams, President; Tel: (801) 734-9416
FOOD GIANT/IGA/MAYFAIR/RED ROOSTER . . . . . . 170 Attwell Dr., Rexdale, ON M9W 6A3   CAN
    Contact: Mr. Ted Moore; Tel: (416) 675-7447
FOOD-N-FUEL . . . . 8500 Lexington Ave., N., New Brighton, MN 55112
    Contact: Mr. Edward Bird; Tel: (612) 786-5151
GIANT EAGLE . . . . .101 Kappa Dr., Pittsburgh, PA 15238
    Contact: President; Tel: (412) 963-2560
GIANT TIGER STORES . . . . 98 George St., Ottawa, ON K1N 5W2   CAN
    Contact: Mr. Svend Pederson; Tel: (613) 238-1201
GREAT LITTLE FOODS STORE . . . . P. O. Box 1073, Goshen, IN 46526
    Contact: President; Tel: (219) 533-1736
HEALTH MART . . . . 1220 Senlac Dr., Carrollton, TX 75006
    Contact: Ms. Shari Pierce, VP Fran.; Tel: (214) 446-4200
KNECHTEL ASSOCIATE STORE . . . . 1644 Highland Rd. W, P.O. Box 1358, Kitchener, ON N2G 4H8   CAN
    Contact: Mr. Don Ridell; Tel: (519) 742-3502
LE$-ON DRUGS . . . . .4722 W. Touhy Ave., Lincolnwood, IL 60646
    Contact: President; Tel: (312) 982-0080
MAC'S CONVENIENCE STORES . . . . 6205 Airport Rd., Mississauga, ON L4V 1E1   CAN
    Contact: Mr. Russell F. Egerdie; Tel: (416) 678-9700
NEXT DOOR FOOD STORES . . . . 5115 E. Pickard St., P. O. Box 385, Mt. Pleasant, MI 48858
    Contact: Mr. David Johnson, President; Tel: (800) 777-9921 (517) 773-9921
NUTMEG PANTRY SUPERETTE . . . . .2030 Straits Trnpk., Middlebury, CT 06762
    Contact: Mr. Al Lussier III; Tel: (203) 758-2421
OKY DOKY FOOD MARTS . . . . 1250 Iowa St., Dubuque, IA 52001
    Contact: Mr. John F. Thompson, President; Tel: (319) 556-8050
OPEN PANTRY FOOD MARTS . . . . 817 S. Main St., Racine, WI 53403
    Contact: Mr. Robert Buhler, President; Tel: (414) 632-3161
PIGGLY WIGGLY . . . . 1991 Corporate Ave., Memphis, TN 38132
    Contact: Ms. Vicki Clement, VP; Tel: (901) 395-8215
SAV-A-STEP FOOD MART . . . . 4265 Roosevelt Ave., Louisville, KY 40213
    Contact: Mr. Joseph Pierce, President; Tel: (502) 367-6421
SHELL PRODUCTS CANADA . . . . Box 394, Campbellville, ON L0P 1B0   CAN
    Contact: Mr. Mark Breslauer; Tel: (416) 441-3800
SHOPPERS DRUG MART . . . . 225 Yorkland Blvd., Willowdale, ON M2J 4Y7   CAN
    Contact: Mr. Marvin Goldberg; Tel: (416) 493-1220
SUGAR CREEK CONVENIENCE STORES & FUEL . . . . . 760 Brooks Ave., Rochester, NY 14619
    Contact: Mr. P. Joseph Crerand; Tel: (716) 436-2691
SUPER VALU STORES/CUB STORES . . . . .P. O. Box 990, Minneapolis, MN 55440
    Contact: Mr. Thomas M. Thueson, Dir. Fran. Dev.; Tel: (612) 828-4000
SUPERMARKETS GENERAL . . . . 200 Milk St., M165, Carteret, NJ 07008
    Contact: President; Tel: (201) 499-4124
TRAILSIDE GENERAL STORE . . . . Box 667, Centerville, UT 84014
    Contact: Ms. Debbie Reese; Tel: (800) 228-8649 (801) 292-2207

UNION PRESCRIPTION CENTERS . . . . 103 W. Michigan St., Milwaukee, WI 53203
Contact: President; Tel: (414) 342-9292

CHAPTER 14

CHILD DEVELOPMENT / EDUCATION / PRODUCTS

A CHOICE NANNY

8950 Rte. 108, # 217
Columbia, MD 21045
TEL: (800) 73-NANNY (410) 730-2356
FAX: (410) 964-5726
Ms. Janice Keel, Fran. Dev.

A CHOICE NANNY is the leader in franchised nanny referral services! The National Chamber of Commerce selected A CHOICE NANNY as a start-up that has "done it right." A CHOICE NANNY franchise matches parents and nannies by a proven system of business. Comprehensive training, on-going support and computer software.

HISTORY: . . . .
Established in 1983;   . . 1st Franchised in 1988
Company-Owned Units (As of 8/31/1992):   . .0
Franchised Units (As of 8/31/1992): 20
Total Units (As of 8/31/1992): 20
Projected New Units for 1993: 12
Distribution: US-20;Can-0;Overseas-0
  North America: . . . . 9 States
  Concentration: . . . .4 in NJ, 4 in MD, 3 in FL
Registered: . . . . FL,IL,MD,NY,VA
. . . .
Type Space: . . . . ;~300-500 SF

FINANCIAL: Earnings Claim: . . .
Cash Investment: $40-50K
Total Investment: $40-50K
Fees: Franchise - $24.9K
  Royalty: 10%, Advert: 3%
Contract Periods (Yrs.): 10/10
Area Development Agreement: . .No
Sub-Franchise Contract: . . . . .No
Expand in Territory: . . . . . . Yes
Passive Ownership: . . . Discouraged
Encourage Conversions: . . . . Yes
Average # Employees: . 1 FT, 2-3 PT

FRANCHISOR TRAINING/SUPPORT:
Financial Assistance Provided: . . . Yes(I)
Site Selection Assistance: . . . . .Yes
Lease Negotiation Assistance: . . . . .Yes
Co-operative Advertising: . . . . .Yes
Training: . . . . . . 1-2 Wks. Headquarters
. . . .
On-Going Support: A,B,C,D,G,H/ 4
EXPANSION PLANS:
US: . . . . .All US
Canada: . . . . .No
Overseas: . . . . No

BELLINI JUVENILE DESIGNER FURNITURE
15 Engle St., # 302
Englewood, NJ 07631
TEL: (800) 332-2229 (201) 871-0370
FAX: (201) 871-7168
Mr. John Sterns, Sales Mgr.

European designer furniture for infants and juveniles, along with offering related accessories and bedding. Geared for the up-scale market.

HISTORY: . . . . IFA	FINANCIAL: Earnings Claim: . .No	FRANCHISOR TRAINING/SUPPORT:
Established in 1982; . . 1st Franchised in 1983	Cash Investment: $50K	Financial Assistance Provided: . . . Yes(I)
Company-Owned Units (As of 8/31/1992): . .7	Total Investment: $135-165K	Site Selection Assistance: . . . . . . .Yes
Franchised Units (As of 8/31/1992): 45	Fees: Franchise - $25K	Lease Negotiation Assistance: . . . .Yes
Total Units (As of 8/31/1992): 52	Royalty: 5%, Advert:	Co-operative Advertising: . . . . . . .Yes
Projected New Units for 1993: 10	Contract Periods (Yrs.): 10/10	Training: . . . . . .2 Wks. Company Store,
Distribution: US-52;Can-0;Overseas-0	Area Development Agreement: . .No	. . . . 1 Wk. Franchisee Location
North America:	Sub-Franchise Contract: . . . . . .No	On-Going Support: C,D,E,G,I/ . . . . . .
Concentration: . . . 14 in CA, 7 in NY, 4 in NJ	Expand in Territory: . . . . Yes	EXPANSION PLANS:
Registered: . . . . CA,FL,IL,MD,NY,VA,WA	Passive Ownership: . . . Not Allowed	US: . . . . All US
. . . .	Encourage Conversions: . . . . .No	Canada: . . . . .No
Type Space: . . . . .SC, RM;~2,500-4,000 SF	Average # Employees:	Overseas: . . . . .Yes

COMPUTERTOTS

10132 Colvin Run Rd., PO Box 340
Great Falls, VA 22066
TEL: (703) 759-2556
FAX: (703) 759-1938
Ms. Mary C. Rogers, CEO

COMPUTERTOTS, a nationally acclaimed program specializing in early computer education, brings classes to thousands of children each week. This home-managed franchise appeals to men and women who wish to build a thriving business while preparing our children for the future.

HISTORY: . . . . IFA	FINANCIAL: Earnings Claim: . Yes	FRANCHISOR TRAINING/SUPPORT:
Established in 1983; . . 1st Franchised in 1988	Cash Investment: . . . .$	Financial Assistance Provided: . . . . .No
Company-Owned Units (As of 8/31/1992): . .1	Total Investment: . . . .$	Site Selection Assistance: . . . . . . .NA
Franchised Units (As of 8/31/1992): 61	Fees: Franchise - $15-19.5K	Lease Negotiation Assistance: . . . .NA
Total Units (As of 8/31/1992): 62	Royalty: 6%or$250, Advert: . . 1%	Co-operative Advertising: . . . . . . .NA
Projected New Units for 1993: 30	Contract Periods (Yrs.): 10/10	Training: . . . . . 5 1/2 Days Headquarters
Distribution: US-62;Can-0;Overseas-0	Area Development Agreement: . .No	. . . .
North America: . . . . 25 States	Sub-Franchise Contract: . . . . . .No	On-Going Support: B,C,D,G,H/ 7
Concentration: . . . 6 in NY, 4 in FL, 4 in OH	Expand in Territory: . . . . .No	EXPANSION PLANS:
Registered: . . . CA,FL,IL,IN,MI,MN,NY,OR	Passive Ownership: . . . Discouraged	US: . . . . All US
. . . . VA,WA,WI	Encourage Conversions: . . . . . NA	Canada: . . . . .No
Type Space: . . . . NA;~ SF	Average # Employees: . . 1 FT, 5 PT	Overseas: . . . . No

GODDARD EARLY LEARNING CENTERS
381 Brooks Rd.
King of Prussia, PA 19406
TEL: (800) 289-2209 (215) 265-5015
FAX: (215) 337-6113
Mr. Alvin Hornstein, Dir. PR

GODDARD PRE-SCHOOLS offer learning programs for children from birth to 12 years of age, primarily for families in which parents work outside of home. Learning varies depending upon age, skills and development of child. Curriculum, facilities and equipment designed in cooperation with Child Life Dept. of the Children's Hospital of Philadelphia, renowned for meeting needs of children.

HISTORY:	FINANCIAL: Earnings Claim: . Yes	FRANCHISOR TRAINING/SUPPORT:
Established in 1988; . . 1st Franchised in 1990	Cash Investment: $45K	Financial Assistance Provided: . . . Yes(I)
Company-Owned Units (As of 8/31/1992): . .3	Total Investment: $160K	Site Selection Assistance: . . . . . . .Yes
Franchised Units (As of 8/31/1992): 6	Fees: Franchise - $25K	Lease Negotiation Assistance: . . . .Yes
Total Units (As of 8/31/1992): 9	Royalty: 7.1-8%, Advert: . . Varies	Co-operative Advertising: . . . . . . .Yes
Projected New Units for 1993: 10	Contract Periods (Yrs.): 15/5	Training: . . . . 3 Wks. Headquarters
Distribution: US-9;Can-0;Overseas-0	Area Development Agreement: . .No	. . . .
North America: . . . . 3 States	Sub-Franchise Contract: . . . . . .No	On-Going Support: B,C,D,G,H,I/ 6
Concentration: . . . . 5 in PA, 3 in NJ, 1 in DE	Expand in Territory: . . . . Yes	EXPANSION PLANS:
Registered: . . . . MD	Passive Ownership: . . . Not Allowed	US: . . . . PA, NJ and DE
. . . .	Encourage Conversions: . . . . . Yes	Canada: . . . . .No
Type Space: FS, Office Space;~5,000-6,000 SF	Average # Employees: . . 8 FT, 4 PT	Overseas: . . . . No

GYM DANDY FOR TOTS +

3290 Tierney Pl.
New York, NY 10465
TEL: (212) 828-2399
FAX:
Mr. Bob Arenholz, Program Dir.

GYM DANDY FOR TOTS + is your fully-equipped tot-size gym. This parent/toddler program combines gross motor development and fine motor through arts and crafts. We are the #1 party business, with themes too many to list. Tots 4 months to 4 years and 4 years to adult in our gymnastic/dance programs!

HISTORY: . . . .
Established in 1983; . . 1st Franchised in 1991
Company-Owned Units (As of 8/31/1992): . .0
Franchised Units (As of 8/31/1992): 7
Total Units (As of 8/31/1992): 7
Projected New Units for 1993: 12
Distribution: US-7;Can-0;Overseas-0
    North America: . . . . 4 States
    Concentration: . . . .5 in NY, 1 in NJ, 1 in PA
Registered: . . . . .All
. . . .
Type Space: . .SF, SC, RM,Church;~2,000 SF

FINANCIAL: Earnings Claim: . . .
Cash Investment: . . . .$
Total Investment: $45K
Fees: Franchise - . . . .$
    Royalty: 6%, Advert: 2%
Contract Periods (Yrs.): 10/10
Area Development Agreement: . Yes
Sub-Franchise Contract: . . . . Yes
Expand in Territory: . . . . . . Yes
Passive Ownership: . . . .
Encourage Conversions: . . . . . .
Average # Employees: . . 2 FT, 2 PT

FRANCHISOR TRAINING/SUPPORT:
Financial Assistance Provided: . . . . .Yes
Site Selection Assistance: . . . . . . .Yes
Lease Negotiation Assistance: . . . .Yes
Co-operative Advertising: . . . . . . .Yes
Training: . . . . .2 Wks. Various Locations
. . . .
On-Going Support: A,B,C,D,E,F,G,H,I/ . .5
EXPANSION PLANS:
    US: . . . . All US
    Canada: . . . . .All Canada
    Overseas: . . . . No

GYMBOREE

577 Airport Blvd., # 400
Burlingame, CA 94010
TEL: (415) 579-0600
FAX: (415) 579-1733
Mr. Bob Campbell, VP

GYMBOREE, the world's largest development play program, offers weekly classes to parents and their children, aged 3 months through 4 years, on custom-designed equipment for infants, toddlers and pre-schoolers. The program is based on sensory integration theory, positive parenting, child development principles and the importance of play.

HISTORY: . . . . IFA
Established in 1976; . . 1st Franchised in 1986
Company-Owned Units (As of 8/31/1992): . .5
Franchised Units (As of 8/31/1992): 447
Total Units (As of 8/31/1992): 452
Projected New Units for 1993: 20
Distribution: . . . US-437;Can-15;Overseas-40
    North America: . . . . 35 States, 5 Provinces
    Concentration: . . . . .CA, NY, NJ
Registered: . . . CA,FL,HI,IL,IN,MD,MI,MN
. . . . NY,OR,RI,VA,WA,AB
Type Space: . . . . ;~1,800 SF

FINANCIAL: Earnings Claim: . .No
Cash Investment: $30-45K
Total Investment: $30-45K
Fees: Franchise - $10-20K
    Royalty: 6%, Advert: 1.8%
Contract Periods (Yrs.): 10/10
Area Development Agreement: . Yes
Sub-Franchise Contract: . . . . . Yes
Expand in Territory: . . . . . . .No
Passive Ownership: . . . Discouraged
Encourage Conversions: . . . . .No
Average # Employees: . . 1 FT, 1 PT

FRANCHISOR TRAINING/SUPPORT:
Financial Assistance Provided: . . . . . No
Site Selection Assistance: . . . . . . .Yes
Lease Negotiation Assistance: . . . No
Co-operative Advertising: . . . . . . .Yes
Training: . . . . 9 Days Headquarters
. . . .
On-Going Support: B,C,D,F,G,h,I/ 9
EXPANSION PLANS:
    US: . . . . All US
    Canada: . . . . .All Canada
    Overseas: . . . . Yes

HAMMETT'S LEARNING WORLD

P.O. Box 9057, Hammett Place
Braintree, MA 02184
TEL: (800) 333-4600 (617) 848-1000
FAX: (617) 843-4901
Mr. Richard A. Krause, VP

Retail stores serve teachers, parents, businesses, hobbyists and whiz kids with educational products, games, toys and office and art supplies. The complete line includes 7,000 items of retail stock supported by a catalog offering 14,000 additional items.

HISTORY: . . . .
Established in 1900; . . 1st Franchised in 1986
Company-Owned Units (As of 8/31/1992): . 31
Franchised Units (As of 8/31/1992): 8
Total Units (As of 8/31/1992): 39
Projected New Units for 1993: . . . .
Distribution: US-39;Can-0;Overseas-0
    North America: . . . . 13 States
    Concentration: . . . . . 3 in FL, 2 in NC, 1 in IL
Registered: . . . . FL,IL,IN,MI,NY
. . . .
Type Space: . . . . ;~3,000 SF

FINANCIAL: Earnings Claim: . . .
Cash Investment: $60-80K
Total Investment: $121-220K
Fees: Franchise - $25K
    Royalty: 6%, Advert: 1%
Contract Periods (Yrs.): 10/5/5
Area Development Agreement: . .No
Sub-Franchise Contract: . . . . . .No
Expand in Territory: . . . . . . Yes
Passive Ownership: . . . Discouraged
Encourage Conversions: . . . . NA
Average # Employees: . 2 FT, 4-6 PT

FRANCHISOR TRAINING/SUPPORT:
Financial Assistance Provided: . . . . .No
Site Selection Assistance: . . . . . . .Yes
Lease Negotiation Assistance: . . . .Yes
Co-operative Advertising: . . . . . . .Yes
Training: . . . . .1 Wk. Headquarters,
. . . 1 Wk. Company-Owned Retail Store
On-Going Support: E,h,I/ 10
EXPANSION PLANS:
    US: . . . . . Southeast and Midwest Only
    Canada: . . . . No
    Overseas: . . . . No

KIDDIE ACADEMY INTERNATIONAL

108 Wheel Rd., # 200
Bel Air, MD 21015
TEL: (800) 5-KIDDIE (410) 515-0788
FAX: (410) 569-9165
Mr. Richard Rohde, VP Fran. Dev.

We provide: site selection, lease negotiation, marketing assistance, on-going consulting, processing accounting and accredited curriculum (including Spanish, computer and kindergarten).

HISTORY: . . . . IFA	FINANCIAL: Earnings Claim: . .No	FRANCHISOR TRAINING/SUPPORT:
Established in 1979; . . 1st Franchised in 1992	Cash Investment: $30K	Financial Assistance Provided: . . . Yes(I)
Company-Owned Units (As of 8/31/1992): . .8	Total Investment: $80-700K	Site Selection Assistance: . . . . .Yes
Franchised Units (As of 8/31/1992): 6	Fees: Franchise - $20K	Lease Negotiation Assistance: . . . . . .Yes
Total Units (As of 8/31/1992): 14	Royalty: 7%, Advert: 0%	Co-operative Advertising: . . . . No
Projected New Units for 1993: 15	Contract Periods (Yrs.): 10/5	Training: . . . . 2 Wks. HQ, 2 Days Grand
Distribution: US-14;Can-0;Overseas-0	Area Development Agreement: Yes/10	. . Opening, 2 Wks. Franchisee Location
North America: . . . . 6 States	Sub-Franchise Contract: . . . . . . .No	On-Going Support: A,B,C,D,E,G,H,I/ .130
Concentration: . . . . .8 in MD	Expand in Territory: . . . . Yes	EXPANSION PLANS:
Registered: . . . .FL,IL,IN,MD,MI,NY,RI,VA	Passive Ownership: . . . Discouraged	US: . . . . All US
. . . . WI,DC	Encourage Conversions: . . . . Yes	Canada: . . . . No
Type Space: . . . . .FS, SC;~6,500 SF	Average # Employees: . .15 FT, 1 PT	Overseas: . . . . No

KIDS' TIME

7101 York Ave.
Edina, MN 55435
TEL: (800) 922-0991 (815) 932-2021
FAX: (815) 937-1442
Mr. Greg Morse, Dir. Fran. Dev.

KIDS' TIME is a supervised child's play center. Located in strip and shopping centers, KIDS' TIME is a drop-in facility that allows parents to bring their children in without prior notice. Parents are given a beeper when they leave. Kids watch movies, play games and may participate in organized activities.

HISTORY:	FINANCIAL: Earnings Claim: . .No	FRANCHISOR TRAINING/SUPPORT:
Established in 1981; . . 1st Franchised in 1990	Cash Investment: $25-30K	Financial Assistance Provided: . . . Yes(I)
Company-Owned Units (As of 8/31/1992): . .2	Total Investment: $89.5-119.5K	Site Selection Assistance: . . . . .Yes
Franchised Units (As of 8/31/1992): 3	Fees: Franchise - $19.5K	Lease Negotiation Assistance: . . . . .Yes
Total Units (As of 8/31/1992): 5	Royalty: 5%, Advert: 3%	Co-operative Advertising: . . . . .NA
Projected New Units for 1993: 5	Contract Periods (Yrs.): 10/10	Training: . . . . .1 Wk. Headquarters,
Distribution: US-5;Can-0;Overseas-0	Area Development Agreement: . .No	. . . . 1 Wk. On-Site
North America: . . . . 2 States	Sub-Franchise Contract: . . . . .No	On-Going Support: C,D,E,H,I/ 3
Concentration: . . . . 4 in MN, 1 in MI	Expand in Territory: . . . . . . Yes	EXPANSION PLANS:
Registered: . . . . IL,MI	Passive Ownership: . . . Discouraged	US: . . . . .37 FTC States + Illinois
. . . .	Encourage Conversions: . . . . NA	Canada: . . . . .No
Type Space: . . . . .SC;~4,000 SF	Average # Employees:	Overseas: . . . . No

KINDERDANCE INTERNATIONAL

2150 Atlantic St., P. O. Box 510881
Melbourne Beach, FL 32951
TEL: (800) 666-1595 (407) 254-3000
FAX: (407) 253-1014
Mr. Bernie Friedman, VP

KINDERDANCE franchisees are trained to teach 4 developmentally unique dance and motor development programs. KINDERDANCE, KINDERGYM, KINDERTOTS and KINDERCOMBO, which are designed for boys and girls ages 2-10. They learn the basics of ballet, tap, gymnastics and creative dance, as well as learning numbers, colors, shapes and words. KINDERDANCE programs are taught in a non-competitive, fun environment at child care centers, etc.

HISTORY:	FINANCIAL: Earnings Claim: . .No	FRANCHISOR TRAINING/SUPPORT:
Established in 1979; . . 1st Franchised in 1985	Cash Investment: $4-5.5K	Financial Assistance Provided: . . . Yes(D)
Company-Owned Units (As of 8/31/1992): . .0	Total Investment: $7-10K	Site Selection Assistance: . . . . .Yes
Franchised Units (As of 8/31/1992): 49	Fees: Franchise - $6-9K	Lease Negotiation Assistance: . . . . .Yes
Total Units (As of 8/31/1992): 49	Royalty: 10-15%, Advert: . . . 3%	Co-operative Advertising: . . . . .Yes
Projected New Units for 1993: 50	Contract Periods (Yrs.): 10/10	Training: . . . . 7 Days Headquarters,
Distribution: US-49;Can-0;Overseas-0	Area Development Agreement: Yes/10	. . . . .3-5 Days Franchisee Area
North America: . . . . 20 States	Sub-Franchise Contract: . . . . . .No	On-Going Support: A,B,C,D,E,F,G,H,I/ . 2
Concentration: . . . 5 in WA, 4 in FL, 3 in CA	Expand in Territory: . . . . Yes	EXPANSION PLANS:
Registered: . . . CA,FL,IL,IN,MD,MI,NY,OR	Passive Ownership: . . . Not Allowed	US: . . . . All US
. . . . VA,WA	Encourage Conversions: . . . . . Yes	Canada: . . . . .No
Type Space: . . . . ;~ SF	Average # Employees: . . 1 FT, 1 PT	Overseas: . . . . No

MISS LITTLE AMERICA

P. O. Box 290837
Port Orange, FL 32129
TEL: (800) 829-8723 (904) 767-2195 C
FAX: (904) 767-2194
Mr. Michael V. Biro, Fran. Dir.

Beauty pageant system for children.

HISTORY:	FINANCIAL: Earnings Claim: . .No	FRANCHISOR TRAINING/SUPPORT:
Established in 1985; . . 1st Franchised in 1989	Cash Investment: $3.9K	Financial Assistance Provided: . . .Yes(D)
Company-Owned Units (As of 8/31/1992): . .1	Total Investment: $3.9-29K	Site Selection Assistance: . . . . .NA
Franchised Units (As of 8/31/1992): 3	Fees: Franchise - $3.9K	Lease Negotiation Assistance: . . . . .NA
Total Units (As of 8/31/1992): 4	Royalty: 25%, Advert:	Co-operative Advertising: . . . . .NA
Projected New Units for 1993: 100	Contract Periods (Yrs.): . . . 5/5/5/5	Training: . . . . 1 Day Headquarters
Distribution: US-4;Can-0;Overseas-0	Area Development Agreement: . .No	. . . .
North America: . . . . 4 States	Sub-Franchise Contract: . . . . . Yes	On-Going Support: b,c,d,h,i/ 3
Concentration: . . . 1 in FL, 1 in GA, 1 in KY	Expand in Territory: . . . . . . Yes	EXPANSION PLANS:
Registered: . . . . .FL	Passive Ownership: . . . Discouraged	US: . . . . All US
. . . .	Encourage Conversions: . . . . . NA	Canada: . . . . .All Canada
Type Space: . . . .;~ SF	Average # Employees: . . 1 FT, 5 PT	Overseas: . . . . No

PEE WEE WORKOUT

34976 Aspenwood Ln.
Willoughby, OH 44094
TEL: (800) 356-6261 (216) 946-7888
FAX:
Ms. Margi Carr, President

PEE WEE WORKOUT teaches healthy living to pre-schoolers. The 30-minute classes consist of 20 minutes of movement set to original music that covers all components of fitness with 10 minutes of a heart/anatomy/nutrition lesson. Trained instructors have weekly visits to day/pre-schools, athletic departments.

HISTORY:	FINANCIAL: Earnings Claim: . .No	FRANCHISOR TRAINING/SUPPORT:
Established in 1986; . . 1st Franchised in 1988	Cash Investment: $2K	Financial Assistance Provided: . . . . .No
Company-Owned Units (As of 8/31/1992): . .1	Total Investment: $2K	Site Selection Assistance: . . . . .No
Franchised Units (As of 8/31/1992): 21	Fees: Franchise - $1.5K	Lease Negotiation Assistance: . . . . .No
Total Units (As of 8/31/1992): 22	Royalty: 10%, Advert: 0%	Co-operative Advertising: . . . . .No
Projected New Units for 1993: 6	Contract Periods (Yrs.): 5/3	Training: . . . . .Video Based
Distribution: US-21;Can-1;Overseas-0	Area Development Agreement: . .No	. . . .
North America: . . . . 9 States	Sub-Franchise Contract: . . . . .No	On-Going Support: G,I/ 2
Concentration: . . . 3 in TX, 2 in OH, 2 in PA	Expand in Territory: . . . . . . Yes	EXPANSION PLANS:
Registered:	Passive Ownership: . . . Discouraged	US: . . . . .All US
. . . .	Encourage Conversions:	Canada: . . . . .All Canada
Type Space: . . . .;~ SF	Average # Employees: . . . . . .1 FT	Overseas: . . . . .Yes

SAF-T-CHILD

401 Friday Mountain Rd.
Austin, TX 78737
TEL: (800) 828-0098 (512) 288-2882
FAX: (512) 288-2898
Mr. Dennis Wagner, VP

Child security and identification products. Proven home business provides exceptional opportunity for profit and emotional satisfaction by helping to prevent missing children through child security and identification products. SAFE-T-CHILD is offered to a ready market of concerned parents through child cares, schools, churches, community organizations and business sponsors. No royalties. Computerization included.

HISTORY:	FINANCIAL: Earnings Claim: . .No	FRANCHISOR TRAINING/SUPPORT:
Established in 1987; . . 1st Franchised in 1992	Cash Investment: $10-12K	Financial Assistance Provided: . . . . .No
Company-Owned Units (As of 8/31/1992): . .1	Total Investment: $10-12K	Site Selection Assistance: . . . . .NA
Franchised Units (As of 8/31/1992): 53	Fees: Franchise - $9.8K	Lease Negotiation Assistance: . . . . .NA
Total Units (As of 8/31/1992): 54	Royalty: 0%, Advert: 0%	Co-operative Advertising: . . . . .NA
Projected New Units for 1993: 48	Contract Periods (Yrs.): 5/15	Training: . . . .
Distribution: US-49;Can-5;Overseas-0	Area Development Agreement: . .No	. . . .
North America: . . . . 25 States, 3 Provinces	Sub-Franchise Contract: . . . . .No	On-Going Support: B,C,d,G,H/ 4
Concentration: . . . . .TX, MI, CA	Expand in Territory: . . . . . . .No	EXPANSION PLANS:
Registered: . . . . .FL,MI,OR	Passive Ownership: . . . Discouraged	US: . . . . All US
. . . .	Encourage Conversions: . . . . . NA	Canada: . . . . .All Canada
Type Space: . . . . . . .Home Based;~NA SF	Average # Employees: . . . . . .1 FT	Overseas: . . . . No

TUTOR TIME

4517 NW 31st Ave.
Ft. Lauderdale, FL 33309
TEL: (800) 275-1235 (305) 730-0332
FAX: (305) 730-7550
Mr. Joseph Geraci, Dir. Fran. Sales

TUTOR TIME is the fastest-growing child care franchise in the USA. We are the exclusive care giver for the children of the Kennedy Space Center (NASA). We provide a turn-key pre-school for qualified people anywhere in the country. We have the most comprehensive training program and our own patented curriculum providing the finest child care and evaluation in the industry.

HISTORY: . . . . IFA
Established in 1980; . . 1st Franchised in 1990
Company-Owned Units (As of 8/31/1992): . .2
Franchised Units (As of 8/31/1992): 22
Total Units (As of 8/31/1992): 24
Projected New Units for 1993: 24
Distribution: US-24;Can-0;Overseas-0
North America: . . . . .1 State
Concentration: . . . . .24 in FL
Registered: . . . . CA,FL,MI,NY
. . . .
Type Space: . . . FS, SC, Off. Park;~8,000 SF

FINANCIAL: Earnings Claim: . .No
Cash Investment: $55-75K
Total Investment: $155-180K
Fees: Franchise - $27.5K
 Royalty: 5%, Advert: 1%
Contract Periods (Yrs.): 10/5
Area Development Agreement: . Yes
Sub-Franchise Contract: . . . . . Yes
Expand in Territory: . . . . Yes
Passive Ownership: . . . Discouraged
Encourage Conversions: . . . . . Yes
Average # Employees: . .3 FT, 17 PT

FRANCHISOR TRAINING/SUPPORT:
Financial Assistance Provided: . . . Yes(I)
Site Selection Assistance: . . . . . . .Yes
Lease Negotiation Assistance: . . . . .Yes
Co-operative Advertising: . . . . .Yes
Training: . . . . 2 Wks. Headquarters,
. . . . 1 Month Franchisee Location
On-Going Support: C,D,E,F,G,H,I/ . . . 40
EXPANSION PLANS:
US: . . . . All US
Canada: . . . . .All Canada
Overseas: . . . . .EUR, S. America

USA BABY

752 N. Larch Ave.
Elmhurst, IL 60126
TEL: (800) 323-4108 (708) 832-9880
FAX: (708) 832-0139
Mr. Todd Levine, Fran. Coord.

USA BABY is America's leading chain of infant and children's furniture retail stores. We've achieved a prominent niche in this fast-growing market by being better than the competition. As a USA BABY store owner, you benefit from national buying power, exclusive merchandise, a comprehensive advertising program and national consumer recognition. Call now for more information.

HISTORY: . . . .
Established in 1975; . . 1st Franchised in 1986
Company-Owned Units (As of 8/31/1992): . .9
Franchised Units (As of 8/31/1992): 33
Total Units (As of 8/31/1992): 42
Projected New Units for 1993: 6
Distribution: US-42;Can-0;Overseas-0
North America: . . . . 21 States
Concentration: . . . . 8 in IL, 5 in NY, 4 in NJ
Registered: . . .CA,FL,IL,IN,MD,MI,MN,NY
. . . . .OR,RI,VA,WA,WI,DC
Type Space: . . . . .SC;~7,500 SF

FINANCIAL: Earnings Claim: . .No
Cash Investment: $75-100K
Total Investment: $125-225K
Fees: Franchise - $7.5-16.5K
 Royalty: 3%, Advert: 1/2%
Contract Periods (Yrs.): 10/10
Area Development Agreement: Yes/Var
Sub-Franchise Contract: . . . . . Yes
Expand in Territory: . . . . Yes
Passive Ownership: . . . Discouraged
Encourage Conversions: . . . . . Yes
Average # Employees: . . 4 FT, 4 PT

FRANCHISOR TRAINING/SUPPORT:
Financial Assistance Provided: . . . . No
Site Selection Assistance: . . . . . . .Yes
Lease Negotiation Assistance: . . . .Yes
Co-operative Advertising: . . . . No
Training: . . . . 2 Wks. Headquarters,
. . . . .1 Wk. On-Site
On-Going Support: a,C,D,E,G,H,I/ 6
EXPANSION PLANS:
US: . . . . .All US
Canada: . . . . No
Overseas: . . . . No

WEE WATCH PRIVATE HOME DAY CARE

25 Valleywood Dr., # 20
Markham, ON L3R 5L9 CAN
TEL: (416) 479-4274 C
FAX: (416) 479-9047
Mr. Terry Fullerton, VP

WEE WATCH is a private, home day care agency, catering to children aged 6 weeks and older. Full-time or part-time. The care takes place in fully-inspected homes containing a trained provider.

HISTORY: . . . .
Established in 1984; . . 1st Franchised in 1987
Company-Owned Units (As of 8/31/1992): . .0
Franchised Units (As of 8/31/1992): 38
Total Units (As of 8/31/1992): 38
Projected New Units for 1993: 6
Distribution: US-0;Can-38;Overseas-0
North America: . . . . 2 Provinces
Concentration: . . . . . . 32 in ON, 6 in BC
Registered: . . . .
. . . .
Type Space: . . . .;~ SF

FINANCIAL: Earnings Claim: . Yes
Cash Investment: $15K
Total Investment: $15K
Fees: Franchise - $6K
 Royalty: 6-8%, Advert: 2%
Contract Periods (Yrs.): 5/20
Area Development Agreement: . .No
Sub-Franchise Contract: . . . . .No
Expand in Territory: . . . . . . .No
Passive Ownership: . . . Not Allowed
Encourage Conversions: . . . . Yes
Average # Employees: . . 2 FT, 1 PT

FRANCHISOR TRAINING/SUPPORT:
Financial Assistance Provided: . . . . .No
Site Selection Assistance: . . . . . . .NA
Lease Negotiation Assistance: . . . . .NA
Co-operative Advertising: . . . . . . .Yes
Training: . . . . 3 Days Headquarters,
. . . . 5 Days On-Site
On-Going Support: B,C,G,H,I/ 8
EXPANSION PLANS:
US: . . . . Master Franchise
Canada: . . . . .All Canada
Overseas: . . . . No

WONDERS OF WISDOM CHILDREN'S CENTERS
3114 Golansky Blvd., # 201
Prince William, VA 22192
TEL: (800) 424-0550 (703) 670-9344
FAX: (703) 670-2851
Ms. E. Gail Scott, VP

Quality childcare, together with a tested developmental educational approach to early education, emphasizing language and social development, motor skills and reading. Programs developed over 25 years by early childhood educators.

HISTORY: . . . . IFA
Established in 1967; . . 1st Franchised in 1989
Company-Owned Units (As of 8/31/1992): . . 1
Franchised Units (As of 8/31/1992): 2
Total Units (As of 8/31/1992): 3
Projected New Units for 1993: 5
Distribution: US-3;Can-0;Overseas-0
  North America: . . . . 3 States
  Concentration: . . . 1 in VA, 1 in NY, 1 in LA
Registered: . . . . FL,MD,MI,NY,OR,VA,DC
. . . .
Type Space: FS,SF,SC,Off.Park;~6,000-7,000 SF

FINANCIAL: Earnings Claim: . .No
Cash Investment: $35K
Total Investment: . . . $110.3-193.5K
Fees: Franchise - $20K
  Royalty: 6%, Advert: 1%
Contract Periods (Yrs.): 10/10
Area Development Agreement: . Yes
Sub-Franchise Contract: . . . . .No
Expand in Territory: . . . . . . Yes
Passive Ownership: . . . Discouraged
Encourage Conversions: . . . . . Yes
Average # Employees: . 12 FT, 15 PT

FRANCHISOR TRAINING/SUPPORT:
Financial Assistance Provided: . . . . . No
Site Selection Assistance: . . . . .Yes
Lease Negotiation Assistance: . . . . .Yes
Co-operative Advertising: . . . . .Yes
Training: . . . . . . 2-3 Wks. Headquarters,
. . . . 1-2 Wks. On-Site
On-Going Support: b,C,d,E,F,G,h,I/ . . . 5
EXPANSION PLANS:
  US: . . . . . Northeast, Southeast and SC
  Canada: . . . . .No
  Overseas: . . . . No

SUPPLEMENTAL LISTING OF FRANCHISORS

BABIES FIRST, A DIAPER SERVICE . . . . .3030 Harbor Ln., # 100, Minneapolis, MN 55447
  Contact: Mr. James Dunlop, VP Fran. Dev.; Tel: (612) 559-7227
BABY NEWS . . . . 23521 Foley St., Hayward, CA 94545
  Contact: Mr. Roger O'Callaghan; Tel: (415) 786-3460
BABY TOYTOWN/4 BABYS ONLY . . . . 8938 E. Valley Blvd., Rosemead, CA 91770
  Contact: Mr. Bernard Zwick; Tel: (818) 280-5410
CAROUSEL SYSTEMS . . . . .381 Brooks Rd., King of Prussia, PA 19406
  Contact: Mr. Joseph Scandone, President; Tel: (215) 265-5015
CHILDREN'S ORCHARD . . . . 253 Low St., Newburyport, MA 01950
  Contact: Ms. Karen Lynch, President; Tel: (800) 999-KIDS (508) 465-7726 C
DIAPER DAN'S DELIVERY . . . . 5008 Herzel Pl., Beltsville, MD 20705
  Contact: Mr. Mark Hill; Tel: (301) 937-1660
DISCOVERY ZONE . . . . .323 W. 8th, # 314, Kansas City, MO 64105
  Contact: Mr. Thayer Bauman, Dir. Fran. Sales; Tel: (816) 472-5437
FIT BY FIVE . . . . 1606 Penfield Rd., Rochester, NY 14625
  Contact: Ms. Betty Perkins-Carpenter, President; Tel: (716) 586-7980
FUTUREKIDS . . . . 5777 W. Century Blvd., # 1555, Los Angeles, CA 90045
  Contact: Mr. Ed Poole, VP Fran. Dev.; Tel: (800) PRO-KIDS (310) 337-7006
GYMSTERS . . . . 5468 Castle Glen Ave., San Jose, CA 95129
  Contact: Ms. Harli Rabow, President; Tel: (800) 456-8955 (408) 996-8955
IDENTIFICATION SERVICES OF CANADA . . . . . . 150 Clark Blvd., # 238, Brampton, ON L6T 4Y8   CAN
  Contact: Mr. Joseph M. Marois; Tel: (416) 796-2211
LEWIS OF LONDON . . . . .25 Power Dr., Hauppauge, NY 11788
  Contact: Mr. Joel Rallo; Tel: (516) 582-8300
LI'L GUYS 'N' GALS DAYCARE . . . . .10850 N. 90th St., Scottsdale, AZ 85260
  Contact: Mr. Tom Trollope, President; Tel: (602) 451-0930
LOLLIPOP LANE PRE-SCHOOL/CHILD CARE . . . 7031 E. Camelback Rd., # 379, Scottsdale, AZ 85251
  Contact: Mr. Jerry Scali, President; Tel: (602) 423-0802
MASTERMIND EDUCATIONAL TECHNOLOGIES . . 465 Milner Ave., # 7, Scarborough, ON M1B 2K4   CAN
  Contact: Mr. Andy Levy; Tel: (416) 321-8984
MUSIC TIME . . . . 915 Front St., San Francisco, CA 94111
  Contact: Ms. Nancy Underhill, Fran. Sales; Tel: (415) 677-9777
PLAYFUL PARENTING . . . . .145 Maple Dr., New Holland, PA 17557
  Contact: Mr. Gary R. Seibert; Tel: (215) 678-0232
PLAYORENA . . . . 125 Mineola Ave., Rosyln Heights, NY 11577
  Contact: Mr. Fred Jaroslow, EVP; Tel: (516) 621-7529
PRIMARY PREP . . . . .159 Sand Pine Dr., Jupiter, FL 33477
  Contact: Ms. Pauline A. McKee, President; Tel: (407) 743-6633

PRIMROSE SCHOOLS . . . . .5131 Roswell Rd., NE, Marietta, GA 30062
    Contact: Mr. Paul Erwin, President; Tel: (800) 745-0728 (404) 998-8329
PRODIGY CHILD DEVELOPMENT CENTERS . . . . . 8601 Dunwoody Pl., # 714, Atlanta, GA 30350
    Contact: President; Tel: (404) 993-7211
QUINBY'S FOR THE CURIOUS CHILD . . . . 3411 California St., San Francisco, CA 94118
    Contact: Ms. Micheline Chau, President; Tel:
SPORTASTIKS . . . . P. O. Box 3271, Champaign, IL 61826
    Contact: Mr. Jim Wilkins, VP; Tel: (217) 352-4269
STORK NEWS OF AMERICA . . . . .5075 Morganton Rd., # 12A, Fayetteville, NC 28314
    Contact: Ms. Kymberli Senecal, Fran. Dir.; Tel: (800) 633-6395 (919) 868-3065
SUPERCLUB SPORTS & FITNESS FOR KIDS . . . . 317 Monticello Ave., Norfolk, VA 23510
    Contact: Mr. Ken Johnson, President; Tel: (804) 463-5437
TEGELER TIME DAY CARE . . . . .P. O. Box 67213, Chestnut Hill, MA 02167
    Contact: Mr. Dean Tegeler, President; Tel: (617) 849-3222
YOUTHLAND ACADEMY . . . . 210 University Dr., # 402, Coral Springs, FL 33071
    Contact: Mr. Bill Landman; Tel: (305) 345-0600

CHAPTER 15

EDUCATION / PERSONAL DEVELOPMENT / TRAINING

AMERICAN COLLEGE PLANNING SERVICE
44F Jeffryn Blvd. W
Deer Park, NY 11729
TEL: (800) 486-2655 (516) 243-5000
FAX: (516) 243-5908
Mr. Randy G. Romano, VP

College financial aid planning and form preparation. ACPS helps parents of college-bound students to qualify and apply for federal, state and college-based financial aid, reducing a family's out of pocket college expenses.

HISTORY: . . . .
Established in 1984; . . 1st Franchised in 1986
Company-Owned Units (As of 8/31/1992): . .1
Franchised Units (As of 8/31/1992): 29
Total Units (As of 8/31/1992): 30
Projected New Units for 1993: 12
Distribution: US-30;Can-0;Overseas-0
 North America: . . . . 9 States
 Concentration: . . . 6 in MA, 4 in CT, 3 in NJ
Registered: . . . .
 . . . .
Type Space: . . . . . Office Space;~1,000 SF

FINANCIAL: Earnings Claim: . .No
Cash Investment: $10-15K
Total Investment: $10-15K
Fees: Franchise - $7.5K
 Royalty: 10%, Advert: 0%
Contract Periods (Yrs.): 10/10
Area Development Agreement: . .No
Sub-Franchise Contract: . . . . .No
Expand in Territory: . . . . . . Yes
Passive Ownership: . . . Discouraged
Encourage Conversions: . . . . . NA
Average # Employees: .2 FT, 5-10 PT

FRANCHISOR TRAINING/SUPPORT:
Financial Assistance Provided: . . . . . No
Site Selection Assistance: . . . . .Yes
Lease Negotiation Assistance: . . . . .Yes
Co-operative Advertising: . . . . No
Training: . . . . 3 Days Home Office,
 . . . . .2 Days Franchisee Location
On-Going Support: a,C,D,G,I/ 10
EXPANSION PLANS:
 US: . . . . .All US
 Canada: . . . . .No
 Overseas: . . . . No

EDUCATIONAL PRODUCT AND SERVICES

| | 1989 | 1990 | 1991 | Percentage Change | |
				90/89	91/90
Total Number of Establishments:					
Company-Owned	841	1,081	1,106	28.54%	2.31%
Franchisee-Owned	10,236	11,458	12,744	11.94%	11.22%
Total	11,077	12,539	13,850	13.20%	10.46%
Ratio of Total Establishments:					
Company-Owned	7.6%	8.6%	8.0%		
Franchisee-Owned	92.4%	91.4%	92.0%		
Total	100.0%	100.0%	100.0%		
Total Sales ($000):					
Company-Owned	540,803	620,020	677,272	14.65%	9.23%
Franchisee-Owned	1,113,527	1,411,379	1,577,733	26.75%	11.79%
Total	1,654,330	2,031,399	2,255,005	22.79%	11.01%
Ratio of Total Sales:					
Company-Owned	32.7%	30.5%	30.0%		
Franchisee-Owned	67.3%	69.5%	70.0%		
Total	100.0%	100.0%	100.0%		
Average Sales Per Unit ($000):					
Company-Owned	643	574	612	-10.81%	6.76%
Franchisee-Owned	109	123	124	13.23%	0.51%
Total	149	162	163	8.48%	0.50%
Relative Average Sales Ratio:	591.1%	465.6%	494.6%		

	Number Of Employees		Employees Per Unit		Avg. Sales Per Employee
Total 1989 Employment:					
Company-Owned	23,534		28.0		$22,980
Franchisee-Owned	44,468		4.3		$25,041
Total	68,002		6.1		$24,328
Relative Employee Performance Ratios:			644.1%		91.8%

	1st Quartile		Median		4th Quartile
Average 1989 Total Investment:					
Company-Owned	$27,500		$82,500		$187,500
Franchisee-Owned	$25,000		$50,000		$100,000
Single Unit Franchise Fee	$12,000		$17,250		$27,500
Mult. Unit Franchise Fee	NA		$20,000		NA
Franchise Start-Up Cost	$15,000		$25,000		$75,000

Source: Franchising In The Economy 1991, IFA Educational Foundation & Horwath International.

ANTHONY ROBBINS & ASSOCIATES

9191 Towne Centre Dr., # 290
San Diego, CA 92122
TEL: (800) 445-8183 (619) 535-9900
FAX:
Ms. Janice Chabza, Compliance

ANTHONY ROBBINS' books and tapes have impacted millions all over the world. As a franchisee of ANTHONY ROBBINS & ASSOCIATES, you are the owner of a full-time seminar and training business. You will be the exclusive marketer of 3 video-based seminars. You also market our complete live seminars and best-selling audiotape series. You will enjoy comprehensive training, coaching and support.

HISTORY: . . . .
Established in 1985; . . 1st Franchised in 1990
Company-Owned Units (As of 8/31/1992): . .0
Franchised Units (As of 8/31/1992): 45
Total Units (As of 8/31/1992): 45
Projected New Units for 1993: 30
Distribution: US-40;Can-5;Overseas-0
  North America: . . . . 28 States, 4 Provinces
  Concentration: . . . 8 in CA, 4 in ON, 3 in TX
Registered: . . . CA,FL,HI,IN,MD,MI,MN,NY
 . . . . OR,RI,WA,WI,DC,AB
Type Space: . . . . NA;~ SF

FINANCIAL: Earnings Claim: . .No
Cash Investment: . . . .$
Total Investment: $49.6-89.2K
Fees: Franchise - $36K
  Royalty: 8%, Advert: 0%
Contract Periods (Yrs.): 5/5
Area Development Agreement: . .No
Sub-Franchise Contract: . . . . .No
Expand in Territory: . . . . . . .No
Passive Ownership: . . . Not Allowed
Encourage Conversions: . . . . NA
Average # Employees: . . . . . .

FRANCHISOR TRAINING/SUPPORT:
Financial Assistance Provided: . . .Yes(D)
Site Selection Assistance: . . . . . . .NA
Lease Negotiation Assistance: . . . . .NA
Co-operative Advertising: . . . . . . .NA
Training: . . . . . . .18 Days Headquarters
 . . . .
On-Going Support: D,G,h,I/ . . . .
EXPANSION PLANS:
  US: . . . . .All US
  Canada: . . . . .Yes
  Overseas: . . . . No

BARBIZON SCHOOLS OF MODELING

1900 Glades Rd., # 300
Boca Raton, FL 33431
TEL: (407) 362-8883
FAX:
Mr. Barry B. Wolff, President

Proprietary, private schools of modeling, personal improvement and related creative arts.

HISTORY: . . . . IFA
Established in 1939; . . 1st Franchised in 1968
Company-Owned Units (As of 8/31/1992): . .0
Franchised Units (As of 8/31/1992): 96
Total Units (As of 8/31/1992): 96
Projected New Units for 1993: 4
Distribution: US-90;Can-2;Overseas-4
  North America: . . . . 40 States
  Concentration: . . . 11 in CA, 7 in NY, 6 in FL
Registered: . . . . .CA,IL,NY
 . . . .
Type Space: . . . .FS, SF, SC, RM;~2,500 SF

FINANCIAL: Earnings Claim: . .No
Cash Investment: $35-45K
Total Investment: $60K
Fees: Franchise - $19-35K
  Royalty: 7.5%, Advert: 2%
Contract Periods (Yrs.): 10
Area Development Agreement: . .No
Sub-Franchise Contract: . . . . .No
Expand in Territory: . . . . . . Yes
Passive Ownership: . . . Discouraged
Encourage Conversions: . . . . .No
Average # Employees: . .5 FT, 10 PT

FRANCHISOR TRAINING/SUPPORT:
Financial Assistance Provided: . . .Yes(D)
Site Selection Assistance: . . . . . . .Yes
Lease Negotiation Assistance: . . . . .Yes
Co-operative Advertising: . . . . . . .NA
Training: . . . . . . .Continuous Training
 . . . .
On-Going Support: C,D,G,H/ 11
EXPANSION PLANS:
  US: . . . . .All US
  Canada: . . . . .All Canada
  Overseas: . . . . Yes

BRITANNICA LEARNING CENTER

310 S. Michigan Ave.
Chicago, IL 60604
TEL: (800) 433-7782 (312) 939-0303
FAX: (312) 939-1680
Mr. James Gurke, Dir. Fran. Dev.

Learning centers for after-school, individual instruction in reading and math for children in K-12. Also includes SAT and ACT preparation and Evelyn Wood Study Skills programs.

HISTORY: . . . .
Established in 1970; . . 1st Franchised in 1983
Company-Owned Units (As of 8/31/1992): . 68
Franchised Units (As of 8/31/1992): 13
Total Units (As of 8/31/1992): 81
Projected New Units for 1993: 15
Distribution: US-81;Can-0;Overseas-0
  North America: . . . . 9 States
  Concentration: . . . 48 in CA, 9 in IL, 8 in NY
Registered: . . . . .All
 . . . .
Type Space: . FS, SF, SC, RM;~1,200-1,800 SF

FINANCIAL: Earnings Claim: . .No
Cash Investment: $51-139K
Total Investment: $85-179.5K
Fees: Franchise - $25-35K
  Royalty: 8% Gross, Advert: 1.5% Gr.
Contract Periods (Yrs.): 5/5
Area Development Agreement: Yes/Var
Sub-Franchise Contract: . . . . .No
Expand in Territory: . . . . . . Yes
Passive Ownership: . . . Discouraged
Encourage Conversions: . . . . Yes
Average # Employees: . 2 FT, 3-6 PT

FRANCHISOR TRAINING/SUPPORT:
Financial Assistance Provided: . . .Yes(D)
Site Selection Assistance: . . . . . . .Yes
Lease Negotiation Assistance: . . . . .Yes
Co-operative Advertising: . . . . . . .Yes
Training: . . . . . 15 Working Days Home
 . . . . Office, 2 Days On-Site
On-Going Support: A,B,C,D,E,F,G,H,I/ 44
EXPANSION PLANS:
  US: . . . . .All US
  Canada: . . . . No
  Overseas: . . . . No

BUTLER LEARNING SYSTEMS

1325 W. Dorothy Ln.
Dayton, OH 45409
TEL: (513) 298-7462
FAX: (513) 298-5022
Mr. Don Butler, President

Choose from 30 proven audio-visual, multi-media, training programs for managers, supervisors, sales professionals and workers. Sell programs and seminars to business, industry, banks, hospitals and public sector. Supplement consulting or build a business. Training available.

HISTORY: . . . .
Established in 1959; . . 1st Franchised in 1977
Company-Owned Units (As of 8/31/1992): . .1
Franchised Units (As of 8/31/1992): . . . . . <u>64</u>
Total Units (As of 8/31/1992): 65
Projected New Units for 1993: 15
Distribution: US-53;Can-7;Overseas-5
 North America: . . . . . 21 States, 6 Provinces
 Concentration: . . . . 5 in OH, 3 in CA
Registered: . . . .
 . . . .
Type Space: . . . . Home Based;~ SF

FINANCIAL: Earnings Claim: . .No
Cash Investment: $10K
Total Investment: $15K
Fees: Franchise - $500
 Royalty: 10%, Advert: 0%
Contract Periods (Yrs.): . . . 1/Infin.
Area Development Agreement: . .No
Sub-Franchise Contract: . . . . .No
Expand in Territory: . . . . . . Yes
Passive Ownership: . . . . .Allowed
Encourage Conversions: . . . . Yes
Average # Employees: . . 1 FT, 1 PT

FRANCHISOR TRAINING/SUPPORT:
Financial Assistance Provided: . . . . .No
Site Selection Assistance: . . . . . . .NA
Lease Negotiation Assistance: . . . . .NA
Co-operative Advertising: . . . . . . .No
Training: . . . . . . 1 Wk. HQ, Yearly at
 . . . . Headquarters
On-Going Support: D,G,H/ 13
EXPANSION PLANS:
US: . . . . All US
Canada: . . . . .All Canada
Overseas: . . . . Yes

CITIZENS AGAINST CRIME

1022 S. Greenville Ave.
Allen, TX 75002
TEL: (800) 466-5566 (214) 390-7033
FAX: (214) 390-7606
Ms. Sheri Thibodeau, Fran. Sales

CITIZENS AGAINST CRIME - A crime prevention safety seminar corporation that has been "Saving Lives Through Education Since 1980." We offer: exclusive territory, impressive earning potential, low investment with financing available, professional and on-going support, recession-proof industry. Qualifications are: entrepreneurial drive, spirit and determination. Public speaking and experience helpful, but not necessary.

HISTORY: . . . . IFA
Established in 1980; . . 1st Franchised in 1986
Company-Owned Units (As of 8/31/1992): . .3
Franchised Units (As of 8/31/1992): . . . . . <u>45</u>
Total Units (As of 8/31/1992): 48
Projected New Units for 1993: 12
Distribution: US-48;Can-0;Overseas-0
 North America: . . . . 26 States
 Concentration: . . . .6 in FL, 4 in TX, 3 in PA
Registered: . . . . All States
 . . . .
Type Space: . . . . . Office Space;~NA SF

FINANCIAL: Earnings Claim: . .No
Cash Investment: $15-30K
Total Investment: $30-50K
Fees: Franchise - . . . . . $17.5K+
 Royalty: 0%, Advert: 0%
Contract Periods (Yrs.): 5/5
Area Development Agreement: Yes/5
Sub-Franchise Contract: . . . . .No
Expand in Territory: . . . . . . Yes
Passive Ownership: . . . Discouraged
Encourage Conversions: . . . . .No
Average # Employees: . . . . . .4 FT

FRANCHISOR TRAINING/SUPPORT:
Financial Assistance Provided: . . .Yes(D)
Site Selection Assistance: . . . . . . .NA
Lease Negotiation Assistance: . . . . No
Co-operative Advertising: . . . . . . .Yes
Training: . . . . . .7 Days National Office,
 . . . . 5 Days Centralized Training Local
On-Going Support: A,B,C,D,F,G,H,I/ . 19
EXPANSION PLANS:
US: . . . . All US
Canada: . . . . .All Canada
Overseas: . . . . Yes

COMPUCOLLEGE SCHOOL OF BUSINESS

5650 Yonge St., # 1400
North York, ON M2M 4G3 CAN
TEL: (416) 733-4452
FAX: (416) 733-4627
Mr. Jerry Stessel, VP

COMPUCOLLEGE BUSINESS SCHOOLS are private schools offering career training at the post-secondary school level. The courses range from general business and accounting to travel, fashion merchandising, etc. The curriculum gives each student the necessary knowledge to gain an entry-level position in his/her chosen field.

HISTORY: . . . . .IFA, CFA
Established in 1976; . . 1st Franchised in 1983
Company-Owned Units (As of 8/31/1992): . .3
Franchised Units (As of 8/31/1992): . . . . . <u>25</u>
Total Units (As of 8/31/1992): 28
Projected New Units for 1993: 4
Distribution: US-0;Can-28;Overseas-0
 North America: . . . . 5 Provinces
 Concentration: . . .19 in ON, 6 in BC, 1 in NS
Registered: . . . .
 . . . .
Type Space: FS, SF, SC, RM;~5,000-6,000 SF

FINANCIAL: Earnings Claim: . .No
Cash Investment: $75-125K
Total Investment: $200-300K
Fees: Franchise - $75K
 Royalty: 7%, Advert: . . . . Varies
Contract Periods (Yrs.): . . .5-10/5
Area Development Agreement: Yes/Var
Sub-Franchise Contract: . . . . . Yes
Expand in Territory: . . . . . . Yes
Passive Ownership: . . . Not Allowed
Encourage Conversions: . . . . Yes
Average # Employees: . . . . .Varies

FRANCHISOR TRAINING/SUPPORT:
Financial Assistance Provided: . . . . .No
Site Selection Assistance: . . . . . . .Yes
Lease Negotiation Assistance: . . . .Yes
Co-operative Advertising: . . . . . . .Yes
Training: . . . . 2 Wks. Headquarters
 . . . . Varies On-Site
On-Going Support: C,D,G,H/ 14
EXPANSION PLANS:
US: . . . . Not at Present
Canada: . . . . .All Canada
Overseas: . . . . Yes

ELS INTERNATIONAL

5761 Buckingham Parkway
Culver City, CA 90230
TEL: (800) 468-8978 (310) 642-0982
FAX: (310) 649-5231
Mr. Richard Cheng, President

ELS INTERNATIONAL franchises English language schools overseas. Our sister division, ELS Language Centers, operates 20 company-owned schools throughout the US. 10 - 20 students per class study business English, conversational English, TOEFL and GMAT preparation and other programs.

HISTORY:	. . . . IFA
Established in 1956;	. . 1st Franchised in 1978
Company-Owned Units (As of 8/31/1992):	. .4
Franchised Units (As of 8/31/1992):	 36
Total Units (As of 8/31/1992):	40
Projected New Units for 1993:	4
Distribution:	. . . . US-1;Can-0;Overseas-39
North America:	. . . . .1 State
Concentration:	. . . . 1 in OK
Registered:	. . . . CA
. . . .	
Type Space:	. . . FS, SF, College;~10,000 SF

FINANCIAL:	Earnings Claim: . .No
Cash Investment:	. . . . $100-200K
Total Investment:	. . . . $150-300K
Fees: Franchise -	. . . . $5-20K
Royalty: 3-5%, Advert:	. . . . . 0%
Contract Periods (Yrs.):	. . . . . 5/5
Area Development Agreement:	. . .
Sub-Franchise Contract:	. . . . .No
Expand in Territory:	. . . . Yes
Passive Ownership:	. . . Discouraged
Encourage Conversions:	. . . . . Yes
Avg. # Employees:	10-15 FT, 5-10 PT

FRANCHISOR TRAINING/SUPPORT:	
Financial Assistance Provided:	. . . . .No
Site Selection Assistance:	. . . . . . .Yes
Lease Negotiation Assistance:	. . . . .No
Co-operative Advertising:	. . . . . . .No
Training:	. . . . .10+ Days Headquarters,
	. .3+ Days Opening, 3+ Days Post-Open.
On-Going Support: C,D,E,G,h/	 3
EXPANSION PLANS:	
US:	. . . . .No
Canada:	. . . . .No
Overseas:	. . . . .Yes

EXECUTRAIN

1000 Abernathy Rd., # 400
Atlanta, GA 30328
TEL: (800) 843-6984 (404) 396-9200
FAX: (404) 698-9180
Ms. Dawn Harbuck, Fran. Sales Rep.

EXECUTRAIN is the nation's leading computer training franchise. Our mission is to increase the effectiveness of individuals through instruction-led, hands-on training programs in a classroom setting.

HISTORY:	. . . .
Established in 1984;	. . 1st Franchised in 1986
Company-Owned Units (As of 8/31/1992):	. .2
Franchised Units (As of 8/31/1992):	 56
Total Units (As of 8/31/1992):	58
Projected New Units for 1993:	6
Distribution:	. . . . . US-54;Can-0;Overseas-4
North America:	. . . . 32 States
Concentration:	. . . .6 in CA, 4 in FL, 3 in CT
Registered:	. . . CA,HI,IL,IN,MD,MI,MN,NY
. . . . .OR,RI,VA,WA,WI,DC	
Type Space:	. Prof. Bus. Park;~2,800-3,200 SF

FINANCIAL:	Earnings Claim: . .No
Cash Investment:	. . . . . . $75K+
Total Investment:	. . . . $145-195K
Fees: Franchise -	. . . . $30K
Royalty: 6-9%, Advert:	. . . . 1.5%
Contract Periods (Yrs.):	. . . . .7/14
Area Development Agreement:	. .No
Sub-Franchise Contract:	. . . . .No
Expand in Territory:	. . . . Yes
Passive Ownership:	. . . Not Allowed
Encourage Conversions:	. . . . .No
Average # Employees:	. . . .8-10 FT

FRANCHISOR TRAINING/SUPPORT:	
Financial Assistance Provided:	. . .Yes(D)
Site Selection Assistance:	. . . . . . .Yes
Lease Negotiation Assistance:	. . . . .Yes
Co-operative Advertising:	. . . . . . .Yes
Training:	. . . . 2 Days Site Location,
	. 5 Days GM HQ, 4-5 Days Training HQ
On-Going Support: b,E,G,H,I/	 30
EXPANSION PLANS:	
US:	. . . . . Midwest, North, Northeast
Canada:	. . . . .All Canada
Overseas:	. . . . . . .GR, UK, MX

GLOBAL DYNAMICS INTERNATIONAL

1600 Kapiolani Blvd., # 1318
Honolulu, HI 96814
TEL: (800) 657-7976 (808) 521-2041
FAX: (808) 941-8435
Mr. Carl P. Worthy, Dir. Fran. Dev.

GLOBAL DYNAMICS offers unique programs in career development to the business community, with over 14,000 graduates to date. The CareerTech Program is an Information (Time) Management Program that teaches individuals how to be organized in the midst of chaos. The SalesTech Program teaches hands-on sales techniques with guaranteed results. The end result is increased productivity and reduction in stress.

HISTORY:	. . . . IFA
Established in 1973;	. . 1st Franchised in 1990
Company-Owned Units (As of 8/31/1992):	. .0
Franchised Units (As of 8/31/1992):	2
Total Units (As of 8/31/1992):	2
Projected New Units for 1993:	
Distribution:	. . . . . . US-1;Can-0;Overseas-1
North America:	. . . . .1 State
Concentration:	. . . . .1 in HI
Registered:	. . . . .CA,FL,HI
. . . .	
Type Space:	. . . . ;~800 SF

FINANCIAL:	Earnings Claim: . .No
Cash Investment:	. . . .$79.2-104.5K
Total Investment:	. . . .$79.2-104.5K
Fees: Franchise -	. . . . $56.4K
Royalty: 8%, Advert:	. . . . . . 2%
Contract Periods (Yrs.):	. . . . . 5/5
Area Development Agreement:	Yes/5
Sub-Franchise Contract:	. . . . .No
Expand in Territory:	. . . . Yes
Passive Ownership:	. . . Not Allowed
Encourage Conversions:	. . . . NA
Average # Employees:	. . . . .3 FT

FRANCHISOR TRAINING/SUPPORT:	
Financial Assistance Provided:	. . . . .No
Site Selection Assistance:	. . . . . . .NA
Lease Negotiation Assistance:	. . . . .Yes
Co-operative Advertising:	. . . . . . .Yes
Training:	. . . . 2 Wks. Headquarters,
	. . . .Minimum 2 Wks. Franchisee Site
On-Going Support: b,C,D,E,F,G,I/	5
EXPANSION PLANS:	
US:	. . . . Northwest and Southwest
Canada:	. . . . .No
Overseas:	. MX,JA,HK,NZ,BZ,AU,Singa.

GLOBAL TALENT

150 Simcoe St.
Toronto, ON M5H 3G4 CAN
TEL: (416) 971-7747 C
FAX: (416) 598-0028
Mr. Peter Stavros, Fran. Dir.

Model training and photography.

HISTORY:	FINANCIAL: Earnings Claim: . .No	FRANCHISOR TRAINING/SUPPORT:
Established in 1992; . . 1st Franchised in 1992	Cash Investment: $30K	Financial Assistance Provided: . . .Yes(D)
Company-Owned Units (As of 8/31/1992): . .1	Total Investment: $50K	Site Selection Assistance: . . . . . . .Yes
Franchised Units (As of 8/31/1992): 2	Fees: Franchise - $25K	Lease Negotiation Assistance: . . . . .Yes
Total Units (As of 8/31/1992): 3	Royalty: 5%, Advert: 3%	Co-operative Advertising: . . . . . . .Yes
Projected New Units for 1993: 4	Contract Periods (Yrs.): 10/5	Training: . . . . 2 Wks. Headquarters,
Distribution: US-0;Can-3;Overseas-0	Area Development Agreement: Yes/10	. . . . .2 Wks. Franchisee Location
North America: . . . . .1 Province	Sub-Franchise Contract: . . . . . Yes	On-Going Support: a,B,C,D,E,G,h,i/ . . 12
Concentration: . . . . 3 in ON	Expand in Territory: . . . . . . Yes	EXPANSION PLANS:
Registered:	Passive Ownership: . . . Not Allowed	US: . . . . .All US
. . . .	Encourage Conversions: . . . . . Yes	Canada: . . . . .All Canada
Type Space: . . . . FS;~3,000 SF	Average # Employees: . . 3 FT, 4 PT	Overseas: . . . . Yes

KOMPUTER KIDS

6600 Busch Blvd., # 101
Columbus, OH 43229
TEL: (800) 659-5437 (614) 888-4900
FAX: (614) 888-4908
Mr. Stan Gebhardt, President

KOMPUTER KIDS is a computer learning course designed for children ranging from pre-school to 16 years of age. This course is designed to join computer knowledge with fun. Personalized classes with 2 children per computer are held for 50 minutes in length. The classes are taught by certified instructors, held in local learning centers and are affordable.

HISTORY:	FINANCIAL: Earnings Claim: . .No	FRANCHISOR TRAINING/SUPPORT:
Established in 1990; . . 1st Franchised in 1991	Cash Investment: $21-22K	Financial Assistance Provided: . . . . .No
Company-Owned Units (As of 8/31/1992): . .0	Total Investment: $21-22K	Site Selection Assistance: . . . . . . .NA
Franchised Units (As of 8/31/1992): 20	Fees: Franchise - $14.5K	Lease Negotiation Assistance: . . . . .No
Total Units (As of 8/31/1992): 20	Royalty: 12.5%, Advert: 0%	Co-operative Advertising: . . . . .No
Projected New Units for 1993: 100	Contract Periods (Yrs.): 10/10	Training: . . . . 2 Days Franchise Training
Distribution: US-20;Can-0;Overseas-0	Area Development Agreement: . .No	. . . . . at HQ, 2 Days Site + 2 Days Site
North America: . . . . 10 States	Sub-Franchise Contract: . . . . . .No	On-Going Support: A,B,C,D,E,G,H,I/ . . 8
Concentration: . . .10 in OH, 2 in TN, 2 in OR	Expand in Territory: . . . . Yes	EXPANSION PLANS:
Registered: . . . . .CA,FL	Passive Ownership: . . . . .Allowed	US: . . . . All US
. . . .	Encourage Conversions:	Canada: . . . . .All Canada
Type Space: . . . . ;~NA SF	Average # Employees: . . 1 FT, 4 PT	Overseas: . . . . .EUR, S. America

LEADERSHIP MANAGEMENT

4567 Lake Shore Dr.
Waco, TX 76710
TEL: (800) 365-7437 (817) 757-4797
FAX: (817) 757-4600
Mr. Gary Mattson, EVP

Career Opportunity. A leading human resource and management development firm is looking for an individual interested in: being self-employed, controlling his/her own financial growth, enjoying freedom and prestige, marketing programs designed to increase productivity, interfacing with corporate decision makers and CEO's. Call (800) 365-7437 or send resume.

HISTORY: . . . . IFA	FINANCIAL: Earnings Claim: . .No	FRANCHISOR TRAINING/SUPPORT:
Established in 1965; . . 1st Franchised in 1965	Cash Investment: . . . .$	Financial Assistance Provided: . . .Yes(D)
Company-Owned Units (As of 8/31/1992): . .0	Total Investment: $30K	Site Selection Assistance: . . . . . . .NA
Franchised Units (As of 8/31/1992): 982	Fees: Franchise - . . . .$	Lease Negotiation Assistance: . . . .NA
Total Units (As of 8/31/1992): 982	Royalty: 0%, Advert: 0%	Co-operative Advertising: . . . . . . .NA
Projected New Units for 1993: 120	Contract Periods (Yrs.): 3/3	Training: . . . . . 1-3 Wks. Headquarters
Distribution: US-982;Can-0;Overseas-0	Area Development Agreement: . .No	. . . .
North America:	Sub-Franchise Contract: . . . . . .No	On-Going Support: D,C,H,I/ 35
Concentration:	Expand in Territory: . . . . . . .No	EXPANSION PLANS:
Registered: . . . . .All States Exc. HI	Passive Ownership: . . . Discouraged	US: . . . . All US
. . . .	Encourage Conversions: . . . . NA	Canada: . . . . .All Canada
Type Space: . . . . ;~ SF	Average # Employees: . . . . .Varies	Overseas: . . . . No

LEE'S INTERNATIONAL SCHOOL OF TENNIS
3321 Greenhill Ln.
Louisville, KY 40206
TEL: (800) BALL-HOG (510) 839-5471
FAX: (510) 547-3245
Ms. Elizabeth Lee, President

Exceptional opportunity to learn from the best - Lee Merriweather, internationally-ranked tennis professional and instructor. Students learn the fundamentals in five 2-hour sessions. Video rental library for reinforcement. On-going relationship with Ms. Merriweather. Franchisees should have some competitive tennis experience.

HISTORY:	FINANCIAL: Earnings Claim: . .No	FRANCHISOR TRAINING/SUPPORT:
Established in 1984; . . 1st Franchised in 1987	Cash Investment: $20-40K	Financial Assistance Provided: . . . . .No
Company-Owned Units (As of 8/31/1992): . .2	Total Investment: $35-65K	Site Selection Assistance: . . . . . . .Yes
Franchised Units (As of 8/31/1992): 2	Fees: Franchise - $22.5K	Lease Negotiation Assistance: . . . .Yes
Total Units (As of 8/31/1992): 4	Royalty: 5%, Advert: 0%	Co-operative Advertising: . . . . . . .Yes
Projected New Units for 1993:	Contract Periods (Yrs.): 5/5	Training: . . . . . . 2 Wks. Headquarters,
Distribution: US-4;Can-0;Overseas-0	Area Development Agreement: . .No	. . . . 2 Wks. On-Site
North America: . . . . 3 States	Sub-Franchise Contract: . . . . .No	On-Going Support: B,D,F,G,i/ 3
Concentration: . . 2 in KY, 1 in CO, 1 IN WA	Expand in Territory: . . . . Yes	EXPANSION PLANS:
Registered: . . . . CA,WA	Passive Ownership: . . . Not Allowed	US: . . . . . .Major Metropolitan Areas
. . . .	Encourage Conversions: . . . . . Yes	Canada: . . . . Major Cities
Type Space: . . . . FS, SF, SC;~800-1,200 SF	Average # Employees: . . 1 FT, 2 PT	Overseas: . . . . .UK, EUR

MODEL MERCHANDISING INTERNATIONAL
111 E. 22nd St.
New York, NY 10010
TEL: (212) 420-0655
FAX: (212) 473-2725
Ms. Charyn Parker, Dir. Fran. Dev.

John Casablancas, Chairman of the Board of Elite Model Management Corp., incorporates his modeling and personal development knowledge in BOE-approved curriculum.

HISTORY: . . . . IFA	FINANCIAL: Earnings Claim: . .No	FRANCHISOR TRAINING/SUPPORT:
Established in 1979; . . 1st Franchised in 1979	Cash Investment: $6.5-27K	Financial Assistance Provided: . . . . .No
Company-Owned Units (As of 8/31/1992): . .0	Total Investment: $100-200K	Site Selection Assistance: . . . . . . .Yes
Franchised Units (As of 8/31/1992): 48	Fees: Franchise - $6.5-27K	Lease Negotiation Assistance: . . . . .No
Total Units (As of 8/31/1992): 48	Royalty: 7%, Advert: 3%	Co-operative Advertising: . . . . . . .Yes
Projected New Units for 1993: 2	Contract Periods (Yrs.): 10/10	Training: . . . . . . 2-3 Days Headquarters
Distribution: US-42;Can-3;Overseas-3	Area Development Agreement: . .No	. . . .
North America: . . . . 24 States, 3 Provinces	Sub-Franchise Contract: . . . . .No	On-Going Support: b,C,D,E,g,h/ 6
Concentration: . . . . .5 in FL, 4 in OH, 3 in PA	Expand in Territory: . . . . Yes	EXPANSION PLANS:
Registered: . . . CA,IL,IN,MD,MI,NY,RI,VA	Passive Ownership: . . . Discouraged	US: . . . . Northwest and Southwest
. . . . WA,WI	Encourage Conversions: . . . . . Yes	Canada: . . . . .No
Type Space: . . . . .SC, RM;~1,800-2,500 SF	Average # Employees: . 4 FT, 6-8 PT	Overseas: . . . . EUR and Far East

NEW HORIZONS COMPUTER LEARNING CENTER
1231 E. Dyer Rd., # 140
Santa Ana, CA 92705
TEL: (714) 556-1220
FAX: (714) 556-4612
Mr. Mark Winburn, Dir. Fran. Sales

NEW HORIZONS is a complete PC and Macintosh training company. Franchisees train in their facilities or the client's. Classes are for any business or individual.

HISTORY: . . . . IFA	FINANCIAL: Earnings Claim: . .No	FRANCHISOR TRAINING/SUPPORT:
Established in 1982; . . 1st Franchised in 1992	Cash Investment: $89-149K	Financial Assistance Provided: . . . . .No
Company-Owned Units (As of 8/31/1992): . .1	Total Investment: $249-435K	Site Selection Assistance: . . . . . . .Yes
Franchised Units (As of 8/31/1992): 13	Fees: Franchise - $20K	Lease Negotiation Assistance: . . . . .No
Total Units (As of 8/31/1992): 14	Royalty: 5%, Advert: 1%	Co-operative Advertising: . . . . .No
Projected New Units for 1993: 12	Contract Periods (Yrs.): 10/5	Training: . . . . 3 Wks. Headquarters,
Distribution: US-12;Can-0;Overseas-2	Area Development Agreement: Yes/2	. . . . 1 Wk. Franchisee Location
North America: . . . . 8 States	Sub-Franchise Contract: . . . . Yes	On-Going Support: B,C,D,G,H,I/ 13
Concentration: . . . . 4 in CA, 2 in TX	Expand in Territory: . . . . . . .No	EXPANSION PLANS:
Registered: . . .CA,IL,MI,MN,NY,OR,WI,DC	Passive Ownership: . . . Not Allowed	US: . . . . All US
. . . .	Encourage Conversions: . . . . Yes	Canada: . . . . .All Canada
Type Space: Office Bldg./Park;~3,000-4,000 SF	Average # Employees: . . . . . .8 FT	Overseas: . . . . .Yes

PRIORITY MANAGEMENT SYSTEMS

500 - 108th Ave. NE, # 1740
Bellevue, WA 98004
TEL: (800) 221-9031 (206) 454-7686
FAX: (206) 454-5506
Mr. Todd Schmick, VP Fran. Dev.

Work with business professionals in the area of effective management skills. This includes meeting management, project planning, decision making, delegation, organization and communication skills development. Both corporate and individual clients are taught a unique process that includes workshops as well as one-on-one consultation.

HISTORY: . . . . IFA	FINANCIAL: Earnings Claim: . .No	FRANCHISOR TRAINING/SUPPORT:
Established in 1984; . . 1st Franchised in 1984	Cash Investment: $7.5K	Financial Assistance Provided: . . . . .Yes
Company-Owned Units (As of 8/31/1992): . .0	Total Investment: $30-45K	Site Selection Assistance: . . . . . . .NA
Franchised Units (As of 8/31/1992): 250	Fees: Franchise - $29.5K	Lease Negotiation Assistance: . . . . .NA
Total Units (As of 8/31/1992): 250	Royalty: 9%, Advert: 1%	Co-operative Advertising: . . . . .NA
Projected New Units for 1993: 45	Contract Periods (Yrs.): 5/5/5	Training: . . . . . . 7 Days Vancouver, BC,
Distribution: . . . US-150;Can-50;Overseas-50	Area Development Agreement: . .No	. . . . 4 Days in Field, 5 Days in Region
North America: . . . . 37 States,10 Provinces	Sub-Franchise Contract: . . . . . .No	On-Going Support: C,D,G,H,I/ 30
Concentration: . 20 in CA, 19 in TX, 10 in NY	Expand in Territory: . . . . Yes	EXPANSION PLANS:
Registered: . . . . .All	Passive Ownership: . . . . . .Allowed	US: . . . . All US
. . . .	Encourage Conversions: . . . . NA	Canada: . . . . .No
Type Space: . . . . ;~ SF	Average # Employees: . . 3 FT, 1 PT	Overseas: . . . . .Yes

SANDLER SYSTEMS

10411 Stevenson Rd.
Stevenson, MD 21153
TEL: (800) 638-5686 (410) 653-1993
FAX: (410) 358-7858
Mr. Phil Goodwin, Fran. Dir.

SANDLER SYSTEMS' unique approach to sales training and sales management training includes selling on-going training, reinforcement, coaching and counseling to companies that cannot afford an internal sales trainer. Our lead generation program eliminates the need for prospecting altogether. Telephone support manager assigned to each franchisee to shorten learning curve dramatically.

HISTORY: . . . . IFA	FINANCIAL: Earnings Claim: . .No	FRANCHISOR TRAINING/SUPPORT:
Established in 1967; . . 1st Franchised in 1984	Cash Investment: $30K	Financial Assistance Provided: . . . . . No
Company-Owned Units (As of 8/31/1992): . .0	Total Investment: $31.5K	Site Selection Assistance: . . . . . . .NA
Franchised Units (As of 8/31/1992): 81	Fees: Franchise - $30K	Lease Negotiation Assistance: . . . .NA
Total Units (As of 8/31/1992): 81	Royalty: $908/Mo., Advert: . . 0%	Co-operative Advertising: . . . . .Yes
Projected New Units for 1993: 70	Contract Periods (Yrs.): 5/10	Training: . . . . . . .3 Days + 3 Additional
Distribution: US-78;Can-2;Overseas-1	Area Development Agreement: . Yes	. . . . Days Headquarters
North America: . . . . 35 States, 2 Provinces	Sub-Franchise Contract: . . . . . .No	On-Going Support: B,C,D,G,H,I/ 15
Concentration: . . . 8 in PA, 9 in MD, 6 in NY	Expand in Territory: . . . . .No	EXPANSION PLANS:
Registered: . . . CA,FL,IL,IN,MD,MI,MN,NY	Passive Ownership: . . . Discouraged	US: . . . . All US
. . . . OR,RI,VA,WI,DC	Encourage Conversions: . . . . NA	Canada: . . . . .All Canada
Type Space: . . . . NA;~NA SF	Average # Employees: . . . . . .1 FT	Overseas: . . . . UK, GR

SYLVAN LEARNING SYSTEMS

9135 Guilford Rd.
Columbia, MD 21046
TEL: (800) 284-8214 (410) 880-0889
FAX: (410) 880-8717
Ms. Charlotte Bentley, Dir. Syst. Dev.

Diagnostic and prescriptive reading, math, writing, college prep, algebra, study skills and readiness instruction for students K-12. After-school teaching with 3:1 ratio, highly motivational, with guaranteed success.

HISTORY: . . . . IFA	FINANCIAL: Earnings Claim: . .No	FRANCHISOR TRAINING/SUPPORT:
Established in 1979; . . 1st Franchised in 1980	Cash Investment: $35-70K	Financial Assistance Provided: . . . . .No
Company-Owned Units (As of 8/31/1992): . .7	Total Investment: $85-120K	Site Selection Assistance: . . . . . . .Yes
Franchised Units (As of 8/31/1992): 444	Fees: Franchise - $19.5-35K	Lease Negotiation Assistance: . . . . .Yes
Total Units (As of 8/31/1992): 451	Royalty: 8-9%, Advert: . . 1.5-5%	Co-operative Advertising: . . . . .Yes
Projected New Units for 1993: 30	Contract Periods (Yrs.): 10/10	Training: . . . . 2 Wks. Headquarters
Distribution: US-424;Can-26;Overseas-1	Area Development Agreement: . .No	. . . .
North America:	Sub-Franchise Contract: . . . . . .No	On-Going Support: B,C,d,E,F,G,h,I/ . .150
Concentration: . .41 in CA, 40 in FL, 34 in TX	Expand in Territory: . . . . Yes	EXPANSION PLANS:
Registered: . . . . All States	Passive Ownership: . . . Discouraged	US: . . . . All US
. . . .	Encourage Conversions: . . . . Yes	Canada: . . . . .All Canada
Type Space: SC, Office Bldg.;~1,000-1,600 SF	Average # Employees: . . 2 FT, 3 PT	Overseas: . . . . No

TELLER TRAINING INSTITUTE

P. O. Box 1758
Mercer Island, WA 98040
TEL: (206) 232-1112
FAX: (206) 232-7490
Mr. David Lonay, President

TELLER TRAINING INSTITUTES recruit, train, and provide job placement for persons seeking entry-level careers in financial institutions. 55,000 graduates nationwide. No competition. No banking or educational experience is necessary to successfully and profitably operate a franchise. Complete franchisee training is provided.

HISTORY: . . . .
Established in 1975; . . 1st Franchised in 1976
Company-Owned Units (As of 8/31/1992): . .1
Franchised Units (As of 8/31/1992): 10
Total Units (As of 8/31/1992): 11
Projected New Units for 1993: 0
Distribution: US-11;Can-0;Overseas-0
  North America: . . . . 7 States
  Concentration: . . .2 in CA, 1 in WA, 1 in MO
Registered: . . . .
. . . .
Type Space: . . . . ;~1,200 SF

FINANCIAL: Earnings Claim: . .No
Cash Investment: $40-60K
Total Investment: $40-60K
Fees: Franchise - $20-30K
  Royalty: 0%, Advert: 0%
Contract Periods (Yrs.): 15/15
Area Development Agreement: . .No
Sub-Franchise Contract: . . . . .No
Expand in Territory: . . . . Yes
Passive Ownership: . . . Not Allowed
Encourage Conversions: . . . . . Yes
Average # Employees: . . 3 FT, 1 PT

FRANCHISOR TRAINING/SUPPORT:
Financial Assistance Provided: . . . . . No
Site Selection Assistance: . . . . .Yes
Lease Negotiation Assistance: . . . . .Yes
Co-operative Advertising: . . . . .No
Training: . . . . 2 Wks. Headquarters,
. . . . 2 Wks. Seattle, WA
On-Going Support: A,B,C,D,E,G,H/ . . . 4
EXPANSION PLANS:
US: . . . . . . Midwest, Select East Coast
Canada: . . . . .No
Overseas: . . . . No

TRAVEL PROFESSIONALS INSTITUTE

10172 Linn Station Rd.
Louisville, KY 40223
TEL: (800) 626-2469 (502) 423-9900
FAX: (502) 423-9914
Mr. John E. Boyce, Dir. Fran. Sales

TRAVEL PROFESSIONALS INSTITUTE provides professional educational training to individuals seeking employment in the travel industry. The curriculum has a long history of a consistently high level of acceptance of its graduates by the industry.

HISTORY: . . . .
Established in 1989; . . 1st Franchised in 1989
Company-Owned Units (As of 8/31/1992): . .1
Franchised Units (As of 8/31/1992): 0
Total Units (As of 8/31/1992): 1
Projected New Units for 1993: 4
Distribution: US-1;Can-0;Overseas-0
  North America: . . . . .1 State
  Concentration: . . . . 1 in KY
Registered: . . . . .FL
. . . .
Type Space: . . . . ;~1,000 SF

FINANCIAL: Earnings Claim: . .No
Cash Investment: $51K
Total Investment: $51K
Fees: Franchise - $19K
  Royalty: 7%, Advert: 0%
Contract Periods (Yrs.): 10/10
Area Development Agreement: . .No
Sub-Franchise Contract: . . . . . Yes
Expand in Territory: . . . . Yes
Passive Ownership: . . . Discouraged
Encourage Conversions: . . . . . Yes
Average # Employees: . . 1 FT, 3 PT

FRANCHISOR TRAINING/SUPPORT:
Financial Assistance Provided: . . . . . No
Site Selection Assistance: . . . . .Yes
Lease Negotiation Assistance: . . . . .Yes
Co-operative Advertising: . . . . .No
Training: . . . . . 5 Days Louisville, KY or
. . . . Denver, CO
On-Going Support: B,C,D,E,H,I/ 6
EXPANSION PLANS:
US: . . . . .All US
Canada: . . . . .No
Overseas: . . . . No

SUPPLEMENTAL LISTING OF FRANCHISORS

A PLUS SOFTWARE . . . . 60 Columbia Pkwy., # 300, Markham, ON L3R 0C9   CAN
    Contact: President; Tel: (416) 940-0764
ALPHABETLAND/CHILD ENRICHMENT CENTERS . . . . 139 Bergen Ave., Cearny, NJ 07032
    Contact: Mr. Russel Rupon, VP; Tel: (201) 488-0446
AMERICAN FLYERS . . . . 821 NW 72nd Terrace, Plantation, FL 33317
    Contact: President; Tel: (305) 584-7910
AMRON SCHOOL OF THE FINE ARTS . . . . .1315 Medlin Rd., Monroe, NC 28112
    Contact: Ms. Norma Williams, President; Tel: (704) 283-4290
ARTHUR MURRAY INTERNATIONAL . . . . . . .1077 Ponce De Leon Blvd., Coral Gables, FL 33134
    Contact: Mr. George B. Theiss, President; Tel: (305) 445-9645
BETTER BIRTH FOUNDATION . . . . 733 Main St., Stone Mt., GA 30083
    Contact: Ms. Brenda Seagraves; Tel: (404) 469-8870
COLLEGE BOUND . . . . 221 Bonita Ave., # 620, Piedmont, CA 94611
    Contact: Mr. Jeff Scharunas; Tel: (502) 839-5471
COLLEGE PREPARATORY SERVICE . . . . 26 Wood Hill Rd., Pittsford, NY 14534
    Contact: President; Tel: (716) 586-7399
COM-CEP USA . . . . .9700 Rodney Parham Rd., Little Rock, AR 72207
    Contact: Mr. Jim Oliver, Dir. Fran. Sales; Tel: (800) 874-1238 (501) 224-3050

FMC COMPANY . . . . Box 491, Union, NJ 07083
    Contact: President; Tel: (201) 964-8928
HMI MODEL & TALENT AGENCIES . . . . 2105 Midland Ave., Scarborough, ON M1P 3E3   CAN
    Contact: Mr. Peter Stavros; Tel: (416) 292-4170
HUNTINGTON LEARNING CENTERS . . . . 660 Kinderkamack Rd., Oradell, NJ 07649
    Contact: Dr. Huntington, President; Tel: (800) 692-8400 (201) 261-8400
INSTITUTE OF LIVING SKILLS . . . . 488 Industrial Way, # A-1, Fallbrook, CA 92028
    Contact: President; Tel: (619) 728-6437
INSTITUTE OF READING DEVELOPMENT . . . . 5 Saddle Ln., Novato, CA 94949
    Contact: Mr. David Soloway; Tel: (415) 386-2000
INT. TRAVEL TRAINING COURSES/ECHOLS . . . . 676 N. Sinclair, # 1950, Chicago, IL 60611
    Contact: President; Tel: (312) 943-5500
JOHN ROBERT POWERS . . . . 175 Andover St., Danvers, MA 01923
    Contact: Mr. Richard Ciummei, President; Tel: (800) 262-2954 (508) 777-8677
LARSON LEARNING INSTITUTE . . . . 1873 S. Bellaire, # 600, Denver, CO 80222
    Contact: President; Tel:
LEARNING FOR EVERYONE . . . . 4194 Pontiac Lake Rd., Waterford, MI 48328
    Contact: Mr. Peter Wehrli, EVP; Tel: (313) 673-5720
SMI INTERNATIONAL . . . . 5000 Lakewood Dr., Waco, TX 76710
    Contact: Mr. Joseph Neglia, Dir. Fran.; Tel: (800) 880-0745 (817) 776-1230
TIME MASTERS-MANAGEMENT TOOLS/SEMINARS . . . . 36 C. Stoffel Dr., Rexdale, ON M9W QA8   CAN
    Contact: Mr. Thom Tyson, President; Tel: (416) 248-5556
TRAVEL TRADE SCHOOL . . . . 7921 South Park Plaza, # 105, Littleton, CO 80120
    Contact: Ms. Adonna Hipple, President; Tel: (303) 795-1825
WILSON LEARNING CORP. . . . . 7500 Flying Cloud Dr., Eden Prairie, MN 55344
    Contact: President; Tel: (612) 944-2880

CHAPTER 16

EMPLOYMENT AND PERSONNEL

AAA EMPLOYMENT

4908-C Creekside Dr.
Clearwater, FL 34620
TEL: (800) 237-2853 (813) 573-0202
FAX: (813) 572-8709
Mr. Joseph M. Kotow, President

AAA EMPLOYMENT emphasizes a full-service general employment agency, specializing in permanent placement at all levels of employment. Applicant-paid and employer-paid positions are handled. Low placement fee with convenient terms sets AAA EMPLOYMENT apart from other agencies, giving them a competitive edge in the employment industry.

HISTORY: . . . . IFA
Established in 1957; . . 1st Franchised in 1977
Company-Owned Units (As of 8/31/1992): . 32
Franchised Units (As of 8/31/1992): 23
Total Units (As of 8/31/1992): 55
Projected New Units for 1993: 10
Distribution: US-55;Can-0;Overseas-0
North America: . . . . 12 States
Concentration: . . . 20 in FL, 7 in GA, 6 in NC
Registered: . . . . FL,IN,MN,OR,VA
. . . .
Type Space: . . FS, SF, SC, RM;~300-500 SF

FINANCIAL: Earnings Claim: . Yes
Cash Investment: $10K
Total Investment: $14-27K
Fees: Franchise - $10K
Royalty: 8%, Advert: 2%
Contract Periods (Yrs.): 10/5
Area Development Agreement: Yes/10
Sub-Franchise Contract: . . . . .No
Expand in Territory: . . . . Yes
Passive Ownership: . . . Discouraged
Encourage Conversions: . . . . . Yes
Average # Employees: . . . . 1-4 FT

FRANCHISOR TRAINING/SUPPORT:
Financial Assistance Provided: . . . . . No
Site Selection Assistance: . . . . .Yes
Lease Negotiation Assistance: . . . . .Yes
Co-operative Advertising: . . . . .No
Training: . . . . . . 2-4 Wks. Headquarters
. . . .
On-Going Support: C,D,E,G,H,I/ 9
EXPANSION PLANS:
US: . . . . All US
Canada: . . . . .No
Overseas: . . . . No

EMPLOYMENT SERVICES

	1989	1990	1991	Percentage Change 90/89	Percentage Change 91/90
Total Number of Establishments:					
Company-Owned	2,654	2,939	3,227	10.74%	9.80%
Franchisee-Owned	3,969	4,569	5,038	15.12%	10.26%
Total	6,623	7,508	8,265	13.36%	10.08%
Ratio of Total Establishments:					
Company-Owned	40.1%	39.1%	39.0%		
Franchisee-Owned	59.9%	60.9%	61.0%		
Total	100.0%	100.0%	100.0%		
Total Sales ($000):					
Company-Owned	2,515,652	2,825,088	3,166,047	12.30%	12.07%
Franchisee-Owned	2,465,837	2,906,728	3,240,350	17.88%	11.48%
Total	4,981,489	5,731,816	6,406,397	15.06%	11.77%
Ratio of Total Sales:					
Company-Owned	50.5%	49.3%	49.4%		
Franchisee-Owned	49.5%	50.7%	50.6%		
Total	100.0%	100.0%	100.0%		
Average Sales Per Unit ($000):					
Company-Owned	948	961	981	1.41%	2.07%
Franchisee-Owned	621	636	643	2.40%	1.10%
Total	752	763	775	1.50%	1.53%
Relative Average Sales Ratio:	152.6%	151.1%	152.5%		

	Number Of Employees	Employees Per Unit	Avg. Sales Per Employee
Total 1989 Employment:			
Company-Owned	185,958	70.1	$13,528
Franchisee-Owned	158,067	39.8	$15,600
Total	344,025	51.9	$14,480
Relative Employee Performance Ratios:		175.9%	86.7%

	1st Quartile	Median	4th Quartile
Average 1989 Total Investment:			
Company-Owned	$75,250	$110,000	$165,000
Franchisee-Owned	$55,000	$70,000	$100,000
Single Unit Franchise Fee	$15,000	$20,000	$25,000
Mult. Unit Franchise Fee	$10,000	$20,000	$45,000
Franchise Start-Up Cost	$25,750	$29,000	$50,000

Source: Franchising In The Economy 1991, IFA Educational Foundation & Horwath International.

AAA MEDICAL SERVICES

3116 E. Shea Blvd., # 247
Phoenix, AZ 85028
TEL: (602) 996-4450
FAX:
Mr. Gerd-D. Linke, Fran. Sales

Professional placement of on-call nurses and on-staffing services.

HISTORY:	FINANCIAL: Earnings Claim: . .No	FRANCHISOR TRAINING/SUPPORT:
Established in 1990; . . 1st Franchised in 1991	Cash Investment: $120K	Financial Assistance Provided: . . . Yes(I)
Company-Owned Units (As of 8/31/1992): . .1	Total Investment: $120K	Site Selection Assistance: . . . . . . .Yes
Franchised Units (As of 8/31/1992): 0	Fees: Franchise - $30K	Lease Negotiation Assistance: . . . .Yes
Total Units (As of 8/31/1992): 1	Royalty: 7-5%, Advert: 0%	Co-operative Advertising: . . . . . . .Yes
Projected New Units for 1993: 3	Contract Periods (Yrs.): 10/10	Training: . . . . . . .1 Wk. Franchisee Site
Distribution: US-1;Can-0;Overseas-0	Area Development Agreement: . .No	. . . .
North America: . . . . .1 State	Sub-Franchise Contract: . . . . .No	On-Going Support: a,B,C,D,E,F,G,H/ . . 2
Concentration: . . . . 1 in GA	Expand in Territory: . . . . Yes	EXPANSION PLANS:
Registered:	Passive Ownership: . . . . . .Allowed	US: . . . . Southwest
. . . .	Encourage Conversions: . . . . . NA	Canada: . . . . .No
Type Space: . . . . Office Suite;~ SF	Average # Employees: . . 3 FT, 4 PT	Overseas: . . . . No

ACCOUNTANTS ON CALL

Park 80 West, Plaza II, 9th Fl.
Saddle Brook, NJ 07662
TEL: (201) 843-0006
FAX: (201) 843-4936
Ms. Linda Krutzsch, VP Operations

ACCOUNTANTS ON CALL is a specialized temporary help service, engaged in providing a full service to the financial area. Placing accounting, bookkeeping and financial personnel to clients on a temporary and permanent basis. We offer exclusive territory, payroll for the temporaries, computerized operational systems and manuals, on- going consulting and training.

HISTORY: . . . . IFA	FINANCIAL: Earnings Claim: . .No	FRANCHISOR TRAINING/SUPPORT:
Established in 1979; . . 1st Franchised in 1979	Cash Investment: $90K	Financial Assistance Provided: . . .Yes(D)
Company-Owned Units (As of 8/31/1992): . 33	Total Investment: $105K	Site Selection Assistance: . . . . . . .Yes
Franchised Units (As of 8/31/1992): 14	Fees: Franchise - $25K	Lease Negotiation Assistance: . . . .Yes
Total Units (As of 8/31/1992): 47	Royalty: 7%, Advert: 0%	Co-operative Advertising: . . . . .No
Projected New Units for 1993: 4	Contract Periods (Yrs.): 20/20	Training: . . . . .12 Days HQ, 2 Wks. Site,
Distribution: US-47;Can-0;Overseas-0	Area Development Agreement: . .No	. . . 2 Daysx3/Yr. Region, Field Training
North America: . . . . 18 States	Sub-Franchise Contract: . . . . .No	On-Going Support: A,B,C,D,E/ 27
Concentration: . . . . . .Primarily CA, NJ, FL	Expand in Territory: . . . . Yes	EXPANSION PLANS:
Registered: . . . . . . .CA,HI,IL,IN,MD,NY	Passive Ownership: . . . . . .Allowed	US: . . . . .All US
. . . .	Encourage Conversions: . . . . . Yes	Canada: . . . . .No
Type Space: . . . . . Office Building;~800 SF	Average # Employees: . . . . . .4 FT	Overseas: . . . . No

ATS PERSONNEL

6440 Atlantic Blvd.
Jacksonville, FL 32211
TEL: (800) 825-4101 (904) 725-5574
FAX: (904) 725-8513
Ms. Donna Buanno, Dir. Fran. Services

ATS PERSONNEL's unique concept offers 4 proven operating systems to each franchisee. With over 14 years' experience, we've perfected systems for the temporary and permanent placement of office, clerical, light industrial, accounting, technical and data processing personnel. For a limited time, all 4 operations are available for one franchise fee.

HISTORY: . . . . IFA	FINANCIAL: Earnings Claim: . .No	FRANCHISOR TRAINING/SUPPORT:
Established in 1978; . . 1st Franchised in 1991	Cash Investment: $30-50K	Financial Assistance Provided: . . .Yes(D)
Company-Owned Units (As of 8/31/1992): . 14	Total Investment: $100-125K	Site Selection Assistance: . . . . . . .Yes
Franchised Units (As of 8/31/1992): 6	Fees: Franchise - $12.5K	Lease Negotiation Assistance: . . . .Yes
Total Units (As of 8/31/1992): 20	Royalty: Varies, Advert: . . . 1/2%	Co-operative Advertising: . . . . .Yes
Projected New Units for 1993: 7	Contract Periods (Yrs.): . . .10/5/5/5	Training: . . . . . . 2 Wks. Headquarters, 1
Distribution: US-20;Can-0;Overseas-0	Area Development Agreement: . .No	. . . . Wk. On-Site, 2 Days 1/4ly On-Site
North America: . . . . 3 States	Sub-Franchise Contract: . . . . .No	On-Going Support: A,B,C,D,E,F,G,H,I/ 50
Concentration: . . . . .GA, SC, TX	Expand in Territory: . . . . Yes	EXPANSION PLANS:
Registered: . . . . .FL	Passive Ownership: . . . Not Allowed	US: . . . . . SE, S. Central, Midwest, Atl
. . . .	Encourage Conversions: . . . . . Yes	Canada: . . . . .No
Type Space: . . . .SF, Office Bldg.;~1,000 SF	Average # Employees: . . . . . .3 FT	Overseas: . . . . No

CAREER ADVANCEMENT SCIENCES

Six Market Square
Pittsburgh, PA 15222
TEL: (412) 281-2005
FAX: (412) 281-2057
Mr. Richard D. Hindman, President

C.A.S. is the only firm of its kind. We provide complete job search assistance services for individuals and corporations, including professional resume preparation, computerized employer research, executive marketing programs, job search consulting and corporate outplacement. All offices are electronically linked to HQ's writing, research and support staff.

HISTORY:	FINANCIAL: Earnings Claim: . .No	FRANCHISOR TRAINING/SUPPORT:
Established in 1962; . . 1st Franchised in 1972	Cash Investment: $5K	Financial Assistance Provided: . . . . .No
Company-Owned Units (As of 8/31/1992): . 12	Total Investment: $5K	Site Selection Assistance: . . . . . . .Yes
Franchised Units (As of 8/31/1992): . . . 30	Fees: Franchise - $0	Lease Negotiation Assistance: . . . . .Yes
Total Units (As of 8/31/1992): 42	Royalty: 0%, Advert: 0%	Co-operative Advertising: . . . . . . .Yes
Projected New Units for 1993: 10	Contract Periods (Yrs.): . . . Infinite	Training: . . . . 1 Wk. Headquarters
Distribution: US-42;Can-0;Overseas-0	Area Development Agreement: . .No	. . . .
North America: . . . . 18 States	Sub-Franchise Contract: . . . . .No	On-Going Support: A,B,C,D,G,h,I/ . . . 12
Concentration:	Expand in Territory: . . . . Yes	EXPANSION PLANS:
Registered:	Passive Ownership: . . . Discouraged	US: . . . . All US
. . . .	Encourage Conversions: . . . . Yes	Canada: . . . . .No
Type Space: . . . . FS;~120 SF	Average # Employees: . . . . 0-1 FT	Overseas: . . . . No

CAREER BLAZERS

590 Fifth Ave.
New York, NY 10036
TEL: (800) 284-3232 (212) 719-3232
FAX: (212) 921-1827
Ms. Barbara Gebhardt, Dir. Fran. Dev.

CAREER BLAZERS offers a personnel service franchise that capitalizes on the financial advantages and natural synergy of a permanent placement agency and a temporary service. Our franchises provide office, clerical and light industrial workers to a wide variety of business, government agencies and non-profit organizations.

HISTORY: . . . . IFA	FINANCIAL: Earnings Claim: . .No	FRANCHISOR TRAINING/SUPPORT:
Established in 1949; . . 1st Franchised in 1987	Cash Investment: $70-85K	Financial Assistance Provided: . . . Yes(I)
Company-Owned Units (As of 8/31/1992): . .7	Total Investment: $95-129K	Site Selection Assistance: . . . . . . .Yes
Franchised Units (As of 8/31/1992): 5	Fees: Franchise - $15-18K	Lease Negotiation Assistance: . . . .Yes
Total Units (As of 8/31/1992): 12	Royalty: 7%, Advert: 1%	Co-operative Advertising: . . . . . . .Yes
Projected New Units for 1993: 2	Contract Periods (Yrs.): 5/5	Training: . . . . . . 15 Days Headquarters,
Distribution: US-12;Can-0;Overseas-0	Area Development Agreement: . .No	. . . . 5 Days On-Site, On-Going
North America: . . . . 5 States	Sub-Franchise Contract: . . . . .No	On-Going Support: A,B,C,D,E,h,I/ . . . 18
Concentration: . . . .6 in NY, 2 in NJ, 1 in CT	Expand in Territory: . . . . Yes	EXPANSION PLANS:
Registered: . . . . MD,NY,RI,VA	Passive Ownership: . . . Discouraged	US: . . . . Eastern Seaboard
. . . .	Encourage Conversions: . . . . Yes	Canada: . . . . .No
Type Space: . . . Class A Off. Bldg;~2,000 SF	Average # Employees: . . . . . .7 FT	Overseas: . . . . No

CAREERS U.S.A

1825 JFK Blvd.
Philadelphia, PA 19103
TEL: (800) 822-8300 (215) 561-3800
FAX: (215) 977-8335
Mr. George Ounjian, President

CAREERS USA is a temporary and permanent placement service, specializing in accounting, technical, light industrial and full office support. CAREERS USA offers a fully-automated computer system that help franchisees manage their business operationally and financially. We finance 100% of temporary payroll, accounts receivable and all billing functions.

HISTORY: . . . . IFA	FINANCIAL: Earnings Claim: . .No	FRANCHISOR TRAINING/SUPPORT:
Established in 1981; . . 1st Franchised in 1987	Cash Investment: $15K	Financial Assistance Provided: . . . Yes(I)
Company-Owned Units (As of 8/31/1992): . 11	Total Investment: $84.5-99.5K	Site Selection Assistance: . . . . . . .Yes
Franchised Units (As of 8/31/1992): 4	Fees: Franchise - $15K	Lease Negotiation Assistance: . . . .Yes
Total Units (As of 8/31/1992): 15	Royalty: Varies, Advert: 0%	Co-operative Advertising: . . . . . . .Yes
Projected New Units for 1993: 4	Contract Periods (Yrs.): 10/5	Training: . . . . 2 Wks. Headquarters,
Distribution: US-15;Can-0;Overseas-0	Area Development Agreement: . .No	. . . . 1 Wk. Franchisee Location
North America: . . . . 8 States	Sub-Franchise Contract: . . . . .No	On-Going Support: A,C,D,E,G,I/ 10
Concentration: . . . .4 in PA, 3 in GA, 2 in NJ	Expand in Territory: . . . . Yes	EXPANSION PLANS:
Registered: . . . . .All	Passive Ownership: . . . Not Allowed	US: . . . . Northeast and Midwest
. . . .	Encourage Conversions: . . . . Yes	Canada: . . . . .No
Type Space: . . . . SC;~1,200 SF	Average # Employees: . . . . . .3 FT	Overseas: . . . . No

COMPUTEMP

4401 N. Federal Hwy., # 202
Boca Raton, FL 33434
TEL: (800) ASK-COMP (407) 362-9104
FAX: (407) 367-9802
Ms. Barbara D. Fleming, President

COMPUTEMP's services are unlike any other temporary personnel services. We specialize in information processing personnel. COMPUTEMP provides temporary staffing options in data processing, micro/PC support and programming/systems support.

HISTORY: . . . . IFA	FINANCIAL: Earnings Claim: . .No	FRANCHISOR TRAINING/SUPPORT:
Established in 1984; . . 1st Franchised in 1991	Cash Investment: . . . . . $80K Min.	Financial Assistance Provided: . . .Yes(D)
Company-Owned Units (As of 8/31/1992): . .3	Total Investment: . . . . .$110K Min.	Site Selection Assistance: . . . . . . .Yes
Franchised Units (As of 8/31/1992): 2	Fees: Franchise - $30K	Lease Negotiation Assistance: . . . . .Yes
Total Units (As of 8/31/1992): 5	Royalty: 7%, Advert: 0%	Co-operative Advertising: . . . . .NA
Projected New Units for 1993: 3	Contract Periods (Yrs.): 5/5	Training: . . . . .10 Days Pre-Opening Co-
Distribution: US-5;Can-0;Overseas-0	Area Development Agreement: . .No	. . Owned Facility,10 Days Post-Opening
North America: . . . . 4 States	Sub-Franchise Contract: . . . . .No	On-Going Support: A,C,D,E,G,H,I/ 3
Concentration: . . . .2 in TX, 1 in CA, 1 in FL	Expand in Territory: . . . . Yes	EXPANSION PLANS:
Registered: . . CA,FL,IL,MD,MI,MN,NY,WA	Passive Ownership: . . . Discouraged	US: . . . . .Major US Markets
. . . . .WI	Encourage Conversions: . . . . . Yes	Canada: . . . . Ontario, BC
Type Space: . . . . .FS;~1,000 SF	Average # Employees: . . 2 FT, 1 PT	Overseas: . . . . No

EAI MEDICAL PERSONNEL SERVICES

5110 N. Central Ave., # 301
Phoenix, AZ 85012
TEL: (800) 736-8066 (602) 266-5704
FAX: (602) 266-5772
Mr. John J. Fagnani, Dir. Fran. Dev.

EAI MEDICAL PERSONNEL SERVICES provides permanent and temporary employees to the growing health care industry. EAI offers its franchisees comprehensive training and on-going support services, marketing materials, protected territories and software to skill match applicants with job orders and manage the financial functions of the unit franchise.

HISTORY:	FINANCIAL: Earnings Claim: . .No	FRANCHISOR TRAINING/SUPPORT:
Established in 1986; . . 1st Franchised in 1989	Cash Investment: . . . $49.9-64.7K	Financial Assistance Provided: . . . Yes(I)
Company-Owned Units (As of 8/31/1992): . .4	Total Investment: . . . $49.9-67.7K	Site Selection Assistance: . . . . . . .Yes
Franchised Units (As of 8/31/1992): 4	Fees: Franchise - $20K	Lease Negotiation Assistance: . . . .Yes
Total Units (As of 8/31/1992): 8	Royalty: 6%, Advert: 2%	Co-operative Advertising: . . . . . . .Yes
Projected New Units for 1993:	Contract Periods (Yrs.): 10/5	Training: . . . . 2 Wks. Headquarters,
Distribution: US-8;Can-0;Overseas-0	Area Development Agreement: . .No	. . . . 5 Days On-Site
North America: . . . . 5 States	Sub-Franchise Contract: . . . . .No	On-Going Support: A,B,C,d,E,G,h,I/ . . .7
Concentration: . . . 3 in CA, 2 in AZ, 1 in TX	Expand in Territory: . . . . .No	EXPANSION PLANS:
Registered: . . . . FL,IL	Passive Ownership: . . . Discouraged	US: . . . . .All US
. . . .	Encourage Conversions: . . . . . Yes	Canada: . . . . .No
Type Space: . . . . .SC, Prof. Bldgs.;~850 SF	Average # Employees: . . 2 FT, 1 PT	Overseas: . . . . No

EXPRESS SERVICES

6300 NW Expressway, # 200
Oklahoma City, OK 73132
TEL: (800) 652-6400 (405) 840-5000
FAX: (405) 720-1040
Mr. Fred Muse, Fran. Exec.

3 divisions, permanent and temporary placement and executive search offer complete coverage of the employment field. With 154 franchises in 33 states, each franchise receives total advertising plus superior training. Complete financing of temporary payroll. Rated in Venture Magazine as 1 of the 10 "best bets" in franchising.

HISTORY: . . . . IFA	FINANCIAL: Earnings Claim: . .No	FRANCHISOR TRAINING/SUPPORT:
Established in 1983; . . 1st Franchised in 1985	Cash Investment: $60-90K	Financial Assistance Provided: . . . . .No
Company-Owned Units (As of 8/31/1992): . .1	Total Investment: $60-90K	Site Selection Assistance: . . . . . . .Yes
Franchised Units (As of 8/31/1992): 159	Fees: Franchise - $12-15K	Lease Negotiation Assistance: . . . . .Yes
Total Units (As of 8/31/1992): 160	Royalty: 8%, Advert: 0%	Co-operative Advertising: . . . . .Yes
Projected New Units for 1993: 30	Contract Periods (Yrs.): 5/5	Training: . . . . . . .11 Days Headquarters
Distribution: US-160;Can-0;Overseas-0	Area Development Agreement: Yes/5	. . . .
North America: . . . . 33 States	Sub-Franchise Contract: . . . . .No	On-Going Support: A,b,C,D,e,f,G,h,I/ . 50
Concentration: . . . 9 in WA, 9 in CO, 8 in OR	Expand in Territory: . . . . Yes	EXPANSION PLANS:
Registered: . . .CA,FL,IL,IN,MD,MN,NY,ND	Passive Ownership: . . . Discouraged	US: . . . . All US, Esp. Southeast
. . . . OR,SD,WA,WI	Encourage Conversions: . . . . Yes	Canada: . . . . .No
Type Space: . . . . .SF, SC;~ SF	Average # Employees: . . . . . .3 FT	Overseas: . . . . No

F-O-R-T-U-N-E FRANCHISE CORP.

655 Third Ave., # 1805
New York, NY 10017
TEL: (800) 886-7839 (212) 697-4314 C
FAX: (212) 286-1877
Mr. Dennis Inziana, EVP

F-O-R-T-U-N-E FRANCHISE CORP. offers a quality middle management/executive recruiting service, utilizing unique, proven methods of operation to achieve its present status of industry leadership. F-O-R-T-U-N-E's reputation is highlighted by its professional service, innovative marketing concepts and sophisticated system of exchange of candidates and job orders, together with an excellent program of support for its franchise offices.

HISTORY: . . . . IFA
Established in 1959; . . 1st Franchised in 1973
Company-Owned Units (As of 8/31/1992): . .0
Franchised Units (As of 8/31/1992): 65
Total Units (As of 8/31/1992): 65
Projected New Units for 1993: 10
Distribution: US-65;Can-0;Overseas-0
North America: . . . . 27 States
Concentration: . . . 6 in CA, 6 in Mi, 5 fin FL
Registered: . . .CA,IL,IN,MD,MI,MN,NY,ND
. . . . RI,SD,VA,WA,WI
Type Space: . Office Building;~750-1,000 SF

FINANCIAL: Earnings Claim: . .No
Cash Investment: $50-70K
Total Investment: $50-70K
Fees: Franchise - $35K
Royalty: 7%, Advert: 1%
Contract Periods (Yrs.): 20/20
Area Development Agreement: . .No
Sub-Franchise Contract: . . . . .No
Expand in Territory: . . . . . . Yes
Passive Ownership: . . . Not Allowed
Encourage Conversions: . . . . NA
Average # Employees: . . . . .3 FT

FRANCHISOR TRAINING/SUPPORT:
Financial Assistance Provided: . . .Yes(D)
Site Selection Assistance: . . . . . . .Yes
Lease Negotiation Assistance: . . . .Yes
Co-operative Advertising: . . . . .NA
Training: . . . . 2 Wks. Headquarters,
. . . . 1 Wk. On-Site
On-Going Support: A,C,D,G,H,I/ 9
EXPANSION PLANS:
US: . . . . .All US
Canada: . . . . .All Canada
Overseas: . . . . EUR

FIRSTAFF

3800 W. 80th St., # 1155
Bloomington, MN 55431
TEL: (800) 477-0088 (612) 893-7555
FAX: (612) 893-7550
Mr. Jim Ginther, President

First modern franchise exclusively in the office support marketplace for permanent and temporary personnel. A full complement of support services are provided, including computerized market analysis, site assistance, comprehensive training, pre-opening services and more!

HISTORY: . . . . IFA
Established in 1967; . . 1st Franchised in 1990
Company-Owned Units (As of 8/31/1992): . .4
Franchised Units (As of 8/31/1992): 2
Total Units (As of 8/31/1992): 6
Projected New Units for 1993: 4
Distribution: US-6;Can-0;Overseas-0
North America: . . . . 3 States
Concentration: . . .4 in MN, 1 in GA, 1 in WA
Registered: . . . CA,FL,IL,IN,MI,MN,WA,WI
. . . .
Type Space: . . . . Office Building;~3,000 SF

FINANCIAL: Earnings Claim: . .No
Cash Investment: $115-200K
Total Investment: $115-200K
Fees: Franchise - $20-50K
Royalty: 7%, Advert: 1-3%
Contract Periods (Yrs.): . . . 4/5/5
Area Development Agreement: . Yes
Sub-Franchise Contract: . . . . .No
Expand in Territory: . . . . . . Yes
Passive Ownership: . . . Discouraged
Encourage Conversions: . . . . Yes
Average # Employees: . . . . 10 FT

FRANCHISOR TRAINING/SUPPORT:
Financial Assistance Provided: . . . .Yes
Site Selection Assistance: . . . . .Yes
Lease Negotiation Assistance: . . . .Yes
Co-operative Advertising: . . . . .No
Training: . . . . 2 Wks. Headquarters,
. . . . 2 Wks. On-Site
On-Going Support: A,B,C,D,E,G,H,I/ . 15
EXPANSION PLANS:
US: . . . . .All US
Canada: . . . . No
Overseas: . . . . No

FIRSTAT NURSING SERVICES

1645 Palm Beach Lakes Blvd., # 450
West Palm Beach, FL 33401
TEL: (800) 845-7828 (407) 684-9000
FAX: (407) 684-9008
Mr. Tom Camplese, VP Mkt. Dev.

Provider of both skilled and unskilled nursing care for patients in the home. Additionally, provide supplemental staffing services to hospitals, nursing homes and rehabilitation centers.

HISTORY: . . . .
Established in 1989; . . 1st Franchised in 1990
Company-Owned Units (As of 8/31/1992): . .3
Franchised Units (As of 8/31/1992): 9
Total Units (As of 8/31/1992): 12
Projected New Units for 1993: 12
Distribution: US-12;Can-0;Overseas-0
North America: . . . . 7 States
Concentration: . . . . 6 in FL
Registered: . . . . .All
. . . .
Type Space: . . . . ;~1,400 SF

FINANCIAL: Earnings Claim: . .No
Cash Investment: $40-50K
Total Investment: $150-190K
Fees: Franchise - $25K
Royalty: 5%, Advert: 0%
Contract Periods (Yrs.): 5/10
Area Development Agreement: . Yes
Sub-Franchise Contract: . . . . .No
Expand in Territory: . . . . . . Yes
Passive Ownership: . . . Not Allowed
Encourage Conversions: . . . . .No
Average # Employees: . . . . .3 FT

FRANCHISOR TRAINING/SUPPORT:
Financial Assistance Provided: . . . Yes(I)
Site Selection Assistance: . . . . . . .Yes
Lease Negotiation Assistance: . . . .Yes
Co-operative Advertising: . . . . . . .Yes
Training: . . . . .1 Wk. Headquarters,
. . . . .2 Wks. Franchisee Location
On-Going Support: B,C,D,E,h,I/ 15
EXPANSION PLANS:
US: . . . . .All US
Canada: . . . . .All Canada
Overseas: . . . . No

FIVE STAR TEMPORARIES

16100 Chesterfield Pkwy. S.
Chesterfield, MO 63017
TEL: (800) 844-3483 (314) 532-2777
FAX:
Mr. Arthur Harter, Jr., President

Supply temporary help to industrial and commercial firms. This includes secretarial, labor, engineering, food processor and professional employees.

HISTORY: . . . .
Established in 1979; . . 1st Franchised in 1992
Company-Owned Units (As of 8/31/1992): . .3
Franchised Units (As of 8/31/1992): 0
Total Units (As of 8/31/1992): 3
Projected New Units for 1993: 5
Distribution: US-3;Can-0;Overseas-0
  North America: . . . . 2 States
  Concentration: . . . . 2 in MO, 1 in IL
Registered: . . . . IL,IN

. . . .
Type Space: . . Office Building;~600-800 SF

FINANCIAL: Earnings Claim: . . Yes
Cash Investment: $10-15K
Total Investment: $60-90K
Fees: Franchise - $5K
  Royalty: 6%, Advert: 1/2%
Contract Periods (Yrs.): . . . . Open
Area Development Agreement: . .No
Sub-Franchise Contract: . . . . .No
Expand in Territory: . . . . . . Yes
Passive Ownership: . . . Discouraged
Encourage Conversions: . . . . . Yes
Average # Employees: . . 4 FT, 2 PT

FRANCHISOR TRAINING/SUPPORT:
Financial Assistance Provided: . . . Yes(I)
Site Selection Assistance: . . . . .Yes
Lease Negotiation Assistance: . . . . .Yes
Co-operative Advertising: . . . . .Yes
Training: . . . . 2 Wks. Headquarters,
. . . . 2 Wks. Franchisee City
On-Going Support: A,b,C,D,E,G,H,I/ . . 10
EXPANSION PLANS:
  US: . . . . Midwest
  Canada: . . . . No
  Overseas: . . . . No

FLEX-STAFF / PRO-TEM

260 Cochituate Rd., # 109
Framingham, MA 01701
TEL: (508) 875-1341
FAX: (508) 879-3441
Mr. Giles A. Powers, President

Our franchise opportunity is reserved for individuals who have a record of management success in the Temporary Services industry. This practice enables us to eliminate the high cost of training those with unrelated backgrounds, as well as replacing those who find they are not right for the industry. As a low-cost operator, we are able to offer our franchise at significantly lower fee levels.

HISTORY: . . . .
Established in 1970; . . 1st Franchised in 1975
Company-Owned Units (As of 8/31/1992): . .1
Franchised Units (As of 8/31/1992): 9
Total Units (As of 8/31/1992): 10
Projected New Units for 1993: 3
Distribution: US-10;Can-0;Overseas-0
  North America: . . . . 5 States
  Concentration: . . . . 7 in FL, 1 in CT, 1 in NJ
Registered: . . . . .FL

. . . .
Type Space: . . . . . FS, SF, SC;~1,250 SF

FINANCIAL: Earnings Claim: . .No
Cash Investment: $15-30K
Total Investment: $25-50K
Fees: Franchise - $1K
  Royalty: Varies, Advert: 0%
Contract Periods (Yrs.): 7/7
Area Development Agreement: . .No
Sub-Franchise Contract: . . . . .No
Expand in Territory: . . . . . . Yes
Passive Ownership: . . . Not Allowed
Encourage Conversions: . . . . . Yes
Average # Employees: . . 2 FT, 2 PT

FRANCHISOR TRAINING/SUPPORT:
Financial Assistance Provided: . . .Yes(D)
Site Selection Assistance: . . . . .Yes
Lease Negotiation Assistance: . . . . .Yes
Co-operative Advertising: . . . . No
Training: . . . . 1 Wk. On-Site
. . . .
On-Going Support: A,C,D/ 7
EXPANSION PLANS:
  US: . . . . All US
  Canada: . . . . No
  Overseas: . . . . No

FLEX-TEAM

265 S. Main St.
Akron, OH 44308
TEL: (800) 759-7673 (216) 762-3838
FAX: (216) 762-7031
Mr. Douglas E. Eilertson, EVP

FLEX-TEAM is a full-service temporary service business, offering rapid response for client requirements for personnel categories including clerical, light industrial, medical, technical and food service. FLEX-TEAM's clients want flexibility for their employee team, allowing them to by-pass problems associated with permanent employment. FLEX-TEAM also offers a lease-to-hire option to its clients.

HISTORY: . . . .
Established in 1985; . . 1st Franchised in 1990
Company-Owned Units (As of 8/31/1992): . .2
Franchised Units (As of 8/31/1992): 0
Total Units (As of 8/31/1992): 2
Projected New Units for 1993: 5
Distribution: US-2;Can-0;Overseas-0
  North America: . . . . .1 State
  Concentration: . . . . 2 in OH
Registered: . . . .

. . . .
Type Space: Class A Off. Bldg;~300-1,000 SF

FINANCIAL: Earnings Claim: . .No
Cash Investment: $25-75K
Total Investment: $25-75K
Fees: Franchise - $15K
  Royalty: 6%, Advert: 0%
Contract Periods (Yrs.): 5/5
Area Development Agreement: . .No
Sub-Franchise Contract: . . . . . Yes
Expand in Territory: . . . . . . .No
Passive Ownership: . . . Not Allowed
Encourage Conversions: . . . . . Yes
Average # Employees: . . . . . .3 FT

FRANCHISOR TRAINING/SUPPORT:
Financial Assistance Provided: . . .Yes(D)
Site Selection Assistance: . . . . .Yes
Lease Negotiation Assistance: . . . . .Yes
Co-operative Advertising: . . . . .Yes
Training: . . . . . . 10 Days Headquarters,
. . . . 4 Days Licensee's Office
On-Going Support: / 15
EXPANSION PLANS:
  US: . . . . All US
  Canada: . . . . No
  Overseas: . . . . No

HAMILTON-RYKER COMPANY, THE

P. O. Box 1068
Martin, TN 38237
TEL: (800) 554-4726 (901) 587-3161
FAX: (901) 587-3195
Mr. Alan R. French, Fran. Mgr.

Temporary and permanent employment service.

HISTORY:	FINANCIAL: Earnings Claim: . .No	FRANCHISOR TRAINING/SUPPORT:
Established in 1971; . . 1st Franchised in 1990	Cash Investment: $18-20K	Financial Assistance Provided: . . . .Yes
Company-Owned Units (As of 8/31/1992): . 11	Total Investment: $60-100K	Site Selection Assistance: . . . . . . .Yes
Franchised Units (As of 8/31/1992): 0	Fees: Franchise - $15K	Lease Negotiation Assistance: . . .Yes
Total Units (As of 8/31/1992): 11	Royalty: 7%, Advert: 0%	Co-operative Advertising: . . . . . . .Yes
Projected New Units for 1993: 6	Contract Periods (Yrs.): 10/10	Training: . . . . .1 Wk. Headquarters,
Distribution: US-11;Can-0;Overseas-0	Area Development Agreement: . .No	. . . . 1 Wk. Branch Office
North America: . . . . 2 States	Sub-Franchise Contract: . . . . .No	On-Going Support: A,B,C,D,E,G,H,I/ . . 2
Concentration: . . . . 9 in TN, 2 in MS	Expand in Territory: . . . . Yes	EXPANSION PLANS:
Registered: . . . . .FL	Passive Ownership: . . . . .Allowed	US: . . . . Southeast
. . . .	Encourage Conversions: . . . . . Yes	Canada: . . . . No
Type Space: . FS, SF, SC, RM;~800-1,000 SF	Average # Employees: . . . . .2 FT	Overseas: . . . . No

HAYES GROUP

4369 Madera Rd.
Irving, TX 75038
TEL: (214) 255-6357
FAX: (214) 255-6357
Ms. Stella Hayes, President

THE HAYES GROUP offers the expertise in permanent, temporary and executive search without the penalty of on-going royalties or the estriction of geographical growth. In addition to the intensive initial training, you can choose our affiliation program on a one-year contract, renewable by your choice.

HISTORY:	FINANCIAL: Earnings Claim: . .No	FRANCHISOR TRAINING/SUPPORT:
Established in 1976; . . 1st Franchised in 1981	Cash Investment: $7.5K	Financial Assistance Provided: . . . . .No
Company-Owned Units (As of 8/31/1992): . .1	Total Investment: $40K	Site Selection Assistance: . . . . . . .Yes
Franchised Units (As of 8/31/1992): 5	Fees: Franchise - $7.5K	Lease Negotiation Assistance: . . . .Yes
Total Units (As of 8/31/1992): 6	Royalty: 0%, Advert: 0%	Co-operative Advertising: . . . . .No
Projected New Units for 1993:	Contract Periods (Yrs.): 1/1	Training: . . . . . 1-3 Wks. Headquarters or
Distribution: US-5;Can-0;Overseas-1	Area Development Agreement: . .No	. . . . On-Site
North America: . . . . 3 States	Sub-Franchise Contract: . . . . .No	On-Going Support: B,C,D,E,G,H,I/ 4
Concentration: . . . 2 in CO, 1 in AZ, 1 in TX	Expand in Territory: . . . . Yes	EXPANSION PLANS:
Registered:	Passive Ownership: . . . . . .Allowed	US: . . . . .All US
. . . .	Encourage Conversions: . . . . . Yes	Canada: . . . . No
Type Space: . . . .;~ SF	Average # Employees: . . . . .2 FT	Overseas: . . . . No

HEALTH FORCE

1600 Stewart Ave., # 700
Westbury, NY 11590
TEL: (800) 879-9243 (516) 683-6000
FAX: (516) 683-1450
Mr. Pat Hiller, Dir. Fran. Dev.

Full-service national temporary health care service to patients at home and staff relief to hospitals and institutions. We offer temporary payroll funding, computer management data, bookkeeping service. HEALTH FORCE allows you the opportunity to be involved in all aspects of temporary health care quickly and easily.

HISTORY: . . . . .IFA	FINANCIAL: Earnings Claim: . .No	FRANCHISOR TRAINING/SUPPORT:
Established in 1975; . . 1st Franchised in 1982	Cash Investment: $100-125K	Financial Assistance Provided: . . . Yes(I)
Company-Owned Units (As of 8/31/1992): . 13	Total Investment: . . . .$	Site Selection Assistance: . . . . . . .Yes
Franchised Units (As of 8/31/1992): 46	Fees: Franchise - $39.5K	Lease Negotiation Assistance: . . . .Yes
Total Units (As of 8/31/1992): 59	Royalty: 12-8.5%, Advert: . . 1/2%	Co-operative Advertising: . . . . . . .Yes
Projected New Units for 1993: 12	Contract Periods (Yrs.): 10/5/5	Training: . . . . 2 Wks. Headquarters,
Distribution: US-59;Can-0;Overseas-0	Area Development Agreement: . .No	. . . . 1 Wk. Franchisee Office
North America: . . . . 23 States	Sub-Franchise Contract: . . . . . .No	On-Going Support: a,b,C,D,E,F,G,H/ . . 60
Concentration: . . 13 in NY, 11 in FL, 7 in CA	Expand in Territory: . . . . Yes	EXPANSION PLANS:
Registered: . . . CA,FL,IL,IN,MD,MI,MN,NY	Passive Ownership: . . . Discouraged	US: . . . . .Midwest and West
. . . . OR,VA,WA,WI,DC	Encourage Conversions: . . . . . Yes	Canada: . . . . No
Type Space: . . . . FS, SF, SC;~800-1,000 SF	Average # Employees: . . 2 FT, 1 PT	Overseas: . . . . No

HEALTHCARE RECRUITERS INTERNATIONAL

5420 LBJ Freeway, LB 4, # 575
Dallas, TX 75240
TEL: (800) 634-1839 (214) 770-2020
FAX: (214) 770-2010
Mr. Bob Roberts, President

Executive recruiting, exclusively for the health care industry. Entry level through CEO. Contingency and retainer fees.

HISTORY:	FINANCIAL: Earnings Claim: . .No	FRANCHISOR TRAINING/SUPPORT:
Established in 1983; . . 1st Franchised in 1985	Cash Investment: . . . .$	Financial Assistance Provided: . . . . .Yes
Company-Owned Units (As of 8/31/1992): . .0	Total Investment: $65-150K	Site Selection Assistance: . . . . . . .Yes
Franchised Units (As of 8/31/1992): 29	Fees: Franchise - $31-48.5K	Lease Negotiation Assistance: . . . . .Yes
Total Units (As of 8/31/1992): 29	Royalty: 10%, Advert: 1%	Co-operative Advertising: . . . . . . .Yes
Projected New Units for 1993: 4	Contract Periods (Yrs.): 5/5	Training: . . . . 2 Wks. Headquarters
Distribution: US-29;Can-0;Overseas-0	Area Development Agreement: . .No	. . . .
North America: . . . . 22 States	Sub-Franchise Contract: . . . . .No	On-Going Support: A,C,D,G,H,I/ 5
Concentration:	Expand in Territory: . . . . . . Yes	EXPANSION PLANS:
Registered: . . . CA,FL,IL,IN,MD,MI,MN,NY	Passive Ownership: . . . Not Allowed	US: . . . . .All US
. . . .	Encourage Conversions: . . . . .NA	Canada: . . . . .Yes
Type Space: . . . . . . Executive Suite;~ SF	Average # Employees: . . 3 FT, 1 PT	Overseas: . . . . No

HOMEWATCH

2865 S. Colorado Blvd.
Denver, CO 80222
TEL: (800) 777-9770 (303) 758-7290
FAX: (303) 757-4403
Mr. Paul A. Sauer, President

HOMEWATCH SERVICES - since 1973. In-home services are the trend of the '90's. Start your own cash business, part-time or full-time, from your home. Services for pets, homes, companion care and handyman services. Minimum cash outlay - fun, easy, profitable business. Training and support provided. No royalty.

HISTORY:	FINANCIAL: Earnings Claim: . .No	FRANCHISOR TRAINING/SUPPORT:
Established in 1973; . . 1st Franchised in 1985	Cash Investment: $10K	Financial Assistance Provided: . . . Yes(I)
Company-Owned Units (As of 8/31/1992): . .4	Total Investment: $16-25K	Site Selection Assistance: . . . . . . .NA
Franchised Units (As of 8/31/1992): 23	Fees: Franchise - $10-19.5K	Lease Negotiation Assistance: . . . . .NA
Total Units (As of 8/31/1992): 27	Royalty: 6%, Advert: 1%	Co-operative Advertising: . . . . . . .Yes
Projected New Units for 1993: 20	Contract Periods (Yrs.): 10/5	Training: . . . . . . 4-5 Days Headquarters
Distribution: US-24;Can-3;Overseas-0	Area Development Agreement: Yes/5	. . . .
North America: . . . . 12 States, 3 Provinces	Sub-Franchise Contract: . . . . . Yes	On-Going Support: A,B,C,D,e,G,H,I/ . . . 4
Concentration: . . . 7 in CO, 4 in AZ, 2 in OH	Expand in Territory: . . . . . . Yes	EXPANSION PLANS:
Registered: . . . . .CA,IL,MI,MN,WA	Passive Ownership: . . . Discouraged	US: . . . All US, Emphasis E & W Coast
. . . .	Encourage Conversions: . . . . . Yes	Canada: . . . . .All Canada
Type Space: . . . . NA;~ SF	Average # Employees: 2 FT, Varies PT	Overseas: . . . . .Yes

HOUSESITTERS, THE

530 Queen St. E.
Toronto, ON M5A 1V2 CAN
TEL: (800) 387-1337 (416) 947-1295
FAX: (416) 947-0075
Ms. Andrea Ballett-Rozak, Bus. Dev.

Property management, home security and child/senior care for travelers provided by bonded and insured sitters on a live-in/live-out basis. Also, hourly babysitting, weekday dog walking and residential cleaning (maid service), corporate relocation. Minimum population base of 100,000.

HISTORY:	FINANCIAL: Earnings Claim: . Yes	FRANCHISOR TRAINING/SUPPORT:
Established in 1981; . . 1st Franchised in 1987	Cash Investment: $10-250K	Financial Assistance Provided: . . .Yes(D)
Company-Owned Units (As of 8/31/1992): . .3	Total Investment: $15-250K	Site Selection Assistance: . . . . . . .NA
Franchised Units (As of 8/31/1992): 31	Fees: Franchise - $10-200K	Lease Negotiation Assistance: . . . . .NA
Total Units (As of 8/31/1992): 34	Royalty: 8%, Advert: 8-5%	Co-operative Advertising: . . . . . . .NA
Projected New Units for 1993: 15	Contract Periods (Yrs.): 5/6/6	Training: . . . . 2 Wks. Headquarters
Distribution: US-0;Can-34;Overseas-0	Area Development Agreement: Yes/5	. . . .
North America: . . . . 5 Provinces	Sub-Franchise Contract: . . . . Yes	On-Going Support: A,B,C,D,E,F,G,h,i/ . 35
Concentration: . . . 16 in ON, 2 in NS, 2 in PQ	Expand in Territory: . . . . . . .No	EXPANSION PLANS:
Registered:	Passive Ownership: . . . Not Allowed	US: . . . . .All US
. . . .	Encourage Conversions: . . . . NA	Canada: . . . . .All Canada
Type Space: . . . . . .Home Based;~NA SF	Average # Employees: . .2 FT, 30 PT	Overseas: . . . . No

INTERIM HEALTHCARE

2050 Spectrum Blvd.
Ft. Lauderdale, FL 33309
TEL: (800) 937-7665 (305) 938-7600
FAX: (305) 938-7775
Mr. Bernie Wollett, Dir. Mkt. Dev.

One of the nation's largest proprietary home health care and hospital staffing services, providing quality patient care by professional nursing personnel. Company provides payroll financing.

HISTORY: . . . .
Established in 1946;   . . 1st Franchised in 1956
Company-Owned Units (As of 8/31/1992): . 84
Franchised Units (As of 8/31/1992): 232
Total Units (As of 8/31/1992): 316
Projected New Units for 1993: 20
Distribution: US-313;Can-3;Overseas-0
  North America: . . . . 44 States, 2 Provinces
  Concentration: . 36 in FL, 26 in NC, 24 in CA
Registered: . . . . All
. . . .
Type Space: . . . . SC;~1,000 SF

FINANCIAL: Earnings Claim: . .No
Cash Investment: $75K
Total Investment: $55-105K
Fees: Franchise - $5K
  Royalty: 6.5%, Advert: . . . 1/4%
Contract Periods (Yrs.): 10/10
Area Development Agreement: . .No
Sub-Franchise Contract: . . . . .No
Expand in Territory: . . . . . . Yes
Passive Ownership: . . . Discouraged
Encourage Conversions: . . . . NA
Average # Employees: . . . . . .3 FT

FRANCHISOR TRAINING/SUPPORT:
Financial Assistance Provided: . . . .
Site Selection Assistance: . . . . .Yes
Lease Negotiation Assistance: . . . . .Yes
Co-operative Advertising: . . . . .Yes
Training: . . . . 2 Wks. Headquarters
. . . .
On-Going Support: A,b,C,D,E,G,H,I/ . .300
EXPANSION PLANS:
US: . . . . All US
Canada: . . . . .All Canada
Overseas: . . . . No

INTERIM PERSONNEL

2050 Spectrum Blvd.
Ft. Lauderdale, Fl 33309
TEL: (800) 937-7665 (305) 938-7600 C
FAX: (305) 938-7775
Mr. John J. Marquez, Dir. Mkt. Dev.

$1.0 billion temporary and full-time personnel services company - office, clerical, data processing, marketing, telemarketing, paratechnical, legal and light industrial. 100% temp payroll funding, including FICA, SUTA, Workers Comp Ins, bonding and liability insurance. Best financially structured franchise in the industry. Our parent company, H & R Block, is the world's largest tax preparer.

HISTORY: . . . . IFA
Established in 1946;   . . 1st Franchised in 1956
Company-Owned Units (As of 8/31/1992): 160
Franchised Units (As of 8/31/1992): 185
Total Units (As of 8/31/1992): 345
Projected New Units for 1993: 20
Distribution: US-340;Can-5;Overseas-0
  North America: . . . . 43 States, 2 Provinces
  Concentration: . . . . 37 in CA, 4 in ON
Registered: . . . . All
. . . .
Type Space: . . . . .SF, SC;~1,000 SF

FINANCIAL: Earnings Claim: . .No
Cash Investment: $50K
Total Investment: $50K
Fees: Franchise - $5K
  Royalty: 25% GP, Advert: . . 1/4%
Contract Periods (Yrs.): 10/5
Area Development Agreement: . .No
Sub-Franchise Contract: . . . . .No
Expand in Territory: . . . . . . Yes
Passive Ownership: . . . Discouraged
Encourage Conversions: . . . . Yes
Average # Employees: . . 1 FT, 1 PT

FRANCHISOR TRAINING/SUPPORT:
Financial Assistance Provided: . . . Yes(I)
Site Selection Assistance: . . . . .Yes
Lease Negotiation Assistance: . . . . .Yes
Co-operative Advertising: . . . . .Yes
Training: . . . . . . 2-3 Wks. Headquarters,
. . . . .2 Wks. Office Site
On-Going Support: a,B,C,D,E,F,G,H,I/ .200
EXPANSION PLANS:
US: . . . . All US
Canada: . . . . .No
Overseas: . . . . No

LABOR WORLD OF AMERICA

8000 N. Federal Hwy.
Boca Raton, FL 33487
TEL: (800) 275-5000 (407) 997-5000
FAX: (800) 275-5000
Mr. Robert Lefcort, COO

LABOR WORLD is the largest company of its type, specializing in the placement of "Blue Collar" temporary personnel, and serving a variety of businesses including, manufacturing, distribution, construction, hotel and food service.

HISTORY: . . . . IFA
Established in 1974;   . . 1st Franchised in 1988
Company-Owned Units (As of 8/31/1992): . .5
Franchised Units (As of 8/31/1992): 24
Total Units (As of 8/31/1992): 29
Projected New Units for 1993: 15
Distribution: US-29;Can-0;Overseas-0
  North America: . . . . 15 States
  Concentration: . . . . 6 in IL, 5 in FL, 2 in GA
Registered: . . . . FL,IL,IN
. . . .
Type Space: . . . . . FS, SF;~1,500-2,000 SF

FINANCIAL: Earnings Claim: . .No
Cash Investment: $50K
Total Investment: $100K
Fees: Franchise - $12-20K
  Royalty: 4-3%, Advert: 1%
Contract Periods (Yrs.): 15/15
Area Development Agreement: . .No
Sub-Franchise Contract: . . . . .No
Expand in Territory: . . . . . . Yes
Passive Ownership: . . . Discouraged
Encourage Conversions: . . . . Yes
Average # Employees: . . . . . .4 FT

FRANCHISOR TRAINING/SUPPORT:
Financial Assistance Provided: . . . Yes(I)
Site Selection Assistance: . . . . .Yes
Lease Negotiation Assistance: . . . . .No
Co-operative Advertising: . . . . .No
Training: . . . . 2 Wks. Various Sites
. . . .
On-Going Support: a,C,D,E,G,H,I/ . . . 25
EXPANSION PLANS:
US: . . . . All US
Canada: . . . . .No
Overseas: . . . . No

LEGALSTAFF

1415 21st St.
Sacramento, CA 95814
TEL: (800) 736-4690 (916) 446-7777
FAX: (916) 446-7404
Ms. Louise Hackett, President

LEGALSTAFF offers a unique, specialized employment agency franchise which provides placement services for all legal personnel, including legal secretaries, paralegals, law clerks and attorneys. The LEGALSTAFF franchisee can meet all law office or legal department staffing needs by providing personnel on either a temporary or permanent basis. A "white collar" business where the franchisee can work with highly-qualified applicants and clients.

HISTORY:	FINANCIAL: Earnings Claim: . .No	FRANCHISOR TRAINING/SUPPORT:
Established in 1973; . . 1st Franchised in 1988	Cash Investment: $45-50K	Financial Assistance Provided: . . . Yes(I)
Company-Owned Units (As of 8/31/1992): . .4	Total Investment: $58-77K	Site Selection Assistance: . . . . .Yes
Franchised Units (As of 8/31/1992): 5	Fees: Franchise - $25K	Lease Negotiation Assistance: . . . . .Yes
Total Units (As of 8/31/1992): 9	Royalty: 4-8%, Advert: 0%	Co-operative Advertising: . . . . .Yes
Projected New Units for 1993:	Contract Periods (Yrs.): 10/5/5	Training: . . . . . . 2 Wks. Headquarters,
Distribution: US-9;Can-0;Overseas-0	Area Development Agreement: . .No	. . . . 1 Wk. Franchisee Office
North America: . . . . 3 States	Sub-Franchise Contract: . . . . .No	On-Going Support: B,C,D,E,G,H,I/ 9
Concentration: . . . 7 in CA, 1 in TX, 1 in PA	Expand in Territory: . . . . . . Yes	EXPANSION PLANS:
Registered: . . . . CA,IL,NY,OR	Passive Ownership: . . . . . .Allowed	US: . . . . .All US
	Encourage Conversions: . . . . . .No	Canada: . . . . .All Canada
Type Space: . . . . FS;~400-600 SF	Average # Employees: . 1-2 FT, 1 PT	Overseas: . . . . No

MANAGEMENT RECRUITERS

1127 Euclid Ave., # 1400
Cleveland, OH 44115
TEL: (800) 875-4000 (216) 696-1122
FAX: (216) 696-3221
Mr. Robert A. Angell, VP Fran. Mktg.

MANAGEMENT RECRUITERS is the world's largest and most professional contingency recruiting firm. Our slogan is apt - "the search and recruiting specialists." Our market is mid-management and professional, the entire gamut of positions from $25,000 - $75,000 per annum and higher.

HISTORY: . . . . .IFA	FINANCIAL: Earnings Claim: . Yes	FRANCHISOR TRAINING/SUPPORT:
Established in 1957; . . 1st Franchised in 1965	Cash Investment: $64-82K	Financial Assistance Provided: . . . . .No
Company-Owned Units (As of 8/31/1992): . 24	Total Investment: $64-82K	Site Selection Assistance: . . . . .Yes
Franchised Units (As of 8/31/1992): 386	Fees: Franchise - $40K	Lease Negotiation Assistance: . . . . .Yes
Total Units (As of 8/31/1992): 410	Royalty: 7%, Advert: 1/2%	Co-operative Advertising: . . . . .No
Projected New Units for 1993: 40	Contract Periods (Yrs.): . . . 5-20/10	Training: . . . . 3 Wks. Headquarters,
Distribution: US-406;Can-4;Overseas-0	Area Development Agreement: . .No	. . . . .3 Wks. Franchisee Location
North America: . . . . 46 States, 2 Provinces	Sub-Franchise Contract: . . . . .No	On-Going Support: C,D,E,G,H,I/ 64
Concentration: . .30 in CA, 30 in FL, 28 in NC	Expand in Territory: . . . . . . Yes	EXPANSION PLANS:
Registered: . . . . .All	Passive Ownership: . . . Discouraged	US: . . . . .All US
	Encourage Conversions: . . . . Yes	Canada: . . . . .All Canada
Type Space: . Office Building;~600-1,000 SF	Average # Employees: . . . 4-6 FT	Overseas: . . . . . AU, UK, NZ, JA

MURPHY GROUP, THE

1211 W. 22nd St., # 200
Oak Brook, IL 60521
TEL: (708) 571-1088
FAX:
Mr. William A. Murphy, II, President

Placement and recruiting of professional and office personnel.

HISTORY:	FINANCIAL: Earnings Claim: . .No	FRANCHISOR TRAINING/SUPPORT:
Established in 1957; . . 1st Franchised in 1975	Cash Investment: $30-50K	Financial Assistance Provided: . . . . .No
Company-Owned Units (As of 8/31/1992): . .4	Total Investment: $50K	Site Selection Assistance: . . . . .NA
Franchised Units (As of 8/31/1992): 7	Fees: Franchise - $15K	Lease Negotiation Assistance: . . . . .Yes
Total Units (As of 8/31/1992): 11	Royalty: 7%, Advert: 0%	Co-operative Advertising: . . . . .Yes
Projected New Units for 1993: 5	Contract Periods (Yrs.): 5/20	Training: . . . . 3 Wks. Headquarters
Distribution: US-11;Can-0;Overseas-0	Area Development Agreement: . .No	
North America: . . . . .1 State	Sub-Franchise Contract: . . . . .No	On-Going Support: a,C,H/ 5
Concentration: . . . . 11 in IL	Expand in Territory: . . . . . . Yes	EXPANSION PLANS:
Registered: IL	Passive Ownership: . . . Not Allowed	US: . . . . .All US
	Encourage Conversions: . . . . . Yes	Canada: . . . . .No
Type Space: . . . . .FS, SF;~1,200 SF	Average # Employees: . . 3 FT, 1 PT	Overseas: . . . . No

NORRELL TEMPORARY SERVICES

3535 Piedmont Rd. NE
Atlanta, GA 30305
TEL: (800) 765-6342 (404) 240-3179
FAX: (404) 240-3084
Ms. Pat Mashura, Fran. Dev. Mgr.

A national temporary help service with a 31-year track record of growth and profitability. Franchising since 1966, NORRELL is committed to providing the highest quality of service available to clients and employees in the temporary help industry. We have one of the most comprehensive support programs in this industry. NORRELL invites you to call and find out how you too can become a franchisee!

HISTORY: . . . . IFA
Established in 1961; . . 1st Franchised in 1966
Company-Owned Units (As of 8/31/1992): 134
Franchised Units (As of 8/31/1992): 93
Total Units (As of 8/31/1992): 227
Projected New Units for 1993: 10
Distribution: US-220;Can-7;Overseas-0
  North America: . . . . 42 States, 2 Provinces
  Concentration: . 22 in FL, 20 in CA, 16 in GA
Registered: . . . . All Except MD
. . . .
Type Space: . . Prof. Bus. Park;~900-1,000 SF

FINANCIAL: Earnings Claim: . Yes
Cash Investment: $20-30K
Total Investment: $50-95K
Fees: Franchise - $0
  Royalty: Varies, Advert: . . . 1/8%
Contract Periods (Yrs.): 15
Area Development Agreement: . .No
Sub-Franchise Contract: . . . . .No
Expand in Territory: . . . . . . Yes
Passive Ownership: . . . Not Allowed
Encourage Conversions: . . . . Yes
Average # Employees: . . . . . .2 FT

FRANCHISOR TRAINING/SUPPORT:
Financial Assistance Provided: . . . . .Yes
Site Selection Assistance: . . . . . . .Yes
Lease Negotiation Assistance: . . . . .Yes
Co-operative Advertising: . . . . . . .Yes
Training: . . . . . 14 Days HQ Service and
. . . . Sales Skills, 4-6 Days Local
On-Going Support: A,B,C,D,E,G,H,I/ .250
EXPANSION PLANS:
US: . . . . All US
Canada: . . . . .All Canada
Overseas: . . . . No

PET-TENDERS

P. O. Box 23622
San Diego, CA 92193
TEL: (619) 283-3033
FAX:
Ms. Cheryl Dagostaro, President

PET-TENDERS is an in-home, pet care service that offers extra services that may appeal to the pet/home-owner who is concerned about home safety, as well as superior pet care, while the owner is away. PET-TENDERS is a unique franchise, ideal for pet lovers only!

HISTORY: . . . .
Established in 1983; . . 1st Franchised in 1990
Company-Owned Units (As of 8/31/1992): . .2
Franchised Units (As of 8/31/1992): 0
Total Units (As of 8/31/1992): 2
Projected New Units for 1993: 2
Distribution: US-2;Can-0;Overseas-0
  North America: . . . . .1 State
  Concentration: . . . . 2 in CA
Registered: . . . . CA
. . . .
Type Space: . . . . Home Based;~ SF

FINANCIAL: Earnings Claim: . .No
Cash Investment: $11.5-13.9K
Total Investment: $11.5-13.9K
Fees: Franchise - $9.5K
  Royalty: 5%, Advert: 2%
Contract Periods (Yrs.): 5/5
Area Development Agreement: . .No
Sub-Franchise Contract: . . . . .No
Expand in Territory: . . . . . . .No
Passive Ownership: . . . Not Allowed
Encourage Conversions: . . . . .No
Average # Employees: . . . .2-20 PT

FRANCHISOR TRAINING/SUPPORT:
Financial Assistance Provided: . . . Yes(I)
Site Selection Assistance: . . . . . . .Yes
Lease Negotiation Assistance: . . . . .NA
Co-operative Advertising: . . . . . . .NA
Training: . . . . . . 3-5 Days Headquarters
. 1
On-Going Support: C,D,h/ 1
EXPANSION PLANS:
US: . . . . All US
Canada: . . . . .All Canada
Overseas: . . . . No

PHARMACISTS: prn

P. O. Box 161
Walpole, MA 02081
TEL: (800) 832-5560 (508) 660-1469
FAX: (508) 668-5663
Ms. Beth J. Leney, VP

PHARMACISTS:prn is a highly specialized temporary service that provides pharmacists and technicians to retail, hospital and home infusion pharmacies on a full- or part-time, as needed, basis. PHARMACISTS: prn also provides permanent placement services and experts consulting services to the pharmacy community. There is only one franchise per state with the exception of Florida, New York, California and Texas.

HISTORY: . . . . IFA
Established in 1987; . . 1st Franchised in 1989
Company-Owned Units (As of 8/31/1992): . .3
Franchised Units (As of 8/31/1992): 7
Total Units (As of 8/31/1992): 10
Projected New Units for 1993: 3
Distribution: US-10;Can-0;Overseas-0
  North America: . . . .
  Concentration: . . . .
Registered: . . . . CA,FL,MI,NY
. . . .
Type Space: . . . .;~ SF

FINANCIAL: Earnings Claim: . .No
Cash Investment: $25K
Total Investment: $45K
Fees: Franchise - $20K
  Royalty: 6%, Advert: 2%
Contract Periods (Yrs.): . . . 10/10
Area Development Agreement: . .No
Sub-Franchise Contract: . . . . .No
Expand in Territory: . . . . . . Yes
Passive Ownership: . . . Discouraged
Encourage Conversions: . . . . Yes
Average # Employees: . . 1 FT, 1 PT

FRANCHISOR TRAINING/SUPPORT:
Financial Assistance Provided: . . .Yes(D)
Site Selection Assistance: . . . . . . .NA
Lease Negotiation Assistance: . . . . .NA
Co-operative Advertising: . . . . . . .NA
Training: . . . . 3 Days Headquarters,
. . . . 2 Days Franchisee Office
On-Going Support: B,C,D,G,H,I/ 3
EXPANSION PLANS:
US: . . . . All US
Canada: . . . . No
Overseas: . . . . No

PROFESSIONAL DYNAMETRIC PROGRAMS / PDP

400 W. Highway 24, # 201, Box 5289
Woodland Park, CO 80866
TEL: (719) 687-6074
FAX:
Mr. Bruce M. Hubby, President

A business-to-business franchise. Independence with lucrative opportunity in the executive management market. Sell, train, consult and service large and small businesses in highly successful and proven programs for: hiring, motivating, stress managing and evaluating programs. Automatic repeat business. Low overhead. No inventory. No leases.

HISTORY: . . . .
Established in 1978; . . 1st Franchised in 1980
Company-Owned Units (As of 8/31/1992): . .0
Franchised Units (As of 8/31/1992): 30
Total Units (As of 8/31/1992): 30
Projected New Units for 1993: 5
Distribution: US-25;Can-4;Overseas-1
 North America: . . . . 14 States, 2 Provinces
 Concentration: . . . 5 in CA, 5 in CO, 3 in TX
Registered: . . . . .CA,FL
 . . . .
Type Space: . . . . Home Based;~ SF

FINANCIAL: Earnings Claim: . .No
Cash Investment: $5-20K
Total Investment: $30-45K
Fees: Franchise - $26.5-29.5K
 Royalty: 0%, Advert: 0%
Contract Periods (Yrs.): 7/3
Area Development Agreement: . .No
Sub-Franchise Contract: . . . . .No
Expand in Territory: . . . . . . Yes
Passive Ownership: . . . Discouraged
Encourage Conversions: . . . . . NA
Average # Employees: . 1-2 FT, 1 PT

FRANCHISOR TRAINING/SUPPORT:
Financial Assistance Provided: . . .Yes(D)
Site Selection Assistance: . . . . . . .NA
Lease Negotiation Assistance: . . . . .NA
Co-operative Advertising: . . . . . . .Yes
Training: . . . . . .5 Days or Longer at HQ
 . . . .
On-Going Support: B,d,F,G,H/ 4
EXPANSION PLANS:
 US: . . . . .All US
 Canada: . . . . .All Canada
 Overseas: . EUR, AU, S. Amer., Pac. Rim

REGIONAL NETWORK OF PERSONNEL CONSULTANTS

1211 W. 22nd St., # 221
Oakbrook, IL 60521
TEL: (708) 571-1088
FAX:
Mr. William A. Murphy, VP

Computerized (currently DEC, migrating to OS2) job order/search assignment sharing and candidate sharing network with production and management reports.

HISTORY: . . . .
Established in 1988; . . 1st Franchised in 1988
Company-Owned Units (As of 8/31/1992): . .2
Franchised Units (As of 8/31/1992): 6
Total Units (As of 8/31/1992): 8
Projected New Units for 1993: 12
Distribution: US-8;Can-0;Overseas-0
 North America: . . . . .1 State
 Concentration: . . . . .8 in IL
Registered: IL
 . . . .
Type Space: . . . . NA;~ SF

FINANCIAL: Earnings Claim: . . .
Cash Investment: $5K
Total Investment: $8K
Fees: Franchise - $5K
 Royalty: 10%, Advert: 0%
Contract Periods (Yrs.): 3/20
Area Development Agreement: . .No
Sub-Franchise Contract: . . . . . Yes
Expand in Territory: . . . . . . Yes
Passive Ownership: . . . . . .Allowed
Encourage Conversions: . . . . . Yes
Average # Employees: . . . . 5-6 FT

FRANCHISOR TRAINING/SUPPORT:
Financial Assistance Provided: . . . . .No
Site Selection Assistance: . . . . No
Lease Negotiation Assistance: . . . . .No
Co-operative Advertising: . . . . . . .Yes
Training: . . . . 2 Days On-Site
 . . . .
On-Going Support: c,d,h/ 4
EXPANSION PLANS:
 US: . . . . .All US
 Canada: . . . . No
 Overseas: . . . . No

REMEDYTEMP

32122 Camino Capistrano
San Juan Capistrano, CA 92675
TEL: (800) 722-TEMP (714) 661-1211
FAX: (714) 248-0813
Mr. Gerry Rhydderch, VP Fran. Dev.

REMEDYTEMP's franchise program provides entrepreneurs with an opportunity to develop a profitable and substantial business in an exclusive market using the proven system, training, marketing and on-going support of one of California's most established and respected temporary help companies.

HISTORY: . . . . IFA
Established in 1968; . . 1st Franchised in 1987
Company-Owned Units (As of 8/31/1992): . 56
Franchised Units (As of 8/31/1992): 30
Total Units (As of 8/31/1992): 86
Projected New Units for 1993: 15
Distribution: US-86;Can-0;Overseas-0
 North America: . . . . 20 States
 Concentration: . . .43 in CA, 4 in AZ, 3 in VA
Registered: . . . CA,FL,HI,IL,IN,MD,MI,MN
 . . . . .NY,OR,RI,VA,WA,WI
Type Space: . . . . . Office Building;~850 SF

FINANCIAL: Earnings Claim: . .No
Cash Investment: $35-50K
Total Investment: $90-125K
Fees: Franchise - $15K
 Royalty: 7.5%, Advert: 1/2%
Contract Periods (Yrs.): 10/10
Area Development Agreement: . .No
Sub-Franchise Contract: . . . . . .No
Expand in Territory: . . . . . . Yes
Passive Ownership: . . . Discouraged
Encourage Conversions: . . . . . Yes
Average # Employees: . . 3 FT, 1 PT

FRANCHISOR TRAINING/SUPPORT:
Financial Assistance Provided: . . . . .Yes
Site Selection Assistance: . . . . . . .Yes
Lease Negotiation Assistance: . . . . .Yes
Co-operative Advertising: . . . . . . .Yes
Training: . . . . 5 Days Headquarters,
 . . . . .5 Days Branch
On-Going Support: A,B,C,D,E,G,H,I/ . . 6
EXPANSION PLANS:
 US: . . . . . .NE, SE, SW and Midwest
 Canada: . . . . .All Canada
 Overseas: . UK, IRE, Holland, Most EUR

RETIREE SKILLS, INC.

1475 W. Prince Rd.
Tucson, AZ 85705
TEL: (602) 888-8310
FAX:
Mr. Robert Rheinhart, President

We are a private temporary help service, specializing in the "Over 50" worker. We have discontinued franchising until the economy improves.

HISTORY:	FINANCIAL: Earnings Claim: . Yes	FRANCHISOR TRAINING/SUPPORT:
Established in 1978; . . 1st Franchised in 1989	Cash Investment: $30K	Financial Assistance Provided: . . . . . No
Company-Owned Units (As of 8/31/1992): . . 1	Total Investment: $30K	Site Selection Assistance: . . . . .Yes
Franchised Units (As of 8/31/1992): 0	Fees: Franchise - $9.5-15K	Lease Negotiation Assistance: . . . . .Yes
Total Units (As of 8/31/1992): 1	Royalty: 4%, Advert: 3%	Co-operative Advertising: . . . . .Yes
Projected New Units for 1993: 1	Contract Periods (Yrs.): . . . 10/10	Training: . . . . 5 Days Headquarters,
Distribution: US-1;Can-0;Overseas-0	Area Development Agreement: . .No	. . . . 5 Days On-Site
North America: . . . . .1 State	Sub-Franchise Contract: . . . . .No	On-Going Support: D,E,G/ 4
Concentration: . . . . 1 in AZ	Expand in Territory: . . . . Yes	EXPANSION PLANS:
Registered:	Passive Ownership: . . . Not Allowed	US: . . . . Southwest
. . . .	Encourage Conversions: . . . . NA	Canada: . . . . .No
Type Space: . . . . SC;~600 SF	Average # Employees: . . 2 FT, 1 PT	Overseas: . . . . No

ROMAC AND ASSOCIATES

183 Middle St., P.O. Box 7469
Portland, ME 04112
TEL: (800) 341-0263 (207) 773-6387
FAX: (207) 774-5326
Ms. Genie A. Beaulieu, Dir. Comm.

Contingency recruiting offices, specializing in the permanent and temporary placement of accounting, banking and financial services personnel. ROMAC offers one of the best training programs in the industry, as well as on-going training support.

HISTORY:	FINANCIAL: Earnings Claim: . .No	FRANCHISOR TRAINING/SUPPORT:
Established in 1966; . . 1st Franchised in 1978	Cash Investment: $100-125K	Financial Assistance Provided: . . .Yes(D)
Company-Owned Units (As of 8/31/1992): . .2	Total Investment: $100-200K	Site Selection Assistance: . . . . . . .Yes
Franchised Units (As of 8/31/1992): 28	Fees: Franchise - $40K	Lease Negotiation Assistance: . . . . .Yes
Total Units (As of 8/31/1992): 30	Royalty: 8%, Advert: 1%	Co-operative Advertising: . . . . .No
Projected New Units for 1993: 8	Contract Periods (Yrs.): 10/10	Training: . . . . 5 Days Headquarters,
Distribution: US-30;Can-0;Overseas-0	Area Development Agreement: . .No	. . . . .15 Days Site
North America: . . . . 23 States	Sub-Franchise Contract: . . . . .No	On-Going Support: b,C,D,G,H,I/ 12
Concentration: . . . .3 in FL, 2 in PA, 2 in TX	Expand in Territory: . . . . Yes	EXPANSION PLANS:
Registered: . . . CA,IL,IN,MI,MN,NY,OR,VA	Passive Ownership: . . . Not Allowed	US: . . . . .All US
. . . . WA,WI	Encourage Conversions: . . . . Yes	Canada: . . . . .No
Type Space: . . . . NA;~ SF	Average # Employees: . . . . .4 FT	Overseas: . . . . No

ROTH YOUNG PERSONNEL SERVICE

535 Fifth Ave., # 710
New York, NY 10017
TEL: (800) 343-8518 (212) 557-4900
FAX: (212) 972-5367
Ms. Carol O'Brien, Dir. Fran. Dev.

ROTH YOUNG PERSONNEL SERVICE, an AmEX corporation, is a permanent placement and recruiting service, specializing in managerial and executive level positions. ROTH YOUNG has been in business since 1964 and offers name recognition and a reputation for client satisfaction. We offer exclusive territory, corporate and on-site training, training materials and on-going telephone support.

HISTORY:	FINANCIAL: Earnings Claim: . .No	FRANCHISOR TRAINING/SUPPORT:
Established in 1964; . . 1st Franchised in 1967	Cash Investment: $30-40K	Financial Assistance Provided: . . . Yes(I)
Company-Owned Units (As of 8/31/1992): . .1	Total Investment: $63-81K	Site Selection Assistance: . . . . .Yes
Franchised Units (As of 8/31/1992): 22	Fees: Franchise - $25K	Lease Negotiation Assistance: . . . . .Yes
Total Units (As of 8/31/1992): 23	Royalty: 3-8%, Advert: 1%	Co-operative Advertising: . . . . .Yes
Projected New Units for 1993: 5	Contract Periods (Yrs.): 10/10	Training: . . . . 2 Wks. Headquarters
Distribution: US-23;Can-0;Overseas-0	Area Development Agreement: . .No	. . . .
North America: . . . . 18 States	Sub-Franchise Contract: . . . . .No	On-Going Support: A,C,D,E,G,H/ 6
Concentration: . . . 2 in TX, 2 in PA, 2 in NY	Expand in Territory: . . . . Yes	EXPANSION PLANS:
Registered: . . . . .All	Passive Ownership: . . . Not Allowed	US: . . . . .All US
. . . .	Encourage Conversions: . . . . Yes	Canada: . . . . .No
Type Space: . . Office Building;~800-1,000 SF	Average # Employees: . 3-4 FT, 1 PT	Overseas: . . . . No

SALES CONSULTANTS

1127 Euclid Ave., # 1400
Cleveland, OH 44115
TEL: (800) 875-4000 (216) 696-1122 C
FAX: (216) 696-3221
Mr. Robert Angell, VP Fran. Mktg.

Our slogan says it all: "Finding and placing sales, sales management and marketing talent is our only business." SALES CONSULTANTS is the world's largest and most professional organization specializing in the search, recruitment and placement of salesmen, saleswomen, sales managers and marketing staff.

HISTORY: . . . . IFA
Established in 1957; . . 1st Franchised in 1965
Company-Owned Units (As of 8/31/1992): . 24
Franchised Units (As of 8/31/1992): 111
Total Units (As of 8/31/1992): 135
Projected New Units for 1993: 10
Distribution: US-134;Can-1;Overseas-0
  North America: . . . . . 37 States, 1 Province
  Concentration: . . 22 in CA, 15 in NJ, 10 in IL
Registered: . . . . .All
. . . .
Type Space: . Office Building;~600-1,000 SF

FINANCIAL: Earnings Claim: . Yes
Cash Investment: $64-82K
Total Investment: $64-82K
Fees: Franchise - $40K
  Royalty: 7%, Advert: 1/2%
Contract Periods (Yrs.): . . . 5-20/10
Area Development Agreement: . .No
Sub-Franchise Contract: . . . . .No
Expand in Territory: . . . . . . Yes
Passive Ownership: . . . Discouraged
Encourage Conversions: . . . . Yes
Average # Employees: . . . . 4-6 FT

FRANCHISOR TRAINING/SUPPORT:
Financial Assistance Provided: . . . . .No
Site Selection Assistance: . . . . . . .Yes
Lease Negotiation Assistance: . . . . .Yes
Co-operative Advertising: . . . . .No
Training: . . . . . . 3 Wks. Headquarters,
. . . . .3 Wks. Franchisee Location
On-Going Support: C,D,E,G,H,I/ 64
EXPANSION PLANS:
  US: . . . . .All US
  Canada: . . . . .All Canada
  Overseas: . . . . AU, NZ, UK, HA

SANFORD ROSE ASSOCIATES

265 S. Main St.
Akron, OH 44308
TEL: (800) 759-7673 (216) 762-6211
FAX: (216) 762-7031
Mr. Douglas R. Eilertson, EVP

"Executive Search" is distinct within the SRA organization! We provide a highly-reliable service to fill critical openings with our corporate clients. Only the most qualified candidates are presented. Our adaptability allows us to work at virtually all professional levels developing repeat business!

HISTORY: . . . . IFA
Established in 1959; . . 1st Franchised in 1970
Company-Owned Units (As of 8/31/1992): . .1
Franchised Units (As of 8/31/1992): 75
Total Units (As of 8/31/1992): 76
Projected New Units for 1993: 10
Distribution: US-76;Can-0;Overseas-0
  North America: . . . . 24 States
  Concentration: . . .21 in OH, 6 in PA, 6 in NY
Registered: . . . CA,FL,IL,IN,MD,MI,NY,OR
. . . . .RI,SD,VA,WI
Type Space: Class A Off. Bldg;~500-1,000 SF

FINANCIAL: Earnings Claim: . .No
Cash Investment: $40-50K
Total Investment: $50-75K
Fees: Franchise - $29.5K
  Royalty: 8-3%, Advert: 0%
Contract Periods (Yrs.): . . . Infinite
Area Development Agreement: . .No
Sub-Franchise Contract: . . . . .No
Expand in Territory: . . . . . . Yes
Passive Ownership: . . . Not Allowed
Encourage Conversions: . . . . .No
Average # Employees: .1-10 FT, 1 PT

FRANCHISOR TRAINING/SUPPORT:
Financial Assistance Provided: . . .Yes(D)
Site Selection Assistance: . . . . . . .Yes
Lease Negotiation Assistance: . . . . .Yes
Co-operative Advertising: . . . . .NA
Training: . . . . 3 Wks. Headquarters,
. . . . 2 Wks. On-Site
On-Going Support: A,B,C,D,E,F,G,H,I/ . .
EXPANSION PLANS:
  US: . . . . .All US
  Canada: . . . . No
  Overseas: . . . . No

SNELLING PERSONNEL SERVICES

12801 N. Central Expy., # 700
Dallas, TX 75243
TEL: (800) 766-5556 (214) 239-7575
FAX: (214) 239-6881
Mr. Rick Spragins, SVP

Unlimited expansion opportunities in the fast-growing personnel services industry. Offers full-service permanent and temporary help franchises nationwide. Extensive training and on-going support, exclusive national computerized network. Cost-effective funding program for payroll and billing.

HISTORY: . . . . IFA
Established in 1951; . . 1st Franchised in 1956
Company-Owned Units (As of 8/31/1992): . .0
Franchised Units (As of 8/31/1992): 373
Total Units (As of 8/31/1992): 373
Projected New Units for 1993: 70
Distribution: US-465;Can-0;Overseas-7
  North America: . . . . 47 States
  Concentration: . . . .
Registered: . . . .
. . . .
Type Space: Office Building;~1,000-1,500 SF

FINANCIAL: Earnings Claim: . .No
Cash Investment: $66-99K
Total Investment: $66-99K
Fees: Franchise - $3K
  Royalty: 4.5-7%, Advert: . . . 0-3%
Contract Periods (Yrs.): . . .Lifetime
Area Development Agreement: . .No
Sub-Franchise Contract: . . . . .No
Expand in Territory: . . . . . . Yes
Passive Ownership: . . . Discouraged
Encourage Conversions: . . . . Yes
Average # Employees: . . . . 3-8 FT

FRANCHISOR TRAINING/SUPPORT:
Financial Assistance Provided: . . . . .No
Site Selection Assistance: . . . . . . .Yes
Lease Negotiation Assistance: . . . . .Yes
Co-operative Advertising: . . . . .No
Training: . . . 2 Wks. HQ,1 Wk. Pre-Open-
. . .ing, 3 Days Post-Opening, On-Going
On-Going Support: a,b,C,D,E,G,h,I/ . . 99
EXPANSION PLANS:
  US: . . . . .All US
  Canada: . . . . .All Canada
  Overseas: . . . . .Yes

STAFF BUILDERS

1981 Marcus Ave.
Lake Success, NY 11042
TEL: (800) 342-5782 (516) 327-3380
FAX: (516) 358-5678
Mr. Ed Teixeira, SVP Fran.

Full-service health care services, providing temporary employment. Benefits of financing temporary payroll and accounts receivable, initial and continuous training, computerization, centralized management and risk control.

HISTORY: . . . . IFA	FINANCIAL: Earnings Claim: . . .	FRANCHISOR TRAINING/SUPPORT:
Established in 1961; . . 1st Franchised in 1966	Cash Investment: $15-50K	Financial Assistance Provided: . . . . . No
Company-Owned Units (As of 8/31/1992): . 24	Total Investment: $75-115K	Site Selection Assistance: . . . . .Yes
Franchised Units (As of 8/31/1992): 80	Fees: Franchise - $25K	Lease Negotiation Assistance: . . . . . .Yes
Total Units (As of 8/31/1992): 104	Royalty: Varies, Advert: 0%	Co-operative Advertising: . . . . .No
Projected New Units for 1993:	Contract Periods (Yrs.): 10/5	Training: . . . . . . 2-3 Wks. Headquarters
Distribution: US-114;Can-0;Overseas-0	Area Development Agreement: . .No	. . . .
North America: . . . . 29 States	Sub-Franchise Contract: . . . . .No	On-Going Support: A,b,C,D,E,G,h,I/ . . . .
Concentration: . 27 in NY, 21 in CA, 14 in OH	Expand in Territory: . . . . . . Yes	EXPANSION PLANS:
Registered: . . . . All States	Passive Ownership: . . . Discouraged	US: . . . . All US
. . . .	Encourage Conversions: . . . . Yes	Canada: . . . . .Yes
Type Space: . . . .;~ SF	Average # Employees: . . 4 FT, 1 PT	Overseas: . . . . Yes

T. L. C. NURSING CENTERS

P. O. Box 767519
Roswell, GA 30076
TEL: (404) 594-1153
FAX:
Mr. Bill Wimbish, President

The T.L.C. NURSING CENTER is a private-duty, nurse-placement service devoted primarily to the home health care market, but which is fully capable of furnishing staffing assistance to doctors, hospitals and other institutions. Each Center maintains a Registry of nurses, homemakers, sitters, etc. to which it sub-contracts positions it has obtained through advertising and marketing of its services.

HISTORY:	FINANCIAL: Earnings Claim: . .No	FRANCHISOR TRAINING/SUPPORT:
Established in 1984; . . 1st Franchised in 1984	Cash Investment: $12-35K	Financial Assistance Provided: . . .Yes(D)
Company-Owned Units (As of 8/31/1992): . .1	Total Investment: $20-50K	Site Selection Assistance: . . . . . . .Yes
Franchised Units (As of 8/31/1992): 5	Fees: Franchise - $5-20K	Lease Negotiation Assistance: . . . .Yes
Total Units (As of 8/31/1992): 6	Royalty: 8%, Advert: 2%	Co-operative Advertising: . . . . . . .Yes
Projected New Units for 1993:	Contract Periods (Yrs.): 5/5	Training: . . . . .1 Wk. Headquarters,
Distribution: US-6;Can-0;Overseas-0	Area Development Agreement: Yes/5	. . . . .1 Wk. Operating Center
North America: . . . . 2 States	Sub-Franchise Contract: . . . . .No	On-Going Support: c,d,h/ 3
Concentration: . . . . 5 in GA, 1 in PA	Expand in Territory: . . . . . . Yes	EXPANSION PLANS:
Registered: . . . . .FL,MI	Passive Ownership: . . . . . .Allowed	US: . . . . All US
. . . .	Encourage Conversions: . . . . Yes	Canada: . . . . .No
Type Space: . . . .;~ SF	Average # Employees: . . 1 FT, 1 PT	Overseas: . . . . No

TALENT TREE PERSONNEL SERVICES

9703 Richmond Ave.
Houston, TX 77042
TEL: (800) 827-8733 (713) 789-1818
FAX: (713) 780-0722
Mr. Ike Steele, Mgr. Fran. Dev.

As a high-quality temporary service, TALENT TREE addresses the human resource challenges of the 90's through innovative, creative solutions to the ever-complex problems of long-term strategic planning. Flexibility and customization are the cornerstone to our operating system.

HISTORY: . . . . IFA	FINANCIAL: Earnings Claim: . .No	FRANCHISOR TRAINING/SUPPORT:
Established in 1976; . . 1st Franchised in 1990	Cash Investment: $20-25K	Financial Assistance Provided: . . . Yes(I)
Company-Owned Units (As of 8/31/1992): 120	Total Investment: $75-125K	Site Selection Assistance: . . . . . . .Yes
Franchised Units (As of 8/31/1992): 16	Fees: Franchise - $10K	Lease Negotiation Assistance: . . . . .Yes
Total Units (As of 8/31/1992): 136	Royalty: Varies, Advert: 0%	Co-operative Advertising: . . . . . . .Yes
Projected New Units for 1993: 16	Contract Periods (Yrs.): . . .10/5/5/5	Training: . . . . . . .3-6 Days HQ Training
Distribution: US-136;Can-0;Overseas-0	Area Development Agreement: . .No	. . . Center, 3 Days Each 1st & 2nd Wks.
North America: . . . . 25 States	Sub-Franchise Contract: . . . . .No	On-Going Support: A,B,C,D,E,G,h/ . .358
Concentration: . .29 in CA, 12 in TX, 11 in FL	Expand in Territory: . . . . . . Yes	EXPANSION PLANS:
Registered: . . .CA,FL,HI,IN,MD,MI,MN,NY	Passive Ownership: . . . Discouraged	US: . . . . All US
. . . . OR,RI,VA,WI,DC	Encourage Conversions: . . . . . Yes	Canada: . . . . .No
Type Space: . . . . .FS, SF;~1,200 SF	Average # Employees: . . . . 2-3 FT	Overseas: . . . . .MX

TEMPFORCE

1600 Stewart Ave., # 700
Westbury, NY 11590
TEL: (800) 275-2750 (516) 683-6000
FAX: (516) 683-1540
Mr. Charles Martin, Dir. Fran. Dev.

TEMPFORCE temporary help service, specializing in office support and light industrial. Full payroll funding, computer data management, bookkeeping services, promotional aids, extensive training and field support, pre-opening, site selection, office layout and staff assistance. Full computerization.

HISTORY: . . . .
Established in 1960; . . 1st Franchised in 1975
Company-Owned Units (As of 8/31/1992): . .5
Franchised Units (As of 8/31/1992): 42
Total Units (As of 8/31/1992): 47
Projected New Units for 1993: 12
Distribution: US-47;Can-0;Overseas-0
    North America: . . . . 26 States
    Concentration: . . . 16 in NY, 4 in IL, 4 in FL
Registered: . . . . .All
. . . .
Type Space: . FS, SF, SC, RM;~800-1,200 SF

FINANCIAL: Earnings Claim: . .No
Cash Investment: $60-110K
Total Investment: $60-110K
Fees: Franchise - $7.5K
    Royalty: 8.5-6.5%, Advert: . . . 1%
Contract Periods (Yrs.): 30/5
Area Development Agreement: . . .
Sub-Franchise Contract: . . . . .No
Expand in Territory: . . . . . . Yes
Passive Ownership: . . . Discouraged
Encourage Conversions: . . . . Yes
Average # Employees: . . . . 2-3 FT

FRANCHISOR TRAINING/SUPPORT:
Financial Assistance Provided: . . .Yes(D)
Site Selection Assistance: . . . . . . .Yes
Lease Negotiation Assistance: . . . .Yes
Co-operative Advertising: . . . . . . .Yes
Training: . . . . 2 Wks. Headquarters,
. . . . .1 Wk. On-Site, On-Going
On-Going Support: A,C,D,E,G,H,I/ . . . 50
EXPANSION PLANS:
US: . . . . .All US
Canada: . . . . .No
Overseas: . . . . No

TEMPS & CO.

245 Peachtree Center Ave., # 2500
Atlanta, GA 30303
TEL: (800) 438-6086 (404) 659-5236
FAX: (404) 659-7139
Mr. Harlan T. Medford, VP/COO

TEMPS & CO. offers client companies a full range of personnel services, including both temporary and permanent placement. Fully-automated cross training and skills enhancement programs are provided.

HISTORY: . . . .
Established in 1972; . . 1st Franchised in 1988
Company-Owned Units (As of 8/31/1992): . 10
Franchised Units (As of 8/31/1992): 10
Total Units (As of 8/31/1992): 20
Projected New Units for 1993: 5
Distribution: US-20;Can-0;Overseas-0
    North America: . . . . 5 States
    Concentration: . . . 7 in GA, 4 in TN, 3 in SC
Registered: . . . .
. . . .
Type Space: . . . . .SF, SC;~ SF

FINANCIAL: Earnings Claim: . Yes
Cash Investment: $25-30K
Total Investment: $50-90K
Fees: Franchise - $12.5K
    Royalty: Varies, Advert: . . Varies
Contract Periods (Yrs.): 5/5
Area Development Agreement: Yes/5
Sub-Franchise Contract: . . . . . Yes
Expand in Territory: . . . . Yes
Passive Ownership: . . . . . .Allowed
Encourage Conversions: . . . . Yes
Average # Employees: . . 2 FT, 1 PT

FRANCHISOR TRAINING/SUPPORT:
Financial Assistance Provided: . . . . .Yes
Site Selection Assistance: . . . . . . .Yes
Lease Negotiation Assistance: . . . .Yes
Co-operative Advertising: . . . . . . .Yes
Training: . . . . 2 Wks. Headquarters
. . . .
On-Going Support: A,B,C,D,E,F,G,H,I/ 20
EXPANSION PLANS:
US: . . . . .All US
Canada: . . . . .No
Overseas: . . . . No

TIME SERVICES /
TIME TEMPORARIES
6422 Lima Rd.
Ft. Wayne, IN 46818
TEL: (800) 837-8463 (219) 489-2020
FAX:
Mr. Thomas C. Ward

Temporary employment - technical, clerical and industrial. TIME TEMPORARIES is a growth company offering franchisees exclusive territories in major markets. Specialization is in the technical fields - i.e. engineers and programmers. On-line operations, search and retrieval systems and centralized payroll and billing.

HISTORY: . . . .
Established in 1981; . . 1st Franchised in 1982
Company-Owned Units (As of 8/31/1992): . .7
Franchised Units (As of 8/31/1992): 2
Total Units (As of 8/31/1992): 9
Projected New Units for 1993: 3
Distribution: US-9;Can-0;Overseas-0
    North America: . . . . 3 States
    Concentration: . . . . 5 in IN, 2 in OH, 1 in MI
Registered: . . . . .FL,IN,VA
. . . .
Type Space: . . . . Office Building;~750+ SF

FINANCIAL: Earnings Claim: . .No
Cash Investment: $50-75K
Total Investment: $50-75K
Fees: Franchise - $20K
    Royalty: Varies, Advert: 0%
Contract Periods (Yrs.): 10/5/5
Area Development Agreement: . .No
Sub-Franchise Contract: . . . . .No
Expand in Territory: . . . . Yes
Passive Ownership: . . . . . .Allowed
Encourage Conversions: . . . . Yes
Average # Employees: . . . . . .4 FT

FRANCHISOR TRAINING/SUPPORT:
Financial Assistance Provided: . . . . .No
Site Selection Assistance: . . . . . . .Yes
Lease Negotiation Assistance: . . . .Yes
Co-operative Advertising: . . . . . . .Yes
Training: . . . . 2 Wks. Headquarters,
. . . . 1 Wk. Grand Opening, 2 Days/Mo.
On-Going Support: a,b,C,D,E,F,G,H/ . . 30
EXPANSION PLANS:
US: . . . . Midwest
Canada: . . . . .No
Overseas: . . . . No

TODAYS TEMPORARY

18111 Preston Rd., # 800
Dallas, TX 75252
TEL: (800) 822-7868 (214) 380-9380
FAX: (214) 250-3732
Mr. Kevin Roberts, Mgr. Fran. Dev.

TODAYS TEMPORARY is a national temporary help company, awarding franchisees an exclusive major market territory. Franchisees control profitability by providing temporary help service to clients, emphasizing quality service. Emphasis is on high-skilled clerical and office automation applications.

HISTORY: . . . . IFA	FINANCIAL: Earnings Claim: . .No	FRANCHISOR TRAINING/SUPPORT:
Established in 1982; . . 1st Franchised in 1983	Cash Investment: $80-120K	Financial Assistance Provided: . . . Yes(I)
Company-Owned Units (As of 8/31/1992): . 22	Total Investment: $80-120K	Site Selection Assistance: . . . . .Yes
Franchised Units (As of 8/31/1992): 21	Fees: Franchise - $0	Lease Negotiation Assistance: . . . .Yes
Total Units (As of 8/31/1992): 43	Royalty: Varies, Advert: . . Varies	Co-operative Advertising: . . . . .Yes
Projected New Units for 1993: 1	Contract Periods (Yrs.): 5/25	Training: . . . . . . 3 Wks. Headquarters
Distribution: US-43;Can-0;Overseas-0	Area Development Agreement: . .No	. . . .
North America: . . . . 15 States	Sub-Franchise Contract: . . . . .No	On-Going Support: A,B,C,D,E,F,G,H,I/ 50
Concentration: . . . 18 in TX, 6 in FL, 3 in NJ	Expand in Territory: . . . . . . Yes	EXPANSION PLANS:
Registered: . . . CA,FL,IL,IN,MD,MI,MN,NY	Passive Ownership: . . . Not Allowed	US: . . . . All US
. . . . .OR,RI,VA,WA,WI,DC	Encourage Conversions: . . . . Yes	Canada: . . . . .No
Type Space: . . .Class A Off. Bldg;~1,200 SF	Average # Employees: . . . . .2 FT	Overseas: . . . . No

TRC TEMPORARY SERVICES

100 Ashford Center N., # 500
Atlanta, GA 30338
TEL: (800) 488-8008 (404) 392-1411
FAX: (404) 393-2742
Mr. Robert Gallagher, VP Fran. Div.

TRC is a full-service, national temporary help company, offering a support program second to none, with exceptional markets available. We specialize in the placement of temporary employees in secretarial, clerical, light industrial, data processing, word processing and more.

HISTORY: . . . . IFA	FINANCIAL: Earnings Claim: . .No	FRANCHISOR TRAINING/SUPPORT:
Established in 1980; . . 1st Franchised in 1984	Cash Investment: . . . .$	Financial Assistance Provided: . . . . .No
Company-Owned Units (As of 8/31/1992): . 19	Total Investment: $75-125K	Site Selection Assistance: . . . . .Yes
Franchised Units (As of 8/31/1992): 24	Fees: Franchise - $0	Lease Negotiation Assistance: . . . . .No
Total Units (As of 8/31/1992): 43	Royalty: 45% GM, Advert: . . . 0%	Co-operative Advertising: . . . . .Yes
Projected New Units for 1993: 8	Contract Periods (Yrs.): 30	Training: . . . . .23 Days On-Site, 21 Days
Distribution: US-43;Can-0;Overseas-0	Area Development Agreement: . .No	. . . . . . .Headquarters, 3 Days/Quarter
North America: . . . . 13 States	Sub-Franchise Contract: . . . . .No	On-Going Support: A,B,C,D,E,G,H/ . . .9
Concentration: . . . .5 in CA, 3 in FL, 3 in MI	Expand in Territory: . . . . . . Yes	EXPANSION PLANS:
Registered: . . . . .CA,FL,MI,NY,OR,RI,WA	Passive Ownership: . . . Not Allowed	US: . . . . All US
. . . .	Encourage Conversions: . . . . Yes	Canada: . . . . .No
Type Space: . . . . . FS, SF, SC;~1,000 SF	Average # Employees: . . . . . .4 FT	Overseas: . . . . No

WESTERN TEMPORARY SERVICES

301 Lennon Ln.
Walnut Creek, CA 94598
TEL: (800) USA-TEMP (510) 930-5345
FAX: (510) 256-1515
Mr. Terry Slocum, Sr. VP

Full-service temporary personnel firm. Match your skills with the dynamic temporary help or supplemental health-care fields. WESTERN offers two-week training, temporary payroll and accounts receivable financing, start-up and volume incentives, QWIZ testing and tutorials and more. Franchises available in select cities. 350 offices worldwide. Office, light industrial, medical, technical, marketing and accounting personnel.

HISTORY:	FINANCIAL: Earnings Claim: . .No	FRANCHISOR TRAINING/SUPPORT:
Established in 1948; . . 1st Franchised in 1963	Cash Investment: $50-75K	Financial Assistance Provided: . . . Yes(I)
Company-Owned Units (As of 8/31/1992): 225	Total Investment: $75-150K	Site Selection Assistance: . . . . .No
Franchised Units (As of 8/31/1992): 124	Fees: Franchise - $10-50K	Lease Negotiation Assistance: . . . . .No
Total Units (As of 8/31/1992): 349	Royalty: Varies, Advert: . . . 0%	Co-operative Advertising: . . . . .Yes
Projected New Units for 1993: 50	Contract Periods (Yrs.): . . . . Indef.	Training: . . . . 7 Days Headquarters,
Distribution: US-309;Can-0;Overseas-40	Area Development Agreement: . .No	. . . . 2-3 Days On-Site
North America: . . . . 44 States	Sub-Franchise Contract: . . . . .No	On-Going Support: A,B,C,D,E,G,H/ . .175
Concentration: . . 55 in CA, 19 in IL, 13 in NJ	Expand in Territory: . . . . . . Yes	EXPANSION PLANS:
Registered: . . . . . All States Exc. ND & DC	Passive Ownership: . . . Not Allowed	US: . . . . All US
. . . .	Encourage Conversions: . . . . Yes	Canada: . . . . .No
Type Space: . . . . FS;~800-1,000 SF	Average # Employees: . . 2 FT, 1 PT	Overseas: . . . . No

SUPPLEMENTAL LISTING OF FRANCHISORS

1ST AGENCY PROFESSIONALS . . . . . . .P. O. Box 1174, 511 Wilson NW, Grand Rapids, MI 49501
    Contact: Ms. Michele Sobczak, Dir. Fran. Sales; Tel: (616) 791-1151
ABRAHAM & LONDON EXECUTIVE PLACEMENT . . . . . . P.O. Box 4945, Chatsworth, CA 91313
    Contact: President; Tel: (800) 258-0860
ACCOUNTANTS EXPRESS . . . . 3111 Camino Del Rio N., # 604, San Diego, CA 92108
    Contact: Mr. Philip Weston; Tel: (800) 326-TEMP
ADIA PERSONNEL SERVICES . . . . 64 Willow Pl., Menlo Park, CA 94025
    Contact: Mr. James Ahern, VP Fran. Ops.; Tel: (800) 366-ADIA (415) 324-0696 C
AGENCY NURSING NETWORK . . . . One Knowlton St., Beverly, MA 01915
    Contact: Ms. JoAnne Rainville, President; Tel: (800) 729-8353 (508) 922-8353
ALL DAY LABOR . . . . 151 Mary Esther Cut-Off, # 402A, Mary Esther, FL 32569
    Contact: Mr. Gunnar Davis, President; Tel: (904) 244-0035
ALLAN & PARTNERS . . . . 428 Forbes Ave., # 603, Pittsburgh, PA 15219
    Contact: Mr. Allan Hyman; Tel: (412) 391-9400
ALPHA PERSONNEL SYSTEM . . . . 535 Fifth Ave., # 710, New York, NY 10017
    Contact: Ms. Carol O'Brien, Dir. Fran. Dev.; Tel: (800) 343-8518 (212) 557-4900 C
ANY SITUATION . . . . .P. O. Box 340, Bala Cynwyd, PA 19004
    Contact: Ms. Helen Tucker, President; Tel: (215) 247-8001
ATLANTIC PERSONNEL SERVICES . . . . .4806 Shelly Dr., Wilmington, NC 28405
    Contact: Mr. Jim Smith, EVP; Tel: (919) 392-5898
AUTOMOTIVE CAREERS PLACEMENT . . . . P. O. Box 1109, Hartford, CT 06143
    Contact: Mr. Joseph Holstein; Tel:
BAILEY EMPLOYMENT SERVICE . . . . 51 Shelton Rd., Monroe, CT 06468
    Contact: Mr. Shelly Leighton, President; Tel: (203) 261-2908
BAKER & BAKER EMPLOYMENT SERVICE . . . . P.O. Box 364, Athens, TN 37303
    Contact: Ms. Kathleen Baker, President; Tel: (615) 745-8805
BURNETT PERSONNEL SERVICES . . . . 9800 Richmond, # 800, Houston, TX 77042
    Contact: Mr. Rusty Burnett, President; Tel: (800) 364-4777 (713) 977-4777
BUSINESS & PROFESSIONAL CONSULTANTS . . 3255 Wilshire Blvd., 17th Fl., Los Angeles, CA 90010
    Contact: Mr. W. A. LaPerch, President; Tel: (213) 380-8200
BUSINESS TESTING SERVICE . . . . 4544 IDS Center, Minneapolis, MN 55402
    Contact: President; Tel: (612) 349-6789
CAREER EMPLOYMENT SERVICES . . . . 1600 Stewart Ave., Westbury, NY 11390
    Contact: Mr. Edward Grant, President; Tel: (516) 683-6000
COSMOPOLITAN PERSONNEL SERVICES . . . . 330 Seventh Ave., New York, NY 10001
    Contact: Mr. Elmer Maack, VP; Tel: (212) 736-0700
DIVISION 10 . . . . 535 Fifth Ave., # 710, New York, NY 10017
    Contact: Mr. Bill Beck, Dir. Ops.; Tel: (800) 343-8518 (212) 557-4900 C
DIVISION 10 TEMPS . . . . 535 Fifth Ave., # 710, New York, NY 10017
    Contact: Ms. Carol O'Brien, Dir. Fran. Dev.; Tel: (800) 343-8518 (212) 557-4900 C
DR. PERSONNEL . . . . 9785 S. Chanteclair Ct., Highlands Ranch, CO 80126
    Contact: Mr. George Formnarino, President; Tel: (303) 791-7643
DRAKE INTERNATIONAL . . . . 55 Bloor St. W., 4th Fl., Totonto, ON M4M 1A5   CAN
    Contact: Ms. Carolyn Grossi; Tel: (416) 476-2829
DRAKE OFFICE OVERLOAD . . . . 10866 Wilshire Blvd., # 925, Los Angeles, CA 90024
    Contact: Ms. Tamara Forman; Tel: (415) 249-0850
DUNHILL PERSONNEL SYSTEM . . . . 1000 Woodbury Rd., Woodbury, NY 11797
    Contact: Mr. Mark Brunkhorst, Dir. Sales; Tel: (516) 364-8800
DYNAMIC TEMPORARY SERVICES . . . . 3535 Piedmont Rd., NE, Atlanta, GA 30305
    Contact: Mr. Mark Guyette, Reg. Mgr.; Tel: (800) 257-2328 (404) 266-2256
EMPLOYMENT USA . . . . .153 Broadway, Providence, RI 02903
    Contact: President; Tel: (401) 351-5590
ENGINEERING CORPORATION OF AMERICA . . . . .2657 37 S. W., Seattle, WA 98116
    Contact: President; Tel: (206) 932-0654
ESSEX PERSONNEL . . . . .507 Fifth Ave., 2nd Fl., New York, NY 10017
    Contact: President; Tel: (212) 490-2410
EXECUTIVE PROTEMPS . . . . 7915 FM, 1960 West, # 175, Houston, TX 77070
    Contact: President; Tel: (713) 955-0400
FRIEND OF THE FAMILY . . . . 895 Mt. Vernon Hwy., Atlanta, GA 30327
    Contact: Mr. Les Rager; Tel: (404) 255-2848

G. A. S. TECHNICAL SERVICES . . . . 6001 Savoy, # 505, Houston, TX 77036
    Contact: Mr. David Glass, President; Tel: (800) 879-4314 (713) 978-6508
GILBERT LANE PERSONNEL SERVICE . . . . 221 Main St., Hartford, CT 06106
    Contact: Mr. Howard Specter, President; Tel: (203) 278-7700
HOMECALL . . . . 92 Thomas Johnson Dr., # 150, Frederick, MD 21701
    Contact: Mr. Artie Esworthy, Jr.; Tel: (301) 694-6846
HOMECARE HELPING HAND . . . . 116 Franklin, West Union, IA 52175
    Contact: Mr. Ronald Garceau, President; Tel:
HRI SERVICES . . . . 140 Wood Rd., # 205, Braintree, MA 02184
    Contact: President; Tel: (617) 848-9110
ITT EDUCATIONAL SERVICES . . . . . .3500 Depauw Blvd., P. O. Box 68888, Indianapolis, IN 46268
    Contact: President; Tel: (317) 875-7160
JOBMATE . . . . .P. O. Drawer 959, Ridgeland, MS 39158
    Contact: Mr. Harold Van Devender, Chairman; Tel: (601) 977-9715
JOBS   260 Cochituate Rd., # 109, Franmingham, MA 01701 . . . .
    Contact: Mr. G. A. Powers, President; Tel: (508) 875-1341
LIFETIME MEDICAL NURSING SERVICES . . . . P.O. Box 1468, Pawtucket, RI 02862
    Contact: Ms. Marie Issa, President; Tel: (800) 333-6877 (401) 728-7823
MANPOWER TEMPORARY SERVICES . . . . 5301 N. Ironwood Rd., Milwaukee, WI 53201
    Contact: Mr. William J. Gallagher; Tel: (414) 961-1000
MANPOWER TEMPORARY SERVICES (CANADA)24 Eglinton St. W., P.O. Box 788,#K, Toronto, ON M4R 2G8   CAN
    Contact: Ms. Maureen Quinn; Tel: (416) 480-2222
MARKETSEARCH . . . . .216 N. Green Bay Rd., # 111, Thiensville, WI 53092
    Contact: President; Tel: (414) 242-4103
NANNY CONNECTION, THE . . . . 1054 Sunnyhills Rd., Oakland, CA 94710
    Contact: Ms. O. Robin Sweet, President; Tel: (714) 597-1334
NAT'L. INST. OF SANITATION & MAINTEN. . . .1512 Western Ave., P. O. Box 1273, Seattle, WA 98111
    Contact: Mr. W. R. Griffin; Tel: (206) 682-9748
NETREX INTERNATIONAL . . . . 5420 LBJ Freeway, # 575, LB4, Dallas, TX 75240
    Contact: Mr. Frank Cooksey; Tel: (800) 634-1839 (214) 770-2525
NURSEFINDERS . . . . 1200 Copeland Rd., # 200, Arlington, TX 76011
    Contact: Ms. Debra Ebel, Dir. Fran. Sales; Tel: (800) 445-0459 (817) 469-1055
NURSES PRN . . . . 9300 SW 87 Ave., # 3, Miami, FL 33176
    Contact: Mr. Russ Brewer, VP; Tel: (305) 598-2288
OLSTEN SERVICES . . . . .One Merrick Ave., Westbury, NY 11590
    Contact: Mr. Vincent Mirizio, Reg. Dir.; Tel: (800) 645-8866 (516) 832-8200
PARKER PAGE ASSOCIATES . . . . .P.O. Box 6353, Bellevue, WA 98008
    Contact: President; Tel: (800) 426-0342
PERSONNEL ONE . . . . .770 S. Dixie Hwy., Coral Gables, FL 33146
    Contact: Mr. Dee Trujillo Spiegel, President; Tel: (305) 662-2500
PERSONNEL POOL OF AMERICA . . . . 2050 Spectrum Blvd., Ft. Lauderdale, FL 33309
    Contact: Mr. Ray Marcy, President; Tel: (800) 937-7665 (305) 938-7600
PHYSICIANS EXEC. MANAGEMENT CENTERS . . . .4830 Kennedy Blvd., # 648, Tampa, FL 33609
    Contact: President; Tel: (813) 287-1800
PROMAX PERSONNEL SYSTEMS . . . . 345 Madison Ave., 10th Fl., New York, NY 10002
    Contact: Mr. Gary Fleisher, President; Tel: (212) 682-2232
RAINY DAY PEOPLE . . . . 2035 Wagner Rd., Glenview, IL 60025
    Contact: President; Tel: (312) 885-2717
RENT-A-MOM . . . . .1873 Bellaire St., # 600, Denver, CO 80222
    Contact: President; Tel: (303) 782-1867
RETAIL RECRUITERS/SPECTRA PROF. SEARCH . . 1445 Wampanoag Trail, # 105, Riverside, RI 02915
    Contact: Mr. Jacques Lapointe, President; Tel:
SARA CARE . . . . 1612 Lee Trevino, # A, El Paso, TX 79936
    Contact: Ms. Sara Addis, Founder; Tel: (800) 351-CARE (915) 593-5071
SCIENCETEMPS . . . . P. O. Box 965, Cranford, NJ 07016
    Contact: President; Tel: (201) 272-1997
SEARCH AND PLACEMENT SERVICES . . . . First and Penn Streets, Pittsfield, MA 01210
    Contact: President; Tel: (800) 428-WORK (413) 499-2498
SENIORS FOR BUSINESS . . . . 55 Eglinton Ave., E., # 803, Toronto, ON M4P 1G8   CAN
    Contact: President; Tel: (416) 481-4579
SHANNON TEMPORARY SERVICES . . . . . 415 Walnut St., P. O. Box 702, Coshocton, OH 43812
    Contact: President; Tel: (614) 622-2600
SITTERS ON SITE . . . . 2875 Northwind Dr., # 111, East Lansing, MI 48823
    Contact: Ms. Karen L. Kayes; Tel: (517) 337-9690
SITTERS UNLIMITED . . . . 23015 Del Lago, # D2, Laguna Hills, CA 92653
    Contact: Ms. Andrea Blumenthal, President; Tel: (800) 328-1191 (714) 752-2366

TALENT FORCE . . . . 2970 Clairmont Rd., # 1000, Atlanta, GA 30329
    Contact: Mr. Michael Walker, Dir. Dev.; Tel: (800) 777-5455 (404) 325-7000
TGIF PEOPLEWORKS . . . . P.O. Box 828, Old Lyme, CT 06371
    Contact: Ms. Joanne Kobar, President; Tel: (203) 434-1262
TRAVEL BUDDY . . . . P. O. Box 31146, Minneapolis, MN 55431
    Contact: Ms. Dona M. Risdall, Director; Tel: (612) 881-5364
UNIFORCE TEMPORARY SERVICES . . . . .1335 Jericho Tpk., New Hyde Park, NY 11040
    Contact: Ms. Rosemary Maniscalco, EVP; Tel: (516) 437-3300
UNITED PERSONNEL SYSTEMS . . . . 555 Pointe Dr., Bldg. 3, # 300, Brea, CA 92621
    Contact: Mr. Jay M. Finkelman, EVP; Tel: (800) 669-4887CA (800) 255-8122
VIP COMPANION CARE . . . . 801 James St., Syracuse, NY 13203
    Contact: President; Tel: (315) 685-8951
WINSTON FRANCHISE CORP. . . . . 535 5th Ave., 7th Fl., New York, NY 10017
    Contact: Mr. Sy Kye, President; Tel: (212) 557-5000
WOODBURY PERSONNEL ASSOCIATES . . . . 375 N. Broadway, Jericho, NY 11753
    Contact: Mr. Louis Copt, President; Tel: (800) 342-2140 (516) 938-7910 C

For a full explanation of the data provided in

the Franchisor Format, please refer to Chapter 2,

"How To Use The Data."

CHAPTER 17

RETAIL FOOD:
DONUTS / COOKIES / BAKERY

BAGEL BUILDERS FAMOUS OVEN FRESH BAGELS
P. O. Box 694
Bellmawr, NJ 08099
TEL: (609) 232-BAKE
FAX: (609) 228-9322
Mr. Rocco Fiorentino, Fran. Dir.

Bagel bakery and salad cafe with cappuccino, espresso, muffins, cookies, etc.

HISTORY: . . . .
Established in 1985; . . 1st Franchised in 1991
Company-Owned Units (As of 8/31/1992): . .5
Franchised Units (As of 8/31/1992): 2
Total Units (As of 8/31/1992): 7
Projected New Units for 1993: 5
Distribution: US-7;Can-0;Overseas-0
  North America: . . . . 3 States
  Concentration: . . . .3 in PA, 3 in NJ, 1 in NC
Registered: . . . .
. . . .
Type Space: . . . . . . SF, SC, RM;~1,800 SF

FINANCIAL: Earnings Claim: . Yes
Cash Investment: $100K
Total Investment: $150-250K
Fees: Franchise - $18.5K
  Royalty: 4%, Advert: 1%
Contract Periods (Yrs.): 10/10
Area Development Agreement: Yes/10
Sub-Franchise Contract: . . . . . .No
Expand in Territory: . . . . Yes
Passive Ownership: . . . . . .Allowed
Encourage Conversions: . . . . . Yes
Average # Employees: . . 8 FT, 6 PT

FRANCHISOR TRAINING/SUPPORT:
Financial Assistance Provided: . . . Yes(I)
Site Selection Assistance: . . . . .Yes
Lease Negotiation Assistance: . . . . .Yes
Co-operative Advertising: . . . . .Yes
Training: . . . . . . 2 Wks. Deptford, NJ, 2
  . . .Wks. Moorestown, NJ, 2 Wks. Phila.
On-Going Support: a,b,C,D,E,F,G,H/ . . 10
EXPANSION PLANS:
  US: . . . . East Coast
  Canada: . . . . .No
  Overseas: . . . . No

RETAILING – FOOD (NON–CONVENIENCE)

	1989	1990	1991	Percentage Change 90/89	91/90
Total Number of Establishments:					
Company-Owned	3,210	3,389	3,546	5.58%	4.63%
Franchisee-Owned	17,854	21,122	21,832	18.30%	3.36%
Total	21,064	24,511	25,378	16.36%	3.54%
Ratio of Total Establishments:					
Company-Owned	15.2%	13.8%	14.0%		
Franchisee-Owned	84.8%	86.2%	86.0%		
Total	100.0%	100.0%	100.0%		
Total Sales ($000):					
Company-Owned	1,389,493	1,504,322	1,646,039	8.26%	9.42%
Franchisee-Owned	8,611,630	10,201,502	10,529,297	18.46%	3.21%
Total	10,001,123	11,705,824	12,175,336	17.05%	4.01%
Ratio of Total Sales:					
Company-Owned	13.9%	12.9%	13.5%		
Franchisee-Owned	86.1%	87.1%	86.5%		
Total	100.0%	100.0%	100.0%		
Average Sales Per Unit ($000):					
Company-Owned	433	444	464	2.55%	4.58%
Franchisee-Owned	482	483	482	0.13%	−0.14%
Total	475	478	480	0.58%	0.46%
Relative Average Sales Ratio:	89.7%	91.9%	96.2%		

	Number Of Employees	Employees Per Unit	Avg. Sales Per Employee
Total 1989 Employment:			
Company-Owned	30,386	9.5	$45,728
Franchisee-Owned	187,750	10.5	$45,868
Total	218,136	10.4	$45,848
Relative Employee Performance Ratios:		90.0%	99.7%

	1st Quartile	Median	4th Quartile
Average 1989 Total Investment:			
Company-Owned	$107,250	$130,000	$180,000
Franchisee-Owned	$100,000	$125,000	$175,000
Single Unit Franchise Fee	$15,000	$20,000	$23,500
Mult. Unit Franchise Fee	$10,000	$17,500	$25,000
Franchise Start-Up Cost	$40,000	$50,000	$75,000

Source: Franchising In The Economy 1991, IFA Educational Foundation & Horwath International.

BAGEL CONNECTION, THE

1408 Whalley Ave.
New Haven, CT 06515
TEL: (203) 387-0595
FAX: (203) 387-6611
Mr. Mark Merrill, Fran. Sales

These are not ordinary bagel shops. They are 50-75 seat, fast-food restaurants serving 36 varieties of New York-style bagels, appetizers, sandwiches, salads, beverages, gourmet coffees, desserts and more. Cost-efficient Area Development is encouraged. Bake bagels in the first store and supply your own expansion outlets.

HISTORY:	FINANCIAL: Earnings Claim: . .No	FRANCHISOR TRAINING/SUPPORT:
Established in 1983; . . 1st Franchised in 1990	Cash Investment: $0-100K	Financial Assistance Provided: . . .Yes(D)
Company-Owned Units (As of 8/31/1992): . .2	Total Investment: $132-300K	Site Selection Assistance: . . . . . . .Yes
Franchised Units (As of 8/31/1992): 2	Fees: Franchise - $30K	Lease Negotiation Assistance: . . . .Yes
Total Units (As of 8/31/1992): 4	Royalty: 5%, Advert: 2%	Co-operative Advertising: . . . . . . .Yes
Projected New Units for 1993: 4	Contract Periods (Yrs.): . . . 10/10	Training: . . . . 4 Wks. Combined at Exist-
Distribution: US-4;Can-0;Overseas-0	Area Development Agreement: Yes/10	. . . . . .ing Stores and Franchisee Store
North America: . . . . .1 State	Sub-Franchise Contract: . . . . .No	On-Going Support: C,D,E/ 4
Concentration: . . . . 4 in CT	Expand in Territory: . . . . . . .No	EXPANSION PLANS:
Registered:	Passive Ownership: . . . . .Allowed	US: . . . . MA, CT and NJ
. . . .	Encourage Conversions: . . . . .No	Canada: . . . . .No
Type Space: . . . . FS, SC;~1,800-2,500 SF	Average # Employees: . . . 16-20 PT	Overseas: . . . . No

BAGELSMITH BAGEL

RD # 3, Box 393-G
Hampton, NJ 08827
TEL: (908) 730-8600
FAX: (908) 730-8165
Mr. Wayne Smith, President

What makes us special is, of course, our BAGELSMITH BAGEL. But we are also famous for our delicatessen, featuring only high-quality products. Whether in our restaurants or in our convenience food stores, we provide our customers with high-quality products, friendly, knowledgeable service, in a clean, pleasant, family- oriented environment.

HISTORY:	FINANCIAL: Earnings Claim: . .No	FRANCHISOR TRAINING/SUPPORT:
Established in 1979; . . 1st Franchised in 1983	Cash Investment: $37-45K	Financial Assistance Provided: . . . . .No
Company-Owned Units (As of 8/31/1992): . .2	Total Investment: $185-225K	Site Selection Assistance: . . . . . . .Yes
Franchised Units (As of 8/31/1992): 21	Fees: Franchise - $25K	Lease Negotiation Assistance: . . . .Yes
Total Units (As of 8/31/1992): 23	Royalty: 4%, Advert: 1%	Co-operative Advertising: . . . . . . .Yes
Projected New Units for 1993: 3	Contract Periods (Yrs.): 10/5	Training: . . . . . .Approximately 120-140
Distribution: US-23;Can-0;Overseas-0	Area Development Agreement: . .No	. . . . .Hours at Headquarters
North America: . . . . 3 States	Sub-Franchise Contract: . . . . .No	On-Going Support: C,D,E,G,H/ 6
Concentration: . . . 19 in NJ, 3 in PA, 1 in FL	Expand in Territory: . . . . Yes	EXPANSION PLANS:
Registered: . . . . .FL	Passive Ownership: . . . Discouraged	US: . . . . .Northeast NJ
. . . .	Encourage Conversions: . . . . .No	Canada: . . . . .No
Type Space: . . . . .FS, SC;~2,000 SF	Average # Employees:	Overseas: . . . . No

BLUE CHIP COOKIES

124 Beale St., # 401
San Francisco, CA 94105
TEL: (800) 888-YUMM (415) 546-3840
FAX: (415) 546-9717
Mr. Ivan Steeves, President

Gourmet bakery retail store, located primarily in regional malls and/or high-traffic areas. Our expanded product menu provides breakfast items, as well as quality bakery items throughout the day, along with beverages to meet the consumer needs.

HISTORY:	FINANCIAL: Earnings Claim: . .No	FRANCHISOR TRAINING/SUPPORT:
Established in 1983; . . 1st Franchised in 1984	Cash Investment: $30K	Financial Assistance Provided: . . . Yes(I)
Company-Owned Units (As of 8/31/1992): . 18	Total Investment: $170-196K	Site Selection Assistance: . . . . .Yes
Franchised Units (As of 8/31/1992): 36	Fees: Franchise - $29.5K	Lease Negotiation Assistance: . . . . .Yes
Total Units (As of 8/31/1992): 54	Royalty: 4%, Advert: 0%	Co-operative Advertising: . . . . .No
Projected New Units for 1993: 6	Contract Periods (Yrs.): 10/10	Training: . . . . 2 Wks. Headquarters
Distribution: US-54;Can-0;Overseas-0	Area Development Agreement: Yes/10	. . . .
North America: . . . . 9 States	Sub-Franchise Contract: . . . . . Yes	On-Going Support: C,D,E,G,h,I/ . . . . . .
Concentration: . . 27 in CA, 7 in OH, 6 in WA	Expand in Territory: . . . . . . .No	EXPANSION PLANS:
Registered: . . . . .CA,FL,NY,WA	Passive Ownership: . . . . . .Allowed	US: . . . . Upper NY, FL, South
. . . .	Encourage Conversions: . . . . NA	Canada: . . . . .No
Type Space: . RM, Outlet Center;~600-800 SF	Average # Employees:	Overseas: . . . . No

BODACIOUS BUNS

10250 Santa Monica Blvd.
Los Angeles, CA 90067
TEL: (310) 470-0031
FAX: (310) 470-7522
Ms. Janet Taylor, Founder

Specialty bakery and coffee bar. Large gourmet cinnamon buns in 7 flavors, baked on premises along with muffins, scones and croissants. Flavored coffees, wide range of specialty coffee drinks, cappuccino/espresso bar and light, healthy lunch.

HISTORY: . . . . IFA	FINANCIAL: Earnings Claim: . .No	FRANCHISOR TRAINING/SUPPORT:
Established in 1987; . . 1st Franchised in 1991	Cash Investment: $50-75K	Financial Assistance Provided: . . . Yes(I)
Company-Owned Units (As of 8/31/1992): . .1	Total Investment: $125-250K	Site Selection Assistance: . . . . . . .Yes
Franchised Units (As of 8/31/1992): 2	Fees: Franchise - $25K	Lease Negotiation Assistance: . . . . .No
Total Units (As of 8/31/1992): 3	Royalty: 5%, Advert: 2%	Co-operative Advertising: . . . . . . .No
Projected New Units for 1993: 4	Contract Periods (Yrs.): 5/5	Training: . . . . 7 Days Headquarters,
Distribution: US-3;Can-0;Overseas-0	Area Development Agreement: . .No	. . . . . . .5-7 Days Franchisee Location
North America: . . . . .1 State	Sub-Franchise Contract: . . . . .No	On-Going Support: C,D,E,F,G/ 1
Concentration: . . . . 3 in CA	Expand in Territory: . . . . . . Yes	EXPANSION PLANS:
Registered: . . . . CA	Passive Ownership: . . . Not Allowed	US: . . . . .West, Southwest
. . . .	Encourage Conversions: . . . . .No	Canada: . . . . .No
Type Space: . . . . . SF, RM;~800-1,200 SF	Average # Employees: . 2 FT, 5-9 PT	Overseas: . . . . No

CINDY'S CINNAMON ROLLS

1432 S. Mission Rd., # G
Fallbrook, CA 92028
TEL: (800) HOT-ROLL (619) 723-1121
FAX: (619) 723-4143
Mr. Tom Harris, President

Fresh-baked cinnamon rolls and muffins. All shops in major shopping malls. Great family business. All products made in the shop and baked fresh all day.

HISTORY:	FINANCIAL: Earnings Claim: . .No	FRANCHISOR TRAINING/SUPPORT:
Established in 1985; . . 1st Franchised in 1986	Cash Investment: $140K	Financial Assistance Provided: . . . . .No
Company-Owned Units (As of 8/31/1992): . .0	Total Investment: $140K	Site Selection Assistance: . . . . . . .Yes
Franchised Units (As of 8/31/1992): 38	Fees: Franchise - $25K	Lease Negotiation Assistance: . . . . .Yes
Total Units (As of 8/31/1992): 38	Royalty: 5%, Advert: 0%	Co-operative Advertising: . . . . . . .No
Projected New Units for 1993: 4	Contract Periods (Yrs.): 10/10	Training: . . . . 1 Wk. Atlanta, GA or
Distribution: US-38;Can-2;Overseas-0	Area Development Agreement: . .No	. . . . Syracuse, NY
North America: . . . . 18 States, 2 Provinces	Sub-Franchise Contract: . . . . .No	On-Going Support: C,D,E,F,G,H/ . . . . . .
Concentration: . . . 5 in CA, 4 in NY, 4 in GA	Expand in Territory: . . . . . . Yes	EXPANSION PLANS:
Registered: . . . . .All	Passive Ownership: . . . Discouraged	US: . . . . .All US
. . . .	Encourage Conversions: . . . . . Yes	Canada: . . . . .All Canada
Type Space: . . . . RM;~700 SF	Average # Employees: . .10 FT, 4 PT	Overseas: . . . . No

COMPANY'S COMING

#440 - 1121 Centre St. N.
Calgary, AB T2E 7K6 CAN
TEL: (403) 230-1151 C
FAX: (403) 230-2182
Ms. Janine Hunka, Fran. Sales Mgr.

COMPANY'S COMING features over 65 varieties of freshly-baked goods, including muffins, brownies, carrot cakes, all baked daily, plus over 20 varieties of Gourmet Liquid Coffees, which are all grounds for success.

HISTORY: . . . . .CFA	FINANCIAL: Earnings Claim: . Yes	FRANCHISOR TRAINING/SUPPORT:
Established in 1986; . . 1st Franchised in 1988	Cash Investment: $50-65K	Financial Assistance Provided: . . . Yes(I)
Company-Owned Units (As of 8/31/1992): . .0	Total Investment: $125-175K	Site Selection Assistance: . . . . . . .Yes
Franchised Units (As of 8/31/1992): 21	Fees: Franchise - $25K	Lease Negotiation Assistance: . . . .Yes
Total Units (As of 8/31/1992): 21	Royalty: 8%, Advert: 0%	Co-operative Advertising: . . . . . . .Yes
Projected New Units for 1993: 21	Contract Periods (Yrs.): 10/10	Training: . . . .
Distribution: US-0;Can-21;Overseas-0	Area Development Agreement: . .No	.
North America: . . . . 7 Provinces	Sub-Franchise Contract: . . . . .No	On-Going Support: C,D,E,f,G,h/ 12
Concentration: . . . 9 in AB, 6 in ON, 4 in BC	Expand in Territory: . . . . . . Yes	EXPANSION PLANS:
Registered: . . . . AB	Passive Ownership: . . . Discouraged	US: . . . . .No
. . . .	Encourage Conversions: . . . . . Yes	Canada: . . . . .Yes
Type Space: . . . . SF, SC, RM;~600 SF	Average # Employees: . . 3 FT, 5 PT	Overseas: . . . . No

COOKIE FACTORY OF AMERICA

17 W 705 E. Butterfield Rd., # E
Oakbrook Terrace, IL 60181
TEL: (800) 626-6204 (708) 629-0800
FAX:
Mr. Michael D. Simpson, President

The franchisee has the right to operate a store under the name COOKIE FAC-TORY BAKERY or COOKIE FACTORY EXPRESS, which specializes in the on-premises baking and sale at retail of a wide assortment of cookies, pastries, muffins, danish and other authorized bakery and other food products and beverages. These stores may be operated as separate stores and as leased departments of major department stores.

HISTORY:	FINANCIAL: Earnings Claim: . .No	FRANCHISOR TRAINING/SUPPORT:
Established in 1974; . . 1st Franchised in 1986	Cash Investment: $20-40K	Financial Assistance Provided: . . . . .No
Company-Owned Units (As of 8/31/1992): . .1	Total Investment: $80-175K	Site Selection Assistance: . . . . . . .Yes
Franchised Units (As of 8/31/1992): 32	Fees: Franchise - $25K	Lease Negotiation Assistance: . . . .Yes
Total Units (As of 8/31/1992): 33	Royalty: 6%, Advert: 0%	Co-operative Advertising: . . . . . . .No
Projected New Units for 1993: 2	Contract Periods (Yrs.): 10/10	Training: . . . . .Duration Varies at
Distribution: US-33;Can-0;Overseas-0	Area Development Agreement: . .No	. . . . Chicago Area Store
North America:	Sub-Franchise Contract: . . . . .No	On-Going Support: B,C,D,E,F,G,H,I/ . . .5
Concentration: . . . . 12 in IL, 9 in MI, 4 in IN	Expand in Territory: . . . . . . Yes	EXPANSION PLANS:
Registered: . . . . IL,IN,MI,MN,WI	Passive Ownership: . . . Discouraged	US: . . . . .Midwest
. . . .	Encourage Conversions: . . . . . Yes	Canada: . . . . .No
Type Space: . . . . .RM;~600-900 SF	Average # Employees: . . 4 FT, 2 PT	Overseas: . . . . .No

COOKIES BY GEORGE

200 Ontario St.
Kingston, ON K7L 2Y9 CAN
TEL: (613) 546-3377
FAX: (613) 549-4998
Mr. Don Landon, VP/GM

Retail sales of gourmet, fresh-baked cookies and accompanying gift packages. Other items include the Loafer, our version of a muffin, and beverages. Ideal product for corporate gift giving. Delivery.

HISTORY:	FINANCIAL: Earnings Claim: . .No	FRANCHISOR TRAINING/SUPPORT:
Established in 1983; . . 1st Franchised in 1985	Cash Investment: $50K	Financial Assistance Provided: . . . . .No
Company-Owned Units (As of 8/31/1992): . .3	Total Investment: $120-150K	Site Selection Assistance: . . . . . . .Yes
Franchised Units (As of 8/31/1992): 35	Fees: Franchise - $19K	Lease Negotiation Assistance: . . . .Yes
Total Units (As of 8/31/1992): 38	Royalty: 5%, Advert: 2%	Co-operative Advertising: . . . . . . .Yes
Projected New Units for 1993: 6	Contract Periods (Yrs.): 10/5/5	Training: . . . . 2 Wks. Headquarters
Distribution: US-0;Can-38;Overseas-0	Area Development Agreement: . .No	
North America: . . . . 7 Provinces	Sub-Franchise Contract: . . . . .No	On-Going Support: B,C,d,E,G,h/ 12
Concentration: . . 11 in BC, 10 in AB, 8 in ON	Expand in Territory: . . . . . . Yes	EXPANSION PLANS:
Registered: . . . . AB	Passive Ownership: . . . Discouraged	US: . . . . .All US
. . . .	Encourage Conversions: . . . . NA	Canada: . . . . .Yes
Type Space: . . . .FS, SF, RM;~500-1,000 SF	Average # Employees: . . 2 FT, 4 PT	Overseas: . . . . .Yes

CREATIVE CROISSANTS

2712-D Transportation Ave.
National City, CA 91950
TEL: (800) 735-3182 (619) 474-3388 C
FAX: (619) 474-3390
Mr. Michael Epstein, Mgr. Mktg. Relat.

Our focus is serving freshly-tossed garden salads, freshly-made sandwiches, soups, baked potatoes, dessert, croissants, danishes, muffins, gourmet coffees and cappuccinos. All served in a European cafe motif.

HISTORY: . . . . IFA	FINANCIAL: Earnings Claim: . .No	FRANCHISOR TRAINING/SUPPORT:
Established in 1986; . . 1st Franchised in 1988	Cash Investment: $50-60K	Financial Assistance Provided: . . . . .No
Company-Owned Units (As of 8/31/1992): . .3	Total Investment: $99-140K	Site Selection Assistance: . . . . . . .Yes
Franchised Units (As of 8/31/1992): 26	Fees: Franchise - $17.5K	Lease Negotiation Assistance: . . . .Yes
Total Units (As of 8/31/1992): 29	Royalty: 4.5%, Advert: 2%	Co-operative Advertising: . . . . . . .Yes
Projected New Units for 1993: 8	Contract Periods (Yrs.): 15/15	Training: . . . . . . 10 Days Headquarters,
Distribution: US-29;Can-0;Overseas-0	Area Development Agreement: Yes/15	. . . . 5 Days On-Site
North America: . . . . 2 States	Sub-Franchise Contract: . . . . . Yes	On-Going Support: C,D,E,G,H,I/ 4
Concentration: . . . . . . .28 in CA, 1 in AZ	Expand in Territory: . . . . . . Yes	EXPANSION PLANS:
Registered: . . . . CA,MD,NY,VA	Passive Ownership: . . . Discouraged	US: . . . . .Florida
. . . .	Encourage Conversions: . . . . . Yes	Canada: . . . . .Yes
Type Space: SF, RM, High Rise;~600-1,200 SF	Average # Employees: . . 2 FT, 2 PT	Overseas: . . . . .Yes

DONUT DELITE CAFE

77 Bessemer Rd., # 19
London, ON N6E 1P9 CAN
TEL: (519) 668-6868
FAX: (519) 668-1127
Mr. Joe Garagozzo, President

Excellent turn-key donut operation to include light lunches and soups.

HISTORY:	FINANCIAL: Earnings Claim: . .No	FRANCHISOR TRAINING/SUPPORT:
Established in 1984; . . 1st Franchised in 1985	Cash Investment: $50K	Financial Assistance Provided: . . . Yes(I)
Company-Owned Units (As of 8/31/1992): . .2	Total Investment: $120-150K	Site Selection Assistance: . . . . . . .Yes
Franchised Units (As of 8/31/1992): 28	Fees: Franchise - $20K	Lease Negotiation Assistance: . . . . .Yes
Total Units (As of 8/31/1992): 30	Royalty: 5%, Advert: 2%	Co-operative Advertising: . . . . . . .Yes
Projected New Units for 1993: 4	Contract Periods (Yrs.): 10/5	Training: . . . . . 3 Wks. or Until Ready at
Distribution: US-0;Can-30;Overseas-0	Area Development Agreement: . .No	. . . . Franchisee Site
North America: . . . . .1 Province	Sub-Franchise Contract: . . . . .No	On-Going Support: a,B,C,D,E,F,G,H,I/ . . 7
Concentration: . . . . 30 in ON	Expand in Territory: . . . . . . Yes	EXPANSION PLANS:
Registered:	Passive Ownership: . . . Discouraged	US: . . . . All US
. . . .	Encourage Conversions: . . . . NA	Canada: . . . . .All Canada
Type Space: . . . . . FS, SC;~1,500-2,000 SF	Average # Employees: . . 6 FT, 4 PT	Overseas: . . . . EUR

HOL 'N ONE CAFE

6390 Beresford St.
Burnaby, BC V5E 1B6 CAN
TEL: (604) 435-4242
FAX:
Mr. Larry Seller, Mgr. Ops.

Outlets specialize in donuts, muffins and a menu consisting of home-style hamburgers, sandwiches and soups.

HISTORY:	FINANCIAL: Earnings Claim: . .No	FRANCHISOR TRAINING/SUPPORT:
Established in 1955; . . 1st Franchised in 1965	Cash Investment: $30-40K	Financial Assistance Provided: . . . . .No
Company-Owned Units (As of 8/31/1992): . .4	Total Investment: $150K	Site Selection Assistance: . . . . . . .Yes
Franchised Units (As of 8/31/1992): 5	Fees: Franchise - $20K	Lease Negotiation Assistance: . . . . .Yes
Total Units (As of 8/31/1992): 9	Royalty: 3%, Advert: 1%	Co-operative Advertising: . . . . . . .Yes
Projected New Units for 1993:	Contract Periods (Yrs.): 10/10	Training: . . . . . . .1 Wk. Company Store
Distribution: US-0;Can-9;Overseas-0	Area Development Agreement: . .No	. . . .
North America: . . . . .1 Province	Sub-Franchise Contract: . . . . .No	On-Going Support: B,C,d,e,f/ 6
Concentration: . . . . 10 in BC	Expand in Territory: . . . . . . Yes	EXPANSION PLANS:
Registered: . . . . AB	Passive Ownership: . . . Discouraged	US: . . . . .No
. . . .	Encourage Conversions: . . . . Yes	Canada: . . . . BC and Alberta
Type Space: . . . . SC, RM;~1,200 SF	Average # Employees: . . 3 FT, 4 PT	Overseas: . . . . No

JOLLY PIRATE DONUTS

3923 E. Broad St.
Columbus, OH 43213
TEL: (614) 235-4501
FAX:
Mr. Robert W. Maloney, Devel. Dir.

Retail donuts, coffee, sandwiches and soft drinks.

HISTORY: . . . . IFA	FINANCIAL: Earnings Claim: . .No	FRANCHISOR TRAINING/SUPPORT:
Established in 1961; . . 1st Franchised in 1970	Cash Investment: $40-60K	Financial Assistance Provided: . . . . .No
Company-Owned Units (As of 8/31/1992): . .3	Total Investment: $300-400K	Site Selection Assistance: . . . . . . .Yes
Franchised Units (As of 8/31/1992): 15	Fees: Franchise - $25K	Lease Negotiation Assistance: . . . . .Yes
Total Units (As of 8/31/1992): 18	Royalty: 4%, Advert: 4%	Co-operative Advertising: . . . . . . .Yes
Projected New Units for 1993: 2	Contract Periods (Yrs.): 20/20	Training: . . . . 6 Wks. Minimum HQ
Distribution: US-18;Can-0;Overseas-0	Area Development Agreement: . .No	. . . .
North America: . . . . 3 States	Sub-Franchise Contract: . . . . .No	On-Going Support: C,D,E,H/ 7
Concentration: . . 15 in OH, 2 in WV, 1 in KY	Expand in Territory: . . . . . . Yes	EXPANSION PLANS:
Registered:	Passive Ownership: . . . Not Allowed	US: . . . . Midwest
. . . .	Encourage Conversions: . . . . Yes	Canada: . . . . .No
Type Space: . . . . .FS;~1,800 SF	Average # Employees: . .5 FT, 12 PT	Overseas: . . . . No

LE MUFFIN PLUS

675 W. Peachtree St., NE
Atlanta, GA 30308
TEL: (404) 876-3858
FAX: (404) 394-5096
Mr. Albert Brull, President

Muffin, cookie, coffee shops. A contemporary European design in the heart of America.

HISTORY:	FINANCIAL: Earnings Claim: . .No	FRANCHISOR TRAINING/SUPPORT:
Established in 1985; . . 1st Franchised in 1986	Cash Investment: . . . . $Varies	Financial Assistance Provided: . . . . . No
Company-Owned Units (As of 8/31/1992): . .4	Total Investment: . . . . $Varies	Site Selection Assistance: . . . . . . .Yes
Franchised Units (As of 8/31/1992): 20	Fees: Franchise - $25K	Lease Negotiation Assistance: . . . . .Yes
Total Units (As of 8/31/1992): 24	Royalty: 8%, Advert: 0-2%	Co-operative Advertising: . . . . .NA
Projected New Units for 1993: 6	Contract Periods (Yrs.): . . . . Lease	Training: . . . . .1-2 Wks. Company Store,
Distribution: US-1;Can-23;Overseas-0	Area Development Agreement: . .No	. . . . .As Required Franchisee Location
North America: . . . . . .1 State, 2 Provinces	Sub-Franchise Contract: . . . . .No	On-Going Support: C,D,E,H,I/ 5
Concentration: . . .22 in PQ, 1 in ON, 1 in GA	Expand in Territory: . . . . Yes	EXPANSION PLANS:
Registered:	Passive Ownership: . . . Discouraged	US: . . . . Southeast
. . . .	Encourage Conversions: . . . . .No	Canada: . . . . .Quebec & Ontario
Type Space: . RM, Office Bldg.;~450-600 SF	Average # Employees: . . . . .Varies	Overseas: . . . . No

MANHATTAN BAGEL COMPANY

675 Line Rd.
Aberdeen, NJ 07747
TEL: (908) 583-8182
FAX: (908) 583-8456
Mr. Colin Gaffney, Fran. Dir.

MANHATTAN BAGEL offers a very easy to operate, up-scale, sit-down/take-out bagel deli. The bagels, spreads, deli meats and drinks are of the highest quality, serving going to work customers, as well as breakfast and lunch.

HISTORY: . . . . IFA	FINANCIAL: Earnings Claim: . .No	FRANCHISOR TRAINING/SUPPORT:
Established in 1987; . . 1st Franchised in 1988	Cash Investment: $80-170K	Financial Assistance Provided: . . . Yes(I)
Company-Owned Units (As of 8/31/1992): . .0	Total Investment: $120-200K	Site Selection Assistance: . . . . . . .Yes
Franchised Units (As of 8/31/1992): 16	Fees: Franchise - $30K	Lease Negotiation Assistance: . . . .Yes
Total Units (As of 8/31/1992): 16	Royalty: 5%, Advert: 1/2%	Co-operative Advertising: . . . . No
Projected New Units for 1993: 15	Contract Periods (Yrs.): . . . . Lease	Training: . . . . . . .30 Days Nearest Store
Distribution: US-16;Can-0;Overseas-0	Area Development Agreement: . .No	5
North America: . . . . 3 States	Sub-Franchise Contract: . . . . .No	On-Going Support: C,D,E,F,G/ 5
Concentration: . . . 13 in NJ, 2 in CT, 1 in PA	Expand in Territory: . . . . Yes	EXPANSION PLANS:
Registered:	Passive Ownership: . . . Discouraged	US: . . . . Northeast
. . . .	Encourage Conversions: . . . . . Yes	Canada: . . . . No
Type Space: . . . FS, SF, SC;~1,200-1,600 SF	Average # Employees: . . 2 FT, 6 PT	Overseas: . . . . No

MICHEL'S BAKERY & CAFE

13685 W. Bayshore Dr., # 200
Traverse City, MI 49684
TEL: (616) 922-0359
FAX: (616) 922-0921
Mr. Michael D. Simpson, President

MICHEL'S BAKERY & CAFE units feature fresh-baked goods, including muffins, croissants, cinnamon rolls and cookies, plus freshly-prepared sandwiches, soups and salads. A MICHEL'S store has the unique opportunity to create sales in 3 ways - quality bakery snacks (i.e. cookies), meals (i.e. sandwiches, salads, etc.) and special- occasion decorated/gift cookies.

HISTORY:	FINANCIAL: Earnings Claim: . .No	FRANCHISOR TRAINING/SUPPORT:
Established in 1991; . . 1st Franchised in 1991	Cash Investment: $30-50K	Financial Assistance Provided: . . . Yes(I)
Company-Owned Units (As of 8/31/1992): . .3	Total Investment: $100-195K	Site Selection Assistance: . . . . . . .Yes
Franchised Units (As of 8/31/1992): 4	Fees: Franchise - $25K	Lease Negotiation Assistance: . . . .Yes
Total Units (As of 8/31/1992): 7	Royalty: 6%, Advert: 1%	Co-operative Advertising: . . . . No
Projected New Units for 1993: 10	Contract Periods (Yrs.): . . . 10/10	Training: . . . . 2 Wks. In-Store
Distribution: US-7;Can-0;Overseas-0	Area Development Agreement: . .No	
North America: . . . . 3 States	Sub-Franchise Contract: . . . . .No	On-Going Support: C,D,E,H,I/ 8
Concentration: . . . . 4 in IL, 2 in MI, 1 in MN	Expand in Territory: . . . . Yes	EXPANSION PLANS:
Registered: . . . . IL,IN,MI,MN	Passive Ownership: . . . Discouraged	US: . . . . All US
. . . .	Encourage Conversions: . . . . . Yes	Canada: . . . . No
Type Space: . . . .FS, SF, SC, RM;~1,500 SF	Average # Employees: . . 1 FT, 4 PT	Overseas: . . . . No

MISTER C'S DONUTS & MORE

8261 Woodbine Ave.
Markham, ON L3R 8Z5 CAN
TEL: (416) 470-2020
FAX: (416) 470-2023
Mr. Sidney Feder, Chairman

A cafe-style bake shop, offering coffee, donuts, muffins and light lunches 24 hours a day, 7 days a week.

HISTORY: . . . .
Established in 1986; . . 1st Franchised in 1986
Company-Owned Units (As of 8/31/1992): . .3
Franchised Units (As of 8/31/1992): 68
Total Units (As of 8/31/1992): 71
Projected New Units for 1993: 14
Distribution: US-0;Can-71;Overseas-0
  North America: . . . . .1 Province
  Concentration: . . . . 71 in ON
Registered: . . . .
  . . . .
Type Space: . . . . .FS, SC;~2,000 SF

FINANCIAL: Earnings Claim: . .No
Cash Investment: $65K
Total Investment: $165-190K
Fees: Franchise - $15K
  Royalty: 4%, Advert: 2%
Contract Periods (Yrs.): 10/10
Area Development Agreement: Yes/10
Sub-Franchise Contract: . . . . .No
Expand in Territory: . . . . Yes
Passive Ownership: . . . Not Allowed
Encourage Conversions: . . . . .No
Average # Employees: . . 6 FT, 6 PT

FRANCHISOR TRAINING/SUPPORT:
Financial Assistance Provided: . . .Yes(D)
Site Selection Assistance: . . . . . . .Yes
Lease Negotiation Assistance: . . . .Yes
Co-operative Advertising: . . . . . . .Yes
Training: . . . . 3 Wks. Headquarters,
  . . . . 2 Wks. On-Site
On-Going Support: B,C,D,E,F,G,H/ . . 16
EXPANSION PLANS:
  US: . . . . .No
  Canada: . . . . Master/Area Fran
  Overseas: . . . . No

MMMARVELOUS MMMUFFINS

Shipp Centre, 3300 Bloor W., Box 54
Etobicoke, ON M8X 2X3 CAN
TEL: (416) 236-0055
FAX: (416) 236-0054
Ms. Patricia Phelan, Mgr. Fran.

Muffins baked on premises.

HISTORY: . . . .
Established in 1979; . . 1st Franchised in 1980
Company-Owned Units (As of 8/31/1992): . .3
Franchised Units (As of 8/31/1992): 104
Total Units (As of 8/31/1992): 107
Projected New Units for 1993: . . . .
Distribution: US-0;Can-107;Overseas-0
  North America: . . . . 10 Provinces
  Concentration: . 47 in ON, 19 in AB, 14 in PQ
Registered: . . . . AB
  . . . .
Type Space: . . . . RM;~ SF

FINANCIAL: Earnings Claim: . . .
Cash Investment: $40-60K
Total Investment: $185K
Fees: Franchise - $25K
  Royalty: 7%, Advert: 2%
Contract Periods (Yrs.): 10
Area Development Agreement: . .No
Sub-Franchise Contract: . . . . Yes
Expand in Territory: . . . . Yes
Passive Ownership: . . . Not Allowed
Encourage Conversions:
Average # Employees: . 3 FT, 4-5 PT

FRANCHISOR TRAINING/SUPPORT:
Financial Assistance Provided: . . . Yes(I)
Site Selection Assistance: . . . . . . .Yes
Lease Negotiation Assistance: . . . .Yes
Co-operative Advertising: . . . . . . .Yes
Training: . . . . .5 Days Toronto, ON
  . . . .
On-Going Support: C,D,E,F,G,H/ 60
EXPANSION PLANS:
  US: . . . . .No
  Canada: . . . . .All Canada
  Overseas: . . . . No

MONSIEUR FELIX
& MR. NORTON COOKIES
4100 Thimens Blvd.
St-Laurent, PQ H4R 1X4 CAN
TEL: (800) 463-7055 (514) 333-4118
FAX: (514) 333-7277
Ms. Tina Sheldon, Fran. Dir.

Gourmet chocolate chunk cookies in 12 decadent flavors, with innovative gift packaging, exclusively designed and trademarked for retail sale, as well as home or office delivery.

HISTORY: . . . . .CFA
Established in 1985; . . 1st Franchised in 1990
Company-Owned Units (As of 8/31/1992): . .8
Franchised Units (As of 8/31/1992): 10
Total Units (As of 8/31/1992): 18
Projected New Units for 1993: 10
Distribution: US-0;Can-18;Overseas-0
  North America: . . . . 2 Provinces
  Concentration: . . . . . .17 in PQ, 1 in ON
Registered: . . . .
  . . . .
Type Space: . . . . .SF, SC;~1,000 SF

FINANCIAL: Earnings Claim: . .No
Cash Investment: $60-75K
Total Investment: $150-175K
Fees: Franchise - $25K
  Royalty: 5%, Advert: 6%
Contract Periods (Yrs.): 10/5/5
Area Development Agreement: Yes/Var
Sub-Franchise Contract: . . . . .No
Expand in Territory: . . . . Yes
Passive Ownership: . . . Not Allowed
Encourage Conversions: . . . . NA
Average # Employees: . 1 FT, 5-8 PT

FRANCHISOR TRAINING/SUPPORT:
Financial Assistance Provided: . . . Yes(I)
Site Selection Assistance: . . . . . . .Yes
Lease Negotiation Assistance: . . . .Yes
Co-operative Advertising: . . . . . . .Yes
Training: . . . . 2 Wks. Headquarters,
  . . . . .1 Wk. On-Site
On-Going Support: A,B,C,D,E,F,G,H,I/ 17
EXPANSION PLANS:
  US: . . . . .No
  Canada: . . . . .Ontario & Quebec
  Overseas: . . . . No

MRS. FIELDS COOKIES

333 Main St., P. O. Box 4000
Park City, UT 84060
TEL: (801) 645-2398
FAX: (801) 645-2223
Mr. Keith M. Gerson, Sr. Dir. Fran.

MRS. FIELDS COOKIES, the #1 leader in the cookie and bakery segment (over 700 stores in 7 countries), is offering special individuals with demonstrated management experience an opportunity to share in its recipe for success. MRS. FIELDS is world-renowned for its commitment to quality products and services. Qualified franchisees will share in our national brand recognition operating systems, proven product line, complete training, field support, etc.

HISTORY: . . . . IFA
Established in 1977; . . 1st Franchised in 1990
Company-Owned Units (As of 8/31/1992): 384
Franchised Units (As of 8/31/1992): 337
Total Units (As of 8/31/1992): 721
Projected New Units for 1993: 25
Distribution: . . . US-675;Can-12;Overseas-34
North America: . . . . 36 States, 5 Provinces
Concentration: . . . . CA, IL, NY
Registered: . . . . All States Exc. MN
. . . .
Type Space: . . . SF, SC, RM, Kiosk;~500 SF

FINANCIAL: Earnings Claim: . .No
Cash Investment: $7-35K
Total Investment: $35-250K
Fees: Franchise - $0-25K
Royalty: 6%, Advert: 0-2%
Contract Periods (Yrs.): 7/5/5
Area Development Agreement: Yes/Var
Sub-Franchise Contract: . . . . . Yes
Expand in Territory: . . . . . . Yes
Passive Ownership: . . . Discouraged
Encourage Conversions: . . . . . Yes
Average # Employees: . . 2 FT, 4 PT

FRANCHISOR TRAINING/SUPPORT:
Financial Assistance Provided: . . . . . No
Site Selection Assistance: . . . . .Yes
Lease Negotiation Assistance: . . . . .Yes
Co-operative Advertising: . . . . .No
Training: . . . . 9 Days Headquarters,
. . . . 9 Days On-Site, On-Going Region
On-Going Support: A,B,C,D,e,F,G,h,I/ . 82
EXPANSION PLANS:
US: . . . . All US
Canada: . . . . .All Canada
Overseas: . JA, AU, W. EUR, Asia

MY FAVORITE MUFFIN

15 Engle St., # 302
Englewood, NJ 07631
TEL: (800) 332-2229 (201) 871-0370
FAX: (201) 871-7168
Mr. John Sterns, Sales Mgr.

Specialty bakery, offering muffins, frozen yogurt, gourmet coffee and related menu offerings.

HISTORY: . . . . IFA
Established in 1987; . . 1st Franchised in 1987
Company-Owned Units (As of 8/31/1992): . .2
Franchised Units (As of 8/31/1992): 24
Total Units (As of 8/31/1992): 26
Projected New Units for 1993: 12
Distribution: US-26;Can-0;Overseas-0
North America: . . . .
Concentration: . . . 8 in NJ, 6 in FL, 5 in NY
Registered: . . . . .FL,IL,NY,VA
. . . .
Type Space: . .SC, RM, Kiosk;~500-1,000 SF

FINANCIAL: Earnings Claim: . .No
Cash Investment: $60K
Total Investment: . . . $140.5-306K
Fees: Franchise - $25K
Royalty: 5%, Advert: 0%
Contract Periods (Yrs.): . . . 10/10
Area Development Agreement: . Yes
Sub-Franchise Contract: . . . . .No
Expand in Territory: . . . . . . Yes
Passive Ownership: . . . Not Allowed
Encourage Conversions: . . . . .No
Average # Employees: . . 2 FT, 4 PT

FRANCHISOR TRAINING/SUPPORT:
Financial Assistance Provided: . . . Yes(I)
Site Selection Assistance: . . . . . . .Yes
Lease Negotiation Assistance: . . . .Yes
Co-operative Advertising: . . . . . . .Yes
Training: . . . .1 Wk. HQ, 1 Wk. Company
. . . . .Store, 1 Wk. Franchisee Location
On-Going Support: C,D,E,G,H,I/ . . . . . .
EXPANSION PLANS:
US: . . . . All US
Canada: . . . . .All Canada
Overseas: . . . . Yes

ROBIN'S DONUTS

725 Hewitson St.
Thunder Bay, ON P7B 6B5 CAN
TEL: (807) 623-4453
FAX: (807) 623-4682
Mr. Ron Whitehead, Fran. Sales

Since 1975, ROBIN'S DONUTS has grown to be the largest grossing donut chain in Western Canada. The success of its approximate 170 locations now coast-to-coast relates to its proven system, based on providing consistent, high-quality donuts, coffee, sub and kaiser sandwiches, soups, salads and other related products in a clean environment to our most important asset - the customer.

HISTORY: . . . . .CFA
Established in 1975; . . 1st Franchised in 1978
Company-Owned Units (As of 8/31/1992): . .2
Franchised Units (As of 8/31/1992): 167
Total Units (As of 8/31/1992): 169
Projected New Units for 1993: 25
Distribution: US-0;Can-169;Overseas-0
North America: . . . . 7 Provinces
Concentration: . 57 in ON, 40 in MB, 30 in AB
Registered: . . . . AB
. . . .
Type Space: . . . FS, SC End Unit;~2,000 SF

FINANCIAL: Earnings Claim: . .No
Cash Investment: $220K
Total Investment: $220K
Fees: Franchise - $35K
Royalty: 4%, Advert: 3%
Contract Periods (Yrs.): . . . 10/10
Area Development Agreement: Yes/25
Sub-Franchise Contract: . . . . .No
Expand in Territory: . . . .
Passive Ownership: . . . Not Allowed
Encourage Conversions: . . . . NA
Average # Employees: . . . 12-14 PT

FRANCHISOR TRAINING/SUPPORT:
Financial Assistance Provided: . . . . .No
Site Selection Assistance: . . . . . . .Yes
Lease Negotiation Assistance: . . . .Yes
Co-operative Advertising: . . . . .NA
Training: . . . . 4 Wks. Headquarters
On-Going Support: B,C,D,E,F,G,H/ . . 30
EXPANSION PLANS:
US: . . . . No
Canada: . . . . .All Canada
Overseas: . . . . No

TIM HORTON DONUTS

874 Sinclair Rd.
Oakville, ON L6K 2Y1 CAN
TEL: (416) 845-6511
FAX: (416) 845-0265
Ms. Louise O'Connor, Dir. Fran.

TIM HORTON'S is Canada's largest franchised retail, coffee, donuts and specialty baked goods chain, with over 600 stores in Canada and the USA. The franchisee purchases a turn-key operation, the right to use TIM HORTON'S trademarks and tradenames, as well as a comprehensive 7-week training program and on-going operational and marketing support.

HISTORY: . . . .
Established in 1964; . . 1st Franchised in 1965
Company-Owned Units (As of 8/31/1992): . 21
Franchised Units (As of 8/31/1992): 579
Total Units (As of 8/31/1992): 600
Projected New Units for 1993: 100
Distribution: . . . US-6;Can-594;Overseas-0
 North America: . . . . 2 States, 11 Provinces
 Concentration: . . 316 in ON, 65 in NS, 65 PQ
Registered: . . . . AB
. . . .
Type Space: . . . . FS, RM;~2,650 SF

FINANCIAL: Earnings Claim: . .No
Cash Investment: $85K
Total Investment: $250-310K
Fees: Franchise - $15K
 Royalty: 3%, Advert: 4%
Contract Periods (Yrs.): 10/10
Area Development Agreement: . Yes
Sub-Franchise Contract: . . . . . .No
Expand in Territory: . . . . Yes
Passive Ownership: . . . Not Allowed
Encourage Conversions: . . . . . Yes
Average # Employees: .22 FT and PT

FRANCHISOR TRAINING/SUPPORT:
Financial Assistance Provided: . . . Yes(I)
Site Selection Assistance: . . . . . . .Yes
Lease Negotiation Assistance: . . . . .Yes
Co-operative Advertising: . . . . . . .Yes
Training: . . . .7 Wks. HQ Training Centre
. . . .
On-Going Support: B,C,D,E,F,G,H/ . .290
EXPANSION PLANS:
 US: . . . . Northeast
 Canada: . . . . .All Canada
 Overseas: . . . . No

WHOLE DONUT, THE

894 New Britain Ave.
Hartford, CT 06106
TEL: (203) 953-3569 C
FAX: (203) 953-1692
Mr. Frank Gencarelli, President

WHOLE DONUT SHOPS are approximately 1,800 SF. All products are made on premises. Donuts, cookies, muffins, fruit squares and other baked goods. The WHOLE DONUT also serves deli sandwiches, hot dogs, chili salad platters and soups. Most new shops have drive-thru windows.

HISTORY: . . . .
Established in 1981; . . 1st Franchised in 1984
Company-Owned Units (As of 8/31/1992): . 10
Franchised Units (As of 8/31/1992): 27
Total Units (As of 8/31/1992): 37
Projected New Units for 1993: . . . .
Distribution: US-37;Can-0;Overseas-0
 North America: . . . . 4 States
 Concentration: . . . . NY, New England
Registered: . . . . NY
. . . .
Type Space: . . . . .FS, SC;~1,800 SF

FINANCIAL: Earnings Claim: . . Yes
Cash Investment: $80-100K
Total Investment: $165K
Fees: Franchise - $20K
 Royalty: 5%, Advert: 2%
Contract Periods (Yrs.): 8/8
Area Development Agreement: Yes/10
Sub-Franchise Contract: . . . . . .No
Expand in Territory: . . . . . . Yes
Passive Ownership: . . . Not Allowed
Encourage Conversions: . . . . .No
Average # Employees: . . 4 FT, 7 PT

FRANCHISOR TRAINING/SUPPORT:
Financial Assistance Provided: . . . . .No
Site Selection Assistance: . . . . . . .Yes
Lease Negotiation Assistance: . . . .Yes
Co-operative Advertising: . . . . . . .Yes
Training: . . . . 6 Wks. Headquarters
. . . .
On-Going Support: b,E,F,G,H/ 7
EXPANSION PLANS:
 US: . . . . . . .New England and NY
 Canada: . . . . No
 Overseas: . . . . No

SUPPLEMENTAL LISTING OF FRANCHISORS

ALL MY MUFFINS . . . . P.O. Box 852, Hillside, IL 60162
 Contact: Mr. Paul Bernstein, VP; Tel: (312) 447-7400
BAGEL NOSH .32 E. 23rd St., New York, NY 10010
 Contact: Mr. Leo Vittorio, President; Tel: (212) 598-0411
BAGELAND ENTERPRISES . . . . .1501 SW 5th, # C, Pompano Beach, FL 33069
 Contact: Mr. Carl Handwerker; Tel: (305) 973-8787
BAKER BOY BAKE SHOP . . . . .RR #1, Box 704, W. Industrial Park, Dickinson, ND 58601
 Contact: Mr. Guy Moos, Fran. Dir.; Tel: (701) 225-4444
BAKER'S DOZEN DONUTS . . . . 1224 Dundas St. E., # 13, Mississauga, ON L4Y 4A2 CAN
 Contact: Mr. Joe Farrugia; Tel: (416)274-1825
BAVARIAN STRUDEL SHOPPES . . . . 79 Parkingway, P. O. Box 7169, Quincy, MA 02169
 Contact: President; Tel: (617) 984-0405
BEST BAGELS IN TOWN . . . . 480-19 Patchogue Holbrook Rd., Holbrook, NY 11741
 Contact: President; Tel:
BREAD & CHEESE CUPBOARD . . . . 7 Timberlea Lane, Cape May Court Hous, NJ 08210
 Contact: Ms. Sue Wilson, President; Tel: (609) 465-3813
BUNS MASTER BAKERY SYSTEMS . . . . . .6505 E. Mississauga Rd. N., Mississauga, ON L5N 1A6 CAN
 Contact: Mr. Richard W. Desrochers; Tel: (416) 858-1336

CHEESECAKE, ETC. . . . . 400 Swallow Dr., Miami Springs, FL 33166
    Contact: Mr. Bill Wolar, President; Tel: (305) 887-0258
CINNABON . . . . 936 N. 34th, # 206, Seattle, WA 98103
    Contact: Mr. James Radloff, VP Franchising; Tel: (206) 548-1032
COUNTRY STYLE DONUTS (CANADA) . . 2 E. Beaver Creek Rd., Bldg. #1, Richmond Hill, ON L4B 2N3   CAN
    Contact: Mr. Girts Steinhards; Tel: (416) 764-7066
DAVID'S COOKIES . . . . 200 Bullfinch Dr., P. O. Box 9008, Andover, MA 01810
    Contact: Mr. Anthony S. Parete, VP Devel.; Tel: (508) 975-1283
DAWN DONUT SYSTEMS . . . . .G-4300 W. Pierson Rd., Flint, MI 48504
    Contact: Mr. Bill Morin, Dir. Franchising; Tel: (313) 733-0760
DIXIE CREAM DONUT SHOP . . . . .P. O. Box 3013, Bowling Green, KY 42102
    Contact: Mr. Paul Manning, President; Tel: (502) 782-6109
DK'S DONUTS . . . . 4103 West State, Boise, ID 83702
    Contact: Mr. Scott Jones; Tel: (208) 342-6447
DONUT HOLE, THE . . . . W. Industrial Park, RR1, Box 704, Dickinson, ND 58601
    Contact: Mr. Guy M. Moos, Dir. Fran.; Tel: (701) 225-4444
DONUT INN . . . . .6355 Topanga Canyon Rd., # 403, Woodland Hills, CA 91367
    Contact: Mr. Arthur Pfefferman, President; Tel: (800) 766-8002 (818) 888-2220
DUNKIN' DONUTS (CANADA) . . . . .3773 Cote Vertu, Lachine, PQ H8T 1A5   CAN
    Contact: Mr. Neil Guanci; Tel: (514) 636-5165
DUNKIN' DONUTS OF AMERICA . . . . .P. O. Box 317, Randolph, MA 02368
    Contact: Mr. Lawrence Hantman, SVP; Tel: (800) 543-3000 (617) 961-4000
DUTCH MASTER DONUTS . . . . 747 Don Mills Rd., Toronto, ON M3C 1T2   CAN
    Contact: Mr. Harry Foiros; Tel: (416) 424-4743
FASTER FORM . . . . One Faster Form Circle, New Hartford, NY 13413
    Contact: President; Tel: (315) 768-7806
FOSTER'S DONUTS . . . . .40 W. Cochran St., # 200, Simi Valley, CA 93065
    Contact: Mr. Tom Murphy, President; Tel: (805) 522-2144
GLENDALE SYSTEMS . . . . .69-16 Metropolitan Ave., Middle Village, NY 11379
    Contact: Mr. Horst Herink, President; Tel: (718) 441-9300
GREAT HARVEST . . . . 28 S. Montana, Dillon, MT 59725
    Contact: Mr. Peter Wakeman, President; Tel: (800) 442-0424 (406) 683-6842
KRISPY KREME DOUGHNUT . . . . 1814 Ivy Ave., Winston-Salem, NC 27102
    Contact: Mr. Scott Livengood, Sr. VP; Tel: (919) 725-2981
LE PATE 1221 Date St., Montebello, CA 90640 . . . .
    Contact: President; Tel: (213) 888-2929
MARIA'S FRANCHISE CORP. . . . . 185 Canal St., New York, Ny 10013
    Contact: President; Tel: (212) 219-1607
MILLIONS OF MUFFINS . . . . .100 Sea Beach Dr., Stamford, CT 06902
    Contact: Ms. Melissa Engel, VP; Tel: (800) YEAH-MOM (203) 324-9188
MRS. POWELL'S BAKERY EATERY . . . . . . 500 Franklin Village Dr., # 106, Franklin, MA 02081
    Contact: Mr. James Lennon, Fran. Dev.; Tel: (508) 520-3787 C
NEAL'S COOKIES . . . . 5700 Savoy, Houston, TX 77036
    Contact: Mr. Neal Elinoff, President; Tel: (713) 784-2722
ORIGINAL GREAT AMERICAN COOKIE COMPANY . . . 4685 Frederick Dr., SW, Atlanta, GA 30336
    Contact: Ms. Betty W. Ansley, VP; Tel: (800) 336-2447 (404) 696-1700
PARADISE BAKERY . . . . 201 Lomas Santa Fe, # 460, Solana Beach, CA 92075
    Contact: Mr. Roy S. Bream, Dir. Fran.; Tel: (619) 792-9449
PARADISE DONUT SHOPS . . . . 211 Thompson Blvd., Sedalia, MO 65301
    Contact: Mr. John White; Tel: (816) 826-8981
SOUTHERN MAID DONUT FLOUR COMPANY . . . . 3615 Cavalier Dr., Garland, TX 75042
    Contact: Ms. Doris Franklin, VP; Tel: (214) 272-6425
SPROLL'S OLD COUNTRY BREAD . . . . 35 Alexandra Blvd., Toronto, ON M4R 1L8   CAN
    Contact: Mr. S. MacKneson, President; Tel: (416) 488-3687 C
STROSSNER'S BAKERY . . . . 1626 East North St., Greenville, SC 29607
    Contact: President; Tel: (803) 233-2990
SWEET ROSIE'S COOKIES . . . . .2-A Wellesley St., W., Toronto, ON M4Y 1E7   CAN
    Contact: Mr. Robert Gumieniak; Tel: (416) 923-9112
T. J. CINNAMONS . . . . 1010 W. 39th St., Kansas City, MO 64111
    Contact: Mr. Kim Stanley, Fran. Sales Coord.; Tel: (816) 931-9341
TASTEE DONUTS . . . . 5600 Mournes St., Harahan, LA 70123
    Contact: Mr. Robert Santopadre, Dir. Fran. Sales; Tel: (504) 734-5333
TREATS BAKERY/CAFE . . . . 1064 E. Main St., # 303, Meriden, CT 06450
    Contact: Mr. Bruce J. Major, VP Fran. Dev.; Tel: (800) 624-0010 (203) 235-2944
TREATS INTERNATIONAL . . . . 418 Preston St., Ottawa, ON K1S 4N2   CAN
    Contact: Mr. Ira Lyons; Tel: (416) 968-0311 (613) 563-4073

VICTORIA'S BAKE SHOP/FORTY CARROTS . . . . P.O. Box 74910, Los Angeles, CA 90004
    Contact: President; Tel:
WINCHELL'S DONUT HOUSE . . . . 16424 Valley View Ave., La Mirada, CA 90637
    Contact: Ms. Cynthia R. Freels; Tel: (714) 670-5300
YUM YUM DONUTS . . . . 18830 E. San Jose Ave., City of Industry, CA 91748
    Contact: Mr. Frank Watase, Chairman; Tel: (818) 961-4000

For Information On Renting Our

Custom Franchisor Mailing List

Or Franchisor Data Base,

Please Refer To Page IX

CHAPTER 18

RETAIL FOOD:
ICE CREAM / YOGURT / GELATO

ALL AMERICAN FROZEN YOGURT SHOPS
4800 SW Macadam Ave., # 301
Portland, OR 97201
TEL: (503) 224-6199 C
FAX: (503) 224-5042
Mr. C. R. Duffie, Jr., President

Regional mall and specialty center based, up-scale franchisor. Shops in Western half of US. Looking for owner/operators in US and Canada for major shopping centers and specialty retail centers. Great "add-on" business for existing food and/or service operation.

HISTORY: . . . .
Established in 1986;   . . 1st Franchised in 1988
Company-Owned Units (As of 8/31/1992): . 15
Franchised Units (As of 8/31/1992): 9
Total Units (As of 8/31/1992): 24
Projected New Units for 1993: . . . .
Distribution: US-24;Can-0;Overseas-0
  North America: . . . . 6 States
  Concentration: . . . 9 in WA, 6 in OR, 4 in CO
Registered: . . . . CA,HI,MI,OR,WA
. . . .
Type Space: . . . . RM;~ SF

FINANCIAL: Earnings Claim: . .No
Cash Investment: $20-35K
Total Investment: $100-132K
Fees: Franchise - $16-20K
  Royalty: 5%, Advert: 1%
Contract Periods (Yrs.): 10/10
Area Development Agreement: Yes/Var
Sub-Franchise Contract: . . . . . .No
Expand in Territory: . . . . Yes
Passive Ownership: . . . Discouraged
Encourage Conversions: . . . . . Yes
Average # Employees: . 1 FT, 6-8 PT

FRANCHISOR TRAINING/SUPPORT:
Financial Assistance Provided: . . . Yes(I)
Site Selection Assistance: . . . . .Yes
Lease Negotiation Assistance: . . . . .Yes
Co-operative Advertising: . . . . .Yes
Training: . . . . .1 Wk. Headquarters,
. . . . .1 Wk. Store Location
On-Going Support: a,B,C,D,E,f,G,H/ . . 25
EXPANSION PLANS:
  US: . . . . All US
  Canada: . . . . .Yes
  Overseas: . . . . No

BASKIN-ROBBINS USA

31 Baskin-Robbins Pl.
Glendale, CA 91201
TEL: (800) 331-0031 (818) 956-0031
FAX: (818) 548-8218
Mr. Keith Emerson, Dir. Fran. Dev.

BASKIN-ROBBINS, the world's largest (over 3,500 locations) and best known (97% name recognition) franchisor of ice cream stores, is currently expanding it location base nationwide. 45 years of successful operation, coupled with No Franchise Fee and low royalties make B-R a good choice. 3 weeks' training, intense field support, quarterly promotional kits, national advertising, and a full range of products make B-R the intelligent choice.

HISTORY: . . . . IFA	FINANCIAL: Earnings Claim: . .No	FRANCHISOR TRAINING/SUPPORT:
Established in 1945; . . 1st Franchised in 1948	Cash Investment: $60K	Financial Assistance Provided: . . . Yes(I)
Company-Owned Units (As of 8/31/1992): . 21	Total Investment: . . . $142.4-187.5K	Site Selection Assistance: . . . . . . .Yes
Franchised Units (As of 8/31/1992): 3487	Fees: Franchise - $0	Lease Negotiation Assistance: . . . . .Yes
Total Units (As of 8/31/1992): 3508	Royalty: 1/2%, Advert: . . 3.0-4.5%	Co-operative Advertising: . . . . . . .Yes
Projected New Units for 1993: 100	Contract Periods (Yrs.): 5/5	Training: . . . . 3 Wks. Headquarters
Distribution: US-2212;Can-200;Overseas-1096	Area Development Agreement: . .No	. . . .
North America: . . . . 47 States	Sub-Franchise Contract: . . . . . Yes	On-Going Support: A,B,C,D,E,F,G,H,I/ 130
Concentration: . 500 in CA, 203 in IL, 188 NY	Expand in Territory: . . . . Yes	EXPANSION PLANS:
Registered: . . . . .All	Passive Ownership: . . . Discouraged	US: . . . . All US
. . . .	Encourage Conversions: . . . . . Yes	Canada: . . . . Separate Entity
Type Space: . . . . . . FS, SC, RM;~1,000 SF	Average # Employees: . . . .7-15 PT	Overseas: . . S. America, IT, Eastern EUR

BLOMMER'S ICE CREAM & SAM'S SUBS

5900 N. Port Washington Rd.
Milwaukee, WI 53217
TEL: (414) 276-2740 C
FAX: (414) 271-8623
Mr. Peter Blommer, President

A combined food and ice cream operation, located in food courts in major regional malls. Two store fronts but one back kitchen, one manager, one lease and interchangeable crews. Two uses in one space for efficiency and cost cutting.

HISTORY:	FINANCIAL: Earnings Claim: . .No	FRANCHISOR TRAINING/SUPPORT:
Established in 1987; . . 1st Franchised in 1989	Cash Investment: $100K	Financial Assistance Provided: . . . . . No
Company-Owned Units (As of 8/31/1992): . .4	Total Investment: $100-160K	Site Selection Assistance: . . . . . . .Yes
Franchised Units (As of 8/31/1992): 4	Fees: Franchise - $22.5K	Lease Negotiation Assistance: . . . .Yes
Total Units (As of 8/31/1992): 8	Royalty: 4%, Advert: 1%	Co-operative Advertising: . . . . No
Projected New Units for 1993: 2	Contract Periods (Yrs.): 5-10/5	Training: . . . . 2 Wks. Headquarters
Distribution: US-8;Can-0;Overseas-0	Area Development Agreement: Yes/10	. . . .
North America: . . . . 4 States	Sub-Franchise Contract: . . . . . .No	On-Going Support: C,D,E,F/ 2
Concentration: . . . . 5 in WI, 1 in IL, 1 in IA	Expand in Territory: . . . . Yes	EXPANSION PLANS:
Registered: . . . . IL,IN,MN,WI	Passive Ownership: . . . . . .Allowed	US: . . . . Midwest
. . . .	Encourage Conversions: . . . . . Yes	Canada: . . . . No
Type Space: . . . . RM;~800 SF	Average # Employees: 3-4 FT, 6-10 PT	Overseas: . . . . No

BRESLER'S ICE CREAM & YOGURT SHOPS

999 E. Touhy Ave., # 333
Des Plaines, IL 60018
TEL: (800) 535-3333 (708) 298-1100
FAX: (708) 298-0697
Mr. Howard Marks, VP, Dir. Fran. Dev.

Treat shop for the family, featuring private recipes of premium ice cream and gourmet yogurts. Specialty items include Lite Yogurts made without sugar, fat or cholesterol, and low-fat ice creams. Other menu items include assorted fresh fruits and candy toppings, sundaes, shakes, soft drinks, coffee, cakes and pies.

HISTORY: . . . . IFA	FINANCIAL: Earnings Claim: . .No	FRANCHISOR TRAINING/SUPPORT:
Established in 1930; . . 1st Franchised in 1963	Cash Investment: $30-50K	Financial Assistance Provided: . . . Yes(I)
Company-Owned Units (As of 8/31/1992): . .6	Total Investment: $130-165K	Site Selection Assistance: . . . . . . .Yes
Franchised Units (As of 8/31/1992): 250	Fees: Franchise - $15K	Lease Negotiation Assistance: . . . .Yes
Total Units (As of 8/31/1992): 256	Royalty: 6%, Advert: 3%	Co-operative Advertising: . . . . . . .Yes
Projected New Units for 1993: 25	Contract Periods (Yrs.): . . 10/Varies	Training: . . . . 2 Wks. Headquarters
Distribution: US-250;Can-0;Overseas-0	Area Development Agreement: Yes/Var	. . . .
North America: . . . . 30 States	Sub-Franchise Contract: . . . . . Yes	On-Going Support: C,D,E,F,G,H,I/ . . . 31
Concentration: . . 40 in IL, 35 in FL, 17 in CA	Expand in Territory: . . . . Yes	EXPANSION PLANS:
Registered: . . .CA,IL,IN,MD,MI,MN,NY,OR	Passive Ownership: . . . . . .Allowed	US: . . . . .All US
. . . . RI,WA,WI	Encourage Conversions: . . . . . Yes	Canada: . . . . .All Canada
Type Space: . FS, SF, SC, RM;~500-1,200 SF	Average # Employees: . . . .6-10 PT	Overseas: . . . . All Overseas

CARVEL ICE CREAM BAKERY

20 Batterson Park Rd.
Farmington, CT 06032
TEL: (800) 322-4848 (203) 677-6811
FAX: (203) 677-8211
Mr. Thomas Kornacki, Dir. Fran. Rctmnt.

CARVEL ICE CREAM BAKERY's manufacture and sell at retail ice cream and sugar-free, low fat yogurt desserts. CARVEL products are designed to compete not only in the frozen dessert markets, but in the $13 billion dollar retail bakery market. Franchise operators can open branch units in malls, tourist areas and beaches for no additional licensing fees

HISTORY: . . . . IFA	FINANCIAL: Earnings Claim: . .No	FRANCHISOR TRAINING/SUPPORT:
Established in 1934; . . . 1st Franchised in 1947	Cash Investment: $75-150K	Financial Assistance Provided: . . .Yes(D)
Company-Owned Units (As of 8/31/1992): . 16	Total Investment: $170-300K	Site Selection Assistance: . . . . . . .Yes
Franchised Units (As of 8/31/1992): 270	Fees: Franchise - $10-20K	Lease Negotiation Assistance: . . . .Yes
Total Units (As of 8/31/1992): 286	Royalty: Varies, Advert: . . Varies	Co-operative Advertising: . . . . .No
Projected New Units for 1993: 30	Contract Periods (Yrs.): 10/10	Training: . . . . 2 Wks. Headquarters
Distribution: US-283;Can-3;Overseas-0	Area Development Agreement: . .No	. . . .
North America: . . . . . 13 States, 1 Province	Sub-Franchise Contract: . . . . . .No	On-Going Support: C,D,E,G,H/ 60
Concentration: . . 240 in NY, 110 in NJ, 65 FL	Expand in Territory: . . . . Yes	EXPANSION PLANS:
Registered: . . . . .FL,MD,NY,VA	Passive Ownership: . . . Not Allowed	US: . . . . . East Coast Exc. NC, SC, GA
. . . .	Encourage Conversions: . . . . . NA	Canada: . . . . .No
Type Space: . . . . . . FS, SF, SC;~1,200 SF	Average # Employees: . . 2 FT, 6 PT	Overseas: . . . . No

EMACK & BOLIO'S ICE CREAM AND YOGURT

P. O. Box 703
Brookline Village, MA 02147
TEL: (617) 739-7995
FAX: (617) 232-2753
Mr. Robert Rook, President

We supply manuals, prototype books, ad slicks, training and telephone evaluations at no charge. We provide you with 17 years' experience and award-winning ice cream and hard, no-fat yogurts in outrageous flavors. No soft-serve equipment needed.

HISTORY:	FINANCIAL: Earnings Claim: . .No	FRANCHISOR TRAINING/SUPPORT:
Established in 1975; . . 1st Franchised in 1977	Cash Investment: $50-75K	Financial Assistance Provided: . . . . No
Company-Owned Units (As of 8/31/1992): . .0	Total Investment: $75K	Site Selection Assistance: . . . . . . .NA
Franchised Units (As of 8/31/1992): 23	Fees: Franchise - $0	Lease Negotiation Assistance: . . . .Yes
Total Units (As of 8/31/1992): 23	Royalty: 0%, Advert: 0%	Co-operative Advertising: . . . . .No
Projected New Units for 1993: 10	Contract Periods (Yrs.): 10/10	Training: . . . . 1 Wk. Headquarters
Distribution: US-23;Can-0;Overseas-0	Area Development Agreement: Yes/20	. . . .
North America: . . . . 5 States	Sub-Franchise Contract: . . . . . Yes	On-Going Support: B,F,G/ 2
Concentration: . . 14 in MA, 4 in NM, 2 in TN	Expand in Territory: . . . . Yes	EXPANSION PLANS:
Registered:	Passive Ownership: . . . Discouraged	US: . . . . All US
. . . .	Encourage Conversions: . . . . . Yes	Canada: . . . . .No
Type Space: . . . . SF, RM;~750 SF	Average # Employees: . . 4 FT, 4 PT	Overseas: . . . . No

FRESHENS PREMIUM YOGURT AND ICE CREAM

2849 Paces Ferry Rd., # 750
Atlanta, GA 30339
TEL: (404) 433-0983
FAX: (404) 431-9081
Ms. Laurie Lanser, Dir. Fran. Dev.

Premium soft-serve yogurt and gourmet hand-dipped ice cream, along with other frozen dessert specialties. All yogurt and ice cream flavors are 100% natural and are kosher certified. FRESHENS also features other tandem concepts, including gourmet coffee under the River Roast Coffee Co. name and baked goods, plus soft-baked pretzels under the Pretzel Logic name.

HISTORY: . . . . IFA	FINANCIAL: Earnings Claim: . .No	FRANCHISOR TRAINING/SUPPORT:
Established in 1985; . . 1st Franchised in 1986	Cash Investment: $50-60K	Financial Assistance Provided: . . .Yes(I)
Company-Owned Units (As of 8/31/1992): . .9	Total Investment: $165-185K	Site Selection Assistance: . . . . . . .Yes
Franchised Units (As of 8/31/1992): 200	Fees: Franchise - $4-25K	Lease Negotiation Assistance: . . . .Yes
Total Units (As of 8/31/1992): 209	Royalty: 4%, Advert: 4%	Co-operative Advertising: . . . . . . .Yes
Projected New Units for 1993: 45	Contract Periods (Yrs.): 10/10	Training: . . . . . 10 Days HQ (Full Store
Distribution: US-207;Can-0;Overseas-2	Area Development Agreement: Yes/3	. . . Program), 3 Days HQ (Mini-Store)
North America: . . . . 32 States	Sub-Franchise Contract: . . . . . Yes	On-Going Support: B,C,D,E,F,G,H,I/ . . 25
Concentration: . 27 in FL, 19 in GA, 19 in NY	Expand in Territory: . . . . Yes	EXPANSION PLANS:
Registered: . . . CA,FL,IL,IN,MD,MI,MN,NY	Passive Ownership: . . . Discouraged	US: . . . . All US
. . . . ND,RI,VA,DC	Encourage Conversions: . . . . . Yes	Canada: . . . . .All Canada
Type Space: . SF, SC, RM, Other;~50-550 SF	Average # Employees: . . 2 FT, 6 PT	Overseas: . . . . .Yes

GELATO AMARE

11504 Hyde Pl.
Raleigh, NC 27614
TEL: (919) 847-4435
FAX: (919) 870-1090
Mr. John Franklin, President

GELATO AMARE stores feature all-natural, no-fat, no-cholesterol, sugar-free frozen yogurt and low-fat, homemade Italian ice cream and ices, as well as cookies, coffees, espresso, soups, salads and sandwiches.

HISTORY: . . . .
Established in 1983; . . 1st Franchised in 1986
Company-Owned Units (As of 8/31/1992): . .1
Franchised Units (As of 8/31/1992): 12
Total Units (As of 8/31/1992): 13
Projected New Units for 1993: 2
Distribution: US-13;Can-0;Overseas-0
 North America: . . . . 3 States
 Concentration: . . . . 3 in NC
Registered: . . . . .CA,FL,IL,MI,NY
. . . .
Type Space: . . . . ;~1,200 SF

FINANCIAL: Earnings Claim: . .No
Cash Investment: $30-60K
Total Investment: $90-160K
Fees: Franchise - $18.9K
 Royalty: 5%, Advert: 2%
Contract Periods (Yrs.): 10/5/5
Area Development Agreement: . Yes
Sub-Franchise Contract: . . . . .No
Expand in Territory: . . . . . . Yes
Passive Ownership: . . . . . .Allowed
Encourage Conversions: . . . . Yes
Average # Employees: . . 1 FT, 6 PT

FRANCHISOR TRAINING/SUPPORT:
Financial Assistance Provided: . . . . . No
Site Selection Assistance: . . . . .Yes
Lease Negotiation Assistance: . . . . .Yes
Co-operative Advertising: . . . . .No
Training: . . . . 2 Wks. Headquarters
. . . .
On-Going Support: C,d,E/ 6
EXPANSION PLANS:
 US: . . . . .All US
 Canada: . . . . .All Canada
 Overseas: . . . . .Yes

GORIN'S HOMEMADE ICE CREAM

158 Oak St.
Avondale Estates, GA 30002
TEL: (404) 292-0043
FAX: (404) 292-0081
Mr. Marvin B. Young, Fran. Dev.

Over 33 location serving our own ice cream, soft and hard yogurt, hot and cold sandwiches, salads, drinks. Our ice cream is of high quality and the ingredients are hand-stirred with each barrel.

HISTORY: . . . .
Established in 1981; . . 1st Franchised in 1983
Company-Owned Units (As of 8/31/1992): . .6
Franchised Units (As of 8/31/1992): 27
Total Units (As of 8/31/1992): 33
Projected New Units for 1993: 6
Distribution: US-33;Can-0;Overseas-0
 North America: . . . . 11 States
 Concentration: . . .22 in GA, 2 in NC, 1 in AL
Registered: . . . .
. . . .
Type Space: . . . . FS, SF, SC, RM;~600+ SF

FINANCIAL: Earnings Claim: . .No
Cash Investment: $100-175K
Total Investment: $100-175K
Fees: Franchise - $21.5K
 Royalty: 5%, Advert: 2%
Contract Periods (Yrs.): 10/10
Area Development Agreement: Yes/Var
Sub-Franchise Contract: . . . . .No
Expand in Territory: . . . . . . Yes
Passive Ownership: . . . Discouraged
Encourage Conversions: . . . . Yes
Average # Employees: . . 9 FT, 5 PT

FRANCHISOR TRAINING/SUPPORT:
Financial Assistance Provided: . . . . . No
Site Selection Assistance: . . . . .Yes
Lease Negotiation Assistance: . . . . .Yes
Co-operative Advertising: . . . . .Yes
Training: . . . . 2 Wks. Headquarters
. . . .
On-Going Support: B,C,D,E,F,h/ 15
EXPANSION PLANS:
 US: . . . . Southeast
 Canada: . . . . No
 Overseas: . . . . No

HAAGEN-DAZS

Glenpointe Centre E.
Teaneck, NJ 07666
TEL: (201) 684-2076
FAX: (201) 684-2243
Mr. Alan Guinn, Devel. Mgr.

HAAGEN-DAZS offers franchisees an outstanding opportunity to sell premier super-premium ice creams and yogurts, with natural product line extensions, to discriminating customers. HAAGEN-DAZS features all-natural products with no additives, stabilizers or extenders. Our retail shops reflect an up-scale, sophisticated look of the 90's. We aggressively seek franchisees who share our vision and direction.

HISTORY: . . . . IFA
Established in 1961; . . 1st Franchised in 1977
Company-Owned Units (As of 8/31/1992): . .2
Franchised Units (As of 8/31/1992): 239
Total Units (As of 8/31/1992): 241
Projected New Units for 1993: 35
Distribution: US-241;Can-0;Overseas-0
 North America: . . . . 32 States
 Concentration: . . 62 in NY, 31 in CA, 29 in FL
Registered: . . . CA,FL,HI,IL,MD,MI,MN,NY
. . . . OR,VA,WA,WI,DC
Type Space: . . . SF, SC, RM;~700-1,000 SF

FINANCIAL: Earnings Claim: . .No
Cash Investment: $100-150K
Total Investment: $150-200K
Fees: Franchise - $35K
 Royalty: 0%, Advert: . . $2.7K/Yr
Contract Periods (Yrs.): 10/10
Area Development Agreement: Yes/Var
Sub-Franchise Contract: . . . . .No
Expand in Territory: . . . . . . Yes
Passive Ownership: . . . Not Allowed
Encourage Conversions: . . . . Yes
Average # Employees: .2 FT, 7-10 PT

FRANCHISOR TRAINING/SUPPORT:
Financial Assistance Provided: . . . Yes(I)
Site Selection Assistance: . . . . .Yes
Lease Negotiation Assistance: . . . . .Yes
Co-operative Advertising: . . . . .Yes
Training: . . . . . . .10 Days Headquarters
. . . .
On-Going Support: B,C,D,E,F,G,H/ . . . .
EXPANSION PLANS:
 US: . . . . . . .Emphasis on Major Cities
 Canada: . . . . No
 Overseas: . . . . No

HIGH WHEELER ICE CREAM PARLOUR/RESTAURANT

5192 West Main St.
Kalamazoo, MI 49009
TEL: (616) 345-0950
FAX: (616) 345-6887
Mr. Roger Buchholtz, President

Large turn-of-the-century, family-oriented ice cream parlour restaurants, featuring an extensive ice cream creation menu and over 45 flavors of ice cream, gourmet hamburgers, lunches and dinners. Further enhanced by an old-fashioned candy and bake shoppe where fudge, chocolates, candies, brownies, cookies and breads are made in view of the customers.

HISTORY: . . . .
Established in 1975; . . 1st Franchised in 1986
Company-Owned Units (As of 8/31/1992): . .2
Franchised Units (As of 8/31/1992): 4
Total Units (As of 8/31/1992): 6
Projected New Units for 1993: 1
Distribution: US-6;Can-0;Overseas-0
  North America: . . . . 3 States
  Concentration: . . . . 2 in MI, 2 in FL, 2 in IL
Registered: . . . .
. . . .
Type Space: . . . . FS;~6,000 SF

FINANCIAL: Earnings Claim: . .No
Cash Investment: $100K
Total Investment: $1MM
Fees: Franchise - $35K
  Royalty: 4%, Advert: 1%
Contract Periods (Yrs.): 20/20
Area Development Agreement: Yes/10
Sub-Franchise Contract: . . . Yes
Expand in Territory: . . . . . . Yes
Passive Ownership: . . . Discouraged
Encourage Conversions: . . . . Yes
Average # Employees: . .3 FT, 50 PT

FRANCHISOR TRAINING/SUPPORT:
Financial Assistance Provided: . . . Yes(I)
Site Selection Assistance: . . . . . . .Yes
Lease Negotiation Assistance: . . . .Yes
Co-operative Advertising: . . . . . . .Yes
Training: . . . . 8 Wks. Headquarters
. . . .
On-Going Support: a,B,C,D,E,F,G,H,I/ . 10
EXPANSION PLANS:
US: . . . . Midwest, S'east, VA, KY, TN
Canada: . . . . .All Canada
Overseas: . . . . .Yes

ICE CREAM CHURN

P. O. Box 1569
Byron, GA 31008
TEL: (800) 822-2967 (912) 956-5880
FAX: (912) 956-1864
Mr. Lee Anderson, VP

ICE CREAM CHURN's concept is to add an old-fashioned ice cream parlor within another existing location, such as delis, bakeries, video stores, convenience stores, truckstops. ICE CREAM CHURN sets up location, trains employees, installs exterior signs and supports location with on-going promotions and training. 32 flavors of ice cream and yogurt are available.

HISTORY: . . . .
Established in 1973; . . 1st Franchised in 1979
Company-Owned Units (As of 8/31/1992): . .0
Franchised Units (As of 8/31/1992): 511
Total Units (As of 8/31/1992): 511
Projected New Units for 1993: 115
Distribution: US-511;Can-0;Overseas-0
  North America: . . . . 26 States
  Concentration: . . 117 in FL, 83 in AR, 42 AL
Registered: . . . . . .FL,IL,IN,MD,RI,VA,DC
. . . .
Type Space: . . . . Existing Business;~135 SF

FINANCIAL: Earnings Claim: . . Yes
Cash Investment: $5K
Total Investment: $5-16.5K
Fees: Franchise - $5K
  Royalty: $1/Tub, Advert: . $.25/Tub
Contract Periods (Yrs.): 10/5
Area Development Agreement: Yes/3
Sub-Franchise Contract: . . . . Yes
Expand in Territory: . . . . . . Yes
Passive Ownership: . . . . . .Allowed
Encourage Conversions: . . . . Yes
Average # Employees: . . . . . .1 PT

FRANCHISOR TRAINING/SUPPORT:
Financial Assistance Provided: . . . . .Yes
Site Selection Assistance: . . . . . . .Yes
Lease Negotiation Assistance: . . . .NA
Co-operative Advertising: . . . . . . .Yes
Training: . . . . .As Needed
. . . .
On-Going Support: D,E,F,G,I/ 7
EXPANSION PLANS:
US: . . . . . .Seeking Master Franchisees
Canada: . . . . .All Canada
Overseas: . . . . .Yes

ICE CREAM CLUB, THE

278 S. Ocean Blvd.
Manalapan, FL 33462
TEL: (800) 535-7711 (407) 533-6668
FAX:
Mr. Richard Draper, President

Premium homemade ice cream, yogurt and fat-free, sugar-free diet desserts. Up-scale interiors. A pleasure to operate, fun business. Complete opening assistance. Financing plans available. Low initial investment.

HISTORY: . . . .
Established in 1982; . . 1st Franchised in 1984
Company-Owned Units (As of 8/31/1992): . .3
Franchised Units (As of 8/31/1992): 13
Total Units (As of 8/31/1992): 16
Projected New Units for 1993: 2
Distribution: US-16;Can-0;Overseas-0
  North America: . . . . 3 States
  Concentration: . . . 13 in FL, 3 in NY, 2 in IL
Registered: . . . . FL,IL,NY
. . . .
Type Space: . . . . SC;~800 SF

FINANCIAL: Earnings Claim: . .No
Cash Investment: $60-90K
Total Investment: $60-90K
Fees: Franchise - $20K
  Royalty: 0%, Advert: 0%
Contract Periods (Yrs.): 5/5
Area Development Agreement: Yes/Var
Sub-Franchise Contract: . . . . . .No
Expand in Territory: . . . . . . Yes
Passive Ownership: . . . Discouraged
Encourage Conversions: . . . . Yes
Average # Employees: .2 FT, 4-10 PT

FRANCHISOR TRAINING/SUPPORT:
Financial Assistance Provided: . . . Yes(I)
Site Selection Assistance: . . . . . . .Yes
Lease Negotiation Assistance: . . . .Yes
Co-operative Advertising: . . . . . . .NA
Training: . . . . .2-3 Days Headquarters or
. . . . .Franchisee Store
On-Going Support: B,C,D,E,F,G,H,I/ . . .7
EXPANSION PLANS:
US: . . . . East of Mississippi
Canada: . . . . .No
Overseas: . . . . .No

ISLAND FREEZE

P. O. Box 10883
Honolulu, HI 96815
TEL: (808) 922-0030
FAX: (808) 923-3054
Ms. Catherine A. Peoples, VP

ISLAND FREEZE features DoleWhip, the non-dairy, fruit-based soft serve dessert which contains NO cholesterol, butterfat or lactose and is low in sodium. DoleWhip is served in cups, cones, shakes, and smoothies. Fruits, juices and other Dole products are also served. Units are flexible and range in size from 80-175 or more SF. The ISLAND FREEZE concept is simple - serve a superior product in a streamlined system with attractive, up-beat decor.

HISTORY:	FINANCIAL: Earnings Claim: . .No	FRANCHISOR TRAINING/SUPPORT:
Established in 1986; . . 1st Franchised in 1989	Cash Investment: $39.5-114K	Financial Assistance Provided: . . . . . No
Company-Owned Units (As of 8/31/1992): . .3	Total Investment: $39.5-114K	Site Selection Assistance: . . . . .Yes
Franchised Units (As of 8/31/1992): 1	Fees: Franchise - $18.5K	Lease Negotiation Assistance: . . . . .Yes
Total Units (As of 8/31/1992): 4	Royalty: 5%, Advert: 1%	Co-operative Advertising: . . . . .Yes
Projected New Units for 1993: 5	Contract Periods (Yrs.): 5/5	Training: . . . . . . .1 Wk. Headquarters,
Distribution: US-4;Can-0;Overseas-0	Area Development Agreement: . Yes	. . . . .3 Days Franchisee Store
North America: . . . . 2 States	Sub-Franchise Contract: . . . . Yes	On-Going Support: a,C,D,E,f/ 2
Concentration: . . . . .3 in HI, 1 in AL	Expand in Territory: . . . . . . Yes	EXPANSION PLANS:
Registered: . . . . FL,HI	Passive Ownership: . . . . .Allowed	US: . . . . .All US
. . . .	Encourage Conversions: . . . . Yes	Canada: . . . . .All Exc. Alberta
Type Space: . . . . RM;~100 SF	Average # Employees: . . 1 FT, 4 PT	Overseas: . . . . .Yes

LOVE'S YOGURT

1830 Techny Ct.
Northbrook, IL 60062
TEL: (708) 480-9200
FAX: (708) 480-0280
Mr. RoBert Silverstein, President

LOVE'S YOGURT AND SALADS offers a unique soft-serve frozen yogurt and salad bar concept. The emphasis is toward healthy, quality foods with salads prepared daily, in addition to soups, chili, baked potatoes with toppings, and freshly-baked muffins. Personalized service is our specialty.

HISTORY:	FINANCIAL: Earnings Claim: . .No	FRANCHISOR TRAINING/SUPPORT:
Established in 1987; . . 1st Franchised in 1988	Cash Investment: $100K	Financial Assistance Provided: . . . Yes(I)
Company-Owned Units (As of 8/31/1992): . .3	Total Investment: $160-200K	Site Selection Assistance: . . . . . . .Yes
Franchised Units (As of 8/31/1992): 8	Fees: Franchise - $20K	Lease Negotiation Assistance: . . . . .Yes
Total Units (As of 8/31/1992): 11	Royalty: 4%, Advert: 2%	Co-operative Advertising: . . . . .Yes
Projected New Units for 1993: 5	Contract Periods (Yrs.): 15/15	Training: . . . . .1 Wk. Headquarters,
Distribution: US-11;Can-0;Overseas-0	Area Development Agreement: . .No	. . . . 1 Wk. Site, 1 Wk. Franchisee Site
North America: . . . . 2 States	Sub-Franchise Contract: . . . . .No	On-Going Support: B,C,D,E,F,H,I/ . . . 10
Concentration: . . . . .10 in IL, 1 in IN	Expand in Territory: . . . . . . Yes	EXPANSION PLANS:
Registered: . . . . IL,IN	Passive Ownership: . . . Not Allowed	US: . . . . .Midwest
. . . .	Encourage Conversions: . . . . .No	Canada: . . . . .No
Type Space: . . . . .SF, SC;~1,800 SF	Average # Employees: . . 3 FT, 3 PT	Overseas: . . . . . . EUR, SE Asia

MARBLE SLAB CREAMERY

3100 S. Gessner, # 230
Houston, TX 77063
TEL: (713) 780-3601
FAX: (713) 780-0264
Mr. Ronald J. Hankamer, President

Retail ice cream stores, featuring super-premium homemade ice cream, cones baked fresh daily, fresh frozen yogurt, frozen pies and cakes, homemade cookies and brownies. Ice cream is custom designed for customer on frozen marble slab and made daily in the store.

HISTORY:	FINANCIAL: Earnings Claim: . .No	FRANCHISOR TRAINING/SUPPORT:
Established in 1983; . . 1st Franchised in 1984	Cash Investment: $30-50K	Financial Assistance Provided: . . . . .No
Company-Owned Units (As of 8/31/1992): . .3	Total Investment: $125-150K	Site Selection Assistance: . . . . . . .Yes
Franchised Units (As of 8/31/1992): 24	Fees: Franchise - $19-25K	Lease Negotiation Assistance: . . . . .Yes
Total Units (As of 8/31/1992): 27	Royalty: 5/6%, Advert: 1%	Co-operative Advertising: . . . . .Yes
Projected New Units for 1993: 8	Contract Periods (Yrs.): 20/20	Training: . . . . . 10-14 Days Franchisor
Distribution: US-27;Can-0;Overseas-0	Area Development Agreement: Yes/Var	. . .Location, 6-8 Days Franchisee Site
North America: . . . . 2 States	Sub-Franchise Contract: . . . . .No	On-Going Support: B,C,D,E,H/ 5
Concentration: . . . . .25 in TX, 2 in LA	Expand in Territory: . . . . . . .No	EXPANSION PLANS:
Registered: . . . . .FL	Passive Ownership: . . . Discouraged	US: . . . . . Southwest, South, Southeast
. . . .	Encourage Conversions: . . . . Yes	Canada: . . . . .No
Type Space: . . . . . .SC, RM;~500-1,000 SF	Average # Employees: . . 2 FT, 6 PT	Overseas: . . . . No

NATURALLY YOGURT / SPEEDSTERS CAFE

P. O. Box 511
San Ramon, CA 94583
TEL: (510) 268-1363
FAX:
Mr. Sheldon Feinberg, VP

NATURALLY YOGURT is a quality, fresh frozen yogurt operation. Clean, high-tech graphics in a unique presentation offering a wide range of toppings, sundaes, shakes, smoothies and other specialty items. SPEEDSTERS is an expanded menu concept in keeping with today's yuppie movement, offering fresh salads, homemade soups, baked potatoes and a complete yogurt presentation that leads up to the tag line "Fun, Fast, First Class."

HISTORY:	FINANCIAL: Earnings Claim: . .No	FRANCHISOR TRAINING/SUPPORT:
Established in 1983; . . 1st Franchised in 1985	Cash Investment: $65-100K	Financial Assistance Provided: . . . . .No
Company-Owned Units (As of 8/31/1992): . .0	Total Investment: $155-180K	Site Selection Assistance: . . . . . . .Yes
Franchised Units (As of 8/31/1992): 15	Fees: Franchise - $20K	Lease Negotiation Assistance: . . . . .Yes
Total Units (As of 8/31/1992): 15	Royalty: Varies, Advert: 0%	Co-operative Advertising: . . . . .NA
Projected New Units for 1993: 5	Contract Periods (Yrs.): 15/10	Training: . . . . 2 Wks. Company-Owned
Distribution: US-15;Can-0;Overseas-0	Area Development Agreement: Yes/15	. . . . .Store
North America: . . . . .1 State	Sub-Franchise Contract: . . . . . Yes	On-Going Support: B,C,D,E,F,G/ 4
Concentration: . . . . 15 in CA	Expand in Territory: . . . . Yes	EXPANSION PLANS:
Registered: . . . . CA	Passive Ownership: . . . Discouraged	US: . . . . .All US
. . . .	Encourage Conversions: . . . . . Yes	Canada: . . . . .All Canada
Type Space: . . . . . FS, SF, RM;~2,000+ SF	Average # Employees: . . 1 FT, 6 PT	Overseas: . . . . .Pacific Rim

ORIGINAL WALT'S, THE

1616 W. Jefferson St.
Joliet, IL 60435
TEL: (800) 786-1856 (815) 725-9258 C
FAX:
Mr. Michael P. Dillon, President

THE ORIGINAL WALT'S franchise provides you with the triple opportunity to profit from the sale of ice cream, soft-serve ice milk and frozen yogurt! High-profile and distinctive free-standing drive-ins with drive-thru windows and strip and regional mall shops serve all the traditional fountain favorites, plus WALT'S unique products, such as WALT'S Original Rainbow Cone, WALT'S Wizzard, Jumbo Turtle Sundaes, Chocolate Lover's Rainbow Cone, etc.

HISTORY:	FINANCIAL: Earnings Claim: . . .	FRANCHISOR TRAINING/SUPPORT:
Established in 1926; . . 1st Franchised in 1992	Cash Investment: . . . .$	Financial Assistance Provided: . . . . .No
Company-Owned Units (As of 8/31/1992): . .1	Total Investment: $75-200K	Site Selection Assistance: . . . . . . .Yes
Franchised Units (As of 8/31/1992): 0	Fees: Franchise - $15-25K	Lease Negotiation Assistance: . . . .Yes
Total Units (As of 8/31/1992): 1	Royalty: 5%, Advert: 0-5%	Co-operative Advertising: . . . . . . .Yes
Projected New Units for 1993:	Contract Periods (Yrs.): . . . . Indef.	Training: . . . . 1 Wk. Headquarters
Distribution: US-1;Can-0;Overseas-0	Area Development Agreement: Yes/Var	. . . .
North America: . . . . .1 State	Sub-Franchise Contract: . . . . . .No	On-Going Support: B,C,D,E,F,G,H,I/ . . .3
Concentration: . . . . .1 in IL	Expand in Territory: . . . . Yes	EXPANSION PLANS:
Registered: IL	Passive Ownership: . . . . . .Allowed	US: . . . . IL, AZ, NV and TX
. . . .	Encourage Conversions: . . . . . Yes	Canada: . . . . .No
Type Space: . . . . ;~ SF	Average # Employees: .1 FT, 8-10 PT	Overseas: . . . . No

STEVE'S HOMEMADE ICE CREAM

200 Bullfinch Dr., P. O. Box 9008
Andover, MA 01810
TEL: (800) 528-0727 (508) 975-1945
FAX: (508) 686-2390
Mr. Anthony S. Parete, VP Devel.

Combination franchises are fast becoming the smart direction to take for the entrepreneurial-minded small businessman. You make the choice of any 3 of our nationally-known trademarks: up-scale, super-premium STEVE'S ICE CREAM, HEIDI'S Frozen Yogurt, or the more traditional favorite, SWENSEN'S ICE CREAM and HEIDI'S, plus, through a special agreement, DAVID'S COOKIES.

HISTORY: . . . . IFA	FINANCIAL: Earnings Claim: . . .	FRANCHISOR TRAINING/SUPPORT:
Established in 1972; . . 1st Franchised in 1973	Cash Investment: $50-60K	Financial Assistance Provided: . . . Yes(I)
Company-Owned Units (As of 8/31/1992): . .0	Total Investment: . . . .$	Site Selection Assistance: . . . . . . .Yes
Franchised Units (As of 8/31/1992): 23	Fees: Franchise - $25K	Lease Negotiation Assistance: . . . . .Yes
Total Units (As of 8/31/1992): 23	Royalty: 6%, Advert: 1.5%	Co-operative Advertising: . . . . .No
Projected New Units for 1993: 15	Contract Periods (Yrs.): . . 10/Varies	Training: . . . . . . .2 Wks. Scottsdale, AZ
Distribution: US-23;Can-0;Overseas-0	Area Development Agreement: . .No	. . . .
North America: . . . . .9 States	Sub-Franchise Contract: . . . . . .No	On-Going Support: B,C,D,E,F,G,H,I/ . . . .
Concentration: . . . 7 in MA, 4 in FL, 3 in CA	Expand in Territory: . . . . Yes	EXPANSION PLANS:
Registered: . . . . .CA,MD,NY,RI,VA	Passive Ownership: . . . Discouraged	US: . . . . .All US
. . . .	Encourage Conversions: . . . . . Yes	Canada: . . . . .No
Type Space: . . . SF, SC, RM;~500-1,200 SF	Average # Employees:	Overseas: . . . . .Yes

SWENSON'S ICE CREAM COMPANY

200 Bullfinch Dr., P. O. Box 9008
Andover, MA 01810
TEL: (800) 528-0727 (508) 975-1283
FAX: (508) 686-2390
Mr. Anthony S. Parete, VP Devel.

Combination franchises are fast becoming the smart direction to take for the entrepreneurial-minded small businessman. You make the choice of any 3 of our nationally-know trademarks: Up-scale, super-premium STEVE'S ICE CREAM, HEIDI'S Frozen Yogurt, or, the more traditional favorite, SWENSEN'S ICE CREAM and HEIDI'S, plus, through a special agreement, DAVID'S COOKIES.

HISTORY: . . . . IFA	FINANCIAL: Earnings Claim: . . .	FRANCHISOR TRAINING/SUPPORT:
Established in 1948; . . 1st Franchised in 1963	Cash Investment: $50-60K	Financial Assistance Provided: . . . Yes(I)
Company-Owned Units (As of 8/31/1992): . .6	Total Investment: . . . .$	Site Selection Assistance: . . . . . . .Yes
Franchised Units (As of 8/31/1992): 247	Fees: Franchise - $25K	Lease Negotiation Assistance: . . . .Yes
Total Units (As of 8/31/1992): 253	Royalty: 6%, Advert: 1%	Co-operative Advertising: . . . . . . .No
Projected New Units for 1993: 15	Contract Periods (Yrs.): 10	Training: . . . . . .2 Wks. Scottsdale, AZ
Distribution: . . . US-134;Can-0;Overseas-119	Area Development Agreement: . .No	. . . .
North America: . . . . 25 States	Sub-Franchise Contract: . . . . .No	On-Going Support: B,C,D,E,F,G,H,I/ . . . .
Concentration: . 54 in CA, 13 in AZ, 10 in TX	Expand in Territory: . . . . . . Yes	EXPANSION PLANS:
Registered: . . . . . . CA,IL,MD,NY,RI,VA	Passive Ownership: . . . Discouraged	US: . . . . All US
. . . .	Encourage Conversions: . . . . . Yes	Canada: . . . . .No
Type Space: . . . SF, SC, RM;~500-1,200 SF	Average # Employees:	Overseas: . . . . .Yes

TCBY
- THE COUNTRY'S BEST YOGURT
1100 TCBY Tower, 425 W. Capitol Ave.
Little Rock, AR 72201
TEL: (501) 688-8229
FAX: (501) 688-8251
Ms. Evelyn Simone, Dir. Fran. Sales

TCBY stores offer soft-serve premium frozen yogurt as a treat, dessert, snack or light meal. TCBY stores may be established in a variety of locations, including strip shopping centers, free-standing buildings (with or without drive-thru windows) or regional shopping malls.

HISTORY: . . . . IFA	FINANCIAL: Earnings Claim: . .No	FRANCHISOR TRAINING/SUPPORT:
Established in 1981; . . 1st Franchised in 1982	Cash Investment: . . . $120-261.2K	Financial Assistance Provided: . . . . .No
Company-Owned Units (As of 8/31/1992): 169	Total Investment: . . . $120-261.2K	Site Selection Assistance: . . . . . . .Yes
Franchised Units (As of 8/31/1992): 1480	Fees: Franchise - $20K	Lease Negotiation Assistance: . . . . .No
Total Units (As of 8/31/1992): 1649	Royalty: 4%, Advert: 3%	Co-operative Advertising: . . . . . . .Yes
Projected New Units for 1993:	Contract Periods (Yrs.): 10/10	Training: . . . . . . .10 Days Headquarters
Distribution: . . US-1591;Can-14;Overseas-44	Area Development Agreement: . .No	. . . .
North America: . . . . 50 States, 3 Provinces	Sub-Franchise Contract: . . . . . Yes	On-Going Support: B,C,D,E,G,H,I/ . . . . .
Concentration: . .120 in TX, 100 in FL, 94 NY	Expand in Territory: . . . . Yes	EXPANSION PLANS:
Registered: . . . . .All	Passive Ownership: . . . Discouraged	US: . . . . All US
. . . .	Encourage Conversions: . . . . . .No	Canada: . . . . .All Canada
Type Space: . . . . .SC;~1,200 SF	Average # Employees: . . 2 FT, 6 PT	Overseas: AU,EUR,UK,NZ,Asia,C&S Am.

WHITE MOUNTAIN CREAMERY

1576 Bardstown Rd.
Louisville, KY 40205
TEL: (502) 456-2663
FAX: (502) 456-2056
Mr. Charles G. Ducas, VP Fran. Dev.

WHITE MOUNTAIN CREAMERY is a unique concept, featuring the on-site production of super-premium ice cream, yogurt and gourmet bakery goods. Come grow with us - we offer three fast-moving product lines under one roof.

HISTORY:	FINANCIAL: Earnings Claim: . .No	FRANCHISOR TRAINING/SUPPORT:
Established in 1985; . . 1st Franchised in 1987	Cash Investment: $50-65K	Financial Assistance Provided: . . . Yes(I)
Company-Owned Units (As of 8/31/1992): . .6	Total Investment: $125-150K	Site Selection Assistance: . . . . . . .Yes
Franchised Units (As of 8/31/1992): 29	Fees: Franchise - $10-20K	Lease Negotiation Assistance: . . . .Yes
Total Units (As of 8/31/1992): 35	Royalty: 4%, Advert: 1%	Co-operative Advertising: . . . . . . .Yes
Projected New Units for 1993: 5	Contract Periods (Yrs.): 10/10	Training: . . . . . 10-14 Days Headquarters
Distribution: US-35;Can-0;Overseas-0	Area Development Agreement: Yes/Var	. . . .
North America: . . . . 14 States	Sub-Franchise Contract: . . . . . .No	On-Going Support: C,D,E,F,G,h/ 11
Concentration: . . . 9 in KY, 4 in PA, 5 in MD	Expand in Territory: . . . . Yes	EXPANSION PLANS:
Registered: . . . .CA,FL,HI,IL,IN,MD,NY,WI	Passive Ownership: . . . Not Allowed	US: . . . . All US
. . . .	Encourage Conversions: . . . . . Yes	Canada: . . . . .No
Type Space: . . . . .SC, RM;~1,200-1,500 SF	Average # Employees: . .2 FT, 10 PT	Overseas: . . . . No

YOGEN FRUZ INTERNATIONAL OF CANADA
7500 Woodbine Ave., # 303
Markham, ON L3R 1A8 CAN
TEL: (416) 479-8762
FAX: (416) 479-5235
Mr. Michael Serruya, President

Fresh fruit-blended frozen yogurt.

HISTORY: . . . . IFA	FINANCIAL: Earnings Claim: . .No	FRANCHISOR TRAINING/SUPPORT:
Established in 1986; . . 1st Franchised in 1987	Cash Investment: $30K	Financial Assistance Provided: . . . Yes(I)
Company-Owned Units (As of 8/31/1992): . .5	Total Investment: $75-100K	Site Selection Assistance: . . . . . . .Yes
Franchised Units (As of 8/31/1992): 162	Fees: Franchise - $25K	Lease Negotiation Assistance: . . . . .Yes
Total Units (As of 8/31/1992): 167	Royalty: 6%, Advert: 2%	Co-operative Advertising: . . . . .Yes
Projected New Units for 1993: 30	Contract Periods (Yrs.): 10/10	Training: . . . . 1 Wk. Toronto, ON
Distribution: . . . US-20;Can-105;Overseas-42	Area Development Agreement: . .No	. . . .
North America: . . . . 5 States, 10 Provinces	Sub-Franchise Contract: . . . . . Yes	On-Going Support: B,C,D,E,F,H/ 22
Concentration: . . . . 45 in ON, 7 in NY	Expand in Territory: . . . . Yes	EXPANSION PLANS:
Registered: . . CA,FL,IL,MD,MN,NY,RI,WA	Passive Ownership: . . . Discouraged	US: . . . . All US
. . . . DC	Encourage Conversions: . . . . . Yes	Canada: . . . . .All Canada
Type Space: . . . . RM;~300 SF	Average # Employees: . . 2 FT, 4 PT	Overseas: . FR,SP,IT,ISR,Egypt,Belg,Sing

YOGURTY'S YOGURT DISCOVERY

7500 Woodbine Ave.
Markham, ON L3R 1A8 CAN
TEL: (416) 479-8762
FAX: (416) 479-5235
Mr. Michael Serruya, President

Soft-serve yogurt franchise, specializing in frozen yogurt desserts, fountain items, hot and cold beverages and fashion apparel.

HISTORY:	FINANCIAL: Earnings Claim: . .No	FRANCHISOR TRAINING/SUPPORT:
Established in 1987; . . 1st Franchised in 1988	Cash Investment: $40K	Financial Assistance Provided: . . . Yes(I)
Company-Owned Units (As of 8/31/1992): . .3	Total Investment: $120-150K	Site Selection Assistance: . . . . . . .Yes
Franchised Units (As of 8/31/1992): 33	Fees: Franchise - $25K	Lease Negotiation Assistance: . . . . .Yes
Total Units (As of 8/31/1992): 36	Royalty: 4%, Advert: 2%	Co-operative Advertising: . . . . .Yes
Projected New Units for 1993: 4	Contract Periods (Yrs.): 10/10	Training: . . . . Headquarters
Distribution: US-0;Can-36;Overseas-0	Area Development Agreement: . .No	. . . .
North America:	Sub-Franchise Contract: . . . . . Yes	On-Going Support: B,C,D,E,F,G,H/ . . .7
Concentration: . . 24 in ON, 5 in BC, 3 in MB	Expand in Territory: . . . . Yes	EXPANSION PLANS:
Registered:	Passive Ownership: . . . . .Allowed	US: . . . . No
. . . .	Encourage Conversions: . . . . . Yes	Canada: . . . . .All Canada
Type Space: . . . . . . SF, SC, RM;~400 SF	Average # Employees: . .4 FT, 15 PT	Overseas: . . . . Yes

SUPPLEMENTAL LISTING OF FRANCHISORS

ABBOTT'S FROZEN CUSTARD . . . . 4791 Lake Ave., Rochester, NY 14612
      Contact: President; Tel: (716) 865-7400
ANA BELL'S CREAMERY . . . . 2800 Manse Ave., Lincoln, NE 68502
      Contact: President; Tel:
BASKIN-ROBBINS ICE CREAM OF CANADA . . . . . 91 Skyway Ave., # 200, Rexdale, ON M9W 6R5   CAN
      Contact: Ms. Sue Buckles; Tel: (416) 675-3131
BEN AND JERRY'S . . . . P. O. Box 240, Route 100, Waterbury, VT 05676
      Contact: Mr. Lee Holden, Comm. Co-ord.; Tel: (802) 244-5676
BO DEE'S YUMMIES . . . . 3520 Hwy. 6, South, Sugarland, TX 77478
      Contact: Mr. Mike Sheikh, Franchise Consultant; Tel: (715) 836-8983
BOY BLUE OF AMERICA . . . . 10919 W. Janesville Rd., Hales Corners, WI 53130
      Contact: Mr. Theanne R. Panos; Tel: (414) 425-5160
CALIFORNIA YOGURT COMPANY . . . . 2401 Vista Way, # E, Oceanside, CA 92054
      Contact: Mr. Roy Ring, Franchise Development; Tel: (619) 439-5650
CARBERRY'S HOMEMADE ICE CREAM PARLORS . . . . . . .42 Rose St., Merritt Island, FL 32953
      Contact: Mr. Steven R. Carberry, Director; Tel: (407) 452-8900
DIPPER DAN ICE CREAM & YOGURT SHOPPES . . . . . . P.O. Box 47068, St. Petersburg, FL 33743
      Contact: Mr. Leo L. LaBonte, EVP; Tel: (813) 323-7927

DIXIE DEE ICE CREAM . . . . 55 Newkirk Rd. N, Richmond Hill, ON L4C 3G4   CAN
    Contact: President; Tel: (416) 883-5558
DOUBLE RAINBOW DESSERT CAFE . . . . 275 S. Van Ness Ave., San Francisco, CA 94103
    Contact: Ms. Leslie Cass, Dir. Fran.; Tel: (800) 543-5885 (415) 861-5858
FROOTY YOGOURT . . . . 1253 McGill College Ave., # 500, Montreal, PQ H3B 2Y5   CAN
    Contact: Mr. Nick Peronace, VP Fran.; Tel: (514) 393-3180
FRUSEN GLADJE . . . . 200 Andover Business Park, # 1000, Andover, MA 01810
    Contact: Mr. Michael Newport, VP; Tel: (508) 975-1283
GREAT MIDWESTERN ICE CREAM CO., THE . . . 209 North 16th St., P.O. Box 1717, Fairfield, IA 52556
    Contact: President; Tel: (515) 472-7595
HANDLE'S ICE CREAM . . . . 3931 Handles Court, Youngstown, OH 44512
    Contact: President; Tel: (216) 788-0356
HAWAIIAN FREEZE . . . . P. O. Box 21987, 2403 E. Waco Dr., Waco, TX 76705
    Contact: Mr. Fred Lupfer, President; Tel: (800) 284-1472 (817) 867-1472
HEIDI'S FROZEN YOGURT SHOPPES . . . . 200 Bullfinch Dr., P.O. Box 9008, Andover, MA 01810
    Contact: Mr. Anthony S. Parete, VP Devel.; Tel: (508) 975-1283
HELEN HUTCHLEYS . . . . P.O. Box 80995, Station C, Canton, OH 44708
    Contact: Mr. Michael Parsons; Tel: (216) 477-4515
HILLARY'S GOURMET . . . . 328 Sussex Blvd., Broomall, PA 19008
    Contact: Mr. Lou Termini, President; Tel: (215) 558-0660
HUCKLEBERRY THIN . . . . 123 Franklin Corner Rd., # 203, Lawrenceville, NJ 08648
    Contact: Mr. Edward M. Bernstein, President; Tel: (609) 895-9676
I CAN'T BELIEVE IT'S YOGURT! . . . . P. O. Box 809112, Dallas, TX 75380
    Contact: Ms. Julie Brice, CEO; Tel: (800) 722-5848 (214) 392-3012
ICE CREAM WORLD . . . . 3512 Hamilton Blvd., Allentown, PA 18103
    Contact: Mr. Ed Dawson, Dir. of Sales; Tel: (215) 439-8591
ISLAND SNOW HAWAII . . . . 229 Paokalani Ave, Honolulu, HI 96815
    Contact: Mr. David Corrao, President; Tel: (808) 926-1815
J. HIGBY'S YOGURT & TREAT SHOPPES . . . . . 11344 Coloma Rd., # 750, Gold River, CA 95670
    Contact: Mr. Berch Richard, Dir. Fran. Dev.; Tel: (800) 678-9648 (916) 635-2929
LARRY'S ICE CREAM & YOGURT PARLORS . . . . 999 E. Touhy Ave., # 333, Des Plaines, IL 60018
    Contact: Mr. Howard Marks, VP; Tel: (800) 424-6285 (708) 298-1135
LARRY'S INDUSTRIES . . . . 999 E. Touhy Ave., # 333, Des Plaines, Il 60018
    Contact: Mr. Howard Marks, Dir. Fran. Dev.; Tel: (800) 424-6285 (708) 298-1135
LEE'S ICE CREAM . . . . 1125 DeSoto Rd., Baltimore, MD 21223
    Contact: Mr. Leon Garfield, President; Tel: (800) 824-3477 (301) 525-8320
MAIN STREET ICE CREAM PARLOURS . . . . 765 123 Ave., St. Petersburg, FL 33706
    Contact: President; Tel:
MOUNTAIN SNOW . . . . 948 Riverview Dr., Morgantown, WV 26505
    Contact: Ms. Iona Lee Bucklew, President; Tel: (304) 599-2233
MS. MUFFET'S YOGURT SHOPS . . . . P. O. Box 447, Wrightsville Beach, NC 28480
    Contact: Mr. Bernie J. Pisczek, VP; Tel: (919) 256-2900
NIBBLE-LO'S . . . . P. O. Box 276289, Boca Raton, FL 33427
    Contact: Mr. Arthur Lenowitz, President; Tel: (800) 962-1996
NIELSEN'S FROZEN CUSTARD . . . . P. O. Box 731, Bountiful, UT 84010
    Contact: Mr. Doug Nielsen, President; Tel: (800) 322-NFCI (801) 292-2998
PENGUIN'S PLACE FROZEN YOGURT . . . . . . 325 E. Hillcrest Dr., # 130, Thousand Oaks, CA 91360
    Contact: Ms. Marci Higgins, Fran. Sales Asst.; Tel: (805) 495-3608
ROYELTY YOGURT . . . . 2601 E. Oakland Pk. Blvd., # 201, Ft. Lauderdale, FL 33306
    Contact: Mr. David Siegel, Dir. Fran. Sales; Tel: (305) 561-0189
SAMS SUBS & BLOOMERS ICE CREAM . . . . 5900 N. Port Washington Rd., Milwaukee, WI 53217
    Contact: Mr. Peter Bloomer; Tel: (414) 276-2740
SKINNY DIP . . . . 1218 Fox Run Dr., Charlotte, NC 28212
    Contact: Mr. D. J. Marcom; Tel: (704) 568-6472 (704) 376-0275
STRAWBERRY HILL ICE CREAM . . . . 8456 Castleton Corner Dr., Indianapolis, IN 46250
    Contact: Ms. Tammy Smith; Tel: (317) 849-4165
SUNBURST ICE CREAM . . . . 1146 Grand Ave., S. Hempstead, NY 11550
    Contact: President; Tel:
TASTES YOGURT EMPORIUM . . . . 300 John St., Thornhill, ON L3T 5W4   CAN
    Contact: Mr. Arthur J. Clabby, President; Tel: (416) 731-7175 C
TWISTEE TREAT . . . . 7904 Esttero Blvd., Ft. Myers Beach, FL 33931
    Contact: Mr. Andrew Brennan; Tel: (813) 765-4906
USA DESSERTS / OASIS ICE CREAM . . . . 1512 Business Loop 70 W., Columbia, MO 65202
    Contact: Mr. Marc Kirchoff, President; Tel: (314) 449-4040
WHIRLA-WHIP SYSTEMS . . . . 9359 G Court, Omaha, NE 68127
    Contact: Mr. Duke Fischer, EVP/GM; Tel: (402) 592-7799

YOGEN FRUZ . . . . 2362 Maya Palm Dr. W., Boca Raton, FL 33432
    Contact: Mr. Tom Bryant, President; Tel: (407) 368-5179
YOGURT FANTASTIK . . . . 1936 County Line Rd., Huntington Valley, PA 19006
    Contact: Mr. Chris Crane; Tel: (215) 953-1102
YOGURT STATION, THE . . . . 437 S. Cataract Ave., # 2, San Dimas, CA 91773
    Contact: Mr. George Reuben; Tel: (714) 592-2564
YUMMY YOGURT . . . . 1010 17th St. NW, Washington, DC 20036
    Contact: Mr. Abi Soltani, President; Tel: (202) 659-9858
ZACK'S FAMOUS FROZEN YOGURT . . . . . 4400 Silas Creek Pkwy., # 302, Winston Salem, NC 27104
    Contact: Ms. Carol Lynch, Ops. Mgr.; Tel: (919) 768-9446

CHAPTER 19

RETAIL FOOD: SPECIALTY FOODS

AUNTIE ANNE'S

5325 Lincoln Hwy.
Gap, PA 17527
TEL: (717) 442-4766
FAX: (717) 442-4139
Mr. David Hood, Dir. Fran.

AUNTIE ANNE'S is a unique food service concept, offering hand-rolled soft pretzels. Our product, available in several varieties, is made from scratch in each store, in full view of the customer. Our focus in on quality operations and intensive franchisee support.

HISTORY: . . . .
Established in 1988; . . 1st Franchised in 1989
Company-Owned Units (As of 8/31/1992): . .4
Franchised Units (As of 8/31/1992): 97
Total Units (As of 8/31/1992): 101
Projected New Units for 1993: 45
Distribution: US-101;Can-0;Overseas-0
  North America: . . . . 13 States
  Concentration: . . 60 in PA, 11 in NY, 7 in NJ
Registered: . . . FL,IN,MD,MI,NY,RI,VA,DC
. . . .
Type Space: . . . . RM;~450 SF

FINANCIAL: Earnings Claim: . Yes
Cash Investment: $50-70K
Total Investment: $75-130K
Fees: Franchise - $15K
  Royalty: 5%, Advert: 1%
Contract Periods (Yrs.): 5/5
Area Development Agreement: . .No
Sub-Franchise Contract: . . . . .No
Expand in Territory: . . . . Yes
Passive Ownership: . . . Discouraged
Encourage Conversions: . . . . .No
Average # Employees: . . 2 FT, 6 PT

FRANCHISOR TRAINING/SUPPORT:
Financial Assistance Provided: . . . . . No
Site Selection Assistance: . . . . .Yes
Lease Negotiation Assistance: . . . . .Yes
Co-operative Advertising: . . . . No
Training: . . . . 9 Days Headquarters,
. . . . .7 Days Franchisee Store
On-Going Support: B,C,D,E,G,H/ . . . 35
EXPANSION PLANS:
  US: . . . . NE, SE and Midwest
  Canada: . . . . No
  Overseas: . . . . No

BAHAMA BUCK'S ORIGINAL SHAVED ICE
670 N. Jentilly Ln., # 202
Chandler, AZ 85226
TEL: (602) 940-1194 C
FAX:
Mr. Blake Buchanan, President

BAHAMA BUCK'S ORIGINAL SHAVED ICE COMPANY is a unique, soft-serve, frozen dessert franchise. BAHAMA BUCK'S offers its Original Shaved Ice in over 80 flavors and specializes in 10% natural lemonades and limeades, as well as a variety of non-alcoholic beverages. BAHAMA BUCK'S creates a fun, tropical atmosphere that attracts people of all ages.

HISTORY:	FINANCIAL: Earnings Claim: . Yes	FRANCHISOR TRAINING/SUPPORT:
Established in 1989; . . 1st Franchised in 1992	Cash Investment: $25K	Financial Assistance Provided: . . . . . No
Company-Owned Units (As of 8/31/1992): . . 1	Total Investment: $40-50K	Site Selection Assistance: . . . . .Yes
Franchised Units (As of 8/31/1992): 0	Fees: Franchise - $15K	Lease Negotiation Assistance: . . . . .Yes
Total Units (As of 8/31/1992): 1	Royalty: $250/Mo., Advert: $100/Mo.	Co-operative Advertising: . . . . .Yes
Projected New Units for 1993: 12	Contract Periods (Yrs.): . . . 10/10	Training: . . . . .5 Days Phoenix, AZ
Distribution: US-1;Can-0;Overseas-0	Area Development Agreement: Yes/10	. . . .
North America: . . . . .1 State	Sub-Franchise Contract: . . . . . Yes	On-Going Support: B,C,D,E,F,h,I/ 2
Concentration: . . . . 1 in TX	Expand in Territory: . . . . . . Yes	EXPANSION PLANS:
Registered:	Passive Ownership: . . . . . .Allowed	US: . . . . Southern Regions
. . . .	Encourage Conversions: . . . . NA	Canada: . . . . .No
Type Space: . . . . .FS, SC;~1,300 SF	Average # Employees: . .1 FT, 12 PT	Overseas: . . . . No

BAIN'S DELI

210 Goddard Blvd., # 204
King of Prussia, PA 19406
TEL: (800) 969-1910 (215) 337-1817
FAX: (215) 337-2396
Mr. Ross P. Lederer, VP Fran. Ops.

We're America's largest shopping center deli chain. If you choose BAIN'S DELI, you will have a corporation with over 80 years of history, the right to utilize our substantial buying power and the knowledge that only generations of experience can provide. A tradition since 1910.

HISTORY:	FINANCIAL: Earnings Claim: . .No	FRANCHISOR TRAINING/SUPPORT:
Established in 1910; . . 1st Franchised in 1990	Cash Investment: $50-188K	Financial Assistance Provided: . . . Yes(I)
Company-Owned Units (As of 8/31/1992): . 42	Total Investment: $134-188K	Site Selection Assistance: . . . . .Yes
Franchised Units (As of 8/31/1992): 43	Fees: Franchise - $25K	Lease Negotiation Assistance: . . . . .Yes
Total Units (As of 8/31/1992): 85	Royalty: 5%, Advert: 1%	Co-operative Advertising: . . . . .No
Projected New Units for 1993: 75	Contract Periods (Yrs.): 10/10	Training: . . . . . . 2 Wks. in Pennsylvania
Distribution: US-85;Can-0;Overseas-0	Area Development Agreement: Yes/Var	. . . . and Florida
North America: . . . . 15 States	Sub-Franchise Contract: . . . . Yes	On-Going Support: B,C,D,E,F,G,H,I/ . . 14
Concentration: . . . . PA, FL, NJ	Expand in Territory: . . . . . . Yes	EXPANSION PLANS:
Registered: . . . CA,FL,IL,IN,MD,MI,MN,NY	Passive Ownership: . . . . . .Allowed	US: . . . . .All US
. . . . .OR,RI,VA,WA,WI,DC,AB	Encourage Conversions: . . . . Yes	Canada: . . . . .All Canada
Type Space: . . . . FS,SF,SC,RM,Airpt;~ SF	Average # Employees: . . 6 FT, 6 PT	Overseas: . . . . . . Western EUR

BOURBON STREET CANDY COMPANY
420 S. Third St.
Jacksonville Beach, FL 32250
TEL: (904) 247-7768 C
FAX: (904) 247-0687
Mr. Blaine McGrath, President

Specialty retail candy franchise. Stores carry a wide selection of candies and confectioneries, including related gift items such as novelty items, stuffed animals, tins, baskets and candy containers. Stores are bulk self-serve operations.

HISTORY: . . . . IFA	FINANCIAL: Earnings Claim: . .No	FRANCHISOR TRAINING/SUPPORT:
Established in 1990; . . 1st Franchised in 1990	Cash Investment: $50-130K	Financial Assistance Provided: . . . Yes(I)
Company-Owned Units (As of 8/31/1992): . .1	Total Investment: $50-130K	Site Selection Assistance: . . . . .Yes
Franchised Units (As of 8/31/1992): 10	Fees: Franchise - $15K	Lease Negotiation Assistance: . . . . .No
Total Units (As of 8/31/1992): 11	Royalty: 5%, Advert: 1%	Co-operative Advertising: . . . . .Yes
Projected New Units for 1993: 30	Contract Periods (Yrs.): 10/10	Training: . . . . .1 Wk. Home Office,
Distribution: US-11;Can-0;Overseas-0	Area Development Agreement: Yes/10	. . . . 7-10 Days Store Opening
North America: . . . . 4 States	Sub-Franchise Contract: . . . . .No	On-Going Support: b,C,D,E,G/ 7
Concentration: . . . . 7 in FL, 2 in NJ, 1 in PA	Expand in Territory: . . . . . . Yes	EXPANSION PLANS:
Registered: . . . . . .FL,IL,MD,NY,VA,WA	Passive Ownership: . . . . . .Allowed	US: . . . . .All US
. . . .	Encourage Conversions:	Canada: . . . . .Vancouver
Type Space: . . . . .RM;~~1,000 SF	Average # Employees: . . 2 FT, 1 PT	Overseas: . . . . No

CANDYLAND

3522 Charlotte St.
Pittsburgh, PA 15201
TEL: (412) 687-3725
FAX: (412) 687-0091
Mr. Mark Lando, Fran. Consult.

Self-serve bulk candy. Specializes in candy and related gift items. Does not carry coffees, popcorns or nuts. This concept allows for reduced spoilage and smaller, more profitable stores than other bulk candy operations.

HISTORY:	FINANCIAL: Earnings Claim: . Yes	FRANCHISOR TRAINING/SUPPORT:
Established in 1991; . . 1st Franchised in 1992	Cash Investment: $50-75K	Financial Assistance Provided: . . . . . No
Company-Owned Units (As of 8/31/1992): . .2	Total Investment: $105-125K	Site Selection Assistance: . . . . .Yes
Franchised Units (As of 8/31/1992): 1	Fees: Franchise - $30K	Lease Negotiation Assistance: . . . . .Yes
Total Units (As of 8/31/1992): 3	Royalty: 6%, Advert: 1%	Co-operative Advertising: . . . . .NA
Projected New Units for 1993: 25	Contract Periods (Yrs.): 10/5	Training: . . . . .1 Wk. Headquarters,
Distribution: US-3;Can-0;Overseas-0	Area Development Agreement: . Yes	. . . . 1 Wk. On-Site for Opening
North America: . . . . 3 States	Sub-Franchise Contract: . . . . . Yes	On-Going Support: B,C,D,E,F,G,H/ . . . 8
Concentration: . . . . 2 in MO, 1 in TX	Expand in Territory: . . . . Yes	EXPANSION PLANS:
Registered: . . . . .All	Passive Ownership: . . . . .Allowed	US: . . . . All US
. . . .	Encourage Conversions: . . . . . Yes	Canada: . . . . .All Canada
Type Space: . . . . RM;~800 SF	Average # Employees: . . 2 FT, 3 PT	Overseas: . . . . .Yes

COFFEE BEANERY, THE

G-3429 Pierson Pl.
Flushing, MI 48473
TEL: (313) 733-1020
FAX: (313) 733-1536
Mr. Kevin Shaw, Dir. Fran. Dev.

Retail - specialty gourmet coffee and tea.

HISTORY: . . . . IFA	FINANCIAL: Earnings Claim: . Yes	FRANCHISOR TRAINING/SUPPORT:
Established in 1976; . . 1st Franchised in 1985	Cash Investment: $50K	Financial Assistance Provided: . . . Yes(I)
Company-Owned Units (As of 8/31/1992): . 26	Total Investment: $73-433K	Site Selection Assistance: . . . . .Yes
Franchised Units (As of 8/31/1992): 46	Fees: Franchise - $25K	Lease Negotiation Assistance: . . . . .Yes
Total Units (As of 8/31/1992): 72	Royalty: 6%, Advert: 1%	Co-operative Advertising: . . . . No
Projected New Units for 1993: 43	Contract Periods (Yrs.): . . 8-10/8-10	Training: . . . . 1 Wk. Headquarters, 1 Wk.
Distribution: US-72;Can-0;Overseas-0	Area Development Agreement: . .No	. . . . . Corporate Store, 2 Wks. On-Site
North America: . . . . 22 States	Sub-Franchise Contract: . . . . . .No	On-Going Support: C,D,E,G,H,I/ 30
Concentration: . . . 19 in MI, 9 in OH, 7 in PA	Expand in Territory: . . . . Yes	EXPANSION PLANS:
Registered: . . . CA,HI,IL,IN,MD,MI,MN,NY	Passive Ownership: . . . Not Allowed	US: . . . . All US
. . . . .ND,RI,SD,VA,WA,WI	Encourage Conversions: . . . . . Yes	Canada: . . . . No
Type Space: SF, SC, RM; Airpt;~500-2,000 SF	Average # Employees: . . 2 FT, 5 PT	Overseas: . . . . No

DOOR 2 DOOR

1240 W. 14 Mile Rd.
Clawson, MI 48017
TEL: (313) 288-3631
FAX: (313) 288-3227
Mr. Kirk Scott, President

DOOR 2 DOOR is the national leader in third-party restaurant delivery services. Using state-of-the-art technology, all phases of the operation are automated with easy to learn computers. Let us show you how to capitalize on the fastest-growing segment of the $130 billion restaurant industry - Delivery!

HISTORY:	FINANCIAL: Earnings Claim: . Yes	FRANCHISOR TRAINING/SUPPORT:
Established in 1988; . . 1st Franchised in 1991	Cash Investment: $100-150K	Financial Assistance Provided: . . . . . No
Company-Owned Units (As of 8/31/1992): . .1	Total Investment: $200K	Site Selection Assistance: . . . . .Yes
Franchised Units (As of 8/31/1992): 3	Fees: Franchise - $25K	Lease Negotiation Assistance: . . . . . No
Total Units (As of 8/31/1992): 4	Royalty: 5%, Advert: 3%	Co-operative Advertising: . . . . .Yes
Projected New Units for 1993: 12	Contract Periods (Yrs.): 5/20	Training: . . . . .1 Wk. Headquarters,
Distribution: US-4;Can-0;Overseas-0	Area Development Agreement: Yes/2	. . . . 1 Wk. Franchisee Site
North America: . . . . 3 States	Sub-Franchise Contract: . . . . . .No	On-Going Support: A,B,C,D,E,F,H/ . . 10
Concentration: . . . 2 in MI, 1 in MA, 1 in KY	Expand in Territory: . . . . Yes	EXPANSION PLANS:
Registered: . . . . .All	Passive Ownership: . . . . . .Allowed	US: . . . . All US
. . . .	Encourage Conversions: . . . . . Yes	Canada: . . . . .All Canada
Type Space: . . . . Industrial Park;~2,500 SF	Average # Employees: . 10 FT, 15 PT	Overseas: . . . . No

FUDGE COMPANY, THE

103 Belvedere Ave.
Charlevoix, MI 49720
TEL: (616) 547-4612
FAX: (616) 547-4678
Mr. R. L. Hoffman, President

FUDGE COMPANY's all natural, homemade fudge is delicious! Our candy is cooked in copper kettles and creamed on marble slabs, in full view of public. The showmanship of making fudge provides unique, enjoyable and profitable operation. FUDGE COMPANY provides equipment, franchisee provides building/location.

HISTORY:	FINANCIAL: Earnings Claim: . .No	FRANCHISOR TRAINING/SUPPORT:
Established in 1977; . . 1st Franchised in 1983	Cash Investment: $15-35K	Financial Assistance Provided: . . . . .No
Company-Owned Units (As of 8/31/1992): . .1	Total Investment: $25-45K	Site Selection Assistance: . . . . . . .Yes
Franchised Units (As of 8/31/1992): 5	Fees: Franchise - $12-15K	Lease Negotiation Assistance: . . . .Yes
Total Units (As of 8/31/1992): 6	Royalty: 3%, Advert: 0%	Co-operative Advertising: . . . . .NA
Projected New Units for 1993: 1	Contract Periods (Yrs.): . . . 10/10	Training: . . . . . . 1-2 Wks. Headquarters,
Distribution: US-6;Can-0;Overseas-0	Area Development Agreement: Yes/10	. . . . .7-10 Days On-Site
North America: . . . . 5 States	Sub-Franchise Contract: . . . . . Yes	On-Going Support: C,D,E,F/ 2
Concentration: . . . 2 in AZ, 1 in AK, 1 in OR	Expand in Territory: . . . . . . Yes	EXPANSION PLANS:
Registered: . . . . .FL,HI,MI,OR,DC	Passive Ownership: . . . Discouraged	US: . . . . All US
. . . .	Encourage Conversions: . . . . . Yes	Canada: . . . . .All Canada
Type Space: . . . . RM, Resort Area;~500 SF	Average # Employees: . 1 FT, 3-4 PT	Overseas: . . . . . . EUR, JA, UK

GLORIA JEAN'S COFFEE BEAN

1001 Asbury Dr.
Buffalo Grove, IL 60089
TEL: (800) 333-0050 (708) 808-0580 C
FAX: (708) 808-0593
Mr. Jim Ludwig, VP Fran. Dev.

America's largest retail gourmet coffee franchisor, offers the highest-quality gourmet coffees, teas and accessories. Our unique store design and exclusive coffee bean counter are the focal points of our nationally-honored company. Each store has up to 64 varieties of coffees, plus a complete line of signature teas, along with a complete line of state-of-the-art coffee and tea accessories.

HISTORY: . . . . IFA	FINANCIAL: Earnings Claim: . Yes	FRANCHISOR TRAINING/SUPPORT:
Established in 1979; . . 1st Franchised in 1986	Cash Investment: $60-70K	Financial Assistance Provided: . . . Yes(I)
Company-Owned Units (As of 8/31/1992): . .4	Total Investment: $126-220K	Site Selection Assistance: . . . . . . .Yes
Franchised Units (As of 8/31/1992): 175	Fees: Franchise - $19.5K	Lease Negotiation Assistance: . . . . .Yes
Total Units (As of 8/31/1992): 179	Royalty: 6%, Advert: 1%	Co-operative Advertising: . . . . .Yes
Projected New Units for 1993: 50	Contract Periods (Yrs.): . . . . Lease	Training: . . . . . . 10 Days Headquarters,
Distribution: US-178;Can-0;Overseas-1	Area Development Agreement: Yes/Var	. . . . .9 Days Pre-Opening
North America: . . . . 29 States	Sub-Franchise Contract: . . . . .No	On-Going Support: A,B,C,D,E,F,G,H,I/ 18
Concentration: . . .27 in CA, 24 in IL, 7 in TX	Expand in Territory: . . . . . . Yes	EXPANSION PLANS:
Registered: . . . . All States	Passive Ownership: . . . Discouraged	US: . . . . All US
. . . .	Encourage Conversions: . . . . Yes	Canada: . . . . .All Canada
Type Space: . . . . RM;~800-1,200 SF	Average # Employees: . . 2 FT, 3 PT	Overseas: . UK, JA, AU, EUR, MX

GOURMET CUP, THE

P. O. Box 490, 2265 W. Railway St.
Abbotsford, BC V2S 5Z5 CAN
TEL: (604) 852-8771
FAX: (604) 859-1711
Mr. Wolfgang Lehmann, Dir. Fran.

Contemporary retail outlet catering to coffee and tea lovers. Extensive selection of fresh-roasted gourmet coffees and gourmet teas, specialty drinks and pastries; complementary merchandise, including mugs and brewing equipment.

HISTORY:	FINANCIAL: Earnings Claim: . . .	FRANCHISOR TRAINING/SUPPORT:
Established in 1985; . . 1st Franchised in 1985	Cash Investment: $35-80K	Financial Assistance Provided: . . . . .No
Company-Owned Units (As of 8/31/1992): . .2	Total Investment: $100-225K	Site Selection Assistance: . . . . . . .Yes
Franchised Units (As of 8/31/1992): 45	Fees: Franchise - $25K	Lease Negotiation Assistance: . . . . .Yes
Total Units (As of 8/31/1992): 47	Royalty: 8%, Advert: 0%	Co-operative Advertising: . . . . .NA
Projected New Units for 1993: 12	Contract Periods (Yrs.): 5/5	Training: . . . . .1 Wk. On-Site
Distribution: US-0;Can-47;Overseas-0	Area Development Agreement: . .No	
North America: . . . . 7 Provinces	Sub-Franchise Contract: . . . . .No	On-Going Support: C,D,E,G,I/ 7
Concentration: . 14 in ON, 11 in AB, 10 in BC	Expand in Territory: . . . . . . .No	EXPANSION PLANS:
Registered: . . . . AB	Passive Ownership: . . . Discouraged	US: . . . . .No
. . . .	Encourage Conversions:	Canada: . . . . .All Canada
Type Space: . . RM, Shopping Ctrs;~300-500 SF	Average # Employees: . . 2 FT, 3 PT	Overseas: . . . . No

GRABBAJABBA

1121 Centre St. N., # 440
Calgary, AB T2E 7K6 CAN
TEL: (403) 230-1151 C
FAX: (403) 230-2182
Ms. Janine Hunka, Fran. Sales Mgr.

Up-scale European coffee house, specializing in over 40 varieties of gourmet liquid coffees, cappuccino and other specialty coffees. European sandwiches, soups, salads, Italian gelato and decadent desserts and pastries.

HISTORY: . . . . .CFA
Established in 1987; . . 1st Franchised in 1990
Company-Owned Units (As of 8/31/1992): . .0
Franchised Units (As of 8/31/1992): 17
Total Units (As of 8/31/1992): 17
Projected New Units for 1993: 6
Distribution: US-0;Can-17;Overseas-0
North America: . . . . 4 Provinces
Concentration: . . .10 in AB, 2 in BC, 2 in ON
Registered: . . . . AB
. . . .
Type Space: . . . . . .SF, SC, RM;~1,100 SF

FINANCIAL: Earnings Claim: . . Yes
Cash Investment: $60-85K
Total Investment: $150-225K
Fees: Franchise - $25K
Royalty: 8%, Advert: 0%
Contract Periods (Yrs.): 10/10
Area Development Agreement: . .No
Sub-Franchise Contract: . . . . .No
Expand in Territory: . . . . . . Yes
Passive Ownership: . . . Discouraged
Encourage Conversions: . . . . Yes
Average # Employees: . . 3 FT, 4 PT

FRANCHISOR TRAINING/SUPPORT:
Financial Assistance Provided: . . . Yes(I)
Site Selection Assistance: . . . . . . .Yes
Lease Negotiation Assistance: . . . . .Yes
Co-operative Advertising: . . . . . . .Yes
Training: . . . .
On-Going Support: C,D,E,f,G,h/ 12
EXPANSION PLANS:
US: . . . . No
Canada: . . . . .All Canada
Overseas: . . . . No

GREAT EARTH VITAMINS

2850 Ocean park Blvd., # 290
Santa Monica, CA 90405
TEL: (800) 374-7328 (310) 314-8700
FAX: (310) 314-8701
Mr. Stuart A. Benson, Chairman

GREAT EARTH VITAMINS offers franchises to retailers interested in selling health and fitness products. GREAT EARTH VITAMINS stores sell all-natural vitamins, minerals, body building and diet products.

HISTORY: . . . .
Established in 1971; . . 1st Franchised in 1979
Company-Owned Units (As of 8/31/1992): . .2
Franchised Units (As of 8/31/1992): 116
Total Units (As of 8/31/1992): 118
Projected New Units for 1993: 50
Distribution: US-116;Can-0;Overseas-0
North America: . . . . 14 States
Concentration: . . 88 in CA, 9 in TX, 3 in WA
Registered: . . . . .All
. . . .
Type Space: . . . . RM;~500-800 SF

FINANCIAL: Earnings Claim: . .No
Cash Investment: $20K
Total Investment: $50-75K
Fees: Franchise - $30K
Royalty: 6%, Advert: . . $150/Mo.
Contract Periods (Yrs.): 10/5/5
Area Development Agreement: Yes/Var
Sub-Franchise Contract: . . . . .No
Expand in Territory: . . . . . . Yes
Passive Ownership: . . . . . .Allowed
Encourage Conversions: . . . . Yes
Average # Employees: . . 2 FT, 1 PT

FRANCHISOR TRAINING/SUPPORT:
Financial Assistance Provided: . . .Yes(D)
Site Selection Assistance: . . . . . . .Yes
Lease Negotiation Assistance: . . . . .Yes
Co-operative Advertising: . . . .
Training: . . . . . 2-3 Wks. Headquarters
. . . .
On-Going Support: C,D,E,G,H,I/ 14
EXPANSION PLANS:
US: . . . . .All US
Canada: . . . . .Yes
Overseas: . . . . .Yes

HAM SUPREME SHOPS

P.O. Box 07009
Detroit, MI 48207
TEL: (800) 783-HAMS (313) 259-HAMS C
FAX: (313) 259-4219
Mr. Don Bonanno, President

Turn-key franchise opportunity, featuring private-labeled, supreme spiral-sliced, fire-glazed hams, whole smoked turkeys, BBQ ribs, Canadian and hickory-smoked bacons. In addition, 7 outstanding party trays, 6 over-stuffed sandwiches, deli - complete with meats, cheeses, salads, homemade soups and baked beans.

HISTORY: . . . . .IFA
Established in 1986; . . 1st Franchised in 1986
Company-Owned Units (As of 8/31/1992): . .1
Franchised Units (As of 8/31/1992): 11
Total Units (As of 8/31/1992): 12
Projected New Units for 1993: 5
Distribution: US-12;Can-0;Overseas-0
North America: . . . . 5 States
Concentration: . . . 5 in CA, 4 in OH, 1 in MI
Registered: . . . . CA,IL,MI
. . . .
Type Space: . . . FS, SF, SC;~1,500-2,000 SF

FINANCIAL: Earnings Claim: . .No
Cash Investment: $100-125K
Total Investment: $142-208K
Fees: Franchise - $20K
Royalty: 5%, Advert: 2%
Contract Periods (Yrs.): 5/5
Area Development Agreement: Yes/Var
Sub-Franchise Contract: . . . . .No
Expand in Territory: . . . . . . Yes
Passive Ownership: . . . Discouraged
Encourage Conversions: . . . . NA
Average # Employees: . . 2 FT, 1 PT

FRANCHISOR TRAINING/SUPPORT:
Financial Assistance Provided: . . . . .No
Site Selection Assistance: . . . . . . .Yes
Lease Negotiation Assistance: . . . . .Yes
Co-operative Advertising: . . . . .NA
Training: . . . . 1 Wk. Headquarters, 1 Wk.
. . .Pre-Opening, 3 Days Grand Opening
On-Going Support: C,D,E,G,h,I/ 6
EXPANSION PLANS:
US: . . . . All US
Canada: . . . . No
Overseas: . . . . No

HEAVENLY HAM

8800 Roswell Rd., # 135
Atlanta, GA 30350
TEL: (800) 899-2228 (404) 993-2232
FAX: (404) 587-3529
Mr. R. Hutch Hodgson, President

Paradise Food franchises retail HEAVENLY HAM STORES, selling fully-baked, spiral sliced, honey and spice glazed HEAVENLY HAM with "a taste that is out of this world." The stores also sell smoked turkey, ribs, condiments and delicious take-away sandwiches. Call today for information!

HISTORY:	FINANCIAL: Earnings Claim: . .No	FRANCHISOR TRAINING/SUPPORT:
Established in 1984; . . 1st Franchised in 1984	Cash Investment: $30-60K	Financial Assistance Provided: . . . . No
Company-Owned Units (As of 8/31/1992): . .1	Total Investment: $84-134K	Site Selection Assistance: . . . . . . .Yes
Franchised Units (As of 8/31/1992): 54	Fees: Franchise - $25K	Lease Negotiation Assistance: . . . .Yes
Total Units (As of 8/31/1992): 55	Royalty: 5%, Advert: 1%	Co-operative Advertising: . . . . . . .No
Projected New Units for 1993: 15	Contract Periods (Yrs.): . . . 10/10	Training: . . . . .1 Wk. Headquarters,
Distribution: US-55;Can-0;Overseas-0	Area Development Agreement: Yes/10	. . . . 5 Days Site, On-Going
North America: . . . . 21 States	Sub-Franchise Contract: . . .No	On-Going Support: C,D,E,F,G,H/ 5
Concentration: . . . 7 in SC, 6 in MD, 7 in FL	Expand in Territory: . . . . . . Yes	EXPANSION PLANS:
Registered: . . . CA,FL,IL,IN,MD,MI,MN,NY	Passive Ownership: . . . Not Allowed	US: . . . . All US
. . . . VA,WI	Encourage Conversions: . . . . .No	Canada: . . . . .No
Type Space: . . . . .SC;~2,000 SF	Average # Employees: . . 2 FT, 2 PT	Overseas: . . . . No

HOUSE OF COFFEE

4 Garden Rd.
Little Silver, NJ 07739
TEL: (908) 741-7347
FAX: (908) 741-7602
Mr. Ronald S. Hari, Dir. Fran.

The only franchise system that roasts its own coffee. We bake all our own desserts. Coffee house and cafe in the European style, with entertainment. Gift baskets also for mailing. Stocking various gifts related to coffees.

HISTORY:	FINANCIAL: Earnings Claim: . Yes	FRANCHISOR TRAINING/SUPPORT:
Established in 1988; . . 1st Franchised in 1989	Cash Investment: $35K	Financial Assistance Provided: . . . Yes(I)
Company-Owned Units (As of 8/31/1992): . .1	Total Investment: $150K	Site Selection Assistance: . . . . . . .Yes
Franchised Units (As of 8/31/1992): 2	Fees: Franchise - $20K	Lease Negotiation Assistance: . . . .Yes
Total Units (As of 8/31/1992): 3	Royalty: 5%, Advert: 0%	Co-operative Advertising: . . . . . . .Yes
Projected New Units for 1993: 3	Contract Periods (Yrs.): . . . 10/10	Training: . . . . 2 Wks. Headquarters
Distribution: US-3;Can-0;Overseas-0	Area Development Agreement: .No	. . . .
North America: . . . . 2 States	Sub-Franchise Contract: . . . . .No	On-Going Support: A,B,C,D,E,F,G,h/ . .6
Concentration: . . . . .2 in NJ, 1 in PA	Expand in Territory: . . . . . . Yes	EXPANSION PLANS:
Registered: . . . . CA,FL,IL,IN,MD,MI,NY,RI	Passive Ownership: . . . Discouraged	US: . . . . All US
. . . . VA,WI	Encourage Conversions: . . . . NA	Canada: . . . . .No
Type Space: . . . . .SF, SC;~1,200 SF	Average # Employees: . . 3 FT, 6 PT	Overseas: . . . . No

JAKE'S TAKE N' BAKE PIZZA

620 High St.
San Luis Obispo, CA 93401
TEL: (805) 543-3339
FAX:
Mr. Willis Reeser, President

We sell unbaked pizzas, cookie dough, salads, hard ice cream and soft drinks. Every product is to-go. Labor is low. Product is usually out the door in 5 minutes.

HISTORY:	FINANCIAL: Earnings Claim: . .No	FRANCHISOR TRAINING/SUPPORT:
Established in 1984; . . 1st Franchised in 1986	Cash Investment: $35-45K	Financial Assistance Provided: . . . . No
Company-Owned Units (As of 8/31/1992): . .0	Total Investment: . . . .$	Site Selection Assistance: . . . . . . .Yes
Franchised Units (As of 8/31/1992): 17	Fees: Franchise - $10K	Lease Negotiation Assistance: . . . .Yes
Total Units (As of 8/31/1992): 17	Royalty: 3%, Advert: 1%	Co-operative Advertising: . . . . No
Projected New Units for 1993: 2	Contract Periods (Yrs.): 10/5	Training: . . . . . . 14 Days Headquarters,
Distribution: US-17;Can-0;Overseas-0	Area Development Agreement: .No	. . . . .5 Days Franchisee Store
North America: . . . . .1 State	Sub-Franchise Contract: . . . . .No	On-Going Support: b,C,D,E,F/ 3
Concentration: . . . . 17 in CA	Expand in Territory: . . . . . . Yes	EXPANSION PLANS:
Registered: . . . . CA	Passive Ownership: . . . Discouraged	US: . . . . California Only
	Encourage Conversions: . . . . NA	Canada: . . . . .No
Type Space: . . . . SC;~600-800 SF	Average # Employees: . . 2 FT, 4 PT	Overseas: . . . . No

JASON'S DELI

363 N. Sam Houston Pkwy., E., # 1100
Houston, TX 77060
TEL: (713) 820-7876
FAX: (713) 591-0150
Mr. Steve Simmons, VP Fran.

A modified New York-style deli.

HISTORY:	FINANCIAL: Earnings Claim: . Yes	FRANCHISOR TRAINING/SUPPORT:
Established in 1976; . . 1st Franchised in 1983	Cash Investment: . . . .$155K+	Financial Assistance Provided: . . . . .No
Company-Owned Units (As of 8/31/1992): . 21	Total Investment: $313-335K	Site Selection Assistance: . . . . . . .Yes
Franchised Units (As of 8/31/1992): 3	Fees: Franchise - $20K	Lease Negotiation Assistance: . . . .Yes
Total Units (As of 8/31/1992): 24	Royalty: 4%, Advert: 2%	Co-operative Advertising: . . . . .NA
Projected New Units for 1993: 3	Contract Periods (Yrs.): 20/10	Training: . . . . . 8-10 Wks.+ Headquarters
Distribution: US-24;Can-0;Overseas-0	Area Development Agreement: Yes/10	. . . .
North America: . . . . 2 States	Sub-Franchise Contract: . . . . .No	On-Going Support: C,D,E,G,H/ . . . . . .
Concentration: . . . . . . .22 in TX, 2 in AZ	Expand in Territory: . . . . . . Yes	EXPANSION PLANS:
Registered: . . . . .FL	Passive Ownership: . . . Not Allowed	US: . . . . SW, S and SE Only
. . . .	Encourage Conversions: . . . . . NA	Canada: . . . . .No
Type Space: . . . . .FS, SC;~3,500 SF	Avg. # Employees:30-32 FT, Varies PT	Overseas: . . . . No

KATIE MCGUIRE'S PIE & BAKE SHOPPE

17682 Sampson Ln.
Huntington Beach, CA 92647
TEL: (714) 847-0325
FAX:
Ms. Katie Bass, President

Home-style pies, muffins, cookies, cheesecakes, plus small cafe of quiche, chicken pot pies, soups and sandwiches. Products supplied from a central commissary to be freshly baked in store. No baking experience is required.

HISTORY:	FINANCIAL: Earnings Claim: . .No	FRANCHISOR TRAINING/SUPPORT:
Established in 1982; . . 1st Franchised in 1984	Cash Investment: $22.5K	Financial Assistance Provided: . . . . .No
Company-Owned Units (As of 8/31/1992): . .0	Total Investment: $100-150K	Site Selection Assistance: . . . . . . .Yes
Franchised Units (As of 8/31/1992): 20	Fees: Franchise - $22.5K	Lease Negotiation Assistance: . . . .Yes
Total Units (As of 8/31/1992): 20	Royalty: 6%, Advert: 2%	Co-operative Advertising: . . . . .No
Projected New Units for 1993: 6	Contract Periods (Yrs.): 10/5	Training: . . . . .1 Wk. Headquarters,
Distribution: US-20;Can-0;Overseas-0	Area Development Agreement: Yes/10	. . . . 2 Wks. On-Site
North America: . . . . .1 State	Sub-Franchise Contract: . . . . .No	On-Going Support: B,C,D,E,F,G,H,I/ . . . 6
Concentration: . . . . 20 in CA	Expand in Territory: . . . . . . Yes	EXPANSION PLANS:
Registered: . . . . CA	Passive Ownership: . . . Discouraged	US: . . . . California Only
. . . .	Encourage Conversions: . . . . . Yes	Canada: . . . . .No
Type Space: . . . . .SC;~1,200 SF	Average # Employees: . . . . .12 FT	Overseas: . . . . No

KERNELS POPCORN

40 Eglinton Ave. E., # 250
Toronto, ON M4P 3A2 CAN
TEL: (416) 487-4194 C
FAX: (416) 487-3920
Ms. Bernice Sinopoli, Ops. Admin.

KERNELS is the largest retail popcorn chain in North America, selling a premium selection of popcorn of over 50 flavors. The marketing of the product is both sharp and entertaining. Our franchisees are, for the most part, owner/operators who love popcorn!

HISTORY:	FINANCIAL: Earnings Claim: . .No	FRANCHISOR TRAINING/SUPPORT:
Established in 1983; . . 1st Franchised in 1984	Cash Investment: $110-150K	Financial Assistance Provided: . . . . .No
Company-Owned Units (As of 8/31/1992): . 17	Total Investment: $110-150K	Site Selection Assistance: . . . . . . .Yes
Franchised Units (As of 8/31/1992): 46	Fees: Franchise - $25K	Lease Negotiation Assistance: . . . .Yes
Total Units (As of 8/31/1992): 63	Royalty: 8%, Advert: 1%	Co-operative Advertising: . . . . . . .Yes
Projected New Units for 1993: 5	Contract Periods (Yrs.): . . . . Lease	Training: . . . Approximately 10 Days HQ
Distribution: US-4;Can-59;Overseas-0	Area Development Agreement: .No	. . . .
North America: . . . . . 3 States, 7 Provinces	Sub-Franchise Contract: . . . . .No	On-Going Support: B,C,D,E,G,H/ . . . . .
Concentration: . . .34 in ON, 8 in AB, 6 in PQ	Expand in Territory: . . . . . . .No	EXPANSION PLANS:
Registered:	Passive Ownership: . . . Not Allowed	US: . . . . .No
. . . .	Encourage Conversions: . . . . . .No	Canada: . . . . All Exc. NF, PEI
Type Space: . . . . RM;~ SF	Average # Employees: . . 2 FT, 6 PT	Overseas: . . . . No

KID'S KORNER FRESH PIZZA

P. O. Box 9288
Waukegan, IL 60079
TEL: (708) 249-8606
FAX:
Ms. Katheen Gulko, VP

We offer an extremely affordable opportunity in one of the fastest growing segments of our economy. We are the originator of the unique "We make 'em, you bake 'em at home" concept with an exceptionally broad customer base. Highest-quality product at a very low price.

HISTORY:	FINANCIAL: Earnings Claim: . .No	FRANCHISOR TRAINING/SUPPORT:
Established in 1977; . . 1st Franchised in 1978	Cash Investment: $25-45K	Financial Assistance Provided: . . . . .No
Company-Owned Units (As of 8/31/1992): . .0	Total Investment: $25-45K	Site Selection Assistance: . . . . . . .Yes
Franchised Units (As of 8/31/1992): 29	Fees: Franchise - $12.5K	Lease Negotiation Assistance: . . . .Yes
Total Units (As of 8/31/1992): 29	Royalty: 4%, Advert: 1.5%	Co-operative Advertising: . . . . . . .Yes
Projected New Units for 1993:	Contract Periods (Yrs.): 10/10	Training: . . . . . . 3-7 Days Headquarters,
Distribution: US-29;Can-0;Overseas-0	Area Development Agreement: Yes/10	. . . . 3-7 Days On-Site
North America:	Sub-Franchise Contract: . . . . .No	On-Going Support: C,D,E,F,G,H,I/ 4
Concentration: . . . 21 in WI, 3 in MN, 2 in IL	Expand in Territory: . . . . Yes	EXPANSION PLANS:
Registered: . . . CA,FL,IL,IN,MI,MN,ND,SD	Passive Ownership: . . . . . .Allowed	US: . . . . Most of US
. . . . VA,WI	Encourage Conversions: . . . . Yes	Canada: . . . . .All Canada
Type Space: . . . . . FS, SF, SC;~500-800 SF	Average # Employees: . 1 FT, 3-5 PT	Overseas: . . . . .Yes

KILWIN'S CHOCOLATES

355 N. Division Rd.
Petoskey, MI 49770
TEL: (616) 347-3800
FAX: (616) 347-6951
Mr. Don McCarty, VP

KILWIN'S CHOCOLATES AND ICE CREAM is a family of confectionery stores that give old-fashioned enjoyment to customers by providing quality products, turn-of-the-century store atmosphere and over 40 years of experience. Modern business systems provide efficiency and simplicity of operation while knowledgeable, experienced franchise personnel are committed to your success.

HISTORY: . . . . IFA	FINANCIAL: Earnings Claim: . .No	FRANCHISOR TRAINING/SUPPORT:
Established in 1946; . . 1st Franchised in 1981	Cash Investment: $50-100K	Financial Assistance Provided: . . . . .No
Company-Owned Units (As of 8/31/1992): . .0	Total Investment: $100-150K	Site Selection Assistance: . . . . . . .Yes
Franchised Units (As of 8/31/1992): 24	Fees: Franchise - $20K	Lease Negotiation Assistance: . . . .Yes
Total Units (As of 8/31/1992): 24	Royalty: 5%, Advert: 0%	Co-operative Advertising: . . . . . . .No
Projected New Units for 1993: 3	Contract Periods (Yrs.): 10/10	Training: . . . . .1 Wk. Min. Headquarters,
Distribution: US-24;Can-0;Overseas-0	Area Development Agreement: Yes/2	. . . . 1 Wk. Min. Franchisee Store
North America: . . . . 8 States	Sub-Franchise Contract: . . . . .No	On-Going Support: C,D,E,G,H/ 3
Concentration: . . . 15 in MI, 2 in NC, 2 in IL	Expand in Territory: . . . . Yes	EXPANSION PLANS:
Registered: . . . . .FL,IL,IN,MI,RI,WI	Passive Ownership: . . . Not Allowed	US: . . . . Midwest and Southeast
. . . .	Encourage Conversions: . . . . Yes	Canada: . . . . .No
Type Space: . .SF,RM,Resort/Tour;~1,500 SF	Average # Employees: . .2 FT, 10 PT	Overseas: . . . . No

MAISON DU POPCORN

188 Washington St.
Norwich, CT 06360
TEL: (203) 886-0360
FAX:
Mr. Bill Abate, Bus. Mgr.

Gourmet popcorn, yogurt, soft-serve ice cream, gelato, snow cones, pretzels, etc.

HISTORY:	FINANCIAL: Earnings Claim: . .No	FRANCHISOR TRAINING/SUPPORT:
Established in 19; . . . 1st Franchised in 1988	Cash Investment: $120K	Financial Assistance Provided: . . . . .No
Company-Owned Units (As of 8/31/1992): . .2	Total Investment: $100-150K	Site Selection Assistance: . . . . . . .Yes
Franchised Units (As of 8/31/1992): 6	Fees: Franchise - $20K	Lease Negotiation Assistance: . . . .Yes
Total Units (As of 8/31/1992): 8	Royalty: 6%, Advert: 0%	Co-operative Advertising: . . . . . . .Yes
Projected New Units for 1993: 4	Contract Periods (Yrs.): . . . 10/5-10	Training: . . . . 5 Days Headquarters,
Distribution: US-8;Can-0;Overseas-0	Area Development Agreement: . .No	. . . . 2 Wks. Franchisee Site
North America: . . . . 6 States	Sub-Franchise Contract: . . . . . .No	On-Going Support: D,E,F,G/ 3
Concentration: . . . 3 in MA, 2 in NH, 2 in CT	Expand in Territory: . . . . Yes	EXPANSION PLANS:
Registered: . . . . MN,NY	Passive Ownership: . . . Not Allowed	US: . . . . All US
. . . .	Encourage Conversions: . . . . . NA	Canada: . . . . .All CAN, Esp. PQ
Type Space: . . FS, SF, SC, RM;~600-800 SF	Average # Employees: . .1 FT, 10 PT	Overseas: . . . . .Yes

MANHATTAN FRIES

124 Rubidge St.
Peterborough, ON K9J 3N4 CAN
TEL: (705) 742-5947
FAX: (705) 742-8132
Mr. Ken Purvey, President

Fresh-cut (skin on) french fries, finger foods, such as popcorn shrimp, clam strips, chicken fish, gravy, soft drinks, coffees, etc.

HISTORY:	FINANCIAL: Earnings Claim: . Yes	FRANCHISOR TRAINING/SUPPORT:
Established in 1987; . . 1st Franchised in 1988	Cash Investment: $25K	Financial Assistance Provided: . . . . . No
Company-Owned Units (As of 8/31/1992): . .1	Total Investment: $100K	Site Selection Assistance: . . . . . . .Yes
Franchised Units (As of 8/31/1992): 9	Fees: Franchise - $25K	Lease Negotiation Assistance: . . . .Yes
Total Units (As of 8/31/1992): 10	Royalty: 6%, Advert: 0%	Co-operative Advertising: . . . . . . .No
Projected New Units for 1993:	Contract Periods (Yrs.): . . . 10/5-10	Training: . . . . 2 Wks. Min. Headquarters
Distribution: US-0;Can-10;Overseas-0	Area Development Agreement: . .No	. . . .
North America: . . . . 3 Provinces	Sub-Franchise Contract: . . . . .No	On-Going Support: A,C,D/ 2
Concentration: . . . 8 in ON, 1 in NS, 1 in MB	Expand in Territory: . . . . . . Yes	EXPANSION PLANS:
Registered:	Passive Ownership: . . . Not Allowed	US: .No
. . . .	Encourage Conversions: . . . . . Yes	Canada: . . . . .Yes
Type Space: . . . . RM;~250-300 SF	Average # Employees: . . 2 FT, 3 PT	Overseas: . . . . No

MOMA'S FAMILY FAVORITE
U-BAKE PIZZA
5770 Hopkins Rd.
Richmond, VA 23234
TEL: (800) 777-7522 (804) 271-7522
FAX: (804) 271-7594
Mr. Gerard L. Daly, VP

Join MOMA'S family of successful entrepreneurs in the fastest-growing segment of the $25 billion pizza industry. We create customized, gourmet, fresh bake-at-home pizza and yogurt to the delight of our customers. The Freshest Idea In Pizza offers an affordable franchise opportunity.

HISTORY:	FINANCIAL: Earnings Claim: . .No	FRANCHISOR TRAINING/SUPPORT:
Established in 1987; . . 1st Franchised in 1988	Cash Investment: $15-20K	Financial Assistance Provided: . . . Yes(I)
Company-Owned Units (As of 8/31/1992): . .5	Total Investment: $40-60K	Site Selection Assistance: . . . . . . .Yes
Franchised Units (As of 8/31/1992): 7	Fees: Franchise - $15K	Lease Negotiation Assistance: . . . .Yes
Total Units (As of 8/31/1992): 12	Royalty: 5%, Advert: 2%	Co-operative Advertising: . . . . . . .Yes
Projected New Units for 1993: 40	Contract Periods (Yrs.): 10/10	Training: . . . . 7 Days Headquarters
Distribution: US-12;Can-0;Overseas-0	Area Development Agreement: Yes/10	. . . .
North America: . . . . 4 States	Sub-Franchise Contract: . . . . . Yes	On-Going Support: a,B,C,D,E,F,G,h,I/ . .4
Concentration: . . . . 5 in GA, 4 in AL	Expand in Territory: . . . . . . Yes	EXPANSION PLANS:
Registered: . . . . FL,IL,IN,VA,DC	Passive Ownership: . . . . . .Allowed	US: . . . . .All US
. . . .	Encourage Conversions: . . . . . Yes	Canada: . . . . .Yes
Type Space: . . . . . FS, SF, SC;~500-900 SF	Average # Employees: . 1-2 FT, 5 PT	Overseas: . . EUR and Pacific Rim

MOXIE JAVA INTERNATIONAL

199 E. 52nd St.
Boise, ID 83714
TEL: (208) 322-7773
FAX: (208) 322-6226
Ms. Patricia Hoffman, Fran. Dev.

MOXIE JAVA - Espresso Bar/Cafe. Serving espresso drinks, coffee, other beverages, pastries, muffins and desserts.

HISTORY:	FINANCIAL: Earnings Claim: . Yes	FRANCHISOR TRAINING/SUPPORT:
Established in 1990; . . 1st Franchised in 1992	Cash Investment: . . . .$	Financial Assistance Provided: . . . . .NA
Company-Owned Units (As of 8/31/1992): . .4	Total Investment: $112-151K	Site Selection Assistance: . . . . . . .Yes
Franchised Units (As of 8/31/1992): 1	Fees: Franchise - $26.5K	Lease Negotiation Assistance: . . . .Yes
Total Units (As of 8/31/1992): 5	Royalty: 5/5%, Advert: 1%	Co-operative Advertising: . . . . . . .Yes
Projected New Units for 1993: 10	Contract Periods (Yrs.): 5/5	Training: . . . . 7 Days Headquarters,
Distribution: US-5;Can-0;Overseas-0	Area Development Agreement: . . .	. . . . 5 Days On-Site
North America: . . . . .1 State	Sub-Franchise Contract:	On-Going Support: A,B,C,D,E,G,I/ . . . 15
Concentration: . . . . .5 in ID	Expand in Territory: . . . . . . Yes	EXPANSION PLANS:
Registered: . . . . CA	Passive Ownership:	US: . . . . . . Northwest and Southwest
. . . .	Encourage Conversions:	Canada: . . . . .No
Type Space: . . . . . SF, SC;~600-1,200 SF	Average # Employees: . . . . .Varies	Overseas: . . . . No

MR. BULKY TREATS AND GIFTS

755 W. Big Beaver, # 1600
Troy, MI 48084
TEL: (313) 244-9000
FAX: (313) 244-9365
Mr. Gerard C. Ales, Dir. Fran. Sales

Up-scale retail centers located in major malls coast to coast. Offer self-service merchandise centers, featuring a dazzling array of quality, mouth-watering domestic and international candies, and snacks sold by the ounce or pound. Stores also merchandise a wide selection of gifts and treats, over 1,000 individually selected items from around the world. Ranked as the #1 bulk candy retailer.

HISTORY:	FINANCIAL: Earnings Claim: . .No	FRANCHISOR TRAINING/SUPPORT:
Established in 1983; . . 1st Franchised in 1984	Cash Investment: $30K	Financial Assistance Provided: . . . Yes(I)
Company-Owned Units (As of 8/31/1992): . 53	Total Investment: $150-250K	Site Selection Assistance: . . . . . . .Yes
Franchised Units (As of 8/31/1992): 70	Fees: Franchise - $30K	Lease Negotiation Assistance: . . . . .Yes
Total Units (As of 8/31/1992): 123	Royalty: 6%, Advert: 0%	Co-operative Advertising: . . . . .NA
Projected New Units for 1993: 55	Contract Periods (Yrs.): 10/5	Training: . . . . 2 Wks. On-Site
Distribution: US-123;Can-0;Overseas-0	Area Development Agreement: Yes/5+	. . . .
North America: . . . . 17 States	Sub-Franchise Contract: . . . . . Yes	On-Going Support: C,D,E,F,G,H/ 50
Concentration: . . 18 in OH, 9 in MO, 7 in MI	Expand in Territory: . . . . . . Yes	EXPANSION PLANS:
Registered: . . . . All States	Passive Ownership: . . . Discouraged	US: . . . . All US
. . . .	Encourage Conversions: . . . . . NA	Canada: . . . . .All Canada
Type Space: . . . . RM;~1,500-1,800 SF	Average # Employees: . 3 FT, 6-8 PT	Overseas: . . . . . .MX, EUR, UK

MR. MUGS

196 Dalhousie St., Box 124
Brantford, ON N3T 5M3 CAN
TEL: (519) 752-9890
FAX: (519) 752-0978
Mr. Ron Hewitt, Fran. Dir.

An exciting concept in the coffee and donut industry, offering the customer a deli-bar section, featuring made-from-scratch chili, soups, salads and sandwiches. Fresh muffins and baked goods prepared daily. All locations show exceptional acceptance of product lines and store design concept.

HISTORY:	FINANCIAL: Earnings Claim: . Yes	FRANCHISOR TRAINING/SUPPORT:
Established in 1984; . . 1st Franchised in 1986	Cash Investment: $50-70K	Financial Assistance Provided: . . . . .No
Company-Owned Units (As of 8/31/1992): . .1	Total Investment: $180-195K	Site Selection Assistance: . . . . . . .Yes
Franchised Units (As of 8/31/1992): 22	Fees: Franchise - $20K	Lease Negotiation Assistance: . . . . .Yes
Total Units (As of 8/31/1992): 23	Royalty: 4%, Advert: 2%	Co-operative Advertising: . . . . .Yes
Projected New Units for 1993: 5	Contract Periods (Yrs.): 10/10	Training: . . . . 4 Wks. Headquarters,
Distribution: US-2;Can-21;Overseas-0	Area Development Agreement: Yes/10	. . . . 2 Wks. Franchisee Site
North America: . . . . . .1 State, 2 Provinces	Sub-Franchise Contract: . . . . . .No	On-Going Support: B,C,D,E,F,G,H,I/ . . 10
Concentration: . . . 20 in ON, 2 in MI, 1 in PQ	Expand in Territory: . . . . Yes	EXPANSION PLANS:
Registered: . . . . CA,FL,NY	Passive Ownership: . . . Discouraged	US: . . . . All US
. . . .	Encourage Conversions: . . . . . Yes	Canada: . . . . .All Canada
Type Space: . . . . SC;~1,800 SF	Average # Employees: . . 9 FT, 7 PT	Overseas: . . . . No

MURPHY'S PIZZA

385 Bel Marin Keys Blvd., # C
Novato, CA 94949
TEL: (415) 883-0701
FAX: (415) 883-0812
Mr. Robert Graham, President

MURPHY'S PIZZA and PAPA ALDO'S sell the highest-quality products at the lowest possible price. Everything is made from scratch on the premises.

HISTORY:	FINANCIAL: Earnings Claim: . .No	FRANCHISOR TRAINING/SUPPORT:
Established in 1981; . . 1st Franchised in 1986	Cash Investment: $75-100K	Financial Assistance Provided: . . . . .No
Company-Owned Units (As of 8/31/1992): . .8	Total Investment: $75-100K	Site Selection Assistance: . . . . . . .Yes
Franchised Units (As of 8/31/1992): 97	Fees: Franchise - $17.5K	Lease Negotiation Assistance: . . . . .Yes
Total Units (As of 8/31/1992): 105	Royalty: 5%, Advert: 1%	Co-operative Advertising: . . . . .Yes
Projected New Units for 1993: 20	Contract Periods (Yrs.): 10/10	Training: . . . . 2 Wks. Headquarters,
Distribution: US-105;Can-0;Overseas-0	Area Development Agreement: . .No	. . . . 2 Wks. Portland, OR
North America: . . . . 3 States	Sub-Franchise Contract: . . . . . .No	On-Going Support: B,C,D,E,F,G,H,I/ . . 17
Concentration: . 57 in OR, 34 in CA, 12 in WA	Expand in Territory: . . . . Yes	EXPANSION PLANS:
Registered: . . . . .CA,OR,WA	Passive Ownership: . . . Not Allowed	US: . . .West Coast Only-CA,OR,WA,ID
. . . .	Encourage Conversions: . . . . . Yes	Canada: . . . . No
Type Space: . . . . . FS, SF, SC;~1,000 SF	Average # Employees: . . 1 FT, 7 PT	Overseas: . . . . No

PAPA ALDO'S INTERNATIONAL

4356 SW Multnomah Blvd.
Portland, OR 97219
TEL: (503) 246-7272
FAX: (503) 245-3654
Mr. Jerry Kenney, VP Ops.

PAPA ALDO'S is the largest take and bake pizza shop chain in the country. We specialize in the highest-quality pizza with terrific price/value for the customers. We also have take and bake lasagna and calzone. Low investment.

HISTORY:	FINANCIAL: Earnings Claim: . .No	FRANCHISOR TRAINING/SUPPORT:
Established in 1981; . . 1st Franchised in 1982	Cash Investment: $17.5K	Financial Assistance Provided: . . . . . No
Company-Owned Units (As of 8/31/1992): . .5	Total Investment: $70-110K	Site Selection Assistance: . . . . . . .Yes
Franchised Units (As of 8/31/1992): 58	Fees: Franchise - $17.5K	Lease Negotiation Assistance: . . . . .Yes
Total Units (As of 8/31/1992): 63	Royalty: 5%, Advert: 1%	Co-operative Advertising: . . . . . . .Yes
Projected New Units for 1993: 6	Contract Periods (Yrs.): 10/5	Training: . . . . 1 Wk. Headquarters
Distribution: US-63;Can-0;Overseas-0	Area Development Agreement: . .No	. . . .
North America: . . . . 3 States	Sub-Franchise Contract: . . . . .No	On-Going Support: B,C,D,E,F,G,H,I/ . . . 5
Concentration:	Expand in Territory:	EXPANSION PLANS:
Registered: . . . . OR,WI	Passive Ownership: . . . Not Allowed	US: . . . . Northwest
. . . .	Encourage Conversions: . . . . Yes	Canada: . . . . No
Type Space: . . . . .SC;~1,000 SF	Average # Employees: . 1 FT, 4-6 PT	Overseas: . . . . No

PERFECT PORTIONS FROZEN FOODS

440 Niagara St.
Welland, ON L3C 1L5 CAN
TEL: (416) 735-2000
FAX: (416) 735-5825
Mr. Andre Champagne, President

Retail/wholesale frozen foods - portion control, sizes individually wrapped. Oven-ready, micro-wavable or BBQ ready. Saves families and singles time and money purchasing in this way. Vegetables, meats, seafoods, finger foods, specialty items, etc. No line ups at supermarket. Excellent quality foods. Credit cards accepted. Turn-key.

HISTORY: . . . . .CFA	FINANCIAL: Earnings Claim: . .No	FRANCHISOR TRAINING/SUPPORT:
Established in 1984; . . 1st Franchised in 1985	Cash Investment: $60K	Financial Assistance Provided: . . . Yes(I)
Company-Owned Units (As of 8/31/1992): . .2	Total Investment: $225K	Site Selection Assistance: . . . . . . .Yes
Franchised Units (As of 8/31/1992): 12	Fees: Franchise - $30K	Lease Negotiation Assistance: . . . . .Yes
Total Units (As of 8/31/1992): 14	Royalty: 4%, Advert: 4%	Co-operative Advertising: . . . . . . .Yes
Projected New Units for 1993: 6	Contract Periods (Yrs.): 10/10	Training: . . . . .1 Wk. at Site
Distribution: US-0;Can-14;Overseas-0	Area Development Agreement: . .No	. . . .
North America: . . . . .1 Province	Sub-Franchise Contract: . . . . .No	On-Going Support: B,C,D,E,F,G,H/ . . . 8
Concentration: . . . . 14 in ON	Expand in Territory: . . . . . . Yes	EXPANSION PLANS:
Registered:	Passive Ownership: . . . Discouraged	US: . . . . .No
. . . .	Encourage Conversions: . . . . Yes	Canada: . . . . .Ontario
Type Space: . . . . .SC;~1,200 SF	Average # Employees: . . 2 FT, 2 PT	Overseas: . . . . No

PICCOLO'S PIZZA

421 No. I St.
Madera, CA 93637
TEL: (209) 673-0435
FAX: (209) 675-3544
Mr. Steven L. Frazier, President

PICCOLO'S Take 'n Bake Pizza is a hot concept in step with today's lifestyle. PICCOLO'S PIZZA sells value, convenience and quality. PICCOLO'S PIZZA has been in the business since 1983, making it one of the first and most experienced operators in the business.

HISTORY:	FINANCIAL: Earnings Claim: . .No	FRANCHISOR TRAINING/SUPPORT:
Established in 1983; . . 1st Franchised in 1985	Cash Investment: $20-30K	Financial Assistance Provided: . . . . .No
Company-Owned Units (As of 8/31/1992): . .6	Total Investment: $50-75K	Site Selection Assistance: . . . . . . .Yes
Franchised Units (As of 8/31/1992): 14	Fees: Franchise - $7.5K	Lease Negotiation Assistance: . . . . .Yes
Total Units (As of 8/31/1992): 20	Royalty: 3.5%, Advert: 1.5%	Co-operative Advertising: . . . . . . .Yes
Projected New Units for 1993: 3	Contract Periods (Yrs.): 5/5	Training: . . . . . . 1 Wk. Company Store,
Distribution: US-18;Can-0;Overseas-2	Area Development Agreement: Yes/Var	. . . . 1 Wk. Franchisee Store
North America: . . . . 4 States	Sub-Franchise Contract: . . . . . Yes	On-Going Support: b,C,D,E,G,h/ 9
Concentration: . . . 16 in CA, 1 in SD, 1 in AL	Expand in Territory: . . . . . . Yes	EXPANSION PLANS:
Registered: . . . . CA,SD	Passive Ownership: . . . Not Allowed	US: . . . . All US
. . . .	Encourage Conversions: . . . . Yes	Canada: . . . . .All Canada
Type Space: . . . . FS, SF, SC;~800-1,200 SF	Average # Employees: . . 1 FT, 6 PT	Overseas: . . . . JA, KO, CH

POP'N STUFF

631 Parkway, Baskins Sq. Mall, # A-8
Gatlinburg, TN 37738
TEL: (800) 735-5440 (615) 436-7230
FAX: (615) 436-7230
Mr. Larry G. Hammond, President

POP'N STUFF is a specialty popcorn, candy, coffee and gift store that sells to the public and to companies on both a retail and wholesale level, as well as mail order.

HISTORY:	FINANCIAL: Earnings Claim: . Yes	FRANCHISOR TRAINING/SUPPORT:
Established in 1987; . . 1st Franchised in 1988	Cash Investment: $40K	Financial Assistance Provided: . . . . .No
Company-Owned Units (As of 8/31/1992): . .1	Total Investment: $85-150K	Site Selection Assistance: . . . . . . .Yes
Franchised Units (As of 8/31/1992): 0	Fees: Franchise - $5K	Lease Negotiation Assistance: . . . . .Yes
Total Units (As of 8/31/1992): 1	Royalty: 5.5%, Advert: 1%	Co-operative Advertising: . . . . . . .Yes
Projected New Units for 1993: 6	Contract Periods (Yrs.): . . . 10/10	Training: . . . . Up to 30 Days Head-
Distribution: US-1;Can-0;Overseas-0	Area Development Agreement: Yes/10	. . . . quarters
North America: . . . . .1 State	Sub-Franchise Contract: . . . . . Yes	On-Going Support: a,B,C,E,F,G,h,I/ . . . 2
Concentration: . . . . 1 in TN	Expand in Territory: . . . . Yes	EXPANSION PLANS:
Registered: . . . . . . Registration in Process	Passive Ownership: . . . . .Allowed	US: . . . . .All US
. . . .	Encourage Conversions: . . . . Yes	Canada: . . . . .All Canada
Type Space: . . RM,Specialty Mall;~1,500 SF	Average # Employees: . . 2 FT, 4 PT	Overseas: . . . . No

SANGSTER'S HEALTH CENTRE

P.O. Box 996
Yorkton, SK S3N 2X3 CAN
TEL: (306) 783-9177
FAX: (306) 783-3331
Mr. R. Sangster, President

SANGSTER'S HEALTH CENTRES offer quality, name-brand vitamins along with assorted bulk nuts and candies. All major health companies are also carried. Increased buying power gives maximum profits.

HISTORY:	FINANCIAL: Earnings Claim: . . .	FRANCHISOR TRAINING/SUPPORT:
Established in 1971; . . 1st Franchised in 1978	Cash Investment: $10K	Financial Assistance Provided: . . . . . No
Company-Owned Units (As of 8/31/1992): . .5	Total Investment: $50-75K	Site Selection Assistance: . . . . . . .Yes
Franchised Units (As of 8/31/1992): 8	Fees: Franchise - $15K	Lease Negotiation Assistance: . . . .Yes
Total Units (As of 8/31/1992): 13	Royalty: 5%, Advert: 2%	Co-operative Advertising: . . . . . . .Yes
Projected New Units for 1993: 3	Contract Periods (Yrs.): 5/5	Training: . . . . .1-2 Wks.
Distribution: US-0;Can-13;Overseas-0	Area Development Agreement: .No	. . . .
North America: . . . . 3 Provinces	Sub-Franchise Contract: . . . . .No	On-Going Support: B,D,E,F,G,I/ 20
Concentration: . . .10 in SK, 2 in MB, 1 in AB	Expand in Territory: . . . . Yes	EXPANSION PLANS:
Registered: . . . . AB	Passive Ownership: . . . Discouraged	US: . . . . No
. . . .	Encourage Conversions: . . . . Yes	Canada: . . . . .All Canada
Type Space: . . . . RM;~600 SF	Average # Employees: . . 1 FT, 2 PT	Overseas: . . . . No

SCHLOTZSKY'S DELI

200 W. Fourth St.
Austin, TX 78701
TEL: (800) 950-8419 (512) 480-9871
FAX: (512) 477-2897
Mr. Kelly Arnold, Natl. Sales Mgr.

SCHLOTZSKY'S DELI is a franchised restaurant serving a menu of sandwiches, pizza and salads on SCHLOTZSKY'S baked-fresh daily sourdough bread. Restaurants are designed to provide fresh, clean environments, with in-store bakery. The design is estimated to cost $120,000 with a sales to investment ratio in excess of 2.5 to 1.

HISTORY:	FINANCIAL: Earnings Claim: . Yes	FRANCHISOR TRAINING/SUPPORT:
Established in 1971; . . 1st Franchised in 1977	Cash Investment: $40-60K	Financial Assistance Provided: . . . Yes(I)
Company-Owned Units (As of 8/31/1992): . .1	Total Investment: $120-190K	Site Selection Assistance: . . . . . . .Yes
Franchised Units (As of 8/31/1992): 256	Fees: Franchise - $15K	Lease Negotiation Assistance: . . . . .Yes
Total Units (As of 8/31/1992): 257	Royalty: 6%, Advert: 1%	Co-operative Advertising: . . . . . . .Yes
Projected New Units for 1993: 100	Contract Periods (Yrs.): 20/10	Training: . . . . . .2 Wks. TX Site, 2 Wks.
Distribution: US-255;Can-2;Overseas-0	Area Development Agreement: Yes/50	. . . . . .Las Vegas, 2 Wks. Atlanta, GA
North America: . . . . 25 States, 2 Provinces	Sub-Franchise Contract: . . . . . Yes	On-Going Support: B,C,D,E,F,G,H/ . . 33
Concentration: . .132 in TX, 17 in OK, 14 NM	Expand in Territory: . . . . Yes	EXPANSION PLANS:
Registered: . . . . . . All States Exc. RI & SD	Passive Ownership: . . . Not Allowed	US: . . . . .All US
. . . .	Encourage Conversions: . . . . Yes	Canada: . . . . .All Canada
Type Space: . . . .FS, SF, SC, RM;~1,600 SF	Average # Employees: . .2 FT, 12 PT	Overseas: . . . . EUR, Pacific Rim

SECOND CUP, THE

3300 Bloor St. W., Box 54
Etobicoke, ON M8X 2X3 CAN
TEL: (416) 236-0053
FAX: (416) 236-0054
Ms. Patricia Phelan,, Mgr. of Fran.

Specialty coffees and teas.

HISTORY:	FINANCIAL: Earnings Claim: . . .	FRANCHISOR TRAINING/SUPPORT:
Established in 1975; . . 1st Franchised in 1975	Cash Investment: $60-80K	Financial Assistance Provided: . . . Yes(I)
Company-Owned Units (As of 8/31/1992): . .2	Total Investment: $175-220K	Site Selection Assistance: . . . . . . .Yes
Franchised Units (As of 8/31/1992): 172	Fees: Franchise - $20K	Lease Negotiation Assistance: . . . . .Yes
Total Units (As of 8/31/1992): 174	Royalty: 9%, Advert: 2%	Co-operative Advertising: . . . . . . .Yes
Projected New Units for 1993: 14	Contract Periods (Yrs.): 10	Training: . . . . . .14 Days Headquarters
Distribution: US-0;Can-174;Overseas-0	Area Development Agreement: . .No	. . . .
North America: . . . . 10 Provinces	Sub-Franchise Contract: . . . . .No	On-Going Support: C,D,E,F,G,H/ 60
Concentration: . . . . ON, AB, BC	Expand in Territory: . . . . Yes	EXPANSION PLANS:
Registered: . . . . AB	Passive Ownership: . . . Not Allowed	US: . . . . .No
. . . .	Encourage Conversions:	Canada: . . . . BC and Ontario
Type Space: . . . . SF, RM;~ SF	Average # Employees: 3-4 FT, 8-9 PT	Overseas: . . . . No

SMOOTHIE KING

2725 Mississippi Ave., # 7
Metairie, LA 70003
TEL: (504) 467-4006
FAX: (504) 469-1274
Mr. Richard Leveille, Jr., Fran. Dir.

Nutritional fruit formulas that are low in calories and have no cholesterol or saturated fat, as well as weight-gain formulas. Full line of vitamin, protein and diet supplements and all the latest trends in sports medicine.

HISTORY: . . . . IFA	FINANCIAL: Earnings Claim: . .No	FRANCHISOR TRAINING/SUPPORT:
Established in 1973; . . 1st Franchised in 1988	Cash Investment: $62-101K	Financial Assistance Provided: . . . . .No
Company-Owned Units (As of 8/31/1992): . .0	Total Investment: $62-101K	Site Selection Assistance: . . . . .Yes
Franchised Units (As of 8/31/1992): 26	Fees: Franchise - $15K	Lease Negotiation Assistance: . . . . .Yes
Total Units (As of 8/31/1992): 26	Royalty: 5%, Advert: 2%	Co-operative Advertising: . . . . .Yes
Projected New Units for 1993: 20	Contract Periods (Yrs.): 5/5	Training: . . . . .1 Wk. Headquarters,
Distribution: US-26;Can-0;Overseas-0	Area Development Agreement: Yes/Var	. . . . .1 Wk. On-Site
North America: . . . . 2 States	Sub-Franchise Contract: . . . . .No	On-Going Support: B,C,D,E,G,H/ 7
Concentration: . . . . . . .25 in LA, 1 in TX	Expand in Territory: . . . . Yes	EXPANSION PLANS:
Registered: . . . . .FL	Passive Ownership: . . . Discouraged	US: . . . . .All US
. . . .	Encourage Conversions: . . . . . .No	Canada: . . . . .No
Type Space: . . . . . FS, SF, SC;~1,200 SF	Average # Employees: . . 4 FT, 6 PT	Overseas: . . . . No

STEAK-OUT

8210 Stephanie Dr.
Huntsville, AL 35802
TEL: (205) 883-2300
FAX: (205) 883-4300
Ms. Shannon Belew, Fran. Licensing

We specialize in delivering charbroiled steaks, burgers and chicken, and, if you're wondering, the food is always piping hot - we guarantee it! People absolutely love our combination of quality food and service and free delivery.

HISTORY:	FINANCIAL: Earnings Claim: . Yes	FRANCHISOR TRAINING/SUPPORT:
Established in 1986; . . 1st Franchised in 1987	Cash Investment: $114-164K	Financial Assistance Provided: . . . Yes(I)
Company-Owned Units (As of 8/31/1992): . .4	Total Investment: $114-164K	Site Selection Assistance: . . . . . . .Yes
Franchised Units (As of 8/31/1992): 32	Fees: Franchise - $21.5K	Lease Negotiation Assistance: . . . . .Yes
Total Units (As of 8/31/1992): 36	Royalty: 4%, Advert: 2%	Co-operative Advertising: . . . . . . .NA
Projected New Units for 1993: 24	Contract Periods (Yrs.): 10/10	Training: . . . . . .8-10 Wks. Headquarters
Distribution: US-36;Can-0;Overseas-0	Area Development Agreement: Yes/Var	. . . .
North America: . . . . 8 States	Sub-Franchise Contract: . . . . .No	On-Going Support: C,D,E,G,H/ 17
Concentration: . . . 11 in AL, 7 in FL, 6 in TN	Expand in Territory: . . . . Yes	EXPANSION PLANS:
Registered: . . . . .FL,IN,VA	Passive Ownership: . . . Discouraged	US: . . . . . . .SE, SW and Mid-Atlantic
. . . .	Encourage Conversions: . . . . . NA	Canada: . . . . .No
Type Space: . . . . .FS, SC;~1,400 SF	Average # Employees: . .6 FT, 14 PT	Overseas: . . . . No

STUFF 'N TURKEY

15 Engle St., # 302
Englewood, NJ 07631
TEL: (800) 332-2229 (201) 871-0370
FAX: (201) 871-7168
Mr. John Sterns, Sales Mgr.

Specialty deli operation, offering fresh-roasted turkey dishes and sandwiches, along with fresh-glazed ham dishes. Also offers related menu items.

HISTORY: . . . .
Established in 1986; . . 1st Franchised in 1987
Company-Owned Units (As of 8/31/1992): . .7
Franchised Units (As of 8/31/1992): 14
Total Units (As of 8/31/1992): 21
Projected New Units for 1993: 12
Distribution: US-21;Can-0;Overseas-0
North America: . . . .
Concentration: . . . 4 in FL, 3 in VA, 2 in MD
Registered: . . . . . CA,FL,IL,MD,MI,NY,VA
. . . .
Type Space: . . . . . . .SC, RM; ~500-750 SF

FINANCIAL: Earnings Claim: . .No
Cash Investment: $50-60K
Total Investment: $163-193K
Fees: Franchise - $25K
Royalty: 5%, Advert: 0%
Contract Periods (Yrs.): . . . 20/10
Area Development Agreement: . Yes
Sub-Franchise Contract: . . . . .No
Expand in Territory: . . . . . . Yes
Passive Ownership: . . . Not Allowed
Encourage Conversions: . . . . .No
Average # Employees: . . 2 FT, 5 PT

FRANCHISOR TRAINING/SUPPORT:
Financial Assistance Provided: . . . Yes(I)
Site Selection Assistance: . . . . . . .Yes
Lease Negotiation Assistance: . . . . .Yes
Co-operative Advertising: . . . . . . .Yes
Training: . . . .1 Day HQ, 1 Wk. Company
. . . . .Store, 1 Wk. Franchisee Location
On-Going Support: C,D,E,G,H,I/ . . . . .
EXPANSION PLANS:
US: . . . . .All US
Canada: . . . . .All Canada
Overseas: . . . . No

TEA MASTERS
- AN INTERNATIONAL CAFE

789 Don Mills Rd., # 606
Don Mills, ON M3C 1T5 CAN
TEL: (416) 429-4242
FAX: (416) 429-0078
Mr. Sid Gladstone, Fran. Dir.

An up-scale gourmet store (take-out and/or eat-in) selling high-quality gourmet coffees and teas, fresh baked goods, desserts, sandwiches, soups and salads. Also, gourmet coffee beans and teas by weight and pre-packaged, plus an assortment of giftware and accessories.

HISTORY: . . . .
Established in 1979; . . 1st Franchised in 1983
Company-Owned Units (As of 8/31/1992): . .6
Franchised Units (As of 8/31/1992): 15
Total Units (As of 8/31/1992): 21
Projected New Units for 1993: 4
Distribution: US-0;Can-21;Overseas-0
North America: . . . . .1 Province
Concentration: . . . . 21 in ON
Registered: . . . .
. . . .
Type Space: SF, RM, Off. Bldg; ~500-1,500 SF

FINANCIAL: Earnings Claim: . .No
Cash Investment: $60-110K
Total Investment: $150-225K
Fees: Franchise - $25K
Royalty: 6%, Advert: 2%
Contract Periods (Yrs.): 10/5
Area Development Agreement: . .No
Sub-Franchise Contract: . . . . . .No
Expand in Territory: . . . . . . Yes
Passive Ownership: . . . Discouraged
Encourage Conversions: . . . . . Yes
Average # Employees: 4-7 FT, 2-4 PT

FRANCHISOR TRAINING/SUPPORT:
Financial Assistance Provided: . . . Yes(I)
Site Selection Assistance: . . . . . . .Yes
Lease Negotiation Assistance: . . . .Yes
Co-operative Advertising: . . . . . . .Yes
Training: . . . . 1 1/2 Wks. Corporate
. . . Store, 1/2 Wk. HQ, 1 1/2 Wks. Site
On-Going Support: a,B,C,D,E,F,G,H/ . .6
EXPANSION PLANS:
US: . . . . .No
Canada: . . . . .Ontario
Overseas: . . . . No

THINNY DELITES

100 Old York Rd., # A-700
Jenkintown, PA 19046
TEL: (215) 887-9770
FAX: (215) 887-0499
Mr. Ron Greber, CEO

Healthy fast foods and "non-fat ice cream."

HISTORY: . . . .
Established in 1987; . . 1st Franchised in 1989
Company-Owned Units (As of 8/31/1992): . .1
Franchised Units (As of 8/31/1992): 7
Total Units (As of 8/31/1992): 8
Projected New Units for 1993: 6
Distribution: US-8;Can-0;Overseas-0
North America: . . . . .1 State
Concentration: . . . . 8 in PA
Registered: . . . . .FL
. . . .
Type Space: FS, SF, SC, RM; ~1,200-1,800 SF

FINANCIAL: Earnings Claim: . .No
Cash Investment: $40K
Total Investment: $103-139K
Fees: Franchise - $12K
Royalty: 3%, Advert: 3%
Contract Periods (Yrs.): 15/10
Area Development Agreement: Yes/15
Sub-Franchise Contract: . . . . . Yes
Expand in Territory: . . . . . . .No
Passive Ownership: . . . Discouraged
Encourage Conversions: . . . . NA
Average # Employees: . . 2 FT, 4 PT

FRANCHISOR TRAINING/SUPPORT:
Financial Assistance Provided: . . . Yes(I)
Site Selection Assistance: . . . . . . .Yes
Lease Negotiation Assistance: . . . .Yes
Co-operative Advertising: . . . . . . .Yes
Training: . . . . . . 10 Days Headquarters,
. . . . .10 Days On-Site
On-Going Support: C,D,E,F,G,H/ 8
EXPANSION PLANS:
US: . . . . Northeast
Canada: . . . . No
Overseas: . . . . No

WEE-BAG-IT DELIVERY EMPORIUMS

2200 Corporate Blvd., NW, # 317
Boca Raton, FL 33431
TEL: (800) 533-7161 (407) 994-3994
FAX: (407) 994-4334
Mr. David M. Klein, President

Unique franchise makes and delivers quality, up-scale breakfast, lunch and dinner to the home and office. Also provides corporate catering. Eclectic, healthy foods - soups, salads, sandwiches, hot entrees and hot and cold breakfasts.

HISTORY:	FINANCIAL: Earnings Claim: . Yes	FRANCHISOR TRAINING/SUPPORT:
Established in 1989; . . 1st Franchised in 1990	Cash Investment: $67-134K	Financial Assistance Provided: . . . . .No
Company-Owned Units (As of 8/31/1992): . .2	Total Investment: $67-134K	Site Selection Assistance: . . . . .Yes
Franchised Units (As of 8/31/1992): 2	Fees: Franchise - $15K	Lease Negotiation Assistance: . . . . .Yes
Total Units (As of 8/31/1992): 4	Royalty: 5%, Advert: 2%	Co-operative Advertising: . . . . . . .Yes
Projected New Units for 1993: 5	Contract Periods (Yrs.): 10/5/5	Training: . . . . 3 Wks. Headquarters
Distribution: US-4;Can-0;Overseas-0	Area Development Agreement: Yes/2	. . . .
North America: . . . . .1 State	Sub-Franchise Contract: . . . . .No	On-Going Support: C,D,E,F,h,I/ 5
Concentration: . . . . 4 in FL	Expand in Territory: . . . . Yes	EXPANSION PLANS:
Registered: . . . . .FL,IL,MD	Passive Ownership: . . . Discouraged	US: . . . . NE, SE, TX and Midwest
. . . .	Encourage Conversions: . . . . . Yes	Canada: . . . . .Yes
Type Space: . SF, SC, Hi-Rise;~800-1,200 SF	Average # Employees: . 4 FT, 4-6 PT	Overseas: . . . . EUR

SUPPLEMENTAL LISTING OF FRANCHISORS

ALPEN PANTRY . . . . 1748 Independence Blvd., # C6, Sarasota, FL 33580
    Contact: President; Tel:
AMERICAN BULK FOOD . . . . .22451 Michigan Ave., Dearborn, MI 48124
    Contact: Mr. Martin Benson; Tel: (313) 277-1010
BARNIE'S COFFEE & TEA COMPANY . . . . .340 N. Primrose Dr., Orlando, FL 32803
    Contact: Mr. Rick Sickles; Tel: (407) 894-1418
BOARDWALK PEANUT SHOPPE . . . . . P.O. Box 749, 10th St. & Boardwalk, Ocean City, NJ 08226
    Contact: Mr. Leo Yeager, III, President; Tel: (800) 527-2430 (609) 399-3359
BROWN BAG DELI . . . . 701 Smithfield St., # 400, Pittsburgh, PA 15222
    Contact: President; Tel: (412) 566-1795
BULK BARN FOODS . . . . 230 Ferrier St., Markham, ON L3R 2Z5   CAN
    Contact: Ms. Paula Rodrigues; Tel: (416) 477-5916
BYGONE DAZE CONCEPTS . . . . .1418 Wakenhurst Cres., Oakville, ON L6J 6P8   CAN
    Contact: Mr. Phil Passy; Tel: (416) 829-0040
CALIFORNIA SMOOTHIE . . . . 1700 Rte. 23, # 120, Wayne, NJ 07470
    Contact: Mr. Robert Keilt, President; Tel: (201) 696-7200 (305) 325-8385
CANDY EXPRESS . . . . 8601 Georgia Ave., # 501, Silver Spring, MD 20910
    Contact: Mr. Joel Rosenberg; Tel: (800) 658-8848 (301) 587-5500
CAROLE'S CHEESECAKE COMPANY . . . . .1272 Castlefield Ave., Toronto, ON M6B 1G3   CAN
    Contact: Mr. Michael Ch. Ogus, EVP; Tel: (416) 256-0000
CHEESE SHOP INTERNATIONAL . . . . 255 Greenwich Ave., Greenwich, CT 06830
    Contact: Mr. James Stevens, President; Tel: (203) 661-1090
COFFEE MERCHANT, THE . . . . P.O. Box 2159, Sandpoint, ID 83864
    Contact: President; Tel:
COFFEE WAY, THE . . . . .123 Rexdale Blvd., Rexdale, ON M9W 1P3   CAN
    Contact: Mr. Roger G. Garneau; Tel: (416) 741-4144
DEAN'S CHOCOLATES & CAPPUCCINO BAR . . . . . . .7621 Vantage Way, Delta, BC V4G 1A6   CAN
    Contact: Mr. Henry Hudel, VP; Tel: (604) 946-1116
DEL'S POPCORN SHOP . . . . 142 Merchant St., Decatur, IL 62523
    Contact: Ms. Trudy Jacobs, Mgr.; Tel: (217) 429-0037
DESSERT CART, THE . . . . 600 Upland Ave., Upland, PA 19015
    Contact: Mr. James Kelly; Tel: (215) 499-7453
EDELWIESS DELICATESSEN . . . . 7 - 3331 Viking Way, Richmond, BC V6V 1X7   CAN
    Contact: Mr. Wayne Hampton; Tel: (604) 270-2360 (604) 275-DELI
ERNIE'S LIQUORS . . . . P. O. Box 525, Rutherford, CA 94573
    Contact: Mr. Ernie Van Asperen; Tel: (707) 963-9573
FANNY FARMER CANDY SHOPS . . . . 5885 Grant Ave., Cleveland, OH 44105
    Contact: President; Tel: (617) 275-1300

FIGARO'S FRESH-TO-BAKE PIZZA . . . . . 1500 Liberty St., SE, P.O. Box 12575, Salem, OR 97309
    Contact: Mr. Ken Robertson, President; Tel: (503) 371-9318
FLYING FRUIT FANTASY . . . . 16 S. Frederick, # 400, Baltimore, MD 21202
    Contact: Mr. Robert Groth, President; Tel: (301) 539-1711
FOREMOST LIQUOR STORES . . . . 5252 N. Broadway, Chicago, IL 60640
    Contact: Ms. Gail Zelitzky, President; Tel: (800) 621-5150 (312) 334-0077
FRONTIER FRUIT & NUT CO. . . . . 3823 Wadsworth Rd., Norton, OH 44203
    Contact: Mr. Raymond J. Karee, President; Tel: (216) 825-7835
GIULIO'S DELI EXPRESS . . . . 1117 E. Walnut St., Carson, CA 90746
    Contact: Mr. Howard J. Kastle; Tel: (213) 537-7700
HICKORY FARMS OF OHIO . . . . 1505 Holland Rd., Maumee, OH 43537
    Contact: Mr. Richard A. Steinbock; Tel: (419) 893-7611
HOUSE OF ALMONDS . . . . .11344 Coloma Rd., # 750, Gold River, CA 96815
    Contact: Mr. Berch Richard, Dir. Fran. Dev.; Tel: (800) 678-9648 (916) 635-2929
INTERNATIONAL CONNOISSEUR, THE . . . . . 201 Torance Blvd., Redondo Beach, CA 90277
    Contact: Mr. Sanford French, President; Tel: (213) 374-9768
JERKY HUT . . . . Hamlet Rt. 934, Seaside, OR 97138
    Contact: President; Tel: (800) 223-5759
KARMELKORN . . . . P.O. Box 39286, Minneapolis, MN 55439
    Contact: Mr. John Hyduke, VP Fran. Dev.; Tel: (612) 830-0312
KAYSERS HEALTH BARS . . . . 3890 La Cumbre Plaza Ln., Santa Barbara, CA 93105
    Contact: Mr. Terry M. Staten, President; Tel: (800)242-FLIP(CA) (805)682-3747
KELLY'S COFFEE & FUDGE FACTORY . . . . 15251 Barranca Pkwy., Irvine, CA 92718
    Contact: Mr. Terry Kelly, President; Tel: (714) 727-3764
LIBERTY PRODUCTS . . . . 329 Parkridge Ave., Orange Park, FL 32065
    Contact: Mr. Robert Haitt; Tel: (904) 272-5598
LOGAN FARMS HONEY GLAZED HAM . . . . . . 10001 Westheimer, # 1040, Houston, TX 77042
    Contact: Mr. Pink Logan, President; Tel: (800) 833-HAMS (713) 781-3773
LOLLYPOPS UNLIMITED . . . . 1409 Tatum Dr., Newburn, NC 28560
    Contact: President; Tel:
M & M MEAT SHOPS . . . . 640 Trillium Dr., Kichener, ON N2R 1E6   CAN
    Contact: Mr. Greg Voisin; Tel: (519) 895-1075
MOM'S BAKE AT HOME PIZZA . . . . 4457 Main St., Philadelphia, PA 19127
    Contact: Mr. Nicholas Castellolli; Tel: (215) 596-7763
MORROW CANDY & YOGURT . . . . .11344 Coloma Rd., # 750, Gold River, CA 95670
    Contact: Mr. Berch Richard, Dir. Fran. Dev.; Tel: (800) 678-9648 (916) 635-2929
MRS. EMM'S ALL NATURAL HEALTH STORES . . . . . 1907 Greentree Rd., Cherry Hill, NJ 08003
    Contact: Mr. Al Hirsh; Tel: (609) 424-7711
NIXON'S DELI . . . . 6426 Baum Dr., # E, Knoxville, TN 37919
    Contact: President; Tel:
NUT KETTLE CANDY KITCHEN, THE . . . . 7723 Summerset Blvd., Paramont, CA 90723
    Contact: Ms. Sally J. White, Dir. Ops.; Tel: (800) 677-1968 (310) 633-6200
NUT MAN, THE . . . . 47 Heisser Ln., Farmingdale, NY 11735
    Contact: Mr. David Goldberg, EVP; Tel: (800) 229-4053 (516) 454-6460
NUTTER'S BULK & NATURAL FOODS . . . # 107 - 1601 Dunmore Rd., SE, Medicine Hat, AB T1A 1Z8   CAN
    Contact: Mr. Donald Cranston; Tel: (403) 529-1664
OLDE WORLD CHEESE SHOP . . . . .3333 S. Pasadena Ave., S. Pasadena, FL 33707
    Contact: Mr. Jud Scott; Tel: (813) 360-6931
OMA'S SOFT PRETZELS . . . . 1120 Fairview Ave., Wyomissing, PA 19610
    Contact: Mr. Robert Logan; Tel: (215) 374-5785
PICOLO'S . . . . 300 Lenora St., # B 357, Seattle, WA 98121
    Contact: Mr. Bill Southwell, President; Tel:
PICOLO'S PIZZA . . . . 421 N. I St., Madera, CA 93637
    Contact: Mr. Stephen L. Frazier; Tel: (209) 673-0435
POPS-U-BAKE PIZZA TO GO/JOHNNY QUIK . . . . . . 7955 N. Cedar Ave., Fresno, CA 93710
    Contact: Mr. Ernie Beal; Tel: (209) 432-1405
POTATO MANIA . . . . .600 Broadway, # 690, Kansas City, MO 64105
    Contact: Mr. Larry K. Childers; Tel: (816) 421-1855
PRIMMERS' COUNTRY STORE . . . . 406 West 9th St., Vinton, IA 52349
    Contact: President; Tel: (319) 472-3582
RALPH ROTTEN'S NUT POUND . . . . 790 New York Ave., Huntington, NY 11743
    Contact: Mr. Irving K. Schwartz, VP/Counsel; Tel: (516) 421-4343
RANELLI'S DELI & SANDWICH SHOP . . . . 2134 Warrior Rd., Birmingham, AL 35208
    Contact: Mr. Frank Ranelli, President; Tel: (205) 785-4196
ROCKY MOUNTAIN CHOCOLATE FACTORY . . . P. O. Box 2408, 265 Turner Dr., Durango, CO 81302
    Contact: Mr. Franklin Crail, President; Tel: (303) 259-0554

SEATECH CORP. . . . . 5305 Shilshole Ave., NW, Seattle, WA 98107
    Contact: President; Tel: (206) 782-6007
STRICTLY SUGARLESS CANDIES . . . . .2516 Indian Ridge Dr., Glenview, IL 60025
    Contact: Mr. Norm Lieber; Tel: (708) 205-0020
SWISS COLONY STORES . . . . 1 Alpine Ln., Monroe, WI 53566
    Contact: Mr. Eugene Curran, Exec. Dir. Fran.; Tel: (608) 328-8555
TAKEOUT TAXI . . . . .1175 Herndon Pkwy., # 150, Herndon, VA 22070
    Contact: Ms. Pat Caldwell-Wilson, Fran. Dev.; Tel: (800) 374-3773 (703) 689-4800
TRA-HANS CANDIES . . . . 530 E. Central Blvd., # 1105, Orlando, FL 32801
    Contact: President; Tel:
TREETOP . . . . P. O. Box 248, Selah, WA 98942
    Contact: President; Tel:
TROPIK SUN FRUIT & NUT . . . . .910 Sherwood Dr., # 13, Lake Bluff, IL 60044
    Contact: Mr. Lou Garriott, Dir. Fran. Sales; Tel: (708) 234-3407
TUDOR'S BISCUIT WORLD . . . . P. O. Box 3603, Charleston, VW 25336
    Contact: President; Tel: (304) 343-4026
U. S. SNACK FOODS . . . . P. O. Box 1180, Seaside, OR 97138
    Contact: President; Tel: (503) 738-9066
WIFE SAVER . . . . 2751 New Barton Chapel Rd., Augusta, GA 30906
    Contact: President; Tel: (404) 798-5897

For a full explanation of the data provided in

the Franchisor Format, please refer to Chapter 2,

"How To Use The Data."

CHAPTER 20

RETAIL FOOD:
QUICK SERVICE / TAKE-OUT

1 POTATO 2

5640 International Pkwy.
New Hope, MN 55428
TEL: (800) 333-8034 (612) 537-3833
FAX: (612) 537-4241
Mr. Todd D. King, VP Fran.

1 POTATO 2 owns and franchises restaurants specializing in baked potato entrees with a variety of hot toppings, and several snack potato items. The restaurants are located exclusively in regional shopping malls and downtown office centers.

HISTORY: . . . .
Established in 1977;   . . 1st Franchised in 1984
Company-Owned Units (As of 8/31/1992):   . 24
Franchised Units (As of 8/31/1992): 40
Total Units (As of 8/31/1992): 64
Projected New Units for 1993: 8
Distribution: US-64;Can-0;Overseas-0
  North America: . . . . 22 States
  Concentration: . . 14 in CA, 9 in MN, 6 in WI
Registered: . . CA,IL,MD,MI,MN,NY,OR,WI
. . . .
Type Space: . . . . RM;~550 SF

FINANCIAL: Earnings Claim: . Yes
Cash Investment: $40-80K
Total Investment: $110-160K
Fees: Franchise - $20K
  Royalty: 4.5%, Advert: . . . 1.25%
Contract Periods (Yrs.): 10/10
Area Development Agreement: Yes/Var
Sub-Franchise Contract: . . . . . .No
Expand in Territory: . . . . .No
Passive Ownership: . . . Discouraged
Encourage Conversions: . . . . . Yes
Average # Employees: 2-3 FT, 6-8 PT

FRANCHISOR TRAINING/SUPPORT:
Financial Assistance Provided: . . .Yes(D)
Site Selection Assistance: . . . . .Yes
Lease Negotiation Assistance: . . . . .Yes
Co-operative Advertising: . . . . .Yes
Training: . . . . . . .14 Days Headquarters
. . . .
On-Going Support: a,B,C,D,E,F,G,H,I/ . 15
EXPANSION PLANS:
US: . . Midwest,Farwest,NE,NW,Mid-At
Canada: . . . . .No
Overseas: . . . . No

RESTAURANTS – ALL TYPES

	1989	1990	1991	Percentage Change 90/89	Percentage Change 91/90
Total Number of Establishments:					
Company–Owned	27,596	29,152	30,533	5.64%	4.74%
Franchisee–Owned	64,359	70,188	72,780	9.06%	3.69%
Total	91,955	99,340	103,313	8.03%	4.00%
Ratio of Total Establishments:					
Company–Owned	30.0%	29.3%	29.6%		
Franchisee–Owned	70.0%	70.7%	70.4%		
Total	100.0%	100.0%	100.0%		
Total Sales ($000):					
Company–Owned	25,490,936	27,901,355	30,498,783	9.46%	9.31%
Franchisee–Owned	44,622,772	49,954,288	54,998,628	11.95%	10.10%
Total	70,113,708	77,855,643	85,497,411	11.04%	9.82%
Ratio of Total Sales:					
Company–Owned	36.4%	35.8%	35.7%		
Franchisee–Owned	63.6%	64.2%	64.3%		
Total	100.0%	100.0%	100.0%		
Average Sales Per Unit ($000):					
Company–Owned	924	957	999	3.61%	4.37%
Franchisee–Owned	693	712	756	2.65%	6.18%
Total	762	784	828	2.79%	5.59%
Relative Average Sales Ratio:	133.2%	134.5%	132.2%		

	Number Of Employees	Employees Per Unit	Avg. Sales Per Employee
Total 1989 Employment:			
Company–Owned	859,934	31.2	$29,643
Franchisee–Owned	2,027,421	31.5	$22,010
Total	2,887,355	31.4	$24,283
Relative Employee Performance Ratios:		98.9%	134.7%

	1st Quartile	Median	4th Quartile
Average 1989 Total Investment:			
Company–Owned	$162,300	$350,000	$654,000
Franchisee–Owned	$140,000	$267,500	$500,000
Single Unit Franchise Fee	$17,250	$20,000	$32,500
Mult. Unit Franchise Fee	$12,500	$17,500	$30,000
Franchise Start–Up Cost	$45,000	$80,000	$130,000

Source: Franchising In The Economy 1991, IFA Educational Foundation & Horwath International.

A & W RESTAURANTS

17197 N. Laurel Park Dr.
Livonia, MI 48152
TEL: (800) 222-2337 (313) 462-0029
FAX: (313) 462-1017
Mr. J. Bryan Stephens, Fran. Sales Dir.

Through the years, A & W has undergone many changes to keep pace with a changing world. With the changes, we have become stronger. Our current direction is designed to fit today's demand for smaller, non-traditional sites, i.e. shopping malls, offices, universities and convenience stores. Our menu consists of high-quality fast food. Burgers, chicken, fries and beverages.

HISTORY: . . . .
Established in 1919; . . 1st Franchised in 1925
Company-Owned Units (As of 8/31/1992): . 12
Franchised Units (As of 8/31/1992): 704
Total Units (As of 8/31/1992): 716
Projected New Units for 1993: 24
Distribution: US-641;Can-0;Overseas-75
  North America: . . . . 34 States
  Concentration: . .76 in MI, 57 in CA, 63 in WI
Registered: . . . CA,FL,IL,IN,MD,MI,MN,NY
 . . . . OR,RI,VA,WA,WI,DC
Type Space: . . . . . .FS, RM;~400-1,700 SF

FINANCIAL: Earnings Claim: . Yes
Cash Investment: $50-75K
Total Investment: $100-450K
Fees: Franchise - $15K
  Royalty: 4%, Advert: 4%
Contract Periods (Yrs.): . . . 20/20
Area Development Agreement: . .No
Sub-Franchise Contract: . . . . . .No
Expand in Territory: . . . . Yes
Passive Ownership: . . . . . .Allowed
Encourage Conversions: . . . . . Yes
Average # Employees: . . . .

FRANCHISOR TRAINING/SUPPORT:
Financial Assistance Provided: . . . . .No
Site Selection Assistance: . . . . .No
Lease Negotiation Assistance: . . . . .Yes
Co-operative Advertising: . . . . .Yes
Training: . . . . . .1 Wk. Corporate Office,
 . . . . 5 Wks. OJT in Restaurants
On-Going Support: B,C,D,E,G,H,I/ . . . 48
EXPANSION PLANS:
US: . . . . .Midwest and West
Canada: . . . . Canadian Entity
Overseas: Separate Overseas Entity

BALDINOS GIANT JERSEY SUBS

760 Elaine St.
Hinesville, GA 31313
TEL: (912) 368-2822
FAX: (912) 369-3923
Mr. Bill Baer, President/CEO

Quality submarine sandwiches with in-store bakery. All subs sliced fresh as ordered in full view of customer, served on freshly-baked rolls. Built for volume business at a "fast food" pace by use of multi-production lines. Variety of 20 hot and cold subs and freshly-baked gourmet cookies.

HISTORY: . . . .
Established in 1975; . . 1st Franchised in 1984
Company-Owned Units (As of 8/31/1992): . .6
Franchised Units (As of 8/31/1992): 19
Total Units (As of 8/31/1992): 25
Projected New Units for 1993: 3
Distribution: US-25;Can-0;Overseas-0
  North America: . . . . 3 States
  Concentration: . . .13 in GA, 9 in NC, 3 in SC
Registered: . . . . .FL
 . . . .
Type Space: . . . . . . FS;~1,800-2,000 SF

FINANCIAL: Earnings Claim: . .No
Cash Investment: $50-75K
Total Investment: $90-150K
Fees: Franchise - $10K
  Royalty: 4.5%, Advert: 1/2%
Contract Periods (Yrs.): . . . 15/10
Area Development Agreement: Yes/15+
Sub-Franchise Contract: . . . . . Yes
Expand in Territory: . . . . Yes
Passive Ownership: . . . . . Discouraged
Encourage Conversions: . . . . . . Yes
Average # Employees: . .8 FT, 12 PT

FRANCHISOR TRAINING/SUPPORT:
Financial Assistance Provided: . . . . .No
Site Selection Assistance: . . . . .Yes
Lease Negotiation Assistance: . . . . .Yes
Co-operative Advertising: . . . . .Yes
Training: . . . . 4 Wks. Headquarters
 . . . .
On-Going Support: B,C,D,E,F,G,H,I/ . . . 4
EXPANSION PLANS:
US: . . . . .GA, SC, NC and FL
Canada: . . . . .No
Overseas: . . . . No

BASSETT'S ORIGINAL TURKEY

P. O. Box 40016
Philadelphia, PA 19106
TEL: (800) 282-8875 (215) 922-4614
FAX: (215) 922-7182
Mr. Roger Bassett, President

Join the exciting new franchise of the 1990's, featuring fresh roasted turkey. At BASSETT'S, we use only the highest-quality ingredients to make our sandwiches and platters. You must see it and taste it to believe it!

HISTORY: . . . . .IFA
Established in 1983; . . 1st Franchised in 1989
Company-Owned Units (As of 8/31/1992): . .4
Franchised Units (As of 8/31/1992): 8
Total Units (As of 8/31/1992): 12
Projected New Units for 1993: 10
Distribution: US-12;Can-0;Overseas-0
  North America: . . . . 5 States
  Concentration: . . . .8 in PA, 1 in FL, 1 in VA
Registered: . . . . . . .CA,FL,IL,MD,NY,VA
 . . . .
Type Space: . . . . .FS;~2,000 SF

FINANCIAL: Earnings Claim: . Yes
Cash Investment: $45-75K
Total Investment: $168-311K
Fees: Franchise - $21K
  Royalty: 5%, Advert: 1%
Contract Periods (Yrs.): . . . 15/10
Area Development Agreement: . Yes/5
Sub-Franchise Contract: . . . . . .No
Expand in Territory: . . . . Yes
Passive Ownership: . . . Discouraged
Encourage Conversions: . . . . . Yes
Average # Employees: . . 5 FT, 5 PT

FRANCHISOR TRAINING/SUPPORT:
Financial Assistance Provided: . . . Yes(I)
Site Selection Assistance: . . . . .Yes
Lease Negotiation Assistance: . . . . .Yes
Co-operative Advertising: . . . . .Yes
Training: . . . . .7 Days Penn Center,
 . . . . .10 Days On-Site
On-Going Support: B,C,D,E,G,H,I/ 4
EXPANSION PLANS:
US: . . . . .Northeast and South
Canada: . . . . .No
Overseas: . . . . No

BEEFY'S

P. O. Box 18412
Knoxville, TN 37928
TEL: (615) 689-7394
FAX:
Mr. Charles R. Montgomery

Double drive-thru restaurant with walk-up window and picnic tables, specializing in quality 1/4 lb. hamburgers, grilled chicken sandwiches, crispy fries and soft drinks at reasonable prices. Unique building design, using modular or on-site construction.

HISTORY: . . . .
Established in 1984; . . 1st Franchised in 1985
Company-Owned Units (As of 8/31/1992): . .1
Franchised Units (As of 8/31/1992): 21
Total Units (As of 8/31/1992): 22
Projected New Units for 1993: 10
Distribution: US-22;Can-0;Overseas-0
  North America: . . . . 6 States
  Concentration: . . .12 in TN, 3 in KY, 3 in AL
Registered: . . . . CA,FL,IL,IN,NY,ND,VA
. . . .
Type Space: . . . . FS;~17,000 SF

FINANCIAL: Earnings Claim: . .No
Cash Investment: $50-60K
Total Investment: $195-225K
Fees: Franchise - $10K
  Royalty: 3%, Advert: 1%
Contract Periods (Yrs.): 20/10
Area Development Agreement: Yes/20
Sub-Franchise Contract: . . . . . Yes
Expand in Territory: . . . . . . Yes
Passive Ownership: . . . Discouraged
Encourage Conversions: . . . . . .No
Average # Employees: . .3 FT, 15 PT

FRANCHISOR TRAINING/SUPPORT:
Financial Assistance Provided: . . . Yes(I)
Site Selection Assistance: . . . . . . .Yes
Lease Negotiation Assistance: . . . . .Yes
Co-operative Advertising: . . . . . . .Yes
Training: . . . . 3 Wks. Headquarters
. . . .
On-Going Support: C,D,E,G,H,I/ 7
EXPANSION PLANS:
  US: . . . . .All US
  Canada: . . . . .No
  Overseas: . . . . No

BENNETT'S PIT BAR-B-QUE

6551 S. Revere Pkwy., # 285
Englewood, CO 80111
TEL: (303) 792-3088
FAX: (303) 792-5801
Mr. Jim W. Conway, VP Fran.

Real hickory-smoked Bar-B-Que. Both full-service and food court. Franchise opportunities. Full support systems, training, design and purchasing.

HISTORY: . . . .
Established in 1984; . . 1st Franchised in 1989
Company-Owned Units (As of 8/31/1992): . .5
Franchised Units (As of 8/31/1992): 19
Total Units (As of 8/31/1992): 24
Projected New Units for 1993: 8
Distribution: US-24;Can-0;Overseas-0
  North America: . . . . 7 States
  Concentration: . . . 9 in CO, 4 in CA, 4 in TN
Registered: . . . CA,FL,IL,IN,MD,MI,NY,WI
. . . . VA
Type Space: . . . . . .FS, RM;~550-6,400 SF

FINANCIAL: Earnings Claim: . . Yes
Cash Investment: $50-200K
Total Investment: $300-660K
Fees: Franchise - $25K
  Royalty: 4-5%, Advert: 1%
Contract Periods (Yrs.): 10/10
Area Development Agreement: Yes/Var
Sub-Franchise Contract: . . . . . Yes
Expand in Territory: . . . . . . Yes
Passive Ownership: . . . Discouraged
Encourage Conversions: . . . . . Yes
Average # Employees:2-10 FT, 4-40 PT

FRANCHISOR TRAINING/SUPPORT:
Financial Assistance Provided: . . . . .Yes
Site Selection Assistance: . . . . . . .Yes
Lease Negotiation Assistance: . . . . .Yes
Co-operative Advertising: . . . . .No
Training: . . . . . . .8 Wks. Full Service, 4
  . . . Wks. Limited Service, Both Denver
On-Going Support: a,B,C,D,E,F,/ 10
EXPANSION PLANS:
  US: . . . . .All US
  Canada: . . . . .Yes
  Overseas: . . . . Yes

BLIMPIE

1775 The Exchange, # 215
Atlanta, GA 30339
TEL: (800) 447-6256 (404) 984-2707
FAX: (404) 980-9176
Mr. Dennis G. Fuller, VP

National submarine sandwich chain, serving fresh-sliced, high-quality meats and cheeses on fresh-baked bread. Also offering an assortment of fresh-made salads and other quality products. Over 60% growth in last 3 years. Opening one new restaurant every 3 days. Offering single, multi-unit and Area Development opportunities.

HISTORY: . . . .
Established in 1964; . . 1st Franchised in 1971
Company-Owned Units (As of 8/31/1992): . .0
Franchised Units (As of 8/31/1992): 497
Total Units (As of 8/31/1992): 497
Projected New Units for 1993: 225
Distribution: US-497;Can-0;Overseas-0
  North America: . . . . 35 States
  Concentration: . . 115 in NY, 89 in GA, 41 FL
Registered: . . . .CA,FL,HI,IL,IN,MI,MN,NY
. . . . OR,RI,WA,WI
Type Space: FS, SF, SC, RM;~1,000-1,200 SF

FINANCIAL: Earnings Claim: . .No
Cash Investment: $50-60K
Total Investment: $90-120K
Fees: Franchise - $18K
  Royalty: 6%, Advert: 3%
Contract Periods (Yrs.): . . .20/Open
Area Development Agreement: Yes/50
Sub-Franchise Contract: . . . . . Yes
Expand in Territory: . . . . . . Yes
Passive Ownership: . . . . . .Allowed
Encourage Conversions: . . . . NA
Average # Employees: . . 3 FT, 1 PT

FRANCHISOR TRAINING/SUPPORT:
Financial Assistance Provided: . . . Yes(I)
Site Selection Assistance: . . . . . . .Yes
Lease Negotiation Assistance: . . . . .Yes
Co-operative Advertising: . . . . .Yes
Training: . . . . .1 Wk. Headquarters,
  . . . . 2 Wks. Region, 2 Wks. In-Store
On-Going Support: C,D,E,F,G,h,I/ . . . 46
EXPANSION PLANS:
  US: . . . . .All US
  Canada: . . . . .All Canada
  Overseas: . . UK, GR, Pacific Rim

BOARDWALK FRIES

8307 Main St.
Ellicott City, MD 21212
TEL: (410) 465-5020
FAX: (301) 465-5213
Mr. J. Alan Hansen, Fran. Sales Rep.

Unique fast-food concept, specializing in fresh-cut fries, burgers, hot dogs, grilled chicken and fresh-squeezed lemonade. Mall locations available in food court and in-lines, with an exciting sit-down concept. The largest retail french fry chain in the US. Offers unlimited opportunity for the dedicated owner/operator. Declare your independence and join the industry leader today.

HISTORY: . . . . IFA
Established in 1981; . . 1st Franchised in 1985
Company-Owned Units (As of 8/31/1992): . 10
Franchised Units (As of 8/31/1992): 66
Total Units (As of 8/31/1992): 76
Projected New Units for 1993: 12
Distribution: US-76;Can-0;Overseas-0
North America: . . . . 17 States
Concentration: . . .18 in MD, 9 in CA, 9 in FL
Registered: . . . . . CA,FL,IL,MD,MI,VA,DC
. . . .
Type Space: . . . Food Court, RM;~Varies SF

FINANCIAL: Earnings Claim: . .No
Cash Investment: $45-112K
Total Investment: $90-225K
Fees: Franchise - $25K
Royalty: 7%, Advert: 2%
Contract Periods (Yrs.): 10/10
Area Development Agreement: Yes/Var
Sub-Franchise Contract: . . . . . .No
Expand in Territory: . . . . Yes
Passive Ownership: . . . Not Allowed
Encourage Conversions: . . . . . Yes
Average # Employees: . . 4 FT, 8 PT

FRANCHISOR TRAINING/SUPPORT:
Financial Assistance Provided: . . . . . No
Site Selection Assistance: . . . . .Yes
Lease Negotiation Assistance: . . . . .Yes
Co-operative Advertising: . . . . .Yes
Training: . . . . . 11 Days Corporate Office
. . . . and On-The-Job Training
On-Going Support: B,C,D,E,F,G,H/ . . 30
EXPANSION PLANS:
US: . . . . . Mid-Atlantic, CA, Southeast
Canada: . . . . .No
Overseas: . . . . AU, JA, MX

BOX LUNCH, THE

P. O. Box 666
Truro, MA 02666
TEL: (508) 349-3509
FAX: (508) 349-3661
Mr. Owen MacNutt, President

THE BOX LUNCH sandwich shops produce rolled pita sandwiches of a very high quality to the broad lunch market. Young and old marvel at our speed, quality and cleanliness. The rolled sandwiches are made to order in seconds from fresh ingredients.

HISTORY: . . . .
Established in 1977; . . 1st Franchised in 1981
Company-Owned Units (As of 8/31/1992): . .1
Franchised Units (As of 8/31/1992): 7
Total Units (As of 8/31/1992): 8
Projected New Units for 1993: 2
Distribution: US-8;Can-0;Overseas-0
North America: . . . . 2 States
Concentration: . . . . 7 in MA, 1 in ME
Registered: . . . .
. . . .
Type Space: . . . FS, SF, SC;~1,000-1,200 SF

FINANCIAL: Earnings Claim: . .No
Cash Investment: $70-85K
Total Investment: $70-85K
Fees: Franchise - $15K
Royalty: 4.5%, Advert: 2%
Contract Periods (Yrs.): . . . 20/Life
Area Development Agreement: . Yes
Sub-Franchise Contract: . . . . Yes
Expand in Territory: . . . . . . Yes
Passive Ownership: . . . Discouraged
Encourage Conversions: . . . . NA
Average # Employees:2-20 FT, 2-20 PT

FRANCHISOR TRAINING/SUPPORT:
Financial Assistance Provided: . . . . .NA
Site Selection Assistance: . . . . .Yes
Lease Negotiation Assistance: . . . . .Yes
Co-operative Advertising: . . . . .Yes
Training: . . . . . . 6-8 Wks. Headquarters
. . . .
On-Going Support: B,C,D,E,G,H/ 5
EXPANSION PLANS:
US: . . . . New England
Canada: . . . . .No
Overseas: . . . . No

BREADEAUX PISA

Frederick Ave. at 23rd, PO Box 6158
St. Joseph, MO 64506
TEL: (816) 364-1088
FAX: (816) 364-3739
Mr. John R. Jarrett, CEO

BREADEAUX PISA is a rapidly growing, carry-out pizza franchise. Pizzas are made with a unique french bread style crust and all-natural ingredients. Menu includes gourmet and dessert pizzas. Average investment is one of the lowest in the industry.

HISTORY: . . . . IFA
Established in 1985; . . 1st Franchised in 1985
Company-Owned Units (As of 8/31/1992): . .2
Franchised Units (As of 8/31/1992): 77
Total Units (As of 8/31/1992): 79
Projected New Units for 1993: 30
Distribution: US-79;Can-0;Overseas-0
North America: . . . . 6 States
Concentration: . . .52 in IA, 8 in NE, 8 in MO
Registered: . . . . IL,MN,SD,WI
. . . .
Type Space: . . . . SF, SC;~Varies SF

FINANCIAL: Earnings Claim: . .No
Cash Investment: $35-50K
Total Investment: $65-100K
Fees: Franchise - $15K
Royalty: 5%, Advert: 3%
Contract Periods (Yrs.): . . . 10/10
Area Development Agreement: . Yes
Sub-Franchise Contract: . . . . .No
Expand in Territory: . . . . . . Yes
Passive Ownership: . . . Not Allowed
Encourage Conversions: . . . . NA
Average # Employees: 2-4 FT, 6-10 PT

FRANCHISOR TRAINING/SUPPORT:
Financial Assistance Provided: . . . Yes(I)
Site Selection Assistance: . . . . .Yes
Lease Negotiation Assistance: . . . . .No
Co-operative Advertising: . . . . .No
Training: . . . . .1 Wk. Headquarters,
. . . . .1 Wk. On-Site, On-Going
On-Going Support: a,B,C,D,E,F,G,H/ . . .
EXPANSION PLANS:
US: . . . . Midwest Only
Canada: . . . . .No
Overseas: . . . . No

BROWN'S CHICKEN & PASTA

2809 Butterfield Rd., # 360
Oakbrook, IL 60154
TEL: (708) 571-5300
FAX: (708) 571-5378
Mr. Frank Portillo, Jr., President

Fast-food restaurant, offering fried chicken, pasta, sandwiches and salads.

HISTORY: . . . .
Established in 1964; . . 1st Franchised in 1965
Company-Owned Units (As of 8/31/1992): . 25
Franchised Units (As of 8/31/1992): 82
Total Units (As of 8/31/1992): 107
Projected New Units for 1993: 2
Distribution: US-107;Can-0;Overseas-0
  North America: . . . . 4 States
  Concentration: . . . . 98 in IL, 6 in FL, 2 in IN
Registered: . . . . FL,IL,IN,WI
. . . .
Type Space: . . . . . FS, SC;~1,500-2,500 SF

FINANCIAL: Earnings Claim: . Yes
Cash Investment: $100-150K
Total Investment: $160-675K
Fees: Franchise - $25K
  Royalty: 5% Max., Advert: 4%
Contract Periods (Yrs.): 15/5
Area Development Agreement: . .No
Sub-Franchise Contract: . . . . .No
Expand in Territory: . . . . . . .No
Passive Ownership: . . . Not Allowed
Encourage Conversions: . . . . . Yes
Average # Employees: . .3 FT, 10 PT

FRANCHISOR TRAINING/SUPPORT:
Financial Assistance Provided: . . . Yes(I)
Site Selection Assistance: . . . . .Yes
Lease Negotiation Assistance: . . . . .Yes
Co-operative Advertising: . . . . .Yes
Training: . . . 8 Wks. HQ. (Once a Week),
  . . . . . 8 Wks. Various Training Stores
On-Going Support: a,B,c,d,e,f,G,H/ . . . 30
EXPANSION PLANS:
  US: . . . . Midwest
  Canada: . . . . No
  Overseas: . . . . No

BURGER BROTHERS

456 Main St.
Penticton, BC V2A 5C5 CAN
TEL: (604) 492-5600
FAX: (604) 492-5600
Mr. Frank Webb, President

Fast food from free-standing, drive-thru modular buildings with drive-thru and interior seats. Broiled hamburgers and chicken, crispy coated fries, desserts and breakfast. Outstanding quality food and service. Computerized cash systems. Ideal for small communities. Nutrition and environmental concerns reflected in food and packaging.

HISTORY: . . . .
Established in 1986; . . 1st Franchised in 1987
Company-Owned Units (As of 8/31/1992): . .1
Franchised Units (As of 8/31/1992): 7
Total Units (As of 8/31/1992): 8
Projected New Units for 1993: 5
Distribution: US-0;Can-8;Overseas-0
  North America: . . . . 2 Provinces
  Concentration: . . . . 7 in BC, 1 in AB
Registered: . . . . WA
. . . .
Type Space: . . . . FS;~1,150 SF

FINANCIAL: Earnings Claim: . .No
Cash Investment: $112.5-150K
Total Investment: $200-365K
Fees: Franchise - $12.5K
  Royalty: 4%, Advert: 0%
Contract Periods (Yrs.): 15/15
Area Development Agreement: Yes/15
Sub-Franchise Contract: . . . . . Yes
Expand in Territory: . . . . Yes
Passive Ownership: . . . Discouraged
Encourage Conversions: . . . . . .No
Average # Employees: . .8 FT, 10 PT

FRANCHISOR TRAINING/SUPPORT:
Financial Assistance Provided: . . . Yes(I)
Site Selection Assistance: . . . . .Yes
Lease Negotiation Assistance: . . . . .Yes
Co-operative Advertising: . . . . .Yes
Training: . . . . 2 Wks. Headquarters
. . . .
On-Going Support: C,D,E,F,G,H,I/ 3
EXPANSION PLANS:
  US: . . . . .All US
  Canada: . . . . .All Canada
  Overseas: . . . . .Asia, AU, EUR

BURGER KING CORPORATION

17777 Old Cutler Rd.
Miami, FL 33157
TEL: (800) 258-6696 (305) 378-7303
FAX: (305) 378-7383
Mr. Frank Paci, Sr. Dir. Fran.

BURGER KING is a highly-recognized worldwide brand, with over 6,400 points of distribution. New, lower cost facility design and flexible ownership guidelines continue to make BURGER KING an attractive franchise investment.

HISTORY: . . . . IFA
Established in 1954; . . 1st Franchised in 1956
Company-Owned Units (As of 8/31/1992): 1058
Franchised Units (As of 8/31/1992): 5326
Total Units (As of 8/31/1992): 6384
Projected New Units for 1993: 400
Distribution: . US-5559;Can-197;Overseas-628
  North America: . . . . 50 States,10 Provinces
  Concentration: . 559 in CA, 441 in FL, 341 NY
Registered: . . . . .All
. . . .
Type Space: FS,SF,SC,RM,Kiosk;~120-2,800 SF

FINANCIAL: Earnings Claim: . .No
Cash Investment: $180-250K
Total Investment: . . . $200K-1.0MM
Fees: Franchise - $40K
  Royalty: 3.5%, Advert: 4%
Contract Periods (Yrs.): 20
Area Development Agreement: . .No
Sub-Franchise Contract: . . . . . .No
Expand in Territory: . . . . Yes
Passive Ownership: . . . . .Allowed
Encourage Conversions: . . . . . Yes
Average # Employees: . .3 FT, 50 PT

FRANCHISOR TRAINING/SUPPORT:
Financial Assistance Provided: . . . Yes(I)
Site Selection Assistance: . . . . .Yes
Lease Negotiation Assistance: . . . . .Yes
Co-operative Advertising: . . . . . . .Yes
Training: . . . . 5 Wks. 22 Regional
. . . . .Centers
On-Going Support: B,C,D,E,G,h,I/ . . .650
EXPANSION PLANS:
  US: . . . . All US
  Canada: . . . . .All Canada
  Overseas: . Operate in 41 Countries

CAFE SALADS ETC.

4300 N. Miller Rd., # 143
Scottsdale, AZ 85251
TEL: (800) 472-5170 (602) 946-2939 C
FAX: (602) 946-1061
Mr. Robert L. Drake, President

We are one of the very few franchises that specializes in salads as main entrees. Our customers have the pleasure of being served in lieu of them having to stand in line and build their own salad at a salad bar. Grease is not on our menu because we are a health-oriented restaurant! We don't require costly hoods or exhaust systems. This opens the door to many locations not available to other restaurants. Investment is low. Training is easy.

HISTORY:	FINANCIAL: Earnings Claim: . .No	FRANCHISOR TRAINING/SUPPORT:
Established in 1992; . . 1st Franchised in 1992	Cash Investment: $25-75K	Financial Assistance Provided: . . . Yes(I)
Company-Owned Units (As of 8/31/1992): . .0	Total Investment: $50-129K	Site Selection Assistance: . . . . . . .Yes
Franchised Units (As of 8/31/1992): 0	Fees: Franchise - $10K	Lease Negotiation Assistance: . . . .Yes
Total Units (As of 8/31/1992): 0	Royalty: 5%, Advert: 1.5%	Co-operative Advertising: . . . . . . .No
Projected New Units for 1993: 15	Contract Periods (Yrs.): 15/5	Training: . . . . 2 Wks. Headquarters,
Distribution: US-0;Can-0;Overseas-0	Area Development Agreement: Yes/15	. . . . . . .2 Wks. Franchisee Restaurant
North America:	Sub-Franchise Contract: . . . . . .No	On-Going Support: B,C,D,E,F,G,I/ 4
Concentration:	Expand in Territory: . . . . Yes	EXPANSION PLANS:
Registered:	Passive Ownership: . . . . . .Allowed	US: . . . . All US
. . . .	Encourage Conversions: . . . . . Yes	Canada: . . . . .No
Type Space: . . . SF, SC, RM;~500-3,000 SF	Average # Employees: 2-5 FT, 5-15 PT	Overseas: . . . . No

CAFE SUPREME

1233 Rue de la Montagne, # 201
Montreal, PQ H3G 1Z2 CAN
TEL: (514) 875-9803
FAX: (514) 875-9899
Mr. Sam Huq, GM

Combining the European cafe tradition with quality, convenience and attractive surroundings. The right ingredients for North American taste.

HISTORY: . . . . .CFA	FINANCIAL: Earnings Claim: . . .	FRANCHISOR TRAINING/SUPPORT:
Established in 1979; . . 1st Franchised in 1980	Cash Investment: $75K	Financial Assistance Provided: . . . . .No
Company-Owned Units (As of 8/31/1992): . .2	Total Investment: $150-250K	Site Selection Assistance: . . . . . . .Yes
Franchised Units (As of 8/31/1992): 35	Fees: Franchise - $25K	Lease Negotiation Assistance: . . . .Yes
Total Units (As of 8/31/1992): 37	Royalty: 5%, Advert: 2%	Co-operative Advertising: . . . . . . .Yes
Projected New Units for 1993: 5	Contract Periods (Yrs.): 5-10/5	Training: . . . . 3 Wks. Headquarters
Distribution: US-0;Can-37;Overseas-0	Area Development Agreement: . .No	. . . .
North America: . . . . 3 Provinces	Sub-Franchise Contract: . . . . . Yes	On-Going Support: C,D,E/ 5
Concentration: . . .34 in PQ, 2 in ON, 1 in NB	Expand in Territory: . . . . Yes	EXPANSION PLANS:
Registered:	Passive Ownership:	US: . . . . .No
. . . .	Encourage Conversions: . . . . .No	Canada: . . . . .Ontario
Type Space: SF, RM, Off. Bldg;~500-1,200 SF	Average # Employees: . 2-3 FT, 2 PT	Overseas: . . . . No

CAP'N TACO

P. O. Box 415
North Olmsted, OH 44070
TEL: (216) 676-9100
FAX:
Mr. Raymond Brown, Chairman

CAP'N TACO has developed a unique niche in fast-food marketing: our service is 35 seconds, our dining room is full-service, our price structure is competitive with the quick-service segment. We are Mexican, however, our restaurants are theme-oriented - multi-TV's, pictures, games, promotions. Our food is also different from most - we use only white mild cheese and a unique blend of secret spices that makes our beef "spreadable."

HISTORY:	FINANCIAL: Earnings Claim: . Yes	FRANCHISOR TRAINING/SUPPORT:
Established in 1976; . . 1st Franchised in 1987	Cash Investment: $15K	Financial Assistance Provided: . . . Yes(I)
Company-Owned Units (As of 8/31/1992): . .2	Total Investment: $95-120K	Site Selection Assistance: . . . . . . .Yes
Franchised Units (As of 8/31/1992): 2	Fees: Franchise - $15K	Lease Negotiation Assistance: . . . .Yes
Total Units (As of 8/31/1992): 4	Royalty: 5%, Advert: 2%	Co-operative Advertising: . . . . . . .Yes
Projected New Units for 1993: 2	Contract Periods (Yrs.): 10/10	Training: . . . . . 2 Wks. Brook Park, OH,
Distribution: US-2;Can-0;Overseas-0	Area Development Agreement: . .No	. . . . .Plus Annual Classes
North America: . . . . .1 State	Sub-Franchise Contract: . . . . . .No	On-Going Support: b,C,D,E,F,G,H/ 4
Concentration: . . . . 2 in OH	Expand in Territory: . . . . Yes	EXPANSION PLANS:
Registered:	Passive Ownership: . . . Not Allowed	US: . . . . All US
. . . .	Encourage Conversions: . . . . . Yes	Canada: . . . . .No
Type Space: . . . .FS, SF, SC, RM;~1,800 SF	Average # Employees: . .2 FT, 10 PT	Overseas: . . . . No

CAPTAIN D'S SEAFOOD

1717 Elm Hill Pike
Nashville, TN 37210
TEL: (800) 346-9637 (615) 391-9325
FAX: (615) 391-9765
Mr. Larry F. Stein, Dir. Fran.

Quick-service dine-in or take-out seafood restaurant, serving baked, broiled and fried fish, shrimp and chicken entrees with a variety of vegetables and desserts.

HISTORY: . . . . IFA	FINANCIAL: Earnings Claim: . Yes	FRANCHISOR TRAINING/SUPPORT:
Established in 1969; . . 1st Franchised in 1969	Cash Investment: $175K	Financial Assistance Provided: . . . . .No
Company-Owned Units (As of 8/31/1992): 357	Total Investment: $495-690K	Site Selection Assistance: . . . . .Yes
Franchised Units (As of 8/31/1992): . . . 288	Fees: Franchise - $25K	Lease Negotiation Assistance: . . . .Yes
Total Units (As of 8/31/1992): 645	Royalty: 3%, Advert: 6%	Co-operative Advertising: . . . . .Yes
Projected New Units for 1993: 30	Contract Periods (Yrs.): 20/20	Training: . . . . 6 Wks. Headquarters
Distribution: US-645;Can-0;Overseas-0	Area Development Agreement: Yes/Var	. . . .
North America: . . . . 25 States	Sub-Franchise Contract: . . . . . .No	On-Going Support: a,b,C,d,e,F,G,h,I/ . . . .
Concentration: . 93 in GA, 85 in TN, 63 in AL	Expand in Territory: . . . . Yes	EXPANSION PLANS:
Registered: . . . . All States	Passive Ownership: . . . . . .Allowed	US: . . . . NE, NW, SW and W
. . . .	Encourage Conversions: . . . . .No	Canada: . . . . .All Exc. Alberta
Type Space: . . . . .FS;~2,200 SF	Average # Employees: . . . . 20 FT	Overseas: . . . . . Starting in 1992

CAPTAIN TONY'S PIZZA
& PASTA EMPORIUM

2990 Culver Rd.
Rochester, NY 14622
TEL: (800) 332-TONY (716) 467-2250
FAX: (716) 467-0784
Mr. Michael J. Martella, President

Pizza and pasta take-out, delivery, full-service. Low franchise fee. Low royalty. High emphasis on quality, variety and service.

HISTORY:	FINANCIAL: Earnings Claim: . .No	FRANCHISOR TRAINING/SUPPORT:
Established in 1985; . . 1st Franchised in 1986	Cash Investment: $50K	Financial Assistance Provided: . . . . .No
Company-Owned Units (As of 8/31/1992): . .0	Total Investment: $50-200K	Site Selection Assistance: . . . . .Yes
Franchised Units (As of 8/31/1992): 18	Fees: Franchise - $9.5K	Lease Negotiation Assistance: . . . . .No
Total Units (As of 8/31/1992): 18	Royalty: 4-5%, Advert: 2%	Co-operative Advertising: . . . . .Yes
Projected New Units for 1993: 3	Contract Periods (Yrs.): 20/5	Training: . . . . . . .Up to 3 Wks. Training
Distribution: US-15;Can-0;Overseas-3	Area Development Agreement: Yes/20	. . . . . . Center, Up to 1 Wk. On-Site
North America: . . . . 5 States	Sub-Franchise Contract: . . . . . Yes	On-Going Support: C,D,E,G,H,I/ 4
Concentration: . . . 6 in NY, 5 in CA, 3 in OH	Expand in Territory: . . . . Yes	EXPANSION PLANS:
Registered: . . . . . CA,FL,IL,MD,MI,NY,VA	Passive Ownership: . . . Discouraged	US: . . . . .All US
. . . .	Encourage Conversions: . . . . . Yes	Canada: . . . . .Ontario
Type Space: . . . . .SF, SC;~1,200 SF	Average # Employees: . .2 FT, 10 PT	Overseas: . . . .~ EUR

CASSANO'S PIZZA & SUBS

1700 E. Stroop Rd.
Dayton, OH 45429
TEL: (513) 294-8400
FAX: (513) 294-8107
Mr. Nelson Barksdale, Fran. Rep.

CASSANO'S PIZZA & SUBS is an independently-owned chain of pizza & sub shops located primarily in Ohio, also in KY, IL and MO. The menu at CASSANO'S restaurants features pizza prepared to customers' orders from a selection of a variety of ingredients, as well as Italian food. CASSANO'S provides on-premises dining and take-out service, but all items are available for delivery. Some sell party supplies.

HISTORY: . . . . IFA	FINANCIAL: Earnings Claim: . Yes	FRANCHISOR TRAINING/SUPPORT:
Established in 1953; . . 1st Franchised in 1962	Cash Investment: $50-75K	Financial Assistance Provided: . . . . .No
Company-Owned Units (As of 8/31/1992): . 49	Total Investment: $128-258K	Site Selection Assistance: . . . . .Yes
Franchised Units (As of 8/31/1992): 11	Fees: Franchise - $10K	Lease Negotiation Assistance: . . . . .Yes
Total Units (As of 8/31/1992): 60	Royalty: 4%, Advert: 1/2%	Co-operative Advertising: . . . . .Yes
Projected New Units for 1993: 20	Contract Periods (Yrs.): 10/5/5	Training: . . . . 4 Wks. Dayton, OH
Distribution: US-60;Can-0;Overseas-0	Area Development Agreement: Yes/10	. . . .
North America: . . . . 4 States	Sub-Franchise Contract: . . . . . .No	On-Going Support: B,C,D,E,F,G,H,I/ . . 35
Concentration: . . 56 in OH, 2 in KY, 1 in MO	Expand in Territory: . . . . Yes	EXPANSION PLANS:
Registered: IL	Passive Ownership: . . . Not Allowed	US: . . . . .Midwest Region
. . . .	Encourage Conversions: . . . . . Yes	Canada: . . . . No
Type Space: . . FS, SC, RM;~1,500-2,200 SF	Average # Employees: . . 8 FT, 7 PT	Overseas: . . . . No

CHEEBURGER CHEEBURGER

2413 Periwinkle Way
Sanibel, FL 33957
TEL: (813) 472-6111
FAX: (813) 472-5620
Ms. Tina M. Bailey, Dir. Training

New concept. Fun and easy. No experience needed. Low start-up costs compared to most restaurants.

HISTORY:	FINANCIAL: Earnings Claim: . .No	FRANCHISOR TRAINING/SUPPORT:
Established in 1986; . . 1st Franchised in 1990	Cash Investment: $100-150K	Financial Assistance Provided: . . . . .NA
Company-Owned Units (As of 8/31/1992): . .2	Total Investment: $100-150K	Site Selection Assistance: . . . . . . .Yes
Franchised Units (As of 8/31/1992): 7	Fees: Franchise - $13.5K	Lease Negotiation Assistance: . . . . . No
Total Units (As of 8/31/1992): 9	Royalty: 4.5-4%, Advert: 0%	Co-operative Advertising: . . . . .NA
Projected New Units for 1993: 3	Contract Periods (Yrs.): 10/5	Training: . . . . .7-12 Days Various
Distribution: US-9;Can-0;Overseas-0	Area Development Agreement: Yes/Var	. . . . .Locations
North America: . . . . 2 States	Sub-Franchise Contract: . . . . . .No	On-Going Support: b,C,D,E,F,G,I/ 5
Concentration: . . . . .8 in FL, 1 in AL	Expand in Territory: . . . . . . .Yes	EXPANSION PLANS:
Registered: . . . . .FL	Passive Ownership: . . . Discouraged	US: . . . . .Florida
. . . .	Encourage Conversions: . . . . . NA	Canada: . . . . .No
Type Space: . . . . .FS, SC;~2,000 SF	Average # Employees:12-14 FT, 3-5 PT	Overseas: . . . . No

CHEF'S FRIED CHICKEN

20 Audobon Oaks
Lafayette, LA 70506
TEL: (318) 233-1621
FAX:
Mr. Lee Shelton, President

Fast-food service, specializing in fried chicken, catfish, shrimp and hamburgers. We offer many side orders to complement our main dishes. We offer drive-thru, as well as sit-down service. Our products have the distinctive cajun taste. Once you try our products, you will be convinced we have the best.

HISTORY:	FINANCIAL: Earnings Claim: . .No	FRANCHISOR TRAINING/SUPPORT:
Established in 1970; . . 1st Franchised in 1974	Cash Investment: $75K	Financial Assistance Provided: . . . . .NA
Company-Owned Units (As of 8/31/1992): . .0	Total Investment: $75-250K	Site Selection Assistance: . . . . . . .Yes
Franchised Units (As of 8/31/1992): 8	Fees: Franchise - $20K	Lease Negotiation Assistance: . . . . .Yes
Total Units (As of 8/31/1992): 8	Royalty: 4%, Advert: 2%	Co-operative Advertising: . . . . . . .NA
Projected New Units for 1993: 2	Contract Periods (Yrs.): . . . 15/15	Training: . . . . 2 Wks. Headquarters
Distribution: US-8;Can-0;Overseas-0	Area Development Agreement: Yes/15	. . . .
North America: . . . . .1 State	Sub-Franchise Contract: . . . . . Yes	On-Going Support: E,F/ . . . .
Concentration: . . . . 8 in LA	Expand in Territory: . . . . . . .No	EXPANSION PLANS:
Registered:	Passive Ownership: . . . Discouraged	US: . . . . .All US
. . . .	Encourage Conversions: . . . Yes	Canada: . . . . .No
Type Space: . . . . FS, RM;~1,600 SF	Average # Employees: . . 6 FT, 3 PT	Overseas: . . . . No

CHICAGO'S PIZZA

1111 N. Broadway
Greenfield, IN
TEL: (317) 462-9878
FAX:
Mr. Robert L. McDonald, CEO

Franchise designed for owner/operator. Flexibility allowed to insure success. Can be adapted to large and small operations. Inside dining/carry-out/delivery.

HISTORY:	FINANCIAL: Earnings Claim: . . .	FRANCHISOR TRAINING/SUPPORT:
Established in 1979; . . 1st Franchised in 1981	Cash Investment: $50K	Financial Assistance Provided: . . . . .No
Company-Owned Units (As of 8/31/1992): . .1	Total Investment: $300K	Site Selection Assistance: . . . . . . .Yes
Franchised Units (As of 8/31/1992): 9	Fees: Franchise - $7K	Lease Negotiation Assistance: . . . . .Yes
Total Units (As of 8/31/1992): 10	Royalty: 4%, Advert: 2%	Co-operative Advertising: . . . . .Yes
Projected New Units for 1993: 4	Contract Periods (Yrs.): 10/10	Training: . . . . . . 4 Wks. Indianapolis, IN
Distribution: US-10;Can-0;Overseas-0	Area Development Agreement: Yes/1	. . . .
North America: . . . . .1 State	Sub-Franchise Contract: . . . . . .No	On-Going Support: C,D,E,F,I/ 4
Concentration: . . . . 10 in IN	Expand in Territory: . . . . Yes	EXPANSION PLANS:
Registered: . . . . .IN	Passive Ownership: . . . Not Allowed	US: . . . . .Indiana Only
. . . .	Encourage Conversions: . . . . Yes	Canada: . . . . .No
Type Space: . . . . . FS, SC;~1,500-3,000 SF	Average # Employees:	Overseas: . . . . No

CHICKEN A-PEEL

915 Market St.
St. Louis, MO 63102
TEL: (314) 231-0400
FAX:
Mr. Al Genovese, President

Up-scale fast-food restaurant, specializing in skinless chicken. We offer fried, roasted and charbroiled chicken. Listed Number 1 in NRN and R & I in 1991 as the Up and Comer.

HISTORY:		FINANCIAL: Earnings Claim: . .No	FRANCHISOR TRAINING/SUPPORT:
Established in 1987; . . 1st Franchised in 1990		Cash Investment: $60K	Financial Assistance Provided: . . .Yes(D)
Company-Owned Units (As of 8/31/1992): . .2		Total Investment: $120K	Site Selection Assistance: . . . . . . .Yes
Franchised Units (As of 8/31/1992): 8		Fees: Franchise - $20K	Lease Negotiation Assistance: . . . . .Yes
Total Units (As of 8/31/1992): 10		Royalty: 4%, Advert: 3%	Co-operative Advertising: . . . . .Yes
Projected New Units for 1993: 30		Contract Periods (Yrs.): . . . 10/10	Training: . . . . . 2-3 Wks. Headquarters
Distribution: US-10;Can-0;Overseas-0		Area Development Agreement: Yes/10	
North America: . . . . 2 States		Sub-Franchise Contract: . . . . Yes	On-Going Support: B,C,D,E,f,G,h/ 3
Concentration: . . . . 2 in MO, 1 in MI		Expand in Territory: . . . . . . Yes	EXPANSION PLANS:
Registered: . . . . CA,MI		Passive Ownership: . . . . .Allowed	US: . . . . All US
		Encourage Conversions: . . . . Yes	Canada: . . . . .Yes
Type Space: . . . .FS, SF, SC, RM;~1,600 SF		Average # Employees: . . 2 FT, 8 PT	Overseas: . . . . .MX

CICI'S PIZZA

1414 W. Randol Mill Rd., # 200
Arlington, TX 76012
TEL: (817) 461-6000
FAX: (817) 461-1333
Mr. Dick Pryor, Fran. Dir.

CICI'S is the most exciting restaurant concept to come along in years! We offer our customers an all-you-can-eat buffet of pizza, pasta, salad and dessert for only $2.99. The great, low price is combined with terrific service, excellent quality and family atmosphere. All of this combines to make CICI'S a regular stop for our customers.

HISTORY:		FINANCIAL: Earnings Claim: . .No	FRANCHISOR TRAINING/SUPPORT:
Established in 1984; . . 1st Franchised in 1990		Cash Investment: $60-70K	Financial Assistance Provided: . . . Yes(I)
Company-Owned Units (As of 8/31/1992): . 10		Total Investment: $150-250K	Site Selection Assistance: . . . . . . .Yes
Franchised Units (As of 8/31/1992): 25		Fees: Franchise - $25K	Lease Negotiation Assistance: . . . . .Yes
Total Units (As of 8/31/1992): 35		Royalty: 4%, Advert: 3%	Co-operative Advertising: . . . . .Yes
Projected New Units for 1993: 35		Contract Periods (Yrs.): . . . 10/10	Training: . . . . . . 4 Wks. Headquarters
Distribution: US-35;Can-0;Overseas-0		Area Development Agreement: Yes/10	
North America: . . . . .1 State		Sub-Franchise Contract: . . . . .No	On-Going Support: b,C,D,E,F,h/ 9
Concentration: . . . . 35 in TX		Expand in Territory: . . . . . . Yes	EXPANSION PLANS:
Registered:		Passive Ownership: . . . Discouraged	US: . . . . . . Southwest, Consider All
		Encourage Conversions: . . . . .No	Canada: . . . . .No
Type Space: . . . . .FS, SC;~3,500 SF		Average # Employees: . 10 FT, 10 PT	Overseas: . . . . No

CONGRESS ROTISSERIE

231 Westmont
West Hartford, CT 06117
TEL: (203) 521-6149
FAX: (203) 521-9294
Mr. Thomas Griffin, Dir. Fran.

CONGRESS ROTISSERIE serves custom-made sandwiches, rotisserie chicken and a variety of homemade soups, salads and desserts. All breads and pastries are baked fresh each morning and we're known for our specially-made dressings. Stores are designed for carry-out service, with limited seating facilities, where appropriate. Freshness and quality of all food products is carefully monitored to ensure customer satisfaction.

HISTORY:		FINANCIAL: Earnings Claim: . .No	FRANCHISOR TRAINING/SUPPORT:
Established in 1986; . . 1st Franchised in 1992		Cash Investment: $30-70K	Financial Assistance Provided: . . . . .No
Company-Owned Units (As of 8/31/1992): . .6		Total Investment: $90-225K	Site Selection Assistance: . . . . . . .Yes
Franchised Units (As of 8/31/1992): 1		Fees: Franchise - $15-20K	Lease Negotiation Assistance: . . . . .Yes
Total Units (As of 8/31/1992): 7		Royalty: 4%, Advert:	Co-operative Advertising: . . . . .Yes
Projected New Units for 1993: 10		Contract Periods (Yrs.): . . . 10/10	Training: . . . . 3 Wks. Headquarters
Distribution: US-7;Can-0;Overseas-0		Area Development Agreement: . .No	
North America: . . . . 2 States		Sub-Franchise Contract: . . . . .No	On-Going Support: a,B,C,D,E,F,H/ . . . 10
Concentration: . . . . 6 in CT, 1 in PA		Expand in Territory: . . . . . . Yes	EXPANSION PLANS:
Registered:		Passive Ownership: . . . Not Allowed	US: . . . . Northeast
		Encourage Conversions: . . . . .No	Canada: . . . . .No
Type Space: FS, SF, SC, RM;~1,000-2,000 SF		Average # Employees: . .4 FT, 10 PT	Overseas: . . . . No

COUSINS SUBMARINES

N83 W13400 Leon Rd.
Menomonee Falls, WI 53051
TEL: (800) 238-9736 (414) 253-7700
FAX: (414) 253-7710
Mr. David K. Kilby, VP Fran. Dev.

Uniquely-developed submarine sandwich operation with over 20 years' experience. Volume-oriented, fast-service concept in an up-scale, in-line strip or free-standing location - some with drive-up windows. Outstanding fresh-baked bread and the finest- quality ingredients go into our hot subs, delicious soups and garden-fresh salads. Now franchising opportunities for a select group of single and multi- unit franchise owners. Area Developments avail.

HISTORY: . . . . IFA
Established in 1972; . . 1st Franchised in 1985
Company-Owned Units (As of 8/31/1992): . 45
Franchised Units (As of 8/31/1992): 74
Total Units (As of 8/31/1992): 119
Projected New Units for 1993: 25
Distribution: US-119;Can-0;Overseas-0
North America: . . . . 3 States
Concentration: . . . . .39 in WI
Registered: . . . . FL,IL,IN,MI,MN,WI
. . . .
Type Space: . . . . . . FS, SF, SC;~1,600 SF

FINANCIAL: Earnings Claim: . .No
Cash Investment: $50-100K
Total Investment: $160-360K
Fees: Franchise - $18.5K
Royalty: 5-4%, Advert: 2%
Contract Periods (Yrs.): 15/15
Area Development Agreement: Yes/Var
Sub-Franchise Contract: . . . . . Yes
Expand in Territory: . . . . . . Yes
Passive Ownership: . . . Not Allowed
Encourage Conversions: . . . . . No
Average # Employees: . .6 FT, 14 PT

FRANCHISOR TRAINING/SUPPORT:
Financial Assistance Provided: . . . Yes(I)
Site Selection Assistance: . . . . . . .Yes
Lease Negotiation Assistance: . . . . .Yes
Co-operative Advertising: . . . . . . .Yes
Training: . . . . . . 4 Wks. Headquarters,
. . . . 10 Days New Restaurant
On-Going Support: B,C,D,E,G,H,I/ . . . . .
EXPANSION PLANS:
US: . . . . Northwest
Canada: . . . . Will Consider
Overseas: . . . . . . Will Consider

CULTURES FRESH FOOD RESTAURANTS

145 Davenport Rd.
Toronto, ON M5R IJ1 CAN
TEL: (416) 968-1440
FAX: (416) 968-6353
Franchise Department

CULTURES is a "fresh food" concept, in which all products are prepared fresh on the premises every day. Salad, soup, sandwiches, a wide variety of baked goods and frozen yogurt specialties make up a Healthy Menu. We are dedicated to providing a "better for you" customer experience by offering great tasting, fresh food. F.A.S.T - friendly, attentive, speedy, thoughtful.

HISTORY: . . . . .CFA
Established in 1977; . . 1st Franchised in 1978
Company-Owned Units (As of 8/31/1992): . 22
Franchised Units (As of 8/31/1992): 39
Total Units (As of 8/31/1992): 61
Projected New Units for 1993: 1
Distribution: US-0;Can-61;Overseas-0
North America: . . . . 5 Provinces
Concentration: . . 52 in ON, 5 in PQ, 2 in MB
Registered: . . . . AB
. . . .
Type Space: . . . . . . SF, RM;~1,200 SF

FINANCIAL: Earnings Claim: . Yes
Cash Investment: $50-100K
Total Investment: $125-225K
Fees: Franchise - $35K
Royalty: 5%, Advert: 2%
Contract Periods (Yrs.): 10/5
Area Development Agreement: . .No
Sub-Franchise Contract: . . . . .No
Expand in Territory: . . . . . . Yes
Passive Ownership: . . . Discouraged
Encourage Conversions: . . . . .No
Average # Employees: 2-8 FT, 6-12 PT

FRANCHISOR TRAINING/SUPPORT:
Financial Assistance Provided: . . . Yes(I)
Site Selection Assistance: . . . . . . .Yes
Lease Negotiation Assistance: . . . .Yes
Co-operative Advertising: . . . . . . .No
Training: . . . . 1 Wk. Headquarters
. . . . . 5 Wks. Corporate Training Store
On-Going Support: B,C,D,E,F,G,H/ . . . .
EXPANSION PLANS:
US: . . . . No
Canada: . . . . .All Canada
Overseas: . . . . No

D'ANGELO SANDWICH SHOPS

321 Manley St.
West Bridgewater, MA 02379
TEL: (800) 848-4422 (508) 583-2116
FAX: (508) 588-3462
Mr. Roy A. Jemison, VP & GM

D'ANGELO SANDWICH SHOPS offer a broad menu of subs, pitas, salads, soup and ice cream/frozen yogurts - including grilled on-premise items. We operate our own bakery (in-store bake-off), meat processing plant and distribution company. D'ANGELO has been in business 25 years and operates 120 restaurants and franchises 40

HISTORY: . . . . IFA
Established in 1967; . . 1st Franchised in 1988
Company-Owned Units (As of 8/31/1992): 120
Franchised Units (As of 8/31/1992): 40
Total Units (As of 8/31/1992): 160
Projected New Units for 1993: 30
Distribution: . . . US-160;Can-0;Overseas-0
North America: . . . . 8 States
Concentration: . 94 in MA, 20 in NH, 19 in RI
Registered: . . . . IL,MD,NY,RI,VA
. . . .
Type Space: . . . . . . SC;~2,000-2,400 SF

FINANCIAL: Earnings Claim: . Yes
Cash Investment: $55-65K
Total Investment: $272-331K
Fees: Franchise - $25-35K
Royalty: 5.2%, Advert: . . . 2.0%
Contract Periods (Yrs.): 20/0
Area Development Agreement: Yes/5+
Sub-Franchise Contract: . . . .No
Expand in Territory: . . . . . . Yes
Passive Ownership: . . . Not Allowed
Encourage Conversions: . . . . Yes
Average # Employees: . .3 FT, 15 PT

FRANCHISOR TRAINING/SUPPORT:
Financial Assistance Provided: . . . Yes(I)
Site Selection Assistance: . . . . . . .Yes
Lease Negotiation Assistance: . . . . .Yes
Co-operative Advertising: . . . . . . .NA
Training: . . . . . 4 Concentrated Wks. HQ
. . . .
On-Going Support: B,C,D,E,F,G,H,I/ . . 99
EXPANSION PLANS:
US: . . . . East Coast
Canada: . . . . No
Overseas: . . . . No

DADDY-O'S EXPRESS DRIVE-THRU

6917 Collins Ave., P. O. Box 414177
Miami Beach, FL 33141
TEL: (800) 487-2729 (305) 866-1904
FAX: (305) 866-0252
Mr. James D. Brockman, VP

A double drive-thru hamburger chain, featuring flame-broiled burgers, bologna, chili dogs, chicken, as well as fries, shakes and drinks. Backed by Arby's, an industry leader in fast food, makes DADDY-O'S the vehicle for success in the 90's and beyond.

HISTORY: . . . .
Established in 1990; . . 1st Franchised in 1990
Company-Owned Units (As of 8/31/1992): . .0
Franchised Units (As of 8/31/1992): 9
Total Units (As of 8/31/1992): 9
Projected New Units for 1993: 15
Distribution: US-9;Can-0;Overseas-0
  North America: . . . . 4 States
  Concentration: . . . .4 in OH, 3 in IL, 1 in GA
Registered: . . . . All States Exc. NY
. . . .
Type Space: . . . . .FS;~ SF

FINANCIAL: Earnings Claim: . .No
Cash Investment: . . . .$
Total Investment: . . . .$
Fees: Franchise - . . . .$
  Royalty: 4%, Advert: 2%
Contract Periods (Yrs.): 20
Area Development Agreement: Yes/5
Sub-Franchise Contract: . . . . .No
Expand in Territory: . . . . . . .No
Passive Ownership: . . . Discouraged
Encourage Conversions: . . . . . .No
Average # Employees: . 10 FT, 20 PT

FRANCHISOR TRAINING/SUPPORT:
Financial Assistance Provided: . . . Yes(I)
Site Selection Assistance: . . . . . . .Yes
Lease Negotiation Assistance: . . . . .Yes
Co-operative Advertising: . . . . . . .Yes
Training: . . . . 1 Wk. HQ - Owner,
  . . . . .1 Wk. Var. Locations - Managers
On-Going Support: B,C,D,E,G,H/ . . .130
EXPANSION PLANS:
US: . . . . .All US
Canada: . . . . No
Overseas: . . . . No

DAIRY QUEEN CANADA

5245 Harvester Rd., P.O. Box 430
Burlington, ON L7R 3Y3 CAN
TEL: (416) 639-1492
FAX: (416) 681-3623
Ms. Jennifer Lang, Fran. Dev. Mgr.

Fast food restaurant, featuring soft-serve products.

HISTORY: . . . .
Established in 1929; . . 1st Franchised in 1929
Company-Owned Units (As of 8/31/1992): . .0
Franchised Units (As of 8/31/1992): . . . . <u>428</u>
Total Units (As of 8/31/1992): 428
Projected New Units for 1993: 12
Distribution: US-0;Can-428;Overseas-0
  North America: . . . . 10 Provinces
  Concentration: . . 146 in ON, 78 in AB, 75 BC
Registered: . . . . AB
. . . .
Type Space: . . . . FS;~3,000 SF

FINANCIAL: Earnings Claim: . .No
Cash Investment: $150-350K
Total Investment: . . . $400K-1.2MM
Fees: Franchise - $30K
  Royalty: 4%, Advert: 3-6%
Contract Periods (Yrs.): . . . . . NA
Area Development Agreement: . .No
Sub-Franchise Contract: . . . . .No
Expand in Territory: . . . . Yes
Passive Ownership: . . . Not Allowed
Encourage Conversions: . . . . . Yes
Average # Employees: . 20 FT, 40 PT

FRANCHISOR TRAINING/SUPPORT:
Financial Assistance Provided: . . . . .No
Site Selection Assistance: . . . . . . .Yes
Lease Negotiation Assistance: . . . . .Yes
Co-operative Advertising: . . . . . . .Yes
Training: . . . . 2 Wks. Headquarters
. . . .
On-Going Support: A,B,C,D,E,F,G,H,I/ 59
EXPANSION PLANS:
US: . . . . .No
Canada: . . . . .All Canada
Overseas: . . . . Yes

DAVE'S PIZZA

#6 - 5579 - 47 St.
Red Deer, AB T4N 1S1 CAN
TEL: (403) 346-7511
FAX: (403) 343-1844
Mr. Dave Nobles, President

21 varieties of pizza, spaghetti, lasagna, subs or full menu. All pizza crusts, sauce, lasagna, spaghetti sauce prepared in central food plant. Allows franchise outlet more flexibility, less equipment, easy to order, more control, less waste, easy to repair and more time to promote business.

HISTORY: . . . .
Established in 1971; . . 1st Franchised in 1980
Company-Owned Units (As of 8/31/1992): . .1
Franchised Units (As of 8/31/1992): . . . . .<u>7</u>
Total Units (As of 8/31/1992): 8
Projected New Units for 1993: 6
Distribution: US-0;Can-8;Overseas-0
  North America: . . . . .1 Province
  Concentration: . . . . 8 in AB
Registered: . . . . AB
. . . .
Type Space: . . . . .SC, RM;~500-4,000 SF

FINANCIAL: Earnings Claim: . .No
Cash Investment: $25-100K
Total Investment: $60-250K
Fees: Franchise - $6.5K
  Royalty: 2.5%, Advert: . . . 1%
Contract Periods (Yrs.): 5/5
Area Development Agreement: Yes/2
Sub-Franchise Contract: . . . . .No
Expand in Territory: . . . . . . Yes
Passive Ownership: . . . . .Allowed
Encourage Conversions: . . . . NA
Average # Employees: . . 4 FT, 3 PT

FRANCHISOR TRAINING/SUPPORT:
Financial Assistance Provided: . . . . .No
Site Selection Assistance: . . . . . . .Yes
Lease Negotiation Assistance: . . . . .Yes
Co-operative Advertising: . . . . . . .Yes
Training: . . . . .2 Wks. Operating Outlets,
. . . . .1-2 Wks. New Location
On-Going Support: A,B,c,D,E,F,i/ 6
EXPANSION PLANS:
US: . . . . .No
Canada: . . . . .AB, Some BC
Overseas: . . . . .China

DEL TACO

345 Baker St.
Costa Mesa, CA 92626
TEL: (714) 540-8914
FAX: (714) 641-3612
Franchise Development Dept.

DEL TACO is an established leader in the exploding Mexican quick-service category. We offer prospective franchisees, who have the financial means, a multi-unit development agreement that gives them exclusive development rights in a designated territory for a set period.

HISTORY: . . . . IFA	FINANCIAL: Earnings Claim: . .No	FRANCHISOR TRAINING/SUPPORT:
Established in 1964; . . 1st Franchised in 1967	Cash Investment: $150K	Financial Assistance Provided: . . . . .No
Company-Owned Units (As of 8/31/1992): 215	Total Investment: $220-400K	Site Selection Assistance: . . . . . . .Yes
Franchised Units (As of 8/31/1992): 81	Fees: Franchise - $25K	Lease Negotiation Assistance: . . . . .Yes
Total Units (As of 8/31/1992): 296	Royalty: 5%, Advert: 4%	Co-operative Advertising: . . . . . . .Yes
Projected New Units for 1993: 15	Contract Periods (Yrs.): 20/15	Training: . . . . . 10-12 Wks. Southern CA
Distribution: US-296;Can-0;Overseas-0	Area Development Agreement: Yes/Var	. . . .
North America: . . . . 6 States	Sub-Franchise Contract: . . . . .No	On-Going Support: C,D,E,G,h/ 116
Concentration: . . 273 in CA, 11 in UT, 10 NV	Expand in Territory: . . . . Yes	EXPANSION PLANS:
Registered: . . . . CA	Passive Ownership: . . . Discouraged	US: . . . . .All US
. . . .	Encourage Conversions: . . . . . .No	Canada: . . . . .Yes
Type Space: . . . . . FS, RM;~+/- 2,000 SF	Average # Employees: . .4 FT, 20 PT	Overseas: . . . . No

DEL'S LEMONADE AND REFRESHMENTS

1260 Oaklawn Ave.
Cranston, RI 02920
TEL: (401) 463-6190
FAX: (401) 463-7931
Mr. Joe Padula, VP

All-natural soft frozen lemonade, first all-natural frozen DEL'S light lemonade (1/2 calories), soft pretzels, nachos, popcorn, pizza, etc. New products to be discussed at meetings.

HISTORY:	FINANCIAL: Earnings Claim: . .No	FRANCHISOR TRAINING/SUPPORT:
Established in 1948; . . 1st Franchised in 1963	Cash Investment: $30K	Financial Assistance Provided: . . . . .No
Company-Owned Units (As of 8/31/1992): . .2	Total Investment: $60-85K	Site Selection Assistance: . . . . . . .Yes
Franchised Units (As of 8/31/1992): 33	Fees: Franchise - $15-25K	Lease Negotiation Assistance: . . . .Yes
Total Units (As of 8/31/1992): 35	Royalty: Varies, Advert: . . Varies	Co-operative Advertising: . . . . . . .Yes
Projected New Units for 1993: 6	Contract Periods (Yrs.): 5/5/5	Training: . . . . .1 Wk. or Less Head-
Distribution: US-35;Can-0;Overseas-0	Area Development Agreement: . .No	. . . . . .quarters or Franchisee Location
North America: . . . . 10 States	Sub-Franchise Contract: . . . . . Yes	On-Going Support: C,D,E,F/ 5
Concentration: . . . 25 in RI, 4 in MA, 2 in CA	Expand in Territory: . . . . Yes	EXPANSION PLANS:
Registered: . . . . CA,RI,VA	Passive Ownership: . . . . . .Allowed	US: . . . . .All US
. . . .	Encourage Conversions: . . . . . NA	Canada: . . . . .No
Type Space: . . . . .FS, SC;~1,000 SF	Average # Employees: . . 1 FT, 2 PT	Overseas: . . . . No

DIAMOND DAVE'S TACO COMPANY

201 S. Clinton St., # 281
Iowa City, IA 52240
TEL: (319) 337-7690
FAX: (319) 337-4707
Mr. Stanley J. White, President

DIAMOND DAVE'S TACO COMPANY is a regional restaurant chain, featuring great family-priced Mexican/American cuisine. Opportunities include full-service restaurant/bar concept and fast-food concept. Locations available in enclosed regional malls, strip centers and free-standing units.

HISTORY:	FINANCIAL: Earnings Claim: . .No	FRANCHISOR TRAINING/SUPPORT:
Established in 1980; . . 1st Franchised in 1982	Cash Investment: $25-75K	Financial Assistance Provided: . . . . .NA
Company-Owned Units (As of 8/31/1992): . .2	Total Investment: $100-250K	Site Selection Assistance: . . . . . . .Yes
Franchised Units (As of 8/31/1992): 30	Fees: Franchise - $15K	Lease Negotiation Assistance: . . . .Yes
Total Units (As of 8/31/1992): 32	Royalty: 4%, Advert: 1%	Co-operative Advertising: . . . . . . .Yes
Projected New Units for 1993: 6	Contract Periods (Yrs.): 10/10	Training: . . . . 2-4 Wks. Local Restaurant
Distribution: US-32;Can-0;Overseas-0	Area Development Agreement: . Yes	. . . .
North America: . . . . 5 States	Sub-Franchise Contract: . . . . .No	On-Going Support: C,D,E,F,G,H,I/ 3
Concentration: . . . . 10 in IL, 9 in WI, 8 in IA	Expand in Territory: . . . . Yes	EXPANSION PLANS:
Registered: . . . . .IL,IN,MN,WI	Passive Ownership: . . . Discouraged	US: . . . . Midwest Only
. . . .	Encourage Conversions: . . . . Yes	Canada: . . . . .No
Type Space: . . . . .SC, RM;~2,000-2,500 SF	Average # Employees: . .5 FT, 10 PT	Overseas: . . . . No

DONATOS PIZZA

935 Taylor Station Rd.
Blacklick, OH 43004
TEL: (800) 366-2867 (614) 476-4663
FAX: (614) 476-1933
Mr. Kevin King, Dir. Fran.

DONATOS PIZZA is a retail outlet, specializing in the sale of pizza and other products and featuring carry-out, dine-in and delivery services. DONATOS PIZZA is devoted to promoting goodwill through product, principle and people. DONATOS PIZZA requires employment in store operations of the recipes, production advertising, promotion and business methods and techniques developed, adopted and approved by franchisor. Assistance and services provided.

HISTORY:	IFA
Established in 1963;	. . 1st Franchised in 1991
Company-Owned Units (As of 8/31/1992):	. 34
Franchised Units (As of 8/31/1992):	3
Total Units (As of 8/31/1992):	 37
Projected New Units for 1993:	 20
Distribution:	US-37;Can-0;Overseas-0
North America:	. . . . .1 State
Concentration:	. . . . 37 in OH
Registered:	. . . . .IL,IN,MI,WA
Type Space:	. . . . FS, SC;~1,200-2,600 SF

FINANCIAL: Earnings Claim:	. Yes
Cash Investment:	. . . . . . $62.5K
Total Investment:	. . . . $240-300K
Fees: Franchise -	. . . . . . $15K
Royalty: 4%, Advert:	. . . . . . 4%
Contract Periods (Yrs.):	20
Area Development Agreement:	. Yes
Sub-Franchise Contract:	. . . . .No
Expand in Territory:	. . . . . . .No
Passive Ownership:	. . . Discouraged
Encourage Conversions:	. . . . . .
Avg. # Employees: 10-15 FT, 15-35 PT	

FRANCHISOR TRAINING/SUPPORT:	
Financial Assistance Provided:	. . . . .NA
Site Selection Assistance:	. . . . . . .Yes
Lease Negotiation Assistance:	. . . . .Yes
Co-operative Advertising:	. . . . . . .Yes
Training:	. . . . . .28 Days Headquarters
On-Going Support: b,C,D,E,G,h,I/	. . . 50
EXPANSION PLANS:	
US:	. . . . OH, IN, KY, PA, TN
Canada:	. . . . .No
Overseas:	. . . . No

DOUBLE DEAL PIZZA

2646 Palma Dr., # 165
Ventura, CA 93003
TEL: (805) 644-0144
FAX: (805) 644-6163
Mr. Philip Scarletta, President

DOUBLE DEAL PIZZA is a value-added take-out and delivery pizza and Italian food concept. Our pricing allows the customer to benefit not only from the convenience of delivered pizza, but the added benefit of receiving two pizzas for one price. The products are priced to be at a competitive advantage in the market, while providing the operator the opportunity for profitable business.

HISTORY:	
Established in 1974;	. . 1st Franchised in 1987
Company-Owned Units (As of 8/31/1992):	. .1
Franchised Units (As of 8/31/1992):	29
Total Units (As of 8/31/1992):	30
Projected New Units for 1993:	 12
Distribution:	US-30;Can-0;Overseas-0
North America:	. . . . .1 State
Concentration:	. . . . 30 in CA
Registered:	. . . . CA
Type Space:	. . . . SC;~800-1,100 SF

FINANCIAL: Earnings Claim:	. .No
Cash Investment:	. . . . . . $30-45K
Total Investment:	. . . . . . $60-95K
Fees: Franchise -	. . . . $15K
Royalty: 4%, Advert:	. . . . . . 3%
Contract Periods (Yrs.):	. . . . 10/10
Area Development Agreement:	Yes/10
Sub-Franchise Contract:	. . . . . Yes
Expand in Territory:	. . . . Yes
Passive Ownership:	. . . Discouraged
Encourage Conversions:	. . . . . Yes
Average # Employees:	.2 FT, 6-12 PT

FRANCHISOR TRAINING/SUPPORT:	
Financial Assistance Provided:	. . . Yes(I)
Site Selection Assistance:	. . . . . . .Yes
Lease Negotiation Assistance:	. . . . .Yes
Co-operative Advertising:	. . . . . . .Yes
Training:	. . . . 2 Wks. Headquarters
On-Going Support: b,C,D,E,F,G,H/	 2
EXPANSION PLANS:	
US:	. . . . Western US
Canada:	. . . . .All Canada
Overseas:	. . . . No

EDWARDO'S NATURAL PIZZA RESTAURANTS

4415 W. Harrison St., # 510
Hillside, IL 60162
TEL: (800) 944-3393 (708) 449-8500
FAX: (708) 449-8732
Mr. Frank D. Knowles, VP Fran.

EDWARDO'S features award-winning pizza that has been critically acclaimed by customers and food critics, a wide variety of salads and pastas and a full-service bar. Our signature stuffed pizza, made with fresh, natural ingredients, has long been a Midwest favorite. The bright open decor with modern posters and mirrors is attractive for family dining.

HISTORY:	
Established in 1978;	. . 1st Franchised in 1991
Company-Owned Units (As of 8/31/1992):	. 17
Franchised Units (As of 8/31/1992):	7
Total Units (As of 8/31/1992):	 24
Projected New Units for 1993:	 15
Distribution:	US-24;Can-0;Overseas-0
North America:	. . . . 4 States
Concentration:	. . . 14 in IL, 3 in WI, 2 in MN
Registered:	. . . . .CA,FL,IL,IN,MI,MN,WI
Type Space:	. . . . .FS, SC;~4,000 SF

FINANCIAL: Earnings Claim:	. Yes
Cash Investment:	. . . . . $270-550K
Total Investment:	. . . . . $270-550K
Fees: Franchise -	. . . . $25K
Royalty: 5%, Advert:	. . . . . . 1%
Contract Periods (Yrs.):	. . . . 10/10
Area Development Agreement:	Yes/Var
Sub-Franchise Contract:	. . . . . .No
Expand in Territory:	. . . . Yes
Passive Ownership:	. . . . . .Allowed
Encourage Conversions:	. . . . . Yes
Average # Employees:	. 10 FT, 60 PT

FRANCHISOR TRAINING/SUPPORT:	
Financial Assistance Provided:	. . . . .No
Site Selection Assistance:	. . . . . . .Yes
Lease Negotiation Assistance:	. . . . .Yes
Co-operative Advertising:	. . . . . . .Yes
Training:	. . . . . . 4-6 Wks. Headquarters
On-Going Support: a,B,C,D,E,F,h,I/	. . 30
EXPANSION PLANS:	
US:	. . . . All US
Canada:	. . . . .No
Overseas:	. . EUR and Pacific Rim

EVERYTHING YOGURT
AND SALAD CAFE
90 Western Ave.
Staten Island, NY 10303
TEL: (800) 999-5835 (718) 816-7800
FAX: (718) 816-1330
Mr. Raymond C. Habib, Dir. Fran.

Our cafes offer a wide variety of frozen yogurt sundaes and shakes, with a choice of 20 toppings. In addition, the menu includes an assortment of 8 healthy salads, freshly prepared in front of the customer. Soups, sandwiches and "Bananas" frosty fruit shakes complement the menu.

HISTORY: . . . . IFA
Established in 1976; . . 1st Franchised in 1981
Company-Owned Units (As of 8/31/1992): . .8
Franchised Units (As of 8/31/1992): 271
Total Units (As of 8/31/1992): 279
Projected New Units for 1993: 30
Distribution: US-279;Can-0;Overseas-0
  North America: . . . . 21 States
  Concentration: . 62 in NY, 44 in NJ, 23 in MD
Registered: . . . CA,FL,IL,MI,NY,WA,WI,DC
. . . .
Type Space: . . RM, Downtown Ctrs;~800 SF

FINANCIAL: Earnings Claim: . .No
Cash Investment: $60-75K
Total Investment: $225-250K
Fees: Franchise - $31K
  Royalty: 5%, Advert: 1%
Contract Periods (Yrs.): 10/10
Area Development Agreement: Yes/10
Sub-Franchise Contract: . . . . .No
Expand in Territory: . . . . Yes
Passive Ownership: . . . Discouraged
Encourage Conversions: . . . . . Yes
Average # Employees: . .2 FT, 15 PT

FRANCHISOR TRAINING/SUPPORT:
Financial Assistance Provided: . . . Yes(I)
Site Selection Assistance: . . . . . . .Yes
Lease Negotiation Assistance: . . . . .Yes
Co-operative Advertising: . . . . . . .Yes
Training: . . . . . . .15 Days Headquarters
. . . .
On-Going Support: B,C,D,E,F,G,H,I/ . . 37
EXPANSION PLANS:
US: . . . . .East and West Coast
Canada: . . . . No
Overseas: . . . . No

FAJITA JUNCTION TEX-MEX CAFE

9801 McCullough
San Antonio, TX 78216
TEL: (800) 833-8989 (512) 340-8989
FAX: (512) 340-0202
Mr. Dan A. Rowe, Dir. Fran.

Authentic Tex-Mex-style Mexican fast food in an up-scale cafe setting. Has the look and feel of a traditional Mexican restaurant, with the service and restaurant operating techniques of a major fast-food chain. Famous for our many popular Mexican dishes, all prepared in an open grill kitchen. Serve margaritas, beer and wine plus full beverage bar. FAJITA JUNCTION has a value menu to compete with Taco Bell, etc. as well as a complete up-scale menu.

HISTORY: . . . .
Established in 1985; . . 1st Franchised in 1987
Company-Owned Units (As of 8/31/1992): . 26
Franchised Units (As of 8/31/1992): 4
Total Units (As of 8/31/1992): 30
Projected New Units for 1993: 25
Distribution: US-30;Can-0;Overseas-0
  North America: . . . . 2 States
  Concentration: . . . . . 29 in TX, 1 in FL
Registered: . . . .
. . . .
Type Space: . . . . FS;~2,500 SF

FINANCIAL: Earnings Claim: . Yes
Cash Investment: . . . .$
Total Investment: . . . .$
Fees: Franchise - $15-25K
  Royalty: 5%, Advert: 3%
Contract Periods (Yrs.): 20/20
Area Development Agreement: . Yes
Sub-Franchise Contract: . . . . .No
Expand in Territory: . . . . Yes
Passive Ownership: . . . Discouraged
Encourage Conversions: . . . . . Yes
Average # Employees: . . . .

FRANCHISOR TRAINING/SUPPORT:
Financial Assistance Provided: . . .Yes(D)
Site Selection Assistance: . . . . . . .Yes
Lease Negotiation Assistance: . . . . .Yes
Co-operative Advertising: . . . . . . .Yes
Training: . . . . . 10-21 Days San Antonio,
. . . . .10-21 Days Dallas
On-Going Support: A,B,C,D,E,F,G,H,I/ 20
EXPANSION PLANS:
US: . . . TX,AL,GA,KY,TN,VA,NC,CA
Canada: . . . . No
Overseas: . . . . No

FAMILY PIZZA

Bay 10 - 318 - 105st
Saskatoon, SK S7N 1Z3 CAN
TEL: (306) 955-0215 C
FAX: (306) 955-0215
Mr. Hal Schmidt, President

Two-for-one oriented. 39 minute guarantee or your order is free. Take-out and delivery only.

HISTORY: . . . . .CFA
Established in 1983; . . 1st Franchised in 1986
Company-Owned Units (As of 8/31/1992): . .3
Franchised Units (As of 8/31/1992): 9
Total Units (As of 8/31/1992): 12
Projected New Units for 1993: 6
Distribution: US-0;Can-12;Overseas-0
  North America: . . . . .1 Province
  Concentration: . . . . .12 in SK
Registered: . . . . AB
. . . .
Type Space: . . . . .SC;~1,000 SF

FINANCIAL: Earnings Claim: . Yes
Cash Investment: $40K
Total Investment: $65-70K
Fees: Franchise - $15K
  Royalty: 4%, Advert: 5%
Contract Periods (Yrs.): 5/5
Area Development Agreement: Yes/5
Sub-Franchise Contract: . . . . . .No
Expand in Territory: . . . . .No
Passive Ownership: . . . Not Allowed
Encourage Conversions: . . . . .No
Average # Employees: . . 4 FT, 4 PT

FRANCHISOR TRAINING/SUPPORT:
Financial Assistance Provided: . . . .
Site Selection Assistance: . . . . .Yes
Lease Negotiation Assistance: . . . . .Yes
Co-operative Advertising: . . . . . . .Yes
Training: . . . . 2 Wks. Headquarters,
. . . . 1-2 Months On-Site
On-Going Support: A,B,C,D,E,F,G,H,I/ .3
EXPANSION PLANS:
US: . . . . No
Canada: . . . . .BC, AB, MB
Overseas: . . . . No

FATBURGER

11110 W. Ohio Ave., # 108
Los Angeles, CA 90025
TEL: (310) 914-1830
FAX: (310) 914-1838
Mr. Forest Hamilton, President

Quick service restaurant.

HISTORY: . . . . IFA
Established in 1952; . . 1st Franchised in 1980
Company-Owned Units (As of 8/31/1992): . .3
Franchised Units (As of 8/31/1992): 16
Total Units (As of 8/31/1992): 19
Projected New Units for 1993: 20
Distribution: US-19;Can-0;Overseas-0
North America: . . . . 2 States
Concentration: . . . . . . 17 in CA, 2 in NV
Registered: . . . . .CA,HI
. . . .
Type Space: . . . . . FS, SC;~1,200-2,000 SF

FINANCIAL: Earnings Claim: . .No
Cash Investment: $150K
Total Investment: $150-250K
Fees: Franchise - $25K
Royalty: 6%, Advert: 3%
Contract Periods (Yrs.): 10/5/5
Area Development Agreement: Yes/15
Sub-Franchise Contract: . . . . . .
Expand in Territory: . . . . . . Yes
Passive Ownership: . . . Not Allowed
Encourage Conversions: . . . . . Yes
Average # Employees: . . 6 FT, 4 PT

FRANCHISOR TRAINING/SUPPORT:
Financial Assistance Provided: . . . . . No
Site Selection Assistance: . . . . . . .Yes
Lease Negotiation Assistance: . . . . .Yes
Co-operative Advertising: . . . . . . .Yes
Training: . . . . . . 6-8 Wks. Headquarters
. . . .
On-Going Support: A,B,C,D,E,F/ 10
EXPANSION PLANS:
US: . . . . .All US
Canada: . . . . .No
Overseas: . . . . No

FATSO'S HOMEMADE HAMBURGERS

1446 Don Mills Rd., # 200
North York, ON M3B 3N3 CAN
TEL: (416) 447-4584
FAX: (416) 444-0001
Mr. Steve Georgopoulos, President

We are the leaders in the homemade hamburger business with our hamburgers weighing 6 ounces (fresh). We also have salads, steak, soup, chili, chicken, hot dogs and also a variety of breakfast. All fresh food in a fast-food concept.

HISTORY: . . . .
Established in 1984; . . 1st Franchised in 1988
Company-Owned Units (As of 8/31/1992): . .1
Franchised Units (As of 8/31/1992): 5
Total Units (As of 8/31/1992): 6
Projected New Units for 1993: 3
Distribution: US-0;Can-6;Overseas-0
North America: . . . . .1 Province
Concentration: . . . . 6 in ON
Registered: . . . .
. . . .
Type Space: . . . . .FS, SC;~2,000 SF

FINANCIAL: Earnings Claim: . .No
Cash Investment: $75K
Total Investment: $175-200K
Fees: Franchise - $20K
Royalty: 5%, Advert: 2%
Contract Periods (Yrs.): 10/10
Area Development Agreement: . .No
Sub-Franchise Contract: . . . . . Yes
Expand in Territory: . . . . . . Yes
Passive Ownership: . . . Discouraged
Encourage Conversions: . . . . Yes
Average # Employees: . . 6 FT, 6 PT

FRANCHISOR TRAINING/SUPPORT:
Financial Assistance Provided: . . . . .Yes
Site Selection Assistance: . . . . . . .Yes
Lease Negotiation Assistance: . . . .Yes
Co-operative Advertising: . . . . . . .Yes
Training: . . . . .4 Wks. Off-Site,
. . . . 2 Wks. On-Site
On-Going Support: a,B,C,D,E,F,G,H/ . .6
EXPANSION PLANS:
US: .No
Canada: . . . . .Yes
Overseas: . . . . No

FLAMERS CHARBROILED HAMBURGERS

126 W. Adams St., # 500
Jacksonville, FL 32202
TEL: (904) 632-1997
FAX: (904) 356-0710
Mr. Paul Martinez, VP Mktg.

Fast-food burger chain - gourmet - up-scale.

HISTORY: . . . .
Established in 1987; . . 1st Franchised in 1988
Company-Owned Units (As of 8/31/1992): . 11
Franchised Units (As of 8/31/1992): 31
Total Units (As of 8/31/1992): 42
Projected New Units for 1993: 24
Distribution: US-42;Can-0;Overseas-0
North America: . . . . 17 States
Concentration: . . . .9 in DC, 8 in FL, 5 in PA
Registered: . . . . . CA,FL,MD,NY,VA,DC
. . . .
Type Space: . . . . RM, Office Bldg.;~600 SF

FINANCIAL: Earnings Claim: . Yes
Cash Investment: $60-90K
Total Investment: $130-175K
Fees: Franchise - $25K
Royalty: 5%, Advert: 1%
Contract Periods (Yrs.): . . . 10/10
Area Development Agreement: Yes/15
Sub-Franchise Contract: . . . . . Yes
Expand in Territory: . . . . . . Yes
Passive Ownership: . . . . .Allowed
Encourage Conversions: . . . . Yes
Average # Employees: . . 4 FT, 7 PT

FRANCHISOR TRAINING/SUPPORT:
Financial Assistance Provided: . . . Yes(I)
Site Selection Assistance: . . . . . . .Yes
Lease Negotiation Assistance: . . . . .Yes
Co-operative Advertising: . . . . .Yes
Training: . . . . .2 Wks. FL,
. . . . 2 Wks. On-Site
On-Going Support: B,C,D,E,F,G,H/ . . 11
EXPANSION PLANS:
US: . . . . .All US
Canada: . . . . .Toronto, Alberta
Overseas: . . . . UK, GR

FOUR STAR PIZZA

125 S. Service Rd., P. O. Box 265
Jericho, NY 11753
TEL: (800) 527-0225 (516) 334-8400 C
FAX: (516) 334-8575
Franchise Development

FOUR STAR PIZZA's commitment to quality, evident in the fresh, wholesome ingredients used in our pizza, special sandwiches & wings, as well as our outstanding national avg. delivery time of 18 minutes, carries over into the franchise program. Through the franchise program at FOUR STAR PIZZA, you can experience the satisfaction of operating your own business, while having access to the services and support of an experienced and progressive franchisor.

HISTORY: . . . .
Established in 1981; . . 1st Franchised in 1985
Company-Owned Units (As of 8/31/1992): . .1
Franchised Units (As of 8/31/1992): 58
Total Units (As of 8/31/1992): 59
Projected New Units for 1993: 15
Distribution: US-54;Can-0;Overseas-5
North America: . . . . 15 States
Concentration: . . .34 in PA, 9 in CA, 6 in OH
Registered: . . . . .CA,FL,IL,MD,NY,ND,VA
. . . .
Type Space: . . . . . . FS, SF, SC;~1,000 SF

FINANCIAL: Earnings Claim: . .No
Cash Investment: $40K
Total Investment: $65-85K
Fees: Franchise - $9K
Royalty: 5%, Advert: 3%
Contract Periods (Yrs.): 10/10
Area Development Agreement: Yes/25
Sub-Franchise Contract: . . . . .No
Expand in Territory: . . . . Yes
Passive Ownership: . . . Not Allowed
Encourage Conversions: . . . . . Yes
Average # Employees: .5-7 FT, 10 PT

FRANCHISOR TRAINING/SUPPORT:
Financial Assistance Provided: . . . Yes(I)
Site Selection Assistance: . . . . . . .Yes
Lease Negotiation Assistance: . . . .Yes
Co-operative Advertising: . . . . . . .Yes
Training: . . . . 2 Wks. Headquarters
. . . .
On-Going Support: B,C,D,E,F,G,H,I/ . . . .
EXPANSION PLANS:
US: .All US
Canada: . . . . .All Canada
Overseas: . EUR, Asia, S. America

FOX'S PIZZA DEN

3243 Old Frankstown Rd.
Pittsburgh, PA 15239
TEL: (412) 733-7888 C
FAX:
Mr. James R. Fox, President

FOX'S PIZZA DEN believes in the philosophy . . . You earned it, you keep it! No percentage charged. FOX's gives you a pizza franchise, a sandwich franchise and wedgie franchise - all for one low price. FOX's truly gives you the opportunity to be your own boss.

HISTORY: . . . .
Established in 1971; . . . 1st Franchised in 1974
Company-Owned Units (As of 8/31/1992): . .0
Franchised Units (As of 8/31/1992): 143
Total Units (As of 8/31/1992): 143
Projected New Units for 1993: 20
Distribution: US-143;Can-0;Overseas-0
North America: . . . . 6 States
Concentration: . 105 in PA, 10 in MD, 10 WV
Registered: . . . . .MD,NY,VA
. . . .
Type Space: . . . . SF;~1,000 SF

FINANCIAL: Earnings Claim: . .No
Cash Investment: $40-60K
Total Investment: $40-60K
Fees: Franchise - $8K
Royalty: $200/Mo., Advert: . . 0%
Contract Periods (Yrs.): 5/5
Area Development Agreement: Yes/3
Sub-Franchise Contract: . . . . . Yes
Expand in Territory: . . . . Yes
Passive Ownership: . . . Discouraged
Encourage Conversions: . . . . . Yes
Average # Employees: . . 2 FT, 8 PT

FRANCHISOR TRAINING/SUPPORT:
Financial Assistance Provided: . . . Yes(I)
Site Selection Assistance: . . . . . . .Yes
Lease Negotiation Assistance: . . . .Yes
Co-operative Advertising: . . . . . . .Yes
Training: . . . . .10 Days On-Site
. . . .
On-Going Support: B,C,D,E,F,G,I/ 1
EXPANSION PLANS:
US: . . . . Northeast
Canada: . . . . .No
Overseas: . . . . No

GALLUCCI'S PIZZERIA

2845 NW Hwy. 101
Lincoln City, OR 97367
TEL: (503) 994-3538
FAX: (503) 994-3542
Ms. Sharon Wright, CEO

GALLUCCI'S PIZZERIA was started in 1974 by Sharon Gallucci Wright on the Central Oregon coast. People drive hours just to eat GALLUCCI PIZZA because its quality is superior to all other pizzas. GALLUCCI's has been featured in Pizza Today 4 times and its owner has been involved in seminars at the National Association of Pizza Operators' convention.

HISTORY: . . . .
Established in 1974; . . . 1st Franchised in 1989
Company-Owned Units (As of 8/31/1992): . .0
Franchised Units (As of 8/31/1992): 1
Total Units (As of 8/31/1992): 1
Projected New Units for 1993:
Distribution: US-1;Can-0;Overseas-0
North America: . . . . .1 State
Concentration: . . . . 1 in OR
Registered: . . . . OR,WA
. . . .
Type Space: . .FS, SF, SC, RM;~2,000 Min. SF

FINANCIAL: Earnings Claim: . .No
Cash Investment: . . . . . . $~65K
Total Investment: $100-175K
Fees: Franchise - $15K
Royalty: 5%, Advert: 1%
Contract Periods (Yrs.): . . . .Varies
Area Development Agreement: . .No
Sub-Franchise Contract: . . . . .No
Expand in Territory: . . . . Yes
Passive Ownership: . . . Not Allowed
Encourage Conversions: . . . . NA
Average # Employees: . . . . .Varies

FRANCHISOR TRAINING/SUPPORT:
Financial Assistance Provided: . . . . .NA
Site Selection Assistance: . . . . . . .Yes
Lease Negotiation Assistance: . . . .Yes
Co-operative Advertising: . . . . . . .Yes
Training: . . . . 2 Wks. Min. Headquarters
. . . .
On-Going Support: B,C,D,E,F,G,H/ . . .2
EXPANSION PLANS:
US: . . . . .All US
Canada: . . . . .No
Overseas: . . . . .Yes

GIFF'S SUB SHOP

634 Eglin Pkwy.
Ft. Walton Beach, FL 32548
TEL: (904) 863-9011
FAX:
Mr. Lance Arnette, President

Fast food service - GIFF'S SUB SHOP is an opportunity to take a proven method, work hard and make a good living. We have over 30 subs, featuring our world famous "Fighter Pilot" steak sub. We believe good food, prepared to our customers' taste, at a good price, will succeed.

HISTORY:	FINANCIAL: Earnings Claim: . Yes	FRANCHISOR TRAINING/SUPPORT:
Established in 1977; . . 1st Franchised in 1983	Cash Investment: $25-30K	Financial Assistance Provided: . . . . . No
Company-Owned Units (As of 8/31/1992): . .1	Total Investment: $25-30K	Site Selection Assistance: . . . . . . .Yes
Franchised Units (As of 8/31/1992): 6	Fees: Franchise - $10.5K	Lease Negotiation Assistance: . . . . .Yes
Total Units (As of 8/31/1992): 7	Royalty: 4%, Advert: 2%	Co-operative Advertising: . . . . . . .Yes
Projected New Units for 1993: 5	Contract Periods (Yrs.): 20/20	Training: . . . . .1 Wk. Headquarters,
Distribution: US-7;Can-0;Overseas-0	Area Development Agreement: Yes/20	. . . . .1 Wk. Grand Opening
North America: . . . . .1 State	Sub-Franchise Contract: . . . . Yes	On-Going Support: C,D,E,F,G,H/ 3
Concentration: . . . . 7 in FL	Expand in Territory: . . . . . . Yes	EXPANSION PLANS:
Registered: . . . . .FL	Passive Ownership: . . . Discouraged	US: . . . . .All US
. . . .	Encourage Conversions: . . . . . Yes	Canada: . . . . .No
Type Space: . . . . .FS, SF, SC, RM;~800 SF	Average # Employees: . . 2 FT, 1 PT	Overseas: . . . . No

GODFATHER'S PIZZA

9140 W. Dodge Rd., # 300
Omaha, NE 68114
TEL: (800) 456-8347 (402) 391-1452
FAX: (402) 392-2357
Mr. Bruce N. Cannon, Dir. Fran. Dev.

GODFATHER'S PIZZA is consistently recognized by consumers and independent research as having a superior quality product. Couple this with consistent operations, innovative new products, attention to service and full support services and GODFATHER'S PIZZA is positioned to retain its reputation for high quality and service.

HISTORY:	FINANCIAL: Earnings Claim: . Yes	FRANCHISOR TRAINING/SUPPORT:
Established in 1973; . . 1st Franchised in 1974	Cash Investment: $55-120K	Financial Assistance Provided: . . . . .No
Company-Owned Units (As of 8/31/1992): 161	Total Investment: $72-291K	Site Selection Assistance: . . . . . . .Yes
Franchised Units (As of 8/31/1992): 364	Fees: Franchise - $7.5-15K	Lease Negotiation Assistance: . . . . No
Total Units (As of 8/31/1992): 525	Royalty: 5%, Advert: 0%	Co-operative Advertising: . . . . . . .Yes
Projected New Units for 1993: 35	Contract Periods (Yrs.): 15/10	Training: . . . . 5 Wks. Headquarters
Distribution: US-522;Can-3;Overseas-0	Area Development Agreement: Yes/5	. . . .
North America: . . . . 39 States	Sub-Franchise Contract: . . . . .No	On-Going Support: B,C,D,E,F,G,H,I/ . . 99
Concentration: . 72 in WA, 47 in IA, 45 in MN	Expand in Territory: . . . . . . Yes	EXPANSION PLANS:
Registered: . . .CA,IL,IN,MD,MI,MN,ND,SD	Passive Ownership: . . . Discouraged	US: . . . . .All US
. . . . .WA,WI	Encourage Conversions: . . . . . Yes	Canada: . . . . .No
Type Space: . . . . .FS, SC;~3,500 SF	Average # Employees:6-8 FT, 12-20 PT	Overseas: . . . . No

GOLD STAR CHILI

5204 Beechmont Ave.
Cincinnati, OH 45230
TEL: (513) 231-4541
FAX: (513) 624-4415
Mr. Raymond P. Peterson, VP Fran.

Cincinnati-style chili and hot dogs.

HISTORY:	FINANCIAL: Earnings Claim: . .No	FRANCHISOR TRAINING/SUPPORT:
Established in 1965; . . 1st Franchised in 1965	Cash Investment: $30-80K	Financial Assistance Provided: . . . . .No
Company-Owned Units (As of 8/31/1992): . .6	Total Investment: $100-350K	Site Selection Assistance: . . . . . . .Yes
Franchised Units (As of 8/31/1992): 92	Fees: Franchise - $10-20K	Lease Negotiation Assistance: . . . . No
Total Units (As of 8/31/1992): 98	Royalty: 5%, Advert: 4%	Co-operative Advertising: . . . . . . .Yes
Projected New Units for 1993: 15	Contract Periods (Yrs.): 20/20	Training: . . . . 2 Wks. Headquarters,
Distribution: US-98;Can-0;Overseas-0	Area Development Agreement: Yes/10	2 Wks. Local
North America: . . . . 4 States	Sub-Franchise Contract: . . . . Yes	On-Going Support: a,C,D,E,G,H,I/ . . . 80
Concentration: . 70 in OH, 22 in KY, 12 in CO	Expand in Territory: . . . . . . .No	EXPANSION PLANS:
Registered: . . . . .CA,IN,MI	Passive Ownership: . . . Discouraged	US: . . . . Cincinnati + 200 Miles
. . . .	Encourage Conversions: . . . . . Yes	Canada: . . . . .No
Type Space: . . . FS, SF, SC, RM;~1,600+ SF	Average # Employees: . . . 10-20 FT	Overseas: . . . . No

GOLDEN FRIED CHICKEN

4835 LBJ Freeway, # 525
Dallas, TX 75244
TEL: (214) 458-9555
FAX: (214) 458-9872
Mr. Victor F. Erwin, EVP

GOLDEN FRIED CHICKEN is a fast-food fried chicken restaurant, offering indoor dining, drive-thru and carry-out service. GFC's menu consists of fresh Golden Fried Chicken, Golden Tenders, country-style biscuits, gravy, french fries, cole-slaw, mashed potatoes, corn on the cob and fountain soft drinks.

HISTORY: . . . . IFA
Established in 1967; . . 1st Franchised in 1972
Company-Owned Units (As of 8/31/1992): . .4
Franchised Units (As of 8/31/1992): 72
Total Units (As of 8/31/1992): 76
Projected New Units for 1993: 10
Distribution: US-76;Can-0;Overseas-0
  North America: . . . . 3 States
  Concentration: . . .70 in TX, 5 in OK, 1 in AR
Registered: . . . .
  . . . .
Type Space: . . . . . . FS;~1,600-1,900 SF

FINANCIAL: Earnings Claim: . Yes
Cash Investment: $25-50K
Total Investment: $250-500K
Fees: Franchise - $10K
  Royalty: 4%, Advert: 1/2%
Contract Periods (Yrs.): 20/0
Area Development Agreement: . .No
Sub-Franchise Contract: . . . . .No
Expand in Territory: . . . . . . Yes
Passive Ownership: . . . Discouraged
Encourage Conversions: . . . . Yes
Average # Employees: . 3 FT, 6-8 PT

FRANCHISOR TRAINING/SUPPORT:
Financial Assistance Provided: . . . . .No
Site Selection Assistance: . . . . . . .Yes
Lease Negotiation Assistance: . . . . .Yes
Co-operative Advertising: . . . . . . .Yes
Training: . . . . . .2 Wks. Company Store,
  . . . . As Needed On-Site (Pre-Opening)
On-Going Support: B,C,D,E,G,H/ . . . 10
EXPANSION PLANS:
US: . . . . Southwest
Canada: . . . . .No
Overseas: . . . . Yes

GREAT WRAPS!

158 Oak St.
Avondale Estates, GA 30002
TEL: (404) 299-5081
FAX: (404) 292-0081
Mr. Marvin Young, Fran. Dev.

Fast food - Mediterranean hot grilled pita sandwiches, serving gyros, chicken, steak wrapped in pita bread. Also serving salads, fries and soft drinks. Over 45 locations in 13 states. Selling points: low food costs, simple operation, food cooked to order. Terrific alternative to burgers, pizza and chicken.

HISTORY: . . . .
Established in 1974; . . 1st Franchised in 1980
Company-Owned Units (As of 8/31/1992): . .1
Franchised Units (As of 8/31/1992): 44
Total Units (As of 8/31/1992): 45
Projected New Units for 1993: 15
Distribution: US-45;Can-0;Overseas-0
  North America: . . . . 13 States
  Concentration: . . 19 in GA, 10 in FL, 4 in NC
Registered: . . . . CA,FL,IL,NY,VA
  . . . .
Type Space: . . . . . FS, SC, RM;~600+ SF

FINANCIAL: Earnings Claim: . .No
Cash Investment: $100-200K
Total Investment: $120-200K
Fees: Franchise - $25K
  Royalty: 5%, Advert: 2%
Contract Periods (Yrs.): 10/10
Area Development Agreement: Yes/Var
Sub-Franchise Contract: . . . . .No
Expand in Territory: . . . . . . Yes
Passive Ownership: . . . Discouraged
Encourage Conversions: . . . . Yes
Average # Employees: . .15 FT, 7 PT

FRANCHISOR TRAINING/SUPPORT:
Financial Assistance Provided: . . . . .No
Site Selection Assistance: . . . . . . .Yes
Lease Negotiation Assistance: . . . .Yes
Co-operative Advertising: . . . . . . .Yes
Training: . . . . 2-3 Wks. Headquarters
  . . . .
On-Going Support: B,C,D,E,F,h/ 15
EXPANSION PLANS:
US: . . . . . All US, Mainly Metro Areas
Canada: . . . . .No
Overseas: . . . . No

GRECO PIZZA DONAIR

105 Walker St.
Truro, NS B2N 5G9 CAN
TEL: (800) 565-4389 (902) 893-4141
FAX: (902) 895-7635
Mr. Chris MacDougall, Dir. Dev.

Atlantic Canada's largest home delivery pizza chain, specializing in pizza, donair products, oven sub sandwiches and pita-wrapped sandwiches.

HISTORY: . . . . .CFA
Established in 1977; . . 1st Franchised in 1981
Company-Owned Units (As of 8/31/1992): . .6
Franchised Units (As of 8/31/1992): 45
Total Units (As of 8/31/1992): 51
Projected New Units for 1993: 2
Distribution: US-0;Can-51;Overseas-0
  North America: . . . . 4 Provinces
  Concentration: . . 21 in NB, 20 in NS, 5 in NF
Registered: . . . .
  . . . .
Type Space: . . . .FS, SF, SC, RM;~1,200 SF

FINANCIAL: Earnings Claim: . .No
Cash Investment: $40K
Total Investment: $110-140K
Fees: Franchise - $15K
  Royalty: 5%, Advert: 3%
Contract Periods (Yrs.): 10/10
Area Development Agreement: Yes/Var
Sub-Franchise Contract: . . . . . Yes
Expand in Territory: . . . . . . Yes
Passive Ownership: . . . Discouraged
Encourage Conversions: . . . . Yes
Average # Employees: . .5 FT, 10 PT

FRANCHISOR TRAINING/SUPPORT:
Financial Assistance Provided: . . . Yes(I)
Site Selection Assistance: . . . . . . .Yes
Lease Negotiation Assistance: . . . . .Yes
Co-operative Advertising: . . . . . . .Yes
Training: . . . . . 4 Wks. Correspondence,
  . . 2 Days Headquarters, 3 Wks. On-Site
On-Going Support: a,b,C,D,E,F,G,h,I/ . 19
EXPANSION PLANS:
US: . . . . .No
Canada: . . . . .PQ, Atlantic CAN
Overseas: . . . . No

GREEN BURRITO, THE

2831 E. Miraloma Ave.
Anaheim, CA 92806
TEL: (714) 632-1672
FAX: (714) 632-2783
Mr. Robert F. Dooley, VP Fran. Dev.

Full-service food, full-service quality and quantity at a fast-food price. GREEN BURRITO fills a unique niche, providing large portions of high-quality food at reasonable fast-food prices in a fast-food environment.

HISTORY: . . . .
Established in 1980; . . 1st Franchised in 1988
Company-Owned Units (As of 8/31/1992): . 11
Franchised Units (As of 8/31/1992): 41
Total Units (As of 8/31/1992): 52
Projected New Units for 1993: 30
Distribution: US-52;Can-0;Overseas-0
North America: . . . . .1 State
Concentration: . . . . 52 in CA
Registered: . . . . CA
. . . .
Type Space: . FS Drive-thru;~1,800-2,000 SF

FINANCIAL: Earnings Claim: . .No
Cash Investment: $60K
Total Investment: $250-320K
Fees: Franchise - $25K
Royalty: 5%, Advert: 1%
Contract Periods (Yrs.): 10/5/5
Area Development Agreement: . .No
Sub-Franchise Contract: . . . . .No
Expand in Territory: . . . . . . .No
Passive Ownership: . . . Discouraged
Encourage Conversions: . . . . .No
Average # Employees: . . 8 FT, 4 PT

FRANCHISOR TRAINING/SUPPORT:
Financial Assistance Provided: . . . Yes(I)
Site Selection Assistance: . . . . . . .Yes
Lease Negotiation Assistance: . . . . .Yes
Co-operative Advertising: . . . . . . .Yes
Training: . . . . .2 Wks. Various Locations
. . . .
On-Going Support: b,C,D,E,G,H/ 22
EXPANSION PLANS:
US: . . . . California
Canada: . . . . No
Overseas: . . . . No

GRINDERS AND SUCH

3200 Whipple Ave., NW
Canton, OH 44718
TEL: (216) 477-3977
FAX: (216) 477-7977
Mr. Dennis Hosterman, VP Ops.

Full-service restaurant, featuring high-quality Grinder sandwiches, homemade soups, desserts and salads. This moderately-priced menu is served in a new Nathanson-designed decor.

HISTORY: . . . . IFA
Established in 1976; . . 1st Franchised in 1978
Company-Owned Units (As of 8/31/1992): . .2
Franchised Units (As of 8/31/1992): 1
Total Units (As of 8/31/1992): 3
Projected New Units for 1993: 2
Distribution: US-3;Can-0;Overseas-0
North America: . . . . .1 State
Concentration: . . . . 3 in OH
Registered: . . . .
. . . .
Type Space: . . . . FS, SC;~4,200+ SF

FINANCIAL: Earnings Claim: . .No
Cash Investment: $150K
Total Investment: . . . . $.3-1.5MM
Fees: Franchise - $25K
Royalty: 4%, Advert: 1/2%
Contract Periods (Yrs.): 10/10
Area Development Agreement: . .No
Sub-Franchise Contract: . . . . .No
Expand in Territory: . . . . Yes
Passive Ownership: . . . Not Allowed
Encourage Conversions: . . . . Yes
Average # Employees: . 18 FT, 22 PT

FRANCHISOR TRAINING/SUPPORT:
Financial Assistance Provided: . . . . . No
Site Selection Assistance: . . . . No
Lease Negotiation Assistance: . . . . No
Co-operative Advertising: . . . . . . .Yes
Training: . . . . .3 Wks. Classes HQ,
. . . . 9 Wks. On-Site
On-Going Support: C,D,E,F,G,H/ 6
EXPANSION PLANS:
US: . . . . Ohio Only
Canada: . . . . No
Overseas: . . . . No

HAPPY JOE'S PIZZA & ICE CREAM PARLOR

2705 Commerce Dr.
Bettendorf, IA 52722
TEL: (319) 332-8811
FAX: (319) 332-5822
Mr. Larry Whitty, President

Pizza and ice cream in a fun, family atmosphere. Birthday party packages available. Very involved with special programs for youth in the community. Diversified pizza, pasta, sandwiches, salad bar and ice cream menu, candy, soft drinks and beer. Several parlors offer Family Fun Centers with Redemption Games.

HISTORY: . . . .
Established in 1972; . . 1st Franchised in 1973
Company-Owned Units (As of 8/31/1992): . 16
Franchised Units (As of 8/31/1992): 36
Total Units (As of 8/31/1992): 52
Projected New Units for 1993: 3
Distribution: US-52;Can-0;Overseas-0
North America: . . . . 6 States
Concentration: . . . 27 in IA, 11 in IL, 9 in WI
Registered: . . . . IL,WI
. . . .
Type Space: . . . . .FS, RM;~1,800-3,500 SF

FINANCIAL: Earnings Claim: . .No
Cash Investment: . . . . . . $75K+
Total Investment: . . . .$160K+
Fees: Franchise - $10K
Royalty: 6%, Advert: 3%
Contract Periods (Yrs.): . . 15/10/15
Area Development Agreement: Yes/15
Sub-Franchise Contract: . . . . .No
Expand in Territory: . . . . Yes
Passive Ownership: . . . Discouraged
Encourage Conversions: . . . . Yes
Average # Employees: . . . . . 31 FT

FRANCHISOR TRAINING/SUPPORT:
Financial Assistance Provided: . . . . . No
Site Selection Assistance: . . . . .Yes
Lease Negotiation Assistance: . . . . .Yes
Co-operative Advertising: . . . . . . .Yes
Training: . . . . 6 Wks. Headquarters
. . . .
On-Going Support: A,B,C,D,E,F,G,H,I/ 20
EXPANSION PLANS:
US: . . . . .All US
Canada: . . . . No
Overseas: . . . . Yes

HARDEE'S FOOD SYSTEMS

1233 Hardee's Blvd.
Rocky Mount, NC 27801
TEL: (800) 346-2243 (919) 977-8889
FAX: (919) 977-5730
Ms. Debbie Arrington, Dir. Corp. Dev.

Only a HARDEE'S franchise offers the diverse menu variety and service that today's customers demand. From breakfast biscuits, to our fresh fried chicken, to Frisco Burgers, to salads, roast beef and other specialty sandwiches, or great desserts, HARDEE'S has it all. And HARDEE'S offers the markets and franchise opportunities to grow with America's fast-food appetite.

HISTORY:	IFA
Established in 1960;	1st Franchised in 1961
Company-Owned Units (As of 8/31/1992):	1253
Franchised Units (As of 8/31/1992):	2745
Total Units (As of 8/31/1992):	3998
Projected New Units for 1993:	100
Distribution:	US-3940;Can-0;Overseas-58
North America:	42 States, 11 Provinces
Concentration:	371 in NC, 251 in VA, 234 IL
Registered:	All States
Type Space:	FS, SF, SC, RM;~40,000 SF

FINANCIAL: Earnings Claim:	Yes
Cash Investment:	$200-300K
Total Investment:	$.5-1.8MM
Fees: Franchise -	$15K
Royalty: 3.5-4%, Advert:	5%
Contract Periods (Yrs.):	20/5-20
Area Development Agreement:	Yes
Sub-Franchise Contract:	No
Expand in Territory:	Yes
Passive Ownership:	Not Allowed
Encourage Conversions:	No
Average # Employees:	~15 FT, ~25 PT

FRANCHISOR TRAINING/SUPPORT:

Financial Assistance Provided:	No
Site Selection Assistance:	Yes
Lease Negotiation Assistance:	Yes
Co-operative Advertising:	Yes
Training:	6-18 Wks. - Varies By Area
On-Going Support: b,C,D,E,H,i/	500

EXPANSION PLANS:

US:	SE, NE, SW, NW and Midwest
Canada:	No
Overseas:	MX, BZ, SE Asia, S. America

HEROS SIMPLY SUBSATIONAL

P. O. Box 21676
Billings, MT 59104
TEL: (406) 252-5884 C
FAX: (406) 256-1930
Mr. Bob Wiseman, VP

Submarine sandwiches, soups, salads. An operation that offers very sophisticated marketing, a totally unique menu, high-quality products and service. Whole markets available. The HERO'S name opens the door to innovative promotions, tie-ins and memorable advertising.

HISTORY:	
Established in 1986;	1st Franchised in 1991
Company-Owned Units (As of 8/31/1992):	6
Franchised Units (As of 8/31/1992):	1
Total Units (As of 8/31/1992):	7
Projected New Units for 1993:	30
Distribution:	US-7;Can-0;Overseas-0
North America:	2 States
Concentration:	5 in MT, 2 in WA
Registered:	WA
Type Space:	FS, SC, RM;~1,400 SF

FINANCIAL: Earnings Claim:	No
Cash Investment:	$50-65K
Total Investment:	$50-65K
Fees: Franchise -	$15K
Royalty: 5%, Advert:	3%
Contract Periods (Yrs.):	10/10
Area Development Agreement:	Yes/20
Sub-Franchise Contract:	No
Expand in Territory:	Yes
Passive Ownership:	Allowed
Encourage Conversions:	Yes
Average # Employees:	2 FT, 6 PT

FRANCHISOR TRAINING/SUPPORT:

Financial Assistance Provided:	No
Site Selection Assistance:	Yes
Lease Negotiation Assistance:	Yes
Co-operative Advertising:	Yes
Training:	2 Wks. Headquarters
On-Going Support: a,B,C,D,E,G,H/	4

EXPANSION PLANS:

US:	Northwest
Canada:	No
Overseas:	No

HO-LEE-CHOW

3135 S. State St.
Ann Arbor, MI 48108
TEL: (800) 241-2469 (313) 769-3020 C
FAX: (313) 662-7110
Ms. Amy Jones, Dir. Fran. Dev.

HO-LEE-CHOW is the new Chinese delivery concept of the 90's which caters to consumer demands by combining the most popular ethnic food, the convenience of delivery and lighter, healthier fare with no MSG added. Everything is keyed to fast preparation and safe, convenient delivery. The franchise stores are clean, sharp and efficient. The store system is based on consistency, reliable, computerized ordering and delivery at a value.

HISTORY:	IFA
Established in 1989;	1st Franchised in 1990
Company-Owned Units (As of 8/31/1992):	5
Franchised Units (As of 8/31/1992):	24
Total Units (As of 8/31/1992):	29
Projected New Units for 1993:	40
Distribution:	US-8;Can-20;Overseas-1
North America:	6 States, 4 Provinces
Concentration:	18 in ON, 3 in MI, 2 in DC
Registered:	All Except SD
Type Space:	SC;~1,200 SF

FINANCIAL: Earnings Claim:	Yes
Cash Investment:	$95-120K
Total Investment:	$159-254K
Fees: Franchise -	$25K
Royalty: 5.5%, Advert:	2-4%
Contract Periods (Yrs.):	10/10
Area Development Agreement:	Yes/Var
Sub-Franchise Contract:	No
Expand in Territory:	Yes
Passive Ownership:	Allowed
Encourage Conversions:	Yes
Average # Employees:	3-5 FT, 10-15 PT

FRANCHISOR TRAINING/SUPPORT:

Financial Assistance Provided:	Yes(I)
Site Selection Assistance:	Yes
Lease Negotiation Assistance:	Yes
Co-operative Advertising:	Yes
Training:	3 Days Headquarters, 3 Wks. Intensive HQ, 2 Wks. Opening
On-Going Support: C,D,E,F,G,H,I/	25

EXPANSION PLANS:

US:	All US
Canada:	All Canada
Overseas:	MX, UK, Israel

HOBEE'S CALIFORNIA RESTAURANTS
4224 El Camino Real
Palo Alto, CA 94306
TEL: (415) 493-7117
FAX: (415) 493-0756
Mr. Ed Fike, VP

Full-service, sit-down restaurant, specializing in healthier, California-style foods. Ambiance is relaxed and service is friendly. Restaurants encouraged to participate in community events rather than advertise.

HISTORY: . . . .
Established in 1974; . . . 1st Franchised in 1986
Company-Owned Units (As of 8/31/1992): . .4
Franchised Units (As of 8/31/1992): 7
Total Units (As of 8/31/1992): 11
Projected New Units for 1993: 2
Distribution: US-11;Can-0;Overseas-0
North America: . . . . .1 State
Concentration: . . . . 11 in CA
Registered: . . . . CA
. . . .
Type Space: . . . . . . SC;~3,500-5,000 SF

FINANCIAL: Earnings Claim: . .No
Cash Investment: . . . . $Varies
Total Investment: . . . . . . $Varies
Fees: Franchise - . . . . $Varies
Royalty: 5%, Advert: . . . 0% Now
Contract Periods (Yrs.): 10/10
Area Development Agreement: Yes/10
Sub-Franchise Contract: . . . . .No
Expand in Territory: . . . .
Passive Ownership: . . . Discouraged
Encourage Conversions: . . . . . Yes
Average # Employees: . .5 FT, 25 PT

FRANCHISOR TRAINING/SUPPORT:
Financial Assistance Provided: . . . . .No
Site Selection Assistance: . . . . . . .Yes
Lease Negotiation Assistance: . . . .Yes
Co-operative Advertising: . . . . . . .Yes
Training: . . . . 5 Days-2 Wks. Pre-
. . . . . Training, Up to 1 Month On-Site
On-Going Support: A,B,C,d,e,F,G,H,I/ . . 3
EXPANSION PLANS:
US: . . . . California Only
Canada: . . . . No
Overseas: . . . . No

HOOTERS OF AMERICA
4501 Circle 75 Pkwy. NW, # E-5110
Atlanta, GA 30339
TEL: (404) 951-2040
FAX: (404) 956-8526
Ms. Kay Sassi, Fran. Dev. Asst.

Full-service, casual restaurant, offering chicken wings, seafood, wine and beer.

HISTORY: . . . . IFA
Established in 1984; . . 1st Franchised in 1988
Company-Owned Units (As of 8/31/1992): . 26
Franchised Units (As of 8/31/1992): 52
Total Units (As of 8/31/1992): 78
Projected New Units for 1993: 50
Distribution: US-78;Can-0;Overseas-0
North America: . . . . 22 States
Concentration: . . . 27 in FL, 9 in GA, 8 in TX
Registered: . . . . FL,MI,MN,ND,RI,VA,WA
. . . .
Type Space: . . FS, SC, RM;~4,000-6,000 SF

FINANCIAL: Earnings Claim: . .No
Cash Investment: $500K
Total Investment: $2.5-3.0MM
Fees: Franchise - $75K
Royalty: 6%, Advert: 1%
Contract Periods (Yrs.): 20
Area Development Agreement: . .No
Sub-Franchise Contract: . . . . .No
Expand in Territory: . . . . Yes
Passive Ownership: . . . . . .Allowed
Encourage Conversions: . . . . Yes
Average # Employees: . .6 FT, 45 PT

FRANCHISOR TRAINING/SUPPORT:
Financial Assistance Provided: . . . . .No
Site Selection Assistance: . . . . . . .Yes
Lease Negotiation Assistance: . . . . .No
Co-operative Advertising: . . . . . . .Yes
Training: . . . . 10 Wks. Headquarters
. . . .
On-Going Support: B,C,d,e,F,H/ 22
EXPANSION PLANS:
US: . . . . . . NW, W, NJ, New England
Canada: . . . . No
Overseas: . . . . No

HUBB'S
7738 Industrial St.
W. Melbourne, FL 32904
TEL: (407) 728-8900
FAX: (407) 728-1126
Mr. Dave Ungar, VP

Largest selection of imported beers - 39. Home of colossal sandwiches. A place you always meet a friend.

HISTORY: . . . .
Established in 1982; . . 1st Franchised in 1992
Company-Owned Units (As of 8/31/1992): . .3
Franchised Units (As of 8/31/1992): 2
Total Units (As of 8/31/1992): 5
Projected New Units for 1993: 8
Distribution: US-5;Can-0;Overseas-0
North America: . . . . .1 State
Concentration: . . . . 5 in FL
Registered: . . . . .FL,MI
. . . .
Type Space: . . . . .SC;~4,000 SF

FINANCIAL: Earnings Claim: . .No
Cash Investment: $100-150K
Total Investment: $100-300K
Fees: Franchise - $50K
Royalty: $500+/Mo, Advert $400/Mo.
Contract Periods (Yrs.): . . 20/20/20
Area Development Agreement: Yes/5
Sub-Franchise Contract: . . . . .No
Expand in Territory: . . . . . . Yes
Passive Ownership: . . . Discouraged
Encourage Conversions: . . . . .No
Average # Employees: . .6 FT, 10 PT

FRANCHISOR TRAINING/SUPPORT:
Financial Assistance Provided: . . . . .No
Site Selection Assistance: . . . . . . .Yes
Lease Negotiation Assistance: . . . .Yes
Co-operative Advertising: . . . . . . .Yes
Training: . . . . . . 4-6 Wks. Headquarters
On-Going Support: a,B,C,D,E,f,G,h,i/ . . 5
EXPANSION PLANS:
US: . . . . All US
Canada: . . . . No
Overseas: . . . . No

HUNKY BILL'S HOUSE OF PEROGIES
1613 Nanaimo St.
Vancouver, BC V7A 2B1 CAN
TEL: (604) 251-1185
FAX:
Mr. Bill Konyk, President

Ukranian and Canadian food. Perogies, cabbage rolls, Ukranian sausage, schnitzel, BBQ back ribs, borsht soup. Unique menu. Easy to learn. All Ukranian food supplied.

HISTORY:	FINANCIAL: Earnings Claim: . Yes	FRANCHISOR TRAINING/SUPPORT:
Established in 1967; . . 1st Franchised in 1970	Cash Investment: $10K	Financial Assistance Provided: . . . Yes(I)
Company-Owned Units (As of 8/31/1992): . .4	Total Investment: $100K	Site Selection Assistance: . . . . .No
Franchised Units (As of 8/31/1992): 0	Fees: Franchise - $10K	Lease Negotiation Assistance: . . . .Yes
Total Units (As of 8/31/1992): 4	Royalty: 4%, Advert: 2%	Co-operative Advertising: . . . . . . .Yes
Projected New Units for 1993: 1	Contract Periods (Yrs.): 5/5	Training: . . . . . . 4 Wks. Headquarters
Distribution: US-0;Can-4;Overseas-0	Area Development Agreement: . .No	. . . .
North America: . . . . .1 Province	Sub-Franchise Contract: . . . . . Yes	On-Going Support: / 4
Concentration: . . . . 4 in BC	Expand in Territory: . . . . Yes	EXPANSION PLANS:
Registered:	Passive Ownership: . . . Not Allowed	US: . . . . Northwest
. . . .	Encourage Conversions: . . . . . Yes	Canada: . . . . Western Canada
Type Space: . . . . . FS, SC;~1,500-2,000 SF	Average # Employees: . . 7 FT, 4 PT	Overseas: . . . . No

INTERSTATE DAIRY QUEEN

4601 Willard Ave.
Chevy Chase, MD 20815
TEL: (301) 913-5923
FAX: (301) 913-5424
Mr. Walt Tellegen, President

Fast-food franchisor, specializing in highway-type operations.

HISTORY:	FINANCIAL: Earnings Claim: . .No	FRANCHISOR TRAINING/SUPPORT:
Established in 1977; . . 1st Franchised in 1977	Cash Investment: $75-100K	Financial Assistance Provided: . . . Yes(I)
Company-Owned Units (As of 8/31/1992): . .3	Total Investment: $300-550K	Site Selection Assistance: . . . . . . .Yes
Franchised Units (As of 8/31/1992): 92	Fees: Franchise - $25K	Lease Negotiation Assistance: . . . .Yes
Total Units (As of 8/31/1992): 95	Royalty: 4%, Advert: 3-5%	Co-operative Advertising: . . . . No
Projected New Units for 1993: 8	Contract Periods (Yrs.): . . . Infinite	Training: . . . . 2 Wks. Headquarters
Distribution: US-95;Can-0;Overseas-0	Area Development Agreement: . .No	. . . . (Tuition of $975)
North America: . . . . 22 States	Sub-Franchise Contract: . . . . . .No	On-Going Support: B,C,D,e,G,H,I/ 8
Concentration: . . 21 in GA, 14 in FL, 8 in NC	Expand in Territory: . . . . Yes	EXPANSION PLANS:
Registered: . . . CA,FL.IL,IN,MD,MI,NY,DC	Passive Ownership: . . . . . .Allowed	US: . . . . Eastern US + NM, CA, IL, IN
. . . .	Encourage Conversions: . . . . . Yes	Canada: . . . . No
Type Space: . . . . FS;~800-2,500 SF	Average # Employees: . . . 15-35 PT	Overseas: . . . . No

JERRY'S SUBS - PIZZA

15942 Shady Grove Rd.
Gaithersburg, MD 20877
TEL: (301) 921-8777
FAX: (301) 948-3508
Ms. Kathleen McDonald, Dir. Fran. Dev.

High-volume, high-traffic locations are selected, featuring our "over-stuffed" subs and fresh-dough pizza. Decor is bright and up-scale and provides a warm, friendly family environment.

HISTORY:	FINANCIAL: Earnings Claim: . .No	FRANCHISOR TRAINING/SUPPORT:
Established in 1954; . . 1st Franchised in 1981	Cash Investment: $50-75K	Financial Assistance Provided: . . . . .Yes
Company-Owned Units (As of 8/31/1992): . .1	Total Investment: $150-225K	Site Selection Assistance: . . . . . . .Yes
Franchised Units (As of 8/31/1992): 73	Fees: Franchise - $25K	Lease Negotiation Assistance: . . . . .Yes
Total Units (As of 8/31/1992): 74	Royalty: 5%, Advert: 3%	Co-operative Advertising: . . . . . . .Yes
Projected New Units for 1993: 10	Contract Periods (Yrs.): 20	Training: . . . . . 10 Wks. Aspen Hill, MD
Distribution: US-74;Can-0;Overseas-0	Area Development Agreement: Yes/20	. . . .
North America: . . . . 5 States	Sub-Franchise Contract: . . . . . .No	On-Going Support: C,D,E,F,G,H/ 15
Concentration: . .38 in MD, 24 in VA, 4 in DC	Expand in Territory: . . . . Yes	EXPANSION PLANS:
Registered: . . . . MD,VA	Passive Ownership: . . . Discouraged	US: . . . . .Mid-Atlantic Only
. . . .	Encourage Conversions: . . . . Yes	Canada: . . . . No
Type Space: . . . . SC, RM;~1,800 SF	Average # Employees: . .2 FT, 14 PT	Overseas: . . . . No

JUICY LUCY'S DRIVE THRU

2235 First St., # 206
Ft. Myers, FL 33901
TEL: (800) 654-6817 (813) 332-0022
FAX: (813) 332-1262
Ms. Suzanne M. Grady, President

Double drive-thru restaurants, featuring fresh, never frozen, hamburgers, freshly-prepared specialty sandwiches, as well as breakfast. Voted Best Hamburger in Southwest Florida in 1990 and 1991.

HISTORY: . . . .
Established in 1988; . . 1st Franchised in 1991
Company-Owned Units (As of 8/31/1992): . .4
Franchised Units (As of 8/31/1992): 3
Total Units (As of 8/31/1992): 7
Projected New Units for 1993: 14
Distribution: US-7;Can-0;Overseas-0
North America: . . . . .1 State
Concentration: . . . . 7 in FL
Registered: . . . . .All
. . . .
Type Space: . . . . FS;~25,000 SF

FINANCIAL: Earnings Claim: . .No
Cash Investment: $75-250K
Total Investment: $550-650K
Fees: Franchise - $25K
Royalty: 5%, Advert: 1.5%
Contract Periods (Yrs.): . . . 20/20
Area Development Agreement: Yes/5
Sub-Franchise Contract: . . . . .No
Expand in Territory: . . . . . . Yes
Passive Ownership: . . . Discouraged
Encourage Conversions: . . . . . NA
Average # Employees: . .8 FT, 20 PT

FRANCHISOR TRAINING/SUPPORT:
Financial Assistance Provided: . . . . . No
Site Selection Assistance: . . . . .Yes
Lease Negotiation Assistance: . . . . .Yes
Co-operative Advertising: . . . . No
Training: . . . . 3 Wks. Headquarters
On-Going Support: C,D,E,H,I/ 7
EXPANSION PLANS:
US: . . . . Southeast
Canada: . . . . .No
Overseas: . . . . No

KENTUCKY FRIED CHICKEN

P. O. Box 32070
Louisville, KY 40232
TEL: (800) 544-5774 (502) 456-8525
FAX: (502) 456-8255
Mr. Walter J. Simon, VP Fran. Dev.

KENTUCKY FRIED CHICKEN is the industry leader in the quick-service chicken segment. With over 30 years' experience in restaurant franchising, KFC is considered one of the world's premier franchise companies. New build and acquisition opportunities are available throughout the KFC worldwide franchise system.

HISTORY: . . . . IFA
Established in 1952; . . 1st Franchised in 1952
Company-Owned Units (As of 8/31/1992): 2223
Franchised Units (As of 8/31/1992): 5971
Total Units (As of 8/31/1992): 8194
Projected New Units for 1993: 200
Distribution: . . US-4980;Can-0;Overseas-3214
North America: . . . . 50 States
Concentration: . . . .
Registered: . . . . .All
. . . .
Type Space: . . . . FS;~2,400 SF

FINANCIAL: Earnings Claim: . .No
Cash Investment: $150K
Total Investment: $600-800K
Fees: Franchise - $20K
Royalty: 4%, Advert: 4.5%
Contract Periods (Yrs.): . . . 20/10
Area Development Agreement: . .No
Sub-Franchise Contract: . . . . .No
Expand in Territory: . . . . . . .No
Passive Ownership: . . . Not Allowed
Encourage Conversions: . . . . . Yes
Average # Employees: . .3 FT, 20 PT

FRANCHISOR TRAINING/SUPPORT:
Financial Assistance Provided: . . . . . No
Site Selection Assistance: . . . . .Yes
Lease Negotiation Assistance: . . . No
Co-operative Advertising: . . . . .Yes
Training: . . . . . 6 Wks. KFC Restaurant,
. . . . Plus Orientation
On-Going Support: B,C,d,E,F,G,H,I/ . . 12
EXPANSION PLANS:
US: . . . . All US
Canada: . . . . .All Canada
Overseas: . . . . Yes

KRYSTAL RESTAURANTS
& KRYSTAL KWIK

One Union Square, 10th Fl.
Chattanooga, TN 37402
TEL: (800) 458-5912 (615) 757-1577
FAX: (615) 757-5616
Mr. Bill Fort, Dir. Fran. Sales

The company franchises both full-size KRYSTAL RESTAURANTS and double drive-thru KRYSTAL KWIK RESTAURANTS. Both feature the unique KRYSTAL BURGER, which is prepared on a grill and topped with steamed onions to give it its mouth-watering flavor.

HISTORY: . . . . IFA
Established in 1932; . . 1st Franchised in 1990
Company-Owned Units (As of 8/31/1992): 232
Franchised Units (As of 8/31/1992): 12
Total Units (As of 8/31/1992): 244
Projected New Units for 1993: 42
Distribution: US-244;Can-0;Overseas-0
North America: . . . . 7 States
Concentration: . . . . TN, GA, AL
Registered: . . . . .FL
. . . .
Type Space: . . . . FS, RM;~ SF

FINANCIAL: Earnings Claim: . .No
Cash Investment: $100-150K
Total Investment: $325-950K
Fees: Franchise - $32.5K
Royalty: 4.5%, Advert: . . . 4+1%
Contract Periods (Yrs.): . . . 10/10
Area Development Agreement: . Yes
Sub-Franchise Contract: . . . . .No
Expand in Territory: . . . . Yes
Passive Ownership: . . . Not Allowed
Encourage Conversions: . . . . . Yes
Average # Employees: 8/Shift

FRANCHISOR TRAINING/SUPPORT:
Financial Assistance Provided: . . . . . No
Site Selection Assistance: . . . . .Yes
Lease Negotiation Assistance: . . . . .Yes
Co-operative Advertising: . . . . .Yes
Training: . . . . 5 Wks. Headquarters,
. . . .
On-Going Support: C,D,E,G,H,I/ . . . . . .
EXPANSION PLANS:
US: . . . . Southeastern US only
Canada: . . . . .No
Overseas: . . . . No

LE CROISSANT SHOP

227 W. 40th St.
New York, NY 10018
TEL: (212) 719-5940
FAX: (212) 944-0269
Mr. Jacques Pelletier, VP

French bakery cafe - specialty croissants, bread, soups, french sandwiches and gourmet salads.

HISTORY:	FINANCIAL: Earnings Claim: . .No	FRANCHISOR TRAINING/SUPPORT:
Established in 1981; . . 1st Franchised in 1984	Cash Investment: $100K	Financial Assistance Provided: . . . .
Company-Owned Units (As of 8/31/1992): . .4	Total Investment: $200-300K	Site Selection Assistance: . . . .
Franchised Units (As of 8/31/1992): 34	Fees: Franchise - $22.5K	Lease Negotiation Assistance: . . . .
Total Units (As of 8/31/1992): 38	Royalty: 5%, Advert: 2%	Co-operative Advertising: . . . .
Projected New Units for 1993: 5	Contract Periods (Yrs.): 10/5/5	Training: . . . . 4 Wks. Headquarters
Distribution: US-20;Can-0;Overseas-18	Area Development Agreement: Yes/10	
North America: . . . . 4 States	Sub-Franchise Contract:	On-Going Support: /
Concentration: . . . 16 in NY, 1 in PA, 1 in FL	Expand in Territory:	EXPANSION PLANS:
Registered:	Passive Ownership:	US: . . . . East Coast
. . . .	Encourage Conversions:	Canada: . . . . .No
Type Space: . . . . SF;~1,000 SF	Average # Employees: . . . . . 10 FT	Overseas: . . . . No

LITTLE CAESARS PIZZA

2211 Woodward Ave., Fox Office Ctr.
Detroit, MI 48201
TEL: (800) 447-1544 (313) 983-6000
FAX: (313) 983-6494
Mr. Gary Jensen, Dir. Fran. Sales

LITTLE CAESARS PIZZA is the world's largest carry-out pizza chain, as well as one of the fastest-growing companies in the industry. The LITTLE CAESARS system developed over 30 years of experience in the restaurant business, and gives its franchisees the means to provide their customers with a quality product, great value and fast service.

HISTORY: . . . . IFA	FINANCIAL: Earnings Claim: . .No	FRANCHISOR TRAINING/SUPPORT:
Established in 1959; . . 1st Franchised in 1961	Cash Investment: . . . .$	Financial Assistance Provided: . . . Yes(I)
Company-Owned Units (As of 8/31/1992): 1000	Total Investment: $140-180K	Site Selection Assistance: . . . . .Yes
Franchised Units (As of 8/31/1992): 3100	Fees: Franchise - $20K	Lease Negotiation Assistance: . . . . .Yes
Total Units (As of 8/31/1992): 4100	Royalty: , Advert:	Co-operative Advertising: . . . . . . .Yes
Projected New Units for 1993: 650	Contract Periods (Yrs.):	Training: . . . . . 7 Wks. Headquarters
Distribution: . . US-3925;Can-160;Overseas-15	Area Development Agreement: . .No	. . . .
North America:	Sub-Franchise Contract: . . . . .No	On-Going Support: B,C,D,E,G,H,I/ . . . . .
Concentration:	Expand in Territory: . . . . . . Yes	EXPANSION PLANS:
Registered: . . . . .All	Passive Ownership: . . . Discouraged	US: . . . . All US
. . . .	Encourage Conversions:	Canada: . . . . .All Canada
Type Space: . . . . ;~ SF	Average # Employees:	Overseas: . . . . .Yes

LITTLE KING RESTAURANTS

10842 Old Mill Rd., # 2
Omaha, NE 68154
TEL: (800) 228-2148 (402) 330-5030 C
FAX: (402) 330-3276
Mr. Curtis W. Paterson, President

Fast-food deli and pizza, featuring "The Royal Treat" sub sandwiches, deli-style sandwiches, pizza, soups, salads, yogurt, desserts. Full-line menu. All breads baked fresh in store daily. Ideal for food courts, strip malls, free-standing with drive-thru.

HISTORY: . . . . IFA	FINANCIAL: Earnings Claim: . .No	FRANCHISOR TRAINING/SUPPORT:
Established in 1969; . . 1st Franchised in 1972	Cash Investment: $55-125K	Financial Assistance Provided: . . . . .No
Company-Owned Units (As of 8/31/1992): . 10	Total Investment: $55-125K	Site Selection Assistance: . . . . .Yes
Franchised Units (As of 8/31/1992): 95	Fees: Franchise - $9.5K	Lease Negotiation Assistance: . . . .Yes
Total Units (As of 8/31/1992): 105	Royalty: 6%, Advert: 2%	Co-operative Advertising: . . . . . . .Yes
Projected New Units for 1993: 100	Contract Periods (Yrs.): 15/15	Training: . . . . 2 Wks. Headquarters,
Distribution: US-105;Can-0;Overseas-0	Area Development Agreement: Yes/15	. . . . .2 Wks. Franchisee Store
North America: . . . . 26 States	Sub-Franchise Contract: . . . . .No	On-Going Support: C,D,E,F,G,H,I/ . . . 12
Concentration: . . . . ND, NC, CA	Expand in Territory: . . . . . . Yes	EXPANSION PLANS:
Registered: . . . . .All	Passive Ownership: . . . . . .Allowed	US: . . . . All US
. . . .	Encourage Conversions: . . . . . Yes	Canada: . . . . .All Canada
Type Space: . FS,SF,SC,RM,Court;~1,200 SF	Average # Employees: . . 2 FT, 3 PT	Overseas: . . . . No

LOS RIOS MEXICAN FOODS

835 Supertest Rd., # 200
North York, ON M3J 2M9 CAN
TEL: (416) 665-4077
FAX: (416) 665-1483
Mr. Nick Lattanzio, Fran. Dir.

LOS RIOS, an original Canadian concept in its 9th year, is a unique Mexican fast-food restaurant. Designed to provide today's consumer with a delicious food alternative, consisting of high-quality foods prepared fresh on site. LOS RIOS is continuing expansion through high-volume food court locations.

HISTORY: . . . .
Established in 1983; . . 1st Franchised in 1985
Company-Owned Units (As of 8/31/1992): . .0
Franchised Units (As of 8/31/1992): 14
Total Units (As of 8/31/1992): 14
Projected New Units for 1993: 4
Distribution: US-0;Can-14;Overseas-0
North America: . . . . 2 Provinces
Concentration: . . . . .12 in ON, 2 in PQ
Registered: . . . .
. . . .
Type Space: . . . . RM, Food Courts;~400 SF

FINANCIAL: Earnings Claim: . .No
Cash Investment: $50K
Total Investment: $130K
Fees: Franchise - $25K
Royalty: 6%, Advert: 2%
Contract Periods (Yrs.): 10/5
Area Development Agreement: Yes/10
Sub-Franchise Contract: . . . . .No
Expand in Territory: . . . . . . Yes
Passive Ownership: . . . Not Allowed
Encourage Conversions: . . . . Yes
Average # Employees: . 3-4 FT, 6 PT

FRANCHISOR TRAINING/SUPPORT:
Financial Assistance Provided: . . . Yes(I)
Site Selection Assistance: . . . . . . .Yes
Lease Negotiation Assistance: . . . .Yes
Co-operative Advertising: . . . . . . .Yes
Training: . . . . . . .4-6 Wks. Headquarters,
. . . . 4-6 Wks. Existing New Unit
On-Going Support: C,D,E,F,G,H,I/ . . . 20
EXPANSION PLANS:
US: . . . . Northwest and North
Canada: . . . . .All Canada
Overseas: . . . . No

MAGIC WOK

2060 W. Laskey Rd.
Toledo, OH 43613
TEL: (800) 447-8998 (419) 471-0696
FAX: (419) 471-0405
Mr. John Byron, VP

Chinese fast food with drive-thru, take-out and home delivery operation with minimal amount of seating.

HISTORY: . . . . IFA
Established in 1983; . . 1st Franchised in 1991
Company-Owned Units (As of 8/31/1992): . .3
Franchised Units (As of 8/31/1992): 17
Total Units (As of 8/31/1992): 20
Projected New Units for 1993: 16
Distribution: US-20;Can-0;Overseas-0
North America: . . . . 2 States
Concentration: . . . . .16 in OH, 4 in MI
Registered: . . . . .MI
. . . .
Type Space: . FS, SF, SC, RM;~600-1,600 SF

FINANCIAL: Earnings Claim: . .No
Cash Investment: $55-70K
Total Investment: $75-125K
Fees: Franchise - $12.5K
Royalty: 6%, Advert: 2%
Contract Periods (Yrs.): 10/10
Area Development Agreement: Yes/10
Sub-Franchise Contract: . . . . .No
Expand in Territory: . . . . . . Yes
Passive Ownership: . . . Discouraged
Encourage Conversions: . . . . . Yes
Average # Employees: . . 4 FT, 8 PT

FRANCHISOR TRAINING/SUPPORT:
Financial Assistance Provided: . . . . .No
Site Selection Assistance: . . . . . . .Yes
Lease Negotiation Assistance: . . . .Yes
Co-operative Advertising: . . . . . . .Yes
Training: . . . . 2 Wks. Headquarters
. . . .
On-Going Support: A,B,C,d,E,F,G,h,I/ . 10
EXPANSION PLANS:
US: . . . . All US
Canada: . . . . .All Canada
Overseas: . . . . .Yes

MAID-RITE

3112 University Ave.
Des Moines, IA 50311
TEL: (515) 279-5022
FAX:
Mr. Clayton Blue, Owner

Double-ground, loose meat sandwich, using 100% USDA choice ground chuck. A special seasoning that enhances the flavor of beef is used in the cooking process (cooker used separates the grease from the meat). Also features a lightly-breaded pork tenderloin.

HISTORY: . . . .
Established in 1926; . . 1st Franchised in 1926
Company-Owned Units (As of 8/31/1992): . .3
Franchised Units (As of 8/31/1992): 160
Total Units (As of 8/31/1992): 163
Projected New Units for 1993: 30
Distribution: US-163;Can-0;Overseas-0
North America: . . . . 8 States
Concentration: . . 80 in IA, 25 in IL, 10 in MO
Registered: . . . . FL,IL,IN,OR,SD
. . . .
Type Space: FS, SF, SC, RM;~1,000-1,500 SF

FINANCIAL: Earnings Claim: . .No
Cash Investment: $20K
Total Investment: $30-70K
Fees: Franchise - $10-15K
Royalty: 6%, Advert: 2%
Contract Periods (Yrs.): 10/10
Area Development Agreement: Yes/10
Sub-Franchise Contract: . . . . . Yes
Expand in Territory: . . . . . . Yes
Passive Ownership: . . . . .Allowed
Encourage Conversions: . . . . Yes
Average # Employees: . . 3 FT, 2 PT

FRANCHISOR TRAINING/SUPPORT:
Financial Assistance Provided: . . . Yes(I)
Site Selection Assistance: . . . . . . .NA
Lease Negotiation Assistance: . . . . .No
Co-operative Advertising: . . . . . . .NA
Training: . . . . As Required On-Site
. . . .
On-Going Support: B,C,D,E,F,G,H/ . . . .
EXPANSION PLANS:
US: . . . . All US
Canada: . . . . No
Overseas: . . . . No

MARCO'S PIZZA

5254 Monroe St.
Toledo, OH 43623
TEL: (419) 885-4844
FAX:
Mr. Ken R. Switzer, Dir. Admin.

MARCO'S PIZZA sells the most popular pizza in its Ohio and Michigan markets due to its high product quality, excellent service and strong brand image. Our highly-refined MARCO'S PIZZA system and strong franchise support provide great opportunities for those with prior food experience.

HISTORY:	FINANCIAL: Earnings Claim: . Yes	FRANCHISOR TRAINING/SUPPORT:
Established in 1978; . . 1st Franchised in 1979	Cash Investment: $35-50K	Financial Assistance Provided: . . . Yes(I)
Company-Owned Units (As of 8/31/1992): . 17	Total Investment: $90-125K	Site Selection Assistance: . . . . Yes
Franchised Units (As of 8/31/1992): 34	Fees: Franchise - $12K	Lease Negotiation Assistance: . . . . . Yes
Total Units (As of 8/31/1992): 51	Royalty: 5%, Advert: 1.5%	Co-operative Advertising: . . . . Yes
Projected New Units for 1993: 10	Contract Periods (Yrs.): 10/10	Training: . . . . 90 Days Headquarters
Distribution: US-51;Can-0;Overseas-0	Area Development Agreement: . Yes	
North America: . . . . 2 States	Sub-Franchise Contract: . . . . . . No	On-Going Support: B,C,D,E,F,G,H/ . . 18
Concentration: . . . . .44 in OH, 7 in MI	Expand in Territory: . . . . No	EXPANSION PLANS:
Registered: . . . . IN,MI	Passive Ownership: . . . Not Allowed	US: . . . . Ohio and Michigan
. . . .	Encourage Conversions: . . . . . No	Canada: . . . . No
Type Space: . . . . SC;~1,400 SF	Average # Employees: . .8 FT, 16 PT	Overseas: . . . . No

MARY'S PIZZA SHACK

P. O. Box 1049
Boyes Hot Springs, CA 95416
TEL: (707) 938-3602
FAX: (707) 938-5976
Mr. Cullen Williamson, President

We distinguish ourselves from other pizza restaurants by offering a complete menu of Italian specialties, soups and salads, as well as award-winning pizzas in an open family environment. With over 30 years of experience in operating high-volume restaurants, we have a lot to offer our franchisees.

HISTORY: . . . . IFA	FINANCIAL: Earnings Claim: . .No	FRANCHISOR TRAINING/SUPPORT:
Established in 1959; . . 1st Franchised in 1990	Cash Investment: $100-200K	Financial Assistance Provided: . . . . . No
Company-Owned Units (As of 8/31/1992): . .9	Total Investment: $400-450K	Site Selection Assistance: . . . . Yes
Franchised Units (As of 8/31/1992): 2	Fees: Franchise - $30K	Lease Negotiation Assistance: . . . . Yes
Total Units (As of 8/31/1992): 11	Royalty: 5%, Advert: 3%	Co-operative Advertising: . . . . Yes
Projected New Units for 1993: 1	Contract Periods (Yrs.): 20/10	Training: . . . . 5 Wks. Headquarters,
Distribution: US-11;Can-0;Overseas-0	Area Development Agreement: Yes/Var	. . . . 3 Wks. On-Site
North America: . . . . .1 State	Sub-Franchise Contract: . . . . . .No	On-Going Support: C,D,E,H/ 11
Concentration: . . . . 10 in CA	Expand in Territory: . . . . . . .No	EXPANSION PLANS:
Registered: . . . . CA	Passive Ownership: . . . Not Allowed	US: . . . . Northern California
. . . .	Encourage Conversions: . . . . . Yes	Canada: . . . . No
Type Space: . . . FS, SF, SC;~3,000-4,000 SF	Average # Employees: . .8 FT, 27 PT	Overseas: . . . . No

MAZZIO'S PIZZA

4441 S. 72nd E. Ave.
Tulsa, OK 74137
TEL: (918) 663-8880
FAX: (918) 664-2518
Mr. Steve Davis, Dir. Fran. Ops./Dev.

MAZZIO'S is a family pizza restaurant, specializing in offering a great-tasting pizza at low everyday prices. The decor is decidedly up-scale, featuring nostalgia and up-to-date colors and restaurant decorating schemes. The base building is 3,200 SF with video games plus a TV room. Home delivery is available in most locations. MAZZIO'S also features a signature 30-item plus salad bar.

HISTORY: . . . . IFA	FINANCIAL: Earnings Claim: . Yes	FRANCHISOR TRAINING/SUPPORT:
Established in 1961; . . 1st Franchised in 1969	Cash Investment: $200K	Financial Assistance Provided: . . . . .NA
Company-Owned Units (As of 8/31/1992): . 86	Total Investment: $600-800K	Site Selection Assistance: . . . . Yes
Franchised Units (As of 8/31/1992): 118	Fees: Franchise - $20K	Lease Negotiation Assistance: . . . . No
Total Units (As of 8/31/1992): 204	Royalty: 3%, Advert: 1%	Co-operative Advertising: . . . . Yes
Projected New Units for 1993: 10	Contract Periods (Yrs.): 20/5	Training: . . . . 16 Wks. Headquarters
Distribution: US-204;Can-0;Overseas-0	Area Development Agreement: Yes/20	. . . .
North America:	Sub-Franchise Contract: . . . . . .No	On-Going Support: B,C,d,E,f,G,h/ . . . 41
Concentration: . 84 in OK, 36 in TX, 20 in AR	Expand in Territory: . . . . Yes	EXPANSION PLANS:
Registered: . . . . IL,IN,MI,VA	Passive Ownership: . . . Not Allowed	US: . . . . Lower Midwest
. . . .	Encourage Conversions: . . . . . Yes	Canada: . . . . No
Type Space: . . . . .FS, SC;~3,500 SF	Average # Employees: 3 FT, 15-20 PT	Overseas: . . . . No

MCDONALD'S CORPORATION

One McDonald's Plaza, Kroc Dr.
Oak Brook, IL 60521
TEL: (708) 575-6196
FAX: (708) 575-5645
Licensing Dept.

World's leading food service organization, serving 22 million customers a day, with annual sales of over $20 billion. 84% of MCDONALD'S restaurants are franchised. Restaurants are franchised by 2 methods: Conventional purchase or leasing program, depending on amount of funds available to invest.

HISTORY: . . . . IFA
Established in 1955; . . 1st Franchised in 1955
Company-Owned Units (As of 8/31/1992): 3491
Franchised Units (As of 8/31/1992): 9093
Total Units (As of 8/31/1992): 12584
Projected New Units for 1993: . . . .
Distribution: US-8807;Can-644;Overseas-3133
 North America: . . . . 50 States
 Concentration: . . . .
Registered: . . . . .All
. . . .
Type Space: . . . .;~ SF

FINANCIAL: Earnings Claim: . Yes
Cash Investment: $75-175K
Total Investment: $550K
Fees: Franchise - $22.5K
 Royalty: 3.5%, Advert: 4%
Contract Periods (Yrs.): 20
Area Development Agreement: . .No
Sub-Franchise Contract: . . . . .No
Expand in Territory: . . . . . . .No
Passive Ownership: . . . Not Allowed
Encourage Conversions: . . . . .No
Average # Employees: . .8 FT, 51 PT

FRANCHISOR TRAINING/SUPPORT:
Financial Assistance Provided: . . . . .No
Site Selection Assistance: . . . . . . .NA
Lease Negotiation Assistance: . . . . .NA
Co-operative Advertising: . . . . .Yes
Training: . . . . . .2 Yrs. Local Restaurant,
 . . 4 Wks. Regional Offices, 2 Wks. HQ
On-Going Support: B,C,D,E,F,G,H/ . . 99
EXPANSION PLANS:
 US: . . . . All US
 Canada: . . . . .All Canada
 Overseas: . . . . .Yes

MELLOW MUSHROOM PIZZA

695 North Ave., NE
Atlanta, GA 30308
TEL: (404) 524-6133
FAX:
Mr. Nick Nicholson, Sec./Treas.

MELLOW MUSHROOM is a neighborhood-style pizzeria where quality of food is accented and the atmosphere is relaxed and casual. We offer good food at a fair price and emphasis is placed on the healthfulness of our product. Streamlined menu, consisting of pizza, sandwiches and salads, helps eliminate waste. This eases inventory control and increases profits.

HISTORY: . . . .
Established in 1975; . . 1st Franchised in 1987
Company-Owned Units (As of 8/31/1992): . .0
Franchised Units (As of 8/31/1992): 15
Total Units (As of 8/31/1992): 15
Projected New Units for 1993: . . . .
Distribution: US-15;Can-0;Overseas-0
 North America: . . . . .1 State
 Concentration: . . . . 15 in GA
Registered: . . . .
. . . .
Type Space: . . . . .All Sites Poss.;~1,500 SF

FINANCIAL: Earnings Claim: . .No
Cash Investment: $40-100K
Total Investment: $50-100K
Fees: Franchise - $25K
 Royalty: 5%, Advert: 1%
Contract Periods (Yrs.): 15
Area Development Agreement: . .No
Sub-Franchise Contract: . . . . .No
Expand in Territory: . . . . . . Yes
Passive Ownership: . . . Discouraged
Encourage Conversions: . . . . Yes
Average # Employees: . . 5 FT, 5 PT

FRANCHISOR TRAINING/SUPPORT:
Financial Assistance Provided: . . . . .No
Site Selection Assistance: . . . . . . .Yes
Lease Negotiation Assistance: . . . .Yes
Co-operative Advertising: . . . . . . .Yes
Training: . . . . . . 1-2 Wks. Headquarters
. . . .
On-Going Support: a,b,C,D,E,F/ 6
EXPANSION PLANS:
 US: . . . . Southeast
 Canada: . . . . .No
 Overseas: . . . . No

MIAMI SUBS

6300 NW 31st Ave.
Ft. Lauderdale, FL 33309
TEL: (305) 973-0000
FAX: (305) 973-7616
Mr. Donald Perlyn, EVP Fran. Dev.

MIAMI SUBS is a quick-service restaurant concept, featuring fresh food, cooked-to-order, providing a diverse menu with exceptional quality of moderately-priced items designed to encourage frequent visits. Our bright, lively, distinctive decor creates both daytime and evening appeal.

HISTORY: . . . . IFA
Established in 1983; . . 1st Franchised in 1986
Company-Owned Units (As of 8/31/1992): . 13
Franchised Units (As of 8/31/1992): 80
Total Units (As of 8/31/1992): 93
Projected New Units for 1993: 90
Distribution: US-93;Can-0;Overseas-0
 North America: . . . . 8 States
 Concentration: . . . 78 in FL, 5 in PA, 2 in IN
Registered: . . . . All States
. . . .
Type Space: . . . . FS;~3,000 SF

FINANCIAL: Earnings Claim: . . .
Cash Investment: $125-175K
Total Investment: $275-350K
Fees: Franchise - $25K
 Royalty: 4%, Advert: 1%
Contract Periods (Yrs.): . . . 20/20
Area Development Agreement: Yes/Var
Sub-Franchise Contract: . . . . .No
Expand in Territory: . . . . . . Yes
Passive Ownership: . . . Not Allowed
Encourage Conversions: . . . . Yes
Average # Employees: . 10 FT, 15 PT

FRANCHISOR TRAINING/SUPPORT:
Financial Assistance Provided: . . . Yes(I)
Site Selection Assistance: . . . . . . .Yes
Lease Negotiation Assistance: . . . . .Yes
Co-operative Advertising: . . . . .NA
Training: . . . . . .5 Wks. Florida Certified
. . . . Training Center
On-Going Support: B,C,D,E,F,G,H/ . . 30
EXPANSION PLANS:
 US: . . . . .All US
 Canada: . . . . .No
 Overseas: . . . . No

MOM'S PIZZA

4457-59 Main St.
Philadelphia, PA 19127
TEL: (215) 482-1044
FAX:
Mr. Nicholas Castellucci, President

MOM'S PIZZA franchise "Bake at Home" pizza stores. The franchisee purchases his supplies from the main office. The franchisee then retails a fresh, hand-made gourmet pizza, which is baked the customer's convenience, in the convenience of his home.

HISTORY:	FINANCIAL: Earnings Claim: . .No	FRANCHISOR TRAINING/SUPPORT:
Established in 1961; . . 1st Franchised in 1981	Cash Investment: $55K	Financial Assistance Provided: . . . . .No
Company-Owned Units (As of 8/31/1992): . .0	Total Investment: $55K	Site Selection Assistance: . . . . . . .Yes
Franchised Units (As of 8/31/1992): 20	Fees: Franchise - $15K	Lease Negotiation Assistance: . . . .Yes
Total Units (As of 8/31/1992): 20	Royalty: 0%, Advert: 0%	Co-operative Advertising: . . . . . . .No
Projected New Units for 1993: 2	Contract Periods (Yrs.): 10/10	Training: . . . . . As Needed Headquarters,
Distribution: US-20;Can-0;Overseas-0	Area Development Agreement: . .No	. . . . .7 Days Existing Franchise
North America: . . . . 2 States	Sub-Franchise Contract: . . . . .No	On-Going Support: B,E,F/ 9
Concentration: . . . . 14 in PA, 6 in NJ	Expand in Territory: . . . . Yes	EXPANSION PLANS:
Registered:	Passive Ownership: . . . Not Allowed	US: . . . . .Pennsylvania and New Jersey
. . . .	Encourage Conversions: . . . . .No	Canada: . . . . .No
Type Space: . . . . .SC;~800 SF	Average # Employees: . . 1 FT, 2 PT	Overseas: . . . . No

MR. GATTI'S

444 Sidney Baker S., P. O. Box 1522
Kerrville, TX 78028
TEL: (512) 257-2000
FAX: (512) 257-2003
Mr. Joel Longtin, CFO

Restaurants that sell "The Best Pizza in Town - Honest!" We also have pasta dishes, sandwiches and a wonderful salad bar, along with bread sticks (cheese and cinnamon) and dessert pizzas. Most restaurants have 3 rooms: quiet dining, big-screen TV and a Good Times Room for small children.

HISTORY:	FINANCIAL: Earnings Claim: . .No	FRANCHISOR TRAINING/SUPPORT:
Established in 1969; . . 1st Franchised in 1974	Cash Investment: . . . . $~150K	Financial Assistance Provided: . . . . .No
Company-Owned Units (As of 8/31/1992): . 74	Total Investment: $150-400K	Site Selection Assistance: . . . . . . .Yes
Franchised Units (As of 8/31/1992): 171	Fees: Franchise - $25K	Lease Negotiation Assistance: . . . .Yes
Total Units (As of 8/31/1992): 245	Royalty: 4%, Advert: 1/2-2%	Co-operative Advertising: . . . . . . .Yes
Projected New Units for 1993: 8	Contract Periods (Yrs.): 20/10	Training: . . . . .Minimum 6 Wks. Various
Distribution: US-245;Can-0;Overseas-0	Area Development Agreement: Yes/Var	. . . . Locations
North America: . . . . 13 States	Sub-Franchise Contract: . . . . .No	On-Going Support: B,C,D,E,F,H/ 48
Concentration: . . 131 in TX, 40 in KY, 20 TN	Expand in Territory: . . . . Yes	EXPANSION PLANS:
Registered: . . . . .FL,IN,VA	Passive Ownership: . . . Not Allowed	US: . . . . Southwest, Midwest,Southeast
. . . .	Encourage Conversions: . . . . . Yes	Canada: . . . . .No
Type Space: . . . .FS, SF, SC, RM;~3,600 SF	Average # Employees: . . 5 FT, 5 PT	Overseas: . . . . No

MR. GOODCENTS

612 W. 47th
Kansas City, MO 64112
TEL: (816) 561-1359
FAX: (816) 561-0819
Mr. Don Burget, VP

Quick-service sub and pasta restaurant.

HISTORY:	FINANCIAL: Earnings Claim: . .No	FRANCHISOR TRAINING/SUPPORT:
Established in 1989; . . 1st Franchised in 1990	Cash Investment: $25-35K	Financial Assistance Provided: . . . . .No
Company-Owned Units (As of 8/31/1992): . .2	Total Investment: $70-90K	Site Selection Assistance: . . . . . . .Yes
Franchised Units (As of 8/31/1992): 10	Fees: Franchise - $12.5K	Lease Negotiation Assistance: . . . .Yes
Total Units (As of 8/31/1992): 12	Royalty: 5%, Advert: 2.5%	Co-operative Advertising: . . . . . . .Yes
Projected New Units for 1993: 15	Contract Periods (Yrs.): 10/10	Training: . . . . . . 30 Days Minimum HQ
Distribution: US-12;Can-0;Overseas-0	Area Development Agreement: . .No	
North America: . . . . 2 States	Sub-Franchise Contract: . . . . .No	On-Going Support: A,B,C,D,E,F,G/ . . .8
Concentration: . . . . 10 in KS, 2 in MO	Expand in Territory: . . . . Yes	EXPANSION PLANS:
Registered:	Passive Ownership: . . . Not Allowed	US: . . . . Midwest
. . . .	Encourage Conversions: . . . . .No	Canada: . . . . .No
Type Space: . . . . . . SC;~1,500-2,000 SF	Average # Employees: 2-5 FT, 8-10 PT	Overseas: . . . . No

MR. JIM'S PIZZA

2995 LBJ Freeway, # 104
Dallas, TX 75234
TEL: (800) 583-5960 (214) 241-9293
FAX: (214) 241-9296
Mr. Chris Bowman, Exec. Dir.

A fast-growing, carry-out/delivery pizza company. The crust is the difference!

HISTORY: . . . .
Established in 1975; . . 1st Franchised in 1981
Company-Owned Units (As of 8/31/1992): . .1
Franchised Units (As of 8/31/1992): 45
Total Units (As of 8/31/1992): 46
Projected New Units for 1993: 4
Distribution: US-46;Can-0;Overseas-0
  North America: . . . . 3 States
  Concentration: . . .44 in TX, 1 in LA, 1 in VA
Registered: . . . . VA
. . . .
Type Space: . . . . SC;~800-1,200 SF

FINANCIAL: Earnings Claim: . Yes
Cash Investment: $45-65K
Total Investment: $45-65K
Fees: Franchise - $10K
  Royalty: 4%, Advert: 1%
Contract Periods (Yrs.): 15/15
Area Development Agreement: Yes/15
Sub-Franchise Contract: . . . . .No
Expand in Territory: . . . . . . Yes
Passive Ownership: . . . Discouraged
Encourage Conversions: . . . . Yes
Average # Employees: . .10 FT, 5 PT

FRANCHISOR TRAINING/SUPPORT:
Financial Assistance Provided: . . . . .No
Site Selection Assistance: . . . . . . .Yes
Lease Negotiation Assistance: . . . .Yes
Co-operative Advertising: . . . . . . .Yes
Training: . . . .300 Hours Training Store,
  . . 10 Days On-Site, Various Classes HQ
On-Going Support: C,D,E,F,G,H,I/ 4
EXPANSION PLANS:
  US: . . . . All US
  Canada: . . . . .All Canada
  Overseas: . . . . No

MRS. VANELLI'S PIZZA & ITALIAN FOODS

2133 Royal Windsor Dr., # 23
Mississauga, ON L5J 1K5 CAN
TEL: (416) 823-8883
FAX: (416) 823-5255
Mr. Nik Jurkovic, Dir. Fran.

Located in high-volume food courts, serving traditional Italian dishes - i.e. specializing in freshly-prepared pizza, pasta, soup, salad, Italian-style submarines. Located in urban and regional shopping centers across Canada.

HISTORY: . . . .
Established in 1981; . . 1st Franchised in 1983
Company-Owned Units (As of 8/31/1992): . .4
Franchised Units (As of 8/31/1992): 75
Total Units (As of 8/31/1992): 79
Projected New Units for 1993: 10
Distribution: US-0;Can-79;Overseas-0
  North America: . . . . 7 Provinces
  Concentration: . . 52 in ON, 12 in BC, 5 in AB
Registered: . . . . AB
. . . .
Type Space: . . . . RM;~360 SF

FINANCIAL: Earnings Claim: . . .
Cash Investment: $40-60K
Total Investment: $175-225K
Fees: Franchise - $25K
  Royalty: 6%, Advert: 2%
Contract Periods (Yrs.): . . 10-5/10-5
Area Development Agreement: Yes/15
Sub-Franchise Contract: . . . . . Yes
Expand in Territory: . . . . . . Yes
Passive Ownership: . . . Not Allowed
Encourage Conversions: . . . . Yes
Average # Employees: . 2 FT, 3-4 PT

FRANCHISOR TRAINING/SUPPORT:
Financial Assistance Provided: . . . Yes(I)
Site Selection Assistance: . . . . . . .Yes
Lease Negotiation Assistance: . . . . .Yes
Co-operative Advertising: . . . . . . .Yes
Training: . . . . 1 Wk. Headquarters, 1 Wk.
  . . . . . . Toronto Site, 1 Wk. On-Site
On-Going Support: A,B,C,D,E,F,G,H,I/ 31
EXPANSION PLANS:
  US: . . . . All US
  Canada: . . . . .All Canada
  Overseas: . . . . Yes

MY FRIEND'S PLACE

106 Hammond Dr.
Atlanta, GA 30328
TEL: (404) 843-2803
FAX: (404) 843-0371
Ms. Rosalind C. Katz, VP

A quality franchise opportunity for your financial independence and future. Our restaurants cater to the quality-oriented customer interested in a quick, yet light and healthy lunch, specializing in sandwiches, salads, soups, quiches and homemade desserts. MY FRIEND'S PLACE is a "Fresh Food Express!"

HISTORY: . . . . IFA
Established in 1980; . . 1st Franchised in 1990
Company-Owned Units (As of 8/31/1992): . .3
Franchised Units (As of 8/31/1992): 3
Total Units (As of 8/31/1992): 6
Projected New Units for 1993: 4
Distribution: US-6;Can-0;Overseas-0
  North America: . . . . 1 State
  Concentration: . . . . 6 in GA
Registered: . . . .
. . . .
Type Space: . . . . .SC, RM;~400-1,500 SF

FINANCIAL: Earnings Claim: . .No
Cash Investment: $45K
Total Investment: $45-77K
Fees: Franchise - $15K
  Royalty: Flat, Advert: . . . . Flat
Contract Periods (Yrs.): 15/10
Area Development Agreement: .No
Sub-Franchise Contract: . . . . . Yes
Expand in Territory: . . . . . . Yes
Passive Ownership: . . . Not Allowed
Encourage Conversions: . . . . Yes
Average # Employees: . . 2 FT, 2 PT

FRANCHISOR TRAINING/SUPPORT:
Financial Assistance Provided: . . . . .No
Site Selection Assistance: . . . . . . .Yes
Lease Negotiation Assistance: . . . .Yes
Co-operative Advertising: . . . . . . .Yes
Training: . . . . . . .10 Business Days HQ,
  . . . . 5 Business Days Franchisee Site
On-Going Support: b,C,d,E,f/ 4
EXPANSION PLANS:
  US: . . . Southeast Only,GA,FL,AL,NC
  Canada: . . . . No
  Overseas: . . . . No

NATHAN'S FAMOUS

1400 Old Country Rd., # 400
Westbury, NY 11590
TEL: (800) NATHANS (516) 338-8500
FAX: (516) 338-7220
Mr. Carl Paley, VP Fran. Devel.

Features 8 prototypes from kiosk to free-standing. 76 years of quality food service. Highly supportive company with professional staff to guide and assist.

HISTORY:	FINANCIAL: Earnings Claim: . .No	FRANCHISOR TRAINING/SUPPORT:
Established in 1916; . . 1st Franchised in 1979	Cash Investment: $150-200K	Financial Assistance Provided: . . . Yes(I)
Company-Owned Units (As of 8/31/1992): . .8	Total Investment: $300-650K	Site Selection Assistance: . . . . . . .Yes
Franchised Units (As of 8/31/1992): 83	Fees: Franchise - $30K	Lease Negotiation Assistance: . . . .Yes
Total Units (As of 8/31/1992): 91	Royalty: 4%, Advert: 3%	Co-operative Advertising: . . . . . . .Yes
Projected New Units for 1993: 35	Contract Periods (Yrs.): . . . 20/15	Training: . . . . 2 Wks. Headquarters,
Distribution: US-91;Can-0;Overseas-0	Area Development Agreement: Yes/20	. . . .
North America: . . . . 12 States	Sub-Franchise Contract: . . . . .No	On-Going Support: C,D,E,F,H,I/ . . . . . .
Concentration: . . . . NY, NJ, FL	Expand in Territory: . . . . . . Yes	EXPANSION PLANS:
Registered: . . . CA,FL,HI,IL,IN,MD,MI,MN	Passive Ownership: . . . Discouraged	US: . . . . Eastern & Mid-Atlantic, West
. . . . .NY,RI,VA,WA,WI,DC	Encourage Conversions: . . . . Yes	Canada: . . . . .Yes
Type Space: . FS, SF, SC, RM;~750-3,000 SF	Average # Employees: . .8 FT, 10 PT	Overseas: . . . . .Yes

NEW HAVEN PIZZA

470 E. Main St.
Branford, CT 06405
TEL: (203) 483-9955 C
FAX: (203) 483-9959
Mr. Richard F. DeMichele, President

Full-service, take-out pizza, serving New Haven-style pizza.

HISTORY:	FINANCIAL: Earnings Claim: . .No	FRANCHISOR TRAINING/SUPPORT:
Established in 1990; . . 1st Franchised in 1990	Cash Investment: $50K	Financial Assistance Provided: . . . Yes(I)
Company-Owned Units (As of 8/31/1992): . .1	Total Investment: $200-250K	Site Selection Assistance: . . . . . . .Yes
Franchised Units (As of 8/31/1992): 2	Fees: Franchise - $15K	Lease Negotiation Assistance: . . . .Yes
Total Units (As of 8/31/1992): 3	Royalty: 4%, Advert: 0%	Co-operative Advertising: . . . . . . .Yes
Projected New Units for 1993: 3	Contract Periods (Yrs.): . . . 10/20	Training: . . . . 2 Wks. Headquarters
Distribution: US-3;Can-0;Overseas-0	Area Development Agreement: . .No	. . . .
North America: . . . . .1 State	Sub-Franchise Contract: . . . . .No	On-Going Support: A,C,D,E,H/ 2
Concentration: . . . . 3 in CT	Expand in Territory: . . . . . . Yes	EXPANSION PLANS:
Registered:	Passive Ownership: . . . Discouraged	US: . . . . Northeast
. . . .	Encourage Conversions: . . . . .No	Canada: . . . . .No
Type Space: . . . . . FS, SF, SC;~2,000 SF	Average # Employees: . . 3 FT, 3 PT	Overseas: . . . . No

NEW YORK FRIES

560 Inverness Rd.
Lisle, IL 60532
TEL: (800) 447-7027 (708) 852-8240
FAX: (708) 852-8261
Mr. Gary R. Dobson, VP Fran. Dev.

This is definitely freedom from ordinary franchises. The menu is simple! We offer extraordinary fresh-cut french fries with a range of exquisite toppings. The locations are situated in food courts found in the best US mega-malls. The concept is simple and controllable. It appeals to seasoned operators wanting to expand their holdings or to budding entrepreneurs.

HISTORY: . . . . IFA	FINANCIAL: Earnings Claim: . .No	FRANCHISOR TRAINING/SUPPORT:
Established in 1984; . . 1st Franchised in 1985	Cash Investment: . . . .$	Financial Assistance Provided: . . . . .No
Company-Owned Units (As of 8/31/1992): . .7	Total Investment: $140-170K	Site Selection Assistance: . . . . . . .Yes
Franchised Units (As of 8/31/1992): 55	Fees: Franchise - $25K	Lease Negotiation Assistance: . . . . .Yes
Total Units (As of 8/31/1992): 62	Royalty: 6%, Advert: 1.5%	Co-operative Advertising: . . . . . . .Yes
Projected New Units for 1993: 10	Contract Periods (Yrs.): . . . 10/5/5	Training: . . . . .1 Wk. Headquarters
Distribution: US-5;Can-57;Overseas-0	Area Development Agreement: Yes/2	. . . . Up to 1 Wk. On-Site
North America:	Sub-Franchise Contract: . . . . .No	On-Going Support: b,C,D,E,G,h/ . . . . . .
Concentration: 5 in MI, 1 in WA, ON, BC, AB	Expand in Territory: . . . . . . Yes	EXPANSION PLANS:
Registered: . . . . . .IL,MI,NY,VA,WA,AB	Passive Ownership: . . . Discouraged	US: . . . . .All US
. . . .	Encourage Conversions: . . . . Yes	Canada: . . . . .All Canada
Type Space: . .RM, Food Courts;~300-400 SF	Average # Employees: 3-5 FT, 1-3 PT	Overseas: . . . . Open

OLD FLORIDA BAR-B-Q

3009 Skidaway Rd.
Savannah, GA 31404
TEL: (912) 356-1156
FAX:
Mr. Bill Claus, President

OLD FLORIDA BAR-B-Q offers top-quality southern BBQ, with full service or take-out only, in a laid-back country atmosphere. Drive-thru, take-out, catering and delivery add immensely to the volume. Buffalo wings, fish and burgers complement the delicious BBQ menu, all with cholesterol-conscious quality in mind.

HISTORY:	FINANCIAL: Earnings Claim: . .No	FRANCHISOR TRAINING/SUPPORT:
Established in 1985; . . 1st Franchised in 1991	Cash Investment: $50-80K	Financial Assistance Provided: . . . . .No
Company-Owned Units (As of 8/31/1992): . .1	Total Investment: $50-80K	Site Selection Assistance: . . . . . . .Yes
Franchised Units (As of 8/31/1992): 1	Fees: Franchise - $12.5K	Lease Negotiation Assistance: . . . .Yes
Total Units (As of 8/31/1992): 2	Royalty: 3%, Advert: 2%	Co-operative Advertising: . . . . . . .Yes
Projected New Units for 1993: 1	Contract Periods (Yrs.): 10/5/5	Training: . . . . 3 Wks. Headquarters,
Distribution: US-2;Can-0;Overseas-0	Area Development Agreement: Yes/10	. . . . 2 Wks. On-Site, On-Going
North America: . . . . 2 States	Sub-Franchise Contract: . . . . .No	On-Going Support: C,D,E,F,H/ . . . .
Concentration: . . . . 1 in FL, 1 in GA	Expand in Territory: . . . . . . Yes	EXPANSION PLANS:
Registered: . . . . .FL	Passive Ownership: . . . Discouraged	US: . . . . East and Midwest
. . . .	Encourage Conversions: . . . . Yes	Canada: . . . . .All Canada
Type Space: . . . . FS or In-Line;~2,300+ SF	Average # Employees: . .10 FT, 2 PT	Overseas: . . . . UK, Sweden

ORANGE JULIUS CANADA

5245 Harvester Rd., P. O. Box 430
Burlington, ON L7R 3Y3 CAN
TEL: (416) 639-1492
FAX: (416) 681-3623
Mr. Jim Douglas, Fran. Dev. Mgr.

Fast-food operation, featuring hot dogs and the brand drink made from freshly-squeezed orange juice, and other flavors.

HISTORY: . . . . IFA	FINANCIAL: Earnings Claim: . .No	FRANCHISOR TRAINING/SUPPORT:
Established in 1926; . . 1st Franchised in 1948	Cash Investment: $50-75K	Financial Assistance Provided: . . . . No
Company-Owned Units (As of 8/31/1992): . .0	Total Investment: $150-200K	Site Selection Assistance: . . . . . . .Yes
Franchised Units (As of 8/31/1992): 107	Fees: Franchise - $30K	Lease Negotiation Assistance: . . . .Yes
Total Units (As of 8/31/1992): 107	Royalty: 6%, Advert: 3%	Co-operative Advertising: . . . . . . .Yes
Projected New Units for 1993: 5	Contract Periods (Yrs.): . . . . . NA	Training: . . . . . 1 Wk. Minneapolis, MN
Distribution: US-0;Can-107;Overseas-0	Area Development Agreement: . .No	. . . .
North America: . . . . 8 Provinces	Sub-Franchise Contract: . . . . .No	On-Going Support: A,B,C,D,E,F,G,H,I/ 59
Concentration: . 45 in BC, 29 in AB, 24 in ON	Expand in Territory: . . . . . . Yes	EXPANSION PLANS:
Registered: . . . . AB	Passive Ownership: . . . Not Allowed	US: . . . . No
. . . .	Encourage Conversions: . . . . Yes	Canada: . . . . .All Canada
Type Space: . . . . RM;~200-300 SF	Average # Employees: . .5 FT, 10 PT	Overseas: . . . . No

PANDA EXPRESS

143 Pasadena Ave.
S. Pasadena, CA 91030
TEL: (213) 257-8183
FAX: (213) 257-0631
Mr. William Yu, Asst. Secty.

Gourmet Chinese food services.

HISTORY:	FINANCIAL: Earnings Claim: . .No	FRANCHISOR TRAINING/SUPPORT:
Established in 1973; . . 1st Franchised in 1990	Cash Investment: $226.7K	Financial Assistance Provided: . . . .NA
Company-Owned Units (As of 8/31/1992): . 58	Total Investment: $274-493K	Site Selection Assistance: . . . . . . .Yes
Franchised Units (As of 8/31/1992): 0	Fees: Franchise - $28.5K	Lease Negotiation Assistance: . . . .Yes
Total Units (As of 8/31/1992): 58	Royalty: 6%, Advert: 1%	Co-operative Advertising: . . . . . . .Yes
Projected New Units for 1993: 30	Contract Periods (Yrs.): 10/5/5	Training: . . . . 45 Days Various Locations
Distribution: US-58;Can-0;Overseas-0	Area Development Agreement: . .No	. . . .
North America: . . . . 13 States	Sub-Franchise Contract: . . . . .No	On-Going Support: a,b,C,D,E,F,H/ . . . 65
Concentration: . . . 39 in CA, 3 in HI, 3 in NJ	Expand in Territory: . . . . . . Yes	EXPANSION PLANS:
Registered: . . . . . CA,HI,MI,MN,ND,RI,WI	Passive Ownership: . . . Discouraged	US: . . . . .All US
. . . .	Encourage Conversions: . . . . NA	Canada: . . . . No
Type Space: . . . . SC, RM;~1,000 SF	Average # Employees: . .10 FT, 8 PT	Overseas: . . . . JA

PAPA DOM'S READY PIZZA

60 Walnut Ave., # 100
Clark, NJ 07066
TEL: (908) 815-7815
FAX: (908) 815-7810
Mr. Larry Meigs, fRAN. sALES dIR.

Gourmet-style pizzas, strombolis, subs. Home delivery. We offer financing assistance, site selection, comprehensive training. Area Developers welcome.

HISTORY:	FINANCIAL: Earnings Claim: . .No	FRANCHISOR TRAINING/SUPPORT:
Established in 1989; . . . 1st Franchised in 1990	Cash Investment: $19.5-24.5K	Financial Assistance Provided: . . . Yes(I)
Company-Owned Units (As of 8/31/1992): . .1	Total Investment: $58.5-74K	Site Selection Assistance: . . . . . . .Yes
Franchised Units (As of 8/31/1992): 177	Fees: Franchise - $12.5K	Lease Negotiation Assistance: . . . . .Yes
Total Units (As of 8/31/1992): 178	Royalty: $200/Wk., Advert: . . 2%	Co-operative Advertising: . . . .
Projected New Units for 1993: 25	Contract Periods (Yrs.): 10/10	Training: . . . . .1 Wk. Headquarters,
Distribution: US-178;Can-0;Overseas-0	Area Development Agreement: Yes/20	. . . . 1 Wk. Franchisee Location
North America:	Sub-Franchise Contract: . . . . .No	On-Going Support: B,C,D,E,F,G,h,I/ . . 10
Concentration:	Expand in Territory: . . . . Yes	EXPANSION PLANS:
Registered: . . . . FL,NY	Passive Ownership: . . . Discouraged	US: . . . . All US
. . . .	Encourage Conversions: . . . . . NA	Canada: . . . . .All Canada
Type Space: . . . FS, SC, RM;~800-1,000 SF	Average # Employees: . . 5 FT, 3 PT	Overseas: . . . . UK, KO

PAPA GINO'S

600 Providence Hwy.
Dedham, MA 02026
TEL: (800) 365-4466 (617) 461-1200 C
FAX: (617) 461-1896
Mr. Richard L. Whitman, VP Fran.

New England's largest privately-owned Italian pizza restaurant chain now offers the opportunity of a lifetime - own your own PAPA GINO'S franchise for under $300,000. Our new 1,700-2,100 SF shopping center franchise model combines eat-in, take-out and delivery for a great investment.

HISTORY: . . . . .IFA	FINANCIAL: Earnings Claim: . Yes	FRANCHISOR TRAINING/SUPPORT:
Established in 1968; . . 1st Franchised in 1992	Cash Investment: $60-75K	Financial Assistance Provided: . . . . .No
Company-Owned Units (As of 8/31/1992): 218	Total Investment: $285-430K	Site Selection Assistance: . . . . .Yes
Franchised Units (As of 8/31/1992): 0	Fees: Franchise - $25K	Lease Negotiation Assistance: . . . .Yes
Total Units (As of 8/31/1992): 218	Royalty: 4.5%, Advert: 2%	Co-operative Advertising: . . . . .Yes
Projected New Units for 1993:	Contract Periods (Yrs.): 10/10	Training: . . . . 4 Wks. Headquarters,
Distribution: US-218;Can-0;Overseas-0	Area Development Agreement: Yes/10	. . . . Includes OJT
North America:	Sub-Franchise Contract: . . . . .No	On-Going Support: C,D,E,G,H/ 85
Concentration:	Expand in Territory: . . . . Yes	EXPANSION PLANS:
Registered: . . . . MI,MN,NY,RI,VA	Passive Ownership: . . . Discouraged	US: . . . . . . S. New England, NY, SE
. . . .	Encourage Conversions: . . . . . Yes	Canada: . . . . No
Type Space: . . . . . . SC;~1,700-2,100 SF	Average # Employees: . .3 FT, 20 PT	Overseas: . . . . No

PASTEL'S

1121 Centre St. N., # 440
Calgary, AB T2E 7K6 CAN
TEL: (403) 230-1151 C
FAX: (403) 230-2182
Ms. Janine Hunka, Fran. Sales Mgr.

PASTEL'S features a full menu of the finest-quality gourmet sandwiches, a mouth-watering array of specialty salads and hearty homemade soups, all prepared with fresh, healthy ingredients and presented with style.

HISTORY: . . . . .CFA	FINANCIAL: Earnings Claim: . Yes	FRANCHISOR TRAINING/SUPPORT:
Established in 1980; . . 1st Franchised in 1982	Cash Investment: $75-95K	Financial Assistance Provided: . . . Yes(I)
Company-Owned Units (As of 8/31/1992): . .0	Total Investment: $160-250K	Site Selection Assistance: . . . . .Yes
Franchised Units (As of 8/31/1992): 18	Fees: Franchise - $25K	Lease Negotiation Assistance: . . . . .Yes
Total Units (As of 8/31/1992): 18	Royalty: 5%, Advert: 0%	Co-operative Advertising: . . . . .Yes
Projected New Units for 1993: 18	Contract Periods (Yrs.): 10/10	Training: . . . .
Distribution: US-0;Can-18;Overseas-0	Area Development Agreement: . .No	
North America: . . . . .1 Province	Sub-Franchise Contract: . . . . .No	On-Going Support: C,D,E,f,G,h/ 12
Concentration: . . . . 18 in BC	Expand in Territory: . . . . Yes	EXPANSION PLANS:
Registered: . . . . AB	Passive Ownership: . . . Discouraged	US: . . . . No
. . . .	Encourage Conversions: . . . . . Yes	Canada: . . . . .All Canada
Type Space: . . . . . . SF, SC, RM;~1,100 SF	Average # Employees: . . 5 FT, 5 PT	Overseas: . . . . No

PENN STATION STEAK & SUB

8510 Morningcalm Dr.
Cincinnati, OH 45255
TEL: (513) 474-5957
FAX:
Mr. Jeff Osterfeld, President

PENN STATION specializes in quality food, prepared fresh before your eyes. We sell original "Philadelphia cheesesteaks," fresh-cut fries, fresh-squeezed lemonade and over-stuffed cold subs. Store locations include strip centers, shopping malls, downtown areas and college campuses.

HISTORY:	FINANCIAL: Earnings Claim: . Yes	FRANCHISOR TRAINING/SUPPORT:
Established in 1983; . . 1st Franchised in 1988	Cash Investment: $30K	Financial Assistance Provided: . . . . . No
Company-Owned Units (As of 8/31/1992): . .1	Total Investment: $115-180K	Site Selection Assistance: . . . . . . .Yes
Franchised Units (As of 8/31/1992): 10	Fees: Franchise - $17.5K	Lease Negotiation Assistance: . . . . .Yes
Total Units (As of 8/31/1992): 11	Royalty: 6%, Advert: . . . . Co-op	Co-operative Advertising: . . . . .No
Projected New Units for 1993: 6	Contract Periods (Yrs.): . . . 5/5/5/5	Training: . . . . . 7-10 Days Headquarters,
Distribution: US-11;Can-0;Overseas-0	Area Development Agreement: . .No	. . . . .7-10 Days On-Site
North America: . . . . 2 States	Sub-Franchise Contract: . . . . . Yes	On-Going Support: B,C,D,E,F,G,H/ . . .2
Concentration: . . . . .9 in OH, 2 in IN	Expand in Territory: . . . . . . Yes	EXPANSION PLANS:
Registered: . . . . .IN	Passive Ownership: . . . Discouraged	US: . . . . Midwest
. . . .	Encourage Conversions: . . . . . Yes	Canada: . . . . .No
Type Space: . . . . . FS, SC, RM;~1,500 SF	Average # Employees: . . 4 FT, 8 PT	Overseas: . . . . No

PETER PIPER PIZZA

2321 W. Royal Palm Rd.
Phoenix, AZ 85021
TEL: (800) 899-3425 (602) 995-1975
FAX: (602) 995-8857
Mr. John F. Baillon, Dir. Fran. Sales

PETER PIPER PIZZA fills a unique niche in the fast-food industry pizza segment. PETER PIPER PIZZA offers take-out, delivery or casual dine-in, with a variety of games and fun for the family. Quality pizza, at a great value. Menu includes regular, pan and express lunch pizza, salad, beer and soft drinks.

HISTORY:	FINANCIAL: Earnings Claim: . .No	FRANCHISOR TRAINING/SUPPORT:
Established in 1973; . . 1st Franchised in 1977	Cash Investment: $140-200K	Financial Assistance Provided: . . . . .No
Company-Owned Units (As of 8/31/1992): . 37	Total Investment: $325-510K	Site Selection Assistance: . . . . . . .Yes
Franchised Units (As of 8/31/1992): 79	Fees: Franchise - $25K	Lease Negotiation Assistance: . . . .Yes
Total Units (As of 8/31/1992): 116	Royalty: 5%, Advert: 5%	Co-operative Advertising: . . . . . . .Yes
Projected New Units for 1993: 6	Contract Periods (Yrs.): 10/10	Training: . . . . 3 Wks. Minimum HQ
Distribution: US-116;Can-0;Overseas-0	Area Development Agreement: Yes/Var	. . . .
North America: . . . . 8 States	Sub-Franchise Contract: . . . . . Yes	On-Going Support: B,C,D,E,F,H,I/ . . . 30
Concentration: . 46 in AZ, 32 in TX, 10 in UT	Expand in Territory:	EXPANSION PLANS:
Registered:	Passive Ownership: . . . Discouraged	US: . . . . Southwest & Southeast
. . . .	Encourage Conversions: . . . . . Yes	Canada: . . . . .All Canada
Type Space: . . . . .FS, SC;~5,000 SF	Average # Employees: . .5 FT, 25 PT	Overseas: . . . . .JA, MX

PIZZA FACTORY

P.O. Box 989
Oakhurst, CA 93644
TEL: (209) 683-3377
FAX: (209) 683-6879
Mr. Ron Willey, VP

"We Toss 'Em, They're Awesome." PIZZA FACTORY has a proven track record with 73 restaurants in 7 states, The franchisee has a strong support system which includes site location, negotiating lease, on-site training and on-going support from headquarters. Call for brochure. Serving homemade pizza, pasta, sandwiches, beer and wine.

HISTORY:	FINANCIAL: Earnings Claim: . .No	FRANCHISOR TRAINING/SUPPORT:
Established in 1979; . . 1st Franchised in 1985	Cash Investment: $65-80K	Financial Assistance Provided: . . . . .No
Company-Owned Units (As of 8/31/1992): . .3	Total Investment: $100K	Site Selection Assistance: . . . . . . .Yes
Franchised Units (As of 8/31/1992): 70	Fees: Franchise - $20K	Lease Negotiation Assistance: . . . . .Yes
Total Units (As of 8/31/1992): 73	Royalty: 3%, Advert: 1%	Co-operative Advertising: . . . . . . .Yes
Projected New Units for 1993: 15	Contract Periods (Yrs.): 20	Training: . . . . 325 Hours Training Stores
Distribution: US-73;Can-0;Overseas-0	Area Development Agreement: Yes/Var	. . . . Training Fee: $2,500
North America: . . . . 7 States	Sub-Franchise Contract: . . . . .No	On-Going Support: C,D,E,G,H,I/ 3
Concentration: . . .52 in CA, 7 in WA, 5 in ID	Expand in Territory: . . . . . . Yes	EXPANSION PLANS:
Registered: . . . . .CA,FL,OR,WA	Passive Ownership: . . . Discouraged	US: . . . . .W, SW, NW and SE (Florida)
. . . .	Encourage Conversions: . . . . . Yes	Canada: . . . . .No
Type Space: . . . . .SC;~2,400 SF	Average # Employees: 3 FT, 12-15 PT	Overseas: . . . . No

PIZZA INN

5050 Quorum Dr., # 500
Dallas, TX 75240
TEL: (800) 880-9955 (214) 638-7250
FAX: (214) 702-9510
Mr. Monty Whitehurst, VP Fran. Dev.

Dine-in, carry-out or delivery. 3 styles of pizza crusts - thin, Chicago and New York-style. Menu carries pizza, pasta, sandwiches, salads and desserts. Lunch and dinner buffets. Marketing, advertising, site selection and training assistance/programs.

HISTORY:	FINANCIAL: Earnings Claim:	FRANCHISOR TRAINING/SUPPORT:
. . . . IFA	. . .	
Established in 1960; . . 1st Franchised in 1963	Cash Investment: $75-150K	Financial Assistance Provided: . . . . . No
Company-Owned Units (As of 8/31/1992): . 14	Total Investment: $100-300K	Site Selection Assistance: . . . . .Yes
Franchised Units (As of 8/31/1992): 420	Fees: Franchise - $7.5-20K	Lease Negotiation Assistance: . . . . .No
Total Units (As of 8/31/1992): 434	Royalty: 4%, Advert: 1.5%	Co-operative Advertising: . . . . .Yes
Projected New Units for 1993: 60	Contract Periods (Yrs.): . . . 20/20	Training: . . . . 5 Wks. at Certified
Distribution: US-434;Can-0;Overseas-23	Area Development Agreement: Yes/Var	. . . . Training Store
North America: . . . . 25 States	Sub-Franchise Contract: . . . . . Yes	On-Going Support: B,C,D,E,H,I/ 99
Concentration:	Expand in Territory: . . . . . . Yes	EXPANSION PLANS:
Registered: . . . . All Except CA, NY, IL	Passive Ownership: . . . . . .Allowed	US: . . . . All US
. . . .	Encourage Conversions: . . . . Yes	Canada: . . . . .All Canada
Type Space: . . . .FS, SC, RM, KI;~2,990 SF	Average # Employees: . 30 FT, 10 PT	Overseas: . . . . .Yes

PIZZA ONE

200 Montego Bay
Mr. Clemens, MI 48043
TEL: (313) 468-1200
FAX:
Ms. Suzanne M. LaTour, VP

PIZZA ONE is growing at a fast pace. We specialize in 2 for 1 round or deep-dish, and free delivery too! We carry a variety of subs and salads. In 1993, we will be starting our new fine specialty pizzas, including our We Make, You Bake. The officers of PIZZA ONE are very active in daily operations, which we feel is very important to understand in today's market.

HISTORY:	FINANCIAL: Earnings Claim: . .No	FRANCHISOR TRAINING/SUPPORT:
. . . .		
Established in 1984; . . 1st Franchised in 1986	Cash Investment: $50K	Financial Assistance Provided: . . . . .NA
Company-Owned Units (As of 8/31/1992): . 41	Total Investment: $50-100K	Site Selection Assistance: . . . . .Yes
Franchised Units (As of 8/31/1992): 18	Fees: Franchise - $10K	Lease Negotiation Assistance: . . . . .Yes
Total Units (As of 8/31/1992): 59	Royalty: 3%, Advert: . . . $.08/Box	Co-operative Advertising: . . . . .Yes
Projected New Units for 1993: 20	Contract Periods (Yrs.): . . . 10/10	Training: . . . . . . .300 Hours at Training
Distribution: US-59;Can-0;Overseas-0	Area Development Agreement: Yes/5	. . . . Locations
North America: . . . . 2 States	Sub-Franchise Contract: . . . . . .No	On-Going Support: A,B,C,D,E,F,G,H/ . . 5
Concentration: . . . . 57 in MI, 2 in FL	Expand in Territory: . . . . . . Yes	EXPANSION PLANS:
Registered: . . . . .FL,MI	Passive Ownership: . . . Discouraged	US: . . . . All US
. . . .	Encourage Conversions: . . . . Yes	Canada: . . . . .Yes
Type Space: . . . .FS, SF, SC, RM;~1,000 SF	Average # Employees: . 2 FT, 6-8 PT	Overseas: . . . . .Yes

PIZZA PIT

4253 Argosy Court
Madison, WI 53714
TEL: (608) 221-6777
FAX: (608) 221-6771
Mr. Kerry P. Cook, VP

Free home delivery and carry-out of handcrafted pizzas and specialty sandwiches. Units also adaptable to inside seating with prepared salads, expanded menu and/or pizza by the slice. Single and multiple-unit programs available.

HISTORY:	FINANCIAL: Earnings Claim: . .No	FRANCHISOR TRAINING/SUPPORT:
. . . .		
Established in 1969; . . 1st Franchised in 1982	Cash Investment: $40-50K	Financial Assistance Provided: . . . . .No
Company-Owned Units (As of 8/31/1992): . 12	Total Investment: $100-230K	Site Selection Assistance: . . . . .Yes
Franchised Units (As of 8/31/1992): 17	Fees: Franchise - $16-17.5K	Lease Negotiation Assistance: . . . . .Yes
Total Units (As of 8/31/1992): 29	Royalty: 4.5%, Advert: 1%	Co-operative Advertising: . . . . .Yes
Projected New Units for 1993: 12	Contract Periods (Yrs.): 10	Training: . . . . . . 4-6 Wks. Headquarters
Distribution: US-29;Can-0;Overseas-0	Area Development Agreement: Yes/10	. . . .
North America: . . . . 3 States	Sub-Franchise Contract: . . . . . .No	On-Going Support: B,C,D,E,F,G,H/ . . 99
Concentration: . . . 18 in WI, 3 in IA, 1 in CA	Expand in Territory: . . . . . . Yes	EXPANSION PLANS:
Registered: . . . . CA,FL,IL,IN,WI	Passive Ownership: . . . Discouraged	US: . . . . .West and Midwest
. . . .	Encourage Conversions: . . . . Yes	Canada: . . . . .No
Type Space: . . . . SC;~1,500+ SF	Average # Employees: . . 6 FT, 9 PT	Overseas: . . . . .No

PIZZA PIZZA

580 Jarvis St.
Toronto, ON M4Y 2H9 CAN
TEL: (800) 263-5556 (416) 967-1010
FAX: (416) 967-0891
Mr. Sebastian Fuschini, Fran. Dir.

Established in 1967, PIZZA PIZZA has developed the successful formula for customer satisfaction and retention through its quality product, convenient service, recognized trademark and the computerized one number ordering system.

HISTORY: . . . . .CFA	FINANCIAL: Earnings Claim: . .No	FRANCHISOR TRAINING/SUPPORT:
Established in 1968; . . 1st Franchised in 1975	Cash Investment: $40-60K	Financial Assistance Provided: . . . . .Yes
Company-Owned Units (As of 8/31/1992): . .8	Total Investment: $125-150K	Site Selection Assistance: . . . . . . .Yes
Franchised Units (As of 8/31/1992): 237	Fees: Franchise - $20K	Lease Negotiation Assistance: . . . . .Yes
Total Units (As of 8/31/1992): 245	Royalty: 6%, Advert: 6%	Co-operative Advertising: . . . . . . .Yes
Projected New Units for 1993: 40	Contract Periods (Yrs.): . . . 5/5/5/5	Training: . . . . . 12-15 Wks. Headquarters
Distribution: US-0;Can-245;Overseas-0	Area Development Agreement: . . .	. . . .
North America: . . . . 2 Provinces	Sub-Franchise Contract: . . . . Yes	On-Going Support: A,B,C,D,E,F,G,H,I/ 150
Concentration: . . . . . . 240 in ON, 5 in PQ	Expand in Territory: . . . . . . Yes	EXPANSION PLANS:
Registered: . . . . AB	Passive Ownership: . . . Not Allowed	US: . . . . No
. . . .	Encourage Conversions: . . . . . NA	Canada: . . . . .All Canada
Type Space: . . . . Various;~1,000 SF	Average # Employees: . 4 FT, 3-5 PT	Overseas: . . . . . . Far East, EUR

PIZZA ROYALE

1720 St-Michel
Sillery, PQ G1S 1J3 CAN
TEL: (418) 682-5744
FAX: (418) 682-2684
Mr. Rejean Sanson, President

PIZZA ROYALE is a chain of Italian restaurants, specializing in pizza cooked in an open wood oven fire in the serving area. It also offers a salad bar and a pasta bar. Take-out orders and delivery are also available. Healthy food and warm atmosphere are the main features of a concept that has proven successful over the years.

HISTORY:	FINANCIAL: Earnings Claim: . . .	FRANCHISOR TRAINING/SUPPORT:
Established in 1980; . . 1st Franchised in 1985	Cash Investment: $100-150K	Financial Assistance Provided: . . . Yes(I)
Company-Owned Units (As of 8/31/1992): . .3	Total Investment: $300-400K	Site Selection Assistance: . . . . . . .Yes
Franchised Units (As of 8/31/1992): 12	Fees: Franchise - $30K	Lease Negotiation Assistance: . . . . .Yes
Total Units (As of 8/31/1992): 15	Royalty: 3%, Advert: 2%	Co-operative Advertising: . . . . . . .Yes
Projected New Units for 1993: 24	Contract Periods (Yrs.): 10/10	Training: . . . . 2 Wks. Headquarters,
Distribution: US-0;Can-15;Overseas-0	Area Development Agreement: . .No	. . . . 2 Wks. On-Site
North America: . . . . .1 Province	Sub-Franchise Contract: . . . . Yes	On-Going Support: B,C,d,E,F,H/ 50
Concentration: . . . . .15 in PQ	Expand in Territory: . . . . . . Yes	EXPANSION PLANS:
Registered:	Passive Ownership: . . . Discouraged	US: . . . . NW, Master Franchises Avail.
. . . .	Encourage Conversions: . . . . . Yes	Canada: . . . . .PQ, ON, Master F
Type Space: . . . . . . FS, SC, RM;~3,500 SF	Average # Employees: . .20 FT, 5 PT	Overseas: . . . . No

PIZZAS BY MARCHELLONI

1051 Essington Rd., # 130
Joliet, IL 60435
TEL: (800) HOTPIE 4 (815) 729-4494
FAX: (815) 729-4508
Mr. Hass Aslami, President

PIZZAS BY MARCHELLONI is a pizza delivery/carry-out restaurant, offering a simple and limited menu. Dine-in capability is optional. When you become the owner of a PBM franchise, you get more than an exciting concept, you get a complete business system, tested and refined, enabling you to have your business up and running as quickly and easily as possible.

HISTORY:	FINANCIAL: Earnings Claim: . .No	FRANCHISOR TRAINING/SUPPORT:
Established in 1986; . . 1st Franchised in 1989	Cash Investment: $32-112K	Financial Assistance Provided: . . . . . No
Company-Owned Units (As of 8/31/1992): . .6	Total Investment: $32-112K	Site Selection Assistance: . . . . . . .Yes
Franchised Units (As of 8/31/1992): 42	Fees: Franchise - $18.5K	Lease Negotiation Assistance: . . . . .Yes
Total Units (As of 8/31/1992): 48	Royalty: 5%, Advert: 1%	Co-operative Advertising: . . . . . . .Yes
Projected New Units for 1993: 12	Contract Periods (Yrs.): 10/10	Training: . . . . 14 Days Headquarters
Distribution: US-48;Can-0;Overseas-0	Area Development Agreement: Yes/10	. . . .
North America: . . . . .1 State	Sub-Franchise Contract: . . . . . .No	On-Going Support: B,C,D,E,F,G,H,I/ . . . 6
Concentration: . . . . 48 in IL	Expand in Territory: . . . . . . Yes	EXPANSION PLANS:
Registered: . . . . FL,IL,IN,OR,WI	Passive Ownership: . . . . . .Allowed	US: . . . . .IL, IN, IA, WI, MO and KS
. . . .	Encourage Conversions: . . . . . Yes	Canada: . . . . No
Type Space: . . . . SC;~900-1,200 SF	Average # Employees: . .2 FT, 18 PT	Overseas: . . . . No

PLUS ONE PIZZA

Carry-out/delivery pizza.

P. O. Box 516, 9100 Jeffrey Dr.
Cambridge, OH 43725
TEL: (614) 432-6066
FAX: (614) 439-1331
Mr. Robert D. Fettes, President

HISTORY:	FINANCIAL: Earnings Claim: . .No	FRANCHISOR TRAINING/SUPPORT:
Established in 1978; . . 1st Franchised in 1989	Cash Investment: $30K	Financial Assistance Provided: . . . . . No
Company-Owned Units (As of 8/31/1992): . 13	Total Investment: $65-85K	Site Selection Assistance: . . . . .Yes
Franchised Units (As of 8/31/1992): 4	Fees: Franchise - $15K	Lease Negotiation Assistance: . . . .Yes
Total Units (As of 8/31/1992): 17	Royalty: 5%, Advert: 2%	Co-operative Advertising: . . . . .No
Projected New Units for 1993: 3	Contract Periods (Yrs.): 10/5	Training: . . . . 2 Wks. Local Store
Distribution: US-17;Can-0;Overseas-0	Area Development Agreement: . Yes	
North America: . . . . 3 States	Sub-Franchise Contract: . . . . . Yes	On-Going Support: B,C,E,H/ 8
Concentration: . . 11 in OH, 5 in WV, 1 in PA	Expand in Territory: . . . . . . Yes	EXPANSION PLANS:
Registered:	Passive Ownership: . . . Discouraged	US: . . . . .OH, KY, PA, WV
. . . .	Encourage Conversions: . . . . . .No	Canada: . . . . .No
Type Space: . . . . . . FS, SF, SC;~1,000 SF	Average # Employees: . . 8 FT, 4 PT	Overseas: . . . . No

PORT OF SUBS

A fast-service restaurant, offering a wide variety of submarine-type sandwiches, hot sandwiches and related items. Sandwiches are made-to-order to customer's specifications, using the freshest-quality meats and cheeses and fresh bread baked on premises.

100 Washington St., # 200
Reno, NV 89503
TEL: (800) 245-0245 (702) 322-7901
FAX: (702) 322-6093
Ms. Patricia Larson, President

HISTORY: . . . . IFA	FINANCIAL: Earnings Claim: . .No	FRANCHISOR TRAINING/SUPPORT:
Established in 1972; . . 1st Franchised in 1986	Cash Investment: $50-60K	Financial Assistance Provided: . . . Yes(I)
Company-Owned Units (As of 8/31/1992): . 10	Total Investment: $127-165K	Site Selection Assistance: . . . . .Yes
Franchised Units (As of 8/31/1992): 54	Fees: Franchise - $16K	Lease Negotiation Assistance: . . . .Yes
Total Units (As of 8/31/1992): 64	Royalty: 5.5%, Advert: 1%	Co-operative Advertising: . . . . .Yes
Projected New Units for 1993: 12	Contract Periods (Yrs.): 10/10	Training: . . . . . 2 1/2 Wks. Headquarters
Distribution: US-64;Can-0;Overseas-0	Area Development Agreement: Yes/Var	. . . .
North America: . . . . 4 States	Sub-Franchise Contract: . . . . . .No	On-Going Support: B,C,D,E,F,G,h,I/ . . 17
Concentration: . . 35 in NV, 23 in CA, 4 in AZ	Expand in Territory: . . . . . . Yes	EXPANSION PLANS:
Registered: . . . . CA,HI,WA	Passive Ownership: . . . . . .Allowed	US: . . . . . Northwest, Southwest, West
. . . .	Encourage Conversions: . . . . Yes	Canada: . . . . .No
Type Space: . . . . . . FS, SF, SC;~1,200 SF	Average # Employees: . 2 FT, 4-6 PT	Overseas: . . . . No

POTTS' HOT DOGS

Fast-food restaurant, mainly hot dogs and breakfast.

P. O. Box 08195
Ft. Myers, FL 33908
TEL: (813) 482-5432 C
FAX:
Mr. Bill Potts, President

HISTORY:	FINANCIAL: Earnings Claim: . .No	FRANCHISOR TRAINING/SUPPORT:
Established in 1984; . . 1st Franchised in 1984	Cash Investment: $10K	Financial Assistance Provided: . . . . .No
Company-Owned Units (As of 8/31/1992): . .7	Total Investment: $50K	Site Selection Assistance: . . . . .Yes
Franchised Units (As of 8/31/1992): 6	Fees: Franchise - $15K	Lease Negotiation Assistance: . . . .Yes
Total Units (As of 8/31/1992): 13	Royalty: 4%, Advert: 2%	Co-operative Advertising: . . . . .Yes
Projected New Units for 1993: 0	Contract Periods (Yrs.): 5/5	Training: . . . . . 100 Hrs. Bethlehem, PA,
Distribution: US-13;Can-0;Overseas-0	Area Development Agreement: . .No	. . . . .100 Hrs. Headquarters
North America: . . . . 3 States	Sub-Franchise Contract: . . . . . .No	On-Going Support: B,D,E,H/ . . . .
Concentration: . . . . 7 in PA, 5 in FL, 1 in NJ	Expand in Territory: . . . . . . Yes	EXPANSION PLANS:
Registered: . . . . .FL	Passive Ownership: . . . Discouraged	US: . . . . .All US
. . . .	Encourage Conversions: . . . . Yes	Canada: . . . . .No
Type Space: . . . . . FS, SC, RM;~1,500 SF	Average # Employees: . . 4 FT, 2 PT	Overseas: . . . . No

PUDGIE'S FAMOUS CHICKEN

7600 Jericho Tnpk., # 206
Woodbury, NY 11797
TEL: (800) 992-4425 (516) 364-6340
FAX: (516) 364-6348
Mr. Howard J. Kane, Dir. Fran. Dev.

PUDGIES'S FAMOUS CHICKEN is America's fastest-growing food franchise. We specialize in skinless fried chicken and serve only the highest-quality ribs, seafood and other items. Our stores are clean, efficiently designed and friendly. PUDGIE'S is "the lighter choice, naturally."

HISTORY: . . . .
Established in 1981; . . 1st Franchised in 1989
Company-Owned Units (As of 8/31/1992): . .3
Franchised Units (As of 8/31/1992): 128
Total Units (As of 8/31/1992): 131
Projected New Units for 1993: 50
Distribution: US-131;Can-0;Overseas-0
North America: . . . . 12 States
Concentration: . . . . 65 in NY, 9 in NJ
Registered: . . . FL,IL,IN,MD,NY,RI,VA,DC
. . . .
Type Space: . . . . . SF, SC, RM;~1,000 SF

FINANCIAL: Earnings Claim: . .No
Cash Investment: $100K
Total Investment: $175-200K
Fees: Franchise - $30K
Royalty: 5%, Advert: 3%
Contract Periods (Yrs.): . . . 10/10
Area Development Agreement: Yes/10
Sub-Franchise Contract: . . . . .No
Expand in Territory: . . . . . . Yes
Passive Ownership: . . . Discouraged
Encourage Conversions: . . . . . Yes
Average # Employees: 1-2 FT, 3-10 PT

FRANCHISOR TRAINING/SUPPORT:
Financial Assistance Provided: . . . Yes(I)
Site Selection Assistance: . . . . . . .Yes
Lease Negotiation Assistance: . . . .Yes
Co-operative Advertising: . . . . . . .Yes
Training: . . . . . 4-6 Wks. at Long Island,
. . . . . Edison, NJ and/or Margate, FL
On-Going Support: A,B,C,D,E,F,G,H,I/ 30
EXPANSION PLANS:
US: . . . . All US
Canada: . . . . .All Canada
Overseas: . . . . Yes

QUIK WOK RESTAURANT

4099 McEwen Dr., # 150
Dallas, TX 75244
TEL: (214) 386-0044
FAX: (214) 386-0148
Mr. Paul M. Lee

Chinese fast food is the last fast-food frontier. In an age in which people are increasingly concerned about eating healthy food, the large consumer attraction of QUIK WOK RESTAURANT is that it offers the opportunity to enjoy the most popular traditional Chinese dishes prepared fresh and cooked to order. QUIK WOK dishes are free from MSG and are low in other food additives. People the world over love Chinese food.

HISTORY: . . . .
Established in 1980; . . 1st Franchised in 1990
Company-Owned Units (As of 8/31/1992): . .0
Franchised Units (As of 8/31/1992): 14
Total Units (As of 8/31/1992): 14
Projected New Units for 1993: 5
Distribution: US-14;Can-0;Overseas-0
North America: . . . . .1 State
Concentration: . . . . 14 in TX
Registered: . . . .
. . . .
Type Space: . . . FS, RM, Flexible;~1,500 SF

FINANCIAL: Earnings Claim: . .No
Cash Investment: $75-150K
Total Investment: $125-350K
Fees: Franchise - $20K
Royalty: 5%, Advert: 2.5%
Contract Periods (Yrs.): . . . 10/10
Area Development Agreement: Yes/20
Sub-Franchise Contract: . . . . .No
Expand in Territory: . . . . . . Yes
Passive Ownership: . . . Discouraged
Encourage Conversions: . . . . . Yes
Average # Employees: . . 4 FT, 5 PT

FRANCHISOR TRAINING/SUPPORT:
Financial Assistance Provided: . . . . . No
Site Selection Assistance: . . . . . . .Yes
Lease Negotiation Assistance: . . . .Yes
Co-operative Advertising: . . . . No
Training: . . . . . . 3-4 Wks. Headquarters
. . . .
On-Going Support: c,d,E,G,h/ 6
EXPANSION PLANS:
US: . . . . Midwest and West Coast
Canada: . . . . No
Overseas: . . . . No

RALLY'S HAMBURGERS

10002 Shelbyville Rd., # 150
Louisville, KY 40223
TEL: (800) 928-9999 (502) 245-8900
FAX: (502) 245-7407
Mr. Edward C. Binzel, Sr. VP

"America's fastest-growing hamburger chain," according to Restaurant Business Magazine, July, 1990 and July, 1991. RALLY'S is a double drive-thru hamburger restaurant with walk-up windows and outside seating.

HISTORY: . . . . IFA
Established in 1985; . . 1st Franchised in 1986
Company-Owned Units (As of 8/31/1992): 150
Franchised Units (As of 8/31/1992): 232
Total Units (As of 8/31/1992): 382
Projected New Units for 1993: 89
Distribution: US-382;Can-0;Overseas-0
North America: . . . . 24 States
Concentration: . . . . Midwest, Southest
Registered: . . . . . All States Exc. HI,N&SD
. . . .
Type Space: . . . . . . FS;~16,000-20,000 SF

FINANCIAL: Earnings Claim: . .No
Cash Investment: . . . . .$150K Min.
Total Investment: . . . . .$350K Min.
Fees: Franchise - $20K
Royalty: 4%, Advert: 4%
Contract Periods (Yrs.): . .15/5/5/5
Area Development Agreement: Yes/Var
Sub-Franchise Contract: . . . . .No
Expand in Territory: . . . . . . Yes
Passive Ownership: . . . Discouraged
Encourage Conversions: . . . . . .
Average # Employees: . . . . .30 FT

FRANCHISOR TRAINING/SUPPORT:
Financial Assistance Provided: . . . . .NA
Site Selection Assistance: . . . . . . .Yes
Lease Negotiation Assistance: . . . .NA
Co-operative Advertising: . . . . . . .Yes
Training: . . . . . .5-12 Wks. Headquarters
. . . .
On-Going Support: B,C,D,E,G,H/ . . . . .
EXPANSION PLANS:
US: . . . SE, MW, SW, CA, Mid-Atlantic
Canada: . . . . Yes-Limited
Overseas: . . . . No

RAX RESTAURANTS

4150 Tuller Rd.
Dublin, OH 43017
TEL: (800) 766-3669 (614) 766-2500
FAX: (614) 766-4706
Mr. G. Bill Burton, VP RE Dev.

Quick-service restaurants, offering a broad menu of specialty sandwiches, hot-topped potatoes, shakes and a 50+ item salad bar with your own Mexican entrees, hot pastas and salads.

HISTORY: . . . .
Established in 1978; . . 1st Franchised in 1978
Company-Owned Units (As of 8/31/1992): 119
Franchised Units (As of 8/31/1992): 160
Total Units (As of 8/31/1992): 279
Projected New Units for 1993: 36
Distribution: US-278;Can-0;Overseas-1
North America: . . . . 29 States, 2 Provinces
Concentration: . . 101 in OH, 55 in PA, 48 IN
Registered: . . . . All Except HI and WI
. . . .
Type Space: . . . . FS;~30,000 SF

FINANCIAL: Earnings Claim: . .No
Cash Investment: $50-125K
Total Investment: $550-800K
Fees: Franchise - $30K
Royalty: 4%, Advert: 4%
Contract Periods (Yrs.): 20
Area Development Agreement: Yes/3-5
Sub-Franchise Contract: . . . . Yes
Expand in Territory: . . . . . . Yes
Passive Ownership: . . . Not Allowed
Encourage Conversions: . . . . . Yes
Average # Employees: 2-3 FT, 30+ PT

FRANCHISOR TRAINING/SUPPORT:
Financial Assistance Provided: . . . Yes(I)
Site Selection Assistance: . . . . . . .Yes
Lease Negotiation Assistance: . . . . .Yes
Co-operative Advertising: . . . . . . .Yes
Training: . . . . . . 5 Wks. Headquarters
. . . .
On-Going Support: B,C,D,E,G,H,I/ . . . 22
EXPANSION PLANS:
US: . . . . . .Midwest, Pacific Northwest
Canada: . . . . .All Canada
Overseas: . . . . No

RENZIOS

P. O. Box 2190, 701 W. Hampden Ave.
Englewood, CO 80150
TEL: (800) 888-3139 (303) 781-3139
FAX: (303) 781-3441
Mr. Thomas D. Rentzios, President

Unique Greek fast-food restaurants, operating in mall food courts and strip malls. RENZIOS fills the space between typical fast-food and the full-service restaurant, offering traditional Greek recipes and featuring the wholesome Gyros Sandwich. For those who want more in a meal, there are lean meat platters, Gyros Salad or lamb kabob. Authentic Greek pastries. You'll have all the right ingredients for success.

HISTORY: . . . .
Established in 1979; . . 1st Franchised in 1989
Company-Owned Units (As of 8/31/1992): . 10
Franchised Units (As of 8/31/1992): 2
Total Units (As of 8/31/1992): 12
Projected New Units for 1993: 3
Distribution: US-12;Can-0;Overseas-0
North America: . . . . 4 States
Concentration: . . . 5 in CO, 3 in MT, 2 in NV
Registered: . . . . CA,MN,WA,WI
. . . .
Type Space: . . . .Shopping Centers;~500 SF

FINANCIAL: Earnings Claim: . .No
Cash Investment: $20-30K
Total Investment: $18-150K
Fees: Franchise - $18K
Royalty: 5%, Advert: 0%
Contract Periods (Yrs.): 10/5/5
Area Development Agreement: . .No
Sub-Franchise Contract: . . . . .No
Expand in Territory: . . . . . . Yes
Passive Ownership: . . . . .Allowed
Encourage Conversions: . . . . Yes
Average # Employees: . . 2 FT, 4 PT

FRANCHISOR TRAINING/SUPPORT:
Financial Assistance Provided: . . . Yes(I)
Site Selection Assistance: . . . . . . .Yes
Lease Negotiation Assistance: . . . .Yes
Co-operative Advertising: . . . . . . .Yes
Training: . . . . . . 21 Days Headquarters,
. .7 Days Franchisee Location,On-Going
On-Going Support: B,D,E,F,G,H/ 4
EXPANSION PLANS:
US: . . . . .All US
Canada: . . . . .No
Overseas: . .JA, KO, Taiwan, Hong Kong

ROCKY ROCOCO PAN STYLE PIZZA

2122 Luann Ln., # 15
Madison, WI 53713
TEL: (800) 888-7625 (608) 276-6760
FAX: (608) 276-6773
Mr. Thomas R. Hester, President

"Pizza By The Slice" and signature pan-style pizza sets ROCKY'S apart from the other pizza guys. A fun restaurant with great food works in free-standing locations, in-line enclosed malls and food court locations.

HISTORY: . . . .
Established in 1974; . . 1st Franchised in 1982
Company-Owned Units (As of 8/31/1992): . 20
Franchised Units (As of 8/31/1992): 30
Total Units (As of 8/31/1992): 50
Projected New Units for 1993: 2
Distribution: US-50;Can-0;Overseas-0
North America: . . . . 6 States
Concentration: . . . 39 in WI, 7 in MN, 1 in IL
Registered: . . . .
. . . .
Type Space: . . . .FS, SF, RM;~600-3,500 SF

FINANCIAL: Earnings Claim: . .No
Cash Investment: $50-250K
Total Investment: . . . . .$.2-1.0MM
Fees: Franchise - $15-25K
Royalty: 3.5-5%, Advert: . . . 2-5%
Contract Periods (Yrs.): . .5-15/5-15
Area Development Agreement: . .No
Sub-Franchise Contract: . . . . . Yes
Expand in Territory: . . . . . . Yes
Passive Ownership: . . . Discouraged
Encourage Conversions: . . . . . Yes
Average # Employees: . .5 FT, 20 PT

FRANCHISOR TRAINING/SUPPORT:
Financial Assistance Provided: . . . . .No
Site Selection Assistance: . . . . . . .Yes
Lease Negotiation Assistance: . . . .Yes
Co-operative Advertising: . . . . . . .Yes
Training: . . . . . . 2 Wks. Headquarters,
. . . . 2 Wks. Milwaukee, WI
On-Going Support: B,C,E,G,h,I/ 12
EXPANSION PLANS:
US: . . . . Midwest
Canada: . . . . .No
Overseas: . . . . No

ROLI BOLI

15 Engle St., # 302
Englewood, NJ 07631
TEL: (800) 332-2229 (201) 871-0370
FAX: (201) 871-7168
Mr. John Sterns, Sales Manager

Specialty sandwich - combines a french bread dough stuffed with a selection of 24 different ingredients to choose from, along with related items.

HISTORY: . . . .
Established in 1987; . . 1st Franchised in 1987
Company-Owned Units (As of 8/31/1992): . .3
Franchised Units (As of 8/31/1992): 10
Total Units (As of 8/31/1992): 13
Projected New Units for 1993: 12
Distribution: US-13;Can-0;Overseas-0
North America: . . . . 6 States
Concentration: . . . .8 in NJ, 1 in CA, 1 in NC
Registered: . . . . CA,FL,NY
. . . .
Type Space: .RM, Hi-Vol. Cmrs;~500-900 SF

FINANCIAL: Earnings Claim: . .No
Cash Investment: $50-75K
Total Investment: $130-195K
Fees: Franchise - $20K
Royalty: 5%, Advert: . . . .
Contract Periods (Yrs.): . . . 10/10
Area Development Agreement: . Yes
Sub-Franchise Contract: . . . . .No
Expand in Territory: . . . . . . Yes
Passive Ownership: . . . Not Allowed
Encourage Conversions: . . . . NA
Average # Employees: . . 2 FT, 4 PT

FRANCHISOR TRAINING/SUPPORT:
Financial Assistance Provided: . . . Yes(I)
Site Selection Assistance: . . . . . . .Yes
Lease Negotiation Assistance: . . . . .Yes
Co-operative Advertising: . . . . . . .Yes
Training: . . . . . .2 Wks. Company Store,
. . . . 1 Wk. Franchisee Location
On-Going Support: C,D,E,G,I/ . . . .
EXPANSION PLANS:
US: . . . . .All US
Canada: . . . . .All Canada
Overseas: . . . . .Yes

SEAFOOD AMERICA

645 Mearns Rd.
Warminster, PA 18974
TEL: (215) 672-2211
FAX: (215) 675-8324
Mr. Robert J. Brennan, President

SEAFOOD AMERICA is a fast-food, take-out seafood store unique in both product and design. The products are primarily seafood items designed for quick service and maximum profits. Some products are prepared on the premises, but most are commissary-based.

HISTORY: . . . .
Established in 1979; . . 1st Franchised in 1980
Company-Owned Units (As of 8/31/1992): . .1
Franchised Units (As of 8/31/1992): 19
Total Units (As of 8/31/1992): 20
Projected New Units for 1993: 3
Distribution: US-20;Can-0;Overseas-0
North America: . . . . 2 States
Concentration: . . . . 17 in PA, 3 in NJ
Registered: . . . .
. . . .
Type Space: . . . . .SC;~1,600 SF

FINANCIAL: Earnings Claim: . .No
Cash Investment: $40-60K
Total Investment: $100-130K
Fees: Franchise - $10K
Royalty: 1%, Advert: 1%
Contract Periods (Yrs.): . . . 10/10
Area Development Agreement: Yes/20
Sub-Franchise Contract: . . . . .No
Expand in Territory: . . . . . . .No
Passive Ownership: . . . Discouraged
Encourage Conversions: . . . . .No
Average # Employees: . . 2 FT, 8 PT

FRANCHISOR TRAINING/SUPPORT:
Financial Assistance Provided: . . . Yes(I)
Site Selection Assistance: . . . . . . .Yes
Lease Negotiation Assistance: . . . . .Yes
Co-operative Advertising: . . . . . . .Yes
Training: . . . . . . .2 Wks. Existing Store,
. . . . 4 Wks. On-Site
On-Going Support: a,B,C,D,E,F,h,I/ . . . 6
EXPANSION PLANS:
US: . . . . . . Pennsylvania and NJ Only
Canada: . . . . .No
Overseas: . . . . No

SELECT SANDWICH

50 Gervais Dr., # 506
Toronto, ON M3C 1Z3 CAN
TEL: (416) 391-1244 C
FAX: (416) 391-5244
Ms. Carol Kahn, Dir. Franchising

Custom-made sandwiches, soups, salads, muffins baked on premises. Hot specials. Catering to business. Breakfast and lunch. 5 days per week, 7 AM - 6 PM.

HISTORY: . . . . .CFA
Established in 1981; . . 1st Franchised in 1983
Company-Owned Units (As of 8/31/1992): . .3
Franchised Units (As of 8/31/1992): 34
Total Units (As of 8/31/1992): 37
Projected New Units for 1993: 6
Distribution: US-0;Can-37;Overseas-0
North America: . . . . .1 Province
Concentration: . . . . 37 in ON
Registered: . . . .
. . . .
Type Space: . . . . . . SF, Other;~2,000 SF

FINANCIAL: Earnings Claim: . .No
Cash Investment: $75K
Total Investment: $220-275K
Fees: Franchise - $30K
Royalty: 6%, Advert: 2%
Contract Periods (Yrs.): 10/5
Area Development Agreement: .No
Sub-Franchise Contract: . . . . .No
Expand in Territory: . . . . . . Yes
Passive Ownership: . . . Not Allowed
Encourage Conversions: . . . . NA
Average # Employees: . . 3 FT, 2 PT

FRANCHISOR TRAINING/SUPPORT:
Financial Assistance Provided: . . . Yes(I)
Site Selection Assistance: . . . . . . .NA
Lease Negotiation Assistance: . . . . .NA
Co-operative Advertising: . . . . . . .Yes
Training: . . . . . . 4-6 Wks. Headquarters
. . . .
On-Going Support: C,D,E,F,G,H/ 8
EXPANSION PLANS:
US: . . . . No
Canada: . . . . .Ontario
Overseas: . . . . No

SOBIK'S SUBS

266 W. State Rd. 434
Longwood, FL 32751
TEL: (407) 339-8400
FAX: (407) 339-0720
Mr. Robin L. Webb, Dir. Fran. Sales

SOBIK'S SUBS is a fast-food restaurant concept, featuring submarine and specialty sandwiches and salads for eat-in or take-out. We have 40+ SOBIK'S SUB SHOPS in Central Florida and have just sold our first Master Franchise for the Southwest Coast of Florida. Our concept stresses quality, ease of operation and speed of service.

HISTORY: . . . .
Established in 1969; . . 1st Franchised in 1981
Company-Owned Units (As of 8/31/1992): . .6
Franchised Units (As of 8/31/1992): . . . . <u>397</u>
Total Units (As of 8/31/1992): 43
Projected New Units for 1993: 12
Distribution: US-43;Can-0;Overseas-0
North America: . . . . .1 State
Concentration: . . . . .43 in FL
Registered: . . . . .FL
. . . .
Type Space: . . . . .SC;~1,200 SF

FINANCIAL: Earnings Claim: . .No
Cash Investment: $20-40K
Total Investment: $65-90K
Fees: Franchise - $15K
Royalty: 4%, Advert: 4%
Contract Periods (Yrs.): . . . 10/10
Area Development Agreement: Yes/10
Sub-Franchise Contract: . . . . . Yes
Expand in Territory: . . . . . Yes
Passive Ownership: . . . Discouraged
Encourage Conversions: . . . . .No
Average # Employees: . . 2 FT, 4 PT

FRANCHISOR TRAINING/SUPPORT:
Financial Assistance Provided: . . . . .No
Site Selection Assistance: . . . . . . .Yes
Lease Negotiation Assistance: . . . . .Yes
Co-operative Advertising: . . . . . . .Yes
Training: . . . . .2 Wks. Orlando, FL

On-Going Support: B,C,D,E,G,H/ . . . 10
EXPANSION PLANS:
US: . . . . .All US
Canada: . . . . .No
Overseas: . . . . No

SONIC DRIVE IN

120 Robert S. Kerr Ave.
Oklahoma City, OK 73102
TEL: (800) 676-6656 (405) 232-4334
FAX: (405) 272-8292
Mr. Roy S. Lemaire, Dir. Fran. Mktg.

Fast-food, drive-in restaurants, featuring hamburgers, coney dogs and onion rings. Service is build around electronic ordering and order delivery by car hops. Founded in 1959, SONIC DRIVE INS are still heavy in the nostalgia of the 50's.

HISTORY: . . . . IFA
Established in 1959; . . 1st Franchised in 1959
Company-Owned Units (As of 8/31/1992): 110
Franchised Units (As of 8/31/1992): . . . <u>1027</u>
Total Units (As of 8/31/1992): 1137
Projected New Units for 1993: 80
Distribution: US-1137;Can-0;Overseas-0
North America: . . . . 21 States
Concentration: . 314 in TX, 137 in OK, 85 AR
Registered: . . . . .CA,FL,IN,VA
. . . .
Type Space: . . . . FS;~25,000 SF

FINANCIAL: Earnings Claim: . .No
Cash Investment: $38-68K
Total Investment: $300-550K
Fees: Franchise - $15K
Royalty: 1-4%, Advert: . . . 3-4%
Contract Periods (Yrs.): . . . 15/15
Area Development Agreement: Yes/Var
Sub-Franchise Contract: . . . . .No
Expand in Territory: . . . . . . Yes
Passive Ownership: . . . Discouraged
Encourage Conversions: . . . . .No
Average # Employees: . 35 FT and PT

FRANCHISOR TRAINING/SUPPORT:
Financial Assistance Provided: . . . Yes(I)
Site Selection Assistance: . . . . . . .Yes
Lease Negotiation Assistance: . . . . .Yes
Co-operative Advertising: . . . . . . .Yes
Training: . . . .6 Days + OJT Headquarters
. . . .
On-Going Support: a,B,C,D,E,F,G,H,I/ . 80
EXPANSION PLANS:
US: . . . . Southeast
Canada: . . . . .No
Overseas: . . . . No

SPINNER'S PIZZA & SUBS

630 N. Highway 67
Cedar Hill, TX 75104
TEL: (214) 299-5656 C
FAX: (214) 299-5659
Mr. Ernest Hagler, VP Fran. Dev.

SPINNER'S PIZZA is seeking individuals to become owner/operators of delivery/take-out units specializing in the highest-quality products with an emphasis on superior customer service. Our strength is training individuals without business/food experience and making them a part of our success. People-oriented!

HISTORY: . . . .
Established in 1983; . . 1st Franchised in 1986
Company-Owned Units (As of 8/31/1992): . .6
Franchised Units (As of 8/31/1992): 22
Total Units (As of 8/31/1992): 28
Projected New Units for 1993: 15
Distribution: US-28;Can-0;Overseas-0
North America: . . . . .1 State
Concentration: . . . . 28 in TX
Registered: . . . .
. . . .
Type Space: . . . . .SC;~1,000 SF

FINANCIAL: Earnings Claim: . .No
Cash Investment: $35-40K
Total Investment: $75-100K
Fees: Franchise - $12.5K
Royalty: 4%, Advert: 2%
Contract Periods (Yrs.): 5/5
Area Development Agreement: Yes/5
Sub-Franchise Contract: . . . . .No
Expand in Territory: . . . . . . Yes
Passive Ownership: . . . Discouraged
Encourage Conversions: . . . . Yes
Average # Employees:3-5 FT, 10-20 PT

FRANCHISOR TRAINING/SUPPORT:
Financial Assistance Provided: . . . Yes(I)
Site Selection Assistance: . . . . . . .Yes
Lease Negotiation Assistance: . . . . .Yes
Co-operative Advertising: . . . . . . .Yes
Training: . . . . . . ~500 Hours Dallas/Fort
. . . . Worth Area
On-Going Support: b,C,D,E,G,h/ 5
EXPANSION PLANS:
US: . . . . . . .TX and Contiguous States
Canada: . . . . .No
Overseas: . . . . No

SPORTS DOG

145 Cedar Ln.
Englewood, NJ 07631
TEL: (800) 524-5873 (201) 568-1999
FAX: (201) 568-5446
Mr. Gary Occhiogrosso, Dir. Fran.

Fast-food restaurant, serving hot dogs, nachos, fries and other stadium-type foods in a ballpark atmosphere. SPORTS DOG stores also offer for sale sports memorabilia, sports merchandise and collectible items. All stores feature "In Store" appearances by nationally-recognized sports celebrities.

HISTORY: . . . .
Established in 1991; . . 1st Franchised in 1991
Company-Owned Units (As of 8/31/1992): . .0
Franchised Units (As of 8/31/1992): 73
Total Units (As of 8/31/1992): 73
Projected New Units for 1993: 75
Distribution: US-73;Can-0;Overseas-0
North America: . . . .
Concentration: . . . .
Registered: . . . .
. . . .
Type Space: . . . . . . SF, SC;~350-1,800 SF

FINANCIAL: Earnings Claim: . .No
Cash Investment: $12.5K
Total Investment: $40-50K
Fees: Franchise - $12.5K
Royalty: 6%, Advert: 2%
Contract Periods (Yrs.): 10/5
Area Development Agreement: Yes/10
Sub-Franchise Contract: . . . . Yes
Expand in Territory: . . . . . . Yes
Passive Ownership: . . . . . .Allowed
Encourage Conversions: . . . . . Yes
Average # Employees: . . 2 FT, 1 PT

FRANCHISOR TRAINING/SUPPORT:
Financial Assistance Provided: . . . . .Yes
Site Selection Assistance: . . . . . . .Yes
Lease Negotiation Assistance: . . . . .Yes
Co-operative Advertising: . . . . . . .Yes
Training: . . . . . . 80 Hours Headquarters
. . . .
On-Going Support: A,B,C,D,E,F,G,H,I/ . 6
EXPANSION PLANS:
US: . . . . All US
Canada: . . . . .All Canada
Overseas: . . . . . . EEC and Asia

STEAK ESCAPE, THE

222 Neilston St.
Columbus, OH 43215
TEL: (614) 224-0300
FAX: (614) 224-6460
Mr. Stanley L. Ames, Dir. Fran. Dev.

Selected as one of INC. Magazine's and Entrepreneur Magazine's top 500 businesses, THE STEAK ESCAPE takes a fresh approach to fast food. Specializing in fresh grilled sandwiches, specialty salads and fresh-cut fries, THE STEAK ESCAPE is located primarily in large regional mall food courts.

HISTORY: . . . .
Established in 1982; . . 1st Franchised in 1983
Company-Owned Units (As of 8/31/1992): . .3
Franchised Units (As of 8/31/1992): 91
Total Units (As of 8/31/1992): 94
Projected New Units for 1993: 20
Distribution: US-90;Can-0;Overseas-4
North America: . . . . 27 States
Concentration: . . . 6 in OH, 6 in CA, 6 in TN
Registered: . . . CA,FL,IL,IN,MD,MI,MN,NY
. . . . .OR,VA,WA,WI
Type Space: . .RM, Food Courts;~600-900 SF

FINANCIAL: Earnings Claim: . .No
Cash Investment: $100-120K
Total Investment: $200-250K
Fees: Franchise - $20K
Royalty: 6%, Advert: 1/2%
Contract Periods (Yrs.): 10/10
Area Development Agreement: . .No
Sub-Franchise Contract: . . . . .No
Expand in Territory: . . . . . . .No
Passive Ownership: . . . Discouraged
Encourage Conversions: . . . . . Yes
Average # Employees: . . 7 FT, 9 PT

FRANCHISOR TRAINING/SUPPORT:
Financial Assistance Provided: . . . . .NA
Site Selection Assistance: . . . . . . .Yes
Lease Negotiation Assistance: . . . .Yes
Co-operative Advertising: . . . . . . .Yes
Training: . . . . . . 4-6 Wks. Headquarters,
. . . . . 10-14 Days Franchisee Location
On-Going Support: B,C,D,E,G,h/ 20
EXPANSION PLANS:
US: . . . . All US
Canada: . . . . .All Canada
Overseas: . . . . Asia, EUR

STUFT PIZZA

1040 Calle Cordillera, # 103
San Clemente, CA 92672
TEL: (714) 361-2522
FAX: (714) 361-2501
Mr. Bill Boie, VP

STUFT PIZZA takes pizza to gourmet quality. STUFT uses only the freshest vegetables, highest-quality mozzarella and premium meats. The dough is made fresh daily and hand thrown for each order. Completing the popular pie is STUFT'S special sauce of secret ingredients developed by founder Jack Bertram.

HISTORY: . . . .
Established in 1976; . . 1st Franchised in 1985
Company-Owned Units (As of 8/31/1992): . .3
Franchised Units (As of 8/31/1992): 32
Total Units (As of 8/31/1992): 35
Projected New Units for 1993: 6
Distribution: US-35;Can-0;Overseas-0
North America: . . . . 2 States
Concentration: . . . . 33 in CA, 2 in OR
Registered: . . . . CA,OR
. . . .
Type Space: . . . .FS, SF, SC, RM;~2,500 SF

FINANCIAL: Earnings Claim: . Yes
Cash Investment: $100-500K
Total Investment: $100-500K
Fees: Franchise - $25K
Royalty: 3%, Advert: 1%
Contract Periods (Yrs.): 20/20
Area Development Agreement: Yes/5
Sub-Franchise Contract: . . . . .No
Expand in Territory: . . . . . . Yes
Passive Ownership: . . . Discouraged
Encourage Conversions: . . . . . Yes
Average # Employees: . .4 FT, 18 PT

FRANCHISOR TRAINING/SUPPORT:
Financial Assistance Provided: . . . . .No
Site Selection Assistance: . . . . . . .Yes
Lease Negotiation Assistance: . . . .Yes
Co-operative Advertising: . . . . . . .Yes
Training: . . . . 2 Wks. in Store,
. . . . 1 Wk. On-Site with Company Rep.
On-Going Support: C,D,E,G,H/ 3
EXPANSION PLANS:
US: . . . . CA, Western States
Canada: . . . . No
Overseas: . . . . No

TACO CASA

P. O. Box 4542
Topeka, KS 66604
TEL: (913) 267-2548
FAX: (913) 267-2652
Mr. James F. Reiter, President

TACO CASA offers Mexican fast-food restaurants, serving taco's, tostadas, burritos, sanchos, enchiladas, sachiladas, chili, chili burritos and various other entree items. Operates primarily in enclosed shopping centers. Free-standing units have drive-thru facilities. The attractive initial investment greatly enhances the return on investment.

HISTORY:	FINANCIAL: Earnings Claim: . Yes	FRANCHISOR TRAINING/SUPPORT:
Established in 1964; . . 1st Franchised in 1976	Cash Investment: $30-70K	Financial Assistance Provided: . . . . . No
Company-Owned Units (As of 8/31/1992): . .1	Total Investment: $90-400K	Site Selection Assistance: . . . . Yes
Franchised Units (As of 8/31/1992): 20	Fees: Franchise - $15K	Lease Negotiation Assistance: . . . . Yes
Total Units (As of 8/31/1992): 21	Royalty: 4%, Advert: 1.5%	Co-operative Advertising: . . . . . . Yes
Projected New Units for 1993: 3	Contract Periods (Yrs.): 20	Training: . . . . 2 Wks. Headquarters
Distribution: US-21;Can-0;Overseas-0	Area Development Agreement: . Yes	. . . .
North America: . . . . 6 States	Sub-Franchise Contract: . . . . . .No	On-Going Support: a,B,C,D,E,F,G,h,I/ . . 5
Concentration: . . . 5 in MS, 4 in KY, 2 in KS	Expand in Territory: . . . . . . Yes	**EXPANSION PLANS:**
Registered:	Passive Ownership: . . . Discouraged	US: . . . . Southeast
. . . .	Encourage Conversions: . . . . . Yes	Canada: . . . . No
Type Space: . . FS, SC, RM;~1,200-2,000 SF	Average # Employees: . .3 FT, 15 PT	Overseas: . . . . .Pacific Rim

TACO GRANDE

P. O. Box 780066
Wichita, KS 67278
TEL: (316) 636-2242
FAX: (316) 636-2282
Mr. John Wylie, President

TACO GRANDE offers a limited-menu Mexican restaurant, featuring drive-thru service. Our recipes are authentic Mexican recipes and we have been in successful operation for over 32 years. We offer excellent products, training and a cost-efficient and labor-saving building design.

HISTORY:	FINANCIAL: Earnings Claim: . .No	FRANCHISOR TRAINING/SUPPORT:
Established in 1960; . . 1st Franchised in 1966	Cash Investment: $45K	Financial Assistance Provided: . . . . . No
Company-Owned Units (As of 8/31/1992): . 11	Total Investment: $250-450K	Site Selection Assistance: . . . . Yes
Franchised Units (As of 8/31/1992): 17	Fees: Franchise - $20K	Lease Negotiation Assistance: . . . . No
Total Units (As of 8/31/1992): 28	Royalty: 3%, Advert: 2%	Co-operative Advertising: . . . . . . Yes
Projected New Units for 1993: 5	Contract Periods (Yrs.): 15/15	Training: . . . . 4 Wks. Headquarters
Distribution: US-28;Can-0;Overseas-0	Area Development Agreement: Yes/5	. . . .
North America: . . . . 5 States	Sub-Franchise Contract: . . . . . Yes	On-Going Support: C,D,E,G,h/ 4
Concentration: . . . 16 in KS, 8 in IN, 2 in MI	Expand in Territory: . . . . . . Yes	**EXPANSION PLANS:**
Registered: . . . . IN,MI	Passive Ownership: . . . Discouraged	US: . . . . All US
. . . .	Encourage Conversions: . . . . . .No	Canada: . . . . No
Type Space: . . . . FS, SC;~15,000 Min. SF	Average # Employees: . 10 FT, 20 PT	Overseas: . . . . No

TACO JOHN'S

P. O. Box 1589
Cheyenne, WY 82003
TEL: (307) 635-0101
FAX: (307) 638-0603
Mr. Mike Brunetti, Sr. Sales

Mexican fast-food, free-standing, regional malls and shopping centers. Sit-down or take-out. High quality and broad variety menu, featuring: tacos, burritos, enchiladas, chimichangas, nachos, taco salads, potato ole's, taco burgers, Sierra chicken sandwich and combination platters. Rated #1 in our segment the last 3 years by Entrepreneur Magazine.

HISTORY: . . . . IFA	FINANCIAL: Earnings Claim: . .No	FRANCHISOR TRAINING/SUPPORT:
Established in 1968; . . 1st Franchised in 1969	Cash Investment: . . . .$	Financial Assistance Provided: . . . . . No
Company-Owned Units (As of 8/31/1992): . 10	Total Investment: . . . .$	Site Selection Assistance: . . . . Yes
Franchised Units (As of 8/31/1992): 424	Fees: Franchise - $19.5K	Lease Negotiation Assistance: . . . . Yes
Total Units (As of 8/31/1992): 434	Royalty: 4%, Advert: 3%	Co-operative Advertising: . . . . . . Yes
Projected New Units for 1993: 30	Contract Periods (Yrs.): . . 20/10/10	Training: . . . . 6 Wks. Headquarters
Distribution: . . . US-434;Can-0;Overseas-0	Area Development Agreement: Yes/Var	. . . .
North America: . . . . 32 States	Sub-Franchise Contract: . . . . . .No	On-Going Support: a,B,C,D,E,f,G,H,I/ . 50
Concentration: . . 62 in Mn, 54 in IA, 35 in SD	Expand in Territory: . . . . . . Yes	**EXPANSION PLANS:**
Registered: . . . . .All States Exc. HI	Passive Ownership: . . . Discouraged	US: . . . . All US
. . . .	Encourage Conversions: . . . . Yes	Canada: . . . . No
Type Space: . . . . . FS, SC, RM;~Varies SF	Average # Employees: . . . 15-25 FT	Overseas: . . . . No

TACO LOCO MEXICAN CAFE

P. O. Box 30334, 349-B Tremont Ave.
Charlotte, NC 28230
TEL: (704) 375-9450
FAX:
Mr. Curtis Randolph, President

Mexican fast food. Serve beer where allowed. Specialize in taking existing units and converting into TACO LOCO theme. Includes simplified menu (value meal items and 10 dinners), salsa bar and colorful atmosphere. No one unit has exceeded total cash investment of $90,000. Stores are proven in malls, strip centers and free- standing units.

HISTORY:	FINANCIAL: Earnings Claim: . .No	FRANCHISOR TRAINING/SUPPORT:
Established in 1984; . . 1st Franchised in 1991	Cash Investment: $60-90K	Financial Assistance Provided: . . .Yes(D)
Company-Owned Units (As of 8/31/1992): . .0	Total Investment: $60-90K	Site Selection Assistance: . . . . . . .Yes
Franchised Units (As of 8/31/1992): 6	Fees: Franchise - $9.5K	Lease Negotiation Assistance: . . . .Yes
Total Units (As of 8/31/1992): 6	Royalty: 4%, Advert: 3%	Co-operative Advertising: . . . . . . .Yes
Projected New Units for 1993: 2	Contract Periods (Yrs.): 15/5	Training: . . . . . . 10 Days Headquarters,
Distribution: US-6;Can-0;Overseas-0	Area Development Agreement: . .No	. . . . 5 Days On-Site (More if Required)
North America:	Sub-Franchise Contract: . . . . .No	On-Going Support: b,C,E,d,F/ 2
Concentration:	Expand in Territory: . . . . . . Yes	EXPANSION PLANS:
Registered:	Passive Ownership: . . . Discouraged	US: . . . . . . .All US, Esp. VA and WV
. . . .	Encourage Conversions: . . . . Yes	Canada: . . . . .No
Type Space: . . . FS, SC, RM;~450-2,200 SF	Average # Employees: . . 5 FT, 4 PT	Overseas: . . . . No

TACO MAKER, THE

3544 Lincoln Ave., # C
Ogden, UT 84409
TEL: (801) 621-7486
FAX: (801) 621-0139
Mr. Gil Craig, VP Sales

International Mexican fast-food franchise, specializing in fast, friendly service and a complete menu with made-from-scratch and fresh ingredients. Centralized purchasing, corporate marketing and promotional support and progressive store design provide for the most comprehensive and fun investment opportunity. Available in free- standing, mall or strip central locations.

HISTORY:	FINANCIAL: Earnings Claim: . .No	FRANCHISOR TRAINING/SUPPORT:
Established in 1978; . . 1st Franchised in 1978	Cash Investment: $50-125K	Financial Assistance Provided: . . . . .No
Company-Owned Units (As of 8/31/1992): . .0	Total Investment: $75-500K	Site Selection Assistance: . . . . . . .Yes
Franchised Units (As of 8/31/1992): 86	Fees: Franchise - $22.5K	Lease Negotiation Assistance: . . . .Yes
Total Units (As of 8/31/1992): 86	Royalty: 5%, Advert: 3%	Co-operative Advertising: . . . . .No
Projected New Units for 1993: 12	Contract Periods (Yrs.): 15/15	Training: . . . . . . 30 Days Headquarters,
Distribution: US-38;Can-1;Overseas-47	Area Development Agreement: Yes/15	. . . . 14 Days Store Training
North America: . . . . . 14 States, 1 Province	Sub-Franchise Contract: . . . . . Yes	On-Going Support: B,C,D,E,F,G,H/ . . 13
Concentration: . . . 8 in UT, 5 in NY, 3 in MA	Expand in Territory: . . . . Yes	EXPANSION PLANS:
Registered:	Passive Ownership: . . . Discouraged	US: . . . . NE, UT and Puerto Rico
. . . .	Encourage Conversions: . . . . Yes	Canada: . . . . .No
Type Space: . . . FS, SF, SC, RM;~Varies SF	Average # Employees: 5-6 FT, 5-20 PT	Overseas: . . . . Yes

TACO MAYO

10405 Greenbriar Pl., # B
Oklahoma City, OK 73159
TEL: (405) 691-8226
FAX: (405) 691-2572
Mr. Randy K. Earhart, President

Quick-service Mexican-style restaurants with a limited menu. Inside dining and drive-thru service. Low start-up costs. "The max in Tex-Mex taste."

HISTORY:	FINANCIAL: Earnings Claim: . .No	FRANCHISOR TRAINING/SUPPORT:
Established in 1978; . . 1st Franchised in 1980	Cash Investment: $30-40K	Financial Assistance Provided: . . . . .No
Company-Owned Units (As of 8/31/1992): . 17	Total Investment: $80-100K	Site Selection Assistance: . . . . . . .Yes
Franchised Units (As of 8/31/1992): 43	Fees: Franchise - $7.5K	Lease Negotiation Assistance: . . . . .Yes
Total Units (As of 8/31/1992): 60	Royalty: 3.5%, Advert: 3%	Co-operative Advertising: . . . . .Yes
Projected New Units for 1993: 9	Contract Periods (Yrs.): 10/10	Training: . . . . 4 Wks. Headquarters
Distribution: US-60;Can-0;Overseas-0	Area Development Agreement: Yes/10	. . . .
North America: . . . . 5 States	Sub-Franchise Contract: . . . . .No	On-Going Support: B,C,D,E,F,G,h/ 8
Concentration: . . .45 in OK, 8 in TX, 3 in AR	Expand in Territory: . . . . . . .No	EXPANSION PLANS:
Registered:	Passive Ownership: . . . Discouraged	US: . . . . Southwest Only
. . . .	Encourage Conversions: . . . . Yes	Canada: . . . . .No
Type Space: . . . . FS;~1,600 SF	Average # Employees: 8-10 FT, 6-8 PT	Overseas: . . . . .No

TACO TIME

3880 W. 11th Ave.
Eugene, OR 97402
TEL: (800) 547-8907 (503) 687-8222
FAX: (503) 343-5208
Mr. Jim Thomas, SVP Dev.

TACO TIME is a dynamic leader in the Mexican fast-food business. Outstanding food products feature quality-fresh ingredients and exciting menu items.

HISTORY: . . . . IFA	FINANCIAL: Earnings Claim: . .No	FRANCHISOR TRAINING/SUPPORT:
Established in 1959; . . 1st Franchised in 1961	Cash Investment: $70K	Financial Assistance Provided: . . . . .No
Company-Owned Units (As of 8/31/1992): . .3	Total Investment: $129-219K	Site Selection Assistance: . . . . . . .Yes
Franchised Units (As of 8/31/1992): 284	Fees: Franchise - $18K	Lease Negotiation Assistance: . . . . .Yes
Total Units (As of 8/31/1992): 287	Royalty: 5%, Advert: 2.5%	Co-operative Advertising: . . . . . . .Yes
Projected New Units for 1993: 12	Contract Periods (Yrs.): . . . 15/10	Training: . . . . . . 5 Wks. Headquarters
Distribution: US-201;Can-84;Overseas-2	Area Development Agreement: Yes/5	. . . .
North America: . . . . 20 States, 8 Provinces	Sub-Franchise Contract: . . . . . Yes	On-Going Support: C,d,E,G,h,I/ 22
Concentration: . 69 in OR, 37 in AB, 36 in UT	Expand in Territory: . . . . .No	EXPANSION PLANS:
Registered: . . . . . . All States Exc. RI & SD	Passive Ownership: . . . Not Allowed	US: . . . . All US
. . . .	Encourage Conversions: . . . . Yes	Canada: . . . . Western Province
Type Space: . . FS, SC, RM;~1,500-2,160 SF	Average # Employees: . .5 FT, 30 PT	Overseas: .Master Franchises - Asia

TASTEE-FREEZ INTERNATIONAL

48380 Van Dyke
Utica, MI 48317
TEL: (313) 739-5520
FAX: (313) 739-8351
Mr. James Brasier, President

TASTEE-FREEZ offers its traditional menu of soft-serve desserts along with a core menu of hamburgers, hot dogs and fries (optional fried chicken and breakfast programs). Most recently, this menu has been augmented with a 14% gourmet dipped ice cream manufactured in the store. TASTEE-FREEZ is entering its 41st year of franchising.

HISTORY: . . . . IFA	FINANCIAL: Earnings Claim: . .No	FRANCHISOR TRAINING/SUPPORT:
Established in 1950; . . 1st Franchised in 1950	Cash Investment: $50-150K	Financial Assistance Provided: . . . Yes(I)
Company-Owned Units (As of 8/31/1992): . .0	Total Investment: $125-450K	Site Selection Assistance: . . . . . . .Yes
Franchised Units (As of 8/31/1992): 400	Fees: Franchise - $10-25K	Lease Negotiation Assistance: . . . . .Yes
Total Units (As of 8/31/1992): 400	Royalty: 4%, Advert: 2%	Co-operative Advertising: . . . . .Yes
Projected New Units for 1993: 12	Contract Periods (Yrs.): . . . 10/10	Training: . . . . . . 3-4 Days Headquarters,
Distribution: US-388;Can-12;Overseas-0	Area Development Agreement: .No	. . . . 10-14 Days On-Site
North America: . . . . 38 States, 4 Provinces	Sub-Franchise Contract: . . . . . Yes	On-Going Support: C,D,E,G,H/ 15
Concentration: . . 34 in IL, 33 in VA, 29 in PA	Expand in Territory:	EXPANSION PLANS:
Registered: . . . . FL,IN,MI,ND,VA	Passive Ownership: . . . Discouraged	US: . . . . All US
. . . .	Encourage Conversions: . . . . Yes	Canada: . . . . .All Canada
Type Space: . . . . . . .FS, SC;~1,600 SF	Average # Employees:	Overseas: . . . Singapore, Malaysia

TIPPY'S TACO HOUSE

Box 665
Winnsboro, TX 75494
TEL: (214) 629-7800
FAX: (214) 342-6001
Mr. W. L. Locklier, Owner

Excellent Tex-Mex food packaged to go or eat in. We give owner-operator a lot of leeway to use his own drive and initiative to be innovative within guidelines laid out by parent company. We are available at any time for advice or guidance.

HISTORY:	FINANCIAL: Earnings Claim: . .No	FRANCHISOR TRAINING/SUPPORT:
Established in 1958; . . 1st Franchised in 1968	Cash Investment: $30K	Financial Assistance Provided: . . . . .No
Company-Owned Units (As of 8/31/1992): . .0	Total Investment: $100K	Site Selection Assistance: . . . . . . .Yes
Franchised Units (As of 8/31/1992): 22	Fees: Franchise - $15K	Lease Negotiation Assistance: . . . . .Yes
Total Units (As of 8/31/1992): 22	Royalty: 3%, Advert: 0%	Co-operative Advertising: . . . . .No
Projected New Units for 1993: 5	Contract Periods (Yrs.): . . . 20/20	Training: . . . . . Varies - Nearest Author-
Distribution: US-22;Can-0;Overseas-0	Area Development Agreement: . Yes	. . . . ized Location
North America: . . . . 7 States	Sub-Franchise Contract: . . . . . .No	On-Going Support: C,D,E,F,G/ . . . .
Concentration:	Expand in Territory: . . . . Yes	EXPANSION PLANS:
Registered: . . . . VA	Passive Ownership: . . . Discouraged	US: . . . . All US
. . . .	Encourage Conversions: . . . . Yes	Canada: . . . . .All Canada
Type Space: FS, SF, SC, RM;~1,500-2,000 SF	Average # Employees: . . . . . .5 FT	Overseas: . . . . .Yes

TOGO'S EATERY

900 E. Campbell, # 1
Campbell, CA 95008
TEL: (408) 377-1754
FAX: (408) 377-4130
Ms. Valerie Konomos, Fran. Coord.

We are an operation specializing in high-quality, fast-service sandwich restaurants. Unique in style, service and decor with a product that offers more variety and quality than traditional fast-food, with an emphasis on healthy food.

HISTORY:	
Established in 1972; . . 1st Franchised in 1977	
Company-Owned Units (As of 8/31/1992): . .8	
Franchised Units (As of 8/31/1992): 138	
Total Units (As of 8/31/1992): 146	
Projected New Units for 1993: 12	
Distribution: US-146;Can-0;Overseas-0	
North America: . . . . 4 States	
Concentration: . . 142 in CA, 1 in NV, 2 in OR	
Registered: . . . . .CA,OR,WA	
Type Space: . . . . . FS, SF, SC;~1,400 SF	

FINANCIAL: Earnings Claim: . .No
Cash Investment: $90-160K
Total Investment: . . . .$
Fees: Franchise - $10-25K
Royalty: 5%, Advert: 2%
Contract Periods (Yrs.): . . . 10/10
Area Development Agreement: Yes/5
Sub-Franchise Contract: . . . . .No
Expand in Territory: . . . . . . Yes
Passive Ownership: . . . Not Allowed
Encourage Conversions: . . . . .No
Average # Employees: . .2 FT, 25 PT

FRANCHISOR TRAINING/SUPPORT:
Financial Assistance Provided: . . . . .No
Site Selection Assistance: . . . . . . .Yes
Lease Negotiation Assistance: . . . . .Yes
Co-operative Advertising: . . . . . . .Yes
Training: . . . . 2 Wks. Headquarters,
. . . . 2 Wks. in Store
On-Going Support: C,D,E,G,H/ 18
EXPANSION PLANS:
US: . . . . West Coast
Canada: . . . . .No
Overseas: . . . . No

TROLL'S SEAFOOD

#602 - 535 Thurlow St.
Vancouver, BC V6E 3L2 CAN
TEL: (604) 684-3331
FAX:
Mr. Geoffrey Hair, Dir. Fran.

Known for its famous fish and chips, this well-established company has been making tasty chowders, calamari, fish and chicken burgers for 45 years. TROLL'S is established in strip plazas and stand-alone locations and has a friendly, active decor.

HISTORY:
Established in 1947; . . 1st Franchised in 1988
Company-Owned Units (As of 8/31/1992): . .0
Franchised Units (As of 8/31/1992): 15
Total Units (As of 8/31/1992): 15
Projected New Units for 1993: . . . .
Distribution: US-0;Can-15;Overseas-0
North America: . . . .
Concentration: . . . .
Registered: . . . .
Type Space: . . . . .SF, SC;~1,250 SF

FINANCIAL: Earnings Claim: . Yes
Cash Investment: $35-50K
Total Investment: $100-180K
Fees: Franchise - $18.5K
Royalty: 7%, Advert: 2%
Contract Periods (Yrs.): 5-10
Area Development Agreement: Yes/10
Sub-Franchise Contract: . . . . . Yes
Expand in Territory: . . . . . . Yes
Passive Ownership: . . . Not Allowed
Encourage Conversions: . . . . . Yes
Average # Employees: . . 3 FT, 5 PT

FRANCHISOR TRAINING/SUPPORT:
Financial Assistance Provided: . . . . .No
Site Selection Assistance: . . . . .Yes
Lease Negotiation Assistance: . . . . .Yes
Co-operative Advertising: . . . . .No
Training: . . . . . . 2 Wks. Headquarters or
. . . . .Store
On-Going Support: a,C,D,E,G/ 3
EXPANSION PLANS:
US: . . . . . Territorial Rights - All US
Canada: . . . . .All Canada
Overseas: . . . . . . .AU, NZ, MX

TUBBY'S SUB SHOPS

34500 Doreka Dr.
Fraser, MI 48026
TEL: (800) 752-0644 (313) 296-1270
FAX: (313) 296-3045
Mr. O. Thomas Boland, VP Fran. Dev.

TUBBY'S SUB SHOPS offers the individual an opportunity to own and manage his/her own business. TUBBY'S is well known for top-quality food products, complete training and efficient operations. Hot, grilled sandwiches on fresh-daily rolls set TUBBY'S apart from other sub sandwich competitors.

HISTORY:
Established in 1968; . . 1st Franchised in 1978
Company-Owned Units (As of 8/31/1992): . .1
Franchised Units (As of 8/31/1992): 61
Total Units (As of 8/31/1992): 62
Projected New Units for 1993: 12
Distribution: US-62;Can-0;Overseas-0
North America: . . . . 4 States
Concentration: . . . .59 in MI, 1 in IL, 1 in FL
Registered: . . . . .FL,IL,IN,MI
Type Space: FS, SF, SC, RM;~1,200-1,800 SF

FINANCIAL: Earnings Claim: . .No
Cash Investment: $35-95K
Total Investment: $85-37.5K
Fees: Franchise - $17.5K
Royalty: 5%, Advert: 2.5%
Contract Periods (Yrs.): . . . 10/10
Area Development Agreement: Yes/5+
Sub-Franchise Contract: . . . . . Yes
Expand in Territory: . . . . . . Yes
Passive Ownership: . . . Not Allowed
Encourage Conversions: . . . . . Yes
Average # Employees: . . 4 FT, 8 PT

FRANCHISOR TRAINING/SUPPORT:
Financial Assistance Provided: . . . Yes(I)
Site Selection Assistance: . . . . .Yes
Lease Negotiation Assistance: . . . . .Yes
Co-operative Advertising: . . . . .Yes
Training: . . . . 4 Wks. Headquarters,
. . . . 1 Wk. Opening, On-Going On-Site
On-Going Support: B,C,D,E,F,G,H,I/ . . 12
EXPANSION PLANS:
US: . . . . All US
Canada: . . . . .Ontario
Overseas: . . . . No

WENDY'S RESTAURANTS OF CANADA

6715 Airport Rd., # 301
Mississauga, ON L4V 1X2 CAN
TEL: (416) 677-7023
FAX: (416) 677-5297
Mr. George Lathouras, VP Devel.

WENDY'S offers a wide variety of high-quality items. Fresh, never frozen, hamburgers prepared while you wait, whole breast of chicken, chili, baked potatoes, fresh salads and frosty dairy dessert.

HISTORY: . . . . IFA	FINANCIAL: Earnings Claim: . .No	FRANCHISOR TRAINING/SUPPORT:
Established in 1969; . . 1st Franchised in 1975	Cash Investment: $300-500K	Financial Assistance Provided: . . .Yes(D)
Company-Owned Units (As of 8/31/1992): . 82	Total Investment: . . . . .$.3-1.0MM	Site Selection Assistance: . . . . . . .Yes
Franchised Units (As of 8/31/1992): 71	Fees: Franchise - $40K	Lease Negotiation Assistance: . . . . . .Yes
Total Units (As of 8/31/1992): 153	Royalty: 4%, Advert: 6%	Co-operative Advertising: . . . . .Yes
Projected New Units for 1993: 25	Contract Periods (Yrs.): . . 20/Varies	Training: . . . . 12 Wks. Regional Training
Distribution: US-0;Can-153;Overseas-0	Area Development Agreement: Yes/Var	. . Center, 2 Wks. Toronto Headquarters
North America: . . . . 10 Provinces	Sub-Franchise Contract: . . . . . Yes	On-Going Support: C,D,E,G,h/ 57
Concentration: . 80 in ON, 24 in BC, 22 in AB	Expand in Territory: . . . . Yes	EXPANSION PLANS:
Registered: . . . . AB	Passive Ownership: . . . Not Allowed	US: .No
. . . .	Encourage Conversions: . . . . . Yes	Canada: . . . . .All Canada
Type Space: . . . . . . FS, RM;~40,000 SF	Average # Employees: . .4 FT, 60 PT	Overseas: . . . . No

WIENERSCHNITZEL

4440 Von Karman Ave.
Newport Beach, CA 92660
TEL: (800) 432-3316 (714) 752-5800
FAX: (714) 851-2618
Mr. Alan F. Gallup, Dir. Fran. Sales

WIENERSCHNITZEL, one of the pioneers of the fast-food business, has succeeded and prospered by insisting on the highest quality standards, fast, efficient service and economical prices. WIENERSCHNITZEL has expanded to over 288 company-owned and franchised units. With 30 years of success behind us, we are in a unique position to take advantage of the consumers' ever-increasing demand for convenience, quality and value.

HISTORY:	FINANCIAL: Earnings Claim: . .No	FRANCHISOR TRAINING/SUPPORT:
Established in 1961; . . 1st Franchised in 1963	Cash Investment: $60K	Financial Assistance Provided: . . . . .No
Company-Owned Units (As of 8/31/1992): . 90	Total Investment: $600K	Site Selection Assistance: . . . . . . .Yes
Franchised Units (As of 8/31/1992): 198	Fees: Franchise - $30K	Lease Negotiation Assistance: . . . .Yes
Total Units (As of 8/31/1992): 288	Royalty: 5%, Advert: 4%	Co-operative Advertising: . . . . .Yes
Projected New Units for 1993: 5	Contract Periods (Yrs.): 20/10	Training: . . . .
Distribution: US-288;Can-0;Overseas-0	Area Development Agreement: Yes/20	. . . .
North America: . . . . 9 States	Sub-Franchise Contract: . . . . .No	On-Going Support: B,C,D,E,F,H,I/ . . . 65
Concentration: . . 224 in CA, 23 in TX, 13 AZ	Expand in Territory: . . . . Yes	EXPANSION PLANS:
Registered: . . . . CA	Passive Ownership: . . . . .Allowed	US: . . . . .Yes
. . . .	Encourage Conversions: . . . . Yes	Canada: . . . . .No
Type Space: FS, SF, SC, RM;~15,000-25,000 SF	Average # Employees: . .6 FT, 14 PT	Overseas: . . . . .Yes

WINGS TO DO

1256 S. Little Creek Rd.
Dover, DE 19901
TEL: (302) 734-5512
FAX: (302) 734-5812
Mr. James F. Tisack, EVP

Specialty, eat-in or take-out restaurant, serving cooked-to-order Authentic Buffalo-style Wings with complementary side dishes.

HISTORY:	FINANCIAL: Earnings Claim: . .No	FRANCHISOR TRAINING/SUPPORT:
Established in 1987; . . 1st Franchised in 1990	Cash Investment: $40-65K	Financial Assistance Provided: . . . . .No
Company-Owned Units (As of 8/31/1992): . .3	Total Investment: $60-65K	Site Selection Assistance: . . . . . . .Yes
Franchised Units (As of 8/31/1992): 40	Fees: Franchise - $15K	Lease Negotiation Assistance: . . . . .Yes
Total Units (As of 8/31/1992): 43	Royalty: 3%, Advert: 2%	Co-operative Advertising: . . . . .Yes
Projected New Units for 1993: 40	Contract Periods (Yrs.): 10/5	Training: . . . . .1 Wk. Headquarters,
Distribution: US-33;Can-0;Overseas-0	Area Development Agreement: Yes/5	. . . . .2 Wks. Franchisee Store
North America: . . . . 9 States	Sub-Franchise Contract: . . . . .No	On-Going Support: C,D,E,F,G,H/ 10
Concentration: . .11 in DE, 10 in PA, 4 in MD	Expand in Territory: . . . . Yes	EXPANSION PLANS:
Registered: . . . . FL,MD,NY,RI,VA	Passive Ownership: . . . . .Allowed	US: . . . . East of Mississippi
. . . .	Encourage Conversions: . . . . Yes	Canada: . . . . .No
Type Space: . . . . SC;~800-1,200 SF	Average # Employees: . . 3 FT, 2 PT	Overseas: . . . . No

SUPPLEMENTAL LISTING OF FRANCHISORS

30 MINUTE PIZZA . . . . 7188 W. Sunset Blvd., # 200, Los Angeles, CA 90046
    Contact: Mr. F. Bonnanno, President; Tel: (213) 278-8211
A. L. VAN HOUTTE . . . . 6045 Boul. Des Grandes Prairies, St. Leonard, PQ H1P 1A5   CAN
    Contact: Mr. Claude Martin, Asst. Dir. Fran.; Tel: (514) 327-3110
ABBY'S PIZZA INNS . . . . 2722 N. E. Stephens, Roseburg, OR 97470
    Contact: Mr. Buck Kessler, GM; Tel: (503) 689-0019
AIDA'S FALAFEL . . . . 1921 Queen St. E., Toronto, ON M4L 1H3   CAN
    Contact: Mr. Laik Ali Khan; Tel: (416) 466-4486
AL'S CHICAGO'S #1 ITALIAN BEEF . . . . . . .22 W. 140 North Ave., Glenellyn, IL 60137
    Contact: Mr. Terry G. Pacelli, President; Tel: (708) 858-9090
ALL AMERICAN HERO . . . . P. O. Box 1127, Gulf Breeze, FL 32562
    Contact: Mr. David Sapp, President; Tel: (305) 486-7000
ALL V'S SANDWICHES . . . . 26 W. Dry Creek Circle, # 390, Littleton, CO 80120
    Contact: Mr. Kenneth Cox, President; Tel: (303) 850-7774
AMECI PIZZA & PASTA - IN & OUT . . . . . . .6603 B Independence Ave., Canoga Park, CA 91303
    Contact: Mr. Nick Andrisano, President; Tel: (800) 339-9239 (818) 712-0110
AMIGOS 2546 S. 48th, # 6, P. O. Box 6189, Lincoln, NE 68506 . . . .
    Contact: Mr. Joseph Field, VP; Tel: (402) 488-8500
ANDY'S OF AMERICA . . . . .11521 W. Markhan, Little Rock, AR 72211
    Contact: Mr. Garland Street, President; Tel: (501) 221-1020
APPETITO'S . . . . 4611 N. 12th St., # 200, Phoenix, AZ 85014
    Contact: Mr. Richard L. Schnakenberg, President; Tel: (602) 279-7704
ARBY'S P. O. Box 414177, Miami, FL 33141 . . . .
    Contact: Mr. Gaylon Smith, SVP; Tel: (800) 554-1388 (305) 866-1904
ARMAN'S SYSTEMS . . . . 6165 Central Ave., Portage, IN 46368
    Contact: President; Tel: (219) 930-0300
ARMAND'S CHICAGO PIZZERIA . . . . 4231 Wisconsin Ave., NW, Wahington, DC 20016
    Contact: Mr. Lou Newmyer; Tel: (202) 363-6268
ARTHUR TREACHERS FISH & CHIPS . . . . .5121 Mahoning Ave., Youngstown, OH 44515
    Contact: Mr. James R. Cataland, President; Tel: (216) 792-2252
ASTOR RESTAURANT GROUP . . . . 740 Broadway, # 602, New York, NY 10003
    Contact: Mr. Charles Leaness, SVP; Tel: (212) 673-5900
ASTRO PIZZA . . . . 45 Stanford Rd., Piscataway, NJ 08845
    Contact: President; Tel: (201) 463-7662
AU NATURAL GOURMET PIZZA . . . . .3050 Biscayne Blvd., # 610, Miami, FL 33137
    Contact: Mr. Reese Victor, President; Tel: (305) 576-8077
AUNT CHILOTTA TACOS . . . . .133 Coon Rapids Blvd., Coon Rapids, MN 55433
    Contact: Mr. Robert Schachtschneider; Tel: (612) 780-1874
AURELIO'S IS PIZZA . . . . 18162 Harwood Ave., Homewood, IL 60430
    Contact: Mr. Aurelio, President; Tel: (708) 798-8050
BACK YARD BURGERS . . . . .4245 Cherry Center Dr., # 4, Memphis, TN 38118
    Contact: Mr. Charles Saba, VP Fran. Devel.; Tel: (901) 367-0888
BAR-B-CUTIE . . . . 6426 Baum Dr., # E, Knoxville, TN 37919
    Contact: President; Tel:
BERT'S HAMBURGERS AND FRIES . . . . P. O. Box 21685, Waco, TX 76702
    Contact: Mr. Bob Pryor, Fran. Dir.; Tel: (817) 757-2378
BIB'S BURGERS . . . . 8192 College Pkwy., SW, # 12, Fort Myers, FL 33919
    Contact: President; Tel: (813) 275-4199
BIG AL'S . . . . 6750 West 93rd St., Overland Park, KS 66210
    Contact: President; Tel: (913) 381-9638
BIG CHEESE PIZZA CORPORATION . . . . 1130 Haskell, Wichita, KS 67213
    Contact: Mr. Vern H. Schroeder, Secty./Treas.; Tel:
BIG FRANK'S CHICAGO STYLE HOT DOGS . . . . 5502 Kirby Dr., Houston, TX 77005
    Contact: Mr. Harry Fleming, President; Tel: (713) 664-3647
BLACK-EYED PEA . . . . 8115 Preston Rd., Lock Box 7, # 80, Dallas, TX 75225
    Contact: Mr. Ted J. Papit, President; Tel: (214) 363-9513
BLIMPIE ASSOCIATES . . . . Seven Penn Plaza, New York, NY 10001
    Contact: Mr. Joseph Dornbush, President; Tel: (212) 279-7100
BOJANGLES' FAMOUS CHICKEN 'N BISCUITS . . . . P. O. Box 240239, Charlotte, NC 28224
    Contact: Mr. Eric Newman, VP/General Counsel; Tel: (800) 366-9921 (704) 527-2675

BOSTON CHICKEN ROTISSERIE . . . . 230 Western Ave., # 502, Boston, MA 02134
    Contact: Mr. Maurice Rowe, Dir. Fran. Dev.; Tel: (617) 783-2585
BOXCAR INDUSTRIES USA . . . . 1820 Independence Sq., Dunwoody, GA 30338
    Contact: President; Tel: (404) 320-2077
BOZ HOT DOGS . . . . 770 E. 142nd St., Dolton, IL 60419
    Contact: Mr. Donald Hart, President; Tel: (708) 841-3747 (312) 468-3647
BRIGHAM'S . . . . 30 Mill St., Millbrook Park, Arlington, MA 02174
    Contact: Mr. John Haywood, EVP; Tel: (800) BRIGHAM (617) 648-9000 C
BROADWAY STATION RESTAURANTS . . . . . 1802 Wooddale Dr., # 210, Woodbury, MN 55125
    Contact: Mr. Charles Cudd, President; Tel: (612) 731-0800
BROWNIES RECIPE FRIED CHICKEN . . . . . . 3650 Bonneville Pl., # 110, Burnaby, BC V5C 6A8   CAN
    Contact: Mr. Herb Wudy, President; Tel: (604) 291-6060 C
BTG EXPRESS/BURGERS TO GO . . . . 5508 Windmill Ct., Lansing, MI 48917
    Contact: Mr. Charles Miller, President; Tel: (616) 968-8044
BUBBA'S BREAKAWAY . . . . 200 Sullivan Ave., South Windsor, CT 06074
    Contact: Mr. Ron Jordan, President; Tel: (814) 237-4616
BUMPERS OF AMERICA . . . . P.O. Box 700, Greenwood, MS 38930
    Contact: Ms. Jane L. Moss; Tel: (601) 453-6601
BURGER EXPRESS . . . . 11511 Katy Freeway, # 520, Houston, TX 77079
    Contact: President; Tel: (713) 556-0751
BURGER KING (CANADA) . . . . 201 City Centre Dr., 8th Fl., Mississauga, ON L5B 2T4   CAN
    Contact: Mr. Ted Young; Tel: (416) 273-5000
BUSCEMI'S PIZZA & SUB SHOPPE . . . . 30362 Gratiot Ave., Roseville, MI 48066
    Contact: Mr. Anthony Buscemi, President; Tel: (313) 296-5560
CAFFE' CLASSICO . . . . 910 E. Birch St., # 350, Brea, CA 92621
    Contact: Mr. Doug Lubbe, Natl. Fran. Mgr.; Tel: (714) 256-8937
CAJUN JOE'S PREMIUM CHICKEN . . . . 325 Bic Dr., Milford, CT 06460
    Contact: Mr. Keith Cross, Fran. Sales. Mgr.; Tel: (800) 888-4848 (203) 877-4281
CAL DE FRANCE . . . . 8201 Greensboro Dr., # 1200, McLean, VA 22102
    Contact: President; Tel: (703) 442-9205
CAPITAL PIZZA . . . . 5834 Ridgewood Rd., Jackson, MS 39211
    Contact: President; Tel: (601) 957-2140
CAPT. SUBMARINE . . . . 69 Viceroy Rd., # 1, Concord, ON L4K 2L6   CAN
    Contact: Mr. Jack Goldstein, President; Tel: (416) 669-6966
CARA OPERATIONS LIMITED . . . . 230 Bloor St. W., Toronto, ON M5S 1T8   CAN
    Contact: Ms. Irene Fong; Tel: (416) 962-4571
CARBONE'S PIZZERIA . . . . 55 E. Wentworth Ave., W. St. Paul, MN 55118
    Contact: Mr. Richard Carbone; Tel: (612) 455-0522
CARL'S JR. RESTAURANTS . . . . 1200 N. Harbor Blvd., Anaheim, CA 92803
    Contact: Mr. Rory Murphy, VP Franchising; Tel: (714) 774-5796
CATFISH CHARLIE . . . . P. O. Box 2503, Gulfport, MS 39507
    Contact: President; Tel: (601) 868-3322
CENTRAL PARK USA . . . . 6100 Bldg., #3800, Eastgate Ctr., Chattanooga, TN 37411
    Contact: Mr. Robert Davenport, Jr., VP; Tel: (615) 622-1874
CHANTECLER CHAR-B.Q. CHICKEN 'N' RIB . . . . . . 39 Pinnacle Rd., Toronto, ON M2L 2V6   CAN
    Contact: Mr. J. V. Durbano; Tel: (416) 441-3351
CHARLIE WOO'S . . . . 884 Oakwood Rd., Charleston, WV 25314
    Contact: Mr. Daniel Sadd, President; Tel: (304) 346-1115
CHATEAU ST. JEROME . . . . P. O. Box 5125, Armdale, NS B3L 4M7   CAN
    Contact: Mr. Richard Morse, Fran. Dev.; Tel: (902) 454-5511
CHECKERBOARD PIZZA . . . . 12891 73rd Ave. N., Maple Grove, MN 55369
    Contact: Mr. Jim Provinzino, President; Tel: (612) 424-5814
CHECKERS PIZZA . . . . 659 West Main Rd., Middletown, RI 02840
    Contact: President; Tel:
CHEF'S TAKEOUT . . . . 111 N. Victory, Burbank, CA 91502
    Contact: Mr. Tom Hanson, Sr., President; Tel: (818) 841-2203
CHEZ MAX . . . . 25 B Bather St., Toronto, ON M5V 2P1   CAN
    Contact: Mr. Ian McClennon, President; Tel: (800) 387-8942 (416) 366-8031
CHICAGO FRANK'S . . . . 133 Edinboro St., Newton, MA 02160
    Contact: Mr. Thomas Giancristiano; Tel: (617) 964-8353
CHICK-FIL-A . . . . 5200 Buffington Rd., Atlanta, GA 30349
    Contact: President; Tel: (404) 765-8050
CHICKEN DELIGHT INTERNATIONAL . . . . 395 Berry St., Winnipeg, MB R3J 1N6   CAN
    Contact: Mr. Robert Ritchie, Dir. Mktg.; Tel: (204) 885-7570
CHICKEN QUICKLY . . . . 10 W. Pearce St., Richmond Hill, ON L4B 1B6   CAN
    Contact: Mr. Stan Vyner; Tel: (416) 764-7815

CHICKEN USA . . . . 2490 Dixie Hwy., Pontiac, MI 48055
    Contact: President; Tel: (313) 858-8710
CHOP CHOP . . . . 4943 Fairhaven Way, Roswell, GA 30075
    Contact: Mr. Cameron Kimmel, Dir. Fran.; Tel: (404) 587-0769
CHURCH'S CHICKEN . . . . 1333 S. Clearview Pkwy., Jefferson, LA 70121
    Contact: Mr. Terrel T. Rhoten, VP Sales; Tel: (800) 848-8248 (504) 735-9392
CLUB SANDWICH . . . . 107 Cherry St., New Canaan, CT 06840
    Contact: Mr. Mickey DeVito, President; Tel: (203) 966-4053
COLONEL LEE'S ENTERPRISES . . . . 3080 E. 50th St., Vernon, CA 90058
    Contact: Colonel John C. Lee, President; Tel: (213) 588-2158
COUCH'S BARBEQUE . . . . 5323 - 27 E. Nettleton, Jonesboro, AR 72410
    Contact: Ms. Beth Couch, President; Tel: (501) 932-0710
CRISPY CREPES . . . . 35 Alexandria Blvd., Toronto, ON M4R 1L8   CAN
    Contact: President; Tel: (416) 488-3687
CRUSTY'S USA / DINO'S . . . . .19215 W. 8 Mile Rd., Detroit, MI 48219
    Contact: Mr. John E. Ray, President; Tel: (313) 537-5252
DAIRY BELLE FREEZE . . . . 832 N. Hillview Dr., Milpitas, CA 95035
    Contact: Mr. Steven H. Foodere, EVP; Tel: (408) 263-2612
DAIRY CHEER STORES . . . . .2914 Forgey St., Ashland, KY 41101
    Contact: Mr. W. Culbertson, President; Tel: (606) 324-5061
DAIRY QUEEN . . . . P. O. Box 39286, Minneapolis, MN 55439
    Contact: Mr. John P. Hyduke, VP Fran. Dev.; Tel: (612) 830-0312
DE BEST CHINESE BUFFET . . . . P. O. Box 51374, Knoxville, TN 37950
    Contact: President; Tel:
DEAN FOODS COMPANY . . . . .3600 N. River Rd., Franklin Park, IL 60131
    Contact: President; Tel: (312) 625-6200
DELIVERY EMPORIUM . . . . 2200 Corporate Blvd., # 317, Boca Raton, FL 33431
    Contact: Mr. John Cotugno, President; Tel: (800) 533-7161 (407) 994-3994
DESIGNER PIZZA . . . . 15125 Ventura Blvd., # 200, Sherman Oaks, CA 91423
    Contact: Mr. Kent Rhodes, Mktg. Dir.; Tel: (818) 784-2000
DIMARTINO'S NEW ORLEANS MUFFULETTAS . . . . . . .1788 Carol Sue Ave., Gretna, LA 70056
    Contact: Mr. Peter S. DiMartino; Tel:
DIMATTIIO'S PIZZA & PASTA . . . . 15490 Ventura Blvd., Sherman Oaks, CA 91403
    Contact: Mr. Gary DiMattio; Tel:
DINNER VENDOR . . . . .16 Office Park Cir., # 13, Birmingham, AL 35223
    Contact: President; Tel:
DOLE SUNFRESH EXPRESS . . . . .10900 Wilshire Blvd., Los Angeles, CA 90024
    Contact: Mr. Robert Puccio, President; Tel: (213) 824-1500
DON CHERRY'S GRAPEVINE RESTAURANTS . . . . . . 88 Wilson St. W., Ancaster, ON L9G 1N2   CAN
    Contact: Mr. Richard J. Scully; Tel: (416) 648-7717
DOSANKA FOODS . . . . 440 W. 47th St., New York, NY 10036
    Contact: Mr. Mac Hidaka, VP; Tel: (212) 757-8690
DRUSILLA SEAFOOD RESTAURANT . . . . 3482 Drusilla Ln., # D, Baton Rouge, LA 70809
    Contact: Mr. Frank J. Fresina, EVP Sales; Tel: (504) 927-8844
EUIE'S BURGERS . . . . 630 Meadowood Dr., Broken Arrow, OK 74011
    Contact: Mr. Bob Sparks; Tel: (800) 888-1305 (918) 451-2677
EXPRESS BURGER . . . . 19th & Pioneer Ave., # 301, Cheyenne, WY 82001
    Contact: Mr. David Ferrari, President; Tel: (307) 638-6815
EZ TAKE OUT BURGERS . . . . 420 Iris St., Corona del Mar, CA 92625
    Contact: Mr. Andrew Costa, President; Tel: (714) 673-1121
FAMOUS DILL BURGER . . . . 600 5th Ave. Plaza, Des Moines, IA 50309
    Contact: Ms. Phyllis Tasler; Tel: (515) 245-4206
FAST STICKS . . . . P. O. Drawer 53905, Fayetteville, NC 28305
    Contact: Ms. Jeanie Smith, Exec. Scty.; Tel: (919) 484-9999
FAST TRACK USA . . . . .138 McGehee Dr., Baton Rouge, LA 70815
    Contact: Mr. Mitch Richardson; Tel: (504) 272-2841
FLOOKYS HOT DOGS . . . . 8732 Corbin, Northridge, CA 91324
    Contact: Mr. Stan Houston, VP Sales; Tel: (818) 775-1844
FLUKY'S . . . . 1768 W. Devon Ave., Chicago, IL 60660
    Contact: Mr. Jason M. Drexler, Admin. Dir.; Tel: (312) 761-1173
FOODMAKER . . . . 9330 Balboa Ave., San Diego, CA 92123
    Contact: Mr. William Thelen, VP; Tel: (619) 571-2200
FOSTERS FREEZE INTERNATIONAL . . . 1052 Grand Ave., # C, P.O. Box 266, Arroyo Grande, CA 93420
    Contact: Mr. Dennis G. Poletti, Dir. Fran. Lic.; Tel: (800) 628-5600 (805) 481-9577
FRANK & STEIN DOGS & DRAFTS . . . . P. O. Box 20608, Roanoke, VA 24018
    Contact: Mr. Charles Caldwell; Tel: (703) 989-1425

FRYDAY'S CHICKEN . . . . .24225 West 9 Mile Rd., # 214, Southfield, MI 48034
    Contact: President; Tel: (313) 354-1070
GINA'S PIZZA/EZ TAKE OUT BURGER . . . . . 1721 Whittier Ave., # C, Costa Mesa, CA 92627
    Contact: Mr. Michael Mooslin; Tel: (714) 631-8741
GIOVANNI'S PIZZA BY THE SLICE . . . . P.O. Drawer 738, Waco, TX 76714
    Contact: Mr. John Diebolt, President; Tel: (817) 772-9242
GOEMON . . . . 1 Kendall Sq., # 100, Cambridge, MA 02139
    Contact: Ms. Kim Douwes, Director; Tel: (617) 577-1030
GOLDEN SKILLET FRIED CHICKEN . . . . 5701 GreenValley Dr., Bloomington, MN 55437
    Contact: Mr. Tom Winterick, Managing Dir.; Tel: (612) 830-0202
GRANDMA LEE'S INTERNATIONAL . . . . 1200 Aerowood Dr., Mississauga, ON L4W 2S7   CAN
    Contact: Mr. Rick Maj, Fran. Dir.; Tel: (416) 625-5055
GRANDY'S . . . . 997 Grandy Ln., Lewisville, TX 75067
    Contact: Mr. Wm. Fred Bartliff, VP Fran.; Tel: (214) 317-8143
GREAT GRUNTS . . . . .3321 Greenhill Lane, Louisville, KY 40207
    Contact: Ms. Roberta Elder; Tel: (502) 839-5471
GUNG HO ORIENTAL STIR FRY . . . . 7803 Glenroy Rd., # 310, Bloomington, MN 55439
    Contact: Mr. Keith Lindstrom, Dir. Fran. Dev.; Tel: (800) 424-6947 (612) 835-3555
HAPPI HOUSE RESTAURANTS . . . . .2901 Moorpark Ave., # 255, San Jose, CA 95128
    Contact: Mr. Carlo Besio, President; Tel: (408) 244-0665
HARTZ CHICKEN . . . . 14409 Cornerstone Village Dr., Houston, TX 77014
    Contact: Mr. Steve Jaspersen, VP Franchising; Tel: (713) 580-3752
HEAVENLY HOT DOGS . . . . .P. O. Box 503, Cape Coral, FL 33910
    Contact: Mr. Lee Lanktree, President; Tel: (813) 945-2300
HEAVY DUTY PIZZA . . . . . 113 - 115 Cushman Rd., Unit 21, St. Catharines, ON L2M 6S9   CAN
    Contact: Mr. Denis Blanchard, President; Tel: (416) 641-1111
HENNY O'ROURKES . . . . .8510 Morningcalm Dr., Cincinnati, OH 45255
    Contact: Mr. Jeff Osterfeld, President; Tel: (513) 231-0181
HENRY MOFFETT CHICKEN PIES . . . . . .16506 Lakewood Blvd., Bellflower, CA 90706
    Contact: President; Tel: (213) 925-5061
HOGS ON THE HILL . . . . 2001 Fourteenth St., NW, 2nd Fl., Washington, DC 20009
    Contact: Mr. Charles Kim, President; Tel: (800) 626-4611 (202) 332-4647
HOOKERS HAMBURGERS/J. J. HOOKERS . . . . . 26133 US Hwy. 19 N., # 204, Clearwater, FL 34623
    Contact: Ms. Marion Davidson; Tel: (813) 443-3200
HOP TOO'S . . . . .4901 NW 17th Wat, # 405, Ft. Lauderdale, FL 33309
    Contact: Mr. Mike Flynn, Dir. Fran.; Tel: (305) 776-7400
HOSS'S 764 Plaza, Duncansville, PA 16635 . . . .
    Contact: President; Tel: (814) 695-7600
HOT DOG CHARLIE'S . . . . 626 Second Ave., Troy, NY 12182
    Contact: Mr. John Fentekes; Tel: (518) 235-2485
HOT DOG ON A STICK . . . . 777 S. Pacific Coast Hwy., # 114, Solana Beach, CA 92075
    Contact: Ms. Dorothy Calhoun, Secty./Treas.; Tel: (619) 755-3049
HUNGRY HOWIE'S PIZZA & SUBS . . . . 35301 Schoolcraft Rd., Livonia, MI 48150
    Contact: Mr. Anthony P. Noga, Dir. Fran. Dev.; Tel: (800) 624-8122 (313) 422-1717
IDEAL SERVICES . . . . P. O. Box 328, Greeley, CO 80632
    Contact: President; Tel: (303) 352-9318
IN 'N' OUT CHICKEN EXPRESSE . . . . 19215 W. Eight Mile Rd., Detroit, MI 48219
    Contact: Mr. Richard Marczak; Tel: (313) 255-0100
INTERNATIONAL DAIRY QUEEN . . . . P. O. Box 35286, Minneapolis, MN 55435
    Contact: Mr. William Zucco, General Counsel; Tel: (612) 830-0308
INTERNATIONAL MULTIFOODS . . . . Multifoods Tower, P. O. Box 2942, Minneapolis, MN 55402
    Contact: Ms. Susan Burns, VP Franchising; Tel: (612) 340-3300
ISAAC'S DELI . . . . 44 N. Queen St., Lancaster, PA 17603
    Contact: President; Tel: (717) 394-0623
ITALO'S PIZZA SHOP . . . . .3560 Middlebranch Rd., N.E., Canton, OH 44705
    Contact: Mr. Italo Ventura; Tel: (216) 455-7443
IVARS Pier 54, Seattle, WA 98104 . . . .
    Contact: President; Tel: (206) 587-6500
IZZY'S PIZZA RESTAURANTS . . . . .110 3rd Ave., SE, Albany, OR 97321
    Contact: Mr. Fred Jansen, President; Tel: (503) 926-8693
JACK IN THE BOX . . . . .P. O. Box 783, San Diego, CA 92112
    Contact: Mr. Jerry K. Prinds, Dir. Fran. Sale; Tel: (800) 876-5225 (619) 571-2200
JACK'S FAMOUS DELIS . . . . 7315 Wisconsin Ave., # 609E, Bethesda, MD 20817
    Contact: Mr. Jordan Feinberg, President; Tel: (800) 726-4015 (301) 961-8585
JACK'S OF LOMBARD . . . . 1105 E. Lombard St., Baltimore, MD 21202
    Contact: President; Tel:

JAKE'S PIZZA . . . . 1204 Carnegie St., Rolling Meadows, IL 60008
    Contact: Mr. John Flowers, President; Tel: (708) 398-2200
JERSEY MIKE'S SUBMARINES & SALADS . . . . . . 2627 Hwy. 70, Manasquan (Wall), NJ 08736
    Contact: Mr. Michael J. Manzo; Tel: (201) 528-7676
JIFFY SHOPPES SUBS & PIZZA . . . . 8543 Ashwood Dr., Capitol Heights, MD 20743
    Contact: President; Tel: (301) 336-4600
JIMBOY'S TACOS . . . . 3112 O St., # 2, Sacramento, CA 95816
    Contact: Mr. Scott Knudson, President; Tel: (800) 248-8226 (619) 454-1614
JOHNNY ROCKETS . . . . 1888 Century park E., # 224, Los Angeles, CA 90067
    Contact: Mr. Carl Jeffers, VP Franchising; Tel: (213) 556-8811
JOHNNY'S PIZZA HOUSE . . . . 2920 N. 7th St., W. Monroe, LA 91291
    Contact: President; Tel:
JOYCE'S SUBS . . . . 1527 Havana St., Aurora, CO 80010
    Contact: Mr. David Meaux, President; Tel: (303) 344-1674
JR.'S HOT DOGS INTERNATIONAL . . . . P. O. Box 65209, Tucson, AZ 85740
    Contact: Mr. Roy Vander Wall, Sr., President; Tel: (602) 322-3644
JRECK SUBS . . . . P.O. Box 6, Watertown, NY 13601
    Contact: Mr. H. Thomas Swartz, President; Tel: (315) 782-0760
JUICE CLUB . . . . 17 Chorro St., # C, San Luis Obispo, CA 93405
    Contact: Mr. Kirk Perron, President; Tel: (805) 549-0232
JUST BURGERS . . . . 1523 Ludington St., P. O. Box 1048, Escanaba, MI 49829
    Contact: Mr. John R. Taylor; Tel: (800) 678-1225 (517) 694-2800
KACHINA KITCHENS . . . . 2437 Cherokee Rd., NW, Albuquerque, NM 87107
    Contact: President; Tel: (505) 345-7322
KAJUN KITCHEN . . . . .P. O. Box 22206, Alexandria, VA 22304
    Contact: President; Tel:
KRUMBLY BURGERS . . . . 9 Newfield Ct., St. Louis, MO 63011
    Contact: Mr. Jack Baker, President; Tel: (314) 391-7038
LA PIZZA LOCA . . . . .7920 Orangethorpe Ave., # 202, Buena Park, CA 90620
    Contact: President; Tel:
LAROSA'S PIZZERIAS . . . . .2334 Boudinot Ave., Cincinnati, OH 45238
    Contact: Mr. Stewart A. Smetts, Mktg. Dir; Tel: (513) 347-5660
LEE'S FAMOUS RECIPE CHICKEN . . . . 1727 Elm Hill Pike, Nashville, TN 37210
    Contact: Mr. Dave Bogart, VP Fran. Ops.; Tel: (800) 346-9637 (615) 391-9325
LEISUREFEST VILLAGE . . . . 5303 1/2 95th St., Oaklawn, IL 60453
    Contact: Mr. William Stickfaden, President; Tel: (312) 422-7671
LINDY - GERTIE'S . . . . 8437 Park Ave., Burr Ridge, IL 60521
    Contact: Mr. Joseph Yesutis; Tel: (708) 323-8003
LITTLE BAKERY CAFE, THE . . . . P. O. Box 134, Concord, ON L4K 1B2   CAN
    Contact: Mr. Paul Tang; Tel: (416) 737-4833
LITTLE ITALIAN ENTERPRISES . . . . 373 E. Bailey Rd., Naperville, IL 60565
    Contact: President; Tel:
LITTLE JOHN'S / LOBSTER JOHN'S . . . . 704 Walnut St., 8-B, Hattiesburg, MS 39401
    Contact: President; Tel: (601) 582-3007
LOEB   1430 Blair Pl., Box 8387, Ottawa, ON K1G 3K8 . . . . CAN
    Contact: Mr. Richard Laniel, VP Admin.; Tel: (613) 747-3305
LONG JOHN SILVER'S . . . . P.O. Box 11988, 111 Jerrico Dr., Lexington, KY 40579
    Contact: Mr. Bruce C. Cotton, SVP; Tel: (606) 263-6341
LUISA'S ITALIAN PIZZERIA . . . . .470 South Main St., Manchester, NH 03102
    Contact: President; Tel: (603) 623-1717
MAJOR MAGIC'S ALL STAR PIZZA . . . . 35255 Gratiot Ave., Mt. Clemens, MI 48043
    Contact: President; Tel: (313) 792-6933
MAMA MIA! PASTA/LIMIT UP . . . . 30 S. Wacker, # 1601, Chicago, IL 60606
    Contact: President; Tel: (312) 559-0355
MANCHU WOK . . . . 400 Fairway Dr., # 106, Deerfield Beach, FL 33441
    Contact: Mr. Harry Grindrod, VP Development; Tel: (800) 423-4009 (305) 481-9555
MARY BROWN'S FRIED CHICKEN . . . . 250 Shields Court, Markham, ON L3R 9W7   CAN
    Contact: Mr. Nigel Beattie, VP Fran. Dev.; Tel: (416) 513-0044
MCDONALD'S RESTAURANTS OF CANADA . . . . . . McDonald's Place, Toronto, ON M3C 3L4   CAN
    Contact: Mr. Kenneth Fong; Tel: (416) 446-3384
MIKE SCHMIDT'S PHILADELPHIA HOAGIES . . . . . . .800 Bustleton Pike, Richboro, PA 18954
    Contact: Mr. Michael Speeney; Tel: (215) 887-0202
MINUTE MAN OF AMERICA . . . . .P.O. Box 828, Little Rock, AR 72203
    Contact: Mr. John Jenkins, President; Tel: (501) 376-8271

MISSISSIPPI JACKS . . . . 949 Kapiolani Blvd., # 102, Honolulu, HI 96814
    Contact: Mr. Hiro Ariga, President; Tel:
MOUNTAIN FRANCHISING . . . . 430 Greggory Ln., Boulder, CO 80302
    Contact: President; Tel: (303) 938-1462
MR. BURGER . . . . P. O. Box 8248, Amarillo, TX 79109
    Contact: Mr. Robert Coleman, Fran. Dir.; Tel: (806) 355-9936
MR. CHICKEN . . . . P. O. Box 23051, Cleveland, OH 44123
    Contact: Mr. Michael Simens, Dir. Franch. Ops.; Tel: (216) 585-4800
MR. HERO / MR. PHILLY . . . . .5755 Granger Rd., 2nd Fl., Independence, OH 44131
    Contact: Mr. Bill Plautz, VP Bus. Devel.; Tel: (800) 837-9599 (216) 842-6000
MR. SUBMARINE / MR. SUB . . . .# 300 - 720 Spadina Ave., Toronto, ON M5S 2T9   CAN
    Contact: Ms. Wendy MacKinnon; Tel: (416) 962-6232
MR. TACO . . . . P. O. Box 305, 604 Willis, Noble, OK 73068
    Contact: Mr. John Horn; Tel: (800) 888-1305 (405) 872-5170
MRS. MARTY'S DELI . . . . .24 N. Cliffe Dr., Wilmington, DE 19809
    Contact: Mr. Melvin D. Messinger; Tel: (800) 992-0243
NATURE'S TABLE . . . . .135 W. Central Blvd., # 1100, Orlando, FL 32801
    Contact: Ms. Sherra Hedrick, President; Tel: (800) 762-2552 (407) 648-0433
NECTARY, THE . . . . 1221 Nicollet Mall, # 711, Minneapolis, MN 55403
    Contact: President; Tel:
NEW ORLEANS FAMOUS FRIED CHICKEN . . . . P. O. Box 700, Greenwood, MS 38930
    Contact: Mr. S. L. Sethi; Tel: (601) 453-6601
NEW YORK BURRITO . . . . 1950 Union St., Lakewood, CO 80215
    Contact: Mr. Robert Palmer, Dir. Fran.; Tel: (303) 980-5118
NEW YORK PIZZA SYSTEMS . . . . 404 S. Figueroa St., # 478, Los Angeles, CA 90071
    Contact: President; Tel: (213) 488-1004
NOVA SANDWICH CORP. . . . . 10 Plastics Ave., Etobicoke, ON M8Z 4B7   CAN
    Contact: Mr. Dieter Hoefel; Tel: (416) 255-1919
OLGA'S KITCHEN . . . . 1940 Northwood Dr., Troy, MI 48084
    Contact: Mr. Robert McRae, Dir. Fran. Ops.; Tel: (313) 362-0001
ORANGE JULIUS OF AMERICA . . . . P.O. Box 35286, Minneapolis, MN 55435
    Contact: Mr. John Hyduke, VP Fran. Dev.; Tel: (800) 634-4384 (612) 830-0200
OREAN THE HEALTH EXPRESS . . . . 1320 North Vine St., Hollywood, CA 90028
    Contact: Mr. Orean C. Thomas, President; Tel: (213) 463-7482
ORIGINAL HAMBURGER STAND . . . . .4440 Von Karman Ave., Newport Beach, CA 92660
    Contact: Mr. Allen Gallup, Dir. Fran. Sales; Tel: (714) 752-5800
ORIGINAL PANCAKE HOUSE . . . . 1826 SW Dewitt, Portland, OR 97201
    Contact: President; Tel: (503) 245-9676
OTTOMANELLI'S CAFE . . . . 15 Engle St., # 302, Englewood, NJ 07631
    Contact: Mr. John Sterns; Tel: (800) 332-2229 (201) 871-0370
P-WEE'S, PIZZA, PASTA & MORE . . . . . P.O. Box 4381, Postal Station D, Hamilton, ON L8V 4L8   CAN
    Contact: Mr. Dan Fratoni, President; Tel: (416) 648-1434
P. D. QUIX . . . . 520 Brickhaven Dr., # 200, Raleigh, NC 27612
    Contact: Mr. Irving H. Tabler, President; Tel: (919) 833-6660
PAGLIAI'S PIZZA . . . . 602 East First, Madrid, IA 50156
    Contact: President; Tel:
PAPA RICARDO'S . . . . 9 Prestbury Sq., Newark, DE 19713
    Contact: Ms. LIsa Lelii; Tel: (302) 368-6069
PARTNERS II PIZZA . . . . Aberdeen Village Center, Peachtree City, GA 30269
    Contact: Mr. John N. Owen; Tel: (404) 487-2091
PASTA LOVERS TRATTORIAS . . . . .120 International Pkwy., # 262, Heathrow, FL 32746
    Contact: Mr. Jeff Osterfeld; Tel: (513) 474-5957
PASTA PLUS . . . . 607 Main St., Avoca, PA 18641
    Contact: President; Tel: (717) 457-9632
PAUL REVERE'S PIZZA . . . . .1570 - 42nd St. NE, # C, Cedar Rapids, IA 52402
    Contact: Mr. Stanley White, VP Fran. Sales; Tel: (319) 395-9113
PEDRO'S TACOS OF CALIFORNIA . . . . 31721 Camino Capristrano, San Juan Capistrano, CA 92675
    Contact: Mr. Edward McNary, Owner; Tel: (714) 496-9414
PENGUIN POINT FRANCHISE SYSTEMS . . . . .P.O. Box 975, Warsaw, IN 46580
    Contact: Mr. W.E. Stouder, Vice President; Tel:
PENN'S GOLDEN NUGGETS . . . . Country Club Rd., Canton, MS 39046
    Contact: President; Tel:
PETRO'S CHILI & CHIPS . . . . P. O. Box 51374, Knoxville, TN 37950
    Contact: President; Tel:
PHILADELPHIA STEAK & SUB . . . . 1700 Rte. 23, Wayne, NJ 07470
    Contact: Mr. Mike Flynn, VP Dev.; Tel: (201) 696-7200

PHILLY MIGNON . . . . P.O. Box 1464, Morristown, NJ 07960
    Contact: President; Tel:
PIETRO'S PIZZA PARLORS . . . . .407 Cernon St., Vacaville, CA 95688
    Contact: President; Tel:
PIRELLI'S PIZZERIA . . . . 10 E. 22nd St., # 115, Lombard, IL 60148
    Contact: Mr. Randall Errington, President; Tel: (708) 932-8878
PITA FEAST INTERNATIONAL . . . . .11660 Olympic Blvd., Los Angeles, CA 90064
    Contact: Mr. Avi Datner, President; Tel: (213) 479-0205
PIZZA COOKERY FRANCHISE CORP. . . . . 6209 Toganga Canyon Blvd., Woodland Hills, CA 91367
    Contact: President; Tel: (818) 887-4770
PIZZA DEPOT . . . . .56 North York Rd.. 1st Fl., Willow Grove, PA 19090
    Contact: President; Tel: (215) 657-3540
PIZZA LITE . . . . .9951 SW 142nd Ave., Miami, FL 33186
    Contact: Mr. Robert Friesmuth, President; Tel: (800) 228-LITE (305) 386-7878
PIZZA MAN, HE DELIVERS . . . . . . 6930-1/2 Tujunga Ave., North Hollywood, CA 91605
    Contact: Mr. James Dalton, President; Tel: (818) 766-4395
PIZZA NOW! . . . . 9393 N. 90th St., Scottsdale, AZ 85258
    Contact: Ms. Kathleen M. Young, AVP; Tel: (513) 821-7788 (602) 596-1166
PIZZA RACK FRANCHISE SYSTEMS . . . . 2130 Market Ave. N., Canton, OH 44714
    Contact: Mr. William Cundiff, President; Tel: (216) 454-9498
PIZZA RANCH, THE . . . . .1112 Main St., Box 532, Hull, IA 51239
    Contact: Mr. Lawrence Vander Esch, President; Tel: (712) 439-1150 C
PIZZA UN-LIMITED . . . . 1774 Cobblestone Ct., Red Wing, MN 55066
    Contact: President; Tel: (612) 854-6434
PLUMLEY BAR-B-QUE . . . . 10715 W. Sardis Rd., Bauxite, AR 72011
    Contact: President; Tel: (501) 332-2333
POFOLKS . . . . P. O. Box 17406, Nashville, TN 37217
    Contact: Mr. Rob Fayard, Dir. Fran. Ops.; Tel: (800) 876-3655 (615) 366-0900
PONY EXPRESS PIZZA . . . . 931 Baxter Ave., Louisville, KY 40204
    Contact: Mr. Kenneth Lamb, President; Tel: (502) 451-9945
PONY EXPRESS PIZZA . . . . 931 Baxter Ave., Louisville, KY 40204
    Contact: President; Tel:
POOR BOY SUBMARINE SHOPS . . . . 1506 Beaverdam Rd., P. O. Box 3097, Point Pleasant, NJ 08742
    Contact: Mr. Victor Merlo, President; Tel: (201) 295-9294
POPEYES FAMOUS FRIED CHICKEN . . . . . . 1333 S. Clearview Pkwy., # 413, Jefferson, LA 70121
    Contact: Mr. William A. Copeland, SVP; Tel: (800) 848-8248 (504) 733-4300
PREMIATO PIZZERIA . . . . 10 E. 22nd St., # 115, Lombard, IL 60148
    Contact: Mr. H. Randall Errington, President; Tel: (708) 932-8878
PRESTO PASTA . . . . .67 Fishkill, P. O. Box 288, Beacon, NY 12508
    Contact: President; Tel: (914) 838-1200
PRO PORTION FOODS . . . . 45 Jefryn Blvd. W., Deer Park, NY 11729
    Contact: Ms. Janet Micheletti; Tel: (516) 667-4500
RED RIVER BAR-B-QUE . . . . 100 N. Meadows Dr., Wexford, PA 15090
    Contact: Mr. Ronald A. Sofranko; Tel: (412) 934-0300
RIBBY'S EXPRESS BARBECUE . . . . 8080 N. Central Expy., # 500, Box 65, Dallas, TX 75206
    Contact: Mr. David A. Vernon, Dir. Fran. Devel.; Tel: (800) 527-6832 (214) 891-8400
RICHIE D'S . . . . .800 Bustleton Pike, Richboro, PA 18954
    Contact: President; Tel: (215) 322-6655
RICKY'S DAIRY BAR/TUBBY'S SUB SHOPS . . . . 34500 Doreka Dr., Fraser, MI 48026
    Contact: Mr. Thomas Pagenes, Exec. Fran. Dir.; Tel: (313) 296-1270
RICKY'S WORLD FAMOUS WINGS . . . . 210 University Dr., # 402, Coral Springs, FL 33071
    Contact: Mr. Bill Landman; Tel: (305) 345-0600
ROY ROGERS RESTAURANTS . . . . 1803 Research Blvd., # LLY, Rockville, MD 20850
    Contact: Mr. Al Schnitzlein, VP Fran.; Tel: (800) 346-2243 (301) 251-8777
RUBY'S 1721 Whittier St., Costa Mesa, CA 92627 . . . .
    Contact: Mr. Mike Mooslin; Tel: (714) 631-8555
RUMA'S DELI . . . . 11182 South Town Square, St. Louis, MO 63123
    Contact: President; Tel: (314) 892-9983
RUNZA DRIVE-INNS OF AMERICA . . . . P. O. Box 6042, Lincoln, NE 68506
    Contact: Mr. Ronald Owens; Tel: (402) 423-2394
RUSTY'S PIZZA PARLOR . . . . 1027 Garden St., Santa Barbara, CA 93101
    Contact: Mr. Roger Duncan, President; Tel: (805) 963-9127
SALVATORE SCALLOPINI . . . . .27190 Dequindre, Warren, MI 48092
    Contact: Mr. Lawrence J. Bongiovanni, President; Tel: (313) 573-8960
SAMMI'S DELI . . . . 2400 Ashland Rd., # E7, Columbia, SC 29201
    Contact: Mr. Hassan Addahoumi; Tel: (803) 798-7972

SANDWICH FACTORY, THE . . . . .5498 Mahoning Ave., # 10, Youngstown, OH 44515
    Contact: Ms. Sue Eckhert; Tel: (216) 793-4084
SBARRO CANADA . . . . 500 Hood Rd., Markham, ON L3R 0P6   CAN
    Contact: Mr. Lloyd E. Dove; Tel: (416) 946-7150
SCOLA'S SANDWICH SHOPPES . . . . .8 Eugene Rd., Burlington, MA 01803
    Contact: President; Tel: (617) 272-1082
SCOOTER'S/KEN'S/MAZZIO'S PIZZA . . . . 4441 S. 72nd E. Ave., Tulsa, OK 74145
    Contact: Mr. Bradford Williams, Sr. VP Fran.; Tel: (918) 663-8880
SCOTTIO PIZZA . . . . 1895 Greentree Rd., Cherry Hill, NJ 08003
    Contact: Mr. John Scotto, President; Tel: (609) 424-4260
SEAWEST SUB SHOPS . . . . One Lake Bellevue Dr., # 107, Bellevue, WA 98005
    Contact: Mr. Bernie J. Kane, Chairman; Tel: (206) 453-5216
SIR PIZZA INTERNATIONAL . . . . 700 S. Madison St., Muncie, IN 47302
    Contact: President; Tel:
SKATS RESTAURANTS . . . . P. O. Box 749, 874 Country Club Dr., Rocky Mount, NC 27802
    Contact: Mr. Ernest Renaud, President; Tel: (919) 937-2036
SKOLNIKS BAGEL BAKERY RESTAURANT . . . . . 10801 Electron Dr., # 308, Louisville, KY 40299
    Contact: Mr. Robert Holmberg, CFO; Tel: (800) 999-7565 (502) 267-7667
SPAGHETTI BENDER . . . . P. O. Box 4381, Station D, Hamilton, ON L8V 4L8   CAN
    Contact: President; Tel: (416) 648-1434
SPAGHETTI SHOP, THE . . . . 8 Henson Place, # B, P.O. Box 1807, Champaign, IL 61824
    Contact: Mr. James Teaters, President; Tel: (217) 356-4200
SPOONER'S PIZZERIA . . . . 9319 Cincinnati-Columbus Rd., # 12, West Chester, OH 45069
    Contact: President; Tel: (513) 779-1087
STOXY'S STEAKS . . . . 1210 Northbrook Dr., # 370, Trevose, PA 19053
    Contact: Mr. Stephen J. Izzi; Tel: (215) 953-8314
SUB STATION II . . . . 425 N. Main St., P. O. Drawer 2260, Sumter, SC 29150
    Contact: Ms. Susan L. Hackett, VP; Tel: (803) 773-4711
SUPER SUBWAY . . . . .7052 Society Center, Dayton, OH 45414
    Contact: President; Tel: (513) 898-0996
TACO BELL (CANADA) . . . . . . 10 Four Seasons Pl., # 500, Etobicoke, ON M9B 6H7   CAN
    Contact: Mr. John Beauparlant; Tel: (416) 626-8011
TACO BELL . . . . 17901 Von Karman, Irvine, CA 92714
    Contact: Mr. Ronnie Volkening, Dir. Gov. Affairs; Tel: (714) 863-4603
TACO TABER . . . . P. O. Box 305, Noble, OK 73068
    Contact: Mr. Floyd Taber, President; Tel: (405) 872-5170
TACO TICO . . . . 3715 Northside Pkwy., NW, # 700, Atlanta, GA 30327
    Contact: Mr. David Lubinski, VP; Tel: (214) 634-8226
TAQUITOS REAL . . . . P. O. Box 43876, Tuscon, AZ 85733
    Contact: President; Tel: (602) 241-9108
TOM'S HOUSE OF PIZZA . . . . .7730 Macleod Tr. S., Calgary, AB T2F 2T1   CAN
    Contact: Mr. Robert Collins; Tel: (403) 252-0111
TONY LENA'S . . . . 304 Squire Rd., Revere, MA 01906
    Contact: Mr. Tony Lena, President; Tel: (617) 289-9133
TROTA'S PIZZA . . . . 2580 Queen City Ave., Cincinnati, OH 45238
    Contact: President; Tel: (513) 661-2407
UNO'S ITALIAN EATERY . . . . 111 Eglinton Ave. E., # 300, Toronto, ON M4P 1H4   CAN
    Contact: President; Tel: (416) 489-6622
VERN'S DOG HOUSE . . . . 1257 NYS Rte. 96N, Waterloo, NY 13156
    Contact: Mr. Vern Sessler, President; Tel: (315) 539-3379
VINET'S PIZZA . . . . 4738 N. Harlem, Harwood Heights, IL 60656
    Contact: President; Tel: (312) 867-7770
VITO'S NEW YORK PIZZA CO. . . . . . . 732 W. New Orleans, Broken Arrow, OK 74011
    Contact: Mr. Phil Kruse; Tel: (918) 455-4000
WAITERS ON WHEELS, INTERNATIONAL . . . . . 425 Divisadero St., # 303, San Francisco, CA 94117
    Contact: Mr. Kevin Murphy, Dir. Fran.; Tel: (800) 343-9433 (707) 942-0443
WALLYBURGER EXPRESS DRIVE-THRU . . . . . 4305 N. State Line Ave., Texarkana, TX 75501
    Contact: President; Tel:
WENDY'S INTERNATIONAL . . . . 4288 W. Dublin-Granville Rd., Dublin, OH 43017
    Contact: Ms. Barbara Langsdon, Dir. Natl. Sales; Tel: (614) 764-3100
WHATABURGER . . . . .4600 Parkdale Dr., P. O. Box 6220, Corpus Christi, TX 78411
    Contact: Mr. Thomas Dobson, VP; Tel: (512) 851-0650
WHITE CASTLE INTERNATIONAL . . . . 555 W. Goodale St., P. O. Box 1498, Columbus, OH 43216
    Contact: Mr. Robert D. Hays, SVP; Tel: (614) 228-5781
WIENER ENTERPRISES . . . . P. O. Box 23607, Harahan, LA 70183
    Contact: President; Tel: (504) 733-7055

WIENER KING CORPORATION . . . . P. O. Box 149, Easton, PA 18044
    Contact: President; Tel:
WING MACHINE . . . . 1925 Yonge St., 2nd Fl., Toronto, ON M4S 1Z3   CAN
    Contact: Mr. Radford Cook; Tel: (416) 961-1000
WING WAGON . . . . 71 Public Square, Watertown, NY 13601
    Contact: Mr. Charles G. Wert, President; Tel: (800) 836-7815 (315) 788-4580
YOUR PIZZA SHOP . . . . 2800 Fulton Dr. NW, Canton, OH 44718
    Contact: Mr. Jon Keefer, President; Tel: (216) 453-0203
YU-CHU'S . . . . 348 Shephard Ave. E., Willowdale, ON M2N 3B4   CAN
    Contact: Mr. Gary Swernik, President; Tel: (416) 733-2000 C
ZIPPS DRIVE THRU . . . . 393 N. Euclid St., # 200, St. Louis, MO 63108
    Contact: Mr. Bob Gontram, President; Tel: (314) 361-1122

CHAPTER 21

RETAIL FOOD:
RESTAURANT / FAMILY-STYLE

ALBERT'S FAMILY RESTAURANT

10544 - 114 St.
Edmonton, AB T5H 3J7 CAN
TEL: (403) 429-1259 C
FAX: (403) 426-7391
Mr. David Gibson, EVP

ALBERT'S FAMILY RESTAURANT is a 32-year old chain that is now franchising. We offer a complete turn-key package which includes design, construction, set-up, operating system and on-going operations and advertising support. The system is easy to learn and the cash flow is excellent.

HISTORY: . . . . .CFA
Established in 1980; . . 1st Franchised in 1990
Company-Owned Units (As of 8/31/1992): . 10
Franchised Units (As of 8/31/1992): 6
Total Units (As of 8/31/1992): 16
Projected New Units for 1993: 8
Distribution: US-0;Can-16;Overseas-0
North America: . . . . 2 Provinces
Concentration: . . . . .14 in AB, 2 in BC
Registered: . . . . AB
. . . .
Type Space: . . . . RM;~4,500 SF

FINANCIAL: Earnings Claim: . .No
Cash Investment: $150K
Total Investment: $350K
Fees: Franchise - $25K
Royalty: 5%, Advert: 2%
Contract Periods (Yrs.): 15/0
Area Development Agreement: . .No
Sub-Franchise Contract: . . . . . .No
Expand in Territory: . . . . . . Yes
Passive Ownership: . . . Not Allowed
Encourage Conversions: . . . . . Yes
Average # Employees: . 25 FT, 15 PT

FRANCHISOR TRAINING/SUPPORT:
Financial Assistance Provided: . . . . . No
Site Selection Assistance: . . . . .Yes
Lease Negotiation Assistance: . . . . .Yes
Co-operative Advertising: . . . . .Yes
Training: . . . . 4 Wks. Headquarters
. . . .
On-Going Support: C,D,E,F/ 450
EXPANSION PLANS:
US: . . . . Minnesota
Canada: . . . . .All Canada
Overseas: . . . . No

BARN'RDS OLD FASHIONED ROAST BEEF
412 First National Bank Bldg.
Council Bluffs, IA 51501
TEL: (712) 323-3484
FAX: (712) 323-8717
Mr. Samuel B. Marvin, President

Old fashioned roast beef - "Real food for busy people." BARN'RDS' story is lite, natural, delicious, great sandwiches, 95% fat-free, baked, not fried, natural, not reconstituted. Soups, chili, buns, salads prepared fresh daily. High return on investment, sales per man hour, return on equity.

HISTORY: . . . .
Established in 1981; . . 1st Franchised in 1981
Company-Owned Units (As of 8/31/1992): . .1
Franchised Units (As of 8/31/1992): 2
Total Units (As of 8/31/1992): 3
Projected New Units for 1993: 1
Distribution: US-3;Can-0;Overseas-0
  North America: . . . . 2 States
  Concentration: . . . . 2 in IA, 1 in KS
Registered: . . . .
. . . .
Type Space: . FS, SF, SC, RM;~650-2,400 SF

FINANCIAL: Earnings Claim: . .No
Cash Investment: $50K
Total Investment: $90-580K
Fees: Franchise - $15-25K
  Royalty: 4%, Advert: 0%
Contract Periods (Yrs.): 10/10
Area Development Agreement: Yes/Var
Sub-Franchise Contract: . . . . Yes
Expand in Territory: . . . . . . Yes
Passive Ownership: . . . Discouraged
Encourage Conversions: . . . . Yes
Average # Employees: .4 FT, 8-12 PT

FRANCHISOR TRAINING/SUPPORT:
Financial Assistance Provided: . . . . . No
Site Selection Assistance: . . . . Yes
Lease Negotiation Assistance: . . . . Yes
Co-operative Advertising: . . . . No
Training: . . . . .30 Days Headquarters
. . . .
On-Going Support: a,B,C,D,E,f,G,h,i/ . . 2
EXPANSION PLANS:
  US: . . . . Midwest and Southwest
  Canada: . . . . No
  Overseas: . . . . No

BEEFSTEAK CHARLIE'S

234 W. 48th St.
New York, NY 10036
TEL: (212) 262-1400
FAX: (212) 582-3760
Mr. Kewal K. Chopra, EVP

BEEFSTEAK CHARLIE'S sets itself apart from the crowd by offering the unique selling proposition of a warm, comfortable atmosphere where diners can enjoy a variety of beef, ribs, chicken or fish entrees that include UNLIMITED SHRIMP, SALAD BAR AND DRINKS, all at a very affordable price. This "winning recipe" gives BEEFSTEAK CHARLIE'S an unusually large and diverse market appeal.

HISTORY: . . . .
Established in 1972; . . 1st Franchised in 1972
Company-Owned Units (As of 8/31/1992): . .9
Franchised Units (As of 8/31/1992): 9
Total Units (As of 8/31/1992): 18
Projected New Units for 1993: 2
Distribution: US-18;Can-0;Overseas-0
  North America: . . . . 7 States
  Concentration: . . .12 in NY, 3 in FL, 1 in MD
Registered: . . . . FL,MD,NY
. . . .
Type Space: . . . . .FS, SC;~5,000 SF

FINANCIAL: Earnings Claim: . .No
Cash Investment: $150-200K
Total Investment: $300-375K
Fees: Franchise - $25K
  Royalty: 5%, Advert: 3%
Contract Periods (Yrs.): 10/10
Area Development Agreement: Yes/10
Sub-Franchise Contract: . . . . Yes
Expand in Territory: . . . . . . Yes
Passive Ownership: . . . Not Allowed
Encourage Conversions: . . . . Yes
Average # Employees: . 15 FT, 20 PT

FRANCHISOR TRAINING/SUPPORT:
Financial Assistance Provided: . . . . . No
Site Selection Assistance: . . . . Yes
Lease Negotiation Assistance: . . . . Yes
Co-operative Advertising: . . . . Yes
Training: . . . 4 Wks. Sheepshead Bay, NY
. . . .
On-Going Support: a,C,D,e,f,G,H/ . . . 15
EXPANSION PLANS:
  US: . . . . All US
  Canada: . . . . .Yes
  Overseas: . . . . GR, UK

BENIHANA OF TOKYO

8685 NW 53 Terrace, P.O. Box 020210
Miami, FL 33102
TEL: (305) 593-0770
FAX: (305) 592-6371
Mr. Michael W. Kata, VP

The BENIHANA STEAKHOUSE chain is known throughout the world for their top-quality food and service. Each guest's meal is prepared right before his eyes by an entertaining chef who introduces all the ingredients before he masterfully cooks. Every meal served includes soup, salad, hibachi shrimp appetizer, hibachi vegetables, an entree, white rice, bean sprouts and green tea. Recognized as America's Most Popular Full Service Restaurant.

HISTORY: . . . .
Established in 1964; . . 1st Franchised in 1970
Company-Owned Units (As of 8/31/1992): . 38
Franchised Units (As of 8/31/1992): 12
Total Units (As of 8/31/1992): 50
Projected New Units for 1993: 2
Distribution: US-45;Can-1;Overseas-4
  North America: . . . . 21 States, 1 Province
  Concentration: . . .12 in CA, 6 in FL, 3 in NY
Registered: . . . . CA,HI,NY
. . . .
Type Space: . . . . FS;~6,000+ SF

FINANCIAL: Earnings Claim: . .No
Cash Investment: $500-600K
Total Investment: . . . $1.2-1.8MM
Fees: Franchise - $50K
  Royalty: 6%, Advert: 1/2%
Contract Periods (Yrs.): . 15/Varies
Area Development Agreement: Yes/15
Sub-Franchise Contract: . . . . . .No
Expand in Territory: . . . . . . .No
Passive Ownership: . . . Discouraged
Encourage Conversions: . . . . Yes
Average # Employees: . .35 FT, 7 PT

FRANCHISOR TRAINING/SUPPORT:
Financial Assistance Provided: . . . . . No
Site Selection Assistance: . . . . Yes
Lease Negotiation Assistance: . . . . No
Co-operative Advertising: . . . . Yes
Training: . . . . . 12-15 Wks. Headquarters
. . . .
On-Going Support: a,C,d,E,F,H,I/ . . . 60
EXPANSION PLANS:
  US: PA,MD,MI,OH,AZ,TX,NY(NotNYC)
  Canada: . . . . .All Canada
  Overseas: . . EUR and Pacific Rim

BINO'S FAMILY RESTAURANT

6962 Buller Ave.
Burnaby, BC V5J 4S3 CAN
TEL: (604) 435-3044
FAX:
Mr. Kevin Turner, Development

Family restaurant with versatile menu, serving breakfast, lunch or dinner - 24 hours per day.

HISTORY:	FINANCIAL: Earnings Claim: . .No	FRANCHISOR TRAINING/SUPPORT:
Established in 1972; . . 1st Franchised in 1977	Cash Investment: $150K	Financial Assistance Provided: . . . . .No
Company-Owned Units (As of 8/31/1992): . .0	Total Investment: $300-350K	Site Selection Assistance: . . . . .Yes
Franchised Units (As of 8/31/1992): 19	Fees: Franchise - $25K	Lease Negotiation Assistance: . . . . .Yes
Total Units (As of 8/31/1992): 19	Royalty: 4%, Advert: 1%	Co-operative Advertising: . . . . .NA
Projected New Units for 1993: 2	Contract Periods (Yrs.): . . . .Varies	Training: . . . . .1 Wk. Headquarters,
Distribution: US-0;Can-19;Overseas-0	Area Development Agreement: . .No	. . . . 6 Wks. On-Site
North America: . . . . .1 Province	Sub-Franchise Contract: . . . . .No	On-Going Support: b,C,D,E,h/ 7
Concentration: . . . . 19 in BC	Expand in Territory: . . . . . . .No	EXPANSION PLANS:
Registered:	Passive Ownership: . . . Discouraged	US: . . . . .No
. . . .	Encourage Conversions: . . . . . Yes	Canada: . . . . .All Canada
Type Space: . . SF, SC, RM;~3,000-4,000 SF	Average # Employees: 12+ FT,10+ PT	Overseas: . . . . No

BOBBY RUBINO'S PLACE FOR RIBS

900 NE 26th Ave.
Ft. Lauderdale, FL 33304
TEL: (305) 565-1888
FAX: (305) 565-9771
Mr. Jerry Moniz, Dir. of Operations

BOBBY RUBINO'S PLACE FOR RIBS is a leader in the family barbecue dinnerhouse segment, meeting the needs of today's consumers by adhering to the practice of serving the best barbecue ribs, chicken and shrimp, steak, prime rib and more in a clean and friendly environment at reasonable prices. BOBBY RUBINO'S is committed to producing maximum results in everything we do, a commitment that will enhance a franchisee's investment.

HISTORY:	FINANCIAL: Earnings Claim: . .No	FRANCHISOR TRAINING/SUPPORT:
Established in 1978; . . 1st Franchised in 1982	Cash Investment: . . . . . $.5-1.5MM	Financial Assistance Provided: . . . . .No
Company-Owned Units (As of 8/31/1992): . 11	Total Investment: . . . . . $.5-1.5MM	Site Selection Assistance: . . . . .Yes
Franchised Units (As of 8/31/1992): 9	Fees: Franchise - $50K	Lease Negotiation Assistance: . . . . .NA
Total Units (As of 8/31/1992): 20	Royalty: 4%, Advert: 2%	Co-operative Advertising: . . . . .Yes
Projected New Units for 1993: 3	Contract Periods (Yrs.): 15/10	Training: . . . . 4 Wks. Headquarters
Distribution: US-19;Can-1;Overseas-0	Area Development Agreement: Yes/15	. . . .
North America: . . . . . .3 States, 1 Province	Sub-Franchise Contract: . . . . .No	On-Going Support: C,D,E,F/ 6
Concentration: . . . 12 in FL, 4 in NY, 1 in PA	Expand in Territory: . . . . . . Yes	EXPANSION PLANS:
Registered: . . . . CA,FL,NY	Passive Ownership: . . . Not Allowed	US: . . . . .All US
. . . .	Encourage Conversions: . . . . . Yes	Canada: . . . . .All Canada
Type Space: . . . . FS;~6,500 SF	Average # Employees: . 50 FT, 10 PT	Overseas: . . . . Yes

BOSTON BEANERY RESTAURANT & TAVERN

265 High St., # 600
Morgantown, WV 26505
TEL: (304) 292-2035
FAX: (304) 292-2057
Mr. Michael J. Forte, Chairman/CEO

BOSTON BEANERY is a new restaurant concept serving the casual theme market. Menu features include stacked deli sandwiches, homemade soups, specialty salads and full-scale dinners. Design is an 1890's Boston Tavern with an oak bar, custom tile and hardwood floors. Unique employee benefits and training programs.

HISTORY:	FINANCIAL: Earnings Claim: . .No	FRANCHISOR TRAINING/SUPPORT:
Established in 1984; . . 1st Franchised in 1988	Cash Investment: $78.5-138K	Financial Assistance Provided: . . . . .No
Company-Owned Units (As of 8/31/1992): . .2	Total Investment: $196-345K	Site Selection Assistance: . . . . .Yes
Franchised Units (As of 8/31/1992): 3	Fees: Franchise - $20K	Lease Negotiation Assistance: . . . . .Yes
Total Units (As of 8/31/1992): 5	Royalty: 5.5%, Advert: 2%	Co-operative Advertising: . . . . .No
Projected New Units for 1993: 3	Contract Periods (Yrs.): 10/2	Training: . . . . 60 Days Morgantown, WV
Distribution: US-5;Can-0;Overseas-0	Area Development Agreement: Yes/3	. . . .
North America: . . . . 4 States	Sub-Franchise Contract: . . . . . Yes	On-Going Support: a,C,D,E,f,H/ 4
Concentration: . . . 2 in WV, 2 in VA, 1 in PA	Expand in Territory: . . . . . . Yes	EXPANSION PLANS:
Registered: . . . . FL,VA	Passive Ownership: . . . Discouraged	US: . . . . Southeast and PA
. . . .	Encourage Conversions: . . . . . Yes	Canada: . . . . .No
Type Space: . . . . .SC;~4,000 SF	Average # Employees: . 25 FT, 35 PT	Overseas: . . . . No

BOSTON PIZZA

#200 - 5500 Parkwood Way
Richmond, BC V6V 2M4 CAN
TEL: (604) 270-1108
FAX: (614) 270-4168
Mr. Bernie Skene, Dir. Fran.

We are an up-scale pizza and pasta restaurant that is unique in as much as we appeal to four sectors of the general public: 1) the families for early evening business, 2) business people in a hurry at lunch, 3) after the movies or show for cocktails and finger foods and 4) take-out and delivery of most items. All at reasonable prices.

HISTORY: . . . . IFA, CFA
Established in 1963; . . 1st Franchised in 1968
Company-Owned Units (As of 8/31/1992): . .1
Franchised Units (As of 8/31/1992): 100
Total Units (As of 8/31/1992): 101
Projected New Units for 1993: 8
Distribution: US-0;Can-96;Overseas-5
  North America: . . . . 5 Provinces
  Concentration: . . 45 in AB, 33 in BC, 9 in ON
Registered: . . . . AB
. . . .
Type Space: . . . . FS;~4,000 SF

FINANCIAL: Earnings Claim: . Yes
Cash Investment: $225-250K
Total Investment: $575-700K
Fees: Franchise - $35K
  Royalty: 7%, Advert: 2.5%
Contract Periods (Yrs.): 10/5
Area Development Agreement: . Yes
Sub-Franchise Contract: . . . . .No
Expand in Territory: . . . . . . Yes
Passive Ownership: . . . Not Allowed
Encourage Conversions: . . . . .No
Average # Employees: . 20 FT, 30 PT

FRANCHISOR TRAINING/SUPPORT:
Financial Assistance Provided: . . . Yes(I)
Site Selection Assistance: . . . . . . .Yes
Lease Negotiation Assistance: . . . .Yes
Co-operative Advertising: . . . . . . .Yes
Training: . . . Minimum 6 Wks. Corporate
  . . . . Store, Richmond, BC
On-Going Support: A,B,C,D,E,F,G,H/ . 23
EXPANSION PLANS:
  US: . . . . All US
  Canada: . . . . .All Canada
  Overseas: . . . . EUR, Asia

BRIDGEMAN'S RESTAURANTS

6009 Wayzata Blvd.
Minneapolis, MN 55416
TEL: (612) 593-1455
FAX: (612) 541-1101
Ms. Mary McKee, Fran. Dev.

A full-service, family-style restaurant, featuring our famous ice cream specialty treats. BRIDGEMAN'S will also award franchise opportunities based on our Dip Shoppe concept. The Dip Shoppe, strong in a food court setting, offers ice cream treats along with a limited sandwich menu.

HISTORY: . . . .
Established in 1936; . . 1st Franchised in 1967
Company-Owned Units (As of 8/31/1992): . .6
Franchised Units (As of 8/31/1992): 10
Total Units (As of 8/31/1992): 16
Projected New Units for 1993: 4
Distribution: US-16;Can-0;Overseas-0
  North America: . . . . 3 States
  Concentration: . . . 20 in MN, 1 in IA, 1 in WI
Registered: . . . . MN,ND
. . . .
Type Space: . . . . . . FS, SC, RM;~4,000 SF

FINANCIAL: Earnings Claim: . Yes
Cash Investment: . . . .$
Total Investment: . . . $113.1-635.3K
Fees: Franchise - $9-25K
  Royalty: 2%, Advert: 2%
Contract Periods (Yrs.): 10/10
Area Development Agreement: . .No
Sub-Franchise Contract: . . . . .No
Expand in Territory: . . . . . . Yes
Passive Ownership: . . . . . .Allowed
Encourage Conversions: . . . . Yes
Average # Employees: . 10 FT, 30 PT

FRANCHISOR TRAINING/SUPPORT:
Financial Assistance Provided: . . . . . No
Site Selection Assistance: . . . . . . .Yes
Lease Negotiation Assistance: . . . . No
Co-operative Advertising: . . . . . . .Yes
Training: . . . . . . 3-6 Weeks (Or Longer)
  . . . at Headquarters or Designated Area
On-Going Support: B,C,D,E,G,H,/ . . . . .
EXPANSION PLANS:
  US: . . . .Midwest, MN, IA, ND, SD, WI
  Canada: . . . . No
  Overseas: . . . . No

CHARLEY'S STEAKERY

1912 N. High St.
Columbus, OH 43201
TEL: (614) 251-6536
FAX: (614) 291-7133
Mr. James A. Kisling, Dir. Fran. Dev.

CHARLEY'S STEAKERY features award-winning Philadelphia cheesesteak sandwiches, hand-cut fries and fresh-squeezed lemonade. All are prepared on the spot, right in front of the customer.

HISTORY: . . . .
Established in 1986; . . 1st Franchised in 1991
Company-Owned Units (As of 8/31/1992): . .3
Franchised Units (As of 8/31/1992): 12
Total Units (As of 8/31/1992): 15
Projected New Units for 1993: 20
Distribution: US-15;Can-0;Overseas-0
  North America: . . . . 8 States
  Concentration: . . . 5 in OH, 3 in PA, 2 in WV
Registered: . . . . . .MI -Pending in 6 States
. . . .
Type Space: FS, RM,Food Court;~450-1,200 SF

FINANCIAL: Earnings Claim: . .No
Cash Investment: $75K
Total Investment: $100-150K
Fees: Franchise - $15K
  Royalty: 4%, Advert: 1%
Contract Periods (Yrs.): . . 5-10/5-10
Area Development Agreement: . Yes
Sub-Franchise Contract: . . . . .No
Expand in Territory: . . . . . . Yes
Passive Ownership: . . . Discouraged
Encourage Conversions: . . . . Yes
Average # Employees: . . 5 FT, 4 PT

FRANCHISOR TRAINING/SUPPORT:
Financial Assistance Provided: . . . . . No
Site Selection Assistance: . . . . . . .Yes
Lease Negotiation Assistance: . . . . .Yes
Co-operative Advertising: . . . . . . .Yes
Training: . . . . . .2 Wks. Corporate Store,
  . . . . .4 Days in Franchise Store
On-Going Support: C,D,E,F,G/ 5
EXPANSION PLANS:
  US: . . . . All US
  Canada: . . . . .Yes
  Overseas: . . . . .Yes

CHARLIE BARLIE'S

P. O. Box 6608
Louisville, KY 40206
TEL: (510) 839-5471
FAX: (510) 547-3245
Mr. Charles Willis, President

A truly unique dining experience, specializing in Mom's frizzled beef, wonderful Southern fried chicken, creamed sweetbreads and many other family recipes - all served in elegant Southern style. 16 units currently operating in Kentucky and Tennessee, with 5 additional units under construction. Unparalleled support from home office before and after opening. "You can't beat Mom's cooking and hospitality."

HISTORY:	FINANCIAL: Earnings Claim: . .No	FRANCHISOR TRAINING/SUPPORT:
Established in 1984; . . 1st Franchised in 1986	Cash Investment: $110-240K	Financial Assistance Provided: . . . Yes(I)
Company-Owned Units (As of 8/31/1992): . .4	Total Investment: $225-425K	Site Selection Assistance: . . . . . . .Yes
Franchised Units (As of 8/31/1992): 12	Fees: Franchise - $25K	Lease Negotiation Assistance: . . . . . . .Yes
Total Units (As of 8/31/1992): 16	Royalty: 6%, Advert: 1%	Co-operative Advertising: . . . . . . .Yes
Projected New Units for 1993: 2	Contract Periods (Yrs.): 10/10	Training: . . . . 8 Wks. Headquarters,
Distribution: US-16;Can-0;Overseas-0	Area Development Agreement: Yes/10	. . . . . . 3 Wks. Pre-0pening, On-Going
North America: . . . . 3 States	Sub-Franchise Contract: . . . . . .No	On-Going Support: A,B,C,D,E,F,G,H,I/ 21
Concentration: . . . 10 in KY, 4 in TN, 2 in IN	Expand in Territory: . . . . .No	EXPANSION PLANS:
Registered: . . . . .IN	Passive Ownership: . . . Not Allowed	US: . . . . .South and Southeast
. . . .	Encourage Conversions: . . . . . Yes	Canada: . . . . No
Type Space: . . . . . . FS;~3,000-4,000 SF	Average # Employees: . .7 FT, 23 PT	Overseas: . . . . No

CHOWDER'S FAMOUS FISH & SEAFOOD

3811 Illinois Rd., # 210
Ft. Wayne, IN 46804
TEL: (219) 432-5247 C
FAX: (219) 436-6443
Mr. Greg Racine, President

Full-service and quick-service family-style fish and seafood restaurant, featuring CHOWDER'S one of a kind "Famous Fish." Additionally, CHOWDER'S offers a full menu of salads, sandwiches, lunch specials, soups and desserts. Dinner entrees include fish, seafood, beef, pork and poultry. The restaurants are easy to learn and the operations require no special equipment or personnel.

HISTORY:	FINANCIAL: Earnings Claim: . .No	FRANCHISOR TRAINING/SUPPORT:
Established in 1976; . . 1st Franchised in 1989	Cash Investment: $37-250K	Financial Assistance Provided: . . . . . No
Company-Owned Units (As of 8/31/1992): . .4	Total Investment: $118-998K	Site Selection Assistance: . . . . . . .Yes
Franchised Units (As of 8/31/1992): 4	Fees: Franchise - $15K	Lease Negotiation Assistance: . . . .Yes
Total Units (As of 8/31/1992): 8	Royalty: 3%, Advert: 0%	Co-operative Advertising: . . . . . . .NA
Projected New Units for 1993: 8	Contract Periods (Yrs.): 15/10	Training: . . . 2 Wks. Company Restaurant
Distribution: US-8;Can-0;Overseas-0	Area Development Agreement: Yes/Var	. . . . . . .2 Wks. Franchisee Restaurant
North America: . . . . 3 States	Sub-Franchise Contract: . . . . . .No	On-Going Support: B,C,D,E,F,H,I/ 1
Concentration: . . . 6 in IN, 1 in MI, 1 in FL	Expand in Territory: . . . . Yes	EXPANSION PLANS:
Registered: . . . . FL,IN,MI	Passive Ownership: . . . Discouraged	US: . . . . IN, OH, MI and FL
. . . .	Encourage Conversions: . . . . . Yes	Canada: . . . . .No
Type Space: . . . . . FS, SF, SC;~6,500 SF	Avg. # Employees: 5-15 FT, 10-25 PT	Overseas: . . . . No

COUNTRY KITCHEN

1101, 10909 Jasper Ave.
Edmonton, AB T5J 3L9 CAN
TEL: (403) 496-9225
FAX: (403) 424-9604
Mr. V. Lorne Humphreys, President

Contemporary family dinner and country pub concept.

HISTORY: . . . . IFA	FINANCIAL: Earnings Claim: . .No	FRANCHISOR TRAINING/SUPPORT:
Established in 1989; . . 1st Franchised in 1989	Cash Investment: $50-250K	Financial Assistance Provided: . . . . .No
Company-Owned Units (As of 8/31/1992): . .1	Total Investment: . . . $150K-1.0MM	Site Selection Assistance: . . . . . . .Yes
Franchised Units (As of 8/31/1992): 5	Fees: Franchise - $40K	Lease Negotiation Assistance: . . . .Yes
Total Units (As of 8/31/1992): 6	Royalty: 5%, Advert: 1%	Co-operative Advertising: . . . . . . .Yes
Projected New Units for 1993: 2	Contract Periods (Yrs.): 20/20	Training: . . . . .30 Days On-Site
Distribution: US-0;Can-6;Overseas-0	Area Development Agreement: Yes/20	. . . .
North America: . . . . 3 Provinces	Sub-Franchise Contract: . . . . . Yes	On-Going Support: B,C,D,E,F,G,H/ . . . 2
Concentration: . . . 4 in SK, 1 in AB, 1 in MB	Expand in Territory: . . . . Yes	EXPANSION PLANS:
Registered: . . . . AB	Passive Ownership: . . . . . .Allowed	US: . . . . .No
. . . .	Encourage Conversions: . . . . . Yes	Canada: . . . . AB, MB, SK, BC
Type Space: . . FS, SC, RM;~3,300-4,900 SF	Average # Employees: . 20 FT, 20 PT	Overseas: . . . . No

COUNTRY KITCHEN RESTAURANT AND LODGING

P. O. Box 59159, Carlson Pkwy.
Minneapolis, MN 55459
TEL: (800) 477-4200 (612) 449-1300
FAX: (612) 449-1338
Mr. Michael Squires, SVP Dev.

COUNTRY KITCHEN franchises two entities: COUNTRY KITCHEN RESTAURANTS, 3-meal family dining and COUNTRY LODGING BY CARLSON, warm and cozy limited-service lodging properties.

HISTORY: . . . . IFA	FINANCIAL: Earnings Claim: . .No	FRANCHISOR TRAINING/SUPPORT:
Established in 1939; . . 1st Franchised in 1987	Cash Investment: $50-350K	Financial Assistance Provided: . . . Yes(I)
Company-Owned Units (As of 8/31/1992): . .0	Total Investment: . . . $250K-1.5MM	Site Selection Assistance: . . . . . . .Yes
Franchised Units (As of 8/31/1992): 237	Fees: Franchise - $20-25K	Lease Negotiation Assistance: . . . . .Yes
Total Units (As of 8/31/1992): 237	Royalty: 3-4%, Advert: 1-3%	Co-operative Advertising: . . . . No
Projected New Units for 1993:	Contract Periods (Yrs.): 20	Training: . . . . Training at Both
Distribution: US-231;Can-6;Overseas-0	Area Development Agreement: Yes/Var	. . . . . Corporate Offices and On-Site
North America: . . . . 21 States, 3 Provinces	Sub-Franchise Contract: . . . . . Yes	On-Going Support: C,D,E,G,H,I/ 39
Concentration: . . . . MN, WI, MO	Expand in Territory: . . . . Yes	EXPANSION PLANS:
Registered: . . . . .All	Passive Ownership:	US: . . . . .All US
. . . .	Encourage Conversions: . . . . . Yes	Canada: . . . . .All Canada
Type Space: . . . . . .FS, SF, SC, RM;~ SF	Average # Employees:	Overseas: . . . . .Yes

DAMON'S - THE PLACE FOR RIBS

P. O. Box 6747
Hilton Head Island, SC 29938
TEL: (803) 686-6909
FAX: (803) 785-6628
Mr. Daryl Magid, Dir. Development

DAMON'S THE PLACE FOR RIBS, a full-service restaurant, specializing in barbecue ribs, fried onion loaf, prime rib and other signature items. Full beverage service. Open 7 days, serving lunch and dinner. Also, DAMON'S CLUBHOUSE(S), same great DAMON'S food, and interactive sports programming, and CAFE DAMON'S.

HISTORY: . . . . IFA	FINANCIAL: Earnings Claim: . .No	FRANCHISOR TRAINING/SUPPORT:
Established in 1979; . . 1st Franchised in 1982	Cash Investment: $100-150K	Financial Assistance Provided: . . . . .Yes
Company-Owned Units (As of 8/31/1992): . .9	Total Investment: $385-800K	Site Selection Assistance: . . . . . . .Yes
Franchised Units (As of 8/31/1992): 36	Fees: Franchise - $50K	Lease Negotiation Assistance: . . . . .Yes
Total Units (As of 8/31/1992): 45	Royalty: 4%, Advert: 1/2%	Co-operative Advertising: . . . . .Yes
Projected New Units for 1993: 3	Contract Periods (Yrs.): 5/5	Training: . . . . .6-8 Wks. in Various
Distribution: US-44;Can-0;Overseas-1	Area Development Agreement: Yes/10	. . . . Regions
North America: . . . . 12 States	Sub-Franchise Contract: . . . . . Yes	On-Going Support: a,B,C,d,E,G,h/ . . . 14
Concentration: . . . . 15 in OH, 7 in IN	Expand in Territory: . . . . Yes	EXPANSION PLANS:
Registered: . . . . FL,IN	Passive Ownership: . . . Discouraged	US: . . . . Midwest and Southeast
. . . .	Encourage Conversions: . . . . . Yes	Canada: . . . . .Yes
Type Space: . . . . . FS, SC;~2,500-8,500 SF	Average # Employees: . 16 FT, 25 PT	Overseas: . . . . .Yes

EDO JAPAN

602 Manitou Rd., SE
Calgary, AB T2G 4C5 CAN
TEL: (403) 287-3822
FAX: (403) 243-6143
Mr. S. K. Ikuta, President

We are in the business of franchising teppan-style food in kiosks in mall food courts.

HISTORY:	FINANCIAL: Earnings Claim: . . .	FRANCHISOR TRAINING/SUPPORT:
Established in 1977; . . 1st Franchised in 1986	Cash Investment: . . . .$	Financial Assistance Provided: . . . . .Yes
Company-Owned Units (As of 8/31/1992): . 13	Total Investment: $170-200K	Site Selection Assistance: . . . . . . .Yes
Franchised Units (As of 8/31/1992): 57	Fees: Franchise - $20K	Lease Negotiation Assistance: . . . . . No
Total Units (As of 8/31/1992): 70	Royalty: 6%, Advert:	Co-operative Advertising: . . . . .Yes
Projected New Units for 1993:	Contract Periods (Yrs.): 10/5	Training: . . . . 3 Days On-Site
Distribution: US-18;Can-52;Overseas-0	Area Development Agreement: . Yes	. . . .
North America: . . . . 9 States, 4 Provinces	Sub-Franchise Contract: . . . . . Yes	On-Going Support: B,C,D,E,F/ . . . . . .
Concentration: . . 25 in AB, 14 in ON, 7 in CA	Expand in Territory: . . . . Yes	EXPANSION PLANS:
Registered: . . . . CA,FL,MD,WA,AB	Passive Ownership: . . . . . .Allowed	US: . . . . .All US
. . . .	Encourage Conversions: . . . . . NA	Canada: . . . . .All Canada
Type Space: . . Mall Food Court;~500-700 SF	Average # Employees: . . 3 FT, 3 PT	Overseas: . . . . No

ELIAS BROTHERS RESTAURANTS

4199 Marcy
Warren, MI 48091
TEL: (800) 837-3003 (313) 755-8113
FAX: (313) 757-4737
Mr. Ronald Johnston, SVP

A full-service family restaurant, featuring a wide menu selection at breakfast and weekend dinner.

HISTORY:	FINANCIAL: Earnings Claim: . .No	FRANCHISOR TRAINING/SUPPORT:
Established in 1938; . . 1st Franchised in 1954	Cash Investment: $150K	Financial Assistance Provided: . . . Yes(I)
Company-Owned Units (As of 8/31/1992): 141	Total Investment: . . . . $.4-1.5MM	Site Selection Assistance: . . . . . . .Yes
Franchised Units (As of 8/31/1992): 817	Fees: Franchise - $25K	Lease Negotiation Assistance: . . . . .Yes
Total Units (As of 8/31/1992): 958	Royalty: 3%, Advert: 3%	Co-operative Advertising: . . . . . . .Yes
Projected New Units for 1993: 22	Contract Periods (Yrs.): . . .20/Open	Training: . . . . 10 Wks. at Various
Distribution: US-885;Can-8;Overseas-65	Area Development Agreement: Yes/Var	. . . . .Locations
North America: . . . . . 29 States, 1 Province	Sub-Franchise Contract: . . . . Yes	On-Going Support: B,C,D,E,F,G,H,I/ . .100
Concentration: . 196 in MI, 148 in OH, 110 CA	Expand in Territory: . . . . . . Yes	EXPANSION PLANS:
Registered: . . . . .All	Passive Ownership: . . . Discouraged	US: . . . . All US
. . . .	Encourage Conversions: . . . . . NA	Canada: . . . . .Ontario
Type Space: . . . . FS;~60,000 SF	Average # Employees: . 35 FT, 20 PT	Overseas: . . . East and West Block

FAT BOY'S BAR-B-Q

1550 W. King St.
Cocoa, FL 32926
TEL: (407) 636-1000
FAX: (407) 632-2964
Mr. Glenn A. Summers, President

FAT BOY'S BAR-B-Q restaurants are full-service, sit-down type restaurants. Over 30 years in business, using secret recipes for beef, ribs, pork chicken plus many other specialty items, including world-famous barbecue beans. Open for breakfast, lunch and dinner. Building is Southwest adobe style.

HISTORY:	FINANCIAL: Earnings Claim: . .No	FRANCHISOR TRAINING/SUPPORT:
Established in 1958; . . 1st Franchised in 1968	Cash Investment: $125-200K	Financial Assistance Provided: . . . Yes(I)
Company-Owned Units (As of 8/31/1992): . .1	Total Investment: $200-900K	Site Selection Assistance: . . . . . . .Yes
Franchised Units (As of 8/31/1992): 24	Fees: Franchise - $25K	Lease Negotiation Assistance: . . . . .Yes
Total Units (As of 8/31/1992): 25	Royalty: 3%, Advert: 1%	Co-operative Advertising: . . . . . . .Yes
Projected New Units for 1993: 6	Contract Periods (Yrs.): 20/20	Training: . . . Minimum 400 Hrs. Training
Distribution: US-25;Can-0;Overseas-0	Area Development Agreement: Yes/20	. . . . at Headquarters
North America: . . . . .1 State	Sub-Franchise Contract: . . . . .No	On-Going Support: a,B,C,D,E,f,G,H/ . . . 6
Concentration: . . . . .25 in FL	Expand in Territory: . . . . . . Yes	EXPANSION PLANS:
Registered: . . . . All Except CA and NY	Passive Ownership: . . . Discouraged	US: . . . . Southeast
. . . .	Encourage Conversions: . . . . Yes	Canada: . . . . No
Type Space: . . . . FS;~50,000 SF	Average # Employees: . 15 FT, 10 PT	Overseas: . . . . No

FIFTH QUARTER STEAK HOUSE

1717 Elm Hill Pike, # B-3
Nashville, TN 37210
TEL: (800) 346-9637 (615) 391-9325
FAX: (615) 391-9765
Mr. Jeffrey L. Heston, Dir. Fran.

A casual-themed, up-scale, full-service steakhouse restaurant, featuring quality beef, seafood and chicken, a 70-item salad bar and "fix your own" Caesar salad, along with choice vegetables and desserts.

HISTORY:	FINANCIAL: Earnings Claim: . .No	FRANCHISOR TRAINING/SUPPORT:
Established in 1973; . . 1st Franchised in 1992	Cash Investment: $500K	Financial Assistance Provided: . . . Yes(I)
Company-Owned Units (As of 8/31/1992): . 10	Total Investment: $1.7-2.0MM	Site Selection Assistance: . . . . . . .Yes
Franchised Units (As of 8/31/1992): 0	Fees: Franchise - $30K	Lease Negotiation Assistance: . . . . .Yes
Total Units (As of 8/31/1992): 10	Royalty: 3%, Advert: 5%	Co-operative Advertising: . . . . . . .Yes
Projected New Units for 1993: 1	Contract Periods (Yrs.): 20/20	Training: . . . . . . 6-8 Wks. Headquarters
Distribution: US-10;Can-0;Overseas-0	Area Development Agreement: Yes/Var	
North America: . . . . 5 States	Sub-Franchise Contract: . . . . . .No	On-Going Support: a,B,C,D,E,F/ 400
Concentration: . . . 3 in AL, 3 in KY, 2 in TN	Expand in Territory: . . . . . . Yes	EXPANSION PLANS:
Registered:	Passive Ownership: . . . . .Allowed	US: . . . . All US
. . . .	Encourage Conversions: . . . . . Yes	Canada: . . . . No
Type Space: . . . . FS;~70,000 SF	Average # Employees: . . . . .75 FT	Overseas: . . . . No

FRIENDLY BANNERS RESTAURANTS

#203 - 1965 W. 4th Ave.
Vancouver, BC V6J 1M8 CAN
TEL: (604) 737-7748
FAX: (604) 737-7993
Mr. Bernie Primack, Devel. Mgr.

A family-oriented restaurant, open for breakfast, lunch and dinner and specializing in ice cream desserts.

HISTORY:	FINANCIAL: Earnings Claim: . .No	FRANCHISOR TRAINING/SUPPORT:
Established in 1969; . . 1st Franchised in 1969	Cash Investment: $125K	Financial Assistance Provided: . . . Yes(I)
Company-Owned Units (As of 8/31/1992): . .2	Total Investment: $250K	Site Selection Assistance: . . . . .Yes
Franchised Units (As of 8/31/1992): 10	Fees: Franchise - $30K	Lease Negotiation Assistance: . . . . .Yes
Total Units (As of 8/31/1992): 12	Royalty: 3%, Advert: 2%	Co-operative Advertising: . . . . . . .Yes
Projected New Units for 1993: 3	Contract Periods (Yrs.): 10/10	Training: . . . . . . 6-8 Wks. Headquarters
Distribution: US-0;Can-12;Overseas-0	Area Development Agreement: Yes/10	. . . . (Depending on Experience)
North America: . . . . .1 Province	Sub-Franchise Contract: . . . . . Yes	On-Going Support: C,D,E,F,G,H/ 4
Concentration: . . . . 12 in BC	Expand in Territory: . . . . Yes	EXPANSION PLANS:
Registered:	Passive Ownership: . . . Not Allowed	US: . . . . . . Washington, Oregon Areas
. . . .	Encourage Conversions: . . . . . Yes	Canada: . . . . ON, Nova Scotia
Type Space: . . . . . FS, SC, RM;~4,000 SF	Average # Employees: . 25 FT, 25 PT	Overseas: . . . . No

FUDDRUCKERS

One Corporate Pl., 55 Ferncroft Rd.
Danvers, MA 01923
TEL: (508) 774-9115
FAX: (508) 774-8485
Mr. Leo H. Skellchock, VP Dev.

FUDDRUCKERS is a casual family restaurant, serving freshly-prepared 1/3 and 1/2 pound hamburgers, chicken, fish and steak sandwiches, hot dogs, salads, fun foods and beverages. On-premise bakery and butcher shop ensures freshness. Our full produce bar permits guests to "build your own" to their liking. Drink refills are free.

HISTORY:	FINANCIAL: Earnings Claim: . .No	FRANCHISOR TRAINING/SUPPORT:
Established in 1980; . . 1st Franchised in 1983	Cash Investment: $350-500K	Financial Assistance Provided: . . . . .No
Company-Owned Units (As of 8/31/1992): . 54	Total Investment: . . . . $.6-1.5MM	Site Selection Assistance: . . . . . . .Yes
Franchised Units (As of 8/31/1992): 82	Fees: Franchise - $50K	Lease Negotiation Assistance: . . . . .No
Total Units (As of 8/31/1992): 136	Royalty: 5%, Advert: 0%	Co-operative Advertising: . . . . . . .Yes
Projected New Units for 1993: 10	Contract Periods (Yrs.): 10/10	Training: . . . . . . 6 Wks. Houston, TX,
Distribution: US-120;Can-6;Overseas-10	Area Development Agreement: . .No	. . . . 6 Wks. Annapolis, MD
North America: . . . . 29 States, 4 Provinces	Sub-Franchise Contract: . . . . . .No	On-Going Support: B,C,D,E,F,G,H/ . . 25
Concentration: . . .24 in TX, 12 in CA, 9 in IL	Expand in Territory: . . . . Yes	EXPANSION PLANS:
Registered: . . . . .All	Passive Ownership: . . . Discouraged	US: . . . . .All US
. . . .	Encourage Conversions: . . . . . Yes	Canada: . . . . .All Canada
Type Space: . . . . . FS, SC, RM;~55,000 SF	Average # Employees: . 25 FT, 15 PT	Overseas: EUR, AU, C & S America, Asia

GIORGIO RESTAURANTS

222 St. Lawrence Blvd.
Montreal, PQ H2Y 2Y3 CAN
TEL: (514) 845-4221
FAX: (514) 844-0071
Ms. Sylvie Paradis, Fran. Dir.

GIORGIO is a chain of Italian restaurants. The concept was developed towards the end of the 1970's in the specialty restaurant field. It positions itself as a responsive and innovative approach to new-style dining in a relaxing and comfortable environment. GIORGIO means quality, low price, quantity, ambiance and speedy service.

HISTORY:	FINANCIAL: Earnings Claim: . .No	FRANCHISOR TRAINING/SUPPORT:
Established in 1977; . . 1st Franchised in 1985	Cash Investment: $200-300K	Financial Assistance Provided: . . . . .No
Company-Owned Units (As of 8/31/1992): . 13	Total Investment: . . . . . . $1.2 MM	Site Selection Assistance: . . . . . . .Yes
Franchised Units (As of 8/31/1992): 16	Fees: Franchise - $30K	Lease Negotiation Assistance: . . . . .Yes
Total Units (As of 8/31/1992): 29	Royalty: 5%, Advert: 4%	Co-operative Advertising: . . . . . . .Yes
Projected New Units for 1993: 2	Contract Periods (Yrs.): 10/10	Training: . . . . . . 8 Wks. Headquarters
Distribution: US-0;Can-29;Overseas-0	Area Development Agreement: . .No	
North America: . . . . .1 Province	Sub-Franchise Contract: . . . . . .No	On-Going Support: C,d,e,G,h/ 30
Concentration: . . . . 29 on PQ	Expand in Territory: . . . . Yes	EXPANSION PLANS:
Registered:	Passive Ownership: . . . Discouraged	US: . . . . .All US
. . . .	Encourage Conversions: . . . . . Yes	Canada: . . . . .Ontario & Quebec
Type Space: . . . . . . FS, SC, RM;~4,500 SF	Average # Employees: . 25 FT, 25 PT	Overseas: . . . . No

GOLDEN CORRAL FAMILY STEAKHOUSE
5151 Glenwood Ave.
Raleigh, NC 27612
TEL: (800) 284-5673 (919) 781-9310
FAX: (919) 881-4485
Mr. Peter J. Charland, Dir. Fran. Dev.

We offer nearly 20 years of proven success in the family steakhouse market segment. The metromarket concept features in-store bakery, dessert bar and our Golden Choice Buffet, in addition to our up-dated core menu. The layout of our metro market restaurant, as well as our expanded food offering, enables each customer to define his own experience each time he visits a GOLDEN CORRAL.

HISTORY: . . . . IFA	FINANCIAL: Earnings Claim: . Yes	FRANCHISOR TRAINING/SUPPORT:
Established in 1973; . . 1st Franchised in 1986	Cash Investment: $300K	Financial Assistance Provided: . . . . .No
Company-Owned Units (As of 8/31/1992): 342	Total Investment: $1.8-2.3MM	Site Selection Assistance: . . . . .Yes
Franchised Units (As of 8/31/1992): 84	Fees: Franchise - . . . .$	Lease Negotiation Assistance: . . . . .No
Total Units (As of 8/31/1992): 426	Royalty: 4%, Advert: 2%	Co-operative Advertising: . . . . . . .No
Projected New Units for 1993: 25	Contract Periods (Yrs.): 15/5	Training: . . . . .12 Wks. Headquarters
Distribution: US-426;Can-0;Overseas-0	Area Development Agreement: Yes/Var	. . . .
North America: . . . . 38 States	Sub-Franchise Contract: . . . . .No	On-Going Support: C,D,E,G/ 190
Concentration: . . . . TX, OK, NC	Expand in Territory: . . . . Yes	EXPANSION PLANS:
Registered: . . . . .All	Passive Ownership: . . . Not Allowed	US: . . . . All US
. . . .	Encourage Conversions: . . . . .No	Canada: . . . . .No
Type Space: . . . . FS;~11,000 SF	Average # Employees: 140 FT, 40 PT	Overseas: . . . . No

GOLDEN GRIDDLE FAMILY RESTAURANTS
505 Consumers Rd., # 1000
Willowdale, ON M2J 4V8 CAN
TEL: (416) 493-3800
FAX: (416) 493-3889
Mr. Bill Hood, Dir. Fran. Dev.

120 - 180 seat family restaurant, full-service, licensed and menu for all three meal occasions with outstanding variety. Signature items are pancakes, waffles, egg dishes, up-scale decor package.

HISTORY: . . . . .CFA	FINANCIAL: Earnings Claim: . Yes	FRANCHISOR TRAINING/SUPPORT:
Established in 1964; . . 1st Franchised in 1976	Cash Investment: $165K	Financial Assistance Provided: . . . . .No
Company-Owned Units (As of 8/31/1992): . .0	Total Investment: $365-400K	Site Selection Assistance: . . . . . . .Yes
Franchised Units (As of 8/31/1992): 58	Fees: Franchise - $50K	Lease Negotiation Assistance: . . . .Yes
Total Units (As of 8/31/1992): 58	Royalty: 5%, Advert: 3%	Co-operative Advertising: . . . . . . .Yes
Projected New Units for 1993: 6	Contract Periods (Yrs.): 10/10	Training: . . . . 6 Wks. Headquarters,
Distribution: US-0;Can-58;Overseas-0	Area Development Agreement: Yes/5	. . . . .6 Wks. Location
North America: . . . . .1 Province	Sub-Franchise Contract: . . . . Yes	On-Going Support: a,B,C,d,E,G,h/ . . . 21
Concentration: . . . . 55 in ON	Expand in Territory: . . . . Yes	EXPANSION PLANS:
Registered:	Passive Ownership: . . . Not Allowed	US: . . . . Northeast
. . . .	Encourage Conversions: . . . . . Yes	Canada: . . . . .All Canada
Type Space: . . . . .SF, SC;~3,000 SF	Average # Employees: . . . .6-12 PT	Overseas: UK, MX, JA, Hong Kong

GROUND ROUND, THE

P. O. Box 9078, 35 Braintree Hill
Braintree, MA 02184
TEL: (617) 380-3116
FAX: (617) 380-3233
Mr. Ed Daly, Dir. Fran. Dev.

Full-service, casual theme, family restaurant. Variety of menu offerings, sandwiches, seafood, appetizers, steaks, ribs, chicken, burgers. Alcoholic beverages available.

HISTORY:	FINANCIAL: Earnings Claim: . Yes	FRANCHISOR TRAINING/SUPPORT:
Established in 1969; . . 1st Franchised in 1970	Cash Investment: $250-500K	Financial Assistance Provided: . . . . .No
Company-Owned Units (As of 8/31/1992): 158	Total Investment: . . . . .$.4-1.3MM	Site Selection Assistance: . . . . . . .Yes
Franchised Units (As of 8/31/1992): 43	Fees: Franchise - $40K	Lease Negotiation Assistance: . . . . .No
Total Units (As of 8/31/1992): 201	Royalty: 3%, Advert: 2%	Co-operative Advertising: . . . . . . .Yes
Projected New Units for 1993: 25	Contract Periods (Yrs.): . . . 20/20	Training: . . . . . 8-10 Wks. Regional Unit
Distribution: US-200;Can-1;Overseas-0	Area Development Agreement: . .No	. . . .
North America:	Sub-Franchise Contract: . . . . . .No	On-Going Support: B,C,D,E,G,H/ . . .100
Concentration:	Expand in Territory: . . . . Yes	EXPANSION PLANS:
Registered:	Passive Ownership: . . . Not Allowed	US: . . . . . Primarily Midwest/Northeast
. . . .	Encourage Conversions: . . . . . Yes	Canada: . . . . .No
Type Space: . . . . . FS, SC, RM;~5,500 SF	Average # Employees: . 75 FT, 25 PT	Overseas: . . . . No

HARVEST RESTAURANT & BAKERY

5200 DTC Pkwy., # 270
Englewood, CO 80111
TEL: (303) 355-7708
FAX: (303) 779-4127
Mr. Randall L. Pike, President

A unique table-service restaurant, serving breakfast, lunch and dinner, 7 days a week. Offering a well-balanced, healthy-oriented menu. The restaurant prepares most recipes from scratch in its own kitchen, using fresh and natural ingredients.

HISTORY: . . . .
Established in 1976; . . 1st Franchised in 1990
Company-Owned Units (As of 8/31/1992): . .2
Franchised Units (As of 8/31/1992): 7
Total Units (As of 8/31/1992): 9
Projected New Units for 1993: 4
Distribution: US-9;Can-0;Overseas-0
North America: . . . .
Concentration: . . . .
Registered: . . . . CA,WA
. . . .
Type Space: FS, SF, SC, RM;~3,000-6,000 SF

FINANCIAL: Earnings Claim: . .No
Cash Investment: $50-150K
Total Investment: $125-600K
Fees: Franchise - $35K
  Royalty: 3-5%, Advert: 0%
Contract Periods (Yrs.): 20/20
Area Development Agreement: Yes/5
Sub-Franchise Contract: . . . . .No
Expand in Territory: . . . . . . Yes
Passive Ownership: . . . Discouraged
Encourage Conversions: . . . . Yes
Average # Employees: . . . .

FRANCHISOR TRAINING/SUPPORT:
Financial Assistance Provided: . . . . .No
Site Selection Assistance: . . . . . . .Yes
Lease Negotiation Assistance: . . . .Yes
Co-operative Advertising: . . . . . . .NA
Training: . . . . . . 2-6 Wks. Headquarters
. . . .
On-Going Support: C,D,E,H/ 10
EXPANSION PLANS:
US: . . . . All US
Canada: . . . . .No
Overseas: . . . . No

HENNING'S FISH HOUSE

1885 Allison Park Dr.
Richland Center, WI 53581
TEL: (608) 585-4262
FAX:
Mr. Gary J. Henning, President

Full-service restaurant, specializing in seafood, with bar-b-q ribs, steak and chicken. 50% carry-outs. Restaurants located in existing buildings with low overhead and investment in mind.

HISTORY: . . . .
Established in 1973; . . 1st Franchised in 1989
Company-Owned Units (As of 8/31/1992): . .2
Franchised Units (As of 8/31/1992): 0
Total Units (As of 8/31/1992): 2
Projected New Units for 1993: 5
Distribution: US-2;Can-0;Overseas-0
North America: . . . . 2 States
Concentration: . . . . .WI
Registered: . . . . IL,WI
. . . .
Type Space: . . . .FS, SF, SC, RM;~1,200 SF

FINANCIAL: Earnings Claim: . .No
Cash Investment: $15-30K
Total Investment: $30-150K
Fees: Franchise - $7.5K
  Royalty: 5%, Advert: 1/2%
Contract Periods (Yrs.): 10/10
Area Development Agreement: . .No
Sub-Franchise Contract: . . . . .No
Expand in Territory: . . . . . . Yes
Passive Ownership: . . . Discouraged
Encourage Conversions: . . . . Yes
Average # Employees: . . 3 FT, 7 PT

FRANCHISOR TRAINING/SUPPORT:
Financial Assistance Provided: . . . . . No
Site Selection Assistance: . . . . . . .Yes
Lease Negotiation Assistance: . . . .Yes
Co-operative Advertising: . . . . . . .Yes
Training: . . . . . 4-8 Wks. Company Store
. . . .
On-Going Support: a,b,C,D,E,f,G,H/ . . . 2
EXPANSION PLANS:
US: . . . . .Wisconsin and Illinois
Canada: . . . . .No
Overseas: . . . . No

HOTLICKS

3522 Charlotte St.
Pittsburgh, PA 15201
TEL: (412) 687-3725
FAX: (412) 687-0091
Mr. Mark R. Lando, President

HOTLICKS is an up-scale mesquite grille, specializing in imported baby back ribs and other Tex-Mex dishes. Emphasis on a fun atmosphere with outstanding service. A selection of salads, secret recipe potatoes and great desserts complement the best ribs in town with sauces totally unique and unduplicated anywhere.

HISTORY: . . . .
Established in 1989; . . 1st Franchised in 1990
Company-Owned Units (As of 8/31/1992): . .2
Franchised Units (As of 8/31/1992): 2
Total Units (As of 8/31/1992): 4
Projected New Units for 1993: 6
Distribution: US-24;Can-0;Overseas-0
North America: . . . . .1 State
Concentration: . . . . 4 in PA
Registered: . . . . .All
. . . .
Type Space: . . . . FS, RM;~3,000 SF

FINANCIAL: Earnings Claim: . .No
Cash Investment: $150K
Total Investment: $250-600K
Fees: Franchise - $20K
  Royalty: 4%, Advert: 1%
Contract Periods (Yrs.): 10/5
Area Development Agreement: Yes/10
Sub-Franchise Contract: . . . . . Yes
Expand in Territory: . . . . . . Yes
Passive Ownership: . . . Discouraged
Encourage Conversions: . . . . Yes
Average # Employees: . .5 FT, 20 PT

FRANCHISOR TRAINING/SUPPORT:
Financial Assistance Provided: . . . . .No
Site Selection Assistance: . . . . . . .Yes
Lease Negotiation Assistance: . . . .Yes
Co-operative Advertising: . . . . . . .Yes
Training: . . . . 3 Wks. Headquarters,
. . . . .2 Wks.On-Site
On-Going Support: B,C,D,E,f,G,H/ . . . 5
EXPANSION PLANS:
US: . . . . All US
Canada: . . . . .All Canada
Overseas: . . . . AU, JA, UK

HUDSON'S GRILL

5528 Everglades St., # A
Ventura, CA 93003
TEL: (805) 644-6756
FAX:
Mr. Davis J. Beckman, SVP

Casual, family-oriented, full-service restaurant with full bar. Simple, but effective, menu featuring hamburgers, salads, sandwiches, appetizers, chicken and desserts for lunch, dinner or late night.

HISTORY:	FINANCIAL: Earnings Claim: . .No	FRANCHISOR TRAINING/SUPPORT:
Established in 1984; . . 1st Franchised in 1990	Cash Investment: $150K	Financial Assistance Provided: . . . . .No
Company-Owned Units (As of 8/31/1992): . 17	Total Investment: $350-750K	Site Selection Assistance: . . . . . . .Yes
Franchised Units (As of 8/31/1992): 5	Fees: Franchise - $25K	Lease Negotiation Assistance: . . . . .Yes
Total Units (As of 8/31/1992): 22	Royalty: 4%, Advert: 1%	Co-operative Advertising: . . . . . . .Yes
Projected New Units for 1993: 3	Contract Periods (Yrs.): 20/0	Training: . . . . . .6-12 Wks. Headquarters
Distribution: US-22;Can-0;Overseas-0	Area Development Agreement: Yes/Var	. . . .
North America: . . . . 3 States	Sub-Franchise Contract: . . . . .No	On-Going Support: C,d,E,F,G,H/ 11
Concentration: . . .17 in CA, 4 in TX, 1 in OR	Expand in Territory: . . . . . . Yes	EXPANSION PLANS:
Registered: . . . . .CA,OR,WA	Passive Ownership: . . . Discouraged	US: . . . . Western US
. . . .	Encourage Conversions: . . . . .No	Canada: . . . . .No
Type Space: FS, SC (End Cap);~3,500-5,000 SF	Average # Employees: . 15 FT, 25 PT	Overseas: . . . . No

HUMPTY'S EGG PLACE

Box 364, Station T
Calgary, AB T2H 2G6 CAN
TEL: (403) 269-4675
FAX: (403) 266-1973
Mr. Tim Walsh, Fran. Mktg.

Family restaurant, open 24 hours, specializing in breakfast, but also offering dinner entrees, gourmet burgers and deli sandwiches.

HISTORY:	FINANCIAL: Earnings Claim: . .No	FRANCHISOR TRAINING/SUPPORT:
Established in 1978; . . 1st Franchised in 1982	Cash Investment: $60-100K	Financial Assistance Provided: . . . Yes(I)
Company-Owned Units (As of 8/31/1992): . .7	Total Investment: $250-325K	Site Selection Assistance: . . . . . . .Yes
Franchised Units (As of 8/31/1992): 23	Fees: Franchise - $25K	Lease Negotiation Assistance: . . . . .Yes
Total Units (As of 8/31/1992): 30	Royalty: 5%, Advert: 2%	Co-operative Advertising: . . . . . . .Yes
Projected New Units for 1993: 10	Contract Periods (Yrs.): 10/5	Training: . . . . 3 Wks. Headquarters.
Distribution: US-0;Can-30;Overseas-0	Area Development Agreement: Yes/20	. . . . 2 Wks. On-Site.
North America: . . . . 4 Provinces	Sub-Franchise Contract: . . . . .No	On-Going Support: B,C,D,E,F,H,I/ 8
Concentration: . . . 18 in AB,6 in SK, 3 in BC	Expand in Territory: . . . . . . Yes	EXPANSION PLANS:
Registered: . . . . AB	Passive Ownership: . . . Discouraged	US: . . . . Midwest
. . . .	Encourage Conversions: . . . . . Yes	Canada: . . . . BC,AB,SK,MB,ON
Type Space: . . . . . FS, SC, RM;~3,400 SF	Average # Employees: . 15 FT, 17 PT	Overseas: . . . . No

JB'S RESTAURANTS

1010 W. 2610 South
Salt Lake City, UT 84119
TEL: (801) 974-4300
FAX: (801) 974-4385
Mr. George Gehling, VP

JB'S is a full-service family restaurant, serving breakfast, lunch and dinner. Our menu features a variety of high-quality offerings, from pot roast and honey-baked chicken to a great line of burgers, sandwiches, salads and breakfast favorites, all complemented by our breakfast buffet and salad bar. JB'S great food, outstanding service and comfortable dining rooms have made us a favorite in the Inter-mountain West.

HISTORY:	FINANCIAL: Earnings Claim: . .No	FRANCHISOR TRAINING/SUPPORT:
Established in 1961; . . 1st Franchised in 1990	Cash Investment: $100-300K	Financial Assistance Provided: . . . . .No
Company-Owned Units (As of 8/31/1992): 131	Total Investment: . . . $350K-1.0MM	Site Selection Assistance: . . . . . . .Yes
Franchised Units (As of 8/31/1992): 4	Fees: Franchise - $25K	Lease Negotiation Assistance: . . . . .Yes
Total Units (As of 8/31/1992): 135	Royalty: 4%, Advert: 3.5%	Co-operative Advertising: . . . . . . .Yes
Projected New Units for 1993: 10	Contract Periods (Yrs.): 20/20	Training: . . . . . . 4-7 Wks. Headquarters,
Distribution: US-135;Can-0;Overseas-0	Area Development Agreement: Yes/Var	. . . . 2-3 Wks. On-Site at Opening
North America: . . . . 10 States	Sub-Franchise Contract: . . . . .No	On-Going Support: C,D,E,G,H,I/ 60
Concentration: . . .43 in AZ, 23 in UT, 9 in ID	Expand in Territory: . . . . . . Yes	EXPANSION PLANS:
Registered: . . . . OR,WA	Passive Ownership: . . . Discouraged	US: . . . . W, SW, Mountain States
. . . .	Encourage Conversions: . . . . Yes	Canada: . . . . Western Province
Type Space: . . . . FS;~5,000 SF	Average # Employees: . 20 FT, 30 PT	Overseas: . . . . No

JOHNNY APPLESEED RESTAURANT

10,000 Ashbridge Pl.
Richmond, VA 23233
TEL: (804) 740-9643
FAX: (804) 741-7809
Mr. Ashton. L. Trice, President

Family restaurant, full-service, with apple product gift shop.

HISTORY:	FINANCIAL: Earnings Claim: . .No	FRANCHISOR TRAINING/SUPPORT:
Established in 1973; . . 1st Franchised in 1988	Cash Investment: $75-200K	Financial Assistance Provided: . . . Yes(I)
Company-Owned Units (As of 8/31/1992): . .4	Total Investment: . . . $700K-1.5MM	Site Selection Assistance: . . . . . . .Yes
Franchised Units (As of 8/31/1992): 3	Fees: Franchise - $25K	Lease Negotiation Assistance: . . . . .Yes
Total Units (As of 8/31/1992): 7	Royalty: 4%, Advert: 2%	Co-operative Advertising: . . . . . . .Yes
Projected New Units for 1993: 2	Contract Periods (Yrs.): 10/10	Training: . . . .6 Wks. Fredericksburg, VA
Distribution: US-7;Can-0;Overseas-0	Area Development Agreement: Yes/10	. . . .
North America: . . . . 3 States	Sub-Franchise Contract: . . . . Yes	On-Going Support: a,b,C,D,E,f,G,h,i/ . . . 5
Concentration:	Expand in Territory: . . . . . . Yes	EXPANSION PLANS:
Registered: . . . . FL,MD,VA	Passive Ownership: . . . . .Allowed	US: . . . . All US
. . . .	Encourage Conversions: . . . . Yes	Canada: . . . . No
Type Space: . . . . FS;~3,500 SF	Average # Employees: . .5 FT, 10 PT	Overseas: . . . . No

K-BOB'S STEAKHOUSES

800 Rankin Rd. NE
Albuquerque, NM 87107
TEL: (800) 225-8403 (505) 345-8403
FAX: (505) 345-0492
Mr. Ed Tinsley, III, President

K-BOB'S caters to small, rural communities with populations of less than 25,000 people. It has dedicated its effort to serving the needs of the K-BOB'S licensees and aiding them in efficiently delivering "the food that America loves" to their patrons. It concentrates on expanding with committed owner/operators in rural markets with good highway count and with the potential sales achievement of $800,000 to $1 million annually.

HISTORY:	FINANCIAL: Earnings Claim: . Yes	FRANCHISOR TRAINING/SUPPORT:
Established in 1966; . . 1st Franchised in 1992	Cash Investment: $75K	Financial Assistance Provided: . . .Yes(D)
Company-Owned Units (As of 8/31/1992): . .1	Total Investment: $100-300K	Site Selection Assistance: . . . . . . .Yes
Franchised Units (As of 8/31/1992): 47	Fees: Franchise - $10K	Lease Negotiation Assistance: . . . . .Yes
Total Units (As of 8/31/1992): 48	Royalty: 3%, Advert: 1%	Co-operative Advertising: . . . . . . .Yes
Projected New Units for 1993: 3	Contract Periods (Yrs.): 20/10	Training: . . . . 1-3 Wks. Truth or
Distribution: US-48;Can-0;Overseas-0	Area Development Agreement: . .No	. . . . Consequences, NM
North America: . . . . 5 States	Sub-Franchise Contract: . . . . .No	On-Going Support: a,b,C,D,E,f,G,H,I/ . . 7
Concentration: . .28 in TX, 11 in NM, 4 in CO	Expand in Territory: . . . . . . Yes	EXPANSION PLANS:
Registered:	Passive Ownership: . . . Not Allowed	US: . . . . .Southwest and Midwest
. . . .	Encourage Conversions: . . . . Yes	Canada: . . . . No
Type Space: . . . . FS;~6,000 SF	Average # Employees: . 20 FT, 10 PT	Overseas: . . . . No

KELSEY'S RESTAURANTS

450 S. Service Rd. W.
Oakville, ON L6K 2H4 CAN
TEL: (416) 842-5510
FAX: (416) 842-5603
Mr. Toby Singlehurst, Dir. Fran.

Licensed, full-service, casual dining. Offering lunch, dinner and late night menu with a wide variety of food items, offering great value with large portions ranging in price from $1.95 - 14.95. The atmosphere is warm, service is fast, friendly and efficient. We also cater to family dining. Stand-up bar also available.

HISTORY:	FINANCIAL: Earnings Claim: . .No	FRANCHISOR TRAINING/SUPPORT:
Established in 1978; . . 1st Franchised in 1983	Cash Investment: . . . . .$200K Min.	Financial Assistance Provided: . . . . .Yes
Company-Owned Units (As of 8/31/1992): . 21	Total Investment: $650K	Site Selection Assistance: . . . . . . .Yes
Franchised Units (As of 8/31/1992): 16	Fees: Franchise - $50K	Lease Negotiation Assistance: . . . . .Yes
Total Units (As of 8/31/1992): 37	Royalty: 5%, Advert: 0%	Co-operative Advertising: . . . . .NA
Projected New Units for 1993: 6	Contract Periods (Yrs.): 10/10	Training: . . . . Minimum 12 Wks. at
Distribution: US-1;Can-36;Overseas-0	Area Development Agreement: . Yes	. . . . .Various Locations
North America: . . . . 4 Provinces	Sub-Franchise Contract: . . . . . .No	On-Going Support: A,B,C,D,E,F,G,H/ . .8
Concentration: . . 32 in ON, 2 in MB, 1 in SK	Expand in Territory: . . . . . . .No	EXPANSION PLANS:
Registered: . . . . AB	Passive Ownership: . . . Discouraged	US: . . . . FL and NY
. . . .	Encourage Conversions: . . . . Yes	Canada: . . . . .All Canada
Type Space: . . . . . FS, In-Line;~5,500 SF	Average # Employees: . 25 FT, 35 PT	Overseas: . . . . No

LA ROSA MEXICAN RESTAURANT

226 W. Third St.
Davenport, IA 52801
TEL: (319) 326-4095
FAX: (319) 326-4097
Mr. Walter Newport

Family-style restaurants, specializing in unique recipes and methods for the preparation, display and service of premium quality tacos, tostados, enchiladas, burritos and other Mexican food.

HISTORY:	FINANCIAL: Earnings Claim: . .No	FRANCHISOR TRAINING/SUPPORT:
Established in 1973; . . 1st Franchised in 1973	Cash Investment: $25-50K	Financial Assistance Provided: . . . . .No
Company-Owned Units (As of 8/31/1992): . .2	Total Investment: $100-160K	Site Selection Assistance: . . . . . . .Yes
Franchised Units (As of 8/31/1992): 9	Fees: Franchise - $10K	Lease Negotiation Assistance: . . . .Yes
Total Units (As of 8/31/1992): 11	Royalty: 4%, Advert: 3%	Co-operative Advertising: . . . . . . .Yes
Projected New Units for 1993: 1	Contract Periods (Yrs.): 10/5	Training: . . . . . . 2 Wks. Headquarters
Distribution: US-11;Can-0;Overseas-0	Area Development Agreement: .No	
North America: . . . . 2 States	Sub-Franchise Contract: . . . . . .No	On-Going Support: C,D,E,H/ 4
Concentration: . . . . 7 in IA, 4 in IL	Expand in Territory: . . . . Yes	EXPANSION PLANS:
Registered: IL	Passive Ownership: . . . Discouraged	US: . . . . Midwest
. . . .	Encourage Conversions: . . . . . NA	Canada: . . . . .No
Type Space: . . . . . FS, SF, SC;~2,500 SF	Average # Employees: . .12 FT, 6 PT	Overseas: . . . . No

MADE IN JAPAN JAPANESE RESTAURANTS

2133 Royal Windsor Dr., # 23
Mississauga, ON L5J 1K5 CAN
TEL: (416) 823-8883
FAX: (416) 823-5255
Mr. Nik Jurkovic, Dir. Fran./Dev.

Fresh-food restaurants, located primarily in food courts of regional shopping malls, specializing in freshly-prepared Japanese-style foods prepared in front of customers. For example: teriyaki steak, chicken or shrimp with freshly-grilled vegetables and steamed rice.

HISTORY: . . . . .CFA	FINANCIAL: Earnings Claim: . . .	FRANCHISOR TRAINING/SUPPORT:
Established in 1986; . . 1st Franchised in 1987	Cash Investment: $40-60K	Financial Assistance Provided: . . . Yes(I)
Company-Owned Units (As of 8/31/1992): . .2	Total Investment: $150-200K	Site Selection Assistance: . . . . . . .Yes
Franchised Units (As of 8/31/1992): 40	Fees: Franchise - $25K	Lease Negotiation Assistance: . . . .Yes
Total Units (As of 8/31/1992): 42	Royalty: 6%, Advert: 2%	Co-operative Advertising: . . . . . . .Yes
Projected New Units for 1993: 10	Contract Periods (Yrs.): . . . 10/5-10	Training: . . . . .1 Wk. Toronto, ON,
Distribution: US-0;Can-42;Overseas-0	Area Development Agreement: Yes/10	. . . 1 Wk. Headquarters, 1 Wk. On-Site
North America: . . . . 7 Provinces	Sub-Franchise Contract: . . . . . Yes	On-Going Support: A,B,C,D,E,F,G,H,I/ 27
Concentration: . . .26 in ON, 8 in PQ, 1 in AB	Expand in Territory: . . . . Yes	EXPANSION PLANS:
Registered: . . . . AB	Passive Ownership: . . . Not Allowed	US: . . . . All US
. . . .	Encourage Conversions: . . . . . Yes	Canada: . . . . .All Canada
Type Space: . . . . .RM;~325-425 SF	Average # Employees: . . 3 FT, 5 PT	Overseas: . . . . Yes

MARIE CALLENDER PIE SHOPS

1100 Town & Country Rd., # 1300
Orange, CA 92668
TEL: (800) 776-7437 (714) 542-3355
FAX: (714) 542-8078
Mr. Gerald K. Tanaka, VP

The MARIE CALLENDER name is synonymous with fresh-baked, premium-quality pies, served with a full-line menu of sandwiches, pastas, salads and pot pies in a homey, authentic American setting. The company is positioned in the top tier of the family-style restaurant market, one of the fastest-growing segments of the restaurant industry.

HISTORY:	FINANCIAL: Earnings Claim: . .No	FRANCHISOR TRAINING/SUPPORT:
Established in 1964; . . 1st Franchised in 1965	Cash Investment: $300-400K	Financial Assistance Provided: . . . . .No
Company-Owned Units (As of 8/31/1992): . 82	Total Investment: $1.0-1.75MM	Site Selection Assistance: . . . . . . .Yes
Franchised Units (As of 8/31/1992): 79	Fees: Franchise - $50K	Lease Negotiation Assistance: . . . .No
Total Units (As of 8/31/1992): 161	Royalty: 5%, Advert: 0%	Co-operative Advertising: . . . . . . .Yes
Projected New Units for 1993: 1	Contract Periods (Yrs.): 15/5	Training: . . . . 12 Wks. Various Locations
Distribution: US-161;Can-0;Overseas-0	Area Development Agreement: .No	. . . .
North America: . . . . 17 States	Sub-Franchise Contract: . . . . . .No	On-Going Support: a,B,C,D,E,F,g,H,I/ . 77
Concentration: . 117 in CA, 11 in AZ, 6 in UT	Expand in Territory: . . . . .No	EXPANSION PLANS:
Registered: . . . . CA	Passive Ownership: . . . . .Allowed	US: . . . . . West, Northwest, Southwest
. . . .	Encourage Conversions: . . . . . Yes	Canada: . . . . .Yes
Type Space: . . . . FS;~5,900 SF	Avg. # Employees: 12-15 FT, 60-70 PT	Overseas: . . . . .Pacific Rim

MARKET STREET BUFFET & BAKERY

17090 N. Dallas Pkwy.
Dallas, TX 75248
TEL: (800) 247-8325 (214) 407-9700
FAX:
Purchasing Dept.

Family-style buffet, featuring scattered hot and cold food bars and display bakery. Top quality home-style foods at one low price.

HISTORY:	FINANCIAL: Earnings Claim: . .No	FRANCHISOR TRAINING/SUPPORT:
Established in 1992; . . 1st Franchised in 1992	Cash Investment: $105-125K	Financial Assistance Provided: . . . . .No
Company-Owned Units (As of 8/31/1992): . .0	Total Investment: . . . . . $.7-1.2MM	Site Selection Assistance: . . . . .Yes
Franchised Units (As of 8/31/1992): 5	Fees: Franchise - $30K	Lease Negotiation Assistance: . . . . .Yes
Total Units (As of 8/31/1992): 5	Royalty: 2%, Advert: 1/2%	Co-operative Advertising: . . . . .NA
Projected New Units for 1993: 13	Contract Periods (Yrs.): 20/10	Training: . . . . . . .10 Wks. Headquarters
Distribution: US-5;Can-0;Overseas-0	Area Development Agreement: Yes/Var	. . . .
North America: . . . . 5 States	Sub-Franchise Contract: . . . . .No	On-Going Support: C,D,E,h,I/ 31
Concentration: . . . 1 in FL, 1 in VA, 1 in NC	Expand in Territory: . . . . .No	EXPANSION PLANS:
Registered:	Passive Ownership: . . . Discouraged	US: . . . . .All US
. . . .	Encourage Conversions: . . . . . Yes	Canada: . . . . .No
Type Space: . . FS, SF, SC;~8,000-10,000 SF	Average # Employees: . 60 FT, 30 PT	Overseas: . . . . No

MELTING POT RESTAURANTS, THE

P. O. Box 270059
Tampa, FL 33688
TEL: (813) 881-0055
FAX: (813) 889-9361
Mr. Robert Johnston, President

Specialty restaurant franchise. Unique fondue entrees prepared in an intimate atmosphere tableside. Perhaps the most unique full-service restaurant in North America today. Superior track record in the industry.

HISTORY:	FINANCIAL: Earnings Claim: . .No	FRANCHISOR TRAINING/SUPPORT:
Established in 1984; . . 1st Franchised in 1985	Cash Investment: $40-60K	Financial Assistance Provided: . . . . .No
Company-Owned Units (As of 8/31/1992): . .4	Total Investment: $89-150K	Site Selection Assistance: . . . . .Yes
Franchised Units (As of 8/31/1992): 21	Fees: Franchise - $15.6K	Lease Negotiation Assistance: . . . . .Yes
Total Units (As of 8/31/1992): 25	Royalty: 4%, Advert: 0%	Co-operative Advertising: . . . . .Yes
Projected New Units for 1993: 10	Contract Periods (Yrs.): 10/10	Training: . . . .Minimum of 150 Hours HQ
Distribution: US-25;Can-0;Overseas-0	Area Development Agreement: . .No	. . . .
North America: . . . . 5 States	Sub-Franchise Contract: . . . . .No	On-Going Support: C,D,E,G,H,I/ 9
Concentration: . . .21 in FL, 2 in NC, 2 in GA	Expand in Territory: . . . . . . Yes	EXPANSION PLANS:
Registered: . . . . MD	Passive Ownership: . . . Not Allowed	US: . . . . .Eastern US
. . . .	Encourage Conversions: . . . . . Yes	Canada: . . . . .All Canada
Type Space: . . . . .SF, SC;~3,000 SF	Average # Employees: . .3 FT, 16 PT	Overseas: . . . . No

MICKEY FINN'S SPORTS CAFE

2211 Peoples Rd., # A
Bellevue, WA 68005
TEL: (402) 292-2056
FAX: (402) 292-9712
Mr. Clyde Pittman, President

Restaurant/sports bar.

HISTORY:	FINANCIAL: Earnings Claim: . . .	FRANCHISOR TRAINING/SUPPORT:
Established in 1981; . . 1st Franchised in 1989	Cash Investment: . . . .$	Financial Assistance Provided: . . . Yes(I)
Company-Owned Units (As of 8/31/1992): . .1	Total Investment: $100-175K	Site Selection Assistance: . . . . .Yes
Franchised Units (As of 8/31/1992): 6	Fees: Franchise - $15K	Lease Negotiation Assistance: . . . . .Yes
Total Units (As of 8/31/1992): 7	Royalty: 5%, Advert: 2%	Co-operative Advertising: . . . . .Yes
Projected New Units for 1993: 4	Contract Periods (Yrs.): 20/10	Training: . . . . .Restaurant
Distribution: US-7;Can-0;Overseas-0	Area Development Agreement: . Yes	. . . .
North America: . . . . 2 States	Sub-Franchise Contract: . . . . . Yes	On-Going Support: B,C,D,E,F,H/ 4
Concentration: . . . . .6 in NE, 1 in IA	Expand in Territory: . . . . . . Yes	EXPANSION PLANS:
Registered:	Passive Ownership: . . . Discouraged	US: . . . . .All US
. . . .	Encourage Conversions: . . . . . Yes	Canada: . . . . .Yes
Type Space: . . . . .FS, SC;~4,000 SF	Average # Employees: . .7 FT, 10 PT	Overseas: . . . . Yes

MIKES RESTAURANTS

8250 Decarie Blvd.
Montreal, PQ H4P 2P5 CAN
TEL: (514) 341-5544
FAX: (514) 341-5635
Mr. Neil Zeidel, Sr. VP

MIKES RESTAURANTS, a wholly-owned subsidiary of M-Corp, Inc., is a franchise management company, operating through licensees, 120 family-style Italian restaurants, featuring pizza, hot submarine sandwiches and pastas, and offering a full turn-key to new franchisees.

HISTORY:	FINANCIAL: Earnings Claim: . . .	FRANCHISOR TRAINING/SUPPORT:
Established in 1967; . . 1st Franchised in 1972	Cash Investment: $75-175K	Financial Assistance Provided: . . . Yes(I)
Company-Owned Units (As of 8/31/1992): . .6	Total Investment: $225-525K	Site Selection Assistance: . . . . . . .Yes
Franchised Units (As of 8/31/1992): 120	Fees: Franchise - $45K	Lease Negotiation Assistance: . . . .Yes
Total Units (As of 8/31/1992): 126	Royalty: 8%, Advert: 0%	Co-operative Advertising: . . . . .Yes
Projected New Units for 1993:	Contract Periods (Yrs.): 20	Training: . . . . . .6 Wks. Training Rest.,
Distribution: US-0;Can-126;Overseas-0	Area Development Agreement: Yes/20	. . . . .2 Wks. New Restaurant
North America: . . . . 2 Provinces	Sub-Franchise Contract: . . . .No	On-Going Support: C,D,E,F,G,H/ 39
Concentration: . . . . . . 125 in PQ, 1 in ON	Expand in Territory: . . . . . . Yes	EXPANSION PLANS:
Registered:	Passive Ownership: . . . Not Allowed	US: . . . . No
. . . .	Encourage Conversions: . . . . .No	Canada: . . . . .Yes
Type Space: . . . . ;~ SF	Average # Employees: . 15 FT, 20 PT	Overseas: . . . . No

MOUNTAIN MIKE'S PIZZA

1014 Second St., 3rd Fl.
Old Sacramento, CA 95814
TEL: (800) 982-MIKE (916) 441-4493
FAX: (916) 441-4493
Mr. Ernie L. Stewart, President

A family-style, sit-down pizza restaurant with a relaxed, casual atmosphere, featuring a unique thick crust pizza with mountains of toppings. Other menu items include over-baked sandwiches, hamburgers, salad, a limited pasta line and beverages, including wine and beer where permitted. All menu items can be taken out and most locations offer delivery. This is a hands-on, no-frills franchise. We do everything we can to minimize the initial investment.

HISTORY:	FINANCIAL: Earnings Claim: . .No	FRANCHISOR TRAINING/SUPPORT:
Established in 1978; . . 1st Franchised in 1979	Cash Investment: $90K	Financial Assistance Provided: . . . Yes(I)
Company-Owned Units (As of 8/31/1992): . .1	Total Investment: $112.4-209K	Site Selection Assistance: . . . . . . .Yes
Franchised Units (As of 8/31/1992): 76	Fees: Franchise - $15K	Lease Negotiation Assistance: . . . .Yes
Total Units (As of 8/31/1992): 77	Royalty: 5% Gross, Advert: . 2%	Co-operative Advertising: . . . . . . .Yes
Projected New Units for 1993: 65	Contract Periods (Yrs.): . . . 15/10	Training: . . . .5 Wks. Company-Owned or
Distribution: US-75;Can-0;Overseas-2	Area Development Agreement: . . .	. . . . .Franchised Location
North America: . . . . .1 State	Sub-Franchise Contract: . . . . Yes	On-Going Support: C,D,E,G,H,I/ 14
Concentration: . . . . 75 in CA	Expand in Territory: . . . . . . Yes	EXPANSION PLANS:
Registered: . . . . .CA,FL	Passive Ownership: . . . Discouraged	US: . . . . .West and Northwest
. . . .	Encourage Conversions: . . . . Yes	Canada: . . . . .All Canada
Type Space: . .SF,SC, Neigh. Ctr;~2,500 SF	Average # Employees: . .3 FT, 12 PT	Overseas: . JA, CH, KO, EUR, UK

MR. MIKE'S RESTAURANTS AND STEAKHOUSES

#5 - 8765 Ash St.
Vancouver, BC V6P 6T3 CAN
TEL: (604) 322-7044 C
FAX: (604) 322-3143
Mr. Roger Newton, VP

A family-style, self-serve restaurant, featuring steaks, chicken and seafood. Offering a 60+ item soup-salad-dessert bar. Basically, everything from soup to nuts. Franchising since early 1960's.

HISTORY:	FINANCIAL: Earnings Claim: . .No	FRANCHISOR TRAINING/SUPPORT:
Established in 1962; . . 1st Franchised in 1964	Cash Investment: $100-150K	Financial Assistance Provided: . . . Yes(I)
Company-Owned Units (As of 8/31/1992): . .2	Total Investment: $180-250K	Site Selection Assistance: . . . . . . .Yes
Franchised Units (As of 8/31/1992): 24	Fees: Franchise - $25K	Lease Negotiation Assistance: . . . .Yes
Total Units (As of 8/31/1992): 26	Royalty: 4%, Advert: 4%	Co-operative Advertising: . . . . . . .Yes
Projected New Units for 1993: 2	Contract Periods (Yrs.): 10/5	Training: . . . . .1-2 Wks. Company Store,
Distribution: US-0;Can-26;Overseas-0	Area Development Agreement: .No	. . . . 2-4 Wks. On-Site
North America: . . . . .1 Province	Sub-Franchise Contract: . . . . . Yes	On-Going Support: a,B,C,D,E,F,G,H/ . .8
Concentration: . . . . 26 in BC	Expand in Territory: . . . . . . Yes	EXPANSION PLANS:
Registered:	Passive Ownership: . . . Not Allowed	US: . . . . .Northwest
. . . .	Encourage Conversions: . . . . Yes	Canada: . . . . .BC and Yukon
Type Space: . . . .FS, SF, SC, RM;~2,000 SF	Average # Employees: . . 8 FT, 6 PT	Overseas: . Orient Opportunities Exist

MR. STEAK

P. O. Box 17130
Denver, CO 80217
TEL: (800) 727-8325 (303) 293-0200
FAX: (303) 293-0299
Mr. Robert Hoadley, VP

A full-service restaurant, specializing in the sale of broiled steak, chicken and seafood.

HISTORY:	FINANCIAL: Earnings Claim: . .No	FRANCHISOR TRAINING/SUPPORT:
Established in 1962; . . 1st Franchised in 1962	Cash Investment: $150-200K	Financial Assistance Provided: . . . . .No
Company-Owned Units (As of 8/31/1992): . .1	Total Investment: $300K	Site Selection Assistance: . . . . .Yes
Franchised Units (As of 8/31/1992): 45	Fees: Franchise - $30K	Lease Negotiation Assistance: . . . . .Yes
Total Units (As of 8/31/1992): 46	Royalty: 4%, Advert: 1%	Co-operative Advertising: . . . . .Yes
Projected New Units for 1993: 6	Contract Periods (Yrs.): 10/10	Training: . . . . 7 Wks. Headquarters,
Distribution: US-46;Can-0;Overseas-0	Area Development Agreement: . .No	. . . . .Various Locations
North America: . . . . 32 States	Sub-Franchise Contract: . . . . . .No	On-Going Support: B,C,D,E,G,H,I/ . . . 10
Concentration: . . . .5 in CO, 4 in OH, 3 in IL	Expand in Territory: . . . . . . .No	EXPANSION PLANS:
Registered: . . . . .Refiling in Progress	Passive Ownership: . . . Discouraged	US: . . . . .Northwest and West
. . . .	Encourage Conversions: . . . . . Yes	Canada: . . . . .No
Type Space: . . . . FS;~40,000 SF	Average # Employees: . 10 FT, 30 PT	Overseas: . . . . No

PACINI

910 rue Belanger Est, # 204
Montreal, PQ H2S 3P4 CAN
TEL: (514) 276-5818
FAX: (514) 276-8147
Mr. Alain Villeneuve, EVP

Italian-style, full-service restaurant - attractive and warm atmosphere. Unique selling point: Bread Bar, where customers toast a choice of breads on a grill. An all-you-can-eat pasta and Caesar salad concept. Pasta dishes are the highlight of the menu. PACINI also offers pizza, chicken, veal, seafood, fish and a wide variety of tasty salads and desserts. Many dishes are approved by the Quebec Heart Association.

HISTORY:	FINANCIAL: Earnings Claim: . .No	FRANCHISOR TRAINING/SUPPORT:
Established in 1980; . . 1st Franchised in 1986	Cash Investment: $50-200K	Financial Assistance Provided: . . . Yes(I)
Company-Owned Units (As of 8/31/1992): . 15	Total Investment: $650K	Site Selection Assistance: . . . . .Yes
Franchised Units (As of 8/31/1992): 21	Fees: Franchise - $35K	Lease Negotiation Assistance: . . . . .Yes
Total Units (As of 8/31/1992): 36	Royalty: 5%, Advert: 4%	Co-operative Advertising: . . . . .Yes
Projected New Units for 1993: 8	Contract Periods (Yrs.): 10/10	Training: . . . . 11 Wks. Headquarters
Distribution: US-0;Can-36;Overseas-0	Area Development Agreement: Yes/10	. . . .
North America: . . . . .1 Province	Sub-Franchise Contract: . . . . . Yes	On-Going Support: B,C,d,E,G,H/ 650
Concentration: . . . . .36 in PQ	Expand in Territory: . . . . . . .No	EXPANSION PLANS:
Registered:	Passive Ownership: . . . Not Allowed	US: . . . . New England
. . . .	Encourage Conversions: . . . . . Yes	Canada: . . . . .Quebec,Maritimes
Type Space: . . . . .FS, SF;~4,500 SF	Average # Employees: . 20 FT, 15 PT	Overseas: . . . . FR

PANCAKE COTTAGE FAMILY RESTAURANTS

P. O. Box 1909
N. Massapequa, NY 11758
TEL: (516) 271-0221
FAX: (516) 271-0449
Mr. Chris Levano, VP Fran. Dev.

Established in 1964, PANCAKE COTTAGE is a time-proven restaurant concept, specializing in a variety of pancakes and waffles. It is now offering franchise opportunities ranging from food courts in malls to full-service restaurants in free-standing buildings. THE PANCAKE COTTAGE menu services every time of day plus dessert. Conversions of existing restaurants are welcome.

HISTORY: . . . . IFA	FINANCIAL: Earnings Claim: . .No	FRANCHISOR TRAINING/SUPPORT:
Established in 1964; . . 1st Franchised in 1971	Cash Investment: $100K	Financial Assistance Provided: . . . Yes(I)
Company-Owned Units (As of 8/31/1992): . .0	Total Investment: $150-450K	Site Selection Assistance: . . . . .Yes
Franchised Units (As of 8/31/1992): 21	Fees: Franchise - $35K	Lease Negotiation Assistance: . . . . .Yes
Total Units (As of 8/31/1992): 21	Royalty: 5%, Advert: 2-3%	Co-operative Advertising: . . . . .Yes
Projected New Units for 1993: 10	Contract Periods (Yrs.): 10/10	Training: . . . . . .1-3 Months at Company
Distribution: US-21;Can-0;Overseas-0	Area Development Agreement: . .No	. . . . Unit or Franchised Unit
North America: . . . . 3 States	Sub-Franchise Contract: . . . . . .No	On-Going Support: B,C,D,E,G,H/ . . . 10
Concentration: . . .19 in NY, 1 in MD, 1 in FL	Expand in Territory: . . . . Yes	EXPANSION PLANS:
Registered: . . . . . .FL,MD,MI,NY,VA,AB	Passive Ownership: . . . . . .Allowed	US: . . . . .Northeast and Southeast
. . . .	Encourage Conversions: . . . . . Yes	Canada: . . . . Eastern Prov.
Type Space: . FS, SF, SC, RM;~500-3,000 SF	Avg. # Employees: 10-25 FT, 3-10 PT	Overseas: . . . . No

PANTRY FAMILY RESTAURANTS

202 - 15463 104th Ave.
Surrey, BC V3R 1N9 CAN
TEL: (604) 584-4115
FAX: (604) 584-0104
Mr. Mike Hoffmann, President

A full-menu family restaurant chain, offering breakfast, lunch or dinner. Served anytime of day, 7 days a week.

HISTORY: . . . . .CFA	FINANCIAL: Earnings Claim: . Yes	FRANCHISOR TRAINING/SUPPORT:
Established in 1975; . . 1st Franchised in 1976	Cash Investment: . . . .$	Financial Assistance Provided: . . . . .No
Company-Owned Units (As of 8/31/1992): . .3	Total Investment: $350-400K	Site Selection Assistance: . . . . . . .Yes
Franchised Units (As of 8/31/1992): 19	Fees: Franchise - $40K	Lease Negotiation Assistance: . . . . .Yes
Total Units (As of 8/31/1992): 21	Royalty: 4.5%, Advert: 2.5%	Co-operative Advertising: . . . . . . .Yes
Projected New Units for 1993: 2	Contract Periods (Yrs.):	Training: . . . . Minimum 6 Wks. at
Distribution: US-0;Can-22;Overseas-0	Area Development Agreement: . .No	. . . . Franchisee Restaurant
North America: . . . . .1 Province	Sub-Franchise Contract: . . . . . .No	On-Going Support: B,C,E,H/ 12
Concentration: . . . . 22 in ON	Expand in Territory: . . . . Yes	EXPANSION PLANS:
Registered:	Passive Ownership: . . . Not Allowed	US: . . . . .No
. . . .	Encourage Conversions: . . . . . Yes	Canada: . . . . .BC
Type Space: FS, SC, RM, Hotel;~4,000-4,500 SF	Average # Employees: . 25 FT, 15 PT	Overseas: . . . . No

PARGO'S

1717 Elm Hill Pike
Nashville, TN 37210
TEL: (800) 346-9637 (615) 391-9325
FAX: (615) 391-9765
Mr. Jeffrey L. Heston, Dir. Fran.

Full-service, casual theme dining restaurant, featuring appetizers, chicken, steak, seafood and the service of liquor.

HISTORY:	FINANCIAL: Earnings Claim: . .No	FRANCHISOR TRAINING/SUPPORT:
Established in 1983; . . 1st Franchised in 1990	Cash Investment: $500K	Financial Assistance Provided: . . . . .No
Company-Owned Units (As of 8/31/1992): . .8	Total Investment: $1.4-1.6MM	Site Selection Assistance: . . . . . . .Yes
Franchised Units (As of 8/31/1992): 1	Fees: Franchise - $30K	Lease Negotiation Assistance: . . . . .Yes
Total Units (As of 8/31/1992): 9	Royalty: 3%, Advert: 5%	Co-operative Advertising: . . . . . . .Yes
Projected New Units for 1993:	Contract Periods (Yrs.): 20/20	Training: . . . . . . 4-8 Wks. Headquarters
Distribution: US-9;Can-0;Overseas-0	Area Development Agreement: Yes/Var	. . . .
North America: . . . . 3 States	Sub-Franchise Contract: . . . . .No	On-Going Support: a,b,C,d,e,F,G,h,I/ . . . .
Concentration: . . . 4 in VA, 3 in TN, 2 in MD	Expand in Territory: . . . . Yes	EXPANSION PLANS:
Registered: . . . . All States	Passive Ownership: . . . . . .Allowed	US: . . . . .All US
. . . .	Encourage Conversions: . . . . .No	Canada: . . . . .No
Type Space: . . . . FS;~6,000 SF	Average # Employees: . . . . 100 FT	Overseas: . . . . No

PEPE'S MEXICAN RESTAURANT

1325 W. 15th St.
Chicago, IL 60608
TEL: (312) 733-2500
FAX: (312) 733-2564
Mr. Edwin A. Ptak, Corp. Counsel

A full-service Mexican restaurant, serving a complete line of Mexican food, with liquor, beer and wine. Complete training and help in remodeling, site selection, equipment purchasing and running the restaurant provided.

HISTORY: . . . . .IFA	FINANCIAL: Earnings Claim: . Yes	FRANCHISOR TRAINING/SUPPORT:
Established in 1967; . . 1st Franchised in 1968	Cash Investment: $30-100K	Financial Assistance Provided: . . . . .Yes
Company-Owned Units (As of 8/31/1992): . .2	Total Investment: $75-300K	Site Selection Assistance: . . . . . . .Yes
Franchised Units (As of 8/31/1992): 57	Fees: Franchise - $15K	Lease Negotiation Assistance: . . . . .Yes
Total Units (As of 8/31/1992): 59	Royalty: 4%, Advert: 3%	Co-operative Advertising: . . . . . . .Yes
Projected New Units for 1993: 5	Contract Periods (Yrs.): 10/10	Training: . . . . 4 Wks. Headquarters
Distribution: US-59;Can-0;Overseas-0	Area Development Agreement: Yes/Var	. . . .
North America: . . . . 2 States	Sub-Franchise Contract: . . . . . .No	On-Going Support: B,C,D,E,F,G,H/ . . 15
Concentration: . . . . 47 in IL, 12 in IN	Expand in Territory: . . . . .No	EXPANSION PLANS:
Registered: . . . . IL,IN,MI,WI	Passive Ownership: . . . Discouraged	US: . . . . .Midwest
. . . .	Encourage Conversions: . . . . . Yes	Canada: . . . . .No
Type Space: . . . . . FS, SF, SC;~3,000 SF	Average # Employees: . . 8 FT, 5 PT	Overseas: . . . . No

PERKINS FAMILY RESTAURANTS

6075 Poplar Ave., # 800
Memphis, TN 38119
TEL: (800) 877-7375 (901) 766-6400
FAX: (901) 766-6482
Mr. Phil Joseph, Sr. Dir. Fran. Dev.

PERKINS FAMILY RESTAURANTS is a full-service, family-style restaurant, offering a broad menu of breakfast, lunch and dinner entrees. 60% of the stores are open 24 hours a day, 7 days a week.

HISTORY: . . . . .IFA, CFA	**FINANCIAL:** Earnings Claim: . .No	**FRANCHISOR TRAINING/SUPPORT:**
Established in 1958; . . 1st Franchised in 1958	Cash Investment: $250K	Financial Assistance Provided: . . . . .No
Company-Owned Units (As of 8/31/1992): 117	Total Investment: . . . $1.1-1.9MM	Site Selection Assistance: . . . . .Yes
Franchised Units (As of 8/31/1992): 290	Fees: Franchise - $35K	Lease Negotiation Assistance: . . . . .Yes
Total Units (As of 8/31/1992): 407	Royalty: 4%, Advert: 4%	Co-operative Advertising: . . . . .Yes
Projected New Units for 1993: 30	Contract Periods (Yrs.): . . . 20/10	Training: . . . . Varies
Distribution: US-402;Can-5;Overseas-0	Area Development Agreement: Yes/Var	. . . .
North America: . . . . 29 States, 2 Provinces	Sub-Franchise Contract: . . . . .No	On-Going Support: b,C,D,e,F,G,H,I/ . . . 4
Concentration: . 58 in MN, 52 in OH, 41 in PA	Expand in Territory: . . . . . . Yes	**EXPANSION PLANS:**
Registered: . . . FL,IL,IN,MD,MI,MN,NY,ND	Passive Ownership: . . . Discouraged	US: . . . . SE, SW and Midwest
. . . . .SD,VA,WA,WI	Encourage Conversions: . . . . . Yes	Canada: . . . . .All Canada
Type Space: . . . . FS;~5,800 SF	Average # Employees: 35 FT, 40+ PT	Overseas: . . . . No

---

PHILADELPHIA BAR & GRILL

2211 Peoples Rd., # A
Bellevue, NE 68005
TEL: (402) 292-2056
FAX: (402) 292-9712
Mr. Clyde Pittman, President

Full-service bar and restaurant.

HISTORY:	**FINANCIAL:** Earnings Claim: . . .	**FRANCHISOR TRAINING/SUPPORT:**
Established in 1981; . . 1st Franchised in 1985	Cash Investment: . . . .$	Financial Assistance Provided: . . . . .Yes
Company-Owned Units (As of 8/31/1992): . .1	Total Investment: $100-180K	Site Selection Assistance: . . . . .Yes
Franchised Units (As of 8/31/1992): 7	Fees: Franchise - $15K	Lease Negotiation Assistance: . . . . .Yes
Total Units (As of 8/31/1992): 8	Royalty: 5%, Advert: 2%	Co-operative Advertising: . . . . .Yes
Projected New Units for 1993: 4	Contract Periods (Yrs.): 20/10	Training: . . . . .Restaurant
Distribution: US-8;Can-0;Overseas-0	Area Development Agreement: . Yes	. . . .
North America: . . . . 3 States	Sub-Franchise Contract: . . . . . Yes	On-Going Support: B,C,D,E,F,H/ 4
Concentration: . . . 5 in NE, 2 in IA, 1 in MN	Expand in Territory: . . . . Yes	**EXPANSION PLANS:**
Registered: . . . . MN	Passive Ownership: . . . Discouraged	US: . . . . All US
. . . .	Encourage Conversions: . . . . . Yes	Canada: . . . . .Yes
Type Space: . . . . .FS, SC;~4,000 SF	Average # Employees: . .7 FT, 10 PT	Overseas: . . . . .Yes

---

PIZZA DELIGHT

Box 2070, Station A
Moncton, NB E1C 8H7 CAN
TEL: (506) 853-0990
FAX: (506) 853-4131
Mr. Malcolm Houser, EVP

Family restaurants, featuring pizza and pasta.

HISTORY:	**FINANCIAL:** Earnings Claim: . .No	**FRANCHISOR TRAINING/SUPPORT:**
Established in 1968; . . 1st Franchised in 1969	Cash Investment: $75-150K	Financial Assistance Provided: . . . . .No
Company-Owned Units (As of 8/31/1992): . .3	Total Investment: $250-350K	Site Selection Assistance: . . . . . . .Yes
Franchised Units (As of 8/31/1992): 147	Fees: Franchise - $30K	Lease Negotiation Assistance: . . . .Yes
Total Units (As of 8/31/1992): 150	Royalty: 6%, Advert: 3%	Co-operative Advertising: . . . . .Yes
Projected New Units for 1993: 16	Contract Periods (Yrs.): 10/10	Training: . . . . 2 Wks. Existing Unit,
Distribution: US-0;Can-150;Overseas-0	Area Development Agreement: Yes/3-6	. . . . .2-4 Wks. Franchise Site
North America: . . . . 6 Provinces	Sub-Franchise Contract: . . . . . Yes	On-Going Support: B,C,D,E,F,G,H/ . . 30
Concentration: . 55 in ON, 40 in NB, 23 in NS	Expand in Territory: . . . . .No	**EXPANSION PLANS:**
Registered:	Passive Ownership: . . . . . .Allowed	US: . . . . New England
. . . .	Encourage Conversions: . . . . . Yes	Canada: . . . . ON, PQ, Atlantic
Type Space: . . . . FS;~2,000 SF	Average # Employees:3-6 FT, 15-25 PT	Overseas: . . . . No

PONDEROSA STEAKHOUSE

P. O. Box 578
Dayton, OH 45401
TEL: (800) 543-9670
FAX: (513) 454-2525
Mr. Edward Day, Dir. Fran. Sales

The franchisor's primary business is a modified full-service, family affordable steakhouse restaurant, open 7 days a week for lunch and dinner. The restaurant features a value-priced menu which includes beef entrees, seafood entrees, chicken entrees and the Grand Buffet. Many PONDEROSA STEAKHOUSES offer breakfast.

HISTORY: . . . . IFA
Established in 1965; . . 1st Franchised in 1966
Company-Owned Units (As of 8/31/1992): 380
Franchised Units (As of 8/31/1992): . . . 406
Total Units (As of 8/31/1992): 786
Projected New Units for 1993: 40
Distribution: US-752;Can-9;Overseas-25
 North America: . . . . 31 States, 4 Provinces
 Concentration: . 139 in OH, 73 in NY,72 in IN
Registered: . . . . All States
. . . .
Type Space: . . . . FS;~55,000 SF

FINANCIAL: Earnings Claim: . .No
Cash Investment: $100-300K
Total Investment: . . . . $.8-1.3MM
Fees: Franchise - $30K
 Royalty: 4.8%, Advert: 4%
Contract Periods (Yrs.): . . . 20/20
Area Development Agreement: Yes/15
Sub-Franchise Contract: . . . . Yes
Expand in Territory: . . . . . . Yes
Passive Ownership: . . . Discouraged
Encourage Conversions: . . . . Yes
Average # Employees: . 15 FT, 50 PT

FRANCHISOR TRAINING/SUPPORT:
Financial Assistance Provided: . . . Yes(I)
Site Selection Assistance: . . . . . . .Yes
Lease Negotiation Assistance: . . . . No
Co-operative Advertising: . . . . . . .Yes
Training: . . . . 5 Wks. in Field,
 . . . 1 Wk. Headquarters, 3 Wks. Field
On-Going Support: B,C,D,E,G,H,I/ . . 45
EXPANSION PLANS:
US: . . . . All US
Canada: . . . . .All Canada
Overseas: . . . . Yes

RED HOT & BLUE, MEMPHIS PIT BAR-B-QUE

1600 Wilson Blvd.
Arlington, VA 22209
TEL: (703) 276-8833
FAX: (703) 528-4789
Mr. Robert Friedman, President

RED HOT & BLUE RESTAURANTS have won numerous awards for their authentic Memphis-style BBQ ribs, "Pulled Pork," chicken and beef brisket. Customers enjoy blues music and memorabilia and fast, friendly service. The Hard Rock Cafe of Blues.

HISTORY: . . . . IFA
Established in 1988; . . 1st Franchised in 1990
Company-Owned Units (As of 8/31/1992): . .3
Franchised Units (As of 8/31/1992): 10
Total Units (As of 8/31/1992): 13
Projected New Units for 1993: 10
Distribution: US-13;Can-0;Overseas-0
 North America: . . . . 5 States
 Concentration: . . . 3 in VA, 2 in MD, 2 in NJ
Registered: . . . . FL,IL,MD,VA,DC
. . . .
Type Space: . . . . .FS, SC;~5,000 SF

FINANCIAL: Earnings Claim: . .No
Cash Investment: $400-500K
Total Investment: $400-500K
Fees: Franchise - $20K
 Royalty: 5%, Advert: 2%
Contract Periods (Yrs.): . . . 20/10
Area Development Agreement: Yes/Var
Sub-Franchise Contract: . . . . .No
Expand in Territory: . . . . . . .No
Passive Ownership: . . . Discouraged
Encourage Conversions: . . . Yes
Average # Employees: . 30 FT, 20 PT

FRANCHISOR TRAINING/SUPPORT:
Financial Assistance Provided: . . . . .No
Site Selection Assistance: . . . . . . .Yes
Lease Negotiation Assistance: . . . .Yes
Co-operative Advertising: . . . . No
Training: . . . . 3 Wks. Headquarters
. . . .
On-Going Support: C,D,E,G,h/ 4
EXPANSION PLANS:
US: . . . . .South and Northeast
Canada: . . . . No
Overseas: . . . . No

RED ROBIN INTERNATIONAL

28 Executive Park, # 200
Irvine, CA 92714
TEL: (714) 756-2121
FAX: (714) 756-2540
Mr. Madison Jobe, VP Fran./Mktg.

Restaurant chain. Our motto: "To serve great food and drink at a value price while creating happy guests." While this philosophy has been the driving force behind the success of RED ROBIN INTERNATIONAL, the key to the on-going prosperity of the chain is its ability to evolve and change with the times.

HISTORY: . . . . IFA
Established in 1969; . . 1st Franchised in 1979
Company-Owned Units (As of 8/31/1992): . 33
Franchised Units (As of 8/31/1992): 20
Total Units (As of 8/31/1992): 53
Projected New Units for 1993: 13
Distribution: US-40;Can-13;Overseas-0
 North America: . . . . 10 States, 2 Provinces
 Concentration: . 11 in CA, 10 in WA, 4 in NY
Registered: . CA,FL,MD,MD,MN,NY,VA,DC
. . . . AB
Type Space: . . . . .SC;~6,300 SF

FINANCIAL: Earnings Claim: . .No
Cash Investment: $500K
Total Investment: . . . $1.0-2.5MM
Fees: Franchise - $25K
 Royalty: 4.5%, Advert: . . . 1/2%
Contract Periods (Yrs.): . . . 20/10
Area Development Agreement: Yes/10
Sub-Franchise Contract: . . . . .No
Expand in Territory: . . . . . . Yes
Passive Ownership: . . . Discouraged
Encourage Conversions: . . . . Yes
Average # Employees: . 50 FT, 50 PT

FRANCHISOR TRAINING/SUPPORT:
Financial Assistance Provided: . . . Yes(I)
Site Selection Assistance: . . . . . . .Yes
Lease Negotiation Assistance: . . . . .Yes
Co-operative Advertising: . . . . . . .Yes
Training: . . . . 10 Days at Various
 . . Locations for Front/Back Office Emp
On-Going Support: a,b,C,D,E,G,H/ . . . 61
EXPANSION PLANS:
US: . . . . All US
Canada: . . . . No
Overseas: . . . . MX, AU, JA

RICKY'S RESTAURANTS

#104 - 12824 Anvil Way
Surrey, BC V3W 8E7 CAN
TEL: (604) 597-7272
FAX: (604) 597-8874
Mr. Ron Hildebrand, SVP

RICKY'S RESTAURANTS ("A Family's Favorite Eating/Meeting Place") is an aggressive, value-oriented restaurant on the cutting edge of the family restaurant business in the Northwest. Big on Service. Big on Quality. Small on Price. Has and will help the franchise look forward to many prosperous years ahead.

HISTORY:	FINANCIAL: Earnings Claim: . Yes	FRANCHISOR TRAINING/SUPPORT:
Established in 1979; . . 1st Franchised in 1987	Cash Investment: $150-200K	Financial Assistance Provided: . . . Yes(I)
Company-Owned Units (As of 8/31/1992): . .4	Total Investment: $300-475K	Site Selection Assistance: . . . . . . .Yes
Franchised Units (As of 8/31/1992): 12	Fees: Franchise - $40K	Lease Negotiation Assistance: . . . .Yes
Total Units (As of 8/31/1992): 16	Royalty: 3%, Advert: 2.5%	Co-operative Advertising: . . . . . . .Yes
Projected New Units for 1993: 12	Contract Periods (Yrs.): 5/10	Training: . . . . . . 2 Wks. Company Store,
Distribution: US-1;Can-15;Overseas-0	Area Development Agreement: . Yes	. . . . 30 Days On Location (New Store)
North America: . . . . . . 1 State, 1 Province	Sub-Franchise Contract: . . . . . Yes	On-Going Support: A,B,C,D,E,F,G,H/ . 10
Concentration: . . . . 15 in BC, 1 in WA	Expand in Territory: . . . . . . Yes	EXPANSION PLANS:
Registered:	Passive Ownership: . . . Discouraged	US: . . . . Northwest (WA and OR)
. . . .	Encourage Conversions: . . . . . Yes	Canada: . . . . BC and AB
Type Space: . . . . FS, SC;~3,000-4,000 SF	Average # Employees: . 20 FT, 15 PT	Overseas: . . . . No

ROUND TABLE PIZZA RESTAURANT

655 Montgomery St., 7th Fl.
San Francisco, CA 94111
TEL: (800) 866-5866 (415) 392-7500
FAX: (415) 362-7967
Mr. Jake Brown, Dir. Fran. Sales

ROUND TABLE FRANCHISE CORP. offers franchisees the opportunity to establish and operate a ROUND TABLE PIZZA RESTAURANT, which provides the public with pizza and related products in a wholesome, family restaurant setting. ROUND TABLE PIZZA is the nation's fourth largest pizza franchise chain, providing restaurant, take-out and delivery service.

HISTORY: . . . . IFA	FINANCIAL: Earnings Claim: . .No	FRANCHISOR TRAINING/SUPPORT:
Established in 1959; . . 1st Franchised in 1962	Cash Investment: $100K	Financial Assistance Provided: . . . . . No
Company-Owned Units (As of 8/31/1992): . .1	Total Investment: $300K	Site Selection Assistance: . . . . . . .Yes
Franchised Units (As of 8/31/1992): 569	Fees: Franchise - $25K	Lease Negotiation Assistance: . . . .Yes
Total Units (As of 8/31/1992): 570	Royalty: 4%, Advert: 3%	Co-operative Advertising: . . . . . . .Yes
Projected New Units for 1993: 15	Contract Periods (Yrs.): 15/15	Training: . . . . 4 Wks. Headquarters
Distribution: US-556;Can-0;Overseas-14	Area Development Agreement: Yes/Var	. . . .
North America: . . . . 9 States	Sub-Franchise Contract: . . . . . Yes	On-Going Support: C,D,E,G,H,I/ 71
Concentration:	Expand in Territory: . . . . Yes	EXPANSION PLANS:
Registered: . . . . CA,HI,OR,WA	Passive Ownership: . . . Discouraged	US: . . . . Northwest and Southwest
. . . .	Encourage Conversions: . . . . . Yes	Canada: . . . . No
Type Space: . . . . SC, RM;~2,800 SF	Average # Employees:5-7 FT, 10-15 PT	Overseas: . . . . No

SALADELLY RESTAURANTS

Coulter Ave. & St. James St.
Ardmore, PA 19003
TEL: (215) 642-0453
FAX:
Mr. Steve Byer, Chairman

Limited-menu, full-service restaurant, featuring a superb SALADELLY Saladbar and a limited selection of hot, grilled entrees. SALADELLY'S average about 110 seats in attractive, comfortable dining settings.

HISTORY:	FINANCIAL: Earnings Claim: . .No	FRANCHISOR TRAINING/SUPPORT:
Established in 1978; . . 1st Franchised in 1986	Cash Investment: $100-150K	Financial Assistance Provided: . . . . .No
Company-Owned Units (As of 8/31/1992): . .6	Total Investment: $275K	Site Selection Assistance: . . . . . . .Yes
Franchised Units (As of 8/31/1992): 2	Fees: Franchise - $25K	Lease Negotiation Assistance: . . . .Yes
Total Units (As of 8/31/1992): 8	Royalty: 4%, Advert: 2%	Co-operative Advertising: . . . . . . .Yes
Projected New Units for 1993: 1	Contract Periods (Yrs.): 10/5	Training: . . . . 6 Wks. Headquarters
Distribution: US-8;Can-0;Overseas-0	Area Development Agreement: Yes/Var	. . . .
North America: . . . . .1 State	Sub-Franchise Contract: . . . . . Yes	On-Going Support: C,D,E/ 5
Concentration: . . . . 8 in PA	Expand in Territory: . . . . Yes	EXPANSION PLANS:
Registered:	Passive Ownership: . . . Not Allowed	US: . . . . Northeast
. . . .	Encourage Conversions: . . . . Yes	Canada: . . . . .No
Type Space: . . . . .SF, SC;~2,700 SF	Average # Employees: . 10 FT, 20 PT	Overseas: . . . . No

SANDWICH TREE RESTAURANTS

602 - 535 Thurlow St.
Vancouver, BC V6E 3L2 CAN
TEL: (800) 663-8733 (604) 684-3314
FAX: (604) 684-2542
Mr. George Moen, President

Famous for our custom sandwiches, creative salads, hearty soups and much more, SANDWICH TREE is a limited-hours operation located in shopping centres, commercial towers and industrial centres. Our quality food, served in our attractive surroundings, make SANDWICH TREE a number one investment opportunity.

HISTORY: . . . . IFA	FINANCIAL: Earnings Claim: . Yes	FRANCHISOR TRAINING/SUPPORT:
Established in 1978; . . 1st Franchised in 1979	Cash Investment: $35-55K	Financial Assistance Provided: . . . Yes(I)
Company-Owned Units (As of 8/31/1992): . .2	Total Investment: $90-120K	Site Selection Assistance: . . . . . . .Yes
Franchised Units (As of 8/31/1992): 68	Fees: Franchise - $27.5K	Lease Negotiation Assistance: . . . . .Yes
Total Units (As of 8/31/1992): 70	Royalty: 5%, Advert: 3%	Co-operative Advertising: . . . . . . .Yes
Projected New Units for 1993: 6	Contract Periods (Yrs.): 5/5/5	Training: . . . . 3 Wks. Headquarters,
Distribution: US-0;Can-70;Overseas-0	Area Development Agreement: Yes/10	. . . . 1 Wk. Toronto, 1 Wk. Halifax, NS
North America: . . . . 8 Provinces	Sub-Franchise Contract: . . . . . Yes	On-Going Support: a,B,C,D,E,F,G,H,I/ . 15
Concentration: . . .35 in BC, 9 in ON, 9 in NS	Expand in Territory: . . . . . . Yes	EXPANSION PLANS:
Registered: . . . . AB	Passive Ownership: . . . Discouraged	US: . . . . .No
. . . .	Encourage Conversions: . . . . . Yes	Canada: . . . . .All Canada
Type Space: . . .SF, RM, Ind. Park;~1,800 SF	Average # Employees: . . 4 FT, 7 PT	Overseas: . . . . No

SBARRO, THE ITALIAN EATERY

763 Larkfield Rd.
Commack, NY 11725
TEL: (800) 766-4949 (516) 864-0200
FAX: (516) 462-9058
Mr. David Gaines, Dir. Fran. Licensing

Fast-food Italian restaurants.

HISTORY:	FINANCIAL: Earnings Claim: . .No	FRANCHISOR TRAINING/SUPPORT:
Established in 1959; . . 1st Franchised in 1977	Cash Investment: $150K	Financial Assistance Provided: . . . . .No
Company-Owned Units (As of 8/31/1992): . .2	Total Investment: $250-600K	Site Selection Assistance: . . . . . . .Yes
Franchised Units (As of 8/31/1992): 118	Fees: Franchise - $35K	Lease Negotiation Assistance: . . . .Yes
Total Units (As of 8/31/1992): 120	Royalty: 5%, Advert: 1%	Co-operative Advertising: . . . . .No
Projected New Units for 1993: 110	Contract Periods (Yrs.): 10	Training: . . . . . . 1-4 Wks. Headquarters
Distribution: US-89;Can-9;Overseas-22	Area Development Agreement: Yes/5	. . . .
North America: . . . . 26 States	Sub-Franchise Contract: . . . . . Yes	On-Going Support: C,D,E/ 150
Concentration: . . .14 in IL, 13 in PA, 8 in NY	Expand in Territory: . . . . . . Yes	EXPANSION PLANS:
Registered: . . . . .All	Passive Ownership: . . . Not Allowed	US: . . . . .All US
. . . .	Encourage Conversions: . . . . . .No	Canada: . . . . No
Type Space: . . . . SF, Non-Tradit.;~1,680 SF	Average # Employees: 8 FT, 15-20 PT	Overseas: . . . . .Yes

SHAKEY'S PIZZA RESTAURANTS

651 Gateway Blvd., # 1200
S. San Francisco, CA 94080
TEL: (800) 444-9268 (415) 873-0640
FAX: (415) 737-2191
Ms. Jean R. Lyles, Fran. Dev.

Family-oriented pizza restaurant, featuring chicken, salad bar, lunch buffet and all-day service.

HISTORY: . . . . IFA	FINANCIAL: Earnings Claim: . .No	FRANCHISOR TRAINING/SUPPORT:
Established in 1954; . . 1st Franchised in 1958	Cash Investment: $150K	Financial Assistance Provided: . . . . .No
Company-Owned Units (As of 8/31/1992): . 20	Total Investment: $350-500K	Site Selection Assistance: . . . . . . .Yes
Franchised Units (As of 8/31/1992): 371	Fees: Franchise - $25K	Lease Negotiation Assistance: . . . .Yes
Total Units (As of 8/31/1992): 391	Royalty: 4.5%, Advert: 2%	Co-operative Advertising: . . . . . . .Yes
Projected New Units for 1993: 20	Contract Periods (Yrs.): 20/20	Training: . . . . . .4 Wks. Co. Training Rest.
Distribution: . . . US-179;Can-0;Overseas-212	Area Development Agreement: Yes/20	. . . . . .2 Wks. Classroom Training HQ
North America: . . . . 21 States	Sub-Franchise Contract: . . . . . Yes	On-Going Support: B,C,D,E,G,H,I/ . . . 36
Concentration: . 94 in CA, 19 in WA, 10 in WI	Expand in Territory: . . . . . . Yes	EXPANSION PLANS:
Registered: . . CA,IL,IN,MD,MN,VA,WA,WI	Passive Ownership: . . . Discouraged	US: . . . . All US, Primarily W/Midwest
. . . .	Encourage Conversions: . . . . . Yes	Canada: . . . . .No
Type Space: . . . . FS, SF, SC;~ SF	Average # Employees: . . . . .Varies	Overseas: . .JA,MX,KO,HK,TH,PH,Sing

SHONEY'S RESTAURANTS

1717 Elm Hill Pike
Nashville, TN 37210
TEL: (800) 346-9637 (615) 391-9325
FAX: (615) 391-9765
Mr. Jeffrey L. Heston, Dir. Fran.

Full-service family restaurant, featuring original breakfast bar.

HISTORY: . . . . IFA	FINANCIAL: Earnings Claim: . .No	FRANCHISOR TRAINING/SUPPORT:
Established in 1959; . . 1st Franchised in 1971	Cash Investment: $150K	Financial Assistance Provided: . . . . .No
Company-Owned Units (As of 8/31/1992): 317	Total Investment: . . . $1.0-1.5MM	Site Selection Assistance: . . . . . . .Yes
Franchised Units (As of 8/31/1992): 514	Fees: Franchise - $30K	Lease Negotiation Assistance: . . . . .Yes
Total Units (As of 8/31/1992): 831	Royalty: 3.5%, Advert: 5%	Co-operative Advertising: . . . . . . .Yes
Projected New Units for 1993:	Contract Periods (Yrs.): 20/20	Training: . . . . . . 4-8 Wks. Headquarters
Distribution: US-831;Can-0;Overseas-0	Area Development Agreement: . Yes	. . . .
North America:	Sub-Franchise Contract: . . . . .No	On-Going Support: a,b,C,d,e,F,G,h,I/ . . . .
Concentration:	Expand in Territory: . . . . . . Yes	EXPANSION PLANS:
Registered: . . . . .All	Passive Ownership: . . . . .Allowed	US: . . . . . . .NE, NW, W and Midwest
. . . .	Encourage Conversions: . . . . .No	Canada: . . . . .No
Type Space: . . . . FS;~45,000 SF	Average # Employees: . . . . 70 FT	Overseas: . . . . No

SHOOTER ON THE WATER

3033 NE 32nd Ave.
Ft. Lauderdale, FL 33308
TEL: (305) 566-2855
FAX: (305) 566-2953
Mr. Melvin Burge, EVP

Up-scale, waterfront family-type restaurant and entertainment complex, catering to singles, family and boating clientele, offering valet service for boat docking and auto's. Outside dining patio, swimming pool, plus over 120 menu items.

HISTORY:	FINANCIAL: Earnings Claim: . .No	FRANCHISOR TRAINING/SUPPORT:
Established in 1982; . . 1st Franchised in 1985	Cash Investment: . . . .$	Financial Assistance Provided: . . . . .No
Company-Owned Units (As of 8/31/1992): . .3	Total Investment: $1.1-1.5MM	Site Selection Assistance: . . . . . . .Yes
Franchised Units (As of 8/31/1992): 4	Fees: Franchise - $100K	Lease Negotiation Assistance: . . . .Yes
Total Units (As of 8/31/1992): 7	Royalty: 4%, Advert: 1%	Co-operative Advertising: . . . . . . .Yes
Projected New Units for 1993: 2	Contract Periods (Yrs.): 15/10	Training: . . . . . 2-3 Months Headquarters
Distribution: US-7;Can-0;Overseas-0	Area Development Agreement: . .No	
North America: . . . . 3 States	Sub-Franchise Contract: . . . . . .No	On-Going Support: C,D,E,F,H/ 15
Concentration: . . . 3 in OH, 3 in FL, 1 in NY	Expand in Territory: . . . . Yes	EXPANSION PLANS:
Registered: . . . . .CA,FL,IL,MI,NY,RI,VA	Passive Ownership: . . . . . .Allowed	US: . . . . All US
. . . .	Encourage Conversions: . . . . . Yes	Canada: . . . . .Ontario
Type Space: . . . . FS;~9,000 SF	Average # Employees: . . . . 210 FT	Overseas: . . . . UK, MX

SICILY'S PIZZA

4635 S. Sherwood Forest Blvd.
Baton Rouge, LA 70816
TEL: (504) 291-0650
FAX: (504) 291-8097
Ms. Fusun Dogu, Mktg. Dir.

Up-scale, family restaurant, with the main attraction being the BUFFET ITALIANO - a buffet that features not only varieties of pizza, but salad, soup, fruit bar, spaghetti, fettuccini, 3 types of lasagna - all home-made with special sauces. Eggplant italiano, broccoli casserole, antipasti and pasta salads and dessert pizza are all special, popular items of the buffet.

HISTORY:	FINANCIAL: Earnings Claim: . Yes	FRANCHISOR TRAINING/SUPPORT:
Established in 1975; . . 1st Franchised in 1985	Cash Investment: $20-30K	Financial Assistance Provided: . . . . .No
Company-Owned Units (As of 8/31/1992): . .1	Total Investment: $60-80K	Site Selection Assistance: . . . . . . .Yes
Franchised Units (As of 8/31/1992): 18	Fees: Franchise - $10K	Lease Negotiation Assistance: . . . . .Yes
Total Units (As of 8/31/1992): 19	Royalty: 4%, Advert: 2-4%	Co-operative Advertising: . . . . . . .Yes
Projected New Units for 1993:	Contract Periods (Yrs.): 5/5	Training: . . . .3 Months Baton Rouge, LA
Distribution: US-13;Can-0;Overseas-6	Area Development Agreement: . .No	. . . .
North America: . . . . 2 States	Sub-Franchise Contract: . . . . . .No	On-Going Support: D,E,H/ 3
Concentration: . . . . 12 in LA, 1 in MS	Expand in Territory: . . . . Yes	EXPANSION PLANS:
Registered:	Passive Ownership: . . . Discouraged	US: . . . . All US
. . . .	Encourage Conversions: . . . . .No	Canada: . . . . .No
Type Space: . . . . .SC;~2,000 SF	Average # Employees:2-3 FT, 12-14 PT	Overseas: . . . . .Yes

SIRLOIN STOCKADE FAMILY STEAKHOUSES

2908 N. Plum
Hutchinson, KS 67502
TEL: (316) 669-9372
FAX: (316) 669-0531
Ms. Judy Froese, Dir. Fran. Dev.

SIRLOIN STOCKADE FAMILY STEAKHOUSES feature a selection of top-quality steaks, chicken and fish, and a self-service salad, hot food and dessert bar, at affordable prices. Free-standing buildings of approx. 10,000 SF, seating 360-400; 70,000 SF of land required.

HISTORY: . . . .
Established in 1984; . . 1st Franchised in 1984
Company-Owned Units (As of 8/31/1992): . .6
Franchised Units (As of 8/31/1992): 72
Total Units (As of 8/31/1992): 78
Projected New Units for 1993: 10
Distribution: US-77;Can-0;Overseas-1
  North America: . . . . 12 States
  Concentration: . 21 in TX, 14 in KS, 10 in OK
Registered: . . . . CA,IL,IN,MN,SD,VA,WI
. . . .
Type Space: . . . . FS;~70,000 SF

FINANCIAL: Earnings Claim: . .No
Cash Investment: $350-500K
Total Investment: $1-1.8MM
Fees: Franchise - $15K
  Royalty: 3%, Advert: 1%
Contract Periods (Yrs.): 15/15
Area Development Agreement: Yes/Var
Sub-Franchise Contract: . . . . .No
Expand in Territory: . . . . . . .No
Passive Ownership: . . . Discouraged
Encourage Conversions: . . . . .No
Average # Employees: . 20 FT, 50 PT

FRANCHISOR TRAINING/SUPPORT:
Financial Assistance Provided: . . . . .No
Site Selection Assistance: . . . . . . .Yes
Lease Negotiation Assistance: . . . . .No
Co-operative Advertising: . . . . .No
Training: . . . . . . 8 Wks. Training Store,
  . . . Opening Wk. at Site, On-Going Site
On-Going Support: B,C,D,E,G,h,i/ . . . 13
EXPANSION PLANS:
US: . . . . All US
Canada: . . . . No
Overseas: . . . . No

SIZZLER RESTAURANTS INTERNATIONAL

12655 W. Jefferson Blvd.
Los Angeles, CA 90066
TEL: (310) 827-2300
FAX: (310) 823-1451
Mr. James S. McGinnis, VP Fran. Dev.

SIZZLER RESTAURANTS operates moderately-priced, limited service restaurants, offering steak, seafood and chicken entrees accompanied by our recently expanded salad and dessert bars. Our concept continues to evolve with customer needs and changes.

HISTORY: . . . .
Established in 1958; . . 1st Franchised in 1968
Company-Owned Units (As of 8/31/1992): 282
Franchised Units (As of 8/31/1992): 441
Total Units (As of 8/31/1992): 723
Projected New Units for 1993: 27
Distribution: US-639;Can-5;Overseas-79
  North America: . . . . 35 States
  Concentration: . . 273 in CA, 40 in FL, 28 AZ
Registered: . . . . .All
. . . .
Type Space: . . . . FS;~6,500 SF

FINANCIAL: Earnings Claim: . .No
Cash Investment: $350-500K
Total Investment: $1.5-2.0MM
Fees: Franchise - $30K
  Royalty: 4.5%, Advert: 4%
Contract Periods (Yrs.): 20
Area Development Agreement: Yes/5
Sub-Franchise Contract: . . . . .No
Expand in Territory: . . . . Yes
Passive Ownership: . . . Not Allowed
Encourage Conversions: . . . . Yes
Average # Employees: 8 FT, 40-50 PT

FRANCHISOR TRAINING/SUPPORT:
Financial Assistance Provided: . . . . . No
Site Selection Assistance: . . . . . . .Yes
Lease Negotiation Assistance: . . . .Yes
Co-operative Advertising: . . . . . . .Yes
Training: . . . . . 10 Wks. Training Unit, 2
  . . Wks. Internship,2 Wks. Headquarters
On-Going Support: C,D,E,G,H/ 310
EXPANSION PLANS:
US: . . . . Midwest and Northeast
Canada: . . . . .No
Overseas: . . . . .EUR, S. America

ST-HUBERT BAR B-Q

2 Place Laval, # 500
Laval, PQ H7N 5N6 CAN
TEL: (514) 668-4500
FAX: (514) 668-9037
Mr. Jacques Guilbert, Mgr. Fran. Ser

ST-HUBERT is a family-style restaurant, offering roasted chicken and Bar-B-Q ribs. Table service, take-out and home delivery in certain areas.

HISTORY: . . . .
Established in 1951; . . 1st Franchised in 1967
Company-Owned Units (As of 8/31/1992): . 22
Franchised Units (As of 8/31/1992): 81
Total Units (As of 8/31/1992): 103
Projected New Units for 1993: 0
Distribution: US-0;Can-103;Overseas-0
  North America: . . . . 3 Provinces
  Concentration: . . 82 in PQ, 18 in ON, 3 in NB
Registered: . . . .
. . . .
Type Space: . . . . FS;~5,200 SF

FINANCIAL: Earnings Claim: . .No
Cash Investment: $200-400K
Total Investment: . . . . . $.7-1.3MM
Fees: Franchise - $40K
  Royalty: 4%, Advert: 3%
Contract Periods (Yrs.): . . . 20/10
Area Development Agreement: Yes/10
Sub-Franchise Contract: . . . . .No
Expand in Territory: . . . . Yes
Passive Ownership: . . . Not Allowed
Encourage Conversions: . . . . Yes
Average # Employees: . 23 FT, 32 PT

FRANCHISOR TRAINING/SUPPORT:
Financial Assistance Provided: . . . . .No
Site Selection Assistance: . . . . . . .NA
Lease Negotiation Assistance: . . . .NA
Co-operative Advertising: . . . . . . .Yes
Training: . . . . 7 Wks. Montreal, PQ
. . . .
On-Going Support: b,c,d,e,G,H,I/ . . . 99
EXPANSION PLANS:
US: . . . . .No
Canada: . . . . .No
Overseas: . . . . No

STEAK EXPRESS

6465 Millcreek Dr., # 205
Mississauga, ON L5N 5R3 CAN
TEL: (800) 387-8335 (416) 567-4180
FAX: (416) 567-5355
Mr. George Kostopoulos, Dir. Fran.

STEAK EXPRESS - frozen, boxed food opens the entrepreneurial doors for potential franchisees from all trades and professions. Your quality products are selected from all the basic food categories, supplied by suppliers who service finer restaurants, packaged for convenience, placed in a user-friendly, self-service retail store.

HISTORY:	FINANCIAL: Earnings Claim: . Yes	FRANCHISOR TRAINING/SUPPORT:
Established in 1987; . . 1st Franchised in 1987	Cash Investment: $70K	Financial Assistance Provided: . . . Yes(I)
Company-Owned Units (As of 8/31/1992): . .2	Total Investment: $150K	Site Selection Assistance: . . . . . . .Yes
Franchised Units (As of 8/31/1992): 7	Fees: Franchise - $30K	Lease Negotiation Assistance: . . . . .Yes
Total Units (As of 8/31/1992): 9	Royalty: 2%, Advert: 3%	Co-operative Advertising: . . . . . . .Yes
Projected New Units for 1993: 6	Contract Periods (Yrs.): 10/5	Training: . . . . . . 10 Days Headquarters,
Distribution: US-0;Can-9;Overseas-0	Area Development Agreement: . .No	. . . .5 Days Various Stores, 5 Days Site
North America: . . . . .1 Province	Sub-Franchise Contract: . . . . .No	On-Going Support: B,C,D,E,F,G,H/ . . . 5
Concentration: . . . . 9 in ON	Expand in Territory: . . . . . . Yes	EXPANSION PLANS:
Registered:	Passive Ownership: . . . Discouraged	US: . . . . No
. . . .	Encourage Conversions: . . . . . NA	Canada: . . . . .Ontario
Type Space: . . . . SC, RM;~1,500 SF	Average # Employees: . . 1 FT, 2 PT	Overseas: . . . . No

STRAW HAT PIZZA

6400 Village Pkwy.
Dublin, CA 94568
TEL: (510) 829-1500
FAX: (510) 833-9215
Mr. Jack T. Wood, President

THE STRAW HAT Co-operative is unique because we are offering memberships, where the franchisees own the franchisor. The benefits are: you will be a member; you will have more flexibility in running your restaurant; you will pay very low assessment and marketing fees; you will receive a broad package of support services. Growth will come from new owners willing to devote considerable time, energy and resources to build a successful business.

HISTORY:	FINANCIAL: Earnings Claim: . .No	FRANCHISOR TRAINING/SUPPORT:
Established in 1987; . . 1st Franchised in 1987	Cash Investment: $50-100K	Financial Assistance Provided: . . . . No
Company-Owned Units (As of 8/31/1992): . .0	Total Investment: $50-400K	Site Selection Assistance: . . . . No
Franchised Units (As of 8/31/1992): 85	Fees: Franchise - $10K	Lease Negotiation Assistance: . . . . No
Total Units (As of 8/31/1992): 85	Royalty: 1%, Advert: 1/2%	Co-operative Advertising: . . . . . . .Yes
Projected New Units for 1993: 5	Contract Periods (Yrs.):	Training: . . . . 30 Days California
Distribution: US-85;Can-0;Overseas-0	Area Development Agreement: . .No	. . . .
North America: . . . . 4 States	Sub-Franchise Contract: . . . . .No	On-Going Support: C,D,E,F,G,H/ 4
Concentration: . . 76 in CA, 5 in NV, 3 in WA	Expand in Territory: . . . . . . Yes	EXPANSION PLANS:
Registered: . . . . CA	Passive Ownership: . . . Discouraged	US: . . . . Northwest
. . . .	Encourage Conversions: . . . . . Yes	Canada: . . . . .No
Type Space: . . . . . SF, SC;~1,100-3,600 SF	Average # Employees:4-8 FT, 10-20 PT	Overseas: . . . . No

SUBWAY SANDWICHES & SALADS

325 Bic Dr.
Milford, CT 06460
TEL: (800) 888-4848 (203) 877-4281
FAX: (203) 876-6688
Franchise Sales Dept.

The world's largest submarine sandwich chain is also the world's fastest-growing franchise! SUBWAY added over 5,000 units in the last 5 years, and now has over 7,000 units in all 50 states and 10 countries. Find out the reasons for this remarkable growth. Call today for a free franchise brochure.

HISTORY: . . . . .IFA, CFA	FINANCIAL: Earnings Claim: . .No	FRANCHISOR TRAINING/SUPPORT:
Established in 1965; . . 1st Franchised in 1974	Cash Investment: $24.1-40.2K	Financial Assistance Provided: . . .Yes(D)
Company-Owned Units (As of 8/31/1992): . .3	Total Investment: $48.2-80.4K	Site Selection Assistance: . . . . . . .Yes
Franchised Units (As of 8/31/1992): 6184	Fees: Franchise - $10K	Lease Negotiation Assistance: . . . . .Yes
Total Units (As of 8/31/1992): 6187	Royalty: 8%, Advert: 2.5%	Co-operative Advertising: . . . . .NA
Projected New Units for 1993: 1100	Contract Periods (Yrs.): 20/20	Training: . . . . 2 Wks. Headquarters
Distribution: . . US-5853;Can-297;Overseas-37	Area Development Agreement: . .No	. . . .
North America: . . . . 50 States,10 Provinces	Sub-Franchise Contract: . . . . . Yes	On-Going Support: C,D,E,F,G,h,I/ . . . 99
Concentration:	Expand in Territory: . . . . . . Yes	EXPANSION PLANS:
Registered: . . . . .All	Passive Ownership: . . . Discouraged	US: . . . .NE, Midwest, Pac. NW, N. CA
. . . .	Encourage Conversions: . . . . . Yes	Canada: . . . . .All Canada
Type Space: . . . . .SC;~1,000 SF	Average # Employees: . . 2 FT, 6 PT	Overseas: . . . . .Yes

TOBY'S GOODEATS

83 Bloor St. W., 2nd Fl.
Toronto, ON M5S 1M1 CAN
TEL: (416) 927-0323
FAX: (416) 927-7678
Mr. Jody Ortved

TOBY'S GOODEATS RESTAURANTS offer a broad-based menu, anchored by gourmet hamburgers, featuring table service in an atmosphere of comfort and nostalgia.

HISTORY:	FINANCIAL: Earnings Claim: . Yes	FRANCHISOR TRAINING/SUPPORT:
Established in 1976; . . 1st Franchised in 1990	Cash Investment: $150-200K	Financial Assistance Provided: . . . . .No
Company-Owned Units (As of 8/31/1992): . 12	Total Investment: $375-550K	Site Selection Assistance: . . . . . . .Yes
Franchised Units (As of 8/31/1992): 0	Fees: Franchise - $45K	Lease Negotiation Assistance: . . . .Yes
Total Units (As of 8/31/1992): 12	Royalty: 5%, Advert: 2%	Co-operative Advertising: . . . . . . .NA
Projected New Units for 1993: 4	Contract Periods (Yrs.): 10/5	Training: . . . . . . 10 Wks. In a Corporate
Distribution: US-0;Can-12;Overseas-0	Area Development Agreement: . Yes	. . . . .Store
North America: . . . . .1 Province	Sub-Franchise Contract: . . . . Yes	On-Going Support: a,C,D,E/ 12
Concentration: . . . . 12 in ON	Expand in Territory: . . . . . . Yes	EXPANSION PLANS:
Registered:	Passive Ownership: . . . Discouraged	US: . . . . .No
. . . .	Encourage Conversions: . . . . Yes	Canada: . . . . .All Canada
Type Space: . . . . . . SF, RM;~2,500 SF	Average # Employees: . 10 FT, 20 PT	Overseas: . . . . No

TODDLE HOUSE DINER

540 New Haven Ave., # 207
Milford, CT 06460
TEL: (800) 535-6387 (203) 876-6441
FAX: (203) 876-6444
Mr. Vin Forleo, Mgr. Fran. Sales

TODDLE HOUSE DINERS is a national 24-hour, full-service restaurant serving America's favorites. Perhaps the original diner concept chain, TODDLE HOUSE is also known as "America's 24-Hour Host."

HISTORY: . . . . IFA	FINANCIAL: Earnings Claim: . .No	FRANCHISOR TRAINING/SUPPORT:
Established in 1931; . . 1st Franchised in 1992	Cash Investment: . . . .$45-50K Min.	Financial Assistance Provided: . . . Yes(I)
Company-Owned Units (As of 8/31/1992): . 40	Total Investment: $42,9-219.2K	Site Selection Assistance: . . . . . . .No
Franchised Units (As of 8/31/1992): 0	Fees: Franchise - $18.5K	Lease Negotiation Assistance: . . . . .No
Total Units (As of 8/31/1992): 40	Royalty: 4%, Advert: 2-4%	Co-operative Advertising: . . . . . . .Yes
Projected New Units for 1993: 50	Contract Periods (Yrs.): . . .15/5/5/5	Training: . . . . 4 Wks. Headquarters
Distribution: US-40;Can-0;Overseas-0	Area Development Agreement: Yes/Var	. . . .
North America: . . . . 10 States	Sub-Franchise Contract: . . . . .No	On-Going Support: C,D,E,F,G,I/ 4
Concentration: . . 9 in LA, 7 in TX, 7 in TN	Expand in Territory: . . . . . Yes	EXPANSION PLANS:
Registered: . . . CA,FL,HI,IL,MD,MI,NY,OR	Passive Ownership: . . . Not Allowed	US: . . . . .All US
. . . . RI,WA,WI	Encourage Conversions: . . . . Yes	Canada: . . . . .No
Type Space: . . . . .SC;~1,300 SF	Average # Employees: . .10 FT, 5 PT	Overseas: . . . . No

TONY ROMA'S
- A PLACE FOR RIBS

10,000 North Central Expy., # 900
Dallas, TX 75231
TEL: (214) 891-7600
FAX: (214) 696-6321
Mr. Dale Ross, VP Fran. Dev.

TONY ROMA'S is the largest dinnerhouse chain specializing in BBQ ribs and chicken, famous onion ring loaf. We have a special niche in the industry. Great price/value relationship, high-quality food products, with full bar service. Also offering take-out and delivery.

HISTORY:	FINANCIAL: Earnings Claim: . .No	FRANCHISOR TRAINING/SUPPORT:
Established in 1972; . . 1st Franchised in 1979	Cash Investment: $300K	Financial Assistance Provided: . . . . .No
Company-Owned Units (As of 8/31/1992): . 17	Total Investment: $600-900K	Site Selection Assistance: . . . . . . .Yes
Franchised Units (As of 8/31/1992): 130	Fees: Franchise - $50K	Lease Negotiation Assistance: . . . .Yes
Total Units (As of 8/31/1992): 147	Royalty: 4%, Advert: 1/2%	Co-operative Advertising: . . . . . . .Yes
Projected New Units for 1993: 15	Contract Periods (Yrs.): . . . 20/20	Training: . . . . 6 Wks. Headquarters,
Distribution: US-122;Can-9;Overseas-16	Area Development Agreement: Yes/Var	. . . . 6 Wks. LA, 10-12 Days On-Site
North America: . . . . 16 States, 5 Provinces	Sub-Franchise Contract: . . . . .No	On-Going Support: C,D,E,F,G,H,I/ . . . 65
Concentration: . 47 in CA, 17 in FL, 11 in NY	Expand in Territory: . . . . . Yes	EXPANSION PLANS:
Registered: . . . . .All	Passive Ownership: . . . Discouraged	US: . . . . . Midwest, N'east & Southeast
. . . .	Encourage Conversions: . . . . Yes	Canada: . . . . .All Canada
Type Space: . FS, SC, Hotel;~4,500-5,500 SF	Average # Employees: . 50 FT, 10 PT	Overseas: . . . . .UK, SP

WESTERN SIZZLIN

17090 N. Dallas Pkwy.
Dallas, TX 75248
TEL: (800) 247-8325 (214) 407-9700
FAX: (214) 250-1205
Franchising Dept.

Family budget steakhouse that serves USDA choice steaks, chicken and fish entrees, also featuring multiple scattered food bars and a bakery.

HISTORY: . . . .
Established in 1962; . . 1st Franchised in 1966
Company-Owned Units (As of 8/31/1992): . .2
Franchised Units (As of 8/31/1992): 368
Total Units (As of 8/31/1992): 370
Projected New Units for 1993: 15
Distribution: US-364;Can-3;Overseas-3
North America: . . . . . 24 States, 1 Province
Concentration: . 38 in VA, 34 in AR, 34 in NC
Registered: . . . . MD
. . . .
Type Space: . . . .FS, SF, SC, RM;~7,000 SF

FINANCIAL: Earnings Claim: . . No
Cash Investment: $250K
Total Investment: . . . . . $.7-1.4MM
Fees: Franchise - $25K
Royalty: 3%, Advert: 1/2%
Contract Periods (Yrs.): 20/10
Area Development Agreement: Yes/Var
Sub-Franchise Contract: . . . . . Yes
Expand in Territory: . . . . . . .No
Passive Ownership: . . . Discouraged
Encourage Conversions: . . . . . Yes
Average # Employees: . 40 FT, 20 PT

FRANCHISOR TRAINING/SUPPORT:
Financial Assistance Provided: . . . . . No
Site Selection Assistance: . . . . .Yes
Lease Negotiation Assistance: . . . . .Yes
Co-operative Advertising: . . . . No
Training: . . . . . 10 Wks. Jackson, TN, 10
. . .Wks. Hillsborough, NC, 10 Wks. CO
On-Going Support: C,D,E,G,h,I/ 36
EXPANSION PLANS:
US: . . . . All US
Canada: . . . . .All Canada
Overseas: . . . . .Yes

SUPPLEMENTAL LISTING OF FRANCHISORS

ACROSS THE STREET RESTAURANTS . . . . United Founders Tower, #300, Oklahoma City, OK 73112
    Contact: President; Tel:
AMERICAN CAFE, THE . . . . 7911 Braygreen Rd., Laurel, MD 20707
    Contact: Mr. Regis T. Robbins, Dir. Fran.; Tel: (301) 497-6921
APPLEBEE'S/CREATIVE FOOD 'N FUN . . . . .400 Northcreek, # 700, 3715 N'side, Atlanta, GA 30327
    Contact: Mr. Steven R. Wolk, Dir. Fran.; Tel: (404) 261-7100
BIG BOY FAMILY RESTAURANT SYSTEMS . . . . 4199 Marcy St., Warren, MI 48091
    Contact: Mr. Ron Johnston; Tel: (313) 759-6000
BIG DADDY'S RESTAURANTS . . . . 2841 Cypress Creek Rd., Ft. Lauderdale, FL 33309
    Contact: President; Tel: (305) 531-8881
BJ'S KOUNTRY KITCHEN . . . . 4323 N. Golden State Blvd., # 5, Fresno, CA 93722
    Contact: Mr. Gary Honeycutt, Chairman; Tel: (209) 275-1981
BOLL WEEVIL SYSTEMS . . . . 9350 Trade Pl., # C, San Diego, CA 92126
    Contact: Mr. Sean Richardson; Tel: (619) 695-7072
BONANZA FAMILY RESTAURANTS . . . . . 8080 N. Central Expwy., #500, Box 65, Dallas, TX 75206
    Contact: Mr. Sam Wyly, Chairman; Tel: (800) 527-6832 (214) 891-8400
BRICK OVEN BEANERY . . . . .1007 E. Colfax Ave., Denver, CO 80218
    Contact: Mr. Ross Johnson, President; Tel:
BYERS RESTAURANTS . . . . 160 - 05 Rt. #110, Huntington Station, NY 11746
    Contact: Mr. Ed Byers, President; Tel: (516) 673-8815
CASEY'S . . . . .10 Kingsbridge Garden Circle, # 600, Mississauga, ON L5R 3K6   CAN
    Contact: Mr. Caz Wisniewski, EVP; Tel: (416) 568-0000
CASWELL'S NEW ENGLAND SEAFOOD . . . . 15 Engle St., # 302, Englewood, NJ 07631
    Contact: Mr. John Sterns, Fran. Sales Dir.; Tel: (800) 332-2229 (201) 871-0370
CAZ'S FISH & CHIP SHOPPE/SEA GRILLE . . . 481 N. Service Rd. W., # 16, Oakville, ON L6M 2V6   CAN
    Contact: Mr. Douglas E. Casimiri, President; Tel: (416) 847-7424 C
CEDAR RIVER SEAFOOD RESTAURANTS . . . . 11570 San Jose Blvd., # 12, Jacksonville, FL 32223
    Contact: Mr. Crawford Johnston, President; Tel: (904) 268-7827
CHAMPIONS SPORTS BAR . . . . .200 N. Glebe Rd., # 808, Arlington, VA 22203
    Contact: Mr. Stan Levy, VP; Tel: (703) 241-1000
CHECKERS RESTAURANTS . . . . 3001 Division St., # 100, Metairie, LA 70002
    Contact: President; Tel: (504) 885-7324
CHELSEA STREET PUBS . . . . 8802 Shoal Creek Blvd., Austin, TX 78766
    Contact: Mr. Norman Crohn, President; Tel: (800) 252-9227 (512) 454-7739
CHILI'S GRILL & BAR . . . . 6820 LBJ Fwy., # 200, Dallas, TX 75240
    Contact: Mr. Norman Brinker, President; Tel: (214) 770-9501
CLASSIC QUICHE CAFE . . . . 330 Queen Anne Rd., Teaneck, NJ 07666
    Contact: Ms. Sandra Cappola, President; Tel: (201) 692-0150 C

COCO'S 17461 Derian Ave., # 200, Irvine, CA 92714 . . . .
    Contact: Mr. Kenneth Harris, President; Tel: (800) 221-6300 (714) 757-7932
COUNTRY MANOR RESTAURANTS . . . . . . 6975 Pronway Ave., NW, North Canton, OH 44720
    Contact: President; Tel: (216) 499-0070
COUNTRYS KITCHEN (CANADA) . . . . 10909 Jasper Ave., # 1101, Edmonton, AB T5J 3L9   CAN
    Contact: Mr. V. Lorne Humphreys; Tel: (403) 429-2663
CUCOS MEXICAN RESTAURANTE . . . . .3009 25th St., Metairie, LA 70002
    Contact: Mr. Vincent Liuzza, President; Tel: (800) 888-2826 (504) 835-0306 C
DANVER'S INTERNATIONAL . . . . P. O. Box 41379, Memphis, TN 38104
    Contact: Mr. T. Berry, Fran. Dir.; Tel: (901) 725-6450
DENNY'S . . . . 3345 Michelsen, # 200, Irvine, CA 92715
    Contact: Ms. Lynette McKee, Dir. Fran. Dev.; Tel: (714) 251-5000
DINING CONCEPTS . . . . 5665 N. Blackstone, Fresno, CA 93710
    Contact: President; Tel: (209) 252-7344
DIXIE LEE CHICKEN & SEAFOOD . . . . P. O. Box 5239, Massena, NY 13662
    Contact: President; Tel:
DOMINO'S PIZZA . . . . .P. O. Box 997, Ann Arbor, MI 48106
    Contact: Mr. Gary McCausland, VP; Tel: (313) 930-3614
DON CARLOS MEXICAN RESTAURANTE . . . . . . P. O. Box 718, Dearborn Heights, MI 48217
    Contact: Mr. Carlos Shaffran; Tel: (313) 427-6800
DRUTHER'S INTERNAT'L./COOKER CONCEPTS . . . . . 2440 Grinstead Dr., Louisville, KY 40204
    Contact: Mr. Thomas S. Hensley, President; Tel: (502) 458-0040
EAST SIDE MARIO'S . . . . . . .10 Kingsbridge Garden Circle, # 600, Mississauga, ON L5R 3K6   CAN
    Contact: Mr. Caz Wisniewski, EVP; Tel: (416) 568-0000
EAT AT JOE'S DINER . . . . P. O. Box 500, Yonkers, NY 10704
    Contact: President; Tel: (914) 337-6584
EL CHICO . . . . 12200 Stemmons Fwy., # 100, Dallas, TX 75234
    Contact: Mr. Wes Jablonski, Dir. Fran.; Tel: (800) 877-1985 (214) 241-5500
ELEPHANT AND CASTLE, THE . . . . P. O. Box 10240, Pacific Centre, Vancouver, BC V7Y 1E7   CAN
    Contact: Mr. Jeffrey M. Barnett, Managing Dir.; Tel: (604) 684-6451
ELMER'S PANCAKE & STEAK HOUSE . . . . P. O. Box 16595, Portland, OR 97216
    Contact: Mr. Herman Goldberg, President; Tel: (800) 325-5188 (503) 252-1485
FLAP JACK SHACK . . . . 3980 U.S. 31 S., Traverse City, MI 49684
    Contact: Ms. Virginia Burley, President; Tel: (616) 941-8280
FORTE RESTAURANTS . . . . 265 High St., # 600, Morgantown, WV 26505
    Contact: President; Tel: (304) 292-2035
FRANKIE'S FAMILY RESTAURANTS . . . . 643 Lakewood Rd., Waterbury, CT 06704
    Contact: Mr. Frank Caiazzo, President; Tel: (203) 756-2935
FRED P. OTT'S BAR & GRILL . . . 4210 Shawnee Mission Pkwy., # 300A, Shawnee Mission, KS 66205
    Contact: Mr. Avery Murray, VP Fran.; Tel: (913) 384-4700
FRESHER COOKER, THE . . . . P. O. Box 4999, Louisville, KY 42204
    Contact: President; Tel:
GARFIELD'S RESTAURANT & PUB . . .3240 W. Britton Rd., Bldg. 2S,# 202, Oklahoma City, OK 73120
    Contact: Mr. Vincent F. Orza, President; Tel: (405) 755-3607
GOLDEN EGG OMELET HOUSE . . . . 807 Grant Ave., Novato, CA 94947
    Contact: President; Tel: (415) 897-7707
GOLDEN GREEK RESTAURANTS . . . . 499 NW 70th Ave., # 120, Plantation, FL 33317
    Contact: Mr. Greg Lane; Tel: (305) 587-1581
GOOD TIMES RESTAURANTS . . . . .2121 30th St., Boulder, CO 80301
    Contact: Mr. Gerry Northrup, Dir. Fran.; Tel: (303) 449-3441
GRANNY FEELGOOD'S NATURAL FOODS REST. . . . . . . 190 SE 1st Ave., Miami, FL 33131
    Contact: Mr. Irving Fields; Tel: (305) 358-6233
GREEK'S PIZZERIA . . . . 1600 University Ave., Muncie, IN 47303
    Contact: Mr. Chris Karamesines; Tel: (317) 284-4900
GREENSTREETS HAMBURGER GRILL & BAR . . . . . . 72 Garden Dr., Burnsville, MN 55337
    Contact: Mr. Gordon Weber; Tel: (612) 934-1703
H. R. H. DUMPLIN'S . . . . .112 E. Center St., P. O. Box 1668, Sikeston, MO 63801
    Contact: Mr. David A. York, President; Tel: (314) 471-8006
HACIENDA MEXICAN RESTAURANT . . . . 3302 Mishawaka Ave., Mishawaka, IN 46615
    Contact: Mr. Dean A. Goodwin, VP Ops.; Tel: (800) 541-3227 (219) 234-3700
HARVEY'S RESTAURANTS/SWISS CHALET . . . . . . 230 Bloor St., W., Toronto, ON M5S 1T8   CAN
    Contact: Ms. Irene Fong; Tel: (416) 926-4571
HENPECKERS . . . . 11098 Biscayne Blvd., # 403, Miami, FL 33161
    Contact: Mr. Donn R. Wilson, President; Tel: (800) 888-7888 (305) 895-9398
HUDDLE HOUSE . . . . .P. O. Box 906, Scottsdale, GA 30079
    Contact: Mr. Ed Bloom; Tel: (800) 476-4833 (404) 377-8131

INTERNATIONAL HOUSE OF PANCAKES/IHOP . . . . 525 N. Brand Blvd., 3rd Fl., Glendale, CA 91203
    Contact: Mr. Richard Herzer, President; Tel: (818) 240-6055
J. T. CROC 'N BERRYS BAR & GRILL . . . . .3333 S. Pasadena Ave., S. Pasadena, FL 33702
    Contact: Mr. Jud Scott; Tel: (813) 360-6931
KETTLE RESTAURANTS . . . . P.O. Box 2964, Houston, TX 77252
    Contact: Mr. Philip Weaver, VP Fran.; Tel: (713) 524-3464
LAZZARINO'S RESTAURANTS . . . . .362 Turnpike St., Stoughton, MA 02072
    Contact: President; Tel:
LE PEEP RESTAURANTS . . . . 4 W. Dry Creek Circle, # 201, Littleton, CO 80210
    Contact: Mr. Anthony E. Doyle, SVP Fran. Dev.; Tel: (303) 730-6300
LIL' DUFFER FAMILY RESTAURANTS . . . . . . 2208 Hancock, P.O. Box 368, Bellevue, NE 68005
    Contact: President; Tel: (402) 291-2040
LOG JAM RESTAURANT . . . . P. O. Box 236, Spring Lake, MI 49456
    Contact: President; Tel: (616) 842-5225
LOSURDO FOODS . . . . 20 Owens Rd., Hackensack, NJ 07601
    Contact: President; Tel:
LOVE'S GREAT RIB RESTAURANTS . . . . . . 3195-C Airport Loop Dr., # B, Costa Mesa, CA 92626
    Contact: Mr. Ronald C. Mesker, President; Tel: (714) 435-3550
MACAYO MEXICAN RESTAURANT . . . . 4001 N. Central Ave., Phoenix, AZ 85012
    Contact: Mr. Stephen Johnson, President; Tel: (800) 622-4797 (602) 264-1831
MANCINI'S RESTAURANT . . . . R. D. 1, Box 383X, Uniontown, PA 15401
    Contact: President; Tel: (412) 438-2810
MARITA'S CANTINA . . . . 210 Carnegie Center, # 103, Princeton, NJ 08540
    Contact: Mr. Mitchell Landis, President; Tel: (609) 452-2838
MAURICE'S GOURMET BBQ PIGGIE PARK 1600 Charleston Hwy., P. O. Box 6847, W. Columbia, SC 29171
    Contact: Mr. Maurice Bessinger, President; Tel: (800) MAURICE (803) 791-5887
MIFFY'S RESTAURANT . . . . Box 540, Don Mills, ON M3C 2T6   CAN
    Contact: Mr. Ernest Ng, Marketing Manager; Tel: (416) 587-3001
NOODLE DELIGHT . . . . .85 W. Wilmot St., # 6, Richmond Hill, ON L4B 1K7   CAN
    Contact: Mr. Alfred P. Lam, CEO; Tel: (416) 886-9700 (416) 886-9701
NUMERO UNO PIZZA & ITALIAN RESTAURANTS . . . 8214 Van Nuys Blvd., Panorama City, CA 91402
    Contact: Mr. Ronald J. Gelet, President; Tel: (818) 781-4448
O'TOOLE'S ROADHOUSE RESTAURANTS . . . . 585 Aero Dr., Buffalo, NY 14225
    Contact: Mr. Stephen F. Leous, Dir. Fran.; Tel: (716) 633-9771
O'TOOLES ROADHOUSE (CANADA) . . . . .70 Galaxy Blvd., Etobicoke, ON M9W 4Y6   CAN
    Contact: Mr. Bruce Dimytosh; Tel: (416) 674-0016
OYSTER KRACKER SEAFOOD/KRACKER SEAFOOD . 7515 NCNB Bank Tower, # 300, Dallas, TX 75231
    Contact: Mr. William H. Hensley, Co-Pres.; Tel: (214) 691-3452
PANCHO'S MEXICAN RESTAURANT . . . . 2881 Lamar Ave., Memphis, TN 38114
    Contact: President; Tel:
PANNEKOEKEN HUIS FAMILY RESTAURANTS . . . . 6517 Cecilia Circle, Edina, MN 55435
    Contact: Ms. Jeannie O'Neel, Fran. Sales/Mktg.; Tel: (612) 944-8090
PANTRY FAMILY RESTAURANTS, THE . . . . # 202 - 15463 104th Ave., Surrey, BC V3R 1N9   CAN
    Contact: Mr. Mike Hoffmann, President; Tel: (604) 584-4115
PAT AND MARIO'S . . . . .10 Kingsbridge Garden Circle, # 600, Mississauga, ON L5R 3K6   CAN
    Contact: Mr. Caz Wisniewski, EVP; Tel: (416) 568-0000
PEWTER MUG . . . . 207 Frankfort Ave., Cleveland, OH 44113
    Contact: Mr. Robert Wertheim; Tel: (216) 621-3636
PEWTER POT FAMILY RESTAURANTS . . . . .P.O. Box 1267, Salem, NH 03079
    Contact: Mr. Bruce R. Butterworth, President; Tel: (617) 272-6360
PHILADELPHIA MIKE'S RESTAURANT . . . . 7732 Wisconsin Ave., Bethesda, MD 20814
    Contact: President; Tel: (301) 565-0103
PIZZA HUT . . . . 9111 E. Douglas, P.O. Box 428, Wichita, KS 67201
    Contact: Mr. Larry Whitt; Tel: (316) 681-9805
PIZZA HUT (CANADA)/TACO BELL (CAN) . . . . 10 Four Seasons Pl., # 500, Etobicoke, ON M9B 6H7   CAN
    Contact: Mr. Roland Walton; Tel: (416) 626-8011
PIZZERIA UNO . . . . 100 Charles Park Rd., Boston, MA 02132
    Contact: Mr. Greggory P. Keenan, VP Dev.; Tel: (617) 323-9200
POUR LA FRANCE! CAFE & BAKERY . . . . 411 E. Main St., Aspen, CO 81611
    Contact: Mr. John Bennett; Tel: (303) 920-1152
PRIME RESTAURANT SYSTEMS . . . . 10 Kingsbridge Garden Cir., # 600, Mississauga, ON L5R 3K6   CAN
    Contact: Mr. C. W. Wisniewski; Tel: (416) 568-0000
PUDLEY'S BURGER/SALOON . . . . 390 El Camino Real, Belmont, CA 94002
    Contact: Mr. Richard Mazzoni; Tel: (415) 593-1144
RALPH & KACOO RESTAURANT . . . . .6110 Blue Bonnet Blvd., Baton Rouge, LA 70809
    Contact: President; Tel:

RESTAURANT ENTERPRISES GROUP . . . . .17461 Derian Ave., Irvine, CA 92714
    Contact: Mr. Kenneth Harris, President; Tel: (714) 757-7932
REX FRANCHISING SYSTEMS . . . . 2007 W. Houston, Broken Arrow, OK 74012
    Contact: Ms. Dollie McFarland, President; Tel: (800) (918) 258-0061
SERGIO'S MEXICAN RESTAURANT . . . . 16 Broadway, # 212, Fargo, ND 59102
    Contact: President; Tel: (701) 237-5151
SHOWBIZ PIZZA PLACE / CHUCK E. CHEESE . . . 4441 W. Airport Fwy., Box 152077, Irving, TX 75015
    Contact: Mr. Gregory Walker, Dir. Fran. Dev.; Tel: (214) 258-8507
SKIPPER JACK'S . . . . 1507 W. Beverly Blvd., Montebello, CA 90640
    Contact: Mr. Michael C. Lao, CEO; Tel: (213) 727-7187
SMITTY'S PANCAKE HOUSE . . . .# 600 - 501 18th Ave. SW, Calgary, AB T2S 0C7   CAN
    Contact: Mr. Walter Chan, President; Tel: (403) 229-3838
SONNY'S REAL PIT BAR B Q . . . . 3631 SW Archer Rd., Gainesville, FL 32608
    Contact: Mr. Frank Scharf, Dir. Mktg.; Tel: (904) 376-9721
SOUP AND SALAD SYSTEMS/SOUP EXCHANGE . . . .2645 Financial Ct., # A, San Diego, CA 92117
    Contact: Ms. Susan Menne; Tel: (619) 581-6700
SPOONS GRILL & BAR . . . . 4410 El Camino Real, # 201, Los Altos, CA 94022
    Contact: Ms. Tish Gilbert; Tel: (415) 941-6400
STARK'S FAMILY RESTAURANTS . . . . . E. Rusk & Austin Sts., Box 1990, Jacksonville, TX 75766
    Contact: President; Tel:
STASH & STELLA'S . . . . 585 Aero Dr., Buffalo, NY 14225
    Contact: Mr. Stephen F. Leous, Dir. Fran.; Tel: (716) 633-9771
STEAK & BURGER RESTAURANTS . . . . 230 Bloor St. W., Toronto, ON M5S 1T8   CAN
    Contact: Ms. Irene Fong; Tel: (416) 962-4571
STRINGS - THE PASTA PLACE . . . . .11344 Coloma Rd., # 545, Gold River, CA 95670
    Contact: Mr. Terry W. Odneal, Dir. Fran. Sales; Tel: (800) 464-0646 (916) 635-3990
T.G.I. FRIDAY'S / DALTS . . . . P.O. Box 809062, Dallas, TX 75380
    Contact: Mr. Wallace Doolin, SVP; Tel: (214) 450-5400
TEXAS LOOSEY'S CHILI PARLOR & SALOON . . . . . . P. O. Box 1697, Temecula, CA 92390
    Contact: Mr. Ron Walton, President; Tel: (714) 676-0323
TEXAS TOM'S . . . . .P.O. Box 4592, Kansas City, MO 64124
    Contact: President; Tel: (816) 214-5592
UNCLE BARNEY'S FAMILY RESTAURANTS . . . . Plaza 94, Hudson, WI 54016
    Contact: President; Tel:
UNCLE TONY'S PIZZA & PASTA . . . . 1800 Post Rd., Warwick, RI 02886
    Contact: Mr. Edward Carosi, President; Tel: (401) 738-1321
VILLAGE INN RESTAURANT . . . . 400 W. 48th Ave., Denver, CO 80216
    Contact: Mr. Robert Kaltenbach, EVP; Tel: (303) 296-2121
WAFFLETOWN U.S.A. . . . . 3110 High St., Portsmouth, VA 23707
    Contact: Mr. George Proferes, President; Tel: (804) 399-6612
WARD'S RESTAURANTS . . . . 7 Professional Pkwy., # 103, Hattiesburg, MS 39402
    Contact: Mr. Kenneth Hrdlica, President; Tel: (800) 748-9273 (601) 584-9273
WAREHOUSE RESTAURANT . . . . 4519 Admiralty Way, # 206, Marina del Rey, CA 90292
    Contact: President; Tel: (213) 823-0919
WESTERN STEER FAMILY STEAKHOUSE/WSMP . . .WSMP Dr., P. O. Box 399, Claremont, NC 28610
    Contact: Mr. Kenneth L. Moser, VP Fran.; Tel: (800) 438-9207 (704) 459-7626
YOUR PLACE RESTAURANTS . . . . 2133 Lincoln Hwy. E., Lancaster, PA 17538
    Contact: Mr. Joe Egenrieder, Jr.; Tel: (717) 393-5622

CHAPTER 22

FURNITURE / APPLIANCE
REFINISHING AND REPAIR

BATCREST

2425 S. Progress Dr.
Salt Lake City, UT 84119
TEL: (800) 826-6790 (801) 972-1110
FAX: (801) 977-0328
Mr. Lloyd Peterson, SVP Mktg./Sales

Now you can discover there is a lot of money in bathtubs, sinks and tiles. Homeowners are constantly making changes and improving their homes, and the bathroom in the #1 place to start. BATHCREST offers you a unique, profitable business opportunity that is low risk, low start-up and has very little competition. You'll save the homeowner up to 80% of conventional replacement.

HISTORY: . . . .
Established in 1979; . . 1st Franchised in 1985
Company-Owned Units (As of 8/31/1992): . .1
Franchised Units (As of 8/31/1992): 172
Total Units (As of 8/31/1992): 173
Projected New Units for 1993: 24
Distribution: US-164;Can-9;Overseas-0
 North America: . . . . 40 States, 3 Provinces
 Concentration: . . 24 in CA, 12 in NJ, 10 in FL
Registered: . . . . NY
. . . .
Type Space: . . . . NA;~ SF

FINANCIAL: Earnings Claim: . .No
Cash Investment: . . . .$
Total Investment: $10-35K
Fees: Franchise - $3.5K
 Royalty: 0%, Advert: 0%
Contract Periods (Yrs.): . . On-Going
Area Development Agreement: . .No
Sub-Franchise Contract: . . . . . .No
Expand in Territory: . . . . .No
Passive Ownership: . . . . . . .Allowed
Encourage Conversions: . . . . . NA
Average # Employees: . . 3 FT, 1 PT

FRANCHISOR TRAINING/SUPPORT:
Financial Assistance Provided: . . . Yes(I)
Site Selection Assistance: . . . . .NA
Lease Negotiation Assistance: . . . . .NA
Co-operative Advertising: . . . . .NA
Training: . . . . 1 Wk. Headquarters
. . . .
On-Going Support: b,C,G,H,I/ 12
EXPANSION PLANS:
US: . . . . .All US
Canada: . . . . .Yes
Overseas: . . . . No

CREATIVE COLORS INTERNATIONAL

5550 W. 175th St.
Tinley Park, IL 60477
TEL: (800) 933-2656 (708) 614-7786 C
FAX: (708) 614-6685
Ms. JoAnn Foster, President

Mobile units provide repair and color restoration in all markets having leather, fabric, vinyl, plastics and fiberglass.

HISTORY:	FINANCIAL: Earnings Claim: . Yes	FRANCHISOR TRAINING/SUPPORT:
Established in 1990; . . 1st Franchised in 1991	Cash Investment: $17.5K	Financial Assistance Provided: . . . Yes(I)
Company-Owned Units (As of 8/31/1992): . .1	Total Investment: $40-55K	Site Selection Assistance: . . . . . . .NA
Franchised Units (As of 8/31/1992): 9	Fees: Franchise - $17.5K	Lease Negotiation Assistance: . . . . .NA
Total Units (As of 8/31/1992): 10	Royalty: 6%, Advert: 0%	Co-operative Advertising: . . . . . . .Yes
Projected New Units for 1993: 8	Contract Periods (Yrs.): 5/5/5/5	Training: . . . . 2 Wks. Home Office,
Distribution: US-10;Can-0;Overseas-0	Area Development Agreement: . .No	. . . . Up to 2 Wks. Territory
North America: . . . . 4 States	Sub-Franchise Contract: . . . . . .No	On-Going Support: A,B,C,D,E,G,H,I/ . . 5
Concentration: . . . . .5 in IL, 3 in IN, 1 in MI	Expand in Territory: . . . . Yes	EXPANSION PLANS:
Registered: . . . . IL,IN,MI,NY	Passive Ownership: . . . . . .Allowed	US: . . . . Eastern US and Southeast
. . . .	Encourage Conversions: . . . . . NA	Canada: . . . . .No
Type Space: . . . . Mobile Unit;~NA SF	Average # Employees: . . . . . .1 FT	Overseas: . . . . No

DR. VINYL & ASSOCIATES

13665 E. 42nd Terrace South
Independence, MO 64055
TEL: (800) 531-6600 (816) 478-0800
FAX: (816) 478-3065
Mr. Tom Buckley, Jr., President

Vinyl, leather and velour, fabric repair and coloring, auto windshield repair, dashboard and hard plastic repair, vinyl and striping and protective molding to new and used car dealers.

HISTORY:	FINANCIAL: Earnings Claim: . .No	FRANCHISOR TRAINING/SUPPORT:
Established in 1972; . . 1st Franchised in 1980	Cash Investment: $15-40K	Financial Assistance Provided: . . .Yes(D)
Company-Owned Units (As of 8/31/1992): . .6	Total Investment: $25-40K	Site Selection Assistance: . . . . . . .NA
Franchised Units (As of 8/31/1992): 100	Fees: Franchise - $20K	Lease Negotiation Assistance: . . . . .NA
Total Units (As of 8/31/1992): 106	Royalty: 4-7%, Advert: 1%	Co-operative Advertising: . . . . . . .Yes
Projected New Units for 1993: 15	Contract Periods (Yrs.): 10/10	Training: . . . . . 2 Wks. Kansas City, MO,
Distribution: US-103;Can-1;Overseas-2	Area Development Agreement: Yes/10	. . . . 1 Wk. Territory
North America: . . . . 28 States	Sub-Franchise Contract: . . . . . Yes	On-Going Support: A,B,C,D,G,H,I/ . . 12
Concentration: . . . 15 in MO, 8 in IL, 6 in NE	Expand in Territory: . . . . Yes	EXPANSION PLANS:
Registered: . . . CA,FL,HI,IL,IN,MD,MI,MN	Passive Ownership: . . . . . .Allowed	US: . . . . .All US
. . . . NY,OR,VA,WA,WI	Encourage Conversions: . . . . . NA	Canada: . . . . .All Canada
Type Space: . . . . ;~ SF	Average # Employees: . . . . . .1 FT	Overseas: . . . . . SP, UK, FR, JA

MARBLE RENEWAL

6805 W. 12th St.
Little Rock, AR 72204
TEL: (501) 663-2080 C
FAX: (501) 663-2401
Mr. Gary Perritt, President

Restoration and continuing maintenance of marble, granite, other polished stones and hardwood floors, using proprietary processes, chemicals and equipment. Now franchising nationwide and internationally in North American and Caribbean.

HISTORY:	FINANCIAL: Earnings Claim: . .No	FRANCHISOR TRAINING/SUPPORT:
Established in 1989; . . 1st Franchised in 1989	Cash Investment: $30-44K	Financial Assistance Provided: . . . Yes(I)
Company-Owned Units (As of 8/31/1992): . .1	Total Investment: $44-97K	Site Selection Assistance: . . . . . . .NA
Franchised Units (As of 8/31/1992): 15	Fees: Franchise - $17.5K	Lease Negotiation Assistance: . . . . .No
Total Units (As of 8/31/1992): 16	Royalty: 8,6,5%, Advert: 0%	Co-operative Advertising: . . . . . . .Yes
Projected New Units for 1993: 35	Contract Periods (Yrs.): 10/10	Training: . . . . 3 Days Headquarters,
Distribution: US-15;Can-1;Overseas-0	Area Development Agreement: . .No	. . . . 3-4 Days On-Site
North America:	Sub-Franchise Contract: . . . . . .No	On-Going Support: b,D,E,G,h/ 5
Concentration:	Expand in Territory: . . . . . . .No	EXPANSION PLANS:
Registered: . . . . FL,MI,OR,WA	Passive Ownership: . . . Not Allowed	US: . . . . . All Exc. Where Not Register.
. . . .	Encourage Conversions: . . . . . .No	Canada: . . . . All Exc. Alberta
Type Space: . . . . ;~ SF	Average # Employees: . . 2 FT, 2 PT	Overseas: . . . Caribbean, Bermuda

MIRACLE METHOD

3732 W. Century Blvd., # 6
Inglewood, CA 90303
TEL: (800) 444-8827 (310) 671-4995
FAX: (310) 671-1146
Mr. Richard Crites, President

Homes, apartments and hotels need improvements to their fixtures and tile in bathrooms and kitchens. Replacement of these fixtures costs thousands, refinishing them costs only hundreds! Plus, 30-50% of all fixtures are damaged during installation by the contractors and need repair. YOU can fulfill this existing demand in your area.

HISTORY:	FINANCIAL: Earnings Claim: . .No	FRANCHISOR TRAINING/SUPPORT:
Established in 1978; . . 1st Franchised in 1979	Cash Investment: $18-21K	Financial Assistance Provided: . . .Yes(D)
Company-Owned Units (As of 8/31/1992): . .0	Total Investment: $18-21K	Site Selection Assistance: . . . . . . .NA
Franchised Units (As of 8/31/1992): 128	Fees: Franchise - $11.5K	Lease Negotiation Assistance: . . . . .NA
Total Units (As of 8/31/1992): 128	Royalty: 5-7.5%, Advert: 3%	Co-operative Advertising: . . . . .NA
Projected New Units for 1993: 12	Contract Periods (Yrs.): 5/5	Training: . . . . . . 2-3 Wks. Headquarters,
Distribution: US-58;Can-0;Overseas-70	Area Development Agreement: . .No	. . . . 1-2 Wks. On-Site
North America: . . . . 16 States	Sub-Franchise Contract: . . . . Yes	On-Going Support: C,d,E,G,H,I/ 8
Concentration: . . 32 in CA, 3 in MA, 3 in TX	Expand in Territory: . . . . . . .No	EXPANSION PLANS:
Registered: . . . . CA,OR,RI,WA	Passive Ownership: . . . Not Allowed	US: . . . . All US
. . . .	Encourage Conversions: . . . . . Yes	Canada: . . . . .All Canada
Type Space: . . . . Home Based;~ SF	Average # Employees: . . . . . .4 FT	Overseas: . . . . Yes

PERMA-GLAZE

1638 S. Research Loop Rd., # 160
Tucson, AZ 85710
TEL: (800) 332-7397 (602) 722-9718
FAX: (602) 296-4393
Mr. Dale R. Young, President

Specialize in restoration/refinishing of bathroom/kitchen fixtures, wall tile, appliances, etc. Refinishable materials include porcelain, fiberglass, acrylic, cultured marble, formica, appliances, shower enclosures, most building materials. Decorative colors available. All work under warranty, residential or commercial. Services include chip repairs, fiberglass/acrylic repairs.

HISTORY: . . . . IFA	FINANCIAL: Earnings Claim: . .No	FRANCHISOR TRAINING/SUPPORT:
Established in 1978; . . 1st Franchised in 1981	Cash Investment: $27.5K	Financial Assistance Provided: . . . Yes(I)
Company-Owned Units (As of 8/31/1992): . .1	Total Investment: $29.5K	Site Selection Assistance: . . . . . . .Yes
Franchised Units (As of 8/31/1992): 157	Fees: Franchise - $29.5K	Lease Negotiation Assistance: . . . . .NA
Total Units (As of 8/31/1992): 158	Royalty: 0%, Advert: 0%	Co-operative Advertising: . . . . No
Projected New Units for 1993: 35	Contract Periods (Yrs.): 10/10	Training: . . . . . . 5-6 Days Headquarters,
Distribution: US-141;Can-10;Overseas-7	Area Development Agreement: . .No	. . . . . . 3 Days in Field, On Location
North America: . . . . 35 States, 2 Provinces	Sub-Franchise Contract: . . . . .No	On-Going Support: B,C,D,E,F,G,H,I/ . . . 6
Concentration: . . 23 in CA, 7 in TX, 6 in WA	Expand in Territory: . . . . . . Yes	EXPANSION PLANS:
Registered: . . . . All States	Passive Ownership: . . . . . .Allowed	US: . . . . All US
. . . .	Encourage Conversions: . . . . . Yes	Canada: . . . . .All Canada
Type Space: . . . . Home Based;~ SF	Average # Employees: . . . . . .2 FT	Overseas: . . . . Yes

PJR TUB & TILE RESTORATION

3398 Sanford Dr.
Marietta, GA 30066
TEL: (404) 429-0232
FAX:
Mr. Larry Stevens, President

Restore ugly, stained tub and tile, no spraying, no odors. Can use the same day. Approved by major hotel chains.

HISTORY:	FINANCIAL: Earnings Claim: . .No	FRANCHISOR TRAINING/SUPPORT:
Established in 1973; . . 1st Franchised in 1973	Cash Investment: . . . .$	Financial Assistance Provided: . . . . .Yes
Company-Owned Units (As of 8/31/1992): . .1	Total Investment: $1.3-3.0K	Site Selection Assistance: . . . . . . .Yes
Franchised Units (As of 8/31/1992): 54	Fees: Franchise - . . . .$	Lease Negotiation Assistance: . . . . .NA
Total Units (As of 8/31/1992): 55	Royalty: 20% Chem, Advert: . . 5%	Co-operative Advertising: . . . . .Yes
Projected New Units for 1993:	Contract Periods (Yrs.):	Training: . . . .
Distribution: US-54;Can-1;Overseas-0	Area Development Agreement: . .No	
North America: . . . . . 25 States, 1 Province	Sub-Franchise Contract: . . . . . Yes	On-Going Support: B,C,D,G,I/ 3
Concentration: . . . .4 in FL, 4 in VA, 3 in TN	Expand in Territory: . . . . Yes	EXPANSION PLANS:
Registered:	Passive Ownership: . . . Discouraged	US: . . . . All US
. . . .	Encourage Conversions: . . . . . Yes	Canada: . . . . .All Canada
Type Space: . . . . NA;~ SF	Average # Employees: . . . . . .2 FT	Overseas: . . . . No

PROFUSION SYSTEMS

2851 S. Parker Rd., # 650
Aurora, CO 80014
TEL: (800) 777-3873 (303) 337-1949
FAX: (303) 337-0790
Mr. David Lowe, Fran. Sales

Plastic, leather, vinyl, velour and formica/laminate repair service that works with hotels, restaurants, airports, hospitals and any business that has plastic, vinyl, leather or formica/laminate furniture. The unique repair system produces un-noticeable repairs with a lifetime warranty.

HISTORY:	FINANCIAL: Earnings Claim: . .No	FRANCHISOR TRAINING/SUPPORT:
Established in 1980; . . 1st Franchised in 1982	Cash Investment: $15-30K	Financial Assistance Provided: . . .Yes(D)
Company-Owned Units (As of 8/31/1992): . .0	Total Investment: $20-40K	Site Selection Assistance: . . . . .NA
Franchised Units (As of 8/31/1992): 184	Fees: Franchise - $20.5K	Lease Negotiation Assistance: . . . .
Total Units (As of 8/31/1992): 184	Royalty: 6%, Advert: 0%	Co-operative Advertising: . . . . .No
Projected New Units for 1993: 50	Contract Periods (Yrs.): 10/10	Training: . . . . 9 Days Headquarters,
Distribution: . . . US-149;Can-10;Overseas-25	Area Development Agreement: . .No	. . . . 4 Days Franchisee Site
North America: . . . . . . 35 States, 4 Provinces	Sub-Franchise Contract: . . . . .No	On-Going Support: A,B,C,D,F,G,H,I/ . .9
Concentration: . . .11 in CA, 7 in CO, 7 in OH	Expand in Territory: . . . . . . Yes	EXPANSION PLANS:
Registered: . . . . . All States Exc. ND & VA	Passive Ownership: . . . Discouraged	US: . . . . All US
. . . .	Encourage Conversions: . . . . .No	Canada: . . . . .All Canada
Type Space: . . . . ;~ SF	Average # Employees: . . 3 FT, 1 PT	Overseas: . . . . .Yes

RE-BATH

1055 S. Country Club Dr., Bldg. 2
Mesa, AZ 85210
TEL: (800) 426-4573 (602) 844-1575
FAX: (602) 964-8365
Mr. Bill Ginalski, VP

Franchisee sells and installs custom-molded acrylic bathtub liners, shower bases and wall surround systems for homes, apartments, condos and commercial establishments. Proven products and installation services with over 250,000 installations during the past 13 years.

HISTORY:	FINANCIAL: Earnings Claim: . .No	FRANCHISOR TRAINING/SUPPORT:
Established in 1979; . . . 1st Franchised in 1991	Cash Investment: . . . . . $15K Min.	Financial Assistance Provided: . . . . .NA
Company-Owned Units (As of 8/31/1992): . .1	Total Investment: $16-27.5K	Site Selection Assistance: . . . . .NA
Franchised Units (As of 8/31/1992): . . . 26	Fees: Franchise - . . . . . $10K Min.	Lease Negotiation Assistance: . . . . .Yes
Total Units (As of 8/31/1992): 27	Royalty: $25/Unit, Advert: . . . 0%	Co-operative Advertising: . . . . . . .Yes
Projected New Units for 1993: 22	Contract Periods (Yrs.): 10/10	Training: . . . . 6 Days Headquarters
Distribution: US-27;Can-0;Overseas-0	Area Development Agreement: . .No	. . . .
North America: . . . . 8 States	Sub-Franchise Contract: . . . . .No	On-Going Support: B,C,D,E,G,H,I/ 4
Concentration: . . . . 2 in FL	Expand in Territory: . . . . . . .No	EXPANSION PLANS:
Registered: . . . CA,FL,HI,IL,MI,MN,NY,OR	Passive Ownership: . . . Discouraged	US: . . . . All US
. . . . WA,WI	Encourage Conversions: . . . . . Yes	Canada: . . . . No
Type Space: . . . . NA;~NA SF	Average # Employees: . . . . . .3 FT	Overseas: . . . . No

REPAIR-IT

7950 E. Redfield Rd., # 120
Scottsdale, AZ 85260
TEL: (602) 596-0262
FAX: (602) 991-1418
Mr. Brook Carey, COO

Our wholesale distributors supply hundreds of retail outlets in protected territories with Liquid Leather and over 20 other patented products to repair vinyl, leather, windshield glass, formica, etc.

HISTORY:	FINANCIAL: Earnings Claim: . Yes	FRANCHISOR TRAINING/SUPPORT:
Established in 1992; . . 1st Franchised in 1992	Cash Investment: . . . .$	Financial Assistance Provided: . . . . .Yes
Company-Owned Units (As of 8/31/1992): . .1	Total Investment: $30K	Site Selection Assistance: . . . . .NA
Franchised Units (As of 8/31/1992): 0	Fees: Franchise - $15K	Lease Negotiation Assistance: . . . . No
Total Units (As of 8/31/1992): 1	Royalty: 0%, Advert: 2%	Co-operative Advertising: . . . . .NA
Projected New Units for 1993: 18	Contract Periods (Yrs.): 10/10	Training: . . . . . 3 Days Management HQ,
Distribution: US-1;Can-0;Overseas-0	Area Development Agreement: . .No	. . . . 7 Days Technical HQ
North America: . . . . .1 State	Sub-Franchise Contract: . . . . .No	On-Going Support: B,G,I/ 3
Concentration: . . . . 1 in AZ	Expand in Territory: . . . . . . Yes	EXPANSION PLANS:
Registered:	Passive Ownership: . . . . . .Allowed	US: . . . . All US
. . . .	Encourage Conversions: . . . NA	Canada: . . . . .All Canada
Type Space: . . .Warehouse/Office;~1,500 SF	Average # Employees: . . 2 FT, 2 PT	Overseas: . . . . No

SPR BATHTUB & COUNTERTOP REFINISHING
3398 Sanford Dr.
Marietta, GA 30066
TEL: (800) 476-9271 (404) 429-0232
FAX: (404) 424-2355
Mr. Larry Stevens, Sr., President

Countertop and bathtub recoloring. Decorating services to offer for color changes in kitchen appliances, cabinets, countertops and baths, vanity, tubs, etc.

HISTORY: . . . .
Established in 1973; . . 1st Franchised in 1973
Company-Owned Units (As of 8/31/1992): . .1
Franchised Units (As of 8/31/1992): 13
Total Units (As of 8/31/1992): 14
Projected New Units for 1993:
Distribution: US-14;Can-0;Overseas-0
  North America: . . . . 9 States
  Concentration: . . . 3 in VA, 2 in MT, 2 in FL
Registered: . . . .
. . . .
Type Space: . . . . . .Home Based;~NA SF

FINANCIAL: Earnings Claim: . .No
Cash Investment: . . . .$
Total Investment: $20K
Fees: Franchise - . . . .$
  Royalty: 20% Chem, Advert: . . 5%
Contract Periods (Yrs.): . . . .
Area Development Agreement: . .No
Sub-Franchise Contract: . . . . Yes
Expand in Territory: . . . . . . Yes
Passive Ownership: . . . Discouraged
Encourage Conversions: . . . . Yes
Average # Employees: . . . . .2 FT

FRANCHISOR TRAINING/SUPPORT:
Financial Assistance Provided: . . . . .Yes
Site Selection Assistance: . . . .
Lease Negotiation Assistance: . . . . .NA
Co-operative Advertising: . . . . . . .Yes
Training: . . . . . 1-2 Wks. Headquarters

On-Going Support: B,C,D,G,I/ 3
EXPANSION PLANS:
  US: . . . . All US
  Canada: . . . . .All Canada
  Overseas: . . . . No

SPR CHIP REPAIR

3398 Sanford Dr.
Marietta, GA 30066
TEL: (800) 476-9271 (404) 429-0232
FAX: (404) 424-2355
Mr. Larry Stevens, Sr., President

Repair chips, cracks, burns and holes in porcelain, fiberglass, acrylic, cultured marble, etc.

HISTORY: . . . .
Established in 1973; . . 1st Franchised in 1973
Company-Owned Units (As of 8/31/1992): . .1
Franchised Units (As of 8/31/1992): 17
Total Units (As of 8/31/1992): 18
Projected New Units for 1993: . . . .
Distribution: US-17;Can-1;Overseas-0
  North America: . . . . . 11 States, 1 Province
  Concentration: . . . .4 in VA, 3 in FL, 3 in TN
Registered: . . . .
. . . .
Type Space: . . . . . .Home Based;~NA SF

FINANCIAL: Earnings Claim: . .No
Cash Investment: . . . .$
Total Investment: . . . . . . $.5-1.3K
Fees: Franchise - . . . .$
  Royalty: 20% Chem, Advert: . . 5%
Contract Periods (Yrs.): . . . .
Area Development Agreement: . .No
Sub-Franchise Contract: . . . . Yes
Expand in Territory: . . . . . . Yes
Passive Ownership: . . . Discouraged
Encourage Conversions: . . . . Yes
Average # Employees: . . . . .2 FT

FRANCHISOR TRAINING/SUPPORT:
Financial Assistance Provided: . . . . .Yes
Site Selection Assistance: . . . . No
Lease Negotiation Assistance: . . . . .NA
Co-operative Advertising: . . . . . . .Yes
Training: . . . . . 1-2 Wks. Headquarters
. . . .
On-Going Support: B,C,D,G,I/ 3
EXPANSION PLANS:
  US: . . . . All US
  Canada: . . . . .All Canada
  Overseas: . . . . No

SURFACE SPECIALISTS

2362 175th Ln., NW
Andover, MN 55304
TEL: (612) 753-2807 C
FAX: (612) 753-6360
Mr. Wayne McClosky, President

Repair, refinish acrylic spas, fiberglass tubs and showers, porcelain tubs, cultured marble, formica countertops, repair and welding of PVC, ABS, acrylic and Rovel spas and pool steps. Factory authorized warranty service for 34 manufacturers. Service work for apartment complexes and major hotel/motel chains. Excellent opportunity.

HISTORY: . . . .
Established in 1981; . . 1st Franchised in 1982
Company-Owned Units (As of 8/31/1992): . .1
Franchised Units (As of 8/31/1992): 18
Total Units (As of 8/31/1992): 19
Projected New Units for 1993: 4
Distribution: US-19;Can-0;Overseas-0
  North America: . . . . 12 States
  Concentration: . . . 3 in WI, 3 in MN, 3 in FL
Registered: . . . . . CA,FL,IL,MI,MN,ND,WI
. . . .
Type Space: . . . . ;~NA SF

FINANCIAL: Earnings Claim: . .No
Cash Investment: $10.5K
Total Investment: $10-20.5K
Fees: Franchise - $10-14.5K
  Royalty: 5%, Advert: 1%
Contract Periods (Yrs.): . . . 10/10
Area Development Agreement: . .No
Sub-Franchise Contract: . . . . . .No
Expand in Territory: . . . . . . Yes
Passive Ownership: . . . Discouraged
Encourage Conversions: . . . . Yes
Average # Employees: . . 2 FT, 2 PT

FRANCHISOR TRAINING/SUPPORT:
Financial Assistance Provided: . . .Yes(D)
Site Selection Assistance: . . . . . . .NA
Lease Negotiation Assistance: . . . . .NA
Co-operative Advertising: . . . . . . .Yes
Training: . . . . . . 3-4 Wks. Headquarters
On-Going Support: B,C,d,G,H/ 4
EXPANSION PLANS:
  US: . . . . All US
  Canada: . . . . No
  Overseas: . . . . No

WORLDWIDE REFINISHING SYSTEMS

1010 University parks Dr.
Waco, TX 76707
TEL: (800) 538-9099 (817) 756-2282
FAX: (817) 756-2938
Mr. Charles Wallis, EVP

Resurface, repair and recolor bathtubs, sinks, toilets, showers (fiberglass or tile), wall tile, countertops of formica, tile, wood or steel and appliances in the kitchen and bath. This includes similar surfaces in commercial and industrial settings. This refinishing save customers 75% of replacement cost. Work guaranteed.

HISTORY:	
Established in 1971; 1st Franchised in 1974	
Company-Owned Units (As of 8/31/1992): 0	
Franchised Units (As of 8/31/1992): 456	
Total Units (As of 8/31/1992): 456	
Projected New Units for 1993: 120	
Distribution: US-351;Can-17;Overseas-88	
North America: 49 States, 5 Provinces	
Concentration: 34 in TX, 24 in CA, 15 in IL	
Registered: All	
Type Space: ;~NA SF	

FINANCIAL: Earnings Claim: No
Cash Investment: $18-35K
Total Investment: $25-50K
Fees: Franchise - $9.5-20K
Royalty: 5%, Advert: 2%
Contract Periods (Yrs.): 10/10
Area Development Agreement: Yes/1
Sub-Franchise Contract: No
Expand in Territory: Yes
Passive Ownership: Discouraged
Encourage Conversions: Yes
Average # Employees: 3 FT, 1 PT

FRANCHISOR TRAINING/SUPPORT:
Financial Assistance Provided: Yes(I)
Site Selection Assistance: NA
Lease Negotiation Assistance: NA
Co-operative Advertising: NA
Training: 2 Wks. Headquarters
On-Going Support: B,C,D,E,F,G,H,I/ 21
EXPANSION PLANS:
US: All US
Canada: All Canada
Overseas: Yes

SUPPLEMENTAL LISTING OF FRANCHISORS

BATH GENIE . . . . 69 River St., Marlboro, MA 01752
    Contact: Mr. John Foley, President; Tel: (800) ALL-TUBS (508) 481-8338
CHEM-CLEAN FURNITURE RESTORATION . . . . .RR #2, Box 285, Freeport, ME 04032
    Contact: President; Tel: (207) 865-9007
DIP 'N STRIP . . . . 2141 S. Platte River Dr., Denver, CO 80223
    Contact: Mr. E. Roger Schuyler, President; Tel: (303) 781-8300
MARBLELIFE . . . . 39 Old Ridgebury Rd., # G-2, Danbury, CT 06817
    Contact: Mr. Joe Bojnowski, President; Tel: (800) 825-8262 (203) 794-2615
MOBILE TRIM TEAM . . . . 1239 Braselton Hwy., Lawrenceville, GA 30243
    Contact: Mr. Ken Clark, President; Tel: (404) 339-1086 C
PERMA CERAM ENTERPRISES . . . . 65 Smithtown Blvd., Smithtown, NY 11787
    Contact: Mr. Joseph A. Tumolo, President; Tel: (800) 645-5039 (516) 724-1205
POLY-TUB-RESTORATION . . . . 3398 Sanford Dr., Marietta, GA 30066
    Contact: Mr. Larry Stevens, President; Tel: (800) 476-9271 (404) 429-0232
PORCELAIN PATCH & GLAZE . . . . 140 Watertown St., Watertown, MA 02172
    Contact: President; Tel: (617) 924-9100
PORCELITE INTERNATIONAL . . . . .15745 Crabbs Branch Way, Rockville, MD 20855
    Contact: Mr. H. D. Bernardi; Tel: (800) 638-5959 (301) 921-1099
SPEEDY VINYL . . . . 5468 Dundas St. W., # 551, Toronto, ON M9B 6E3   CAN
    Contact: Mr. Dennis Kwasnicki; Tel: (416) 234-0731
WESTERN VINYL REPAIR . . . . 2851 S. Parker Rd., # 650, Aurora, CO 80014
    Contact: Mr. Guy Jenkins, Marketing Director; Tel: (303) 337-1949

CHAPTER 23

HAIRSTYLING SALONS

ACCENT HAIR SALON

211 S. Main St., # 720
Dayton, OH 45402
TEL: (513) 461-0394
FAX: (513) 223-3221
Mr. Claude Patmon, President

America's #1 choice for total black hair care, featuring convenient walk-in service, 7 Days per week, attractive mall locations, affordable prices and a full range of black hair care services. A carefully-planned salon system, designed with today's black woman in mind.

HISTORY: . . . .
Established in 1981; . . 1st Franchised in 1987
Company-Owned Units (As of 8/31/1992): . .2
Franchised Units (As of 8/31/1992): 11
Total Units (As of 8/31/1992): 13
Projected New Units for 1993: 4
Distribution: US-13;Can-0;Overseas-0
 North America: . . . . 6 States
 Concentration: . . .5 in OH, 4 in MD, 1 in GA
Registered: . . . . MD,MI
. . . .
Type Space: . . . . RM;~2,000 SF

FINANCIAL: Earnings Claim: . .No
Cash Investment: $35-40K
Total Investment: $125-140K
Fees: Franchise - $20K
 Royalty: 5%, Advert: 5%
Contract Periods (Yrs.): 10/10
Area Development Agreement: Yes/5
Sub-Franchise Contract: . . . . . .No
Expand in Territory: . . . . Yes
Passive Ownership: . . . Discouraged
Encourage Conversions: . . . . . Yes
Average # Employees: . . . . .19 FT

FRANCHISOR TRAINING/SUPPORT:
Financial Assistance Provided: . . . Yes(I)
Site Selection Assistance: . . . . .Yes
Lease Negotiation Assistance: . . . . .Yes
Co-operative Advertising: . . . . .Yes
Training: . . . . 3 Wks. Headquarters,
 . . . . 2 Wks. Franchised Unit
On-Going Support: C,D,E,F,H/ 4
EXPANSION PLANS:
US: . . . . Midwest, East, Southeast
Canada: . . . . No
Overseas: . . . . No

CITY LOOKS SALONS INTERNATIONAL
300 Industrial Blvd., NE
Minneapolis, MN 55413
TEL: (612) 331-8500
FAX: (612) 331-2821
Ms. Julie Langenbrunner, Sales Admin.

CITY LOOKS SALONS INTERNATIONAL provides private, individual consultation and styling in tasteful, comfortable surroundings, filling a need for clients who place a strong emphasis on full-service, personalized hair care. CITY LOOKS franchises generate deep customer loyalty and up-scale sales.

HISTORY: . . . .
Established in 1963; . . 1st Franchised in 1968
Company-Owned Units (As of 8/31/1992): . .3
Franchised Units (As of 8/31/1992): 71
Total Units (As of 8/31/1992): 74
Projected New Units for 1993: 10
Distribution: US-72;Can-0;Overseas-2
  North America: . . . . 9 States
  Concentration: . . 42 in MN, 11 in WI, 8 in IA
Registered: . . . . .All
. . . .
Type Space: . . . . . SF, SC, RM;~1,000 SF

FINANCIAL: Earnings Claim: . .No
Cash Investment: $6.6-13.8K
Total Investment: $59.5-126K
Fees: Franchise - $12.5K
  Royalty: 4%, Advert: 4%
Contract Periods (Yrs.): 15/15
Area Development Agreement: Yes/Var
Sub-Franchise Contract: . . . . .No
Expand in Territory: . . . .
Passive Ownership: . . . . . .Allowed
Encourage Conversions: . . . . . Yes
Average # Employees: . . . . . 10 FT

FRANCHISOR TRAINING/SUPPORT:
Financial Assistance Provided: . . . Yes(I)
Site Selection Assistance: . . . . . . .Yes
Lease Negotiation Assistance: . . . . .Yes
Co-operative Advertising: . . . . .Yes
Training: . . . . 1 Wk. Headquarters, 1 Wk.
 . . . . On-Site, On-Going Training
On-Going Support: C,d,e,G,h,I/ 66
EXPANSION PLANS:
  US: . . . . All US
  Canada: . . . . .Yes
  Overseas: . . . . Yes

COMMAND PERFORMANCE STYLING SALONS
P. O. Box 3000-266
Georgetown, TX 78627
TEL: (800) 872-4247 (512) 869-1201
FAX: (512) 869-0366
Ms. Jackie Ellason

COMMAND PERFORMANCE Hairstyling Salons: nationwide, excellent training and support systems. Computerized point-of-sale information system. Under new ownership since 11/1991. Franchisor principals have been franchisees since 1976. Emphasis on consistent, client-oriented quality, caring experience for our clients.

HISTORY: . . . .
Established in 1975; . . 1st Franchised in 1976
Company-Owned Units (As of 8/31/1992): . 12
Franchised Units (As of 8/31/1992): 140
Total Units (As of 8/31/1992): 152
Projected New Units for 1993: 12
Distribution: US-152;Can-0;Overseas-0
  North America: . . . . 34 States
  Concentration: . . . 22 in CA, 19 in TX, 13 i NY
Registered: . . . .
. . . .
Type Space: . . . . SC, RM;~1,500 SF

FINANCIAL: Earnings Claim: . .No
Cash Investment: $25-50K
Total Investment: $75-125K
Fees: Franchise - $25K
  Royalty: 6%, Advert: 0%
Contract Periods (Yrs.): 10/10
Area Development Agreement: . .No
Sub-Franchise Contract: . . . . .No
Expand in Territory: . . . . . . Yes
Passive Ownership: . . . . . .Allowed
Encourage Conversions: . . . . . Yes
Average # Employees: . . 6 FT, 4 PT

FRANCHISOR TRAINING/SUPPORT:
Financial Assistance Provided: . . . . . No
Site Selection Assistance: . . . . . . .Yes
Lease Negotiation Assistance: . . . . .Yes
Co-operative Advertising: . . . . No
Training: . . . . 10 Days Austin, TX,
 . . . . 10 Days Rochester, NY
On-Going Support: B,c,d,E,G,h,I/ 6
EXPANSION PLANS:
  US: . . . . All US
  Canada: . . . . No
  Overseas: . . . . No

COST CUTTERS FAMILY HAIR CARE

300 Industrial Blvd. NE
Minneapolis, MN 55413
TEL: (800) 858-2266 (612) 331-8500
FAX: (612) 331-2821
Ms. Julie Langenbrunner, Sales Admin.

COST CUTTERS franchises provide low-cost, no frills, hair services for the family, with each service being offered at a separate price. The franchisor created COST CUTTERS to meet the demand for providing the public with quality hair products and services at a moderate price.

HISTORY: . . . .
Established in 1963; . . 1st Franchised in 1968
Company-Owned Units (As of 8/31/1992): . .2
Franchised Units (As of 8/31/1992): 482
Total Units (As of 8/31/1992): 484
Projected New Units for 1993: 40
Distribution: US-482;Can-2;Overseas-0
  North America: . . . . . 33 States, 1 Province
  Concentration: . 90 in WI, 80 in MN, 38 in CA
Registered: . . . . .All
. . . .
Type Space: . . . SF, SC, RM;~900-1,200 SF

FINANCIAL: Earnings Claim: . .No
Cash Investment: $6.6-13.8K
Total Investment: $59.9-99.3K
Fees: Franchise - $19.5K
  Royalty: 6%, Advert: 4%
Contract Periods (Yrs.): 15/15
Area Development Agreement: Yes/Var
Sub-Franchise Contract: . . . . .No
Expand in Territory: . . . . Yes
Passive Ownership: . . . . . .Allowed
Encourage Conversions: . . . . Yes
Average # Employees: . . . . . 10 FT

FRANCHISOR TRAINING/SUPPORT:
Financial Assistance Provided: . . . Yes(I)
Site Selection Assistance: . . . . . . .Yes
Lease Negotiation Assistance: . . . . .Yes
Co-operative Advertising: . . . . .Yes
Training: . . . . .1 Wk. Headquarters,
 . . . . 1 Wk. On-Site, On-Going Training
On-Going Support: C,d,E,G,h,I/ 66
EXPANSION PLANS:
  US: . . . . All US
  Canada: . . . . .Quebec
  Overseas: . . . . Yes

FAMILY HAIRCUT STORE

398 Hebron Ave.
Glastonbury, CT 06033
TEL: (800) 343-9531 (203) 659-1430
FAX: (203) 657-9813
Mr. Mike Lepson, VP

FAMILY HAIRCUT STORE is a family-oriented haircare franchise that has served hundreds of thousands of satisfied customers in the Northeast. As a result of our success with company-owned stores, we have developed a turn-key package, and personal on-going support system that allows individuals from various backgrounds to take advantage of the growth potential offered by the haircare industry.

HISTORY: . . . .
Established in 1985; . . 1st Franchised in 1987
Company-Owned Units (As of 8/31/1992): . .4
Franchised Units (As of 8/31/1992): 22
Total Units (As of 8/31/1992): 26
Projected New Units for 1993: 6
Distribution: US-26;Can-0;Overseas-0
  North America: . . . . 3 States
  Concentration: . . . . .20 in CT
Registered: . . . .
. . . .
Type Space: . . . . .SC;~1,200 SF

FINANCIAL: Earnings Claim: . Yes
Cash Investment: $20K
Total Investment: $60-99K
Fees: Franchise - $23K
  Royalty: 6%, Advert: 0%
Contract Periods (Yrs.): 10
Area Development Agreement: Yes/10
Sub-Franchise Contract: . . . . .No
Expand in Territory: . . . . . . Yes
Passive Ownership: . . . Discouraged
Encourage Conversions: . . . . .No
Average # Employees: 5-8 FT, 2-4 PT

FRANCHISOR TRAINING/SUPPORT:
Financial Assistance Provided: . . . . .Yes
Site Selection Assistance: . . . . . . .Yes
Lease Negotiation Assistance: . . . . .Yes
Co-operative Advertising: . . . . .Yes
Training: . . . . .1 Wk. Headquarters,
. . . . .3 Days On-Site (Start-Up)
On-Going Support: B,C,D,E,G,I/ 5
EXPANSION PLANS:
  US: . . . . Northeast
  Canada: . . . . No
  Overseas: . . . . No

FIRST CHOICE HAIRCUTTERS

6465 Millcreek Dr., # 205
Mississauga, ON L5N 5R3 CAN
TEL: (800) 387-8335 (416) 567-4180
FAX: (416) 567-5335
Mr. George Kostopoulos, President

We are a chain of price-value, full-service family hair care shops, offering excellent franchisee service in training, advertising, management expertise, R & D and field support. Our proven concept offers exclusive territories, excellent growth potential, a cash business with virtually no inventory and a strong base of franchisees.

HISTORY: . . . . .CFA
Established in 1980; . . 1st Franchised in 1982
Company-Owned Units (As of 8/31/1992): . 75
Franchised Units (As of 8/31/1992): 151
Total Units (As of 8/31/1992): 226
Projected New Units for 1993: 20
Distribution: US-55;Can-171;Overseas-0
  North America: . . . . . 3 States, 9 Provinces
  Concentration: . . 109 in ON, 29 in OH, 19 FL
Registered: . . . . FL,IL,AB
. . . .
Type Space: . . . . .SC;~1,000 SF

FINANCIAL: Earnings Claim: . .No
Cash Investment: $35-40K
Total Investment: $75-80K
Fees: Franchise - $25K
  Royalty: 6%, Advert: 2%
Contract Periods (Yrs.): 10/5
Area Development Agreement: Yes/15
Sub-Franchise Contract: . . . . .No
Expand in Territory: . . . . . . Yes
Passive Ownership: . . . Discouraged
Encourage Conversions: . . . . Yes
Average # Employees: 4-6 FT, 2-4 PT

FRANCHISOR TRAINING/SUPPORT:
Financial Assistance Provided: . . . Yes(I)
Site Selection Assistance: . . . . . . .Yes
Lease Negotiation Assistance: . . . . .Yes
Co-operative Advertising: . . . . .Yes
Training: . . . .1-2 Wks. Classroom at HQ,
. . . . . 10-13 Days On-Site - Practical
On-Going Support: B,C,D,E,F,G,H,I/ . . . .
EXPANSION PLANS:
  US: . . . . .Northeast, Southest, Midwest
  Canada: . . . . .All Canada
  Overseas: . . . . No

GREAT CLIPS

3800 W. 80th St., # 400
Minneapolis, MN 55431
TEL: (800) 999-5959 (612) 893-9088
FAX: (612) 893-9784
Ms. Kimberly MacDonald, Fran. Dev.

High-volume haircutting salon, specializing in haircuts for the entire family. Unique, attractive décor, with quality, comprehensive advertising programs. Strong, hands-on support to franchisees, excellent training programs. We offer real value to our customers. Tremendous growth opportunities.

HISTORY: . . . .
Established in 1982; . . 1st Franchised in 1983
Company-Owned Units (As of 8/31/1992): . .0
Franchised Units (As of 8/31/1992): 235
Total Units (As of 8/31/1992): 235
Projected New Units for 1993: 300
Distribution: US-235;Can-0;Overseas-0
  North America: . . . . 11 States
  Concentration: .61 in MN, 53 in CO, 43 in MO
Registered: . . . . FL,IN,MN,WI
. . . .
Type Space: . . . . . . SC;~1,000-1,200 SF

FINANCIAL: Earnings Claim: . .No
Cash Investment: $20-30K
Total Investment: $71-97K
Fees: Franchise - $17.5K
  Royalty: 6%, Advert: 5%
Contract Periods (Yrs.): 10/10
Area Development Agreement: . .No
Sub-Franchise Contract: . . . . . .No
Expand in Territory: . . . . . . .No
Passive Ownership: . . . Discouraged
Encourage Conversions: . . . . . .No
Average # Employees: 6-10 FT, 2-4 PT

FRANCHISOR TRAINING/SUPPORT:
Financial Assistance Provided: . . . . . .No
Site Selection Assistance: . . . . .Yes
Lease Negotiation Assistance: . . . . .Yes
Co-operative Advertising: . . . . .Yes
Training: . . . . . 3-5 Days HQ-Franchisee,
. . . . .4-5 Days Training Center-Stylists
On-Going Support: B,C,d,E,f,G,h/ . . . 16
EXPANSION PLANS:
  US: . . . . .Midwest, Southwest, SE, NW
  Canada: . . . . No
  Overseas: . . . . No

HEADSTART HAIR CARE SALONS

405 Valley Ave.
Birmingham, AL 35209
TEL: (800) 783-7915 (205) 277-3161 C
FAX: (205) 279-6220
Ms. Janice P. Blake, Fran. Dev.

HEADSTART HAIR CARE SALONS offer a unique, no appointment necessary concept that really fits the needs of the 90's family. A concept with a strong emphasis on customer service. We offer convenient hours and 7 days per week service. All major lines of hair care products offered. Services include cuts, styles, perms and color.

HISTORY:	FINANCIAL: Earnings Claim: . .No	FRANCHISOR TRAINING/SUPPORT:
Established in 1983; . . 1st Franchised in 1989	Cash Investment: $50-75K	Financial Assistance Provided: . . . Yes(I)
Company-Owned Units (As of 8/31/1992): . 21	Total Investment: $60-85K	Site Selection Assistance: . . . . . . .Yes
Franchised Units (As of 8/31/1992): 8	Fees: Franchise - $12.5K	Lease Negotiation Assistance: . . . . .Yes
Total Units (As of 8/31/1992): 29	Royalty: 6%, Advert: 2%	Co-operative Advertising: . . . . . . .Yes
Projected New Units for 1993: 12	Contract Periods (Yrs.): 10/10	Training: . . . . 1 Wk. On-Site,
Distribution: US-29;Can-0;Overseas-0	Area Development Agreement: . .No	. . . . On-Going
North America: . . . . .1 State	Sub-Franchise Contract: . . . . .No	On-Going Support: a,b,C,D,E,F,G,H,I/ . . 8
Concentration: . . . . 29 in AL	Expand in Territory: . . . . .No	EXPANSION PLANS:
Registered:	Passive Ownership: . . . . . .Allowed	US: . . . . Southwest
. . . .	Encourage Conversions: . . . . Yes	Canada: . . . . No
Type Space: . . . . . . SC;~1,200-1,400 SF	Average # Employees: . . . . . .8 FT	Overseas: . . . . No

LEMON TREE, A UNISEX HAIRCUTTING ESTABLISHMENT

3301 Hempstead Tnpk.
Levittown, NY 11756
TEL: (800) 345-9156 (516) 735-2828 C
FAX: (516) 735-1851
Mr. John L. Wagner, VP

LEMON TREE FAMILY HAIRCUTTERS offers complete haircare and grooming services to men, women and children at affordable prices. LEMON TREE offers franchise opportunities to individuals who have a strong desire to become financially independent. LEMON TREE offers some financing on the initial franchise fee and a portion of the equipment package. For a total investment of $26,000-35,000, a dream can become a reality.

HISTORY:	FINANCIAL: Earnings Claim: . .No	FRANCHISOR TRAINING/SUPPORT:
Established in 1974; . . 1st Franchised in 1976	Cash Investment: $19-26K	Financial Assistance Provided: . . .Yes(D)
Company-Owned Units (As of 8/31/1992): . .0	Total Investment: $28-40K	Site Selection Assistance: . . . . . . .Yes
Franchised Units (As of 8/31/1992): 85	Fees: Franchise - $7.5K	Lease Negotiation Assistance: . . . .Yes
Total Units (As of 8/31/1992): 85	Royalty: 6%, Advert: . . $400/Mo.	Co-operative Advertising: . . . . . . .Yes
Projected New Units for 1993: 6	Contract Periods (Yrs.): 15/15	Training: . . . . 5 Days Headquarters,
Distribution: US-85;Can-0;Overseas-0	Area Development Agreement: . .No	. . . . 5 Days On-Site
North America: . . . . 6 States	Sub-Franchise Contract: . . . . .No	On-Going Support: A,C,D,E,F,G,H,I/ . . 6
Concentration: . . 74 in NY, 4 in PA, 4 in MD	Expand in Territory: . . . . Yes	EXPANSION PLANS:
Registered: . . . . FL,MD,NY,VA	Passive Ownership: . . . . . .Allowed	US: . . . . Northwest, MD, VA, CT, NJ
. . . .	Encourage Conversions: . . . . Yes	Canada: . . . . No
Type Space: . . . . FS, SF, SC;~800-1,200 SF	Average # Employees: . . 5 FT, 2 PT	Overseas: . . . . No

MARYANN'S HAIRCRAFT

1581 W. Main St.
Willimantic, CT 06226
TEL: (203) 228-0081 C
FAX: (203) 228-1987
Mr. Louis Haddad, Jr., President

MARYANN'S HAIRCRAFT offers a complete image enhancement center. Easy to operate, multi-level profit centers integrate to yield high margins, client and staff loyalty and unparalleled opportunity. Emphasis on core services and products. Custom training in systems that generate success in a full-price environment.

HISTORY:	FINANCIAL: Earnings Claim: . .No	FRANCHISOR TRAINING/SUPPORT:
Established in 1977; . . 1st Franchised in 1987	Cash Investment: $15-50K	Financial Assistance Provided: . . . Yes(I)
Company-Owned Units (As of 8/31/1992): . .3	Total Investment: $50-100K	Site Selection Assistance: . . . . . . .Yes
Franchised Units (As of 8/31/1992): 0	Fees: Franchise - $5K	Lease Negotiation Assistance: . . . .Yes
Total Units (As of 8/31/1992): 3	Royalty: 5%, Advert: 1.5%	Co-operative Advertising: . . . . . . .Yes
Projected New Units for 1993: 2	Contract Periods (Yrs.): 10/10	Training: . . . . .1 Wk. Headquarters,
Distribution: US-3;Can-0;Overseas-0	Area Development Agreement: Yes/10	. . . . .1 Wk. On-Site
North America: . . . . .1 State	Sub-Franchise Contract: . . . . . Yes	On-Going Support: a,B,C,D,E,F,g,h/ . . . 4
Concentration: . . . . 3 in CT	Expand in Territory: . . . . Yes	EXPANSION PLANS:
Registered: . . . . .FL	Passive Ownership: . . . . . .Allowed	US: . . . . Northeast and Florida
. . . .	Encourage Conversions: . . . . Yes	Canada: . . . . No
Type Space: . . . . SF;~600-1,200 SF	Average # Employees: . . 5 FT, 3 PT	Overseas: . . . . No

SNIP N' CLIP HAIRCUT SHOPS

9300 Metcalf, Glenwood Pl., # 205
Overland Park, KS 66212
TEL: (800) 622-6804 (913) 649-9303
FAX: (913) 649-0416
Mr. Dain R. Zinn, Dir. Mktg.

Budget family haircuts is the fastest-growing segment of the hair care business. SNIP N' CLIP is looking for franchise owners that want to own multiple units while keeping their current job. We offer one of the lowest-cost total turn-key packages to get owners in business quickly.

HISTORY: . . . .
Established in 1975; . . 1st Franchised in 1986
Company-Owned Units (As of 8/31/1992): . 40
Franchised Units (As of 8/31/1992): 22
Total Units (As of 8/31/1992): 62
Projected New Units for 1993: 12
Distribution: US-62;Can-0;Overseas-0
  North America: . . . . 9 States
  Concentration: . . 31 in KS, 20 in MO, 4 in IL
Registered: . . . . .FL
. . . .
Type Space: . . . . .SC;~1,000 SF

FINANCIAL: Earnings Claim: . .No
Cash Investment: $15-35K
Total Investment: $45-55K
Fees: Franchise - $10K
  Royalty: 5%, Advert: 1%
Contract Periods (Yrs.): 5/5
Area Development Agreement: Yes/5
Sub-Franchise Contract: . . . . .No
Expand in Territory: . . . . Yes
Passive Ownership: . . . . .Allowed
Encourage Conversions: . . . . . Yes
Average # Employees: . . 5 FT, 5 PT

FRANCHISOR TRAINING/SUPPORT:
Financial Assistance Provided: . . . . . No
Site Selection Assistance: . . . . .Yes
Lease Negotiation Assistance: . . . . .Yes
Co-operative Advertising: . . . . No
Training: . . . . 3 Days Headquarters,
. . . . 5 Days On-Site
On-Going Support: B,C,D,E,f,G,H,I/ . . . 5
EXPANSION PLANS:
US: . . . . Mid States
Canada: . . . . No
Overseas: . . . . No

SUPERCUTS

555 Northgate Dr.
San Rafael, CA 94903
TEL: (800) 999-2887 (415) 472-1170
FAX: (415) 492-0982
Mr. Ken Zimmermann, Dir. Fran. Sales

SUPERCUTS shops provide affordable, stylish, custom haircare for men, women and children. SUPERCUTS' success is founded on the simple concept of the precision, mistake-proof, guaranteed haircut made possible by technical advances pioneered by SUPERCUTS and supported by a training program unrivaled in the industry.

HISTORY: . . . .
Established in 1975; . . 1st Franchised in 1979
Company-Owned Units (As of 8/31/1992): . 57
Franchised Units (As of 8/31/1992): 640
Total Units (As of 8/31/1992): 697
Projected New Units for 1993: 100
Distribution: . . . US-697;Can-0;Overseas-0
  North America: . . . . 36 States + PR
  Concentration: . . 199 in CA, 90 in TX, 66 FL
Registered: . . . .CA,FL,HI,IL,IN,MD,MI,NY
. . . . .OR,RI,VA,WA,WI,DC
Type Space: . . . . .SC;~1,200 SF

FINANCIAL: Earnings Claim: . Yes
Cash Investment: $75K
Total Investment: $100-125K
Fees: Franchise - $25K
  Royalty: 10%, Advert: 5%
Contract Periods (Yrs.): 10/10
Area Development Agreement: . Yes
Sub-Franchise Contract: . . . . .No
Expand in Territory: . . . . Yes
Passive Ownership: . . . Discouraged
Encourage Conversions: . . . . .No
Average # Employees: . . 7 FT, 5 PT

FRANCHISOR TRAINING/SUPPORT:
Financial Assistance Provided: . . . Yes(I)
Site Selection Assistance: . . . . . . .Yes
Lease Negotiation Assistance: . . . .Yes
Co-operative Advertising: . . . . No
Training: . . . . 5 Days Headquarters,
. . . . . . 5 Days Stylist Training Locally
On-Going Support: C,d,E,G,H/ 145
EXPANSION PLANS:
US: . . . . NE, SE and Midwest
Canada: . . . . No
Overseas: . . . . No

WE CARE HAIR

325 Bic Dr.
Milford, CT 06460
TEL: (800) 888-4848 (203) 877-4281
FAX: (203) 876-6688
Franchise Sales Dept.

WE CARE HAIR is a hair salon franchise designed for the entrepreneur. It provides high quality, low cost hair care. No salon experience necessary, multi-unit ownership encouraged. WE CARE HAIR now has over 120 units in 27 states.

HISTORY: . . . . IFA
Established in 1985; . . 1st Franchised in 1986
Company-Owned Units (As of 8/31/1992): . .3
Franchised Units (As of 8/31/1992): 69
Total Units (As of 8/31/1992): 72
Projected New Units for 1993: 70
Distribution: US-72;Can-0;Overseas-0
  North America: . . . . 35 States
  Concentration: . . . .
Registered: . . . . All States
. . . .
Type Space: . . . . SC, RM;~1,000 SF

FINANCIAL: Earnings Claim: . .No
Cash Investment: $25-50K
Total Investment: $48-96K
Fees: Franchise - $7.5K
  Royalty: 8%, Advert: 4%
Contract Periods (Yrs.): 20
Area Development Agreement: . Yes
Sub-Franchise Contract: . . . . .No
Expand in Territory: . . . . . . Yes
Passive Ownership: . . . . . .Allowed
Encourage Conversions: . . . . Yes
Average # Employees: . . . . . .8 FT

FRANCHISOR TRAINING/SUPPORT:
Financial Assistance Provided: . . .Yes(D)
Site Selection Assistance: . . . . . . .Yes
Lease Negotiation Assistance: . . . .Yes
Co-operative Advertising: . . . .
Training: . . . . . . 2 Wks. Bridgeview, IL
. . . .
On-Going Support: E,G,I/ . . . .
EXPANSION PLANS:
US: . . . . All US
Canada: . . . . .All Canada
Overseas: . . . . No

SUPPLEMENTAL LISTING OF FRANCHISORS

BARBERS, HAIRSTYLING FOR MEN & WOMEN . . . . 730 Carla Ln., Minneapolis, MN 55109
    Contact: Mr. Joe Francis, Chairman; Tel: (800) 433-1884 (612) 331-8500
BARRY LEONARD CRIMPERS . . . . .24 N. Cliffe Dr., Wilmington, DE 19809
    Contact: Mr. Melvin D. Messinger; Tel: (800) 992-0243
BOCA BEAUTY SALON . . . . 210 University Dr., Coral Springs, FL 33071
    Contact: Mr. Bill Landman; Tel: (305) 345-0600
CALL N' CUT . . . . 880 Wilson Ave., North York, ON M3K 1E7   CAN
    Contact: Mr. Joseph Pampena, EVP; Tel: (416) 630-5001
CUSTOM CUTS . . . . 13850 Manchester Rd., St. Louis, MO 63011
    Contact: Mr. Bob Hanson, President; Tel: (314) 391-1717
DAVID ALAN'S CUTS FOR KIDS/C.A.P. CTR. . . . . 15 Engle St., # 302, Englewood, NJ 07631
    Contact: Mr. John Sterns, Sales Dir.; Tel: (800) 332-2229 (201) 871-0370
EASY HAIR . . . . 1257-H Kennestone Circle, Marietta, GA 30066
    Contact: Mr. Don Westbrook, President; Tel: (404) 426-0254
ELAN HAIR DESIGN . . . . 3 River Run, East Greenwich, RI 02905
    Contact: President; Tel: (401) 884-6525
FANTASTIC SAM'S . . . . P.O. Box 18845, 3180 Old Getwell Rd., Memphis, TN 38181
    Contact: Mr. Paul Rivard, Dir. Fran.; Tel: (800) 844-7267 (901) 363-8624 C
FOR PEANUTS ONLY . . . . 427 St. Paul Ave., Branford, ON N3R 4N8   CAN
    Contact: Mr. Harold Osborne, Pres.; Tel: (519) 752-8073
GIORGIO'S / HAIR SENSATIONS . . . . .142 Mineola Ave., Roslyn Heights, NY 11577
    Contact: Mr. Georgio Castriota, President; Tel: (800) 753-5788 (516) 621-4970
GREAT CUTS . . . . 800 W. Cummings Pk., # 6600, Woburn, MA 01801
    Contact: Mr. Robert Silverman, President; Tel: (617) 938-4707
GREAT EXPECTATIONS / HAIRCRAFTERS . . . 125 S. Service Rd., P. O. Box 265, Jericho, NY 11753
    Contact: Mr. Don vonLiebermann, VP; Tel: (800) 992-0139 (516) 334-8400
HAIR CLUB FOR MEN . . . . .185 Madison Ave., # 1300, New York, NY 10016
    Contact: Mr. George Haggerty, President; Tel: (212) 779-4236
HAIR PERFORMERS, THE . . . . 7327 W. 90th St., Bridgeview, IL 60455
    Contact: Mr. John Amico; Tel: (800) 323-8309 (708) 430-2552
JOAN M. CABLE'S LA FEMMINA SALON . . . 3301 Hempstead Tpk.-Levittown, Long Island, NY 11756
    Contact: Mr. John L. Wagner; Tel: (800) 345-9156 (516) 735-2828
LORD'S & LADY'S HAIR SALONS . . . . 450 Belgrade Ave., Boston, MA 02132
    Contact: Mr. Michael Barsamian; Tel: (617) 323-4700 (617) 323-4714
MAGICUTS . . . . 5430 Beach Blvd., Buena Park, CA 90621
    Contact: Ms. Heather Brown, Dir. Comm.; Tel: (800) 661-2887 (416) 470-2887
MAGICUTS (CANADA) . . . . 3780 14th Ave., # 106, Markham, ON L3R 9Y5   CAN
    Contact: Mr. Brian Luborsky, President; Tel: (800) 661-2887 (416) 470-2887
PRO-CUTS . . . . 3716 Rufe Snow Dr., Fort Worth, TX 76180
    Contact: Mr. Donald H. Stone, VP; Tel: (800) 542-2887 (817) 595-4171
THIRD DIMENSION CUTS . . . . 8015 Broadway, Everett, WA 98203
    Contact: Mr. Mel Hoelzle, President; Tel: (206) 355-2247

For a full explanation of the data provided in

the Franchisor Format, please refer to Chapter 2,

"How To Use The Data."

CHAPTER 24

HEALTH / FITNESS / BEAUTY

AMERICAN MEDICAL WEIGHT ASSOCIATION
750 E. Washington
Medina, OH 44256
TEL: (216) 722-5928
FAX: (216) 722-5928
Ms. Jo Meadows, President

AMERICAN MEDICAL WEIGHT ASSOCIATION offers you an opportunity to become part of a growing organization in the business of weight loss. Our program consists of medical supervision, a well-balanced diet and behavior modification. We promote a lifestyle change. Thousands have lost weight on our program. We are a super service organization and also provide a product to enhance our program. Great growth opportunities!

HISTORY: . . . .
Established in 1985; . . 1st Franchised in 1985
Company-Owned Units (As of 8/31/1992): . .0
Franchised Units (As of 8/31/1992): 2
Total Units (As of 8/31/1992): 2
Projected New Units for 1993: 4
Distribution: US-2;Can-0;Overseas-0
 North America: . . . . 2 States
 Concentration: . . . .
Registered: . . . .
. . . .
Type Space: . . . . .SC;~1,000 SF

FINANCIAL: Earnings Claim: . .No
Cash Investment: $100K
Total Investment: $150K
Fees: Franchise - . . . .$
 Royalty: 7%, Advert: 1%
Contract Periods (Yrs.): 5/5
Area Development Agreement: . Yes
Sub-Franchise Contract: . . . . . .
Expand in Territory: . . . . Yes
Passive Ownership: . . . Discouraged
Encourage Conversions: . . . . . Yes
Average # Employees: . . 2 FT, 2 PT

FRANCHISOR TRAINING/SUPPORT:
Financial Assistance Provided: . . . . .No
Site Selection Assistance: . . . . .Yes
Lease Negotiation Assistance: . . . . .Yes
Co-operative Advertising: . . . . .No
Training: . . . . .1 Wk. Headquarters,
 . . . . .1 Wk. On-Site, On-Going
On-Going Support: b,d,E,G/ 3
EXPANSION PLANS:
 US: . . . . Southwest
 Canada: . . . . .All Canada
 Overseas: . . . . .Yes

BEAUX VISAGES

270 Mount Hope Dr.
Albany, NY 12202
TEL: (518) 465-1420
FAX: (518) 465-0364
Mr. John H. Dennis, EVP

Purveyor of exclusive line of European skin care products and services.

HISTORY: . . . . IFA	FINANCIAL: Earnings Claim: . .No	FRANCHISOR TRAINING/SUPPORT:
Established in 1985; . . 1st Franchised in 1989	Cash Investment: $50-75K	Financial Assistance Provided: . . . . .No
Company-Owned Units (As of 8/31/1992): . .8	Total Investment: $125-150K	Site Selection Assistance: . . . . . . .Yes
Franchised Units (As of 8/31/1992): 11	Fees: Franchise - $25K	Lease Negotiation Assistance: . . . . .Yes
Total Units (As of 8/31/1992): 19	Royalty: 6%, Advert: 2-5%	Co-operative Advertising: . . . . . . .Yes
Projected New Units for 1993: 5	Contract Periods (Yrs.): 10/10	Training: . . . . 6 Wks. Headquarters
Distribution: US-19;Can-0;Overseas-0	Area Development Agreement: Yes/Var	. . . .
North America: . . . . 6 States	Sub-Franchise Contract: . . . . . .No	On-Going Support: a,B,C,d,E,F,G,H/ . . 12
Concentration: . . . .9 in CT, 3 in NY, 3 in NJ	Expand in Territory: . . . . Yes	EXPANSION PLANS:
Registered: . . . . .MD,NY,VA	Passive Ownership: . . . . . .Allowed	US: . . . . .Eastern US
. . . .	Encourage Conversions: . . . . . .No	Canada: . . . . .Ontario
Type Space: . . . . . . SC;~2,000-3,000 SF	Average # Employees: . . . . 5-7 FT	Overseas: . . . . No

BENEFICIAL HEALTH AND BEAUTY

1780 West 5th S.
Salt Lake City, UT 84104
TEL: (800) 367-0990 (801) 973-7778
FAX: (801) 973-8836
Ms. Linda T. Nelson, President

BENEFICIAL HEALTH AND BEAUTY CENTERS are "urban mini-health spas," offering a total wellness and fitness program in each local community. We offer programs that aid in body cleansing, weight-loss, nutrition, body contouring, skin care, massage, personal exercise trainers and many complementary programs.

HISTORY: . . . . IFA	FINANCIAL: Earnings Claim: . .No	FRANCHISOR TRAINING/SUPPORT:
Established in 1981; . . 1st Franchised in 1990	Cash Investment: $30-80K	Financial Assistance Provided: . . . . .No
Company-Owned Units (As of 8/31/1992): . .0	Total Investment: $100K	Site Selection Assistance: . . . . . . .Yes
Franchised Units (As of 8/31/1992): 13	Fees: Franchise - $15K	Lease Negotiation Assistance: . . . . .Yes
Total Units (As of 8/31/1992): 13	Royalty: 3%, Advert: 4%	Co-operative Advertising: . . . . . . .Yes
Projected New Units for 1993: 13	Contract Periods (Yrs.): 10/5	Training: . . . . 2 Days Local Area, 4 Days
Distribution: US-11;Can-0;Overseas-2	Area Development Agreement: Yes/10	. . . Practical SLC, UT, Weekly On-Site
North America: . . . . 3 States	Sub-Franchise Contract: . . . . . .No	On-Going Support: B,C,D,E,F,G,h,I/ . . .7
Concentration: . . . 4 in CA, 2 HI, 2 Singapore	Expand in Territory: . . . . . . Yes	EXPANSION PLANS:
Registered: . . .CA,HI,IL,MI,MN,NY,ND,OR	Passive Ownership: . . . Discouraged	US: . . . . All US
. . . . WA,WI	Encourage Conversions: . . . . . Yes	Canada: . . . . .All Canada
Type Space: . . . . . . SF, SC, RM;~1,200 SF	Average # Employees: . . 2 FT, 2 PT	Overseas: . . . . .Yes

BEVERLY HILLS WEIGHT LOSS CLINIC

200 Highpoint Ave.
Portsmouth, RI 02871
TEL: (800) 285-4500 (401) 683-6620
FAX: (401) 683-6885
Mr. O. J. Mulkey, President

BEVERLY HILLS CLINICS are medically supervised. Patients must have lab work performed and doctor approval before starting the program. Our patients are taught to modify their eating habits and eat regular store-bought food from the start. The company takes pride in its success with weight loss and especially with maintaining the loss.

HISTORY:	FINANCIAL: Earnings Claim: . .No	FRANCHISOR TRAINING/SUPPORT:
Established in 1986; . . 1st Franchised in 1989	Cash Investment: $45K	Financial Assistance Provided: . . . Yes(I)
Company-Owned Units (As of 8/31/1992): . .0	Total Investment: $50-75K	Site Selection Assistance: . . . . . . .Yes
Franchised Units (As of 8/31/1992): 97	Fees: Franchise - $15K	Lease Negotiation Assistance: . . . . .Yes
Total Units (As of 8/31/1992): 97	Royalty: 8%, Advert: 1.5%	Co-operative Advertising: . . . . . . .Yes
Projected New Units for 1993: 20	Contract Periods (Yrs.): 5/5	Training: . . . . 2 Wks. Headquarters
Distribution: US-44;Can-53;Overseas-0	Area Development Agreement: Yes/5	. . . .
North America: . . . . . 9 States, 2 Provinces	Sub-Franchise Contract: . . . . . Yes	On-Going Support: B,C,D,E,G,H,I/ 9
Concentration: . . . . VA, NC, KY	Expand in Territory: . . . . . . Yes	EXPANSION PLANS:
Registered: . . . . FL,MD,RI,VA	Passive Ownership: . . . Discouraged	US: . . . . .All US
. . . .	Encourage Conversions: . . . . . Yes	Canada: . . . . .All Canada
Type Space: . . . . . . .SF, SC;~1,000 SF	Average # Employees:	Overseas: . . . . No

BIOGIME SKIN CARE CENTERS

1665 Townhurst, # 100
Houston, TX 77043
TEL: (800) 882-3535 (303) 721-1662
FAX: (800) 536-1610
Mr. John Riemann, President

Specialty stores, featuring an exclusive line of All Natural BIOGIME brand skin and body care products. Complete franchise support from set-up to integrated television promotional campaigns.

HISTORY: . . . .
Established in 1983; . . 1st Franchised in 1991
Company-Owned Units (As of 8/31/1992): . .2
Franchised Units (As of 8/31/1992): 6
Total Units (As of 8/31/1992): 8
Projected New Units for 1993: 12
Distribution: US-8;Can-0;Overseas-0
North America: . . . . 7 States
Concentration: . . . . 3 in CA, 2 in TX
Registered: . . . . .CA,HI
. . . .
Type Space: . . . . .SC;~750 SF

FINANCIAL: Earnings Claim: . . Yes
Cash Investment: $70-100K
Total Investment: $80-109K
Fees: Franchise - $15K
Royalty: 2%, Advert: 0%
Contract Periods (Yrs.): 10/10
Area Development Agreement: . .No
Sub-Franchise Contract: . . . . .No
Expand in Territory: . . . . . . Yes
Passive Ownership: . . . Discouraged
Encourage Conversions: . . . . .No
Average # Employees: . . . . .2 FT

FRANCHISOR TRAINING/SUPPORT:
Financial Assistance Provided: . . . . .Yes
Site Selection Assistance: . . . . . . .Yes
Lease Negotiation Assistance: . . . . .Yes
Co-operative Advertising: . . . . .No
Training: . . . . 1 Wk. Existing Store,
. . . . 1 Wk. New Store
On-Going Support: A,B,C,D,E,G,H,I/ . . 6
EXPANSION PLANS:
US: . . . . .All US
Canada: . . . . .All Canada
Overseas: . . . . .Yes

BODY SHOP, THE

45 Horsehill Rd.
Cedar Knolls, NJ 07927
TEL: (201) 984-9200
FAX: (201) 984-8437
Ms. Susan A. Jones, Fran. Select. Mgr.

International skin and hair care company that focuses on business as a source for profits and principles.

HISTORY: . . . .
Established in 1976; . . 1st Franchised in 1977
Company-Owned Units (As of 8/31/1992): . 15
Franchised Units (As of 8/31/1992): 88
Total Units (As of 8/31/1992): 103
Projected New Units for 1993: 45
Distribution: US-103;Can-0;Overseas-0
North America: . . . . 40 States
Concentration: . 15 in CA, 10 in NY, 10 in FL
Registered: . . . . .All
. . . .
Type Space: . . . . SF, RM;~800 SF

FINANCIAL: Earnings Claim: . .No
Cash Investment: $300-350K
Total Investment: $300-350K
Fees: Franchise - $40K
Royalty: 0-5%, Advert: 0%
Contract Periods (Yrs.): 15/5
Area Development Agreement: . .No
Sub-Franchise Contract: . . . . .No
Expand in Territory: . . . . . . .No
Passive Ownership: . . . Not Allowed
Encourage Conversions: . . . . NA
Avg. # Employees: 210 Hrs. per Week

FRANCHISOR TRAINING/SUPPORT:
Financial Assistance Provided: . . . . . No
Site Selection Assistance: . . . . . . .Yes
Lease Negotiation Assistance: . . . . .Yes
Co-operative Advertising: . . . . .No
Training: . . . . 6 Wks. Headquarters
. . . .
On-Going Support: a,b,C,d,E,F,G,H,I/ . .200
EXPANSION PLANS:
US: . . . . .All US
Canada: . . . . Separate Entity
Overseas: . . . . . .Separate Entity

CALLANETICS

1600 Stout St., # 555
Denver, CO 80202
TEL: (800) 8-CALLAN (303) 572-7517
FAX: (303) 572-7614
Ms. Elizabeth S. Bennett, President

Make a difference in people's lives. The fastest-growing, women-owned franchise company seeks franchisees to teach CALLANETICS classes, The Chanel of exercise, and manage studios. Small classes produce phenomenal results. Improve your bottom line.

HISTORY: . . . . IFA
Established in 1990; . . 1st Franchised in 1990
Company-Owned Units (As of 8/31/1992): . .1
Franchised Units (As of 8/31/1992): 84
Total Units (As of 8/31/1992): 85
Projected New Units for 1993: 80
Distribution: US-64;Can-0;Overseas-21
North America: . . . .
Concentration: . . . . . . 10 in CO, 8 in CA
Registered: . . . CA,FL,HI,IL,IN,MD,MI,MN
. . . . .NY,OR,RI,WA,WI,DC
Type Space: . . . . Varies;~1,000 SF

FINANCIAL: Earnings Claim: . .No
Cash Investment: $30-45K
Total Investment: $35-50K
Fees: Franchise - $18.8K
Royalty: 12%, Advert: 4%
Contract Periods (Yrs.): . . . 10/10
Area Development Agreement: . Yes
Sub-Franchise Contract: . . . . .No
Expand in Territory: . . . .
Passive Ownership: . . . Discouraged
Encourage Conversions: . . . . .No
Average # Employees: . . 2 FT, 1 PT

FRANCHISOR TRAINING/SUPPORT:
Financial Assistance Provided: . . . . . No
Site Selection Assistance: . . . . . . .Yes
Lease Negotiation Assistance: . . . . .Yes
Co-operative Advertising: . . . . .Yes
Training: . . . . . . 10 Days Headquarters,
. . . . . . 25 Days at Home Pre-Training
On-Going Support: G,H,I/ 21
EXPANSION PLANS:
US: . . . . .All US
Canada: . . . . .All Canada
Overseas: . . . . .Yes

CAROL BLOCK

7701 Bull Valley Rd.
McHenry, IL 60050
TEL: (800) HAIRLES (815) 344-0488
FAX: (815) 344-2503
Mr. Neal Rohr

D'PLUME is the state-of-the-art in equipment that removes superfluous hair permanently. D'PLUME remove hair with laser-like technology, high intensity light - no needles - no pain - no scarring. In the age of AIDS, D'PLUME eliminates the risk of infection from needle stick injuries.

HISTORY: . . . . IFA	FINANCIAL: Earnings Claim: . .No	FRANCHISOR TRAINING/SUPPORT:
Established in 1937; . . 1st Franchised in 1986	Cash Investment: $30K	Financial Assistance Provided: . . . Yes(I)
Company-Owned Units (As of 8/31/1992): . 15	Total Investment: $100K	Site Selection Assistance: . . . . . . .Yes
Franchised Units (As of 8/31/1992): 9	Fees: Franchise - $22.7K	Lease Negotiation Assistance: . . . . .Yes
Total Units (As of 8/31/1992): 24	Royalty: 10%, Advert: 3%	Co-operative Advertising: . . . . . . .Yes
Projected New Units for 1993:	Contract Periods (Yrs.): . . . 15/15	Training: . . . . . . 3 Wks. Headquarters
Distribution: US-14;Can-0;Overseas-10	Area Development Agreement: Yes/15	. . . .
North America: . . . . 2 States	Sub-Franchise Contract: . . . . Yes	On-Going Support: A,B,C,D,E,F,G,H,I/ . .
Concentration: . . . . 13 in IL, 1 in WI	Expand in Territory: . . . . . . Yes	EXPANSION PLANS:
Registered: IL	Passive Ownership: . . . . . .Allowed	US: . . . . All US
. . . .	Encourage Conversions: . . . . .No	Canada: . . . . All Exc. Alberta
Type Space: . . . FS, SF, SC;~1,200-1,500 SF	Average # Employees: . . . . 3-6 FT	Overseas: . . . UK, Brazil, Taiwan

DIET CENTER

921 Penn Ave., 9th Fl.
Pittsburgh, PA 15222
TEL: (800) 333-2581 (412) 338-8700
FAX: (412) 338-8743
Ms. Mary McClain, Dir Fran. Admin./Dev.

DIET CENTER offers one of the most innovative weight management programs available in the industry today. Recognizing that scale weight and the one-size-fits-all approach are no longer acceptable, DIET CENTER relies on body composition analysis to individualize caloric intake and to monitor changes in fat and lean tissue. DIET CENTER, INC. has franchises throughout the US and Canada.

HISTORY: . . . . IFA	FINANCIAL: Earnings Claim: . .No	FRANCHISOR TRAINING/SUPPORT:
Established in 1972; . . 1st Franchised in 1975	Cash Investment: $39.5-58K	Financial Assistance Provided: . . . . .Yes
Company-Owned Units (As of 8/31/1992): . .0	Total Investment: $39.5-58K	Site Selection Assistance: . . . . No
Franchised Units (As of 8/31/1992): 1361	Fees: Franchise - $18K	Lease Negotiation Assistance: . . . . . No
Total Units (As of 8/31/1992): 1361	Royalty: 8%, Advert: 8%	Co-operative Advertising: . . . . No
Projected New Units for 1993: 90	Contract Periods (Yrs.): 10/5	Training: . . . . . 3-5 Days HQ, 1-5 Days
Distribution: US-1275;Can-85;Overseas-1	Area Development Agreement: . .No	. . . . Regional Training, Home Study
North America: . . . . 50 States, 9 Provinces	Sub-Franchise Contract: . . . . Yes	On-Going Support: B,C,D,e,G,H,I/ . . . 37
Concentration: . . 184 in CA, 85 in NY, 79 TX	Expand in Territory: . . . . . . Yes	EXPANSION PLANS:
Registered: . . . CA,FL,HI,IL,IN,MD,MI,MN	Passive Ownership: . . . Not Allowed	US: . . . . All US
. . . . .NY,ND,RI,WA,WI,DC	Encourage Conversions: . . . . . NA	Canada: . . . . .All Canada
Type Space: . . . FS, SF, SC;~1,000-1,200 SF	Average # Employees: . . . . .3 FT	Overseas: . . . . No

DIET LIGHT

300 Market St., # 101
Lebanon, OR 97355
TEL: (800) 248-7712 (503) 259-3573
FAX: (503) 259-3506
Ms. Kathy Bengston, President

DIET LIGHT is a complete weight loss system that incorporates individual counseling with delicious gourmet meals. The Delight Entrees are vacuum-sealed, contain no additives or preservatives and require no refrigeration. One day a week clients can eat out or plan their own meals to learn lifestyle changes by making good choices.

HISTORY:	FINANCIAL: Earnings Claim: . .No	FRANCHISOR TRAINING/SUPPORT:
Established in 1983; . . 1st Franchised in 1988	Cash Investment: . . . .$	Financial Assistance Provided: . . . . .Yes
Company-Owned Units (As of 8/31/1992): . .6	Total Investment: $25-35K	Site Selection Assistance: . . . . . . .Yes
Franchised Units (As of 8/31/1992): 7	Fees: Franchise - $15K	Lease Negotiation Assistance: . . . . .Yes
Total Units (As of 8/31/1992): 13	Royalty: 0%, Advert: 2%	Co-operative Advertising: . . . . . . .Yes
Projected New Units for 1993: 6	Contract Periods (Yrs.): 23/5	Training: . . . . . . 3-5 Days Headquarters
Distribution: US-13;Can-0;Overseas-0	Area Development Agreement: Yes/23	. . . .
North America: . . . . 2 States	Sub-Franchise Contract: . . . . .No	On-Going Support: B,G,H,I/ 3
Concentration: . . . . 12 in OR, 1 in WA	Expand in Territory: . . . . . . Yes	EXPANSION PLANS:
Registered: . . . . OR,WA	Passive Ownership: . . . Discouraged	US: . . . . Northwest
. . . .	Encourage Conversions:	Canada: . . . . No
Type Space: . . . SF, SC, RM;~600-1,200 SF	Average # Employees: . . 1 FT, 2 PT	Overseas: . . . . No

DOCTORS & NURSES WEIGHT CONTROL CENTER

2 N. Palafot St., # 200
Pensacola, FL 32501
TEL: (800) 367-6391 (904) 433-9797
FAX: (904) 433-4149
Mr. David Owens, VP

Professionally-supervised weight control program, utilizing store-bought foods and nutritional, high-energy weight control supplements.

HISTORY: . . . .
Established in 1987; . . 1st Franchised in 1987
Company-Owned Units (As of 8/31/1992): . .1
Franchised Units (As of 8/31/1992): 29
Total Units (As of 8/31/1992): 30
Projected New Units for 1993: 15
Distribution: US-30;Can-0;Overseas-0
  North America: . . . . 7 States
  Concentration: . . . .7 in FL, 6 in GA, 3 in TN
Registered: . . . . .CA,VA,WA
. . . .
Type Space: FS, SF, SC, RM;~1,000-1,500 SF

FINANCIAL: Earnings Claim: . .No
Cash Investment: $25.5-35K
Total Investment: $35-66K
Fees: Franchise - $25.5K
  Royalty: 10%, Advert: 2%
Contract Periods (Yrs.): 5/5
Area Development Agreement: Yes/5
Sub-Franchise Contract: . . . . Yes
Expand in Territory: . . . . . . Yes
Passive Ownership: . . . Discouraged
Encourage Conversions: . . . . Yes
Average # Employees: . . 2 FT, 1 PT

FRANCHISOR TRAINING/SUPPORT:
Financial Assistance Provided: . . . Yes(I)
Site Selection Assistance: . . . . . . .Yes
Lease Negotiation Assistance: . . . . .Yes
Co-operative Advertising: . . . . . . .Yes
Training: . . . . 2 Wks. Headquarters
. . . .
On-Going Support: B,C,d,E,F,G,h,I/ . . 17
EXPANSION PLANS:
US: . . . . All US
Canada: . . . . .No
Overseas: . . . . No

E-Z TAN PROFESSIONAL TANNING SALONS

21073 Powerline Rd., # 63
Boca Raton, FL 33433
TEL: (407) 479-2105
FAX: (407) 479-4246
Ms. Lisa Brackett, Director

E-Z TAN PROFESSIONAL TANNING SALONS offer a state-of-the-art indoor tanning center. Our computerized systems give you the controls you need with ease of operation. Product mix includes tanning lotions, accessories and swimwear. A proven track record. Assistance every step of the way makes for a winning combination.

HISTORY: . . . .
Established in 1984; . . 1st Franchised in 1991
Company-Owned Units (As of 8/31/1992): . .0
Franchised Units (As of 8/31/1992): 6
Total Units (As of 8/31/1992): 6
Projected New Units for 1993: 24
Distribution: US-6;Can-0;Overseas-0
  North America: . . . . .1 State
  Concentration: . . . . 6 in FL
Registered: . . . . .FL
. . . .
Type Space: . . . . .SC;~1,200 SF

FINANCIAL: Earnings Claim: . Yes
Cash Investment: $30K
Total Investment: $75K
Fees: Franchise - $15K
  Royalty: 6%, Advert: 1%
Contract Periods (Yrs.): . . . 10/10
Area Development Agreement: Yes/10
Sub-Franchise Contract: . . . . .No
Expand in Territory: . . . . . . Yes
Passive Ownership: . . . . . .Allowed
Encourage Conversions: . . . . Yes
Average # Employees: . . 1 FT, 2 PT

FRANCHISOR TRAINING/SUPPORT:
Financial Assistance Provided: . . . Yes(I)
Site Selection Assistance: . . . . . . .Yes
Lease Negotiation Assistance: . . . . .Yes
Co-operative Advertising: . . . . . . .Yes
Training: . . . . 7 Days Headquarters
. . . .
On-Going Support: A,B,C,d,E,F,h/ 4
EXPANSION PLANS:
US: . . . . All US, SE Aggressively
Canada: . . . . .All Canada
Overseas: . . . . No

ELIZABETH GRADY FACE FIRST

360 Merrimack St., Riverwalk Bldg.#9
Lawrence, MA 01843
TEL: (800) FACIALS (508) 975-7115
FAX: (508) 975-7547
Mr. John P. Walsh, President

Largest chain of skin care salons in the US, offering unique services, including specialized and prescribed facial treatments, make-up instructions and application, waxing services (hair removal), paraffin treatments (for softening and hydrating), manicures and pedicures. Also, free skin care consultations available.

HISTORY: . . . .
Established in 1974; . . 1st Franchised in 1982
Company-Owned Units (As of 8/31/1992): . .9
Franchised Units (As of 8/31/1992): 15
Total Units (As of 8/31/1992): 24
Projected New Units for 1993: 12
Distribution: US-24;Can-0;Overseas-0
  North America: . . . . 3 States
  Concentration: . .19 in MA, 3 ion NH, 2 in CT
Registered: . . . . CA,FL,MD
. . . .
Type Space: . . . . .SC;~1,000 SF

FINANCIAL: Earnings Claim: . .No
Cash Investment: $15-30K
Total Investment: $90-133K
Fees: Franchise - $25K
  Royalty: 6%, Advert: 3%
Contract Periods (Yrs.): . . . 10/10
Area Development Agreement: . .No
Sub-Franchise Contract: . . . . .No
Expand in Territory: . . . . . . .No
Passive Ownership: . . . . . .Allowed
Encourage Conversions: . . . . Yes
Average # Employees: . . 3 FT, 2 PT

FRANCHISOR TRAINING/SUPPORT:
Financial Assistance Provided: . . . . .Yes
Site Selection Assistance: . . . . . . .Yes
Lease Negotiation Assistance: . . . . .Yes
Co-operative Advertising: . . . . . . .Yes
Training: . . . . . 30 Days Company Salon,
. . . . .30 Days On-Site
On-Going Support: B,C,D,I/ 10
EXPANSION PLANS:
US: . . . . All US
Canada: . . . . .All Canada
Overseas: . . . . . . EUR, Far East

EUROPEAN TANSPA

5002 Main St.
Downers Grove, IL 60515
TEL: (708) 963-2626
FAX:
Ms. Joyce Cocogliato, President

Largest nationwide chain of tanning salons.

HISTORY:	FINANCIAL: Earnings Claim: . . .	FRANCHISOR TRAINING/SUPPORT:
Established in 1982; . . 1st Franchised in 1982	Cash Investment: . . . .$	Financial Assistance Provided: . . . . . No
Company-Owned Units (As of 8/31/1992): . .2	Total Investment: $25-30K	Site Selection Assistance: . . . . .Yes
Franchised Units (As of 8/31/1992): 102	Fees: Franchise - $7.5K	Lease Negotiation Assistance: . . . .Yes
Total Units (As of 8/31/1992): 104	Royalty: /Bed Hr., Advert: . . . 0%	Co-operative Advertising: . . . . . . .Yes
Projected New Units for 1993:	Contract Periods (Yrs.): 10/5	Training: . . . . Site Visits and
Distribution: US-104;Can-0;Overseas-0	Area Development Agreement: . .No	. . . . Seminars at Headquarters
North America:	Sub-Franchise Contract: . . . . .No	On-Going Support: B,C,D,E,G,H,I/ . . . . .
Concentration:	Expand in Territory: . . . . . . Yes	EXPANSION PLANS:
Registered: . . . . .IL,IN,MN,WI	Passive Ownership: . . . . .Allowed	US: . . . . Midwest
. . . .	Encourage Conversions: . . . Yes	Canada: . . . . .No
Type Space: . . . . . .FS, SF, SC, RM;~ SF	Average # Employees: . . 2 FT, 2 PT	Overseas: . . . . No

FORMU-3 WEIGHT LOSS CENTERS

4790 Douglas Circle, NW
Canton, OH 44718
TEL: (800) 525-6315 (216) 499-3334
FAX: (216) 499-8231
Mr. Walter E. Poston, VP Fran. Dev.

FORMU-3's competitive edge: Affordability. An affordable franchise opportunity for the average person in an economy where franchises cost upwards of $100,000. FORMU-3's low total investment of $29,375-60,400 provides a viable, cost-effective business opportunity. Additionally, the cost of the weight loss program is 35-70% less than other national weight loss programs. Our program is based on real grocery store food and 1-on-1 counseling.

HISTORY: . . . . .IFA	FINANCIAL: Earnings Claim: . .No	FRANCHISOR TRAINING/SUPPORT:
Established in 1982; . . 1st Franchised in 1983	Cash Investment: $19.6-42.5K	Financial Assistance Provided: . . . . .Yes
Company-Owned Units (As of 8/31/1992): . 34	Total Investment: $29.4-60.4K	Site Selection Assistance: . . . . .Yes
Franchised Units (As of 8/31/1992): 261	Fees: Franchise - $17.9K	Lease Negotiation Assistance: . . . .Yes
Total Units (As of 8/31/1992): 295	Royalty: 5%, Advert: 1%	Co-operative Advertising: . . . . . . .Yes
Projected New Units for 1993: 75	Contract Periods (Yrs.): 10/10	Training: . . . . . 5 Days Basic and 5 Days
Distribution: US-295;Can-0;Overseas-0	Area Development Agreement: Yes/2-3	. . . . . . Franchisee Orientation at HQ
North America: . . . . 26 States	Sub-Franchise Contract: . . . . .No	On-Going Support: C,D,E,G,H/ 55
Concentration: . .81 in OH, 29 in PA, 25 in MI	Expand in Territory: . . . . . . Yes	EXPANSION PLANS:
Registered: . . . CA,FL,IL,IN,MD,MI,MN,NY	Passive Ownership: . . . Discouraged	US: . . . . .All US
. . . . SD,VA,WI	Encourage Conversions: . . . . .No	Canada: . . . . .Yes
Type Space: SF,SC,Prof. Bldg.;~700-1,000 SF	Average # Employees: . . 2 FT, 2 PT	Overseas: . . . . .Yes

GNC FRANCHISING

921 Penn Ave.
Pittsburgh, PA 15222
TEL: (800) 766-7099 (412) 288-2071
FAX: (412) 288-2033
Mr. Michael A. Lando, Sr. Sales Dir.

GENERAL NUTRITION CORPORATION is committed to becoming the leading provider of products, services and information in the self-care and personal health enhancement market.

HISTORY: . . . . .IFA	FINANCIAL: Earnings Claim: . Yes	FRANCHISOR TRAINING/SUPPORT:
Established in 1936; . . 1st Franchised in 1988	Cash Investment: $50-60K	Financial Assistance Provided: . . .Yes(D)
Company-Owned Units (As of 8/31/1992): 977	Total Investment: $110-140K	Site Selection Assistance: . . . . .Yes
Franchised Units (As of 8/31/1992): 263	Fees: Franchise - $17.5K	Lease Negotiation Assistance: . . . .Yes
Total Units (As of 8/31/1992): 1240	Royalty: 5-6%, Advert: 2%	Co-operative Advertising: . . . . . . .NA
Projected New Units for 1993: 120	Contract Periods (Yrs.): 10/5/5	Training: . . . . 1 Wk. Local Store,
Distribution: US-192;Can-0;Overseas-8	Area Development Agreement: . .No	. . . . 1 Wk. HQ, 1 Wk. Franchisee Unit
North America: . . . . 35 States	Sub-Franchise Contract: . . . . .No	On-Going Support: C,D,E,F,G,h,I/ . . . 18
Concentration: . . 15 in NY, 13 in CA, 5 in FL	Expand in Territory: . . . . . . Yes	EXPANSION PLANS:
Registered: . . . . .All	Passive Ownership: . . . Not Allowed	US: . . . . .All US
. . . .	Encourage Conversions: . . . . Yes	Canada: . . . . .All Canada
Type Space: . . . . . .SF, SC, RM;~1,250 SF	Average # Employees: . . 2 FT, 3 PT	Overseas: . Emphasis of S/C America,Asia

GOODEBODIES THE NATURAL INVESTMENT

1001 S. Bayshore Dr., # 2402
Miami, FL 33131
TEL: (800) 966-3993 (305) 358-1903
FAX: (305) 358-9797
Ms. Shawn Nightingale, VP

Retailer of natural skin, bath and body products, which do not test on animals or use any by-products. Our packaging is recyclable and we have a recycling program.

HISTORY:	FINANCIAL: Earnings Claim: . .No	FRANCHISOR TRAINING/SUPPORT:
Established in 1989; . . 1st Franchised in 1991	Cash Investment: $30-100K	Financial Assistance Provided: . . . . . No
Company-Owned Units (As of 8/31/1992): . .6	Total Investment: $150-200K	Site Selection Assistance: . . . . .Yes
Franchised Units (As of 8/31/1992): 16	Fees: Franchise - $30K	Lease Negotiation Assistance: . . . . .Yes
Total Units (As of 8/31/1992): 22	Royalty: 2.5%, Advert: 1%	Co-operative Advertising: . . . . .Yes
Projected New Units for 1993: 10	Contract Periods (Yrs.): 10/5/5	Training: . . . . 2 Wks. Headquarters
Distribution: US-7;Can-0;Overseas-15	Area Development Agreement: Yes/10	
North America: . . . . 5 States	Sub-Franchise Contract: . . . . .No	On-Going Support: A,B,C,D,E,F,h,I/ . . . .
Concentration: . . . .2 in FL, 1 in NY, 1 in CT	Expand in Territory: . . . . . . Yes	EXPANSION PLANS:
Registered: . . . . All States	Passive Ownership: . . . Discouraged	US: . . . . All US
. . . .	Encourage Conversions: . . . . . Yes	Canada: . . . . .All Canada
Type Space: . . . . RM;~700 SF	Average # Employees: . . 3 FT, 2 PT	Overseas: . . . . Yes

GOUBAUD

280 Smith St.
Farmingdale, NY 11735
TEL: (516) 420-8000
FAX:
Mr. Emil Backstrom, GM

Skin care and cosmetics.

HISTORY:	FINANCIAL: Earnings Claim: . .No	FRANCHISOR TRAINING/SUPPORT:
Established in 1946; . . 1st Franchised in 1950	Cash Investment: $10-20K	Financial Assistance Provided: . . . . . No
Company-Owned Units (As of 8/31/1992): . .2	Total Investment: $20-40K	Site Selection Assistance: . . . . .Yes
Franchised Units (As of 8/31/1992): 40	Fees: Franchise - $0	Lease Negotiation Assistance: . . . . .No
Total Units (As of 8/31/1992): 42	Royalty: 0%, Advert: 5%	Co-operative Advertising: . . . . .Yes
Projected New Units for 1993: 10	Contract Periods (Yrs.): . . . 1/Infin.	Training: . . . . As Necessary Headquarters
Distribution: US-42;Can-0;Overseas-0	Area Development Agreement: . .No	. . . .
North America:	Sub-Franchise Contract: . . . . .No	On-Going Support: A,B,C,D,E,F,G,H,I/ 10
Concentration:	Expand in Territory: . . . . . . Yes	EXPANSION PLANS:
Registered:	Passive Ownership: . . . . . .Allowed	US: . . . . All US
. . . .	Encourage Conversions: . . . . . Yes	Canada: . . . . .All Canada
Type Space: . . . . SF;~3,000 SF	Average # Employees: . . 1 FT, 2 PT	Overseas: . . . . No

HAIR REPLACEMENT SYSTEMS

400 S. Dixie Highway
Hallandale, FL 33009
TEL: (800) 327-7971 (305) 457-0050 C
FAX: (305) 457-0054
Mr. Jules Borenstein, President

Sales on men's and women's custom-made, non-surgical hair replacements. Emphasis is on quality product and excellent marketing programs, including TV, newspaper, radio and other print campaigns. We retain our own in-house art department and top NYC creative talent. HRS manufactures in its own factory, allowing us to sell products and franchises at a highly competitive price.

HISTORY: . . . . IFA	FINANCIAL: Earnings Claim: . .No	FRANCHISOR TRAINING/SUPPORT:
Established in 1981; . . 1st Franchised in 1984	Cash Investment: $50-100K	Financial Assistance Provided: . . . Yes(I)
Company-Owned Units (As of 8/31/1992): . .0	Total Investment: $50-200K	Site Selection Assistance: . . . . .Yes
Franchised Units (As of 8/31/1992): 46	Fees: Franchise - . . . . . $6.5K Min.	Lease Negotiation Assistance: . . . . .Yes
Total Units (As of 8/31/1992): 46	Royalty: 6%, Advert: 0%	Co-operative Advertising: . . . . No
Projected New Units for 1993: 8	Contract Periods (Yrs.): 5/5	Training: . . . . 2 Wks. Headquarters,
Distribution: US-41;Can-5;Overseas-0	Area Development Agreement: Yes/Var	. . . . 4 Days Franchisee Site, As Needed
North America: . . . . 17 States, 2 Provinces	Sub-Franchise Contract: . . . . . Yes	On-Going Support: B,c,d,E,G,H,I/ . . . 11
Concentration: . . . 8 in NY, 4 in PA, 4 in ON	Expand in Territory: . . . . . . Yes	EXPANSION PLANS:
Registered: . . . .CA,FL,IL,IN,MI,MN,NY,RI	Passive Ownership: . . . Discouraged	US: . . . . All US
. . . . .VA,WA,WI,AB	Encourage Conversions: . . . . . Yes	Canada: . . . . .All Canada
Type Space: . . . . Office Building;~1,500 SF	Average # Employees: . . 2 FT, 1 PT	Overseas: . . . . . UK, FR, GR, IT

INCHES-A-WEIGH NORTH AMERICA

P. O. Box 59346
Birmingham, AL 35259
TEL: (800) 241-8663 (205) 879-8663
FAX: (205) 879-2106
Mr. Chris Yates, President

INCHES-A-WEIGH WEIGHT LOSS CENTERS offers a complete "figure cor-
rection" program for ladies 30-95 years of age. We are the affordable alternative
to Jenny Craig and Nutri/System. We offer an innovative approach of weight loss
and exercise, which is our true point of difference.

HISTORY:	FINANCIAL: Earnings Claim: . .No	FRANCHISOR TRAINING/SUPPORT:
Established in 1985; . . 1st Franchised in 1986	Cash Investment: $45-50K	Financial Assistance Provided: . . . . .Yes
Company-Owned Units (As of 8/31/1992): . .5	Total Investment: $45-50K	Site Selection Assistance: . . . . . . .Yes
Franchised Units (As of 8/31/1992): 40	Fees: Franchise - $29.5K	Lease Negotiation Assistance: . . . .Yes
Total Units (As of 8/31/1992): 45	Royalty: 4%, Advert: 0%	Co-operative Advertising: . . . . . . .Yes
Projected New Units for 1993: 24	Contract Periods (Yrs.): 7/7	Training: . . . . . . 10 Days Headquarters
Distribution: US-42;Can-1;Overseas-2	Area Development Agreement: . .No	
North America: . . . . . 20 States, 1 Province	Sub-Franchise Contract: . . . .No	On-Going Support: C,D,E,G,H,I/ 11
Concentration: . . . 10 in AL, 5 in NC, 5 in PR	Expand in Territory: . . . . . Yes	EXPANSION PLANS:
Registered: . . . . IL,NY,VA	Passive Ownership: . . . Discouraged	US: . . . . TX, CA and FL
. . . .	Encourage Conversions: . . . . . Yes	Canada: . . . . .All Canada
Type Space: . . . . . . SC;~1,200-1,400 SF	Average # Employees: . . . . .4 FT	Overseas: . . . . All

INVISIONS

161 Gaither Dr., # 201
Mt. Laurel, NJ 08054
TEL: (609) 273-9800
FAX: (609) 273-7950
Mr. Timothy Leogrande, Dir. Fran. Dev.

Approximately 40% of all men (and some women) will experience some form
of noticeable hair loss. INVISIONS franchises serve this market. With the
aging of the Baby Boomers generation, we expect continued growth and
profitability.

HISTORY: . . . . IFA	FINANCIAL: Earnings Claim: . .No	FRANCHISOR TRAINING/SUPPORT:
Established in 1987; . . 1st Franchised in 1990	Cash Investment: $35K	Financial Assistance Provided: . . . . .NA
Company-Owned Units (As of 8/31/1992): . .6	Total Investment: $136-176K	Site Selection Assistance: . . . . . . .Yes
Franchised Units (As of 8/31/1992): 8	Fees: Franchise - $35K	Lease Negotiation Assistance: . . . .Yes
Total Units (As of 8/31/1992): 14	Royalty: 12%, Advert: 3%	Co-operative Advertising: . . . . . . .NA
Projected New Units for 1993: 10	Contract Periods (Yrs.): . . . 10/10	Training: . . . . . 2 Wks. Headquarters,
Distribution: US-12;Can-2;Overseas-0	Area Development Agreement: . .No	. . . . 1 Wk. On-Site
North America: . . . 10 States, 2 Provinces	Sub-Franchise Contract: . . . . .No	On-Going Support: A,B,C,D,E,H/ . . . 25
Concentration: . . . . 3 in NJ	Expand in Territory: . . . . . . Yes	EXPANSION PLANS:
Registered: . . . . . CA,FL,IL,NY,OR,RI,WI	Passive Ownership: . . . . .Allowed	US: . . . . Midwest, Central US
. . . .	Encourage Conversions: . . . . NA	Canada: . . . . .All Canada
Type Space: . . . . . Business Park;~2,400 SF	Average # Employees: . .12 FT, 3 PT	Overseas: . . . . No

JAZZERCISE

2808 Roosevelt St.
Carlsbad, CA 92008
TEL: (800) FIT IS IT (619) 434-2101
FAX: (619) 434-8958
Ms. Maureen Brown, Fran. Services

JAZZERCISE is the #1 Fitness Program in the world. All routines are
choreographed by Judi Sheppard Misset and screened by an in-house exercise
physiologist for safety and effectiveness. All JAZZERCISE instructors are pre-
screened and carefully trained in dance technique, marketing and business operations. All instructors are certified by JAZZERCISE, INC.

HISTORY:	FINANCIAL: Earnings Claim: . .No	FRANCHISOR TRAINING/SUPPORT:
Established in 1969; . . 1st Franchised in 1983	Cash Investment: $2K	Financial Assistance Provided: . . . . .No
Company-Owned Units (As of 8/31/1992): . .0	Total Investment: $2K	Site Selection Assistance: . . . . . . .Yes
Franchised Units (As of 8/31/1992): 4677	Fees: Franchise - $650	Lease Negotiation Assistance: . . . . .No
Total Units (As of 8/31/1992): 4677	Royalty: 20%, Advert: 0%	Co-operative Advertising: . . . . . . .Yes
Projected New Units for 1993: 700	Contract Periods (Yrs.): 5/5	Training: . . . . .2-3 Days Workshop
Distribution: . US-4377;Can-150;Overseas-150	Area Development Agreement: Yes/Var	. . . . . . Preceded by Video Training
North America: . . . . 50 States, 5 Provinces	Sub-Franchise Contract: . . . . . Yes	On-Going Support: C,D,G,H,I/ 85
Concentration:	Expand in Territory: . . . . . . Yes	EXPANSION PLANS:
Registered: . . . . .All	Passive Ownership: . . . Not Allowed	US: . . . . .All US
. . . .	Encourage Conversions: . . . . . .No	Canada: . . . . .All Canada
Type Space: . . . .;~ SF	Average # Employees: . 1 FT, 1-2 PT	Overseas: . . . . .Yes

JENNY CRAIG WEIGHT LOSS CENTRES
445 Marine View Dr., # 300
Del Mar, CA 92014
TEL: (619) 259-7000
FAX: (619) 259-2812
Mr. Gary Hawk, VP Fran. Dev.

JENNY CRAIG offers a proven structure for success in the dynamic weight loss industry. Our program provides personal counseling, great-tasting Jenny's Cuisine and a supportive, motivating environment. Seeking franchisees with a proven record of developing and motivating talent, dedication to client service and making a profit.

HISTORY:	IFA
Established in 1983; 1st Franchised in 1986	
Company-Owned Units (As of 8/31/1992):	473
Franchised Units (As of 8/31/1992):	224
Total Units (As of 8/31/1992):	697
Projected New Units for 1993:	100
Distribution: US-585;Can-11;Overseas-101	
North America:	37 States
Concentration: 140 in CA, 43 in IL, 25 FL	
Registered:	All
Type Space:	SC;~2,500 SF

FINANCIAL: Earnings Claim:	No
Cash Investment:	$150K
Total Investment:	$150K
Fees: Franchise -	$50K
Royalty: 7%, Advert:	0%
Contract Periods (Yrs.):	10/10
Area Development Agreement:	No
Sub-Franchise Contract:	No
Expand in Territory:	Yes
Passive Ownership:	Not Allowed
Encourage Conversions:	NA
Average # Employees:	6 FT, 2 PT

FRANCHISOR TRAINING/SUPPORT:	
Financial Assistance Provided:	No
Site Selection Assistance:	Yes
Lease Negotiation Assistance:	Yes
Co-operative Advertising:	No
Training:	6 Wks. in San Diego
On-Going Support: A,B,C,D,E,F,H/	99
EXPANSION PLANS:	
US:	Midwest, South, S'east, NE
Canada:	Yes
Overseas:	No

LADY OF AMERICA

100 Glenborough Dr., # 1210
Houston, TX 77067
TEL: (800) 833-LADY (713) 876-1956
FAX: (713) 876-1603
Mr. Roger Wittenberns, President

This chain of ultra-modern fitness centers positions its locations in neighborhood retail centers. The company features collection of monthly dues from its members by electronic funds transfer. Often referred to as the McDonald's of fitness.

HISTORY:	
Established in 1984; 1st Franchised in 1986	
Company-Owned Units (As of 8/31/1992):	9
Franchised Units (As of 8/31/1992):	43
Total Units (As of 8/31/1992):	52
Projected New Units for 1993:	15
Distribution: US-52;Can-0;Overseas-0	
North America:	1 State
Concentration:	40 in TX
Registered:	
Type Space:	FS, SF, SC;~3,100 SF

FINANCIAL: Earnings Claim:	No
Cash Investment:	$40K
Total Investment:	$99K
Fees: Franchise -	$25K
Royalty: 10-5%, Advert:	2-5%
Contract Periods (Yrs.):	10/5
Area Development Agreement:	Yes/1
Sub-Franchise Contract:	No
Expand in Territory:	Yes
Passive Ownership:	Allowed
Encourage Conversions:	Yes
Average # Employees:	2 FT, 7 PT

FRANCHISOR TRAINING/SUPPORT:	
Financial Assistance Provided:	Yes(D)
Site Selection Assistance:	Yes
Lease Negotiation Assistance:	Yes
Co-operative Advertising:	Yes
Training:	35 Hours Headquarters, 30 Days Pre-Sale Site, On-Going
On-Going Support: a,c,d,E,G,H,I/	38
EXPANSION PLANS:	
US:	All US
Canada:	All Canada
Overseas:	Yes

LIFE TREND WEIGHT LOSS AND EXERCISE CENTER
106 W. 31st St.
Independence, MO 64055
TEL: (800) 821-3126 (816) 254-0805
FAX: (816) 254-1557
Mr. Glen Henson, VP

Our LIFE TREND TANNING AND TONING CENTERS are combined with a small exercise center, which leads to permanent weight loss. We provide many options, I.E., Isokinetic exercisers, treadmills and bikes, toning tables, body wraps and tanning beds. We provide full training and follow-up.

HISTORY:	
Established in 1977; 1st Franchised in 1979	
Company-Owned Units (As of 8/31/1992):	0
Franchised Units (As of 8/31/1992):	350
Total Units (As of 8/31/1992):	350
Projected New Units for 1993:	25
Distribution: US-300;Can-20;Overseas-30	
North America: 30 States, 5 Provinces	
Concentration: 40 in ME, 30 in KS, 26 in NE	
Registered:	All
Type Space:	SC;~ SF

FINANCIAL: Earnings Claim:	No
Cash Investment:	$20-30K
Total Investment:	$25-35K
Fees: Franchise -	$1K
Royalty: 0%, Advert:	0%
Contract Periods (Yrs.):	10/10
Area Development Agreement:	No
Sub-Franchise Contract:	No
Expand in Territory:	Yes
Passive Ownership:	Discouraged
Encourage Conversions:	No
Average # Employees:	1 FT, 2 PT

FRANCHISOR TRAINING/SUPPORT:	
Financial Assistance Provided:	Yes(D)
Site Selection Assistance:	No
Lease Negotiation Assistance:	No
Co-operative Advertising:	No
Training:	3 Days Headquarters
On-Going Support: E,G,H,I/	6
EXPANSION PLANS:	
US:	All US
Canada:	All Canada
Overseas:	Yes

NAILS 'N LASHES STUDIO

Box 340
Sharon, ON L0G 1V0 CAN
TEL: (416) 473-5774
FAX:
Mr. Irving Fine, President

Application of artificial acrylic fingernails and eyelashes (only).

HISTORY:	FINANCIAL: Earnings Claim: . .No	FRANCHISOR TRAINING/SUPPORT:
Established in 1970; . . 1st Franchised in 1973	Cash Investment: $15-25K	Financial Assistance Provided: . . . . .No
Company-Owned Units (As of 8/31/1992): . .0	Total Investment: $15-25K	Site Selection Assistance: . . . . . . .Yes
Franchised Units (As of 8/31/1992): 21	Fees: Franchise - $5-15K	Lease Negotiation Assistance: . . . .Yes
Total Units (As of 8/31/1992): 21	Royalty: 0%, Advert: 0%	Co-operative Advertising: . . . . . . .Yes
Projected New Units for 1993:	Contract Periods (Yrs.): . .Unlimited	Training: . . . . 6 Wks. Franchisee Site
Distribution: US-1;Can-20;Overseas-0	Area Development Agreement: Yes/Unl	. . . .
North America: . . . . . .1 State, 3 Provinces	Sub-Franchise Contract: . . . .No	On-Going Support: B,D,E/ 1
Concentration: . . .13 in ON, 6 in BC, 1 in AB	Expand in Territory: . . . . Yes	EXPANSION PLANS:
Registered:	Passive Ownership: . . . Not Allowed	US: . . . . .No
. . . .	Encourage Conversions: . . . . NA	Canada: . . . . .Yes
Type Space: . . . . FS, SF, SC;~400-600 SF	Average # Employees: . . . . 2-3 FT	Overseas: . . . . No

NUSHAPE FIGURE SPAS

150 Simcoe St.
Toronto, ON M5H 3G4 CAN
TEL: (416) 598-7727 C
FAX: (416) 598-0028
Mr. Peter Stauros, Fran. Dir.

Weight loss and body-toning treatments.

HISTORY:	FINANCIAL: Earnings Claim: . .No	FRANCHISOR TRAINING/SUPPORT:
Established in 1992; . . 1st Franchised in 1992	Cash Investment: $20K	Financial Assistance Provided: . . .Yes(D)
Company-Owned Units (As of 8/31/1992): . .1	Total Investment: $40K	Site Selection Assistance: . . . . .Yes
Franchised Units (As of 8/31/1992): 3	Fees: Franchise - $15K	Lease Negotiation Assistance: . . . . .Yes
Total Units (As of 8/31/1992): 4	Royalty: 5%, Advert: 3%	Co-operative Advertising: . . . . . . .Yes
Projected New Units for 1993: 4	Contract Periods (Yrs.): 10/5	Training: . . . . 2 Wks. Headquarters,
Distribution: US-0;Can-4;Overseas-0	Area Development Agreement: Yes/10	. . . . .2 Wks. Franchisee Location
North America: . . . . .1 Province	Sub-Franchise Contract: . . . . Yes	On-Going Support: a,B,C,D,E,G,h,i/ . . .4
Concentration: . . . . 4 in ON	Expand in Territory: . . . . . . Yes	EXPANSION PLANS:
Registered:	Passive Ownership: . . . Not Allowed	US: . . . . .All US
. . . .	Encourage Conversions: . . . . Yes	Canada: . . . . .All Canada
Type Space: . . . . FS;~1,000 SF	Average # Employees: . . 1 FT, 2 PT	Overseas: . . . . .Yes

OUR WEIGH

3340 Poplar, # 136
Memphis, TN 38104
TEL: (901) 458-7546
FAX:
Ms. Helen K. Seale, President

A unique weight control group, consisting of 30-minute meetings, behavior modification, exercise and, most important, a nutritional diet that allows members to eat what they like and not have to eat foods they don't like. First in the field to introduce "food rewards" and free weekly weigh-in upon reaching desired weight.

HISTORY:	FINANCIAL: Earnings Claim: . .No	FRANCHISOR TRAINING/SUPPORT:
Established in 1974; . . 1st Franchised in 1974	Cash Investment: $1.5K	Financial Assistance Provided: . . . . .No
Company-Owned Units (As of 8/31/1992): . 11	Total Investment: $3K	Site Selection Assistance: . . . . No
Franchised Units (As of 8/31/1992): 1	Fees: Franchise - $1.5K	Lease Negotiation Assistance: . . . . .No
Total Units (As of 8/31/1992): 12	Royalty: $1.5K, Advert: 0%	Co-operative Advertising: . . . . No
Projected New Units for 1993: 2	Contract Periods (Yrs.):	Training: . . . . 2 Wks. Headquarters
Distribution: US-12;Can-0;Overseas-0	Area Development Agreement: . Yes	. . . .
North America: . . . . 3 States	Sub-Franchise Contract: . . . . .No	On-Going Support: / 1
Concentration: . . . .6 in TN, 5 in MI, 1 in AR	Expand in Territory: . . . . . . Yes	EXPANSION PLANS:
Registered:	Passive Ownership: . . . Discouraged	US: . . . . .All US
. . . .	Encourage Conversions: . . . . .No	Canada: . . . . No
Type Space: . . . . ;~Varies SF	Average # Employees: . . . . .2 PT	Overseas: . . . . No

PHYSICIANS WEIGHT LOSS CENTERS
395 Springside Dr.
Akron, OH 44333
TEL: (216) 666-7952
FAX: (216) 666-6180
Ms. Dianne Riffle, Fran. Dev.

Supervised weight reduction business, offering the consumer a comprehensive program utilizing individualized treatment, personal care, counseling and weight maintenance.

HISTORY: . . . .
Established in 1979; . . 1st Franchised in 1980
Company-Owned Units (As of 8/31/1992): . 15
Franchised Units (As of 8/31/1992): 156
Total Units (As of 8/31/1992): 171
Projected New Units for 1993: 25
Distribution: US-161;Can-10;Overseas-0
 North America: . . . . 23 States, 3 Provinces
 Concentration: . . 36 in OH, 14 in FL, 12 in IN
Registered: . . . . . FL,IL,IN,MD,MI,VA,DC
. . . .
Type Space: . . . . SC;~1,200 SF

FINANCIAL: Earnings Claim: . .No
Cash Investment: $40-80K
Total Investment: $40-80K
Fees: Franchise - $7.5K
 Royalty: 10%, Advert: $250/Wk.
Contract Periods (Yrs.): . . . 3/5/5/5
Area Development Agreement: . .No
Sub-Franchise Contract: . . . . .No
Expand in Territory: . . . . . . Yes
Passive Ownership: . . . Not Allowed
Encourage Conversions: . . . . Yes
Average # Employees: 2-3 FT, 1-2 PT

FRANCHISOR TRAINING/SUPPORT:
Financial Assistance Provided: . . .Yes(D)
Site Selection Assistance: . . . . . . .Yes
Lease Negotiation Assistance: . . . . .Yes
Co-operative Advertising: . . . . . . .Yes
Training: . . . . . . 2 Wks. Headquarters,
 . . . . . .2 Wks. Centers Throughout US
On-Going Support: A,B,C,D,E,F,G,h/ . 45
EXPANSION PLANS:
US: . . . . .All US
Canada: . . . . .All Canada
Overseas: . . . . No

POTIONS & LOTIONS

10201 N. 21st Ave., # 8
Phoenix, AZ 85251
TEL: (800) 456-3765 (602) 944-6642
FAX: (602) 395-9518
Ms. Sharon Muir, President

Personal body care product retail stores with over 200 fragrances in perfumes, lotions, bath beads and crystals, soaps and bath accouterments. P-h balanced, environmentally friendly, cruelty-free.

HISTORY: . . . .
Established in 1975; . . 1st Franchised in 1989
Company-Owned Units (As of 8/31/1992): . .8
Franchised Units (As of 8/31/1992): 5
Total Units (As of 8/31/1992): 13
Projected New Units for 1993: 10
Distribution: US-13;Can-0;Overseas-0
 North America: . . . . 6 States
 Concentration: . . . 6 in AZ, 2 in CO, 2 in UT
Registered: . . . . .CA,MD,MI,OR,VA
. . . .
Type Space: . . . . RM;~700-800 SF

FINANCIAL: Earnings Claim: . .No
Cash Investment: $147-307K
Total Investment: $147-307K
Fees: Franchise - $25K
 Royalty: 5%, Advert: 2%
Contract Periods (Yrs.): . . . 10/10
Area Development Agreement: Yes/Var
Sub-Franchise Contract: . . . . .No
Expand in Territory: . . . . . . Yes
Passive Ownership: . . . Discouraged
Encourage Conversions: . . . . Yes
Average # Employees: . . 2 FT, 1 PT

FRANCHISOR TRAINING/SUPPORT:
Financial Assistance Provided: . . . . .No
Site Selection Assistance: . . . . . . .Yes
Lease Negotiation Assistance: . . . . .Yes
Co-operative Advertising: . . . . . . .Yes
Training: . . . . . . .10 Days Headquarters
On-Going Support: b,C,D,E,G,H,I/ . . . 10
EXPANSION PLANS:
US: . . . . .All US
Canada: . . . . .All Canada
Overseas: . . . . .Yes

SUNBANQUE ISLAND TANNING

2533A Yonge St.
Toronto, ON M4P 2H9 CAN
TEL: (416) 488-5838
FAX: (416) 488-3712
Mr. Joel Giusto, Chairman

SUNBANQUE ISLAND TANNING is a full-service suntan salon with complete and exclusive inventory control and management.

HISTORY: . . . .
Established in 1983; . . 1st Franchised in 1984
Company-Owned Units (As of 8/31/1992): . .4
Franchised Units (As of 8/31/1992): 11
Total Units (As of 8/31/1992): 15
Projected New Units for 1993: 10
Distribution: US-7;Can-8;Overseas-0
 North America: . . . . . . 1 State, 1 Province
 Concentration: . . . . .8 in ON, 7 in MA
Registered: . . . .
. . . .
Type Space: . . . . .FS, SF;~1,000 SF

FINANCIAL: Earnings Claim: . Yes
Cash Investment: $10-20K
Total Investment: $30-40K
Fees: Franchise - $5K
 Royalty: 3%, Advert: 5%
Contract Periods (Yrs.): 5/5
Area Development Agreement: Yes/5
Sub-Franchise Contract: . . . . . Yes
Expand in Territory: . . . . Yes
Passive Ownership: . . . Discouraged
Encourage Conversions: . . . . . Yes
Average # Employees: . . 2 FT, 1 PT

FRANCHISOR TRAINING/SUPPORT:
Financial Assistance Provided: . . .Yes(D)
Site Selection Assistance: . . . . . . .Yes
Lease Negotiation Assistance: . . . . .Yes
Co-operative Advertising: . . . . . . .Yes
Training: . . . . . . 1-2 Wks. Headquarters
. . . .
On-Going Support: A,B,C,D,E,F,G,H/ . .5
EXPANSION PLANS:
US: . . . . .All US
Canada: . . . . .All Canada
Overseas: . . . . Yes

TOP OF THE LINE COSMETICS AND FRAGRANCES
Plaza 1000, Main St., # 202
Voorhees, N3 08043
TEL: (609) 751-3303 C
FAX: (609) 751-0920
Mr. Richard Comp, Partner

Retail sales of nationally-advertised fragrance and cosmetic brands at a discount. Stores are in factory outlet centers and regional malls throughout the country. Full training provided. No experience necessary.

HISTORY: . . . .
Established in 1983; . . 1st Franchised in 1989
Company-Owned Units (As of 8/31/1992): . 23
Franchised Units (As of 8/31/1992): 4
Total Units (As of 8/31/1992): 27
Projected New Units for 1993: 10
Distribution: US-27;Can-0;Overseas-0
North America: . . . . 19 States
Concentration: . . . 2 in VA, 2 in MI, 2 in NY
Registered: . . . . CA,FL,NY
. . . .
Type Space: SC, Factory Outlt;~800-1,500 SF

FINANCIAL: Earnings Claim: . .No
Cash Investment: . . . . $Varies
Total Investment: $90-125K
Fees: Franchise - $25K
Royalty: 5%, Advert: 1%
Contract Periods (Yrs.): 5/5
Area Development Agreement: . .No
Sub-Franchise Contract: . . . . .No
Expand in Territory: . . . . . . Yes
Passive Ownership: . . . . .Allowed
Encourage Conversions: . . . . NA
Average # Employees: . . 2 FT, 2 PT

FRANCHISOR TRAINING/SUPPORT:
Financial Assistance Provided: . . . Yes(I)
Site Selection Assistance: . . . . . . .Yes
Lease Negotiation Assistance: . . . .Yes
Co-operative Advertising: . . . . No
Training: . . . . . . 2 Wks. Company Store
. . . . and On-Site
On-Going Support: A,B,C,D,E,F,G,h,I/ . 10
EXPANSION PLANS:
US: . . . . .All US, Emph. on West Coast
Canada: . . . . .No
Overseas: . . . . No

TRADE SECRET

130 Henry St., P. O. Box 58
Dousman, WI 53118
TEL: (800) 462-6092 (414) 965-2196
FAX:
Mr. Bryan Patzkowski, VP Fran. Dev.

Pioneer at the new concept retail products salon, featuring a full retail presentation of professional hair care products, cosmetics, nail supplies and limited service (4 chairs).

HISTORY: . . . . IFA
Established in 1983; . . 1st Franchised in 1988
Company-Owned Units (As of 8/31/1992): . 24
Franchised Units (As of 8/31/1992): 50
Total Units (As of 8/31/1992): 74
Projected New Units for 1993: 15
Distribution: US-74;Can-0;Overseas-0
North America: . . . . 20 States
Concentration: . . . 16 in WI, 11 in IL, 7 in FL
Registered: . . . . . CA,IL,IN,MD,MI,VA,WI
. . . .
Type Space: . . . . RM;~800 SF

FINANCIAL: Earnings Claim: . .No
Cash Investment: $50K
Total Investment: $100-130K
Fees: Franchise - $27.5K
Royalty: 6%, Advert: 2%
Contract Periods (Yrs.): . . . . Lease
Area Development Agreement: . .No
Sub-Franchise Contract: . . . . .No
Expand in Territory: . . . . . . .No
Passive Ownership: . . . Not Allowed
Encourage Conversions: . . . .No
Average # Employees: . . 3 FT, 3 PT

FRANCHISOR TRAINING/SUPPORT:
Financial Assistance Provided: . . . Yes(I)
Site Selection Assistance: . . . . . . .Yes
Lease Negotiation Assistance: . . . .Yes
Co-operative Advertising: . . . . . . .Yes
Training: . . . . 5 Days Headquarters,
. . . . 8 Days Shop Site
On-Going Support: C,D,E,G,H,I/ 12
EXPANSION PLANS:
US: . . . . .All US
Canada: . . . . .No
Overseas: . . . . No

VOLPE NAILS

1 N. Page Ave., P. O. Box 7339
Endicott, NY 13760
TEL: (800) 848-6573 (607) 786-5051 C
FAX: (607) 786-9023
Ms. Maureen Volpe, President

We are presently the only nail salon franchise, with over 65 salons on the East Coast. We have the best education in the industry - plus state-of-the-art equipment and products. We totally develop your salon, from site and employee selection to grand opening and filling your appointment book! Offering clients the most pampering atmosphere while servicing all nail needs from the most therapeutic to the most artistic!

HISTORY: . . . .
Established in 1980; . . 1st Franchised in 1989
Company-Owned Units (As of 8/31/1992): . .3
Franchised Units (As of 8/31/1992): 62
Total Units (As of 8/31/1992): 65
Projected New Units for 1993: 30
Distribution: US-65;Can-0;Overseas-0
North America: . . . . 9 States
Concentration: . .30 in NY, 12 in PA, 6 in MA
Registered: . . . . FL,NY,VA
. . . .
Type Space: . . . . .SC;~1,000 SF

FINANCIAL: Earnings Claim: . . .
Cash Investment: $30-60K
Total Investment: $60-100K
Fees: Franchise - $25K
Royalty: Flat Fee, Advert: $100/Mo.
Contract Periods (Yrs.): 10/10
Area Development Agreement: . .No
Sub-Franchise Contract: . . . . .No
Expand in Territory: . . . . . . .No
Passive Ownership: . . . Discouraged
Encourage Conversions: . . . . Yes
Average # Employees: . . . .6-10 FT

FRANCHISOR TRAINING/SUPPORT:
Financial Assistance Provided: . . .Yes(D)
Site Selection Assistance: . . . . . . .Yes
Lease Negotiation Assistance: . . . . .Yes
Co-operative Advertising: . . . . . . .Yes
Training: . . . . . 4 Wks. Headquarters, 1-2
. . . . Wks. On-Site or 6 Wks. On-site
On-Going Support: A,B,C,d,E,F,G,h,I/ . . 8
EXPANSION PLANS:
US: . . . . All US, Esp. Northeast
Canada: . . . . Not Yet But Soon
Overseas: . . . . .Not Yet

WILLIE'S PLACE

221 Bonita Ave., # 203
Piedmont, CA 94611
TEL: (800) CLOS-CUT (510) 839-5471
FAX: (510) 547-3245
Dr. Willie Free, President

Unique opportunity in the highly profitable, growth business of removing un-
wanted facial and body hair. Specializing in "Pat's Bikini Cuts," guaranteed to
last 3 months. Custom merkin fitting. Free initial consultation. Average customer
spends $225 per year for services. Great customer loyalty. Complete turn-key
operation. Initial investment under $25,000.

HISTORY:	**FINANCIAL:** Earnings Claim: . Yes	**FRANCHISOR TRAINING/SUPPORT:**
Established in 1982; . . 1st Franchised in 1986	Cash Investment: $25-45K	Financial Assistance Provided: . . .Yes(D)
Company-Owned Units (As of 8/31/1992): . .3	Total Investment: $35-75K	Site Selection Assistance: . . . . .Yes
Franchised Units (As of 8/31/1992): 4	Fees: Franchise - $12K	Lease Negotiation Assistance: . . . . .Yes
Total Units (As of 8/31/1992): 7	Royalty: 4%, Advert. . . 1%	Co-operative Advertising: . . . . .Yes
Projected New Units for 1993: 3	Contract Periods (Yrs.): 10/10	Training: . . . . 4 Wks. Headquarters,
Distribution: US-6;Can-1;Overseas-0	Area Development Agreement: Yes/10	. . . . 2 Wks. On-Site
North America: . . . . . .3 States, 1 Province	Sub-Franchise Contract: . . . . .No	On-Going Support: A,C,D,G,H,I/ 5
Concentration: . . . 3 in CA, 2 in KY, 1 in TN	Expand in Territory: . . . . . . .No	**EXPANSION PLANS:**
Registered: . . . . .CA,OR,AB	Passive Ownership: . . . Discouraged	US: . . . . .All US
. . . .	Encourage Conversions: . . . . .Yes	Canada: . . . . BC and Ontario
Type Space: FS, SF, SC, RM;~1,500-1,800 SF	Average # Employees: . . 2 FT, 3 PT	Overseas: . . . . UK, EUR, JA, AU

SUPPLEMENTAL LISTING OF FRANCHISORS

ALOETTE COSMETICS . . . . 1301 Wright's Lane, West Chester, PA 19380
    Contact: Ms. Susan Graybill, VP Fran. Ops.; Tel: (215) 692-0600
ALOETTE COSMETICS OF CANADA . . . . 89 Edilcan Dr., Concord, ON L4K 3S6   CAN
    Contact: Mr. Bob Mundy; Tel: (416) 738-6775
BODY DESIGN BY GILDA STUDIOS . . . . 11755 Exposition Blvd., Los Angeles, CA 90064
    Contact: President; Tel: (213) 477-0418
CHRISTINE VALMY . . . . 260 Fifth Line, New York City, NY 10001
    Contact: Ms. Joan Kennedy; Tel: (201) 575-1050
CLEAN AND LEAN - LAUNDRY AND FITNESS . . . . . 770 Sycamore Ave., # J428, Vista, CA 92083
    Contact: Mr. Rob Shively; Tel: (619) 598-1030
DERMACULTURE CLINIC . . . . 1936 W. 135th St., Gardena, CA 90249
    Contact: Mr. Donald James, President; Tel: (213) 538-1300
DIET WORKSHOP, THE . . . . 10 Brookline Pl. W., # 107, Brookline, MA 02146
    Contact: Ms. Rennie Shepen, President; Tel: (617) 739-2222
DOCTORS WEIGHT LOSS . . . . 4400 Bayou Blvd., # 49, Pensacola, FL 32503
    Contact: Ms. Peggy Oakley; Tel: (904) 478-2334
FACE UP PROFESSIONAL SKIN CARE CENTERS . . . . 888 W. 16th St., Newport Beach, CA 92663
    Contact: President; Tel: (714) 631-0149
FEMININE WAY INTERNATIONAL . . . . 24 Inglewood Dr., Hamilton, ON L8P 2T5   CAN
    Contact: Ms. Barbara Gordon, CEO; Tel: (416) 523-4506
FIFTH SEASON, THE . . . . 18518 Detroit Ave., Lakewood, OH 44107
    Contact: Mr. Mike Matynka, President; Tel: (216) 228-7869
FITNESS ON WHEELS . . . . 1185 S. Milwaukee St., Denver, CO 80210
    Contact: President; Tel:
FITNESS TREND . . . . 106 West 31st St., Independence, MO 64055
    Contact: Mr. Glen E. Henson, VP; Tel: (816) 254-0805
FRANKIE JENNINGS INTERNATIONAL . . . . P. O. Box 42575, Atlanta, GA 30311
    Contact: President; Tel: (404) 767-5801
GALLIMORE ENTERPRISES . . . . 19 Railside Rd., Toronto, ON M3R 1B2   CAN
    Contact: President; Tel: (416) 449-2447
GODDESSE OF LAS VEGAS NAIL SUPPLY . . . . . . 310 Shaw Rd., # H, S. San Francisco, CA 94080
    Contact: Mr. Ed Collantes, President; Tel: (800) NAIL-BIS (415) 876-0300
HEALTH CLUBS OF AMERICA . . . . Box 4098, Waterville, CT 06714
    Contact: Mr. Gregg Nolan, Franchise Director; Tel: (203) 879-4675
HOLLYWOOD WEIGHT LOSS CLINICS . . . . 45-47 E. Penn St., Uniontown, PA 15401
    Contact: President; Tel:
JACQUIE'S PLACE . . . . 450 Fairway Dr., # 204, Deerfield Beach, FL 33441
    Contact: Mr. Harold Glickman; Tel: (407) 368-3417

JENEAL STUDIOS .3798 Westchase, Houston, TX 77042
    Contact: Dr. Jerry O'Neal, Ph.D, President; Tel: (800) 7JE-NEAL (713) 781-2263 C
JERRYANN ELECTROLYSIS . . . . P. O. Box 97, Cold Spring Harbor, NY 11724
    Contact: Ms. Ann Paduano; Tel: (516) 931-9400
JUDITH SANS SKIN CARE . . . . 3853 Oakcliff Industrial Ct., Atlanta, GA 30340
    Contact: President; Tel: (404) 449-7196
LANA GRAY INTERNATIONAL . . . . 7590 E. Gray Rd., # 201, Scottsdale, AZ 85260
    Contact: President; Tel:
LES CONSULTANTS CHEV'HAIR . . . . 221 St. Georges, St-Barnabe Nord, PQ G0X 2K0   CAN
    Contact: Mr. Gaston Gelinas, President; Tel: (819) 264-2116
LORRAINE'S TROPI-TAN/TROPI-TAN . . . . G-4290 Miller Rd., Flint, MI 48507
    Contact: Mr. Vince Lorraine; Tel: (313) 230-0090
MERLE NORMAN COSMETICS . . . . 9130 Bellanca Ave., Los Angeles, CA 90045
    Contact: Mr. Bob Deutsch, VP; Tel: (800) 421-6648 (213) 337-2200
NECTAR BEAUTY SHOPS . . . . .2367 Anson Dr., Mississauga, ON L5S 1G1   CAN
    Contact: Mr. Barry Johnson; Tel: (416) 673-7984
NU-CONCEPT BODY WRAP . . . . 603 Cleveland St., Elyria, OH 44035
    Contact: Mr. Dennis Doman; Tel: (216) 365-7378
NU-LIFE NUTRITION . . . . .621 Williams St., Kewanee, IL 61443
    Contact: President; Tel: (309) 853-5600
NUTRA BOLIC WEIGHT REDUCTION . . . . 4790 Douglas Circle NW, Canton, OH 44718
    Contact: Mr. Dennis Kline, Natl. Marketing Dir.; Tel: (216) 499-3334
NUTRI/SYSTEM . . . . 380 Sentry Pkwy., Blue Bell, PA 19411
    Contact: Mr. Joel D. Rosen, Director; Tel: (800) 777-7892 (215) 940-3000
PERMANENT WEIGHT CONTROL CENTERS . . . . 99 Cherry St., # B, Milford, CT 06460
    Contact: Ms. Gae Adams; Tel: (203) 877-1702
R. X. SOLEIL . . . . 490 Young St., Toronto, ON M4Y 1X5   CAN
    Contact: Mr. Lucien Dugal; Tel: (416) 920-2730
SLENDER CENTER . . . . 6515 Grand Teton Plaza, # 241, Madison, WI 53719
    Contact: Ms. Jean Geurink, President; Tel: (608) 833-1477 C
SLIM TAN TOTAL BEAUTY CENTERS . . . . 8040 E. Mill Plain Blvd., Vancouver, WA 98664
    Contact: Ms. Marie Bell, President; Tel: (206) 693-4118
STOP SMOKING PLAN . . . . P.O. Box 232, E. Amherst, NY 14051
    Contact: Mrs. Fredrica A. Nixon, President; Tel: (716) 688-4573
SUDDENLY SUN . . . . 3681 Green Rd., # 212, Beachwood, OH 44122
    Contact: Ms. Terri Mrklas, President; Tel: (800) 858-1851 (216) 524-0999
TRIMLINES AMERICA . . . . .912 Drew St., # 104, Clearwater, FL 34615
    Contact: President; Tel:
WEIDER FRANCHISING . . . . 15375 Barranca Pkwy., # B-209, Irvine, CA 92718
    Contact: Mr. Mike Hays, President; Tel: (714) 753-8353
WEIGH TO GO . . . . .2311 205th St., # 103, Torrance, CA 90501
    Contact: Mr. Doyle Wellbrock, VP Franchise Mktg.; Tel: (213) 533-0221
WOMEN AT LARGE FITNESS SALON . . . . 1020 S. 48th Ave., Yakima, WA 98908
    Contact: Ms. Sharlyne Powell, Pres./CEO; Tel: (509) 965-0115
WOMEN'S WORKOUT WORLD . . . . 16015 Harlem Ave., Tinsley Park, IL 60477
    Contact: Ms. Shari Whitley, President; Tel: (708) 429-7766

CHAPTER 25

LAUNDRY AND DRY CLEANING

A-1 DISCOUNT CLEANERS

1000 Shelard Pkwy., # 560
Minneapolis, MN 55426
TEL: (800) 234-3726 (612) 541-1385
FAX: (612) 542-2246
Mr. John Campbell, CEO

A-1 DISCOUNT CLEANERS is a true discount cleaners, with the most modern and up-to-date equipment package that is balanced for a fast, even through-put rate to insure efficient and economical operation and greater profitability.

HISTORY: . . . .
Established in 1987; . . 1st Franchised in 1990
Company-Owned Units (As of 8/31/1992): . .2
Franchised Units (As of 8/31/1992): 4
Total Units (As of 8/31/1992): 6
Projected New Units for 1993: 12
Distribution: US-6;Can-0;Overseas-0
 North America: . . . . 4 States
 Concentration: . . . . 3 in NE, 2 in OH
Registered: . . . . CA,MD
. . . .
Type Space: . . . . SC;~3,000 SF

FINANCIAL: Earnings Claim: . .No
Cash Investment: $8-9K
Total Investment: $138-154K
Fees: Franchise - $10K
 Royalty: 5%, Advert: 1.5%
Contract Periods (Yrs.): 15/15
Area Development Agreement: Yes/15
Sub-Franchise Contract: . . . . . Yes
Expand in Territory: . . . . Yes
Passive Ownership: . . . Discouraged
Encourage Conversions: . . . . .No
Average # Employees: . . 4 FT, 3 PT

FRANCHISOR TRAINING/SUPPORT:
Financial Assistance Provided: . . . Yes(I)
Site Selection Assistance: . . . . . . .Yes
Lease Negotiation Assistance: . . . . .Yes
Co-operative Advertising: . . . . .NA
Training: . . . . .1 Wk. Headquarters,
 . . . . .1 Wk. On-Site
On-Going Support: C,D,E,F,G,/ 2
EXPANSION PLANS:
 US: . . . . .All US
 Canada: . . . . .All Canada
 Overseas: . . . . No

COMET ONE-HOUR CLEANERS

406 W. Division St. (Hwy. 80)
Arlington, TX 76011
TEL: (817) 461-3555
FAX: (817) 861-4779
Mr. Randy Bench, Sales Rep.

We offer a turn-key opportunity in the laundry and dry cleaning business. Site evaluation, complete training and installation are just a few of the services that COMET offers. There is only a one time per year franchise fee required of $1,000 as opposed to other franchisors that require a % of your gross income per year.

HISTORY: . . . . IFA	FINANCIAL: Earnings Claim: . .No	FRANCHISOR TRAINING/SUPPORT:
Established in 1960; . . 1st Franchised in 1967	Cash Investment: $50-80K	Financial Assistance Provided: . . . Yes(I)
Company-Owned Units (As of 8/31/1992): . 10	Total Investment: $130-150K	Site Selection Assistance: . . . . . . .Yes
Franchised Units (As of 8/31/1992): 265	Fees: Franchise - $10K	Lease Negotiation Assistance: . . . . .Yes
Total Units (As of 8/31/1992): 275	Royalty: $1K/Yr., Advert: . . . 0%	Co-operative Advertising: . . . . . . .Yes
Projected New Units for 1993: 15	Contract Periods (Yrs.): 1/1	Training: . . . . . . 1-2 Wks. at Nearby
Distribution: US-275;Can-0;Overseas-0	Area Development Agreement: . .No	. . . . Regional Unit
North America: . . . . 14 States	Sub-Franchise Contract: . . . . . .No	On-Going Support: D,E,F/ 13
Concentration: . . . 14 in TN, 13 in NM, TX	Expand in Territory: . . . . . . Yes	EXPANSION PLANS:
Registered: . . . . CA	Passive Ownership: . . . Discouraged	US: . . . . All US
. . . .	Encourage Conversions: . . . . . NA	Canada: . . . . .No
Type Space: . . .FS, SC (End Cap);~1,800 SF	Average # Employees: . . 5 FT, 2 PT	Overseas: . . . . .MX

DRYCLEAN - U.S.A.

12515 N. Kendall Dr., # 400
Miami, FL 33186
TEL: (305) 270-0000
FAX: (305) 271-1119
Mr. Jack Keilt, VP Fran. Dev.

Subsidiary of the largest dry cleaning company in the world. Offers complete turn-key franchise opportunities. Complete training and support to franchisees. Franchises available in the US and internationally.

HISTORY: . . . . IFA	FINANCIAL: Earnings Claim: . .No	FRANCHISOR TRAINING/SUPPORT:
Established in 1976; . . . 1st Franchised in 19	Cash Investment: $50-70K	Financial Assistance Provided: . . . Yes(I)
Company-Owned Units (As of 8/31/1992): 100	Total Investment: $100-240K	Site Selection Assistance: . . . . . . .Yes
Franchised Units (As of 8/31/1992): 190	Fees: Franchise - . . . .$	Lease Negotiation Assistance: . . . . .Yes
Total Units (As of 8/31/1992): 290	Royalty: 3-5%, Advert: 3%	Co-operative Advertising: . . . . . . .Yes
Projected New Units for 1993: 15	Contract Periods (Yrs.): . . . 10/10	Training: . . . . 3 Wks. Headquarters
Distribution: US-177;Can-0;Overseas-13	Area Development Agreement: Yes/5+	. . . .
North America: . . . . 10 States	Sub-Franchise Contract: . . . . . .No	On-Going Support: b,C,d,E,G/ 30
Concentration: . . . . .CA, FL, TX	Expand in Territory: . . . . . . Yes	EXPANSION PLANS:
Registered: . .CA,FL,MD,MI,NY,OR,VA,WA	Passive Ownership: . . . Discouraged	US: . . . . All US
. . . .	Encourage Conversions: . . . . . Yes	Canada: . . . . .All Canada
Type Space: . . . . . . SF, SC, RM;~1,200 SF	Average # Employees: . . 3 FT, 2 PT	Overseas: . EUR, C & S America, SE Asia

DUDS 'N SUDS

3000 Justin Dr., # G
Des Moines, IA 50325
TEL: (800) 383-6421 (515) 270-3837
FAX: (515) 270-6656
Ms. Jadine Anderson, Dir. Fran.

DUDS 'N SUDS is the leader in franchise laundry centers. Our market is growing and so is our company. Don't miss out on this profitable service business. DUDS 'N SUDS is a combination self-service laundry and snack bar entertainment center.

HISTORY:	FINANCIAL: Earnings Claim: . Yes	FRANCHISOR TRAINING/SUPPORT:
Established in 1982; . . 1st Franchised in 1983	Cash Investment: $40-70K	Financial Assistance Provided: . . .Yes(D)
Company-Owned Units (As of 8/31/1992): . .0	Total Investment: $160-220K	Site Selection Assistance: . . . . . . .Yes
Franchised Units (As of 8/31/1992): 70	Fees: Franchise - $25K	Lease Negotiation Assistance: . . . . .Yes
Total Units (As of 8/31/1992): 70	Royalty: 5%, Advert: 2%	Co-operative Advertising: . . . . . . .Yes
Projected New Units for 1993: 25	Contract Periods (Yrs.): . . . 10/10	Training: . . . . .1 Wk. Headquarters,
Distribution: US-67;Can-2;Overseas-1	Area Development Agreement: Yes/20	. . . . 1 Wk. Store Location
North America: . . . . . 30 States, 1 Province	Sub-Franchise Contract: . . . . . .No	On-Going Support: B,C,D,E,F,G,H,I/ . . 14
Concentration: . . .11 in IA, 8 in MO, 5 in CA	Expand in Territory: . . . . . . Yes	EXPANSION PLANS:
Registered: . . CA,FL,IL,MI,MN,NY,OR,WA	Passive Ownership: . . . Discouraged	US: . . . . All US
. . . . .WI	Encourage Conversions: . . . . . Yes	Canada: . . . . .All Canada
Type Space: . . . . .SC;~2,800 SF	Average # Employees: . . 1 FT, 7 PT	Overseas: . . . . .UK, JA

JIM DANDY DISCOUNT DRY CLEANERS
15155 Stagg St.
Van Nuys, CA 91405
TEL: (800) 635-0516 (818) 782-8166
FAX: (818) 782-4749
Ms. Mary Anne Leiker, Real Estate

JIM DANDY INTERNATIONAL allows entry into the multi-billion dollar dry cleaning industry. A unique opportunity in "Profit-Based Discount Dry Cleaning." This franchise was organized for the explicit purpose of satisfying consumer demand for convenient, quality dry cleaning, coupled with discount pricing.

HISTORY: . . . .
Established in 1986; . . 1st Franchised in 1989
Company-Owned Units (As of 8/31/1992): . .1
Franchised Units (As of 8/31/1992): 7
Total Units (As of 8/31/1992): 8
Projected New Units for 1993: 5
Distribution: US-8;Can-0;Overseas-0
  North America: . . . .
  Concentration: . . . .
Registered: . . . . CA,FL,OR
. . . .
Type Space: . . . . .SC;~1,500 SF

FINANCIAL: Earnings Claim: . .No
Cash Investment: $75K
Total Investment: $195K
Fees: Franchise - $0
  Royalty: 3%, Advert: 0%
Contract Periods (Yrs.): 10/5
Area Development Agreement: .No
Sub-Franchise Contract: . . . . .No
Expand in Territory: . . . . . . Yes
Passive Ownership: . . . Discouraged
Encourage Conversions: . . . . .No
Average # Employees: . . . . . .6 FT

FRANCHISOR TRAINING/SUPPORT:
Financial Assistance Provided: . . . . .Yes
Site Selection Assistance: . . . . . . .Yes
Lease Negotiation Assistance: . . . .Yes
Co-operative Advertising: . . . . .No
Training: . . . . . . .1 Wk. Headquarters,
. . . . 2 Wks. On-Site
On-Going Support: C,D,E,F,H,I/ 5
EXPANSION PLANS:
  US: . . . . .All US
  Canada: . . . . .No
  Overseas: . . . . .Yes

LONDON CLEANERS

21 Amber St., # 12
Markham, ON L3R 4Z3 CAN
TEL: (416) 475-1350
FAX: (416) 475-7249
Mr. Mark Kuzu, VP

Dry cleaning and alterations.

HISTORY: . . . .
Established in 1974; . . 1st Franchised in 1982
Company-Owned Units (As of 8/31/1992): . .2
Franchised Units (As of 8/31/1992): 17
Total Units (As of 8/31/1992): 19
Projected New Units for 1993: 3
Distribution: US-0;Can-19;Overseas-0
  North America: . . . . .1 Province
  Concentration: . . . . 18 in ON
Registered: . . . .
. . . .
Type Space: . . . . . .SF, SC, RM;~400 SF

FINANCIAL: Earnings Claim: . . .
Cash Investment: $40-60K
Total Investment: $50-80K
Fees: Franchise - $30-40K
  Royalty: 5%, Advert: 2%
Contract Periods (Yrs.): 10/5
Area Development Agreement: .No
Sub-Franchise Contract: . . . . .No
Expand in Territory: . . . .
Passive Ownership: . . . .
Encourage Conversions: . . . . NA
Average # Employees: . . 1 FT, 1 PT

FRANCHISOR TRAINING/SUPPORT:
Financial Assistance Provided: . . . Yes(I)
Site Selection Assistance: . . . . . . .Yes
Lease Negotiation Assistance: . . . . .Yes
Co-operative Advertising: . . . . .Yes
Training: . . . . 3 Wks. at Main Plant
. . . .
On-Going Support: B,C,D,E,f/ 1
EXPANSION PLANS:
  US: . . . . .All US
  Canada: . . . . .BC
  Overseas: . . . . No

PRESSED FOR TIME

48 Mechanic St.
Newton, MA 02164
TEL: (800) 423-8711 (617) 630-9026
FAX: (617) 630-9028
Mr. James Markson, President

PRESSED FOR TIME is an exciting franchise concept that capitalizes on the ever-increasing demand for more leisure time. It's simple and profitable. A mobile dry cleaning pick-up/delivery service with low overhead and high repeat business. Franchisees in protected territories serve executives and staff in local businesses and office buildings. We provide training and support and arrange for professional cleaning plants.

HISTORY: . . . . IFA
Established in 1987; . . 1st Franchised in 1990
Company-Owned Units (As of 8/31/1992): . .1
Franchised Units (As of 8/31/1992): 65
Total Units (As of 8/31/1992): 66
Projected New Units for 1993: 24
Distribution: US-40;Can-1;Overseas-25
  North America: . . . . 19 States
  Concentration: . . 22 in CA, 2 in NJ, 2 in PA
Registered: . . . CA,FL,IL,MD,MI,MN,OR,RI
. . . . .VA,WA,DC
Type Space: . . . . NA;~NA SF

FINANCIAL: Earnings Claim: . .No
Cash Investment: $12-15K
Total Investment: $12-15K
Fees: Franchise - $9.5K
  Royalty: 3.5%, Advert: . . $30/Mo./
Contract Periods (Yrs.): 10/10
Area Development Agreement: .No
Sub-Franchise Contract: . . . . .No
Expand in Territory: . . . . . . Yes
Passive Ownership: . . . Discouraged
Encourage Conversions: . . . . . Yes
Average # Employees: . . . . . .1 FT

FRANCHISOR TRAINING/SUPPORT:
Financial Assistance Provided: . . . . .NA
Site Selection Assistance: . . . . . . .NA
Lease Negotiation Assistance: . . . . .NA
Co-operative Advertising: . . . . .NA
Training: . . . . 1-2 Days Headquarters,
. . . . 1-2 Days With Existing Franchisee
On-Going Support: B,c,d,G,H,I/ . . . . .
EXPANSION PLANS:
  US: . . . . .All US
  Canada: . . . . All Exc. Alberta
  Overseas: . . . . UK

**WEDDING GOWN SPECIALISTS/
RESTORATION**
1799 Briarcliff Rd. NE
Atlanta, GA 30306
TEL: (800) 543-8987 (404) 875-8281
FAX: (404) 847-0189
Mr. Gary Webster, Founder

For established professional dry cleaners, an added specialty of restoring yellowed/stained wedding gowns to true color. No additional equipment, space or staffing required for those already handling wedding gowns. Restoration is just one more step to your current procedure. Each unit operates under license to provide services under national trade name and logo.

HISTORY: . . . .
Established in 1987; . . 1st Franchised in 1987
Company-Owned Units (As of 8/31/1992): . .1
Franchised Units (As of 8/31/1992): 89
Total Units (As of 8/31/1992): 90
Projected New Units for 1993: 20
Distribution: US-78;Can-11;Overseas-1
  North America: . . . . 27 States, 4 Provinces
  Concentration: . . . .6 in OH, 5 in IL, 4 in TN
Registered: . . . . .All
. . . .
Type Space: . . . .FS, SF, SC, RM;~25-50 SF

FINANCIAL: Earnings Claim: . .No
Cash Investment: $1-45K
Total Investment: $1-45K
Fees: Franchise - $1-45K
  Royalty: 20%, Advert: . . . 0%
Contract Periods (Yrs.): 1/1
Area Development Agreement: . .No
Sub-Franchise Contract: . . . . .No
Expand in Territory: . . . . . . Yes
Passive Ownership: . . . Discouraged
Encourage Conversions: . . . . .No
Average # Employees: . . . . . .1 PT

FRANCHISOR TRAINING/SUPPORT:
Financial Assistance Provided: . . . . .No
Site Selection Assistance: . . . . . . .No
Lease Negotiation Assistance: . . . . .No
Co-operative Advertising: . . . . . . .Yes
Training: . . . . Not Required
. . . .
On-Going Support: D,g,h,I/ 2
EXPANSION PLANS:
US: . . . . .All US
Canada: . . . . .All Canada
Overseas: . . . . . .All Free World

SUPPLEMENTAL LISTING OF FRANCHISORS

AMERIVEND . . . . 4101 SW 73rd Ave., Miami, FL 33155
  Contact: Mr. Ralph Geronimo, VP; Tel: (800) 780-WASH (305) 264-6060
APPARELMASTER . . . . 2786 Crescentville Rd., Box 62687, Cincinnati, OH 45262
  Contact: Ms. Liz Remle, President; Tel: (800) 543-1678 (513) 772-7721 C
APPEARANCE PROFESSIONALS, THE . . . . . 13665 E. 42nd Terrace, # H, Independence, MO 64055
  Contact: Mr. Tom Buckley, President; Tel: (800) 872-7951 (816) 478-0800
CANDUDS LAUNDRY SYSTEMS . . . . 908 Magnetic Dr., Downsview, ON M3J 2C4   CAN
  Contact: Mr. Thomas Manol; Tel: (416) 739-0237
CLEAN 'N' PRESS . . . . .101 Union St., San Francisco, CA 94111
  Contact: Ms. Sandra Lipkowitz, EVP & COO; Tel: (800) 237-1711 (415) 362-1700
DRY CLEANING WORLD/LAUNDRY WORLD . . . . 1234 Brittain Rd., Akron, OH 44310
  Contact: Mr. Jerry Freeman; Tel: (216) 633-0013
ELASCO 276 Hamilton St., Rahway, NJ 07065 . . . .
  Contact: Mr. Neil Slofkis, VP; Tel: (800) 221-6948 (908) 388-3388
EXECUTIVE IMAGE CLEANERS . . . . 1333 W. 120th Ave., # 222, Denver, CO 80234
  Contact: Mr. Chuck Yerbic, President; Tel: (303) 457-2700
HIS AND HERS IRONING SERVICE . . . . 10841 W. 155th Terrace, Overland Park, KS 66221
  Contact: Mr. Kenneth Mairs, President; Tel: (913) 897-5757 C
KING KOIN . . . . 5700 W. 36th St., Minneapolis, MN 55416
  Contact: President; Tel: (612) 929-0661
KNIGHT CLEANERS . . . . 1650 Helen St., Gaylord, MI 49735
  Contact: Mr. Daren Nowaczyk, President; Tel: (800) 227-9557MI (517) 732-7102
LAU WEST WASH HOUSE . . . . P. O. Box 835, Somerset, PA 15501
  Contact: President; Tel: (814) 443-3356
LAUNDRY BAR . . . . 11333 N. 92nd St., # 2052, Scottsdale, AZ 85260
  Contact: President; Tel: (602) 990-7152
ONE HOUR MARTINIZING DRY CLEANING . . . . 2005 Ross Ave., Cincinnati, OH 45212
  Contact: Mr. Frank Flack, President; Tel: (800) 827-0207 (513) 731-5500
OPERA COMPANY . . . . 5757 Corporate Blvd., # 304, Baton Rouge, LA 70808
  Contact: Mr. Boolus J. Boohaker; Tel: (504) 927-8013
PILGRIM CLEANERS & LAUNDERERS . . . . 4201 Lakeland Ave. N., Minneapolis, MN 55422
  Contact: Mr. Gene J. Bemel, VP; Tel: (612) 533-1293
SKETCHLEY CLEANERS . . . . 1 Concord Gate, # 600, North York, ON M3C 3N6   CAN
  Contact: Ms. Maureen Haroldsen; Tel: (416) 449-8180
STAR CLEANERS . . . . 2502 Rocky Point Rd., # 655, Tampa, FL 33607
  Contact: Mr. Gene Rutherford; Tel: (800) 743-7827 (813) 286-2220
SUNDAY BEST! . . . . P. O. Box 7169, Boston, MA 02169
  Contact: Mr. Thomas Gilmore; Tel: (617) 984-0405

WASH BOWL COIN LAUNDRY . . . . 4101 SW 73rd. Ave., Miami, FL 33155
Contact: President; Tel: (305) 264-6060

For Information On Renting Our

Custom Franchisor Mailing List

Or Franchisor Data Base,

Please Refer To Page IX

CHAPTER 26

LAWN AND GARDEN

EMERALD GREEN LAWN CARE

5300 Dupont Circle, P. O. Box G
Milford, OH 45150
TEL: (800) 783-0981 (513) 248-0981 C
FAX: (513) 831-1428
Mr. Jim Miller, General Manager

With an EMERALD GREEN franchise, you can count on being backed by our superior lawn care system - a system that will build your business through time. It only takes a modest equipment cost and a small franchise fee to share the EMERALD GREEN success formula.

HISTORY: . . . .
Established in 1984; . . 1st Franchised in 1985
Company-Owned Units (As of 8/31/1992): . .2
Franchised Units (As of 8/31/1992): 12
Total Units (As of 8/31/1992): 14
Projected New Units for 1993: . . . .
Distribution: US-14;Can-0;Overseas-0
North America: . . . . 8 States
Concentration: . . . .5 in OH, 4 in PA, 2 in NJ
Registered: . . . . .IL,IN,MD,MI
. . . .
Type Space: . . . . ;~ SF

FINANCIAL: Earnings Claim: . .No
Cash Investment: $20-40K
Total Investment: $50-70K
Fees: Franchise - $7.5-10K
Royalty: 8.5%, Advert: 0%
Contract Periods (Yrs.): 15/1
Area Development Agreement: . .No
Sub-Franchise Contract: . . . . .No
Expand in Territory: . . . . . . .Yes
Passive Ownership: . . . Not Allowed
Encourage Conversions: . . . . . Yes
Average # Employees: . . . . . .2 FT

FRANCHISOR TRAINING/SUPPORT:
Financial Assistance Provided: . . . Yes(I)
Site Selection Assistance: . . . . .NA
Lease Negotiation Assistance: . . . . .NA
Co-operative Advertising: . . . . .Yes
Training: . . . . . 1 Wk. Company-Owned
. . . . . . Branch, As Needed, On-Going
On-Going Support: B,C,D,F,g,H,I/ . . . 10
EXPANSION PLANS:
US: . . . . .Primarily Midwest, N and SE
Canada: . . . . No
Overseas: . . . . No

ENVIRO MASTERS LAWN CARE

Box 178
Caledon East, ON L0N 1E0 CAN
TEL: (416) 584-9592
FAX:
Mr. Martin Fielding, President

Organic and environmentally considerate lawn care service. Our franchisees benefit from bulk buying with no product mark-ups and no royalties until your second year of business. If you dream of starting your own business and would like to be part of an exciting new concept of organic lawn care, call today!

HISTORY:	FINANCIAL: Earnings Claim: . Yes	FRANCHISOR TRAINING/SUPPORT:
Established in 1987; . . 1st Franchised in 1991	Cash Investment: $20K	Financial Assistance Provided: . . . . . No
Company-Owned Units (As of 8/31/1992): . .3	Total Investment: $20-30K	Site Selection Assistance: . . . . .Yes
Franchised Units (As of 8/31/1992): 14	Fees: Franchise - $10-12K	Lease Negotiation Assistance: . . . . No
Total Units (As of 8/31/1992): 17	Royalty: 5%, Advert: 2%	Co-operative Advertising: . . . . .Yes
Projected New Units for 1993: 6	Contract Periods (Yrs.): . . . 10/10	Training: . . . . 2 Wks. On-Site
Distribution: US-1;Can-16;Overseas-0	Area Development Agreement: Yes/10	. . . .
North America: . . . . . . 1 State, 1 Province	Sub-Franchise Contract: . . . . .No	On-Going Support: B,C,D,E,F,G,H,I/ . . . 2
Concentration: . . . . 16 in ON	Expand in Territory: . . . . . . Yes	EXPANSION PLANS:
Registered:	Passive Ownership: . . . . . .Allowed	US: . . . . All US
. . . .	Encourage Conversions: . . . . NA	Canada: . . . . .All Canada
Type Space: . . . . . . .Home Based;~NA SF	Average # Employees: . . 2 FT, 1 PT	Overseas: . . . . No

LAWN DOCTOR

142 Hwy. 34, Box 512
Matawan, NJ 07747
TEL: (800) 631-5660 (908) 583-4700
FAX: (908) 583-8254
Mr. Edward L. Reid, Natl. Fran. Dir.

Largest franchise automated lawn care company in the US. Franchisees operate using the company's patented equipment, providing service at 1,000 SF a minute. Company provides complete classroom training and field support in business systems, operating procedures and analysis of lawn problems.

HISTORY: . . . . IFA	FINANCIAL: Earnings Claim: . . .	FRANCHISOR TRAINING/SUPPORT:
Established in 1967; . . 1st Franchised in 1967	Cash Investment: $25.5K	Financial Assistance Provided: . . .Yes(D)
Company-Owned Units (As of 8/31/1992): . .1	Total Investment: $30.5K	Site Selection Assistance: . . . . . . .NA
Franchised Units (As of 8/31/1992): 290	Fees: Franchise - $0	Lease Negotiation Assistance: . . . .NA
Total Units (As of 8/31/1992): 291	Royalty: 10%, Advert: 0%	Co-operative Advertising: . . . . . . .Yes
Projected New Units for 1993:	Contract Periods (Yrs.): . . . 20/10	Training: . . . . . . 2 Wks. Headquarters
Distribution: US-291;Can-0;Overseas-0	Area Development Agreement: . .No	. . . .
North America: . . . . 30 States	Sub-Franchise Contract: . . . . .No	On-Going Support: A,B,C,D,G,H,I/ . . 50
Concentration: . .67 in NJ, 65 in NY, 29 in PA	Expand in Territory: . . . . . . .No	EXPANSION PLANS:
Registered: . . . FL,HI,IL,IN,MD,MI,MN,NY	Passive Ownership: . . . . . .Allowed	US: . . . . All US Exc. CA
. . . . .RI,SD,VA,WI	Encourage Conversions: . . . . .No	Canada: . . . . No
Type Space: . . . . ;~ SF	Average # Employees: . . . . . .3 PT	Overseas: . . . . No

NATURALAWN OF AMERICA

5705 Industry Ln., # H
Frederick, MD 21701
TEL: (800) 989-5444 (301) 694-5440
FAX: (301) 846-0320
Mr. Beecher E. Smith, VP Ops.

The NATURALAWN franchise is a total system package, covering business planning, marketing and technical and operational functions. We deliver a service to mostly residential customers that consists of a natural, organic-based fertilization program in conjunction with a specially-designed Integrated Pest Management Program as opposed to the traditional chemical fertilization programs with indiscriminate pesticide applications.

HISTORY: . . . . IFA	FINANCIAL: Earnings Claim: . .No	FRANCHISOR TRAINING/SUPPORT:
Established in 1987; . . 1st Franchised in 1989	Cash Investment: $30-60K	Financial Assistance Provided: . . . Yes(I)
Company-Owned Units (As of 8/31/1992): . .3	Total Investment: $75-100K	Site Selection Assistance: . . . . . . .Yes
Franchised Units (As of 8/31/1992): 19	Fees: Franchise - $29.5K	Lease Negotiation Assistance: . . . . No
Total Units (As of 8/31/1992): 22	Royalty: 7-9%, Advert: 0%	Co-operative Advertising: . . . . . . .Yes
Projected New Units for 1993: 15	Contract Periods (Yrs.): . . . 10/10/5	Training: . . . . . . 4-5 Days Headquarters
Distribution: US-22;Can-0;Overseas-0	Area Development Agreement: . .No	
North America: . . . . 12 States	Sub-Franchise Contract: . . . . .No	On-Going Support: B,C,D,F,G,H,I/ 5
Concentration: . . 4 in MD, 3 in VA, 3 in PA	Expand in Territory: . . . . . . Yes	EXPANSION PLANS:
Registered: . . . . IN,MI,MN,VA	Passive Ownership: . . . . . .Allowed	US: . . . . . East of Miss., Cent. Time Zn
. . . .	Encourage Conversions: . . . . Yes	Canada: . . . . No
Type Space: Warehouse/Office;~1,500-2,000 SF	Average # Employees: . . 5 FT, 1 PT	Overseas: . . . . No

NITRO-GREEN PROFESSIONAL LAWN & TREE CARE

2791 F. N. Texas St., # 300
Fairfield, CA 94533
TEL: (800) 982-5296 (707) 428-5296
FAX: (707) 425-9811
Mr. Roger Albrecht, President

Professional lawn and tree care services to residential and commercial properties. We offer "pesticide-free programs."

HISTORY:	FINANCIAL:	FRANCHISOR TRAINING/SUPPORT:
HISTORY: . . . . IFA	FINANCIAL: Earnings Claim: . .No	FRANCHISOR TRAINING/SUPPORT:
Established in 1977; . . . 1st Franchised in 1979	Cash Investment: \$25-46K	Financial Assistance Provided: . . .Yes(D)
Company-Owned Units (As of 8/31/1992): . .2	Total Investment: \$35K	Site Selection Assistance: . . . . .Yes
Franchised Units (As of 8/31/1992): 38	Fees: Franchise - \$17.4K	Lease Negotiation Assistance: . . . . . . .NA
Total Units (As of 8/31/1992): 40	Royalty: 7%, Advert: 0%	Co-operative Advertising: . . . . No
Projected New Units for 1993: 7	Contract Periods (Yrs.): 20/10	Training: . . . . 2 Wks. Headquarters,
Distribution: US-40;Can-0;Overseas-0	Area Development Agreement: . .No	. . . . 1 Wk. Franchisee Location
North America: . . . . 14 States	Sub-Franchise Contract: . . . . . .No	On-Going Support: B,C,D,E,F,G,H,I/ . . . 3
Concentration: . . . 8 in MT, 6 in CO, 5 in ND	Expand in Territory: . . . . Yes	EXPANSION PLANS:
Registered: . . . . CA,MN,ND,OR,SD	Passive Ownership: . . . Discouraged	US: . . . . West, Midwest and South
. . . .	Encourage Conversions: . . . . . Yes	Canada: . . . . .No
Type Space: . . . . NA;~NA SF	Average # Employees: . . 1 FT, 1 PT	Overseas: . . . . No

NUTRITE

P. O. Box 1000
Brossard, PQ J4Z 3N2 CAN
TEL: (514) 462-2555 C
FAX: (514) 462-3634
M. Jacques Cardinal, Mktg. Mgr.

Your venture . . . If you dream of starting your own business, or want to add new services to an existing business, you should think seriously about owning a NUTRITE LAWN CARE franchise. The bottom line is . . . A NUTRITE franchise is a wise investment. Join the NUTRITE group now!

HISTORY:	FINANCIAL:	FRANCHISOR TRAINING/SUPPORT:
HISTORY:	FINANCIAL: Earnings Claim: . Yes	FRANCHISOR TRAINING/SUPPORT:
Established in 1967; . . 1st Franchised in 1984	Cash Investment: \$40K	Financial Assistance Provided: . . . . . No
Company-Owned Units (As of 8/31/1992): . .0	Total Investment: \$40K	Site Selection Assistance: . . . . . . .Yes
Franchised Units (As of 8/31/1992): 38	Fees: Franchise - \$10K	Lease Negotiation Assistance: . . . . . No
Total Units (As of 8/31/1992): 38	Royalty: \$3.5K/Yr, Advert: . . . 0%	Co-operative Advertising: . . . . No
Projected New Units for 1993: 0	Contract Periods (Yrs.): 5/5	Training: . . . . . . .No Limit On Location
Distribution: US-0;Can-38;Overseas-0	Area Development Agreement: . .No	. . . .
North America: . . . . 3 Provinces	Sub-Franchise Contract: . . . . . .No	On-Going Support: A,B,C,D,F,G,h,i/ . . 30
Concentration: . . . 30 in PQ, 7 in ON, 1 in NS	Expand in Territory: . . . . . . .No	EXPANSION PLANS:
Registered: . . . . CA	Passive Ownership: . . . . . .Allowed	US: . . . . .No
. . . .	Encourage Conversions: . . . . . Yes	Canada: . . . . .Yes
Type Space: . . . . ;~ SF	Average # Employees: . . . . . .2 FT	Overseas: . . . . No

SERVICEMASTER LAWN CARE (CAN)

4210 Midland Ave.
Scarborough, ON M1V 4S6 CAN
TEL: (416) 291-2596 C
FAX: (416) 291-6792
Mr. Robert G. Goodwin, VP Mktg.

Lawn care.

HISTORY:	FINANCIAL:	FRANCHISOR TRAINING/SUPPORT:
HISTORY: . . . . .IFA, CFA	FINANCIAL: Earnings Claim: . Yes	FRANCHISOR TRAINING/SUPPORT:
Established in 1973; . . . 1st Franchised in 1990	Cash Investment: \$24.5K	Financial Assistance Provided: . . .Yes(D)
Company-Owned Units (As of 8/31/1992): . .1	Total Investment: \$30K	Site Selection Assistance: . . . . .Yes
Franchised Units (As of 8/31/1992): 5	Fees: Franchise - \$17.5K	Lease Negotiation Assistance: . . . . .Yes
Total Units (As of 8/31/1992): 6	Royalty: 8%, Advert: 0%	Co-operative Advertising: . . . . .Yes
Projected New Units for 1993: 8	Contract Periods (Yrs.): 5/5	Training: . . . . 2 Wks. Headquarters,
Distribution: US-0;Can-6;Overseas-0	Area Development Agreement: Yes/10	. . . . 1 Wk. Memphis, TN
North America: . . . . .1 Province	Sub-Franchise Contract: . . . . . Yes	On-Going Support: C,D,E,F,G,g,h,I/ . . . 7
Concentration: . . . . 6 in ON	Expand in Territory: . . . . Yes	EXPANSION PLANS:
Registered:	Passive Ownership: . . . Discouraged	US: . . . . .No
. . . .	Encourage Conversions: . . . . . Yes	Canada: . . . . .All Canada
Type Space: . . . . NA;~NA SF	Average # Employees: . . 3 FT, 3 PT	Overseas: . . . . No

SPRING-GREEN LAWN AND TREE CARE
11927 Spaulding School Dr.
Plainfield, IL 60544
TEL: (800) 435-4051 (815) 436-8777 C
FAX: (815) 436-9056
Mr. Bill Tichnor, Dir. Fran. Dev.

SPRING-GREEN LAWN CARE offers high-quality, professional lawn, tree and shrub care services to residential and commercial customers. Primary focus is on highly-efficient application processes for fertilization and other lawn health and beautification services. SPRING-GREEN's on-going support and training focuses on getting and keeping customers, emphasizing a unique computer system for efficiency.

HISTORY: . . . . .IFA
Established in 1977; . . 1st Franchised in 1977
Company-Owned Units (As of 8/31/1992): . 12
Franchised Units (As of 8/31/1992): 120
Total Units (As of 8/31/1992): 132
Projected New Units for 1993: 5
Distribution: US-132;Can-0;Overseas-0
  North America: . . . . 22 States
  Concentration: . . 28 in IL, 14 in WI, 14 in PA
Registered: . . . IL,IN,MD,MI,MN,NY,OR,RI
. . . . VA,WA,WI
Type Space: . . . . ;~ SF

FINANCIAL: Earnings Claim: . Yes
Cash Investment: $18-25K
Total Investment: $22-52K
Fees: Franchise - $12.9K
  Royalty: 6-9%, Advert: 2%
Contract Periods (Yrs.): 10/10
Area Development Agreement: . .No
Sub-Franchise Contract: . . . . .No
Expand in Territory: . . . . Yes
Passive Ownership: . . . Discouraged
Encourage Conversions: . . . . . Yes
Average # Employees: . . 2 FT, 3 PT

FRANCHISOR TRAINING/SUPPORT:
Financial Assistance Provided: . . . Yes(I)
Site Selection Assistance: . . . . .Yes
Lease Negotiation Assistance: . . . . .Yes
Co-operative Advertising: . . . . .Yes
Training: . . . . .30-Hr Pre-training Course
. . . . . 1 Wk. Natl. Ctr., 4 Days On-Site
On-Going Support: A,B,C,D,E,F,G,H,I/ 15
EXPANSION PLANS:
  US: . . . . NW, SE, E and Midwest
  Canada: . . . . No
  Overseas: . . . . No

SUPER LAWNS

15901 Derwood Rd., P. O. Box 5677
Rockville, MD 20855
TEL: (800) 44-LAWN1 (301) 948-8181
FAX: (301) 948-8461
Mr. Ron Miller, President

Our system is a modern, profitable approach to lawncare. One person or any, dependent upon your desire to succeed. We offer complete training and constant assistance in all areas of business. We'll try to keep you "One step ahead of the competition."

HISTORY: . . . .
Established in 1979; . . 1st Franchised in 1979
Company-Owned Units (As of 8/31/1992): . .2
Franchised Units (As of 8/31/1992): 22
Total Units (As of 8/31/1992): 24
Projected New Units for 1993: 3
Distribution: US-24;Can-0;Overseas-0
  North America: . . . . 4 States
  Concentration: . . 11 in MD, 6 in VA, 3 in DE
Registered: . . . . .MD,VA
. . . .
Type Space: . . . . NA;~NA SF

FINANCIAL: Earnings Claim: . .No
Cash Investment: $30-40K
Total Investment: $60K
Fees: Franchise - $17.5K
  Royalty: 10% Max., Advert: . . 0%
Contract Periods (Yrs.): 20/5
Area Development Agreement: . .No
Sub-Franchise Contract: . . . . .No
Expand in Territory: . . . .
Passive Ownership: . . . Not Allowed
Encourage Conversions: . . . . .No
Average # Employees: . 1-2 FT, 1 PT

FRANCHISOR TRAINING/SUPPORT:
Financial Assistance Provided: . . .Yes(D)
Site Selection Assistance: . . . . .Yes
Lease Negotiation Assistance: . . . . .NA
Co-operative Advertising: . . . . .NA
Training: . . . . .Home Office
. . . .
On-Going Support: b,C,D,F,H,I/ 3
EXPANSION PLANS:
  US: . . . . East of Mississippi
  Canada: . . . . No
  Overseas: . . . . No

WEED MAN

2399 Royal Windsor Dr.
Mississauga, ON L5J 1K9 CAN
TEL: (416) 823-8550
FAX: (416) 823-4594
Mr. Kent Jackson, Mktg. Mgr.

Professional lawn care services. Seasonal home/mobile franchise.

HISTORY: . . . . .CFA
Established in 1970; . . 1st Franchised in 1976
Company-Owned Units (As of 8/31/1992): . .1
Franchised Units (As of 8/31/1992): 106
Total Units (As of 8/31/1992): 107
Projected New Units for 1993: 6
Distribution: US-2;Can-105;Overseas-0
  North America: . . . . 6 Provinces
  Concentration: . . 2 in PQ, 2 in BC, 2 in Marit
Registered: . . . .
. . . .
Type Space: . . . . NA;~ SF

FINANCIAL: Earnings Claim: . Yes
Cash Investment: $25K
Total Investment: $75K
Fees: Franchise - $25K
  Royalty: 6-7%, Advert: 1-2%
Contract Periods (Yrs.): 10/10
Area Development Agreement: Yes/25
Sub-Franchise Contract: . . . . . Yes
Expand in Territory: . . . . Yes
Passive Ownership: . . . Discouraged
Encourage Conversions: . . . . .No
Average # Employees: . . 3 FT, 6 PT

FRANCHISOR TRAINING/SUPPORT:
Financial Assistance Provided: . . . . .No
Site Selection Assistance: . . . . .Yes
Lease Negotiation Assistance: . . . . .NA
Co-operative Advertising: . . . . .Yes
Training: . . . . 1 Wk. Headquarters
. . . .
On-Going Support: B,C,D,E,G,H/ . . . 10
EXPANSION PLANS:
  US: . . . . .No
  Canada: . . . . .All Canada
  Overseas: . . . . . AU, UK, Ireland

SUPPLEMENTAL LISTING OF FRANCHISORS

A-PERM-O-GREEN LAWN . . . . P.O. Box 561687, Dallas, TX 75356
    Contact: Mr. Tommy Isbell; Tel: (214) 263-1370
BAREFOOT GRASS LAWN SERVICE . . . . 1018 Proprietors Rd., Worthington, OH 43085
    Contact: Mr. Mark Long, Franchise Mgr.; Tel: (614) 846-1800
CHEMLAWN SERVICES CORPORATION . . . . 8275 N. High St., Columbus, OH 43235
    Contact: Mr. Bruce Fowler, GM; Tel: (614) 888-3572
EQUIS LANDSCAPING . . . . 8336 76th Ave. N., Seminole, FL 33543
    Contact: President; Tel: (813) 392-6675
FASGRAS INTERNATIONAL . . . . 13751 Travilah Rd., Rockville, MD 20850
    Contact: Mr. Mark A. Johnson, Mktg./Fran. Dir; Tel: (800) 777-5862 (301) 340-0805
GREEN KEEPERS INTERNATIONAL . . . . .10821 Canal St., Largo, FL 34647
    Contact: President; Tel:
GREENS ALIVE INTERNATIONAL . . . . 35 Alexandra Blvd., Toronto, ON M4R 1L8   CAN
    Contact: Mr. Stephen MacKneson, Fran. Dir.; Tel: (416) 488-3687 C
J. K. CUTTER . . . . P. O. Box 2254 Square One, Mississauga, ON L5B 3C7   CAN
    Contact: Mr. Kirk Jackson; Tel: (416) 896-7010
LAWN MASTERS, THE . . . . .Box 178, Caledon East, ON L0N 1E0   CAN
    Contact: Mr. Marty Fielding, Mgr.; Tel: (416) 584-9592 C
LAWNMASTER OF AMERICA . . . . 3850 NW 2nd Ave., # 22, Boca Raton, FL 33432
    Contact: President; Tel: (305) 394-6557
LIQUI-GREEN LAWN CARE . . . . 9601 N. Allen Rd., Peoria, IL 61615
    Contact: Mr. C. Millard Dailey, Director; Tel: (800) 747-5211 (309) 243-5211
MR. TREES . . . . 343 San Anselmo Ave., San Anselmo, CA 94960
    Contact: Mr. Tripp Curtis, President; Tel: (800) 634-3337 (415) 485-5455
NUTRI-LAWN INTERNATIONAL . . . . 2319 McGillivray Blvd., PO Box 128, Winnipeg, MB R3Y 1G5   CAN
    Contact: Mr. Dick Nelles; Tel: (204) 895-4232
OMNI-TECH . . . . P. O. Box 5055, Thibodaux, LA 70302
    Contact: President; Tel: (504) 446-2003
SERVICEMASTER LAWNCARE . . . . 855 Ridge Lake Blvd., Memphis, TN 38120
    Contact: Mr. Bob Morris, Dir. Mkt. Expansion; Tel: (800) 228-2814 (901) 684-7500
U. S. LAWNS . . . . .1930 Silver Star Rd., Orlando, FL 32804
    Contact: Mr. Bill Neetz, VP & GM; Tel: (407) 294-1401 C
USA/CAN ACID LIQUID FERTILIZER . . . . 8582 Katy Fwy., # 200, Houston, TX 77024
    Contact: President; Tel: (800) 255-9548

CHAPTER 27

MAID SERVICES AND
HOME CLEANING

CLASSY MAIDS USA

P. O. Box 160879
Altamonte Springs, FL 32716
TEL: (800) 445-5238 (407) 862-0493
FAX:
Mr. William Olday, President

Professional home cleaning service with latest state-of-the-art computer management program. Proven training and marketing program. Protected territory. Grand Opening Program gets you off to fast start. Carpet cleaning and commercial cleaning. Annual marketing program. No experience needed.

HISTORY: . . . .
Established in 1980; . . 1st Franchised in 1985
Company-Owned Units (As of 8/31/1992): . .0
Franchised Units (As of 8/31/1992): 12
Total Units (As of 8/31/1992): 12
Projected New Units for 1993: 3
Distribution: US-12; Can-0; Overseas-0
  North America: . . . . 5 States
  Concentration: . . . 3 in WI, 2 in PA, 1 in MN
Registered: . . . . FL,HI
. . . .
Type Space: . . . . NA;~NA SF

FINANCIAL: Earnings Claim: . .No
Cash Investment: $4-8K
Total Investment: $8-14K
Fees: Franchise - $5.9-9.5K
  Royalty: 6%, Advert: 0%
Contract Periods (Yrs.): 10/10
Area Development Agreement: Yes/10
Sub-Franchise Contract: . . . . . .No
Expand in Territory: . . . . Yes
Passive Ownership: . . . Discouraged
Encourage Conversions: . . . . . Yes
Average # Employees: .1 FT, 6-10 PT

FRANCHISOR TRAINING/SUPPORT:
Financial Assistance Provided: . . .Yes(D)
Site Selection Assistance: . . . . . . .NA
Lease Negotiation Assistance: . . . . .NA
Co-operative Advertising: . . . . . . .Yes
Training: . . . . . . 4-5 Days New Smyrna
. . . . Beach, FL
On-Going Support: c,d,G,h,I/ 3
EXPANSION PLANS:
US: . . . . All US
Canada: . . . . All Exc. Alberta
Overseas: . . . . No

CUSTOM MAID (AZ)

1608 N. Miller Rd., # 5
Scottsdale, AZ 85257
TEL: (800) 888-6876 (602) 941-2993
FAX:
Mr. Frank Hronek, President

CUSTOM MAID provides quality home cleaning on a regularly-scheduled basis. The maids learn CUSTOM MAID methods and procedures, which optimize efficiency and help assure quality. CUSTOM MAID offers you a complete package of operating manuals, training videos, office forms and 5 days of comprehensive training.

HISTORY:	FINANCIAL: Earnings Claim: . . .	FRANCHISOR TRAINING/SUPPORT:
Established in 1985; . . 1st Franchised in 1989	Cash Investment: $500-5K	Financial Assistance Provided: . . . . . No
Company-Owned Units (As of 8/31/1992): . .1	Total Investment: $500-5K	Site Selection Assistance: . . . . .NA
Franchised Units (As of 8/31/1992): 10	Fees: Franchise - $2.9K	Lease Negotiation Assistance: . . . . . No
Total Units (As of 8/31/1992): 11	Royalty: 0%, Advert: 0%	Co-operative Advertising: . . . . .NA
Projected New Units for 1993: 24	Contract Periods (Yrs.): . . . Indefin.	Training: . . . . 5 Days Headquarters
Distribution: US-11;Can-0;Overseas-0	Area Development Agreement: . .No	. . . .
North America: . . . . 8 States	Sub-Franchise Contract: . . . . .No	On-Going Support: I/ 2
Concentration: . . . . 2 in TX, 2 in AZ	Expand in Territory: . . . . Yes	EXPANSION PLANS:
Registered:	Passive Ownership: . . . . . .Allowed	US: . . . . .All US
. . . .	Encourage Conversions: . . . . . Yes	Canada: . . . . No
Type Space: . . . . ;~ SF	Average # Employees: .1 FT, 2-24 PT	Overseas: . . . . No

HOME CLEANING CENTERS OF AMERICA

11111 W. 95th St.
Overland Park, KS 66214
TEL: (800) 767-1118 (913) 599-6453
FAX: (913) 599-6454
Mr. Mike Calhoon, President

Primarily a conventional home cleaning service for the two income family, with secondary emphasis on carpet, window and small office cleaning. Strong appeal to franchisees who are looking for an individualized business plan which will yield predictable results.

HISTORY:	FINANCIAL: Earnings Claim: . .No	FRANCHISOR TRAINING/SUPPORT:
Established in 1981; . . 1st Franchised in 1984	Cash Investment: $20-30K	Financial Assistance Provided: . . . Yes(I)
Company-Owned Units (As of 8/31/1992): . .0	Total Investment: $20-30K	Site Selection Assistance: . . . . . . .Yes
Franchised Units (As of 8/31/1992): 18	Fees: Franchise - $15.5K	Lease Negotiation Assistance: . . . .Yes
Total Units (As of 8/31/1992): 18	Royalty: 4.5-5%, Advert: 0%	Co-operative Advertising: . . . . . . .Yes
Projected New Units for 1993: 6	Contract Periods (Yrs.): . . 10/Varies	Training: . . . . 5 Days Headquarters
Distribution: US-18;Can-0;Overseas-0	Area Development Agreement: Yes/Var	. . . .
North America: . . . . 5 States	Sub-Franchise Contract: . . . . .No	On-Going Support: B,C,D,E,G,H/ 3
Concentration: . . . . 4 in MO, 3 in KS	Expand in Territory: . . . . Yes	EXPANSION PLANS:
Registered: . . . . .IN	Passive Ownership: . . . Discouraged	US: . . . . .All US
. . . .	Encourage Conversions: . . . . . NA	Canada: . . . . No
Type Space: . . . . .SC;~700 SF	Average # Employees: . . . . . 10 FT	Overseas: . . . . No

HOMEMAID SERVICES

1020 Sunset Dr.
Bountiful, UT 84010
TEL: (800) 658-8439 (801) 298-2795
FAX:
Ms. Karen Henderson, VP

Unique opportunity, low investment, flexible development plan, unlimited income potential without franchise restrictions. No royalties! Many extra profit centers, such as wall washing, carpet and upholstery cleaning, window and blind cleaning. We teach four businesses for one fee.

HISTORY:	FINANCIAL: Earnings Claim: . Yes	FRANCHISOR TRAINING/SUPPORT:
Established in 1985; . . 1st Franchised in 1989	Cash Investment: $15-20K	Financial Assistance Provided: . . .Yes(D)
Company-Owned Units (As of 8/31/1992): . .2	Total Investment: $15-20K	Site Selection Assistance: . . . . . . .Yes
Franchised Units (As of 8/31/1992): 3	Fees: Franchise - $12K	Lease Negotiation Assistance: . . . .NA
Total Units (As of 8/31/1992): 5	Royalty: 0%, Advert: 0%	Co-operative Advertising: . . . . .No
Projected New Units for 1993: 12	Contract Periods (Yrs.): 10/10	Training: . . . . .1 Wk. Headquarters,
Distribution: US-5;Can-0;Overseas-0	Area Development Agreement: Yes/10	. . . . 1 Wk. On-Site
North America: . . . . 2 States	Sub-Franchise Contract: . . . . Yes	On-Going Support: C,D,E,F,G,h,I/ 4
Concentration: . . . . 4 in UT, 1 in WI	Expand in Territory: . . . . Yes	EXPANSION PLANS:
Registered: . . . . .All	Passive Ownership: . . . . . .Allowed	US: . . . . .All US
. . . .	Encourage Conversions: . . . . Yes	Canada: . . . . .All Canada
Type Space: . . . . Home Based;~ SF	Average # Employees: . . . . 3-6 FT	Overseas: . . . . No

MAID BRIGADE SERVICES

850 Indian Trail Rd.
Atlanta, GA 30247
TEL: (800) 722-MAID (404) 564-2400
FAX: (404) 279-9668
Mr. Don M. Hay, President

America's largest independently-owned maid service. Costs less than half its nearest competitor and yet you still get outstanding training, start-up package, training videos, advertising manuals and our exclusive Micro Maid software.

HISTORY: . . . .
Established in 1979; . . 1st Franchised in 1980
Company-Owned Units (As of 8/31/1992): . .5
Franchised Units (As of 8/31/1992): 220
Total Units (As of 8/31/1992): 225
Projected New Units for 1993: 30
Distribution: US-130;Can-94;Overseas-1
North America: . . . . 24 States, 8 Provinces
Concentration: . 30 in VA, 16 in MD, 13 in TN
Registered: . . .CA,FL,IN,MD,MI,NY,OR,VA
. . . . WA
Type Space: Small Office/Home;~200-1,000 SF

FINANCIAL: Earnings Claim: . .No
Cash Investment: $10K
Total Investment: $18.5K
Fees: Franchise - $8.5K
Royalty: 5-6-7%, Advert: 2%
Contract Periods (Yrs.): 10/10
Area Development Agreement: . .No
Sub-Franchise Contract: . . . . . Yes
Expand in Territory: . . . . Yes
Passive Ownership: . . . . . .Allowed
Encourage Conversions: . . . . .No
Average # Employees: . . . . . 12 FT

FRANCHISOR TRAINING/SUPPORT:
Financial Assistance Provided: . . . Yes(I)
Site Selection Assistance: . . . . . . .Yes
Lease Negotiation Assistance: . . . .Yes
Co-operative Advertising: . . . . . . .Yes
Training: . . . .
. . . .
On-Going Support: B,C,D,E,F,G,H,I/ . . 6
EXPANSION PLANS:
US: . . . . All US
Canada: . . . . .Yes
Overseas: . . . . Yes

MAID EASY

43 Orchard Ln.
Glastonbury, CT 06033
TEL: (203) 659-2953
FAX:
Ms. Patricia Brubaker, Fran. Dev.

MAID EASY, with the only "one maid custom matched" to your home concept, has developed a comprehensive, yet streamlined system with a heavy emphasis on professional marketing and business management. No expensive office and auto requirements to decrease your profits. Complete programs for advertising, training, computerized systems and maximum support after opening.

HISTORY: . . . .
Established in 1981; . . 1st Franchised in 1987
Company-Owned Units (As of 8/31/1992): . .0
Franchised Units (As of 8/31/1992): 3
Total Units (As of 8/31/1992): 3
Projected New Units for 1993: 10
Distribution: US-3;Can-0;Overseas-0
North America: . . . . .1 State
Concentration: . . . . 3 in CT
Registered: . . . .
. . . .
Type Space: . . . . ;~500 SF

FINANCIAL: Earnings Claim: . .No
Cash Investment: $11K
Total Investment: $17-20K
Fees: Franchise - $8K
Royalty: 4%, Advert: 2%
Contract Periods (Yrs.): 10/10
Area Development Agreement: . .No
Sub-Franchise Contract: . . . . .No
Expand in Territory: . . . . . . Yes
Passive Ownership: . . . Discouraged
Encourage Conversions: . . . . Yes
Average # Employees: 1 FT, 10-20 PT

FRANCHISOR TRAINING/SUPPORT:
Financial Assistance Provided: . . . Yes(I)
Site Selection Assistance: . . . . . . .Yes
Lease Negotiation Assistance: . . . .Yes
Co-operative Advertising: . . . . . . .Yes
Training: . . . . 1 Wk. Headquarters
. . . .
On-Going Support: A,B,C,D,E,F,G,H,I/ . .2
EXPANSION PLANS:
US: . . . . All US
Canada: . . . . .No
Overseas: . . . . No

MAID TO PERFECTION

134 Nunnery Ln.
Baltimore, MD 21228
TEL: (800) 648-6243 (410) 747-0891
FAX: (410) 747-9483
Mr. Michael Katzenberger, CEO

A systematic approach to residential and light commercial cleaning on a high-volume basis. MAID TO PERFECTION is an up-scale maid service, providing customized cleaning to customers with supervised mini-teams or individuals who are fully insured, bonded and uniformed. The most unique cleaning concept in the industry.

HISTORY: . . . .
Established in 1980; . . 1st Franchised in 1990
Company-Owned Units (As of 8/31/1992): . .1
Franchised Units (As of 8/31/1992): 11
Total Units (As of 8/31/1992): 12
Projected New Units for 1993: 10
Distribution: US-12;Can-0;Overseas-0
North America: . . . . .1 State
Concentration: . . . . 12 in MD
Registered: . . . . MD,VA
. . . .
Type Space: . . . . NA;~ SF

FINANCIAL: Earnings Claim: . .No
Cash Investment: . . . .$
Total Investment: . . . $25.5-32.8K
Fees: Franchise - $18.5K
Royalty: 7%, Advert: 0%
Contract Periods (Yrs.): 10/5
Area Development Agreement: Yes/10
Sub-Franchise Contract: . . . .
Expand in Territory: . . . . . . .No
Passive Ownership: . . . Discouraged
Encourage Conversions: . . . . Yes
Average # Employees: . .10 FT, 2 PT

FRANCHISOR TRAINING/SUPPORT:
Financial Assistance Provided: . . . .
Site Selection Assistance: . . . . . . .NA
Lease Negotiation Assistance: . . . .NA
Co-operative Advertising: . . . . . . .Yes
Training: . . . . . . 5-7 Days Headquarters
. . . .
On-Going Support: C,D,E,F,G,H,I/ 5
EXPANSION PLANS:
US: .Yes
Canada: . . . . .No
Overseas: . . . . No

MAIDS IN WAITING

P. O. Box 1361
Glastonbury, CT 06033
TEL: (203) 657-3729
FAX:
Ms. Laurie Ann Lima, President

Complete training and support for residential and commercial cleaning. Full maid services training. Many avenues from which to profit.

HISTORY:	FINANCIAL: Earnings Claim: . .No	FRANCHISOR TRAINING/SUPPORT:
Established in 1982; . . 1st Franchised in 1986	Cash Investment: $15K	Financial Assistance Provided: . . .Yes(D)
Company-Owned Units (As of 8/31/1992): . .1	Total Investment: . . . .$	Site Selection Assistance: . . . . . . .Yes
Franchised Units (As of 8/31/1992): 1	Fees: Franchise - $8.5K	Lease Negotiation Assistance: . . . . .NA
Total Units (As of 8/31/1992): 2	Royalty: 7%, Advert: 2%	Co-operative Advertising: . . . . . . .Yes
Projected New Units for 1993: 2	Contract Periods (Yrs.): 5/5	Training: . . . . . . .40 Hours/30 Days HQ
Distribution: US-2;Can-0;Overseas-0	Area Development Agreement: . .No	. . . .
North America: . . . . .1 State	Sub-Franchise Contract: . . . . . Yes	On-Going Support: B,F,G,h/ 1
Concentration: . . . . 2 in CT	Expand in Territory: . . . . Yes	EXPANSION PLANS:
Registered:	Passive Ownership: . . . Not Allowed	US: . . . . All US
. . . .	Encourage Conversions: . . . . . Yes	Canada: . . . . .No
Type Space: . . . . NA;~ SF	Average # Employees: . . . . .2 PT	Overseas: . . . . No

MAIDS, THE

4820 Dodge St.
Omaha, NE 68132
TEL: (800) THE-MAID (402) 558-5555 C
FAX: (402) 558-4112
Ms. Danielle Bishop, President

Fortune, Success and USA Today single out THE MAIDS as one of North America's best franchise opportunities. They like our decade of 500% growth in customer sales in one of America's hottest markets -residential cleaning. They also like our fanatical commitment to our franchisees' success.

HISTORY: . . . . IFA	FINANCIAL: Earnings Claim: . .No	FRANCHISOR TRAINING/SUPPORT:
Established in 1979; . . 1st Franchised in 1981	Cash Investment: $13.5-23.5K	Financial Assistance Provided: . . . Yes(I)
Company-Owned Units (As of 8/31/1992): . .0	Total Investment: $31.5-41.5K	Site Selection Assistance: . . . . . . .Yes
Franchised Units (As of 8/31/1992): 192	Fees: Franchise - $17.5K	Lease Negotiation Assistance: . . . . No
Total Units (As of 8/31/1992): 192	Royalty: 7%, Advert: 4%	Co-operative Advertising: . . . . . . .Yes
Projected New Units for 1993: 30	Contract Periods (Yrs.): 10/10	Training: . . . . .12 Days Headquarters
Distribution: US-183;Can-9;Overseas-0	Area Development Agreement: Yes/10	. . . .
North America: . . . . 35 States, 2 Provinces	Sub-Franchise Contract: . . . . . Yes	On-Going Support: A,B,C,d,F,G,h,I/ . . 22
Concentration: . 16 in CA, 16 in PA, 14 in NY	Expand in Territory: . . . . Yes	EXPANSION PLANS:
Registered: . . . . .All	Passive Ownership: . . . Discouraged	US: . . . . All US
. . . .	Encourage Conversions: . . . . Yes	Canada: . . . . .All Canada
Type Space: . . . . Flexible;~200 SF	Average # Employees: .1 FT, 8-10 PT	Overseas: . . . . JA, EUR

MERRY MAIDS

11117 Mill Valley Rd.
Omaha, NE 68154
TEL: (800) 798-8000 (402) 498-0331 C
FAX: (402) 498-0142
Mr. Robert Burdge, Mkt. Expansion Mgr.

MERRY MAIDS is the largest and most successful company in the maid service industry. The company's commitment to training and on-going support is unmatched. MERRY MAIDS is ranked among the nation's hottest and fastest-growing franchises in Success, Money and Entrepreneur. MERRY MAIDS provides the most comprehensive computer software package and equipment and supply package in the industry.

HISTORY: . . . . .IFA, CFA	FINANCIAL: Earnings Claim: . .No	FRANCHISOR TRAINING/SUPPORT:
Established in 1980; . . 1st Franchised in 1981	Cash Investment: $30-35K	Financial Assistance Provided: . . .Yes(D)
Company-Owned Units (As of 8/31/1992): . .2	Total Investment: $30-35K	Site Selection Assistance: . . . . .Yes
Franchised Units (As of 8/31/1992): 653	Fees: Franchise - $19.5K	Lease Negotiation Assistance: . . . . . No
Total Units (As of 8/31/1992): 655	Royalty: 7%, Advert: 0%	Co-operative Advertising: . . . . .Yes
Projected New Units for 1993: 100	Contract Periods (Yrs.): 5/5	Training: . . . . .1 Wk. Headquarters,
Distribution: . . . US-593;Can-12;Overseas-50	Area Development Agreement: . .No	. . . . .4 Wks. Buddy System
North America: . . . . 48 States, 5 Provinces	Sub-Franchise Contract: . . . . .No	On-Going Support: A,B,C,D,E,F,G,H,I/ 35
Concentration: . . 106 in CA, 38 in IL, 27 MA	Expand in Territory: . . . . Yes	EXPANSION PLANS:
Registered: . . . . All States Exc. DC	Passive Ownership: . . . Discouraged	US: . . . . All US
. . . .	Encourage Conversions: . . . . Yes	Canada: . . . . .All Canada
Type Space: . . . .SF, W/H, Off. Ctr;~900 SF	Average # Employees: . .2 FT, 12 PT	Overseas: . . . . .Yes

MINI MAID SERVICE SYSTEMS OF CANADA
188 Shorting Rd.
Scarborough, ON M1S 3S7 CAN
TEL: (416) 298-7288
FAX: (416) 298-8445
Mr. Fred Romito, President

Team of 4 maids clean, using own supplies and equipment. All fully-trained, uniformed, insured and bonded. Arrive at customer homes in identifiable station wagons for professional image. Strong support programs from home office assures successful operation.

HISTORY: . . . .
Established in 1979; . . 1st Franchised in 1979
Company-Owned Units (As of 8/31/1992): . 23
Franchised Units (As of 8/31/1992): 78
Total Units (As of 8/31/1992): 101
Projected New Units for 1993: 3
Distribution: US-0;Can-101;Overseas-0
North America: . . . . 7 Provinces
Concentration: . . 20 in ON, 14 in BC, 9 in PQ
Registered: . . . . AB
. . . .
Type Space: . . . . ;~ SF

FINANCIAL: Earnings Claim: . .No
Cash Investment: $14K
Total Investment: $14K
Fees: Franchise - $10K
Royalty: 6%, Advert: 2%
Contract Periods (Yrs.): 10/10
Area Development Agreement: Yes/5
Sub-Franchise Contract: . . . . . Yes
Expand in Territory: . . . . . . Yes
Passive Ownership: . . . Not Allowed
Encourage Conversions: . . . . .No
Average # Employees: . . . . .6 FT

FRANCHISOR TRAINING/SUPPORT:
Financial Assistance Provided: . . . . . No
Site Selection Assistance: . . . . .NA
Lease Negotiation Assistance: . . . . .NA
Co-operative Advertising: . . . . .Yes
Training: . . . . .1 Wk. Headquarters,
. . . . Annual Seminars
On-Going Support: B,C,D,G,H,I/ 5
EXPANSION PLANS:
US: . . . . No
Canada: . . . . .All Canada
Overseas: . . . . ;~ No

MINI MAID SERVICES, THE
1341 Canton Rd. NE, # c-1
Marietta, GA 30066
TEL: (800) 627-6464 (404) 421-1588
FAX: (404) 421-1586
Mr. Jim Deitz, Mktg. Dir.

Residential team cleaning.

HISTORY: . . . .
Established in 1973; . . 1st Franchised in 1976
Company-Owned Units (As of 8/31/1992): . .0
Franchised Units (As of 8/31/1992): 106
Total Units (As of 8/31/1992): 106
Projected New Units for 1993: 6
Distribution: US-106;Can-0;Overseas-0
North America: . . . . 24 States
Concentration: . . . .7 in PA, 6 in TX, 5 in AL
Registered: . . . .
. . . .
Type Space: . . . . NA;~NA SF

FINANCIAL: Earnings Claim: . .No
Cash Investment: $12.5-22K
Total Investment: $19.8-22K
Fees: Franchise - $12.5K
Royalty: $350/Mo., Advert: . . 0%
Contract Periods (Yrs.): 5/5
Area Development Agreement: . .No
Sub-Franchise Contract: . . . . . Yes
Expand in Territory: . . . . . . Yes
Passive Ownership: . . . . . .Allowed
Encourage Conversions: . . . . .No
Average # Employees: . . . . .4 FT

FRANCHISOR TRAINING/SUPPORT:
Financial Assistance Provided: . . . . . No
Site Selection Assistance: . . . . No
Lease Negotiation Assistance: . . . . .NA
Co-operative Advertising: . . . . .NA
Training: . . . . .1 Wk. Headquarters,
. . . . 2-5 Days Pre-Training Home
On-Going Support: b,C,D,G,h/ 2
EXPANSION PLANS:
US: . . . . .All US
Canada: . . . . .No
Overseas: . . . . Open for Inquiries

MOLLY MAID
540 Avis Dr., # B
Ann Arbor, MI 48108
TEL: (800) 289-4600 (313) 996-1555 C
FAX: (313) 996-1906
Mr. David Hutchinson, Fran. Dev. Coord.

MOLLY MAID is distinguished by its high-profile image and its affiliation with Johnson Wax. Inc Magazine rated MOLLY MAID as one of the 500 fastest-growing, privately-held companies in the US for 3 consecutive years and it is continually rated as one of the best low investment franchise by numerous entrepreneurial publications.

HISTORY: . . . . IFA
Established in 1979; . . 1st Franchised in 1979
Company-Owned Units (As of 8/31/1992): . .0
Franchised Units (As of 8/31/1992): 277
Total Units (As of 8/31/1992): 277
Projected New Units for 1993: 36
Distribution: . . . US-59;Can-162;Overseas-56
North America: . . . .
Concentration: . . 15 in MI, 10 in CA, 6 in VA
Registered: . . . CA,FL,IL,IN,MD,MI,NY,OR
. . . . .VA,WA,DC
Type Space: . . . . NA;~NA SF

FINANCIAL: Earnings Claim: . .No
Cash Investment: $20-24K
Total Investment: $25-34.5K
Fees: Franchise - $14.5K
Royalty: 3-5%, Advert: 0-2%
Contract Periods (Yrs.): 10/5
Area Development Agreement: . .No
Sub-Franchise Contract: . . . . .No
Expand in Territory: . . . .
Passive Ownership: . . . Not Allowed
Encourage Conversions: . . . . . Yes
Average # Employees: . . . . . 12 FT

FRANCHISOR TRAINING/SUPPORT:
Financial Assistance Provided: . . . Yes(I)
Site Selection Assistance: . . . . . . .Yes
Lease Negotiation Assistance: . . . . .NA
Co-operative Advertising: . . . . No
Training: . . . . .5 Days Franchise Support
. . . . Center
On-Going Support: A,B,C,D,G,h,I/ 8
EXPANSION PLANS:
US: . . . . .All US
Canada: . . . . .All Canada
Overseas: . . . . JA

WORKENDERS

P. O. Box 810455
Boca Raton, FL 33481
TEL: (800) 634-1717 (407) 997-5717
FAX: (407) 997-5755
Mr. Gary Goranson, President

A residential cleaning service based on the Team Cleaning/Speed Cleaning concept developed by Speed Cleaning author Jeff Campbell, who has been operating in San Francisco's most famous housecleaning service since 1979 and whose 10 teams clean homes over 15,000 times annually. THE WORKENDERS System achieves high-quality cleaning in a far more efficient manner.

HISTORY:	IFA
Established in 1991;	1st Franchised in 1991
Company-Owned Units (As of 8/31/1992):	0
Franchised Units (As of 8/31/1992):	31
Total Units (As of 8/31/1992):	31
Projected New Units for 1993:	100
Distribution:	US-31;Can-0;Overseas-0
North America:	18 States
Concentration:	5 in TX, 4 in FL, 4 in OH
Registered:	FL,MI,OR
Type Space:	NA;~ SF

FINANCIAL: Earnings Claim: No
Cash Investment: $5-15K
Total Investment: $5-27K
Fees: Franchise - $1.5-7.5K
    Royalty: 4%, Advert: 2%
Contract Periods (Yrs.): 10/10
Area Development Agreement: No
Sub-Franchise Contract: No
Expand in Territory: Yes
Passive Ownership: Discouraged
Encourage Conversions: Yes
Avg. # Employees:2-3 People per Team

FRANCHISOR TRAINING/SUPPORT:
Financial Assistance Provided: Yes(D)
Site Selection Assistance: NA
Lease Negotiation Assistance: NA
Co-operative Advertising: NA
Training: 2 Days Headquarters

On-Going Support: b,G,H,I/ 6
EXPANSION PLANS:
US: All US
Canada: All Exc. Alberta
Overseas: No

SUPPLEMENTAL LISTING OF FRANCHISORS

CLOVERFIELD'S-CLEANING AMERICA'S HOMES . 4007 Country Club Rd., Winston-Salem, NC 27104
    Contact: Ms. Glenda Vogler; Tel: (919) 760-3455
CUSTOM CARE FOR HOMES . 7127 E. Becker Ln., # 132, Scottsdale, AZ 85254
    Contact: Mr. Mark Johnson; Tel: (602) 947-2868
CUSTOM MAID (MI) . 30455 Greenfield Rd., Southfield, MI 48076
    Contact: Mr. Robert Toliver, President; Tel: (313) 258-6243 C
CUSTOM MAIDS . 4217 W. 21st, Amarillo, TX 79106
    Contact: Mr. William R. Mangiameli, President; Tel: (800) 530-4778 (806) 355-1651
DAY'S EASE . 473 Charing Cross Dr., Grand Blanc, MI 48439
    Contact: Ms. Sally Tartoni; Tel:
DIAL-A-MAID . 823 Oakdale Rd., Johnson City, NY 13790
    Contact: Mr. Dennis Coughlin, President; Tel: (607) 798-8871 C
EXPRESS MAID . P. O. Box 2500, Williamsport, PA 17703
    Contact: Mr. Jeff A. Carey, President; Tel: (800) 333-MAID (717) 321-MAID
GUARANTEE GIRLS . 6210 Hollyfield Dr., Baton Rouge, LA 70809
    Contact: Ms. Ellen K. Folks, President; Tel: (800) 735-4475 (504) 293-8682
MAID AROUND . 496 Red Chimney Dr., Warwick, RI 02886
    Contact: President; Tel: (401) 885-0003
MAID ELITE . 310 S. Main St., P. O. Box 381998, Duncanville, TX 75138
    Contact: Mr. Charles Smith, CEO; Tel: (214) 709-1900
MAID IN HEAVEN . P. O. Box 204, Woodbridge, VA 22194
    Contact: Mr. Michael Tigner, President; Tel: (800) 678-6243 (703) 680-1705
MAID MASTERS . 18002 Irvine Blvd., # 202, Tustin, CA 92680
    Contact: Mr. Terry Lewis; Tel: (714) 832-5270
MAID OF GOLD . 951 Government St., # 804, Mobile, AL 36609
    Contact: Mr. A. L. Lundy, President; Tel: (800) 451-5371 (205) 348-2296
MCMAID . 10 W. Kinzie St., Chicago, IL 60565
    Contact: Mr. John Chesny, Fran. Sales Mgr.; Tel: (800) 444-6250 (312) 321-6250
NATIONS MAID . 5213 Ridge Rd., Cheyenne, WY 82009
    Contact: President; Tel: (307) 635-4197
SPARKLING MAID . 7936 E. Arapahoe Ct., Englewood, CO 80112
    Contact: Ms. Eileen T. Marin; Tel: (303) 770-6059
SUN SERVICES WINDOW CLEANING . 35 High St., Belfast, ME 04915
    Contact: Mr. Michael Hurley; Tel: (207) 338-1975
TREND TIDY'S MAID SERVICE . 380 Esna Park Dr., Markham, ON L3R 1H5   CAN
    Contact: Mr. David Bewsey, President; Tel: (416) 479-TIDY

CHAPTER 28

MAINTENANCE / CLEANING / SANITATION

AMERICAN AIR CARE

4751 Lydell Rd.
Cheverly, MD 20781
TEL: (800) 878-8700 (301) 772-2000
FAX: (301) 322-8446
Mr. Eric C. Moreno, VP Ops.

AMERICAN AIR CARE is a leader in professional commercial and residential air duct cleaning. We are a service organization backed by over 30 years of experience. We are committed to excellence and have time-tested systems to keep our franchises on track. We are looking for a select number of qualified business people to share our success. With exclusive territories, realistic costs and a virtually unlimited market, now is the time to tap the industry.

HISTORY: . . . . IFA
Established in 1961; . . 1st Franchised in 1991
Company-Owned Units (As of 8/31/1992): . .1
Franchised Units (As of 8/31/1992): 2
Total Units (As of 8/31/1992): 3
Projected New Units for 1993: . . . .
Distribution: US-3;Can-0;Overseas-0
  North America: . . . . .1 State
  Concentration: . . . . .3 in MD
Registered: . . . . MD,RI,VA,DC
. . . .
Type Space: . . . . Warehouse;~500 SF

FINANCIAL: Earnings Claim: . Yes
Cash Investment: $40-60K
Total Investment: $104-184K
Fees: Franchise - $25.5K
  Royalty: 7-10%, Advert: 1%
Contract Periods (Yrs.): 5/5/5
Area Development Agreement: . .No
Sub-Franchise Contract: . . . . .No
Expand in Territory: . . . . . . Yes
Passive Ownership: . . . Discouraged
Encourage Conversions: . . . . . NA
Average # Employees: . . 3 FT, 3 PT

FRANCHISOR TRAINING/SUPPORT:
Financial Assistance Provided: . . . Yes(I)
Site Selection Assistance: . . . . .Yes
Lease Negotiation Assistance: . . . . .Yes
Co-operative Advertising: . . . . .Yes
Training: . . . . . 2-3 Wks. Franchisee Site
. . . .
On-Going Support: A,B,C,d,e,G,H,I/ . . . 5
EXPANSION PLANS:
  US: . . . . East Coast
  Canada: . . . . .No
  Overseas: . . . . No

AMERICAN ENTERPRISES

P. O. Box 2374
Kailua-Kona, HI 96745
TEL: (800) 247-3001 (808) 329-2001
FAX:
Mr. Ray E. Dille, President

A new chemical discovery and carpet cleaning system (Rinse Out and Thermal Rinse System) has literally enabled this system to outperform, outclean and underprice any and all wet or dry carpet cleaning systems used in the world today, making all others obsolete! Actually take over any city or town in the world in this business.

HISTORY:	FINANCIAL: Earnings Claim: . .No	FRANCHISOR TRAINING/SUPPORT:
Established in 1982; . . 1st Franchised in 1985	Cash Investment: $15-20K	Financial Assistance Provided: . . . . .No
Company-Owned Units (As of 8/31/1992): . .1	Total Investment: $17-25K	Site Selection Assistance: . . . . . . .Yes
Franchised Units (As of 8/31/1992): 0	Fees: Franchise - $12.5K	Lease Negotiation Assistance: . . . .NA
Total Units (As of 8/31/1992): 1	Royalty: 8%, Advert: 0%	Co-operative Advertising: . . . . . . .Yes
Projected New Units for 1993: 4	Contract Periods (Yrs.): . . . .Varies	Training: . . . . 2 Wks. Headquarters,
Distribution: US-1;Can-0;Overseas-0	Area Development Agreement: . Yes	. . . . .30 Days Franchisee Site
North America: . . . . .1 State	Sub-Franchise Contract: . . . . . Yes	On-Going Support: D,E,I/ 1
Concentration: . . . . .1 in HI	Expand in Territory: . . . . . . .Yes	EXPANSION PLANS:
Registered: . . . . .HI	Passive Ownership: . . . Not Allowed	US: . . . . Northwest and Southwest
. . . .	Encourage Conversions: . . . . . .No	Canada: . . . . .All Canada
Type Space: . . . . . . Home Based;~400 SF	Average # Employees: . . 1 FT, 3 PT	Overseas: . EUR, AU, NZ, and Asia

AMERICAN LEAK DETECTION / LEAK BUSTERS

888 Research Dr.,# 109, PO Box 1701
Palm Springs, CA 92263
TEL: (800) 755-6697 (619) 320-9991 C
FAX: (619) 320-1288
Mr. Richard Rennick, President

Use of highly sophisticated electronic equipment to locate concealed water, gas or sewer leaks in swimming pools, spas, fountain, under concrete slabs, roadways and parking lots.

HISTORY: . . . . .IFA	FINANCIAL: Earnings Claim: . Yes	FRANCHISOR TRAINING/SUPPORT:
Established in 1975; . . 1st Franchised in 1984	Cash Investment: . . . . . . $20K+	Financial Assistance Provided: . . .Yes(D)
Company-Owned Units (As of 8/31/1992): . .2	Total Investment: . . . . . . $25K+	Site Selection Assistance: . . . . . . .NA
Franchised Units (As of 8/31/1992): 130	Fees: Franchise - . . . . $25K+	Lease Negotiation Assistance: . . . .NA
Total Units (As of 8/31/1992): 132	Royalty: 8-10%, Advert: 0%	Co-operative Advertising: . . . . . . .NA
Projected New Units for 1993: 6	Contract Periods (Yrs.): . . . 5-10/10	Training: . . . . . . 6-8 Wks. Headquarters
Distribution: US-126;Can-0;Overseas-6	Area Development Agreement: . .No	. . . .
North America: . . . . 15 States	Sub-Franchise Contract: . . . . .No	On-Going Support: b,C,G,h/ 7
Concentration: . .57 in CA, 21 in TX, 20 in FL	Expand in Territory: . . . . . . .Yes	EXPANSION PLANS:
Registered: . . . CA,FL,HI,IL,IN,MD,NY,OR	Passive Ownership: . . . Not Allowed	US: . . . . . . .All US, Exc. CA and HI
. . . . .VA,WA	Encourage Conversions: . . . . Yes	Canada: . . . . .All Canada
Type Space: . . . . NA;~ SF	Average # Employees: . . 1 FT, 1 PT	Overseas: . . . . Yes

AMERICLEAN

6602 S. Frontage Rd.
Billings, MT 59102
TEL: (800) 827-9111 (406) 652-1960
FAX: (406) 652-7710
Mr. Robert Pearson, President

Service business, offering flood, fire, smoke, vandalism, odor, etc. Disaster restoration to insurance adjusters, commercial and residential property owners. Also offers exclusive liquid dry-cleaning process for carpeting, upholstery and draperies, plus acoustical ceiling cleaning and other specialty processes.

HISTORY:	FINANCIAL: Earnings Claim: . Yes	FRANCHISOR TRAINING/SUPPORT:
Established in 1979; . . 1st Franchised in 1980	Cash Investment: $30K	Financial Assistance Provided: . . . Yes(I)
Company-Owned Units (As of 8/31/1992): . .1	Total Investment: $13-79K	Site Selection Assistance: . . . . . . .Yes
Franchised Units (As of 8/31/1992): 29	Fees: Franchise - $15-45K	Lease Negotiation Assistance: . . . .Yes
Total Units (As of 8/31/1992): 30	Royalty: 1-8.5%, Advert: 0%	Co-operative Advertising: . . . . . . .No
Projected New Units for 1993: 2	Contract Periods (Yrs.): 10/5	Training: . . . . 2 Wks. Headquarters,
Distribution: US-30;Can-0;Overseas-0	Area Development Agreement: . .No	. . . . 1 Wk. Franchisee Location
North America: . . . . 19 States	Sub-Franchise Contract: . . . . .No	On-Going Support: A,C,D,E,G,H,I/ 5
Concentration: . . . . 5 in MT, 4 in FL, 3 in ID	Expand in Territory: . . . . . . .Yes	EXPANSION PLANS:
Registered: . . . . .FL,MI	Passive Ownership: . . . . . .Allowed	US: . . . . . . Northwest, Central and SW
. . . .	Encourage Conversions: . . . . . Yes	Canada: . . . . .No
Type Space: . . . . . Shop/Office;~4,000+ SF	Average # Employees: 5-7 FT, 1-10 PT	Overseas: . . . . No

BEE-CLEAN

4140 - 97th St.
Edmonton, AB T6E 5Y6 CAN
TEL: (403) 462-0069
FAX:
Mr. Jim Malott, GM

BEE-CLEAN franchisees are managers who oversee their janitorial service business.

HISTORY:	FINANCIAL: Earnings Claim: . .No	FRANCHISOR TRAINING/SUPPORT:
Established in 1967; . . 1st Franchised in 1972	Cash Investment: $5-50K	Financial Assistance Provided: . . . . .Yes
Company-Owned Units (As of 8/31/1992): . .7	Total Investment: $10-150K	Site Selection Assistance: . . . . . . .Yes
Franchised Units (As of 8/31/1992): 24	Fees: Franchise - $3.5-12.5K	Lease Negotiation Assistance: . . . .NA
Total Units (As of 8/31/1992): 31	Royalty: 2-6%, Advert: 0%	Co-operative Advertising: . . . . . . .Yes
Projected New Units for 1993: 2	Contract Periods (Yrs.): 15/15	Training: . . . . 10 Days-3 Months On-Site
Distribution: US-0;Can-31;Overseas-0	Area Development Agreement: . .No	. . . .
North America: . . . . 5 Provinces	Sub-Franchise Contract: . . . . .No	On-Going Support: a,b,c,D,G,h/ 7
Concentration: . . .14 in AB, 9 in BC, 5 in SK	Expand in Territory: . . . . . . Yes	EXPANSION PLANS:
Registered: . . . . AB	Passive Ownership: . . . Discouraged	US: . . . . No
. . . .	Encourage Conversions: . . . . Yes	Canada: . . . . .All Canada
Type Space: Warehouse, Office;~200-2,000 SF	Average # Employees:	Overseas: . . . . No

BLIND CLEANING EXPRESS

3728 Overland Ave.
Los Angeles, CA 90034
TEL: (310) 287-2255
FAX: (310) 287-2642
Mr. Bob Eckert, Fran. Dev.

There's a new window of opportunity in the service industry called BLIND CLEANING EXPRESS. BCE offers a unique mobile and in-store service for cleaning, repairs, sales and installation of all kinds of blinds. Our system offers complete support to help you enjoy the advantages of business ownership in a unique niche of the huge cleaning/maintenance service industry that services residential, commercial and industrial clients. Third party financing.

HISTORY:	FINANCIAL: Earnings Claim: . Yes	FRANCHISOR TRAINING/SUPPORT:
Established in 1989; . . 1st Franchised in 1992	Cash Investment: . . . $41.8-64.5K	Financial Assistance Provided: . . . Yes(I)
Company-Owned Units (As of 8/31/1992): . .1	Total Investment: $75-100K	Site Selection Assistance: . . . . . . .Yes
Franchised Units (As of 8/31/1992): 0	Fees: Franchise - $16K	Lease Negotiation Assistance: . . . .Yes
Total Units (As of 8/31/1992): 1	Royalty: 4-8%, Advert: 2%	Co-operative Advertising: . . . . . . .Yes
Projected New Units for 1993: 12	Contract Periods (Yrs.): . . . 5/5/5/5	Training: . . . . . . 1 Wk. Min. Corporate,
Distribution: US-1;Can-0;Overseas-0	Area Development Agreement: . .No	. . . . 4 Days Min. On-Site
North America: . . . . .1 State	Sub-Franchise Contract: . . . . .No	On-Going Support: B,C,D,E,F,G,H,I/ . . .4
Concentration: . . . . 1 in CA	Expand in Territory: . . . . . . .No	EXPANSION PLANS:
Registered: . . . . CA	Passive Ownership: . . . Discouraged	US: . . . . California
. . . .	Encourage Conversions: . . . . Yes	Canada: . . . . No
Type Space: . . . SF, Light Indust.;~1,000 SF	Average # Employees: . . 2 FT, 2 PT	Overseas: . . . . JA

BUILDING SERVICES OF AMERICA

126 Indian Ave.
Lawrence, KS 66046
TEL: (800) 272-2741 (913) 749-0936
FAX: (913) 749-3993
Mr. Michael Jenkins, VP

BUILDING SERVICES OF AMERICA has a proven master franchise program that can be a very successful opportunity for larger metropolitan areas. A master franchise sells associate franchises with guaranteed accounts and charges finders fees for additional accounts. The master franchise markets professional "White Glove" cleaning services.

HISTORY:	FINANCIAL: Earnings Claim: . .No	FRANCHISOR TRAINING/SUPPORT:
Established in 1978; . . 1st Franchised in 1992	Cash Investment: $8-10K	Financial Assistance Provided: . . .Yes(D)
Company-Owned Units (As of 8/31/1992): . .1	Total Investment: $25-40K	Site Selection Assistance: . . . . . . .Yes
Franchised Units (As of 8/31/1992): 0	Fees: Franchise - $25K	Lease Negotiation Assistance: . . . . .No
Total Units (As of 8/31/1992): 1	Royalty: 4%, Advert: 0%	Co-operative Advertising: . . . . . . .No
Projected New Units for 1993: 8	Contract Periods (Yrs.): 10/10	Training: . . . . .1 Wk. Headquarters,
Distribution: US-1;Can-0;Overseas-0	Area Development Agreement: . .No	. . . . . 1 Wk. Area or Master Franchise
North America: . . . . .1 State	Sub-Franchise Contract: . . . . Yes	On-Going Support: C,D,E,G,h,I/ 6
Concentration: . . . . 1 in KS	Expand in Territory: . . . . . . Yes	EXPANSION PLANS:
Registered:	Passive Ownership: . . . . . .Allowed	US: . . . . All US
. . . .	Encourage Conversions: . . . . Yes	Canada: . . . . .All Canada
Type Space: . . . . NA;~ SF	Average # Employees: . . . . 1-4 FT	Overseas: . . . . No

CEILING DOCTOR

5151 Beltline Rd., # 950
Dallas, TX 75240
TEL: (214) 702-8046 C
FAX: (214) 702-9466
Mr. Rob Forrest, Chairman

CEILING DOCTOR is the world leader in specialty cleaning. Your role as franchisee is that of a manager and supervisor with employees doing the actual cleaning work. Plans are to establish 1,000 franchises by 1996.

HISTORY: . . . . IFA	FINANCIAL: Earnings Claim: . .No	FRANCHISOR TRAINING/SUPPORT:
Established in 1984; . . 1st Franchised in 1986	Cash Investment: $19.5K	Financial Assistance Provided: . . . . .NA
Company-Owned Units (As of 8/31/1992): . .1	Total Investment: $19.5K	Site Selection Assistance: . . . . . . .NA
Franchised Units (As of 8/31/1992): 87	Fees: Franchise - $10K	Lease Negotiation Assistance: . . . . .NA
Total Units (As of 8/31/1992): 88	Royalty: 8%, Advert: 2%	Co-operative Advertising: . . . . .Yes
Projected New Units for 1993: 48	Contract Periods (Yrs.): 5/45	Training: . . . . 7 Days Headquarters
Distribution: . . . US-20;Can-25;Overseas-43	Area Development Agreement: Yes/50	. . . .
North America: . . . . 13 States,10 Provinces	Sub-Franchise Contract: . . . . . .No	On-Going Support: C,D,F,G,H,I/ 5
Concentration: . . .13 in ON, 3 in CA, 3 in TN	Expand in Territory: . . . . Yes	EXPANSION PLANS:
Registered: . . . . .All	Passive Ownership: . . . Discouraged	US: . . . . All US
. . . .	Encourage Conversions: . . . . . Yes	Canada: . . . . .All Canada
Type Space: . . . . Home Based;~ SF	Average # Employees: . . 1 FT, 3 PT	Overseas: . EUR, S. America, Asia

CHEM-DRY

3330 Cameron Park Dr., # 700
Cameron Park, CA 95682
TEL: (800) 841-6583 (916) 677-0231
FAX: (916) 677-2908
Mr. Michael Mastous, Natl. Fran. Dir.

A unique carpet, drapery and upholstery cleaning service, utilizing a patented, non-toxic cleaning solution which is guaranteed to remove virtually all stains, including the so-called "impossible" stains like red soft drinks, indelible ink, etc. Generally dries in one hour or less.

HISTORY:	FINANCIAL: Earnings Claim: . .No	FRANCHISOR TRAINING/SUPPORT:
Established in 1977; . . 1st Franchised in 1978	Cash Investment: $5K	Financial Assistance Provided: . . . . .Yes
Company-Owned Units (As of 8/31/1992): . .0	Total Investment: $10K	Site Selection Assistance: . . . . . . .NA
Franchised Units (As of 8/31/1992): 3014	Fees: Franchise - $6.7K	Lease Negotiation Assistance: . . . . .Yes
Total Units (As of 8/31/1992): 3014	Royalty: 175/Mo., Advert: . . 0%	Co-operative Advertising: . . . . .NA
Projected New Units for 1993: 250	Contract Periods (Yrs.): 5/5	Training: . . . . . . .Home Study on Video
Distribution: . . US-2221;Can-69;Overseas-724	Area Development Agreement: . .No	. . . .
North America: . . . . 50 States, 7 Provinces	Sub-Franchise Contract: . . . . . .No	On-Going Support: B,D,G,H/ 51
Concentration: 443 in CA, 137 in TX, 136 WA	Expand in Territory: . . . . Yes	EXPANSION PLANS:
Registered: . . . . .All	Passive Ownership: . . . . . .Allowed	US: . . . . All US
. . . .	Encourage Conversions: . . . . . .No	Canada: . . . . .All
Type Space: . . . . NA;~ SF	Average # Employees: . . . . . .3 FT	Overseas: . . . . .Yes

CHEMSTATION INTERNATIONAL

3201 Encrete Ln.
Dayton, OH 45439
TEL: (513) 294-8265
FAX: (513) 294-5360
Mr. Joseph Novostat, Dir. Ops.

CHEMSTATION is engaged in the business of selling franchises for the operation of CHEMSTATION dealerships. The dealerships are "bulk" suppliers of industrial strength cleaners to industrial and commercial clients. Dealerships offer their customers a considerable savings through the use of permanent storage tanks and blending pumps. Chemicals are non-hazardous.

HISTORY: . . . . IFA	FINANCIAL: Earnings Claim: . .No	FRANCHISOR TRAINING/SUPPORT:
Established in 1983; . . 1st Franchised in 1984	Cash Investment: $80-125K	Financial Assistance Provided: . . . Yes(I)
Company-Owned Units (As of 8/31/1992): . .1	Total Investment: $175-290K	Site Selection Assistance: . . . . .NA
Franchised Units (As of 8/31/1992): 19	Fees: Franchise - $20K	Lease Negotiation Assistance: . . . . .No
Total Units (As of 8/31/1992): 20	Royalty: 4%, Advert: 2%	Co-operative Advertising: . . . . .No
Projected New Units for 1993: 5	Contract Periods (Yrs.): 10/5	Training: . . . . . . 1-2 Wks. Headquarters,
Distribution: US-20;Can-0;Overseas-0	Area Development Agreement: . .No	. . . . Indefinite On-Site
North America: . . . . 18 States	Sub-Franchise Contract: . . . . . .No	On-Going Support: A,C,D,E,F,G,h,I/ . . 15
Concentration: . . . . 4 in OH, 3 in MI	Expand in Territory: . . . . Yes	EXPANSION PLANS:
Registered: . . . . IL,IN,MD,MI	Passive Ownership: . . . . . .Allowed	US: . . . . All US
. . . .	Encourage Conversions: . . . . . NA	Canada: . . . . .Yes
Type Space: . . . . . . NA;~3,000-5,000 SF	Average # Employees: . . . . 3-5 FT	Overseas: . . . . No

CLEAN TEAM

210 University Dr., # 402
Coral Springs, FL 33071
TEL: (305) 345-0600
FAX: (305) 345-9213
Mr. Bill Lendman, Dir. Mktg.

Unique opportunity in a recession-proof industry - commercial window cleaning. This low-cost, high-profit business operates with almost no overhead, minimal employees and an income opportunity unparalleled when compared to total investment required.

HISTORY:	FINANCIAL: Earnings Claim: . .No	FRANCHISOR TRAINING/SUPPORT:
Established in 1983; . . 1st Franchised in 1992	Cash Investment: . . . .$	Financial Assistance Provided: . . . Yes(I)
Company-Owned Units (As of 8/31/1992): . .1	Total Investment: $35-63K	Site Selection Assistance: . . . . . . .Yes
Franchised Units (As of 8/31/1992): 0	Fees: Franchise - $15K	Lease Negotiation Assistance: . . . .Yes
Total Units (As of 8/31/1992): 1	Royalty: 5%, Advert: 1%	Co-operative Advertising: . . . . . . .Yes
Projected New Units for 1993: 6	Contract Periods (Yrs.): 10/10	Training: . . . . 2 Wks. Headquarters
Distribution: US-1;Can-0;Overseas-0	Area Development Agreement: . .No	. . . .
North America: . . . . .1 State	Sub-Franchise Contract: . . . . .No	On-Going Support: B,C,D,E,F,H/ 6
Concentration: . . . . 1 in FL	Expand in Territory: . . . . Yes	EXPANSION PLANS:
Registered:	Passive Ownership: . . . Discouraged	US: . . . . .All US
. . . .	Encourage Conversions: . . . . . Yes	Canada: . . . . .No
Type Space: . . . . . . Warehouse;~500 SF	Average # Employees: . . 6 FT, 3 PT	Overseas: . . . . No

CLEAN UP SYSTEMS

P. O. Box 86310
North Vancouver, BC V7L 4K6 CAN
TEL: (604) 980-4561
FAX:
Mr. Bert Woldring, Owner

The Science of Cleaning and Protecting Surfaces. Specialty cleaning of all ceilings, walls, interior and exterior surfaces, special cleaning of computers, telephones and all equipment. Computerized operation makes us the best, easiest and most profitable. Personal attention means success with every franchise. Join our special family of success.

HISTORY:	FINANCIAL: Earnings Claim: . Yes	FRANCHISOR TRAINING/SUPPORT:
Established in 1981; . . 1st Franchised in 1983	Cash Investment: $5-30K	Financial Assistance Provided: . . .Yes(D)
Company-Owned Units (As of 8/31/1992): . .0	Total Investment: $5-30K	Site Selection Assistance: . . . . . . .NA
Franchised Units (As of 8/31/1992): 7	Fees: Franchise - $7-30K	Lease Negotiation Assistance: . . . .NA
Total Units (As of 8/31/1992): 7	Royalty: 4.5-6%, Advert: 1.5%	Co-operative Advertising: . . . . . . .NA
Projected New Units for 1993:	Contract Periods (Yrs.): 10/89	Training: . . . . 4 Wks. Headquarters
Distribution: US-0;Can-7;Overseas-0	Area Development Agreement: Yes/99	. . . .
North America: . . . . 5 Provinces	Sub-Franchise Contract: . . . . .No	On-Going Support: a,C,D,F,G,h/ 2
Concentration: . . . 2 in BC, 1 in PQ, 1 in ON	Expand in Territory: . . . . Yes	EXPANSION PLANS:
Registered:	Passive Ownership: . . . Not Allowed	US: . . . . .No
. . . .	Encourage Conversions: . . . . . Yes	Canada: . . . . .All Canada
Type Space: . . . . . . Home Based;~100 SF	Average # Employees: 1-2 FT, 4-5 PT	Overseas: . . . . .Yes

CLEANING CONSULTANT SERVICES

1512 Western Ave., P. O. Box 1273
Seattle, WA 98111
TEL: (800) 622-4221 (206) 682-9748
FAX: (206) 622-6876
Mr. William R. Griffin, President

Our consultants provide information services for custodial managers and business owners in the following areas: budget and workload analysis, inventory management, quality inspections, scheduling, supply and equipment data, technical support, training materials and programs and small business services.

HISTORY:	FINANCIAL: Earnings Claim: . .No	FRANCHISOR TRAINING/SUPPORT:
Established in 1976; . . 1st Franchised in 1984	Cash Investment: $5K	Financial Assistance Provided: . . . . .No
Company-Owned Units (As of 8/31/1992): . .2	Total Investment: $5K	Site Selection Assistance: . . . . . . .NA
Franchised Units (As of 8/31/1992): 3	Fees: Franchise - $2.5K	Lease Negotiation Assistance: . . . .NA
Total Units (As of 8/31/1992): 5	Royalty: $50/Mo., Advert:	Co-operative Advertising: . . . . . . .Yes
Projected New Units for 1993: 8	Contract Periods (Yrs.): 5/5	Training: . . . . 1 Wk. Headquarters
Distribution: US-5;Can-0;Overseas-0	Area Development Agreement: Yes/5	. . . .
North America: . . . . 4 States	Sub-Franchise Contract: . . . . . Yes	On-Going Support: C,d,I/ 10
Concentration: . . . . .WA, CA	Expand in Territory: . . . . .No	EXPANSION PLANS:
Registered: . . . . .All	Passive Ownership: . . . Not Allowed	US: . . . . .All US
. . . .	Encourage Conversions: . . . . . .No	Canada: . . . . .No
Type Space: . . . . . . Home/Office;~NA SF	Average # Employees: . . 1 FT, 1 PT	Overseas: . . . . . . MX, JA, EUR

CLEANNET USA

9861 Broken Land Pkwy., # 208
Columbia, MD 21046
TEL: (800) 735-8838 (410) 720-6444
FAX: (410) 720-5307
Mr. John A. Zsidisin, VP

Full-service, turn-key commercial office cleaning franchise, offering guaranteed customer accounts, training, equipment, supplies, localized office support, quality control back-up, billing/invoicing and guaranteed payment for services provided.

HISTORY: . . . .
Established in 19; . . . 1st Franchised in 1987
Company-Owned Units (As of 8/31/1992): . .1
Franchised Units (As of 8/31/1992): **681**
Total Units (As of 8/31/1992): 682
Projected New Units for 1993: 480
Distribution: . . . US-682;Can-0;Overseas-0
  North America: . . . . 9 States
  Concentration: . 201 in MD, 137 in NJ, 88 CA
Registered: . . CA,FL,IL,MD,MI,MN,NY,VA
. . . . WA,WI,DC
Type Space: . . . . NA;~ SF

FINANCIAL: Earnings Claim: . .No
Cash Investment: $1.8-25K
Total Investment: $3.0-28.4K
Fees: Franchise - . . . . . .$Included
  Royalty: 10-13%, Advert: . . . 0%
Contract Periods (Yrs.): 10/10
Area Development Agreement: Yes/10
Sub-Franchise Contract: . . . . . Yes
Expand in Territory: . . . . . . Yes
Passive Ownership: . . . Discouraged
Encourage Conversions: . . . . .No
Average # Employees: 1-2 FT, 0-10 PT

FRANCHISOR TRAINING/SUPPORT:
Financial Assistance Provided: . . .Yes(D)
Site Selection Assistance: . . . . . . .NA
Lease Negotiation Assistance: . . . . .NA
Co-operative Advertising: . . . . . . .NA
Training: . . . . . . .3 Days On-Site Plus
  . . Minimum Once Per Month Follow-Up
On-Going Support: A,B,C,D,E,F/ 16
EXPANSION PLANS:
US: . . . . .60 Largest MSA's
Canada: . . . . .Ontario
Overseas: . . . . Yes

COLOR YOUR CARPET

2465 Ridgecrest Ave.
Orange Park, FL 32065
TEL: (800) 321-6567 (904) 272-6567
FAX: (904) 272-6750
Ms. Connie D'Imperio, President

The only full-time carpet dyeing service. One-step, on-site dyeing and color restoration for 85% of all carpets. Rated the #1 service franchise "Up and Coming for the 90's" by the Arthur Andersen accounting firm. Multiple and master franchise territories open. Competition invisible or non-existent.

HISTORY: . . . .
Established in 1979; . . 1st Franchised in 1988
Company-Owned Units (As of 8/31/1992): . .1
Franchised Units (As of 8/31/1992): **76**
Total Units (As of 8/31/1992): 77
Projected New Units for 1993: 24
Distribution: US-49;Can-28;Overseas-0
  North America: . . . . 11 States, 3 Provinces
  Concentration: . 16 in BC, 12 in PA, 12 in MD
Registered: . . . . FL,HI,MD,MI,OR
. . . .
Type Space: . . . . NA;~ SF

FINANCIAL: Earnings Claim: . .No
Cash Investment: $22-31K
Total Investment: $25-45K
Fees: Franchise - $15K
  Royalty: 3%, Advert: 0%
Contract Periods (Yrs.): 5/5
Area Development Agreement: Yes/15
Sub-Franchise Contract: . . . . Yes
Expand in Territory: . . . . . . Yes
Passive Ownership: . . . . .Allowed
Encourage Conversions: . . . . .No
Average # Employees: . . 1 FT, 1 PT

FRANCHISOR TRAINING/SUPPORT:
Financial Assistance Provided: . . . Yes(I)
Site Selection Assistance: . . . . . . .Yes
Lease Negotiation Assistance: . . . . .NA
Co-operative Advertising: . . . . . . .NA
Training: . . . . 2 Wks. Home Study, 1 Wk.
  . . . Jacksonville, FL, 1 Wk. Raleigh, NC
On-Going Support: B,C,D,G,h,I/ 1
EXPANSION PLANS:
US: . . . . All US
Canada: . . . . .All Canada
Overseas: . . . . UK, AU, MX, JA

COLOR-GLO INTERNATIONAL

7111 Ohms Ln.
Minneapolis, MN 55439
TEL: (800) 333-8523 (612) 835-1338
FAX: (612) 835-1395
Mr. Scott Smith, VP

Low-overhead mobile business, providing exclusive color and surface restoration service for leather, cloth, vinyl, plastic, etc. To auto dealers, fleets, boats, RV's, aircraft, business - anywhere. Savings of up to 98% over replacement. Vast ready market awaits motivated individual desiring extremely high income, full-time or part-time.

HISTORY: . . . .
Established in 1976; . . . 1st Franchised in 1985
Company-Owned Units (As of 8/31/1992): . .3
Franchised Units (As of 8/31/1992): **318**
Total Units (As of 8/31/1992): 321
Projected New Units for 1993: 20
Distribution: . . . US-294;Can-12;Overseas-15
  North America: . . . . 50 States, 3 Provinces
  Concentration: . . . 8 in FL, 7 in MN, 6 in OH
Registered: . . . . .All
. . . .
Type Space: . . . .;~ SF

FINANCIAL: Earnings Claim: . . .
Cash Investment: $4.9-17K
Total Investment: $5.6-25K
Fees: Franchise - $2.5K
  Royalty: 0%, Advert: 0%
Contract Periods (Yrs.): 10/5
Area Development Agreement: Yes/5
Sub-Franchise Contract: . . . . . Yes
Expand in Territory: . . . . . . Yes
Passive Ownership: . . . . .Allowed
Encourage Conversions: . . . Yes
Average # Employees: . . . . .Varies

FRANCHISOR TRAINING/SUPPORT:
Financial Assistance Provided: . . .Yes(D)
Site Selection Assistance: . . . . . . .Yes
Lease Negotiation Assistance: . . . . .Yes
Co-operative Advertising: . . . . . . .Yes
Training: . . . . .3 Days Central Area
. . . .
On-Going Support: A,B,C,D,E,F,G,H,I/ 11
EXPANSION PLANS:
US: . . . . .All US
Canada: . . . . .Yes
Overseas: . . . . .Yes

COLORKING INTERNATIONAL

13726 Lookout Rd.
San Antonio, TX 78233
TEL: (800) 852-9587 (512) 646-6677 C
FAX: (512) 646-6670
Mr. Randy Massey, VP Fran. Recruit.

Comprehensive program for On Location carpet and upholstery dyeing/cleaning/color repair/disaster and restoration service business. Complete training program, combining one week classroom training, on-the-job and home study exercises, business management and technical support hotline, comprehensive manual and national convention.

HISTORY: . . . .
Established in 1990; . . 1st Franchised in 1990
Company-Owned Units (As of 8/31/1992): . .0
Franchised Units (As of 8/31/1992): 9
Total Units (As of 8/31/1992): 9
Projected New Units for 1993:
Distribution: US-9;Can-0;Overseas-0
  North America: . . . . 5 States
  Concentration: . . . . 4 in TX, 2 in NJ, 1 in FL
Registered: . . . . .FL
. . . .
Type Space: . . . .;~ SF

FINANCIAL: Earnings Claim: . .No
Cash Investment: . . . . $7K+
Total Investment: . . . . . . $23K+
Fees: Franchise - . . . . . . $15K+
  Royalty: 2-7%, Advert: 2%
Contract Periods (Yrs.): 5/5
Area Development Agreement: .No
Sub-Franchise Contract: . . . . .No
Expand in Territory: . . . . . . Yes
Passive Ownership: . . . Not Allowed
Encourage Conversions: . . . . Yes
Average # Employees: . 1-2 FT, 5 PT

FRANCHISOR TRAINING/SUPPORT:
Financial Assistance Provided: . . .Yes(D)
Site Selection Assistance: . . . . . . .Yes
Lease Negotiation Assistance: . . . .NA
Co-operative Advertising: . . . . . . .Yes
Training: . . . . 1 Wk. Headquarters
. . . .
On-Going Support: B,C,G,H,I/ 5
EXPANSION PLANS:
US: . . . . .FTC Disclosure States
Canada: . . . . No
Overseas: . . . . No

CONSOL CARPET CLEANING

298 Tosca Dr., P. O. Box 630
Stoughton, MA 02072
TEL: (800) 826-0112 (617) 341-0168
FAX: (617) 341-3440
Mr. Robert G. Melchionno, VP

National company offers carpet cleaning and maintenance franchises with guaranteed exclusive territory sized to meet your financial capabilities. Unique opportunity. Franchisee is provided with base of prestigious accounts and start-up income. Franchisor offers 15 years' experience in the industry and provides continuous support and training.

HISTORY: . . . .
Established in 1988; . . 1st Franchised in 1988
Company-Owned Units (As of 8/31/1992): . .1
Franchised Units (As of 8/31/1992): 3
Total Units (As of 8/31/1992): 4
Projected New Units for 1993: 5
Distribution: US-4;Can-0;Overseas-0
  North America: . . . . 4 States
  Concentration: . . . . 1 in MA, 1 in IL, 1 in FL
Registered: . . .CA,FL,IL,MD,MI,NY,OR,VA
. . . .
Type Space: . . . . . . HB, Storage Area;~ SF

FINANCIAL: Earnings Claim: . .No
Cash Investment: $7.5-20K
Total Investment: $20-50K
Fees: Franchise - $9.5-22.5K
  Royalty: 7%, Advert: 3%
Contract Periods (Yrs.): 5/5
Area Development Agreement: .No
Sub-Franchise Contract: . . . . .No
Expand in Territory: . . . . . . Yes
Passive Ownership: . . . Not Allowed
Encourage Conversions: . . . . Yes
Average # Employees: . . . . .2 FT

FRANCHISOR TRAINING/SUPPORT:
Financial Assistance Provided: . . .Yes(D)
Site Selection Assistance: . . . . . . .NA
Lease Negotiation Assistance: . . . .NA
Co-operative Advertising: . . . . . . .Yes
Training: . . . . . . 3-6 Days Headquarters,
. . . . . . 1-2 Wks. Franchisee Territory
On-Going Support: A,B,C,D,F,G,h,I/ . . . .
EXPANSION PLANS:
US: . . . NE, MW, SE, CA, Mid-Atlantic
Canada: . . . . No
Overseas: . . . . No

COUSTIC-GLO INTERNATIONAL

7111 Ohms Ln.
Minneapolis, MN 55435
TEL: (800) 333-8523 (612) 835-1338 C
FAX: (612) 835-1395
Mr. Gary Smith, CFO

Providing only complete line of products and services to clean and remove all types of ceiling and wall materials. These exclusive, environmentally-safe products will restore a clean, healthy environment to all buildings, while saving thousands over alternative methods. Very high profit, low overhead business.

HISTORY: . . . . .IFA
Established in 1970; . . 1st Franchised in 1980
Company-Owned Units (As of 8/31/1992): . .1
Franchised Units (As of 8/31/1992): 247
Total Units (As of 8/31/1992): 248
Projected New Units for 1993: 20
Distribution: US-221;Can-8;Overseas-19
  North America: . . . . 50 States, 4 Provinces
  Concentration: . . 13 in FL, 11 in PA, 11 in TX
Registered: . . . . .All
. . . .
Type Space: . . . .;~ SF

FINANCIAL: Earnings Claim: . .No
Cash Investment: $9.8-255K
Total Investment: $12-50K
Fees: Franchise - $12.5K
  Royalty: 5%, Advert: 1%
Contract Periods (Yrs.): 10/5
Area Development Agreement: Yes/10
Sub-Franchise Contract: . . . . . Yes
Expand in Territory: . . . . . . Yes
Passive Ownership: . . . . . .Allowed
Encourage Conversions: . . . . Yes
Average # Employees: . . . . .2 PT

FRANCHISOR TRAINING/SUPPORT:
Financial Assistance Provided: . . . Yes(I)
Site Selection Assistance: . . . . . . .Yes
Lease Negotiation Assistance: . . . .Yes
Co-operative Advertising: . . . . . . .Yes
Training: . . . . 2-3 Days Training On-Site
. . . .
On-Going Support: A,B,C,D,E,F,G,H,I/ 14
EXPANSION PLANS:
US: . . . . All US
Canada: . . . . .Yes
Overseas: . . . . No

COVERALL NORTH AMERICA

3111 Camino Del Rio N., # 1200
San Diego, CA 92108
TEL: (800) 537-3371 (619) 584-1911 C
FAX: (619) 584-4923
Mr. Jack Caughey, Dir. Fran. Sales

COVERALL offers a comprehensive janitorial franchise which includes customer base, equipment and supplies package. Franchisee will provide professional cleaning programs to commercial and industrial buildings. Franchisees can obtain future contracts directly through COVERALL. COVERALL also has a few choice markets left for Master Franchisers.

HISTORY:	IFA
Established in 1985;	1st Franchised in 1985
Company-Owned Units (As of 8/31/1992):	10
Franchised Units (As of 8/31/1992):	2411
Total Units (As of 8/31/1992):	2421
Projected New Units for 1993:	900
Distribution:	US-2243;Can-68;Overseas-110
North America:	22 States, 1 Province
Concentration:	228 in CA, 225 in FL, 219 OH
Registered:	CA,FL,IL,MD,MI,MN,NY,OR
	RI,VA,WA,WI,DC
Type Space:	NA;~NA SF

FINANCIAL:	Earnings Claim:	No
Cash Investment:		$2.5-30K
Total Investment:		$5-42K
Fees: Franchise -		$4.2-33.6K
Royalty: 10%, Advert:		0%
Contract Periods (Yrs.):		10/10
Area Development Agreement:		No
Sub-Franchise Contract:		Yes
Expand in Territory:		Yes
Passive Ownership:		Discouraged
Encourage Conversions:		Yes
Average # Employees:		1 FT, 2 PT

FRANCHISOR TRAINING/SUPPORT:
Financial Assistance Provided: Yes(D)
Site Selection Assistance: NA
Lease Negotiation Assistance: NA
Co-operative Advertising: Yes
Training: 3-4 Wks. Regional Office, 1-2 Wks. On-Site
On-Going Support: A,B,C,D,G,H,I/ 160
EXPANSION PLANS:
US: All US
Canada: All Canada
Overseas: EUR, AU, SE Asia, S.America

FABRI-ZONE CLEANING SYSTEMS

3135 Universal Dr., # 6
Mississauga, ON L4X 2E2 CAN
TEL: (416) 602-7691
FAX: (416) 602-7821
Mr. David S. Collier, President

FABRI-ZONE offers a full-service franchise concept to start part or full-time. Turn-key operation. Offering FABRI-RESTORE, a patented dry cleaning and purification carpet cleaning, steam finishing process. Also cleaning upholstery, drapery, ceilings, insurance restoration, professional marketing and sales programs, technical support, technical support center. Recommended by carpet manufacturers.

HISTORY:	
Established in 1981;	1st Franchised in 1985
Company-Owned Units (As of 8/31/1992):	1
Franchised Units (As of 8/31/1992):	92
Total Units (As of 8/31/1992):	93
Projected New Units for 1993:	20
Distribution:	US-15;Can-70;Overseas-8
North America:	
Concentration:	22 in ON, 14 in AB, 7 in NS
Registered:	AB
Type Space:	NA;~NA SF

FINANCIAL:	Earnings Claim:	No
Cash Investment:		$2-7K
Total Investment:		$15-30K
Fees: Franchise -		$1.5K
Royalty: 5%, Advert:		1%
Contract Periods (Yrs.):		5/5
Area Development Agreement:		Yes
Sub-Franchise Contract:		Yes
Expand in Territory:		Yes
Passive Ownership:		Not Allowed
Encourage Conversions:		Yes
Average # Employees:	1-4 FT, 1-3 PT

FRANCHISOR TRAINING/SUPPORT:
Financial Assistance Provided: Yes
Site Selection Assistance:
Lease Negotiation Assistance: NA
Co-operative Advertising: Yes
Training: 1 Wk. Headquarters or Regional Office
On-Going Support: G,H/ 13
EXPANSION PLANS:
US: No
Canada: All Canada
Overseas: Yes

HEAVEN'S BEST CARPET AND UPHOLSTERY CLEANERS

247 N. 1st E., P. O. Box 607
Rexburg, ID 83440
TEL: (800) 359-2095 (208) 359-1106 C
FAX:
Mr. Cody Howard, President

HEAVEN'S BEST offers the advantage of modern, low-moisture cleaning techniques. Our operators receive professional training, a complete equipment package, all start-up supplies and on-going research and support. These factors, coupled with a low flat rate royalty fee, insure success.

HISTORY:	
Established in 1983;	1st Franchised in 1984
Company-Owned Units (As of 8/31/1992):	4
Franchised Units (As of 8/31/1992):	81
Total Units (As of 8/31/1992):	85
Projected New Units for 1993:	
Distribution:	US-85;Can-0;Overseas-0
North America:	
Concentration:	16 in ID, 9 in KS, 7 in UT
Registered:	CA,IN,OR,WA
Type Space:	;~ SF

FINANCIAL:	Earnings Claim:	No
Cash Investment:		$9.5-25K
Total Investment:		$9.5-25K
Fees: Franchise -		$9.5K
Royalty: $40/Mo., Advert:		0%
Contract Periods (Yrs.):		5/5
Area Development Agreement:		No
Sub-Franchise Contract:		Yes
Expand in Territory:		Yes
Passive Ownership:		Discouraged
Encourage Conversions:		NA
Average # Employees:		1 FT

FRANCHISOR TRAINING/SUPPORT:
Financial Assistance Provided: No
Site Selection Assistance: NA
Lease Negotiation Assistance: NA
Co-operative Advertising: No
Training: 1 Wk. Headquarters
On-Going Support: A,C,d,G,h,I/ 2
EXPANSION PLANS:
US: All US
Canada: No
Overseas: No

JAN-PRO CLEANING SYSTEMS

210 Lonsdale Ave.
Pawtucket, RI 02860
TEL: (401) 727-4040 C
FAX: (401) 727-4171
Mr. Jack LaPointe, President

Franchisor of commercial/janitorial services with guaranteed clients and income.

HISTORY:	FINANCIAL: Earnings Claim: . Yes	FRANCHISOR TRAINING/SUPPORT:
Established in 1991; . . 1st Franchised in 1992	Cash Investment: $1.6-16K	Financial Assistance Provided: . . . Yes(D)
Company-Owned Units (As of 8/31/1992): . . 1	Total Investment: $3.8-36K	Site Selection Assistance: . . . . NA
Franchised Units (As of 8/31/1992): 24	Fees: Franchise - $1.6-16K	Lease Negotiation Assistance: . . . NA
Total Units (As of 8/31/1992): 25	Royalty: 8%, Advert: 1%	Co-operative Advertising: . . . . .Yes
Projected New Units for 1993: 50	Contract Periods (Yrs.): . . . 10/10	Training: . . . . .1 Wk. Headquarters,
Distribution: US-25;Can-0;Overseas-0	Area Development Agreement: . .No	. . . . 2 Wks. On-Site
North America: . . . . 3 States	Sub-Franchise Contract: . . . . .No	On-Going Support: a,C,D,E,F,G,H,I/ . . . 9
Concentration: . . . 14 in RI, 8 in MA, 2 in CT	Expand in Territory: . . . . . . Yes	EXPANSION PLANS:
Registered: . . . . RI	Passive Ownership: . . . Discouraged	US: . . . . .Northeast, Southeast
. . . .	Encourage Conversions: . . . . Yes	Canada: . . . . .Quebec & Ontario
Type Space: . . . . NA;~NA SF	Average # Employees: . . 1 FT, 4 PT	Overseas: . . . . No

JANI-KING

4950 Keller Springs Rd., # 190
Dallas, TX 75248
TEL: (800) 552-5264 (214) 991-0900
FAX: (214) 239-7706
Mr. Scott Gann, Natl. Mktg. Dir.

World's largest and top-ranked commercial cleaning franchisor. Our proven franchise plan offers a specified amount of initial business, depending on the plan purchased. Franchisees benefit from JANI-KING's 23 years of experience in this recession-resistant industry.

HISTORY: . . . . IFA, CFA	FINANCIAL: Earnings Claim: . .No	FRANCHISOR TRAINING/SUPPORT:
Established in 1969; . . 1st Franchised in 1974	Cash Investment: . . . . . $2-14K+	Financial Assistance Provided: . . . Yes(D)
Company-Owned Units (As of 8/31/1992): . 20	Total Investment: . . . . . $6.5-14K+	Site Selection Assistance: . . . . .NA
Franchised Units (As of 8/31/1992): 3491	Fees: Franchise - . . . . . $6.5-14K+	Lease Negotiation Assistance: . . . . .NA
Total Units (As of 8/31/1992): 3511	Royalty: 7-10%, Advert: . . . 1/2%	Co-operative Advertising: . . . . .NA
Projected New Units for 1993:	Contract Periods (Yrs.): . . . 20/20	Training: . . . . . 30 Days Regional Center,
Distribution: . . US-3418;Can-67;Overseas-26	Area Development Agreement: . .No	. . . 1 Wk. Headquarters (As Requested)
North America: . . . . 36 States, 9 Provinces	Sub-Franchise Contract: . . . . . Yes	On-Going Support: A,B,C,D,G,H,I/ . . 40
Concentration: . . 827 in CA, 749 TX, 257 FL	Expand in Territory: . . . . . . .No	EXPANSION PLANS:
Registered: . . . . All States Exc. WI	Passive Ownership: . . . Discouraged	US: . . . . All US
. . . .	Encourage Conversions: . . . . . Yes	Canada: . . . . .All Canada
Type Space: . . . . NA;~NA SF	Average # Employees: . . . . .Varies	Overseas: . . . . .UK, BZ

JANTIZE AMERICA

20300 Superior, # 190
Taylor, MI 48180
TEL: (800) 456-9182 (313) 287-6006
FAX: (313) 287-3230
Mr. Jerry Grabowski, VP

You can own your own business for less than the cost of a new car! A JANTIZE commercial office cleaning franchise has it all - computerized procedures, audio/visual training, on-going assistance, and more!

HISTORY:	FINANCIAL: Earnings Claim: . .No	FRANCHISOR TRAINING/SUPPORT:
Established in 1985; . . 1st Franchised in 1988	Cash Investment: $9-11.5K	Financial Assistance Provided: . . . Yes(D)
Company-Owned Units (As of 8/31/1992): . .1	Total Investment: $20K	Site Selection Assistance: . . . . .Yes
Franchised Units (As of 8/31/1992): 16	Fees: Franchise - $3.5-16K	Lease Negotiation Assistance: . . . . . No
Total Units (As of 8/31/1992): 17	Royalty: 9%, Advert: 1%	Co-operative Advertising: . . . . No
Projected New Units for 1993: 5	Contract Periods (Yrs.): 10/10	Training: . . . . 3-6 Days Headquarters,
Distribution: US-17;Can-0;Overseas-0	Area Development Agreement: . .No	. . . . . . .3 Days Franchisee Location
North America: . . . . 2 States	Sub-Franchise Contract: . . . . . Yes	On-Going Support: a,D,E,G,H,I/ 8
Concentration: . . . . .12 in MI, 1 in VA	Expand in Territory: . . . . .No	EXPANSION PLANS:
Registered: . . . . MI,VA	Passive Ownership: . . . Discouraged	US: . . . . All US
. . . .	Encourage Conversions: . . . . Yes	Canada: . . . . .All Canada
Type Space: . . . .;~ SF	Average # Employees: . . . .3-20 PT	Overseas: . . . . No

LANGENWALTER DYE CONCEPT

4410 E. La Palma Ave.
Anaheim, CA 92807
TEL: (800) 422-4370 (714) 528-7610
FAX: (714) 528-7620
Mr. John Langenwalter, VP

Complete carpet restoration. The franchisees are professionals in taking care of carpet problems, including sun-fading, pet-bleach-chemical stains, etc. and can make complete color changes, saving the customer up to 75% of carpet replacement costs.

HISTORY:	FINANCIAL: Earnings Claim: . .No	FRANCHISOR TRAINING/SUPPORT:
Established in 1975; . . 1st Franchised in 1981	Cash Investment: $17.5K	Financial Assistance Provided: . . . . .No
Company-Owned Units (As of 8/31/1992): . .2	Total Investment: $18-20K	Site Selection Assistance: . . . . . . .NA
Franchised Units (As of 8/31/1992): 130	Fees: Franchise - $16.5K	Lease Negotiation Assistance: . . . .NA
Total Units (As of 8/31/1992): 132	Royalty: Flat, Advert: . . $125/Mo.	Co-operative Advertising: . . . . . . .Yes
Projected New Units for 1993: 10	Contract Periods (Yrs.): 3/3	Training: . . . . 1 Wk. Headquarters
Distribution: US-128;Can-2;Overseas-2	Area Development Agreement: . .No	. . . .
North America: . . . . 28 States	Sub-Franchise Contract: . . . . . Yes	On-Going Support: G,H,I/ 6
Concentration: . . 52 in CA, 5 in OR, 5 in WA	Expand in Territory: . . . . Yes	EXPANSION PLANS:
Registered:	Passive Ownership: . . . Not Allowed	US: . . . . .All US
. . . .	Encourage Conversions:	Canada: . . . . .All Canada
Type Space: . . . . ;~ SF	Average # Employees: 1-2 FT, 2-3 PT	Overseas: . . . . Yes

LASER CHEM

126 Indian Ave.
Lawrence, KS 66046
TEL: (800) 272-2741 (913) 749-0936
FAX: (913) 749-3993
Mr. Dennis R. Jenkins, President

LASER CHEM offers the most advanced carpet and upholstery cleaning system on the market. Carpets are restored to their original lustre and dry within 30 minutes. A full floor care system package provides franchisee with opportunities to service wood, vinyl and other floor surfaces for residential and small business.

HISTORY:	FINANCIAL: Earnings Claim: . .No	FRANCHISOR TRAINING/SUPPORT:
Established in 1978; . . 1st Franchised in 1991	Cash Investment: $3.7K	Financial Assistance Provided: . . .Yes(D)
Company-Owned Units (As of 8/31/1992): . .0	Total Investment: $10K	Site Selection Assistance: . . . . . . .Yes
Franchised Units (As of 8/31/1992): 15	Fees: Franchise - $10K	Lease Negotiation Assistance: . . . . .No
Total Units (As of 8/31/1992): 15	Royalty: $125, Advert: 0%	Co-operative Advertising: . . . . .No
Projected New Units for 1993: 48	Contract Periods (Yrs.): 5/5	Training: . . . . 4 Days Headquarters
Distribution: US-15;Can-0;Overseas-0	Area Development Agreement: . .No	. . . .
North America: . . . . 11 States	Sub-Franchise Contract: . . . . .No	On-Going Support: c,d,G,h,I/ 6
Concentration: . . . 2 in AZ, 2 in KS, 2 in CA	Expand in Territory: . . . . . . .No	EXPANSION PLANS:
Registered: . . . . CA,OR	Passive Ownership: . . . . .Allowed	US: . . . . All US
. . . .	Encourage Conversions: . . . . Yes	Canada: . . . . .All Canada
Type Space: . . . . NA;~NA SF	Average # Employees: . . . . .2 FT	Overseas: . . . . No

LONE DRAINER AND PRONTO!, THE

4660 S. Eastern Ave.
Commerce, CA 90040
TEL: (800) 54-ROOTER (213) 887-6920
FAX: (213) 724-9688
Mr. Russell Taylor, CEO

24-hour drain cleaning, plumbing repair and specialist services. Residential, commercial and industrial customers. Franchisor answers phones and dispatches to franchisee by computer. Exclusive areas - many with existing business, so don't have to start from zero.

HISTORY:	FINANCIAL: Earnings Claim: . .No	FRANCHISOR TRAINING/SUPPORT:
Established in 1986; . . 1st Franchised in 1992	Cash Investment: $15-30K	Financial Assistance Provided: . . .Yes(D)
Company-Owned Units (As of 8/31/1992): . .8	Total Investment: . . . . $70K+	Site Selection Assistance: . . . . . . .NA
Franchised Units (As of 8/31/1992): 150	Fees: Franchise - $6.5K	Lease Negotiation Assistance: . . . . .NA
Total Units (As of 8/31/1992): 158	Royalty: 7%, Advert: 2%	Co-operative Advertising: . . . . . . .NA
Projected New Units for 1993: 10	Contract Periods (Yrs.): 10/5	Training: . . . . 4 Wks. Headquarters
Distribution: . . . US-8;Can-0;Overseas-150	Area Development Agreement: . .No	. . . .
North America: . . . . .1 State	Sub-Franchise Contract: . . . . .No	On-Going Support: A,C,D,e,G,I/ 30
Concentration: . . . . 8 in CA	Expand in Territory: . . . . Yes	EXPANSION PLANS:
Registered: . . . . CA	Passive Ownership: . . . Discouraged	US: . . . . The West
. . . .	Encourage Conversions: . . . . Yes	Canada: . . . . .No
Type Space: . . . . NA;~NA SF	Average # Employees: . . . . .4 FT	Overseas: . . . . No

MR. BUILD HANDI-MAN SERVICES

2049 Silas Deane Hwy., # 207
Rocky Hill, CT 06067
TEL: (800) 899-6965 (203) 257-8101
FAX: (203) 257-8101
Mr. Martin Sudy, VP Sales/Mktg.

MR. BUILD HANDI-MAN SERVICES does small maintenance, repair and renovation work for residences and businesses. Franchisees get protected territories, help in hiring handymen, step-by-step marketing and customized computer lead-tracking and management. A 24-hour toll-free Consumer Action Line and a 1-year work guarantee help reach and sell customers.

HISTORY:	FINANCIAL: Earnings Claim: . . .	FRANCHISOR TRAINING/SUPPORT:
Established in 1989; . . 1st Franchised in 1990	Cash Investment: . . . $26.9-46.4K	Financial Assistance Provided: . . .Yes(D)
Company-Owned Units (As of 8/31/1992): . .0	Total Investment: $60-70K	Site Selection Assistance: . . . . . . .NA
Franchised Units (As of 8/31/1992): 34	Fees: Franchise - $26.9K	Lease Negotiation Assistance: . . . . .NA
Total Units (As of 8/31/1992): 34	Royalty: 7%, Advert: 4%	Co-operative Advertising: . . . . . . .Yes
Projected New Units for 1993: 45	Contract Periods (Yrs.): . . . 20/20	Training: . . . . .1 Wk. Headquarters,
Distribution: US-23;Can-11;Overseas-0	Area Development Agreement: Yes/20	. . . . . . .On-Going Areas and Regions
North America: . . . . . 6 States, 2 Provinces	Sub-Franchise Contract: . . . . Yes	On-Going Support: A,B,C,D,E,G,H,I/ . . 8
Concentration: . . .10 in CT, 5 in BC, 4 in MA	Expand in Territory: . . . . . . Yes	EXPANSION PLANS:
Registered: . . . . IL,IN,NY	Passive Ownership: . . . Not Allowed	US: . . . New England,OH,PA,IN,KY,IL
. . . .	Encourage Conversions: . . . . .No	Canada: . . . . .All Canada
Type Space: . . . . NA;~NA SF	Average # Employees: . . 3 FT, 1 PT	Overseas: . . . . JA

MR. ROOTER

P. O. Box 1309
Waco, TX 76703
TEL: (800) 583-8003 (817) 755-0055
FAX: (817) 757-1667
Mr. Robert Tunmire, President

MR. ROOTER offers franchises for businesses providing drain cleaning and expert plumbing services under the name MR. ROOTER. Its wholly-owned subsidiary, National Manufacturing Co., manufactures sewer and drain cleaning equipment, which it sells to its franchisees and others in the plumbing industry.

HISTORY:	FINANCIAL: Earnings Claim: . .No	FRANCHISOR TRAINING/SUPPORT:
Established in 1968; . . 1st Franchised in 1974	Cash Investment: $15-75K	Financial Assistance Provided: . . . . .Yes
Company-Owned Units (As of 8/31/1992): . .1	Total Investment: $30-300K	Site Selection Assistance: . . . . . . .NA
Franchised Units (As of 8/31/1992): 130	Fees: Franchise - $15K	Lease Negotiation Assistance: . . . .NA
Total Units (As of 8/31/1992): 131	Royalty: 6%, Advert: 2%	Co-operative Advertising: . . . . . . .NA
Projected New Units for 1993: 75	Contract Periods (Yrs.): 10/10	Training: . . . . .1 Wk. Headquarters
Distribution: US-129;Can-1;Overseas-1	Area Development Agreement: Yes/20	. . . .
North America: . . . . 30 States	Sub-Franchise Contract: . . . . .No	On-Going Support: C,D,G,H,I/ 15
Concentration: . . . . .CA, TX, FL	Expand in Territory: . . . . . . Yes	EXPANSION PLANS:
Registered: . . . . .All	Passive Ownership: . . . . . .Allowed	US: . . . . All US
. . . .	Encourage Conversions: . . . . . Yes	Canada: . . . . .All Canada
Type Space: . . . . NA;~ SF	Average # Employees: . . . . . .1 FT	Overseas: . . . . .Yes

NATIONAL LEAK DETECTION

P. O. Box 3191
Palos Verdes Estate, CA 90274
TEL: (310) 377-2699
FAX: (310) 377-5363
Mr. Richard Evans, President

Detection of hidden underground water and gas leaks utilizing sonar, ultrasonic field testing equipment, video inspection of underground pipeline structures and infrared thermography. Specializing in pools, spas, fountains, ponds, slab leaks, leaks in walls, domestic water supply systems, irrigation systems and natural gas supply line systems. Exclusive product - Aqua 2000 only available to our franchisees.

HISTORY: . . . . IFA	FINANCIAL: Earnings Claim: . .No	FRANCHISOR TRAINING/SUPPORT:
Established in 1979; . . 1st Franchised in 1990	Cash Investment: $35K	Financial Assistance Provided: . . .Yes(D)
Company-Owned Units (As of 8/31/1992): . .6	Total Investment: $55K	Site Selection Assistance: . . . . . . .NA
Franchised Units (As of 8/31/1992): 23	Fees: Franchise - $35K	Lease Negotiation Assistance: . . . .NA
Total Units (As of 8/31/1992): 29	Royalty: 8%, Advert: 2%	Co-operative Advertising: . . . . . . .Yes
Projected New Units for 1993: 12	Contract Periods (Yrs.): 5/5	Training: . . . . . . 4-6 Wks. Headquarters
Distribution: US-29;Can-0;Overseas-0	Area Development Agreement: .No	. . . .
North America: . . . . 4 States	Sub-Franchise Contract: . . . . .No	On-Going Support: A,B,C,D,G,H,I/ . . .3
Concentration: . . .26 in CA, 1 in TX, 1 in AZ	Expand in Territory: . . . . . . Yes	EXPANSION PLANS:
Registered: . . . . .CA,FL	Passive Ownership: . . . Not Allowed	US: . . . . All US
. . . .	Encourage Conversions: . . . . NA	Canada: . . . . .All Canada
Type Space: . . . . NA;~NA SF	Average # Employees: . . . . . .1 FT	Overseas: . . . . .Yes

O.P.E.N. CLEANING SYSTEMS

2390 E. Camelback Rd., # 304
Phoenix, AZ 85016
TEL: (800) 777-6736 (602) 224-0594 C
FAX: (602) 468-3788
Mr. Eric Roudi, President

O.P.E.N. provides the opportunity for the small investor to enter the highly profitable and growing field of office cleaning. Each O.P.E.N. franchisee will receive initial cleaning contracts, plus training and full support from the franchisor.

HISTORY:	FINANCIAL: Earnings Claim: . .No	FRANCHISOR TRAINING/SUPPORT:
Established in 1983; . . 1st Franchised in 1983	Cash Investment: $1.7-9K	Financial Assistance Provided: . . .Yes(D)
Company-Owned Units (As of 8/31/1992): . .3	Total Investment: $2.5-11K	Site Selection Assistance: . . . . . . .NA
Franchised Units (As of 8/31/1992): 540	Fees: Franchise - $3-15K	Lease Negotiation Assistance: . . . . . .NA
Total Units (As of 8/31/1992): 543	Royalty: 10%, Advert: 0%	Co-operative Advertising: . . . . . . .NA
Projected New Units for 1993: 150	Contract Periods (Yrs.): . . . 10/10	Training: . . . . 3 Days Headquarters,
Distribution: US-543;Can-0;Overseas-0	Area Development Agreement: Yes/10	. . . 3 Days Seattle, 3 Days Los Angeles
North America: . . . . 3 States	Sub-Franchise Contract: . . . . Yes	On-Going Support: A,b,C,D,G,H,I/ . . . 32
Concentration: . . . . AZ, WA, CA	Expand in Territory: . . . . . . Yes	EXPANSION PLANS:
Registered: . . . . CA,WA	Passive Ownership: . . . Discouraged	US: . . . . .All US
. . . .	Encourage Conversions: . . . . . Yes	Canada: . . . . .All Canada
Type Space: . . . . Home Based;~ SF	Average # Employees: . . 1 FT, 3 PT	Overseas: . . . . AU

PROFESSIONAL CARPET SYSTEMS

5182 Old Dixie Hwy.
Forest Park, GA 30050
TEL: (800) 925-5055 (404) 361-9362 C
FAX: (404) 362-2888
Mr. Mike G. Philips, Dir. Fran. Dev.

PROFESSIONAL CARPET SYSTEMS is the leader in "on-site" carpet re-dyeing, servicing thousands of apartment complexes, hotels and motels worldwide. Services also include carpet cleaning, rejuvenation, repair, water and flood damage restoration and "guaranteed odor control." A total carpet care concept.

HISTORY: . . . . IFA	FINANCIAL: Earnings Claim: . .No	FRANCHISOR TRAINING/SUPPORT:
Established in 1978; . . 1st Franchised in 1979	Cash Investment: $8.5-9.7K	Financial Assistance Provided: . . .Yes(D)
Company-Owned Units (As of 8/31/1992): . .6	Total Investment: $9.7-19.7K	Site Selection Assistance: . . . . . . .Yes
Franchised Units (As of 8/31/1992): 570	Fees: Franchise - $10K	Lease Negotiation Assistance: . . . . .NA
Total Units (As of 8/31/1992): 576	Royalty: 6% or$45, Advert: . . 0%	Co-operative Advertising: . . . . . . .NA
Projected New Units for 1993: 100	Contract Periods (Yrs.): 10/10	Training: . . . . . . 2 Wks. Headquarters
Distribution: . . . US-540;Can-25;Overseas-11	Area Development Agreement: . .No	. . . .
North America: . . . . 47 States, 7 Provinces	Sub-Franchise Contract: . . . . .No	On-Going Support: A,B,C,D,F,G,H,I/ . 50
Concentration: . 25 in CA, 16 in FL, 11 in MA	Expand in Territory: . . . . . . Yes	EXPANSION PLANS:
Registered: . . . . All Except VA	Passive Ownership: . . . Discouraged	US: . . . . .All US
. . . .	Encourage Conversions: . . . . .No	Canada: . . . . .All Canada
Type Space: . . . . Home Based;~ SF	Average # Employees: 1 FT With Truck	Overseas: . . . . .Yes

PROFESSIONAL POLISH

2410 Gravel Rd.
Ft. Worth, TX 76118
TEL: (800) 255-0488 (817) 589-0102
FAX: (817) 590-0240
Mr. Sid Cavanaugh, Dir. Fran. Sales

Janitorial service and lawn service.

HISTORY:	FINANCIAL: Earnings Claim: . Yes	FRANCHISOR TRAINING/SUPPORT:
Established in 1981; . . 1st Franchised in 1986	Cash Investment: $20K	Financial Assistance Provided: . . .Yes(D)
Company-Owned Units (As of 8/31/1992): . .3	Total Investment: $30K	Site Selection Assistance: . . . . . . .Yes
Franchised Units (As of 8/31/1992): 25	Fees: Franchise - $10K	Lease Negotiation Assistance: . . . . .NA
Total Units (As of 8/31/1992): 28	Royalty: 1/2%, Advert: 0%	Co-operative Advertising: . . . . . . .NA
Projected New Units for 1993: 5	Contract Periods (Yrs.): . . . 10/10	Training: . . . . .1 Wk. Headquarters,
Distribution: US-26;Can-1;Overseas-1	Area Development Agreement: . .No	. . . . . . 30 Days Franchisee Location
North America: . . . . 2 States	Sub-Franchise Contract: . . . . .No	On-Going Support: A,B,C,d,E,f,G,h,I/ . . 4
Concentration: . . . . .26 in TX, 2 in NC	Expand in Territory: . . . . . . Yes	EXPANSION PLANS:
Registered: . . . . .FL,AB	Passive Ownership: . . . Not Allowed	US: . . . . Southwest and Southeast
. . . .	Encourage Conversions: . . . . NA	Canada: . . . . .All Canada
Type Space: . . . . Office;~1,100 SF	Average # Employees: . . 2 FT, 2 PT	Overseas: . . . . .Yes

PROPERTY DAMAGE APPRAISERS

6100 Western Pl., # 900
Fort Worth, TX 76107
TEL: (817) 731-5555
FAX:
Mr. John R. Tate, SVP Fran. Ops.

PROPERTY DAMAGE APPRAISERS offers the potential franchisee a complete insurance appraisal business to include administration, accounting, marketing and direct sales assistance. No initial franchise fee is required. A royalty on completed business.

HISTORY: . . . . IFA	FINANCIAL: Earnings Claim: . .No	FRANCHISOR TRAINING/SUPPORT:
Established in 1963; . . 1st Franchised in 1963	Cash Investment: $0	Financial Assistance Provided: . . . . . No
Company-Owned Units (As of 8/31/1992): . .0	Total Investment: $5-15K	Site Selection Assistance: . . . . . . .Yes
Franchised Units (As of 8/31/1992): 190	Fees: Franchise - $0	Lease Negotiation Assistance: . . . . .No
Total Units (As of 8/31/1992): 190	Royalty: 15%, Advert: 0%	Co-operative Advertising: . . . . . . .Yes
Projected New Units for 1993: 20	Contract Periods (Yrs.): 3/5	Training: . . . . 1 Wk. On-Site
Distribution: US-190;Can-0;Overseas-0	Area Development Agreement: . .No	. . . .
North America:	Sub-Franchise Contract: . . . . .No	On-Going Support: A,C,D,E,F,G,h,I/ . . 31
Concentration: . .16 in TX, 15 in CA, 10 in FL	Expand in Territory: . . . . . . Yes	EXPANSION PLANS:
Registered: . . . . All States	Passive Ownership: . . . Not Allowed	US: . . . . .All US
. . . .	Encourage Conversions: . . . . Yes	Canada: . . . . No
Type Space: . . . . ;~ SF	Average # Employees: . . . . .Varies	Overseas: . . . . No

ROTO-ROOTER

300 Ashworth Rd.
West Des Moines, IA 50265
TEL: (515) 223-1343
FAX: (515) 223-4220
Mr. Paul W. Carter, Dir. Fran. Admin.

The nation's largest and most experienced plumbing and sewer repair and drain cleaning franchisor.

HISTORY: . . . . IFA	FINANCIAL: Earnings Claim: . .No	FRANCHISOR TRAINING/SUPPORT:
Established in 1935; . . 1st Franchised in 1935	Cash Investment: $15-75K	Financial Assistance Provided: . . . Yes(I)
Company-Owned Units (As of 8/31/1992): . 84	Total Investment: $25-99K	Site Selection Assistance: . . . . No
Franchised Units (As of 8/31/1992): 520	Fees: Franchise - $1K	Lease Negotiation Assistance: . . . . .NA
Total Units (As of 8/31/1992): 604	Royalty: Varies, Advert: . . Varies	Co-operative Advertising: . . . . .NA
Projected New Units for 1993: 2	Contract Periods (Yrs.): 5/5	Training: . . . . No Training
Distribution: US-582;Can-22;Overseas-0	Area Development Agreement: . .No	. . . .
North America: . . . . 50 States, 5 Provinces	Sub-Franchise Contract: . . . . .No	On-Going Support: C,D,G,h,I/ 25
Concentration: . 48 in CA, 30 in TX, 25 in OH	Expand in Territory: . . . . . . Yes	EXPANSION PLANS:
Registered: . . . .CA,FL,HI,IL,IN,MI,MN,NY	Passive Ownership: . . . Discouraged	US: . . . . . Scattered Rural Areas Only
. . . . ND,OR,SD,VA,WA,WI	Encourage Conversions: . . . . . .No	Canada: . . . . No
Type Space: . . . . NA;~ SF	Average # Employees: . . 3 FT, 1 PT	Overseas: . . . . No

ROTO-STATIC INTERNATIONAL

100 Leek Cres., # 3
Richmond Hill, ON L4B 3E6 CAN
TEL: (416) 886-5560
FAX: (416) 886-5776
Mr. Richard J. Crispi, President

Unique system of carpet cleaning, using Static Attraction principle. Professional water damage restoration and odor removal services. Complete training in Head Office. On-going support systems. A company with a proven past. On-going support.

HISTORY: . . . . .CFA	FINANCIAL: Earnings Claim: . .No	FRANCHISOR TRAINING/SUPPORT:
Established in 1977; . . 1st Franchised in 1977	Cash Investment: $25.7K	Financial Assistance Provided: . . . . .Yes
Company-Owned Units (As of 8/31/1992): . .0	Total Investment: $25.7K	Site Selection Assistance: . . . . . . .NA
Franchised Units (As of 8/31/1992): 110	Fees: Franchise - $5K	Lease Negotiation Assistance: . . . . .NA
Total Units (As of 8/31/1992): 110	Royalty: 5%, Advert: 0%	Co-operative Advertising: . . . . .NA
Projected New Units for 1993: 10	Contract Periods (Yrs.): 50	Training: . . . . .4 Days Toronto, ON
Distribution: US-0;Can-109;Overseas-1	Area Development Agreement: . .No	. . . .
North America: . . . . 9 Provinces	Sub-Franchise Contract: . . . . .No	On-Going Support: C,G,H/ 8
Concentration: . . . . .ON, PQ, BC	Expand in Territory: . . . . . . Yes	EXPANSION PLANS:
Registered: . . . . AB	Passive Ownership: . . . Discouraged	US: . . . . .No
. . . .	Encourage Conversions:	Canada: . . . . .All Canada
Type Space: . . . . ;~ SF	Average # Employees: . . . . 1-2 FT	Overseas: . . . . .UK, FR, GR, AU

RUG DOCTOR PRO

2788 N. Larkin Ave.
Fresno, CA 93727
TEL: (800) 678-7844 (209) 291-5511
FAX: (209) 291-9963
Mr. John T. Mandeville, Natl. Dir.

Full-service carpet, drapery, upholstery and ceiling cleaning and care. Only franchisor-run training school certified by the IICVC. RUG DOCTOR is to carpet cleaning what Kleenex is to tissue. Aggressively delivering the system worldwide. Excellent territories available.

HISTORY: IFA	FINANCIAL: Earnings Claim: No	FRANCHISOR TRAINING/SUPPORT:
Established in 1971; 1st Franchised in 1987	Cash Investment: $3.5-25K	Financial Assistance Provided: Yes(D)
Company-Owned Units (As of 8/31/1992): 1	Total Investment: $9.5-60K	Site Selection Assistance: Yes
Franchised Units (As of 8/31/1992): 54	Fees: Franchise - $3.5-25K	Lease Negotiation Assistance: Yes
Total Units (As of 8/31/1992): 55	Royalty: 3-6%, Advert: 2%	Co-operative Advertising: No
Projected New Units for 1993: 50	Contract Periods (Yrs.): 10/5/5	Training: 6 Days Headquarters
Distribution: US-33;Can-0;Overseas-22	Area Development Agreement: Yes/5	
North America: 11 States	Sub-Franchise Contract: No	On-Going Support: B,C,D,G,H,I/ 6
Concentration: 17 in CA, 2 in IN, 2 in NM	Expand in Territory: Yes	EXPANSION PLANS:
Registered: All	Passive Ownership: Discouraged	US: All US
	Encourage Conversions: Yes	Canada: All Canada
Type Space: NA;~NA SF	Average # Employees: 2 FT	Overseas: Yes

SERV U-1ST

10175 SW Barbur Blvd., Bldg.B,-100BA
Portland, OR 97219
TEL: (503) 244-7628
FAX:
Mr. Bob Rosenkranz, President

SERV U-1ST owners clean up with know-how. We serve you with on-going instruction in janitorial services for buildings. We teach proven technologies for procuring, servicing and keeping our clients. We offer 20 years' experience and our honest reputation.

HISTORY:	FINANCIAL: Earnings Claim: Yes	FRANCHISOR TRAINING/SUPPORT:
Established in 1988; 1st Franchised in 1988	Cash Investment: $1-9K	Financial Assistance Provided: Yes(D)
Company-Owned Units (As of 8/31/1992): 0	Total Investment: $3-36K	Site Selection Assistance: NA
Franchised Units (As of 8/31/1992): 9	Fees: Franchise - $3.4K	Lease Negotiation Assistance: NA
Total Units (As of 8/31/1992): 9	Royalty: Varies, Advert: 0%	Co-operative Advertising: No
Projected New Units for 1993: 2	Contract Periods (Yrs.): 2/2	Training: 8 2-Hour Initial Sessions
Distribution: US-9;Can-0;Overseas-0	Area Development Agreement: No	at Headquarters
North America: 1 State	Sub-Franchise Contract: No	On-Going Support: C,D,H/ 2
Concentration: 9 in OR	Expand in Territory: No	EXPANSION PLANS:
Registered: OR	Passive Ownership: Not Allowed	US: OR Only
	Encourage Conversions: Yes	Canada: No
Type Space: ;~NA SF	Average # Employees: Varies	Overseas: No

SERVICE ONE JANITORIAL

5104 N. Orange Blossom Tr., # 117
Orlando, FL 32810
TEL: (800) 522-7111 (407) 293-7645
FAX: (407) 299-4306
Mr. Steve Rathel, President

Janitorial franchise. We deliver supplies and equipment, training and customers. Turn-key operation. Delivered anywhere in the US.

HISTORY:	FINANCIAL: Earnings Claim: Yes	FRANCHISOR TRAINING/SUPPORT:
Established in 1985; 1st Franchised in 1985	Cash Investment: $6.8K	Financial Assistance Provided: Yes(D)
Company-Owned Units (As of 8/31/1992): 2	Total Investment: $7.5K	Site Selection Assistance: NA
Franchised Units (As of 8/31/1992): 87	Fees: Franchise - $6.8K	Lease Negotiation Assistance: NA
Total Units (As of 8/31/1992): 89	Royalty: $175/Mo., Advert: 0%	Co-operative Advertising: Yes
Projected New Units for 1993: 96	Contract Periods (Yrs.): 5/5	Training: 2 Days Headquarters
Distribution: US-89;Can-0;Overseas-0	Area Development Agreement: Yes/5	2 Days Local City
North America: 16 States	Sub-Franchise Contract: No	On-Going Support: A,C,D,F,G,H,I/ 6
Concentration: 59 in FL, 12 in GA, 9 in NC	Expand in Territory: Yes	EXPANSION PLANS:
Registered: FL,HI,IL,IN,MI,WI	Passive Ownership: Discouraged	US: All US
	Encourage Conversions: NA	Canada: All Canada
Type Space: NA;~NA SF	Average # Employees: 1 FT	Overseas: Yes

SERVICE-TECH CORPORATION

21012 Aurora Rd.
Warrensville Hts., OH 44146
TEL: (800) 992-9302 (216) 663-2600 C
FAX: (216) 663-8804
Mr. Alan Sutton, President

Indoor Air Quality. Opportunity to join 30 years of experience in solving the growing concerns of indoor air pollution. Services offered include air duct cleaning, kitchen exhaust cleaning, vacuum cleaning and specialized cleaning, plus more, to industrial and commercial customers.

HISTORY:	FINANCIAL: Earnings Claim: . .No	FRANCHISOR TRAINING/SUPPORT:
Established in 1960; . . 1st Franchised in 1988	Cash Investment: $20-50K	Financial Assistance Provided: . . . Yes(I)
Company-Owned Units (As of 8/31/1992): . .5	Total Investment: $59-89K	Site Selection Assistance: . . . . .NA
Franchised Units (As of 8/31/1992): 1	Fees: Franchise - $39K	Lease Negotiation Assistance: . . . . .NA
Total Units (As of 8/31/1992): 6	Royalty: 4-6%, Advert: 1%	Co-operative Advertising: . . . . .NA
Projected New Units for 1993: 6	Contract Periods (Yrs.): . . . 10/10+	Training: . . . . 2 Wks. Headquarters,
Distribution: US-6;Can-0;Overseas-0	Area Development Agreement: . .No	. . . . 1 Wk. Franchisee Location
North America: . . . . 2 States	Sub-Franchise Contract: . . . . .No	On-Going Support: B,C,D,H,I/ 35
Concentration: . . . . 4 in OH, 1 in MI	Expand in Territory: . . . . Yes	EXPANSION PLANS:
Registered: . . . . FL,IL,IN,MI	Passive Ownership: . . . Not Allowed	US: . . . . .All US
. . . .	Encourage Conversions: . . . . NA	Canada: . . . . .No
Type Space: . . . . ;~ SF	Average # Employees: . . 4 FT, 2 PT	Overseas: . . . . No

SERVICEMASTER RESIDENTIAL/ COMMERCIAL

855 Ridge Lake Blvd.
Memphis, TN 38120
TEL: (800) 752-6688 (901) 684-7500
FAX: (901) 684-7600
Mr. Don Anderson, President

SERVICEMASTER provides heavy cleaning services for homes, including carpet, upholstery, draperies, windows and disaster restoration. Also janitorial services for the commercial market. As you would expect from a $2.5 billion company, we provide all the research, equipment, supplies, initial and continuous training you will need.

HISTORY: . . . . IFA	FINANCIAL: Earnings Claim: . .No	FRANCHISOR TRAINING/SUPPORT:
Established in 1947; . . 1st Franchised in 1952	Cash Investment: $7-20K	Financial Assistance Provided: . . . . .Yes
Company-Owned Units (As of 8/31/1992): . .0	Total Investment: $16.4-29.9K	Site Selection Assistance: . . . . .NA
Franchised Units (As of 8/31/1992): . . .4169	Fees: Franchise - $8.7-19.7K	Lease Negotiation Assistance: . . . . .NA
Total Units (As of 8/31/1992): 4169	Royalty: 7-10%, Advert: . . 1/2-1%	Co-operative Advertising: . . . . .Yes
Projected New Units for 1993: 225	Contract Periods (Yrs.): 5/5	Training: . . . . . 2 Wks. On-the-Job Train-
Distribution: US-2902;Can-148;Overseas-1119	Area Development Agreement: . .No	. . . ing, 1 Wk. HQ, 2 Wks. Home Study
North America: . . . . 50 States, 9 Provinces	Sub-Franchise Contract: . . . . .No	On-Going Support: B,C,D,G,h,I/ 44
Concentration: . 218 in IL, 207 in CA, 143 PA	Expand in Territory: . . . . Yes	EXPANSION PLANS:
Registered: . . . . .All	Passive Ownership: . . . Discouraged	US: . . . . .All US
. . . .	Encourage Conversions: . . . . .No	Canada: . . . . .All Canada
Type Space: . . . . ;~ SF	Average # Employees:	Overseas: . . . . Yes

SPARKLE WASH

26851 Richmond Rd.
Cleveland, OH 44146
TEL: (800) 321-0770 (216) 464-4212
FAX: (216) 464-8869
Mr. Wallace J. Nido, President

Mobile pressure cleaning and restoration service. Cleaning and restoration of all types of surfaces. Natural wood cleaning and restoration with special preservation sealing and coating.

HISTORY: . . . . IFA	FINANCIAL: Earnings Claim: . . .No	FRANCHISOR TRAINING/SUPPORT:
Established in 1965; . . 1st Franchised in 1967	Cash Investment: . . . . . . $20K+	Financial Assistance Provided: . . . Yes(D)
Company-Owned Units (As of 8/31/1992): . .1	Total Investment: $40-60K	Site Selection Assistance: . . . . .NA
Franchised Units (As of 8/31/1992): 209	Fees: Franchise - . . . . $9K+	Lease Negotiation Assistance: . . . . .NA
Total Units (As of 8/31/1992): 210	Royalty: 5%, Advert: 0%	Co-operative Advertising: . . . . .NA
Projected New Units for 1993: 15	Contract Periods (Yrs.): 5/5/5	Training: . . . . 5 Days Headquarters,
Distribution: US-136;Can-2;Overseas-72	Area Development Agreement: . .No	. . . .Min. 3 Days Franchisee Territory
North America: . . . . 37 States, 2 Provinces	Sub-Franchise Contract: . . . . .No	On-Going Support: B,C,D,F,G,H,I/ . . . 15
Concentration: . .18 in PA, 15 in OH, 13 in FL	Expand in Territory: . . . . Yes	EXPANSION PLANS:
Registered: . . . CA,FL,IL,IN,MD,MI,MN,NY	Passive Ownership: . . . . . .Allowed	US: . . . . .All US
. . . . OR,RS,VA,WA,WI,DC	Encourage Conversions: . . . . . Yes	Canada: . . . . .All Canada
Type Space: . . . . . .Home Based;~300+ SF	Average # Employees: . . 1 FT, 1 PT	Overseas: . . . . Yes

STANLEY STEEMER CARPET CLEANER
5500 Stanley Steemer Pkwy.
Dublin, OH 43017
TEL: (800) 848-7496 (614) 764-2007
FAX: (614) 764-1506
Mr. Philip Ryser, Dir. Fran.

Carpet and upholstery cleaning and related services for both residential and commercial customers. Provides additional services, such as deodorizing, carpet protection, static electricity and water extraction.

HISTORY: . . . . IFA	FINANCIAL: Earnings Claim: . Yes	FRANCHISOR TRAINING/SUPPORT:
Established in 1947; . . 1st Franchised in 1972	Cash Investment: $42-200K	Financial Assistance Provided: . . .Yes(D)
Company-Owned Units (As of 8/31/1992): . 18	Total Investment: $42-200K	Site Selection Assistance: . . . . . . .NA
Franchised Units (As of 8/31/1992): 211	Fees: Franchise - . . . . $15K+	Lease Negotiation Assistance: . . . . .Yes
Total Units (As of 8/31/1992): 229	Royalty: 7%, Advert: 0%	Co-operative Advertising: . . . . . . .Yes
Projected New Units for 1993:	Contract Periods (Yrs.): . . . 20/10	Training: . . . . 2 Wks. Headquarters
Distribution: US-229;Can-0;Overseas-0	Area Development Agreement: .No	. . . .
North America: . . . . 37 States	Sub-Franchise Contract: . . . . .No	On-Going Support: A,B,C,D,G,H,I/ . . 80
Concentration: . . 32 in FL, 20 in OH, 15 in IN	Expand in Territory: . . . . Yes	EXPANSION PLANS:
Registered: . . . . All States	Passive Ownership: . . . . .Allowed	US: . . . . All US
. . . .	Encourage Conversions: . . . . .No	Canada: . . . . .Yes
Type Space: . . . . ;~ SF	Average # Employees: . . . . .3 FT	Overseas: . . . . .Yes

SWISHER HYGIENE

1004 Palmer Plaza Ln.
Charlotte, NC 28211
TEL: (800) 444-4138 (704) 364-7707
FAX: (800) 444-4565
Mr. Jerry Allen, Dir. Fran.

Recession-resistant service business, proven track record, limited capital requirements, unlimited growth potential, national account networking, easy to recruit service personnel. Provide a unique restroom hygiene service and 6 additional revenue/profit services outside the restroom to a diverse range of clients that includes some of the best-known names in America.

HISTORY: . . . . IFA	FINANCIAL: Earnings Claim: . .No	FRANCHISOR TRAINING/SUPPORT:
Established in 1983; . . 1st Franchised in 1990	Cash Investment: $45-75K	Financial Assistance Provided: . . . . .No
Company-Owned Units (As of 8/31/1992): . .2	Total Investment: $35-75K	Site Selection Assistance: . . . . . . .Yes
Franchised Units (As of 8/31/1992): 36	Fees: Franchise - $35-75K	Lease Negotiation Assistance: . . . . .NA
Total Units (As of 8/31/1992): 38	Royalty: 6%, Advert: 2%	Co-operative Advertising: . . . . . . .NA
Projected New Units for 1993: 24	Contract Periods (Yrs.): 10/5	Training: . . . . 2 Wks. Headquarters,
Distribution: US-38;Can-0;Overseas-0	Area Development Agreement: .No	. . . . 1 Wk. On-Site
North America: . . . . 23 States	Sub-Franchise Contract: . . . .No	On-Going Support: a,b,c,d,E,F,G,h,I/ . . 24
Concentration: . . . 6 in FL, 4 IN TX, 3 in CA	Expand in Territory: . . . . Yes	EXPANSION PLANS:
Registered: . . . CA,FL,IL,IN,MD,MI,MN,NY	Passive Ownership: . . . Not Allowed	US: . . . . All US
. . . . .OR,RI,VA,WA,WI,DC	Encourage Conversions: . . . . NA	Canada: . . . . .All Canada
Type Space: . . .Office/Warehouse;~1,000 SF	Average # Employees: . . . . 2-3 FT	Overseas: . . . . .No

TOWER CLEANING SYSTEMS

565 E. Swedesford Rd., # 103
Wayne, PA 19087
TEL: (800) 67-TOWER (215) 293-2000
FAX: (215) 293-9985
Mr. Adam Beck, VP

TOWER CLEANING SYSTEMS offers franchises in the recession-resistant, $30 billion commercial cleaning industry. TOWER provides its franchisees with guaranteed initial cleaning contacts, classroom and on-site training, free equipment and comprehensive accounting services. TOWER also guarantees that its franchisees get paid by their clients.

HISTORY: . . . . IFA	FINANCIAL: Earnings Claim: . .No	FRANCHISOR TRAINING/SUPPORT:
Established in 1988; . . 1st Franchised in 1990	Cash Investment: $1.5K	Financial Assistance Provided: . . . . .Yes
Company-Owned Units (As of 8/31/1992): . .4	Total Investment: . . . .$	Site Selection Assistance: . . . . .NA
Franchised Units (As of 8/31/1992): 241	Fees: Franchise - . . . . $Varies	Lease Negotiation Assistance: . . . . .NA
Total Units (As of 8/31/1992): 245	Royalty: , Advert:	Co-operative Advertising: . . . . . . .NA
Projected New Units for 1993: 350	Contract Periods (Yrs.): 10/10	Training: . . . .
Distribution: US-245;Can-0;Overseas-0	Area Development Agreement: .No	. . . .
North America:	Sub-Franchise Contract: . . . . .No	On-Going Support: A,B,C,D,F,G,H,I/ .100
Concentration: . . 135 in PA, 50 in MD, 40 NJ	Expand in Territory: . . . . Yes	EXPANSION PLANS:
Registered: . . . . All States	Passive Ownership: . . . Discouraged	US: . . . . Northeast
. . . .	Encourage Conversions: . . . . Yes	Canada: . . . . .Ontario
Type Space: . . . . NA;~NA SF	Average # Employees: . . 1 FT, 3 PT	Overseas: . . . . No

ULTRA WASH

2335 Naomi St.
Houston, TX 77054
TEL: (713) 796-2431
FAX: (713) 790-1804
Mr. Brian Peskin, President

State-of-the-art mobile washing franchise, specializing in commercial fleet washing at the customer's location. $25,000-100,000 guaranteed initial sales included. Exclusive areas. Proprietary equipment and detergents.

HISTORY: . . . .
Established in 1981; . . 1st Franchised in 1984
Company-Owned Units (As of 8/31/1992): . .3
Franchised Units (As of 8/31/1992): 36
Total Units (As of 8/31/1992): 39
Projected New Units for 1993: 3
Distribution: US-39;Can-0;Overseas-0
  North America: . . . . 8 States
  Concentration: . . 10 in TX, 8 in CA, 3 in MO
Registered: . . . . .All
. . . .
Type Space: . . . . NA;~NA SF

FINANCIAL: Earnings Claim: . .No
Cash Investment: $12.5-30K
Total Investment: $25-75K
Fees: Franchise - $10K
  Royalty: 8-6%, Advert: 0%
Contract Periods (Yrs.): 5/5
Area Development Agreement: . .No
Sub-Franchise Contract: . . . . . No
Expand in Territory: . . . . . . Yes
Passive Ownership: . . . Not Allowed
Encourage Conversions: . . . . NA
Average # Employees: . . 2 FT, 2 PT

FRANCHISOR TRAINING/SUPPORT:
Financial Assistance Provided: . . .Yes(D)
Site Selection Assistance: . . . . .Yes
Lease Negotiation Assistance: . . . . .Yes
Co-operative Advertising: . . . . .NA
Training: . . . . 2 Wks. Headquarters,
  . . . . . . 1-3 Wks. Franchisee Location
On-Going Support: B,C,D,E,F,G,H/ . . . 5
EXPANSION PLANS:
US: . . . . .All US
Canada: . . . . .No
Overseas: . . . . .Yes

UNIMAX BUILDING SERVICES OF AMERICA

P. O. Box 2461
Clarksville, IN 47130
TEL: (812) 944-0360 C
FAX: (812) 246-6179
Mr. Lloyd E. Pate, CEO

UNIMAX will finance 55% of total package on local franchise. 70% on Master Franchise with approved credit through UNIMAX Financial Service. UNIMAX is a complete carpet and janitorial cleaning service.

HISTORY: . . . .
Established in 1986; . . 1st Franchised in 1986
Company-Owned Units (As of 8/31/1992): . .2
Franchised Units (As of 8/31/1992): 4
Total Units (As of 8/31/1992): 6
Projected New Units for 1993: 20
Distribution: US-6;Can-0;Overseas-0
  North America: . . . . 4 States
  Concentration: . . . 2 in KY, 1 in FL, 1 in NC
Registered: . . . . FL,HI,IL,IN,MD,OR,RI,SD
. . . . VA
Type Space: . . . . Home Based;~ SF

FINANCIAL: Earnings Claim: . . .
Cash Investment: $2-4K
Total Investment: $14.5K
Fees: Franchise - . . . .$
  Royalty: 2%, Advert: 3%
Contract Periods (Yrs.): 3/3
Area Development Agreement: . .No
Sub-Franchise Contract: . . . . . Yes
Expand in Territory: . . . . . . Yes
Passive Ownership: . . . . . .Allowed
Encourage Conversions: . . . . .No
Average # Employees: . . . . . .1 FT

FRANCHISOR TRAINING/SUPPORT:
Financial Assistance Provided: . . .Yes(D)
Site Selection Assistance: . . . . .Yes
Lease Negotiation Assistance: . . . . . No
Co-operative Advertising: . . . . .Yes
Training: . . . . **5 Days Headquarters,**
  . . . . 5 Days On-Site, On-Going
On-Going Support: A,B,C,D,E,F,G,H,I/ 20
EXPANSION PLANS:
US: . . . . .Southeast, KY,TN,NC,SC,FL
Canada: . . . . .No
Overseas: . . . . No

WEST SANITATION SERVICES

25100 S. Normandie Ave.
Harbor City, CA 90710
TEL: (310) 539-6104
FAX: (310) 539-8442
Mr. Graham H. Emery, President

AEROWEST and WESTAIR odor control and sanitation services for industrial and commercial washrooms.

HISTORY: . . . .
Established in 1984; . . 1st Franchised in 1980
Company-Owned Units (As of 8/31/1992): . .0
Franchised Units (As of 8/31/1992): 24
Total Units (As of 8/31/1992): 24
Projected New Units for 1993: 4
Distribution: US-24;Can-0;Overseas-0
  North America: . . . . 10 States
  Concentration: . . . .7 in CA, 5 in NY, 3 in IL
Registered: . . . . CA,IL,NY,WA
. . . .
Type Space: . . . . ;~ SF

FINANCIAL: Earnings Claim: . . .
Cash Investment: $2-12K
Total Investment: $3-20K
Fees: Franchise - $1K
  Royalty: Varies, Advert: . . Varies
Contract Periods (Yrs.): 5/1
Area Development Agreement: . .No
Sub-Franchise Contract: . . . . . .No
Expand in Territory: . . . . . . Yes
Passive Ownership: . . . Discouraged
Encourage Conversions: . . . . NA
Average # Employees: . . . .

FRANCHISOR TRAINING/SUPPORT:
Financial Assistance Provided: . . .Yes(D)
Site Selection Assistance: . . . . .NA
Lease Negotiation Assistance: . . . . .NA
Co-operative Advertising: . . . . .NA
Training: . . . . .1-2 Wks. Franchisee
. . . . Location
On-Going Support: A,B,C,D/ 22
EXPANSION PLANS:
US: . . . . .S. California, NY Metro Area
Canada: . . . . .No
Overseas: . . . . No

**WINCO WINDOW CLEANING &
MAINTENANCE**
P. O. Box 83
Knoxville, IA 50138
TEL: (515) 842-4887
FAX:
Mr. David Wolett, Fran. Dir.

WINCO offers a nationally-registered trademark, copyrighted manuals and workshop. Thorough and complete training, covering 20 profit centers. Window, gutter, chimney cleaning, pest control and janitorial services. On-going support and consultation. WINCO provides information and training essential for a successful business.

HISTORY:		
Established in 1977; . . . 1st Franchised in 1987		
Company-Owned Units (As of 8/31/1992): . .1		
Franchised Units (As of 8/31/1992): 3		
Total Units (As of 8/31/1992): 4		
Projected New Units for 1993:		
Distribution: US-4;Can-0;Overseas-0		
North America: . . . . 3 States		
Concentration: . . . .2 in TX, 1 in IA, 1 in OR		
Registered: . . . . .All		
. . . .		
Type Space: . . . . Home Based;~ SF		

FINANCIAL: Earnings Claim: . Yes
Cash Investment: $3.9K
Total Investment: $3.9K
Fees: Franchise - $3.9K
   Royalty: 0%, Advert: 0%
Contract Periods (Yrs.): . .Unlimited
Area Development Agreement: Yes/Unl
Sub-Franchise Contract: . . . . . Yes
Expand in Territory: . . . . Yes
Passive Ownership: . . . Discouraged
Encourage Conversions: . . . . . Yes
Average # Employees: .6+ FT, 6+ PT

FRANCHISOR TRAINING/SUPPORT:
Financial Assistance Provided: . . . Yes(I)
Site Selection Assistance: . . . . . . .Yes
Lease Negotiation Assistance: . . . .NA
Co-operative Advertising: . . . . . . .NA
Training: . . . . . .7-10 Days Headquarters
. . . .
On-Going Support: A,B,C,D,E,F/ 3
EXPANSION PLANS:
US: . . . . .All US
Canada: . . . . .All Canada
Overseas: . . . . .Yes

SUPPLEMENTAL LISTING OF FRANCHISORS

ACOUSTIC KING . . . . 6330 E. 75th St., # 146, Indianapolis, IN 46250
   Contact: Mr. Kenneth M. Booster, Pressident; Tel: (317) 595-5050
ACTION DUCT CLEANING/CLEAN AIR . . . . . . 1625 Steeles Ave., # 5, Brampton, ON L6T 4T7   CAN
   Contact: Mr. Paul T. Maurer; Tel: (416) 790-6000
AIRE-MASTER OF AMERICA . . . . P. O. Box 2310, Nixa, MO 65714
   Contact: Mr. Jerry P. McCauley; Tel: (417) 725-2691
ALL TEXAS DUCT CLEANING . . . . 1717 Gessner, Houston, TX 77080
   Contact: Mr. Thomas M. St. John; Tel: (713) 465-0450
ALL-PRO ENTERPRISES . . . . 5016 Alta Dr., # 4, Las Vegas, NV 89107
   Contact: President; Tel: (702) 870-7818
AMERICORP . . . . .24 Hill Rd., Parsippany, NJ 07054
   Contact: President; Tel:
AMERISEAL . . . . .3060 Leon Rd., P. O. Box 8645, Jacksonville, FL 32216
   Contact: Mr. Dale Bond, EVP; Tel: (904) 642-5213
ARODAL INTERNATIONAL . . . . 27 Worcester Rd., Rexdale, ON M9W 1K9   CAN
   Contact: Mr. Al Fisher; Tel: (416) 674-8700
BIO-CARE . . . . 1976 Hartog Dr., Campbell, CA 95131
   Contact: Mr. Bob Nardi, Mgr.; Tel: (800) 421-9740 (408) 866-7500
BLUE DIAMOND WINDOW CLEANING (CAN) . . . 2339 Royal Windsor Dr., Mississauga, ON L5J 1K9   CAN
   Contact: Mr. Michael Kernaghan, Dir. Fran. Sales; Tel: (416) 823-8550 (416) 823-0032
BLUE DIAMOND WINDOW CLEANING . . . . 984 Williamsburg Pk., Barrington, IL 60010
   Contact: Mr. Dave Knight; Tel: (708) 526-4282
BRITE SITE . . . . .4616 W. Fullerton Ave., Chicago, IL 60639
   Contact: Mr. Andreas Vassilos, President; Tel: (800) 35-BRITE (312) 772-7300
BUCK-A-STALL PARKING LOT PAINTING . . . . P.O. Box 1156, Madison, TN 37116
   Contact: Mr. Jim Shafer; Tel: (800) 321-BUCK (615) 824-2825
BUDGET PEST CONTROL . . . . .One Parker Pl., Rt. 2, Box 37, Ponca City, OK 74604
   Contact: President; Tel: (405) 762-6614
BUILDING SERVICE & MAINTENANCE . . . . . 575 Airport Blvd., P. O. Box 1978, Gallatin, TN 37066
   Contact: Mr. Richard Isaacson, EVP; Tel: (800) 826-9586 (615) 451-0200
CHEM SEAL . . . . .1052 W. Foxcroft Dr., #A, Box 762, Camp Hill, PA 17011
   Contact: Mr. Norbert K. Flammang, President; Tel: (717) 737-0108 C
CHEMAN MANUFACTURING CORP. . . . . 5679 Monroe St., # 208, Sylvania, OH 43560
   Contact: President; Tel: (419) 882-6950
CLEANING CONSULTANT SERVICES . . . . .1512 Western Ave., P. O. Box 1273, Seattle, WA 98111
   Contact: Mr. William R. Griffin, President; Tel: (800) 622-4221 (206) 682-9748
CLEANING IDEAS .P. O. Box 7268, San Antonio, TX 78207
   Contact: Mr. Charles Davis; Tel: (800) 227-9161 (512) 227-9161

CLEANMARK . . . . 185 Greens Farm Rd., Westport, CT 06880
    Contact: Mr. Helmuth W. Krause, President; Tel: (203) 227-8618
CLEANSERV INDUSTRIES . . . . .3403 Tenth St., # 810, Riverside, CA 92501
    Contact: Mr. George Horoika, President; Tel: (800) 942-0073 (714) 781-0220
CLEANWAY INDUSTRIES . . . . Box 6, Westhampton Beach, NY 11978
    Contact: Mr. Bill Harding; Tel: (800) 332-6996 (516) 288-6300
CLENTECH / ACOUSTIC CLEAN . . . . 2901 Wayzata Blvd., Minneapolis, MN 55405
    Contact: Mr. Jim Knutsen, Sales Rep.; Tel: (800) 328-4650 (612) 374-5852
COIT DRAPERY AND CARPET CLEANERS . . . . 897 Hinckley Rd., Burlingame, CA 94010
    Contact: Mr. Robert Kearn, VP; Tel: (800) 243-8797 (415) 697-5471
COMMCARE CARPET SYSTEMS . . . . 44845 Falcon Place, # 104, Sterling, VA 22170
    Contact: Mr. Ronald Buckman, VP; Tel: (703) 318-7718
COMPU-FRESH . . . . 410 - 145 Chadwick Ct., N. Vancouver, BC V7M 3K1   CAN
    Contact: Mr. Mark Winder; Tel: (604) 984-7878
COVERALL . . . . .2174 N. Gladstone Court, # C, Glendale Heights, IL 60139
    Contact: Mr. Alex Roudi, President; Tel: (800) 537-3371 (708) 924-8700
CRITTER RIDDERS . . . . .809 Rugby Pl., Louisville, KY 40222
    Contact: Mr. Clem Lindsey, President; Tel: (502) 423-0575
DOCTOR STEAM CLEAN . . . . 4289 Thom Gardens, Mississauga, ON L5Z 2B4   CAN
    Contact: Mr. D. Hubert; Tel: (416) 820-1599
DUCT CLEANING SYSTEMS . . . . 1717 Gessner, Houston, TX 77080
    Contact: Mr. Thomas M. St. John, VP Sales/Mktg.; Tel: (713) 465-0359
DURACLEAN INTERNATIONAL . . . . 2151 Waukegan Rd., Deerfield, IL 60015
    Contact: Mr. Irl Marshall, President; Tel: (800) 251-7070 (708) 945-2000 C
DYMAC DYES & CHEMICALS . . . . 17701 Avalon Blvd., # 158, Carson, CA 90746
    Contact: President; Tel: (213) 513-8070
DYNO-ROD . . . . 4660 S. Eastern Ave., Commerce, CA 90040
    Contact: Mr. Russell Taylor, President; Tel: (213) 724-4960
ELDON DRAPERY CLEANERS . . . . 9291 Arleta Ave., Arleta, CA 91331
    Contact: Mr. Julius Bruck, President; Tel: (818) 899-3573
FILTER CARE . . . . 115 W. 5th St., Grafton, ND 58237
    Contact: President; Tel: (701) 352-3304
FOREST HILL ENTERPRISES . . . . .Rte. 9, Box 1-A, Charlottesville, VA 22901
    Contact: Mr. Walter L. Lumpp, President; Tel: (804) 971-5641 C
GRIMEFIGHTERS . . . . 4694 Ashton Rd., # A, Sarasota, FL 34233
    Contact: President; Tel: (800) 428-6893
HANDYMAN HOUSE CALLS . . . . 640 Northland Rd., # 33, Forest Park, OH 45240
    Contact: Ms. Susan Rupp; Tel: (513) 825-3863
INTERCLEAN SERVICE SYSTEM . . . . 12075 E. 45th Ave., # 200, Denver, CO 80239
    Contact: Mr. Henry H. Zelle; Tel: (303) 373-0533
KING ORGANIZATION, THE . . . . .5275 Arthur Kill Rd., Staten Island, NY 10307
    Contact: Mr. Vincent Acierno, President; Tel: (718) 948-2409
LIEN CHEMICAL COMPANY . . . . 501 W. Lake St., Elmhurst, IL 60126
    Contact: Mr. R. S. Crane, President; Tel: (312) 832-6500
MASTER WORKS INTERNATIONAL . . . . 121 Interstate Blvd., Greenville, SC 29615
    Contact: Mr. Jim Saxion, Fran. Dir.; Tel: (800) 782-9475 (803) 288-1010 C
MASTER-STROKE . . . . .P. O. Box 2129, Peabody, MA 01960
    Contact: Mr. Alex Kulpa, President; Tel: (508) 356-3666
MR. MAINTENANCE . . . . 21401 S. Norwalk Blvd., Hawaiian Gardens, CA 90716
    Contact: President; Tel: (213) 860-3446
NATIONAL CHEMICALS & SERVICES . . . . 691 N. Church Rd., Elmhurst, IL 60126
    Contact: Mr. Michael M. Saks, President; Tel: (800) 888-8407 (708) 832-8407 C
NATIONAL MAINTENANCE CONTRACTORS . . . . 1801 130th Ave. NE, Bellevue, WA 98005
    Contact: Mr. Lyle Graddon, President; Tel: (206) 881-0500
OLIN CORPORATION . . . . 120 Long Ridge Rd., Stamford, CT 06904
    Contact: President; Tel:
OMEX - OFFICE MAINTENANCE EXPERTS . . . . . . 3905 Hartzdale Dr., # 506, Camp Hill, PA 17011
    Contact: Mr. Gerald Boarman; Tel: (800) 827-OMEX
ON-SITE BLIND CLEANING SERVICE . . . . .6110 Rock Spring Dr., Birmingham, MI 48010
    Contact: President; Tel: (313) 433-3881
PROTOUCH MAINTENANCE COMPANY . . . . .100 E. 20th St., Kansas City, MO 64108
    Contact: Mr. Frank Oddo, President; Tel: (800) 356-5755 (816) 842-3956
PUROFIRST INTERNATIONAL . . . . 6436 NW 5th Way, Ft. Lauderdale, FL 33309
    Contact: Ms. Donah Parent, Fran. Dir.; Tel: (800) 247-9047 (305) 771-3121
QUALITY MARKETING . . . . .6278 N. Federal Hwy., # 284, Ft. Lauderdale, FL 33308
    Contact: Mr. Wiliam B. Chappie; Tel: (305) 537-1695

RAINBOW INTERNATL. CARPET DYE/CLEAN . . . . P. O. Box 3146, Waco, TX 76707
    Contact: Mr. Don Dwyer, President; Tel: (817) 756-2122
REDI-NATIONAL PEST ELIMINATORS . . . . .4453 Aurora Ave. N, Seattle, WA 98103
    Contact: Mr. Fred Lewis, President; Tel: (800) 247-0388 (206) 633-1234
RESCUE INDUSTRIES . . . . P.O. Box 85095, San Diego, CA 92138
    Contact: Mr. Roger Benson, President; Tel: (619) 296-2162
SEARS CARPET & UPHOLSTERY CLEANING . . . . .2480 Walkley Rd., 2nd Fl., Ottawa, ON K1G 3R8   CAN
    Contact: Mr. Jeff Hunt, GM; Tel: (613) 521-3898
SERVICEMASTER (CANADA) . . . . 6315 Shawson Dr., Unit 1, Mississauga, ON L5T 1J2   CAN
    Contact: Mr. Gary Franklin; Tel: (416) 670-3766
SERVICEMASTER CORPORATION . . . . 855 Ridge Lake Blvd., Memphis, TN 38120
    Contact: Mr. Dan Kellow, VP Mkt. Expansion; Tel: (800) 752-6688
SERVPRO BUILDING SERVICE/MAINTENANCE . . 575 Airport Blvd., P. O. Box 1978, Gallatin, TN 37066
    Contact: Mr. Richard Isaacson, EVP; Tel: (800) 826-9586 (615) 451-0200
SPOTLESS OFFICE SERVICES . . . . 4040 Brockton Cr., North Vancouver, BC V7G 1E6   CAN
    Contact: Mr. Bob Mussio, President; Tel: (604) 929-4432
STEAMATIC . . . . 1320 S. University Dr., # 400, Fort Worth, TX 76107
    Contact: Mr. Lloyd Swiggum, GM; Tel: (800) 544-1303 (817) 332-1575
STEAMATIC (CANADA) . . . . .6535 Millcreek Dr., Unit 2, Mississauga, ON L5N 2M2   CAN
    Contact: Mr. Bruce Paleczny; Tel: (416) 858-3232
THEE CHIMNEY SWEEP . . . . .36 Vernon Rd. NE, Rome, GA 30165
    Contact: Mr. Gary Trotter, President; Tel: (404) 232-5261
TOTAL ENVIRONMENTAL SERVICE CO. . . . . 413 S. Normandy, Olathe, KS 66061
    Contact: Mr. Kerry Chastain, Marketing; Tel: (800) 359-7928 (913) 764-6622
TOWN & COUNTRY OFFICE & CARPET CARE 2580 San Ramon Valley Blvd. # B208, San Ramon, CA 94583
    Contact: Mr. Theodore F. Prince, President; Tel: (800) 522-3130 (510) 867-3850
TWO TWINS FROM TEXAS . . . . 14252 Culver Dr., A439, Irvine, CA 92714
    Contact: Mr. Steven K. Dale, COO; Tel: (714) 543-5996
U. S. ROOTER . . . . 17023 Batesville Pike Rd., North Little Rock, AR 72120
    Contact: Ms. Pat Ratliff, Sec.; Tel: (501) 835-1500
ULTRASONIC PREDICTABLE MAINTENANCE . . . . 815 Sunrise Ln., Centralia, WA 98531
    Contact: President; Tel:
UNICLEAN SYSTEMS . . . . 642 W. 29th St., N. Vancouver, BC V7N 2K2   CAN
    Contact: Mr. Jack B. Karpowicz, President; Tel: (604) 986-4750
UNIVERSAL SWEEPING SERVICES . . . . 525 Sunol St., San Jose, CA 95126
    Contact: Mr. Gerald Koehler, Fran. Sales; Tel: (800) 647-9337 (408) 295-9688
VALUE LINE MAINTENANCE SYSTEMS . . . . 3801 River Dr. N., Great Falls, MT 59401
    Contact: Mr. William Blackhall, VP Ops.; Tel: (800) 824-4838 (406) 761-4471

CHAPTER 29

MOTELS / HOTELS / CAMPGROUNDS

AMERICINN INTERNATIONAL

620 Mendelssohn Ave., # 125
Golden Valley, MN 55427
TEL: (612) 593-7605
FAX: (612) 593-5159
Mr. John R. Whisnant, VP Fran. Dev.

AMERICINN MOTELS provide the finest quality and friendliest service in lodging today. Our primary market is towns of population under 25,000. AMERICINN MOTELS are in their own niche within this market, that being luxury budget. our company motto is - "Absolutely nobody will equal our quality, service or performance - and that's a promise!"

HISTORY: . . . .
Established in 1979; . . 1st Franchised in 1987
Company-Owned Units (As of 8/31/1992): . .0
Franchised Units (As of 8/31/1992): 34
Total Units (As of 8/31/1992): 34
Projected New Units for 1993: 10
Distribution: US-34;Can-0;Overseas-0
   North America: . . . . 4 States
   Concentration: . .22 in MN, 11 in WI, 1 in ND
Registered: . . . . MN,ND,WI
. . . .
Type Space: . . . . FS;~66,000 SF

FINANCIAL: Earnings Claim: . .No
Cash Investment: $300K
Total Investment: $1.5MM
Fees: Franchise - $15K
   Royalty: 4.5%, Advert: 1%
Contract Periods (Yrs.): 25/0
Area Development Agreement: . .No
Sub-Franchise Contract: . . . . .No
Expand in Territory: . . . . Yes
Passive Ownership: . . . . . .Allowed
Encourage Conversions: . . . . .No
Average # Employees: . . 2 FT, 6 PT

FRANCHISOR TRAINING/SUPPORT:
Financial Assistance Provided: . . . . . No
Site Selection Assistance: . . . . Yes
Lease Negotiation Assistance: . . . . .NA
Co-operative Advertising: . . . . No
Training: . . . . .7-10 Days On-Site
. . . .
On-Going Support: a,B,C,D,E,F,G,H,I/ . . 3
EXPANSION PLANS:
US: . . . . North Central
Canada: . . . . No
Overseas: . . . . No

HOTELS, MOTELS AND CAMPGROUNDS

	1989	1990	1991	Percentage Change 90/89	91/90
Total Number of Establishments:					
Company–Owned	1,232	1,261	1,307	2.35%	3.65%
Franchisee–Owned	8,880	9,785	10,091	10.19%	3.13%
Total	10,112	11,046	11,398	9.24%	3.19%
Ratio of Total Establishments:					
Company–Owned	12.2%	11.4%	11.5%		
Franchisee–Owned	87.8%	88.6%	88.5%		
Total	100.0%	100.0%	100.0%		
Total Sales ($000):					
Company–Owned	6,233,245	6,459,292	7,073,476	3.63%	9.51%
Franchisee–Owned	15,337,833	17,356,349	18,912,699	13.16%	8.97%
Total	21,571,078	23,815,641	25,986,175	10.41%	9.11%
Ratio of Total Sales:					
Company–Owned	28.9%	27.1%	27.2%		
Franchisee–Owned	71.1%	72.9%	72.8%		
Total	100.0%	100.0%	100.0%		
Average Sales Per Unit ($000):					
Company–Owned	5,059	5,122	5,412	1.24%	5.65%
Franchisee–Owned	1,727	1,774	1,874	2.69%	5.66%
Total	2,133	2,156	2,280	1.07%	5.74%
Relative Average Sales Ratio:	292.9%	288.8%	288.8%		

	Number Of Employees	Employees Per Unit	Avg. Sales Per Employee
Total 1989 Employment:			
Company–Owned	161,979	131.5	$38,482
Franchisee–Owned	438,909	49.4	$34,945
Total	600,888	59.4	$35,899
Relative Employee Performance Ratios:		266.0%	110.1%

	1st Quartile	Median	4th Quartile
Average 1989 Total Investment:			
Company–Owned	$650,000	$1,612,500	$4,500,000
Franchisee–Owned	$500,000	$1,500,000	$4,250,000
Single Unit Franchise Fee	$15,500	$20,000	$32,500
Mult. Unit Franchise Fee	$15,000	$20,000	$25,000
Franchise Start–Up Cost	$212,000	$400,000	$600,000

Source: Franchising In The Economy 1991, IFA Educational Foundation & Horwath International.

BEST INNS OF AMERICA

RR #3. P. O. Box 1719
Marion, IL 62959
TEL: (618) 997-5454 C
FAX: (618) 993-5974
Ms. Lynn Brewer, Franchise Development

BEST INNS OF AMERICA and BEST SUITES OF AMERICA are limited service, mid-market motels which have historically run 10-15% higher than national average occupancy rates and which can bring the project in at a reasonably low range per room, with excellent bottom line profits.

HISTORY: . . . .
Established in 1968; . . 1st Franchised in 1968
Company-Owned Units (As of 8/31/1992): . 25
Franchised Units (As of 8/31/1992): 14
Total Units (As of 8/31/1992): 39
Projected New Units for 1993: 7
Distribution: US-39;Can-0;Overseas-0
North America: . . . . 11 States
Concentration: . . . 10 in IL, 2 in GA, 2 in FL
Registered: . . . . CA,FL,IL,IN
. . . .
Type Space: . . . . . . .FS;~2-3.5 Acres SF

FINANCIAL: Earnings Claim: . .No
Cash Investment: . . . $1.5-4.5MM
Total Investment: . . . . . . $Varies
Fees: Franchise - . . . . . $10K Min.
Royalty: 2% Room, Advert:1% Room
Contract Periods (Yrs.): . . . 5/5/5/5
Area Development Agreement: Yes/10
Sub-Franchise Contract: . . . . . Yes
Expand in Territory: . . . . . . Yes
Passive Ownership: . . . . .Allowed
Encourage Conversions: . . . . Yes
Avg. # Employees: . 15-20 FT, 3-5 PT

FRANCHISOR TRAINING/SUPPORT:
Financial Assistance Provided: . . . . . No
Site Selection Assistance: . . . . . . .Yes
Lease Negotiation Assistance: . . . . .Yes
Co-operative Advertising: . . . . . . .Yes
Training: . . . . . 6-12 Wks. Best Location
. . . . to get Best Training
On-Going Support: a,B,C,D,E,F,g,h,i/ . 37
EXPANSION PLANS:
US: . . . . Southwest, Northwest,Midwest
Canada: . . . . .Yes
Overseas: . . . . No

BUDGET HOST INNS

2601 Jacksboro Hwy., # 202
Ft. Worth, TX 76114
TEL: (817) 626-7064
FAX:
Mr. Ray Sawyer, President

Referral chain of affiliated independent inns (a la Best Western) that meet AAA or Mobil Travel Guide, or equivalent, standards and provide moderate room rates for respective market area. BUDGET HOST provides full-service program for advertising, promotion and national account savings on supplies, equipment and services.

HISTORY: . . . .
Established in 1975; . . 1st Franchised in 1976
Company-Owned Units (As of 8/31/1992): . .0
Franchised Units (As of 8/31/1992): 162
Total Units (As of 8/31/1992): 162
Projected New Units for 1993:
Distribution: . . . US-158;Can-4;Overseas-0
North America: . . . . 36 States, 3 Provinces
Concentration: . .11 in CO, 13 in KS, 7 in MO
Registered: . . . .
. . . .
Type Space: . . . . ;~ SF

FINANCIAL: Earnings Claim: . . .
Cash Investment: . . . . $5K+
Total Investment: . . . . $5K+
Fees: Franchise - $1.5K
Royalty: Varies, Advert: . . Varies
Contract Periods (Yrs.): 1/1
Area Development Agreement: .No
Sub-Franchise Contract: . . . . .No
Expand in Territory: . . . . . . Yes
Passive Ownership: . . . . .Allowed
Encourage Conversions: . . . . .No
Average # Employees: . . . .

FRANCHISOR TRAINING/SUPPORT:
Financial Assistance Provided: . . . . . No
Site Selection Assistance: . . . . No
Lease Negotiation Assistance: . . . . . No
Co-operative Advertising: . . . . . . .Yes
Training: . . . .

On-Going Support: B,C,G,H/ 3
EXPANSION PLANS:
US: . . . . .All US
Canada: . . . . .Yes
Overseas: . . . . No

CHOICE HOTELS INTERNATIONAL

10750 Columbia Pike
Silver Spring, MD 20901
TEL: (800) 547-0007 (301) 236-5073
FAX: (301) 681-7478
Mr. Jeff Williams, SVP Devel.

CHOICE HOTELS is the world's largest hotel franchisor, marketing more than 2,800 hotels in 29 countries under the **Comfort, Quality, Clarion, Sleep, Rodeway, Econo Lodge** and **Friendship** brands. CHOICE is a subsidiary of Manor Care, Inc., a public corporation.

HISTORY: . . . .
Established in 1939; . . 1st Franchised in 1960
Company-Owned Units (As of 8/31/1992): . 12
Franchised Units (As of 8/31/1992): 2806
Total Units (As of 8/31/1992): 2818
Projected New Units for 1993: 200
Distribution: . US-2532;Can-100;Overseas-186
North America: . . . . . 49 States, 1 Province
Concentration: . 244 in CA, 207 in FL, 174 VA
Registered: . . . . .All
. . . .
Type Space: . . . . . . FS, Other;~2 Acres SF

FINANCIAL: Earnings Claim: . Yes
Cash Investment: . . . .$
Total Investment: . . . .$
Fees: Franchise - $15-50K
Royalty: 6-7.9%, Advert: . Included
Contract Periods (Yrs.): 20/20
Area Development Agreement: .No
Sub-Franchise Contract: . . . . . Yes
Expand in Territory: . . . . . . Yes
Passive Ownership: . . . . .Allowed
Encourage Conversions: . . . . Yes
Avg. # Employees: 12+ FT, Varies PT

FRANCHISOR TRAINING/SUPPORT:
Financial Assistance Provided: . . . Yes(I)
Site Selection Assistance: . . . . . . .Yes
Lease Negotiation Assistance: . . . . . No
Co-operative Advertising: . . . . . . .Yes
Training: . . . . Varies at On-Site Opening
. . .Marketing Assistance Varies On-Site
On-Going Support: B,C,D,E,G,h/ . . .1200
EXPANSION PLANS:
US: . . . . .All US
Canada: . . . . .All Canada
Overseas: EUR, Asia/Pacific,Latin Amer.

CLUBHOUSE INNS OF AMERICA

7101 College Blvd., # 1150
Overland Park, KS 66210
TEL: (913) 451-1300
FAX: (913) 451-6072
Mr. David H. Aull, President

High quality, moderate-priced courtyard-style hotel. 120-150 rooms. Best located in towns over 100,000 and located near office corridors to attract traveling business people.

HISTORY:	FINANCIAL: Earnings Claim: . . .	FRANCHISOR TRAINING/SUPPORT:
Established in 1984; . . 1st Franchised in 1986	Cash Investment: $1.5MM	Financial Assistance Provided: . . . . .No
Company-Owned Units (As of 8/31/1992): . 14	Total Investment: . . . $6.0-7.5MM	Site Selection Assistance: . . . . . . .Yes
Franchised Units (As of 8/31/1992): 1	Fees: Franchise - $30K	Lease Negotiation Assistance: . . . .NA
Total Units (As of 8/31/1992): 15	Royalty: 4%, Advert: 1.5%	Co-operative Advertising: . . . . . . .No
Projected New Units for 1993: 2	Contract Periods (Yrs.): 15/0	Training: . . . . . 2 Wks. Headquarters for
Distribution: US-15;Can-0;Overseas-0	Area Development Agreement: . Yes	. . . . .Manager
North America: . . . . 9 States	Sub-Franchise Contract: . . . . . .No	On-Going Support: a,b,C,d,e,h,I/ 25
Concentration: . . . 3 in TN, 3 in GA, 3 in KS	Expand in Territory: . . . . Yes	EXPANSION PLANS:
Registered: . . . . .CA,IL,MI,VA	Passive Ownership: . . . . . .Allowed	US: . . . . All US
. . . .	Encourage Conversions: . . . . Yes	Canada: . . . . .No
Type Space: . . . Adequate Land;~130,000 SF	Average # Employees: . . . . 30 FT	Overseas: . . . . No

CONDOTELS INTERNATIONAL

2703 Hwy. 17 S.
N. Myrtle Beach, SC 29582
TEL: (800) 852-6636 (803) 272-8400
FAX: (803) 272-6556
Mr. Raymond L. Mann, Jr., Fran. Anyst.

Operates much as a hotel franchisor except the accommodations provided are condominium homes rather than hotel rooms. Franchisees manage rentals of resort condos for the condo homeowners and provide check-in and daily maid service.

HISTORY:	FINANCIAL: Earnings Claim: . .No	FRANCHISOR TRAINING/SUPPORT:
Established in 1982; . . 1st Franchised in 1989	Cash Investment: $45.2-192.5K	Financial Assistance Provided: . . . . .No
Company-Owned Units (As of 8/31/1992): . .1	Total Investment: $45.2-192.5K	Site Selection Assistance: . . . . . . .Yes
Franchised Units (As of 8/31/1992): 7	Fees: Franchise - $35K	Lease Negotiation Assistance: . . . .No
Total Units (As of 8/31/1992): 8	Royalty: 4%, Advert: 1.5%	Co-operative Advertising: . . . . . . .Yes
Projected New Units for 1993: 4	Contract Periods (Yrs.): 10/5/5	Training: . . . . . . 10 Days Headquarters,
Distribution: US-8;Can-0;Overseas-0	Area Development Agreement: . .No	. . . . 2 Days On-Site
North America: . . . . 4 States	Sub-Franchise Contract: . . . . . .No	On-Going Support: a,b,C,D,E,G,H,I/ . . 15
Concentration: . . . . 4 in SC, 2 in FL, 1 in CA	Expand in Territory: . . . . Yes	EXPANSION PLANS:
Registered: . . . . .CA,FL	Passive Ownership: . . . Discouraged	US: . . . . Southeast and Southwest
. . . .	Encourage Conversions: . . . . Yes	Canada: . . . . .Yes
Type Space: . . . . .SC;~1,500 SF	Average # Employees: . .4 FT, 40 PT	Overseas: . . . . . .MX, Caribbean

ECONOMY LODGING SYSTEMS

26650 Emery Pkwy.
Cleveland, OH 44128
TEL: (800) 932-3300 (216) 464-5055
FAX: (216) 464-2210
Mr. Roger J. Bloss, SVP Dev.

Franchise programs consist of market protection with 100% of marketing and reservation fees being returned to the system. No additional reservation fees, resulting in the lowest total franchise fee in the industry.

HISTORY:	FINANCIAL: Earnings Claim: . Yes	FRANCHISOR TRAINING/SUPPORT:
Established in 1991; . . 1st Franchised in 1992	Cash Investment: . . . .$100K+	Financial Assistance Provided: . . . . .NA
Company-Owned Units (As of 8/31/1992): . 18	Total Investment: . . . . .$.5-5.0MM	Site Selection Assistance: . . . . . . .Yes
Franchised Units (As of 8/31/1992): 161	Fees: Franchise - . . . $150 per Room	Lease Negotiation Assistance: . . . .Yes
Total Units (As of 8/31/1992): 179	Royalty: 4%, Advert: 2%	Co-operative Advertising: . . . . . . .Yes
Projected New Units for 1993: 35	Contract Periods (Yrs.): 10/10	Training: . . . . . . 1-5 Days Headquarters,
Distribution: US-179;Can-0;Overseas-0	Area Development Agreement: . Yes/5	. . . . .1-5 Days Regional
North America: . . . . 22 States	Sub-Franchise Contract: . . . . . Yes	On-Going Support: a,B,C,D,E,G,h,I/ . 2000
Concentration: . .33 in OH, 20 in MI, 14 in FL	Expand in Territory: . . . . Yes	EXPANSION PLANS:
Registered: . . . CA,FL,IL,IN,MD,MI,NY,SD	Passive Ownership: . . . . . .Allowed	US: . . . . Central and West US
. . . . VA,WI,DC	Encourage Conversions: . . . . Yes	Canada: . . . . .No
Type Space: . . . . FS;~1 Acre SF	Average # Employees: . .6 FT, 24 PT	Overseas: . . . . No

EMBASSY SUITES

850 Ridge Lake Blvd., # 400
Memphis, TN 38120
TEL: (901) 680-7200
FAX: (901) 680-7220
Mr. William G. Moeckel, SVP Devel.

Dominating the all-suite market, EMBASSY SUITES targets the up-scale frequent business traveler and weekend/leisure guest attracted to the chain's value, flexibility and space. EMBASSY SUITES' guest satisfaction is one of the highest in the up-scale hotel segment.

HISTORY: . . . . IFA	FINANCIAL: Earnings Claim: . .No	FRANCHISOR TRAINING/SUPPORT:
Established in 1983; . . 1st Franchised in 1985	Cash Investment: . . . . . $.3-4.0MM	Financial Assistance Provided: . . . . . No
Company-Owned Units (As of 8/31/1992): . 38	Total Investment: $17.5-20MM	Site Selection Assistance: . . . . No
Franchised Units (As of 8/31/1992): . . . . . <u>64</u>	Fees: Franchise - $500/Suite	Lease Negotiation Assistance: . . . . .No
Total Units (As of 8/31/1992): 102	Royalty: 4%, Advert: 3.5%	Co-operative Advertising: . . . . .Yes
Projected New Units for 1993: 3	Contract Periods (Yrs.): 20/0	Training: . . . . 3-6 Days Various
Distribution: US-101;Can-1;Overseas-0	Area Development Agreement: . .No	. . .Locations, Training Custom Tailored
North America: . . . . . 31 States, 1 Province	Sub-Franchise Contract: . . . . .No	On-Going Support: A,b,C,D,E,G,h/ . . . 75
Concentration: . . . 14 in CA, 8 in TX, 6 in FL	Expand in Territory: . . . . . . .No	EXPANSION PLANS:
Registered: . . . CA,HI,IL,MI,MN,ND,OR,RI	Passive Ownership: . . . . . .Allowed	US: . . . . .All US
. . . . .SD,VA,WA,WI	Encourage Conversions: . . . . . Yes	Canada: . . . . .ON, PQ, AB
Type Space: . . . . .FS;~3-5 Acres SF	Average # Employees: . . . . 100 FT	Overseas: . . EUR, Asia, C. & S. America

HAMPTON INNS

6800 Poplar Ave., # 200
Memphis, TN 38138
TEL: (901) 758-3100
FAX: (901) 756-9479
Mr. David C. Sullivan, VP Dev./Ops.

HAMPTON INN hotels is one of the fastest-growing, moderately-priced chains. Hotels offer 100% Satisfaction Guarantee, free continental breakfast, free local phone calls, free in-room movie channel, no charge for 3rd or 4th adult and 50% non-smoking room inventory. Development opportunities exist with our standard prototype, our modified prototype designed for communities of 75,000 people or less and conversions. Division of The Promus Companies.

HISTORY: . . . . IFA	FINANCIAL: Earnings Claim: . .No	FRANCHISOR TRAINING/SUPPORT:
Established in 1983; . . 1st Franchised in 1984	Cash Investment: . . . .$	Financial Assistance Provided: . . . . . No
Company-Owned Units (As of 8/31/1992): . 15	Total Investment: $2.5-7.0MM	Site Selection Assistance: . . . . .Yes
Franchised Units (As of 8/31/1992): . . . . <u>300</u>	Fees: Franchise - $300/Room	Lease Negotiation Assistance: . . . . .No
Total Units (As of 8/31/1992): 315	Royalty: 4%, Advert: 4%	Co-operative Advertising: . . . .
Projected New Units for 1993: 45	Contract Periods (Yrs.): 20	Training: . . . .
Distribution: US-315;Can-0;Overseas-0	Area Development Agreement: . .No	. . . .
North America: . . . . 41 States	Sub-Franchise Contract: . . . . .No	On-Going Support: A,C,D,G,h,I/ 82
Concentration: . 27 in NC, 20 in TX, 19 in TN	Expand in Territory: . . . . . . Yes	EXPANSION PLANS:
Registered: . . . . .All	Passive Ownership: . . . . . .Allowed	US: . . . . .All US
. . . .	Encourage Conversions: . . . . . Yes	Canada: . . . . .Yes
Type Space: . . . . FS;~52,000 SF	Average # Employees: . . . . .20 FT	Overseas: . .MX, C & S Amer., Asia, IRE

HAWTHORN SUITES HOTELS

400 Fifth Ave.
Waltham, MA 02154
TEL: (617) 290-0175 C
FAX: (617) 290-0175
Mr. William Begley, VP

HAWTHORN SUITES is an all-suite, limited-service hotel chain designed to meet the needs of the upper mid-scale, extended-stay customer. The building style will be high-rise, mid-rise, as well as garden-style, featuring one and two bedroom suites with separate living room, full kitchen, swimming pool and health/fitness center, full complimentary breakfast and complimentary cocktail hour.

HISTORY:	FINANCIAL: Earnings Claim: . .No	FRANCHISOR TRAINING/SUPPORT:
Established in 1986; . . 1st Franchised in 1986	Cash Investment: $25-40K	Financial Assistance Provided: . . . . .NA
Company-Owned Units (As of 8/31/1992): . .3	Total Investment: . . . . $70K+ /Suite	Site Selection Assistance: . . . . .Yes
Franchised Units (As of 8/31/1992): . . . . . <u>10</u>	Fees: Franchise - . . . . $Varies	Lease Negotiation Assistance: . . . . .No
Total Units (As of 8/31/1992): 13	Royalty: 4%, Advert: 2.5%	Co-operative Advertising: . . . . .Yes
Projected New Units for 1993: 3	Contract Periods (Yrs.): . . 10-15/10	Training: . . . .
Distribution: US-13;Can-0;Overseas-0	Area Development Agreement: . Yes	. . . .
North America: . . . . 7 States	Sub-Franchise Contract: . . . . .No	On-Going Support: a,b,C,D,h,I/ 20
Concentration: . . . . 7 in TX	Expand in Territory: . . . . . . Yes	EXPANSION PLANS:
Registered: . . . . .All	Passive Ownership: . . . . . .Allowed	US: . . . . .All US
. . . .	Encourage Conversions: . . . . . Yes	Canada: . . . . .All Canada
Type Space: . . . . NA;~Varies SF	Average # Employees: . . . 30-40 FT	Overseas: . MX, Carib, EUR, Asia/Pacific

HOLIDAY INNS WORLDWIDE

3 Ravinia Dr., # 2000
Atlanta, GA 30346
TEL: (404) 604-2000
FAX: (404) 604-2107
Mr. Jimmy Thomas, Dir. Fran. Mktg.

HOLIDAY INN, the international hotel business of Bass PLC, is the world's leading hotel chain, with nearly 1,600 hotels and 320,000 rooms in 51 countries or territories. The HOLIDAY INN, HOLIDAY INN CROWNE PLAZA, HOLIDAY INN GARDEN COURT and HOLIDAY INN EXPRESS hotels.

HISTORY: . . . . IFA	FINANCIAL: Earnings Claim: . .No	FRANCHISOR TRAINING/SUPPORT:
Established in 1952; . . 1st Franchised in 1954	Cash Investment: . . . . $250K+	Financial Assistance Provided: . . . Yes(I)
Company-Owned Units (As of 8/31/1992): 216	Total Investment: . . . . . $1.0+MM	Site Selection Assistance: . . . . .NA
Franchised Units (As of 8/31/1992): 1470	Fees: Franchise - . . . . $$400/Room	Lease Negotiation Assistance: . . . . . .NA
Total Units (As of 8/31/1992): 1686	Royalty: 5%, Advert: 2%	Co-operative Advertising: . . . . .Yes
Projected New Units for 1993: 100	Contract Periods (Yrs.): 20/10	Training: . . . . 2-3 Wks. Atlanta,
Distribution: . . US-1402;Can-64;Overseas-220	Area Development Agreement: . .No	. . . . Regional or On-Site
North America: . . . . 50 States, 8 Provinces	Sub-Franchise Contract: . . . . .No	On-Going Support: A,B,C,D,E,F,G,h,I/ . . .
Concentration: . . 128 in FL, 99 in TX, 79 CA	Expand in Territory: . . . . Yes	EXPANSION PLANS:
Registered: . . . . .All	Passive Ownership: . . . . .Allowed	US: . . . . All US
. . . .	Encourage Conversions: . . . . Yes	Canada: . . . . .All Canada
Type Space: . . . . FS;~Varies SF	Average # Employees: . 50 FT, 20 PT	Overseas: . . . . .Yes

HOMEWOOD SUITES

6800 Poplar Ave., # 200
Memphis, TN 38138
TEL: (901) 758-3100
FAX: (901) 756-9479
Mr. David C. Sullivan, VP Devel./Ops.

HOMEWOOD SUITES is a chain of extended stay, all suites hotels, geared for today's business travel market. Development opportunities exist with our standard prototype, modified prototype (which requires less land) and conversions. HOMEWOOD SUITES is a division of The Promus Companies.

HISTORY:	FINANCIAL: Earnings Claim: . .No	FRANCHISOR TRAINING/SUPPORT:
Established in 1989; . . 1st Franchised in 1989	Cash Investment: . . . .$	Financial Assistance Provided: . . . . .No
Company-Owned Units (As of 8/31/1992): . .8	Total Investment: $3-8MM	Site Selection Assistance: . . . . . . .Yes
Franchised Units (As of 8/31/1992): 16	Fees: Franchise - $300/Suite	Lease Negotiation Assistance: . . . . . No
Total Units (As of 8/31/1992): 24	Royalty: 4%, Advert: 4%	Co-operative Advertising: . . . .
Projected New Units for 1993: 3	Contract Periods (Yrs.): 20	Training: . . . .
Distribution: US-24;Can-0;Overseas-0	Area Development Agreement: . .No	. . . .
North America: . . . . 16 States	Sub-Franchise Contract: . . . . .No	On-Going Support: A,C,D,G,h,I/ 82
Concentration: . . . 3 in GA, 3 in OH, 2 in NC	Expand in Territory: . . . . Yes	EXPANSION PLANS:
Registered: . . . . All States	Passive Ownership: . . . . . .Allowed	US: . . . . All US
. . . .	Encourage Conversions: . . . . Yes	Canada: . . . . .Yes
Type Space: . . . . FS;~70,000 SF	Average # Employees: . . . . . 25 FT	Overseas: . . . . .MX

INTER HOTELS AND RESORTS

100 N. Pineapple Ave.
Sarasota, FL 34236
TEL: (800) 468-3750 (813) 957-3200 C
FAX: (813) 955-5599
Mr. Neil Camera, President

Most effective advertising program via electronic and printed media that relates directly to licensee's market through INTER HOTELS AND RESORTS "Inter Media Services." This service requires No Cash Expenditure on Licensee's part and is inclusive of world-wide coverage.

HISTORY:	FINANCIAL: Earnings Claim: . .No	FRANCHISOR TRAINING/SUPPORT:
Established in 1967; . . 1st Franchised in 1967	Cash Investment: . . . .$	Financial Assistance Provided: . . . . .No
Company-Owned Units (As of 8/31/1992): . .0	Total Investment: . . . .$	Site Selection Assistance: . . . . . . .Yes
Franchised Units (As of 8/31/1992): 410	Fees: Franchise - $2.5-15K	Lease Negotiation Assistance: . . . . .Yes
Total Units (As of 8/31/1992): 410	Royalty: 1.9%, Advert: . . . Varies	Co-operative Advertising: . . . . . . .Yes
Projected New Units for 1993: 60	Contract Periods (Yrs.): 1/10	Training: . . . . . .2 Wks. or More On-Site
Distribution: US-10;Can-0;Overseas-400	Area Development Agreement: . Yes	. . . .
North America: . . . . . 2 States, 5 Provinces	Sub-Franchise Contract: . . . . . Yes	On-Going Support: a,B,C,D,E,f,G,H,I/ . 12
Concentration: . . . 2 in FL, 200 in FR, 40 UK	Expand in Territory: . . . . Yes	EXPANSION PLANS:
Registered: . . . . .All	Passive Ownership: . . . . . .Allowed	US: . . . . All US
. . . .	Encourage Conversions: . . . . Yes	Canada: . . . . .All Canada
Type Space: . . . . SF;~Varies SF	Average # Employees: . . . . .Varies	Overseas: . . . . .Yes

KAMPGROUNDS OF AMERICA / KOA

550 N. 31st TWIII, P. O. Box 30558
Billings, MT 59114
TEL: (800) 548-7239 (406) 248-7444
FAX: (406) 248-7414
Mr. David W. Johnson, VP Licensing

KAMPGROUNDS OF AMERICA is America's largest system of campgrounds for recreational vehicles. The average campground contains 100 sites equipped with water and electrical hookups; many sites have sewer hookups. Each campground features clean restrooms with hot showers, a convenience store, laundry equipment and playground equipment. Most have swimming pools.

HISTORY:	IFA
Established in 1961; 1st Franchised in 1962	
Company-Owned Units (As of 8/31/1992): 12	
Franchised Units (As of 8/31/1992): 573	
Total Units (As of 8/31/1992): 585	
Projected New Units for 1993: 12	
Distribution: US-530;Can-55;Overseas-0	
North America: 46 States, 8 Provinces	
Concentration: 38 in CA, 33 in FL, 30 in CO	
Registered: All	
Type Space: NA;~ SF	

FINANCIAL: Earnings Claim: . Yes	
Cash Investment:	$85K+
Total Investment:	$250+K
Fees: Franchise -	$20K
Royalty: 8%, Advert:	2%
Contract Periods (Yrs.):	5/5
Area Development Agreement:	No
Sub-Franchise Contract:	Yes
Expand in Territory:	Yes
Passive Ownership:	Discouraged
Encourage Conversions:	Yes
Average # Employees:	2 FT, 1 PT

FRANCHISOR TRAINING/SUPPORT:
Financial Assistance Provided:	Yes(I)
Site Selection Assistance:	Yes
Lease Negotiation Assistance:	No
Co-operative Advertising:	Yes
Training:	3 Days Headquarters
On-Going Support: B,C,D,E,G,h,I/	72

EXPANSION PLANS:
US:	All US
Canada:	All Exc. Alberta
Overseas:	JA, MX

MASTER HOST INNS/RED CARPET/ SCOTTISH

1152 Spring St., # A
Atlanta, GA 30309
TEL: (800) 247-4677 (404) 873-5924 C
FAX: (404) 872-6358
Ms. Loretta Oliver, Fran. Dev.

Major franchisor of budget, limited-service, full-service and bed & breakfast properties at a fraction of the cost. We assist with marketing, purchasing, quality assurance, housekeeping, advertising, sales, operations and public relations.

HISTORY:	IFA
Established in 1982; 1st Franchised in 1982	
Company-Owned Units (As of 8/31/1992): 0	
Franchised Units (As of 8/31/1992): 350	
Total Units (As of 8/31/1992): 350	
Projected New Units for 1993: 69	
Distribution: US-345;Can-4;Overseas-1	
North America: 33 States, 2 Provinces	
Concentration: 49 in FL, 44 in GA, 27 in TN	
Registered: CA,FL,IL,IN,MD,MI,MN,NY	
ND,RI,SE,VA,WI,AB	
Type Space: ;~ SF	

FINANCIAL: Earnings Claim: . No	
Cash Investment:	$100-400K
Total Investment:	$1.2-4.8MM
Fees: Franchise -	$10-15K
Royalty: 2-3%, Advert:	.05%
Contract Periods (Yrs.):	5/5/5/5
Area Development Agreement:	No
Sub-Franchise Contract:	No
Expand in Territory:	Yes
Passive Ownership:	Allowed
Encourage Conversions:	Yes
Average # Employees:	10 FT, 10 PT

FRANCHISOR TRAINING/SUPPORT:
Financial Assistance Provided:	No
Site Selection Assistance:	No
Lease Negotiation Assistance:	No
Co-operative Advertising:	Yes
Training:	4-5 Days Headquarters,
	1-2 Days Regional
On-Going Support: C,D,G,H,I/	30

EXPANSION PLANS:
US:	West Coast and Northeast
Canada:	Ontario, Alberta
Overseas:	Yes

MICROTEL

One Airport Way, # 200
Rochester, NY 14624
TEL: (716) 436-6000
FAX: (716) 436-1865
Mr. George R. Justus, SVP Fran. Dev.

Hotel franchise, featuring luxury downsize rooms, focused on providing excellent price/value. Rates typically 15-20% below budget competition.

HISTORY:	
Established in 1987; 1st Franchised in 1988	
Company-Owned Units (As of 8/31/1992): 0	
Franchised Units (As of 8/31/1992): 8	
Total Units (As of 8/31/1992): 8	
Projected New Units for 1993: 15	
Distribution: US-8;Can-0;Overseas-0	
North America: 3 States	
Concentration: 5 in KY, 2 in OH, 1 in KY	
Registered: All	
Type Space: FS;~90,000 Land SF	

FINANCIAL: Earnings Claim: . No	
Cash Investment:	$600-750K
Total Investment:	$2.5-3.0MM
Fees: Franchise -	$25K
Royalty: 2.5%, Advert:	0%
Contract Periods (Yrs.):	10/10
Area Development Agreement:	No
Sub-Franchise Contract:	No
Expand in Territory:	Yes
Passive Ownership:	Allowed
Encourage Conversions:	No
Average # Employees:	15 FT, 6 PT

FRANCHISOR TRAINING/SUPPORT:
Financial Assistance Provided:	Yes(I)
Site Selection Assistance:	Yes
Lease Negotiation Assistance:	No
Co-operative Advertising:	No
Training:	2-4 Days Headquarters
On-Going Support: C,D,E,H,I/	12

EXPANSION PLANS:
US:	All US
Canada:	All Canada
Overseas:	W. EUR

NENDELS INNS / VALUE INNS BY NENDEL
520 Pike St., # 1600
Seattle, WA 98101
TEL: (800) 547-0106 (206) 623-4832
FAX: (206) 623-8403
Mr. Gary Maisel, VP Fran. Dev.

NENDELS offers a market-sensitive brand name for independent or new construction hotels. NENDELS franchises NENDELS INNS, SUITES, HOTELS and RESORTS in the mid-priced segment and VALU INNS by NENDELS in the economy segment.

HISTORY:	FINANCIAL: Earnings Claim: . .No	FRANCHISOR TRAINING/SUPPORT:
Established in 1934; . . 1st Franchised in 1986	Cash Investment: $10-20K	Financial Assistance Provided: . . . Yes(I)
Company-Owned Units (As of 8/31/1992): . .0	Total Investment: $25-4,000K	Site Selection Assistance: . . . . . . .Yes
Franchised Units (As of 8/31/1992): 70	Fees: Franchise - $10-20K	Lease Negotiation Assistance: . . . . .No
Total Units (As of 8/31/1992): 70	Royalty: 3.5%, Advert: . . . . Flat	Co-operative Advertising: . . . . . . .Yes
Projected New Units for 1993: 80	Contract Periods (Yrs.): 10/10	Training: . . . . 1 Wk. Seattle, WA
Distribution: US-68;Can-2;Overseas-0	Area Development Agreement: . .No	
North America: . . . . 10 States, 2 Provinces	Sub-Franchise Contract: . . . . . . .No	On-Going Support: A,B,C,D,e,G,H,I/ . . 32
Concentration: . 19 in WA, 18 in CA, 15 in OR	Expand in Territory: . . . . Yes	EXPANSION PLANS:
Registered: . . . . .CA,OR,WA	Passive Ownership: . . . . . .Allowed	US: . . . . All US, Focus on West
	Encourage Conversions: . . . . . Yes	Canada: . . . . BC, AB and SK
Type Space: . . . . FS;~85,000 SF	Average # Employees: . .12 FT, 4 PT	Overseas: . . . . .Pacific Rim

SHERATON INNS
60 State St.
Boston, MA 02109
TEL: (617) 367-3600
FAX: (617) 367-5676
Mr. Mike Getto, VP Dir. Dev.

Hotel chain with hotels, inns, resorts and all-suites in 67 countries worldwide.

HISTORY: . . . . .IFA, CFA	FINANCIAL: Earnings Claim: . .No	FRANCHISOR TRAINING/SUPPORT:
Established in 1937; . . 1st Franchised in 1962	Cash Investment: . . . .$~3MM	Financial Assistance Provided: . . . . .No
Company-Owned Units (As of 8/31/1992): 164	Total Investment: $9MM	Site Selection Assistance: . . . . . . .Yes
Franchised Units (As of 8/31/1992): 258	Fees: Franchise - . . . . $30K+	Lease Negotiation Assistance: . . . .NA
Total Units (As of 8/31/1992): 422	Royalty: 5%, Advert: 1%	Co-operative Advertising: . . . . . . .Yes
Projected New Units for 1993: 9	Contract Periods (Yrs.): 10/10	Training: . . . .
Distribution: US-397;Can-17;Overseas-8	Area Development Agreement: . .No	
North America: . . . . 43 States, 8 Provinces	Sub-Franchise Contract: . . . . . .No	On-Going Support: A,C,D,G,H/ 99
Concentration: . .31 in CA, 30 in FL, 17 in TX	Expand in Territory: . . . . .No	EXPANSION PLANS:
Registered: . . . . All Except HI	Passive Ownership: . . . . . .Allowed	US: . . . . .All US
	Encourage Conversions: . . . . . Yes	Canada: . . . . .All Canada
Type Space: . . . . FS;~Varies SF	Average # Employees: . . . . .Varies	Overseas: . . . . .Worldwide

SHONEY'S INNS
217 W. Main St.
Gallatin, TN 37066
TEL: (615) 452-7200
FAX: (615) 452-7332
Mr. Richard L. Johnson, EVP

SHOLODGE FRANCHISE SYSTEMS, INC. is the franchisor of the SHONEY'S INN brand of motels. Inns are located next to SHONEY'S restaurants, one of the leading restaurant chains in the US.

HISTORY: . . . . IFA	FINANCIAL: Earnings Claim: . Yes	FRANCHISOR TRAINING/SUPPORT:
Established in 1980; . . 1st Franchised in 1980	Cash Investment: . . . . .$.3-1.0MM	Financial Assistance Provided: . . . . .No
Company-Owned Units (As of 8/31/1992): . 18	Total Investment: $1.0-3MM	Site Selection Assistance: . . . . . . .Yes
Franchised Units (As of 8/31/1992): 41	Fees: Franchise - $15K	Lease Negotiation Assistance: . . . . .Yes
Total Units (As of 8/31/1992): 59	Royalty: 3.5%, Advert: 1%	Co-operative Advertising: . . . . . . .Yes
Projected New Units for 1993: 4	Contract Periods (Yrs.): 20/20	Training: . . . . All Training at Head-
Distribution: US-59;Can-0;Overseas-0	Area Development Agreement: Yes/5	. . . . quarters
North America: . . . . 16 States	Sub-Franchise Contract: . . . . . .No	On-Going Support: a,C,D,E,f,G,H,I/ . . 20
Concentration: . . . 12 in GA, 8 in TN, 6 in FL	Expand in Territory: . . . . Yes	EXPANSION PLANS:
Registered: . . . . All States	Passive Ownership: . . . . . .Allowed	US: . . . . .All US
	Encourage Conversions: . . . . . Yes	Canada: . . . . .No
Type Space: . . . . FS;~50,000 SF	Average # Employees: . . . . .20 FT	Overseas: . . . . .No

SUPER 8 MOTELS

1910 Eighth Ave., NE, P. O. Box 4090
Aberdeen, SD 57401
TEL: (800) 843-1960 (605) 225-2272
FAX: (605) 225-5060
Mr. Dale Aasen, EVP Sales/Mktg.

SUPER 8 MOTELS is the nation's largest economy motel chain. SUPER 8 can provide turn-key operation after land had been acquired. Our franchise fees are documented to be the lowest of the major economy motel competitors.

HISTORY: . . . . .IFA, CFA	FINANCIAL: Earnings Claim: . Yes	FRANCHISOR TRAINING/SUPPORT:
Established in 1973; . . 1st Franchised in 1976	Cash Investment: $100-300K	Financial Assistance Provided: . . . Yes(I)
Company-Owned Units (As of 8/31/1992): . 52	Total Investment: . . . . . $.4-3.0MM	Site Selection Assistance: . . . . No
Franchised Units (As of 8/31/1992): 858	Fees: Franchise - $20K	Lease Negotiation Assistance: . . . . .NA
Total Units (As of 8/31/1992): 910	Royalty: 4%, Advert: . . . . 2+1%	Co-operative Advertising: . . . . .No
Projected New Units for 1993: 90	Contract Periods (Yrs.): . . 20/Varies	Training: . . . . 3 Wks. Headquarters,
Distribution: US-899;Can-11;Overseas-0	Area Development Agreement: Yes/Var	. . . . As Needed On-Site
North America: . . . . 49 States, 4 Provinces	Sub-Franchise Contract: . . . . . Yes	On-Going Support: a,B,C,D,e,G,h,I/ .300
Concentration: . . 74 in MN, 51 in IL, 51 in IA	Expand in Territory: . . . . . . Yes	EXPANSION PLANS:
Registered: . . . . .All	Passive Ownership: . . . . . .Allowed	US: . . . . All US
. . . .	Encourage Conversions: . . . . . Yes	Canada: . . . . .All Canada
Type Space: . . . . FS;~35,000+ SF	Average # Employees: . . 6 FT, 6 PT	Overseas: . . . .UK, EUR and Asia

TRAVELODGE

1973 Friendship Dr.
El Cajon, CA 92020
TEL: (800) 947-4357 (619) 258-6580
FAX: (619) 562-6646
Mr. Chris Cullen, Dir. Communications

The first name in economy lodging. A leader in the segment for 45 years, TRAVELODGE is a sales and marketing powerhouse, with the industry's most advanced system and most professional franchise services organization.

HISTORY: . . . . IFA	FINANCIAL: Earnings Claim: . .No	FRANCHISOR TRAINING/SUPPORT:
Established in 1946; . . 1st Franchised in 1966	Cash Investment: . . . .$	Financial Assistance Provided: . . . . .No
Company-Owned Units (As of 8/31/1992): . 50	Total Investment: . . . .$1MM+	Site Selection Assistance: . . . . .Yes
Franchised Units (As of 8/31/1992): 453	Fees: Franchise - $300/RM	Lease Negotiation Assistance: . . . . .No
Total Units (As of 8/31/1992): 503	Royalty: 4%, Advert: 4%	Co-operative Advertising: . . . . .Yes
Projected New Units for 1993: 100	Contract Periods (Yrs.): 20/10	Training: . . . .
Distribution: US-450;Can-53;Overseas-0	Area Development Agreement: Yes/Var	. . . .
North America: . . . . 47 States, 5 Provinces	Sub-Franchise Contract: . . . . . Yes	On-Going Support: A,B,C,D,E,f,G,H,I/ .200
Concentration: . . 160 in CA, 50 in FL, 35 TX	Expand in Territory: . . . . Yes	EXPANSION PLANS:
Registered: . . . . .All	Passive Ownership: . . . Discouraged	US: . . . . All US
. . . .	Encourage Conversions: . . . . . Yes	Canada: . . . . .All Canada
Type Space: . . . . FS;~Varies SF	Average # Employees: . . . . .Varies	Overseas: . . . . AU, MX

YOGI BEAR JELLYSTONE PARK CAMP/RESORTS

6201 Kellogg Ave.
Cincinnati, OH 45230
TEL: (800) 626-3720 (513) 232-6800
FAX: (513) 232-1191
Mr. Rob Schutter, VP/GM

A unique recreation camp-resort for the entire family. Yogi and friends offer daily activities with a full amenity package, clean restrooms and Yogi souvenirs. Each camp-resort is independently owned and operated and maintains system standards.

HISTORY:	FINANCIAL: Earnings Claim: . . .	FRANCHISOR TRAINING/SUPPORT:
Established in 1969; . . 1st Franchised in 1969	Cash Investment: $6-25K	Financial Assistance Provided: . . .Yes(D)
Company-Owned Units (As of 8/31/1992): . .0	Total Investment: $23-250K	Site Selection Assistance: . . . . .Yes
Franchised Units (As of 8/31/1992): 71	Fees: Franchise - $15-23K	Lease Negotiation Assistance: . . . . .Yes
Total Units (As of 8/31/1992): 71	Royalty: 6%, Advert: 1%	Co-operative Advertising: . . . . . . .Yes
Projected New Units for 1993: 5	Contract Periods (Yrs.): . . 5-20/5-10	Training: . . . . . . .2-3 Days Site, 3-4 Days
Distribution: US-68;Can-3;Overseas-0	Area Development Agreement: . .No	. . . Headquarters, 1-3 Days/Yr. On-Site
North America: . . . . 25 States, 2 Provinces	Sub-Franchise Contract: . . . . . .No	On-Going Support: B,C,D,E,G,H,I/ 6
Concentration: . . . . 8 in WI, 8 in VA, 7 in IN	Expand in Territory: . . . . . . .No	EXPANSION PLANS:
Registered: . . . FL,IL,IN,MD,MI,MN,VA,WI	Passive Ownership: . . . Discouraged	US: . . . . All US
. . . .	Encourage Conversions: . . . . . Yes	Canada: . . . . .Yes
Type Space: . . . . ;~ SF	Average # Employees: . .3 FT, 25 PT	Overseas: . . . . No

SUPPLEMENTAL LISTING OF FRANCHISORS

BED & BATH MINI-MOTEL . . . . 1309 W. Abram, # 102, Arlington, TX 76013
    Contact: President; Tel:
BUDGETEL INNS . . . . 212 W. Wisconsin Ave., 11th Fl., Milwaukee, WI 53203
    Contact: Mr. G. Edward Wilson, Dir. Fran.; Tel: (414) 272-6020
CARDINAL LODGING GROUP . . . . 2255 Kimberly Pkwy. E., Columbus, OH 43232
    Contact: Mr. Mark Williams; Tel: (614) 755-6230
CARLSON TRAVEL NETWORK . . . . .12755 State Hwy. 55, Minneapolis, MN 55441
    Contact: Mr. Terry Robertson, EVP; Tel: (612) 449-2278
CARLTON LODGE . . . . 1000 East 80th Pl., Merrillville, IN 46410
    Contact: President; Tel: (219) 736-0288
COMFORT INN . . . . 10750 Columbia Pike, Silver Springs, MD 20901
    Contact: Mr. Frederick Mosser, Sr. VP Devel.; Tel: (301) 236-5080
COMPRI HOTEL SYSTEMS . . . . 410 N. 44th St., # 700, Phoenix, AZ 85008
    Contact: Mr. Edward Pritchard, President; Tel: (800) 4-COMPRI (602) 220-6666
CORPORATE LODGING . . . . .11215 Research Blvd., # 2103, Austin, TX 78759
    Contact: Mr. Warren R. Haskin, II, President; Tel: (512) 345-8822
DAYS INN/DAYS LODGE . . . . .2751 Buford Hwy., NE, Atlanta, GA 30324
    Contact: Mr. Greg Casserly, SVP Fran.; Tel: (404) 325-4000
DOWNTOWNER MOTOR INNS/PASSPORT INNS . 454 Moss Trail, P. O. Box 749, Goodlettsville, TN 37072
    Contact: Mr. Terry Graham, President; Tel: (800) 238-6161 (615) 859-4522
ECONO LODGES OF AMERICA . . . . 10750 Columbia Pike, Silver Spring, MD 20901
    Contact: Mr. Robert Weller, President; Tel: (800) 441-1212
FAIRFIELD INN BY MARRIOTT . . . . 1 Marriott Dr., Washington, DC 20058
    Contact: Mr. Daryl A. Nickel, SVP; Tel: (301) 380-7658
FAMILY INNS OF AMERICA . . . . .P.O. Box 1345, Pigeon Forge, TN 37863
    Contact: Ms. Dee Lundy; Tel: (615) 453-5700 (615) 453-1240
FRIENDSHIP INNS . . . . 6135 Park South Dr., # 304, Charlotte, NC 28210
    Contact: Ms. Abigail Mayer-Reece, COO; Tel: (704) 552-9131
HILTON INNS . . . . 9336 Civic Center Dr., Beverly Hills, CA 90210
    Contact: Mr. Allen Hermansen, SVP; Tel: (213) 278-4321
HOSPITALITY FRANCHISE SYSTEMS . . . . 339 Jefferson Rd., Box 278, Parsippany, NJ 07054
    Contact: Ms. Jeanne Murphy, General Counsel; Tel: (201) 256-9030
HOSPITALITY INTERNATIONAL . . . . . . .1152 Spring St., # A, Atlanta, GA 30309
    Contact: Mr. Don McCroan; Tel: (404) 873-5924
HOWARD JOHNSON FRANCHISE SYSTEMS . . .339 Jefferson Rd., P. O. Box 278, Parsippany, NJ 07054
    Contact: Mr. John D. Snodgrass, President; Tel: (201) 428-9700 (201) 256-9030
INNSUITES INTERNATIONAL INNS/RESORTS . . . . . .1615 E. Northern Ave., Phoenix, AZ 85020
    Contact: Mr. Mark Berg; Tel: (800) 842-4242 (602) 997-6285
KAMP DAKOTA . . . . 103 W. 20th Street S., Brookings, SD 57006
    Contact: President; Tel:
KNIGHTS INN, KNIGHTSTOP, KNIGHTS COURT . . . . .26650 Emery Pkwy., Cleveland, OH 44128
    Contact: Mr. Roger Bloss, VP; Tel: (216) 464-5055
LEISURE INN . . . . 242 E. Woodlawn Ave., Charlotte, NC 28210
    Contact: President; Tel: (704) 525-5454
MIDWAY HOSPITALITY CORPORATION . . . . 1025 S. Moorland Rd., Brookfield, WI 53005
    Contact: President; Tel:
NEW WORLD BED & BREAKFAST . . . . 150 5th Ave., # 711, New York, NY 10011
    Contact: Ms. Laura Tilden, President; Tel: (800) 443-3800 (212) 675-5600
OMNI HOTELS . . . . .6407 Idlewild Rd., # 645, Charlotte, NC 28212
    Contact: President; Tel: (704) 537-4611
PARK INN INTERNATIONAL/PARK PLAZA . . . 4425 W. Airport Fwy., Box 152083, Irving, TX 75062
    Contact: Ms. Cyndee Brock; Tel: (214) 258-1919
PRIME RATE MOTELS . . . . .P.O. Box 1228, St. Cloud, MN 56301
    Contact: President; Tel:
PROMUS COMPANIES . . . . 1023 Cherry Rd., Memphis, TN 38117
    Contact: Mr. Randolph Baker, Dir. Pub. Affairs; Tel: (901) 762-8950
RADISSON HOTELS INTERNATIONAL . . . P. O. Box 59159, Carlson Parkway, Minneapolis, MN 55459
    Contact: Mr. Robert Berkwitz; Tel: (612) 540-5526
RAMADA INNS . . . . .339 Jefferson Rd., P. O. Box 278, Parsippany, NJ 07054
    Contact: Mr. Michael B. Lee, VP Fran. Sales; Tel: (201) 428-9700

RAMADA INNS OF CANADA . . . . 2300 Yonge St., # 1701, Toronto, ON M4P 1E4 CAN
    Contact: Mr. W. David Oliver, VP; Tel: (416) 485-2692
RESIDENCE INN BY MARRIOTT . . . . . . .One Marriott Dr., Dept. 514.01, Washington, DC 20058
    Contact: Mr. Daryl A. Nickel, SVP Fran. Dev.; Tel: (301) 380-7658
RODEWAY INNS INTERNATIONAL . . . . 10750 Columbia Pike, Silver Spring, MD 20901
    Contact: Mr. Sam Apostle, President; Tel: (301) 593-5600
STANLAKE LUXURY BUDGET MOTELS . . . . 6200 S. Syracuse Way, # 125, Englewood, CO 80111
    Contact: Mr. S. J. Lake, President; Tel: (303) 795-7600
STUDIO PLUS OF AMERICA . . . . 1999 Richmond Rd., # 4, Lexington, KY 40502
    Contact: Mr. Norwood Cowgill, Jr., President; Tel: (606) 269-1999
THRIFTY SCOT MOTELS/SUNWOOD INNS . . . . P.O. Box 399, St. Cloud, MN 56302
    Contact: President; Tel:
TREADWAY INNS CORPORATION . . . . . 50 Kenny Place, P.O. Box 1912, Saddle Brook, NJ 07662
    Contact: Ms. Wendy W. Denn; Tel: (201) 881-7900
WANDLYN INNS . . . . 88 Prospect St., P.O. Box 430, Fredericton, NB E3B 4X4 CAN
    Contact: Mr. Gary Llewellyn, President; Tel: (506) 452-0550
WOODFIN SUITES . . . . .9255 Town Center Dr., # 900, San Diego, CA 92121
    Contact: President; Tel:

For a full explanation of the data provided in

the Franchisor Format, please refer to Chapter 2,

"How To Use The Data."

CHAPTER 30

OPTICAL / DENTAL / MEDICAL

AMERICAN VISION CENTERS

90 John St.
New York, NY 10038
TEL: (800) 232-5558 (212) 385-1000 C
FAX: (212) 385-1149
Mr. Seth Poppel, President

AMERICAN VISION CENTERS was the first, and is still the only, large retail optical chain that is all-franchisee. Our franchisees are our only business. As an AVC franchisee, you get the best of both worlds: individual ownership and control with large corporate backing in order to provide quality eyecare and eyewear.

HISTORY: . . . .
Established in 1977;   . . 1st Franchised in 1977
Company-Owned Units (As of 8/31/1992):   . .0
Franchised Units (As of 8/31/1992):   . . . . . <u>53</u>
Total Units (As of 8/31/1992):   53
Projected New Units for 1993: 5
Distribution: US-53;Can-0;Overseas-0
  North America: . . . . 7 States
  Concentration: . . 24 in IL, 15 in NY, 4 in MA
Registered: . . . . .IL,NY
. . . .
Type Space: FS, SF, SC, RM;~1,100-1,900 SF

FINANCIAL: Earnings Claim: . .No
Cash Investment: $25-50K
Total Investment: $75-225K
Fees: Franchise - $10K
  Royalty: 8.5%, Advert: . . . 1.5-6%
Contract Periods (Yrs.): 10/10
Area Development Agreement: . .No
Sub-Franchise Contract: . . . . .No
Expand in Territory: . . . . Yes
Passive Ownership: . . . Not Allowed
Encourage Conversions: . . . . . Yes
Average # Employees: 4-8 FT, 1-3 PT

FRANCHISOR TRAINING/SUPPORT:
Financial Assistance Provided: . . .Yes(D)
Site Selection Assistance: . . . . . . .Yes
Lease Negotiation Assistance: . . . . .Yes
Co-operative Advertising: . . . . . . .Yes
Training: . . . . As Needed at Headquarters
  . . . . As Needed On-Site
On-Going Support: B,C,D,E,G,H,I/   . . . 12
EXPANSION PLANS:
  US: . . . . . Northeast, Midwest, SW, SE
  Canada: . . . . .No
  Overseas: .SP, E. EUR, JA, Taiwan

FIRST OPTOMETRY EYECARE CENTERS
32600 Gratiot Ave.
Roseville, MI 48066
TEL: (313) 296-7800
FAX: (313) 294-2623
Mr. D. M. Borsand, CEO

Sale of visioncare services and optical products - eyeglasses, contact lenses and sunglasses.

HISTORY: . . . .
Established in 1980; . . 1st Franchised in 1981
Company-Owned Units (As of 8/31/1992): . 12
Franchised Units (As of 8/31/1992): 20
Total Units (As of 8/31/1992): 32
Projected New Units for 1993: 3
Distribution: US-32;Can-0;Overseas-0
  North America: . . . .
  Concentration: . . . .
Registered: . . . .
. . . .
Type Space: . . . . .FS, SC;~1,500 SF

FINANCIAL: Earnings Claim: . .No
Cash Investment: $25-35K
Total Investment: $75-100K
Fees: Franchise - $6.5K
  Royalty: 7%, Advert: 5%
Contract Periods (Yrs.): 10/10
Area Development Agreement: Yes/10
Sub-Franchise Contract: . . . . . Yes
Expand in Territory: . . . . Yes
Passive Ownership: . . . Discouraged
Encourage Conversions: . . . . . Yes
Average # Employees: . . 3 FT, 1 PT

FRANCHISOR TRAINING/SUPPORT:
Financial Assistance Provided: . . . Yes(I)
Site Selection Assistance: . . . . . . .Yes
Lease Negotiation Assistance: . . . . . .Yes
Co-operative Advertising: . . . . .Yes
Training: . . . . . . 40 Hours Headquarters
. . . .
On-Going Support: B,C,D,E,F,G,H/ . . 10
EXPANSION PLANS:
US: . . . . Midwest Only
Canada: . . . . No
Overseas: . . . . No

HEMORRHOID CLINIC, THE

25 Weebetook Ln.
Cincinnati, OH 45212
TEL: (800) NO-HEMIS (510) 839-5471
FAX: (510) 547-3256
Dr. Robert D. H. Anning, President

Highly efficient and automated out-patient clinics for hemorrhoid and related rectal procedures. Proprietary laser TECHNIQUES developed by Dr. Anning insure painless, 20-minute procedure and minimal recuperative discomfort. Lucrative business that takes advantage of the fact that 1 in 8 adults requires rectal surgery. 12 wk. training at headquarters clinic. All procedures on video. Excellent opportunity to work with the best!

HISTORY: . . . .
Established in 1987; . . 1st Franchised in 1988
Company-Owned Units (As of 8/31/1992): . .6
Franchised Units (As of 8/31/1992): 8
Total Units (As of 8/31/1992): 14
Projected New Units for 1993: 2
Distribution: US-12;Can-2;Overseas-0
  North America: . . . . . 5 States, 2 Provinces
  Concentration: . . . 3 in OH, 2 in KY, 2 in MS
Registered: . . . . CA,FL,IL
. . . .
Type Space: . . . . . FS, SF;~1,500-2,000 SF

FINANCIAL: Earnings Claim: . Yes
Cash Investment: $80-125K
Total Investment: $140-225K
Fees: Franchise - $25K
  Royalty: 6%, Advert: 1%
Contract Periods (Yrs.): 10/10
Area Development Agreement: Yes/10
Sub-Franchise Contract: . . . . . Yes
Expand in Territory: . . . . Yes
Passive Ownership: . . . Not Allowed
Encourage Conversions: . . . . . Yes
Average # Employees: . . 3 FT, 4 PT

FRANCHISOR TRAINING/SUPPORT:
Financial Assistance Provided: . . . Yes(I)
Site Selection Assistance: . . . . .Yes
Lease Negotiation Assistance: . . . .Yes
Co-operative Advertising: . . . . . . .Yes
Training: . . . . . . 12 Wks. Anning Clinic,
. . . . .3 Wks. On-Site, On-Going Video
On-Going Support: C,D,E,G,H,I/ 12
EXPANSION PLANS:
US: . . . . All US
Canada: . . . . Ontario Only
Overseas: . . . . . . UK, AU, NZ

MEDI STOP

English Creek Ctr., Blackhorse Pike
McKee City, NJ 08232
TEL: (800) 755-MEDI (609) 625-4400
FAX: (609) 646-5523
Mr. Donald DuBeck, Director

MEDI STOP is a family practice - "Your Family Doctor." No appointments, open 7 days, lab, EKG, one-stop medical center.

HISTORY: . . . .
Established in 1989; . . 1st Franchised in 1991
Company-Owned Units (As of 8/31/1992): . .4
Franchised Units (As of 8/31/1992): 0
Total Units (As of 8/31/1992): 4
Projected New Units for 1993: 4
Distribution: US-4;Can-0;Overseas-0
  North America: . . . . .1 State
  Concentration: . . . . 4 in NJ
Registered: . . . .
. . . .
Type Space: . . . . . . FS, SC, RM;~4,800 SF

FINANCIAL: Earnings Claim: . Yes
Cash Investment: . . . .$
Total Investment: $180-250K
Fees: Franchise - $39K
  Royalty: 9%, Advert: 2%
Contract Periods (Yrs.): 10/10
Area Development Agreement: . .No
Sub-Franchise Contract: . . . . .No
Expand in Territory: . . . . Yes
Passive Ownership: . . . Discouraged
Encourage Conversions: . . . . NA
Average # Employees: . . 4 FT, 2 PT

FRANCHISOR TRAINING/SUPPORT:
Financial Assistance Provided: . . . Yes(I)
Site Selection Assistance: . . . . . . .Yes
Lease Negotiation Assistance: . . . .Yes
Co-operative Advertising: . . . . . . .Yes
Training: . . . . . . 30 Days Headquarters,
. . . . .30 Days On-Site
On-Going Support: a,B,C,D,E,F,h/ . . . 18
EXPANSION PLANS:
US: . . . . Mid-Atlantic States
Canada: . . . . No
Overseas: . . . . No

MIRACLE-EAR

4101 Dahlberg Dr.
Golden Valley, MN 55422
TEL: (800) 234-7714 (612) 520-9520
FAX: (612) 520-9575
Ms. Becky Bates, Fran. Licensing

Manufacturer and distributor of hearing instruments.

HISTORY: . . . . IFA	FINANCIAL: Earnings Claim: . .No	FRANCHISOR TRAINING/SUPPORT:
Established in 1948; . . 1st Franchised in 1983	Cash Investment: $20-50K	Financial Assistance Provided: . . . . .No
Company-Owned Units (As of 8/31/1992): . 13	Total Investment: $60-100K	Site Selection Assistance: . . . . . . .Yes
Franchised Units (As of 8/31/1992): 775	Fees: Franchise - $20K	Lease Negotiation Assistance: . . . . .No
Total Units (As of 8/31/1992): 788	Royalty: $38/Aid, Advert: . Varies	Co-operative Advertising: . . . . . . .Yes
Projected New Units for 1993: 250	Contract Periods (Yrs.): 5/5	Training: . . . . . . 2 Wks. Headquarters
Distribution: US-785;Can-0;Overseas-3	Area Development Agreement: . .No	. . . .
North America: . . . . 50 States	Sub-Franchise Contract: . . . . .No	On-Going Support: A,C,D,G,h/ 932
Concentration: . .88 in CA, 69 in FL, 42 in TX	Expand in Territory: . . . . . . Yes	EXPANSION PLANS:
Registered: . . . . .All	Passive Ownership: . . . Discouraged	US: . . . . South
. . . .	Encourage Conversions: . . . . Yes	Canada: . . . . .No
Type Space: . . . . .SF, SF, SC, RM;~650 SF	Average # Employees: . . 5 FT, 2 PT	Overseas: . . JA, Singapore, Thai., Taipei

MOBILITY CENTER

6693 Dixie Hwy.
Bridgeport, MI 48722
TEL: (800) 821-2710 (517) 777-6537 C
FAX: (517) 777-8184
Mr. Richard E. Zimmer, Fran. Ops.

A retail sales and service outlet, carrying products for mobility-impaired individuals or anyone with difficulty walking. For either a residential or commercial use.

HISTORY: . . . . IFA	FINANCIAL: Earnings Claim: . .No	FRANCHISOR TRAINING/SUPPORT:
Established in 1968; . . 1st Franchised in 1984	Cash Investment: $40-50K	Financial Assistance Provided: . . . . .No
Company-Owned Units (As of 8/31/1992): . .3	Total Investment: $80-100K	Site Selection Assistance: . . . . . . .Yes
Franchised Units (As of 8/31/1992): 7	Fees: Franchise - $2K	Lease Negotiation Assistance: . . . .Yes
Total Units (As of 8/31/1992): 10	Royalty: 5-4-3%, Advert: 1%	Co-operative Advertising: . . . . . . .Yes
Projected New Units for 1993: 10	Contract Periods (Yrs.): 10/5	Training: . . . . 7 Days Headquarters,
Distribution: US-10;Can-0;Overseas-0	Area Development Agreement: . .No	. . . . .7-10 Days Franchise Center
North America: . . . . 7 States	Sub-Franchise Contract: . . . . .No	On-Going Support: A,C,D,E,F,G,H,I/ . . 5
Concentration: . . . . 3 in MI, 2 in FL, 1 in TX	Expand in Territory: . . . . . . Yes	EXPANSION PLANS:
Registered: . . . . FL,IL,IN,MI	Passive Ownership: . . . Discouraged	US: . . . . Midwest
. . . .	Encourage Conversions: . . . . Yes	Canada: . . . . .No
Type Space: . . . . SF;~1,800 SF	Average # Employees: . . . . . .3 FT	Overseas: . . . . No

NUVISION

2284 S. Ballenger Hwy., Box 2600
Flint, MI 48501
TEL: (800) 733-5468 (313) 767-0900
FAX: (313) 767-6390
Mr. Patrick Welch, VP Fran.

NUVISION, INC. markets prescription eyewear, contact lenses, sunglasses and related optical products. The company owns and operates a modern ophthalmic laboratory and distribution facility, providing laboratory services and eyecare products to company-operated and franchised stores. Mega-Labs in many locations provide glasses in about an hour. All locations provide optometry services.

HISTORY: . . . . IFA	FINANCIAL: Earnings Claim: . Yes	FRANCHISOR TRAINING/SUPPORT:
Established in 1956; . . 1st Franchised in 1983	Cash Investment: $20-200K	Financial Assistance Provided: . . . . .Yes
Company-Owned Units (As of 8/31/1992): 111	Total Investment: $50K-1.0MM	Site Selection Assistance: . . . . . . .Yes
Franchised Units (As of 8/31/1992): 36	Fees: Franchise - $15K	Lease Negotiation Assistance: . . . .Yes
Total Units (As of 8/31/1992): 147	Royalty: 7%, Advert: 8.5%	Co-operative Advertising: . . . . . . .Yes
Projected New Units for 1993: 5	Contract Periods (Yrs.): . . . 10/10	Training: . . . . On-Going Corporate,
Distribution: US-147;Can-0;Overseas-0	Area Development Agreement: . Yes	. . . . .On-Going Franchisee Site
North America: . . . . 4 States	Sub-Franchise Contract: . . . . .No	On-Going Support: b,C,D,E,G,H,I/ . . . 99
Concentration: . . . . 86 in MI, 18 in IN	Expand in Territory: . . . . . . .No	EXPANSION PLANS:
Registered: . . . . .All	Passive Ownership: . . . Discouraged	US: . . . . MI, IN and NJ
. . . .	Encourage Conversions: . . . . Yes	Canada: . . . . .No
Type Space: FS, SF, SC, RM;~1,200-4,000 SF	Average # Employees:	Overseas: . . . . No

O2 EMERGENCY MEDICAL CARE SERVICE

5950 Pinetree Dr.
W. Bloomfield, MI 48322
TEL: (313) 661-0581
FAX: (313) 661-0581
Mr. Donald M. Stern, President

A sales/marketing franchise that provides an emergency medical program, including emergency oxygen equipment, first aid kits, first aid training and equipment maintenance to all businesses, organizations, facilities and government offices.

HISTORY:	
Established in 1986; . . . 1st Franchised in 1989	
Company-Owned Units (As of 8/31/1992): . . 1	
Franchised Units (As of 8/31/1992): 6	
Total Units (As of 8/31/1992): 7	
Projected New Units for 1993: 6	
Distribution: US-7;Can-0;Overseas-0	
North America: . . . . 3 States	
Concentration: . . . . 3 in MI, 2 in FL, 2 in PA	
Registered: . . . . FL,HI,IN,MI,OR,RI,WA,WI	
Type Space: . . . . ;~300-400 SF	

FINANCIAL: Earnings Claim: . .No	
Cash Investment: $27-30K	
Total Investment: $33-54K	
Fees: Franchise - $12.5K	
Royalty: Varies, Advert: 3%	
Contract Periods (Yrs.): . . 12/12/12	
Area Development Agreement: Yes/10	
Sub-Franchise Contract: . . . . .No	
Expand in Territory: . . . . . . Yes	
Passive Ownership: . . . Discouraged	
Encourage Conversions: . . . . . Yes	
Average # Employees: . . . . . .1 PT	

FRANCHISOR TRAINING/SUPPORT:	
Financial Assistance Provided: . . .Yes(D)	
Site Selection Assistance: . . . . .NA	
Lease Negotiation Assistance: . . . . .NA	
Co-operative Advertising: . . . . .NA	
Training: . . . . Minimum 5 Days	
. . . . Headquarters	
On-Going Support: B,C,D,G,H,I/ 5	
EXPANSION PLANS:	
US: . . . . .All US	
Canada: . . . . .All Exc. Alberta	
Overseas: . . . . .Yes	

PEARLE VISION CENTER

2534 Royal Ln.
Dallas, TX 75229
TEL: (800) PEARLE1 (214) 277-5000
FAX: (214) 277-5979
Mr. Greg A. Downling, Dir. New Bus.

PEARLE VISION operates full-service eyecare centers. As permitted by law, professional eye examinations are provided through affiliated doctors of optometry or ophthalmologists. Quality optical products, both prescription and non-prescription, are dispensed through well-trained opticians and sales associates.

HISTORY: . . . . IFA	
Established in 1961; . . 1st Franchised in 1980	
Company-Owned Units (As of 8/31/1992): 539	
Franchised Units (As of 8/31/1992): 531	
Total Units (As of 8/31/1992): 1070	
Projected New Units for 1993:	
Distribution: . . . US-914;Can-0;Overseas-156	
North America:	
Concentration:	
Registered: . . . . . HI,IL,MI,MN,VA,SD,WI	
Type Space: . . . . . FS, SC, RM;~2,000 SF	

FINANCIAL: Earnings Claim: . .No	
Cash Investment: $46-200K	
Total Investment: . . .$33.2K-3.6MM	
Fees: Franchise - $30K	
Royalty: 7.5%, Advert: 9%	
Contract Periods (Yrs.): . . . 10/10	
Area Development Agreement: . .No	
Sub-Franchise Contract: . . . . . .No	
Expand in Territory: . . . . . . Yes	
Passive Ownership: . . . . . .Allowed	
Encourage Conversions: . . . . . Yes	
Average # Employees: . . 3 FT, 2 PT	

FRANCHISOR TRAINING/SUPPORT:	
Financial Assistance Provided: . . .Yes(D)	
Site Selection Assistance: . . . . . . .Yes	
Lease Negotiation Assistance: . . . . .Yes	
Co-operative Advertising: . . . . .Yes	
Training: . . . . .12-16 Days Headquarters,	
. . . . . 12-16 Days 4 Regional Facilities	
On-Going Support: C,G,h,I/	
EXPANSION PLANS:	
US: . . . . . . All US Exc. CA and WA	
Canada: . . . . .All Canada	
Overseas: . . . . Yes	

PROCARE VISION CENTERS

926 N. 21st St.
Newark, OH 43055
TEL: (614) 366-7011 C
FAX: (614) 366-5453
Dr. Frank Bickle, President

PROCARE provides vision care services and products through franchises owned and operated by licensed vision care professionals.

HISTORY: . . . . IFA	
Established in 1981; . . 1st Franchised in 1985	
Company-Owned Units (As of 8/31/1992): . .1	
Franchised Units (As of 8/31/1992): 19	
Total Units (As of 8/31/1992): 20	
Projected New Units for 1993: 12	
Distribution: US-20;Can-0;Overseas-0	
North America: . . . . 2 States	
Concentration: . . . . . 19 in OH, 1 in WV	
Registered:	
Type Space: . . . . . . FS, SC, RM;~2,000 SF	

FINANCIAL: Earnings Claim: . .No	
Cash Investment: $0-30K	
Total Investment: $30-200K	
Fees: Franchise - $6K	
Royalty: 5%, Advert: 1%	
Contract Periods (Yrs.): . . . 10/10	
Area Development Agreement: . .No	
Sub-Franchise Contract: . . . . . .No	
Expand in Territory: . . . . . . Yes	
Passive Ownership: . . . Not Allowed	
Encourage Conversions: . . . . . Yes	
Average # Employees: . . 3 FT, 2 PT	

FRANCHISOR TRAINING/SUPPORT:	
Financial Assistance Provided: . . . Yes(I)	
Site Selection Assistance: . . . . . . .Yes	
Lease Negotiation Assistance: . . . . .Yes	
Co-operative Advertising: . . . . . . .Yes	
Training: . . . . .1 Wk. Headquarters,	
. . . . 3 Days Franchisee Site	
On-Going Support: B,C,D,E,F,G,H,I/ . . . 7	
EXPANSION PLANS:	
US: . . . . Ohio and West Virginia	
Canada: . . . . No	
Overseas: . . . . No	

READING GLASSES-TO-GO

9131 King Arthur Dr.
Dallas, TX 75247
TEL: (214) 631-6082
FAX: (214) 688-1046
Mr. Robert Granoff, President

An up-scale boutique that sells only non-prescription reading glasses. No optical expertise is needed, just a professional attitude to complement the clean, inviting boutique atmosphere. You stock a huge selection of exclusive, top designer-look reading glasses of the highest optical quality and price ranges from $16 to $49. Your clientele is the enormous 40+ market, plus the 77 million baby boomers joining them.

HISTORY: . . . .
Established in 1987; . . 1st Franchised in 1992
Company-Owned Units (As of 8/31/1992): . .8
Franchised Units (As of 8/31/1992): 0
Total Units (As of 8/31/1992): 8
Projected New Units for 1993: 9
Distribution: US-8;Can-0;Overseas-0
  North America: . . . . 2 States
  Concentration: . . . . 6 in TX, 2 in OK
Registered: . . . . CA,FL,OR,DC
. . . .
Type Space: . . . . .SC;~800 SF

FINANCIAL: Earnings Claim: . .No
Cash Investment: $71.9K
Total Investment: $102.9K
Fees: Franchise - $19K
  Royalty: 6%, Advert: 5%
Contract Periods (Yrs.): 5/5
Area Development Agreement: Yes/5
Sub-Franchise Contract: . . . . .No
Expand in Territory: . . . . . . Yes
Passive Ownership: . . . Not Allowed
Encourage Conversions: . . . . . NA
Average # Employees: . 1 FT, 1/2 PT

FRANCHISOR TRAINING/SUPPORT:
Financial Assistance Provided: . . . . .No
Site Selection Assistance: . . . . . . .Yes
Lease Negotiation Assistance: . . . .Yes
Co-operative Advertising: . . . . . . .No
Training: . . . .10-12 Days Headquarters,
. . . . 7 Days Store Site
On-Going Support: A,B,C,D,E,F,H,I/ . . . 6
EXPANSION PLANS:
  US: . . . . .Southwest
  Canada: . . . . .No
  Overseas: . . . . No

SINGER / SPECS

1909 Chestnut St.
Philadelphia, PA 19103
TEL: (800) 343-4786 (215) 270-8814
FAX: (215) 569-8610
Mr. Alan Singer, President

SINGER/SPECS offers the franchising option which allows professionals to compete with the big optical chains and superstores. Our philosophy allows the owner/operator to retain the commitment to quality care while SINGER/SPECS provides a comprehensive practice management system, including everything from site selection and power buying to proven merchandising and traffic generating techniques.

HISTORY: . . . .
Established in 1946; . . 1st Franchised in 1986
Company-Owned Units (As of 8/31/1992): . .5
Franchised Units (As of 8/31/1992): 26
Total Units (As of 8/31/1992): 31
Projected New Units for 1993: 23
Distribution: US-31;Can-0;Overseas-0
  North America: . . . . 5 States
  Concentration: . . . 16 in PA, 5 in DE, 4 in NJ
Registered: . . . . .MD,NY,VA
. . . .
Type Space: . . Power Center, RM;~1,500 SF

FINANCIAL: Earnings Claim: . .No
Cash Investment: $20-30K
Total Investment: $99-139K
Fees: Franchise - $15K
  Royalty: 7%, Advert: 4%
Contract Periods (Yrs.): 10/5
Area Development Agreement: . .No
Sub-Franchise Contract: . . . . Yes
Expand in Territory: . . . . . . Yes
Passive Ownership: . . . Not Allowed
Encourage Conversions: . . . . Yes
Average # Employees: 2-5 FT, 2-4 PT

FRANCHISOR TRAINING/SUPPORT:
Financial Assistance Provided: . . . . .Yes
Site Selection Assistance: . . . . . . .Yes
Lease Negotiation Assistance: . . . . .Yes
Co-operative Advertising: . . . . . . .Yes
Training: . . . . .7-10 Days Various
. . . . Locations
On-Going Support: C,D,E,F,G,H,I/ . . . 12
EXPANSION PLANS:
  US: . . . . . . East Coast, Midwest, SW
  Canada: . . . . .No
  Overseas: . . . . No

SUPPLEMENTAL LISTING OF FRANCHISORS

ACCU + MED . . . . P. O. Box 6226, Rutland, VT 05701
  Contact: President; Tel: (802) 775-2727
ACI AUDITORY CENTERS . . . . 9203 W. Bluemound Rd., Milwaukee, WI 53226
  Contact: President; Tel: (414) 273-2434
AMERICA'S DOCTORS OF OPTOMETRY . . . . 505 State St., Tracy, MN 56175
  Contact: President; Tel:
AMERICAN PHYSICAL REHABILITATION NETWK 4050 Talmadge Rd., P. O. Box 8864, Toledo, OH 43623
  Contact: Mr. Harvey Bowles, CFO; Tel: (800) 331-3058 (419) 474-0507
AMERICARE DENTAL CENTERS USA . . . . .P. O. Box 35365, Phoenix, AZ 85069
  Contact: Mr. Bernard Serbin; Tel: (602) 995-3368
ARCH CRAFTERS FOOT STORES . . . . 11324 Tuck Ct., # 2, Indianapolis, IN 46229
  Contact: Mr. Mark Shiveley; Tel: (317) 576-0626
BROOKS DENTAL LAB . . . . .7501 Stiller Lake Rd., Pensacola, FL 32506
  Contact: Mr. Ken Brooks, President; Tel: (800) 222-5175 (904) 944-5175
CARDIO-FITNESS CORP. . . . . 444 Madison Ave., New York, NY 10022
  Contact: President; Tel: (212) 319-5400
CARING CONCEPTS . . . . 469 7th Ave., New York, NY 10018
  Contact: Mr. Lawrence Kaplan, President; Tel: (800) 321-2856 (212) 564-3400

CHALL-AIDE MEDICAL PRODUCTS . . . . .P. O. Box 99, Sparta, NJ 07871
    Contact: Mr. Roger Day, VP; Tel: (201) 383-0705
CHS DENTAL LABORATORIES . . . . .955 Dairy Ashford, # 222, Houston, TX 77079
    Contact: Mr. Paul Hilliard, Mktg. Dir.; Tel: (606) 278-1111
CLAFLIN HOME HEALTH CENTERS . . . . . . .486 Silver Spring St., Providence, RI 02904
    Contact: Mr. Richard Westlake, President; Tel: (401) 331-0154
COHEN'S FASHION OPTICAL . . . . 1175 Broadway, Hewlett, NY 11557
    Contact: President; Tel: (516) 295-9494
COMMONWEALTH CLINICAL SYSTEMS . . . . .1650 State Farm Blvd., Charlottesville, VA 22901
    Contact: President; Tel: (804) 977-1867
CONCEPT CARE . . . . 3160 5th Ave. N., # 101, St. Petersburg, FL 33713
    Contact: President; Tel:
CONSUMER DENTAL NETWORK . . . . . . .1401 Dove St., # 290, Newport Beach, CA 92660
    Contact: Mr. Bob Milunas, VP; Tel: (714) 752-8522
D & K OPTICAL . . . . 4415 Poplar Level Rd., PO Box 37410, Louisville, KY 40233
    Contact: President; Tel: (502) 459-6722
D. O. C. OPTICS CORPORATION . . . . 19800 W. Eight Mile Rd., Southfield, MI 48075
    Contact: Mr. Chuck Males, VP; Tel: (313) 354-7100
DENTAL STORE, THE . . . . 1010 Grove Mall, Elk Grove Village, IL 60007
    Contact: President; Tel: (312) 439-0550
DENTAL WORLD CENTER . . . . 900 Elisson Ave., # LL, Westbury, NY 11590
    Contact: President; Tel: (516) 742-4200
DR. SCOTT'S OPTICAL OUTLET . . . . 1323 Jackson St., Omaha, NE 68102
    Contact: Mr. Sheldon Rips, President; Tel: (800) 999-3059 (402) 342-0959
EAR LABS . . . . 405 N. Palm Canyon Dr., Palm Springs, CA 92262
    Contact: Mr. Robert De Castro; Tel:
ELECTRIC MOBILITY CENTER . . . . 1 Mobility Plaza, Sewell, NJ 08080
    Contact: President; Tel:
EYEGLASS EMPORIUM . . . . .8120 Georgia St., Merrillville, IN 46410
    Contact: Mr. Atse Krstevski, President; Tel: (219) 736-1366
EYESUPPLY . . . . 51-00 Northern Blvd., Woodside, NY 11377
    Contact: President; Tel: (718) 429-2020
FAMILY DENTAL CENTER . . . . 3690 Orange Pl., # 310, Beachwood, OH 44122
    Contact: President; Tel: (216) 464-4042
HARMONY HEALTH SERVICES . . . . .1151 E. Warrenville Rd., Naperville, IL 60566
    Contact: President; Tel: (312) 357-4800
HEALTH QUEST CORP. . . . . .315 W. Jefferson Blvd., South Bend, IN 46601
    Contact: President; Tel:
HEALTHCALL . . . . .728 N. 7th St., Milwaukee, WI 53233
    Contact: President; Tel: (800) 558-7130 (414) 278-0606
INDEPENDENT MEDICAL ASSESSMENT GROUP . .1405 Coraopolis Heights Rd., Coraopolis, PA 15108
    Contact: Mr. Mark R. Lando; Tel: (412) 264-7008
JONATHON DENTAL . . . . 5909 Baker Rd., # 575, Minnetonka, MN 55345
    Contact: Mr. Dan Racine; Tel: (612) 936-2222
LIFECALL SYSTEMS . . . . 1300 Admiral Wilson Blvd., Camden, NJ 08101
    Contact: President; Tel: (609) 963-5433
MOTHERTIME . . . . .140 Christie St., Leonia, NJ 07605
    Contact: President; Tel: (201) 585-0846
NUMEDCO . . . . .24 N. Cliffe Dr., Wilmington, DE 19809
    Contact: Mr. Melvin D. Messinger; Tel: (800) 992-0243
OPTICAL FRANCHISING CO. . . . . 1323 Jackson St., Omaha, NE 68102
    Contact: President; Tel: (402) 342-0953
OPTOMETRIC EYE CARE CENTER . . . . 2309 Sunset Ave., Rocky Mount, NC 27804
    Contact: Dr. Blair Harrold, President; Tel: (800) 334-3937 (919) 937-6650
OXYGEN THERAPY INSTITUTE . . . . . . .1835 Moriah Woods Blvd., # 1, Memphis, TN 38117
    Contact: Mr. Jim Van Cleave, President; Tel: (800) 521-4836 (901) 684-1197
ROONEY OPTICAL . . . . .5440 West 164th St., Cleveland, OH 44142
    Contact: President; Tel: (216) 267-5600
SITE FOR SORE EYES . . . . 3512 Breakwater Court, Hayward, CA 94545
    Contact: Mr. Paul Licht, President; Tel: (800) 767-7483 (510) 732-8900
TEXAS STATE OPTICAL . . . . .2534 Royal Ln., Dallas, TX 75229
    Contact: Mr. James T. Rothe, President; Tel: (214) 241-3381 (214) 247-3421
WESTERN MEDICAL SERVICES . . . . 301 Lennon Ln., Walnut Creek, CA 94598
    Contact: Mr. A. Terry Slocum, SVP Fran. Sales; Tel: (800) 872-8367 (510) 930-5300

CHAPTER 31

PET PRODUCTS AND SERVICES

CANINE COUNSELORS

3570 Consumer St., # 8
West Palm Beach, FL 33404
TEL: (800) 456-3647 (407) 863-5370
FAX:
Mr. Robert Ward, President

CANINE COUNSELOR offers a full range of professional dog training and animal behavior training programs. Each franchise has its staff broken into 3 specialties: 1) administrative; 2) sales and public relations; and 3) professional dog training staff. This is a very exciting way to train dogs and a great opportunity to earn excellent income working in the pet industry.

HISTORY: . . . .
Established in 1982; . . 1st Franchised in 1988
Company-Owned Units (As of 8/31/1992): . .1
Franchised Units (As of 8/31/1992): 5
Total Units (As of 8/31/1992): 6
Projected New Units for 1993: 6
Distribution: US-6;Can-0;Overseas-0
North America: . . . . .1 State
Concentration: . . . . 6 in FL
Registered: . . . . .FL
. . . .
Type Space: . . . SF, SC, Exec. Ste;~1,000 SF

FINANCIAL: Earnings Claim: . . .No
Cash Investment: $30-40K
Total Investment: $40-50K
Fees: Franchise - $29K
Royalty: 7%, Advert: 2%
Contract Periods (Yrs.): 10/10
Area Development Agreement: Yes/10
Sub-Franchise Contract: . . . . . .No
Expand in Territory: . . . . Yes
Passive Ownership: . . . Discouraged
Encourage Conversions: . . . . . .No
Average # Employees: . . . . 6-8 FT

FRANCHISOR TRAINING/SUPPORT:
Financial Assistance Provided: . . . . .Yes
Site Selection Assistance: . . . . . . .Yes
Lease Negotiation Assistance: . . . . .Yes
Co-operative Advertising: . . . . .Yes
Training: . . . . 2 Wks. Headquarters,
. . . . .2 Wks. Franchisee Location
On-Going Support: A,B,c,d,E,G,H,I/ . . . 5
EXPANSION PLANS:
US: . . . . . . Southeast and East Coast
Canada: . . . . No
Overseas: . . . . No

CRITTER CARE

1825 Darren Dr.
Baton Rouge, LA 70816
TEL: (504) 273-3356
FAX: (504) 293-2901
Ms. Pamela Runnels, President

CRITTER CARE is a customized concept in the care of pets, home and plants. We make calls to the customer's home to meet their individual needs while they are away. We have developed a profitable, professional home care service that now includes a 1-800-256-3014 national travel line, specializing in animal transportation and people travel services. We have a proprietary pet stain and odor remover. There are 6 additional "value-added" services.

HISTORY:	FINANCIAL: Earnings Claim: . .No	FRANCHISOR TRAINING/SUPPORT:
Established in 1980; . . 1st Franchised in 1984	Cash Investment: $5-15K	Financial Assistance Provided: . . .Yes(D)
Company-Owned Units (As of 8/31/1992): . .3	Total Investment: $3-10K	Site Selection Assistance: . . . . .NA
Franchised Units (As of 8/31/1992): 31	Fees: Franchise - $3-10K	Lease Negotiation Assistance: . . . . .NA
Total Units (As of 8/31/1992): 34	Royalty: 5% Max., Advert: 2% Max.	Co-operative Advertising: . . . . .Yes
Projected New Units for 1993: 12	Contract Periods (Yrs.): 10/5	Training: . . . . . . 5 15-Hr. Days at HQ, 2
Distribution: US-30;Can-0;Overseas-0	Area Development Agreement: . Yes	. . . . . .Days On-Site, 2 Days Annually
North America: . . . . 15 States	Sub-Franchise Contract: . . . . .No	On-Going Support: A,B,C,D,E,f,g,h,I/ . . 5
Concentration: . . . .6 in TX, 6 in PA, 4 in LA	Expand in Territory: . . . . Yes	EXPANSION PLANS:
Registered: . . . . .CA,FL,IL,IN,MN,NY,WA	Passive Ownership: . . . Discouraged	US: . . . . .All US
. . . .	Encourage Conversions: . . . . . Yes	Canada: . . . . .All Canada
Type Space: . . . . ;~ SF	Average # Employees: 4-5 FT, 2-4 PT	Overseas: .UK, FR, IT, JP, AU, GR

DOCKTOR PET CENTERS

355 Middlesex Ave.
Wilmington, MA 01887
TEL: (800) 765-4PET (508) 658-7840
FAX: (508) 657-6193
Mr. Ira Rashap, Dir. Fran. Dev.

Department store for pets. Full line of pets and pet supplies. Located in regional shopping centers. Offering a state-of-the-art program to assure that your puppies come from reputable breeders. Extensive corporate and field support. Strong private label and distribution program.

HISTORY: . . . . IFA	FINANCIAL: Earnings Claim: . .No	FRANCHISOR TRAINING/SUPPORT:
Established in 1937; . . 1st Franchised in 1967	Cash Investment: $50-100K	Financial Assistance Provided: . . . Yes(I)
Company-Owned Units (As of 8/31/1992): . 28	Total Investment: . . . $129.5-280K	Site Selection Assistance: . . . . .Yes
Franchised Units (As of 8/31/1992): 107	Fees: Franchise - $15K	Lease Negotiation Assistance: . . . . .Yes
Total Units (As of 8/31/1992): 135	Royalty: 4.5%, Advert: 1/2%	Co-operative Advertising: . . . . .Yes
Projected New Units for 1993: 15	Contract Periods (Yrs.): 10/10	Training: . . . . 3 Wks. Headquarters
Distribution: US-135;Can-0;Overseas-0	Area Development Agreement: . .No	. . . .
North America: . . . . 30 States	Sub-Franchise Contract: . . . . .No	On-Going Support: B,C,D,E,F,G,H,I/ . . 32
Concentration: . 17 in NY, 16 in MD, 14 in PA	Expand in Territory: . . . . Yes	EXPANSION PLANS:
Registered: . . . . All States Exc. CA	Passive Ownership: . . . . . .Allowed	US: . . . . All US
. . . .	Encourage Conversions: . . . . . Yes	Canada: . . . . .Yes
Type Space: . . . . .SC, RM;~2,000-4,000 SF	Average # Employees: . . 4 FT, 8 PT	Overseas: . . . . No

PET HABITAT

6921 Heather St.
Vancouver, BC V6P 3P5 CAN
TEL: (604) 266-2721 C
FAX: (604) 266-5880
Mr. Ernest Ang, President

Retail pet shop. Very up-scale. Mall locations.

HISTORY:	FINANCIAL: Earnings Claim: . Yes	FRANCHISOR TRAINING/SUPPORT:
Established in 1980; . . 1st Franchised in 1981	Cash Investment: $50K	Financial Assistance Provided: . . . . .Yes
Company-Owned Units (As of 8/31/1992): . .2	Total Investment: $125-200K	Site Selection Assistance: . . . . .Yes
Franchised Units (As of 8/31/1992): 4	Fees: Franchise - $25K	Lease Negotiation Assistance: . . . .Yes
Total Units (As of 8/31/1992): 6	Royalty: 5%, Advert: 2%	Co-operative Advertising: . . . . .Yes
Projected New Units for 1993: 3	Contract Periods (Yrs.): 5/5	Training: . . . . . . .30 Days Headquarters
Distribution: US-0;Can-6;Overseas-0	Area Development Agreement: Yes/1	. . . .
North America: . . . . .1 Province	Sub-Franchise Contract: . . . . Yes	On-Going Support: a,b,C,D,E,F,H/ 6
Concentration: . . . . 6 in BC	Expand in Territory: . . . . Yes	EXPANSION PLANS:
Registered:	Passive Ownership: . . . Discouraged	US: . . . . Northwest
. . . .	Encourage Conversions: . . . . . Yes	Canada: . . . . .All Canada
Type Space: . . . . RM;~1,500 SF	Average # Employees: . . 3 FT, 3 PT	Overseas: . . . . Asia

PET NANNY OF AMERICA

1000 Long Blvd., # 9
Lansing, MI 48911
TEL: (517) 694-4400
FAX:
Ms. Rebecca A. Brevitz, President

PET NANNY franchises provide professional, personalized pet care in the pet's home while owners are away or otherwise unable to provide the care. Home-based operation. PET NANNY franchises are bonded, insured and trained via veterinarian-developed training program. Franchise fee includes exclusive territory, bond, training, operational and marketing materials for approximately first year of operation.

HISTORY:	FINANCIAL: Earnings Claim: . .No	FRANCHISOR TRAINING/SUPPORT:
Established in 1983; . . 1st Franchised in 1985	Cash Investment: $1.4-4.5K	Financial Assistance Provided: . . .Yes(D)
Company-Owned Units (As of 8/31/1992): . .2	Total Investment: . . . $10.1-13.2K	Site Selection Assistance: . . . . . . .Yes
Franchised Units (As of 8/31/1992): 18	Fees: Franchise - $8.7K	Lease Negotiation Assistance: . . . .NA
Total Units (As of 8/31/1992): 20	Royalty: 5%, Advert: 0%	Co-operative Advertising: . . . . . . .Yes
Projected New Units for 1993: 4	Contract Periods (Yrs.): 5/5	Training: . . . . . 4 Days Headquarters
Distribution: US-20;Can-0;Overseas-0	Area Development Agreement: Yes/10	
North America: . . . . 13 States	Sub-Franchise Contract: . . . . . Yes	On-Going Support: C,D,G,H/ . . . .
Concentration: . . . 4 in MI, 4 in OH, 2 in NY	Expand in Territory: . . . . .No	EXPANSION PLANS:
Registered: . . . . . FL,IL,IN,MD,MI,NY,OR	Passive Ownership: . . . . .Allowed	US: . . . . All US
	Encourage Conversions: . . . . . Yes	Canada: . . . . .All Exc. Alberta
Type Space: . . . . . . Home Based;~200 SF	Average # Employees: . 1 FT, 1-5 PT	Overseas: . . . . No

PET VALU

7300 Warden Ave., # 400
Markham, ON L3R 9Z6 CAN
TEL: (416) 946-1200
FAX: (416) 946-0659
Mr. Colin R. Freel, VP Fran. Dev.

PET VALU is a chain of specialty stores that feature exclusively pet foods, supplies and accessories. We concentrate on customer service, provide a wide selection of brands and product sizes, and offer everyday low, low prices on all products.

HISTORY:	FINANCIAL: Earnings Claim: . . Yes	FRANCHISOR TRAINING/SUPPORT:
Established in 1976; . . 1st Franchised in 1987	Cash Investment: $40K	Financial Assistance Provided: . . . . .No
Company-Owned Units (As of 8/31/1992): . 32	Total Investment: $90K	Site Selection Assistance: . . . . . . .Yes
Franchised Units (As of 8/31/1992): 114	Fees: Franchise - $12K	Lease Negotiation Assistance: . . . . .Yes
Total Units (As of 8/31/1992): 146	Royalty: 6%, Advert: 0%	Co-operative Advertising: . . . . . . .Yes
Projected New Units for 1993: 20	Contract Periods (Yrs.): . . . 6/4/5/5	Training: . . . . 3 Wks. Headquarters
Distribution: US-0;Can-146;Overseas-0	Area Development Agreement: . .No	
North America: . . . . .1 Province	Sub-Franchise Contract: . . . . . .No	On-Going Support: a,B,C,D,E,F,H/ . . .187
Concentration: . . . . .146 in ON	Expand in Territory: . . . . Yes	EXPANSION PLANS:
Registered:	Passive Ownership: . . . Not Allowed	US: . . . . .No
	Encourage Conversions: . . . . . Yes	Canada: . . . . .Ontario
Type Space: . . . . .SC;~1,500 SF	Average # Employees: . . 2 FT, 2 PT	Overseas: . . . . No

PET XTRA

7805 Arjons Dr.
San Diego, CA 92126
TEL: (800) 748-5577 (619) 693-3639
FAX: (619) 693-1120
Mr. Russell H. Harris, President

PET XTRA retail stores offer the customer a vast selection of high-quality pet food and accessories at reasonable prices. The franchisee receives a turn-key, modern, efficient, professionally-merchandised retail store. PET XTRA carries pet supplies only - no livestock.

HISTORY:	FINANCIAL: Earnings Claim: . .No	FRANCHISOR TRAINING/SUPPORT:
Established in 1973; . . 1st Franchised in 1984	Cash Investment: $75K	Financial Assistance Provided: . . . . .Yes
Company-Owned Units (As of 8/31/1992): . .7	Total Investment: $125K	Site Selection Assistance: . . . . . . .Yes
Franchised Units (As of 8/31/1992): 19	Fees: Franchise - $15K	Lease Negotiation Assistance: . . . .Yes
Total Units (As of 8/31/1992): 26	Royalty: 6%, Advert: 2%	Co-operative Advertising: . . . . . . .Yes
Projected New Units for 1993: 12	Contract Periods (Yrs.): 10/5	Training: . . . . . . 2 Wks. Headquarters
Distribution: US-26;Can-0;Overseas-0	Area Development Agreement: . Yes	
North America: . . . . 2 States	Sub-Franchise Contract: . . . . . .No	On-Going Support: A,B,C,D,E,F,G,H,I/ 12
Concentration: . . . . 24 in CA	Expand in Territory: . . . . Yes	EXPANSION PLANS:
Registered: . . . . CA,WA	Passive Ownership: . . . Discouraged	US: . . . . All US
	Encourage Conversions: . . . . . .No	Canada: . . . . No
Type Space: . . .Comm. Shop. Ctr.;~2,400 SF	Average # Employees: . . 2 FT, 2 PT	Overseas: . . . . No

SHAMPOO CHEZ

1380 Soquel Ave.
Santa Cruz, CA 95062
TEL: (800) 888-BATH (408) 427-BATH
FAX: (408) 457-2854
Ms. Anne Singer, President

Self-service dog wash, natural non-toxic pet supplies and professional dog and cat grooming.

HISTORY: . . . . IFA	FINANCIAL: Earnings Claim: . .No	FRANCHISOR TRAINING/SUPPORT:
Established in 1983; . . 1st Franchised in 1986	Cash Investment: $25K	Financial Assistance Provided: . . . . . No
Company-Owned Units (As of 8/31/1992): . .1	Total Investment: $60-77K	Site Selection Assistance: . . . . . . .Yes
Franchised Units (As of 8/31/1992): 2	Fees: Franchise - $15K	Lease Negotiation Assistance: . . . .Yes
Total Units (As of 8/31/1992): 3	Royalty: 3.5-5%, Advert: 2%	Co-operative Advertising: . . . . . . .Yes
Projected New Units for 1993: 4	Contract Periods (Yrs.): 10/10	Training: . . . . . 1 Wk. Min. Headquarters
Distribution: US-3;Can-0;Overseas-0	Area Development Agreement: . .No	. . . .
North America: . . . . .1 State	Sub-Franchise Contract: . . . . .No	On-Going Support: A,B,C,D,E,F/ 2
Concentration: . . . . 3 in CA	Expand in Territory: . . . . Yes	EXPANSION PLANS:
Registered: . . . . CA	Passive Ownership: . . . Discouraged	US: . . . . West Coast
. . . .	Encourage Conversions: . . . . . NA	Canada: . . . . .No
Type Space: . . . . . SF, SC;~1,800-2,000 SF	Average # Employees: . . 2 FT, 2 PT	Overseas: . . . . No

SUPPLEMENTAL LISTING OF FRANCHISORS

AQUARIUM WORLD . . . . .2625 Northchase Pkwy., SE, Wilmington, NC 28405
    Contact: President; Tel: (919) 799-8700
CAT'S PAJAMAS, THE . . . . P. O. Box 48, Lincolnville, ME 04849
    Contact: President; Tel: (207) 789-5139
CHERRYBROOK . . . . Box 15, Rte. 57, Broadway, NJ 08808
    Contact: Mr. Wayne Ferguson, President; Tel: (800) 524-0820 (908) 689-7979
DOG BARBER, THE . . . . 40 Skokie Blvd., # 430, Northbrook, IL 60062
    Contact: Ms. Jill Schmidt, Fran. Dir.; Tel: (708) 498-9965
DOG WASH . . . . 5724 SW Green Oaks Blvd., Arlington, TX 76017
    Contact: Ms. Jeannie Powell, VP Fran. Dev.; Tel: (817) 572-5106 C
GOING TO THE DOGS! . . . . 2760 Carousel Dr., # 1607, Glouster, ON K1T 2N4   CAN
    Contact: Ms. Jane Seymour; Tel: (613) 731-6116
KASTLE KEEPER . . . . 6955 Firethorn, Beaumont, TX 77708
    Contact: President; Tel: (409) 899-5434
LEASH & COLLAR, THE . . . . 6493 Aiken Rd., Lockport, NY 14094
    Contact: President; Tel: (716) 694-4035
LICK YOUR CHOPS . . . . .50 Water St., South Norwalk, CT 06854
    Contact: Ms. Susan Goldstein, President; Tel: (203) 854-5001
PET CITY . . . . 1325 S. Cherokee St., Denver, CO 80221
    Contact: President; Tel: (303) 744-6131
PETLAND . . . . .195 N. Hickory St., P.O. Box 1606, Chillicothe, OH 45601
    Contact: Mr. James L. Whitman, EVP; Tel: (800) 221-5935 (614) 775-2464
PETMART, THE PETSMART PEOPLE . . . . 7805 Arjons Dr., San Diego, CA 92126
    Contact: Mr. Russel H. Harris, President; Tel: (800) 748-5577 (619) 693-3639
PETS ARE INN . . . . 27 N. Fourth St., # 500, Minneapolis, MN 55401
    Contact: Mr. Harry Sanders-Greenberg, President; Tel: (800) 248-PETS (612) 339-6255
RUFFINS PET CENTRES . . . . .225 Queen St., Dunnville, ON N1A 1H8   CAN
    Contact: Mr. Mark Reynolds; Tel: (416) 774-7079

CHAPTER 32

PUBLICATIONS

AUTO SHOW WEEKLY

6030 S. Lindbergh Blvd.
St. Louis, MO 63123
TEL: (800) 521-5540 (314) 487-0054
FAX:
Mr. James Smoot, President

AUTO SHOW WEEKLY is a bi-weekly Buy-Sell-Trade magazine that features a spectacular showcase of vehicles for sale by private owners and licensed dealers. It has a full-color cover, entertaining articles and money-saving coupons that combine with the expensive look of a national magazine with the affordable cost of a local newspaper. It is a cost-effective and successful medium for your automotive advertisers.

HISTORY: . . . .
Established in 1991; . . 1st Franchised in 1992
Company-Owned Units (As of 8/31/1992): . .1
Franchised Units (As of 8/31/1992): 0
Total Units (As of 8/31/1992): 1
Projected New Units for 1993: 6
Distribution: US-1;Can-0;Overseas-0
  North America: . . . . .1 State
  Concentration: . . . . .1 in MO
Registered: . . . .
. . . .
Type Space: . . . . . . Office Suite;~1,000 SF

FINANCIAL: Earnings Claim: . .No
Cash Investment: $6-8K
Total Investment: $15-30K
Fees: Franchise - $6K
  Royalty: $75/Wk., Advert: $25/Wk.
Contract Periods (Yrs.): 5/10
Area Development Agreement: . .No
Sub-Franchise Contract: . . . . . .No
Expand in Territory: . . . . . . .Yes
Passive Ownership: . . . Discouraged
Encourage Conversions: . . . . . Yes
Average # Employees: . . 2 FT, 4 PT

FRANCHISOR TRAINING/SUPPORT:
Financial Assistance Provided: . . . . .No
Site Selection Assistance: . . . . . . .Yes
Lease Negotiation Assistance: . . . .Yes
Co-operative Advertising: . . . . . . .Yes
Training: . . . . 2 Wks. Headquarters
. . . .
On-Going Support: A,C,D,E,G,H,I/ 3
EXPANSION PLANS:
US: . . . . Midwest, Mid-South
Canada: . . . . .No
Overseas: . . . . No

BINGO BUGLE NEWSPAPER

P. O. Box 51189
Seattle, WA 98115
TEL: (800) 447-1958 (206) 527-4958 C
FAX: (206) 527-9756
Mr. Warren E. Kraft, Jr., President

The BINGO BUGLE is the nation's largest network of newspapers for bingo players. Listed in Entrepreneur's Annual Top Franchise. Franchise fees range from $1,500 to $6,000. Complete training and support. Relatively high income potential at modest cost. Call 1-800-447-1958 for details.

HISTORY: . . . .
Established in 1979; . . 1st Franchised in 1982
Company-Owned Units (As of 8/31/1992): . .0
Franchised Units (As of 8/31/1992): 66
Total Units (As of 8/31/1992): 66
Projected New Units for 1993: 6
Distribution: US-64;Can-2;Overseas-0
　North America: . . . . 33 States
　Concentration: . . . 12 in CA, 6 in FL, 5 in NY
Registered: . . . CA,FL,IL,IN,MN,NY,ND,OR
. . . . SD,VA
Type Space: . . . . . . Home Based, OB;~ SF

FINANCIAL: Earnings Claim: . .No
Cash Investment: $1.5-6K
Total Investment: $3.5-8K
Fees: Franchise - $1.5-6K
　Royalty: 10%, Advert: 0%
Contract Periods (Yrs.): 5
Area Development Agreement: . .No
Sub-Franchise Contract: . . . . .No
Expand in Territory: . . . . . . .No
Passive Ownership: . . . Discouraged
Encourage Conversions: . . . . NA
Average # Employees: . . 0 FT, 0 PT

FRANCHISOR TRAINING/SUPPORT:
Financial Assistance Provided: . . . . .No
Site Selection Assistance: . . . . . . .NA
Lease Negotiation Assistance: . . . . .NA
Co-operative Advertising: . . . . . . .NA
Training: . . . . .2.5 Days at Headquarters,
. . . . .or Franchisee City
On-Going Support: / 4
EXPANSION PLANS:
　US: . . . . NY, PA, AK +14 Other Cities
　Canada: . . . . .Yes
　Overseas: . . . . No

BRIDE'S DAY MAGAZINE

750 Hamburg Tnpk., # 208
Pompton Lakes, NJ 07442
TEL: (201) 835-6551
FAX: (201) 835-3639
Mr. David A. Gay, Publisher

Community bridal magazine, available free to brides. Profitability from local advertising revenue.

HISTORY: . . . .
Established in 1987; . . 1st Franchised in 1990
Company-Owned Units (As of 8/31/1992): . .2
Franchised Units (As of 8/31/1992): 8
Total Units (As of 8/31/1992): 10
Projected New Units for 1993: 4
Distribution: US-10;Can-0;Overseas-0
　North America: . . . .
　Concentration: . . . 2 in NJ, 2 in PA, 2 in MA
Registered: . . CA,FL,IL,MD,MI,MN,NY,VA
. . . .
Type Space: . . . . NA;~NA SF

FINANCIAL: Earnings Claim: . .No
Cash Investment: $14.9K
Total Investment: $14.9-16.5K
Fees: Franchise - $14.9K
　Royalty: 6%, Advert: 0%
Contract Periods (Yrs.): 5/5
Area Development Agreement: Yes/5
Sub-Franchise Contract: . . . . .No
Expand in Territory: . . . . . . Yes
Passive Ownership: . . . Discouraged
Encourage Conversions: . . . . NA
Average # Employees: . . 1 FT, 1 PT

FRANCHISOR TRAINING/SUPPORT:
Financial Assistance Provided: . . . . .No
Site Selection Assistance: . . . . . . .NA
Lease Negotiation Assistance: . . . .NA
Co-operative Advertising: . . . . . . .NA
Training: . . . . 3 Days Headquarters,
. . . . 2-3 Days On-Site
On-Going Support: A,B,C,D,/ 2
EXPANSION PLANS:
　US: . . . . .All US
　Canada: . . . . No
　Overseas: . . . . No

EXECUTIVE, THE

4518 Valleydale Rd., # 203-F
Birmingham, AL 35242
TEL: (800) 264-EXEC (205) 991-2970
FAX: (205) 991-2564
Mr. Kevin A. Foote, President

THE EXECUTIVE is a coupon-oriented business magazine that is distributed to employees of companies, businesses and residences. The business sells advertising to merchants and professionals wanting to reach an exclusive market of managers, secretaries, workers and others.

HISTORY: . . . .
Established in 1987; . . 1st Franchised in 1989
Company-Owned Units (As of 8/31/1992): . .1
Franchised Units (As of 8/31/1992): 5
Total Units (As of 8/31/1992): 6
Projected New Units for 1993: 4
Distribution: US-8;Can-0;Overseas-0
　North America: . . . . 4 States
　Concentration: . . . . 3 in AL
Registered: . . . . .CA,FL
. . . .
Type Space: . . . . . . Home Based, OB;~ SF

FINANCIAL: Earnings Claim: . Yes
Cash Investment: $15K
Total Investment: $15K
Fees: Franchise - $8-22K
　Royalty: 5%, Advert: 0%
Contract Periods (Yrs.): 5/5
Area Development Agreement: . Yes
Sub-Franchise Contract: . . . . Yes
Expand in Territory: . . . . . . Yes
Passive Ownership: . . . . .Allowed
Encourage Conversions: . . . . Yes
Average # Employees: . . 1 FT, 1 PT

FRANCHISOR TRAINING/SUPPORT:
Financial Assistance Provided: . . . .NA
Site Selection Assistance: . . . . . . .NA
Lease Negotiation Assistance: . . . .NA
Co-operative Advertising: . . . . . . .No
Training: . . . . 3 Days Headquarters
. . . .
On-Going Support: D,E,H/ 1
EXPANSION PLANS:
　US: . . . . .All US
　Canada: . . . . .All Canada
　Overseas: . . . . EUR, Asia

FINDERBINDER/SOURCEBOOK DIRECTORIES

4679 Vista St.
San Diego, CA 92116
TEL: (800) 255-2575 (619) 284-1145
FAX: (619) 284-6290
Mr. Gary Beals, CEO

The FINDERBINDER News Media Directory and the SOURCE BOOK Directory of Clubs and Associations are locally-produced reference books created by existing communications firms, such as an advertising agency or public relations consultants. It is an added profit center that builds public awareness for the local company.

HISTORY:	FINANCIAL: Earnings Claim: . .No	FRANCHISOR TRAINING/SUPPORT:
Established in 1973; . . 1st Franchised in 1978	Cash Investment: $6-12K	Financial Assistance Provided: . . . . .No
Company-Owned Units (As of 8/31/1992): . .2	Total Investment: $10-15K	Site Selection Assistance: . . . . .NA
Franchised Units (As of 8/31/1992): 20	Fees: Franchise - . . . .$	Lease Negotiation Assistance: . . . .NA
Total Units (As of 8/31/1992): 22	Royalty: 5+%, Advert: 0%	Co-operative Advertising: . . . . . . .Yes
Projected New Units for 1993: 3	Contract Periods (Yrs.): . . . Infinite	Training: . . . . 1 Day On-Site
Distribution: US-22;Can-0;Overseas-0	Area Development Agreement: . .No	
North America: . . . . 13 States	Sub-Franchise Contract: . . . . .No	On-Going Support: b,C,D,G,H,I/ 4
Concentration: . . . 4 in CA, 2 in MO, 2 in TX	Expand in Territory: . . . . Yes	EXPANSION PLANS:
Registered: . . . . CA	Passive Ownership: . . . Discouraged	US: . . . . All US
	Encourage Conversions: . . . . . .No	Canada: . . . . .All Canada
Type Space: . . . . Exist. Quarters;~1,000 SF	Average # Employees: . . 2 FT, 2 PT	Overseas: . . . . UK, AU, NZ

HOMES & LAND MAGAZINE

P. O. Box 5018
Tallahassee, FL 32314
TEL: (800) 277-4357 (206) 882-1100
FAX: (904) 574-2525
Mr. Dan Fallon, Natl. Fran. Sales Dir.

HOMES AND LAND MAGAZINE offers an opportunity for the franchisee to build a successful business by selling advertising and other services to the local real estate and building community. H & L has become the largest (over 200 magazines covering over 1,000 cities) and highest-quality real estate magazine franchise by providing a wide range of products, advanced electronic desktop publishing systems, strong training and support, name recognition, etc.

HISTORY: . . . . IFA	FINANCIAL: Earnings Claim: . .No	FRANCHISOR TRAINING/SUPPORT:
Established in 1973; . . 1st Franchised in 1984	Cash Investment: $25-50K	Financial Assistance Provided: . . . . .No
Company-Owned Units (As of 8/31/1992): . .3	Total Investment: $25-50K	Site Selection Assistance: . . . . .NA
Franchised Units (As of 8/31/1992): 199	Fees: Franchise - $20K	Lease Negotiation Assistance: . . . .NA
Total Units (As of 8/31/1992): 202	Royalty: Varies, Advert: 0%	Co-operative Advertising: . . . . . . .Yes
Projected New Units for 1993: 15	Contract Periods (Yrs.): 5/5	Training: . . . . .1 Wk. Headquarters,
Distribution: US-202;Can-0;Overseas-0	Area Development Agreement: . .No	. . . . .Varies On-Site
North America: . . . . 41 States	Sub-Franchise Contract: . . . . .No	On-Going Support: C,D,G,H,I/ 45
Concentration: . .39 in CA, 24 in FL, 17 in NC	Expand in Territory: . . . . Yes	EXPANSION PLANS:
Registered: . . . . All States	Passive Ownership: . . . Discouraged	US: . . . . All US, Emphasis on Midwest
	Encourage Conversions: . . . . . Yes	Canada: . . . . No
Type Space: . . . . NA;~NA SF	Average # Employees: . 1-2 FT, 2 PT	Overseas: . . . . No

RENTAL GUIDE MAGAZINE

P. O. Box 5018
Tallahassee, FL 32314
TEL: (800) 277-4357 (206) 882-1100
FAX: (904) 574-2525
Mr. Tom Scardino, VP

RENTAL GUIDE MAGAZINE offers the successful salesperson an opportunity to build a business through selling advertising and other services to the apartment industry. Demographic projections are that this will be a rapidly-growing segment of the housing industry over the next decade. Be a part of the nationally-known and respected Homes and Land network of community real estate magazines. Extensive benefits.

HISTORY:	FINANCIAL: Earnings Claim: . .No	FRANCHISOR TRAINING/SUPPORT:
Established in 1973; . . 1st Franchised in 1987	Cash Investment: $44-105K	Financial Assistance Provided: . . . . .No
Company-Owned Units (As of 8/31/1992): . .2	Total Investment: $44-105K	Site Selection Assistance: . . . . .NA
Franchised Units (As of 8/31/1992): 29	Fees: Franchise - $20K	Lease Negotiation Assistance: . . . .NA
Total Units (As of 8/31/1992): 31	Royalty: Varies, Advert: 0%	Co-operative Advertising: . . . . . . .Yes
Projected New Units for 1993: 12	Contract Periods (Yrs.): 5/5	Training: . . . . .1 Wk. Headquarters,
Distribution: US-31;Can-0;Overseas-0	Area Development Agreement: . .No	. . . . .Varies On-Site
North America: . . . . 17 States	Sub-Franchise Contract: . . . . .No	On-Going Support: C,D,G,H,I/ 45
Concentration: . . .10 in CA, 4 in WA, 3 in FL	Expand in Territory: . . . . .No	EXPANSION PLANS:
Registered: . . . . All States	Passive Ownership: . . . Discouraged	US: . . . . All US
	Encourage Conversions: . . . . . Yes	Canada: . . . . No
Type Space: . . . . NA;~NA SF	Average # Employees: . . 3 FT, 2 PT	Overseas: . . . . No

TV FACTS OF NORTH AMERICA

Liberty Square
Danvers, MA 01923
TEL: (508) 777-9225
FAX: (617) 595-9237
Ms. Joan Gallagher, Natl. Fran. Dir.

Free weekly TV magazine and shopper's guide.

HISTORY:	FINANCIAL: Earnings Claim: . .No	FRANCHISOR TRAINING/SUPPORT:
HISTORY: . . . . IFA	Cash Investment: $24.5-30K	Financial Assistance Provided: . . . . .NA
Established in 1987; . . 1st Franchised in 1987	Total Investment: $24.5K	Site Selection Assistance: . . . . . . .NA
Company-Owned Units (As of 8/31/1992): . .0	Fees: Franchise - $24.5K	Lease Negotiation Assistance: . . . . .NA
Franchised Units (As of 8/31/1992): 150	Royalty: $60+/Wk., Advert: . . 0%	Co-operative Advertising: . . . . . . .NA
Total Units (As of 8/31/1992): 150	Contract Periods (Yrs.): 10/10	Training: . . . . .1 Wk. Headquarters,
Projected New Units for 1993: 25	Area Development Agreement: . .No	. . . . 5 Days On-Site
Distribution: US-130;Can-20;Overseas-0	Sub-Franchise Contract: . . . . .No	On-Going Support: D,G,H/ 10
North America:	Expand in Territory: . . . . . . .No	EXPANSION PLANS:
Concentration: . . . . FL, MA, ON	Passive Ownership: . . . Discouraged	US: . . . . All US
Registered: . . . . .All	Encourage Conversions: . . . . NA	Canada: . . . . .Ontario
. . . .	Average # Employees: . . 1 FT, 1 PT	Overseas: . . . . No
Type Space: . . . . NA;~NA SF		

TV TIMES

Box 2487
Chapel Hill, NC 27515
TEL: (919) 967-5657
FAX:
Mr. Benjamin F. Saxon, President

Franchisee will be the associate publisher of a weekly TV magazine distributed in his area by local supermarkets and businesses. Magazine is free and is supported by local advertising. Free expert training included. $7,500 - no other fees.

HISTORY:	FINANCIAL: Earnings Claim: . . .	FRANCHISOR TRAINING/SUPPORT:
HISTORY:	Cash Investment: $7.5K	Financial Assistance Provided: . . .Yes(D)
Established in 1976; . . 1st Franchised in 1983	Total Investment: $7.5K	Site Selection Assistance: . . . . . . .Yes
Company-Owned Units (As of 8/31/1992): . .1	Fees: Franchise - $7.5K	Lease Negotiation Assistance: . . . .NA
Franchised Units (As of 8/31/1992): 2	Royalty: 0%, Advert: 0%	Co-operative Advertising: . . . . . . .NA
Total Units (As of 8/31/1992): 3	Contract Periods (Yrs.): 10/10	Training: . . . . 1 Wk. On-Site,
Projected New Units for 1993:	Area Development Agreement: . .No	. . . . Ongoing at Headquarters
Distribution: US-3;Can-0;Overseas-0	Sub-Franchise Contract: . . . . Yes	On-Going Support: B,C,D,H/ 2
North America: . . . . 3 States	Expand in Territory: . . . . . . Yes	EXPANSION PLANS:
Concentration: . . . . 2 in NC, 1 in FL	Passive Ownership: . . . Not Allowed	US: . . . . .Northeast, Southeast
Registered: . . . . .FL	Encourage Conversions: . . . . NA	Canada: . . . . No
. . . .	Average # Employees: . . . . .1 FT	Overseas: . . . . No
Type Space: . . . . ;~ SF		

TV-TRAVEL MAGAZINE

2482 Lorrie Dr., P. O. Box 669051
Marietta, GA 30066
TEL: (404) 977-1468
FAX:
Mr. W. Ken Acree, President

Dining, entertainment and shopping guide directed to the multi-million dollar leisure and business travel market. Furnished free to hotels/motels for placement in guest rooms for maximum readership. Income derived from sale of advertising to appear in guide. This is a home-based, low overhead opportunity with high profit potential. Direct sales ability and creativity are the major ingredients for success. If this sounds like you, investigate!

HISTORY:	FINANCIAL: Earnings Claim: . .No	FRANCHISOR TRAINING/SUPPORT:
HISTORY:	Cash Investment: $15.5K	Financial Assistance Provided: . . . . .No
Established in 1983; . . 1st Franchised in 1989	Total Investment: $20K	Site Selection Assistance: . . . . . . .NA
Company-Owned Units (As of 8/31/1992): . .1	Fees: Franchise - $15.5K	Lease Negotiation Assistance: . . . . .NA
Franchised Units (As of 8/31/1992): 0	Royalty: 0%, Advert: 0%	Co-operative Advertising: . . . . . . .NA
Total Units (As of 8/31/1992): 1	Contract Periods (Yrs.): 5/5	Training: . . . . 3 Days Headquarters
Projected New Units for 1993:	Area Development Agreement: . .No	. . . .
Distribution: US-1;Can-0;Overseas-0	Sub-Franchise Contract: . . . . .No	On-Going Support: B,C,d,G/ 2
North America: . . . . .1 State	Expand in Territory: . . . . . . Yes	EXPANSION PLANS:
Concentration: . . . . 1 in GA	Passive Ownership: . . . Not Allowed	US: . . . . . . Southeast and Southwest
Registered: . . . . .FL	Encourage Conversions: . . . . NA	Canada: . . . . No
. . . .	Average # Employees: . . . . . .2 FT	Overseas: . . . . No
Type Space: . . . . NA;~NA SF		

WEDDING GUIDE, THE

44 Union Blvd., # 650
Lakewood, CO 80228
TEL: (800) 477-0142 (303) 969-8094
FAX: (303) 969-8761
Mr. John Anderson, SVP

THE WEDDING GUIDE is a 4-color planning guide that is given away to brides free through a proven and unique distribution method. The guide is supported by those who are interested in reaching the multi-billion dollar wedding industry through display ads, coupons, direct mail and telemarketing.

HISTORY:	FINANCIAL: Earnings Claim: . .No	FRANCHISOR TRAINING/SUPPORT:
Established in 1985; . . 1st Franchised in 1990	Cash Investment: \$15-30K	Financial Assistance Provided: . . . . .Yes
Company-Owned Units (As of 8/31/1992): . .2	Total Investment: \$17.5-32.5K	Site Selection Assistance: . . . . .NA
Franchised Units (As of 8/31/1992): . . . . . <u>34</u>	Fees: Franchise - \$15-30K	Lease Negotiation Assistance: . . . . .NA
Total Units (As of 8/31/1992): 36	Royalty: 8%, Advert: . . . \$300/Yr.	Co-operative Advertising: . . . . .Yes
Projected New Units for 1993: 20	Contract Periods (Yrs.): 3/2	Training: . . . . 4 Days Headquarters,
Distribution: US-36;Can-0;Overseas-0	Area Development Agreement: Yes/3	. . . . As Needed By Phone
North America: . . . . 23 States	Sub-Franchise Contract: . . . . . .No	On-Going Support: a,b,C,G,h,I/ 7
Concentration: . . . . 4 in CA, 4 in PA, 3 in IL	Expand in Territory: . . . . Yes	EXPANSION PLANS:
Registered: . . . . .FL,MI	Passive Ownership: . . . Discouraged	US: . . . . All US
. . . .	Encourage Conversions: . . . . . Yes	Canada: . . . . .No
Type Space: . . . . . . Home Based;~200 SF	Average # Employees: . . 1 FT, 2 PT	Overseas: . . . . UK

WEDDING PAGES, THE

11106 Mockingbird Dr.
Omaha, NE 68137
TEL: (800) 843-4983 (402) 331-7755
FAX: (402) 331-2887
Mr. Doug Russel, VP

THE WEDDING PAGES represents one of the most dynamic direct marketing tools ever developed to help retailers reach the \$33 billion bridal market. The program is centered around a 250-page wedding planner called THE WEDDING PAGES and the corresponding list of brides-to-be generated through its distribution. Involves sales of advertising in a protected territory.

HISTORY:	FINANCIAL: Earnings Claim: . .No	FRANCHISOR TRAINING/SUPPORT:
Established in 1982; . . 1st Franchised in 1984	Cash Investment: \$15K	Financial Assistance Provided: . . . . . No
Company-Owned Units (As of 8/31/1992): . 15	Total Investment: \$25-65K	Site Selection Assistance: . . . . .NA
Franchised Units (As of 8/31/1992): . . . . . <u>61</u>	Fees: Franchise - \$15K	Lease Negotiation Assistance: . . . .NA
Total Units (As of 8/31/1992): 76	Royalty: 10%, Advert: 0%	Co-operative Advertising: . . . . .NA
Projected New Units for 1993: 2	Contract Periods (Yrs.): 5/5	Training: . . . . 2 Days Headquarters,
Distribution: US-75;Can-1;Overseas-0	Area Development Agreement: . .No	. . . . 1 Wk. Field
North America: . . . . 37 States	Sub-Franchise Contract: . . . . . .No	On-Going Support: A,D,E,G,H,I/ 30
Concentration: . . . .8 in CA, 5 in TX, 4 in FL	Expand in Territory: . . . . Yes	EXPANSION PLANS:
Registered: . . . .FL,HI,IL,MN,NY,RI,VA,WI	Passive Ownership: . . . . . .Allowed	US: . . . . All US
. . . .	Encourage Conversions: . . . . .No	Canada: . . . . .No
Type Space: . . . . ;~ SF	Average # Employees: . . . . .1 FT	Overseas: . . . . No

SUPPLEMENTAL LISTING OF FRANCHISORS

AMATEUR SPORT JOURNAL . . . . P. O. Box 6996, Hollywood, FL 33081
    Contact: Mr. Ed Foley; Tel: (305) 893-6554
ASCEND PUBLISHER'S FRANCHISE . . . . . 1817 North Hills Blvd., # 4500, Knoxville, TN 37917
    Contact: President; Tel:
BINGO SCENE MAGAZINE . . . . 9930 Johnnycake Ridge, # 2E, Mentor, OH 44060
    Contact: Mr. Peter Janes, President; Tel: (216) 639-0057
BUSINESS DIGEST MAGAZINE . . . . 650 Main St., South Portland, ME 04106
    Contact: Mr. Mark Girr, Owner; Tel: (207) 772-1972 C
BUYING & DINING GUIDE . . . . 80 Eighth Ave., New York, NY 10011
    Contact: Mr. Allan Horwitz; Tel: (212) 243-6800
CHANNEL CHOICES WEEKLY T.V. NEWSMAG. . . . . . 36 C Stoffel Dr., Rexdale, ON M9W 1A8 CAN
    Contact: Ms. Stacey Beatty; Tel: (416) 248-5555
EXPRESSIONS, THE WOMAN'S MAGAZINE . . . . . P. O. Box 111, Woodland Park, CO 80866
    Contact: Ms. Karyl Anderson, President; Tel: (719) 687-6013
HOME INC. . . . . P. O. Box 290837, Port Orange, FL 32129
    Contact: Mr. Michael V. Biro; Tel: (800) 829-8723 (904) 767-2195 C
INSIDERS' GUIDES . . . . .P. O. Box 2057, US Hwy. 64, Manteo, NC 27954
    Contact: President; Tel: (919) 473-6100

LORD PUBLISHING . . . . P. O. Box 806, Dover, MA 02030
    Contact: President; Tel: (508) 785-0666
M. A. G. PUBLISHING CO. . . . . 750 Hamburg Tnpk., # 208, Pompton Lakes, NJ 07442
    Contact: Mr. David Gay, Publisher; Tel: (201) 835-6551
NATIONAL BRIDAL PUBLICATIONS . . . . .303 E. Livingston Ave., Columbus, OH 43215
    Contact: Mr. Marvin Brown, President; Tel: (614) 224-1992
PAGE SPECIALTY . . . . 1500 Poplar Ave., # 2170, Memphis, TN 38137
    Contact: President; Tel: (901) 761-3084
PENNYSAVER . . . . 80 Eighth Ave., New York, NY 10011
    Contact: Mr. Allan Horwitz; Tel: (212) 243-6800
PHOTOSHOPPER PUBLICATIONS . . . . 650 Elm St., # 500, Manchester, NH 03101
    Contact: Mr. Walter McAdam, President; Tel: (603) 641-2677
SENIORS CHOICE . . . . 44 Union Blvd., # 650, Lakewood, CO 80228
    Contact: President; Tel: (303) 969-8094
SMALL CITY BUSINESS JOURNALS . . . . .110 Merchants Row, Rutland, VT 05701
    Contact: President; Tel:
TODAY'S SENIORS . . . . 1091 Brevic Pl., Mississauga, ON L4W 3R7   CAN
    Contact: Mr. George Coyle; Tel: (416) 238-0555
TRAVEL MAGAZINE . . . . .P. O. Box 669051, 2482 Lorrie Dr., Marietta, GA 30066
    Contact: President; Tel: (404) 977-1468
TV NEWS MAGAZINE . . . . 80 Eighth Ave., New York, NY 10011
    Contact: Mr. Allan Horwitz; Tel: (212) 243-6800
TV SCENE . . . . 15951 McGregor Blvd., # 2D, Fort Meyers, FL 33908
    Contact: Mr. William Anderson, President; Tel: (813) 466-8707
TV SPOTLIGHT MAGAZINE/TELE-VIDEO . . . . 2213 Mountain View, Hurst, TX 76054
    Contact: President; Tel: (817) 280-0551
YOUR CITY'S OFFICIAL WEDDING GUIDE . . . . .P.O. Box 73042, Metairie, LA 70033
    Contact: Mr. Bob Walker; Tel: (504) 455-6650

CHAPTER 33

REAL ESTATE

ADVANTAGE RADON CONTROL CENTERS
804 Second St. Pike
Southampton, PA 18966
TEL: (800) 535-8378 (215) 953-9200
FAX: (215) 953-8837
Mr. Perry S. Ecksel, CEO

We are a multi-faceted environmental testing and mitigation company, offering franchisees an excellent program for entrance into this quickly-growing industry.

HISTORY:		
Established in 1984; . . . 1st Franchised in 1990	**FINANCIAL:** Earnings Claim: . Yes	**FRANCHISOR TRAINING/SUPPORT:**
Company-Owned Units (As of 8/31/1992): . .4	Cash Investment: $10K	Financial Assistance Provided: . . .Yes(D)
Franchised Units (As of 8/31/1992): 4	Total Investment: $25-40K	Site Selection Assistance: . . . . .Yes
Total Units (As of 8/31/1992): 8	Fees: Franchise - $17.5K	Lease Negotiation Assistance: . . . . .Yes
Projected New Units for 1993: 15	Royalty: 8%, Advert: 3%	Co-operative Advertising: . . . . .Yes
Distribution: US-8;Can-0;Overseas-0	Contract Periods (Yrs.): 15/10	Training: . . . . 2 Wks.+ Executive Offices
North America: . . . . 8 States	Area Development Agreement: Yes/5	. . . . 1 Wk. Franchisee Office
Concentration: . . . 2 in PA, 2 in MD, 2 in DE	Sub-Franchise Contract: . . . . . Yes	On-Going Support: a,B,C,D,E,H,I/ 6
Registered:	Expand in Territory: . . . . . . .Yes	**EXPANSION PLANS:**
. . . .	Passive Ownership: . . . Discouraged	US: . . . . . . .PA, NJ, DE, OH and MD
Type Space: . . . . .Varies;~500 SF	Encourage Conversions: . . . . Yes	Canada: . . . . .No
	Average # Employees: . . 1 FT, 1 PT	Overseas: . . . . No

REAL ESTATE

	1989	1990	1991	Percentage Change 90/89	91/90
Total Number of Establishments:					
Company-Owned	118	118	130	0.00%	10.17%
Franchisee-Owned	15,688	16,322	18,039	4.04%	10.52%
Total	15,806	16,440	18,169	4.01%	10.52%
Ratio of Total Establishments:					
Company-Owned	0.7%	0.7%	0.7%		
Franchisee-Owned	99.3%	99.3%	99.3%		
Total	100.0%	100.0%	100.0%		
Total Sales ($000):					
Company-Owned	68,412	71,882	78,497	5.07%	9.20%
Franchisee-Owned	6,116,090	6,714,781	7,601,768	9.79%	13.21%
Total	6,184,502	6,786,663	7,680,265	9.74%	13.17%
Ratio of Total Sales:					
Company-Owned	1.1%	1.1%	1.0%		
Franchisee-Owned	98.9%	98.9%	99.0%		
Total	100.0%	100.0%	100.0%		
Average Sales Per Unit ($000):					
Company-Owned	580	609	604	5.07%	−0.88%
Franchisee-Owned	390	411	421	5.52%	2.43%
Total	391	413	423	5.50%	2.40%
Relative Average Sales Ratio:	148.7%	148.1%	143.3%		

	Number Of Employees	Employees Per Unit	Avg. Sales Per Employee
Total 1989 Employment:			
Company-Owned	2,581	21.9	$26,506
Franchisee-Owned	204,912	13.1	$29,847
Total	207,493	13.1	$29,806
Relative Employee Performance Ratios:		167.5%	88.8%

	1st Quartile	Median	4th Quartile
Average 1989 Total Investment:			
Company-Owned	NA	$37,500	NA
Franchisee-Owned	$20,000	$25,000	$47,500
Single Unit Franchise Fee	$7,500	$10,000	$15,000
Mult. Unit Franchise Fee	NA	NA	NA
Franchise Start-Up Cost	$10,000	$17,500	$22,500

Source: Franchising In The Economy 1991, IFA Educational Foundation & Horwath International.

AMBIC BUILDING INSPECTION CONSULTANTS
1200 Rt. 130
Robbinsville, NJ 08691
TEL: (800) 88-AMBIC (609) 448-3900
FAX: (609) 426-1230
Mr. David Goldstein, President

AMBIC offers complete training in residential, commercial and industrial inspections and related services, i.e. termite, radon, septic and well tests. Computer training and software and computer updates are included. Actual inspection experience provided. AMBIC offers over 16 years' experience by licensed building inspectors and professional engineers trained in home inspections.

HISTORY: .... IFA	FINANCIAL: Earnings Claim: . .No	FRANCHISOR TRAINING/SUPPORT:
Established in 1987; . . 1st Franchised in 1988	Cash Investment: $21-27K	Financial Assistance Provided: . . . Yes(I)
Company-Owned Units (As of 8/31/1992): . .0	Total Investment: $26-27K	Site Selection Assistance: .... NA
Franchised Units (As of 8/31/1992): 19	Fees: Franchise - $16.5K	Lease Negotiation Assistance: ..... NA
Total Units (As of 8/31/1992): 19	Royalty: 6%, Advert: 3%	Co-operative Advertising: .... NA
Projected New Units for 1993: 6	Contract Periods (Yrs.): 10/10	Training: .... 3 Wks. Headquarters,
Distribution: US-19;Can-0;Overseas-0	Area Development Agreement: . .No	.... 1 Wk. Franchisee Location
North America: .... 4 States	Sub-Franchise Contract: ..... .No	On-Going Support: b,C,D,E,F,G,H,I/ . . . 6
Concentration: . . . 12 in NJ, 4 in PA, 2 in NC	Expand in Territory: .... Yes	EXPANSION PLANS:
Registered: .... CA,FL,MD,NY	Passive Ownership: . . . Discouraged	US: .... All US
. . . .	Encourage Conversions: ..... Yes	Canada: .... .All Canada
Type Space: .... Home Based;~200-300 SF	Average # Employees: ..... .2 FT	Overseas: .... No

APARTMENT SELECTOR

P.O. Box 8355
Dallas, TX 75205
TEL: (800) 324-FREE (214) 361-4420 C
FAX: (214) 361-8677
Mr. Kendall A. Laughlin, Chairman

APARTMENT SELECTOR is the nation's oldest and largest FREE apartment and home rental service. Our fee is paid by apartment owners. Extensive training systems for agents and management. Referral network called Official Relocation Network.

HISTORY:	FINANCIAL: Earnings Claim: . .No	FRANCHISOR TRAINING/SUPPORT:
Established in 1959; . . 1st Franchised in 1982	Cash Investment: $20K	Financial Assistance Provided: ..... No
Company-Owned Units (As of 8/31/1992): . .0	Total Investment: $25K	Site Selection Assistance: .... No
Franchised Units (As of 8/31/1992): 22	Fees: Franchise - $7-10K	Lease Negotiation Assistance: ..... No
Total Units (As of 8/31/1992): 22	Royalty: 5%, Advert: 1%	Co-operative Advertising: .... No
Projected New Units for 1993: 3	Contract Periods (Yrs.): 3/3	Training: .... 1 Wk. Headquarters
Distribution: US-22;Can-0;Overseas-0	Area Development Agreement: . .No	. . . .
North America: .... 5 States	Sub-Franchise Contract: ..... .No	On-Going Support: B,c,d,e,G,h,I/ 3
Concentration: .... 14 in TX, 3 in GA	Expand in Territory: .... Yes	EXPANSION PLANS:
Registered:	Passive Ownership: . . . Discouraged	US: .... South and Southwest
. . . .	Encourage Conversions: ..... Yes	Canada: .... No
Type Space: .... .SC;~1,000 SF	Average # Employees: ..... .1 FT	Overseas: .... No

BETTER HOMES REALTY

P. O. Box 8181, 1556 Parkside Dr.
Walnut Creek, CA 94956
TEL: (800) 642-4428 (510) 937-9001
FAX: (510) 937-9006
Ms. Florence Stevens, VP Ops.

Real estate sales. Strong area identity and market share. Excellent corporate support, strong marketing department. Benefits such as free legal counsel to agents, free educational programs, affiliation with major TV network for listing exposure, E & O coverage, preferred financing available just for BETTER HOMES REALTY clients and 24-hour info-line.

HISTORY:	FINANCIAL: Earnings Claim: . .No	FRANCHISOR TRAINING/SUPPORT:
Established in 1964; . . 1st Franchised in 1969	Cash Investment: .... $	Financial Assistance Provided: . . . Yes(I)
Company-Owned Units (As of 8/31/1992): . .0	Total Investment: .... $	Site Selection Assistance: .... No
Franchised Units (As of 8/31/1992): 66	Fees: Franchise - $10K	Lease Negotiation Assistance: ..... No
Total Units (As of 8/31/1992): 66	Royalty: Varies, Advert: 0%	Co-operative Advertising: .... Yes
Projected New Units for 1993: 12	Contract Periods (Yrs.): 5/5	Training: ....
Distribution: US-66;Can-0;Overseas-0	Area Development Agreement: . .No	. . . .
North America: .... 2 States	Sub-Franchise Contract: ..... Yes	On-Going Support: C,D,G,H,I/ 6
Concentration: .... 65 in CA, 1 in ID	Expand in Territory: .... .No	EXPANSION PLANS:
Registered: .... CA	Passive Ownership: ..... .Allowed	US: .... Northern California
. . . .	Encourage Conversions: .... Yes	Canada: .... No
Type Space: .... ;~NA SF	Average # Employees:	Overseas: .... No

BUYER'S RESOURCE

717 17th St., # 1400
Denver, CO 80202
TEL: (800) 359-4092 (303) 292-5454 C
FAX: (303) 292-5454
Mr. Barry M. Miller, President

BUYER'S RESOURCE, INC. is the industry's leader in the business of protecting consumers who buy real estate. We exclusively represent the best interests of real estate buyers through a national network of exclusive buyer brokerage franchises.

HISTORY: . . . .
Established in 1989; . . 1st Franchised in 1990
Company-Owned Units (As of 8/31/1992): . .0
Franchised Units (As of 8/31/1992): 30
Total Units (As of 8/31/1992): 30
Projected New Units for 1993: 180
Distribution: US-30;Can-0;Overseas-0
  North America: . . . . 10 States
  Concentration: . . . 9 in FL, 8 in CO, 4 in NH
Registered: . . . . All Except AB
. . . .
Type Space: . . . All But Exec. Ste;~1,000 SF

FINANCIAL: Earnings Claim: . .No
Cash Investment: $25-40K
Total Investment: $35-50K
Fees: Franchise - $5-10K
  Royalty: 4%, Advert: 2%
Contract Periods (Yrs.): 5/5
Area Development Agreement: . .No
Sub-Franchise Contract: . . . . .No
Expand in Territory: . . . . . . Yes
Passive Ownership: . . . Discouraged
Encourage Conversions: . . . . . Yes
Average # Employees: . . . 10-20 FT

FRANCHISOR TRAINING/SUPPORT:
Financial Assistance Provided: . . . . .No
Site Selection Assistance: . . . . . . .NA
Lease Negotiation Assistance: . . . .NA
Co-operative Advertising: . . . . . . .Yes
Training: . . . . . . 5 Days Headquarters
. . . .
On-Going Support: C,d,E,G,h,I/ 15
EXPANSION PLANS:
US: . . . . .All US
Canada: . . . . .No
Overseas: . . . . No

BY OWNER REALITY NETWORK

501 W. Appleway, # H
Coeur d'Alene, ID 83814
TEL: (208) 667-6184
FAX:
Ms. Ann Wall, VP

Real estate marketing centers, featuring displays of "By Owner" properties in retail locations. Local and network exposure with no percentage commissions. Broker services and consultation also available. "By Owner's federally registered logo, concept and colorful high-traffic locations, naturally attract sellers and buyers.

HISTORY: . . . .
Established in 1985; . . 1st Franchised in 1986
Company-Owned Units (As of 8/31/1992): . .1
Franchised Units (As of 8/31/1992): 9
Total Units (As of 8/31/1992): 10
Projected New Units for 1993: 10
Distribution: US-9;Can-1;Overseas-0
  North America: . . . . . .3 States, 1 Province
  Concentration: . . . 5 in MT, 2 in ID, 2 in WA
Registered: . . . . MN,NR,OR,WA,AB
. . . .
Type Space: . . . . . . SF, SC, RM;~900 SF

FINANCIAL: Earnings Claim: . .No
Cash Investment: $15-40K
Total Investment: $30-50K
Fees: Franchise - $16.5K
  Royalty: 8%, Advert: 2%
Contract Periods (Yrs.): 5/5
Area Development Agreement: . .No
Sub-Franchise Contract: . . . . . Yes
Expand in Territory: . . . . .No
Passive Ownership: . . . Discouraged
Encourage Conversions: . . . . NA
Average # Employees: . 3-5 FT, 2 PT

FRANCHISOR TRAINING/SUPPORT:
Financial Assistance Provided: . . . Yes(I)
Site Selection Assistance: . . . . . . .Yes
Lease Negotiation Assistance: . . . .Yes
Co-operative Advertising: . . . . . . .Yes
Training: . . . . . . 3-5 Days Headquarters,
. . .2-3 Days On-Site, On-Going Support
On-Going Support: B,C,D,E,G,H,I/ 3
EXPANSION PLANS:
US: . . . . .All US
Canada: . . . . .All Canada
Overseas: . . . . No

CENTURY 21 REAL ESTATE

2601 SE Main St.
Irvine, CA 92714
TEL: (714) 553-2100
FAX: (714) 553-2133
Mr. Duane Mora, VP Fran. Mktg.

Real estate brokerage franchisor, offering conversion and start-up opportunities. Franchisor provides top brand-name awareness in industry. Sales and management training, recruiting assistance and nationwide referral system is also available.

HISTORY: . . . . IFA
Established in 1971; . . 1st Franchised in 1972
Company-Owned Units (As of 8/31/1992): . .0
Franchised Units (As of 8/31/1992): 6280
Total Units (As of 8/31/1992): 6280
Projected New Units for 1993: 430
Distribution: . US-5008;Can-345;Overseas-927
  North America: . . . . 50 States
  Concentration: . . . . CA, NY, TX
Registered: . . . CA,HI,IL,IN,MD,MI,MN,NY
. . . . .ND,OR,RI,SD,VA,WA,WI
Type Space: . . . . . . FS, SF, SC;~Varies SF

FINANCIAL: Earnings Claim: . .No
Cash Investment: $3-500K
Total Investment: $3-500K
Fees: Franchise - . . . . $25.5K Max.
  Royalty: ~6%, Advert: . . . Varies
Contract Periods (Yrs.): 5/5
Area Development Agreement: . . .
Sub-Franchise Contract: . . . . . Yes
Expand in Territory: . . . .
Passive Ownership: . . . Not Allowed
Encourage Conversions: . . . . . Yes
Average # Employees: . . . .

FRANCHISOR TRAINING/SUPPORT:
Financial Assistance Provided: . . . . .Yes
Site Selection Assistance: . . . . . . .Yes
Lease Negotiation Assistance: . . . . .NA
Co-operative Advertising: . . . . . . .Yes
Training: . . . . . 4 1/2 Days Headquarters,
. . . . Addit'l Training Varies By Region
On-Going Support: C,D,E,G,h/ 165
EXPANSION PLANS:
US: . . . . .All US
Canada: . . . . .All Canada
Overseas: . . UK, JA, AU, NZ, MX

CENTURY 21 REAL ESTATE (CANADA)
10551 Shellbridge Way, #135
Richmond, BC V6X 2W9 CAN
TEL: (604) 273-2721
FAX: (604) 273-6663
Mr. Gordon Gerrie, SVP Fran.

CENTURY 21 is a well-established company in Canada. The franchise has a very high consumer awareness and consumer preference with an image of professionalism and dependability. Brokers receive a wide range of support services, including management and business training for themselves and sales training for employees. Exclusive air miles sponsor in real estate category.

HISTORY: . . . . .IFA, CFA
Established in 1976; . . 1st Franchised in 1976
Company-Owned Units (As of 8/31/1992): . .0
Franchised Units (As of 8/31/1992): 408
Total Units (As of 8/31/1992): 408
Projected New Units for 1993: 36
Distribution: US-0;Can-408;Overseas-0
North America: . . . .
Concentration: . . 183 in ON, 56 in AB, 51 PQ
Registered: . . . . AB
. . . .
Type Space: . . . . .SC;~2,500 SF

FINANCIAL: Earnings Claim: . .No
Cash Investment: $50K
Total Investment: $70K
Fees: Franchise - $20K
Royalty: 6%, Advert: . . . . Varies
Contract Periods (Yrs.): 5/5
Area Development Agreement: . .No
Sub-Franchise Contract: . . . . . Yes
Expand in Territory: . . . . . . Yes
Passive Ownership: . . . . . .Allowed
Encourage Conversions: . . . . Yes
Average # Employees: . . . . . 20 FT

FRANCHISOR TRAINING/SUPPORT:
Financial Assistance Provided: . . . . .Yes
Site Selection Assistance: . . . . . . .Yes
Lease Negotiation Assistance: . . . . . No
Co-operative Advertising: . . . . .Yes
Training: . . . . 1 Day Toronto/ Vancouver/
. . . .Montreal, 5 Days Vancouver/Calif.
On-Going Support: A,B,C,D,E,H/ . . . 55
EXPANSION PLANS:
US: .No
Canada: . . . . .All Canada
Overseas: . . . . No

CRITERIUM ENGINEERS

650 Brighton Ave.
Portland, ME 04102
TEL: (800) 242-1969 (207) 828-1969
FAX: (207) 775-4405
Mr. H. Alan Mooney, President

CRITERIUM ENGINEERS is a unique consulting franchise available to registered professional engineers. Company specializes in building inspection and evaluation services for buyers, investors, corporations, attorneys, insurance companies, lenders and government. Services include pre-purchase inspections, insurance investigations, maintenance planning, expert testimony, environmental assessments, design and construction review.

HISTORY: . . . .
Established in 1957; . . 1st Franchised in 1989
Company-Owned Units (As of 8/31/1992): . .1
Franchised Units (As of 8/31/1992): 55
Total Units (As of 8/31/1992): 56
Projected New Units for 1993: 12
Distribution: US-56;Can-0;Overseas-0
North America: . . . . 33 States
Concentration: . . . 5 in CA, 4 in FL, 4 in NJ
Registered: . . . . .CA,FL,IN,OR,RI,VA,WI
. . . .
Type Space: . . . . ;~300 SF

FINANCIAL: Earnings Claim: . .No
Cash Investment: $2.5K
Total Investment: $17.5K
Fees: Franchise - $18K
Royalty: 6%, Advert: 1%
Contract Periods (Yrs.): 15/5
Area Development Agreement: . .No
Sub-Franchise Contract: . . . . .No
Expand in Territory: . . . . . . Yes
Passive Ownership: . . . Not Allowed
Encourage Conversions: . . . . NA
Average # Employees: . . 2 FT, 2 PT

FRANCHISOR TRAINING/SUPPORT:
Financial Assistance Provided: . . . . . No
Site Selection Assistance: . . . . . . .NA
Lease Negotiation Assistance: . . . . No
Co-operative Advertising: . . . . .NA
Training: . . . . 1 Wk. Headquarters
. . . .
On-Going Support: B,C,D,G,H,I/ 5
EXPANSION PLANS:
US: . . . . All Legally Permitted
Canada: . . . . .No
Overseas: . . . . No

EGAL

P. O. Box 226
Paola, KS 66071
TEL: (800) 368-9201 (913) 294-3945 C
FAX:
Mr. Timothy J. Warkins, President

Home inspection and radon screening.

HISTORY: . . . .
Established in 1987; . . 1st Franchised in 1988
Company-Owned Units (As of 8/31/1992): . .0
Franchised Units (As of 8/31/1992): 11
Total Units (As of 8/31/1992): 11
Projected New Units for 1993: 11
Distribution: US-11;Can-0;Overseas-0
North America: . . . . 5 States
Concentration: . . . .4 in KS, 3 in OH, 2 in FL
Registered: . . . . .FL
. . . .
Type Space: . . . . . . .Home Based;~NA SF

FINANCIAL: Earnings Claim: . .No
Cash Investment: $16K
Total Investment: $16K
Fees: Franchise - $12.8K
Royalty: 5%, Advert: 2%
Contract Periods (Yrs.): 10/10
Area Development Agreement: . .No
Sub-Franchise Contract: . . . . .No
Expand in Territory: . . . . . . Yes
Passive Ownership: . . . Discouraged
Encourage Conversions: . . . . .No
Average # Employees: . . . .

FRANCHISOR TRAINING/SUPPORT:
Financial Assistance Provided: . . . . .No
Site Selection Assistance: . . . . .No
Lease Negotiation Assistance: . . . . .NA
Co-operative Advertising: . . . . .Yes
Training: . . . . . . .10 Days Headquarters
. . . .
On-Going Support: b,C,D,G,h,I/ 1
EXPANSION PLANS:
US: . . . . .All US
Canada: . . . . .No
Overseas: . . . . No

GRASSROOTS HOME INSPECTIONS

12 Export Ave.
St. Catharines, ON L2M 7L9 CAN
TEL: (416) 687-1925
FAX: (416) 685-8125
Mr. Graham A. Ashdown, President

Pre-purchase home inspection and reporting services. Exclusive checklist with over 2,000 items linked to computerized report system. Includes inspections for vendor marketing purposes, progress inspections on new homes and environmental tests. We report on special features in a home to give a balanced report.

HISTORY:	FINANCIAL: Earnings Claim: . Yes	FRANCHISOR TRAINING/SUPPORT:
Established in 1990; . . 1st Franchised in 1991	Cash Investment: $15-25K	Financial Assistance Provided: . . . . .NA
Company-Owned Units (As of 8/31/1992): . .0	Total Investment: $15-25K	Site Selection Assistance: . . . . . . .Yes
Franchised Units (As of 8/31/1992): 3	Fees: Franchise - $10K	Lease Negotiation Assistance: . . . .Yes
Total Units (As of 8/31/1992): 3	Royalty: 7%, Advert: 3%	Co-operative Advertising: . . . . . . .Yes
Projected New Units for 1993: 12	Contract Periods (Yrs.): 10/10	Training: . . . . . . 1-2 Wks. Headquarters,
Distribution: US-0;Can-3;Overseas-0	Area Development Agreement: . .No	. . . . 1-2 Wks. Franchisee Site
North America: . . . . .1 Province	Sub-Franchise Contract: . . . . . Yes	On-Going Support: B,C,D,E,G,H/ 2
Concentration: . . . . 3 in ON	Expand in Territory: . . . . Yes	EXPANSION PLANS:
Registered:	Passive Ownership: . . . Discouraged	US: . . . . .Northeast and Southeast
. . . .	Encourage Conversions: . . . . . Yes	Canada: . . . . .All Canada
Type Space: . . . . . .Various Types;~500 SF	Average # Employees: . . 1 FT, 1 PT	Overseas: . . . . No

GROUP TRANS-ACTION BROKERAGE SERVICES

550 Sherbrooke, W., # 775
Montreal, PQ H3A 1B9 CAN
TEL: (514) 288-6777 C
FAX: (514) 288-7543
Mr. Jean-Louis Bernard, GM

Group of independent real estate brokers everywhere in Quebec. Affiliated with PHH Homequity for all relocation services in the world. Complete real estate services.

HISTORY:	FINANCIAL: Earnings Claim: . .No	FRANCHISOR TRAINING/SUPPORT:
Established in 1979; . . 1st Franchised in 1982	Cash Investment: $10K	Financial Assistance Provided: . . . Yes(I)
Company-Owned Units (As of 8/31/1992): . .0	Total Investment: $50K	Site Selection Assistance: . . . . . . .Yes
Franchised Units (As of 8/31/1992): 42	Fees: Franchise - $16.5K	Lease Negotiation Assistance: . . . . .Yes
Total Units (As of 8/31/1992): 42	Royalty: Flat, Advert: . . . . . Flat	Co-operative Advertising: . . . . . . .Yes
Projected New Units for 1993: 6	Contract Periods (Yrs.): . . . . Life	Training: . . . . 1 Wk. Headquarters
Distribution: US-0;Can-42;Overseas-0	Area Development Agreement: . Yes	. . . .
North America: . . . . .1 Province	Sub-Franchise Contract: . . . . . .No	On-Going Support: a,b,c,D,E,f,G,H,i/ . . . 4
Concentration: . . . . .42 in PQ	Expand in Territory: . . . . Yes	EXPANSION PLANS:
Registered: . . . . AB	Passive Ownership: . . . Not Allowed	US: .No
. . . .	Encourage Conversions: . . . . . NA	Canada: . . . . .All Canada
Type Space: . . . . .FS, SF;~2,000 SF	Average # Employees: . . . . . 10 FT	Overseas: . . . . No

H.O.M.E. / HOME OWNERS MARKETING ENTERPRISES

P. O. Box 290837
Port Orange, FL 32129
TEL: (800) 829-8723 (904) 767-2195 C
FAX: (904) 767-2194
Mr. Michael V. Biro, Director

National For Sale By Owner, 900 system. Sold at $88.50. National computer system. Regional franchises only.

HISTORY:	FINANCIAL: Earnings Claim: . .No	FRANCHISOR TRAINING/SUPPORT:
Established in 1990; . . 1st Franchised in 1990	Cash Investment: $1.6K	Financial Assistance Provided: . . . . .NA
Company-Owned Units (As of 8/31/1992): . .0	Total Investment: $1.6-111K	Site Selection Assistance: . . . . .NA
Franchised Units (As of 8/31/1992): 2	Fees: Franchise - $2K	Lease Negotiation Assistance: . . . . .NA
Total Units (As of 8/31/1992): 2	Royalty: , Advert:	Co-operative Advertising: . . . . .NA
Projected New Units for 1993: 30	Contract Periods (Yrs.): 5/5/5	Training: . . . . .1 Day Atlanta,
Distribution: US-2;Can-0;Overseas-0	Area Development Agreement: . .No	. . . . .1 Day Daytona Beach
North America: . . . . 2 States	Sub-Franchise Contract: . . . . . .No	On-Going Support: B,F,G,h,i/ 3
Concentration: . . . . .1 in PA, 1 in FL	Expand in Territory: . . . . Yes	EXPANSION PLANS:
Registered: . . . . .FL	Passive Ownership: . . . Discouraged	US: . . . . All US
. . . .	Encourage Conversions: . . . . . NA	Canada: . . . . .All Canada
Type Space: . . . . ;~ SF	Average # Employees: . .1 FT, 10 PT	Overseas: . . . . .English Speaking

HER REAL ESTATE

4656 Executive Dr.
Columbus, OH 43220
TEL: (800) 848-7400 (614) 459-7400
FAX: (614) 457-6807
Ms. Karen Pemberton, VP

Personalized approach to real estate financing. Brokers keep their own identity and marks of franchisor do not detract or dominate. On-location educational opportunities. Franchisee offered exclusive territory, test-marketed, award-winning marketing tools and techniques. Support program through field representation, continuing education and other unique educational opportunities.

HISTORY:	FINANCIAL: Earnings Claim: . .No	FRANCHISOR TRAINING/SUPPORT:
Established in 1976; . . 1st Franchised in 1981	Cash Investment: . . . .$	Financial Assistance Provided: . . . . . No
Company-Owned Units (As of 8/31/1992): . 23	Total Investment: $9.3-103K	Site Selection Assistance: . . . . .NA
Franchised Units (As of 8/31/1992): 12	Fees: Franchise - $2.5-80K	Lease Negotiation Assistance: . . . . . No
Total Units (As of 8/31/1992): 35	Royalty: 5%, Advert: 1%	Co-operative Advertising: . . . . .Yes
Projected New Units for 1993: 4	Contract Periods (Yrs.): 5/5	Training: . . . . 2 Wks. Headquarters
Distribution: US-35;Can-0;Overseas-0	Area Development Agreement: . .No	. . . .
North America: . . . . .1 State	Sub-Franchise Contract: . . . . . Yes	On-Going Support: b,C,D,E/ 22
Concentration: . . . . 35 in OH	Expand in Territory: . . . . Yes	EXPANSION PLANS:
Registered:	Passive Ownership: . . . Not Allowed	US: . . . . .Ohio Only
. . . .	Encourage Conversions: . . . . Yes	Canada: . . . . .No
Type Space: . . . . NA;~ SF	Average # Employees:	Overseas: . . . . No

---

HOMETREND

603 N. Pacific Coast Hwy.
Solana Beach, CA 92075
TEL: (619) 481-5858
FAX: (619) 481-8022
Mr. Howard L. Behling, President

Real estate management consulting network - complete broker package -including sales and management training, computer with complete software, international/national relocation, home warranties and more.

HISTORY:	FINANCIAL: Earnings Claim: . .No	FRANCHISOR TRAINING/SUPPORT:
Established in 1981; . . 1st Franchised in 1981	Cash Investment: $1-5K	Financial Assistance Provided: . . .Yes(D)
Company-Owned Units (As of 8/31/1992): . .2	Total Investment: $14.5-51K	Site Selection Assistance: . . . . .Yes
Franchised Units (As of 8/31/1992): 80	Fees: Franchise - $12.5-50K	Lease Negotiation Assistance: . . . . .NA
Total Units (As of 8/31/1992): 82	Royalty: 5%, Advert: 1/2%	Co-operative Advertising: . . . . .Yes
Projected New Units for 1993: 50	Contract Periods (Yrs.): 3-15	Training: . . . . 2 Days Headquarters,
Distribution: US-82;Can-0;Overseas-0	Area Development Agreement: Yes/15	. . . . On-Going in Franchise
North America:	Sub-Franchise Contract: . . . . . Yes	On-Going Support: A,B,C,D,E,F,G,h/ . .6
Concentration:	Expand in Territory: . . . . Yes	EXPANSION PLANS:
Registered:	Passive Ownership: . . . . . .Allowed	US: . . . . .All US
. . . .	Encourage Conversions: . . . . Yes	Canada: . . . . .All Canada
Type Space: . . . . . .FS, SF, SC, RM;~ SF	Average # Employees: . . . . .6 FT	Overseas: . . . . . JA, Hong Kong

---

HOUSEMASTER OF AMERICA

421 W. Union Ave.
Bound Brook, NJ 08805
TEL: (800) 526-3939 (201) 469-6565
FAX: (201) 469-9560
Ms. Linda Sigman, Fran. Sales

A home inspection service catering primarily to home buyers. Appealing to men and women alike who are business or marketing minded. Engineers are readily available to perform the inspections, which are backed by an optional warranty. This is a much-needed service and HOUSEMASTER has a proven format for developing and conducting the business.

HISTORY: . . . . IFA	FINANCIAL: Earnings Claim: . .No	FRANCHISOR TRAINING/SUPPORT:
Established in 1976; . . 1st Franchised in 1979	Cash Investment: $20-38K	Financial Assistance Provided: . . . Yes(I)
Company-Owned Units (As of 8/31/1992): . .0	Total Investment: $27-50K	Site Selection Assistance: . . . . . . .NA
Franchised Units (As of 8/31/1992): 131	Fees: Franchise - $17-35K	Lease Negotiation Assistance: . . . . .NA
Total Units (As of 8/31/1992): 131	Royalty: 7.5%, Advert: 2.5%	Co-operative Advertising: . . . . .No
Projected New Units for 1993: 12	Contract Periods (Yrs.): 5/5	Training: . . . . 1 Wk. Tech., 4 Days Sales
Distribution: US-131;Can-0;Overseas-0	Area Development Agreement: . .No	. . . . 1 Day Operations - Headquarters
North America: . . . . 36 States	Sub-Franchise Contract: . . . . . .No	On-Going Support: b,C,G,H,I/ 17
Concentration: . . .15 in NJ, 11 in FL, 8 in NY	Expand in Territory: . . . . .No	EXPANSION PLANS:
Registered: . . . . . CA,IL,IN,MD,MN,NY,RI	Passive Ownership: . . . Not Allowed	US: . . . . .All US
. . . . .SD,VA,WA,WI	Encourage Conversions: . . . . . Yes	Canada: . . . . .All Canada
Type Space: . . . . ;~ SF	Average # Employees: . . 5 FT, 2 PT	Overseas: . . . . AU, NZ, UK

MORTGAGE SERVICE ASSOCIATES

21 Brock St.
North Haven, CT 06473
TEL: (800) 888-8107 (203) 773-3001
FAX: (203) 787-0114
Mr. Joseph D. Raffone, President

A unique approach to the property preservation, servicing and inspection side of mortgage servicing. Our custom software and intensive marketing effort have resulted in a position of industry leadership. Local market control through additional franchises. On-going support is guaranteed as clients are common to all franchises. Immediate cash flow.

HISTORY:	FINANCIAL: Earnings Claim: . .No	FRANCHISOR TRAINING/SUPPORT:
Established in 1946; . . 1st Franchised in 1986	Cash Investment: $15-20K	Financial Assistance Provided: . . . . .Yes
Company-Owned Units (As of 8/31/1992): . .1	Total Investment: $15-20K	Site Selection Assistance: . . . . . . .NA
Franchised Units (As of 8/31/1992): 4	Fees: Franchise - $15K	Lease Negotiation Assistance: . . . . .NA
Total Units (As of 8/31/1992): 5	Royalty: 5-15%, Advert:	Co-operative Advertising: . . . . . . .Yes
Projected New Units for 1993: 6	Contract Periods (Yrs.): 10/10	Training: . . . . 30 Hours Various
Distribution: US-5;Can-0;Overseas-0	Area Development Agreement: . .No	. . . . Locations
North America: . . . . 4 States	Sub-Franchise Contract: . . . . .No	On-Going Support: A,C,D,G,H,I/ 12
Concentration: . . . 2 in VA, 1 in CT, 1 in NY	Expand in Territory: . . . . Yes	EXPANSION PLANS:
Registered:	Passive Ownership: . . . Not Allowed	US: . . . . .All US
. . . .	Encourage Conversions: . . . . . NA	Canada: . . . . .No
Type Space: . . . . Small Office;~150-300 SF	Average # Employees: . . 2 FT, 1 PT	Overseas: . . . . No

NATIONAL PROPERTY INSPECTIONS

236 S. 108th Ave., # 3
Omaha, NE 68154
TEL: (800) 333-9807 (402) 333-9807
FAX: (402) 333-9780
Mr. Roland Bates, President

Residential and commercial property inspections, radon testing and environmental screenings. Exclusive area. Financial assistance provided. Outstanding referral network. One week training provided in Omaha. All training expenses are included in franchise fee. Step-by-step business plan. On-going support.

HISTORY:	FINANCIAL: Earnings Claim: . .No	FRANCHISOR TRAINING/SUPPORT:
Established in 1987; . . 1st Franchised in 1987	Cash Investment: $15K	Financial Assistance Provided: . . .Yes(D)
Company-Owned Units (As of 8/31/1992): . .0	Total Investment: $25K	Site Selection Assistance: . . . . . . .NA
Franchised Units (As of 8/31/1992): 60	Fees: Franchise - $17K	Lease Negotiation Assistance: . . . . .NA
Total Units (As of 8/31/1992): 60	Royalty: 8%, Advert: 0%	Co-operative Advertising: . . . . . . .NA
Projected New Units for 1993: 20	Contract Periods (Yrs.): 10/10	Training: . . . . .1 Wk. Headquarters,
Distribution: US-60;Can-0;Overseas-0	Area Development Agreement: . .No	. . . . On-Going
North America:	Sub-Franchise Contract: . . . . .No	On-Going Support: D,G,H,I/ 6
Concentration: . . . . WI, NY, CA	Expand in Territory: . . . . Yes	EXPANSION PLANS:
Registered: . . . . .All	Passive Ownership: . . . Discouraged	US: . . . . .All US
. . . .	Encourage Conversions: . . . . . Yes	Canada: . . . . .All Canada
Type Space: . . . . NA;~NA SF	Average # Employees: . . . . . .1 FT	Overseas: . . . . No

NATIONAL REAL ESTATE SERVICE NRS

18200 Von Karman Ave., # 670
Irvine, CA 92715
TEL: (800) 246-0646 (714) 250-3311
FAX: (714) 757-0205
Mr. Doug Balog, VP

The NRS program is designed to improve a broker's competitive ability. NRS pioneered concepts such a listing catalogs, personalized marketing materials and an international computerized listing service, including both photographs of the listed properties and the sales representative.

HISTORY: . . . . .IFA	FINANCIAL: Earnings Claim: . . .	FRANCHISOR TRAINING/SUPPORT:
Established in 1979; . . 1st Franchised in 1980	Cash Investment: . . . .$	Financial Assistance Provided: . . . . .Yes
Company-Owned Units (As of 8/31/1992): . .0	Total Investment: . . . .$	Site Selection Assistance: . . . . . . .Yes
Franchised Units (As of 8/31/1992): 197	Fees: Franchise - $16K	Lease Negotiation Assistance: . . . . .Yes
Total Units (As of 8/31/1992): 197	Royalty: $150/Mo., Advert: $45/Mo.	Co-operative Advertising: . . . . . . .Yes
Projected New Units for 1993: 15	Contract Periods (Yrs.): 5/5	Training: . . . . 5 Days Headquarters,
Distribution: US-38;Can-156;Overseas-3	Area Development Agreement: Yes/20	. . . . 2 Days Regional Offices
North America: . . . . . 4 States, 6 Provinces	Sub-Franchise Contract: . . . . . Yes	On-Going Support: C,G,h,I/ 50
Concentration: . 77 in BC, 34 in ON, 28 in AB	Expand in Territory: . . . . Yes	EXPANSION PLANS:
Registered: . . . CA,FL,HI,IL,IN,MI,MN,OR	Passive Ownership: . . . Discouraged	US: . . . . . . CA, AZ, FL, Pacific NW
. . . . WA,AB	Encourage Conversions: . . . . . Yes	Canada: . . . . .All Canada
Type Space: . . . . ;~Varies SF	Average # Employees: . . 2 FT, 1 PT	Overseas: . . . . FR, GR, UK, Asia

NATIONAL TENANT NETWORK

525 SW 1st, # 105
Lake Oswego, OR 97034
TEL: (800) 228-0989 (503) 635-1118
FAX: (503) 635-9392
Mr. Ed Byczynski, President

Tenant performance reporting. Nationally networked mainframe provides instant access to data bases used to provide tenancy profile. Staff is fully trained in credit analysis, fraud detection. Comprehensive profiles are exclusive to NTN. Large territories. Full support and training.

HISTORY:	FINANCIAL: Earnings Claim: . .No	FRANCHISOR TRAINING/SUPPORT:
Established in 1980; . . 1st Franchised in 1987	Cash Investment: $20-30K	Financial Assistance Provided: . . .Yes(D)
Company-Owned Units (As of 8/31/1992): . .3	Total Investment: $40-50K	Site Selection Assistance: . . . . .No
Franchised Units (As of 8/31/1992): 10	Fees: Franchise - $11K	Lease Negotiation Assistance: . . . . .NA
Total Units (As of 8/31/1992): 13	Royalty: 10%, Advert: 0%	Co-operative Advertising: . . . . .Yes
Projected New Units for 1993: 5	Contract Periods (Yrs.): . . . 10/10	Training: . . . . 1 Wk. Franchisee Location
Distribution: US-13;Can-0;Overseas-0	Area Development Agreement: . .No	. . . .
North America: . . . . 12 States	Sub-Franchise Contract: . . . . . .No	On-Going Support: a,C,d,E,F,G,H,I/ . . 10
Concentration: . . . .3 in CA, 2 in NC, 2 in FL	Expand in Territory: . . . . Yes	EXPANSION PLANS:
Registered: . . . . .FL	Passive Ownership: . . . Discouraged	US: . . . . All US
. . . .	Encourage Conversions: . . . . .No	Canada: . . . . .All Canada
Type Space: . . . . FS, Office;~300-500 SF	Average # Employees: . . 2 FT, 1 PT	Overseas: . . . . No

PROPERTY INSPECTION SERVICE

1072 S. Saratoga-Sunnyvale, #B 201
San Jose, CA 95129
TEL: (800) 733-3524 (408) 446-9400
FAX: (408) 446-3528
Mr. Ben Vitcov, President

Providing residential building inspections for home buyers. Inspectors include roof and foundation, as well as plumbing, electrical and heating systems.

HISTORY:	FINANCIAL: Earnings Claim: . .No	FRANCHISOR TRAINING/SUPPORT:
Established in 1981; . . 1st Franchised in 1984	Cash Investment: $20K	Financial Assistance Provided: . . . Yes(I)
Company-Owned Units (As of 8/31/1992): . .0	Total Investment: $20-50K	Site Selection Assistance: . . . . .Yes
Franchised Units (As of 8/31/1992): 11	Fees: Franchise - $16.5K	Lease Negotiation Assistance: . . . . .NA
Total Units (As of 8/31/1992): 11	Royalty: 8%, Advert: 2%	Co-operative Advertising: . . . . .Yes
Projected New Units for 1993: 2	Contract Periods (Yrs.): 5/5	Training: . . . . 3 Wks. Headquarters
Distribution: US-11;Can-0;Overseas-0	Area Development Agreement: . .No	. . . .
North America: . . . . .1 State	Sub-Franchise Contract: . . . . .No	On-Going Support: B,C,D,g,H,I/ 8
Concentration: . . . . 11 in CA	Expand in Territory: . . . . Yes	EXPANSION PLANS:
Registered: . . . . CA	Passive Ownership: . . . Not Allowed	US: . . . . California Only
. . . .	Encourage Conversions: . . . . Yes	Canada: . . . . No
Type Space: . . . . NA;~250 SF	Average # Employees: . . . . .1 PT	Overseas: . . . . No

RE/MAX INTERNATIONAL

5445 DTC Parkway, # 1200
Englewood, CO 80111
TEL: (800) 525-7452 (303) 770-5531
FAX: (303) 796-3599
Ms. Maureen Hardgrove, PR Coord.

RE/MAX (real estate maximums) is an international franchisor of real estate offices. The firm was built on the concept of allowing sales associates to retain the highest possible % of commissions earned in exchange for paying management fees and sharing in the office overhead. RE/MAX was designed and developed for full-time associates, who are supported by a strong regional and national program and who want to develop to their full potential.

HISTORY: . . . . IFA	FINANCIAL: Earnings Claim: . .No	FRANCHISOR TRAINING/SUPPORT:
Established in 1973; . . 1st Franchised in 1975	Cash Investment: . . . . . . $Varies	Financial Assistance Provided: . . . Yes(I)
Company-Owned Units (As of 8/31/1992): . .0	Total Investment: $50-100K	Site Selection Assistance: . . . . .Yes
Franchised Units (As of 8/31/1992): 1877	Fees: Franchise - $15-25K	Lease Negotiation Assistance: . . . . .NA
Total Units (As of 8/31/1992): 1877	Royalty: Varies, Advert: . . Varies	Co-operative Advertising: . . . . .No
Projected New Units for 1993:	Contract Periods (Yrs.): 5/5	Training: . . . . . 40+ Hours Headquarters
Distribution: . . US-1475;Can-399;Overseas-3	Area Development Agreement: . .No	. . . .
North America: . . . . 50 States,12 Provinces	Sub-Franchise Contract: . . . . . Yes	On-Going Support: C,D,G,h,I/ 170
Concentration: . 181 in CA, 170 in ON, 125 IL	Expand in Territory: . . . . Yes	EXPANSION PLANS:
Registered: . . . . .All	Passive Ownership: . . . Not Allowed	US: . . . . All US
. . . .	Encourage Conversions: . . . . Yes	Canada: . . . . .Yes
Type Space: . . . FS, SF, SC, RM;~Varies SF	Average # Employees: . 3-4 FT, 1 PT	Overseas: . . . . .MX

REALTY EXECUTIVES

4427 N. 36th St., # 100
Phoenix, AZ 85018
TEL: (800) 528-0365 (602) 957-0747
FAX: (602) 224-5542
Mr. William A. Powers, CEO

REALTY EXECUTIVES is the originator of the "100% Commission Concept" in real estate, which attracts the top producing agents in the industry and ends the revolving door syndrome that is so common with traditional brokers.

HISTORY:	FINANCIAL: Earnings Claim: . .No	FRANCHISOR TRAINING/SUPPORT:
Established in 1965; . . 1st Franchised in 1973	Cash Investment: $15K	Financial Assistance Provided: . . .Yes(D)
Company-Owned Units (As of 8/31/1992): . 40	Total Investment: $15-100K	Site Selection Assistance: . . . . No
Franchised Units (As of 8/31/1992): 139	Fees: Franchise - $15K	Lease Negotiation Assistance: . . . . No
Total Units (As of 8/31/1992): 179	Royalty: Flat Fee, Advert: $5/Mo/Ag	Co-operative Advertising: . . . . . . .Yes
Projected New Units for 1993: 25	Contract Periods (Yrs.): . . . 5/5/5/5	Training: . . . . 3 Days Headquarters
Distribution: US-177;Can-2;Overseas-0	Area Development Agreement: Yes/5	. . . .
North America: . . . . 32 States, 2 Provinces	Sub-Franchise Contract: . . . . Yes	On-Going Support: A,b,C,d,E,G,h,I/ . . .6
Concentration: . . 52 in AZ, 25 in CA, 13 in IL	Expand in Territory: . . . . . . Yes	EXPANSION PLANS:
Registered: . . . CA,FL,HI,IL,IN,MD,MI,MN	Passive Ownership: . . . . .Allowed	US: . . . . .All US
. . . . NY,RI,SD,VA,WI	Encourage Conversions: . . . . Yes	Canada: . . . . .All Canada
Type Space: Off/Profess.Space;~1,000-3,000 SF	Average # Employees: . . 4 FT, 2 PT	Overseas: . . . . JA, EUR

RESIDENTIAL BUILDING INSPECTORS

701 Fairway Dr.
Clayton, NC 27520
TEL: (919) 553-3959
FAX:
Mr. Claude T. Canipe, President

RBI franchises are independently owned and operated - in business for yourself, but not by yourself. The full line of home inspection services are provided to buyers, sellers and others, including environmental assessments. On-site reporting and warranties provided.

HISTORY:	FINANCIAL: Earnings Claim: . .No	FRANCHISOR TRAINING/SUPPORT:
Established in 1986; . . 1st Franchised in 1989	Cash Investment: $8.5-10.9K	Financial Assistance Provided: . . .Yes(D)
Company-Owned Units (As of 8/31/1992): . .0	Total Investment: $8.5-10.9K	Site Selection Assistance: . . . . No
Franchised Units (As of 8/31/1992): 7	Fees: Franchise - $6.9K	Lease Negotiation Assistance: . . . . No
Total Units (As of 8/31/1992): 7	Royalty: 10%, Advert: 0%	Co-operative Advertising: . . . . No
Projected New Units for 1993: 2	Contract Periods (Yrs.): . . . 20/20	Training: . . . . 2 Days On-Site
Distribution: US-7;Can-0;Overseas-0	Area Development Agreement: .No	. . . .
North America: . . . . 6 States	Sub-Franchise Contract: . . . . .No	On-Going Support: C,G/ 2
Concentration:	Expand in Territory: . . . . . . Yes	EXPANSION PLANS:
Registered:	Passive Ownership: . . . . .Allowed	US: . . . . .All US
. . . .	Encourage Conversions: . . . . NA	Canada: . . . . .All Canada
Type Space: . . . . NA;~ SF	Average # Employees: . . . . .1 FT	Overseas: . . . . No

ROOM-MATE REFERRAL SERVICE CENTERS

P. O. Box 760328
Oklahoma City, OK 73176
TEL: (405) 692-0947 C
FAX:
Ms. Florence S. Cook, CEO

A service company that handles the placement of persons as roommates for economic and a variety of other needs.

HISTORY:	FINANCIAL: Earnings Claim: . .No	FRANCHISOR TRAINING/SUPPORT:
Established in 1979; . . 1st Franchised in 1985	Cash Investment: $3-15K	Financial Assistance Provided: . . .Yes(D)
Company-Owned Units (As of 8/31/1992): . .1	Total Investment: $10-25K	Site Selection Assistance: . . . . . . .Yes
Franchised Units (As of 8/31/1992): 17	Fees: Franchise - $7.5-15K	Lease Negotiation Assistance: . . . .Yes
Total Units (As of 8/31/1992): 18	Royalty: 5%, Advert: 1%	Co-operative Advertising: . . . . . . .Yes
Projected New Units for 1993: 12	Contract Periods (Yrs.): . . . 10/10	Training: . . . . .3-5 Days Franchisee Area
Distribution: US-18;Can-0;Overseas-0	Area Development Agreement: .No	. . . .
North America: . . . . 6 States	Sub-Franchise Contract: . . . . Yes	On-Going Support: D,e,G,H,i/ . . . .
Concentration: . . . 4 in PA, 4 in GA, 4 in TX	Expand in Territory: . . . . . . Yes	EXPANSION PLANS:
Registered:	Passive Ownership: . . . Discouraged	US: . . . . .All US
. . . .	Encourage Conversions: . . . . Yes	Canada: . . . . .All Canada
Type Space: . . . . .SC;~350 SF	Average # Employees: . . . . . .1 PT	Overseas: . . . . .Yes

TERMINIX INTERNATIONAL

855 Ridge Lake Blvd.
Memphis, TN 38120
TEL: (800) 654-7848 (901) 766-1333
FAX: (901) 766-1107
Mr. Bob Morris, Dir. Fran. Recruit.

World's largest structural pest control company, with over 500 service centers nationwide and in several foreign countries, offering termite and pest control services to residential, commercial and industrial customers.

HISTORY:	FINANCIAL: Earnings Claim: . .No	FRANCHISOR TRAINING/SUPPORT:
Established in 1927; . . 1st Franchised in 1927	Cash Investment: $15-27.5K	Financial Assistance Provided: . . .Yes(D)
Company-Owned Units (As of 8/31/1992): 302	Total Investment: $50.9-97.5K	Site Selection Assistance: . . . . .No
Franchised Units (As of 8/31/1992): 212	Fees: Franchise - $25-50K	Lease Negotiation Assistance: . . . . .NA
Total Units (As of 8/31/1992): 514	Royalty: 7%, Advert: 2%	Co-operative Advertising: . . . . .Yes
Projected New Units for 1993: 25	Contract Periods (Yrs.): 5/5	Training: . . . . . . Various By Location of
Distribution: US-514;Can-0;Overseas-0	Area Development Agreement: . .No	. . . . Franchisee
North America: . . . . 49 States	Sub-Franchise Contract: . . . . .No	On-Going Support: B,C,D,G,h,I/ . . . . . .
Concentration: . 49 in NC, 38 in AR, 27 in TX	Expand in Territory: . . . . . . Yes	EXPANSION PLANS:
Registered: . . . . . All States Exc. MD & VA	Passive Ownership: . . . Discouraged	US: . . . . .All US
. . . .	Encourage Conversions: . . . . Yes	Canada: . . . . .No
Type Space: . . . FS, SC, SC;~1,500-2,000 SF	Average # Employees: . . . . .Varies	Overseas: . . . . No

UNITED SERVICES OF AMERICA / EUROPA 2000

P. O. Box 290837
Port Orange, FL 32129
TEL: (800) 829-8723 (904) 767-2195 C
FAX: (904) 767-2194
Mr. Michael V. Biro

International real estate, world-wide, under the USA logo, combining the European market as well as the American, unique in personalized service, enhance present offices, not to change them.

HISTORY:	FINANCIAL: Earnings Claim: . .No	FRANCHISOR TRAINING/SUPPORT:
Established in 1973; . . 1st Franchised in 1990	Cash Investment: . . . . . . $4.5K+	Financial Assistance Provided: . . .Yes(D)
Company-Owned Units (As of 8/31/1992): . .1	Total Investment: $4.5-250K	Site Selection Assistance: . . . . .No
Franchised Units (As of 8/31/1992): 2	Fees: Franchise - $4.5K	Lease Negotiation Assistance: . . . . .NA
Total Units (As of 8/31/1992): 3	Royalty: Flat, Advert: 0%	Co-operative Advertising: . . . . .Yes
Projected New Units for 1993: 60	Contract Periods (Yrs.): . . . 5/5/5/5	Training: . . . . .None
Distribution: US-2;Can-0;Overseas-1	Area Development Agreement: . .No	. . . .
North America:	Sub-Franchise Contract: . . . . .No	On-Going Support: B,d,g,h,i/ 7
Concentration:	Expand in Territory: . . . . . . .No	EXPANSION PLANS:
Registered: . . . . .FL	Passive Ownership: . . . Discouraged	US: . . . . .All US
. . . .	Encourage Conversions: . . . . . Yes	Canada: . . . . .All Canada
Type Space: . . . . ;~ SF	Average # Employees: . . 7 FT, 7 PT	Overseas: . . . . Worldwide

WATERMASTER AMERICA

1255 N. High St.
Columbus, OH 43201
TEL: (800) 444-WATER (614) 291-3141
FAX:
Mr. Jack Bernstein, Fran. Dir.

WATERMASTER AMERICA provides sub-metering services for owners of apartments, shopping centers, mobile home parks, offices and condos. The service includes installation, reading and billing of individual sub-meters, resulting in the elimination of the property owner's water/service expenses.

HISTORY:	FINANCIAL: Earnings Claim: . .No	FRANCHISOR TRAINING/SUPPORT:
Established in 1987; . . 1st Franchised in 1987	Cash Investment: $0	Financial Assistance Provided: . . . . .NA
Company-Owned Units (As of 8/31/1992): . .1	Total Investment: $0	Site Selection Assistance: . . . . . . .NA
Franchised Units (As of 8/31/1992): 4	Fees: Franchise - $5-30K	Lease Negotiation Assistance: . . . . .NA
Total Units (As of 8/31/1992): 5	Royalty: 5%, Advert: 1%	Co-operative Advertising: . . . . .NA
Projected New Units for 1993:	Contract Periods (Yrs.): 10/10	Training: . . . . 1 Wk. Headquarters
Distribution: US-5;Can-0;Overseas-0	Area Development Agreement: . .No	. . . .
North America: . . . . 2 States	Sub-Franchise Contract: . . . . .No	On-Going Support: A,C,D,G,H,I/ 3
Concentration: . . . . 3 in OH	Expand in Territory: . . . . . . Yes	EXPANSION PLANS:
Registered:	Passive Ownership: . . . Discouraged	US: . . . . . . .All Non-Registration States
. . . .	Encourage Conversions: . . . . NA	Canada: . . . . .No
Type Space: . . . . ;~ SF	Average # Employees: . . . . . .1 FT	Overseas: . . . . No

SUPPLEMENTAL LISTING OF FRANCHISORS

A-1 REALTY . . . . 7005 Suburban Arch, Norfolk, VA 23505
    Contact: President; Tel: (703) 853-7795
ALSIDE 3773 State Rd., P. O. Box 2010, Akron, OH 44309 . . . .
    Contact: President; Tel: (216) 929-1811
AMERISPEC HOME INSPECTION SERVICE . . . . . 1855 W. Katella Ave., # 330, Orange, CA 92667
    Contact: Mr. Thomas Carrol, President; Tel: (800) 426-2270 (714) 744-8360
APARTMENT SEARCH INTERNATIONAL . . . . 7900 Xerxes Ave. S., # 2044, Minneapolis, MN 55431
    Contact: Mr. John Appert, EVP; Tel: (800) 830-0509 (612) 830-0509
BETTER HOMES & GARDENS REAL ESTATE . . . . 2000 Grand Ave., Des Moines, IA 50312
    Contact: Mr. Allen Sabbag, President; Tel: (800) 274-7653 (515) 284-3000
BILTMORE MORTGAGE COMPANY . . . . . . 112 S. Tyron 1st Southeastern, Raleigh, NC 28284
    Contact: President; Tel: (919) 847-1070
BUILDING INSPECTOR OF AMERICA . . . . 684 Main St., Wakefield, MA 01880
    Contact: Mr. Larry Finklestone, Dir. Sales; Tel: (800) 321-4677 (617) 246-4215
BUY OWNER INTERNATIONAL . . . . . 1500 W. Cypress Creek Rd., # 105, Ft. Lauderdale, FL 33309
    Contact: Mr. Scott A. Eckert, President; Tel: (800) 771-7777 (305) 771-7771
BUYERS MARKET, THE . . . . 717 17th St., # 1400, Denver, CO 80202
    Contact: Mr. Barry M. Miller, President; Tel: (800) 359-4092 (303) 292-5454
CAMPUS COMMERCIAL PROPERTIES . . . . P. O. Box 8165, Ann Arbor, MI 58107
    Contact: President; Tel: (313) 995-5454
CAYLOR FINANCIAL . . . . .11370 E. Sunnyside Dr., Scottsdale, AZ 85259
    Contact: President; Tel: (602) 948-8555
CENTER COMPANIES, THE . . . . 404 S. Figueroa St., # 606, Los Angeles, CA 90071
    Contact: President; Tel: (213) 687-0680
COLDWELL BANKER AFFILIATES (CANADA) . 3 Robert Speck Pkwy., # 750, Mississauga, ON L4Z 2G5   CAN
    Contact: Mr. Ken Wright; Tel: (416) 566-9240
COLDWELL BANKER RESIDENTIAL AFFILIATES . 27271 Las Ramblas, # 231, Mission Viejo, CA 92691
    Contact: Mr. Roy W. Hibberd, VP; Tel: (800) 854-6800 (714) 367-2075
COMREAL INTERNATIONAL . . . . 8725 NW 18th Terrace, # 200, Miami, FL 33172
    Contact: Mr. Stephen H. Smith, President; Tel: (305) 591-3044
D. A. DURYEE & COMPANY REAL ESTATE . . . . P. O. Box 509, Everett, WA 98206
    Contact: President; Tel: (206) 258-3411
DELTONA CORP. . . . . .3250 SW 3rd Ave., Miami, FL 33129
    Contact: Mr. Joseph Corbin, President; Tel: (305) 854-1111
DIRECT BY OWNER . . . . 14 E. Northwest Hwy., Arlington Heights, IL 60004
    Contact: Mr. Mike Grady; Tel: (708) 870-1700
DISCOUNT REALTY INTERNATIONAL . . . . P.O. Box 7836, Westlake Village, CA 91359
    Contact: Mr. Bob Deutsch, President; Tel: (805) 499-4966
ELECTRONIC REALTY ASSOCIATES / ERA . . . . . . P. O. Box 2974, Shawnee Mission, KS 66201
    Contact: Mr. Robert Purcell; Tel: (800) 728-0999 (913) 432-2600
EXECU*SYSTEMS REAL ESTATE . . . . 4427 North 36th St., # 200, Phoenix, AZ 85018
    Contact: President; Tel: (602) 957-0444
EXECUTRON MORTGAGE NETWORK . . . . . . .2001 Killebrew Dr., # 435, Bloomington, MN 55425
    Contact: President; Tel:
FACTUAL DATA . . . . 736 Whalers Way. Bldg. F, Box 436, Ft. Collins, CO 80522
    Contact: Mr. Jerry Donnan, President; Tel: (800) 759-3400 (303) 226-3600
FELLER REAL ESTATE . . . . 101 W. Garfield Ave., Box 267, Cissna Park, IL 60924
    Contact: Mr. Arthur Feller, Principal; Tel: (8150 457-2175
FIFTY STATES REAL ESTATE . . . . 3504 W. Peoria Ave., Phoenix, AZ 85029
    Contact: President; Tel: (602) 242-6669
GALLERY OF HOMES . . . . 800 Hingham, # 2N, Rockland, MA 02370
    Contact: Mr. Larry Roache, VP Ops.; Tel: (800) 241-8320 (617) 871-0927
HELP-U-SELL . . . . 57 W. 200 S., # 200, PO Box 45828, Salt Lake City, UT 84145
    Contact: Mr. Marv Hoffman, COO; Tel: (800) 366-1177 (801) 355-1177
HOME RATERS . . . . .3080 Skokie Valley Rd., Highland Park, IL 60035
    Contact: President; Tel: (800) 5 RATERS
HOMELIFE REALTY SERVICES . . . . 397 Eglinton Ave. E., Toronto, ON M4P 1M6   CAN
    Contact: Mr. A. Cimerman; Tel: (416) 486-9444
HOMEOWNERS CONCEPT . . . . 951 E. 86th St., # 201, Indianapolis, IN 46240
    Contact: Mr. J. Michael Phillips, President; Tel: (800) 800-9890 (317) 257-9999

HOMEQUEST . . . . 6350 A McDonough Dr., Norcross, GA 30093
    Contact: Mr. Jack Stein; Tel: (404) 447-1111
HYATT REAL ESTATE . . . . .1919 West St., Annapolis, MD 21401
    Contact: President; Tel: (301) 261-8832
INTELLISPECT . . . . P. O. Box 51374, Knoxville, TN 37950
    Contact: President; Tel:
NATIONAL BROKERS REGISTRY / NBR . . . . .560 Brant St., Burlington, ON L7R 2G8   CAN
    Contact: Ms. Lynda D. Prouse, Dir. Mktg.; Tel: (416) 333-1122 C
NATIONAL HOUSING INSPECTIONS . . . . 1817 North Hills Blvd., Knoxville, TN 37917
    Contact: Mr. Brad Raney, VP Marketing; Tel: (615) 525-5017 C
NATIONAL REAL ESTATE SERVICE . . . . . . # 900 - 1075 W. Georgia St., Vancouver, BC V6E 4G8   CAN
    Contact: Mr. Bill Binnie, President; Tel: (604) 685-3474
PORTMAN-BARRY . . . . 1000 Abernathy Rd., # 900, Atlanta, GA 30328
    Contact: President; Tel: (404) 668-2200
PRUDENTIAL REAL ESTATE AFFILIATES . . . . . 3200 Park Center Dr., # 1500, Costa Mesa, CA 92626
    Contact: Ms. Patricia Mansur-Brown; Tel: (714) 966-7900
RADON DETECTION SERVICES . . . . P.O. Box 419, Route 179, Ringoes, NJ 08551
    Contact: Ms. Deborah Fuggazotto, Fran. Dir.; Tel: (201) 788-3080
REAL ESTATE ONE . . . . .745 S. Garfield Ave., Traverse City, MI 49684
    Contact: Mr. Gary L. Pownall, Dir. Fran.; Tel: (616) 946-4040
REALTY 500 . . . . 4600 Kietzke Ln., # M247, Reno, NV 89502
    Contact: Mr. Craig N. Schriber, CEO; Tel: (702) 322-5500
REALTY ONE . . . . 7310 Potomac Dr., Boise, ID 83704
    Contact: Mr. David W. Dildine, President; Tel: (800) 732-5896 (208) 322-2700
REALTY USA/INTERSTATE REFERRAL SERVICE . . . . P.O. Box 402, Rte. 9, Clifton Park, NY 12065
    Contact: Mr. Chris Schmid, President; Tel: (800) 833-4833
REALTY WORLD . . . . 12500 Fair Lakes Circle, # 300, Fairfax, VA 22038
    Contact: Mr. Brian Malone, Fran. Coord.; Tel: (800) 777-5565 (703) 631-9300
REALTY WORLD OF N. CALIFORNIA . . . . 2880 Diamond Blvd., # 500, Concord, CA 94520
    Contact: Mr. Scott LeForce, Dir. Mktg.; Tel: (510) 460-9700
RED CARPET REAL ESTATE SERVICES . . . . 4180 Ruffin Rd., San Diego, CA 92123
    Contact: Mr. Mike DesMarteau, VP Fran. Sales; Tel: (800) 654-7653 (619) 571-7181
RENET FINANCIAL-THE MORTGAGE FRANCHISE . . .2400 E. Katella Ave., # 970, Anaheim, CA 92806
    Contact: Mr. Tom Van Wagoner, Natl. Mktg. Dir; Tel: (714) 385-1244
RENTAL II . . . . 44 Hampton Cres., London, ON N6H 2N8   CAN
    Contact: President; Tel: (519) 473-1294
SELL-U-LAND . . . . 5820 Mirimar Rd., San Diego, CA 92121
    Contact: President; Tel: (619) 455-1600
SMD FRANCHISE CORP. . . . . 2506 35th Ave. SW, Fargo, ND 58104
    Contact: Mr. Peter Mehl, CEO; Tel: (800) 369-9556 (701) 234-9556
STATE WIDE REAL ESTATE SERVICES . . . . P.O. Box 297, Escanaba, MI 49829
    Contact: Mr. Richard J. Langley; Tel: (800) 338-9884 (800) 682-9123MI
U. S. REALTY ADVISORS . . . . .125 S. Wacker Dr., # 3010, Chicago, IL 60606
    Contact: President; Tel: (312) 201-1990
USA REAL ESTATE TEAM . . . . . . 3612 S. Atlantic Ave., USA Bldg., Daytona Beach Shore, FL 32127
    Contact: Mr. Vladislav Michael Biro; Tel: (904) 767-2195
VIDRON OF NEVADA . . . . 2470 Wrondel Way, # 107, Reno, NV 89502
    Contact: President; Tel: (702) 826-7377

CHAPTER 34

RECREATION AND ENTERTAINMENT

ADRENALIN ADVENTURES

1674 Myles
Carson City, NV 89701
TEL: (702) 882-5867
FAX: (702) 883-2344
Mr. Chris Gehr, Fran. Dev. Coord.

Bungee-jumping company, using hot air balloons, cranes and towers. Holders of the world record 2,600' balloon bungee jump. Over 35,000 jumps with a perfect safety record. Only bungee company with FAA supervised engineering.

HISTORY: . . . .
Established in 1990; . . 1st Franchised in 1990
Company-Owned Units (As of 8/31/1992): . . 1
Franchised Units (As of 8/31/1992): 21
Total Units (As of 8/31/1992): 22
Projected New Units for 1993: 20
Distribution: US-21;Can-0;Overseas-1
  North America: . . . . 11 States
  Concentration: . . . .3 in CO, 2 in NJ, 2 in AZ
Registered: . . . .FL,HI,IN,MD,MI,NY,OR,RI
  . . . . SD,VA,WA
Type Space: . . . 3 Acres Open Land;~NA SF

FINANCIAL: Earnings Claim: . .No
Cash Investment: $50-75K
Total Investment: $40-60K
Fees: Franchise - $9.5-16.5K
  Royalty: 8%, Advert: 0%
Contract Periods (Yrs.): . . . 10/10
Area Development Agreement: Yes/10
Sub-Franchise Contract: . . . . .No
Expand in Territory: . . . . . . Yes
Passive Ownership: . . . Discouraged
Encourage Conversions: . . . . .No
Average # Employees: . . 1 FT, 5 PT

FRANCHISOR TRAINING/SUPPORT:
Financial Assistance Provided: . . . . .Yes
Site Selection Assistance: . . . . . . .Yes
Lease Negotiation Assistance: . . . . .Yes
Co-operative Advertising: . . . . .No
Training: . . . . .1 Wk. Colorado,
  . . . . .1 Wk. Franchisee Site, On-Going
On-Going Support: B,C,D,E,G,H/ 8
EXPANSION PLANS:
US: . . . . .All US
Canada: . . . . .All Canada
Overseas: . . . . .Yes

RECREATION, ENTERTAINMENT AND TRAVEL

	1989	1990	1991	Percentage Change 90/89	Percentage Change 91/90
Total Number of Establishments:					
Company-Owned	480	587	705	22.29%	20.10%
Franchisee-Owned	9,322	10,300	10,849	10.49%	5.33%
Total	9,802	10,887	11,554	11.07%	6.13%
Ratio of Total Establishments:					
Company-Owned	4.9%	5.4%	6.1%		
Franchisee-Owned	95.1%	94.6%	93.9%		
Total	100.0%	100.0%	100.0%		
Total Sales ($000):					
Company-Owned	818,929	978,791	1,105,216	19.52%	12.92%
Franchisee-Owned	2,708,687	3,253,133	3,704,017	20.10%	13.86%
Total	3,527,616	4,231,924	4,809,233	19.97%	13.64%
Ratio of Total Sales:					
Company-Owned	23.2%	23.1%	23.0%		
Franchisee-Owned	76.8%	76.9%	77.0%		
Total	100.0%	100.0%	100.0%		
Average Sales Per Unit ($000):					
Company-Owned	1,706	1,667	1,568	-2.27%	-5.98%
Franchisee-Owned	291	316	341	8.70%	8.10%
Total	360	389	416	8.01%	7.08%
Relative Average Sales Ratio:	587.2%	527.9%	459.2%		

	Number Of Employees	Employees Per Unit	Avg. Sales Per Employee
Total 1989 Employment:			
Company-Owned	3,642	7.6	$224,857
Franchisee-Owned	32,184	3.5	$84,163
Total	35,826	3.7	$98,465
Relative Employee Performance Ratios:		219.8%	267.2%

	1st Quartile	Median	4th Quartile
Average 1989 Total Investment:			
Company-Owned	$75,000	$100,000	$185,000
Franchisee-Owned	$70,000	$100,000	$125,000
Single Unit Franchise Fee	$12,500	$25,000	$30,000
Mult. Unit Franchise Fee	NA	NA	NA
Franchise Start-Up Cost	$27,500	$50,000	$60,000

Source: Franchising In The Economy 1991, IFA Educational Foundation & Horwath International.

AMERICAN POOLPLAYERS ASSOCIATION
1000 Lake St. Louis Blvd., # 325
Lake St. Louis, MO 63367
TEL: (314) 625-8611
FAX: (314) 625-2975
Ms. Renee Lyle, Dir. Marketing

APA franchisees run a national network of amateur handicapped pool leagues. No knowledge of pool is required. Complete training and on-going marketing experience is provided. Protected territories. Operate from your home. Work part-time or full-time. Sponsored nationally by Anheuser-Busch since 1980.

HISTORY: . . . . IFA	FINANCIAL: Earnings Claim: . Yes	FRANCHISOR TRAINING/SUPPORT:
Established in 1981; . . 1st Franchised in 1982	Cash Investment: . . . $Varies w/ Pop	Financial Assistance Provided: . . . . . No
Company-Owned Units (As of 8/31/1992): . .0	Total Investment: . . . . $~6.5K	Site Selection Assistance: . . . . . . .NA
Franchised Units (As of 8/31/1992): 215	Fees: Franchise - . . . . $~6.5K	Lease Negotiation Assistance: . . . . .No
Total Units (As of 8/31/1992): 215	Royalty: 20%, Advert: 0%	Co-operative Advertising: . . . . .NA
Projected New Units for 1993:	Contract Periods (Yrs.): 1/5	Training: . . . . 3 Days Headquarters
Distribution: US-213;Can-2;Overseas-0	Area Development Agreement: . .No	. . . .
North America:	Sub-Franchise Contract: . . . . .No	On-Going Support: B,C,D,G,H/ 35
Concentration:	Expand in Territory: . . . . . . .No	EXPANSION PLANS:
Registered: . . . . All Except DC and AB	Passive Ownership: . . . . . .Allowed	US: . . . . . West Coast, Northeast, Other
. . . .	Encourage Conversions: . . . . NA	Canada: . . . . .All Canada
Type Space: . . . . NA;~NA SF	Average # Employees: . . . . . .1 PT	Overseas: . . . . No

ATEC GRAND SLAM U.S.A.

115 Post St., P.O. Box 1317
Santa Cruz, CA 95060
TEL: (800) 547-6273 (408) 425-1484 C
FAX: (408) 425-7832
Mr. David Shepard, VP

ATEC GRAND SLAM U.S.A. is the only known franchisor of baseball and softball automated batting ranges and training academies. Our state-of-the-art training equipment can be used indoor or outdoors and ATEC's Casey and Hummer Pitching Machines are used by all 26 Major League Baseball teams.

HISTORY: . . . . IFA	FINANCIAL: Earnings Claim: . .No	FRANCHISOR TRAINING/SUPPORT:
Established in 1976; . . 1st Franchised in 1982	Cash Investment: . . . .$	Financial Assistance Provided: . . . . . No
Company-Owned Units (As of 8/31/1992): . .0	Total Investment: $90-200K	Site Selection Assistance: . . . . . . .Yes
Franchised Units (As of 8/31/1992): 87	Fees: Franchise - $3-12K	Lease Negotiation Assistance: . . . . .Yes
Total Units (As of 8/31/1992): 87	Royalty: 6%, Advert: 8%	Co-operative Advertising: . . . . .Yes
Projected New Units for 1993: 15	Contract Periods (Yrs.): 10/10	Training: . . . . . . 3 Days Pleasanton, CA,
Distribution: US-86;Can-1;Overseas-0	Area Development Agreement: Yes/Var	. . . . .On-Going at Site & Headquarters
North America: . . . . . 30 States, 1 Province	Sub-Franchise Contract: . . . . . Yes	On-Going Support: b,C,D,E,G,h,I/ . . . 65
Concentration: . . . 9 in CA, 8 in PA, 8 in NY	Expand in Territory: . . . . . .No	EXPANSION PLANS:
Registered: . . . CA,HI,IL,IN,MD,MI,MN,NY	Passive Ownership: . . . Discouraged	US: . . . . .All US
. . . . .RI,VA,WA,,WI,AB	Encourage Conversions: . . . . . Yes	Canada: . . . . .All Canada
Type Space: Lt. Indust., W/H;~15,000-20,000 SF	Average # Employees: . . 3 FT, 2 PT	Overseas: . . . . No

BUD LIGHT DART LEAGUE

1000 Lake St. Louis Blvd., # 325
Lake St. Louis, MO 63367
TEL: (314) 625-8621
FAX: (314) 625-2975
Mr. Glenn Remick, President

Franchised dart league system. Targets vast majority of dart enthusiasts through copyrighted handicap system. Focuses on fun and excitement of weekly competition on a year-round basis. Members of leagues pay franchisees weekly for the administrative service.

HISTORY:	FINANCIAL: Earnings Claim: . .No	FRANCHISOR TRAINING/SUPPORT:
Established in 1990; . . 1st Franchised in 1991	Cash Investment: . . . . .$1.2K + Fee	Financial Assistance Provided: . . . . .No
Company-Owned Units (As of 8/31/1992): . .0	Total Investment: . . . . .$1.2K + Fee	Site Selection Assistance: . . . . . . .NA
Franchised Units (As of 8/31/1992): 46	Fees: Franchise - . . . . $Varies	Lease Negotiation Assistance: . . . . .NA
Total Units (As of 8/31/1992): 46	Royalty: 20%, Advert: 0%	Co-operative Advertising: . . . . .Yes
Projected New Units for 1993: 20	Contract Periods (Yrs.): 1/5	Training: . . . . 3 Days Headquarters
Distribution: US-46;Can-0;Overseas-0	Area Development Agreement: . .No	. . . .
North America:	Sub-Franchise Contract: . . . . . .No	On-Going Support: A,B,C,d,G,H/ 2
Concentration: . . . .9 in IL, 9 in MO, 5 in CA	Expand in Territory: . . . . Yes	EXPANSION PLANS:
Registered: . . . . All States Exc. DC	Passive Ownership: . . . Discouraged	US: . . . . .All US
. . . .	Encourage Conversions: . . . . NA	Canada: . . . . .No
Type Space: . . . . NA;~NA SF	Average # Employees: . . . . . .1 FT	Overseas: . . . . No

CALCULATED COUPLES

3370 N. Hayden Rd., # 123-296
Scottsdale, AZ 85251
TEL: (800) 44-MATCH (602) 494-7783
FAX:
Mr. David E. Gorman, President

Singles matchmaking party service. Patent-pending system matches hundreds of singles each week at each CALCULATED COUPLES party. Replaces dating services. Fun, unique, part-time, all cash singles business.

HISTORY:	FINANCIAL: Earnings Claim: . .No	FRANCHISOR TRAINING/SUPPORT:
Established in 1983; . . 1st Franchised in 1987	Cash Investment: $15-30K	Financial Assistance Provided: . . .Yes(D)
Company-Owned Units (As of 8/31/1992): . .6	Total Investment: $18-49K	Site Selection Assistance: . . . . . . .Yes
Franchised Units (As of 8/31/1992): 7	Fees: Franchise - $15-30K	Lease Negotiation Assistance: . . . .NA
Total Units (As of 8/31/1992): 13	Royalty: 5%, Advert: 0%	Co-operative Advertising: . . . . . . .Yes
Projected New Units for 1993:	Contract Periods (Yrs.): 2/2	Training: . . . . . . 3 Days Headquarters,
Distribution: US-13;Can-0;Overseas-0	Area Development Agreement: . .No	. . . . . . .2 Days Franchisee Location
North America: . . . . 8 States	Sub-Franchise Contract: . . . . .No	On-Going Support: B,C,D,E,G,h,I/ 2
Concentration: . . . .5 in NY, 1 in NJ, 1 in AZ	Expand in Territory: . . . . . . Yes	EXPANSION PLANS:
Registered: . . . . CA,NY	Passive Ownership: . . . Discouraged	US: . . . . .All US
. . . .	Encourage Conversions: . . . . Yes	Canada: . . . . .No
Type Space: . . . . NA;~NA SF	Average # Employees: . . . . .4 PT	Overseas: . . . . No

CLUB NAUTICO INTERNATIONAL

5450 NW 33rd Ave., # 106
Ft. Lauderdale, FL 33309
TEL: (800) NAUTICO (305) 739-9800
FAX: (305) 739-9892
Ms. Gina A. Durnak, VP Mktg.

Each CLUB NAUTICO retail center rents superior quality powerboats to the qualified general public, and sells memberships. The CLUB NAUTICO network focuses on providing the consumer an easy, convenient and affordable alternative to boat ownership which allows the members to enjoy highly preferential rates at any CLUB NAUTICO in the world.

HISTORY: . . . . .IFA	FINANCIAL: Earnings Claim: . .No	FRANCHISOR TRAINING/SUPPORT:
Established in 1984; . . 1st Franchised in 1986	Cash Investment: $80-100K	Financial Assistance Provided: . . . Yes(I)
Company-Owned Units (As of 8/31/1992): . .6	Total Investment: $80-100K	Site Selection Assistance: . . . . . . .Yes
Franchised Units (As of 8/31/1992): 54	Fees: Franchise - $25K	Lease Negotiation Assistance: . . . . .Yes
Total Units (As of 8/31/1992): 60	Royalty: 10%, Advert: 2%	Co-operative Advertising: . . . . . . .Yes
Projected New Units for 1993: 10	Contract Periods (Yrs.): 5/5	Training: . . . . 1 Wk. Headquarters, 1 Wk.
Distribution: US-56;Can-0;Overseas-4	Area Development Agreement: . .No	. . On-Site, 1 Wk. OMC Regional Train.
North America: . . . . 11 States	Sub-Franchise Contract: . . . . . Yes	On-Going Support: A,B,C,d,E,G,H,I/ . . 22
Concentration: . . . 36 in FL, 4 in TX, 4 in CA	Expand in Territory: . . . . . . Yes	EXPANSION PLANS:
Registered: . . . . .All	Passive Ownership: . . . Not Allowed	US: . . . . .All US
. . . .	Encourage Conversions: . . . . Yes	Canada: . . . . .No
Type Space: . . . . . . Waterfront;~150 SF	Average # Employees: . . 3 FT, 1 PT	Overseas: . . . . EUR, Asia

COMPLETE MUSIC

8317 Cass St.
Omaha, NE 68114
TEL: (800) 843-3866 (402) 391-4847 C
FAX: (402) 391-4622
Mr. Gerald E. Maas, President

COMPLETE MUSIC is the leader in disc jockey entertainment, providing dance music for over 1 million people each year. The uniqueness of this business allows owners, who need not be entertainers, to use their skills in management to hire and book their own complete music-trained DJ's for all types of special events.

HISTORY:	FINANCIAL: Earnings Claim: . .No	FRANCHISOR TRAINING/SUPPORT:
Established in 1972; . . 1st Franchised in 1982	Cash Investment: $6-15.5K	Financial Assistance Provided: . . . . .Yes
Company-Owned Units (As of 8/31/1992): . .1	Total Investment: $10-25K	Site Selection Assistance: . . . . . . .NA
Franchised Units (As of 8/31/1992): 98	Fees: Franchise - $3-9.5K	Lease Negotiation Assistance: . . . . .NA
Total Units (As of 8/31/1992): 99	Royalty: 8%, Advert: 2%	Co-operative Advertising: . . . . . . .Yes
Projected New Units for 1993: 24	Contract Periods (Yrs.): . . .Lifetime	Training: . . . . . . 10 Days Headquarters,
Distribution: US-96;Can-3;Overseas-0	Area Development Agreement: . .No	. . . . .4 Days Franchisee Location
North America: . . . . . 25 States, 1 Province	Sub-Franchise Contract: . . . . .No	On-Going Support: B,C,d,F,G,H,i/ 6
Concentration: . . . .9 in NE, 6 in KS, 6 in MI	Expand in Territory: . . . . . . .No	EXPANSION PLANS:
Registered: . . .CA,FL,IL,MD,MI,MN,ND,SD	Passive Ownership: . . . Not Allowed	US: . . . . .Nebraska
. . . .	Encourage Conversions: . . . . NA	Canada: . . . . .All Canada
Type Space: . . . . NA;~NA SF	Average # Employees: . . 1 FT, 3 PT	Overseas: . . . . .No

FUN SERVICES

3815 S. Ashland Ave.
Chicago, IL 60609
TEL: (800) 926-1223 (312) 847-2600
FAX: (312) 847-6127
Mr. Jay Holt, Bus. Devel.

FUN SERVICES provides a wide range of fund raising programs for countless industries. Some of these programs include the original Santa's Secret Shop program, Fun Fair program, Just For Fun exclusive premium and gifts catalogue, cheese, sausage and cookies, company picnics, parties, etc.

HISTORY:	FINANCIAL: Earnings Claim: . .No	FRANCHISOR TRAINING/SUPPORT:
Established in 1965; . . 1st Franchised in 1965	Cash Investment: . . . . . $20K Min.	Financial Assistance Provided: . . .Yes(D)
Company-Owned Units (As of 8/31/1992): . .1	Total Investment: . . . . . $70K Min.	Site Selection Assistance: . . . . . . .Yes
Franchised Units (As of 8/31/1992): 120	Fees: Franchise - $20K	Lease Negotiation Assistance: . . . . .Yes
Total Units (As of 8/31/1992): 121	Royalty: $150/Mo., Advert: . . 0%	Co-operative Advertising: . . . . .No
Projected New Units for 1993: 3	Contract Periods (Yrs.): 10/10	Training: . . . . . . 5 Days Headquarters
Distribution: US-120;Can-1;Overseas-0	Area Development Agreement: .No	. . . .
North America: . . . . . 30 States, 1 Province	Sub-Franchise Contract: . . . . .No	On-Going Support: B,C,d,E,G,H,I/ . . . 20
Concentration: . . . 6 in CA, 4 in MI, 4 in OH	Expand in Territory: . . . . . . Yes	EXPANSION PLANS:
Registered: . . . . IL,IN,VA	Passive Ownership: . . . Discouraged	US: . . . . Various
. . . .	Encourage Conversions: . . . . NA	Canada: . . . . .No
Type Space: . . . .FS, SF, SC;~2,500 Min. SF	Average # Employees: 3-5 FT, 3-5 PT	Overseas: . . . . No

FUN WORKS

3216 Power Blvd.
Metairie, LA 70003
TEL: (504) 887-5678
FAX: (504) 887-4782
Mr. Frank M. Scurlock, President

FUN WORKS is an indoor high-tech amusement facility, catering to today's family. It features physical and educational rides and games. Primary customers are 2-12 year olds. Customers come for family outings, birthday parties and group events. Each store will vary slightly as we design to the site selected. Our unique concept has been perfected and is ready to be expanded through franchising.

HISTORY:	FINANCIAL: Earnings Claim: . .No	FRANCHISOR TRAINING/SUPPORT:
Established in 1986; . . 1st Franchised in 1991	Cash Investment: $50K	Financial Assistance Provided: . . . Yes(I)
Company-Owned Units (As of 8/31/1992): . .0	Total Investment: $225K	Site Selection Assistance: . . . . . . .Yes
Franchised Units (As of 8/31/1992): 3	Fees: Franchise - $25K	Lease Negotiation Assistance: . . . . .Yes
Total Units (As of 8/31/1992): 3	Royalty: 6%, Advert: 1/2%	Co-operative Advertising: . . . . .Yes
Projected New Units for 1993: 5	Contract Periods (Yrs.): 5/10	Training: . . . . . . .1 Wk. Headquarters,
Distribution: US-3;Can-0;Overseas-0	Area Development Agreement: Yes/5	. . . . 1 Wk. Store
North America: . . . . 2 States	Sub-Franchise Contract: . . . . .No	On-Going Support: a,b,C,D,E,F,G,H/ . . 5
Concentration: . . . . 2 in LA, 1 in TN	Expand in Territory: . . . . . . Yes	EXPANSION PLANS:
Registered:	Passive Ownership: . . . Discouraged	US: . . . . .All US
. . . .	Encourage Conversions: . . . . Yes	Canada: . . . . .All Canada
Type Space: FS, SF, SC, RM;~8,000-12,000 SF	Average # Employees: . .3 FT, 12 PT	Overseas: . . . . No

GREAT EXPECTATIONS

16830 Ventura Blvd., # P
Encino, CA 91436
TEL: (818) 788-5200
FAX: (818) 788-5304
Mr. Jeffrey Ullman, President

GREAT EXPECTATIONS is the largest video dating organization in the world. We have more members, more marriages and the highest system sales of any such company in the world.

HISTORY: . . . . IFA	FINANCIAL: Earnings Claim: . .No	FRANCHISOR TRAINING/SUPPORT:
Established in 1976; . . 1st Franchised in 1977	Cash Investment: . . . .$	Financial Assistance Provided: . . . . .Yes
Company-Owned Units (As of 8/31/1992): . .5	Total Investment: $162-292K	Site Selection Assistance: . . . . . . .Yes
Franchised Units (As of 8/31/1992): 37	Fees: Franchise - $55K	Lease Negotiation Assistance: . . . . .Yes
Total Units (As of 8/31/1992): 42	Royalty: 8%, Advert: 0%	Co-operative Advertising: . . . . .Yes
Projected New Units for 1993: 10	Contract Periods (Yrs.): 10/10	Training: . . . . . . 1-2 Wks. Headquarters,
Distribution: US-42;Can-0;Overseas-0	Area Development Agreement: .No	. . . . .4 Wks. Franchisee Location
North America: . . . . 25 States	Sub-Franchise Contract: . . . . .No	On-Going Support: A,B,C,D,E,G,H/ . . 25
Concentration: . . . 9 in CA, 4 in PA, 4 in FL	Expand in Territory: . . . . . . .No	EXPANSION PLANS:
Registered: . . . . . .All States Exc. ND & SD	Passive Ownership: . . . Discouraged	US: . . . . .All US
. . . .	Encourage Conversions: . . . . Yes	Canada: . . . . .All Canada
Type Space: . . . . FS;~3,000+ SF	Average # Employees: . .10 FT, 5 PT	Overseas: . . . . .Yes

GREAT GOLF LEARNING CENTERS

1001 Lower Landing Rd., # 201
Blackwood, NJ 08012
TEL: (609) 232-6029
FAX: (609) 227-9229
Mr. Carl B. Pimental, VP Mktg. Sales

Golf training, featuring a patented product. You've read about us in Entrepreneur and Golf Digest. PGA Magazine said we have "the best, most visible, self-teaching practice method yet devised" and we own the patent on the technology that makes it all possible! Our strength has been proven with thousands of golfers. We serve a growing market and offer proprietary teaching tools. Exclusive areas and more.

HISTORY: . . . .
Established in 1990; . . 1st Franchised in 1991
Company-Owned Units (As of 8/31/1992): . .2
Franchised Units (As of 8/31/1992): 4
Total Units (As of 8/31/1992): 6
Projected New Units for 1993: 50
Distribution: US-6;Can-0;Overseas-0
North America: . . . . 3 States
Concentration: . . . .3 in PA, 2 in NJ, 1 in OH
Registered: . . .CA,FL,HI,MD,MI,NY,OR,VA
. . . . .DC - Pending in 6 Others
Type Space: . . . SC, Ind. Flex Sp.;~4,000 SF

FINANCIAL: Earnings Claim: . .No
Cash Investment: $75-150K
Total Investment: $75-150K
Fees: Franchise - $24.5K
Royalty: 6%, Advert: . . . . Varies
Contract Periods (Yrs.): 15/15
Area Development Agreement: Yes/3
Sub-Franchise Contract: . . . . .No
Expand in Territory: . . . . Yes
Passive Ownership: . . . . .Allowed
Encourage Conversions: . . . . NA
Average # Employees: 2-3 FT, 2-3 PT

FRANCHISOR TRAINING/SUPPORT:
Financial Assistance Provided: . . . .NA
Site Selection Assistance: . . . . . . .Yes
Lease Negotiation Assistance: . . . .No
Co-operative Advertising: . . . . . . .Yes
Training: . . . . 8 Days Headquarters,
. . . . 5 Days Franchisee Site
On-Going Support: b,C,D,G,h,I/ 10
EXPANSION PLANS:
US: . . . . All US
Canada: . . . . All Exc. Alberta
Overseas: . . . . No

MINI PUTT INTERNATIONAL

6135 Metropolitan Blvd. E.
St. Leonard, PQ H1P 1X7 CAN
TEL: (514) 323-9864
FAX: (514) 323-9938
Mr. Rene Deshaies, VP Sales

MINI PUTT INTERNATIONAL offers more than 20 years' experience in evaluating, constructing and managing miniature golf operations. Our leadership in known in Quebec. This expertise will give you what you are looking for - protected area, training programs, promotional support, competition activities and recognition.

HISTORY: . . . .
Established in 1971; . . 1st Franchised in 1971
Company-Owned Units (As of 8/31/1992): . .0
Franchised Units (As of 8/31/1992): 42
Total Units (As of 8/31/1992): 42
Projected New Units for 1993: 6
Distribution: US-0;Can-42;Overseas-0
North America: . . . . .1 Province
Concentration: . . . . .42 in PQ
Registered: . . . .
. . . .
Type Space: . . . . . . SC, RM;~30,000 SF

FINANCIAL: Earnings Claim: . .No
Cash Investment: $75K
Total Investment: $150K
Fees: Franchise - $30K
Royalty: $5,000, Advert: 3%
Contract Periods (Yrs.): 5/5
Area Development Agreement: . .No
Sub-Franchise Contract: . . . . .No
Expand in Territory: . . . . Yes
Passive Ownership: . . . Discouraged
Encourage Conversions: . . . . Yes
Average # Employees: . . 2 FT, 1 PT

FRANCHISOR TRAINING/SUPPORT:
Financial Assistance Provided: . . . .Yes
Site Selection Assistance: . . . . . . .Yes
Lease Negotiation Assistance: . . . .Yes
Co-operative Advertising: . . . . . . .Yes
Training: . . . . 3 Days Headquarters,
. . . . 2 Days On-Site
On-Going Support: B,C,D,E,G,h/ 5
EXPANSION PLANS:
US: . . . . All US
Canada: . . . . .All Canada
Overseas: . . . . No

NETWORK CLUB INTERNATIONAL

1525 Aviation Blvd., # 215
Redondo Beach, CA 90278
TEL: (310) 978-8799 (310) 793-3000
FAX:
Mr. Eric Panitz, President

Video dating service, located in major regional shopping malls. Low overhead and advertising costs and the tremendous benefit of walk-in traffic allow us to provide great service at a fraction of the cost our competitor charges.

HISTORY: . . . .
Established in 1988; . . 1st Franchised in 1990
Company-Owned Units (As of 8/31/1992): . .0
Franchised Units (As of 8/31/1992): 2
Total Units (As of 8/31/1992): 2
Projected New Units for 1993: 6
Distribution: US-2;Can-0;Overseas-0
North America: . . . . .1 State
Concentration: . . . . 2 in CA
Registered: . . . . CA
. . . .
Type Space: . . . . RM;~1,000 SF

FINANCIAL: Earnings Claim: . .No
Cash Investment: $50-80K
Total Investment: $70-140K
Fees: Franchise - $27.5K
Royalty: 7%, Advert: 0%
Contract Periods (Yrs.): . . . 10/10
Area Development Agreement: . .No
Sub-Franchise Contract: . . . . .No
Expand in Territory: . . . . Yes
Passive Ownership: . . . Discouraged
Encourage Conversions: . . . . Yes
Average # Employees: . . 4 FT, 4 PT

FRANCHISOR TRAINING/SUPPORT:
Financial Assistance Provided: . . . Yes(I)
Site Selection Assistance: . . . . . . .Yes
Lease Negotiation Assistance: . . . .Yes
Co-operative Advertising: . . . . . . .Yes
Training: . . . . 1 Wk. Headquarters
. . . .
On-Going Support: b,C,D,E,H/ 2
EXPANSION PLANS:
US: . . . . Western US
Canada: . . . . .Yes
Overseas: . . . . No

PARTY ANIMALS

6625 Williamson Dr.
Atlanta, GA 30328
TEL: (404) 303-7789
FAX: (404) 303-8118
Ms. Cheryl Carter, President

How would you like to wear a big head, make people laugh and add a special touch to business and residential functions? Our costumed characters perform for family and corporate events, painting faces, doing magic, creating theme parties. Provide education and fun for children and wholesome entertainment for adults. Growing list of major corporate clients. Exclusive franchise for your area. Priced by population.

HISTORY:	FINANCIAL: Earnings Claim: . .No	FRANCHISOR TRAINING/SUPPORT:
Established in 1987; . . 1st Franchised in 1990	Cash Investment: $22-86K	Financial Assistance Provided: . . .Yes(D)
Company-Owned Units (As of 8/31/1992): . .1	Total Investment: $22-126K	Site Selection Assistance: . . . . . . .NA
Franchised Units (As of 8/31/1992): 6	Fees: Franchise - $10-100K	Lease Negotiation Assistance: . . . .NA
Total Units (As of 8/31/1992): 7	Royalty: 5%, Advert: 0-2%	Co-operative Advertising: . . . . . . .NA
Projected New Units for 1993: 10	Contract Periods (Yrs.): 5/5	Training: . . . . Up to 5 Days Headquarters
Distribution: US-7;Can-0;Overseas-0	Area Development Agreement: . .No	. . . . .Up to 2 Days On-Site
North America: . . . . .5 States	Sub-Franchise Contract: . . . . .No	On-Going Support: B,c,D,G,h/ 2
Concentration: . . .1 in VA, 1 in GA, 1 in MD	Expand in Territory: . . . . . .Yes	EXPANSION PLANS:
Registered:	Passive Ownership: . . . Not Allowed	US: . . . . .All US
. . . .	Encourage Conversions: . . . . NA	Canada: . . . . .All Canada
Type Space: . . . . . .Home Based;~NA SF	Average # Employees: . .1 FT, 25 PT	Overseas: . . . . No

R AND R SOUND SYSTEMS

100 River Ridge Rd.
Liverpool, NY 13090
TEL: (315) 652-5461
FAX: (315) 454-8836
Mr. Rich Strage, Jr., CEO

Full-service mobile entertainment DJ/Emcee company. Providing music, lighting and video for any event from 2-2,000+. Many packages available. Family business using traditional customer is first practice which made us the #1 DJ company in Upstate NY 4 years in a row. Member ADJA, ASCAP.

HISTORY:	FINANCIAL: Earnings Claim: . .No	FRANCHISOR TRAINING/SUPPORT:
Established in 1980; . . 1st Franchised in 1991	Cash Investment: . . . . $6K+	Financial Assistance Provided: . . . Yes(I)
Company-Owned Units (As of 8/31/1992): . .4	Total Investment: $6-30K	Site Selection Assistance: . . . . . . .NA
Franchised Units (As of 8/31/1992): 0	Fees: Franchise - $2K	Lease Negotiation Assistance: . . . .NA
Total Units (As of 8/31/1992): 4	Royalty: $175/Mo., Advert: . . 0%	Co-operative Advertising: . . . . No
Projected New Units for 1993: 50	Contract Periods (Yrs.): 1/1	Training: . . . . . . 15 Days Post-Sale for
Distribution: US-4;Can-0;Overseas-0	Area Development Agreement: . .No	. . . . Each Unit at Headquarters
North America: . . . . .1 State	Sub-Franchise Contract: . . . . Yes	On-Going Support: B,C,d,F,G,I/ 10
Concentration: . . . . 4 in NY	Expand in Territory: . . . . . .Yes	EXPANSION PLANS:
Registered: . . . . NY	Passive Ownership: . . . Discouraged	US: . . . . .All US
. . . .	Encourage Conversions: . . . . NA	Canada: . . . . .All Canada
Type Space: . . . Home Office/Bldg.;~150 SF	Average # Employees: . . . . . .2 PT	Overseas: . . . . No

RECORDS ON WHEELS /
R.O.W. ENTERTAINMENT
255 Shields Ct.
Markham, ON L3R 8V2 CAN
TEL: (416) 475-3550
FAX: (416) 475-4163
Ms. Rosie Knapp, Fran. Dir.

Independently-owned retail outlet of cassettes, compact disc, videos, laser discs and other related accessories.

HISTORY:	FINANCIAL: Earnings Claim: . .No	FRANCHISOR TRAINING/SUPPORT:
Established in 1974; . . 1st Franchised in 1975	Cash Investment: $75-100K	Financial Assistance Provided: . . . . .No
Company-Owned Units (As of 8/31/1992): . .0	Total Investment: . . . .$	Site Selection Assistance: . . . . . . .Yes
Franchised Units (As of 8/31/1992): 31	Fees: Franchise - $7.5K	Lease Negotiation Assistance: . . . .Yes
Total Units (As of 8/31/1992): 31	Royalty: 0%, Advert: 0%	Co-operative Advertising: . . . . . . .Yes
Projected New Units for 1993:	Contract Periods (Yrs.): 5/5	Training: . . . . 5-10 Days Closest Operat-
Distribution: US-0;Can-31;Overseas-0	Area Development Agreement: . .No	. . . . .ing Franchise
North America: . . . . 3 Provinces	Sub-Franchise Contract: . . . . .No	On-Going Support: B,D,E,F,H/ 25
Concentration: . . 27 in ON, 3 in SK, 1 in MB	Expand in Territory: . . . . . .Yes	EXPANSION PLANS:
Registered:	Passive Ownership: . . . Discouraged	US: . . . . .No
. . . .	Encourage Conversions: . . . . .No	Canada: . . . . .All Canada
Type Space: . .SF, RM, Downtown;~1,000 SF	Average # Employees: . . 2 FT, 1 PT	Overseas: . . . . No

SCORECASTER

P. O. Box 5
Westwood, MA 02090
TEL: (800) 875-FANS (617) FAN-0000
FAX: (617) 329-2217
Mr. Chris Thompson, Fran. Dev. Mgr.

SCORECASTER offers a unique information service to bars, restaurants, clubs and homes. SCORECASTER provides a fully-manufactured electronic scoreboard that simply plugs into a standard outlet and gives the customer instantly-updated sports and lottery information for a small monthly fee. A SCORECASTER instantly updates scores and point spreads for professional basketball, football, hockey and baseball. College football and basketball are covered.

HISTORY:	FINANCIAL: Earnings Claim: . .No	FRANCHISOR TRAINING/SUPPORT:
Established in 1991; . . 1st Franchised in 1991	Cash Investment: $7.1K	Financial Assistance Provided: . . . . . No
Company-Owned Units (As of 8/31/1992): . .1	Total Investment: $7.1-7.7K	Site Selection Assistance: . . . . . . .NA
Franchised Units (As of 8/31/1992): 0	Fees: Franchise - $2.5K	Lease Negotiation Assistance: . . . .NA
Total Units (As of 8/31/1992): 1	Royalty: 0%, Advert: 0%	Co-operative Advertising: . . . . . . .No
Projected New Units for 1993: 12	Contract Periods (Yrs.): 5/5	Training: . . . . . . .No Training Required
Distribution: US-1;Can-0;Overseas-0	Area Development Agreement: . .No	. . . .
North America: . . . . .1 State	Sub-Franchise Contract: . . . . .No	On-Going Support: A,I/ 6
Concentration: . . . . 1 in MA	Expand in Territory: . . . . . . Yes	EXPANSION PLANS:
Registered: . . . . NY	Passive Ownership: . . . . . .Allowed	US: . . . . All US
. . . .	Encourage Conversions: . . . . .No	Canada: . . . . No
Type Space: . . . . . .Home Based;~NA SF	Average # Employees: . . . . . .1 FT	Overseas: . . . . No

WOODY'S WOOD SHOPS

300 Summit St., P. O. Box 40
Hartford, CT 06106
TEL: (800) PSI-UPSS (510) 839-5471
FAX: (510) 547-3245
Mr. Chris Bruiser, President

WOODY'S WOOD SHOPS offer instruction and use of virtually all shop tools in a fully-outfitted wood shop. After detailed instruction and testing, members have full use of shop and related facilities. Open 15 hours/day, 7 days/week. Also sell small tools and all power equipment at cost plus 5%. Members pay front-end fees plus dues.

HISTORY:	FINANCIAL: Earnings Claim: . . Yes	FRANCHISOR TRAINING/SUPPORT:
Established in 1978; . . 1st Franchised in 1980	Cash Investment: $72K	Financial Assistance Provided: . . .Yes(D)
Company-Owned Units (As of 8/31/1992): . 13	Total Investment: $85-185K	Site Selection Assistance: . . . . . . .Yes
Franchised Units (As of 8/31/1992): 26	Fees: Franchise - $22K	Lease Negotiation Assistance: . . . .Yes
Total Units (As of 8/31/1992): 39	Royalty: 6%, Advert: 2%	Co-operative Advertising: . . . . . . .Yes
Projected New Units for 1993: 4	Contract Periods (Yrs.): 15/15	Training: . . . . 3 Wks. Headquarters,
Distribution: US-34;Can-5;Overseas-0	Area Development Agreement: Yes/15	. . . . 2 Wks. On-Site, Opening
North America: . . . . . 7 States, 2 Provinces	Sub-Franchise Contract: . . . . . Yes	On-Going Support: A,C,D,g,H,i/ 21
Concentration: . . . 8 in CA, 4 in OR, 3 in WA	Expand in Territory: . . . . . . .No	EXPANSION PLANS:
Registered: . . . . . CA,IL,FL,OR,WA,WI,AB	Passive Ownership: . . . Discouraged	US: . . . . All US
. . . .	Encourage Conversions: . . . . . Yes	Canada: . . . . Ontario Only
Type Space: . FS, Warehouse;~2,800-3,400 SF	Average # Employees: . . 1 FT, 4 PT	Overseas: . . . . No

SUPPLEMENTAL LISTING OF FRANCHISORS

AIR BOINGO . . . . .1500 E. Kearns Blvd., # E-300, Park City, UT 84060
    Contact: Mr. Tom Woodard, President; Tel: (800) 354-9357 (801) 649-4078

AMERICAN DART LEAGUE . . . . 1000 Lake St. Louis Blvd., # 325, Lake St. Louis, MO 63367
    Contact: Ms. Renee Lyle, Dir. Marketing; Tel: (314) 625-8621

BRUNSWICK CORP. . . . . 525 W. Laketon Ave., Muskegon, MI 44443
    Contact: President; Tel: (616) 725-3486

CANOE OUTPOST . . . . P.O. Box 301, RR #7, Arcadia, FL 33821
    Contact: Mr. D. E. Stout, Exec. Dir.; Tel:

CHAMPIONSHIP MINIATURE GOLF . . . . 1964 Harvest Circle, State College, PA 16803
    Contact: Mr. Kevin M. Ream, President; Tel: (814) 238-4653

CINEMA 'N' DRAFTHOUSE INTERNATIONAL . . . . P. O. Box 28467, Atlanta, GA 30358
    Contact: Mr. John Duffy, VP; Tel: (404) 250-9536

DUFFERIN GAME ROOM STORE . . . . 52 Titan Rd., Etobicoke, ON M8Z 2J8   CAN
    Contact: Mr. Mark Wells; Tel: (416) 239-2761

FORCE-E . . . . .286 SW 12th Ave., Deerfield Beach, FL 33433
    Contact: President; Tel: (305) 426-4120

GARRY ROBERTSON MUSIC SERVICES . . . .# 160 - 208 Provencher Blvd., Winnipeg, MB R2H 3B4   CAN
    Contact: Mr. Garry Robertson, President; Tel: (204) 941-9116

HAUNTED HAYRIDES . . . . 5100 W. Genesee St., Camillus, NY 13031
    Contact: Mr. Ronald A. Brooks, President; Tel: (800) 344-2868 (315) 488-2824
JUNGLE JIM'S PLAYLAND . . . . 9000 Wurzbach, San Antonio, TX 78240
    Contact: Mr. David Pickus; Tel: (512) 692-3555
KIM'S KARATE, USA . . . . 9690 Deereco Rd., Lutherville, MD 21093
    Contact: President; Tel:
KKIC'S FAMILY MARTIAL ARTS CENTER . . . . P. O. Box 3146, Waco, TX 76707
    Contact: Mr. Donald J. Dwyer, Owner; Tel: (817) 756-2122
MATCHMAKER INTERNATIONAL . . . . 5103 Kingston Pike, Box 10963, Knoxville, TN 37939
    Contact: Mr. Louis A. Paravate; Tel: (615) 689-2611
MILLION CONNECTIONS . . . . 2922 E. Chapman Ave., # 100, Orange, CA 92669
    Contact: Mr. Brian Popko; Tel: (714) 771-7902
OUTDOOR OUTLET . . . . .620 E. Monroe St., Riverton, WY 82501
    Contact: President; Tel: (307) 856-6559
PAY 'N PLAY RACQUETBALL OF AMERICA . . . . 23165 Vista Way, El Toro, CA 92630
    Contact: Mr. Bill McClintock; Tel: (714) 951-3991
PRO D. J.'S . . . . 1252 1/2 Remington Rd., Schaumburg, IL 60173
    Contact: Mr. Robert Glen, President; Tel: (800) 843-1357 (708) 843-7767
PUTT-PUTT GOLF COURSES OF AMERICA . . . . . . .P.O. Box 35237, Fayetteville, NC 28303
    Contact: Mr. Bobby Owens, Natl. Fran. Dir.; Tel: (919) 485-7131
SINGLES TODAY INTRODUCTION SERVICES . . . . 1091 Setchfield Ave., Victoria, BC V9B 5A3   CAN
    Contact: Mr. Chris Slater; Tel: (604) 478-9975
STERLING BILLIARD CO. . . . . P. O. Box 1188, Rosman, NC 28772
    Contact: President; Tel: (704) 862-4400
SUN CREATIVE SYSTEM/WOOZ . . . . 500 Orange Dr., Vacaville, CA 95687
    Contact: Ms. Cheryl Esters, Fran. Dir.; Tel: (707) 446-5588
SUNSET ENTERTAINMENT . . . . 3120 49th St. N., St. Petersburg, FL 33710
    Contact: President; Tel: (813) 521-2378
SYBARIS . . . . .600 Ogden Ave., Downers Grove, IL 60515
    Contact: President; Tel: (312) 960-4000
TOGETHER DATING SERVICE . . . . 171 Main St., # 102, Ashland, MA 01721
    Contact: Mr. Brian Pappas; Tel: (508) 881-5925
WHITEY FORD'S GRAND SLAM . . . . 33 Route 46 W., Fairfield, NJ 07006
    Contact: President; Tel: (201) 575-1144

CHAPTER 35

RENTAL SERVICES

AARON'S RENT-TO-OWN

3001 N. Fulton Dr., NE
Atlanta, GA 30363
TEL: (800) 551-6015 (404) 240-6500
FAX: (404) 240-6594
Mr. Todd Evans, Director

AARON'S RENT-TO-OWN is one of the fastest growing rent-to-own companies in the nation specializing in furniture, electronics and appliances. AARON'S RENT-TO-OWN offers our franchisees the expertise, advantage and support of a well-established company, while also giving them the opportunity to be their own boss.

HISTORY: . . . .
Established in 1955; . . 1st Franchised in 1992
Company-Owned Units (As of 8/31/1992): . 32
Franchised Units (As of 8/31/1992): 1
Total Units (As of 8/31/1992): 33
Projected New Units for 1993: 10
Distribution: US-33;Can-0;Overseas-0
  North America: . . . . 8 States
  Concentration: . . . 16 in FL, 9 in GA, 7 in TX
Registered: . . . . VA
. . . .
Type Space: . . . . .SC;~5,000 SF

FINANCIAL: Earnings Claim: . Yes
Cash Investment: $40-60K
Total Investment: . . . $117.3-258.1K
Fees: Franchise - $14.5K
  Royalty: 5%, Advert: 2.5%
Contract Periods (Yrs.): 10/10
Area Development Agreement: Yes/Var
Sub-Franchise Contract: . . . . . .No
Expand in Territory: . . . . Yes
Passive Ownership: . . . . . .Allowed
Encourage Conversions: . . . . . NA
Average # Employees: . . . . . .5 FT

FRANCHISOR TRAINING/SUPPORT:
Financial Assistance Provided: . . . Yes(I)
Site Selection Assistance: . . . . .Yes
Lease Negotiation Assistance: . . . . .Yes
Co-operative Advertising: . . . . .Yes
Training: . . . . .1 Wk. Headquarters,
. . . . 2 Wks. Franchisee Site
On-Going Support: A,B,C,D,E,F,G,h,I/ . 25
EXPANSION PLANS:
US: . . . . Southeast
Canada: . . . . No
Overseas: . . . . No

RENTAL SERVICES: EQUIPMENT

	1989	1990	1991	Percentage Change 90/89	Percentage Change 91/90
Total Number of Establishments:					
Company–Owned	731	784	804	7.25%	2.55%
Franchisee–Owned	1,885	1,962	2,094	4.08%	6.73%
Total	2,616	2,746	2,898	4.97%	5.54%
Ratio of Total Establishments:					
Company–Owned	27.9%	28.6%	27.7%		
Franchisee–Owned	72.1%	71.4%	72.3%		
Total	100.0%	100.0%	100.0%		
Total Sales ($000):					
Company–Owned	229,901	243,001	257,095	5.70%	5.80%
Franchisee–Owned	457,139	488,682	514,093	6.90%	5.20%
Total	687,040	731,683	771,188	6.50%	5.40%
Ratio of Total Sales:					
Company–Owned	33.5%	33.2%	33.3%		
Franchisee–Owned	66.5%	66.8%	66.7%		
Total	100.0%	100.0%	100.0%		
Average Sales Per Unit ($000):					
Company–Owned	315	310	320	−1.45%	3.17%
Franchisee–Owned	243	249	246	2.70%	−1.43%
Total	263	266	266	1.46%	−0.13%
Relative Average Sales Ratio:	129.7%	124.4%	130.2%		

	Number Of Employees	Employees Per Unit	Avg. Sales Per Employee
Total 1989 Employment:			
Company–Owned	4,184	5.7	$54,948
Franchisee–Owned	11,825	6.3	$38,659
Total	16,009	6.1	$42,916
Relative Employee Performance Ratios:		91.2%	142.1%

	1st Quartile	Median	4th Quartile
Average 1989 Total Investment:			
Company–Owned	$75,000	$100,000	$150,000
Franchisee–Owned	$100,000	$130,000	$200,000
Single Unit Franchise Fee	$12,500	$15,250	$22,500
Mult. Unit Franchise Fee	NA	NA	NA
Franchise Start–Up Cost	$32,500	$40,000	$75,000

Source: Franchising In The Economy 1991, IFA Educational Foundation & Horwath International.

FORMALS ETC.

4600 Shreveport Hwy.
Pineville, LA 71360
TEL: (318) 640-3766
FAX: (318) 640-8191
Mr. Sam Brimer, President

Rental of ladies' formalwear, including prom, party, pageant, bridesmaid and bridal gowns. FORMALS ETC. also designs and manufactures one-piece gowns, with emphasis on quality and style. FORMALS ETC. would like to redefine the ladies' formalwear industry. With our experience and commitment to customer service, quality, selection and style, we feel we are in a good position to participate in the growth phase of a new industry!

HISTORY:	FINANCIAL: Earnings Claim: . .No	FRANCHISOR TRAINING/SUPPORT:
Established in 1984; . . 1st Franchised in 1990	Cash Investment: $50-65K	Financial Assistance Provided: . . . . . No
Company-Owned Units (As of 8/31/1992): . .4	Total Investment: . . . .$	Site Selection Assistance: . . . . .Yes
Franchised Units (As of 8/31/1992): 9	Fees: Franchise - $15K	Lease Negotiation Assistance: . . . . .Yes
Total Units (As of 8/31/1992): 13	Royalty: 6%, Advert: 1%	Co-operative Advertising: . . . . .Yes
Projected New Units for 1993: 12	Contract Periods (Yrs.): 10/10	Training: . . . . . . .1 Wk. Company Store
Distribution: US-13;Can-0;Overseas-0	Area Development Agreement: . Yes	. . . .
North America: . . . . 5 States	Sub-Franchise Contract: . . . . . Yes	On-Going Support: d,E,F,G,H/ 3
Concentration: . . . . 4 in LA, 1 in TN, 1 in IL	Expand in Territory: . . . . Yes	EXPANSION PLANS:
Registered: . . . . FL,IL,NY,WA	Passive Ownership: . . . Discouraged	US: . . . . All US
. . . .	Encourage Conversions: . . . . . Yes	Canada: . . . . .All Canada
Type Space: . . . . .SC;~1,700 SF	Average # Employees: . . . . . .3 FT	Overseas: . . . . No

GINGISS FORMALWEAR CENTER

180 N. LaSalle St., # 1111
Chicago, IL 60601
TEL: (800) 621-7125 (312) 236-2333
FAX: (312) 580-7170
Mr. John Heiser, VP

GINGISS FORMALWEAR specializes in the rental and sales of men's formalwear and related accessories. Primarily shopping center locations. Extensive outside PR and sales promotion is necessary.

HISTORY: . . . . .IFA	FINANCIAL: Earnings Claim: . . Yes	FRANCHISOR TRAINING/SUPPORT:
Established in 1936; . . 1st Franchised in 1968	Cash Investment: $50-100K	Financial Assistance Provided: . . . Yes(I)
Company-Owned Units (As of 8/31/1992): . 29	Total Investment: $120-170K	Site Selection Assistance: . . . . .Yes
Franchised Units (As of 8/31/1992): 216	Fees: Franchise - $15K	Lease Negotiation Assistance: . . . . .Yes
Total Units (As of 8/31/1992): 245	Royalty: 6-10%, Advert: 3%	Co-operative Advertising: . . . . .Yes
Projected New Units for 1993: 12	Contract Periods (Yrs.): 10/10	Training: . . . . 2 Wks. Headquarters,
Distribution: US-245;Can-0;Overseas-0	Area Development Agreement: . .No	. . . . .1 Wk. On-Site
North America: . . . . 36 States	Sub-Franchise Contract: . . . . . .No	On-Going Support: b,C,D,E,F,G,H/ . . . 35
Concentration: . . 41 in CA, 37 in TX, 30 in IL	Expand in Territory: . . . . Yes	EXPANSION PLANS:
Registered: . . .CA,IL,IN,MD,MI,MN,NY,OR	Passive Ownership: . . . Not Allowed	US: . . . . All US
. . . . RI,VA,WA,WI	Encourage Conversions: . . . . . Yes	Canada: . . . . No
Type Space: RM, Power Center;~1,000-1,200 SF	Average # Employees: . 1 FT, 3-6 PT	Overseas: . . . . No

JOE RENT ALL

28, rue Vanier
Chateauguay, PQ J6J 3W8 CAN
TEL: (514) 692-6268
FAX: (514) 692-2848
Mr. J. M. Bissonnette, President

Franchising in tools and equipment rental.

HISTORY:	FINANCIAL: Earnings Claim: . . .	FRANCHISOR TRAINING/SUPPORT:
Established in 1979; . . 1st Franchised in 1982	Cash Investment: $50-100K	Financial Assistance Provided: . . . Yes(I)
Company-Owned Units (As of 8/31/1992): . .0	Total Investment: . . . .$	Site Selection Assistance: . . . . .Yes
Franchised Units (As of 8/31/1992): 51	Fees: Franchise - $15K	Lease Negotiation Assistance: . . . . .No
Total Units (As of 8/31/1992): 51	Royalty: 4%, Advert: 3%	Co-operative Advertising: . . . . .Yes
Projected New Units for 1993: 4	Contract Periods (Yrs.): 5/5	Training: . . . . 2 Wks. Headquarters
Distribution: US-0;Can-51;Overseas-0	Area Development Agreement: . Yes	. . . .
North America: . . . . 4 Provinces	Sub-Franchise Contract: . . . . . .No	On-Going Support: A,B,D,E,F,G,H,I/ . . 5
Concentration: . . .42 in PQ, 7 in ON, 1 in NB	Expand in Territory: . . . . Yes	EXPANSION PLANS:
Registered:	Passive Ownership: . . . Discouraged	US: . . . . No
. . . .	Encourage Conversions:	Canada: . . . . .All Canada
Type Space: . . . . ;~1,200-4,000 SF	Average # Employees: . 2 FT, 2-3 PT	Overseas: . . . . Yes

MILITARY RENT-ALL

3545 Motor Ave., # 200
Los Angeles, CA 90034
TEL: (800) 669-2221 (310) 204-2220
FAX: (310) 204-0148
Mr. Matt Feinstein, Dir. Fran. Dev.

Furniture, appliances and electronics rental. Stores on or near military bases.

HISTORY:		
Established in 1969; . . 1st Franchised in 1988	**FINANCIAL:** Earnings Claim: . .No	**FRANCHISOR TRAINING/SUPPORT:**
Company-Owned Units (As of 8/31/1992): . 11	Cash Investment: $50K	Financial Assistance Provided: . . . . .Yes
Franchised Units (As of 8/31/1992): 2	Total Investment: $100-150K	Site Selection Assistance: . . . . . . .Yes
Total Units (As of 8/31/1992): 13	Fees: Franchise - $20K	Lease Negotiation Assistance: . . . . .Yes
Projected New Units for 1993: 12	Royalty: 6%, Advert: . . . Included	Co-operative Advertising: . . . . . . .Yes
Distribution: US-13;Can-0;Overseas-0	Contract Periods (Yrs.): 10/5	Training: . . . . . As Long As Necessary
North America: . . . . 9 States	Area Development Agreement: . .No	. . . . On-Site
Concentration: . . . 4 in TX, 2 in NC, 2 in OK	Sub-Franchise Contract: . . . . Yes	On-Going Support: B,C,D,F,G,I/ 6
Registered: . . . . All States Exc. NY	Expand in Territory: . . . . . . Yes	**EXPANSION PLANS:**
. . . .	Passive Ownership: . . . Discouraged	US: . . . . .All US
	Encourage Conversions:	Canada: . . . . .Yes
Type Space: . . . . . FS, SC;~2,500-3,000 SF	Average # Employees: . 1 FT, 1-2 PT	Overseas: . . . . Yes

NATURAL SETTINGS

Box 1277, RR # 3
Crete, IL 60417
TEL: (800) 722-9422 (708) 755-2233
FAX:
Mr. Stan Woerner, VP Fran. Dev.

NATURAL SETTINGS provides live tropical plant rental and maintenance programs to a wide variety of businesses, organizations and institutions.

HISTORY:		
Established in 1978; . . 1st Franchised in 1988	**FINANCIAL:** Earnings Claim: . Yes	**FRANCHISOR TRAINING/SUPPORT:**
Company-Owned Units (As of 8/31/1992): . .2	Cash Investment: $5K	Financial Assistance Provided: . . .Yes(D)
Franchised Units (As of 8/31/1992): 10	Total Investment: $20K	Site Selection Assistance: . . . . . . .NA
Total Units (As of 8/31/1992): 12	Fees: Franchise - $17.5K	Lease Negotiation Assistance: . . . . .NA
Projected New Units for 1993: 4	Royalty: 8%, Advert: 2%	Co-operative Advertising: . . . . . . .Yes
Distribution: US-12;Can-0;Overseas-0	Contract Periods (Yrs.): 10/20	Training: . . . . 5 Days Headquarters,
North America: . . . . 8 States	Area Development Agreement: . .No	. . . . Forever Local
Concentration: . . . .2 in IL, 2 in FL, 2 in IN	Sub-Franchise Contract: . . . . .No	On-Going Support: A,B,C,D,E,F,G,H,I/ . 4
Registered: . . . . . . FL,IL,IN,MD,MI,RI,WI	Expand in Territory: . . . . . . .No	**EXPANSION PLANS:**
. . . .	Passive Ownership: . . . Not Allowed	US: . . . . .All US
	Encourage Conversions: . . . . . NA	Canada: . . . . .All Canada
Type Space: . . . . ;~ SF	Average # Employees: . . 2 FT, 2 PT	Overseas: . . . . No

PCR PERSONAL COMPUTER RENTALS

2557 Rt. 130
Cranbury, NJ 08512
TEL: (800) 727-7079
FAX: (404) 977-1802
Mr. Skip Kirby, Fran. Dev. Mgr.

PCR PERSONAL COMPUTER RENTALS is a nationwide computer rental company with over 70 franchised computer centers in the US. PCR provides computer rental equipment to clients across the US on a short and long-term basis. Our service includes delivery, installation, pick-up, 24-hour on-call technical support and customer service!

HISTORY:		
Established in 1983; . . 1st Franchised in 1984	**FINANCIAL:** Earnings Claim: . .No	**FRANCHISOR TRAINING/SUPPORT:**
Company-Owned Units (As of 8/31/1992): . .0	Cash Investment: $5-150K	Financial Assistance Provided: . . .Yes(D)
Franchised Units (As of 8/31/1992): 70	Total Investment: $26.5-230.5K	Site Selection Assistance: . . . . . . .Yes
Total Units (As of 8/31/1992): 70	Fees: Franchise - $5-29.5K	Lease Negotiation Assistance: . . . . .Yes
Projected New Units for 1993: 10	Royalty: 7%, Advert: 1%	Co-operative Advertising: . . . . . . .Yes
Distribution: US-70;Can-0;Overseas-0	Contract Periods (Yrs.): 10/10	Training: . . . . 1 Wk. Headquarters
North America: . . . . 25 States	Area Development Agreement: . .No	. . . .
Concentration: . . . 11 in CA, 6 in FL, 5 in TX	Sub-Franchise Contract: . . . . .No	On-Going Support: b,c,d,E,F,G,H,I/ . . 15
Registered: . . . . .All	Expand in Territory: . . . . . . Yes	**EXPANSION PLANS:**
. . . .	Passive Ownership: . . . Discouraged	US: . . . . . All US, Mostly 2ndary Mkts.
	Encourage Conversions: . . . . Yes	Canada: . . . . No
Type Space: . . .Office/Warehouse;~1,500 SF	Average # Employees: . . . . . .3 FT	Overseas: . . . . No

STARLIT SOIREE

8950 W. Olympic Blvd., # 213
Beverly Hills, CA 90211
TEL: (800) 300-GOWN (310) 275-5570 C
FAX:
Mr. Gordon Giles, President

What a great idea! Men rent their formalwear, now ladies can too. We offer an extraordinary ground floor opportunity to join our exciting franchise network in the exquisite world of fashion. Our concept of ladies' designer formalwear rental is rapidly becoming the wave of the future.

HISTORY:	FINANCIAL: Earnings Claim: . .No	FRANCHISOR TRAINING/SUPPORT:
Established in 1986; . . 1st Franchised in 1988	Cash Investment: $75-95K	Financial Assistance Provided: . . . . .No
Company-Owned Units (As of 8/31/1992): . .2	Total Investment: $75-125K	Site Selection Assistance: . . . . . . .Yes
Franchised Units (As of 8/31/1992): 1	Fees: Franchise - $20K	Lease Negotiation Assistance: . . . .Yes
Total Units (As of 8/31/1992): 3	Royalty: 6%, Advert: 10%	Co-operative Advertising: . . . . . . .Yes
Projected New Units for 1993: 2	Contract Periods (Yrs.): 5/5	Training: . . . . . . .1 Wk. Headquarters,
Distribution: US-3;Can-0;Overseas-0	Area Development Agreement: Yes/5	. . . . 1 Wk. Franchisee Location
North America: . . . . 3 States	Sub-Franchise Contract: . . . . .No	On-Going Support: b,C,D,E,F,G,H,I/ . . . 4
Concentration: . . . 1 in AZ, 1 in CA, 1 in TX	Expand in Territory: . . . . . . Yes	EXPANSION PLANS:
Registered: . . . . CA	Passive Ownership: . . . . .Allowed	US: . . . . .All US
. . . .	Encourage Conversions: . . . . Yes	Canada: . . . . .All Canada
Type Space: . . . . .FS, SF;~1,800 SF	Average # Employees: . . 2 FT, 1 PT	Overseas: . . . . No

TAYLOR RENTAL

1000 Stanley Dr., P. O. Box 8000
New Britain, CT 06050
TEL: (203) 229-9100
FAX: (203) 826-3207
Mr. Mark Gelinas, Dir. Fran. Ops.

TAYLOR RENTAL is the largest general rental chain in the rental industry. We offer a full range of support services, including building design and layout, inventory analysis, advertising support, professional field support, computer systems, etc.

HISTORY: . . . . IFA	FINANCIAL: Earnings Claim: . .No	FRANCHISOR TRAINING/SUPPORT:
Established in 1946; . . 1st Franchised in 1963	Cash Investment: $90K	Financial Assistance Provided: . . . . .No
Company-Owned Units (As of 8/31/1992): . 80	Total Investment: $235-275K	Site Selection Assistance: . . . . . . .Yes
Franchised Units (As of 8/31/1992): 232	Fees: Franchise - $20K	Lease Negotiation Assistance: . . . . No
Total Units (As of 8/31/1992): 312	Royalty: 2.75%, Advert: 0%	Co-operative Advertising: . . . . . . .Yes
Projected New Units for 1993: 5	Contract Periods (Yrs.): 5/10	Training: . . . . 1 Wk. Headquarters
Distribution: US-312;Can-0;Overseas-0	Area Development Agreement: Yes/10	. . . .
North America: . . . . 35 States	Sub-Franchise Contract: . . . . .No	On-Going Support: B,C,D,E,f,G,h,I/ . . 37
Concentration: . 39 in MA, 28 in NY, 26 in FL	Expand in Territory: . . . . . . .No	EXPANSION PLANS:
Registered: . . . . .All	Passive Ownership: . . . Discouraged	US: . . . . .All US
. . . .	Encourage Conversions: . . . . .No	Canada: . . . . No
Type Space: . . . . . . FS;~4,000-5,000 SF	Average # Employees: . . 3 FT, 1 PT	Overseas: . . . . No

YARD CARDS

2940 West Main St.
Belleville, IL 62223
TEL: (618) 233-0491
FAX: (618) 277-1594
Mr. Michael Hoepfinger, President

Rental of 8' greeting cards for any and all occasions, including storks to announce new babies, graduation, Valentine's Day, birthday, retirement, Mother's Day, Father's Day and anniversary cards. Can be operated as a home-based business or added on to an existing business.

HISTORY:	FINANCIAL: Earnings Claim: . .No	FRANCHISOR TRAINING/SUPPORT:
Established in 1983; . . 1st Franchised in 1986	Cash Investment: $5-15K	Financial Assistance Provided: . . . . .No
Company-Owned Units (As of 8/31/1992): . .1	Total Investment: $5-23K	Site Selection Assistance: . . . . . . .NA
Franchised Units (As of 8/31/1992): 23	Fees: Franchise - . . . . . .$1K Min.	Lease Negotiation Assistance: . . . .NA
Total Units (As of 8/31/1992): 24	Royalty: 5%, Advert: 2%	Co-operative Advertising: . . . . . . .NA
Projected New Units for 1993: 5	Contract Periods (Yrs.): 20/5/5	Training: . . . . .3 Days
Distribution: US-24;Can-0;Overseas-0	Area Development Agreement: Yes/Var	. . . .
North America: . . . . 12 States	Sub-Franchise Contract: . . . . .No	On-Going Support: B,C,G,h,i/ 2
Concentration: . . . . 8 in IL, 4 in CA, 2 in VA	Expand in Territory: . . . . . . Yes	EXPANSION PLANS:
Registered: . . . . CA,FL,IL,IN,MI,VA	Passive Ownership: . . . Discouraged	US: . . . . .All US
. . . .	Encourage Conversions:	Canada: . . . . No
Type Space: . . . . . . .Home Based;~NA SF	Average # Employees: . . . . 1-2 FT	Overseas: . . . . No

SUPPLEMENTAL LISTING OF FRANCHISORS

A TO Z RENTAL CENTERS . . . . 3550 Cedar Ave. S., Minneapolis, MN 55407
    Contact: President; Tel: (612) 729-2328

AL'S FORMAL WEAR . . . . P. O. Box 379, Bedford, TX 76095
    Contact: Mr. Allen N. Bodzy, President; Tel: (800) 879-1777 (817) 355-4444

COLORTYME . . . . P. O. Box 1781, Athens, TX 75751
    Contact: Mr. James Crysdale, CEO; Tel: (903) 675-9291

FINE ART RENTALS . . . . .24321 La Hermosa, Laguna Niguel, CA 92677
    Contact: Mr. Steve Smith; Tel: (714) 831-0222

NATION-WIDE GENERAL RENTAL CENTERS . . . . 1805 Hembree Rd., # C, Alpharetta, GA 30201
    Contact: Mr. Ike Goodvin, President; Tel: (800) 227-1643 (404) 644-7765

PARTY FASHIONS . . . . .2551 Pacific Coast Hwy., Torrance, CA 90505
    Contact: Mr. Satish C. Mehta, President; Tel: (800) 762-8300 (310) 325-6300 C

PRESIDENT TUXEDO . . . . 32185 Hollingsworth, Warren, MI 48092
    Contact: Mr. Michael Sbrocca, Jr., VP; Tel: (800) 837-TUXS (313) 264-0600

RENTALAND . . . . 2400 Chris Wood Ct., Oakton, VA 22124
    Contact: Mr. Richard J. Guiney, Sr.; Tel: (704) 541-5050

TUBS TO GO . . . . 1815 Weaver St., State College, PA 16803
    Contact: Mr. Ron Tosh, President; Tel: (800) 882-7864 (814) 234-0394 C

UNITED RENT-ALL . . . . 6408 Dearborn Dr., Shawnee Mission, KS 66202
    Contact: Mr. William Heuermann, President; Tel: (818) 704-5404

CHAPTER 36

RETAIL: ART, ART SUPPLIES AND FRAMING

DECK THE WALLS

16825 Northchase Dr., # 910
Houston, TX 77060
TEL: (800) 443-3325 (713) 874-3661
FAX: (713) 874-3650
Ms. Ann Nance, Qualifier

The nation's largest retailer specializing in art and custom framing. DECK THE WALLS has tailored the art gallery concept to meet the needs of mall shoppers. Stores feature prints, posters and frames that complement current decorating styles. Inviting decor and emphasis on skilled personal service make shopping at DECK THE WALLS a quality experience.

HISTORY: . . . . IFA
Established in 1979;   . . 1st Franchised in 1979
Company-Owned Units (As of 8/31/1992):   . .1
Franchised Units (As of 8/31/1992): 195
Total Units (As of 8/31/1992): 196
Projected New Units for 1993: 15
Distribution: . . .   US-196;Can-0;Overseas-0
  North America: . . . . 39 States
  Concentration: . 18 in PA, 18 in TX, 16 in CA
Registered: . . .CA,HI,IL,IN,MD,MN,NY,ND
 . . . . RI,SD,VA,WA,WI
Type Space: . . . . RM;~1,500 SF

FINANCIAL: Earnings Claim: . .No
Cash Investment: $75K
Total Investment: $175-210K
Fees: Franchise - $35K
  Royalty: 6%, Advert: 2%
Contract Periods (Yrs.): 10/10
Area Development Agreement: . .No
Sub-Franchise Contract: . . . . .No
Expand in Territory: . . . . . . Yes
Passive Ownership: . . . Not Allowed
Encourage Conversions: . . . . .No
Average # Employees: . . 2 FT, 2 PT

FRANCHISOR TRAINING/SUPPORT:
Financial Assistance Provided: . . . Yes(I)
Site Selection Assistance: . . . . .Yes
Lease Negotiation Assistance: . . . . .Yes
Co-operative Advertising: . . . . .Yes
Training: . . . . . . .10 Days Headquarters
 . . . .
On-Going Support: C,D,E,G,H,I/ 24
EXPANSION PLANS:
  US: . . . . .All US
  Canada: . . . . .No
  Overseas: . . . . No

RETAILING (NON-FOOD)

	1989	1990	1991	Percentage Change 90/89	Percentage Change 91/90
Total Number of Establishments:					
Company-Owned	13,497	14,151	14,621	4.85%	3.32%
Franchisee-Owned	36,582	40,277	42,414	10.10%	5.31%
Total	50,079	54,428	57,035	8.68%	4.79%
Ratio of Total Establishments:					
Company-Owned	27.0%	26.0%	25.6%		
Franchisee-Owned	73.0%	74.0%	74.4%		
Total	100.0%	100.0%	100.0%		
Total Sales ($000):					
Company-Owned	9,061,059	9,831,140	10,505,085	8.50%	6.86%
Franchisee-Owned	17,608,429	19,433,781	20,879,902	10.37%	7.44%
Total	26,669,488	29,264,921	31,384,987	9.73%	7.24%
Ratio of Total Sales:					
Company-Owned	34.0%	33.6%	33.5%		
Franchisee-Owned	66.0%	66.4%	66.5%		
Total	100.0%	100.0%	100.0%		
Average Sales Per Unit ($000):					
Company-Owned	671	695	718	3.48%	3.42%
Franchisee-Owned	481	483	492	0.24%	2.03%
Total	533	538	550	0.96%	2.34%
Relative Average Sales Ratio:	139.5%	144.0%	145.9%		

	Number Of Employees	Employees Per Unit	Avg. Sales Per Employee
Total 1989 Employment:			
Company-Owned	100,825	7.5	$89,869
Franchisee-Owned	208,120	5.7	$84,607
Total	308,945	6.2	$86,324
Relative Employee Performance Ratios:		131.3%	106.2%

	1st Quartile	Median	4th Quartile
Average 1989 Total Investment:			
Company-Owned	$75,000	$130,000	$200,000
Franchisee-Owned	$97,500	$125,000	$200,000
Single Unit Franchise Fee	$12,500	$15,000	$27,500
Mult. Unit Franchise Fee	$10,000	$17,500	$25,000
Franchise Start-Up Cost	$40,000	$85,000	$75,000

Source: Franchising In The Economy 1991, IFA Educational Foundation & Horwath International.

FASTFRAME USA

30495 Canwood St., # 100
Agoura Hills, CA 91301
TEL: (800) 521-3726 (818) 707-1166
FAX: (818) 707-0164
Mr. John L. Scott, CEO

Chain of retail custom picture framing stores.

HISTORY: . . . . IFA	FINANCIAL: Earnings Claim: . .No	FRANCHISOR TRAINING/SUPPORT:
Established in 1986; . . 1st Franchised in 1987	Cash Investment: $50-100K	Financial Assistance Provided: . . . . .Yes
Company-Owned Units (As of 8/31/1992): . .2	Total Investment: $130-190K	Site Selection Assistance: . . . . . . .Yes
Franchised Units (As of 8/31/1992): 168	Fees: Franchise - $25K	Lease Negotiation Assistance: . . . .Yes
Total Units (As of 8/31/1992): 170	Royalty: 7.5%, Advert: 3%	Co-operative Advertising: . . . . . . .Yes
Projected New Units for 1993: 20	Contract Periods (Yrs.): . . . 10/10	Training: . . . . . 11 Days Training School,
Distribution: . . . US-170;Can-0;Overseas-100	Area Development Agreement: Yes/5	. . . . 2-4 Days On-Site
North America: . . . . 25 States	Sub-Franchise Contract: . . . . . .No	On-Going Support: A,B,C,D,E,G,H,I/ . 16
Concentration: . . . 88 in CA, 9 in IL, 8 in VA	Expand in Territory: . . . . .No	EXPANSION PLANS:
Registered: . . . CA,FL,IL,IN,MD,MI,MN,NY	Passive Ownership: . . . Discouraged	US: . . . . Northeast
. . . . .OR,VA,WA,WI	Encourage Conversions: . . . . . NA	Canada: . . . . No
Type Space: . . . . . . FS, SF, SC;~1,400 SF	Average # Employees: . . . 2-3 FT	Overseas: . . . . . . MX, NZ, EUR

FLAIR-U FRAME IT

321 McDermot Ave., # 300
Winnipeg, MB R3A 0A3 CAN
TEL: (800) 665-2622 (204) 944-8705 C
FAX: (204) 942-3691
Mr. Ted Clifton, President

FLAIR FRAMING offers its customer a a full-range picture framing service that is conducted in a professional but relaxed atmosphere. Our services include custom picture framing, sale of artworks, posters and prints. Sale of related materials and accessories.

HISTORY: . . . . .CFA	FINANCIAL: Earnings Claim: . .No	FRANCHISOR TRAINING/SUPPORT:
Established in 1972; . . 1st Franchised in 1974	Cash Investment: $25K	Financial Assistance Provided: . . . Yes(I)
Company-Owned Units (As of 8/31/1992): . .2	Total Investment: $90K	Site Selection Assistance: . . . . . . .Yes
Franchised Units (As of 8/31/1992): 33	Fees: Franchise - $15K	Lease Negotiation Assistance: . . . .Yes
Total Units (As of 8/31/1992): 35	Royalty: 6.5%, Advert: 2%	Co-operative Advertising: . . . . . . .Yes
Projected New Units for 1993: 3	Contract Periods (Yrs.): . . . 5/5/5/5	Training: . . . . 3 Wks. Headquarters,
Distribution: US-0;Can-35;Overseas-0	Area Development Agreement: . .No	. . . . 1 Wk. On Location
North America: . . . . 5 Provinces	Sub-Franchise Contract: . . . . . .No	On-Going Support: A,C,E,F,G,H,I/ 3
Concentration: . . 11 in ON, 10 in BC, 6 in AB	Expand in Territory: . . . . Yes	EXPANSION PLANS:
Registered: . . . . AB	Passive Ownership: . . . Not Allowed	US: . . . . No
. . . .	Encourage Conversions: . . . . .No	Canada: . . . . .All Canada
Type Space: . . . . SC, RM;~1,500 SF	Average # Employees: . . 2 FT, 3 PT	Overseas: . . . . No

FRAMING EXPERIENCE

1800 Appleby Line
Burlington, ON L7L 6A1 CAN
TEL: (416) 332-6116
FAX: (416) 335-5377
Mr. John Williams, Dir. Retail Dev.

Quality custom and do-it-yourself framing and art stores, corporate and residential art consulting.

HISTORY: . . . . .CFA	FINANCIAL: Earnings Claim: . Yes	FRANCHISOR TRAINING/SUPPORT:
Established in 1974; . . 1st Franchised in 1977	Cash Investment: $20-50K	Financial Assistance Provided: . . . . .Yes
Company-Owned Units (As of 8/31/1992): . .0	Total Investment: $40-110K	Site Selection Assistance: . . . . . . .Yes
Franchised Units (As of 8/31/1992): 37	Fees: Franchise - $18K	Lease Negotiation Assistance: . . . .Yes
Total Units (As of 8/31/1992): 37	Royalty: 5.5%, Advert: 1%	Co-operative Advertising: . . . . . . .Yes
Projected New Units for 1993: 6	Contract Periods (Yrs.): 5/5/5	Training: . . . . .1 Wk. Home Office,
Distribution: US-0;Can-37;Overseas-0	Area Development Agreement: Yes/25	. . . . .3-4 Wks. Training Store
North America: . . . . 4 Provinces	Sub-Franchise Contract: . . . . . Yes	On-Going Support: b,C,D,E,F,G,h,I/ . . .7
Concentration: . . .31 in ON, 5 in BC, 1 in PQ	Expand in Territory: . . . . Yes	EXPANSION PLANS:
Registered: . . . . AB	Passive Ownership: . . . Not Allowed	US: . . . . .No
. . . .	Encourage Conversions: . . . . Yes	Canada: . . . . .AB, BC, ON
Type Space: . . . . . . SF, SC;~800-1,800 SF	Average # Employees: 2-3 FT, 2-3 PT	Overseas: . . . . No

GREAT FRAME UP, THE

9335 Belmont Ave.
Franklin Park, IL 60131
TEL: (800) 553-7263 (708) 671-2530
FAX: (708) 671-2580
Mr. Steve Beller, EVP

We are the high-volume, top-quality, low-priced leaders in the do-it-yourself and custom picture framing industry. We aggressively pursue markets in major cities and suburbs.

HISTORY: . . . . IFA	FINANCIAL: Earnings Claim: . Yes	FRANCHISOR TRAINING/SUPPORT:
Established in 1971; . . 1st Franchised in 1975	Cash Investment: $40K	Financial Assistance Provided: . . . . .Yes
Company-Owned Units (As of 8/31/1992): . .1	Total Investment: $140K	Site Selection Assistance: . . . . . . .Yes
Franchised Units (As of 8/31/1992): 119	Fees: Franchise - $15K	Lease Negotiation Assistance: . . . .Yes
Total Units (As of 8/31/1992): 120	Royalty: 6%, Advert: 2%	Co-operative Advertising: . . . . . . .Yes
Projected New Units for 1993: 20	Contract Periods (Yrs.): . . . . NA	Training: . . . . 5 Wks. Headquarters
Distribution: US-120;Can-0;Overseas-0	Area Development Agreement: . .No	. . . .
North America: . . . . 25 States	Sub-Franchise Contract: . . . . .No	On-Going Support: A,B,C,D,E,F,G,H,I/ . .
Concentration: . . .26 in IL, 20 in CA, 8 in CO	Expand in Territory: . . . . . . Yes	EXPANSION PLANS:
Registered: . . . . All States	Passive Ownership: . . . Discouraged	US: . . . . .All US
. . . .	Encourage Conversions: . . . . Yes	Canada: . . . . .No
Type Space: . . . . .SC;~1,700 SF	Average # Employees: . . . . .2 FT	Overseas: . . . . EUR, JA

KENNEDY STUDIOS

140 Tremont St.
Boston, MA 02111
TEL: (800) 448-0027 (617) 542-0868
FAX: (617) 695-0957
Mr. Kevin G. Richard, GM

Art and framing gallery, offering moderately-priced, limited edition prints and posters of the local area, painted by founder and artist Robert Kennedy, Michele Kennedy and other artists. Franchisee buys direct from KENNEDY's in-house art publishing department. Quality custom picture framing and unique line of artwork sets us apart.

HISTORY:	FINANCIAL: Earnings Claim: . .No	FRANCHISOR TRAINING/SUPPORT:
Established in 1973; . . 1st Franchised in 1983	Cash Investment: $40-90K	Financial Assistance Provided: . . . . .No
Company-Owned Units (As of 8/31/1992): . 14	Total Investment: $42-102K	Site Selection Assistance: . . . . . . .Yes
Franchised Units (As of 8/31/1992): 33	Fees: Franchise - $15-25K	Lease Negotiation Assistance: . . . .Yes
Total Units (As of 8/31/1992): 47	Royalty: 3%, Advert: 0%	Co-operative Advertising: . . . . . . .Yes
Projected New Units for 1993: 3	Contract Periods (Yrs.): 5/5	Training: . . . . .1-2 Wks. Key West,
Distribution: US-47;Can-0;Overseas-0	Area Development Agreement: . .No	. . . . Boston, or Rehobeth, DE
North America: . . . . 9 States	Sub-Franchise Contract: . . . . . .No	On-Going Support: C,D,E,G,H,I/ 8
Concentration: . .20 in MA, 14 in FL, 4 in ME	Expand in Territory: . . . . . . Yes	EXPANSION PLANS:
Registered: . . . . FL,MD,RI,VA,DC	Passive Ownership: . . . Discouraged	US: . . . . . New Eng., FL, SE Coast, DC
. . . .	Encourage Conversions: . . . . Yes	Canada: . . . . .No
Type Space: . . . . Urban/Resort;~1,400 SF	Average # Employees: . . 2 FT, 1 PT	Overseas: . . . . No

SUPPLEMENTAL LISTING OF FRANCHISORS

ART MASTERS INTERNATIONAL GALLERIES . . . . .10 W. 100 S., # 710, Salt Lake City, UT 84060
    Contact: Mr. Brian N. Walker; Tel: (801) 645-8100
FRAME & SAVE . . . . 3126 Dixie Hwy., Erlanger, KY 41018
    Contact: Mr. Chuck Karlosky; Tel: (606) 341-1210
FRAMEWORKS FACTORY . . . . 190 Highway 18, East Brunswick, NJ 08816
    Contact: Mr. Gary Nacht, President; Tel: (201) 247-2220
GRAPHICS GALLERY . . . . 219 Marine Ave., P. O. Box JJ, Balboa Island, CA 92662
    Contact: Ms. Darlene Griffin; Tel: (714) 673-4125
GREAT AMERICAN PICTURE COMPANY . . . . 52 Warehan St., Boston, MA 02118
    Contact: President; Tel: (617) 542-8504
KOENIG ART EMPORIUM . . . . 265 Old Gate Lane, Milford, CT 06460
    Contact: Mr. Anthony Parete, VP Store Devel.; Tel: (800) 367-3500 (203) 877-4541
POSTER GALLERY . . . . P. O. Box 8205, Little Rock, AR 72221
    Contact: Mr. Thomas Galyear, President; Tel: (817) 926-5599 (214) 578-7060

CHAPTER 37

RETAIL: ATHLETIC WEAR AND SPORTING GOODS

A. J. BARNES BICYCLE EMPORIUM

13889 Wellington Trace, # A21
Wellington, FL 33414
TEL: (407) 795-7987 C
FAX: (407) 795-3038
Mr. Mark Biskup, Jr., President

Bicycle retail stores, featuring new, exciting bicycles, parts and accessories, service and rentals in an "old-fashioned retail store." Family-oriented, with reasonable hours of operation. Great family business! Corporate philosophy: "To offer the highest quality bicycle retail franchise in the world."

HISTORY: . . . .
Established in 1989; . . 1st Franchised in 1992
Company-Owned Units (As of 8/31/1992): . .1
Franchised Units (As of 8/31/1992): 1
Total Units (As of 8/31/1992): 2
Projected New Units for 1993: 3
Distribution: US-2;Can-0;Overseas-0
  North America: . . . . 2 States
  Concentration: . . . . 1 in FL, 1 in GA
Registered: . . . . .FL
. . . .
Type Space: . . . . .SC;~1,800 SF

FINANCIAL: Earnings Claim: . .No
Cash Investment: $50K
Total Investment: $55-85K
Fees: Franchise - $15K
  Royalty: 5%, Advert: 1%
Contract Periods (Yrs.): 10/10
Area Development Agreement: . .No
Sub-Franchise Contract: . . . . .No
Expand in Territory: . . . . Yes
Passive Ownership: . . . . . .Allowed
Encourage Conversions: . . . . Yes
Average # Employees: . . 1 FT, 2 PT

FRANCHISOR TRAINING/SUPPORT:
Financial Assistance Provided: . . . . .No
Site Selection Assistance: . . . . .Yes
Lease Negotiation Assistance: . . . . .Yes
Co-operative Advertising: . . . . No
Training: . . . . 2 Wks. Home Office,
  . . .1 Wk. On-Site, Follow-up as Needed
On-Going Support: A,b,C,D,E,F,G,H,I/ . 2
EXPANSION PLANS:
  US: . . . . Southeast
  Canada: . . . . .No
  Overseas: . . . . No

BIKE LINE

1035 Andrew Dr.
West Chester, PA 19380
TEL: (800) 537-2654 (215) 429-4370
FAX: (215) 429-4295
Ms. Terri Kelly, Fran. Support

Full-service bicycle and fitness retail stores. BIKE LINE offers exclusive territories, top-notch training and support, access to name-brand inventory, maximum product quantity discounts, site selection, lease negotiation and site development assistance. We utilize sophisticated advertising and marketing techniques with fully-tested systems, methods and programs. BIKE LINE is the largest independent bicycle chain. Become a part of this fun industry.

HISTORY: . . . . IFA	FINANCIAL: Earnings Claim: . .No	FRANCHISOR TRAINING/SUPPORT:
Established in 1983; . . 1st Franchised in 1991	Cash Investment: $0-60K	Financial Assistance Provided: . . . Yes(I)
Company-Owned Units (As of 8/31/1992): . 18	Total Investment: $90-120K	Site Selection Assistance: . . . . . . .Yes
Franchised Units (As of 8/31/1992): 6	Fees: Franchise - $19.5K	Lease Negotiation Assistance: . . . . .Yes
Total Units (As of 8/31/1992): 24	Royalty: 4%, Advert: 1%	Co-operative Advertising: . . . . .Yes
Projected New Units for 1993: 12	Contract Periods (Yrs.): 10/10	Training: . . . . 2 Wks. at Corporate
Distribution: US-24;Can-0;Overseas-0	Area Development Agreement: . .No	. . . . Headquarters and Training Center
North America: . . . . 3 States	Sub-Franchise Contract: . . . . .No	On-Going Support: B,C,D,E,F,G,h/ . . . 12
Concentration: . . . 19 in PA, 4 in DE, 1 in NJ	Expand in Territory: . . . . Yes	EXPANSION PLANS:
Registered: . . . . .FL,OR	Passive Ownership: . . . Discouraged	US: . . . . .All US
. . . .	Encourage Conversions: . . . . . Yes	Canada: . . . . .No
Type Space: . . . . . FS, SF, SC;~2,500 SF	Average # Employees: . . 1 FT, 1 PT	Overseas: . . . . No

CYCLEFIT

6410 S. College Ave., # C
Ft. Collins, CO 80525
TEL: (800) 530-8825 (303) 223-3399
FAX: (303) 225-1989
Mr. Chuck McNeal, VP Fran. Dev.

Full-service bicycle and fitness equipment store. New and used bicycles and home fitness equipment, parts, accessories and full service. Franchisor offers complete training and continuing support to make you successful in the fun, and growing, bicycle and fitness business.

HISTORY:	FINANCIAL: Earnings Claim: . .No	FRANCHISOR TRAINING/SUPPORT:
Established in 1979; . . 1st Franchised in 1991	Cash Investment: $30-50K	Financial Assistance Provided: . . . Yes(I)
Company-Owned Units (As of 8/31/1992): . .4	Total Investment: $88-186K	Site Selection Assistance: . . . . . . .Yes
Franchised Units (As of 8/31/1992): 1	Fees: Franchise - $24.5K	Lease Negotiation Assistance: . . . . .Yes
Total Units (As of 8/31/1992): 5	Royalty: 5%, Advert: 1.5%	Co-operative Advertising: . . . . .NA
Projected New Units for 1993: 4	Contract Periods (Yrs.): 10/5/5	Training: . . . . 2 Wks. Headquarters,
Distribution: US-5;Can-0;Overseas-0	Area Development Agreement: . .No	. . . . 1 Wk. On-Site
North America: . . . . 2 States	Sub-Franchise Contract: . . . . .No	On-Going Support: a,C,D,E,F,G,H,I/ . . . 4
Concentration: . . . . 3 in CO, 2 in WY	Expand in Territory: . . . . . . .No	EXPANSION PLANS:
Registered:	Passive Ownership: . . . . . .Allowed	US: . . . . . Rocky Mtns., SE, S. Central
. . . .	Encourage Conversions: . . . . .No	Canada: . . . . .No
Type Space: . . .FS, SF, SC,;~4,000-5,000 SF	Average # Employees: 3-4 FT, 3-4 PT	Overseas: . . . . No

CYCLEPATH, THE

6465 Millcreek Ave., # 205
Mississauga, ON L5N 5R3 CAN
TEL: (800) 387-8335 (416) 567-4180
FAX: (416) 567-5355
Mr. George Kostopoulos, Fran. Dev.

THE CYCLEPATH is Canada's foremost retail specialty bicycle franchise, with a successful chain of corporate-owned and franchised stores. We carry an extensive selection of brand name and private label bicycles, parts and accessories, catering to the needs of all cyclists from the racing enthusiast to the recreational cyclist.

HISTORY:	FINANCIAL: Earnings Claim: . Yes	FRANCHISOR TRAINING/SUPPORT:
Established in 1981; . . 1st Franchised in 1988	Cash Investment: $50-100K	Financial Assistance Provided: . . . Yes(I)
Company-Owned Units (As of 8/31/1992): . .2	Total Investment: $135-200K	Site Selection Assistance: . . . . . . .Yes
Franchised Units (As of 8/31/1992): 31	Fees: Franchise - $40K	Lease Negotiation Assistance: . . . . .Yes
Total Units (As of 8/31/1992): 33	Royalty: 0%, Advert: 3%	Co-operative Advertising: . . . . .Yes
Projected New Units for 1993: 6	Contract Periods (Yrs.): 10/10	Training: . . . . . 1 Wk. Classroom at HQ,
Distribution: US-0;Can-33;Overseas-0	Area Development Agreement: . .No	. . . . 1 Wk. Franchisee Store
North America: . . . . 2 Provinces	Sub-Franchise Contract: . . . . .No	On-Going Support: B,C,D,E,F,H/ . . . . . .
Concentration: . . . . 29 in ON, 4 in BC	Expand in Territory: . . . . . . Yes	EXPANSION PLANS:
Registered:	Passive Ownership: . . . Not Allowed	US: . . . . No
. . . .	Encourage Conversions: . . . . Yes	Canada: . . . . .All Canada
Type Space: . . . . .SC;~2,000 SF	Average # Employees: 1-3 FT, 1-4 PT	Overseas: . . . . No

FIELD OF DREAMS

72-027 Desert Dr.
Rancho Mirage, CA 92270
TEL: (619) 773-1796
FAX: (619) 779-0217
Mr. John Hartfield, Natl. Sales

"America's Sports Personality Gift Store" is the only franchised mall-based sports memorabilia, baseball card store in the US. Only autographed items are sold, including bats, gloves, jerseys, pictures and one-of-a-kind items.

HISTORY:	FINANCIAL: Earnings Claim: . .No	FRANCHISOR TRAINING/SUPPORT:
Established in 1990; . . 1st Franchised in 1991	Cash Investment: $60K	Financial Assistance Provided: . . . Yes(I)
Company-Owned Units (As of 8/31/1992): . .0	Total Investment: $145-245K	Site Selection Assistance: . . . . . . .Yes
Franchised Units (As of 8/31/1992): 11	Fees: Franchise - $23-32.5K	Lease Negotiation Assistance: . . . . .Yes
Total Units (As of 8/31/1992): 11	Royalty: 6%, Advert: 4%	Co-operative Advertising: . . . . .NA
Projected New Units for 1993: 18	Contract Periods (Yrs.): 10/5/5	Training: . . . . .1 Wk. Headquarters,
Distribution: US-11;Can-0;Overseas-0	Area Development Agreement: Yes/Var	. . . . .1 Wk. Store Site
North America: . . . . 4 States	Sub-Franchise Contract: . . . . . .No	On-Going Support: B,C,D,E,F,G,h/ 8
Concentration: . . . 9 in CA, 1 in NV, 1 in OR	Expand in Territory: . . . . .No	EXPANSION PLANS:
Registered: . . . . . CA,FL,HI,IL,NY,OR,WA	Passive Ownership: . . . . . .Allowed	US: . . . . All US
. . . .	Encourage Conversions: . . . . . . Yes	Canada: . . . . .Yes
Type Space: . . . . .RM;~900+/- SF	Average # Employees: . 1 FT, 3-4 PT	Overseas: . . . . AU

FLEET FEET

2407 J St.
Sacramento, CA 95816
TEL: (916) 557-1000
FAX: (916) 557-1010
Mr. Tom Raynor, SVP

Retail sports franchise that is committed to developing and selling athletic footwear, apparel and accessories in a highly-promotional way. We seek individuals who follow a fitness lifestyle and love to participate in sports. We sponsor community-oriented events, sell name-brand products in a retail store.

HISTORY:	FINANCIAL: Earnings Claim: . .No	FRANCHISOR TRAINING/SUPPORT:
Established in 1976; . . 1st Franchised in 1979	Cash Investment: $40-50K	Financial Assistance Provided: . . . Yes(I)
Company-Owned Units (As of 8/31/1992): . .0	Total Investment: $125-175K	Site Selection Assistance: . . . . . . .Yes
Franchised Units (As of 8/31/1992): 40	Fees: Franchise - $17.5K	Lease Negotiation Assistance: . . . .Yes
Total Units (As of 8/31/1992): 40	Royalty: 4-2%, Advert: 0%	Co-operative Advertising: . . . . .Yes
Projected New Units for 1993: 6	Contract Periods (Yrs.): 20/20	Training: . . . . 5 Days Headquarters,
Distribution: US-39;Can-0;Overseas-1	Area Development Agreement: . .No	. . . . 5 Days In Store
North America: . . . . 13 States	Sub-Franchise Contract: . . . . .No	On-Going Support: C,D,E,F,G,H,I/ 7
Concentration: . . 20 in CA, 4 in NV, 3 in VA	Expand in Territory: . . . . . . Yes	EXPANSION PLANS:
Registered: . . . . All States	Passive Ownership: . . . Not Allowed	US: . . . . .All US
. . . .	Encourage Conversions: . . . . Yes	Canada: . . . . .No
Type Space: . . . Depends on Area;~1,200 SF	Average # Employees: . . 1 FT, 3 PT	Overseas: . . . . No

GOLF USA

1801 S. Broadway
Edmond, OK 73013
TEL: (405) 341-0009
FAX: (405) 340-8716
Mr. Jim Gould, Dir. Fran./Mktg.

Full-line and discount golf retail store - equipment, accessories and apparel, club repair and hitting ranges.

HISTORY: . . . . IFA	FINANCIAL: Earnings Claim: . .No	FRANCHISOR TRAINING/SUPPORT:
Established in 1986; . . 1st Franchised in 1989	Cash Investment: $35-75K	Financial Assistance Provided: . . . . .No
Company-Owned Units (As of 8/31/1992): . .1	Total Investment: $140-330K	Site Selection Assistance: . . . . .Yes
Franchised Units (As of 8/31/1992): 68	Fees: Franchise - $25-40K	Lease Negotiation Assistance: . . . . .Yes
Total Units (As of 8/31/1992): 69	Royalty: 2%, Advert: 1%	Co-operative Advertising: . . . . .Yes
Projected New Units for 1993: 22	Contract Periods (Yrs.): . . . 20/20	Training: . . . . .1 Wk. Headquarters
Distribution: US-64;Can-0;Overseas-5	Area Development Agreement: . Yes	. . . .
North America: . . . . 28 States	Sub-Franchise Contract: . . . . Yes	On-Going Support: A,B,C,D,E,F,G,H,I/ 16
Concentration: . . . 5 in CA, 4 in NE, 4 in TX	Expand in Territory: . . . . . . Yes	EXPANSION PLANS:
Registered: . . . CA,FL,HI,IL,IN,MD,MI,MN	Passive Ownership: . . . Discouraged	US: . . . . All US
. . . . .NY,OR,RI,VA,WA,WI	Encourage Conversions: . . . . Yes	Canada: . . . . .All Canada
Type Space: . . . .FS, SF, SC;~2,000 Min. SF	Average # Employees: . . 2 FT, 1 PT	Overseas: AU,EUR,Asia,S. Amer., AF, NZ

JUST FOR FEET

485 Sassafras Ln.
Roswell, GA 30076
TEL: (404) 992-9333
FAX: (404) 992-9333
Mr. Tony Bastio, VP Fran. Sales

JUST FOR FEET is the world's largest athletic shoe specialty store. Ranging from 16,000 - 20,000 SF, JFF superstores feature an indoor basketball court, elevated running track, rock climbing walls and much more. Superior service, unequaled service and boutique design for major vendors makes JUST FOR FEET one of the most exciting franchise opportunities of the '90's.

HISTORY: . . . .
Established in 1977; . . 1st Franchised in 1988
Company-Owned Units (As of 8/31/1992): . .3
Franchised Units (As of 8/31/1992): 2
Total Units (As of 8/31/1992): 5
Projected New Units for 1993: 3
Distribution: US-5;Can-0;Overseas-0
North America: . . . . 3 States
Concentration: . . . 2 in OH, 2 in AL, 1 in NV
Registered: . . . . .FL
. . . .
Type Space: . . . . FS, SC;~18,000 SF

FINANCIAL: Earnings Claim: . .No
Cash Investment: $600-750K
Total Investment: . . . $1.2-1.5MM
Fees: Franchise - $110K
Royalty: 2-5%, Advert: 1/2%
Contract Periods (Yrs.): 10/10
Area Development Agreement: Yes/Var
Sub-Franchise Contract: . . . . .No
Expand in Territory: . . . . Yes
Passive Ownership: . . . Not Allowed
Encourage Conversions: . . . . .No
Average # Employees: . 25 FT, 25 PT

FRANCHISOR TRAINING/SUPPORT:
Financial Assistance Provided: . . . . . No
Site Selection Assistance: . . . . .Yes
Lease Negotiation Assistance: . . . . .Yes
Co-operative Advertising: . . . . .Yes
Training: . . . . 2 Wks. Headquarters,
. . . . .3 Wks. Franchisee Location
On-Going Support: a,b,C,D,E,F,H/ 5
EXPANSION PLANS:
US: . . . . All US
Canada: . . . . .No
Overseas: . . . . No

MERLE HARMON'S FAN FAIR

12425 Knoll Rd.
Elm Grove, WI 53122
TEL: (800) 788-0983 (817) 548-0983
FAX: (817) 860-9160
Mr. Keith Harmon, VP Mktg.

MERLE HARMON'S FAN FAIR, the Sports Fan's Gift Shop, is a retail store specializing in the sale of licensed sports apparel. We provide franchisees with merchandise group buying programs, store signage and posters, graphic design services, on-staff experts in all fields of the business, training programs and videos, product updates, exclusive graphics program, MasterCard/Visa discount program, tested systems procedures, store visitation, etc.

HISTORY: . . . . IFA
Established in 1977; . . 1st Franchised in 1982
Company-Owned Units (As of 8/31/1992): . .8
Franchised Units (As of 8/31/1992): 142
Total Units (As of 8/31/1992): 150
Projected New Units for 1993: 20
Distribution: US-150;Can-0;Overseas-0
North America: . . . . 28 States
Concentration: . . 20 in TX, 19 in OH, 16 in IL
Registered: . . . CA,FL,HI,IL,IN,MD,MN,NY
. . . . ND,RI,SD,VA,WI
Type Space: . . . . RM;~1,500 SF

FINANCIAL: Earnings Claim: . .No
Cash Investment: $128-199K
Total Investment: $128-199K
Fees: Franchise - $25K
Royalty: 4-5%, Advert: 1%
Contract Periods (Yrs.): 15/15
Area Development Agreement: . .No
Sub-Franchise Contract: . . . . . .No
Expand in Territory: . . . . Yes
Passive Ownership: . . . . . .Allowed
Encourage Conversions: . . . . . Yes
Average # Employees: . . 2 FT, 2 PT

FRANCHISOR TRAINING/SUPPORT:
Financial Assistance Provided: . . . Yes(I)
Site Selection Assistance: . . . . . . .Yes
Lease Negotiation Assistance: . . . .Yes
Co-operative Advertising: . . . . . . .Yes
Training: . . . . .1 Wk. Headquarters,
. . . . .1 Wk. On-Site For Opening
On-Going Support: C,D,E,G,H,I/ 30
EXPANSION PLANS:
US: . . . . All US
Canada: . . . . .All Canada
Overseas: . EUR, Carib.,S. Amer,Pac. Rim

METAPRO GOLF

330 Versailles Rd., Brighton Pk. Ctr
Frankfort, KY 40601
TEL: (800) 521-2582 (502) 695-7352
FAX:
Mr. Steve Lewis, President

Full-service golf shops. Custom-build golf equipment, complete repair service, bags, shoes and accessories.

HISTORY: . . . .
Established in 1989; . . 1st Franchised in 1992
Company-Owned Units (As of 8/31/1992): . .0
Franchised Units (As of 8/31/1992): 1
Total Units (As of 8/31/1992): 1
Projected New Units for 1993: 2
Distribution: US-1;Can-0;Overseas-0
North America: . . . . .1 State
Concentration: . . . . 1 in KY
Registered: . . . . .FL
. . . .
Type Space: . . . . .SC;~1,500 SF

FINANCIAL: Earnings Claim: . .No
Cash Investment: $45K
Total Investment: $65-97.5K
Fees: Franchise - $15K
Royalty: 3%, Advert: 1%
Contract Periods (Yrs.): 5/5
Area Development Agreement: . .No
Sub-Franchise Contract: . . . . . .No
Expand in Territory: . . . . Yes
Passive Ownership: . . . . . .Allowed
Encourage Conversions: . . . . . Yes
Average # Employees: . . 1 FT, 2 PT

FRANCHISOR TRAINING/SUPPORT:
Financial Assistance Provided: . . . . .No
Site Selection Assistance: . . . . . . .Yes
Lease Negotiation Assistance: . . . . .No
Co-operative Advertising: . . . . .No
Training: . . . . 2 Wks. Headquarters,
. . . . 1 Wk. Repair School
On-Going Support: D,E,h,I/ 2
EXPANSION PLANS:
US: . . . . All US
Canada: . . . . .No
Overseas: . . . . No

NEVADA BOB'S GOLF & TENNIS

3333 E. Flamingo Rd.
Las Vegas, NV 89121
TEL: (702) 451-3333
FAX: (702) 451-9378
Mr. Bob Hulley, Fran. Dir.

Selling discount golf equipment in an attractive atmosphere, specializing in top-of-the-line golf clubs, golf bags and accessories from McGregor, Spalding, Prima, Mizuno, Dunlop. etc. Also, professional advice on all golf equipment given by our professional staff.

HISTORY:	FINANCIAL: Earnings Claim: . .No	FRANCHISOR TRAINING/SUPPORT:
Established in 1974; . . 1st Franchised in 1978	Cash Investment: $130-150K	Financial Assistance Provided: . . . . .NA
Company-Owned Units (As of 8/31/1992): . .4	Total Investment: $260-300K	Site Selection Assistance: . . . . . . .Yes
Franchised Units (As of 8/31/1992): 299	Fees: Franchise - $57.5K	Lease Negotiation Assistance: . . . . .Yes
Total Units (As of 8/31/1992): 303	Royalty: 3%, Advert: 0%	Co-operative Advertising: . . . . .NA
Projected New Units for 1993: 20	Contract Periods (Yrs.): 10/10	Training: . . . . 1 Wk. Headquarters
Distribution: . . . US-235;Can-20;Overseas-48	Area Development Agreement: . .No	. . . .
North America: . . . . 43 States, 2 Provinces	Sub-Franchise Contract: . . . . .No	On-Going Support: B,C,D,E,F,G,H,I/ . . 60
Concentration: . .38 in CA, 20 in TX, 20 in FL	Expand in Territory: . . . . Yes	EXPANSION PLANS:
Registered: . . . . .All	Passive Ownership: . . . Not Allowed	US: . . . . All US
. . . .	Encourage Conversions: . . . . . NA	Canada: . . . . .All Canada
Type Space: . . . . .FS, SC;~4,000 SF	Average # Employees: . . 3 FT, 2 PT	Overseas: . . . . . . AU, NZ, CH

PLAY IT AGAIN SPORTS

1550 Utica Ave. S., # 775
Minneapolis, MN 55416
TEL: (800) 433-2540 (612) 593-0683
FAX: (612) 593-0730
Mr. Steve Gemlo, Exec. Dir. Fran.

New/used retail sporting goods store. Buy-sell-trade and consign used and new sports equipment.

HISTORY: . . . . IFA	FINANCIAL: Earnings Claim: . Yes	FRANCHISOR TRAINING/SUPPORT:
Established in 1983; . . 1st Franchised in 1988	Cash Investment: $40-50K	Financial Assistance Provided: . . . Yes(I)
Company-Owned Units (As of 8/31/1992): . 12	Total Investment: $120-140K	Site Selection Assistance: . . . . .Yes
Franchised Units (As of 8/31/1992): 176	Fees: Franchise - $20K	Lease Negotiation Assistance: . . . . .Yes
Total Units (As of 8/31/1992): 188	Royalty: 5%, Advert: 0%	Co-operative Advertising: . . . . .NA
Projected New Units for 1993: 200	Contract Periods (Yrs.): . . . 10/10	Training: . . . . 8 Days Headquarters
Distribution: US-185;Can-3;Overseas-0	Area Development Agreement: . .No	. . . .
North America: . . . . 46 States, 1 Province	Sub-Franchise Contract: . . . . .No	On-Going Support: b,C,D,E,F,G,H,I/ . . 31
Concentration: . .36 in CA, 21 in MI, 20 in WI	Expand in Territory: . . . . Yes	EXPANSION PLANS:
Registered: . . . . .All	Passive Ownership: . . . Not Allowed	US: . . . . All US
. . . .	Encourage Conversions: . . . . . NA	Canada: . . . . .All Canada
Type Space: . . . . . FS, SF, SC;~2,400 SF	Average # Employees: . . 2 FT, 3 PT	Overseas: . . . . No

PRO GOLF OF AMERICA

31884 Northwestern Hwy.
Farmington Hills, MI 48334
TEL: (800) 521-6388 (313) 737-0560
FAX: (313) 737-9077
Mr. Don Kearns, Dir. Corp. Devel.

Full-line golf equipment and accessory retailer - at discount prices.

HISTORY:	FINANCIAL: Earnings Claim: . .No	FRANCHISOR TRAINING/SUPPORT:
Established in 1961; . . 1st Franchised in 1971	Cash Investment: $200-250K	Financial Assistance Provided: . . . . .No
Company-Owned Units (As of 8/31/1992): . .3	Total Investment: $350-400K	Site Selection Assistance: . . . . . . .Yes
Franchised Units (As of 8/31/1992): 169	Fees: Franchise - $45K	Lease Negotiation Assistance: . . . . .Yes
Total Units (As of 8/31/1992): 172	Royalty: 2%, Advert: 0%	Co-operative Advertising: . . . . .Yes
Projected New Units for 1993: 20	Contract Periods (Yrs.): . . . 30/20	Training: . . . . . . .2 Wks. or More Head-
Distribution: US-152;Can-14;Overseas-6	Area Development Agreement: . .No	. . . . quarters
North America: . . . . 29 States, 2 Provinces	Sub-Franchise Contract: . . . . .No	On-Going Support: C,D,f,G,h,I/ 20
Concentration: . . 20 in FL, 10 in CA, 1 in MI	Expand in Territory: . . . . Yes	EXPANSION PLANS:
Registered: . . . CA,FL,IL,IN,MI,MN,NY,OR	Passive Ownership: . . . Discouraged	US: . . . . All US
. . . . WA,WI	Encourage Conversions: . . . . NA	Canada: . . . . .All Canada
Type Space: . . . . . FS, SC;~4,000-5,000 SF	Average # Employees:	Overseas: . . . . EUR

PRO IMAGE, THE

563 West 500 South, # 330
Bountiful, UT 84010
TEL: (800) 347-1991 (801) 292-8777
FAX: (801) 292-4603
Mr. Mark Gilleland, Mktg. Dir.

Largest and fastest-growing franchisor of "Sport Fan Gift Shops." The stores are located in regional malls and retail licensed, authentic and replica logo'd products from all the professional and college teams. This is the fastest-growing segment of the sporting retail industry. Complete turn-key operation with custom, computerized store system and company warehouse.

HISTORY: . . . . IFA	FINANCIAL: Earnings Claim: . .No	FRANCHISOR TRAINING/SUPPORT:
Established in 1985; . . 1st Franchised in 1985	Cash Investment: . . . .$	Financial Assistance Provided: . . . . . No
Company-Owned Units (As of 8/31/1992): . .1	Total Investment: $95-185K	Site Selection Assistance: . . . . . .Yes
Franchised Units (As of 8/31/1992): 209	Fees: Franchise - $19.5K	Lease Negotiation Assistance: . . . . .Yes
Total Units (As of 8/31/1992): 210	Royalty: 4%, Advert: 3%	Co-operative Advertising: . . . . .No
Projected New Units for 1993: 30	Contract Periods (Yrs.): 10/10	Training: . . . . 4 Days Headquarters
Distribution: US-178;Can-30;Overseas-2	Area Development Agreement: . .No	. . . .
North America: . . . . 45 States, 6 Provinces	Sub-Franchise Contract: . . . . .No	On-Going Support: B,C,D,E,F,G,H,I/ . . 26
Concentration: . . 22 in CA, 13 in TX, 12 in NY	Expand in Territory: . . . . Yes	EXPANSION PLANS:
Registered: . . . . All Except AB	Passive Ownership: . . . . .Allowed	US: . . . . All US
. . . .	Encourage Conversions: . . . . . Yes	Canada: . . . . .All Canada
Type Space: . . . . SC, RM;~1,500 SF	Average # Employees: . . 2 FT, 4 PT	Overseas: . . . . Yes

SHOWCASE / COMPLETE ATHLETE

1850 Delmar Dr.
Folcroft, PA 19032
TEL: (800) 345-1485 (215) 532-7200
FAX: (215) 532-1833
Mr. Gary Adler, CEO

SHOWCASE or THE COMPLETE ATHLETE is one of the nation's largest retailers of sports team-licensed products, specializing in authentic and replica team merchandise. We carry the greatest selection of sports apparel from NFL, NHL, NBA, MLB and the NCAA.

HISTORY:	FINANCIAL: Earnings Claim: . Yes	FRANCHISOR TRAINING/SUPPORT:
Established in 1982; . . 1st Franchised in 1989	Cash Investment: $25-50K	Financial Assistance Provided: . . . Yes(I)
Company-Owned Units (As of 8/31/1992): . 30	Total Investment: $150-175K	Site Selection Assistance: . . . . .Yes
Franchised Units (As of 8/31/1992): 44	Fees: Franchise - $30K	Lease Negotiation Assistance: . . . . .Yes
Total Units (As of 8/31/1992): 74	Royalty: 6-8%, Advert: 1-3%	Co-operative Advertising: . . . . .Yes
Projected New Units for 1993: 20	Contract Periods (Yrs.): 10/5/5	Training: . . . . 2 Wks. Merchandising On-
Distribution: US-74;Can-0;Overseas-0	Area Development Agreement: Yes/3	. . . . Site, 4-6 Wks. Staff Near-By Store
North America: . . . . 15 States	Sub-Franchise Contract: . . . . .No	On-Going Support: A,B,C,D,E,F,H/ . . 41
Concentration: . .21 in NY, 13 in NJ, 13 in PA	Expand in Territory: . . . . Yes	EXPANSION PLANS:
Registered: . . . . CA,MD,MI,MN,NY,RI,VA	Passive Ownership: . . . . .Allowed	US: . . . . . .Northeast and Mid-Atlantic
. . . .	Encourage Conversions: . . . . . Yes	Canada: . . . . .No
Type Space: . . . . RM;~1,300 SF	Average # Employees: 4-5 FT, 2-3 PT	Overseas: . . . . No

SPECTATHLETE

1850 Delmar Dr.
Folcroft, PA 19032
TEL: (800) 345-1485 (2150 532-7200
FAX: (215) 532-1833
Mr. Frank J. Miceli, VP Mktg.

SPECTATHLETE is the leading retailer of authentic and replica sports team apparel licensed from major league baseball, NFL, NBA, NHL and NCAA. Additionally, all our stores carry a complete line of authentic, notarized sports memorabilia.

HISTORY:	FINANCIAL: Earnings Claim: . Yes	FRANCHISOR TRAINING/SUPPORT:
Established in 1982; . . 1st Franchised in 1985	Cash Investment: $100K	Financial Assistance Provided: . . . Yes(I)
Company-Owned Units (As of 8/31/1992): . 31	Total Investment: $225-275K	Site Selection Assistance: . . . . .Yes
Franchised Units (As of 8/31/1992): 38	Fees: Franchise - $30K	Lease Negotiation Assistance: . . . . . .Yes
Total Units (As of 8/31/1992): 69	Royalty: 6-8%, Advert: . . . 1.5-3%	Co-operative Advertising: . . . . .Yes
Projected New Units for 1993: 25	Contract Periods (Yrs.): 10	Training: . . . . 1 Month In-Store
Distribution: US-69;Can-0;Overseas-0	Area Development Agreement: Yes/3-5	. . . .
North America: . . . . 15 States	Sub-Franchise Contract: . . . . .No	On-Going Support: A,B,C,D,E,F,g,h/ . . 45
Concentration: . .26 in NY, 12 in PA, 12 in NJ	Expand in Territory: . . . . Yes	EXPANSION PLANS:
Registered: . . . . . . FL,MD,NY,RI,VA,DC	Passive Ownership: . . . . .Allowed	US: . . . . Northeast Corridor, FL
. . . .	Encourage Conversions: . . . . Yes	Canada: . . . . .No
Type Space: . . . . . .FS, SC, RM;~1,300 SF	Average # Employees: . . 4 FT, 3 PY	Overseas: . . . . No

WORLD CLASS ATHLETE

1814 Franklin St., # 820
Oakland, CA 94612
TEL: (800) SURF-RAT (510) 839-5471
FAX: (510) 547-3245
Mr. Jeff McKee, President

WORLD CLASS ATHLETE offers a unique, specialty sporting goods concept. Product mix concentrates on athletic footwear, running, tennis and swimwear. Emphasis on race sponsorship, training programs and custom fitting. All major lines of footwear, accessories, warm-up suits and bags. Custom re-soling at Company-owned distribution centers.

HISTORY: . . . . .IFA, CFA
Established in 1976; . . 1st Franchised in 1977
Company-Owned Units (As of 8/31/1992): . 15
Franchised Units (As of 8/31/1992): 66
Total Units (As of 8/31/1992): 81
Projected New Units for 1993: 12
Distribution: US-74;Can-7;Overseas-0
 North America: . . . . 15 States, 2 Provinces
 Concentration: . . 25 in CA, 8 in WA, 5 in KY
Registered: . . . CA,FL,HI,IL,MN,MI,NY,OR
 . . . . WA,WI,AB
Type Space: FS, SC, SC, RM;~1,800-2,200 SF

FINANCIAL: Earnings Claim: . Yes
Cash Investment: $75K
Total Investment: $120-225K
Fees: Franchise - $18K
 Royalty: 6%, Advert: 2%
Contract Periods (Yrs.): 15/15
Area Development Agreement: Yes/15
Sub-Franchise Contract: . . . . . Yes
Expand in Territory: . . . . .No
Passive Ownership: . . . Not Allowed
Encourage Conversions: . . . . Yes
Average # Employees: . . 2 FT, 4 PT

FRANCHISOR TRAINING/SUPPORT:
Financial Assistance Provided: . . .Yes(D)
Site Selection Assistance: . . . . . . .Yes
Lease Negotiation Assistance: . . . . .Yes
Co-operative Advertising: . . . . . . .Yes
Training: . . . . 3 Wks. Headquarters,
 . . . . 2 Wks. On-Site, On-Going
On-Going Support: a,B,C,D,E,f,G,H,I/ . 24
EXPANSION PLANS:
 US: .All US
 Canada: . . . . .All Canada
 Overseas: . . . .EUR, UK, AU, NZ

SUPPLEMENTAL LISTING OF FRANCHISORS

ATHLETE'S FOOT, THE . . . . 1950 Vaugn Rd., Kennesaw, GA 30144
 Contact: Mr. Perry Volpone, VP Fran.; Tel: (800) 524-6444 (404) 514-4500
ATHLETIC ATTIC/ATHLETIC LADY . . . . .P. O. Box 14503, Gainesville, FL 32604
 Contact: Mr. Ed McEachron, Dir. Sales Leasing; Tel: (904) 377-5289
BIG BOB'S SPORTS COLLECTIBLES . . . . 282-L Quarry Rd., Milford, CT 06460
 Contact: Mr. Rich Safton, VP; Tel: (800) 432-2027 (203) 874-0061
CLUBHOUSE GOLF . . . . 7321 N. Broadway Extension, Oklahoma City, OK 73116
 Contact: Mr. Gary D. Doublin, EVP; Tel: (405) 840-2882
EXERCISE POWER . . . . 15125 Ventura Blvd., # 200, Sherman Oaks, CA 91423
 Contact: Mr. Kent Rhodes, Mktg. Dir.; Tel: (818) 784-2000
INTERNATIONAL GOLF . . . . .9101 N. Thorndale, Tucson, AZ 85741
 Contact: Mr. Steve Porter, President; Tel: (602) 744-1840
JERCITY135 16 Ave. NW, Calgary, AB T2M 0H3 . . . . CAN
 Contact: Mr. Doug Forrest, President; Tel: (403) 276-4577
LAS VEGAS DISCOUNT . . . . .5325 S. Valley View Blvd., # 10, Las Vegas, NV 89118
 Contact: Mr. Monte Hamilton, Dir. Fran. Sales; Tel: (800) 873-5110 (702) 798-7777
RYAN'S SOCCER INTERNATIONAL . . . . 101 E. Alex. Bell Rd., # 110, Centerville, OH 45459
 Contact: Mr. Robert H. Ryan, President; Tel: (513) 434-7687
SCHWINN CYCLING AND FITNESS . . . . 217 N. Jefferson St., Chicago, IL 60606
 Contact: Mr. Daniel Garramone, Gen. Counsel; Tel: (312) 454-7400
SECOND SOLE . . . . 300 Montgomery St., 3rd Fl., San Francisco, CA 94104
 Contact: Mr. Mark Lando; Tel: (415) 982-8698
SOCCER KICK . . . . 2130 Henderson Mill Rd., Atlanta, GA 30345
 Contact: President; Tel: (404) 939-6355
SPORTS FANTASY . . . . 1028 Front Ave., Athens, GA 31901
 Contact: Mr. Reese Davis, President; Tel: (404) 327-0257
SUNBUMS SURF & SPORT . . . . 724 Middle Ground Blvd., Newport News, VA 23606
 Contact: Mr. Michael Fox, President; Tel: (804) 873-2257

CHAPTER 38

RETAIL: CLOTHING AND SHOES

ALBERT ANDREWS LTD.

10 Newbury St.
Boston, MA 02116
TEL: (800) 543-7848 (617) 247-9090
FAX: (617) 247-2808
Mr. Andrew L. Stern, President

You and your sales consultants present an unlimited selection of custom-tailored clothing to your up-scale clients at their offices. You can start from an in-home office with no inventory. Our program includes a patented computer measuring system, training, extensive support, your exclusive territory and we put you in front of qualified prospects (we telemarket for you).

HISTORY: . . . .
Established in 1990; . . 1st Franchised in 1991
Company-Owned Units (As of 8/31/1992): . .4
Franchised Units (As of 8/31/1992): 2
Total Units (As of 8/31/1992): 6
Projected New Units for 1993: 6
Distribution: US-6;Can-0;Overseas-0
  North America: . . . . 4 States
  Concentration: . . . 3 in MA, 1 in CT, 1 in CA
Registered: . . . . CA,FL,MI,NY
. . . .
Type Space: . . . . . Office in Home;~100 SF

FINANCIAL: Earnings Claim: . .No
Cash Investment: $26.5-70K
Total Investment: $26.5-70K
Fees: Franchise - $19.5-50K
  Royalty: 8%, Advert: 5-15%
Contract Periods (Yrs.): 3/12
Area Development Agreement: . .No
Sub-Franchise Contract: . . . . .No
Expand in Territory: . . . . Yes
Passive Ownership: . . . Not Allowed
Encourage Conversions: . . . . . NA
Average # Employees: . . . . . .3 FT

FRANCHISOR TRAINING/SUPPORT:
Financial Assistance Provided: . . . . . No
Site Selection Assistance: . . . . .NA
Lease Negotiation Assistance: . . . . .NA
Co-operative Advertising: . . . . .NA
Training: . . . . . . 5-6 Days Headquarters,
  . . .1-2 Days Follow-Up at Headquarters
On-Going Support: B,C,I/ 9
EXPANSION PLANS:
  US: . . . . .All US
  Canada: . . . . .No
  Overseas: . . . . No

EASY SPIRIT SHOE STORES

Men's and women's comfort footwear shoe store.

15 Engle St., # 302
Englewood, NJ 07631
TEL: (800) 332-2229 (201) 871-0370
FAX: (201) 871-7168
Mr. Ron Sommers, Fran. Dir. Mr. Sommers

HISTORY:	FINANCIAL: Earnings Claim: . .No	FRANCHISOR TRAINING/SUPPORT:
Established in 1990; . . 1st Franchised in 1992	Cash Investment: $75-100K	Financial Assistance Provided: . . . Yes(I)
Company-Owned Units (As of 8/31/1992): . 20	Total Investment: $267-453K	Site Selection Assistance: . . . . . . .Yes
Franchised Units (As of 8/31/1992): 0	Fees: Franchise - $20K	Lease Negotiation Assistance: . . . . .Yes
Total Units (As of 8/31/1992): 20	Royalty: 4%, Advert: 2%	Co-operative Advertising: . . . . . . .Yes
Projected New Units for 1993: 20	Contract Periods (Yrs.): . . . 10/10	Training: . . . .1 Wk. HQ, 1 Wk. Company
Distribution: US-20;Can-0;Overseas-0	Area Development Agreement: . .No	. . . . .Store, 1 Wk. Franchisee Location
North America:	Sub-Franchise Contract: . . . . . .No	On-Going Support: B,C,D,E,F,G,H,I/ . . . .
Concentration:	Expand in Territory: . . . . . . Yes	EXPANSION PLANS:
Registered: . . . . .All	Passive Ownership: . . . Not Allowed	US: . . . . All US
. . . .	Encourage Conversions: . . . . .No	Canada: . . . . .All Canada
Type Space: . . . . RM;~ SF	Average # Employees: . . . . .4 FT	Overseas: . . . . No

FIFTH AVENUE RESORT WEAR

Our proven, successful concept uses central-corridor kiosks at up-scale retail centers where our franchisee sells high-quality T-shirts and sweats featuring exclusive "Local Color" designs that are created in-house. We research local history, landmarks, themes, etc., and conceptualize 10-15 designs for each market.

125 B MacArthur Ct.
Nicholasville, KY 40356
TEL: (606) 885-6645
FAX: (606) 885-6996
Ms. Dotti Berry, Fran. Rep.

HISTORY:	FINANCIAL: Earnings Claim: . .No	FRANCHISOR TRAINING/SUPPORT:
Established in 1987; . . 1st Franchised in 1990	Cash Investment: $55-65K	Financial Assistance Provided: . . . . .No
Company-Owned Units (As of 8/31/1992): . .5	Total Investment: $55-65K	Site Selection Assistance: . . . . . . .Yes
Franchised Units (As of 8/31/1992): 3	Fees: Franchise - $25K	Lease Negotiation Assistance: . . . . .Yes
Total Units (As of 8/31/1992): 8	Royalty: 4%, Advert: 2%	Co-operative Advertising: . . . . No
Projected New Units for 1993:	Contract Periods (Yrs.): 10/5	Training: . . . . 7 Days Headquarters,
Distribution: US-8;Can-0;Overseas-0	Area Development Agreement: . .No	. . . . .5 Days Franchisee Location
North America: . . . . 3 States	Sub-Franchise Contract: . . .No	On-Going Support: B,C,D,E,F,G,H/ . . 10
Concentration: . . . 3 in KY, 3 in GA, 1 in LA	Expand in Territory: . . . . . . .No	EXPANSION PLANS:
Registered: . . . . .FL	Passive Ownership: . . . . .Allowed	US: . . . . .All US
. . . .	Encourage Conversions: . . . . NA	Canada: . . . . No
Type Space: . . . . . Cart/Kiosk-Malls;~ SF	Average # Employees: . . 2 FT, 2 PT	Overseas: . . . . No

KIDDIE KOBBLER

Children's shoe stores, located in major shopping malls. The extensive marketing program is designed to develop new and repeat business through intensive customer service, selection and value.

68 Robertson Rd.
Nepean, ON K2H 8P5 CAN
TEL: (613) 820-0505
FAX: (416) 665-8250
Mr. Fred Norman, President

HISTORY:	FINANCIAL: Earnings Claim: . .No	FRANCHISOR TRAINING/SUPPORT:
Established in 1951; . . 1st Franchised in 1968	Cash Investment: $100-125K	Financial Assistance Provided: . . . .NA
Company-Owned Units (As of 8/31/1992): . .0	Total Investment: $100-125K	Site Selection Assistance: . . . . . . .Yes
Franchised Units (As of 8/31/1992): 35	Fees: Franchise - $30K	Lease Negotiation Assistance: . . . .Yes
Total Units (As of 8/31/1992): 35	Royalty: 4%, Advert:	Co-operative Advertising: . . . . . . .NA
Projected New Units for 1993: 2	Contract Periods (Yrs.): 10/5	Training: . . . 10-12 Wks. Existing Store
Distribution: US-2;Can-33;Overseas-0	Area Development Agreement: . .No	. . . . 10-12 Days On-Site, 1-2 Days HQ
North America: . . . . . 2 States, 7 Provinces	Sub-Franchise Contract: . . . . .No	On-Going Support: A,C,D,G,H/ 3
Concentration: . . .25 in ON, 2 in NS, 2 in PQ	Expand in Territory: . . . . . . Yes	EXPANSION PLANS:
Registered:	Passive Ownership: . . . Discouraged	US: . . . . New York
. . . .	Encourage Conversions: . . . . Yes	Canada: . . . . .Yes
Type Space: . . . SC, RM;~11,000-12,000 SF	Average # Employees: . . 2 FT, 2 PT	Overseas: . . . . No

KRUG'S BIG & TALL

16 N. Washington Ave.
Bergenfield, NJ 07621
TEL: (201) 387-0100 C
FAX: (201) 387-1619
Mr. Neil Rubin, VP Ops.

KRUG'S BIG & TALL stores provide top-quality clothing and tailoring to the expanding market of big and tall men. KRUG'S BIG & TALL is the only franchise opportunity developed for this market, which is estimated to be 15% of all men in the US.

HISTORY:	FINANCIAL: Earnings Claim: . .No	FRANCHISOR TRAINING/SUPPORT:
Established in 1955; . . 1st Franchised in 1989	Cash Investment: $200K	Financial Assistance Provided: . . . . .No
Company-Owned Units (As of 8/31/1992): . .3	Total Investment: $250-300K	Site Selection Assistance: . . . . . . .Yes
Franchised Units (As of 8/31/1992): 0	Fees: Franchise - $18K	Lease Negotiation Assistance: . . . . .Yes
Total Units (As of 8/31/1992): 3	Royalty: 5%, Advert: 0%	Co-operative Advertising: . . . . . . .Yes
Projected New Units for 1993: 2	Contract Periods (Yrs.): 5/5	Training: . . . . 3 Wks. Headquarters,
Distribution: US-3;Can-0;Overseas-0	Area Development Agreement: . .No	. . . . 3 Days Store Site
North America: . . . . .1 State	Sub-Franchise Contract: . . . . .No	On-Going Support: A,C,D,E,F,G,H/ . . . 5
Concentration: . . . . 3 in NJ	Expand in Territory: . . . . Yes	EXPANSION PLANS:
Registered: . . . . NY	Passive Ownership: . . . Not Allowed	US: . . . . .NY, NJ, CT and PA
. . . .	Encourage Conversions: . . . . . Yes	Canada: . . . . .No
Type Space: . . . . .SC;~3,000 SF	Average # Employees: . . 3 FT, 2 PT	Overseas: . . . . No

LE BATEAU BLANC

475 Boul. de L'Atrium
Charlesbourg, PQ G1H 7H9 CAN
TEL: (418) 627-1846
FAX: (418) 627-4125
Mr. Pierre Yelle, President

LE BATEAU BLANC offers consumers children's fashion of superior workmanship in the latest styles.

HISTORY:	FINANCIAL: Earnings Claim: . .No	FRANCHISOR TRAINING/SUPPORT:
Established in 1975; . . 1st Franchised in 1984	Cash Investment: $25-35K	Financial Assistance Provided: . . . . .No
Company-Owned Units (As of 8/31/1992): . .3	Total Investment: $125K	Site Selection Assistance: . . . . . . .Yes
Franchised Units (As of 8/31/1992): 14	Fees: Franchise - $20K	Lease Negotiation Assistance: . . . .Yes
Total Units (As of 8/31/1992): 17	Royalty: 5%, Advert: 2%	Co-operative Advertising: . . . . . . .Yes
Projected New Units for 1993: 5	Contract Periods (Yrs.): 5/5	Training: . . . . 1 Wk. Franchisee Site
Distribution: US-0;Can-17;Overseas-0	Area Development Agreement: Yes/15	. . . .
North America: . . . . 2 Provinces	Sub-Franchise Contract: . . . . .No	On-Going Support: B,C,d,E,H/ 5
Concentration: . . . . .16 in PQ, 1 in ON	Expand in Territory: . . . . Yes	EXPANSION PLANS:
Registered:	Passive Ownership: . . . Not Allowed	US: . . . . . New England to FL, NE, SE
. . . .	Encourage Conversions: . . . . . Yes	Canada: . . . . Ontario Only
Type Space: . . . . .FS, SF, SC, RM;~950 SF	Average # Employees: . . 2 FT, 2 PT	Overseas: . . . . No

MORGAN'S LEATHER AND LACE

P. O. Box 12488
Oakland, CA 94604
TEL: (510) 839-5471
FAX: (510) 547-3245
Ms. Morgan Rissel, President

Nationally-known lingerie designer Morgan Rissel has established a high-margin chain of retail outlets, featuring the finest in women's and men's undergarments. The unique product mix includes leather, lace, spandex, etc. - all at reasonable prices and of unparalleled quality. Preview shows for otherwise shy male buyers. This $500 million/year industry is skyrocketing, so the potential for ADRIENNE'S LEATHER AND LACE is unlimited.

HISTORY:	FINANCIAL: Earnings Claim: . Yes	FRANCHISOR TRAINING/SUPPORT:
Established in 1987; . . 1st Franchised in 1989	Cash Investment: $85K	Financial Assistance Provided: . . . Yes(I)
Company-Owned Units (As of 8/31/1992): . .2	Total Investment: $125K	Site Selection Assistance: . . . . . . .Yes
Franchised Units (As of 8/31/1992): 2	Fees: Franchise - $20K	Lease Negotiation Assistance: . . . . .Yes
Total Units (As of 8/31/1992): 4	Royalty: 5%, Advert: 1%	Co-operative Advertising: . . . . . . .Yes
Projected New Units for 1993: 4	Contract Periods (Yrs.): 5/5	Training: . . . . 2 Wks. Headquarters,
Distribution: US-4;Can-0;Overseas-0	Area Development Agreement: Yes/5	. . . 1 Wk. Existing Store, 1 Wk. On-Site
North America: . . . . 3 States	Sub-Franchise Contract: . . . . . Yes	On-Going Support: A,B,C,D,E,f,g,h,i/ . . 3
Concentration: . . .2 in CA, 1 in NY, 1 in WA	Expand in Territory: . . . . Yes	EXPANSION PLANS:
Registered: . . . . .NY,WA	Passive Ownership: . . . Not Allowed	US: . . . . .All US
. . . .	Encourage Conversions: . . . . . NA	Canada: . . . . .All Canada
Type Space: . FS, SF, SC, RM;~800-1,200 SF	Average # Employees: . . . 1 FT, 3 PT	Overseas: . . . . No

PANDA SHOES

132 La Belle boul., # 160
Rosemere, PQ J7A 2H1 CAN
TEL: (514) 437-5655
FAX: (514) 437-5296
Ms. Linda Goulet, President

Children's shoe specialist - locations in major malls across Canada - 74 stores. Complete training program, including selling, merchandising, administration, etc. National advertising. Best selection of footwear for kids.

HISTORY:	FINANCIAL: Earnings Claim: . .No	FRANCHISOR TRAINING/SUPPORT:
Established in 1972; . . 1st Franchised in 1974	Cash Investment: $60K	Financial Assistance Provided: . . . . .No
Company-Owned Units (As of 8/31/1992): . .4	Total Investment: $80-125K	Site Selection Assistance: . . . . . . .Yes
Franchised Units (As of 8/31/1992): 58	Fees: Franchise - $25K	Lease Negotiation Assistance: . . . . .Yes
Total Units (As of 8/31/1992): 62	Royalty: 4%, Advert: 1/2%	Co-operative Advertising: . . . . . . .Yes
Projected New Units for 1993: 2	Contract Periods (Yrs.): . . . 5/Lease	Training: . . . . 2 Wks. Toronto, ON,
Distribution: US-0;Can-62;Overseas-0	Area Development Agreement: . .No	. . . . 2 Wks. On-Site (At Opening)
North America: . . . . 6 Provinces	Sub-Franchise Contract: . . . . . .No	On-Going Support: B,C,D,E,F,G,H/ . . . 8
Concentration: . . 38 in PQ, 12 in ON, 9 in BC	Expand in Territory: . . . . . . Yes	EXPANSION PLANS:
Registered:	Passive Ownership: . . . Discouraged	US: .No
. . . .	Encourage Conversions: . . . . . Yes	Canada: . . . . All Exc. Alberta
Type Space: . . . . RM;~800 SF	Average # Employees: . . 3 FT, 2 PT	Overseas: . . . . No

WORK WORLD

#101 - 12827 76th Ave.
Surrey, BC V3W 2V3 CAN
TEL: (604) 590-1841
FAX: (604) 590-0880
Mr. Bernie Bielby, Fran. Sales Dir.

Franchise for work clothes, boots, leisure wear and outer wear.

HISTORY:	FINANCIAL: Earnings Claim: . .No	FRANCHISOR TRAINING/SUPPORT:
Established in 1978; . . 1st Franchised in 1979	Cash Investment: . . . .$	Financial Assistance Provided: . . . Yes(I)
Company-Owned Units (As of 8/31/1992): . .7	Total Investment: $65K	Site Selection Assistance: . . . . . . .Yes
Franchised Units (As of 8/31/1992): 144	Fees: Franchise - $25K	Lease Negotiation Assistance: . . . . .Yes
Total Units (As of 8/31/1992): 151	Royalty: 3.25%, Advert: 3%	Co-operative Advertising: . . . . .NA
Projected New Units for 1993: 16	Contract Periods (Yrs.): 20	Training: . . . . .Training On-Site Prior To
Distribution: US-2;Can-149;Overseas-0	Area Development Agreement: . .No	. . . . and Through Grand Opening
North America:	Sub-Franchise Contract: . . . . .No	On-Going Support: D,E,F,G,H/ 26
Concentration: . . . . BC, ON, AB	Expand in Territory: . . . . . . .No	EXPANSION PLANS:
Registered: . . . . .Registrations Being	Passive Ownership: . . . Not Allowed	US: .No
. . . . .Prepared	Encourage Conversions: . . . . . Yes	Canada: . . . . AB,SK,MB,ON,Mari
Type Space: . . . . SC, RM;~2,000 SF	Average # Employees: . .2 FT, 2+ PT	Overseas: . . . . No

SUPPLEMENTAL LISTING OF FRANCHISORS

ACA JOE . . . . 235 Valley Dr., Brisbane, CA
    Contact: Mr. Val Hornstein, VP; Tel: (800) 969-4563 (415) 467-3888
AGNEW/AGGIES/ASHTON SHOES . . . . .298 Park Road N., Brantford, ON N3T 5T9   CAN
    Contact: Mr. Ed F. Mayne, VP Franchising; Tel: (519) 752-7854
BILL'S P. O. Box 2561, Huntsville, AL 35804 . . . .
    Contact: President; Tel: (205) 533-6600
BLUE JUNCTION / FASHION WAVES . . . . 590 Gordon Baker Rd., Willowdale, ON M2H 3B4   CAN
    Contact: Mr. Tanna Raj; Tel: (416) 490-1719
CALHOUN SPORTSWEAR . . . . 250 Bunting Rd., St. Catharines, ON L2M 3Y1   CAN
    Contact: Mr. M. Myers, President; Tel: (416) 688-6100
CAMP BEVERLY HILLS . . . . .9615 Brighton Way, # 210, Beverly Hills, CA 90210
    Contact: Mr. Neal Wallach; Tel: (213) 858-3925
CELLEBRATIONS . . . . 2023 Samford Dr., Mt. Juliet, TN 37122
    Contact: President; Tel: (615) 754-5776
CHEROKEE . . . . 9545 Wentworth St., Sunland, CA 91040
    Contact: Mr. Dan Zuckerman, EVP; Tel: (213) 875-1002
CONSUMER PRODUCTS OF AMERICA . . . . 10450 SW 187th Terrace, Miami, FL 33157
    Contact: President; Tel: (305) 233-1946

ESPRIT 900 Minnesota St., San Francisco, CA 94107 . . . .
    Contact: Ms. Kathleen Anderson, Legal Counsel; Tel: (415) 648-6900
FASHION IS . . . . .2901 Steeles Ave. W., Downsview, ON M3J 3A5 CAN
    Contact: Mr. Mike Mehta, President; Tel: (416) 661-1212
FASHIONS UNDER $10 . . . . 1036 E. Sibley Blvd., Dolton, IL 60419
    Contact: Mr. Stephen C. Tepper, EVP; Tel: (708) 849-8722
FLORSHEIM SHOE COMPANY . . . . 130 S. Canal St., Chicago, IL 60606
    Contact: President; Tel: (312) 559-2579
JUST PANTS . . . . 3525 W. Peterson Ave., # T-10, Chicago, IL 60659
    Contact: Mr. Bernie Bloomenkranz, Dir. Fran.; Tel: (708) 894-7500
KELLY SHOE SYSTEMS . . . . .269-3L Grand Central Pkwy., Floral Park, NY 11005
    Contact: President; Tel: (718) 204-4875
LADY MADONNA MATERNITY . . . . 7542 W. Villa Theresa Dr., Glendale, CA 85308
    Contact: President; Tel: (602) 995-1792
LANZ 8680 Hayden Place, Culver City, CA 90232 . . . .
    Contact: Mr. Christopher Scharff, Mktg. Dir.; Tel: (800) 421-0731 (213) 558-0200
MAGNIFETE . . . . .31 West 4th, 2nd Fl., Cincinnati, OH 45202
    Contact: Ms. Shelagh M. Watson, President; Tel: (513) 241-4669
MARK'S WORK WEARHOUSE . . . . 1035 64th Ave. SE, # 30, Calgary, AB T2J 2L2 CAN
    Contact: Mr. Kirk Marleau, VP Franchising; Tel: (403) 255-9220
MS. EMMA DESIGNS . . . . 275 Queen St. W., Toronto, ON M5V 1Z9 CAN
    Contact: Ms. Sofia Verna, President; Tel: (416) 598-2471 C
NORMAN HILTON . . . . 35 E. Elizabeth Ave., Linden, NJ 07036
    Contact: Mr. Norman Hilton, Chairman; Tel: (800) 441-8080 (908) 486-2610
OFF CAMPUS . . . . .684 White Plains Rd., Scarsdale, NY 10583
    Contact: Mr. Michael Greenberg; Tel: (914(472-2700
STRIDE RITE . . . . 5 Cambridge Ctr., Cambridge, MA 02421
    Contact: President; Tel: (617) 491-8800
TEAM LOGOS SPORTSWEAR . . . . 2715 Tuller Pkwy., Dublin, OH 43017
    Contact: Mr. Jon Carter, Dir. Mktg.; Tel: (614) 793-0654
THREE LITTLE PIGS . . . . 2901 Bayview Ave., Toronto, ON M2K 1E6 CAN
    Contact: President; Tel: (416) 222-5332
WILD TOPS . . . . .74 Main St., Framingham, MA 01701
    Contact: Mr. Richard S. Gold, President; Tel: (617) 879-9664

For a full explanation of the data provided in
the Franchisor Format, please refer to Chapter 2,

"How To Use The Data."

CHAPTER 39

RETAIL: COMPUTER SALES AND SERVICE

COMPUTER MAINTENANCE SERVICE Repair and maintenance of computer peripherals and PC computers.

P.O. Box 8
San Marcos, TX 78667
TEL: (512) 629-1400
FAX: (512) 353-5333
Mr. Floyd MacKenzie

HISTORY: . . . .
Established in 1986;   . . 1st Franchised in 1987
Company-Owned Units (As of 8/31/1992):   . .1
Franchised Units (As of 8/31/1992): 0
Total Units (As of 8/31/1992): 1
Projected New Units for 1993: 1
Distribution: US-1;Can-0;Overseas-0
  North America: . . . . .1 State
  Concentration: . . . . 1 in TX
Registered: . . . .
. . . .
Type Space: . . . . .SF;~ SF

FINANCIAL: Earnings Claim: . Yes
Cash Investment: $10K
Total Investment: . . . . . . $ 10-20K
Fees: Franchise - . . . .$
  Royalty: 3%, Advert: 1%
Contract Periods (Yrs.): 5/5
Area Development Agreement: . .No
Sub-Franchise Contract: . . . . .No
Expand in Territory: . . . . . . .No
Passive Ownership: . . . Discouraged
Encourage Conversions: . . . . .No
Average # Employees: . . . . .3 FT

FRANCHISOR TRAINING/SUPPORT:
Financial Assistance Provided: . . . . . No
Site Selection Assistance: . . . . .NA
Lease Negotiation Assistance: . . . . .NA
Co-operative Advertising: . . . . .NA
Training: . . . . . Continuous Headquarters
  . . . . and On-Site
On-Going Support: A,B,C,D,F,G,h,I/ . . . 3
EXPANSION PLANS:
  US: . . . . All US
  Canada: . . . . .All Canada
  Overseas: . . . . No

COMPUTER TIME RENTALS

15625 Preston Rd., # 1025
Dallas, TX 75248
TEL: (214) 824-6600
FAX: (214) 490-5405
Mr. Doug Reeder, President

A computer-related service business done from a retail location. Services include hourly rental of IBMs and MACs, laser printing, hardware rental and repair, user support, brokerage of new and used equipment and lease financing.

HISTORY:	FINANCIAL: Earnings Claim: . Yes	FRANCHISOR TRAINING/SUPPORT:
Established in 1957; . . 1st Franchised in 1990	Cash Investment: $25K	Financial Assistance Provided: . . . Yes(I)
Company-Owned Units (As of 8/31/1992): . .1	Total Investment: $75-100K	Site Selection Assistance: . . . . .Yes
Franchised Units (As of 8/31/1992): 0	Fees: Franchise - $20K	Lease Negotiation Assistance: . . . . .Yes
Total Units (As of 8/31/1992): 1	Royalty: 6%, Advert: 2%	Co-operative Advertising: . . . . .Yes
Projected New Units for 1993: 30	Contract Periods (Yrs.): 10/5	Training: . . . . 2 Wks. Headquarters
Distribution: US-1;Can-0;Overseas-0	Area Development Agreement: Yes/10	. . . .
North America: . . . . .1 State	Sub-Franchise Contract: . . . . . .No	On-Going Support: C,D,e,h/ 5
Concentration: . . . . 1 in TX	Expand in Territory: . . . . Yes	EXPANSION PLANS:
Registered:	Passive Ownership: . . . . . .Allowed	US: . . . . Southwest and Midwest
. . . .	Encourage Conversions: . . . . . .No	Canada: . . . . .All Canada
Type Space: . . . . SF;~1,200 SF	Average # Employees: . . 1 FT, 2 PT	Overseas: . . . . .MX

SUPPLEMENTAL LISTING OF FRANCHISORS

AMERICAN COMPUTER SERVICE . . . . 8380 Alban Rd., Springfield, VA 22150
    Contact: President; Tel: (703) 912-8900
CLASSIC CONFIGURATIONS . . . . 11011 S. Wilcrest, Houston, TX 77099
    Contact: Mr. Glenn Kramer, President; Tel: (713) 498-0208
COMPUTER BAY . . . . .4300 W. Brown Deer Rd., Milwaukee, WI 53223
    Contact: Mr. Bob Mahlum; Tel: (414) 357-7705
COMPUTER SERVICE & RENTAL CENTERS . . . . 484 Wrightwood Ave., Elmhurst, IL 60126
    Contact: Mr. Robert Roitblat, Owner; Tel: (800) 942-2772 (708) 279-7700
COMPUTERLAND CORPORATION . . . . 5964 W. Las Positas Blvd., Box 9012, Pleasanton, CA 94588
    Contact: Mr. William Tauscher, President; Tel: (415) 734-4000
DISC ADVANTAGE, THE . . . . P. O. Box 9368, Scottsdale, AZ 85252
    Contact: Mr. James H. Quinn, Jr., Partner; Tel: (801) 277-3940
DISCUS ELECTRONIC TRAINING . . . . 64 Commercial St., Rochester, NY 14614
    Contact: President; Tel: (716) 781-1061
INACOMP COMPUTER CENTERS . . . . 1500 W. Big Beaver, # 100, Troy, MI 48084
    Contact: Mr. Frank Stopa, VP Fran.; Tel: (800) 477-2827 (313) 649-3040
INTELLIGENT ELECTRONICS . . . . 411 Eagleview Blvd., Exton, PA 19341
    Contact: Mr. Joe de Simone, Fran. Dev. Mgr.; Tel: (215) 458-5500
LASERQUIPT INTERNATIONAL . . . . 10300 Bren Rd. East, Minnetonka, MN 55343
    Contact: Mr. Jeffrey T. Gilmer, VP Fran. Ops.; Tel: (800) 777-8444 (612) 942-7033
MICRO AGE COMPUTER STORES/COMPUCENTRE 9001 Louis H. LaFontaine, Ville Danjou, PQ H1J 2C5 CAN
    Contact: Mr. Chris Copeland; Tel: (514) 354-3810
MICROAGE COMPUTER CENTERS . . . . 2308 S. 55th St., Tempe, AZ 85282
    Contact: Ms. Tori Eggleston, Mgr. Fran. Mktg.; Tel: (800) 232-3369 (602) 968-3168
ORANGE MICRO PRINTER STORES . . . . 1400 N. Lakeview Ave., Anaheim, CA 92807
    Contact: President; Tel: (305) 444-9930
RICHARD YOUNG . . . . 508 S. Military Trail, Deerfield Beach, Fl 33442
    Contact: Mr. Crawford G. Paton, VP; Tel: (800) 828-9949 (305) 426-8100
SIMTEL COMPUTER RENTALS . . . . 2899 E. Big Beaver Rd., # 312, Troy, MI 48083
    Contact: Ms. Gail S. Ray, President; Tel: (313) 649-0909
SOFTWARE CITY . . . . 26 W. Forest Ave., Englewood, NJ 07631
    Contact: Mr. Shep Altshuler, President; Tel: (800) 222-0918 (201) 569-8900
SOFTWARE WORKS!, THE . . . . .200 N. Maryland Ave, Glendale, CA 91206
    Contact: President; Tel: (818) 500-1806
TODAYS COMPUTER BUSINESS CENTERS . . . . 411 Eagleview Blvd., Exton, PA 19335
    Contact: Mr. Joseph DeSimone; Tel: (215) 458-5500
VALCOM COMPUTER CENTER . . . . 10810 Farnam Dr., # 200, Omaha, NE 68102
    Contact: President; Tel: (402) 392-3900

CHAPTER 40

RETAIL: FLOWERS AND PLANTS

**BOTANICAL ENVIRONMENTS
SYSTEMS**
9201 Livingston Rd.
Ft. Washington, MD 20744
TEL: (800) 334-2731 (301) 248-4222
FAX: (301) 248-4852
Mr. Mark Fisher, CEO

BOTANICAL ENVIRONMENTS is engaged in the business of selling franchises in the indoor/interior landscaping field. Interior landscaping is the field in which plants and planters are installed into offices, hotels, restaurants, homes, etc. and then cared for by the franchisee.

HISTORY: . . . .
Established in 1982;   . . 1st Franchised in 1989
Company-Owned Units (As of 8/31/1992):   . .5
Franchised Units (As of 8/31/1992): 1
Total Units (As of 8/31/1992): 6
Projected New Units for 1993: 5
Distribution: US-6;Can-0;Overseas-0
 North America: . . . . 2 States
 Concentration: . . . 3 in MD, 2 in VA, 1 in DC
Registered: . . . . .MD,VA,DC
 . . . .
Type Space: . . . . NA;~NA SF

FINANCIAL: Earnings Claim: . .No
Cash Investment: $30-80K
Total Investment: $30-150K
Fees: Franchise - $20K
 Royalty: 10%, Advert: 0%
Contract Periods (Yrs.): 5/5
Area Development Agreement: . .No
Sub-Franchise Contract: . . . . . .No
Expand in Territory: . . . . .No
Passive Ownership: . . . Discouraged
Encourage Conversions: . . . . . Yes
Average # Employees: . . . . . .1 FT

FRANCHISOR TRAINING/SUPPORT:
Financial Assistance Provided: . . . Yes(I)
Site Selection Assistance: . . . . .NA
Lease Negotiation Assistance: . . . . .NA
Co-operative Advertising: . . . .
Training: . . . .
 . . . .
On-Going Support: B,C,D,G,h,I/ 3
EXPANSION PLANS:
 US: . . . . .Mid-Atlantic, Southeast
 Canada: . . . . .No
 Overseas: . . . . No

CONROY'S FLOWERS

6621 E. Pacific Coast Hwy., # 280
Long Beach, CA 90803
TEL: (800) 435-6937 (310) 594-4484
FAX: (310) 594-8253
Mr. Christopher Barr, COO

The nation's largest flower shop franchise in total sales and in sales per unit. This opportunity combines a retail concept proven for nearly 30 years with the most advanced techniques in flower processing, merchandising and customer retention.

HISTORY: . . . . IFA	FINANCIAL: Earnings Claim: . .No	FRANCHISOR TRAINING/SUPPORT:
Established in 1960; . . 1st Franchised in 1974	Cash Investment: $100-300K	Financial Assistance Provided: . . . . .No
Company-Owned Units (As of 8/31/1992): . .0	Total Investment: $225-300K	Site Selection Assistance: . . . . .Yes
Franchised Units (As of 8/31/1992): 94	Fees: Franchise - $75K	Lease Negotiation Assistance: . . . . .Yes
Total Units (As of 8/31/1992): 94	Royalty: 7.75%, Advert: 3%	Co-operative Advertising: . . . . .Yes
Projected New Units for 1993: 6	Contract Periods (Yrs.): 20	Training: . . . . 4 Wks. Southern CA
Distribution: US-94;Can-0;Overseas-0	Area Development Agreement: . .No	. . . .
North America: . . . . 3 States	Sub-Franchise Contract: . . . . .No	On-Going Support: A,C,D,E,G,H/ . . . 34
Concentration: . . 85 in CA, 4 in TX, 1 in NM	Expand in Territory: . . . . . . Yes	EXPANSION PLANS:
Registered: . . . . CA	Passive Ownership: . . . Discouraged	US: . . . . .West + Dallas, TX
. . . .	Encourage Conversions:	Canada: . . . . .No
Type Space: . . . . .FS, SF;~2,000 SF	Average # Employees: 4-5 FT, 2-6 PT	Overseas: . . . . No

FLOWERAMA

3165 W. Airline Hwy.
Waterloo, IA 50613
TEL: (800) 728-6004 (319) 291-6004
FAX: (319) 291-8676
Mr. Charles Nygren, VP Fran.

FLOWERAMA offers franchise opportunities in regional malls and free-standing locations. FLOWERAMA's mass merchandising, cash and carry concept offers its customers quality floral products at affordable prices. Comprehensive training in all areas of shop operations is provided along with continued support to franchise owners.

HISTORY: . . . . IFA	FINANCIAL: Earnings Claim: . Yes	FRANCHISOR TRAINING/SUPPORT:
Established in 1967; . . 1st Franchised in 1972	Cash Investment: $25-100K	Financial Assistance Provided: . . . Yes(I)
Company-Owned Units (As of 8/31/1992): . 16	Total Investment: $60-150K	Site Selection Assistance: . . . . .Yes
Franchised Units (As of 8/31/1992): 66	Fees: Franchise - $17-30K	Lease Negotiation Assistance: . . . . .Yes
Total Units (As of 8/31/1992): 82	Royalty: 5%, Advert: 0%	Co-operative Advertising: . . . . No
Projected New Units for 1993: 6	Contract Periods (Yrs.): . . . Infinite	Training: . . . . . . 10 Days Headquarters,
Distribution: US-82;Can-0;Overseas-0	Area Development Agreement: . .No	. . . . Up to 5 Wks. In Store
North America: . . . . 23 States	Sub-Franchise Contract: . . . . .No	On-Going Support: C,D,E,G,I/ 90
Concentration:	Expand in Territory: . . . . . . Yes	EXPANSION PLANS:
Registered: . . . . FL,IL,IN,WI	Passive Ownership: . . . . .Allowed	US: . . . . .Midwest, Southeast, TX
. . . .	Encourage Conversions: . . . . . Yes	Canada: . . . . .No
Type Space: . . . . . .FS, RM;~600-3,000 SF	Average # Employees: . . 2 FT, 4 PT	Overseas: . . . . No

FOLIAGE DESIGN SYSTEMS

1553 SE Fort King Ave.
Ocala, FL 34471
TEL: (800) 933-7351 (904) 629-7351 C
FAX: (904) 629-0355
Mr. John S. Hagood, President

FOLIAGE DESIGN SYSTEMS is the 2nd largest interior plant maintenance company in the US, according to Interiorscape Magazine. Foliage Design franchisees learn the business from the ground up in an intensive training program at headquarters, followed by 2 different training sessions in the field. Franchisees are taught design, sales and maintenance of interior foliage plants.

HISTORY:	FINANCIAL: Earnings Claim: . .No	FRANCHISOR TRAINING/SUPPORT:
Established in 1971; . . 1st Franchised in 1980	Cash Investment: $18-30K	Financial Assistance Provided: . . . . .No
Company-Owned Units (As of 8/31/1992): . .2	Total Investment: $30-50K	Site Selection Assistance: . . . . .Yes
Franchised Units (As of 8/31/1992): 44	Fees: Franchise - $16-40K	Lease Negotiation Assistance: . . . . .Yes
Total Units (As of 8/31/1992): 46	Royalty: 4%, Advert: 0%	Co-operative Advertising: . . . . .Yes
Projected New Units for 1993: 5	Contract Periods (Yrs.): 20/5	Training: . . . . 2 Wks. Headquarters,
Distribution: US-44;Can-1;Overseas-1	Area Development Agreement: . .No	. . . . 3 Days Field, 4-5 Days Field
North America: . . . . . 17 States, 1 Province	Sub-Franchise Contract: . . . . . Yes	On-Going Support: a,B,C,D,E,F,G,H,I/ . . 6
Concentration: . . . 16 in FL, 5 in AL, 3 in SC	Expand in Territory: . . . . . . Yes	EXPANSION PLANS:
Registered: . . . . . . .FL,HI,IL,MD,MI,VA	Passive Ownership: . . . Discouraged	US: . . . . All US
. . . .	Encourage Conversions: . . . . .No	Canada: . . . . .All Canada
Type Space: . . .Greenhouse, W/H;~2,000 SF	Average # Employees: . . 4 FT, 2 PT	Overseas: . . . . . EUR, Asia, MX

GROWER DIRECT FRESH CUT FLOWERS
4220 - 98 St., # 301
Edmonton, AB T6E 6A1 CAN
TEL: (403) 436-7774
FAX: (403) 436-3336
Mr. Bill Hustler, SVP

Sale of fresh flowers in a unique warehouse-type setting at wholesale prices. 50-60 inventory turns annually. Makes the enjoyment of fresh-cut flowers an everyday event in homes and in the workplace.

HISTORY:	FINANCIAL: Earnings Claim: . Yes	FRANCHISOR TRAINING/SUPPORT:
Established in 1990; . . 1st Franchised in 1991	Cash Investment: $50-60K	Financial Assistance Provided: . . . . . No
Company-Owned Units (As of 8/31/1992): . . 1	Total Investment: $50-60K	Site Selection Assistance: . . . . Yes
Franchised Units (As of 8/31/1992): 64	Fees: Franchise - $15K	Lease Negotiation Assistance: . . . . No
Total Units (As of 8/31/1992): 65	Royalty: 0%, Advert: 1/2%	Co-operative Advertising: . . . . Yes
Projected New Units for 1993: 125	Contract Periods (Yrs.): 10/10	Training: . . . . . 1 1/2 Wks. in Edmonton,
Distribution: US-0;Can-65;Overseas-0	Area Development Agreement: . . .	. . . . Vancouver and Toronto
North America: . . . . 5 Provinces	Sub-Franchise Contract: . . . . . Yes	On-Going Support: C,E,G,h,I/ 11
Concentration: . . 23 in AB, 21 in BC, 8 in ON	Expand in Territory: . . . . Yes	EXPANSION PLANS:
Registered: . . . . AB	Passive Ownership: . . . Discouraged	US: . . . . All US
. . . .	Encourage Conversions: . . . . . NA	Canada: . . . . .BC,ON,PQ, Marit.
Type Space: . . . . SC;~800 SF	Average # Employees: . . 2 FT, 4 PT	Overseas: . . . . UK, AU

SUZANN'S FLOWERS

710 N. Mountain Ave.
Ontario, CA 91762
TEL: (714) 986-0214
FAX: (714) 986-5819
Mr. Norman W. Mathis, President

One of the nation's leading F.T.D florists now offers full-service franchises. Extensive training and on-going support from a successful flower business management team. Proven marketing, production and delivery systems. Direct access to growers/importers. Exclusive custom-formulated preservatives and processing techniques. Be in business with the best!

HISTORY:	FINANCIAL: Earnings Claim: . .No	FRANCHISOR TRAINING/SUPPORT:
Established in 1990; . . 1st Franchised in 1991	Cash Investment: $50-150K	Financial Assistance Provided: . . . . . No
Company-Owned Units (As of 8/31/1992): . . 3	Total Investment: $150-300K	Site Selection Assistance: . . . . Yes
Franchised Units (As of 8/31/1992): 1	Fees: Franchise - $25K	Lease Negotiation Assistance: . . . . Yes
Total Units (As of 8/31/1992): 4	Royalty: 5%, Advert: 2%	Co-operative Advertising: . . . . Yes
Projected New Units for 1993: 1	Contract Periods (Yrs.): 10/10	Training: . . . . .5 Wks. S. California
Distribution: US-4;Can-0;Overseas-0	Area Development Agreement: . .No	
North America: . . . . .1 State	Sub-Franchise Contract:	On-Going Support: b,C,D,e,G,H/ 4
Concentration: . . . . 4 in CA	Expand in Territory: . . . . Yes	EXPANSION PLANS:
Registered: . . . . CA	Passive Ownership: . . . Discouraged	US: . . . . Southern California
. . . .	Encourage Conversions: . . . . . Yes	Canada: . . . . .No
Type Space: . . . . FS;~2,500 SF	Average # Employees: . . 3 FT, 3 PT	Overseas: . . . . No

SUPPLEMENTAL LISTING OF FRANCHISORS

AFFORDABLE LOVE . . . . 7103 Cresswyck Ct., Wexford, PA 15090
    Contact: Mr. Richard L. Finley, President; Tel: (412) 935-3260
ALLEN'S FLOWERS & PLANTS . . . . 741 S. San Pedro St., Los Angeles, CA 90014
    Contact: Mr. Ben Goldman, President; Tel:
BUNING THE FLORIST . . . . 3860 W. Commercial Blvd., Ft. Lauderdale, FL 33309
    Contact: Mr. Edward P. Thal, President; Tel: (305) 463-7660
FLOWERS BY SMITH . . . . 3908 W. Warren Ave., Detroit, MI 48208
    Contact: President; Tel: (313) 898-2340
PARKER INTERIOR PLANTSCAPE . . . . 1325 Terrill Rd., Scotch Plains, NJ 07076
    Contact: Mr. Richard Parker, President; Tel: (800) 526-3672 (908) 322-5552
REDBOOK FLORIST SERVICES . . . . P. O. Box 258, Paragould, AR 72450
    Contact: Mr. David Sluder, VP Cust. Relations; Tel: (800) 643-0100 (501) 236-7731
SHE'S FLOWERS . . . . 21 S. Venice Blvd., # 6, Venice, CA 90291
    Contact: Ms. Helen Shih, President; Tel: (818) FLO-RIST (213) 680-0088
WESLEY BERRY FLOWERS . . . . 15305 Schoolcraft Rd., Detroit, MI 48227
    Contact: Mr. Wesley Berry, II, President; Tel: (800) 356-5690 (313) 273-8590

CHAPTER 41

RETAIL: HOME FURNISHINGS

ATTIC, LTD., THE

3605 N. Willow Knolls Rd.
Peoria, IL 61615
TEL: (309) 692-6109 (309) 692-3317
FAX:
Mr. James M. Tedford, Treasurer

THE ATTIC sells pre-owned home furnishings, accessories and collectibles on a consignment basis. THE ATTIC's mission is to provide a convenient way for area residents to sell and buy quality used home furnishings. Sales are made from an attractive 4,000 SF retail store.

HISTORY: . . . .
Established in 1979; . . 1st Franchised in 1991
Company-Owned Units (As of 8/31/1992): . . 1
Franchised Units (As of 8/31/1992): 0
Total Units (As of 8/31/1992): 1
Projected New Units for 1993: 2
Distribution: US-1;Can-0;Overseas-0
North America: . . . . 1 State
Concentration: . . . . 1 in IL
Registered: IL
. . . .
Type Space: . . . . FS;~3,500-4,000 SF

FINANCIAL: Earnings Claim: . .No
Cash Investment: $33-89K
Total Investment: $144-224K
Fees: Franchise - $15K
Royalty: 10%, Advert: . Minimum
Contract Periods (Yrs.): 10/10
Area Development Agreement: . .No
Sub-Franchise Contract: . . . . .No
Expand in Territory: . . . . . . Yes
Passive Ownership: . . . Not Allowed
Encourage Conversions: . . . . . NA
Average # Employees: . 1 FT, 2-3 PT

FRANCHISOR TRAINING/SUPPORT:
Financial Assistance Provided: . . . . . No
Site Selection Assistance: . . . . .Yes
Lease Negotiation Assistance: . . . . .Yes
Co-operative Advertising: . . . . .No
Training: . . . . 2 Wks. Headquarters,
. . . . 2 Wks. with Franchisee
On-Going Support: a,C,D,E,f,/ 1
EXPANSION PLANS:
US: . . . . All US
Canada: . . . . .No
Overseas: . . . . No

CALIFORNIA CLOSET COMPANY

1700 Montgomery St., # 249
San Francisco, CA 94111
TEL: (415) 433-9999
FAX: (415) 433-2911
Ms. Megan Hall, Fran. Dev. Mgr.

CALIFORNIA CLOSET COMPANY is the leader in customized closet, garage and storage space design, promotion and installation services. As part of this exciting franchise system, you will receive specialized training, management and marketing support. Newsletters, seminars, conventions and a top notch corporate staff keep you current. A formula for success!

HISTORY: . . . . IFA	FINANCIAL: Earnings Claim: . .No	FRANCHISOR TRAINING/SUPPORT:
Established in 1979; . . 1st Franchised in 1982	Cash Investment: $75-200K	Financial Assistance Provided: . . . . .No
Company-Owned Units (As of 8/31/1992): . .4	Total Investment: $75-200K	Site Selection Assistance: . . . . .Yes
Franchised Units (As of 8/31/1992): 96	Fees: Franchise - $40K	Lease Negotiation Assistance: . . . . .Yes
Total Units (As of 8/31/1992): 100	Royalty: 5%, Advert: 5%	Co-operative Advertising: . . . . . . .Yes
Projected New Units for 1993: 4	Contract Periods (Yrs.): 10/10	Training: . . . . 3 Wks. Headquarters
Distribution: US-82;Can-7;Overseas-11	Area Development Agreement: . .No	
North America: . . . . . 33 States, 5 Provinces	Sub-Franchise Contract: . . . . . .No	On-Going Support: B,C,D,E,F,G,H,I/ . . 26
Concentration: . . . 11 in CA, 8 in NY, 6 in FL	Expand in Territory: . . . . Yes	EXPANSION PLANS:
Registered: . . . CA,IL,IN,MD,MI,MN,NY,RI	Passive Ownership: . . . Discouraged	US: . . . . .Various US Locations
. . . . .VA,WA,WI	Encourage Conversions: . . . . . NA	Canada: . . . . .Quebec
Type Space: .Light Industrial;~2,000-6,000 SF	Average # Employees: . . . . . .8 FT	Overseas: . . . . . EUR, Asia, MX

CLOSET FACTORY, THE

12800 S. Broadway
Los Angeles, CA 90061
TEL: (310) 516-7000
FAX: (213) 538-2676
Ms. Nancy Seyfert, VP/Fran. Dir.

Design, manufacture and install custom closet systems, computer furniture, garages, entertainment centers. High-line product, stressing variety of options and accessories and complete customization to client's specifications.

HISTORY: . . . . IFA	FINANCIAL: Earnings Claim: . .No	FRANCHISOR TRAINING/SUPPORT:
Established in 1983; . . 1st Franchised in 1986	Cash Investment: $135-145K	Financial Assistance Provided: . . . Yes(I)
Company-Owned Units (As of 8/31/1992): . .1	Total Investment: $185-195K	Site Selection Assistance: . . . . .Yes
Franchised Units (As of 8/31/1992): 26	Fees: Franchise - $28.5K	Lease Negotiation Assistance: . . . . .Yes
Total Units (As of 8/31/1992): 27	Royalty: 5.75%, Advert: 1%	Co-operative Advertising: . . . . . . .Yes
Projected New Units for 1993: 8	Contract Periods (Yrs.): 5/5	Training: . . . . . 2 Wks. LA or Other City,
Distribution: US-27;Can-0;Overseas-0	Area Development Agreement: . .No	. . . 2 Wks. On-Site, 2 Days Orientation
North America: . . . . 8 States	Sub-Franchise Contract: . . . . . .No	On-Going Support: B,C,D,E,F,G,H/ . . 67
Concentration: . . . 3 in MI, 2 in WI, 2 in IL	Expand in Territory: . . . . Yes	EXPANSION PLANS:
Registered: . . . . .IN,MD,MN,RI,WA	Passive Ownership: . . . Not Allowed	US: . . . . All US
. . . .	Encourage Conversions: . . . . . NA	Canada: . . . . .Yes
Type Space: . . . . Light Industrial;~4,000 SF	Average # Employees: . . 7 FT, 0 PT	Overseas: . . . . Yes

CLOSETS TO GO

9974 SW Arctic Dr.
Beaverton, OR 97005
TEL: (503) 644-7776
FAX: (503) 644-7930
Mr. Jeff Turner, Fran. Dir.

CLOSETS TO GO (portable custom closet and storage systems) offers an innovative way to conquer the storage dilemma. Through pre-manufactured parts, each outlet can assemble any configuration in a matter of minutes. The simplicity of no manufacturing and instant service puts CLOSETS TO GO light-years ahead of the competition.

HISTORY:	FINANCIAL: Earnings Claim: . .No	FRANCHISOR TRAINING/SUPPORT:
Established in 1985; . . 1st Franchised in 1987	Cash Investment: $75-100K	Financial Assistance Provided: . . . . .No
Company-Owned Units (As of 8/31/1992): . .1	Total Investment: $80-144K	Site Selection Assistance: . . . . .Yes
Franchised Units (As of 8/31/1992): 4	Fees: Franchise - $17.5K	Lease Negotiation Assistance: . . . . .Yes
Total Units (As of 8/31/1992): 5	Royalty: 5%, Advert: 2%	Co-operative Advertising: . . . . .NA
Projected New Units for 1993: 1	Contract Periods (Yrs.): 10/5	Training: . . . . 2 Wks. Headquarters,
Distribution: US-5;Can-0;Overseas-0	Area Development Agreement: . .No	. . . . 2 Wks. Franchisee Site, On-Going
North America: . . . . 3 States	Sub-Franchise Contract: . . . . . .No	On-Going Support: B,C,D,E,F,I/ 2
Concentration: . . . 1 in WA, 1 in OR, 1 in CA	Expand in Territory: . . . . .No	EXPANSION PLANS:
Registered: . . . . CA,FL,OR,WA	Passive Ownership: . . . Not Allowed	US: . . . . All US
. . . .	Encourage Conversions: . . . . . Yes	Canada: . . . . All Exc. Alberta
Type Space: . . . . . Business Park;~2,500 SF	Average # Employees: . . 4 FT, 1 PT	Overseas: . . . . JA

CLOSETTEC

55 Providence Hwy.
Norwood, MA 02062
TEL: (617) 769-9997
FAX: (617) 769-9996
Mr. Elliott S. Cubell, VP

CLOSETTEC sells, manufactures and installs residential and commercial storage systems, using the finest wood laminates and exclusive European hardware. We offer comprehensive training, field support, site selection, sales/marketing programs and on-going design assistance to every franchisee.

HISTORY:	FINANCIAL: Earnings Claim: . . .	FRANCHISOR TRAINING/SUPPORT:
Established in 1986; . . 1st Franchised in 1986	Cash Investment: $91-143K	Financial Assistance Provided: . . . Yes(I)
Company-Owned Units (As of 8/31/1992): . .0	Total Investment: $115-171K	Site Selection Assistance: . . . . . . .Yes
Franchised Units (As of 8/31/1992): 32	Fees: Franchise - $30K	Lease Negotiation Assistance: . . . . .Yes
Total Units (As of 8/31/1992): 32	Royalty: 5.5%, Advert: 1%	Co-operative Advertising: . . . . .No
Projected New Units for 1993: 10	Contract Periods (Yrs.): 15/15	Training: . . . . 2 Wks. Headquarters
Distribution: US-32;Can-0;Overseas-0	Area Development Agreement: . .No	. . . .
North America: . . . . 26 States	Sub-Franchise Contract:	On-Going Support: D,F,H,I/ 5
Concentration: . . . 4 in MA, 3 in OH, 3 in PA	Expand in Territory: . . . . . . Yes	EXPANSION PLANS:
Registered: . . . CA,FL,IL,IN,MD,MI,MN,NY	Passive Ownership: . . . Discouraged	US: .All US
. . . . .RI,VA	Encourage Conversions: . . . . . NA	Canada: . . . . .All Canada
Type Space: . . . . Light Industrial;~2,500 SF	Average # Employees: . . . . . .5 FT	Overseas: . . . . .Yes

DECORATING DEN SYSTEMS

7910 Woodmont Ave., # 200
Bethesda, MD 20814
TEL: (800) 428-1366 (301) 652-6393
FAX: (301) 652-9017
Ms. Patti Coons, VP Corp. Dev.

America's first shop-at-home, affordable decorating service. A professionally-trained decorator brings 1,000's of samples to the customer's home or business in a specially-equipped ColorVan.

HISTORY: . . . . IFA	FINANCIAL: Earnings Claim: . .No	FRANCHISOR TRAINING/SUPPORT:
Established in 1970; . . 1st Franchised in 1970	Cash Investment: $7-19K	Financial Assistance Provided: . . . . .Yes
Company-Owned Units (As of 8/31/1992): . .0	Total Investment: $15-30K	Site Selection Assistance: . . . . . . .NA
Franchised Units (As of 8/31/1992): 1138	Fees: Franchise - $7-19K	Lease Negotiation Assistance: . . . . .NA
Total Units (As of 8/31/1992): 1138	Royalty: 6-15%, Advert: . . . 0-2%	Co-operative Advertising: . . . . . . .Yes
Projected New Units for 1993: 300	Contract Periods (Yrs.): 10/10	Training: . . . . 1 Wk. Headquarters
Distribution: . . US-1017;Can-83;Overseas-38	Area Development Agreement: . .No	. . . .
North America: . . . . 50 States, 5 Provinces	Sub-Franchise Contract: . . . . . Yes	On-Going Support: C,D,E,G,H,i/ 45
Concentration: . . 128 in CA, 91 in TX, 69 FL	Expand in Territory: . . . . . . Yes	EXPANSION PLANS:
Registered: . . . . All Except AB	Passive Ownership: . . . Discouraged	US: . . . . All US
. . . .	Encourage Conversions: . . . . . Yes	Canada: . . . . .All Canada
Type Space: . . . . . . .ColorVan, HB;~ SF	Average # Employees: . . 1 FT, 1 PT	Overseas: . . .UK, JA, SC, AU, SP

EXPRESSIONS

3212 W. Esplanade Ave.
Metairie, LA 70002
TEL: (800) 544-4519 (504) 834-9222
FAX: (504) 837-7613
Ms. Lydia James, VP

Selling upholstered furniture is our business - a business that now operates in nearly 50 markets nationwide. Our merchandising formula has carved a niche in the marketplace by offering customers a choice of 150 furniture frame styles and over 700 designer fabrics. Customers pick the frame, the fabric and any special features, and their EXPRESSIONS furniture is custom-crafted and delivered in only 45 days.

HISTORY: . . . . IFA	FINANCIAL: Earnings Claim: . .No	FRANCHISOR TRAINING/SUPPORT:
Established in 1978; . . 1st Franchised in 1983	Cash Investment: $75-80K	Financial Assistance Provided: . . . . .No
Company-Owned Units (As of 8/31/1992): . .2	Total Investment: $220K	Site Selection Assistance: . . . . . . .Yes
Franchised Units (As of 8/31/1992): 45	Fees: Franchise - $30K	Lease Negotiation Assistance: . . . .Yes
Total Units (As of 8/31/1992): 47	Royalty: 3/4/3/2%, Advert: . 9.5%	Co-operative Advertising: . . . . .No
Projected New Units for 1993: 12	Contract Periods (Yrs.): . . . .Varies	Training: . . . . . 10-15 Days Headquarters
Distribution: US-47;Can-0;Overseas-0	Area Development Agreement: Yes/Var	
North America: . . . . 28 States	Sub-Franchise Contract: . . . . . .No	On-Going Support: A,B,C,D,E,G,h,i/ . . 27
Concentration: . . . . 4 in FL, 4 in MI, 3 in CA	Expand in Territory: . . . . . . Yes	EXPANSION PLANS:
Registered: . . . . All States	Passive Ownership: . . . Discouraged	US: . . . . . Concentration of West Coast
. . . .	Encourage Conversions: . . . . . Yes	Canada: . . . . Alberta, Ontario
Type Space: . . . FS, SF, SC;~4,200-6,000 SF	Average # Employees: . . . . .Varies	Overseas: . . . . .MX

FLOOR COVERINGS INTERNATIONAL
5182 Old Dixie Hwy.
Forest Park, GA 30050
TEL: (800) 955-4324 (404) 361-5047 C
FAX: (404) 366-4606
Mr. Phillip R. Green, Mktg. Dir.

The "Carpet Store At Your Door" concept allows the homeowner the convenience of purchasing floor covering at home. Our Carpet Showrooms On Wheels has a store full of samples and allows the customer to coordinate colors with existing decor in the actual lighting of their residence.

HISTORY:	FINANCIAL: Earnings Claim: . .No	FRANCHISOR TRAINING/SUPPORT:
Established in 1985; . . 1st Franchised in 1988	Cash Investment: $18.5K	Financial Assistance Provided: . . . . .NA
Company-Owned Units (As of 8/31/1992): . .0	Total Investment: $18.5-34.5K	Site Selection Assistance: . . . . . . .NA
Franchised Units (As of 8/31/1992): 233	Fees: Franchise - $18.5K	Lease Negotiation Assistance: . . . .NA
Total Units (As of 8/31/1992): 233	Royalty: 5%, Advert: 2%	Co-operative Advertising: . . . . . . .Yes
Projected New Units for 1993: 150	Contract Periods (Yrs.): 10/10	Training: . . . . 1 Wk. Home Study Course,
Distribution: US-216;Can-17;Overseas-0	Area Development Agreement: . .No	. . . . . .1 Wk. Training at Headquarters
North America: . . . . 41 States, 5 Provinces	Sub-Franchise Contract: . . . . .No	On-Going Support: B,C,D,E,G,H,I/ . . . 26
Concentration: . . 25 in PA, 23 in CA, 14 in OH	Expand in Territory: . . . . Yes	EXPANSION PLANS:
Registered: . . . . All States	Passive Ownership: . . . Discouraged	US: . . . . All US
. . . .	Encourage Conversions: . . . . . .No	Canada: . . . . .All Canada
Type Space: . . . . NA;~ SF	Average # Employees: . . . . 1-2 FT	Overseas: . . C/S America, EUR, Far East

FURNITURE WEEKEND

21 W. Main St.
Malone, NY 12953
TEL: (800) 562-1606 (518) 483-1328
FAX:
Mr. Larry Kriff, President

Enter the growing furniture industry, offering brand-name furniture at substantial savings: FURNITURE WEEKEND stores are operating only on the 3 prime selling days - Friday, Saturday and Sunday! Benefits include complete training, simple operation, low overhead, on-going guidance and support, high quality of life through flexible hours.

HISTORY:	FINANCIAL: Earnings Claim: . .No	FRANCHISOR TRAINING/SUPPORT:
Established in 1981; . . 1st Franchised in 1990	Cash Investment: $89-145K	Financial Assistance Provided: . . . . . No
Company-Owned Units (As of 8/31/1992): . .4	Total Investment: $89-145K	Site Selection Assistance: . . . . .Yes
Franchised Units (As of 8/31/1992): 4	Fees: Franchise - $15K	Lease Negotiation Assistance: . . . .Yes
Total Units (As of 8/31/1992): 8	Royalty: 5%, Advert: 1%	Co-operative Advertising: . . . . No
Projected New Units for 1993: 6	Contract Periods (Yrs.): 10/10	Training: . . . . 6 Days Headquarters
Distribution: US-8;Can-0;Overseas-0	Area Development Agreement: . .No	. . . .
North America: . . . . 2 States	Sub-Franchise Contract: . . . . .No	On-Going Support: C,D,E,F,I/ 6
Concentration: . . . . . . 6 in NY, 2 in VT	Expand in Territory: . . . . Yes	EXPANSION PLANS:
Registered: . . . . .NY,RI	Passive Ownership: . . . . . .Allowed	US: . . . . Northeast
. . . .	Encourage Conversions: . . . . . Yes	Canada: . . . . No
Type Space: . . . . .FS, SF;~6,000 SF	Average # Employees: . . 1 FT, 2 PT	Overseas: . . . . No

KING KOIL BEDQUARTERS

770 Transfer Rd., # 13
St. Paul, MN 55114
TEL: (800) 888-6070 (612) 646-6882
FAX:
Mr. Paul Sullivan, Natl. Sales Mgr.

Specialty retailing of sleep products. The BEDQUARTERS program provides the complete formula necessary for the successful sleep specialist. This includes display, marketing, merchandising and advertising direction, in addition to providing the actual merchandise.

HISTORY:	FINANCIAL: Earnings Claim: . .No	FRANCHISOR TRAINING/SUPPORT:
Established in 1982; . . 1st Franchised in 1982	Cash Investment: . . . .$	Financial Assistance Provided: . . . . . No
Company-Owned Units (As of 8/31/1992): . .0	Total Investment: $60-85K	Site Selection Assistance: . . . . . . .NA
Franchised Units (As of 8/31/1992): 200	Fees: Franchise - $5K	Lease Negotiation Assistance: . . . . No
Total Units (As of 8/31/1992): 200	Royalty: 0%, Advert: 0%	Co-operative Advertising: . . . . .Yes
Projected New Units for 1993:	Contract Periods (Yrs.): . . . .Varies	Training: . . . . .On-Going On-Site
Distribution: US-180;Can-20;Overseas-0	Area Development Agreement: . .No	. . . .
North America:	Sub-Franchise Contract: . . . . .No	On-Going Support: C,D,F,G,H,I/ . . . . .
Concentration:	Expand in Territory: . . . . Yes	EXPANSION PLANS:
Registered:	Passive Ownership: . . . . . .Allowed	US: . . . . Most of US
. . . .	Encourage Conversions: . . . . . Yes	Canada: . . . . No
Type Space: . . . . .SC;~3,000 SF	Average # Employees: . 2-3 FT, 1 PT	Overseas: . . . . UK, AU, IR

MOUNTAIN COMFORT FURNISHINGS

507 Summit Blvd.
Frisco, CO 80443
TEL: (303) 668-1414
FAX: (303) 668-5329
Mr. Bill Jarski, President

Complete home furnishings, solid woods and upholstery, specializing in unique hand-crafted mountain contemporary, Southwest and lodge furniture.

HISTORY: . . . .
Established in 1984; . . 1st Franchised in 1992
Company-Owned Units (As of 8/31/1992): . .2
Franchised Units (As of 8/31/1992): 5
Total Units (As of 8/31/1992): 7
Projected New Units for 1993: 8
Distribution: US-7;Can-0;Overseas-0
 North America: . . . . 4 States
 Concentration: . . . . 5 in CO
Registered: . . . . CA,OR
. . . .
Type Space: . . . . . FS, SC;~5,000-8000 SF

FINANCIAL: Earnings Claim: . .No
Cash Investment: $80-140K
Total Investment: . . . $127.7-235.2K
Fees: Franchise - $22.5K
 Royalty: 5%, Advert: 1/5%
Contract Periods (Yrs.): 10/10
Area Development Agreement: . .No
Sub-Franchise Contract: . . . . .No
Expand in Territory: . . . . . . .No
Passive Ownership: . . . . . .Allowed
Encourage Conversions: . . . . Yes
Average # Employees: . . 2 FT, 2 PT

FRANCHISOR TRAINING/SUPPORT:
Financial Assistance Provided: . . .Yes(D)
Site Selection Assistance: . . . . .Yes
Lease Negotiation Assistance: . . . . .Yes
Co-operative Advertising: . . . . .Yes
Training: . . . . 2 Wks. Headquarters
. . . .
On-Going Support: C,D,E,G,H/ 15
EXPANSION PLANS:
 US: . . . . . . West, Southwest, Northeast
 Canada: . . . . .No
 Overseas: . . . . No

NAKED FURNITURE

P. O. Box F
Clarks Summit, PA 18411
TEL: (800) 352-2522 (717) 587-7800
FAX: (717) 586-8587
Mktg. Dept.

NAKED FURNITURE is the nation's largest retailer of custom-finished and ready-to-finish real wood home furnishings. Franchise owners are provided comprehensive pre-opening training and on-going support that covers all aspects of owning and operating a retail home furnishings business. Our expertise is in helping our franchisees to offer their customers the widest possible range of innovative and affordable finishing and decorating choices.

HISTORY: . . . . IFA
Established in 1972; . . 1st Franchised in 1976
Company-Owned Units (As of 8/31/1992): . .2
Franchised Units (As of 8/31/1992): 42
Total Units (As of 8/31/1992): 44
Projected New Units for 1993: 6
Distribution: US-44;Can-0;Overseas-0
 North America: . . . . 13 States
 Concentration: . . . . .9 in MI, 8 in IL, 4 in IN
Registered: . . . FL,IL,IN,MD,MI,MN,NY,RI
. . . . VA,WI
Type Space: . . . FS, SF, SC, RM;~6,500+ SF

FINANCIAL: Earnings Claim: . .No
Cash Investment: $71.5-122.5K
Total Investment: $143-245K
Fees: Franchise - $19.5K
 Royalty: 4%, Advert: 1%
Contract Periods (Yrs.): 10/10
Area Development Agreement: . Yes
Sub-Franchise Contract: . . . . .No
Expand in Territory: . . . . . . Yes
Passive Ownership: . . . . . .Allowed
Encourage Conversions: . . . . Yes
Average # Employees: . . 2 FT, 1 PT

FRANCHISOR TRAINING/SUPPORT:
Financial Assistance Provided: . . . . .No
Site Selection Assistance: . . . . .Yes
Lease Negotiation Assistance: . . . . .Yes
Co-operative Advertising: . . . . .No
Training: . . . . .1 Wk. Headquarters,
. . . . 1 Wk. On-Site
On-Going Support: a,C,D,E,F,G,h,I/ . . 14
EXPANSION PLANS:
 US: . . . . East of Mississippi
 Canada: . . . . .No
 Overseas: . . . . No

NORWALK - THE FURNITURE IDEA

100 Furniture Pkwy.
Norwalk, OH 44857
TEL: (800) 837-2565 (419) 668-4461
FAX: (419) 668-6223
Mr. Bob Young, VP Fran.

Custom-ordered upholstered furniture - delivered in 35 days. Over 2,000 fabrics and leathers are offered on 500 styles. Lifetime product warranty. Beautiful store display makes shopping experience unique in the home furnishings industry.

HISTORY: . . . . IFA
Established in 1902; . . 1st Franchised in 1986
Company-Owned Units (As of 8/31/1992): . .7
Franchised Units (As of 8/31/1992): 18
Total Units (As of 8/31/1992): 25
Projected New Units for 1993: 10
Distribution: US-25;Can-0;Overseas-0
 North America: . . . . 9 States
 Concentration: . . . 8 in FL, 5 in GA, 3 in OH
Registered: . . . . .All
. . . .
Type Space: . . . . . FS, SC;~4,000-5,000 SF

FINANCIAL: Earnings Claim: . .No
Cash Investment: $80-120K
Total Investment: $150-200K
Fees: Franchise - $15K
 Royalty: 0%, Advert: 0%
Contract Periods (Yrs.): 20/5
Area Development Agreement: . Yes
Sub-Franchise Contract: . . . . .No
Expand in Territory: . . . . . . Yes
Passive Ownership: . . . . . .Allowed
Encourage Conversions: . . . . Yes
Average # Employees: . . 2 FT, 2 PT

FRANCHISOR TRAINING/SUPPORT:
Financial Assistance Provided: . . . . .No
Site Selection Assistance: . . . . .Yes
Lease Negotiation Assistance: . . . . .Yes
Co-operative Advertising: . . . . .Yes
Training: . . . . . . .5 Days Atlanta, GA, 5
. . . . Days Franchisee Store, 5 Days HQ
On-Going Support: C,D,E,G,h,I/ 40
EXPANSION PLANS:
 US: . . . . .All US
 Canada: . . . . .Yes
 Overseas: . . . . No

PROGRESSIVE WINDOW FASHIONS INTERNATIONAL
201 N. Front St., # 604
Wilmington, NC 28401
TEL: (919) 251-1435 C
FAX: (919) 251-1445
Mr. Tom DeFrancesco, President

PROGRESSIVE WINDOW FASHIONS is one of the most up-and-coming custom window decorating franchises in America. Our "Window Fashions on Wheels" concept maximizes profits by eliminating costly overhead. PWF's mobile sample van takes a complete line of national brand-name awnings, shutters, blinds, shades and drapes, manually and electrically operated, to the consumer's home/office. Group buying power means the highest quality at the lowest price.

HISTORY: . . . .
Established in 1985; . . 1st Franchised in 1991
Company-Owned Units (As of 8/31/1992): . .1
Franchised Units (As of 8/31/1992): 4
Total Units (As of 8/31/1992): 5
Projected New Units for 1993: 10
Distribution: US-5;Can-0;Overseas-0
North America: . . . . 2 States
Concentration: . . . . 4 in FL, 1 in NC
Registered: . . . . .FL
. . . .
Type Space: . . . . .Mini Cargo Van;~NA SF

FINANCIAL: Earnings Claim: . .No
Cash Investment: $20K
Total Investment: $30-45K
Fees: Franchise - $16.5K
Royalty: 4%, Advert: 0%
Contract Periods (Yrs.): 5/5
Area Development Agreement: . .No
Sub-Franchise Contract: . . . . .No
Expand in Territory: . . . . . . Yes
Passive Ownership: . . . Discouraged
Encourage Conversions: . . . . .No
Average # Employees: . . . . .2 FT

FRANCHISOR TRAINING/SUPPORT:
Financial Assistance Provided: . . . Yes(I)
Site Selection Assistance: . . . . .Yes
Lease Negotiation Assistance: . . . . .NA
Co-operative Advertising: . . . . .Yes
Training: . . . 1 Wk. At Home, 2 Wks. HQ
. . . . 4 Days Site with Representative
On-Going Support: C,D,E,G,h,I/ 5
EXPANSION PLANS:
US: . . . . All US
Canada: . . . . .No
Overseas: . . . . No

SLUMBERLAND INTERNATIONAL

3060 Centerville Rd.
Little Canada, MN 55117
TEL: (612) 482-7500
FAX: (612) 482-0027
Mr. Ken R. Larson, President

SLUMBERLAND is a home furnishing specialty retailer, featuring name-brand mattresses, sleep sofas, reclining chairs, sofas and chairs, daybeds and related bedroom furniture. SLUMBERLAND is a market-driven retailer that outpaces national averages in sales/SF and gross margins.

HISTORY: . . . .
Established in 1967; . . 1st Franchised in 1978
Company-Owned Units (As of 8/31/1992): . 12
Franchised Units (As of 8/31/1992): 18
Total Units (As of 8/31/1992): 30
Projected New Units for 1993: 2
Distribution: US-30;Can-0;Overseas-0
North America: . . . . 6 States
Concentration: . . . . .16 in MN, 8 in IA
Registered: . . . . IL,MN,SD,WI
. . . .
Type Space: . . . . FS, SC;~10,000 SF

FINANCIAL: Earnings Claim: . .No
Cash Investment: . . . .$
Total Investment: $100-200K
Fees: Franchise - $10K
Royalty: 3%, Advert: 0%
Contract Periods (Yrs.): . . . 10/10
Area Development Agreement: . .No
Sub-Franchise Contract: . . . . .No
Expand in Territory: . . . . . . Yes
Passive Ownership: . . . Discouraged
Encourage Conversions: . . . . Yes
Average # Employees: . . 4 FT, 2 PT

FRANCHISOR TRAINING/SUPPORT:
Financial Assistance Provided: . . . . .No
Site Selection Assistance: . . . . .No
Lease Negotiation Assistance: . . . . .Yes
Co-operative Advertising: . . . . .NA
Training: . . . . . . 3-4 Wks. Headquarters
. . . .
On-Going Support: B,c,d,G,H,i/ . . . . . .
EXPANSION PLANS:
US: . . . . .Central Midwest
Canada: . . . . .No
Overseas: . . . . No

SPRING CREST DRAPERY CENTERS

505 W. Lambert Rd.
Brea, CA 92621
TEL: (800) 552-5523 (714) 529-9993
FAX: (714) 529-2093
Mr. Jack Long, President

Prestigious store selling to up-scale clientele, protected territory, little inventory, exclusive products and all the top brands in custom window fashions... and more. Purchasing power of 300 stores, complete training, on-going support from a 36-year-old company consistently ranked #1 in its' franchise category.

HISTORY: . . . . IFA
Established in 1955; . . 1st Franchised in 1968
Company-Owned Units (As of 8/31/1992): . .1
Franchised Units (As of 8/31/1992): 174
Total Units (As of 8/31/1992): 175
Projected New Units for 1993: 6
Distribution: . . . US-142;Can-20;Overseas-13
North America: . . . . 35 States, 5 Provinces
Concentration: . 24 in CA, 12 in OK, 11 in FL
Registered: . . CA,FL,IL,IN,MI,MN,ND,OR
. . . . .SD,VA,WA,WI,AB
Type Space: . . . . .SC;~1,200 SF

FINANCIAL: Earnings Claim: . .No
Cash Investment: $37-55K
Total Investment: $55K
Fees: Franchise - $15K
Royalty: 3%, Advert: 2%
Contract Periods (Yrs.): . . . 10/10
Area Development Agreement: . .No
Sub-Franchise Contract: . . . . .No
Expand in Territory: . . . . . . Yes
Passive Ownership: . . . Discouraged
Encourage Conversions: . . . . Yes
Average # Employees: . . 2 FT, 1 PT

FRANCHISOR TRAINING/SUPPORT:
Financial Assistance Provided: . . . Yes(I)
Site Selection Assistance: . . . . .Yes
Lease Negotiation Assistance: . . . . .Yes
Co-operative Advertising: . . . . .Yes
Training: . . . . 2 Wks. Headquarters,
. . . .2 Wks. On-Site, On-Going On-Site
On-Going Support: C,D,E,G,h,I/ 15
EXPANSION PLANS:
US: . . . . All US
Canada: . . . . .All Canada
Overseas: . . . . Yes

WINDOW-OLOGY

3500 W. Garry Ave.
Santa Ana, CA 92704
TEL: (800) 675-1513 (714) 771-2649 C
FAX:
Mr. John McElroy, President

We are a full-service mobile window covering franchise. We bring the showroom to the customer's door. We are a home-based business with low overhead, no rent, employees or inventory hassles. This is a new concept. You will not find one in every city like you do with yogurt or sandwich shops. We require a modest investment and a great potential for success.

HISTORY: . . . .
Established in 1987; . . 1st Franchised in 1992
Company-Owned Units (As of 8/31/1992): . .2
Franchised Units (As of 8/31/1992): 3
Total Units (As of 8/31/1992): 5
Projected New Units for 1993: . . . .
Distribution: US-5;Can-0;Overseas-0
  North America: . . . . .1 State
  Concentration: . . . . 5 in CA
Registered: . . . . CA
. . . .
Type Space: . . . . Mobile Cargo Van;~ SF

FINANCIAL: Earnings Claim: . .No
Cash Investment: $25K
Total Investment: $25-43K
Fees: Franchise - $15.9K
  Royalty: 5%, Advert: 5%
Contract Periods (Yrs.): 5/5
Area Development Agreement: . .No
Sub-Franchise Contract: . . . . .No
Expand in Territory: . . . . . . .No
Passive Ownership: . . . Not Allowed
Encourage Conversions: . . . . Yes
Average # Employees: . . . . . .1 FT

FRANCHISOR TRAINING/SUPPORT:
Financial Assistance Provided: . . .Yes(D)
Site Selection Assistance: . . . . .Yes
Lease Negotiation Assistance: . . . . .NA
Co-operative Advertising: . . . . .Yes
Training: . . . . . . 60 Hours Headquarters
. . . .
On-Going Support: C,D,E,G,H,I/ 3
EXPANSION PLANS:
US: . . . . .All US
Canada: . . . . .No
Overseas: . . . . No

SUPPLEMENTAL LISTING OF FRANCHISORS

ABBEY CARPET COMPANY . . . . 425 University Ave., # 222, Sacramento, CA 95825
  Contact: Mr. Phil Gutierrez, President; Tel: (916) 925-7213
ARISE FUTON/FUTON USA . . . . 272 N. Bedford Rd., Mt. Kisco, NY 10549
  Contact: Ms. Terri Rae Kuhajda, VP; Tel: (914) 666-2770
BEDDING SHACK LICENSING CORP. . . . . 46 Glenwood Ave., Bridgeport, CT 06610
  Contact: President; Tel:
BOCA RATTAN PREMIUM RATTAN FURNITURE . . . . . 127 Mohawk Ave., Scotia, NY 12302
  Contact: Mr. Richard J. Norelli; Tel: (800) 678-2622 (518) 393-2200
BRACKEN SYSTEMS CARPET/UPHOLSTERY . . . . 2800 North A-1-A, # 103, Ft. Pierce, FL 34949
  Contact: President; Tel:
CACTUS FLOWER . . . . 3020 N. Federal Way Hwy., Bldg. #9, Ft. Lauderdale, FL 33306
  Contact: President; Tel: (305) 561-4161
CARPET TOWN . . . . 937 N. Citrus Ave., Hollywood, CA 90038
  Contact: President; Tel:
CARPETERIA . . . . .28159 Ave. Stanford, Santa Clarita, CA 91355
  Contact: Mr. George Holder, Dir. Fran.; Tel: (800) 356-6763 (805) 295-1000
CARPETLAND USA . . . . 8201 Calumet Ave., Munster, IN 46321
  Contact: Mr. John Booth; Tel: (219) 836-5628
CARPETMAX . . . . .595 Blossom Rd., Rochester, NY 14610
  Contact: Mr. Gary Eidlin, VP Sales; Tel: (800) 331-1744 (716) 654-6310
CLASSY CLOSETS ETC. . . . . 2001 W. Alameda Dr., Tempe, AZ 85282
  Contact: Mr. John Thomas, President; Tel: (800) 992-2448 (602) 438-7343
CLOSET SYSTEMS OF . . . . 99 - 899 Iwaena St., Aiea, HI 96701
  Contact: Mr. Jerry Olinski, President; Tel: (800) 367-8047 (808) 488-0811 C
COMFORTABLES, THE LIVING ROOM STORE . . . . P. O. Box 531, Navesink, NJ 07752
  Contact: Mr. Charles L. Matson; Tel: (201) 291-5888
CONTOUR WINDOW FASHIONS . . . . . # 102-10651 Shellbridge Way, Richmond, BC V6X 2W8 CAN
  Contact: Mr. Michael B. Harrison; Tel: (604) 273-5445
CUSTOM MATTRESS FACTORY OUTLET CTRS. . . . . 3401 Lake Ave., Fort Wayne, IN 46805
  Contact: Mr. John Thistlewaite; Tel: (219) 426-7134
DAKOTA . . . . P. O. Box 120, Webster, SD 57274
  Contact: President; Tel: (605) 345-4646
DIAL-A-TILE . . . . 1604 Highway 35, P. O. Box 71, Oakhurst, NJ 07755
  Contact: Mr. Robert Ballack, President; Tel: (800) 955-8453
DRAPERY FACTORY, THE . . . . 80 Tanforan Ave., # 10, So. San Francisco, CA 94080
  Contact: Mr. A. D. Brown, President; Tel: (800) 637-2731 (415) 583-1300
DWOSKIN'S WALLCOVERINGS . . . . 5903 Peachtree Industrial Blvd., Norcross, GA 30092
  Contact: Mr. Myron Dwoskin, President; Tel: (404) 449-5180 C

FINE DESIGNS SOFA GALLERY . . . . 100 Furniture Pkwy., Norwalk, OH 44857
    Contact: Mr. Bill Gerken, President; Tel: (800) 837-2565 (419) 668-4461
FURNITURE TO GO . . . . 76 Otis St., Westboro, MA 01581
    Contact: President; Tel: (508) 366-0639
G. FRIED CARPETLAND . . . . .800 Old Country Rd., Westbury, NY 11590
    Contact: Mr. Al Fried, President; Tel: (516) 333-3900
GIANT CARPET . . . . 120 Moonachie Ave., Moonachie, NJ 07074
    Contact: Mr. Samuel Rosenberg, President; Tel: (800) 507-0035
HILLSIDE BEDDING . . . . .700 Havemeyer Ave., Bronx, NY 10473
    Contact: Mr. Robert Martire, President; Tel: (800) 873-4BED (212) 597-3300
HOME DECORATING . . . . .8806 Woodlake Dr., Rowlett, TX 75088
    Contact: President; Tel: (214) 412-0117
INNERHOUSE . . . . .P. O. Box 7239, Thousand Oaks, CA 91359
    Contact: Mr. Bernard Weiser, President; Tel: (818) 785-1182
LAURA'S DRAPERIES, BEDSPREADS & MORE . . . . .9331 Katy Fwy., Houston, TX 77024
    Contact: Mr. Harold Nedell, President; Tel: (800) 654-7922 (713) 973-0214
LIBERTY GREEN . . . . P. O. Box 5035, Station 1, Wilmington, NC 28403
    Contact: Mr. Bernie Pisczek, VP Dev.; Tel: (800) 255-9704 (919) 343-9551
LIGHTING UNLIMITED . . . . 131 Cartwright Ave., Toronto, ON M6A 1V4   CAN
    Contact: Mr. John Cole, VP Ops.; Tel: (416) 781-5691 C
LIVING LIGHTING . . . . 4699 Keele St., # 1, Downsview, ON M3J 2N8   CAN
    Contact: Mr. Ted Loyst; Tel: (416) 661-9916
PIER 1 IMPORTS . . . . 301 Commerce St., # 600, Fort Worth, TX 77102
    Contact: President; Tel: (817) 335-7031
SCANDIA DOWN SHOPS . . . . 455 Park Plaza Dr., 2025 First Ave., La Crosse, WI 54601
    Contact: Mr. Kell Larsen, President; Tel: (800) 237-5337 (608) 785-7755
STARMARK . . . . 600 E. 48th St. N., Sioux Falls, SD 57104
    Contact: Mr. Randy Pooley, Natl. Fran. Mgr.; Tel: (605) 335-8600
TMF SYSTEMS . . . . 127 Mohawk Ave., Scotia, NY 12302
    Contact: Mr. Richard Norelli, COO; Tel: (800) 673-2622 (518) 393-2200
TOP DRAWER CUSTOM CLOSETS . . . . 1892 Kentucky Ave., Winter Park, FL 32789
    Contact: Ms. Tania Torruella, President; Tel: (407) 644-9665
TOW-IT 9 S. Washington Ave., Bergenfield, NJ 07621 . . . .
    Contact: President; Tel:
WATERBED EMPORIUM . . . . 1902 W. 3rd St., Cleveland, OH 44113
    Contact: Mr. Ray Salupo, President; Tel: (800) 443-1163 (216) 781-4200
WINDOW WORKS INTERNATIONAL . . . . 6321 Bury Dr., # 2, Eden Prairie, MN 54346
    Contact: Mr. Mike Jorgensen; Tel: (800) 937-2004
WORKBENCH . . . . .470 Park Avenue S., New York, NY 10016
    Contact: Ms. Nancy Pulaski; Tel: (800) 777-7790 (212) 532-7900
WORLD BAZAAR . . . . 4849 Massachusetts Blvd., College Park, GA 30337
    Contact: Mr. Paul Modzelewski; Tel: (404) 994-7979

CHAPTER 42

RETAIL: HOME IMPROVEMENT AND HARDWARE

ALMOST HEAVEN, LTD.

Rt. 5-FS
Renick, WV 24966
TEL: (304) 497-3163 C
FAX: (304) 497-2698
Ms. Stephanie Cleghon

ALMOST HEAVEN is the world's largest manufacturer of hot water health and leisure products. Their line includes hot tubs, spas, steamrooms, saunas and whirlpool baths.

HISTORY: . . . .
Established in 1971; . . 1st Franchised in 1975
Company-Owned Units (As of 8/31/1992): . .0
Franchised Units (As of 8/31/1992): 1590
Total Units (As of 8/31/1992): 1590
Projected New Units for 1993: 150
Distribution: . . US-1130;Can-60;Overseas-400
  North America: . . . .
  Concentration: .60 in MA, 45 in NY, 38 in MD
Registered: . . . . .All
. . . .
Type Space: . . . . FS;~1,000 Min. SF

FINANCIAL: Earnings Claim: . .No
Cash Investment: $5-10K
Total Investment: $10-20K
Fees: Franchise - $0
  Royalty: 0%, Advert: 0%
Contract Periods (Yrs.): 5/5
Area Development Agreement: Yes/5
Sub-Franchise Contract: . . . . . Yes
Expand in Territory: . . . . Yes
Passive Ownership: . . . . . .Allowed
Encourage Conversions: . . . . . Yes
Average # Employees: . . 3 FT, 2 PT

FRANCHISOR TRAINING/SUPPORT:
Financial Assistance Provided: . . . Yes(I)
Site Selection Assistance: . . . . .Yes
Lease Negotiation Assistance: . . . . .Yes
Co-operative Advertising: . . . . .Yes
Training: . . . . 2 Wks. Factory,
. . . . 2 Wks. On-Site
On-Going Support: A,B,C,D,E,F,G,h,I/ . 99
EXPANSION PLANS:
US: . . . . .All US
Canada: . . . . .All Canada
Overseas: . . . . .Yes

AMERICA'S CARPET GALLERY

Innsbrook Corp. Ctr., P.O. Box 70040
Richmond, VA 23255
TEL: (800) 344-7557 (804) 527-1435
FAX: (804) 965-0180
Mr. Neal O'Shea, Dir. Fran. Dev.

Complete and unique retail floorcovering and home decorating franchise. Ideally suited for individuals or couples interested in a quality of life work experience. Product line features DuPont Certified Stainmaster carpets and Mannington flooring. Unique marketing and merchandising concepts include computerized home decorating system - The Gallery Designer - and an extended warranty program - Performance Assurance Program.

HISTORY: . . . . IFA
Established in 1986; . . 1st Franchised in 1992
Company-Owned Units (As of 8/31/1992): . .0
Franchised Units (As of 8/31/1992): 10
Total Units (As of 8/31/1992): 10
Projected New Units for 1993: 20
Distribution: US-10;Can-0;Overseas-0
  North America: . . . . 2 States
  Concentration: . . . . .9 in VA, 1 in WV
Registered: . . . . FL,IL,IN,MD,VA,DC
. . . .
Type Space: . . . . .FS, SC;~4,000 SF

FINANCIAL: Earnings Claim: . .No
Cash Investment: $35K
Total Investment: $100-165K
Fees: Franchise - $15K
  Royalty: 4%, Advert: 4%
Contract Periods (Yrs.): 10/5
Area Development Agreement: Yes/10
Sub-Franchise Contract: . . . . .No
Expand in Territory: . . . . . . Yes
Passive Ownership: . . . . . .Allowed
Encourage Conversions: . . . . Yes
Average # Employees: . . 2 FT, 1 PT

FRANCHISOR TRAINING/SUPPORT:
Financial Assistance Provided: . . . . . No
Site Selection Assistance: . . . . . . .Yes
Lease Negotiation Assistance: . . . . .Yes
Co-operative Advertising: . . . . . . .Yes
Training: . . . . 2 Wks. Headquarters
. . . .
On-Going Support: A,C,D,E,F,h,I/ . . . 10
EXPANSION PLANS:
US: . . . . . Mid-Atlantic and East Coast
Canada: . . . . .No
Overseas: . . . . No

BUY THE YARD

4457 Chesswood Dr.
Downsview, ON M3J 2C2 CAN
TEL: (416) 630-9674
FAX: (416) 630-9166
Ms. Stacy Steinberg, Mgr. Licensing

One-stop decorating stores. We sell fabric, wallpaper, accessories and carpets. We offer shop at home, provided by on-staff designers. And we have custom labor for draperies, bedding, upholstery, slipcovers, etc. Company no longer franchises, but licenses a turn-key operation in Canada and operates an affiliated buying network in the US.

HISTORY: . . . .
Established in 1976; . . 1st Franchised in 1985
Company-Owned Units (As of 8/31/1992): . .5
Franchised Units (As of 8/31/1992): 9
Total Units (As of 8/31/1992): 14
Projected New Units for 1993: 10
Distribution: US-2;Can-12;Overseas-0
  North America: . . . . . 2 States, 2 Provinces
  Concentration: . . . 11 in ON, 1 in TX, 1 in IL
Registered: . . . .
. . . .
Type Space: . . . . NA;~1,000 SF

FINANCIAL: Earnings Claim: . .No
Cash Investment: $50K
Total Investment: $100K
Fees: Franchise - $50K
  Royalty: 0%, Advert: 0%
Contract Periods (Yrs.): 10/5
Area Development Agreement: . .No
Sub-Franchise Contract: . . . . .No
Expand in Territory: . . . . . . .No
Passive Ownership: . . . . . .Allowed
Encourage Conversions: . . . . Yes
Average # Employees: . . 2 FT, 2 PT

FRANCHISOR TRAINING/SUPPORT:
Financial Assistance Provided: . . . . .Yes
Site Selection Assistance: . . . . . . .Yes
Lease Negotiation Assistance: . . . .Yes
Co-operative Advertising: . . . . . . .No
Training: . . . . . 2 Wks. Toronto, ON,
. . . . 2 Wks. Chicago, IL
On-Going Support: B,c,D,E,f/ 12
EXPANSION PLANS:
US: . . . . .All US
Canada: . . . . .All Canada
Overseas: . . . . UK

COLOR TILE

515 Houston St.
Ft. Worth, TX 76102
TEL: (800) 688-8063 (817) 870-9400
FAX: (817) 870-9589
Mr. Gary T. Lomax, VP Fran.

Retail flooring, window and wall covering, name-brand products, nationally recognized name (store and mobile van franchise available).

HISTORY: . . . . IFA
Established in 1953; . . 1st Franchised in 1989
Company-Owned Units (As of 8/31/1992): 777
Franchised Units (As of 8/31/1992): 54
Total Units (As of 8/31/1992): 831
Projected New Units for 1993: 16
Distribution: US-831;Can-0;Overseas-0
  North America: . . . .
  Concentration: . . . . .CA, MI, PA
Registered: . . . CA,FL,IN,MI,MN,NY,OR,RI
. . . . .VA,WA,DC
Type Space: . . . . FS;~4,000-5,000 SF

FINANCIAL: Earnings Claim: . .No
Cash Investment: $12.5-75K
Total Investment: $12.5-218K
Fees: Franchise - $12.5-20K
  Royalty: 6%, Advert: 1-3%
Contract Periods (Yrs.): . . . 3-5/3-5
Area Development Agreement: . .No
Sub-Franchise Contract: . . . . .No
Expand in Territory: . . . . . . .No
Passive Ownership: . . . Discouraged
Encourage Conversions: . . . . Yes
Average # Employees: . . . . 1-5 FT

FRANCHISOR TRAINING/SUPPORT:
Financial Assistance Provided: . . . Yes(I)
Site Selection Assistance: . . . . . . .Yes
Lease Negotiation Assistance: . . . .Yes
Co-operative Advertising: . . . . . . .Yes
Training: . . . . 6 Wks. Closest Color
. . . . Tile Store
On-Going Support: / 7
EXPANSION PLANS:
US: . . . . .All US
Canada: . . . . .No
Overseas: . . . . No

PLUMBING MART

2047 Avenue Rd.
Toronto, ON M5M 4A7 CAN
TEL: (416) 752-4550 C
FAX: (416) 752-4872
Mr. William A. Gibson, President

A bathroom renovation centre, catering to the retail home owner/customer and small contractor/renovator. We cover from do-it-yourself help, the sale of plumbing fixtures and parts to full bathroom renovation contracting.

HISTORY:	FINANCIAL: Earnings Claim: . .No	FRANCHISOR TRAINING/SUPPORT:
Established in 1959; . . 1st Franchised in 1975	Cash Investment: $150K	Financial Assistance Provided: . . . Yes(I)
Company-Owned Units (As of 8/31/1992): . .0	Total Investment: $250K	Site Selection Assistance: . . . . . . .Yes
Franchised Units (As of 8/31/1992): 12	Fees: Franchise - $50K	Lease Negotiation Assistance: . . . . .Yes
Total Units (As of 8/31/1992): 12	Royalty: 5%, Advert: 5%	Co-operative Advertising: . . . . . . .Yes
Projected New Units for 1993: 5	Contract Periods (Yrs.): 10/5	Training: . . . . . 3 Months Existing Store,
Distribution: US-0;Can-12;Overseas-0	Area Development Agreement: . .No	. . . . 3 Months New Store
North America: . . . . .1 Province	Sub-Franchise Contract: . . . . .No	On-Going Support: C,D,E,H/ 5
Concentration: . . . . 12 in ON	Expand in Territory: . . . . . . Yes	EXPANSION PLANS:
Registered:	Passive Ownership: . . . Not Allowed	US: . . . . No
. . . .	Encourage Conversions: . . . . . Yes	Canada: . . . . .Ontario
Type Space: . . . . .SC;~4,000 SF	Average # Employees: . . 3 FT, 2 PT	Overseas: . . . . No

STAINED GLASS OVERLAY

1827 N. Case St.
Orange, CA 92665
TEL: (800) 944-4746 (714) 974-6124
FAX: (714) 974-6529
Ms. Susan L. Pope, VP Fran. Ops.

STAINED GLASS OVERLAY is a rapidly-growing international franchise organization. The foundation of the STAINED GLASS OVERLAY business is the patented process used to manufacture solid, seamless, one-piece stained glass in any design or pattern. Exclusive territories, turn-key package.

HISTORY:	FINANCIAL: Earnings Claim: . .No	FRANCHISOR TRAINING/SUPPORT:
Established in 1974; . . 1st Franchised in 1981	Cash Investment: $45-75K	Financial Assistance Provided: . . . . .No
Company-Owned Units (As of 8/31/1992): . .0	Total Investment: $45-75K	Site Selection Assistance: . . . . . . .Yes
Franchised Units (As of 8/31/1992): 321	Fees: Franchise - $34K	Lease Negotiation Assistance: . . . . . No
Total Units (As of 8/31/1992): 321	Royalty: 5%, Advert: 2%	Co-operative Advertising: . . . . . . .Yes
Projected New Units for 1993: 20	Contract Periods (Yrs.): 5/5	Training: . . . . 6 Days Headquarters
Distribution: . . US-179;Can-11;Overseas-131	Area Development Agreement: . .No	. . . .
North America: . . . . 41 States, 5 Provinces	Sub-Franchise Contract: . . . . .No	On-Going Support: C,d,G,H,I/ 12
Concentration: . . 50 in CA, 10 in FL, 9 in PA	Expand in Territory: . . . . . . Yes	EXPANSION PLANS:
Registered: . . . . .All	Passive Ownership: . . . Discouraged	US: . . . . .All US
. . . .	Encourage Conversions: . . . . . NA	Canada: . . . . .All Canada
Type Space: . . . . .SF;~1,000 SF	Average # Employees: 2-3 FT, 1-2 PT	Overseas: . . . . Asia, EUR

WALLPAPERS TO GO

P. O. Box 4586
Houston, TX 77210
TEL: (800) 843-7094 (713) 874-3686
FAX: (713) 874-3655
Ms. Deborah Steinberg, VP

WALLPAPERS TO GO stores offer high-quality, fashion wallcoverings and related home decor items to the do-it-yourself home decorator, at our everyday low prices. Appealing displays and emphasis on service have set WALLPAPERS TO GO stores apart from the competition.

HISTORY: . . . . IFA	FINANCIAL: Earnings Claim: . Yes	FRANCHISOR TRAINING/SUPPORT:
Established in 1967; . . 1st Franchised in 1967	Cash Investment: $40-80K	Financial Assistance Provided: . . . Yes(I)
Company-Owned Units (As of 8/31/1992): . 22	Total Investment: $121-131K	Site Selection Assistance: . . . . . . .Yes
Franchised Units (As of 8/31/1992): 97	Fees: Franchise - $40K	Lease Negotiation Assistance: . . . . .Yes
Total Units (As of 8/31/1992): 119	Royalty: 8%, Advert: 5%	Co-operative Advertising: . . . . . . .Yes
Projected New Units for 1993: 15	Contract Periods (Yrs.): 10/5/5	Training: . . . . . .7-14 Days Headquarters
Distribution: US-119;Can-0;Overseas-0	Area Development Agreement: . .No	. . . .
North America: . . . . 27 States	Sub-Franchise Contract: . . . . .No	On-Going Support: B,C,D,E,f,G,H,I/ . . 99
Concentration: . . 42 in CA, 14 in TX, 7 in IN	Expand in Territory: . . . . . . Yes	EXPANSION PLANS:
Registered: . . . . .All	Passive Ownership: . . . Not Allowed	US: . . . . .All US
. . . .	Encourage Conversions: . . . . . .No	Canada: . . . . No
Type Space: . . . FS, SF, SC;~2,800-3,200 SF	Average # Employees: . . 3 FT, 3 PT	Overseas: . . . . No

SUPPLEMENTAL LISTING OF FRANCHISORS

AMERICAN HARDWARE SUPPLY CO. . . . . P. O. Box 1510, East Butler, PA 160013
    Contact: Mr. Don Belt, VP Sales/Mktg.; Tel: (412) 283-4567
AMERICAN PAINTING AND PAPERING . . . . 236 S. 108th Ave., # 3, Omaha, NE 68154
    Contact: Mr. Roland Bates; Tel: (800) 933-2508 (402) 333-1685
ARMSTRONG WORLD INDUSTRIES . . . . P.O. Box 3001, Lancaster, PA 17601
    Contact: President; Tel: (717) 397-0611
AUSTIN HARDWOODS . . . . .2119 Goodrich, Austin, TX 78704
    Contact: Mr. Carl Lasner, President; Tel: (512) 442-4001
BEAVER LUMBER COMPANY . . . . 7303 Warden Ave., Markham, ON L3R 5Y6   CAN
    Contact: Mr. William Worden; Tel: (416) 479-2255
BECKERMANN KITCHENS US . . . . 2000 Powell St., # 1650, Emeryville, CA 94608
    Contact: Mr. Jostein Stokkan; Tel: (415) 652-4566
BLINDS ON WHEELS . . . . 4012 Zahm Rd., Belding, MI 48809
    Contact: Mr. Lon Ferguson, President; Tel: (800) 747-9864 (616) 897-0200
CARIBBEAN INTERIOR DESIGN CENTER . . . . . 2240 Woolbright Rd., Boynton Beach, FL 33426
    Contact: Mr. Edward Donatelli, VP; Tel: (407) 738-1278
CLOVERDALE PAINT . . . . 6950 King George Hwy., Surrey, BC V3W 4Z1   CAN
    Contact: Mr. Nick Willis; Tel: (604) 596-6261
COLOR YOUR WORLD . . . . 10 Carson St., Toronto, ON M8W 3R5   CAN
    Contact: Mr. Peter Neubauer; Tel: (416) 259-6296
DAVIS PAINT COMPANY . . . . 1311 Iron St., North Kansas City, MO 64116
    Contact: President; Tel: (816) 471-4447
HOME HARDWARE/HOME ALL BUILDING CENTRE . . . . 34 Henry St. W., St. Jacobs, ON N0B 2N0   CAN
    Contact: President; Tel: (519) 664-2252
INDOOR MAGIC . . . . P.O. Box 34545, Omaha, NE 68134
    Contact: President; Tel:
INTILE DESIGNS . . . . 9716 Old Katy Rd, # 110, Houston, TX 77065
    Contact: Ms. Tracy Cernan, Asst. to President; Tel: (713) 468-8400
JUNIORS TOOLS . . . . 1434 S. Richey, Santa Ana, CA 92705
    Contact: Mr. Mark Skolnick, President; Tel: (714) 588-7152
MATCO TOOLS . . . . 4403 Allen Rd., Stow, OH 44224
    Contact: Mr. Richard King, VP Human Resources; Tel: (216) 929-4949
MR. BUILD PLUS . . . . .276 Turnpike Rd., Westboro, MA 10581
    Contact: Mr. Paul Carlson, Mgr. Fran.; Tel: (800) 242-8453 (203) 657-3607
MR. MINIBLIND . . . . 20341 Irvine Ave., # 1, Santa Ana Heights, CA 92707
    Contact: Ms. Christina Huckins, CEO; Tel: (800) 877-7712 (714) 929-9221
OUR OWN HARDWARE COMPANY . . . . .2300 West Highway 13, Fernsville, MN 55337
    Contact: President; Tel:
QUALITY MARK HOUSE OF PLUMBING/BATH . . . . . . 533 University Ave., Rochester, NY 14607
    Contact: Mr. Jerome Standera, VP; Tel: (716) 442-7380
SNAP-ON-TOOLS . . . . .2801 80th St., Kenosha, WI 53141
    Contact: Mr. Tommy Clark, Dir. Frn.; Tel: (414) 656-4784
STRIPPER WALLPAPER SERVICE . . . . 8092 Windy Sea Circle, Huntington Beach, CA 92647
    Contact: President; Tel: (714) 841-3808
TRUE VALUE HARDWARE . . . . .333 Harvey Rd., Manchester, NH 03103
    Contact: Mr. Ed Giunco, Regional Sales Mgr.; Tel: (603) 669-2221
WALLPAPER AMERICA . . . . .2862 E. Ponce de Leon Ave., Decatur, GA 30036
    Contact: President; Tel:
WALLPAPERS GALORE . . . . .11155 Bluegrass Pkwy., Louisville, KY 40299
    Contact: Mr. Tom Owen, President; Tel: (502) 267-9577

CHAPTER 43

RETAIL: PHOTOGRAPHY PRODUCTS AND SERVICES

ELEGANT IMAGES

15 Engle St., # 302
Englewood, NJ 07631
TEL: (800) 332-2229 (201) 871-0370
FAX: (201) 871-7168
Mr. John Sterns, Sales Mgr.

Complete make-over and photography studio - combines skills of a make-up artist, hair stylist, accessory and wardrobe coordinator and fashion photographer.

HISTORY: . . . .
Established in 1989; . . 1st Franchised in 1991
Company-Owned Units (As of 8/31/1992): . .5
Franchised Units (As of 8/31/1992): 9
Total Units (As of 8/31/1992): 14
Projected New Units for 1993: 10
Distribution: US-14;Can-0;Overseas-0
North America: . . . . 7 States
Concentration: . . . .4 in MD, 3 in CA, 2 in IL
Registered: . . . . CA,IL,MD,NY
. . . .
Type Space: . . . . .RM;~600-1,300 SF

FINANCIAL: Earnings Claim: . .No
Cash Investment: $50K
Total Investment: $136-180K
Fees: Franchise - . . . .$
  Royalty: 5%, Advert: 0%
Contract Periods (Yrs.): 10/10
Area Development Agreement: . Yes
Sub-Franchise Contract: . . . . . .No
Expand in Territory: . . . . Yes
Passive Ownership: . . . Not Allowed
Encourage Conversions: . . . . . .No
Average # Employees: . . 3 FT, 8 PT

FRANCHISOR TRAINING/SUPPORT:
Financial Assistance Provided: . . . Yes(I)
Site Selection Assistance: . . . . .Yes
Lease Negotiation Assistance: . . . . .Yes
Co-operative Advertising: . . . . .Yes
Training: . . . .1 Wk. HQ, 1 Wk. Company
  . . . . .Store, 1 Wk. Franchisee Location
On-Going Support: C,D,E,H,I/ . . . .
EXPANSION PLANS:
US: . . . . All US
Canada: . . . . .All Canada
Overseas: . . . . .Yes

FREEZE FRAME

369 Los Cerritos Ctr.
Cerritos, CA 90701
TEL: (310) 924-5792
FAX: (310) 402-9968
Ms. Laina Sullivan, VP Fran.

FREEZE FRAME is a contemporary "make-over" photography studio founded by Susan Page, former Miss Texas, who has been in the business of helping people reach their beauty potential for over 20 years. FREEZE FRAME has defined itself as the photo studio of the 90's. A quality photo experience - that's our promise!

HISTORY:	FINANCIAL: Earnings Claim: . .No	FRANCHISOR TRAINING/SUPPORT:
Established in 1989; . . 1st Franchised in 1990	Cash Investment: $90-125K	Financial Assistance Provided: . . . Yes(I)
Company-Owned Units (As of 8/31/1992): . .6	Total Investment: $100-160K	Site Selection Assistance: . . . . . . .Yes
Franchised Units (As of 8/31/1992): 6	Fees: Franchise - $15K	Lease Negotiation Assistance: . . . .Yes
Total Units (As of 8/31/1992): 12	Royalty: 5%, Advert: 3%	Co-operative Advertising: . . . . . . .Yes
Projected New Units for 1993: 10	Contract Periods (Yrs.): 10/10	Training: . . . . 2 Wks. Headquarters,
Distribution: US-7;Can-0;Overseas-5	Area Development Agreement: Yes/10	. . . . 1 Wk. Store Location
North America: . . . . .1 State	Sub-Franchise Contract: . . . . Yes	On-Going Support: B,C,D,E,H/ 8
Concentration: . . . . 1 in CA	Expand in Territory: . . . . . . Yes	EXPANSION PLANS:
Registered: . . . . All States	Passive Ownership: . . . Discouraged	US: . . . . .All US
. . . .	Encourage Conversions: . . . . . Yes	Canada: . . . . .No
Type Space: . . . . RM;~900-1,200 SF	Average # Employees: 2-3 FT, 6-8 PT	Overseas: . JA, HK, UK, FR, Asia, Indon.

HEADSHOTS

23316 Nameless Rd.
Leander, TX 78641
TEL: (512) 267-3111
FAX: (512) 267-4668
Ms. Karen Rego, VP

HEADSHOTS is a contemporary photographic studio, specializing in women and beauty. In-depth training provided. Locations are in prime super-regional malls. Creative, profitable business. Exciting! LA Times - "They walk into the mall looking like Kate and Allie and they walk out looking like Alexis and Krystle!"

HISTORY:	FINANCIAL: Earnings Claim: . .No	FRANCHISOR TRAINING/SUPPORT:
Established in 1987; . . 1st Franchised in 1990	Cash Investment: $132-150K	Financial Assistance Provided: . . . . .No
Company-Owned Units (As of 8/31/1992): . .2	Total Investment: $150K	Site Selection Assistance: . . . . . . .Yes
Franchised Units (As of 8/31/1992): 14	Fees: Franchise - $25K	Lease Negotiation Assistance: . . . . .Yes
Total Units (As of 8/31/1992): 16	Royalty: 7%, Advert: 2%	Co-operative Advertising: . . . . .No
Projected New Units for 1993: 12	Contract Periods (Yrs.): 5/10	Training: . . . . . . 10 Days Headquarters,
Distribution: US-16;Can-0;Overseas-0	Area Development Agreement: . .No	. . . . 17 Days Mall Location
North America: . . . . 6 States	Sub-Franchise Contract: . . . . .No	On-Going Support: C,D,E,H/ 5
Concentration: . . . 3 in CA, 2 in HI, 2 in AZ	Expand in Territory: . . . . . . Yes	EXPANSION PLANS:
Registered: . . . . . .All States Exc. ND & SD	Passive Ownership: . . . Not Allowed	US: . . . . .All US
. . . .	Encourage Conversions: . . . . NA	Canada: . . . . .No
Type Space: . . . . RM;~ SF	Average # Employees: . . 7 FT, 7 PT	Overseas: . . . . .No

ONE HOUR MOTO PHOTO & PORTRAIT STUDIO

4444 Lake Center Dr.
Dayton, OH 45426
TEL: (800) 733-6686 (513) 854-6686
FAX: (513) 854-0140
Mr. Paul Pieschel, VP Fran. Dev.

World's largest franchisor one-hour film processor, featuring related add-on imaging services, such as portrait studios, video transfer systems, etc. A company with over 40 years' experience in the industry, now positioned in the exploding growth market of on-site processing stores.

HISTORY: . . . . IFA	FINANCIAL: Earnings Claim: . Yes	FRANCHISOR TRAINING/SUPPORT:
Established in 1981; . . 1st Franchised in 1982	Cash Investment: $45-60K	Financial Assistance Provided: . . . Yes(I)
Company-Owned Units (As of 8/31/1992): . 67	Total Investment: $136K	Site Selection Assistance: . . . . . . .Yes
Franchised Units (As of 8/31/1992): 295	Fees: Franchise - $35K	Lease Negotiation Assistance: . . . . .Yes
Total Units (As of 8/31/1992): 362	Royalty: 6%, Advert: 1/2%	Co-operative Advertising: . . . . . . .Yes
Projected New Units for 1993: 30	Contract Periods (Yrs.): 10/10	Training: . . . . . . .1 Wk. Regional Store,
Distribution: . . . US-302;Can-35;Overseas-25	Area Development Agreement: . Yes	. . . 2 Wks. Headquarters, 1 Wk. On-Site
North America: . . . . . 28 States, 1 Province	Sub-Franchise Contract: . . . . .No	On-Going Support: a,B,C,D,E,f,G,H,I/ . 99
Concentration: . .44 in CA, 33 in NJ, 25 in OK	Expand in Territory: . . . . . . Yes	EXPANSION PLANS:
Registered: . . . . . .All States Exc. ND & SD	Passive Ownership: . . . Discouraged	US: . . . . .All US
. . . .	Encourage Conversions: . . . . Yes	Canada: . . . . .All Canada
Type Space: . . . .FS, SF, SC, RM;~1,400 SF	Average # Employees: 3-4 FT, 3-4 PT	Overseas: . . . . . .E. and W. EUR

ONE HOUR MOTO PHOTO (CANADA)

1315 Lawrence Ave. E., # 509
Don Mills, ON M3A 3R3 CAN
TEL: (800) 463-6686 (416) 443-1900 C
FAX: (416) 443-1653
Mr. Sam Hamam, President

A complete photo-finishing franchise, including on-site photo processing, portrait photography and other imaging services, including the sale of photographic goods and films.

HISTORY: . . . . IFA, CFA
Established in 1986; . . 1st Franchised in 1987
Company-Owned Units (As of 8/31/1992): . .1
Franchised Units (As of 8/31/1992): 34
Total Units (As of 8/31/1992): 35
Projected New Units for 1993: 10
Distribution: US-0;Can-36;Overseas-0
North America: . . . . .1 Province
Concentration: . . . . 36 in ON
Registered: . . . .
. . . . : . . . .
Type Space: . . . .FS, SF, SC, RM;~1,000 SF

FINANCIAL: Earnings Claim: . Yes
Cash Investment: $70-85K
Total Investment: $200-250K
Fees: Franchise - $35K
Royalty: 6%, Advert: 6%
Contract Periods (Yrs.): 10/5/5
Area Development Agreement: . .No
Sub-Franchise Contract: . . . . .No
Expand in Territory: . . . . . . .No
Passive Ownership: . . . Discouraged
Encourage Conversions: . . . . Yes
Average # Employees: . . 3 FT, 3 PT

FRANCHISOR TRAINING/SUPPORT:
Financial Assistance Provided: . . . Yes(I)
Site Selection Assistance: . . . . . . .Yes
Lease Negotiation Assistance: . . . . .Yes
Co-operative Advertising: . . . . . . .Yes
Training: . . . . 1 Wk. Local Store, 2 Wks.
. . . . .Dayton, OH, 1 Wk. On-Site
On-Going Support: a,B,C,D,E,G,H,I/ . . . 8
EXPANSION PLANS:
US: . . . . No
Canada: . . . . .Ontario
Overseas: . . . . No

SPORTS SECTION, THE

3120 Medlock Bridge Rd., Bldg. A
Norcross, GA 30071
TEL: (800) 321-9127 (404) 416-6604
FAX: (404) 416-8302
Ms. Nancy Wood, Fran. Dir.

Entrepreneur will become a business-minded sales and marketing expert while TSS trains him/her in photography. Rated in top 500 national franchises. Great profits. No royalty fees. 3 franchise levels to choose from, starting at $14,500. Operate from home. Send for free pack of information and photos.

HISTORY: . . . . IFA
Established in 1983; . . 1st Franchised in 1984
Company-Owned Units (As of 8/31/1992): . .2
Franchised Units (As of 8/31/1992): 59
Total Units (As of 8/31/1992): 61
Projected New Units for 1993: 24
Distribution: US-58;Can-1;Overseas-2
North America: . . . . 22 States
Concentration: . . . 5 in TX, 5 in GA, 4 in TN
Registered: . . . . FL,IL,MI,AB
. . . .
Type Space: . . . . ;~ SF

FINANCIAL: Earnings Claim: . .No
Cash Investment: $14.5-29.5K
Total Investment: $14.5-29.5K
Fees: Franchise - $14.5-29.5K
Royalty: 0%, Advert: 0%
Contract Periods (Yrs.): 2/5
Area Development Agreement: Yes/Var
Sub-Franchise Contract: . . . . . .No
Expand in Territory: . . . . . . Yes
Passive Ownership: . . . . . .Allowed
Encourage Conversions: . . . . Yes
Average # Employees: . . . . . .2 FT

FRANCHISOR TRAINING/SUPPORT:
Financial Assistance Provided: . . .Yes(D)
Site Selection Assistance: . . . . . . .NA
Lease Negotiation Assistance: . . . . .NA
Co-operative Advertising: . . . . . . .NA
Training: . . . . . . 1-5 Days Site for Sales/
. . . Mktg., 1-5 Days Site - Photography
On-Going Support: D,G,H,I/ 16
EXPANSION PLANS:
US: . . . . .All US
Canada: . . . . .All Canada
Overseas: . . . . .Yes

SUPPLEMENTAL LISTING OF FRANCHISORS

1 HOUR PHOTOWORKS . . . . 43 Manor Dr., Kitchener, ON N2A 2T9 CAN
Contact: Mr. Dave Lamka, President; Tel: (519) 894-5568
AMERICAN FAST PHOTO & CAMERA . . . . 157 S. Pine St., Spartanburg, SC 29302
Contact: Mr. Buddy Jones, President; Tel: (800) 336-1467 (803) 585-3686
BUSCH PHOTO . . . . .713 Arsenal Rd., York, PA 17402
Contact: President; Tel: (717) 755-3721
CELEBRITY PHOTOS . . . . .P. O. Box 1335, South Hanover, MA 02339
Contact: President; Tel: (617) 826-6788
EASTMAN KODAK COMPANY . . . . 343 State St., 1st Fl., Bldg. 6, Rochester, NY 14650
Contact: Mr. Joseph F. Ruh, Counsel; Tel: (716) 724-4000
JAPAN CAMERA CENTRE 1 HOUR PHOTO . . . . .150 Lesmill Rd., Don Mills, ON M3B 2T5 CAN
Contact: Ms. Wendy Maul; Tel: (800) 268-7740 (416) 445-1481
JET PHOTO INTERNATIONAL . . . . .P.O. Box 1609, Minot, ND 58702
Contact: Mr. Patrick S. Ryan; Tel: (701) 852-0327
KITS CAMERAS . . . . 6051 S. 194th St., Kent, WA 98032
Contact: Mr. Mike Greenen, Fran. Div. Mgr.; Tel: (206) 872-3688 C
ONE HOUR PHOTO . . . . 8440 Market St., Youngstown, OH 44512
Contact: Mr. J. Daniel Eicher; Tel: (216) 758-0982

QUICK SHOTS . . . . 1322 Bell Ave., # L, Tustin, CA 92680
    Contact: President; Tel: (714) 259-9113
SPECIAL DELIVERY PHOTOS . . . . 458 Rocky Point Rd., P. O. Box 395, Cordova, TN 38018
    Contact: Mr. Charles Saba, VP; Tel: (901) 753-7079
UNIVERSAL ART . . . . 1525 Hardeman Ln., Cleveland, TN 37311
    Contact: Mr. Reginald Law, VP; Tel: (800) 628-8221 (615) 479-8546
ZELLERS PORTRAIT STUDIO . . . . 158 Principale St., Gatineau, PQ J8T 4H2   CAN
    Contact: Mr. Luc St. Anour, President; Tel: (819) 561-7113

CHAPTER 44

RETAIL: SPECIALTY SHOPS

...IT STORE

122 Cambridge Ave.
Toronto, ON M4K 2L6 CAN
TEL: (416) IT-STORE
FAX:
Mr. Jack Green, President

Canada's leading contemporary card and gift store chain, with 50 locations across Canada.

HISTORY: . . . .
Established in 1981; . . 1st Franchised in 1981
Company-Owned Units (As of 8/31/1992): . 16
Franchised Units (As of 8/31/1992): . . . . . <u>34</u>
Total Units (As of 8/31/1992): 50
Projected New Units for 1993: 3
Distribution: US-0;Can-50;Overseas-0
  North America: . . . . 6 Provinces
  Concentration: . . .38 in On, 4 in MB, 4 in NB
Registered: . . . .
. . . .
Type Space: . . . . RM;~1,000 SF

FINANCIAL: Earnings Claim: . .No
Cash Investment: $50-100K
Total Investment: $100-200K
Fees: Franchise - $25K
  Royalty: 6%, Advert: 1.5%
Contract Periods (Yrs.): 5/5
Area Development Agreement: . .No
Sub-Franchise Contract: . . . . .No
Expand in Territory: . . . . Yes
Passive Ownership: . . . Not Allowed
Encourage Conversions: . . . . . .
Average # Employees: . . 2 FT, 1 PT

FRANCHISOR TRAINING/SUPPORT:
Financial Assistance Provided: . . . . .No
Site Selection Assistance: . . . . . . .Yes
Lease Negotiation Assistance: . . . . .Yes
Co-operative Advertising: . . . . .Yes
Training: . . . . 3 Days Headquarters,
. . . . 2 Wks. Existing Store
On-Going Support: C,D,E,F,G,h/ 8
EXPANSION PLANS:
  US: . . . . No
  Canada: . . . . .All Canada
  Overseas: . . . . No

A NOVEL IDEA

168 Great Rd., Route 2A
Acton, MA 01729
TEL: (508) 263-3158 (508) 452-1755
FAX:
Ms. Annie Adams, President

Up-scale recycled paperback bookstores. We sell in-good-condition paperbacks at half price and we give the public credit for books they bring to us. Product mix includes extensive selection of new children's books, new bargain books, greeting cards, cassettes and other book-related merchandise. We also special order books for customers. Annie Adams has opened over 130 bookstores. She was formerly a franchisor and is now a consultant.

HISTORY:	FINANCIAL: Earnings Claim: . .No	FRANCHISOR TRAINING/SUPPORT:
Established in 1991; . . 1st Franchised in 1991	Cash Investment: $36-62K	Financial Assistance Provided: . . . . .No
Company-Owned Units (As of 8/31/1992): . .2	Total Investment: $36-62K	Site Selection Assistance: . . . . . . .Yes
Franchised Units (As of 8/31/1992): 33	Fees: Franchise - $10K	Lease Negotiation Assistance: . . . .Yes
Total Units (As of 8/31/1992): 35	Royalty: 0%, Advert: 0%	Co-operative Advertising: . . . . . . .Yes
Projected New Units for 1993: 12	Contract Periods (Yrs.):	Training: . . . . .1 Wk. Headquarters.
Distribution: US-34;Can-1;Overseas-0	Area Development Agreement: . .No	. . . . Longer if Client Wishes.
North America: . . . . . 12 States, 1 Province	Sub-Franchise Contract: . . . . .No	On-Going Support: D,E,F,G/ 2
Concentration: . . .16 in MA, 4 in OH, 3 in FL	Expand in Territory: . . . . Yes	EXPANSION PLANS:
Registered:	Passive Ownership: . . . . .Allowed	US: . . . . .All US
. . . .	Encourage Conversions: . . . . . NA	Canada: . . . . .Yes
Type Space: . . . . SC, RM;~1,200 SF	Average # Employees: . . 1 FT, 1 PT	Overseas: . . . . .Yes

BALLOON BOUQUETS

500 23rd St. NW
Washington, DC 20037
TEL: (800) 424-2323 (202) 785-1131
FAX:
Mr. Joseph Del Vecchio, VP

Nationwide balloon delivery and decorating service. Network of franchisees, licensees and subscribers nationwide. BALLOON BOUQUETS Nationwide Delivery Service toll-free telephone number advertised in over 120 telephone books. Customer referrals made to franchisee for exclusive territory.

HISTORY:	FINANCIAL: Earnings Claim: . .No	FRANCHISOR TRAINING/SUPPORT:
Established in 1976; . . 1st Franchised in 1979	Cash Investment: $10-15K	Financial Assistance Provided: . . . . .No
Company-Owned Units (As of 8/31/1992): . .0	Total Investment: $15-20K	Site Selection Assistance: . . . . . . .No
Franchised Units (As of 8/31/1992): 14	Fees: Franchise - . . . . $Varies	Lease Negotiation Assistance: . . . .No
Total Units (As of 8/31/1992): 14	Royalty: 5%, Advert: 3%	Co-operative Advertising: . . . . . . .Yes
Projected New Units for 1993: 0	Contract Periods (Yrs.): 5/5	Training: . . . . 2-3 Days Washington, DC
Distribution: US-14;Can-0;Overseas-0	Area Development Agreement: . .No	. . . .
North America:	Sub-Franchise Contract: . . . . .No	On-Going Support: B,C,D,G,I/ 6
Concentration:	Expand in Territory: . . . . Yes	EXPANSION PLANS:
Registered: . . . . CA,NY,RI,VA	Passive Ownership: . . . Not Allowed	US: . . . . .All US
. . . .	Encourage Conversions: . . . . . Yes	Canada: . . . . .No
Type Space: . . . . ;~ SF	Average # Employees: . . .6FT, 6 PT	Overseas: . . . . No

BASQUETTES OF AMERICA

P. O. Box 278
Sumter, SC 29151
TEL: (803) 773-2356
FAX: (803) 773-9947
Ms. Lana Hoffman, VP

A specialty custom gift basket retail opportunity, focusing on gourmet foods and confections. New modules include gourmet coffee clubs, espresso, cappuccino and dessert bars. Up-scale mini-basketing centers feature croissants, breads, rolls, muffins and cookies.

HISTORY:	FINANCIAL: Earnings Claim: . .No	FRANCHISOR TRAINING/SUPPORT:
Established in 1985; . . 1st Franchised in 1986	Cash Investment: $40K	Financial Assistance Provided: . . . . .No
Company-Owned Units (As of 8/31/1992): . .0	Total Investment: $90K	Site Selection Assistance: . . . . . . .Yes
Franchised Units (As of 8/31/1992): 14	Fees: Franchise - $15K	Lease Negotiation Assistance: . . . .Yes
Total Units (As of 8/31/1992): 14	Royalty: 4%, Advert: 0%	Co-operative Advertising: . . . . . . .No
Projected New Units for 1993: 8	Contract Periods (Yrs.): 20/10	Training: . . . . . . 1 Wk. Hilton Head, SC
Distribution: US-14;Can-0;Overseas-0	Area Development Agreement: Yes/3-5	. . . .
North America: . . . . 6 States	Sub-Franchise Contract: . . . . . Yes	On-Going Support: c,d,E,F,G,H/ 6
Concentration: . . . .7 in SC, 4 in NC, 2 in TN	Expand in Territory: . . . . Yes	EXPANSION PLANS:
Registered: . . . . .FL	Passive Ownership: . . . Not Allowed	US: . . . . Southeast
. . . .	Encourage Conversions: . . . . . NA	Canada: . . . . .No
Type Space: . . . . . . SF, SC, RM;~1,500 SF	Average # Employees: . . 1 FT, 2 PT	Overseas: . . . . .No

BOOK RACK

2703 E. Commercial Blvd.
Ft. Lauderdale, FL 33308
TEL: (305) 771-4310
FAX:
Mr. Fred Darnell, President

Used and new paperback books.

HISTORY: . . . . IFA	FINANCIAL: Earnings Claim: . .No	FRANCHISOR TRAINING/SUPPORT:
Established in 1963; . . 1st Franchised in 1965	Cash Investment: $15K	Financial Assistance Provided: . . . . .No
Company-Owned Units (As of 8/31/1992): . .1	Total Investment: $32K	Site Selection Assistance: . . . . . . .Yes
Franchised Units (As of 8/31/1992): 234	Fees: Franchise - $6K	Lease Negotiation Assistance: . . . . .Yes
Total Units (As of 8/31/1992): 235	Royalty: $50/Mo., Advert: . . . NA	Co-operative Advertising: . . . . . . .NA
Projected New Units for 1993: 35	Contract Periods (Yrs.): . . . . . Life	Training: . . . . 1 Wk. Headquarters
Distribution: US-234;Can-1;Overseas-0	Area Development Agreement: . .No	. . . .
North America: . . . . . 32 States, 1 Province	Sub-Franchise Contract: . . . . .No	On-Going Support: B,D,E,F,G,H/ . . . . . .
Concentration: . . . . CA, FL, TN	Expand in Territory: . . . . . . Yes	EXPANSION PLANS:
Registered: . . . . .All	Passive Ownership: . . . . .Allowed	US: . . . . .All US
. . . .	Encourage Conversions: . . . . Yes	Canada: . . . . No
Type Space: . . . . .SC;~1,200 SF	Average # Employees: . . . . .1 FT	Overseas: . . . . No

CLOCK GALLERY, THE

3400 Pharmacy Ave., # 5
Scarborough, ON M1W 3J8 CAN
TEL: (416) 491-5324
FAX: (416) 492-7239
Mr. Daniel Kesselring, President

Retail sale and service of every type of clock. Our specialty is Grandfather clocks.

HISTORY:	FINANCIAL: Earnings Claim: . .No	FRANCHISOR TRAINING/SUPPORT:
Established in 1977; . . 1st Franchised in 1990	Cash Investment: $40-70K	Financial Assistance Provided: . . . Yes(I)
Company-Owned Units (As of 8/31/1992): . 12	Total Investment: $150-200K	Site Selection Assistance: . . . . . . .Yes
Franchised Units (As of 8/31/1992): 3	Fees: Franchise - $25K	Lease Negotiation Assistance: . . . . .NA
Total Units (As of 8/31/1992): 15	Royalty: 6%, Advert: 4%	Co-operative Advertising: . . . . . . .Yes
Projected New Units for 1993: 1	Contract Periods (Yrs.): 10/5	Training: . . . . . . 2.5 Wks. Headquarters
Distribution: US-0;Can-15;Overseas-0	Area Development Agreement: . .No	. . . .
North America: . . . . 4 Provinces	Sub-Franchise Contract: . . . . .No	On-Going Support: C,D,E,F,H/ 10
Concentration: . . . 9 in ON, 3 in BC, 3 in AB	Expand in Territory: . . . . Yes	EXPANSION PLANS:
Registered: . . . . AB	Passive Ownership: . . . Discouraged	US: . . . . .No
. . . .	Encourage Conversions: . . . . . Yes	Canada: . . . . .All Canada
Type Space: . . . . RM;~700 SF	Average # Employees: . . 1 FT, 2 PT	Overseas: . . . . No

CONNOISSEUR, THE

201 Torrance Blvd.
Redondo Beach, CA 90277
TEL: (310) 374-9768
FAX: (310) 372-9097
Mr. Sandy French, President

Personalized gifts of fine wines, champagnes, gourmet, crystal and special occasion items.

HISTORY:	FINANCIAL: Earnings Claim: . .No	FRANCHISOR TRAINING/SUPPORT:
Established in 1975; . . 1st Franchised in 1989	Cash Investment: $100-125K	Financial Assistance Provided: . . . . .No
Company-Owned Units (As of 8/31/1992): . .1	Total Investment: $100-125K	Site Selection Assistance: . . . . . . .Yes
Franchised Units (As of 8/31/1992): 3	Fees: Franchise - $29.5K	Lease Negotiation Assistance: . . . . .Yes
Total Units (As of 8/31/1992): 4	Royalty: 6%, Advert: 3%	Co-operative Advertising: . . . . .No
Projected New Units for 1993: 10	Contract Periods (Yrs.): 15/15	Training: . . . . 1 Wk. Headquarters
Distribution: US-4;Can-0;Overseas-0	Area Development Agreement: Yes/15	. . . .
North America: . . . . 2 States	Sub-Franchise Contract: . . . . . Yes	On-Going Support: A,B,C,D,E,F,h/ 4
Concentration: . . . . 3 in IL, 1 in CA	Expand in Territory: . . . . Yes	EXPANSION PLANS:
Registered: . . . . .All	Passive Ownership: . . . Discouraged	US: . . . . .All US
. . . .	Encourage Conversions: . . . . .No	Canada: . . . . No
Type Space: . . . . FS, SC, RM;~600-800 SF	Average # Employees: . . 1 FT, 2 PT	Overseas: . . . . No

EXECUTIVE GIFT GALLERY

Box 13876
St. John's, NF A1B 4G7 CAN
TEL: (709) 745-3054
FAX:
Mr. Melvin Slade, Owner

Small office or home-based business. Our marketing program provides up-scale giftware and corporate awards to businesses and personal shoppers. A very lucrative business to start on a small budget.

HISTORY:	FINANCIAL: Earnings Claim: . .No	FRANCHISOR TRAINING/SUPPORT:
Established in 1988; . . 1st Franchised in 1992	Cash Investment: . . . . $3K+	Financial Assistance Provided: . . . . .Yes
Company-Owned Units (As of 8/31/1992): . .1	Total Investment: . . . . $3K+	Site Selection Assistance: . . . . . . .No
Franchised Units (As of 8/31/1992): 0	Fees: Franchise - . . . .$1K+	Lease Negotiation Assistance: . . . .No
Total Units (As of 8/31/1992): 1	Royalty: 10%, Advert: 0%	Co-operative Advertising: . . . . . . .No
Projected New Units for 1993: 20	Contract Periods (Yrs.): 3/3	Training: . . . . . . 2 Days Headquarters
Distribution: US-0;Can-1;Overseas-0	Area Development Agreement: . .No	. . . .
North America: . . . . .1 Province	Sub-Franchise Contract: . . . . .No	On-Going Support: / 2
Concentration: . . . . 1 in Newfoundland	Expand in Territory: . . . . . . Yes	EXPANSION PLANS:
Registered:	Passive Ownership: . . . . .Allowed	US: . . . . All US
. . . .	Encourage Conversions: . . . . .No	Canada: . . . . .All Canada
Type Space: . . . . . Home Based;~200 SF	Average # Employees: . . . . .1 FT	Overseas: . . . . No

EXQUISITE CRAFTS

108 Gleneida Ave.
Carmel, NY 10512
TEL: (914) 225-2606
FAX:
Ms. Marianne Montagna, President

EXQUISITE CRAFTS is a special craft supply store that offers over 30 different departments, as well as workshops and quality-finished crafts and designs. Customer service is a strong point in selling needlecrafts, candy, art supplies, stenciling, flowers, baskets, ribbons, children's crafts, fabrics, paints, wood and dollhouse miniatures in only 1,200 SF of space.

HISTORY:	FINANCIAL: Earnings Claim: . .No	FRANCHISOR TRAINING/SUPPORT:
Established in 1973; . . 1st Franchised in 1988	Cash Investment: $45-55K	Financial Assistance Provided: . . . . .No
Company-Owned Units (As of 8/31/1992): . .1	Total Investment: $45-55K	Site Selection Assistance: . . . . . . .Yes
Franchised Units (As of 8/31/1992): 0	Fees: Franchise - $10K	Lease Negotiation Assistance: . . . .Yes
Total Units (As of 8/31/1992): 1	Royalty: 4%, Advert: 5%	Co-operative Advertising: . . . . . . .Yes
Projected New Units for 1993: 5	Contract Periods (Yrs.): 10/10	Training: . . . . . . .10 Days Headquarters
Distribution: US-1;Can-0;Overseas-0	Area Development Agreement: . .No	. . . .
North America: . . . . .1 State	Sub-Franchise Contract: . . . . .No	On-Going Support: a,C,D,E,F,G,H,I/ . . .2
Concentration: . . . . 1 in NY	Expand in Territory: . . . . . . .No	EXPANSION PLANS:
Registered: . . . . NY	Passive Ownership: . . . Not Allowed	US: . . . . Southeast
. . . .	Encourage Conversions: . . . . . Yes	Canada: . . . . .No
Type Space: . . . . SF;~1,200 SF	Average # Employees: . . 1 FT, 2 PT	Overseas: . . . . .No

FLAG SHOP, THE

1755 West 4th Ave.
Vancouver, BC V6J 1M2 CAN
TEL: (800) 663-8681 (604) 736-8161
FAX: (604) 736-6439
Ms. Doreen Braverman, President

Custom and stock flags and banners, poles, hardware and accessories. Custom design for one-of-a-kind fabric items. Suppliers to major events, all levels of government and major corporations.

HISTORY:	FINANCIAL: Earnings Claim: . Yes	FRANCHISOR TRAINING/SUPPORT:
Established in 1975; . . 1st Franchised in 1981	Cash Investment: $20-50K	Financial Assistance Provided: . . . . .Yes
Company-Owned Units (As of 8/31/1992): . .2	Total Investment: $20-80K	Site Selection Assistance: . . . . . . .Yes
Franchised Units (As of 8/31/1992): 3	Fees: Franchise - $2.5-20K	Lease Negotiation Assistance: . . . .Yes
Total Units (As of 8/31/1992): 5	Royalty: Surcharg, Advert: Surcharg	Co-operative Advertising: . . . . . . .Yes
Projected New Units for 1993: 2	Contract Periods (Yrs.): 10/10	Training: . . . . . . 2 Wks. Headquarters,
Distribution: US-0;Can-5;Overseas-0	Area Development Agreement: . Yes	. . . . 1 Wk. On-Site
North America: . . . . 3 Provinces	Sub-Franchise Contract: . . . . Yes	On-Going Support: A,B,C,D,E,f,G,h,I/ . .8
Concentration: . . . 2 in BC, 2 in AB, 1 in ON	Expand in Territory: . . . . . . Yes	EXPANSION PLANS:
Registered: . . . . AB	Passive Ownership: . . . Not Allowed	US: . . . . . .UFOC Application Pending
. . . .	Encourage Conversions: . . . . NA	Canada: . . . . .All Canada
Type Space: . . . . ;~ SF	Average # Employees: . . 1 FT, 1 PT	Overseas: . . . . . .Open to Inquiries

HOBBYTOWN USA

5930 S. 58th St.
Lincoln, NE 68516
TEL: (402) 434-5050
FAX: (402) 434-5053
Mr. Jim E. Hogg, VP Fran. Services

HOBBYTOWN USA allows you the rare opportunity to work and play at the same time. HOBBYTOWN USA carries radio-controlled vehicles of all types, model trains, adventure games, models, rockets, sports cards and more. HOBBYTOWN USA is the country's largest chain of franchised hobby stores.

HISTORY: . . . . IFA	FINANCIAL: Earnings Claim: . .No	FRANCHISOR TRAINING/SUPPORT:
Established in 1969; . . 1st Franchised in 1986	Cash Investment: $75-100K	Financial Assistance Provided: . . . . .No
Company-Owned Units (As of 8/31/1992): . .2	Total Investment: $150-200K	Site Selection Assistance: . . . . . . .Yes
Franchised Units (As of 8/31/1992): 70	Fees: Franchise - $17.5K	Lease Negotiation Assistance: . . . .Yes
Total Units (As of 8/31/1992): 72	Royalty: 3%, Advert:	Co-operative Advertising: . . . . . . .Yes
Projected New Units for 1993: 25	Contract Periods (Yrs.): 10/10	Training: . . . . 2-3 Wks. at Store Site
Distribution: US-72;Can-0;Overseas-0	Area Development Agreement: . .No	. . . .
North America: . . . . 30 States	Sub-Franchise Contract: . . . . .No	On-Going Support: C,D,E,F,G,I/ 15
Concentration: . . . 8 in CA, 7 in NE, 5 in CO	Expand in Territory: . . . . Yes	EXPANSION PLANS:
Registered: . . . . . . .CA,IL,MD,MI,OR,WA	Passive Ownership: . . . Discouraged	US: . . . . All US
. . . . (Pending in 11 Others)	Encourage Conversions: . . . . . . Yes	Canada: . . . . .No
Type Space: . . . . .SC;~2,500 SF	Average # Employees: 1-2 FT, 2-3 PT	Overseas: . . . . No

IMPOSTERS COPY JEWELRY

651 Gateway Blvd., # 900
South San Francisco, CA 94080
TEL: (800) 999-9010 (415) 588-1800
FAX: (415) 588-1805
Mr. Larry Matthews, VP Fran. Dev.

High-quality reproductions of fine jewelry.

HISTORY: . . . . IFA	FINANCIAL: Earnings Claim: . .No	FRANCHISOR TRAINING/SUPPORT:
Established in 1984; . . 1st Franchised in 1988	Cash Investment: $50K	Financial Assistance Provided: . . . . .No
Company-Owned Units (As of 8/31/1992): . 43	Total Investment: $112-299K	Site Selection Assistance: . . . . . . .Yes
Franchised Units (As of 8/31/1992): 70	Fees: Franchise - $30K	Lease Negotiation Assistance: . . . .Yes
Total Units (As of 8/31/1992): 113	Royalty: 0%, Advert: 3%	Co-operative Advertising: . . . . . . .Yes
Projected New Units for 1993: 30	Contract Periods (Yrs.): . . 10/Varies	Training: . . . . 2 Wks. Headquarters
Distribution: US-113;Can-0;Overseas-0	Area Development Agreement: Yes/Var	
North America: . . . . 27 States	Sub-Franchise Contract: . . . . . .No	On-Going Support: A,B,C,D,E,F,G,H,I/ 65
Concentration: . . .35 in CA, 9 in FL, 7 in MD	Expand in Territory: . . . . Yes	EXPANSION PLANS:
Registered: . . . CA,FL,HI,IL,IN,MD,MI,MN	Passive Ownership: . . . Discouraged	US: . . . . . All Exc. RI, WI, SD and ND
. . . . NY,OR,VA,WA,DC	Encourage Conversions: . . . . . .No	Canada: . . . . .Yes
Type Space: . . . . RM;~600 SF	Average # Employees: . . 2 FT, 3 PT	Overseas: . . . . No

JEWELRY REPAIR ENTERPRISES

1501 Decker Ave., # 107
Stuart, FL 34994
TEL: (800) 359-0407 (407) 221-9207
FAX: (407) 221-9209
Mr. Robert Goldstein, President

Jewelry and watch repairs while you wait. Also watch bands, batteries, engraving, remounts and all supplies for the upkeep of jewelry. Conveniently located in regional malls.

HISTORY:	FINANCIAL: Earnings Claim: . Yes	FRANCHISOR TRAINING/SUPPORT:
Established in 1984; . . 1st Franchised in 1987	Cash Investment: $50K	Financial Assistance Provided: . . .Yes(D)
Company-Owned Units (As of 8/31/1992): . .2	Total Investment: $70K	Site Selection Assistance: . . . . . . .Yes
Franchised Units (As of 8/31/1992): 48	Fees: Franchise - $10K	Lease Negotiation Assistance: . . . .Yes
Total Units (As of 8/31/1992): 50	Royalty: 5%, Advert: 1%	Co-operative Advertising: . . . . .No
Projected New Units for 1993: 12	Contract Periods (Yrs.): 10/10	Training: . . . . .1 Wk. On-Site
Distribution: US-50;Can-0;Overseas-0	Area Development Agreement: Yes/1	. . . .
North America: . . . . 11 States	Sub-Franchise Contract: . . . . .No	On-Going Support: B,C,D,E,F,G,H,I/ . . . 5
Concentration: . . . 13 in TX, 9 in FL, 6 in PA	Expand in Territory: . . . . Yes	EXPANSION PLANS:
Registered: . . . . .FL,IL,MD	Passive Ownership: . . . . . .Allowed	US: . . . . Western US
. . . .	Encourage Conversions: . . . . . Yes	Canada: . . . . .All Canada
Type Space: . . . RM, Kiosk,In-Line;~150 SF	Average # Employees: . . 3 FT, 2 PT	Overseas: . . . . UK

JEWELRY REPAIRS BY US / JEWELRY STORE
East Video Plaza, 339 Rte. 9
Manalapan, NJ 07726
TEL: (908) 780-1500
FAX: (908) 780-1551
Ms. Judy Cowit, Mktg. Dept.

We put men and women into their own jewelry store business. This is a fantastic opportunity to be your own boss and make money at the same time. Some retail experience is necessary. We sell 14 kt jewelry and diamonds as well. The work is clean, 5 days per week, normal working hours and very rewarding.

HISTORY:	FINANCIAL: Earnings Claim: . Yes	FRANCHISOR TRAINING/SUPPORT:
Established in 1984; . . 1st Franchised in 1986	Cash Investment: $125-175K	Financial Assistance Provided: . . . Yes(I)
Company-Owned Units (As of 8/31/1992): . .1	Total Investment: . . . .$	Site Selection Assistance: . . . . . . .Yes
Franchised Units (As of 8/31/1992): 7	Fees: Franchise - $27K	Lease Negotiation Assistance: . . . .Yes
Total Units (As of 8/31/1992): 8	Royalty: 5%, Advert: 1.5%	Co-operative Advertising: . . . . . .Yes
Projected New Units for 1993: 4	Contract Periods (Yrs.): 10/5	Training: . . . . . . 3 Wks. Headquarters
Distribution: US-8;Can-0;Overseas-0	Area Development Agreement: . .No	. . . .
North America: . . . . 8 States	Sub-Franchise Contract: . . . . . .No	On-Going Support: B,C,E,H/ 4
Concentration: . . . . 6 in NJ, 2 in NY	Expand in Territory: . . . . . . Yes	EXPANSION PLANS:
Registered:	Passive Ownership: . . . . .Allowed	US: . . . . .All US
. . . .	Encourage Conversions: . . . . Yes	Canada: . . . . .All Canada
Type Space: . . . . .SC;~800 SF	Average # Employees: . . 2 FT, 1 PT	Overseas: . . . . No

JOHN SIMMONS

36 W. Calhoun Ave.
Memphis, TN 38103
TEL: (901) 526-5567 C
FAX: (901) 526-5605
Mr. Jim Hyatt, III, Asst. to President

Merchandise includes the unusual, the outstanding and the well-priced. We are known for our flair in decorative accessories and gift items. We also specialize in "fun" items, as well as gifts for those who love to entertain.

HISTORY:	FINANCIAL: Earnings Claim: . .No	FRANCHISOR TRAINING/SUPPORT:
Established in 1985; . . 1st Franchised in 1985	Cash Investment: $110-185K	Financial Assistance Provided: . . . . .No
Company-Owned Units (As of 8/31/1992): . .1	Total Investment: $110-185K	Site Selection Assistance: . . . . . . .Yes
Franchised Units (As of 8/31/1992): 4	Fees: Franchise - $15K	Lease Negotiation Assistance: . . . .Yes
Total Units (As of 8/31/1992): 5	Royalty: 4.5%, Advert: 0%	Co-operative Advertising: . . . . . . .NA
Projected New Units for 1993:	Contract Periods (Yrs.): 5/1	Training: . . . . . . 1-3 Days Headquarters,
Distribution: US-5;Can-0;Overseas-0	Area Development Agreement: . .No	. . . .4-7 Days On-Site, 5-7 Days Market
North America: . . . . 4 States	Sub-Franchise Contract: . . . . . Yes	On-Going Support: C,D,E,G,H/ 4
Concentration: . . . .2 in TN, 1 in IN, 1 in VA	Expand in Territory: . . . . . . Yes	EXPANSION PLANS:
Registered: . . . . .IN,VA	Passive Ownership: . . . Discouraged	US: . . . . SE, SW, Midwest
. . . .	Encourage Conversions: . . . . .No	Canada: . . . . .No
Type Space: . . . . .SC;~2,000 SF	Average # Employees: . 2 FT, 1-3 PT	Overseas: . . . . No

KIDS - PRAISE

6987 N. Oracle Rd.
Tucson, AZ 85704
TEL: (602) 579-0852
FAX:
Ms. Sandi Whalon, Fran. Sales

Personalized Christian children's book.

HISTORY:	FINANCIAL: Earnings Claim: . .No	FRANCHISOR TRAINING/SUPPORT:
Established in 1992; . . 1st Franchised in 1992	Cash Investment: $10K	Financial Assistance Provided: . . . . .No
Company-Owned Units (As of 8/31/1992): . .0	Total Investment: $10-15K	Site Selection Assistance: . . . . . . .Yes
Franchised Units (As of 8/31/1992): 2	Fees: Franchise - $7.5K	Lease Negotiation Assistance: . . . .Yes
Total Units (As of 8/31/1992): 2	Royalty: 5%, Advert: 2%	Co-operative Advertising: . . . . . . .Yes
Projected New Units for 1993: 6	Contract Periods (Yrs.): . . . 10/10	Training: . . . . . . 2 Days Franchisee Site
Distribution: US-2;Can-0;Overseas-0	Area Development Agreement: . .No	. . . .
North America: . . . . .1 State	Sub-Franchise Contract: . . . . . .No	On-Going Support: b,C,D,E,F,G,H/ 2
Concentration: . . . . 2 in AZ	Expand in Territory: . . . . . . Yes	EXPANSION PLANS:
Registered:	Passive Ownership: . . . . .Allowed	US: . . . . .All US
. . . .	Encourage Conversions: . . . . .No	Canada: . . . . .Yes
Type Space: . . . . . .Home Based;~NA SF	Average # Employees: . . . . . .1 FT	Overseas: . . . . Yes

LATEX CITY

1814 Franklin St., # 820
Oakland, CA 94612
TEL: (800) LOVE-AID (510) 839-5471
FAX: (510) 547-3245
Dr. David Brown, President

Unique ground-floor specialty retailing opportunity in booming latex novelty aid business. Complete line of proprietary products. Turn-key package includes lease negotiation, fully-stocked inventory, in-store merchandising/display. On-going support. LATEX CITY is ideal for aggressive couples. This is not smut - but a highly profitable, high-margin, fully legal business.

HISTORY:	FINANCIAL: Earnings Claim: . Yes	FRANCHISOR TRAINING/SUPPORT:
Established in 1972; . . 1st Franchised in 1986	Cash Investment: $65K	Financial Assistance Provided: . . .Yes(D)
Company-Owned Units (As of 8/31/1992): . .4	Total Investment: $85-235K	Site Selection Assistance: . . . . . . .Yes
Franchised Units (As of 8/31/1992): 15	Fees: Franchise - $15K	Lease Negotiation Assistance: . . . . .Yes
Total Units (As of 8/31/1992): 19	Royalty: 6%, Advert: 2%	Co-operative Advertising: . . . . . . .Yes
Projected New Units for 1993: 10	Contract Periods (Yrs.): 10/10	Training: . . . . 3 Wks. Headquarters,
Distribution: US-16;Can-2;Overseas-1	Area Development Agreement: Yes/5	. . . . 1 Wk. Plant, 2 Wks. On-Site
North America: . . . . . .9 States, 1 Province	Sub-Franchise Contract: . . . . .No	On-Going Support: A,B,C,D,G,H/ 6
Concentration: . . . 3 in CA, 3 in NY, 2 in OR	Expand in Territory: . . . . . . .No	EXPANSION PLANS:
Registered: . . . . CA,NY,OR,WA,AB	Passive Ownership: . . . Discouraged	US: . . . . .All US
. . . .	Encourage Conversions: . . . . . Yes	Canada: . . . . .Major Cities
Type Space: FS, SF, SC, RM;~1,000-1,400 SF	Average # Employees: . . . . . .2 FT	Overseas: . . . . UK, EUR, JA, AU

LEMSTONE BOOKS

1123 Wheaton Oaks Ct.
Wheaton, IL 60187
TEL: (708) 682-1400
FAX: (708) 682-1828
Mr. Lynn P. Wheaton, Sales Manager

Christian bookstores in regional shopping centers, featuring Bibles, books, music (cassettes, CD's, accompaniment), gifts and greeting cards.

HISTORY:	FINANCIAL: Earnings Claim: . .No	FRANCHISOR TRAINING/SUPPORT:
Established in 1981; . . 1st Franchised in 1982	Cash Investment: $40-60K	Financial Assistance Provided: . . . . No
Company-Owned Units (As of 8/31/1992): . .1	Total Investment: $130-175K	Site Selection Assistance: . . . . . . .Yes
Franchised Units (As of 8/31/1992): 49	Fees: Franchise - $25K	Lease Negotiation Assistance: . . . . .Yes
Total Units (As of 8/31/1992): 50	Royalty: 4%, Advert: 1%	Co-operative Advertising: . . . . . . .Yes
Projected New Units for 1993: 8	Contract Periods (Yrs.): 10/5	Training: . . . . 5 Days Headquarters,
Distribution: US-50;Can-0;Overseas-0	Area Development Agreement: .No	. . . . 5 Days On-Site
North America: . . . . 18 States	Sub-Franchise Contract: . . . . .No	On-Going Support: a,C,D,E,F,G,H/ 8
Concentration: . . .7 in OH, 6 in IL, 6 in TN	Expand in Territory: . . . . . . Yes	EXPANSION PLANS:
Registered: . . .IL,IN,MD,MI,MN,NY,VA,WI	Passive Ownership: . . . Discouraged	US: . . . . Midwest,Mid-Atl,S,SE,NY,NJ
. . . .	Encourage Conversions: . . . . . Yes	Canada: . . . . .No
Type Space: . . . . . .RM;~1,200-1,400 SF	Average # Employees: . . 1 FT, 2 PT	Overseas: . . . . No

LITTLE PROFESSOR BOOK CENTERS

130 S. First St., # 300
Ann Arbor, MI 48104
TEL: (800) 899-6232 (313) 994-1212
FAX: (313) 994-9009
Ms. Deanna Rion, Fran. Dev. Coord.

LITTLE PROFESSOR STORES are full-line, full-service retail book stores. Each store carries a complete selection of books, magazines and book-related sidelines. Franchisor provides complete assistance and counsel needed to open and operate a book store from site selection to store opening through the life of the agreement.

HISTORY: . . . . .IFA	FINANCIAL: Earnings Claim: . Yes	FRANCHISOR TRAINING/SUPPORT:
Established in 1961; . . 1st Franchised in 1969	Cash Investment: . . . . $60K+	Financial Assistance Provided: . . . Yes(I)
Company-Owned Units (As of 8/31/1992): . .1	Total Investment: . . . .$180K+	Site Selection Assistance: . . . . . . .Yes
Franchised Units (As of 8/31/1992): 133	Fees: Franchise - $21K	Lease Negotiation Assistance: . . . . .Yes
Total Units (As of 8/31/1992): 134	Royalty: 3%, Advert: 1/2%	Co-operative Advertising: . . . . . . .Yes
Projected New Units for 1993: 10	Contract Periods (Yrs.): 10/10	Training: . . . . . 10 Days HQ, 5 Days On-
Distribution: US-134;Can-0;Overseas-0	Area Development Agreement: .No	. . . . Site, 2 Days On-Site Follow-Up
North America: . . . . 38 States	Sub-Franchise Contract: . . . . .No	On-Going Support: A,C,D,E,F,H,h,I/ . . 23
Concentration: . . 17 in OH, 10 in MI, 9 in WI	Expand in Territory: . . . . . . Yes	EXPANSION PLANS:
Registered: . . . CA,FL,IL,IN,MD,MI,MN,OR	Passive Ownership: . . . Discouraged	US: . . . . .All US
. . . . RI,SD,VA,WA,WI	Encourage Conversions: . . . . . Yes	Canada: . . . . .No
Type Space: . . . . . . SC;~2,000-4,000 SF	Average # Employees: . . 1 FT, 2 PT	Overseas: . . . . No

MACBIRDIE GOLF GIFTS

5250 W. 73rd St., # H
Minneapolis, MN 55439
TEL: (800) 343-1033 (612) 830-1033 C
FAX: (612) 830-1055
Mr. Bob Haben, Sr., President

Golf is one of the fastest-growing industries worldwide. MACBIRDIE offers a unique way to tap into the virtually untapped golf gift market. We sell impulse golf gifts and apparel in shopping malls, resorts, pro shops and leased space in retail stores. Our kiosks, carts and spinner racks provide year-round sales and profits for the franchisee.

HISTORY:	FINANCIAL: Earnings Claim: . .No	FRANCHISOR TRAINING/SUPPORT:
Established in 1989; . . 1st Franchised in 1992	Cash Investment: $30-50K	Financial Assistance Provided: . . . Yes(I)
Company-Owned Units (As of 8/31/1992): . .1	Total Investment: $70-100K	Site Selection Assistance: . . . . . . .Yes
Franchised Units (As of 8/31/1992): 0	Fees: Franchise - $5-50K	Lease Negotiation Assistance: . . . .Yes
Total Units (As of 8/31/1992): 1	Royalty: 5%, Advert: 1%	Co-operative Advertising: . . . . . . .NA
Projected New Units for 1993: 10	Contract Periods (Yrs.): 5/5	Training: . . . . 1 Wk. Headquarters
Distribution: US-1;Can-0;Overseas-0	Area Development Agreement: Yes/5	
North America: . . . . .1 State	Sub-Franchise Contract: . . . . .No	On-Going Support: B,c,d,f,G,I/ 4
Concentration: . . . . 1 in MN	Expand in Territory: . . . . . . Yes	EXPANSION PLANS:
Registered: . . . . MN	Passive Ownership: . . . Discouraged	US: . . . . . .Midwest, Southwest and SE
	Encourage Conversions: . . . . NA	Canada: . . . . .No
Type Space: . . . . .RM;~Varies SF	Average # Employees: . . 1 FT, 4 PT	Overseas: . . . JA, KO, AU, EUR, Taiwan

MONOGRAMS PLUS

P. O. Box 20608
Waco, TX 76702
TEL: (817) 662-5050 C
FAX: (817) 662-3223
Mr. David Byrd, EVP Devel.

High-tech, computerized monogramming and embroidery. Create unique, personalized gifts in seconds from wide selection of high, brand-name fashion items and accessories. Custom-designed kiosks in select regional mall locations. High profit margin with minimal space requirements. Complete assistance, including start-up, financing, training and on-going support from in-house market research and field management teams.

HISTORY:	FINANCIAL: Earnings Claim: . .No	FRANCHISOR TRAINING/SUPPORT:
Established in 1988; . . 1st Franchised in 1988	Cash Investment: $30-50K	Financial Assistance Provided: . . . Yes(I)
Company-Owned Units (As of 8/31/1992): . .0	Total Investment: $45-80K	Site Selection Assistance: . . . . . . .Yes
Franchised Units (As of 8/31/1992): 84	Fees: Franchise - $27K	Lease Negotiation Assistance: . . . .Yes
Total Units (As of 8/31/1992): 84	Royalty: 6%, Advert: 1%	Co-operative Advertising: . . . . . . .Yes
Projected New Units for 1993: 12	Contract Periods (Yrs.): 10/5	Training: . . . . . . 9 Days Headquarters,
Distribution: US-84;Can-0;Overseas-0	Area Development Agreement: Yes/15	3 Days On-Site
North America:	Sub-Franchise Contract: . . . . .No	On-Going Support: B,C,D,E,G,H,I/ . . . 52
Concentration:	Expand in Territory: . . . . . . .No	EXPANSION PLANS:
Registered: . . . . .All	Passive Ownership: . . . Discouraged	US: . . . . .All US
	Encourage Conversions: . . . . . Yes	Canada: . . . . .All Canada
Type Space: . . . . .RM;~150-700 SF	Average # Employees: 1-2 FT, 2-3 PT	Overseas: . . . . .No

MR. BULB

One Duncan Ave.
Worcester, MA 01603
TEL: (800) 782-BULB (508) 753-4000
FAX: (508) 755-1100
Mr. Dennis K. Brown, Fran. Mktg. Dir.

MR. BULB distributes state-of-the-art lighting and lighting-related products from mobile units. Exclusive territories, no competition, commercial, industrial and retail customers, constant demand, complete training and support, regular business hours. MR. BULB profit center - full range of lighting and related products.

HISTORY:	FINANCIAL: Earnings Claim: . .No	FRANCHISOR TRAINING/SUPPORT:
Established in 1989; . . 1st Franchised in 1990	Cash Investment: $40K	Financial Assistance Provided: . . .Yes(D)
Company-Owned Units (As of 8/31/1992): . .2	Total Investment: $55-65K	Site Selection Assistance: . . . . .NA
Franchised Units (As of 8/31/1992): 2	Fees: Franchise - $23K	Lease Negotiation Assistance: . . . . .NA
Total Units (As of 8/31/1992): 4	Royalty: 5%, Advert: 1%	Co-operative Advertising: . . . . No
Projected New Units for 1993: 30	Contract Periods (Yrs.): . . . 10/10	Training: . . . . .2 Full Wks. Headquarters
Distribution: US-4;Can-0;Overseas-0	Area Development Agreement: Yes/10	
North America: . . . . .2 States	Sub-Franchise Contract: . . . . .Yes	On-Going Support: A,B,C,D,E,F,G,H,I/ . 8
Concentration: . . . . 1 in MA, 1 in NH	Expand in Territory: . . . . . . Yes	EXPANSION PLANS:
Registered:	Passive Ownership: . . . Discouraged	US: . . . . .All US
	Encourage Conversions: . . . . . Yes	Canada: . . . . .No
Type Space: . . . . Home Based;~ SF	Average # Employees: . . . . 1-2 FT	Overseas: . . . . .No

ONE ACCORD

3116 E. Shea Blvd., # 247
Phoenix, AZ 85028
TEL: (602) 996-4450
FAX: (602) 996-4450
Mr. Gerd D. Linke, VP

Christian bookstore.

HISTORY:	FINANCIAL: Earnings Claim: . .No	FRANCHISOR TRAINING/SUPPORT:
Established in 1991; . . 1st Franchised in 1992	Cash Investment: $200K	Financial Assistance Provided: . . . Yes(I)
Company-Owned Units (As of 8/31/1992): . .0	Total Investment: $200-300K	Site Selection Assistance: . . . . . . .Yes
Franchised Units (As of 8/31/1992): 0	Fees: Franchise - $25K	Lease Negotiation Assistance: . . . . .Yes
Total Units (As of 8/31/1992): 0	Royalty: 2%, Advert: 1/2%	Co-operative Advertising: . . . . . . .Yes
Projected New Units for 1993: 2	Contract Periods (Yrs.): 10/10	Training: . . . . 1 Wk. On-Site
Distribution: US-0;Can-0;Overseas-0	Area Development Agreement: . .No	. . . .
North America:	Sub-Franchise Contract: . . . . .No	On-Going Support: a,B,C,D,E,F,G,H/ . . 4
Concentration:	Expand in Territory: . . . . Yes	EXPANSION PLANS:
Registered:	Passive Ownership: . . . . . .Allowed	US: . . . . Southwest
. . . .	Encourage Conversions: . . . . . NA	Canada: . . . . .Yes
Type Space: . . . . SF;~3,500 SF	Average # Employees: . . 3 FT, 3 PT	Overseas: . . . . Yes

PAPER FIRST

4420 Monroe Rd.
Charlotte, NC 28205
TEL: (704) 342-5815
FAX: (704) 342-5818
Mr. Mel Frank, President

Wholesale and retail distribution and sale of paper products, janitorial supplies, catering and party supplies and related items to business and walk-in customers from a store-front, warehouse-type location.

HISTORY:	FINANCIAL: Earnings Claim: . . .	FRANCHISOR TRAINING/SUPPORT:
Established in 1982; . . 1st Franchised in 1988	Cash Investment: $66-95K	Financial Assistance Provided: . . . Yes(I)
Company-Owned Units (As of 8/31/1992): . .1	Total Investment: $75-100K	Site Selection Assistance: . . . . . . .Yes
Franchised Units (As of 8/31/1992): 11	Fees: Franchise - $15K	Lease Negotiation Assistance: . . . . .Yes
Total Units (As of 8/31/1992): 12	Royalty: 2.5-.5%, Advert: . . . 1/2%	Co-operative Advertising: . . . . . . .Yes
Projected New Units for 1993:	Contract Periods (Yrs.): 20/20	Training: . . . . . . Total 140 Hrs. at 3 NC
Distribution: US-12;Can-0;Overseas-0	Area Development Agreement: . .No	. . . . Locations, 80 Hrs. Franchisee Site
North America: . . . . 3 States	Sub-Franchise Contract: . . . . .No	On-Going Support: B,C,D,E,F,G,H,I/ . . . 3
Concentration: . . . 6 in NC, 3 in VA, 1 in SC	Expand in Territory: . . . . Yes	EXPANSION PLANS:
Registered: . . . . FL,MD,VA	Passive Ownership: . . . Not Allowed	US: . . . . . .SE, Midwest, South Central
. . . .	Encourage Conversions: . . . . . Yes	Canada: . . . . .Yes
Type Space: . . . . ;~5,000 SF	Average # Employees: . . 3 FT, 3 PT	Overseas: . . . . No

PAPER WAREHOUSE

7634 Golden Traingle Dr.
Eden Prairie, MN 55344
TEL: (800) 229-1792 (612) 829-5467
FAX: (612) 829-0247
Mr. Vernon Lewis, Dir. Fran.

A unique retail concept, featuring paper goods, party and entertainment paper and plastic, home paper supplies, balloons and party favors. Discount pricing, huge assortment in a warehouse environment. Our concept has unique advantages that other retail concepts do not offer.

HISTORY:	FINANCIAL: Earnings Claim: . .No	FRANCHISOR TRAINING/SUPPORT:
Established in 1983; . . 1st Franchised in 1987	Cash Investment: $50K	Financial Assistance Provided: . . . . .No
Company-Owned Units (As of 8/31/1992): . 35	Total Investment: $90-100K	Site Selection Assistance: . . . . . . .Yes
Franchised Units (As of 8/31/1992): 17	Fees: Franchise - $19K	Lease Negotiation Assistance: . . . . .Yes
Total Units (As of 8/31/1992): 52	Royalty: 3,4,5%, Advert:	Co-operative Advertising: . . . . . . .Yes
Projected New Units for 1993: 10	Contract Periods (Yrs.): 10/10	Training: . . . . 1 Wk. Headquarters
Distribution: US-52;Can-0;Overseas-0	Area Development Agreement: Yes/10	. . . .
North America: . . . . 10 States	Sub-Franchise Contract: . . . . . .No	On-Going Support: B,C,E,G,H,I/ . . . . . .
Concentration: . . 22 in MN, 5 in KS, 5 in MO	Expand in Territory: . . . . Yes	EXPANSION PLANS:
Registered: . . . CA,FL,IL,IN,MI,MN,ND,SD	Passive Ownership: . . . Discouraged	US: . . . . Midwest
. . . . .WI	Encourage Conversions: . . . . . Yes	Canada: . . . . .No
Type Space: . . . . SC;~3,500 SF	Average # Employees: . . 1 FT, 4 PT	Overseas: . . . . No

PAPYRUS

1349 Powell St.
Emeryville, CA 94608
TEL: (800) 872-7978 (510) 428-0166 C
FAX: (510) 428-0615
Ms. Kathleen A. Low, Dir. Fran. Dev.

A unique system, featuring fine greeting cards, stationery, designer's gift wrap and associated products in fine paper. Specializing in superior design and quality. Personalized stationery, invitations, announcements, custom printing and engraving.

HISTORY:	FINANCIAL: Earnings Claim: . Yes	FRANCHISOR TRAINING/SUPPORT:
Established in 1973; . . 1st Franchised in 1988	Cash Investment: $50K	Financial Assistance Provided: . . . . . No
Company-Owned Units (As of 8/31/1992): . 10	Total Investment: . . . $130.5-220.5K	Site Selection Assistance: . . . . Yes
Franchised Units (As of 8/31/1992): 26	Fees: Franchise - $29.5K	Lease Negotiation Assistance: . . . . . . No
Total Units (As of 8/31/1992): 36	Royalty: 6%, Advert: 1%	Co-operative Advertising: . . . . No
Projected New Units for 1993: 10	Contract Periods (Yrs.): 10/5/5	Training: . . . . 12 Days Headquarters
Distribution: US-36;Can-0;Overseas-0	Area Development Agreement: Yes/Var	
North America: . . . . 4 States	Sub-Franchise Contract: . . . . . .No	On-Going Support: A,C,D,E,F,G,H,I/ . . 7
Concentration: . . 32 in CA, 2 in WA, 2 in TX	Expand in Territory: . . . . . . Yes	EXPANSION PLANS:
Registered: . . .CA,FL,IL,MI,MN,OR,WA,DC	Passive Ownership: . . . Discouraged	US: . . . . All US
	Encourage Conversions: . . . . . Yes	Canada: . . . . No
Type Space: . . . . SF, RM;~1,000 SF	Average # Employees: 1-2 FT, 2-3 PT	Overseas: . . . . No

PARTY CITY

1440 Route 46
Parsippany, NJ 07054
TEL: (800) 883-2100 (201) 335-8900
FAX: (201) 316-9578
Mr. Steve Mandell, President

Discount party supply super store. 6,000-8,000 SF stores, offering the largest selection of party supplies at deep discount prices.

HISTORY: . . . . IFA	FINANCIAL: Earnings Claim: . Yes	FRANCHISOR TRAINING/SUPPORT:
Established in 1986; . . 1st Franchised in 1989	Cash Investment: $215-300K	Financial Assistance Provided: . . . Yes(I)
Company-Owned Units (As of 8/31/1992): . .4	Total Investment: $215-345K	Site Selection Assistance: . . . . . . .Yes
Franchised Units (As of 8/31/1992): 15	Fees: Franchise - $25K	Lease Negotiation Assistance: . . . . . .Yes
Total Units (As of 8/31/1992): 19	Royalty: 4%, Advert: 1%	Co-operative Advertising: . . . . . . .Yes
Projected New Units for 1993: 15	Contract Periods (Yrs.): 10/10	Training: . . . . 7 Days Headquarters
Distribution: US-19;Can-0;Overseas-0	Area Development Agreement: . .No	
North America: . . . . 6 States	Sub-Franchise Contract: . . . . . .No	On-Going Support: A,B,C,D,E,F,H/ . . .9
Concentration: . . . . NY, PA, NJ	Expand in Territory: . . . . . . .No	EXPANSION PLANS:
Registered: . . . . .CA,FL,IL,MD,NY,VA,DC	Passive Ownership: . . . Not Allowed	US: . . . . All US
	Encourage Conversions: . . . . . .No	Canada: . . . . .No
Type Space: . . . . .FS, SC;~7,000 SF	Average # Employees: . .3 FT, 10 PT	Overseas: . . . . No

PARTY LAND

842 Red Lion Rd.
Philadelphia, PA 19115
TEL: (215) 676-5550
FAX: (215) 676-5767
Mr. Brian Feller, President

Retail party supplies and balloons for all occasions.

HISTORY:	FINANCIAL: Earnings Claim: . .No	FRANCHISOR TRAINING/SUPPORT:
Established in 1986; . . 1st Franchised in 1988	Cash Investment: . . . .$	Financial Assistance Provided: . . . Yes(I)
Company-Owned Units (As of 8/31/1992): . .1	Total Investment: $75-90K	Site Selection Assistance: . . . . . . .Yes
Franchised Units (As of 8/31/1992): 21	Fees: Franchise - $20K	Lease Negotiation Assistance: . . . .Yes
Total Units (As of 8/31/1992): 22	Royalty: 3-5%, Advert: 1%	Co-operative Advertising: . . . . . . .Yes
Projected New Units for 1993: 6	Contract Periods (Yrs.): 10/5	Training: . . . . . .7-10 Days Headquarters
Distribution: US-22;Can-0;Overseas-0	Area Development Agreement: . .No	
North America: . . . . 3 States	Sub-Franchise Contract: . . . . . .No	On-Going Support: A,B,C,D,E,F,G,H/ . . 5
Concentration: . . . 17 in PA, 4 in NJ, 1 in DE	Expand in Territory: . . . . . . Yes	EXPANSION PLANS:
Registered:	Passive Ownership: . . . . . .Allowed	US: . . . . All US
	Encourage Conversions: . . . . . .No	Canada: . . . . .Yes
Type Space: . . . FS, SF, SC;~2,000-3,000 SF	Average # Employees: . . 1 FT, 4 PT	Overseas: . . . . MX, EUR

PARTY WORLD

10701 Vanowen St.
North Hollywood, CA 91605
TEL: (818) 762-7717
FAX: (818) 509-8676
Mr. Stanley Tauber, President

We specialize in the sale of party supplies, utilizing a marketing strategy unique in the industry. By offering a large variety of selections, depth of stock and heavily discounted prices, we "bring the customer to us." The buying public seeks us out and we become the destination shop.

HISTORY: . . . . IFA
Established in 1979; . . 1st Franchised in 1987
Company-Owned Units (As of 8/31/1992): . 13
Franchised Units (As of 8/31/1992): 7
Total Units (As of 8/31/1992): 20
Projected New Units for 1993: 2
Distribution: US-20;Can-0;Overseas-0
 North America: . . . . .1 State
 Concentration: . . . . 14 in CA
Registered: . . . . CA
. . . .
Type Space: . . . . .FS, SC;~7,000 SF

FINANCIAL: Earnings Claim: . .No
Cash Investment: $100K
Total Investment: $250K
Fees: Franchise - $20K
 Royalty: 4%, Advert: 2%
Contract Periods (Yrs.): 10/10
Area Development Agreement: . .No
Sub-Franchise Contract: . . . . .No
Expand in Territory: . . . . . . .No
Passive Ownership: . . . Not Allowed
Encourage Conversions: . . . . .No
Average # Employees: . . . . .6 FT

FRANCHISOR TRAINING/SUPPORT:
Financial Assistance Provided: . . . Yes(I)
Site Selection Assistance: . . . . . . .Yes
Lease Negotiation Assistance: . . . .Yes
Co-operative Advertising: . . . . . . .Yes
Training: . . . . . . 3 Wks. Northridge, CA

On-Going Support: B,C,D,E,F,H/ 8
EXPANSION PLANS:
 US: . . . . California Only
 Canada: . . . . .No
 Overseas: . . . . No

PINCH-A-PENNY

Box 6025
Clearwater, FL 34618
TEL: (813) 531-8913
FAX: (813) 536-8066
Mr. Fred Thomas, President

PINCH-A-PENNY is the nation's largest retailer of swimming pool, spa and patio supplies.

HISTORY: . . . .
Established in 1974; . . 1st Franchised in 1976
Company-Owned Units (As of 8/31/1992): . .5
Franchised Units (As of 8/31/1992): 86
Total Units (As of 8/31/1992): 91
Projected New Units for 1993: . . . .
Distribution: US-91;Can-0;Overseas-0
 North America: . . . . 2 States
 Concentration: . . . . 90 in FL, 1 in AL
Registered: . . . . .FL
. . . .
Type Space: . . . . .SC;~5,000 SF

FINANCIAL: Earnings Claim: . .No
Cash Investment: . . . .$
Total Investment: $85-400K
Fees: Franchise - $15-200K
 Royalty: 6%, Advert: 4%
Contract Periods (Yrs.): 5/15
Area Development Agreement: . .No
Sub-Franchise Contract: . . . . .No
Expand in Territory: . . . . Yes
Passive Ownership: . . . Discouraged
Encourage Conversions: . . . . .No
Average # Employees: . . . .

FRANCHISOR TRAINING/SUPPORT:
Financial Assistance Provided: . . . . .No
Site Selection Assistance: . . . . . . .Yes
Lease Negotiation Assistance: . . . .Yes
Co-operative Advertising: . . . . .NA
Training: . . . .
. . . .
On-Going Support: A,B,C,D,E,H,I/ . . . . .
EXPANSION PLANS:
 US: . . . . .Yes
 Canada: . . . . .No
 Overseas: . . . . No

REDDING'S AUDIOBOOK SUPERSTORES

2302 N. Scottsdale Rd.
Scottsdale, AZ 85257
TEL: (800) REDDING (602) 650-1776
FAX: (602) 481-0076
Mr. Edvard R. Richards, CEO

Retail audiobooks sale and rental. The world's first audiobook superstore offers over 10,000 audiobook titles for sale and rental through their large, well-lit, professionally merchandised and operated superstores. Plans call for 300 units by 1999.

HISTORY: . . . .
Established in 1989; . . 1st Franchised in 1991
Company-Owned Units (As of 8/31/1992): . .0
Franchised Units (As of 8/31/1992): 2
Total Units (As of 8/31/1992): 2
Projected New Units for 1993: 24
Distribution: US-2;Can-0;Overseas-0
 North America: . . . . .1 State
 Concentration: . . . . 2 in AZ
Registered: . . . . .CA,FL,IL
. . . .
Type Space: . . . . .FS, SC;~3,500 SF

FINANCIAL: Earnings Claim: . .No
Cash Investment: $125-325K
Total Investment: $125-325K
Fees: Franchise - $32.5K
 Royalty: 5%, Advert: 3%
Contract Periods (Yrs.): 10/10
Area Development Agreement: Yes/5
Sub-Franchise Contract: . . . . .No
Expand in Territory: . . . . Yes
Passive Ownership: . . . Discouraged
Encourage Conversions: . . . . . Yes
Average # Employees: . . 2 FT, 8 PT

FRANCHISOR TRAINING/SUPPORT:
Financial Assistance Provided: . . . . .No
Site Selection Assistance: . . . . . . .Yes
Lease Negotiation Assistance: . . . .Yes
Co-operative Advertising: . . . . . . .Yes
Training: . . . . .1 Wk. Headquarters,
. . . . .1 Wk. On-Site
On-Going Support: C,D,E,F,g,h,i/ 3
EXPANSION PLANS:
 US: . . . . .All US
 Canada: . . . . .All Canada
 Overseas: . . . . Yes

RELAX THE BACK STORE

1004 Mopac Circle, # 100
Austin, TX 78746
TEL: (800) 451-5168 (512) 329-8240
FAX: (512) 329-8245
Mr. Ray Orgera, VP Mktg.

Franchisor of quality retail stores, featuring over 300 products for prevention and relief of back pain and related conditions. Products include ergonomically-designed office chairs and workstation accessories, specially-designed home furniture, car seats, specialty sleep products, tools and equipment, travel items and massage devices.

HISTORY:	. . . . IFA
Established in 1984;	. . 1st Franchised in 1989
Company-Owned Units (As of 8/31/1992):	. .0
Franchised Units (As of 8/31/1992):	7
Total Units (As of 8/31/1992):	7
Projected New Units for 1993:	 25
Distribution:	. . . . . . US-7;Can-0;Overseas-0
North America:	. . . . 4 States
Concentration:	. . . 5 in TX, 1 in NE, 1 in MN
Registered:	. . . . . . .CA,FL,IL,MN,OR,WA
. . . .	
Type Space:	. . . . .SC;~2,000 SF

FINANCIAL:	Earnings Claim: . .No
Cash Investment:	. . . . .$68.5-168K
Total Investment:	. . . . .$68.5-168K
Fees: Franchise -	. . . . $15K
Royalty: 4%, Advert:	. . . . . . 1%
Contract Periods (Yrs.):	. . . 10/10
Area Development Agreement:	Yes/10
Sub-Franchise Contract:	. . . . .No
Expand in Territory:	. . . . Yes
Passive Ownership:	. . . Discouraged
Encourage Conversions:	. . . . . NA
Average # Employees:	. . 3 FT, 1 PT

FRANCHISOR TRAINING/SUPPORT:	
Financial Assistance Provided:	. . . . . No
Site Selection Assistance:	. . . . . . .Yes
Lease Negotiation Assistance:	. . . .Yes
Co-operative Advertising:	. . . . .NA
Training:	. . . . 2 Wks. Headquarters,
	. . . . .1 Wk. On-Site
On-Going Support: B,C,D,E,f,I/	 9
EXPANSION PLANS:	
US:	. . . . All US
Canada:	. . . . No
Overseas:	. . . . No

RODAN JEWELERS /
SIMPLY CHARMING

13379B 72 Ave.
Surrey, BC V3W 2N5 CAN
TEL: (604) 572-3883
FAX: (604) 572-3993
Mr. Rob Davidson, President

Retail jewelry stores, specializing in fine gold and silver jewelry, diamonds, watches and full services. Located on key corners in major regional shopping centers. No experience necessary. Full classroom and on-site training with on-going support.

HISTORY:	. . . .
Established in 1976;	. . 1st Franchised in 1982
Company-Owned Units (As of 8/31/1992):	. .2
Franchised Units (As of 8/31/1992):	10
Total Units (As of 8/31/1992):	 12
Projected New Units for 1993:	2
Distribution:	. . . . . US-0;Can-10;Overseas-0
North America:	. . . . .1 Province
Concentration:	. . . . 10 in BC
Registered:	. . . .
. . . .	
Type Space:	. . . . RM;~309-1,300 SF

FINANCIAL:	Earnings Claim: . .No
Cash Investment:	. . . . . .$75-150K
Total Investment:	. . . . . $300-500K
Fees: Franchise -	. . . . . . $50-75K
Royalty: 5-3%, Advert:	. . . 2-2.5%
Contract Periods (Yrs.):	. . 5-7/3-5
Area Development Agreement:	Yes/10
Sub-Franchise Contract:	. . . . .No
Expand in Territory:	. . . . . . .No
Passive Ownership:	. . . Not Allowed
Encourage Conversions:	. . . . . Yes
Average # Employees:	2-3 FT, 3-4 PT

FRANCHISOR TRAINING/SUPPORT:	
Financial Assistance Provided:	. . .Yes(D)
Site Selection Assistance:	. . . . . . .Yes
Lease Negotiation Assistance:	. . . .Yes
Co-operative Advertising:	. . . . . . .Yes
Training:	. . . . . 2 Wks. Headquarters, 4-6
	. . Months Combination HQ and On-Site
On-Going Support: B,C,D,E,h/	 5
EXPANSION PLANS:	
US:	. . . . .No
Canada:	. . . . .BC Only
Overseas:	. . . . No

ROLLING PIN KITCHEN EMPORIUM

4264 Winters Chapel Rd.
Atlanta, GA 30360
TEL: (800) 423-4387 (404) 457-2600
FAX: (404) 457-3110
Ms. Carol Burnett

ROLLING PIN is more than a kitchenware store. It is a virtual kitchen emporium. Product mix includes only well-made cookware, cutlery, gadgets, utensils, bakeware and linens. An extensive selection of gourmet coffee beans are offered. Service, quality and product knowledge are key elements to operation.

HISTORY:	. . . .
Established in 1978;	. . 1st Franchised in 1982
Company-Owned Units (As of 8/31/1992):	. 10
Franchised Units (As of 8/31/1992):	21
Total Units (As of 8/31/1992):	31
Projected New Units for 1993:	6
Distribution:	. . . . . US-31;Can-0;Overseas-0
North America:	. . . .
Concentration:	. . . . .FL, GA, LA
Registered:	. . . . CA,FL,IL,NY,VA
. . . .	
Type Space:	. . . . RM;~2,000 SF

FINANCIAL:	Earnings Claim: . .No
Cash Investment:	. . . .$185K
Total Investment:	. . . . $185-300K
Fees: Franchise -	. . . . $20K
Royalty: 5%, Advert:	. . . . . 1/2%
Contract Periods (Yrs.):	. . . 10/10
Area Development Agreement:	Yes/10
Sub-Franchise Contract:	. . . . .No
Expand in Territory:	. . . . Yes
Passive Ownership:	. . . . . .Allowed
Encourage Conversions:	. . . . . Yes
Average # Employees:	. . 1 FT, 8 PT

FRANCHISOR TRAINING/SUPPORT:	
Financial Assistance Provided:	. . . . .No
Site Selection Assistance:	. . . . . . .Yes
Lease Negotiation Assistance:	. . . .Yes
Co-operative Advertising:	. . . . .NA
Training:	. . . . .1 Wk. Headquarters,
	. . . . 1 Wk. Store Location
On-Going Support: C,D,E,G,H/	 10
EXPANSION PLANS:	
US:	. . . . All US
Canada:	. . . . .No
Overseas:	. . . . No

ROSENBERG JEWELRY

Box 13876
St. John's, NF A1B 4G7 CAN
TEL: (709) 745-3054
FAX:
Mr. Melvin Slade, Owner

Small office or home-based jewelry business. Our marketing program recruits consultants who sell via parties and other methods. As a franchisee, you can expect to run this very profitable franchise from your home or small office.

HISTORY:	FINANCIAL: Earnings Claim: . .No	FRANCHISOR TRAINING/SUPPORT:
Established in 1988; . . 1st Franchised in 1992	Cash Investment: . . . . $3K+	Financial Assistance Provided: . . . . .Yes
Company-Owned Units (As of 8/31/1992): . .1	Total Investment: . . . . $3K+	Site Selection Assistance: . . . . .No
Franchised Units (As of 8/31/1992): 0	Fees: Franchise - . . . . $1K+	Lease Negotiation Assistance: . . . . .No
Total Units (As of 8/31/1992): 1	Royalty: 10%, Advert: 0%	Co-operative Advertising: . . . . .No
Projected New Units for 1993: 20	Contract Periods (Yrs.): 3/3	Training: . . . . 2 Days Headquarters
Distribution: US-0;Can-1;Overseas-0	Area Development Agreement: . .No	
North America: . . . . .1 Province	Sub-Franchise Contract: . . . . .No	On-Going Support: / 2
Concentration: . . . . 1 in NF	Expand in Territory: . . . . . . Yes	EXPANSION PLANS:
Registered:	Passive Ownership: . . . . .Allowed	US: . . . . All US
. . . .	Encourage Conversions: . . . . .No	Canada: . . . . .All Canada
Type Space: . . . . . . Home Based;~200 SF	Average # Employees: . . . . . .1 FT	Overseas: . . . . No

SCRAMBLES

15 Engle St., # 302
Englewood, NJ 07631
TEL: (800) 332-2229 (201) 871-0370
FAX: (201) 871-7168
Mr. John Sterns, Sales Mgr.

Customized and/or hand-painted gifts and accessories for children and adults.

HISTORY:	FINANCIAL: Earnings Claim: . .No	FRANCHISOR TRAINING/SUPPORT:
Established in 1983; . . 1st Franchised in 1986	Cash Investment: $25-50K	Financial Assistance Provided: . . . Yes(I)
Company-Owned Units (As of 8/31/1992): . .2	Total Investment: $117-155K	Site Selection Assistance: . . . . . . .Yes
Franchised Units (As of 8/31/1992): 8	Fees: Franchise - $25K	Lease Negotiation Assistance: . . . . .Yes
Total Units (As of 8/31/1992): 10	Royalty: 6%, Advert: 0%	Co-operative Advertising: . . . . . . .Yes
Projected New Units for 1993: 10	Contract Periods (Yrs.): 10/10	Training: . . . . . . 2 Wks. Company Store,
Distribution: US-10;Can-0;Overseas-0	Area Development Agreement: . .No	. . . . 1 Wk. Franchisee Location
North America: . . . . 5 States	Sub-Franchise Contract: . . . . .No	On-Going Support: C,D,E,F,G,H,I/ . . . . .
Concentration: . . . .6 in NJ, 1 in NY, 1 in CT	Expand in Territory: . . . . . . Yes	EXPANSION PLANS:
Registered: . . . . FL,MD,NY	Passive Ownership: . . . Not Allowed	US: . . . . All US
. . . .	Encourage Conversions: . . . . .No	Canada: . . . . No
Type Space: . . . . SC, RM;~1,500 SF	Average # Employees: . . 2 FT, 4 PT	Overseas: . . . . No

SHEFIELD & SONS

2265 W. Railway St., Box 490
Abbotsford, BC V2S 5Z5 CAN
TEL: (604) 859-1014
FAX: (604) 859-1711
Mr. Wolfgang Lehmann, Dir. Fran.

Retail outlet featuring tobaccos and related products, but also offering a merchandise mix including beverages, confectionery, reading material, giftware and lottery that caters to everyday needs and impulse buying.

HISTORY:	FINANCIAL: Earnings Claim: . . .	FRANCHISOR TRAINING/SUPPORT:
Established in 1976; . . 1st Franchised in 1976	Cash Investment: $24-45K	Financial Assistance Provided: . . . . .No
Company-Owned Units (As of 8/31/1992): . .3	Total Investment: $69-130K	Site Selection Assistance: . . . . . . .Yes
Franchised Units (As of 8/31/1992): 64	Fees: Franchise - $10K	Lease Negotiation Assistance: . . . . .Yes
Total Units (As of 8/31/1992): 67	Royalty: 2%, Advert:	Co-operative Advertising: . . . . . . .NA
Projected New Units for 1993: 5	Contract Periods (Yrs.): 5/5	Training: . . . . .1 Wk. On-Site
Distribution: US-0;Can-67;Overseas-0	Area Development Agreement: . .No	. . . .
North America: . . . . 7 Provinces	Sub-Franchise Contract: . . . . .No	On-Going Support: C,D,E,G,I/ 7
Concentration: . 28 in BC, 20 in ON, 13 in AB	Expand in Territory: . . . . . . Yes	EXPANSION PLANS:
Registered: . . . . AB	Passive Ownership: . . . Discouraged	US: . . . . No
. . . .	Encourage Conversions: . . . . . Yes	Canada: . . . . .All Canada
Type Space: . . RM, Shopping Ctrs;~350-500 SF	Average # Employees: . . 1 FT, 1 PT	Overseas: . . . . No

SOAPBERRY SHOP

50 Galaxy Blvd., # 12
Rexdale, ON M9W 4Y5 CAN
TEL: (416) 674-0248
FAX: (416) 674-0249
Ms. Susan Whyte, Dir. Mktg.

SOAPBERRY SHOP is an environment-conscious company, offering herbal skin, hair and bath preparations through 21 retail concept shops. We care about our customers, the environment and about anti-cruelty in cosmetic manufacturing. Locations are now available in regional shopping centres across the US and Canada.

HISTORY:	FINANCIAL: Earnings Claim: . .No	FRANCHISOR TRAINING/SUPPORT:
Established in 1983; . . 1st Franchised in 1987	Cash Investment: $37K	Financial Assistance Provided: . . . . .No
Company-Owned Units (As of 8/31/1992): . .7	Total Investment: $100-165K	Site Selection Assistance: . . . . . . .Yes
Franchised Units (As of 8/31/1992): 28	Fees: Franchise - $17K	Lease Negotiation Assistance: . . . .Yes
Total Units (As of 8/31/1992): 35	Royalty: 0%, Advert: 3%	Co-operative Advertising: . . . . .NA
Projected New Units for 1993: 20	Contract Periods (Yrs.): 5/5	Training: . . . . . . 2 Wks. Toronto, ON,
Distribution: US-5;Can-30;Overseas-0	Area Development Agreement: . .No	. . . . 2 Wks. On-Site
North America: . . . . . 3 States, 6 Provinces	Sub-Franchise Contract: . . . . .No	On-Going Support: B,C,d,E,G,H/ 6
Concentration: . . . 18 in On, 5 in AB, 2 in FL	Expand in Territory: . . . . Yes	EXPANSION PLANS:
Registered: . . . . CA,FL,AB	Passive Ownership: . . . Not Allowed	US: . . . . All US
. . . .	Encourage Conversions: . . . . . NA	Canada: . . . . AB, BC,Maritimes
Type Space: . . . . RM;~600-800 SF	Average # Employees: . . 2 FT, 6 PT	Overseas: . . . . No

SOX APPEAL

6321 Bury Dr., # 1
Eden Prairie, MN 55346
TEL: (800) 966-7699 (612) 937-6162
FAX: (612) 934-5665
Mr. Jack Abelson, VP Fran. Dev.

SOX APPEAL offers the best selection of socks and hosiery for men, women and children. As a new and exciting specialty store, SOX APPEAL gives the customer a fun and fashionable place to shop. As a business, SOX APPEAL has given its owners a fun and rewarding opportunity.

HISTORY: . . . . IFA	FINANCIAL: Earnings Claim: . .No	FRANCHISOR TRAINING/SUPPORT:
Established in 1984; . . 1st Franchised in 1986	Cash Investment: $100-180K	Financial Assistance Provided: . . . . .No
Company-Owned Units (As of 8/31/1992): . .0	Total Investment: $100-180K	Site Selection Assistance: . . . . . . .Yes
Franchised Units (As of 8/31/1992): 25	Fees: Franchise - $20K	Lease Negotiation Assistance: . . . .Yes
Total Units (As of 8/31/1992): 25	Royalty: 5%, Advert: 1%	Co-operative Advertising: . . . . .NA
Projected New Units for 1993: 10	Contract Periods (Yrs.): 10/10	Training: . . . . . 1 Wk. Minneapolis, MN
Distribution: US-25;Can-0;Overseas-0	Area Development Agreement: Yes/Var	. . . .
North America: . . . . 13 States	Sub-Franchise Contract: . . . . .No	On-Going Support: B,C,D,E,F,G,H,I/ . . . 6
Concentration: . . . 4 in MN, 4 in CO, 3 in CA	Expand in Territory: . . . . Yes	EXPANSION PLANS:
Registered: . . . . All States Exc. NY	Passive Ownership: . . . . . .Allowed	US: . . . . All US
. . . .	Encourage Conversions: . . . . .No	Canada: . . . . No
Type Space: . RM, High Fashion;~400-700 SF	Average # Employees: . . 2 FT, 3 PT	Overseas: . . . . No

SOX CLINIC, THE

9 Maryvale Cres.
Richmond Hill, ON L4C 6P6 CAN
TEL: (416) 886-3537
FAX: (416) 886-2934
Mr. Raj Nathwani, President

THE SOX CLINIC offers a unique hosiery concept. Product mix concentrates on fashion and basic hosiery for men, women and children. Excellent operating system insures growth and profitability.

HISTORY:	FINANCIAL: Earnings Claim: . . .	FRANCHISOR TRAINING/SUPPORT:
Established in 1984; . . 1st Franchised in 1986	Cash Investment: $30-50K	Financial Assistance Provided: . . . Yes(I)
Company-Owned Units (As of 8/31/1992): . .1	Total Investment: $100-130K	Site Selection Assistance: . . . . . . .Yes
Franchised Units (As of 8/31/1992): 10	Fees: Franchise - $25K	Lease Negotiation Assistance: . . . . .Yes
Total Units (As of 8/31/1992): 11	Royalty: 6%, Advert: 2%	Co-operative Advertising: . . . . .Yes
Projected New Units for 1993: 3	Contract Periods (Yrs.): 10/10	Training: . . . . 2 Wks. On-Site
Distribution: US-0;Can-12;Overseas-0	Area Development Agreement: . .No	. . . .
North America: . . . . 5 Provinces	Sub-Franchise Contract: . . . . .No	On-Going Support: C,D,E,F,G,h/ 21
Concentration: . . . 7 in ON, 2 in BC, 1 in PQ	Expand in Territory: . . . . Yes	EXPANSION PLANS:
Registered:	Passive Ownership: . . . Not Allowed	US: . . . . No
. . . .	Encourage Conversions: . . . . Yes	Canada: . . . . .Yes
Type Space: . . . . RM;~600 SF	Average # Employees: . . 2 FT, 2 PT	Overseas: . . . . No

STRICTLY SHOOTING

26 Pinewood Dr.
Monee, IL 60449
TEL: (708) 499-4420
FAX: (708) 499-4421
Mr. Ludwig Sawicki, President

STRICTLY SHOOTING is the only firm to ever offer franchises in the retail firearms and ammunition industry. The franchisee will carry a wide assortment of high-quality new and used handguns, rifles and shotguns, as well as ammunition and accessories. This is an excellent opportunity to combine business with the pleasures of target shooting, trap, skeet, sporting clays and hunting both upland and big game.

HISTORY: . . . . IFA
Established in 1988; . . 1st Franchised in 1992
Company-Owned Units (As of 8/31/1992): . .1
Franchised Units (As of 8/31/1992): 0
Total Units (As of 8/31/1992): 1
Projected New Units for 1993: 8
Distribution: US-1;Can-0;Overseas-0
 North America: . . . . .1 State
 Concentration: . . . . .1 in IL
Registered: . . . . FL,IL,IN,MI,MN,WI
. . . .
Type Space: . . . . Any Type OK;~2,000+ SF

FINANCIAL: Earnings Claim: . .No
Cash Investment: $100-150K
Total Investment: . . . .$225K+
Fees: Franchise - $25K
 Royalty: 5%, Advert: 0%
Contract Periods (Yrs.): 5/5
Area Development Agreement: . .No
Sub-Franchise Contract: . . . . .No
Expand in Territory: . . . . . Yes
Passive Ownership: . . . . .Allowed
Encourage Conversions: . . . . Yes
Average # Employees: . . 2 FT, 2 PT

FRANCHISOR TRAINING/SUPPORT:
Financial Assistance Provided: . . . Yes(I)
Site Selection Assistance: . . . . . . .Yes
Lease Negotiation Assistance: . . . .Yes
Co-operative Advertising: . . . . . . .Yes
Training: . . . . Up to 2 Wks. Headquarters
. . . .
On-Going Support: C,D,E,F,G/ 3
EXPANSION PLANS:
US: . . . . All US
Canada: . . . . .All Exc. Alberta
Overseas: . . . . No

T-SHIRTS PLUS

3630 IH-35 S.
Waco, TX 76706
TEL: (800) 922-7255 (817) 662-5050
FAX: (817) 662-3223
Mr. David Byrd, EVP Devel.

Ranked #1 in its category by Entrepreneur Magazine. Continuing as the industry trendsetter with successful 14-year track record. In-store custom decorating on private label garments. Select regional mall locations available with extensively-researched, contemporary store design. Complete start-up, training, financing assistance and on-going support provided.

HISTORY: . . . .
Established in 1975; . . 1st Franchised in 1976
Company-Owned Units (As of 8/31/1992): . .0
Franchised Units (As of 8/31/1992): **188**
Total Units (As of 8/31/1992): 188
Projected New Units for 1993: 24
Distribution: US-188;Can-0;Overseas-0
 North America: . . . . 47 States
 Concentration: . . . . .CA, TX, FL
Registered: . . . . All States
. . . .
Type Space: . . . . RM;~450-800 SF

FINANCIAL: Earnings Claim: . .No
Cash Investment: $40-45K
Total Investment: $120-150K
Fees: Franchise - $35K
 Royalty: 7%, Advert: 1%
Contract Periods (Yrs.): 15/5/5
Area Development Agreement: Yes/15
Sub-Franchise Contract: . . . . .No
Expand in Territory: . . . . . . .No
Passive Ownership: . . . Discouraged
Encourage Conversions: . . . . Yes
Average # Employees: 1-2 FT, 2-3 PT

FRANCHISOR TRAINING/SUPPORT:
Financial Assistance Provided: . . . Yes(I)
Site Selection Assistance: . . . . . . .Yes
Lease Negotiation Assistance: . . . .Yes
Co-operative Advertising: . . . . . . .Yes
Training: . . . . 5 Days Home Office,
 . . .3 Days Home Office, 3 Days On-Site
On-Going Support: B,C,D,E,G,H,I/ . . . 52
EXPANSION PLANS:
US: . . . . .All US
Canada: . . . . .All Canada
Overseas: . . . . No

TREASURE CACHE, THE

44-F Jeffryn Blvd. W.
Deer park, NY 11729
TEL: (800) 969-5969 (516) 243-5029
FAX: (516) 243-5908
Mr. Richard A. Simeone, President

A retail, arts and crafts store, located in high-traffic malls and/or strip centers. THE TREASURE CACHE leases shelf space to local artisans and crafters.

HISTORY: . . . .
Established in 1991; . . 1st Franchised in 1992
Company-Owned Units (As of 8/31/1992): . .1
Franchised Units (As of 8/31/1992): 0
Total Units (As of 8/31/1992): 1
Projected New Units for 1993: 12
Distribution: US-1;Can-0;Overseas-0
 North America: . . . . .1 State
 Concentration: . . . . .1 in NY
Registered: . . . . FL,NY
. . . .
Type Space: . . . . .Large SC, RM;~1,200 SF

FINANCIAL: Earnings Claim: . .No
Cash Investment: $25K
Total Investment: $40-50K
Fees: Franchise - $12.5K
 Royalty: 6%, Advert: 1%
Contract Periods (Yrs.): 10/10
Area Development Agreement: . .No
Sub-Franchise Contract: . . . .No
Expand in Territory: . . . . . . .No
Passive Ownership: . . . . .Allowed
Encourage Conversions: . . . . NA
Average # Employees: . . 1 FT, 3 PT

FRANCHISOR TRAINING/SUPPORT:
Financial Assistance Provided: . . . Yes(I)
Site Selection Assistance: . . . . . . .Yes
Lease Negotiation Assistance: . . . .Yes
Co-operative Advertising: . . . . . . .Yes
Training: . . . . 3 Days Headquarters,
 . . . . . .3 Days Grand Opening On-Site
On-Going Support: a,B,C,D,E,F,G,H,I/ . .6
EXPANSION PLANS:
US: . . . . Northeast and East
Canada: . . . . Eastern Canada
Overseas: . . . . No

WILD BIRD CENTERS OF AMERICA

7687 MacArthur Blvd.
Cabin John, MD 20818
TEL: (800) 759-WILD (301) 229-9585
FAX: (301) 320-6154
Mr. George Petrides, President

WILD BIRD CENTER retail stores supply and educate backyard bird watchers. Products include birdseed, feeders, houses, baths, binoculars and gifts. Stores offer educational programs to schools and community groups and sponsor birding opportunities. Headquarters publishes customized editions of an educational newsletter for each store.

HISTORY:	FINANCIAL: Earnings Claim: . .No	FRANCHISOR TRAINING/SUPPORT:
Established in 1985; . . 1st Franchised in 1990	Cash Investment: $45-55K	Financial Assistance Provided: . . . Yes(I)
Company-Owned Units (As of 8/31/1992): . .1	Total Investment: $45-55K	Site Selection Assistance: . . . . . . .Yes
Franchised Units (As of 8/31/1992): 26	Fees: Franchise - $18.5K	Lease Negotiation Assistance: . . . .Yes
Total Units (As of 8/31/1992): 27	Royalty: 3-4.5%, Advert: 0%	Co-operative Advertising: . . . . . . .Yes
Projected New Units for 1993: 34	Contract Periods (Yrs.): 5/5	Training: . . . . .10-14 Days Headquarters,
Distribution: US-33;Can-1;Overseas-0	Area Development Agreement: . .No	1-3 Days On-Site
North America: . . . . . 11 States, 1 Province	Sub-Franchise Contract: . . . . .No	On-Going Support: A,B,C,D,E,F,G,H,I/ . 4
Concentration: . . . 8 in MD, 3 in CO, 3 in VA	Expand in Territory: . . . . . . Yes	EXPANSION PLANS:
Registered: . . .CA,IL,IN,MD,MI,OR,VA,WA	Passive Ownership: . . . Discouraged	US: . . . . All US
. . . . .WI	Encourage Conversions: . . . . . .No	Canada: . . . . .All Canada
Type Space: . . . . .SC;~2,000 SF	Average # Employees: . . 1 FT, 2 PT	Overseas: . . . . No

WILD BIRD MARKETPLACE

710 W. Main St., P. O. Box 1184
New Holland, PA 17557
TEL: (800) 962-1031 (717) 354-2841
FAX: (717) 355-0425
Mr. John F. Gardner, President

WILD BIRD MARKETPLACE meets the growing interest in backyard birding, bird watching and related birding activities. Strong emphasis in feed and feeders with commitment to books, gifts, prints, porcelains, binoculars and birding accessories. We encourage input from local artisans and craftpersons.

HISTORY:	FINANCIAL: Earnings Claim: . .No	FRANCHISOR TRAINING/SUPPORT:
Established in 1988; . . 1st Franchised in 1989	Cash Investment: $45K	Financial Assistance Provided: . . . Yes(I)
Company-Owned Units (As of 8/31/1992): . .1	Total Investment: $45-100K	Site Selection Assistance: . . . . . . .Yes
Franchised Units (As of 8/31/1992): 9	Fees: Franchise - $10K	Lease Negotiation Assistance: . . . .Yes
Total Units (As of 8/31/1992): 10	Royalty: 3%, Advert: 1%	Co-operative Advertising: . . . . . . .Yes
Projected New Units for 1993: 15	Contract Periods (Yrs.): 10/5	Training: . . . . 5 Days Headquarters
Distribution: US-10;Can-0;Overseas-0	Area Development Agreement: . .No	. . . .
North America: . . . . 7 States	Sub-Franchise Contract: . . . . .No	On-Going Support: B,C,D,E,F,G,H,I/ . . 2
Concentration: . . . 3 in NY, 2 in OH, 1 in NJ	Expand in Territory: . . . . . . Yes	EXPANSION PLANS:
Registered: . . . . FL,IL,IN,MI,NY,RI	Passive Ownership: . . . . . .Allowed	US: . . . . All US, Emphasis in East
. . . .	Encourage Conversions: . . . . Yes	Canada: . . . . .NB, ON and PQ
Type Space: . . . . . . SC;~1,600-2,000 SF	Average # Employees: . . 1 FT, 1 PT	Overseas: . . . . No

WILD BIRDS UNLIMITED

3003 E. 96th St., # 201
Indianapolis, IN 46240
TEL: (800) 326-4928 (317) 571-7100
FAX: (317) 571-7110
Mr. Paul E. Pickett, Dir. Fran. Sales

WILD BIRDS UNLIMITED offers unique retail shops that specialize in supplying birdseed, feeders and gift items for the popular hobby of backyard bird feeding. This is the perfect occupation for nature enthusiasts.

HISTORY: . . . . IFA	FINANCIAL: Earnings Claim: . .No	FRANCHISOR TRAINING/SUPPORT:
Established in 1981; . . 1st Franchised in 1983	Cash Investment: $50-75K	Financial Assistance Provided: . . . . .No
Company-Owned Units (As of 8/31/1992): . .1	Total Investment: $50-75K	Site Selection Assistance: . . . . . . .Yes
Franchised Units (As of 8/31/1992): 112	Fees: Franchise - $15K	Lease Negotiation Assistance: . . . .Yes
Total Units (As of 8/31/1992): 113	Royalty: 3%, Advert: 0%	Co-operative Advertising: . . . . . . .Yes
Projected New Units for 1993: 25	Contract Periods (Yrs.): 10/5	Training: . . . . . . 5-6 Days Headquarters
Distribution: US-103;Can-10;Overseas-0	Area Development Agreement: . Yes	. . . .
North America: . . . . 20 States, 3 Provinces	Sub-Franchise Contract: . . . . . .No	On-Going Support: C,D,E,G,H,I/ 7
Concentration: . . . 11 in MI, 8 in OH, 7 in IN	Expand in Territory: . . . . . . Yes	EXPANSION PLANS:
Registered: . . .CA,FL,IL,IN,MD,MI,MN,NY	Passive Ownership: . . . Not Allowed	US: . . . . All US
. . . . .OR,VA,WA,WI	Encourage Conversions: . . . . . NA	Canada: . . . . .All Canada
Type Space: . . . . .FS, SC;~1,600 SF	Average # Employees: . . 2 FT, 4 PT	Overseas: . . . . No

SUPPLEMENTAL LISTING OF FRANCHISORS

14 KARAT PLUM, THE . . . . 46022 Alaloa St., # 205, Kaneohe, HI 96744
    Contact: Mr. Joel Brown, President; Tel: (808) 247-1127 C
ANNIE'S BOOK STOP . . . . 168 Great Rd., Acton, MA 01720
    Contact: Ms. Annie Adams, President; Tel: (508) 366-9547
BARGAIN BOOK PUBLICATIONS . . . . .476 Main St., Middlefield, CT 06455
    Contact: Mr. Robert Sherman, Fran. Dir.; Tel: (203) 349-0001
BASS RIVER CHAIRS . . . . #B 10800 Steeles Ave., W., Box 135, Thornhill, ON L4J 7L2   CAN
    Contact: Ms. Robin Shields Teeger; Tel: (416) 731-5574
BATH & A-HALF . . . . .P. O. Box 90343, Gainesville, FL 32607
    Contact: Mr. John Lehrer, VP; Tel: (708) 259-8979 C
BATHTIQUE . . . . 7979 Victor-Pittsford Rd., Victor, NY 14564
    Contact: Mr. Don Seipel, President; Tel: (716) 223-4662
BIGHORN SHEEPSKIN CO./COMIC COLLECT. . . . . . . .11600 Manchaca Rd., Austin, TX 78748
    Contact: Mr. Barry Silverman, President; Tel: (800) 992-1650 (512) 280-1650
BIJOUX TERNER . . . . .7200 NW 7th St., 3rd Fl., Miami, FL 33126
    Contact: Mr. Salomon Terner, President; Tel: (800) 247-8922 (305) 266-9000
BIN & BARREL . . . . .9950 West Park, # 110, Houston, TX 77063
    Contact: Ms. Ann Nance, VP Fran. Dev.; Tel: (713) 782-1101
BLACKBERRY COTTAGE . . . . 3107 Eubank NE, # 5, Albuquerque, NM 87111
    Contact: Mr. Paul Johnson, Dir. Fran.; Tel: (800) 759-3655 (505) 292-3323
BOWL AND BOARD . . . . 12 St. Marks Pl., New York, NY 10003
    Contact: Mr. Charles Fitzgerald, President; Tel:
BOXWORKS, THE . . . . 5209 Linbar Dr., # 641, Nashville, TN 37211
    Contact: Mr. Henry Zoller, President; Tel: (615) 331-8900
BUTTERFIELDS, ETC. . . . . 1250 Capitol of TX Hwy., #1, #260, Austin, TX 78746
    Contact: Mr. Stan Butterfield, President; Tel: (512) 328-6960
CARDWARE STORE, THE . . . . 4025 W. 183rd St., Country Club Hills, IL 60478
    Contact: Ms. Marcia R. Hartford, Fran. Dir.; Tel: (708) 957-9444
CENTRAL DEVELOPMENT . . . . 11324 Q St., Omaha, NE 68137
    Contact: President; Tel: (402) 553-8491
CHEEPERS PARTY GOODS WAREHOUSE . . . . . 1210 Northbrook Dr., # 370, Trevose, PA 19053
    Contact: Mr. Stephen J. Izzi; Tel: (215) 953-8314
CIRCLE GALLERY OF ANIMATION/CARTOON . . . . 303 E. Wacker Dr., Chicago, Il 60601
    Contact: President; Tel:
ECOLOGY HOUSE . . . . P. O. Box 40428, Portland, OR 97240
    Contact: Mr. Paul Derdzinski, President; Tel: (503) 223-1842
EMBRACEABLE ZOO . . . . 500 Old York Rd., Rydal Sq., # 216, Jenkintown, PA 19046
    Contact: Mr. Bart J. Axelrod; Tel: (800) 676-7466 (215) 572-2450
ENERGY SCIENCES . . . . 1335 Piccard Dr., Rockville, MD 20850
    Contact: President; Tel:
EVERFAST . . . . 203 Gale Ln., Kennett Square, PA 19348
    Contact: Mr. William Chissus, Dir. Fran. Rel.; Tel: (215) 444-9700
EVERGOOD PRODUCTS . . . . .175 Lauman Ln., Hicksville, NY 11801
    Contact: President; Tel:
FRIEDMANS MICROWAVE OVENS . . . . 2301 Broadway, Oakland, CA 94612
    Contact: Mr. Duane Tuttle; Tel: (415) 444-1139
GRANDPA'S ROCKER . . . . 6820 S. University Blvd., Littleton, CO 80122
    Contact: Ms. Kathy Cary; Tel: (303) 694-2166
HAPPI-COOK . . . . .1225 Park Place Mall, Memphis, TN 38119
    Contact: Mr. J. Richard Holley, President; Tel: (901) 767-6067
HAPPI-NAMES PERSONALIZED GIFTS . . . . .1225 Park Place Mall, Memphis, TN 38119
    Contact: Mr. J. Richard Holley, President; Tel: (901) 767-6067
HEROES WORLD CENTERS . . . . 961 Route 10, Randolph, NJ 07869
    Contact: President; Tel: (201) 927-4447
HONORE JEWELRY . . . . One Civic Center Plaza, Hartford, CT 06103
    Contact: Mr. Gregg Nolan, Fran. Dir.; Tel: (203) 879-4675
HOUSE OF WATCH BANDS . . . . 29223 Southfield Rd., Southfield, MI 48076
    Contact: President; Tel: (313) 552-0090
JUST BASKETS . . . . 1239 E. Newport Ctr. Dr., # 115, Deerfield Beach, FL 33442
    Contact: President; Tel: (305) 428-0477

KOEHLER GALLERIES . . . . 175 N. Franklin St., Chicago, IL 60606
Contact: President; Tel:
LA BRIDE D'ELEGANCE . . . . .2120 N. Woodlawn, # 364, Wichita, KS 67208
Contact: Mr. Steve Watson; Tel: (316) 681-0121
LE PANIER FOR SPECIAL OCCASIONS . . . . 714 1/2 Lee St., # 10, Charleston, WV 25301
Contact: Mr. Marshall L. Gregg, Dir. Fran.; Tel: (304) 343-1796
LEMSTONE BOOKS . . . . 1123 Wheaton Oaks Ct., Wheaton, IL 60187
Contact: Mr. Lynn P. Wheaton, Sales Manager; Tel: (708) 682-1400
LOVE SHOP, THE . . . . P.O. Box 200, Station A, Vancouver, BC V6C 2V2   CAN
Contact: Mr. Gary Hodge; Tel: (604) 689-7290
MEDICAL DEPOT . . . . .2400 W. Cypress Creek Rd., # 206, Ft. Lauderdale, FL 33309
Contact: Mr. Ralph Leopold, President; Tel: (305) 938-0307
MISS BOJANGLES . . . . 9711 Cortana Pl., Baton Rouge, LA 70815
Contact: Mr. G. Paul Smith; Tel: (504) 923-3565
MONOGRAMS TO GO . . . . .14200 E. Alameda Ave., Aurora, CO 80012
Contact: Ms. Marlenna Krueger; Tel: (303) 366-8812
MOTHER GRIMM'S BEARS . . . . P. O. Box 2226, 727 Beach Dr., Cape May, NJ 08204
Contact: Mr. Jim Grimm, Fran. Dir.; Tel: (800) 488-6980 (408) 778-6990
MUSIC PROMOTIONS . . . . .4366 Indianola Ave., Columbus, OH 43214
Contact: Mr. Dave Stein, Ops. Mgr.; Tel: (614) 262
NAMES 'N THINGS . . . . 2021 N. Highland, Old Hickory Mall, Jackson, TN 38305
Contact: Mr. William Kunz; Tel: (901) 668-3164 (901) 668-0708
NATIONAL DEVELOPMENT GROUP . . . . .74 Main St., Framingham, MA 01701
Contact: Mr. Richard Gold; Tel: (617) 879-9664
NEW ALTERNATIVE, THE . . . . 4724 Lincoln Blvd., # 313, Marina del Rey, CA 90292
Contact: President; Tel: (310) 827-9868
NEWSSTAND EXPRESS . . . . 70 Walnut St., Wellesley, MA 02181
Contact: Mr. William Herp, VP/Dir. Fran.; Tel: (800) 370-5991 (617) 431-5991
ONE STOP PARTY SHOP . . . . .5908 Eastex Fwy., Beaumont, TX 77708
Contact: Mr. Marvin C. Newman, President; Tel: (409) 899-5713
PAINTEMONIUM . . . . P. O. Box 21994, 9740 Scranton, #300, San Diego, CA 92121
Contact: Ms. Melissa Sickels, President; Tel: (619) 458-3203
PAPER OUTLET, THE . . . . 445 Hanover Ave., Allentown, PA 18103
Contact: Mr. Tim Mulligan, Treasurer; Tel: (215) 439-4030
PARTY FAIR . . . . .Pond Rd. Ctr., Rte. # 9, Freehold, NJ 07728
Contact: Mr. David Silverstein; Tel: (201) 974-1116
PERFECT GIFT, THE . . . . 2900 Wilcrest, # 400, Houston, TX 77042
Contact: Mr. Richard Park, VP Ops.; Tel: (800) 789-8976
PERFUMERY, THE . . . . 724 W. 21st St., Houston, TX 77008
Contact: Ms. Donna Taylor; Tel: (713) 880-5818
POT POURRI . . . . 4699 Keele St., # 1, Downsview, ON M3J 2N8   CAN
Contact: Mr. Ted Loyst; Tel: (416) 661-9916
PRESS BOX NEWS-DRIVE-THRU NEWSSTAND . . . . . . 2600 Columbia Ave., Lancaster, PA 17603
Contact: President; Tel: (800) 283-4639 (717) 291-9649
QUICK PAWN SHOP . . . . 4204 Norman Bridge Rd., Montgomery, AL 36105
Contact: Mr. Frank E. Evans, President; Tel: (205) 281-3615
RAFTERS STORES/PANHANDLER/ABINGTONS . . . . 4699 Keele St., # 1, Downsview, ON M3J 2N8   CAN
Contact: Mr. Michael Mayerson, Fran. Dir.; Tel: (416) 661-9916
RECOGNITION EXPRESS . . . . 11305 Rancho Bernardo Rd., # 101, San Diego, CA 92127
Contact: Mr. Jeff Tino, VP Fran. Dev.; Tel: (800) 345-3666 (619) 451-9100
RED ROSE, ARTS & CRAFTS . . . . 79 Parkingway, P. O. Box 7169, Quincy, MA 02169
Contact: President; Tel: (617) 773-0530
SALLY WALLACE BRIDES SHOP . . . . .2210 Pine Terrace, Scotch Plains, NJ 07076
Contact: Mr. John Van Drill, President; Tel:
SAM THE RECORD MAN . . . . 274 Church St., Toronto, ON M5B 1Z5   CAN
Contact: President; Tel: (416) 977-6490
SERENDIPITY ANTIQUES AND FURNITURE . . . . .1430 E. New York Ave., Deland, FL 32724
Contact: Mr. Terry W. Bishop, President; Tel: (800) 428-2837 (904) 736-2837
SHAVER CENTRE FINE BLADE . . . . .3151 rue Joseph Dubreuil, Lachine, PQ H8T 3H6   CAN
Contact: Mr. Germain Langlois; Tel: (514) 636-4512
TIES, ETC. . . . . 2817 E. 3rd Ave., Cherry Creek N., Denver, CO 80206
Contact: Mr. Gerry Northrup, Dir. Fran. Dev.; Tel: (800) 748-1142 (303) 782-1865 C
TIMES SQUARE . . . . Box A160, 465 Davis Dr., # 304, Newmarket, ON L3Y 2P1   CAN
Contact: Mr. George Moore, Fran. Dir.; Tel: (416) 853-3722
TINDER BOX INTERNATIONAL . . . . .25 Parkway, Upper Saddle River, NJ 07458
Contact: Mr. Wayne Best, Dir. Fran. Dev.; Tel: (800) 322-4824 (201) 934-0160

TRILEA SPECIALTY GROUP . . . . 20 Richmond St. E., # 400, Toronto, ON M5C 2Z4   CAN
    Contact: Ms. Shirley Mesbur; Tel: (416) 366-9191
TUPPERWARE . . . . P. O. Box 2353, Orlando, FL 32802
    Contact: President; Tel: (305) 826-4546
UNITED SURGICAL CENTERS . . . . 380 Warwick Ave., Warwick, RI 02888
    Contact: Mr. Stevan Datz, President; Tel: (800) 556-7641 (401) 781-2166
WEDDING BELL BRIDAL BOUTIQUES . . . . 27 W. Judson Ave., Youngstown, OH 44507
    Contact: Mr. Theodore E. Khoury; Tel: (216) 782-1310
WEDDING EXPRESSIONS . . . . .2120 N. Woodlawn, # 364, Wichita, KS 67208
    Contact: Mr. Steve Watson, VP; Tel: (316) 681-0121
WICKS 'N' STICKS . . . . P. O. Box 4586, Houston, TX 77010
    Contact: Mr. Dennis Dickinson, VP; Tel: (800) 231-6337 (713) 874-0800
WONDERFUL WORLD OF WEDDING RINGS . . . . 1790 Hwy. A1A, # 101, Satellite Beach, FL 32937
    Contact: Ms. Barbara Sawczyn, Director; Tel: (407) 773-4164
YAW GALLERY . . . . 550 N. Woodward Ave., Birmingham, MI 48011
    Contact: President; Tel: (313) 647-5470

For Information On Renting Our

Custom Franchisor Mailing List

Or Franchisor Data Base,

Please Refer To Page IX

CHAPTER 45

RETAIL: VIDEO / AUDIO / ELECTRONICS

C & M VIDEO

313 Professional Park Ave.
Effingham, IL 62401
TEL: (800) 323-4586 (217) 347-5651
FAX: (217) 342-5667
Mr. Terry Monroe, President

Our market targets towns with a population of 5,000-50,000. A specialty store for a specialized niche market, offering video cassette rentals with the entertainment business in mind.

HISTORY: . . . .
Established in 1983; . . 1st Franchised in 1984
Company-Owned Units (As of 8/31/1992): . .8
Franchised Units (As of 8/31/1992): 20
Total Units (As of 8/31/1992): 28
Projected New Units for 1993: 12
Distribution: US-28;Can-0;Overseas-0
  North America: . . . . 2 States
  Concentration: . . . . .27 in IL, 1 in IN
Registered: . . . . IL,IN,MI
. . . .
Type Space: . . . . . . FS, SF, SC;~3,000 SF

FINANCIAL: Earnings Claim: . .No
Cash Investment: $45K
Total Investment: $85-125K
Fees: Franchise - $13.5K
  Royalty: 6%, Advert: 1%
Contract Periods (Yrs.): 5/5
Area Development Agreement: Yes/5
Sub-Franchise Contract: . . . . .No
Expand in Territory: . . . . Yes
Passive Ownership: . . . . . .Allowed
Encourage Conversions: . . . . Yes
Average # Employees: . . 2 FT, 4 PT

FRANCHISOR TRAINING/SUPPORT:
Financial Assistance Provided: . . . . . No
Site Selection Assistance: . . . . .Yes
Lease Negotiation Assistance: . . . . .Yes
Co-operative Advertising: . . . . .Yes
Training: . . . . 5 Days Headquarters,
  . . . . .5 Days Franchisee Location
On-Going Support: B,C,D,E,H,I/ 7
EXPANSION PLANS:
  US: . . . . Midwest
  Canada: . . . . No
  Overseas: . . . . No

EDIT POINT

3713 Brewerton Rd.
N. Syracuse, NY 13212
TEL: (800) 424-EDIT (315) 455-6272
FAX:
Mr. Perry Como, Dir. Fran.

Tap the increasing demand by business and consumers for video production, editing & duplication services. An EDIT POINT franchise can offer professional industrial marketing & training videos, special occasion videography, edit suite & camcorder rentals, film/slide/photos transfers and a variety of other video production and post- production services.

HISTORY:	FINANCIAL: Earnings Claim: . .No	FRANCHISOR TRAINING/SUPPORT:
Established in 1988; . . 1st Franchised in 1990	Cash Investment: $14.9K	Financial Assistance Provided: . . . Yes(I)
Company-Owned Units (As of 8/31/1992): . .1	Total Investment: $24.9-112K	Site Selection Assistance: . . . . .Yes
Franchised Units (As of 8/31/1992): 1	Fees: Franchise - $9-15K	Lease Negotiation Assistance: . . . . . No
Total Units (As of 8/31/1992): 2	Royalty: 5%, Advert: 1%	Co-operative Advertising: . . . . .No
Projected New Units for 1993: 5	Contract Periods (Yrs.): 10/10	Training: . . . . . . 15 Days Headquarters,
Distribution: US-2;Can-0;Overseas-0	Area Development Agreement: . .No	. . . . 3 Days On-Site
North America: . . . . .1 State	Sub-Franchise Contract: . . . . .No	On-Going Support: B,C,D,E,G,H,I/ 4
Concentration: . . . . 1 in NY	Expand in Territory: . . . . .No	EXPANSION PLANS:
Registered: . . . . NY	Passive Ownership: . . . Discouraged	US: . . . . .All US
. . . .	Encourage Conversions: . . . . . Yes	Canada: . . . . .No
Type Space: . . . . .SC;~ SF	Average # Employees: . . 2 FT, 2 PT	Overseas: . . . . No

GREG SOUND AND COMMUNICATION

14200 Sullyfield Circle
Chantilly, VA 22021
TEL: (703) 968-0250
FAX: (703) 968-0255
Mr. Greg Tsiopanas, President

GREG SOUND AND COMMUNICATION offers a unique opportunity in mobile electronics. We specialize in high-end brand names of cellular phones, alarm systems and stereo systems. Our 17 years of experience in this industry enables us to offer you extensive on-going support of your franchise. We'll tailor our program to meet your needs and level of expertise.

HISTORY: . . . . IFA	FINANCIAL: Earnings Claim: . .No	FRANCHISOR TRAINING/SUPPORT:
Established in 1975; . . 1st Franchised in 1991	Cash Investment: $30-60K	Financial Assistance Provided: . . . Yes(I)
Company-Owned Units (As of 8/31/1992): . .3	Total Investment: $119-172K	Site Selection Assistance: . . . . .Yes
Franchised Units (As of 8/31/1992): 1	Fees: Franchise - $18.5K	Lease Negotiation Assistance: . . . . .Yes
Total Units (As of 8/31/1992): 4	Royalty: 6%, Advert: 2.5%	Co-operative Advertising: . . . . .Yes
Projected New Units for 1993: 8	Contract Periods (Yrs.): 10/10	Training: . . . . . . 30 Days Headquarters,
Distribution: US-4;Can-0;Overseas-0	Area Development Agreement: . .No	. . . . .30 Days On-Site
North America: . . . . .1 State	Sub-Franchise Contract: . . . . .No	On-Going Support: B,C,D,E,F/ 7
Concentration: . . . . 4 in VA	Expand in Territory: . . . . Yes	EXPANSION PLANS:
Registered: . . . . MD,VA	Passive Ownership:	US: . . . . .All US
. . . .	Encourage Conversions: . . . . . Yes	Canada: . . . . .No
Type Space: . . . . . FS, SC, Other;~3,000 SF	Average # Employees: . . . . . .5 FT	Overseas: . . . . No

INTERNATIONAL VIDEO YEARBOOKS

25 Century Blvd., # 507
Nashville, TN 37214
TEL: (800) 468-2049 (615) 889-3700
FAX: (615) 889-3721
Mr. Jim McCarthy, President

Produce video yearbooks for high schools and middle schools.

HISTORY:	FINANCIAL: Earnings Claim: . .No	FRANCHISOR TRAINING/SUPPORT:
Established in 1988; . . 1st Franchised in 1988	Cash Investment: $50K	Financial Assistance Provided: . . . . .No
Company-Owned Units (As of 8/31/1992): . .0	Total Investment: $50K	Site Selection Assistance: . . . . .NA
Franchised Units (As of 8/31/1992): 46	Fees: Franchise - $35K	Lease Negotiation Assistance: . . . . .NA
Total Units (As of 8/31/1992): 46	Royalty: 10%, Advert: 0%	Co-operative Advertising: . . . . .NA
Projected New Units for 1993: 16	Contract Periods (Yrs.): 25/5	Training: . . . . 2 Wks. Headquarters
Distribution: US-43;Can-3;Overseas-0	Area Development Agreement: . .No	
North America: . . . 21 States, 3 Provinces	Sub-Franchise Contract: . . . . .No	On-Going Support: C,D,E,G,H,I/ 12
Concentration: . . . .5 in OH, 5 in TN, 4 in FL	Expand in Territory: . . . . .No	EXPANSION PLANS:
Registered: . . . CA,FL,IL,IN,MD,MI,MN,NY	Passive Ownership: . . . Not Allowed	US: . . . . .All US
. . . . OR,RI,VA,WA,WI	Encourage Conversions: . . . . . NA	Canada: . . . . .All Canada
Type Space: . . . . . . .Home Based;~NA SF	Average # Employees: . . . . . .2 FT	Overseas: . . . . No

JUMBO VIDEO

1075 N. Service Rd. W., # 101
Oakville, ON L6M 2G2 CAN
TEL: (416) 847-7212
FAX: (416) 847-7276
Mr. John Prittie, VP

Video sales and rental business.

HISTORY: . . . . .CFA	FINANCIAL: Earnings Claim: . .No	FRANCHISOR TRAINING/SUPPORT:
Established in 1987; . . 1st Franchised in 1987	Cash Investment: $250-300K	Financial Assistance Provided: . . . Yes(I)
Company-Owned Units (As of 8/31/1992): . 15	Total Investment: $500-550K	Site Selection Assistance: . . . . . . .Yes
Franchised Units (As of 8/31/1992): 70	Fees: Franchise - $75K	Lease Negotiation Assistance: . . . . .Yes
Total Units (As of 8/31/1992): 85	Royalty: 5%, Advert: 4%	Co-operative Advertising: . . . . .No
Projected New Units for 1993: 20	Contract Periods (Yrs.): . . . . . .No	Training: . . . . . 2 Wks. HQ, 1 Wk. Corp.
Distribution: US-0;Can-85;Overseas-0	Area Development Agreement: . Yes	. . . . . Training Store, 10 Days On-Site
North America: . . . . 7 Provinces	Sub-Franchise Contract: . . . . . .No	On-Going Support: B,C,D,E,F,G,h/ . . . 35
Concentration: . . 70 in ON, 5 in AB, 3 in MB	Expand in Territory: . . . . . . Yes	EXPANSION PLANS:
Registered: . . . . AB	Passive Ownership: . . . Discouraged	US: . . . . No
. . . .	Encourage Conversions: . . . . . Yes	Canada: . . . . .All Canada
Type Space: FS, SF, SC, RM;~6,000-7,000 SF	Average # Employees: . .5 FT, 20 PT	Overseas: . . . . No

LE CLUB INTERNATIONAL VIDEO FILM

350 Elaine
Fabreville (Laval), PQ H7P 2R1 CAN
TEL: (514) 628-1910
FAX: (514) 628-1034
Mrs. Manon Belisle,, Mktg. Director

The support that we are offering, the involvement of all our members and our commitment to professionalism are certainly the facts that have made us the best video franchisor in Canada.

HISTORY:	FINANCIAL: Earnings Claim: . .No	FRANCHISOR TRAINING/SUPPORT:
Established in 1981; . . 1st Franchised in 1982	Cash Investment: $80K	Financial Assistance Provided: . . . Yes(I)
Company-Owned Units (As of 8/31/1992): . .2	Total Investment: $175K	Site Selection Assistance: . . . . . . .Yes
Franchised Units (As of 8/31/1992): 56	Fees: Franchise - $25K	Lease Negotiation Assistance: . . . . .Yes
Total Units (As of 8/31/1992): 58	Royalty: 5%, Advert: 3%	Co-operative Advertising: . . . . .Yes
Projected New Units for 1993: 6	Contract Periods (Yrs.): 10/10	Training: . . . . 2 Wks. On-Site
Distribution: US-0;Can-58;Overseas-0	Area Development Agreement: . .No	. . . .
North America: . . . . .1 Province	Sub-Franchise Contract: . . . . . .No	On-Going Support: B,C,D,E,F,G,H,I/ . . 17
Concentration: . . . . .54 in PQ	Expand in Territory: . . . . Yes	EXPANSION PLANS:
Registered:	Passive Ownership: . . . Discouraged	US: . . . . No
. . . .	Encourage Conversions: . . . . . Yes	Canada: . . . . .Quebec
Type Space: . . . . .SC;~200 SF	Average # Employees: . . 3 FT, 4 PT	Overseas: . . . . No

MARBLES MUSIC & VIDEO

3545 Motor Ave., # 200
Los Angeles, CA 90034
TEL: (800) 669-2221 (310) 204-2220
FAX: (310) 204-0148
Mr. Matt Feinstein, Dir. Fran. Dev.

Total home entertainment store. Video movie rentals, CD's, tapes, laser discs and related merchandise.

HISTORY:	FINANCIAL: Earnings Claim: . . .	FRANCHISOR TRAINING/SUPPORT:
Established in 1989; . . 1st Franchised in 1991	Cash Investment: $50K	Financial Assistance Provided: . . . . .Yes
Company-Owned Units (As of 8/31/1992): . .4	Total Investment: $100-175K	Site Selection Assistance: . . . . . . .Yes
Franchised Units (As of 8/31/1992): 3	Fees: Franchise - $20K	Lease Negotiation Assistance: . . . . .Yes
Total Units (As of 8/31/1992): 7	Royalty: 6%, Advert: . . . Included	Co-operative Advertising: . . . . .Yes
Projected New Units for 1993: 12	Contract Periods (Yrs.): 10/5	Training: . . . . . . As Long As Necessary
Distribution: US-7;Can-0;Overseas-0	Area Development Agreement: . .No	. . . . In-Store Training
North America: . . . . 5 States	Sub-Franchise Contract:	On-Going Support: B,C,D,F,G,I/ 6
Concentration: . . . 2 in NC, 2 in TX, 1 in CO	Expand in Territory: . . . . Yes	EXPANSION PLANS:
Registered: . . . . All States Exc. NY	Passive Ownership: . . . Discouraged	US: . . . . .All US
. . . .	Encourage Conversions:	Canada: . . . . .Yes
Type Space: . . . . . FS, SC;~3,500-5,000 SF	Average # Employees: . 1 FT, 2-3 PT	Overseas: . . . . .Yes

PALMER VIDEO SUPERSTORES

1767 Morris Ave.
Union, NJ 07083
TEL: (908) 686-3030
FAX: (908) 686-2151
Ms. Gert Elster

PALMER VIDEO offers an opportunity in attractive, well-inventoried video superstores based on a professional franchise system. Emphasis on sound operating principles and aggressive marketing concepts to obtain a disproportionate market share. Our top management's on-going support is dedicated to driving customers to our franchised video superstores.

HISTORY:	FINANCIAL: Earnings Claim: . . .	FRANCHISOR TRAINING/SUPPORT:
Established in 1981; . . 1st Franchised in 1982	Cash Investment: $50-100K	Financial Assistance Provided: . . . Yes(I)
Company-Owned Units (As of 8/31/1992): . 32	Total Investment: $200-400K	Site Selection Assistance: . . . . .Yes
Franchised Units (As of 8/31/1992): 41	Fees: Franchise - $39K	Lease Negotiation Assistance: . . . . .Yes
Total Units (As of 8/31/1992): 73	Royalty: 5%, Advert: . . . Varies	Co-operative Advertising: . . . . . . .Yes
Projected New Units for 1993:	Contract Periods (Yrs.): 10/10	Training: . . . . 5 Days Headquarters,
Distribution: US-73;Can-0;Overseas-0	Area Development Agreement: Yes/Var	. . . . .2 Days Field
North America: . . . . 7 States	Sub-Franchise Contract: . . . . . .No	On-Going Support: A,B,C,D,E,g,H,I/ . . 40
Concentration: . . . . 56 in NJ, 6 in IL	Expand in Territory: . . . . . . Yes	EXPANSION PLANS:
Registered: . . . . .CA,IL,NY	Passive Ownership: . . . . . .Allowed	US: . . . .
. . . .	Encourage Conversions: . . . . . Yes	Canada: . . . .
Type Space: . . . . ;~ SF	Average # Employees: . . 2 FT, 6 PT	Overseas: . . . . No

PROVIDEO PRODUCTIONS

8040 E. Morgan Tr., # 8
Scottsdale, AZ 85258
TEL: (602) 948-5579 (602) 948-9310
FAX: (602) 948-5935
Mr. Dean Wiltse, President

One of the brightest franchise opportunities of the 90's is available from PROVIDEO PRODUCTIONS. Prospective franchisees do not need prior experience in videotaping or production. They can start part-time and operate from their home, producing videotapes for business owners, cable television, infomercials, legal depositions, etc. Can later add video duplication, photo and home movie transfer & do-it- yourself video editing. Complete turn-key business.

HISTORY:	FINANCIAL: Earnings Claim: . .No	FRANCHISOR TRAINING/SUPPORT:
Established in 1992; . . 1st Franchised in 1992	Cash Investment: $15-50K	Financial Assistance Provided: . . .Yes(D)
Company-Owned Units (As of 8/31/1992): . .1	Total Investment: $30-100K	Site Selection Assistance: . . . . .Yes
Franchised Units (As of 8/31/1992): 7	Fees: Franchise - $15K	Lease Negotiation Assistance: . . . . .Yes
Total Units (As of 8/31/1992): 8	Royalty: 5%, Advert: 1%	Co-operative Advertising: . . . . . . .Yes
Projected New Units for 1993: 12	Contract Periods (Yrs.): 10/10	Training: . . . . 7 Days Headquarters
Distribution: US-8;Can-0;Overseas-0	Area Development Agreement: Yes/10	. . . .
North America: . . . . 7 States	Sub-Franchise Contract: . . . . . Yes	On-Going Support: B,c,d,E,G,H,I/ 5
Concentration: . . . . 2 in CA	Expand in Territory: . . . . . . Yes	EXPANSION PLANS:
Registered: . . . . .All	Passive Ownership: . . . . . .Allowed	US: . . . . .All US
. . . .	Encourage Conversions: . . . . . Yes	Canada: . . . . Master Fran Only
Type Space: . . . . . Office;~800-1,200 SF	Average # Employees: . 1 FT, 2-4 PT	Overseas: . . .Master Franchise Only

RED GIRAFFE VIDEO

11403 Bluegrass Pkwy., # 400
Louisville, KY 40299
TEL: (502) 266-6740
FAX: (502) 267-8742
Mr. James L. Cannon, Corp. Controller

RED GIRAFFE VIDEO superstores feature a business system designed to put you head and shoulders above other video rental stores. The entire store has been designed to make it easy to satisfy the customers.

HISTORY:	FINANCIAL: Earnings Claim: . .No	FRANCHISOR TRAINING/SUPPORT:
Established in 1986; . . 1st Franchised in 1989	Cash Investment: $200-400K	Financial Assistance Provided: . . . . .No
Company-Owned Units (As of 8/31/1992): . 18	Total Investment: $200-400K	Site Selection Assistance: . . . . .No
Franchised Units (As of 8/31/1992): 1	Fees: Franchise - $15K	Lease Negotiation Assistance: . . . . .No
Total Units (As of 8/31/1992): 19	Royalty: 6%, Advert: 4%	Co-operative Advertising: . . . . . . .Yes
Projected New Units for 1993:	Contract Periods (Yrs.): 20	Training: . . . . 1 Wk. Headquarters
Distribution: US-19;Can-0;Overseas-0	Area Development Agreement: . Yes	. . . .
North America: . . . . 3 States	Sub-Franchise Contract: . . . . . .No	On-Going Support: A,B,C,D,E,F,H,i/ . . . 9
Concentration: . . . 11 in KY, 5 in IN, 3 in OH	Expand in Territory: . . . . . . Yes	EXPANSION PLANS:
Registered: . . . . IL,IN	Passive Ownership: . . . Discouraged	US: . . . . KY, OH and IN Only
. . . .	Encourage Conversions: . . . . . Yes	Canada: . . . . .No
Type Space: . . . . .SC;~5,000 SF	Average # Employees: . .4 FT, 10 PT	Overseas: . . . . .No

STEREO DEN

2300 Lawrence Ave. E., # 14
Scarborough, ON M1P 2R2 CAN
TEL: (416) 750-4250
FAX: (416) 750-4249
Mr. Stephen Yap, President

Retailer of electronic entertainment products, specializing in brand-name products in the categories of stereo, television, video, car audio, telephone and related items and accessories.

HISTORY:	FINANCIAL: Earnings Claim: . .No	FRANCHISOR TRAINING/SUPPORT:
Established in 1977; . . 1st Franchised in 1982	Cash Investment: $75K	Financial Assistance Provided: . . . . .No
Company-Owned Units (As of 8/31/1992): . .6	Total Investment: $125-150K	Site Selection Assistance: . . . . . . .Yes
Franchised Units (As of 8/31/1992): 16	Fees: Franchise - $27K	Lease Negotiation Assistance: . . . .Yes
Total Units (As of 8/31/1992): 22	Royalty: 3%, Advert: 3%	Co-operative Advertising: . . . . . .Yes
Projected New Units for 1993: 4	Contract Periods (Yrs.): 5/5	Training: . . . . .4-6 Wks.
Distribution: US-0;Can-22;Overseas-0	Area Development Agreement: . .No	. . . .
North America: . . . . .1 Province	Sub-Franchise Contract: . . . . .No	On-Going Support: B,C,D,E,F,G,H/ . . . .
Concentration: . . . . 22 in ON	Expand in Territory: . . . . Yes	EXPANSION PLANS:
Registered:	Passive Ownership: . . . Not Allowed	US: . . . . .No
. . . .	Encourage Conversions: . . . . . Yes	Canada: . . . . .Ontario
Type Space: . . . . SC, RM;~2,000 SF	Average # Employees: . . 4 FT, 1 PT	Overseas: . . . . No

TOP FORTY

10333 - 174 St.
Edmonton, AB T5S 1H1 CAN
TEL: (800) 661-9931 (403) 489-2324
FAX: (403) 486-7528
Mr. Al J. Herfst, VP

Retail sales of pre-recorded music (compact discs and cassettes), as well as videos and related accessories. Franchisor provides full turn-key operation, inventory controls and full operational guidance.

HISTORY: . . . . .CFA	FINANCIAL: Earnings Claim: . .No	FRANCHISOR TRAINING/SUPPORT:
Established in 1974; . . 1st Franchised in 1985	Cash Investment: $48-64K	Financial Assistance Provided: . . . . .Yes
Company-Owned Units (As of 8/31/1992): . 19	Total Investment: $120-160K	Site Selection Assistance: . . . . . . .Yes
Franchised Units (As of 8/31/1992): 18	Fees: Franchise - $15K	Lease Negotiation Assistance: . . . .Yes
Total Units (As of 8/31/1992): 37	Royalty: 5%, Advert: 1%	Co-operative Advertising: . . . . . . .Yes
Projected New Units for 1993: 3	Contract Periods (Yrs.): 5/5	Training: . . . . 1 Wk. Headquarters, 1 Wk.
Distribution: US-0;Can-37;Overseas-0	Area Development Agreement: . .No	. . . . In Store, 2 Day Refresher On-Site
North America:	Sub-Franchise Contract: . . . . .No	On-Going Support: B,C,D,E,F,G,H,I/ . . . 7
Concentration: . . 13 in AB, 13 in SK, 7 in BC	Expand in Territory: . . . . Yes	EXPANSION PLANS:
Registered: . . . . AB	Passive Ownership: . . . . . .Allowed	US: . . . . .No
. . . .	Encourage Conversions: . . . . . Yes	Canada: . . . . N & W Canada
Type Space: . . . . RM;~1,200 SF	Average # Employees: . . 2 FT, 3 PT	Overseas: . . . . No

VEND-A-VIDEO

1873 S. Bellaire St., # 600
Denver, CO 80222
TEL: (800) 748-1142 (303) 782-1866
FAX: (303) 756-4299
Mr. Gene R. Yokley, President

Fully-automated video rental store with state-of-the-art machinery and software, featuring no employees or overhead. All transactions by cash or credit card. Aggressive marketing program designed to develop and retain customer base. Individual, multi-unit and area developer franchises available.

HISTORY:	FINANCIAL: Earnings Claim: . .No	FRANCHISOR TRAINING/SUPPORT:
Established in 1991; . . 1st Franchised in 1991	Cash Investment: $30-85K	Financial Assistance Provided: . . . . .No
Company-Owned Units (As of 8/31/1992): . .0	Total Investment: $90-150K	Site Selection Assistance: . . . . . . .Yes
Franchised Units (As of 8/31/1992): 5	Fees: Franchise - $22.5K	Lease Negotiation Assistance: . . . .Yes
Total Units (As of 8/31/1992): 5	Royalty: 6%, Advert: 1%	Co-operative Advertising: . . . . . . .NA
Projected New Units for 1993: 20	Contract Periods (Yrs.): 10/10	Training: . . . . 1 Wk. Headquarters
Distribution: US-4;Can-0;Overseas-1	Area Development Agreement: Yes/10	. . . .
North America: . . . . .1 State	Sub-Franchise Contract: . . . . .No	On-Going Support: C,D,E,G,I/ 4
Concentration: . . . . 4 in CO	Expand in Territory: . . . . Yes	EXPANSION PLANS:
Registered: . . . . .All	Passive Ownership: . . . . . .Allowed	US: . . . . .All US
. . . .	Encourage Conversions: . . . . . NA	Canada: . . . . .No
Type Space: . . . . .FS, SC;~700 SF	Average # Employees: . . . . . .1 PT	Overseas: . . . . .MX

VIDEO BIZ

224 N. Nova Rd.
Ormond Beach, FL 32174
TEL: (800) 672-0851 (904) 676-2148 C
FAX: (904) 672-0851
Mr. Steve Edson, President

Rentals and sales of video tapes and games. Unique rental program encourages multiple tape rental at each visit, which will enhance profitability. Current expansion designed to enter smaller markets and establish market dominance. VIDEO BIZ will finance 50% of franchise fee.

HISTORY:	FINANCIAL: Earnings Claim: . Yes	FRANCHISOR TRAINING/SUPPORT:
Established in 1981; . . 1st Franchised in 1983	Cash Investment: $80-150K	Financial Assistance Provided: . . .Yes(D)
Company-Owned Units (As of 8/31/1992): . .3	Total Investment: $80-150K	Site Selection Assistance: . . . . . . .Yes
Franchised Units (As of 8/31/1992): 160	Fees: Franchise - $15K	Lease Negotiation Assistance: . . . .Yes
Total Units (As of 8/31/1992): 163	Royalty: 0%, Advert: 0%	Co-operative Advertising: . . . . . . .Yes
Projected New Units for 1993: 8	Contract Periods (Yrs.): . . . 10/10	Training: . . . . .10 Days On-Site
Distribution: . . . US-163;Can-0;Overseas-0	Area Development Agreement: Yes/10	
North America: . . . . 38 States	Sub-Franchise Contract: . . . . .No	On-Going Support: B,D,E,F,I/ 3
Concentration: . . . 12 in FL, 8 in NJ, 8 in CA	Expand in Territory: . . . . . . Yes	EXPANSION PLANS:
Registered: . . . . .All	Passive Ownership: . . . . .Allowed	US: . . . . All US
. . . .	Encourage Conversions: . . . . Yes	Canada: . . . . .No
Type Space: . . . . .SC;~1,800 SF	Average # Employees: . . 1 FT, 2 PT	Overseas: . . . . .Yes

VIDEO DATA SERVICES

30 Grove St.
Pittsford, NY 14534
TEL: (800) 836-9461 (716) 385-4773
FAX:
Mr. Stuart Dizak, President

Provide a unique video photography service to business and consumers. Complete package includes all equipment, training, marketing and field assistance. Can be started part-time. Ideal as a family or retirement business. VIDEO DATA SERVICES is the largest video taping service in North America. Also provide film-to-tape transfer.

HISTORY:	FINANCIAL: Earnings Claim: . .No	FRANCHISOR TRAINING/SUPPORT:
Established in 1981; . . 1st Franchised in 1984	Cash Investment: $18K	Financial Assistance Provided: . . . . . No
Company-Owned Units (As of 8/31/1992): . .1	Total Investment: $18K	Site Selection Assistance: . . . . .NA
Franchised Units (As of 8/31/1992): 240	Fees: Franchise - $8K	Lease Negotiation Assistance: . . . . .NA
Total Units (As of 8/31/1992): 241	Royalty: Flat, Advert: 0%	Co-operative Advertising: . . . . .Yes
Projected New Units for 1993: 48	Contract Periods (Yrs.): 10/10	Training: . . . . 4 Days Field,
Distribution: US-239;Can-2;Overseas-0	Area Development Agreement: . .No	. . . . 6 Wks. Training at Home
North America: . . . . 38 States, 2 Provinces	Sub-Franchise Contract: . . . . .No	On-Going Support: B,C,E,F,G,H,I/ 6
Concentration: . . . 12 in CA, 8 in FL, 7 in LA	Expand in Territory: . . . . Yes	EXPANSION PLANS:
Registered: . . . CA,FL,IL,IN,MD,MI,MN,NY	Passive Ownership: . . . Not Allowed	US: . . . . All US
. . . . RI,VA,WA,WI	Encourage Conversions: . . . . .No	Canada: . . . . .Yes
Type Space: . . . . Home Based;~ SF	Average # Employees: . . . . . .2 PT	Overseas: . . . . No

VIDEO UPDATE

287 East 6th St.
St. Paul, MN 55101
TEL: (800) 433-1195 (612) 222-0006
FAX: (612) 297-6629
Mr. John Bedard, President

VIDEO UPDATE has developed the highest-quality retail rental/sales stores in the world. Our merchandising and marketing skills are unsurpassed. We attribute our achievement to our uncompromising commitment to franchisee support.

HISTORY:	FINANCIAL: Earnings Claim: . .No	FRANCHISOR TRAINING/SUPPORT:
Established in 1982; . . 1st Franchised in 1983	Cash Investment: $20-50K	Financial Assistance Provided: . . .Yes(D)
Company-Owned Units (As of 8/31/1992): . 12	Total Investment: $90-260K	Site Selection Assistance: . . . . . . .Yes
Franchised Units (As of 8/31/1992): 40	Fees: Franchise - $19.5K	Lease Negotiation Assistance: . . . .Yes
Total Units (As of 8/31/1992): 52	Royalty: 5%, Advert: 1%	Co-operative Advertising: . . . . . . .Yes
Projected New Units for 1993: 10	Contract Periods (Yrs.): 10	Training: . . . . . . .5 Days Owner's Store
Distribution: US-52;Can-0;Overseas-2	Area Development Agreement: . Yes	. . . .
North America: . . . . 6 States	Sub-Franchise Contract: . . . . .No	On-Going Support: A,B,C,D,E,F,G,H,I/ . .
Concentration: . . . . MN, VA, PA	Expand in Territory: . . . . . . Yes	EXPANSION PLANS:
Registered: . . . . MN	Passive Ownership: . . . . . .Allowed	US: . . . . All US
. . . .	Encourage Conversions: . . . . NA	Canada: . . . . .All Canada
Type Space: . . . FS, SF, SC;~2,000-5,000 SF	Average # Employees: . . 1 FT, 4 PT	Overseas: . . . . .Yes

VIDEOMATIC INTERNATIONAL

2002 Locust Ct.
Ontario, CA 91761
TEL: (800) 542-2002 (714) 923-3333
FAX: (714) 923-3220
Mr. Harold E. Brown, President

VIDEOMATIC Automated Video Stores. No employees. Operates unattended. No cash on-site. Accepts only major credit cards. Rents only top hit, first-release movies. Takes only a few hours per week. Keep your present income. Let VIDEOMATIC earn you a second income. Stocks the same inventory of top hits as the largest superstores, but with the lowest overhead in the industry.

HISTORY: . . . . IFA
Established in 1988; . . 1st Franchised in 1989
Company-Owned Units (As of 8/31/1992): . .0
Franchised Units (As of 8/31/1992): 40
Total Units (As of 8/31/1992): 40
Projected New Units for 1993: 50
Distribution: US-40;Can-0;Overseas-0
North America: . . . . 9 States
Concentration: . . . 14 in CA, 3 in FL, 1 in CO
Registered: . . . .
. . . .
Type Space: . . . . Free Standing SC;~500 SF

FINANCIAL: Earnings Claim: . .No
Cash Investment: $25K
Total Investment: $100-132K
Fees: Franchise - $25K
Royalty: 5%, Advert. 2.5%
Contract Periods (Yrs.): 10/10
Area Development Agreement: . .No
Sub-Franchise Contract: . . . . .No
Expand in Territory: . . . . . . Yes
Passive Ownership: . . . . .Allowed
Encourage Conversions: . . . . Yes
Average # Employees: No Employees

FRANCHISOR TRAINING/SUPPORT:
Financial Assistance Provided: . . . . .No
Site Selection Assistance: . . . . .No
Lease Negotiation Assistance: . . . .Yes
Co-operative Advertising: . . . . .Yes
Training: . . . . . 2-5 Days Site and Office
. . . .
On-Going Support: D,E,H/ 12
EXPANSION PLANS:
US: . . . . All US
Canada: . . . . .All Canada
Overseas: . . . . .Yes

SUPPLEMENTAL LISTING OF FRANCHISORS

ADVENTURELAND VIDEO . . . . 1900 Broadway, New York, NY 10023
    Contact: Mr. Howard Berkowitz, President; Tel: (813) 973-7109
APPLAUSE VIDEO . . . . 2901 W. Cypress Creek Rd., Ft. Lauderdale, FL 33309
    Contact: Mr. Bruce Shackman, President; Tel: (402) 330-1000
BLOCKBUSTER VIDEOS . . . . 901 E. Las Olas Blvd., Ft. Lauderdale, FL 33301
    Contact: Mr. Charles J. Averbook, VP Fran.; Tel: (305) 524-8200
CURTIS MATHES . . . . One Curtis Mathes Pkwy., Box 2160, Athens, TX 75751
    Contact: Mr. Ethan Ristow; Tel: (214) 675-2292
DR. VIDEO . . . . 1131 Bay Ave., Point Pleasant, NJ 08742
    Contact: Mr. Joseph F. DeGraw, Chairman; Tel: (800) 533-5362 (908) 892-8877
FAST FORWARD VIDEO . . . . 2034 Cotner Ave., 4th Fl., Los Angeles, CA 90025
    Contact: President; Tel: (213) 312-1171
FILMED EVENTS NETWORKS . . . . 2725 Contrell Valley Plaza, # 101, Little Rock, AR 72202
    Contact: President; Tel: (501) 664-4900
HOLLYWOOD CONNECTION VIDEO PRODUCTIONS . . 8040 E. Morgon Trail, # 8, Scottsdale, AZ 85258
    Contact: Mr. Dean Wiltse, President; Tel: (602) 948-9310
LASERLAND . . . . 1685 S. Colorado Blvd., # L, Denver, CO 80222
    Contact: Ms. Joy H. Barber, Dir. Fran. Support; Tel: (303) 757-8778
MEGAVIDEO . . . . 220 Commerce Rd., # 220, Ft. Washington, PA 19034
    Contact: Mr. Michael T. Flannery; Tel: (800) 345-2595 (215) 643-9400
MOVIE KING . . . . .Liberty Plaza at Possum Park, Newark, DE 19711
    Contact: Mr. Daniel Herron; Tel: (301) 392-5469
MOVIE WAREHOUSE . . . . P. O. Box 23259, Lexington, KY 40523
    Contact: Mr. James L. Crawford; Tel: (800) 243-3726 (606) 293-6223
MOVIES & MORE . . . . 1429 Warwick Ave., Warwick, RI 02888
    Contact: Mr. Arnold Kornstein, President; Tel: (401) 463-8130
MR. MOVIES . . . . .6566 Edenvale Blvd., Eden Prairie, MN 55346
    Contact: Mr. Michael Jorgensen, President; Tel: (800) 562-7667 (612) 934-7088
NATIONAL VIDEO YEARBOOK . . . . 25 Century Blvd., # 507, Nashville, TN 37214
    Contact: Mr. Jim McCarthy, President; Tel: (800) 552-9103 (615) 889-3700
NEEDLE IN A HAYSTACK . . . . P. O. Box 143, Powell, OH 43065
    Contact: Mr. Jim Bowser, Fran. Sales; Tel: (614) 876-8014
NETWORK VIDEO . . . . .5562 Quail Run, N. Olmsted, OH 44070
    Contact: Mr. Robert F. Bunte; Tel:
RADIO SHACK (CANADA) . . . . P.O. Box 34000, Barrie, ON L4M 4W5   CAN
    Contact: Mr. Andrew Shepard, Dealer Director; Tel: (705) 728-6242
RADIO SHACK DIVISION . . . . 1600 One Tandy Center, Fort Worth, TX 76102
    Contact: Mr. Robert Owens, VP; Tel: (817) 390-3386
STAR TIME FOTO VIDEO . . . . P.O. Box 300, Winnipeg, MB R3C 3A3   CAN

Contact: Mr. Sheldon N. Gale; Tel: (204) 633-1395

TELOS PRODUCTIONS . . . . 67 Alpha Park, Cleveland, OH 44143
Contact: President; Tel: (216) 446-4777

TOP 20 VIDEO . . . . P. O. Box 6962, Ketchikan, AK 99901
Contact: President; Tel: (206) 892-2867

VIDEO 5000 . . . . 211 E. 43rd St., New York, NY 10017
Contact: Mr. Chuck Delaney; Tel: (212) 371-7050

VIDEO FLICKS CANADA . . . . 1654 Avenue Rd., Toronto, ON M5M 3Y1   CAN
Contact: President; Tel: (416) 782-4438

VIDEO GALAXY . . . . 101 West Rd., Vernon, CT 06066
Contact: Mr. William D. Corbin, Dir. Dev.; Tel: (203) 871-7831

VIDEO QUIKLAB . . . . 2121 W. Oakland Park Blvd., Ft. Lauderdale, FL 33311
Contact: Mr. David Bawarsky, Dir. Fran.; Tel: (800) 225-0005 (305) 735-2300

VIDEO VALUE . . . . 350 Keewatin St., # 5, Winnipeg, MB R2X 2R9   CAN
Contact: Mr. I. D. Oiring, President; Tel: (204) 694-2930

VIDTRON TOP 40 DRIVE THRU VIDEO RENTAL . . . . 2109 Wedgewood Dr., Grapevine, TX 76051
Contact: Ms. Cathy O'Connell, Dir. Fran.; Tel:

WEST COAST VIDEO . . . . 9990 Global Rd., Philadelphia, PA 19115
Contact: Mr. John L. Barry, VP Sales; Tel: (800) 433-5171 (215) 677-1000

WEST COAST VIDEO (CANADA) . . . . # 10 - 52 Antares Dr., Nepean, ON K2E 7Z1   CAN
Contact: Ms. Helen McGuire; Tel: (613) 723-9378

ZM VIDEO RENTAL . . . . 3501 Chateau Blvd., # E-2B, Kenner, LA 70065
Contact: Mr. George Brooks; Tel: (504) 464-1417

CHAPTER 46

RETAIL: MISCELLANEOUS

BEN FRANKLIN STORES

500 E. North Ave.
Carol Stream, IL 60188
TEL: (800) 669-6413 (708) 462-6100
FAX: (708) 690-1356
Mr. C. Wayne Pyrant, VP Fran. Sales

BEN FRANKLIN offers one of the most complete, turn-key franchise opportunities to operate your own franchised BEN FRANKLIN CRAFTS STORE or BEN FRANKLIN VARIETY STORE.

HISTORY: . . . . IFA, CFA
Established in 1920; . . 1st Franchised in 1927
Company-Owned Units (As of 8/31/1992): . .5
Franchised Units (As of 8/31/1992): . . . . <u>959</u>
Total Units (As of 8/31/1992): 964
Projected New Units for 1993: 26
Distribution: US-960;Can-0;Overseas-4
  North America: . . . . 47 States
  Concentration: . 91 in MN, 70 in MI, 45 in FL
Registered: . . . . .All
. . . .
Type Space: . . . . SC;~15,000 SF

FINANCIAL: Earnings Claim: . .No
Cash Investment: $150K
Total Investment: . . . $350K-1.0MM
Fees: Franchise - $24K
  Royalty: 2.5%, Advert: 1/2%
Contract Periods (Yrs.): 10
Area Development Agreement: Yes/Var
Sub-Franchise Contract: . . . . . .No
Expand in Territory: . . . . . . Yes
Passive Ownership: . . . . .Allowed
Encourage Conversions: . . . . . Yes
Average # Employees: . . . .

FRANCHISOR TRAINING/SUPPORT:
Financial Assistance Provided: . . . Yes(I)
Site Selection Assistance: . . . . . . .Yes
Lease Negotiation Assistance: . . . . .Yes
Co-operative Advertising: . . . . . . .Yes
Training: . . . . . . 1-2 Wks. Headquarters,
  . . . . .2 Wks. Training Store
On-Going Support: A,B,C,D,E,F,G,H,I/ . .
EXPANSION PLANS:
  US: . . . . All US
  Canada: . . . . No
  Overseas: . . . . No

COBBLESTONE QUALITY SHOE REPAIR
5944 Luther Ln., # 402
Dallas, TX 75225
TEL: (800) 735-6231 (214) 696-4436
FAX: (214) 696-2483
Ms. Janice Proffitt, Natl. Sales Dir.

COBBLESTONE provides quality shoe, boot and luggage repair, on time, at reasonable prices in an attractive shoe setting. COBBLESTONE franchisees are not cobblers. Customers are guaranteed satisfaction! The franchisee is a business person using our high-tech, state-of-the-art Centralized Repair Facilities to handle the toughest jobs. COBBLESTONE and its affiliates are consistently rated "Best Shoe Repair."

HISTORY: . . . .
Established in 1988; . . 1st Franchised in 1989
Company-Owned Units (As of 8/31/1992): . 39
Franchised Units (As of 8/31/1992): 32
Total Units (As of 8/31/1992): 71
Projected New Units for 1993: 100
Distribution: US-71;Can-0;Overseas-0
 North America: . . . . 6 States
 Concentration: . . 58 in TX, 6 in MO, 4 in AZ
Registered: . . . . FL,VA,DC
 . . . .
Type Space: . . . . SC;~600-800 SF

FINANCIAL: Earnings Claim: . Yes
Cash Investment: $48K
Total Investment: $48K
Fees: Franchise - $13.4K
 Royalty: 6%, Advert: 1%
Contract Periods (Yrs.): 10/10
Area Development Agreement: Yes/50
Sub-Franchise Contract: . . . . .No
Expand in Territory: . . . . . . Yes
Passive Ownership: . . . Discouraged
Encourage Conversions: . . . . Yes
Average # Employees: . . . . . .1 FT

FRANCHISOR TRAINING/SUPPORT:
Financial Assistance Provided: . . . Yes(I)
Site Selection Assistance: . . . . . . .Yes
Lease Negotiation Assistance: . . . .Yes
Co-operative Advertising: . . . . . . .Yes
Training: . . . . . . 2-3 Wks. Headquarters,
 . . . . .1-2 Wks. Franchisee Area
On-Going Support: C,D,E,I/ 3
EXPANSION PLANS:
US: . . . . .Southwest, DC, VA, FL
Canada: . . . . .No
Overseas: . . . . No

DOLLAR DISCOUNT STORES

1326 Naamans Creek Rd.
Boothwyn, PA 19061
TEL: (800) 227-5314 (215) 497-1991 C
FAX: (215) 485-6439
Mr. Paul Cohen, President

DOLLAR DISCOUNT STORES feature a wide variety of discount close-out merchandise at rock-bottom prices. Product categories include toys, candy, seasonal products, health and beauty aids, party and paper goods, pet supplies and other new and unusual products.

HISTORY: . . . . IFA
Established in 1982; . . 1st Franchised in 1987
Company-Owned Units (As of 8/31/1992): . .0
Franchised Units (As of 8/31/1992): 32
Total Units (As of 8/31/1992): 32
Projected New Units for 1993: 24
Distribution: US-32;Can-0;Overseas-0
 North America: . . . . 6 States
 Concentration: . . . . .MD, NJ, PA
Registered: . . . . FL,MD,NY,RI,VA
 . . . .
Type Space: . . . . .SC;~ SF

FINANCIAL: Earnings Claim: . .No
Cash Investment: $20-40K
Total Investment: $80-120K
Fees: Franchise - $18K
 Royalty: 2%, Advert: 0%
Contract Periods (Yrs.): 10
Area Development Agreement: . Yes
Sub-Franchise Contract: . . . . .No
Expand in Territory: . . . . . . .No
Passive Ownership: . . . Discouraged
Encourage Conversions: . . . . Yes
Average # Employees: . . 2 FT, 3 PT

FRANCHISOR TRAINING/SUPPORT:
Financial Assistance Provided: . . . Yes(I)
Site Selection Assistance: . . . . . . .Yes
Lease Negotiation Assistance: . . . .Yes
Co-operative Advertising: . . . . . . .No
Training: . . . . 1 Wk. Headquarters
 . . . .
On-Going Support: A,B,C,D,E,F,G,H,I/ 14
EXPANSION PLANS:
US: . . . .PA, NJ, MD, DE, MI and VA
Canada: . . . . .No
Overseas: . . . . No

HEEL QUIK / SEW QUIK

1720 Cumberland Pt. Dr., # 17
Marietta, GA 30067
TEL: (800) 255-8145 (404) 951-9440
FAX: (404) 933-8268
Ms. Colleen Turner, Fran. Dev. Coord.

Instant shoe repair, clothing alterations and monogramming. No failures to date. 670% growth in last 3 years. Ranked #1 in our industry by Entrepreneur Magazine. Listed in top 100 franchises for women by Woman's Enterprise.

HISTORY: . . . . IFA
Established in 1984; . . 1st Franchised in 1985
Company-Owned Units (As of 8/31/1992): . .3
Franchised Units (As of 8/31/1992): 329
Total Units (As of 8/31/1992): 332
Projected New Units for 1993: 100
Distribution: . . . US-131;Can-1;Overseas-200
 North America: . . . . 26 States, 1 Province
 Concentration: . . 15 in GA, 14 in FL, 5 in OH
Registered: . . . .CA,FL,IL,IN,MD,MI,MN,RI
 . . . . VA,WI
Type Space: SC, RM,Superstore;~150-1,000 SF

FINANCIAL: Earnings Claim: . .No
Cash Investment: $6K
Total Investment: $6K
Fees: Franchise - $2.5K
 Royalty: 4%, Advert: 2%
Contract Periods (Yrs.): 15/10
Area Development Agreement: Yes/10
Sub-Franchise Contract: . . . . .No
Expand in Territory: . . . . . . Yes
Passive Ownership: . . . . . .Allowed
Encourage Conversions: . . . . Yes
Average # Employees: . . 3 FT, 1 PT

FRANCHISOR TRAINING/SUPPORT:
Financial Assistance Provided: . . . Yes(I)
Site Selection Assistance: . . . . . . .Yes
Lease Negotiation Assistance: . . . . .Yes
Co-operative Advertising: . . . . . . .Yes
Training: . . . . . . 2-3 Wks. Headquarters
 . . . .
On-Going Support: C,D,E,F,G,H,I/ . . . 21
EXPANSION PLANS:
US: . . . . .All US
Canada: . . . . .All Canada
Overseas: . EUR, Asia, S. Amer,Mdl. East

MONEYSWORTH & BEST QUALITY SHOE REPAIR
80 Galaxy Blvd., # 11
Rexdale, ON M9W 4Y8 CAN
TEL: (800) 363-SHOE (416) 674-6148
FAX: (416) 674-8945
Mr. Rick Vansant, President

Complete shoe repair, while-you-wait, plus full line of MONEYSWORTH and BEST branded shoe care merchandise. Guaranteed customer satisfaction. Locations in major shopping malls. Distinctive turn-of-the-century designed stores, reminiscent of The Good Old Days. Full training at M & B's College; no experience required.

HISTORY:	. . . . .CFA
Established in 1984;	. . 1st Franchised in 1987
Company-Owned Units (As of 8/31/1992):	. 20
Franchised Units (As of 8/31/1992):	 80
Total Units (As of 8/31/1992):	 100
Projected New Units for 1993:	 10
Distribution:	. . . . . US-8;Can-92;Overseas-0
North America:	. . . . . 4 States, 6 Provinces
Concentration:	. .50 in ON, 13 in AB, 5 in MN
Registered:	. . . . MD,RI,VA,DC
. . . .	
Type Space:	. . . . RM;~250 SF

FINANCIAL: Earnings Claim: . Yes
Cash Investment: . . . . $25K+
Total Investment: $60-100K
Fees: Franchise - $10K
 Royalty: 8%, Advert: 1%
Contract Periods (Yrs.): . . . . Lease
Area Development Agreement: . .No
Sub-Franchise Contract: . . . . . .No
Expand in Territory: . . . . . . Yes
Passive Ownership: . . . Not Allowed
Encourage Conversions: . . . . NA
Average # Employees: . 2 FT, 1-2 PT

FRANCHISOR TRAINING/SUPPORT:
Financial Assistance Provided: . . .Yes(D)
Site Selection Assistance: . . . . . . .Yes
Lease Negotiation Assistance: . . . .Yes
Co-operative Advertising: . . . . . .Yes
Training: . . . . . 4-6 Wks. Kelowna, BC,
 . . . . 4-6 Wks. Toronto, ON
On-Going Support: A,B,C,D,E,F,G,H,I/ 110
EXPANSION PLANS:
US: . . . . Northeast
Canada: . . . . All Exc. Alberta
Overseas: . . . . No

SHOE STOP

13625 NE 126th Pl., # 430
Kirkland, WA 98034
TEL: (800) 275-3503 (206) 823-3199
FAX: (206) 823-8992
Mr. E. Michael Pula, President

State-of-the-art equipment and technical training to improve the quality of repairs, while reducing the time it takes. Heels can be replaced in 3 minutes and new soles take about 15 minutes. Repairs can be made while the customer waits.

HISTORY:	. . . .
Established in 1984;	. . 1st Franchised in 1985
Company-Owned Units (As of 8/31/1992):	. 10
Franchised Units (As of 8/31/1992):	 25
Total Units (As of 8/31/1992):	 35
Projected New Units for 1993:	2
Distribution:	. . . . . US-35;Can-0;Overseas-0
North America:	. . . . 5 States
Concentration:	. .15 in WA, 13 in CA, 4 in OR
Registered:	. . . . .CA,OR,WA
. . . .	
Type Space:	. . . SF, SC, RM;~300-600 SF

FINANCIAL: Earnings Claim: . Yes
Cash Investment: $20-40K
Total Investment: $75-130K
Fees: Franchise - $15K
 Royalty: 7%, Advert: . . . .
Contract Periods (Yrs.): . . . 10/10
Area Development Agreement: . .No
Sub-Franchise Contract: . . . . Yes
Expand in Territory: . . . . . . Yes
Passive Ownership: . . . .
Encourage Conversions: . . . . . .
Average # Employees: . . 2 FT, 1 PT

FRANCHISOR TRAINING/SUPPORT:
Financial Assistance Provided: . . . . .No
Site Selection Assistance: . . . . . . .Yes
Lease Negotiation Assistance: . . .Yes
Co-operative Advertising: . . . . . . .Yes
Training: . . . . 4-6 Wks. In-Store
 . . . .
On-Going Support: B,C,D,E,F,G,I/ 5
EXPANSION PLANS:
US: . . . . .Southwest, Northwest,Central
Canada: . . . . No
Overseas: . . . . No

SHOESMITH / SHOEFIXERS

15 Engle St., # 302
Englewood, NJ 07631
TEL: (800) 332-2229 (201) 871-0370
FAX: (201) 871-7168
Mr. John P. Sterns, Sales Mgr.

Instant shoe repair and shoe care.

HISTORY:	. . . .
Established in 1987;	. . 1st Franchised in 1987
Company-Owned Units (As of 8/31/1992):	. .0
Franchised Units (As of 8/31/1992):	 45
Total Units (As of 8/31/1992):	 45
Projected New Units for 1993:	 12
Distribution:	. . . . . US-45;Can-0;Overseas-0
North America:	
Concentration:	. . . 9 in MI, 7 in OH, 5 in MO
Registered:	. . . . . . .IL,IN,MI,NY,VA,WI
. . . .	
Type Space:	. .SC, RM, Kiosk;~300-1,200 SF

FINANCIAL: Earnings Claim: . .No
Cash Investment: $15-34K
Total Investment: $44.5-102.5K
Fees: Franchise - $12.5K
 Royalty: 5%, Advert: 0%
Contract Periods (Yrs.): 10/10
Area Development Agreement: . .No
Sub-Franchise Contract: . . . . . .No
Expand in Territory: . . . . . . Yes
Passive Ownership: . . . Not Allowed
Encourage Conversions: . . . . .No
Average # Employees: . . . .

FRANCHISOR TRAINING/SUPPORT:
Financial Assistance Provided: . . . Yes(I)
Site Selection Assistance: . . . . .Yes
Lease Negotiation Assistance: . . . . .Yes
Co-operative Advertising: . . . . .Yes
Training: . . . . 2 Wks. Headquarters,
 . . . . 1 Wk. Franchisee Location
On-Going Support: E,G,I/ . . . .
EXPANSION PLANS:
US: . . . . All US
Canada: . . . . .All Canada
Overseas: . . . . No

SUPPLY MASTER USA

P. O. Box 156
Sparta, NJ 07871
TEL: (201) 729-5006
FAX:
Mr. Albert T. Owens, President

SUPPLY MASTER USA is a unique mobile distribution of quantity maintenance hardware (bolts, fasteners, connectors) and related quality packages/assortments to the maintenance professional. No mechanical skill required. This is a home-based service industry which can be operated by a man or woman on a full- or part-time basis.

HISTORY:	FINANCIAL: Earnings Claim: . .No	FRANCHISOR TRAINING/SUPPORT:
Established in 1982; . . 1st Franchised in 1990	Cash Investment: $5-15K	Financial Assistance Provided: . . . Yes(I)
Company-Owned Units (As of 8/31/1992): . .2	Total Investment: $25-35K	Site Selection Assistance: . . . . .Yes
Franchised Units (As of 8/31/1992): 0	Fees: Franchise - $5K	Lease Negotiation Assistance: . . . . .Yes
Total Units (As of 8/31/1992): 2	Royalty: 5%, Advert: 2%	Co-operative Advertising: . . . .
Projected New Units for 1993: 5	Contract Periods (Yrs.): 15/15	Training: . . . . . . 1 Wk. Atlantic City, NJ
Distribution: US-2;Can-0;Overseas-0	Area Development Agreement: . Yes	. . . .
North America: . . . . 2 States	Sub-Franchise Contract: . . . . . Yes	On-Going Support: B,C,D,F,G,h/ 2
Concentration: . . . . 1 in NJ	Expand in Territory: . . . . Yes	EXPANSION PLANS:
Registered:	Passive Ownership: . . . Discouraged	US: . . . . .All US
. . . .	Encourage Conversions: . . . . . NA	Canada: . . . . .No
Type Space: . . . . .Home Based, Van;~ SF	Average # Employees: . . 1 FT, 1 PT	Overseas: . . . . No

TAILOR, NEEDLE & THREAD

500 Park Blvd., # 985
Itasca, IL 60143
TEL: (800) 432-5995 (708) 285-0285
FAX: (708) 285-0222
Mr. Richard A. Hovet, Dir. Fran. Dev.

Franchisor specializing in alterations and tailoring of apparel and the retail sale of related products and services in specially-designed retail locations.

HISTORY: . . . . IFA	FINANCIAL: Earnings Claim: . .No	FRANCHISOR TRAINING/SUPPORT:
Established in 1991; . . 1st Franchised in 1991	Cash Investment: $35K	Financial Assistance Provided: . . . Yes(I)
Company-Owned Units (As of 8/31/1992): . .1	Total Investment: $120-160K	Site Selection Assistance: . . . . .Yes
Franchised Units (As of 8/31/1992): 6	Fees: Franchise - $20K	Lease Negotiation Assistance: . . . . .Yes
Total Units (As of 8/31/1992): 7	Royalty: 7%, Advert: 3%	Co-operative Advertising: . . . . .NA
Projected New Units for 1993: 80	Contract Periods (Yrs.): . . . . Lease	Training: . . . . 2 Wks. Headquarters
Distribution: US-7;Can-0;Overseas-0	Area Development Agreement: . Yes	. . . .
North America:	Sub-Franchise Contract: . . . . .No	On-Going Support: A,B,C,D,E,F,G,H,I/ 12
Concentration:	Expand in Territory: . . . . Yes	EXPANSION PLANS:
Registered: . . . . .All	Passive Ownership: . . . . . .Allowed	US: . . . . .All US
. . . .	Encourage Conversions: . . . . . Yes	Canada: . . . . .All Canada
Type Space: . . . . RM;~900 SF	Average # Employees: . . 5 FT, 4 PT	Overseas: . . . . No

SUPPLEMENTAL LISTING OF FRANCHISORS

A BUCK OR TWO STORES . . . . 350 Crestline Rd., # 201, Concord, ON L4K 3Z2 CAN
        Contact: Mr. Amir Raubvogel; Tel: (416) 738-3180
LAROSSA INSTANT SHOE REPAIR . . . . 94 Pleasant St., S. Weymouth, MA 02190
        Contact: Mr. William LaRossa, President; Tel: (617) 227-8499
ORDER FROM HORTER OFFICE SUPPLY . . . . 211 E. Ontario, Chicago, IL 60611
        Contact: Mr. Ken Johnson; Tel: (312) 648-7278
QUICK STITCH TAILOR SHOPPES . . . . 3370 S. Service Rd., Burlington, ON L7N 3M6 CAN
        Contact: Mr. William Jackson, President; Tel: (800) 465-0450 (416) 681-6080
SHINES 'N MORE . . . . 94 Country Place, Cordova, TN 38018
        Contact: Mr. Joseph Gattas; Tel: (901) 756-5803
STEDMANS . . . . 1530 Gamble Pl, Winnipeg, MB R3C 3A9 CAN
        Contact: Mr. Alan Schoemperlen, Fran. Dir.; Tel:

CHAPTER 47

SECURITY AND SAFETY SYSTEMS

ALLIANCE SECURITY SYSTEMS

5 - 140 McGovern Dr.
Cambridge, ON N3H 4R7 CAN
TEL: (519) 650-5353
FAX: (519) 650-1704
Mr. Brien Welwood, Mktg. Mgr.

Security alarm dealership. Complete with training, products and support services. Monitoring station - U.L.C. Approved.

HISTORY: . . . .
Established in 1969; . . 1st Franchised in 1971
Company-Owned Units (As of 8/31/1992): . .1
Franchised Units (As of 8/31/1992): 80
Total Units (As of 8/31/1992): 81
Projected New Units for 1993: 6
Distribution: US-0;Can-81;Overseas-0
 North America: . . . . 4 Provinces
 Concentration: . . .66 in ON, 4 in NF, 3 in AB
Registered: . . . . AB
 . . . .
Type Space: . . Office Bldg., W/H;~1,000 SF

FINANCIAL: Earnings Claim: . Yes
Cash Investment: . . . .$
Total Investment: $10K
Fees: Franchise - $10K
 Royalty: $1.2/Yr., Advert: . . . 0%
Contract Periods (Yrs.): 3/1
Area Development Agreement: .No
Sub-Franchise Contract: . . . . .No
Expand in Territory: . . . . . . Yes
Passive Ownership: . . . Not Allowed
Encourage Conversions: . . . . . Yes
Average # Employees: . 2 FT, 1-2 PT

FRANCHISOR TRAINING/SUPPORT:
Financial Assistance Provided: . . . Yes(I)
Site Selection Assistance: . . . . .NA
Lease Negotiation Assistance: . . . . .Yes
Co-operative Advertising: . . . . No
Training: . . . . 5 Days Headquarters
 . . . .
On-Going Support: B,D,F,G,H,I/ 7
EXPANSION PLANS:
 US: . . . . .All US
 Canada: . . . . .All Canada
 Overseas: . . . . No

CUSTOM HOMEWATCH INTERNATIONAL
1090 Trevor Dr.
Kelowna, BC V1Z 2J8 CAN
TEL: (604) 769-4329
FAX: (604) 769-4329
Mr. Robin Jarman, President

Selling of franchises. House sitting - house checking. We do it all! Plants, pets, yard. Whatever is needed to make the home have a "Lived In" look.

HISTORY: . . . .
Established in 1988; . . 1st Franchised in 1988
Company-Owned Units (As of 8/31/1992): . .0
Franchised Units (As of 8/31/1992): . . . . . <u>52</u>
Total Units (As of 8/31/1992): 52
Projected New Units for 1993: 10
Distribution: US-0;Can-52;Overseas-0
  North America: . . . . 10 Provinces
  Concentration: . . 15 in ON, 11 in AB, 6 in BC
Registered: . . . . AB
. . . .
Type Space: . . . . ;~ SF

FINANCIAL: Earnings Claim: . .No
Cash Investment: $3-6K
Total Investment: $3-10K
Fees: Franchise - $3-6K
  Royalty: 3%, Advert: 2%
Contract Periods (Yrs.): 5
Area Development Agreement: Yes/2
Sub-Franchise Contract: . . . . .No
Expand in Territory: . . . . . . .No
Passive Ownership: . . . . .Allowed
Encourage Conversions: . . . . NA
Average # Employees: . . . . .5 PT

FRANCHISOR TRAINING/SUPPORT:
Financial Assistance Provided: . . . . .No
Site Selection Assistance: . . . . . . .NA
Lease Negotiation Assistance: . . . . .NA
Co-operative Advertising: . . . . . . .Yes
Training: . . . . 2 Days at Various
. . . . Locations
On-Going Support: a,b,d,G,H/ 1
EXPANSION PLANS:
US: . . . . Northwest and Northeast
Canada: . . . . .All Exc. Quebec
Overseas: . . . . Australia

DICTOGRAPH SECURITY SYSTEMS

21 Northfield Ave., P. O. Box 3017
Edison, NJ 08818
TEL: (800) 526-0672 (908) 225-4433
FAX: (908) 417-1945
Mr. Myles Goldberg, Sr. VP

Residential specialists - over 1 million installations nationwide. Company name established in 1902 - recently joined forces with Holmes Group, which has been in business since 1858. Proven training and marketing skills.

HISTORY: . . . . IFA
Established in 1902; . . 1st Franchised in 1948
Company-Owned Units (As of 8/31/1992): . .0
Franchised Units (As of 8/31/1992): . . . . . <u>48</u>
Total Units (As of 8/31/1992): 48
Projected New Units for 1993: 48
Distribution: US-45;Can-0;Overseas-3
  North America: . . . . 3 States
  Concentration: . . . .
Registered: . . . . . . Several in Registration
. . . . Process
Type Space: . . . . SF;~ SF

FINANCIAL: Earnings Claim: . .No
Cash Investment: $100K
Total Investment: $150K
Fees: Franchise - $25-35K
  Royalty: 6%, Advert: 0%
Contract Periods (Yrs.): 5/5
Area Development Agreement: . .No
Sub-Franchise Contract: . . . . .No
Expand in Territory: . . . . . . Yes
Passive Ownership: . . . Discouraged
Encourage Conversions: . . . . Yes
Average # Employees: . . . . . .7 FT

FRANCHISOR TRAINING/SUPPORT:
Financial Assistance Provided: . . . Yes(I)
Site Selection Assistance: . . . . . . .NA
Lease Negotiation Assistance: . . . . .No
Co-operative Advertising: . . . . . . .Yes
Training: . . . . . 1 Wk. Sales, 1 Wk. Tech-
. . . . . nical, 1 Wk General - All at HQ
On-Going Support: C,D,E,G,H,I/ 10
EXPANSION PLANS:
US: . . . . .All US
Canada: . . . . .No
Overseas: . . Caribbean, S. America, EUR

DYNAMARK SECURITY CENTERS

19833 Leitersburg Pike
Hagerstown, MD 21742
TEL: (800) 342-4243 (301) 797-2124
FAX: (301) 797-2189
Mr. Marcus Peters, Dir. Fran. Dev.

A specialist in the marketing, installation and monitoring of residential and commercial security systems. Only about 15% of homes are currently protected and forecasters predict tremendous industry growth. Franchisees also earn on-going income by linking their customers into our DYNAWATCH Central Monitoring Station.

HISTORY: . . . . IFA
Established in 1977; . . 1st Franchised in 1984
Company-Owned Units (As of 8/31/1992): . .0
Franchised Units (As of 8/31/1992): . . . . <u>115</u>
Total Units (As of 8/31/1992): 115
Projected New Units for 1993: 30
Distribution: US-115;Can-0;Overseas-0
  North America: . . . . 34 States
  Concentration: . 16 in PA, 11 in NY, 11 in VA
Registered: . . .CA,IL,IN,MD,MI,MN,NY,ND
. . . . RI,SD,VA,WA,WI
Type Space: . . . . . Small Office;~600 SF

FINANCIAL: Earnings Claim: . .No
Cash Investment: $20K
Total Investment: $42-46K
Fees: Franchise - $15K
  Royalty: $100/Mo., Advert: . . 1%
Contract Periods (Yrs.): 10/10
Area Development Agreement: . .No
Sub-Franchise Contract: . . . . .No
Expand in Territory: . . . . . . Yes
Passive Ownership: . . . Discouraged
Encourage Conversions: . . . . Yes
Average # Employees: . . 1 FT, 1 PT

FRANCHISOR TRAINING/SUPPORT:
Financial Assistance Provided: . . . . .No
Site Selection Assistance: . . . . . . .Yes
Lease Negotiation Assistance: . . . . .No
Co-operative Advertising: . . . . . . .No
Training: . . . . 1 Wk. Headquarters
. . . .
On-Going Support: C,D,E,F,G,H,I/ . . . 60
EXPANSION PLANS:
US: . . . . .All US
Canada: . . . . .All Canada
Overseas: . . . EUR, S. America, Far East

FIRE DEFENSE CENTERS

3919 Morton St.
Jacksonville, FL 32217
TEL: (904) 731-0244 (904) 731-1896
FAX:
Mr. I. A. La Russo, Mktg. Dir.

Sales and service of fire extinguishers, automatic restaurant hood systems, municipal supplies and first aid kits. Everything we sell, we service. Warranty on equipment sold to business and guarantee fire code compliance to business. Provide consultation for businesses to comply with city and state governments.

HISTORY:	FINANCIAL: Earnings Claim: . .No	FRANCHISOR TRAINING/SUPPORT:
Established in 1973; . . 1st Franchised in 1986	Cash Investment: $22-29K	Financial Assistance Provided: . . . . .Yes
Company-Owned Units (As of 8/31/1992): . .2	Total Investment: $22-29K	Site Selection Assistance: . . . . . . .Yes
Franchised Units (As of 8/31/1992): 18	Fees: Franchise - $13.5K	Lease Negotiation Assistance: . . . . .Yes
Total Units (As of 8/31/1992): 20	Royalty: 7%, Advert: 2%	Co-operative Advertising: . . . . . . .Yes
Projected New Units for 1993: 2	Contract Periods (Yrs.): . . .10/5	Training: . . . . . . 2 Wks. Headquarters
Distribution: US-20;Can-0;Overseas-0	Area Development Agreement: .No	
North America: . . . . .1 State	Sub-Franchise Contract: . . . . .No	On-Going Support: A,B,C,D,E,F,G,H,I/ 12
Concentration: . . . . .20 in FL	Expand in Territory: . . . . . . Yes	EXPANSION PLANS:
Registered: . . . . .IL,FL,NY	Passive Ownership: . . . Not Allowed	US: . . . . .All US
	Encourage Conversions: . . . . .No	Canada: . . . . .No
Type Space: . . . . . . Warehouse;~1,000 SF	Average # Employees: . . . . .2 FT	Overseas: . . . . No

PEOPLE'S SECURITY COMPANY

P. O. Box 467, Hwy. 371 North
Brainerd, MN 56401
TEL: (800) 735-1440 (218) 828-4828 C
FAX: (218) 829-2215
Mr. George G. Miller, Genl. Sales Mgr.

Full-service alarm company, providing sales, installation and personal emergency systems. Our primary market is residential and small to medium- sized commercial customers. We offer our basic security system for $195 installed and $19.95 per month. We are a subsidiary of Crow Wing Co-op Power and Light Co.

HISTORY:	FINANCIAL: Earnings Claim: . .No	FRANCHISOR TRAINING/SUPPORT:
Established in 1988; . . 1st Franchised in 1989	Cash Investment: . . . $28.9-48.5K	Financial Assistance Provided: . . . . .No
Company-Owned Units (As of 8/31/1992): . .1	Total Investment: . . . . $Varies	Site Selection Assistance: . . . . . . .NA
Franchised Units (As of 8/31/1992): 7	Fees: Franchise - . . .$12.5K Minimum	Lease Negotiation Assistance: . . . . . No
Total Units (As of 8/31/1992): 8	Royalty: 4%, Advert: 1%	Co-operative Advertising: . . . . No
Projected New Units for 1993: 6	Contract Periods (Yrs.): 20/20	Training: . . . . . . 5 Days/40 Hours HQ
Distribution: US-8;Can-0;Overseas-0	Area Development Agreement: .No	
North America: . . . . 2 States	Sub-Franchise Contract: . . . . . Yes	On-Going Support: a,B,D,f,g,H,I/ 8
Concentration: . . . . .7 in MN, 1 in ND	Expand in Territory: . . . . Yes	EXPANSION PLANS:
Registered: . . . . .MN,ND,SD,WI	Passive Ownership: . . . Discouraged	US: . . . . .All US
	Encourage Conversions: . . . . NA	Canada: . . . . No
Type Space: . . . . NA;~500 SF	Average # Employees: . . 2 FT, 2 PT	Overseas: . . . . No

PROFILES-Personnel and Security Risk Assessment

P. O. Box 880461
San Diego, CA 92168
TEL: (619) 280-3486
FAX: (619) 280-3486
Mr. Phil Sprague, President

Assess an applicant's past and their potential capabilities, attitudes, security risk, alcohol/drug usage, voice analysis for theft detection. From laborers to clerks to management. Asset or liability? Employers want to know. Make money by providing these valuable answers! Send for a demo disk (IBM 5 1/4").

HISTORY:	FINANCIAL: Earnings Claim: . Yes	FRANCHISOR TRAINING/SUPPORT:
Established in 1980; . . 1st Franchised in 1982	Cash Investment: $2-15K	Financial Assistance Provided: . . . Yes(I)
Company-Owned Units (As of 8/31/1992): . .1	Total Investment: $3-20K	Site Selection Assistance: . . . . . . .NA
Franchised Units (As of 8/31/1992): 5	Fees: Franchise - . . . .$	Lease Negotiation Assistance: . . . . . No
Total Units (As of 8/31/1992): 6	Royalty: 2-5%, Advert: 0%	Co-operative Advertising: . . . . .NA
Projected New Units for 1993: 2	Contract Periods (Yrs.): . . . 1-5/1-5	Training: . . . . . . 3-7 Days Headquarters
Distribution: US-6;Can-0;Overseas-0	Area Development Agreement: Yes/1-5	
North America: . . . . 4 States	Sub-Franchise Contract: . . . . .No	On-Going Support: A,G/ 2
Concentration:	Expand in Territory: . . . . . . Yes	EXPANSION PLANS:
Registered: . . . . CA	Passive Ownership: . . . Discouraged	US: . . . . .All US
	Encourage Conversions: . . . . NA	Canada: . . . . .All Canada
Type Space: . . . . Home Based;~ SF	Average # Employees: . . . . 1-2 FT	Overseas: . . . . No

SONITROL

424 N. Washington St.
Alexandria, VA 22314
TEL: (703) 549-3900
FAX: (703) 549-2053
Mr. Chris Cobb, COO

Franchised dealer is granted an area of primary responsibility where he is responsible for sales, installation, monitoring and service of SONITROL security systems for business and residential customers.

HISTORY: . . . . .CFA	
Established in 1960; . . 1st Franchised in 1965	
Company-Owned Units (As of 8/31/1992): . 17	
Franchised Units (As of 8/31/1992): 153	
Total Units (As of 8/31/1992): 170	
Projected New Units for 1993: 5	
Distribution: US-161;Can-3;Overseas-6	
North America: . . . . . 38 States, 1 Province	
Concentration: . . 22 in CA, 13 in FL, 12 in IN	
Registered: . . . . . CA,FL,IL,MD,MI,NY,VA	
. . . .	
Type Space: . . . .FS, Office, W/H;~3,000 SF	

FINANCIAL: Earnings Claim: . .No
Cash Investment: $125-500K
Total Investment: $250-900K
Fees: Franchise - $20-50K
 Royalty: 2.5%, Advert: 3%
Contract Periods (Yrs.): 10/10
Area Development Agreement: . .No
Sub-Franchise Contract: . . . . . Yes
Expand in Territory: . . . . . . Yes
Passive Ownership: . . . Discouraged
Encourage Conversions: . . . . . Yes
Average # Employees: . . . . . 15 FT

FRANCHISOR TRAINING/SUPPORT:
Financial Assistance Provided: . . . . . No
Site Selection Assistance: . . . . . . .Yes
Lease Negotiation Assistance: . . . . . No
Co-operative Advertising: . . . . .No
Training: . . . . 2 Wks. Headquarters,
 . . . . .1 Wk. On-Site
On-Going Support: b,C,d,E,G,h,I/ 9
EXPANSION PLANS:
US: . . . . .All US
Canada: . . . . .All Canada
Overseas: . . . . No

SUPPLEMENTAL LISTING OF FRANCHISORS

ALARMEFORCE INDUSTRIES . . . . 1370 Don Mills Rd., # 205, Don Mills, ON M3B 3N7 CAN
 Contact: Mr. Joel Matlin; Tel: (416) 445-2001
CHAMBERS FRANCHISED SECURITY SYSTEMS . . .1103 Fredericksburg Rd., San Antonio, TX 78201
 Contact: Mr. David Morris, President; Tel: (512) 736-2268
COUNTERFORCE ELECTRONIC SECURITY . . . . . . 1331 W. Central Blvd., Orlando, FL 32805
 Contact: President; Tel: (305) 849-6426
EMERGENCY 24 . . . . 4179 W. Irving Park Rd., Chicago, IL 60641
 Contact: Mr. Dante Monteverde, President; Tel: (312) 725-0222
EMPLOYMENT SCREENING SYSTEMS . . . . 2340 Industrial Blvd., Norman, OK 73069
 Contact: Mr. Ron Henderson, President; Tel: (800) 245-3550
FIREMASTER . . . . 520 Broadway, # 650, Santa Monica, CA 90401
 Contact: Mr. Ronald W. Bogardus, VP; Tel: (800) 944-3473
JADE SECURITY . . . . 137 1/2 Main, New Eagle, PA 15067
 Contact: President; Tel: (412) 258-8555
LOCKS & KEYS . . . . Woburn Mall, Woburn, MA 01801
 Contact: Mr. John Casey, President; Tel: (617) 933-9999
MY ALARM SECURITY RENTAL CENTER . . . . 3701 Hwy. 151 East, Marion, IA 52302
 Contact: Mr. William Ginalski, VP Fran. Dev.; Tel: (800) 835-5378 (319) 377-6343
OUT OF HARM'S WAY . . . . 35 International Blvd., Etobicoke, ON M9W 6H3 CAN
 Contact: Mr. Howard Rose; Tel: (416) 213-0180
RAMTRON PRE-ENTRY ALARM SYSTEMS . . . . . .A-1150 Waverley St., Winnipeg, MB R3T 0P4 CAN
 Contact: Mr. Barry C. Effler, Sec./Treas.; Tel: (800) 235-328) (204) 452-9900
SECURITY TECH/SECURITY TIME . . . . 1025 Gessner, Houston, TX 77055
 Contact: Mr. Bob Moutrie; Tel: (713) 465-8741

CHAPTER 48

SIGNS

AMERICAN SIGN SHOPS

208 Snow Ave.
Raleigh, NC 27603
TEL: (800) 966-2700 (919) 833-9200 C
FAX: (919) 834-5333
Ms. Gwen Richie, Mktg. Asst.

AMERICAN SIGN SHOPS is a computerized retail sign shop, using the latest technology in a low overhead environment. This low overhead and an efficient production system make AMERICAN SIGN SHOPS very profitable on sales.

HISTORY: . . . .
Established in 1985; . . 1st Franchised in 1987
Company-Owned Units (As of 8/31/1992): . .0
Franchised Units (As of 8/31/1992): 22
Total Units (As of 8/31/1992): 22
Projected New Units for 1993: 10
Distribution: US-22;Can-0;Overseas-0
  North America: . . . . 7 States
  Concentration: . . . 10 in NC, 6 in MI, 2 in PA
Registered: . . . . FL,MD,MI,VA
. . . .
Type Space: . . . . . . SC;~1,000-1,200 SF

FINANCIAL: Earnings Claim: . . .No
Cash Investment: $30-35K
Total Investment: $45-55K
Fees: Franchise - $15K
  Royalty: 6%, Advert: 0%
Contract Periods (Yrs.): . . . 10/10
Area Development Agreement: Yes/10
Sub-Franchise Contract: . . . . .No
Expand in Territory: . . . . . . .No
Passive Ownership: . . . Discouraged
Encourage Conversions: . . . . .No
Average # Employees: . . . . . .3 FT

FRANCHISOR TRAINING/SUPPORT:
Financial Assistance Provided: . . . Yes(I)
Site Selection Assistance: . . . . . . .Yes
Lease Negotiation Assistance: . . . . .Yes
Co-operative Advertising: . . . . .No
Training: . . . . .1 Wk. Headquarters,
. . . . .4 Days Store Location
On-Going Support: B,C,D,E,F,G,h,I/ . . . 5
EXPANSION PLANS:
US: . . . . .All US
Canada: . . . . .All Canada
Overseas: . . . Accepting Inquiries

ASI SIGN SYSTEMS

555 W. 25th St.
New York, NY 10001
TEL: (212) 675-8686
FAX: (212) 924-3110
Mr. Tim Jones, Natl. Sales Dir.

ASI franchisees manufacture and sell high-quality architectural signs and sign system planning services to a wide range of clients, including hotels, hospitals and corporate offices. Frequently working with architects and designers, franchisees furnish complete sign systems from exterior building identification through individual name plates.

HISTORY:	FINANCIAL: Earnings Claim: . .No	FRANCHISOR TRAINING/SUPPORT:
Established in 1977; . . 1st Franchised in 1978	Cash Investment: $125-175K	Financial Assistance Provided: . . . Yes(D)
Company-Owned Units (As of 8/31/1992): . .0	Total Investment: $125-175K	Site Selection Assistance: . . . . .Yes
Franchised Units (As of 8/31/1992): 34	Fees: Franchise - $50K	Lease Negotiation Assistance: . . . . .NA
Total Units (As of 8/31/1992): 34	Royalty: 5%, Advert: 1%	Co-operative Advertising: . . . . .No
Projected New Units for 1993: 2	Contract Periods (Yrs.): . . . 10/10	Training: . . . . 5 Days Headquarters,
Distribution: US-32;Can-2;Overseas-0	Area Development Agreement: . .No	. . . . 3 Days On-Site, On-Going
North America: . . . . 25 States, 2 Provinces	Sub-Franchise Contract: . . . . .No	On-Going Support: C,D,E,G,H,I/ 12
Concentration: . . . 3 in TX, 2 in PA, 2 in CA	Expand in Territory: . . . . Yes	EXPANSION PLANS:
Registered: . . . . NY	Passive Ownership: . . . Not Allowed	US: . . . . All US
. . . .	Encourage Conversions: . . . . . NA	Canada: . . . . .Quebec & Ontario
Type Space: . . . . Light Industrial;~5,000 SF	Average # Employees: . . 8 FT, 2 PT	Overseas: . . . .GR, IT, FR and SP

BEST INSTANT SIGN COMPANY

4301 N. Federal Hwy.
Ft. Lauderdale, FL 33308
TEL: (800) 545-2378 (305) 938-8448
FAX: (305) 938-4465
Mr. Orville C. Wright, President

Franchisor provides all the equipment, training and assistance necessary to become successful in this $5 billion a year growth industry. Franchisor is looking for franchisee teams with general business background, preferably in the areas of sales and marketing. Absolutely no computer, artistic or signage experience is required whatsoever!

HISTORY:	FINANCIAL: Earnings Claim: . .No	FRANCHISOR TRAINING/SUPPORT:
Established in 1990; . . 1st Franchised in 1991	Cash Investment: $40-50K	Financial Assistance Provided: . . . Yes(I)
Company-Owned Units (As of 8/31/1992): . .1	Total Investment: $88-105K	Site Selection Assistance: . . . . .Yes
Franchised Units (As of 8/31/1992): 61	Fees: Franchise - $20K	Lease Negotiation Assistance: . . . . .Yes
Total Units (As of 8/31/1992): 62	Royalty: 6%, Advert: . . . . . Flat	Co-operative Advertising: . . . . .NA
Projected New Units for 1993: 50	Contract Periods (Yrs.): 5/5	Training: . . . . 2 Wks. Headquarters
Distribution: US-2;Can-0;Overseas-60	Area Development Agreement: Yes/10	. . . .
North America: . . . . 2 States	Sub-Franchise Contract: . . . . . Yes	On-Going Support: A,B,C,D,E,F,G,H,I/ . 6
Concentration: . . . . 1 in FL, 1 in CA	Expand in Territory: . . . . Yes	EXPANSION PLANS:
Registered: . . . . .All	Passive Ownership: . . . Not Allowed	US: . . . . All US
. . . .	Encourage Conversions: . . . . . Yes	Canada: . . . . All Exc. Alberta
Type Space: . . . . .SC;~1,000 SF	Average # Employees: . . . . . .3 FT	Overseas: . EUR, MX, Orient, S. America

FASTSIGNS

4951 Airport Pkwy., # 530
Dallas, TX 75248
TEL: (800) 827-7446 (214) 702-0171
FAX: (214) 991-6058
Mr. Wes Jablonski

FASTSIGNS is the high-tech choice for transition from executive to entrepreneur in business-to-business industry marketing to corporate, professional and retail. Create top-quality signs, banners and vehicle graphics with computer technology, all in one day. Bright, attractive stores are located in retail centers.

HISTORY: . . . . IFA	FINANCIAL: Earnings Claim: . Yes	FRANCHISOR TRAINING/SUPPORT:
Established in 1985; . . 1st Franchised in 1986	Cash Investment: $40-50K	Financial Assistance Provided: . . . Yes(I)
Company-Owned Units (As of 8/31/1992): . .1	Total Investment: $112-162K	Site Selection Assistance: . . . . .Yes
Franchised Units (As of 8/31/1992): 171	Fees: Franchise - $20K	Lease Negotiation Assistance: . . . . .Yes
Total Units (As of 8/31/1992): 172	Royalty: 5.5%, Advert: 2%	Co-operative Advertising: . . . . .Yes
Projected New Units for 1993: 48	Contract Periods (Yrs.): 20/10	Training: . . . . 3 Wks. Headquarters
Distribution: US-167;Can-1;Overseas-5	Area Development Agreement: Yes/20	. . . .
North America: . . . . 35 States	Sub-Franchise Contract: . . . . . .No	On-Going Support: C,D,E,F,G,H,I/ . . . 30
Concentration: . . 27 in TX, 23 in CA, 12 in IL	Expand in Territory: . . . . .No	EXPANSION PLANS:
Registered: . . . . All States Exc. ND	Passive Ownership: . . . Not Allowed	US: . . . . All US
. . . .	Encourage Conversions: . . . . . .No	Canada: . . . . All Exc. Alberta
Type Space: . . . . . FS, SF, SC,;~1,200 SF	Average # Employees: . . . . . .5 FT	Overseas: . . . . W. EUR and S. America

HIGHTECH SIGNS

1806 Royal Ln.
Dallas, TX 75229
TEL: (800) 829-7446 (214) 869-9630 C
FAX: (214) 869-9542
Mr. Mike B. Hickey, VP Fran. Dev.

HIGHTECH SIGNS is a full-service franchisor, specializing in providing all sign products to business professionals, and utilizing the latest computer technology to create lettering and graphics for application to many surfaces. HIGHTECH SIGN CENTERS are located in high business density commercial parks.

HISTORY: . . . . IFA
Established in 1989; . . 1st Franchised in 1989
Company-Owned Units (As of 8/31/1992): . .0
Franchised Units (As of 8/31/1992): 86
Total Units (As of 8/31/1992): 86
Projected New Units for 1993: 40
Distribution: . . . US-71;Can-1;Overseas-14
North America: . . . . 23 States
Concentration: . . .18 in TX, 7 in GA, 4 in OH
Registered: . . . . .All
. . . .
Type Space: . . . . . Business Park;~1,800 SF

FINANCIAL: Earnings Claim: . .No
Cash Investment: $40-60K
Total Investment: $80-120K
Fees: Franchise - $21.5K
Royalty: 6%, Advert: 1%
Contract Periods (Yrs.): . . .10/5/5
Area Development Agreement: Yes/1-5
Sub-Franchise Contract: . . . . .No
Expand in Territory: . . . . . . Yes
Passive Ownership: . . . Not Allowed
Encourage Conversions: . . . . Yes
Average # Employees: . . 3 FT, 1 PT

FRANCHISOR TRAINING/SUPPORT:
Financial Assistance Provided: . . . Yes(I)
Site Selection Assistance: . . . . . . .Yes
Lease Negotiation Assistance: . . . .Yes
Co-operative Advertising: . . . . . . .Yes
Training: . . . . 2 Wks. Headquarters,
. . . . 1 Wk. Franchisee Location
On-Going Support: B,C,D,E,F,G,h,I/ . . 22
EXPANSION PLANS:
US: . . . . All US
Canada: . . . . .All Canada
Overseas: . . . . SP, MX, UK

KWIK SIGNS

P. O. Box 370
Marion, CT 06444
TEL: (203) 628-2440
FAX: (203) 621-7429
Mr. Mark Merrill, Sales Mgr.

A totally mobile, low overhead, computerized sign making business. No rent, no employees, no utilities, etc. Includes training, manuals, software updates, newsletters and sales materials.

HISTORY: . . . .
Established in 1986; . . 1st Franchised in 1987
Company-Owned Units (As of 8/31/1992): . .1
Franchised Units (As of 8/31/1992): 5
Total Units (As of 8/31/1992): 6
Projected New Units for 1993: 3
Distribution: US-6;Can-0;Overseas-0
North America: . . . . 2 States
Concentration: . . . . .CT, MA
Registered: . . . .
. . . .
Type Space: . . . . . . Mobile Unit;~NA SF

FINANCIAL: Earnings Claim: . .No
Cash Investment: $15K
Total Investment: $60-65K
Fees: Franchise - $15K
Royalty: 7-3%, Advert: 2%
Contract Periods (Yrs.): 5/5
Area Development Agreement: . .No
Sub-Franchise Contract: . . . . .No
Expand in Territory: . . . . . . Yes
Passive Ownership: . . . Discouraged
Encourage Conversions: . . . . NA
Average # Employees: . . . . .1 FT

FRANCHISOR TRAINING/SUPPORT:
Financial Assistance Provided: . . . Yes(I)
Site Selection Assistance: . . . . . . .NA
Lease Negotiation Assistance: . . . .Yes
Co-operative Advertising: . . . . . . .Yes
Training: . . . . .10 Sessions Headquarters,
. . . . 3 Sessions On-Site
On-Going Support: B,E,F,G,H,I/ 3
EXPANSION PLANS:
US: . . . . CT, MA and RI
Canada: . . . . .No
Overseas: . . . . No

NEXT DAY SIGNS

2234 S. Hamilton Rd.
Columbus, OH 43232
TEL: (800) 837-7446 (614) 575-9696
FAX: (614) 575-9699
Mr. Bill Williams

We are the most economical sign franchisor in the business. We offer a 2-week training period to make computer-generated signs, banners, vehicle graphics and lettering. We also teach you how to operate a successful business and offer on-going support as you need it.

HISTORY: . . . .
Established in 1989; . . 1st Franchised in 1989
Company-Owned Units (As of 8/31/1992): . .1
Franchised Units (As of 8/31/1992): 27
Total Units (As of 8/31/1992): 28
Projected New Units for 1993: 40
Distribution: US-28;Can-0;Overseas-0
North America: . . . . . . 13 States, incl. PR
Concentration: . . . .8 in OH, 6 in IN, 3 in CA
Registered: . . . . CA,FL,IL,IN,MI
. . . .
Type Space: . . . . .SF, SC;~1,200 SF

FINANCIAL: Earnings Claim: . .No
Cash Investment: $35-40K
Total Investment: $40-85K
Fees: Franchise - $10K
Royalty: 4%, Advert: 1%
Contract Periods (Yrs.): . . . 10/10
Area Development Agreement: Yes/1-5
Sub-Franchise Contract: . . . . Yes
Expand in Territory: . . . . . . Yes
Passive Ownership: . . . Discouraged
Encourage Conversions: . . . . Yes
Average # Employees: . . . . .3 FT

FRANCHISOR TRAINING/SUPPORT:
Financial Assistance Provided: . . . Yes(I)
Site Selection Assistance: . . . . . . .Yes
Lease Negotiation Assistance: . . . . .Yes
Co-operative Advertising: . . . . . . .Yes
Training: . . . . 2 Wks. Headquarters,
. . . . 3 Days Franchisee Store Site
On-Going Support: G,I/ 3
EXPANSION PLANS:
US: . . . . All US
Canada: . . . . .All Canada
Overseas: . . . . Yes

SIGN BIZ

15375 Barranca Pkwy., # J-108
Irvine, CA 92718
TEL: (800) 633-5580 (714) 727-4445
FAX: (714) 727-4467
Ms. Sherry Suffins, Natl. Sales Dir.

Fastest-growing sign network of full-service sign centers - using latest scanning and automated technology developed in-house. Strengths include direct marketing programs, business building programs, fully proven, national support network and full training.

HISTORY:	FINANCIAL: Earnings Claim: . .No	FRANCHISOR TRAINING/SUPPORT:
Established in 1989; . . 1st Franchised in 1990	Cash Investment: $39K	Financial Assistance Provided: . . . . .No
Company-Owned Units (As of 8/31/1992): . .0	Total Investment: $75-85K	Site Selection Assistance: . . . . . . .Yes
Franchised Units (As of 8/31/1992): 71	Fees: Franchise - $0	Lease Negotiation Assistance: . . . .Yes
Total Units (As of 8/31/1992): 71	Royalty: 0%, Advert: 0%	Co-operative Advertising: . . . . . . .No
Projected New Units for 1993: 30	Contract Periods (Yrs.):	Training: . . . . 6 Days Headquarters
Distribution: US-68;Can-1;Overseas-2	Area Development Agreement: . .No	
North America: . . . . 21 States	Sub-Franchise Contract: . . . . .No	On-Going Support: c,d,E,f,G,H,I/ 5
Concentration: . . . 24 in CA, 6 in FL, 5 in NJ	Expand in Territory: . . . . . . Yes	EXPANSION PLANS:
Registered:	Passive Ownership: . . . . .Allowed	US: . . . . .All US
. . . .	Encourage Conversions: . . . . Yes	Canada: . . . . .All Canada
Type Space: . . . . SF;~1,200-1,400 SF	Average # Employees: . . 4 FT, 2 PT	Overseas: . . . . Yes

SIGN EXPRESS

6 Clarke Circle, P. O. Box 309
Bethel, CT 06801
TEL: (800) 525-7446 (203) 791-0004
FAX: (203) 743-7028
Mr. John Schmuecker, President

SIGN EXPRESS is a computerized signmaking business. Customers include corporations, retail stores, real estate, professional, etc. It is not labor-intensive and does not require expensive retail space. SIGN EXPRESS is a great marketing opportunity and offers 3 weeks' training, 1 week at franchisee location, toll-free line and on- going support.

HISTORY: . . . . IFA	FINANCIAL: Earnings Claim: . .No	FRANCHISOR TRAINING/SUPPORT:
Established in 1985; . . 1st Franchised in 1988	Cash Investment: $50K	Financial Assistance Provided: . . . . .Yes
Company-Owned Units (As of 8/31/1992): . .0	Total Investment: $30-50K	Site Selection Assistance: . . . . . . .Yes
Franchised Units (As of 8/31/1992): 52	Fees: Franchise - $0	Lease Negotiation Assistance: . . . . .Yes
Total Units (As of 8/31/1992): 52	Royalty: Varies, Advert: 0%	Co-operative Advertising: . . . . . . .Yes
Projected New Units for 1993: 15	Contract Periods (Yrs.): 10/10	Training: . . . . 2 Wks. Headquarters,
Distribution: US-20;Can-0;Overseas-32	Area Development Agreement: Yes/10	. . . . 1 Wk. On-Site, 30 & 90 Day Visits
North America: . . . . 10 States	Sub-Franchise Contract: . . . . .No	On-Going Support: C,D,E,G,H,I/ 10
Concentration: . . . 5 in CT, 2 in OH, 2 in TN	Expand in Territory: . . . . . . Yes	EXPANSION PLANS:
Registered: . . . . . .All States Exc. ND & SD	Passive Ownership: . . . Discouraged	US: . . . . .All US
. . . .	Encourage Conversions: . . . . .No	Canada: . . . . .All Canada
Type Space: . . . . . SF, SC;~1,500-2,000 SF	Average # Employees: . . . . .3 FT	Overseas: . S. Amer., Pacific Rim,MX,BZ

SIGNERY, THE

1717 N. Naper Blvd., # 205
Naperville, IL 60563
TEL: (800) 695-4257 (708) 955-0700 C
FAX: (708) 955-0704
Mr. richard Gretz, President

THE SIGNERY shops are fully-formatted, computerized businesses serving primarily business customers of all sizes. THE SIGNERY specializes in wide variety, high quality and prompt service and delivery of its products. We offer extensive training and support services to our franchisees.

HISTORY: . . . . IFA	FINANCIAL: Earnings Claim: . .No	FRANCHISOR TRAINING/SUPPORT:
Established in 1986; . . 1st Franchised in 1986	Cash Investment: $75-80K	Financial Assistance Provided: . . . Yes(I)
Company-Owned Units (As of 8/31/1992): . .1	Total Investment: $100-110K	Site Selection Assistance: . . . . . . .Yes
Franchised Units (As of 8/31/1992): 40	Fees: Franchise - $21.5K	Lease Negotiation Assistance: . . . . .Yes
Total Units (As of 8/31/1992): 41	Royalty: 6%, Advert: 2%	Co-operative Advertising: . . . . . . .Yes
Projected New Units for 1993: 15	Contract Periods (Yrs.): 20/20	Training: . . . . 3 Wks. Headquarters,
Distribution: US-40;Can-0;Overseas-1	Area Development Agreement: Yes/Var	. . . . .1 Wk. In-Store
North America: . . . . 8 States	Sub-Franchise Contract: . . . . . .No	On-Going Support: C,D,E,G,H,I/ 5
Concentration: . . .26 in IL, 3 in WI, 2 in IA	Expand in Territory: . . . . . . Yes	EXPANSION PLANS:
Registered: . . . CA,FL,IL,IN,MD,MI,MN,OR	Passive Ownership: . . . Not Allowed	US: . . . . Midwest and East
. . . . VA,WI	Encourage Conversions: . . . . NA	Canada: . . . . .All Canada
Type Space: . . . . .SC;~1,200 SF	Average # Employees: . . . . . .3 FT	Overseas: . . . . Yes

SIGNS & MORE IN 24

1739 St. Mary's Ave.
Parkersburg, WV 26101
TEL: (800) 358-2358 (304) 424-7446
FAX: (304) 422-7449
Mr. Bruce Bronski, Owner

A sign franchise with a difference. Like other quick sign businesses, we do basic signs, banners, window and vehicle lettering. However, by expanding our lines to include residential and commercial back-lit awnings, complete electrical signage products and sophisticated architectural displays, we are able to offer a complete package of signage products in the marketplace. We also offer all franchise equipment and inventory at our cost.

HISTORY:	FINANCIAL: Earnings Claim: . .No	FRANCHISOR TRAINING/SUPPORT:
Established in 1991; . . 1st Franchised in 1992	Cash Investment: $20-40K	Financial Assistance Provided: . . . . .No
Company-Owned Units (As of 8/31/1992): . .1	Total Investment: $45-99K	Site Selection Assistance: . . . . . . .Yes
Franchised Units (As of 8/31/1992): 1	Fees: Franchise - $13K	Lease Negotiation Assistance: . . . .Yes
Total Units (As of 8/31/1992): 2	Royalty: 6%, Advert: 0%	Co-operative Advertising: . . . . .No
Projected New Units for 1993: 10	Contract Periods (Yrs.): . . . 10/10	Training: . . . . . .2 Wks. Training Center,
Distribution: US-2;Can-0;Overseas-0	Area Development Agreement: . .No	. . . . 1 Wk. On-Site
North America: . . . . 2 States	Sub-Franchise Contract: . . . . .No	On-Going Support: B,C,D,E,F,G,H,I/ . . . 3
Concentration: . . . . .1 in OH, 1 in WV	Expand in Territory: . . . . . Yes	EXPANSION PLANS:
Registered:	Passive Ownership: . . . . . .Allowed	US: . . . . .WV, PA, OH and KY
. . . .	Encourage Conversions: . . . . .No	Canada: . . . . .No
Type Space: . . . . .FS, SC;~1,500 SF	Average # Employees: . . 3 FT, 1 PT	Overseas: . . . . No

SIGNS FIRST

813 Ridge Lake Blvd., # 390
Memphis, TN 38120
TEL: (800) 852-2163 (901) 386-6631
FAX: (901) 388-0675
Mr. Mack Warr, CEO

SIGNS FIRST is a computerized sign shop focused on serving retail, commercial and professional customers. High-profile locations in retail centers offer convenience for both business customers and SIGNS FIRST owners during an 8-5 business day. Your SIGNS FIRST franchisor draws from over 20 years of experience of retail, walk- in sign shop ownership. SIGNS FIRST offers a turn-key operation featuring training and support.

HISTORY:	FINANCIAL: Earnings Claim: . .No	FRANCHISOR TRAINING/SUPPORT:
Established in 1966; . . 1st Franchised in 1989	Cash Investment: $18.8-67.7K	Financial Assistance Provided: . . . . .No
Company-Owned Units (As of 8/31/1992): . .0	Total Investment: $45.5-81.7K	Site Selection Assistance: . . . . . . .Yes
Franchised Units (As of 8/31/1992): 11	Fees: Franchise - $15K	Lease Negotiation Assistance: . . . .Yes
Total Units (As of 8/31/1992): 11	Royalty: 6%, Advert: 0%	Co-operative Advertising: . . . . . . .Yes
Projected New Units for 1993: 12	Contract Periods (Yrs.): . . . 10/10	Training: . . . . . 16 Days Headquarters,
Distribution: US-11;Can-0;Overseas-0	Area Development Agreement: Yes/10	. . . . 5 Days On-Site
North America: . . . . 3 States	Sub-Franchise Contract: . . . . .No	On-Going Support: C,D,E,H,I/ 4
Concentration: . . . 8 in TN, 2 in MS, 1 in AR	Expand in Territory: . . . . . . Yes	EXPANSION PLANS:
Registered: . . . . .FL	Passive Ownership: . . . Discouraged	US: . . . . Southeast
. . . .	Encourage Conversions: . . . . Yes	Canada: . . . . .No
Type Space: . . . . .SC;~1,400 SF	Average # Employees: . . 2 FT, 2 PT	Overseas: . . . . No

SIGNS NOW

P. O. Box 91688
Mobile, AL 36691
TEL: (800) 356-3373
FAX: (205) 661-4275
Mr. Randy Peake, Dir. Fran. Sales

Computerized sign shop with 24-hour turn-around; produces vinyl signs and lettering, including banners, real estate signs, vehicle lettering and graphics, building signs, window lettering, etc. Vinyl products guaranteed for 5 years against fading. Classroom and in-store training for franchisee and one key employee, assistance with site location, building, set-up, opening, advertising and complete on-going support.

HISTORY: . . . . .IFA	FINANCIAL: Earnings Claim: . Yes	FRANCHISOR TRAINING/SUPPORT:
Established in 1984; . . 1st Franchised in 1986	Cash Investment: $40-91K	Financial Assistance Provided: . . . Yes(I)
Company-Owned Units (As of 8/31/1992): . .2	Total Investment: $40-91K	Site Selection Assistance: . . . . . . .Yes
Franchised Units (As of 8/31/1992): 122	Fees: Franchise - $12K	Lease Negotiation Assistance: . . . .Yes
Total Units (As of 8/31/1992): 124	Royalty: 7%, Advert: 2%	Co-operative Advertising: . . . . . . .Yes
Projected New Units for 1993: 70	Contract Periods (Yrs.): . . . 5/5/5/5	Training: . . . . . .2 Wks. Training Center,
Distribution: US-124;Can-0;Overseas-0	Area Development Agreement: . Yes	. . . . 1 Wk. at Store
North America: . . . . 39 States	Sub-Franchise Contract: . . . . Yes	On-Going Support: A,B,C,D,E,F,G,H,I/ 16
Concentration: . . . 14 in FL, 7 in OR, 4 in MI	Expand in Territory: . . . . . . Yes	EXPANSION PLANS:
Registered: . . . CA,FL,HI,IL,IN,MD,MI,MN	Passive Ownership: . . . Discouraged	US: . . . . .All US
. . . . .NY,OR,RI,WA,WI	Encourage Conversions: . . . . .No	Canada: . . . . .All Canada
Type Space: . . . .;~ SF	Average # Employees: . . 1 FT, 1 PT	Overseas: . . . . Yes

SPEEDI-SIGN

P. O. Box 2882, 9 N. Fahm St.
Savannah, GA 31402
TEL: (800) 666-8007 (912) 651-8887 C
FAX: (912) 651-8887
Ms. Karen M. Sills, Mktg. Dir.

Computerized sign shop - provides vinyl-lettered signs and banners for commercial and retail businesses and also to individuals. Package includes equipment, supplies and training to start a retail sign shop. Add-on packages available for paper signs, screen printing, sandblasting and engraving.

HISTORY:	FINANCIAL: Earnings Claim: . .No	FRANCHISOR TRAINING/SUPPORT:
Established in 1987; . . 1st Franchised in 1989	Cash Investment: $25-65K	Financial Assistance Provided: . . . Yes(I)
Company-Owned Units (As of 8/31/1992): . .2	Total Investment: . . . . $65K+	Site Selection Assistance: . . . . . . .Yes
Franchised Units (As of 8/31/1992): 16	Fees: Franchise - $15.5K	Lease Negotiation Assistance: . . . . .Yes
Total Units (As of 8/31/1992): 18	Royalty: 0%, Advert: 0%	Co-operative Advertising: . . . . . . .NA
Projected New Units for 1993: 25	Contract Periods (Yrs.): 5/5	Training: . . . . 10 Working Days Head-
Distribution: US-17;Can-0;Overseas-1	Area Development Agreement: . .No	. . . . quarters
North America: . . . . 10 States	Sub-Franchise Contract: . . . . .No	On-Going Support: C,D,E,G,H,I/ 11
Concentration: . . . 3 in FL, 3 in GA, 2 in NC	Expand in Territory: . . . . . . .No	EXPANSION PLANS:
Registered: . . . CA,FL,IL,IN.MI.MN.NY,ND	Passive Ownership: . . . Discouraged	US: . . . . .All US
. . . . OR,RI,SD,VA,WI,DC	Encourage Conversions: . . . . NA	Canada: . . . . All Exc. Alberta
Type Space: . . . . . . FS, SF, SC;~1,000 SF	Average # Employees: . . 2 FT, 1 PT	Overseas: . . . . No

SPEEDY SIGN-A-RAMA, USA

3450 Northlake Blvd., # 203
Palm Beach Gardens, FL 33403
TEL: (800) 776-8105 (407) 624-8110
FAX: (407) 624-8117
Mr. Raymond Titus, VP

A full-service sign business in a retail format that combines today's technology with one of the largest franchise networks available. There is financing available, copyrighted software and 12 regional offices throughout the US that provide local back-up and support for all SPEEDY SIGN-A-RAMA, USA outlets. Entrepreneur ranked SPEEDY SIGN-A-RAMA, USA #1 in 1990 and 1991.

HISTORY:	FINANCIAL: Earnings Claim: . .No	FRANCHISOR TRAINING/SUPPORT:
Established in 1986; . . 1st Franchised in 1987	Cash Investment: $33-47K	Financial Assistance Provided: . . . Yes(I)
Company-Owned Units (As of 8/31/1992): . .2	Total Investment: $90-120K	Site Selection Assistance: . . . . . . .Yes
Franchised Units (As of 8/31/1992): 144	Fees: Franchise - $29.5K	Lease Negotiation Assistance: . . . . .Yes
Total Units (As of 8/31/1992): 146	Royalty: 6%, Advert: 0%	Co-operative Advertising: . . . . . . .NA
Projected New Units for 1993: 30	Contract Periods (Yrs.): 35/35	Training: . . . . 2 Wks. Headquarters,
Distribution: US-146;Can-0;Overseas-0	Area Development Agreement: . .No	. . . . .2 Wks. On Location
North America: . . . . 21 States	Sub-Franchise Contract: . . . . .No	On-Going Support: B,C,D,E,G,H,I/ . . . 40
Concentration: . . . . .CA, FL, NY	Expand in Territory: . . . . . . .No	EXPANSION PLANS:
Registered: . . . . . . All States Exc. HI & OR	Passive Ownership: . . . Discouraged	US: . . . . .All US
. . . .	Encourage Conversions: . . . . NA	Canada: . . . . .No
Type Space: . . . . . SF, SC;~1,000-1,200 SF	Average # Employees: . . . . 2-3 FT	Overseas: . . . . No

VINYLGRAPHICS SAME DAY SIGNS

1733 Keele St.
Toronto, ON M6M 3W7 CAN
TEL: (800) 265-7446 (416) 656-9988
FAX: (416) 656-3676
Mr. Glenn Kerekes, President

VINYLGRAPHICS is a Canadian franchisor of custom sign centres that offers interior/exterior signage, window lettering, vehicle and boat decoration, magnetic signs and more, to today's business community. The lettering for the signs is generated utilizing state-of-the-art technology and proven vinyl films.

HISTORY:	FINANCIAL: Earnings Claim: . .No	FRANCHISOR TRAINING/SUPPORT:
Established in 1960; . . 1st Franchised in 1990	Cash Investment: $40K	Financial Assistance Provided: . . . Yes(I)
Company-Owned Units (As of 8/31/1992): . .1	Total Investment: $85K	Site Selection Assistance: . . . . . . .Yes
Franchised Units (As of 8/31/1992): 6	Fees: Franchise - $25K	Lease Negotiation Assistance: . . . . .Yes
Total Units (As of 8/31/1992): 7	Royalty: 8%, Advert: 0%	Co-operative Advertising: . . . . . . .Yes
Projected New Units for 1993: 12	Contract Periods (Yrs.): 5/5/5	Training: . . . . 4 Wks. Headquarters
Distribution: US-0;Can-7;Overseas-0	Area Development Agreement: Yes/10	. . . .
North America: . . . . .1 Province	Sub-Franchise Contract: . . . . .No	On-Going Support: a,B,C,D,e,F,G,H,I/ . . 8
Concentration: . . . . 7 in ON	Expand in Territory: . . . . Yes	EXPANSION PLANS:
Registered: . . . . CA	Passive Ownership: . . . Discouraged	US: . . . . .All US
. . . .	Encourage Conversions: . . . . NA	Canada: . . . . .All Canada
Type Space: . . . . .SC;~1,500 SF	Average # Employees: . . . . . .2 FT	Overseas: . . . . . .AU, EUR, Asia

SUPPLEMENTAL LISTING OF FRANCHISORS

OUTDOOR FUN SIGNS . . . . 138 River Corner Rd., Conestoga, PA 17516
        Contact: Ms. Dianne Shiffer, Owner; Tel: (717) 872-6916
PERMASIGN . . . . 2000 Powell St., # 1290, Emeryville, CA 94608
        Contact: President; Tel:
SIGNS BY TOMORROW . . . . .6460 Dobbin Rd., Columbia, MD 21045
        Contact: Ms. Valerie Maione; Tel: (800) 336-4610 (410) 992-7192
SIGNS TO GO . . . . 2433 Montgomery Hwy., Dothan, AL 36303
        Contact: Mr. John Collins, President; Tel: (205) 793-3236

> For a full explanation of the data provided in the Franchisor Format, please refer to Chapter 2,
>
> *"How To Use The Data."*

CHAPTER 49

TRAVEL

**ADMIRAL OF THE FLEET
CRUISE CENTERS**
3430 Pacific Ave. SE, # A-5
Olympia, WA 98501
TEL: (800) 877-7447 (206) 866-7447
FAX: (206) 438-1191
Mr. Bob L. Lovely, CEO

Cruising is the fastest-growing segment of the travel business - and the most profitable. We provide a unique approach to the retail selling of cruises with an emphasis on professionalism and quality service. It's also fun, because "Cruising is our Only Business!"

HISTORY: . . . .
Established in 1986;   . . 1st Franchised in 1986
Company-Owned Units (As of 8/31/1992):   . .5
Franchised Units (As of 8/31/1992): 3
Total Units (As of 8/31/1992): 8
Projected New Units for 1993: 2
Distribution: US-7;Can-0;Overseas-0
  North America: . . . . 4 States
  Concentration: . . . 4 in WA, 3 in WI, 1 in TX
Registered: . . . . .NY,WA
. . . .
Type Space: . . . . .SC;~1,500 SF

FINANCIAL: Earnings Claim: . .No
Cash Investment: $50-75K
Total Investment: $100-150K
Fees: Franchise - $25K
  Royalty: 5%, Advert: 1%
Contract Periods (Yrs.): 15/5
Area Development Agreement: . .No
Sub-Franchise Contract: . . . . .No
Expand in Territory: . . . . . . .No
Passive Ownership: . . . Not Allowed
Encourage Conversions: . . . . .No
Average # Employees: . . 3 FT, 2 PT

FRANCHISOR TRAINING/SUPPORT:
Financial Assistance Provided: . . . . . No
Site Selection Assistance: . . . . .Yes
Lease Negotiation Assistance: . . . . .Yes
Co-operative Advertising: . . . . .NA
Training: . . . . . . 1-2 Wks. Headquarters,
   . . . 1 Wk. On-Site, Free Cruise Seminar
On-Going Support: B,C,D,E,G,H/   . . . . .
EXPANSION PLANS:
  US: . . . . . . .Pacific Coast & Northeast
  Canada: . . . . .No
  Overseas: . . . . No

CRUISE HOLIDAYS INTERNATIONAL

9089 Clairemont Mesa Blvd., # 306
San Diego, CA 92123
TEL: (800) 866-7245 (619) 279-4780
FAX: (619) 279-4788
Ms. Jackie Wessel, Dir. Fran. Sales

Largest franchisor of cruise-only travel agencies. No inventory, easy to operate. Marketing and advertising programs available at no cost. On- going negotiations with major cruise lines for group pricing.

HISTORY: . . . . IFA	FINANCIAL: Earnings Claim: . .No	FRANCHISOR TRAINING/SUPPORT:
Established in 1984; . . 1st Franchised in 1985	Cash Investment: $100K	Financial Assistance Provided: . . . . .No
Company-Owned Units (As of 8/31/1992): . .1	Total Investment: . . . .$	Site Selection Assistance: . . . . . . .Yes
Franchised Units (As of 8/31/1992): 136	Fees: Franchise - $25K	Lease Negotiation Assistance: . . . . .Yes
Total Units (As of 8/31/1992): 137	Royalty: 1%, Advert: 0%	Co-operative Advertising: . . . . . . .Yes
Projected New Units for 1993: 40	Contract Periods (Yrs.): . 7/Ongoing	Training: . . . . 2 Wks. Headquarters,
Distribution: . . . US-94;Can-41;Overseas-2	Area Development Agreement: . .No	. . . . 1 Wk. Cruise Ship
North America: . . . . 26 States, 5 Provinces	Sub-Franchise Contract: . . . . . .No	On-Going Support: B,C,D,E,G,H,I/ . . . 25
Concentration: . 38 in CA, 19 in BC, 13 in ON	Expand in Territory: . . . . Yes	EXPANSION PLANS:
Registered: . . . CA,FL,IL,IN,MD,MI,MN,NY	Passive Ownership: . . . Discouraged	US: . . . . All US
. . . . OR,VA,WA,WI,AB	Encourage Conversions: . . . . . Yes	Canada: . . . . .All Canada
Type Space: . . . . SC;~800-1,000 SF	Average # Employees: . . . . .2 FT	Overseas: . . . . No

CRUISE LINES RESERVATION CENTER

9229 Kaufman Place
Brooklyn, NY 11236
TEL: (718) 763-4259
FAX:
Mr. Bernard Korn, President

Cruise only travel agency.

HISTORY:	FINANCIAL: Earnings Claim: . .No	FRANCHISOR TRAINING/SUPPORT:
Established in 1989; . . 1st Franchised in 1990	Cash Investment: $1-2K	Financial Assistance Provided: . . . . .No
Company-Owned Units (As of 8/31/1992): . .1	Total Investment: $2-3K	Site Selection Assistance: . . . . . . .No
Franchised Units (As of 8/31/1992): 24	Fees: Franchise - . . . . $.5-1K	Lease Negotiation Assistance: . . . . .No
Total Units (As of 8/31/1992): 25	Royalty: 1%, Advert: 0%	Co-operative Advertising: . . . . . . .Yes
Projected New Units for 1993: 50	Contract Periods (Yrs.): 10/10	Training: . . . . 1 Day Headquarters
Distribution: US-25;Can-0;Overseas-0	Area Development Agreement: Yes/20	. . . .
North America: . . . . .1 State	Sub-Franchise Contract: . . . . . Yes	On-Going Support: a,b,c,d,e,f,g,h,i/ . . . 10
Concentration: . . . . 25 in NY	Expand in Territory: . . . . Yes	EXPANSION PLANS:
Registered: . . . . NY	Passive Ownership: . . . . . .Allowed	US: . . . . All US
. . . .	Encourage Conversions: . . . . . Yes	Canada: . . . . .Yes
Type Space: . . . . . Home Based;~100 SF	Average # Employees: . . . . . .1 FT	Overseas: . . . . No

GOLIGER'S TRAVEL

201 - 40 St. Clair Ave. W.
Toronto, ON M4V 1M2 CAN
TEL: (416) 926-0814 C
FAX: (416) 926-9120
Mr. David Snutch

Full-service travel agencies, serving the Canadian corporate and vacation traveler for over 35 years. We offer a unique system of fixed royalty fees and comprehensive training. An exciting "lifestyle" franchise in the world's largest single industry.

HISTORY: . . . . .CFA	FINANCIAL: Earnings Claim: . .No	FRANCHISOR TRAINING/SUPPORT:
Established in 1955; . . 1st Franchised in 1979	Cash Investment: $80K	Financial Assistance Provided: . . . . .Yes
Company-Owned Units (As of 8/31/1992): . .5	Total Investment: $180K	Site Selection Assistance: . . . . . . .Yes
Franchised Units (As of 8/31/1992): 75	Fees: Franchise - $50K	Lease Negotiation Assistance: . . . .Yes
Total Units (As of 8/31/1992): 80	Royalty: Flat, Advert: . . . . . Flat	Co-operative Advertising: . . . . . . .Yes
Projected New Units for 1993: 9	Contract Periods (Yrs.): 10/5	Training: . . . . 2 Wks. Headquarters,
Distribution: US-0;Can-80;Overseas-0	Area Development Agreement: Yes/10+	. . . . 1 Wk. HQ, On-Going Support
North America: . . . . 9 Provinces	Sub-Franchise Contract: . . . . . Yes	On-Going Support: B,C,D,E,G,h,i/ . . . 12
Concentration: . .57 in ON, 6 in BC, 5 in AB	Expand in Territory: . . . . Yes	EXPANSION PLANS:
Registered: . . . . AB	Passive Ownership: . . . Discouraged	US: . . . . No
. . . .	Encourage Conversions: . . . . . Yes	Canada: . . . . .All Canada
Type Space: . . . . ;~ SF	Average # Employees: . . 2 FT, 1 PT	Overseas: . . . . No

INTERNATIONAL TOURS

5810 E. Skelly Dr., # 400
Tulsa, OK 74135
TEL: (800) 777-9691 (918) 665-2300
FAX: (918) 665-6644
Mr. Ron Blaylock, President

Retail travel agency franchisor. Start-up and conversion units. Training, site location, overall direction of new franchisees, training manuals, open house assistance, on-site training, budget and accounting package, preferred supplier program, airline agreement and special cruise program.

HISTORY: . . . .
Established in 1968; . . 1st Franchised in 1970
Company-Owned Units (As of 8/31/1992): . .0
Franchised Units (As of 8/31/1992): 367
Total Units (As of 8/31/1992): 443
Projected New Units for 1993: 89
Distribution: US-367;Can-76;Overseas-0
  North America: . . . . 43 States, 9 Provinces
  Concentration: . 35 in TX, 13 in MO, 11 in KS
Registered: . . . . All Except HI
. . . .
Type Space: . . . . .FS, SF, SC, RM;~750 SF

FINANCIAL: Earnings Claim: . .No
Cash Investment: $25-75K
Total Investment: $100-175K
Fees: Franchise - $34.5K
  Royalty: $275-700, Advert: . . 0%
Contract Periods (Yrs.): 20/25
Area Development Agreement: Yes/1-5
Sub-Franchise Contract: . . . . .No
Expand in Territory: . . . . . . Yes
Passive Ownership: . . . Not Allowed
Encourage Conversions: . . . . Yes
Average # Employees: . . 4 FT, 2 PT

FRANCHISOR TRAINING/SUPPORT:
Financial Assistance Provided: . . . . No
Site Selection Assistance: . . . . . . .Yes
Lease Negotiation Assistance: . . . .Yes
Co-operative Advertising: . . . . .No
Training: . . . . . 3 1/2 Days HQ, 6 Wks.
  . . Training School, 7 Days Agency Loc.
On-Going Support: B,C,D,E,h,I/ 10
EXPANSION PLANS:
US: . . . . .All US
Canada: . . . . .All Canada
Overseas: . . . . .Yes

OTTAWA ALGONQUIN TRAVEL

657 Bronson Ave.
Ottawa, ON K1S 4E7 CAN
TEL: (613) 233-7713 C
FAX: (613) 233-7805
Nr. Ronald C. Greenwood, President

Our mission is to be the dominant travel agency organization in each market in which we are active. This enables us to maximize our advertising, promotion value-added programs, exclusive products, supplier revenues and franchisee profitability. We are the service-oriented department store of travel-related services in each market. Our average sales level per store is substantially higher than the industry average.

HISTORY: . . . . .CFA
Established in 1964; . . 1st Franchised in 1978
Company-Owned Units (As of 8/31/1992): . .2
Franchised Units (As of 8/31/1992): 51
Total Units (As of 8/31/1992): 53
Projected New Units for 1993: 12
Distribution: US-0;Can-53;Overseas-0
  North America: . . . . 3 Provinces
  Concentration: . . 46 in ON, 5 in MB, 3 in PQ
Registered: . . . .
. . . .
Type Space: . . . . RM;~600 SF

FINANCIAL: Earnings Claim: . .No
Cash Investment: $35-100K
Total Investment: $75-200K
Fees: Franchise - $25-35K
  Royalty: 3-9% GP, Advert: 1-5% GP
Contract Periods (Yrs.): . . . 5/5/5/5
Area Development Agreement: . .No
Sub-Franchise Contract: . . . . .No
Expand in Territory: . . . . . . Yes
Passive Ownership: . . . Not Allowed
Encourage Conversions: . . . . Yes
Average # Employees: . 5 FT, 1-2 PT

FRANCHISOR TRAINING/SUPPORT:
Financial Assistance Provided: . . . . .Yes
Site Selection Assistance: . . . . . . .Yes
Lease Negotiation Assistance: . . . . .Yes
Co-operative Advertising: . . . . . . .Yes
Training: . . . . 3 Wks. Headquarters
. . . .
On-Going Support: A,B,C,D,E,G,h,i/ . . 10
EXPANSION PLANS:
US: . . . . .No
Canada: . . . . .All Canada
Overseas: . . . . No

TIX TRAVEL & TICKET AGENCY

48 Burd St., # 203
Nyack-on-Hudson, NY 10960
TEL: (800) TRAVTIX (914) 358-1007
FAX: (800) 2-FAXTIX
Mr. Rich Klein, President

Full-service travel agency, featuring tickets to Sold Out Events worldwide (concerts, sports, theatre), i.e. Super Bowl, US Open, World Series, Kentucky Derby, Phantom of the Opera, Springsteen, etc.

HISTORY: . . . .
Established in 1980; . . 1st Franchised in 1992
Company-Owned Units (As of 8/31/1992): . .1
Franchised Units (As of 8/31/1992): 200
Total Units (As of 8/31/1992): 201
Projected New Units for 1993: 50
Distribution: US-201;Can-0;Overseas-0
  North America: . . . .
  Concentration: . . . .
Registered: . . . .
. . . .
Type Space: . . . . . . Home/Office;~NA SF

FINANCIAL: Earnings Claim: . .No
Cash Investment: . . . . . . $.8-2.5K
Total Investment: . . . . . . $.8-2.5K
Fees: Franchise - . . . . . . $.8-2.5K
  Royalty: % of Com, Advert: . . 0%
Contract Periods (Yrs.): . . . .
Area Development Agreement: . .No
Sub-Franchise Contract: . . . . .No
Expand in Territory: . . . . . . Yes
Passive Ownership: . . . . . .Allowed
Encourage Conversions: . . . .
Average # Employees: . . . . . .1 PT

FRANCHISOR TRAINING/SUPPORT:
Financial Assistance Provided: . . . . .No
Site Selection Assistance: . . . . . . .NA
Lease Negotiation Assistance: . . . . .NA
Co-operative Advertising: . . . . . . .Yes
Training: . . . . Manuals
. . . .
On-Going Support: G,H/ 3
EXPANSION PLANS:
US: . . . . .All US
Canada: . . . . .All Canada
Overseas: . . . . .EUR, AU

TRAVEL AGENTS INTERNATIONAL

111 Second Ave. NE, 15th Fl.
St. Petersburg, FL 33731
TEL: (800) 678-8241 (813) 894-1537
FAX: (813) 894-6318
Mr. C. Glynn Culver, SVP

TRAVEL AGENTS INTERNATIONAL is the leading US-based franchisor of retail travel agencies. The franchise package establishes a professional look, uniform and integrated system and quality control program. It translates to a strong support system for franchise owners and professional-level travel services for the public.

HISTORY:	IFA
Established in 1980; 1st Franchised in 1982	
Company-Owned Units (As of 8/31/1992):	3
Franchised Units (As of 8/31/1992):	380
Total Units (As of 8/31/1992):	383
Projected New Units for 1993:	43
Distribution:	US-340;Can-43;Overseas-0
North America:	40 States, 7 Provinces
Concentration:	25 in CA, 25 in FL, 29in ON
Registered:	All
Type Space:	SC, RM;~800-1,200 SF

FINANCIAL: Earnings Claim:	No
Cash Investment:	$80-110K
Total Investment:	$80-110K
Fees: Franchise -	$44.5K
Royalty: $500/Mo., Advert: $75/Mo.	
Contract Periods (Yrs.):	15
Area Development Agreement:	Yes/10
Sub-Franchise Contract:	No
Expand in Territory:	Yes
Passive Ownership:	Allowed
Encourage Conversions:	Yes
Average # Employees:	3 FT, 1 PT

FRANCHISOR TRAINING/SUPPORT:
Financial Assistance Provided: Yes(D)
Site Selection Assistance: Yes
Lease Negotiation Assistance: Yes
Co-operative Advertising: Yes
Training: 2 Wks. Headquarters, 1 Wk. Houston Computer Training
On-Going Support: A,B,C,D,E,G,H,I/ 92
EXPANSION PLANS:
US: All US
Canada: All Canada
Overseas: No

TRAVEL AGENTS INTERNATIONAL OF CANADA

175 - 5945 Airport Rd.
Mississauga, ON L4V 1R9 CAN
TEL: (800) 234-8241 (416) 671-4114
FAX: (416) 673-3327
Mr. Ash Mukherjee, President/CEO

We have every tool you need to compete effectively in your market place. If you have faith in yourself, you will fall in the 97% of our franchisees who succeed. Call our franchisees. Call theirs before you decide.

HISTORY:	
Established in 1980; 1st Franchised in 1980	
Company-Owned Units (As of 8/31/1992):	1
Franchised Units (As of 8/31/1992):	35
Total Units (As of 8/31/1992):	36
Projected New Units for 1993:	10
Distribution:	US-0;Can-36;Overseas-0
North America:	8 Provinces
Concentration:	26 in ON, 4 in BC, 4 in AB
Registered:	AB
Type Space:	SF, SC, RM;~700 SF

FINANCIAL: Earnings Claim:	Yes
Cash Investment:	$44.5K
Total Investment:	$85K
Fees: Franchise -	$34.5K
Royalty: $385/Mo., Advert: $175/Mo.	
Contract Periods (Yrs.):	10/10
Area Development Agreement:	Yes
Sub-Franchise Contract:	Yes
Expand in Territory:	Yes
Passive Ownership:	Discouraged
Encourage Conversions:	Yes
Average # Employees:	3 FT

FRANCHISOR TRAINING/SUPPORT:
Financial Assistance Provided: Yes(D)
Site Selection Assistance: Yes
Lease Negotiation Assistance: Yes
Co-operative Advertising: Yes
Training: 2 Wks. St. Petersburg, FL 1 Wk. Toronto or Dallas
On-Going Support: A,B,C,D,E,F,G,H,I/ 9
EXPANSION PLANS:
US: Parent Company in US
Canada: All Canada
Overseas: GR, Middle East

TRAVEL NETWORK

560 Sylvan Ave.
Englewood Cliffs, NJ 07632
TEL: (800) TRAV-NET (201) 567-8500 C
FAX: (201) 567-4405
Mr. Michael Y. Brent, COO

Complete start-up assistance (site selection, lease negotiations, staffing, industry accreditation, bonding, store furnishing package, 4-week intensive front-end training), accounting package, complete computerization, on-going, continuous support and training programs locally, on-site in field, plus regional/national meetings/trainings, strong saturated marketing program, high commissions earnings program.

HISTORY:	IFA
Established in 1982; 1st Franchised in 1982	
Company-Owned Units (As of 8/31/1992):	1
Franchised Units (As of 8/31/1992):	249
Total Units (As of 8/31/1992):	250
Projected New Units for 1993:	50
Distribution:	US-232;Can-0;Overseas-18
North America:	32 States, 2 Provinces
Concentration:	30 in NJ, 24 in CA, 20 in NY
Registered:	CA,FL,HI,IL,MD,MI,MN,NY OR,VA,WA,WI,DC
Type Space:	SF, SC;~800-1,000 SF

FINANCIAL: Earnings Claim:	No
Cash Investment:	$45-60K
Total Investment:	$85-100K
Fees: Franchise -	$29.9K
Royalty: Fixed, Advert: $200/Mo.	
Contract Periods (Yrs.):	15/10
Area Development Agreement:	Yes/20
Sub-Franchise Contract:	Yes
Expand in Territory:	Yes
Passive Ownership:	Discouraged
Encourage Conversions:	Yes
Average # Employees:	4 FT, 6 PT

FRANCHISOR TRAINING/SUPPORT:
Financial Assistance Provided: Yes(I)
Site Selection Assistance: Yes
Lease Negotiation Assistance: Yes
Co-operative Advertising: Yes
Training: 1 Wk. NJ, 1 Wk. FL, 1 Wk. TX, 1 Wk. On-Site
On-Going Support: a,B,C,D,E,F,F,G,H,I/ 18
EXPANSION PLANS:
US: All US
Canada: All Canada
Overseas: Yes

TRAVEL PROFESSIONALS INTERNATIONAL

10172 Linn Station Rd., # 360
Louisville, KY 40223
TEL: (800) 626-2469 (502) 423-9900
FAX: (502) 423-9914
Mr. John E. Boyce, Dir. Fran. Sales

A network of full-service travel agencies, founded by agency owners and operators. We provide marketing and sales support and assistance in day- to-day operations. Training is continuous. We have programs designed to allow our agencies to increase their commission potential, and decrease their costs of operations.

HISTORY:	FINANCIAL: Earnings Claim: . .No	FRANCHISOR TRAINING/SUPPORT:
Established in 1982; . . 1st Franchised in 1983	Cash Investment: $75K	Financial Assistance Provided: . . . . .No
Company-Owned Units (As of 8/31/1992): . .1	Total Investment: $100K	Site Selection Assistance: . . . . . . .Yes
Franchised Units (As of 8/31/1992): 51	Fees: Franchise - $11.5-33K	Lease Negotiation Assistance: . . . . .Yes
Total Units (As of 8/31/1992): 52	Royalty: 1-5%, Advert: . . $150/Qtr	Co-operative Advertising: . . . . .Yes
Projected New Units for 1993: 15	Contract Periods (Yrs.): 10/10	Training: . . . . 2 Days HQ - Owners,
Distribution: US-52;Can-0;Overseas-0	Area Development Agreement: . Yes	. . 2 Days HQ - Managers, 10 Days Field
North America: . . . . 20 States	Sub-Franchise Contract: . . . . .No	On-Going Support: A,B,C,D,E,F,G,H,i/ 30
Concentration: . . . 15 in KY, 7 in FL, 5 in AL	Expand in Territory: . . . . . . Yes	EXPANSION PLANS:
Registered: . . . . .CA,FL,IL,MD,VA,WA,WI	Passive Ownership: . . . Discouraged	US: . . . . .All US
. . . .	Encourage Conversions: . . . . . Yes	Canada: . . . . .No
Type Space: . . . . ;~900 Min. SF	Average # Employees: . . 2 FT, 2 PT	Overseas: . . . . No

TRAVEL PROS

3001 N. Rocky Pt. Rd. NE, # 160
Tampa, FL 33607
TEL: (813) 281-5670
FAX: (813) 281-2304
Mr. Bernhard Benet, President

TRAVEL PROS specializes in setting up persons with no prior travel experience in the field of highly lucrative international air and tours. No license or bond or qualified manager needed. Extremely high commissions.

HISTORY:	FINANCIAL: Earnings Claim: . .No	FRANCHISOR TRAINING/SUPPORT:
Established in 1986; . . 1st Franchised in 1989	Cash Investment: $9-15K	Financial Assistance Provided: . . . . .No
Company-Owned Units (As of 8/31/1992): . .1	Total Investment: $15-50K	Site Selection Assistance: . . . . No
Franchised Units (As of 8/31/1992): 300	Fees: Franchise - $9-15K	Lease Negotiation Assistance: . . . . No
Total Units (As of 8/31/1992): 301	Royalty: $500/Mo., Advert: . . 0%	Co-operative Advertising: . . . . No
Projected New Units for 1993: 100	Contract Periods (Yrs.): 5/5	Training: . . . . 2 Days On-Site,
Distribution: US-301;Can-0;Overseas-0	Area Development Agreement: . .No	. . . . .1 Wk. Kansas City
North America: . . . . 30 States	Sub-Franchise Contract: . . . . .No	On-Going Support: A,B,C,D,e,g,H/ 4
Concentration:	Expand in Territory: . . . . . . Yes	EXPANSION PLANS:
Registered: . . . . All States	Passive Ownership: . . . . . .Allowed	US: . . . . .All US
. . . .	Encourage Conversions: . . . . . Yes	Canada: . . . . .All Canada
Type Space: . . . . ;~500 SF	Average # Employees: . . 1 FT, 1 PT	Overseas: . . . . Yes

TRAVELPLEX INTERNATIONAL

655 Metro Pl. S., # 250
Dublin, OH 43017
TEL: (800) 221-9581 (614) 766-6315
FAX: (614) 766-0540
Mr. Darryl Warner, President

Retail travel agency franchise organization, specializing in business and vacation travel arrangements. This unique franchise has been created by working agency owner-managers. A comprehensive training program is provided for all staff levels. TRAVELPLEX INTERNATIONAL provides recruitment services and productive office procedures. Franchisees receive: sales and marketing programs, operational support and effective networking with member agencies.

HISTORY:	FINANCIAL: Earnings Claim: . .No	FRANCHISOR TRAINING/SUPPORT:
Established in 1984; . . 1st Franchised in 1989	Cash Investment: $50K	Financial Assistance Provided: . . . Yes(I)
Company-Owned Units (As of 8/31/1992): . .0	Total Investment: $70-100K	Site Selection Assistance: . . . . . . .Yes
Franchised Units (As of 8/31/1992): 15	Fees: Franchise - $30.9K	Lease Negotiation Assistance: . . . . .Yes
Total Units (As of 8/31/1992): 15	Royalty$400/Mo., Advert: $400/Mo.	Co-operative Advertising: . . . . .Yes
Projected New Units for 1993: 5	Contract Periods (Yrs.): 10/10	Training: . . . . .1 Wk. Headquarters,
Distribution: US-15;Can-0;Overseas-0	Area Development Agreement: Yes/10	. . . . Up to 2 Wks. On-Site
North America: . . . . 4 States	Sub-Franchise Contract: . . . . .No	On-Going Support: b,C,D,E,g,H,I/ 5
Concentration: . . . 7 in OH, 2 in KY, 2 in MO	Expand in Territory: . . . . . . Yes	EXPANSION PLANS:
Registered: . . . . CA,WI	Passive Ownership: . . . Discouraged	US: . . . . .All US
. . . .	Encourage Conversions: . . . . Yes	Canada: . . . . .No
Type Space: SF, SC, Off. Bldg;~1,200-1,800 SF	Average # Employees: . . 4 FT, 2 PT	Overseas: . . . . No

UNIGLOBE TRAVEL (INTERNATIONAL)
1199 W. Pender St., # 900
Vancouver, BC V6E 2R1 CAN
TEL: (604) 662-3800 C
FAX: (604) 662-3878
Ms. Suzanne Kauss, VP Corp. Comm.

A UNIGLOBE franchise owner receives a vast array of services: national TV advertising, brand image, profitability software programs, on-going business consultation, one-to-one agency visits, owners/managers meetings, preferred override programs, plus over 125 days of training/month system-wide, all to get a competitive edge on the travel market. Come and join the #1 travel franchisor in the world.

HISTORY: . . . . IFA
Established in 1980; . . 1st Franchised in 1980
Company-Owned Units (As of 8/31/1992): . .0
Franchised Units (As of 8/31/1992): 767
Total Units (As of 8/31/1992): 767
Projected New Units for 1993: 400
Distribution: . . US-601;Can-134;Overseas-32
  North America: . . . . 47 States,10 Provinces
  Concentration: . .116 in CA, 59 in ON, 55 OH
Registered: . . . . .All
. . . .
Type Space: . . . . Office Building;~1,000 SF

FINANCIAL: Earnings Claim: . .No
Cash Investment: $2.5-60K
Total Investment: $2.5-150K
Fees: Franchise - $47K
  Royalty: 1/2-5%, Advert: . . . $706
Contract Periods (Yrs.): 10/5
Area Development Agreement: . .No
Sub-Franchise Contract: . . . . . Yes
Expand in Territory: . . . . Yes
Passive Ownership: . . . Discouraged
Encourage Conversions: . . . . . Yes
Average # Employees: . . . . 5-7 FT

FRANCHISOR TRAINING/SUPPORT:
Financial Assistance Provided: . . . . .No
Site Selection Assistance: . . . . .Yes
Lease Negotiation Assistance: . . . . .Yes
Co-operative Advertising: . . . . .Yes
Training: . . . . 4 Days Headquarters,
. . . . .Weekly at Regional Centers
On-Going Support: B,C,D,E,G,h,i/ . . . 25
EXPANSION PLANS:
US: . . . . All US
Canada: . . . . .All Canada
Overseas: . .W. EUR, JA, MX, AU

SUPPLEMENTAL LISTING OF FRANCHISORS

CRUISE COMPANY . . . . .2121 4th St., Peru, IL 61354
  Contact: President; Tel: (815) 223-2700
CRUISE OF A LIFETIME USA . . . . .237 Park Ave., 21st Fl., New York, NY 10017
  Contact: Ms. Emilie Zilnicki, Chairman; Tel: (516) 829-SAIL
EMPRESS TRAVEL . . . . 450 Harmon Meadow Blvd., # 1568, Secaucus, NJ 07096
  Contact: Mr. Jack Cygielman, President; Tel: (201) 617-8513
FUGAZY INTERNATIONAL . . . . 717 Fifth Ave., New York, NY 10022
  Contact: President; Tel: (212) 838-7577
GALAXSEA CRUISES . . . . .1400 E. Oakland Park Blvd., # 216, Ft. Lauderdale, FL 33334
  Contact: Ms. Lois Jean Utt, Dir. Ops.; Tel: (800) 821-1072 (305) 564-7072
HARTLEY VACATION CENTERS . . . . P. O. Box 6286, Providence, RI 02940
  Contact: President; Tel: (401) 726-8100
INTERNATIONAL TOURS . . . . .5810 E. Skelly Dr., # 400, Tulsa, OK 74135
  Contact: Mr. Ron Blaylock, President; Tel: (800) 777-9691 (918) 665-2300
MILLION AIR CANADA . . . . .Toronto-Buttonville Airport, Markham, ON L3P 3J9   CAN
  Contact: President; Tel: (416) 477-8000
NEW CREATION WORLDWIDE CRUISE . . . . P. O. Box 574837, Orlando, FL 32857
  Contact: President; Tel: (305) 671-3224
PAL TRAVEL INTERNATIONAL . . . . 3321 Forest Dr., # 7, Columbia, SC 29204
  Contact: Mr. Rick Palyok; Tel: (803) 738-8710
STA TRAVEL . . . . 17 East 45th St., New York, NY 10017
  Contact: President; Tel: (212) 986-9470
TRAVELHOST TRAVEL AGENCIES . . . . .8080 N. Central Expy., # 1450, Dallas, TX 75206
  Contact: Mr. Dawson Granade; Tel: (214) 691-1163

CHAPTER 50

MISCELLANEOUS

ADVANCED TECHNOLOGY SPECIALISTS
Rte. 9, Box 534, Hi-Tech Center
Crossville, TN 38555
TEL: (800) 548-5927 (615) 484-5577
FAX:
Mr. Ric Ordway, Owner

ADVANCED TECHNOLOGY SPECIALISTS has cleaning and preventive products for all electronic equipment. We have training videos to train personnel to do in-house cleaning and maintenance of all electronic equipment. This will save you money on service calls that are unnecessary.

HISTORY: . . . .
Established in 1986;   . . 1st Franchised in 1991
Company-Owned Units (As of 8/31/1992):   . .1
Franchised Units (As of 8/31/1992): 0
Total Units (As of 8/31/1992): 1
Projected New Units for 1993: . . . .
Distribution: US-1;Can-0;Overseas-0
 North America: . . . . .1 State
 Concentration: . . . . 1 in TN
Registered: . . . .
 . . . .
Type Space: . . . . Home Based;~ SF

FINANCIAL: Earnings Claim: . Yes
Cash Investment: $10-20K
Total Investment: . . . . $20K+
Fees: Franchise - $9.9K
 Royalty: 3%, Advert: 1%
Contract Periods (Yrs.): 10/10
Area Development Agreement: . . .
Sub-Franchise Contract: . . . . . .No
Expand in Territory: . . . .
Passive Ownership: . . . . . .Allowed
Encourage Conversions: . . . . .No
Average # Employees: . . . . . .1 FT

FRANCHISOR TRAINING/SUPPORT:
Financial Assistance Provided: . . . . .NA
Site Selection Assistance: . . . . .NA
Lease Negotiation Assistance: . . . . .NA
Co-operative Advertising: . . . . .Yes
Training: . . . . . . 3-5 Days Headquarters,
 . . . . . .Additional Sessions As Needed
On-Going Support: b,C,d,f,G,h,I/ 2
EXPANSION PLANS:
US: . . . . All US
Canada: . . . . .No
Overseas: . . . . No

AIR BROOK LIMOUSINE

Box 123
Rochelle Park, NJ 07662
TEL: (201) 843-6100
FAX: (201) 368-2247
Mr. Conrad Rehill, Fran. Dir.

Ground transportation.

HISTORY:	FINANCIAL: Earnings Claim: . .No	FRANCHISOR TRAINING/SUPPORT:
Established in 1969; . . 1st Franchised in 1971	Cash Investment: $4.5K	Financial Assistance Provided: . . .Yes(D)
Company-Owned Units (As of 8/31/1992): . 25	Total Investment: $10.8-16K	Site Selection Assistance: . . . . .NA
Franchised Units (As of 8/31/1992): 100	Fees: Franchise - $7.5-12.5K	Lease Negotiation Assistance: . . . . .NA
Total Units (As of 8/31/1992): 125	Royalty: 40%, Advert: 0%	Co-operative Advertising: . . . . .NA
Projected New Units for 1993: 25	Contract Periods (Yrs.): 10/10	Training: . . . . . 5 Days Rochelle Park, NJ
Distribution: US-125;Can-0;Overseas-0	Area Development Agreement: . .No	. . . . .No Charge
North America: . . . . .1 State	Sub-Franchise Contract: . . . . .No	On-Going Support: A,B,C,D,G,H,I/ . . 75
Concentration: . . . . 125 in NJ	Expand in Territory: . . . . . . .No	EXPANSION PLANS:
Registered:	Passive Ownership: . . . . .Allowed	US: . . . . NJ Only
. . . .	Encourage Conversions: . . . . . NA	Canada: . . . . .No
Type Space: . . . . ;~NA SF	Average # Employees: . . . . . .1 PT	Overseas: . . . . No

AMERICAN RECYCLING

2150 E. Lake Cook Rd., # 350
Buffalo Grove, IL 60089
TEL: (800) 732-9256 (708) 215-7600
FAX: (708) 215-7666
Mr. Harvey Matarasso, VP Sales

AMERICAN RECYCLING franchises provide recycling of aluminum and non-ferrous metals to the general public and private industry. The first franchise to address the growing recycling movement by offering a solution to America's rising environmental concern.

HISTORY: . . . . IFA	FINANCIAL: Earnings Claim: . . Yes	FRANCHISOR TRAINING/SUPPORT:
Established in 1991; . . 1st Franchised in 1991	Cash Investment: $60-100K	Financial Assistance Provided: . . . . No
Company-Owned Units (As of 8/31/1992): . .2	Total Investment: $7.3-123K	Site Selection Assistance: . . . . .Yes
Franchised Units (As of 8/31/1992): 2	Fees: Franchise - $25K	Lease Negotiation Assistance: . . . . .Yes
Total Units (As of 8/31/1992): 4	Royalty: 7%, Advert: 1%	Co-operative Advertising: . . . . .No
Projected New Units for 1993: 15	Contract Periods (Yrs.): 5/15	Training: . . .3 Days HQ, 3 Wks. Company
Distribution: US-4;Can-0;Overseas-0	Area Development Agreement: . .No	. . . . Operation, 3 Wks. Franchisee Site
North America: . . . . .1 State	Sub-Franchise Contract: . . . . .No	On-Going Support: B,C,D,E,F,I/ 5
Concentration: . . . . .4 in IL	Expand in Territory: . . . . . . .No	EXPANSION PLANS:
Registered: IL	Passive Ownership: . . . . . .Allowed	US: . . . . .Illinois Only
. . . .	Encourage Conversions: . . . . . .No	Canada: . . . . .No
Type Space: . . . . FS;~2,500 SF	Average # Employees: . . 2 FT, 1 PT	Overseas: . . . . No

ARMOLOY CORPORATION

1325 Sycamore Rd.
DeKalb, IL 60115
TEL: (815) 758-6657 C
FAX: (815) 758-0268
Mr. Jerome Bejbl, President

Unique, proprietary chromium alloy metal surface finishing process that extends wear-life, corrosion resistance and improves friction reducing characteristics to all ferrous and non-ferrous finished machine and equipment parts.

HISTORY:	FINANCIAL: Earnings Claim: . Yes	FRANCHISOR TRAINING/SUPPORT:
Established in 1957; . . 1st Franchised in 1969	Cash Investment: $50-100K	Financial Assistance Provided: . . . . .No
Company-Owned Units (As of 8/31/1992): . .2	Total Investment: $250-350K	Site Selection Assistance: . . . . . . .Yes
Franchised Units (As of 8/31/1992): 9	Fees: Franchise - . . . . $50K+	Lease Negotiation Assistance: . . . . .Yes
Total Units (As of 8/31/1992): 11	Royalty: 7%, Advert: 1%	Co-operative Advertising: . . . . .Yes
Projected New Units for 1993: 1	Contract Periods (Yrs.): 15/5	Training: . . . . . 4-6 Wks. Headquarters +
Distribution: US-8;Can-0;Overseas-3	Area Development Agreement: . .No	. . . . As Required at Plant Site
North America: . . . . 7 States	Sub-Franchise Contract: . . . . .No	On-Going Support: C,D,E,F,H,I/ 6
Concentration:	Expand in Territory: . . . . . . Yes	EXPANSION PLANS:
Registered: . . . . .All	Passive Ownership: . . . Discouraged	US: . . . . All US
. . . .	Encourage Conversions: . . . . . .No	Canada: . . . . .All Canada
Type Space: . . . . FS;~ SF	Average # Employees: . . 3 FT, 2 PT	Overseas: . . . . Yes

ATLANTIC MOWER PARTS SUPPLY

13421 SW 14 Pl.
Ft. Lauderdale, FL 33325
TEL: (305) 474-4942
FAX: (305) 475-0414
Mr. Robert J. Bettelli, President

Lawn mower replacement after-market. Parts for national brands (Snapper, Toro, MTD, Murray, etc.).

HISTORY:	FINANCIAL: Earnings Claim: . .No	FRANCHISOR TRAINING/SUPPORT:
Established in 1978; . . 1st Franchised in 1988	Cash Investment: $45K	Financial Assistance Provided: . . . . . No
Company-Owned Units (As of 8/31/1992): . .0	Total Investment: $45K	Site Selection Assistance: . . . . . . .Yes
Franchised Units (As of 8/31/1992): 14	Fees: Franchise - $15.9K	Lease Negotiation Assistance: . . . . .Yes
Total Units (As of 8/31/1992): 14	Royalty: 5%, Advert: 1/2%	Co-operative Advertising: . . . . .No
Projected New Units for 1993: 4	Contract Periods (Yrs.): . . 10/10/10	Training: . . . . 5 Days Headquarters,
Distribution: US-14;Can-0;Overseas-0	Area Development Agreement: Yes/1	. . . . .5 Days Franchisee Area
North America: . . . . 2 States	Sub-Franchise Contract: . . . . Yes	On-Going Support: B,C,D,E/ 3
Concentration: . . . . .Ct, FL	Expand in Territory: . . . . . . Yes	EXPANSION PLANS:
Registered: . . . . .FL	Passive Ownership: . . . . . .Allowed	US: . . . . All US
. . . .	Encourage Conversions: . . . . Yes	Canada: . . . . .No
Type Space: . . . . Warehouse;~250 SF	Average # Employees: . . . . . .1 FT	Overseas: . . . . No

CROWN TROPHY

1 Odell Plaza
Yonkers, NY 10701
TEL: (800) 227-1557 (914) 963-0005
FAX: (914) 963-0181
Mr. Chuck Weisenfeld, President

We provide you with the buying and marketing power of a large corporation and, most of all, the experience of successful leaders in the awards industry. All work is done on premises with state-of-the-art computer engraving equipment.

HISTORY:	FINANCIAL: Earnings Claim: . .No	FRANCHISOR TRAINING/SUPPORT:
Established in 1978; . . 1st Franchised in 1986	Cash Investment: $50K	Financial Assistance Provided: . . . Yes(I)
Company-Owned Units (As of 8/31/1992): . .2	Total Investment: $60-68K	Site Selection Assistance: . . . . . . .Yes
Franchised Units (As of 8/31/1992): 17	Fees: Franchise - $15K	Lease Negotiation Assistance: . . . .Yes
Total Units (As of 8/31/1992): 19	Royalty: 4%, Advert:	Co-operative Advertising: . . . . . . .Yes
Projected New Units for 1993: 5	Contract Periods (Yrs.): 10/5	Training: . . . . 2 Wks. Headquarters,
Distribution: US-19;Can-0;Overseas-0	Area Development Agreement: .No	. . . . .1 Wk. On-Site
North America: . . . . 6 States	Sub-Franchise Contract: . . . . .No	On-Going Support: B,C,D,E,F,H,I/ . . . 10
Concentration: . . . 10 in NY, 3 in NJ, 2 in CT	Expand in Territory: . . . . . . Yes	EXPANSION PLANS:
Registered: . . . . FL,MD,NY,RI	Passive Ownership: . . . Discouraged	US: . . . . .Northeast and South
. . . .	Encourage Conversions: .No	Canada: . . . . .No
Type Space: . . . . SF;~1,000 SF	Average # Employees: . . 1 FT, 2 PT	Overseas: . . . . No

CUSTOM ETCH INTERNATIONAL

520 W. Hwy. 436, # 1180
Altamonte Springs, CA 32714
TEL: (800) 288-ETCH (407) 774-0800 C
FAX: (407) 774-8103
Mr. K. J. Wari, President

We offer a system to custom etch glass items on a commercial level. Our system provides a step-by-step procedure to glass engraving, including making the mask needed for any type of design. No special skills required. Computer knowledge is helpful.

HISTORY:	FINANCIAL: Earnings Claim: . .No	FRANCHISOR TRAINING/SUPPORT:
Established in 1992; . . 1st Franchised in 1992	Cash Investment: $25K	Financial Assistance Provided: . . . Yes(I)
Company-Owned Units (As of 8/31/1992): . .1	Total Investment: . . . . . . $+/- 50K	Site Selection Assistance: . . . . . . .Yes
Franchised Units (As of 8/31/1992): 1	Fees: Franchise - $20K	Lease Negotiation Assistance: . . . .Yes
Total Units (As of 8/31/1992): 2	Royalty: $3.00, Advert: . . . $2.00	Co-operative Advertising: . . . . . . .NA
Projected New Units for 1993: 6	Contract Periods (Yrs.): 10/10	Training: . . . . 2 Wks. On-Site
Distribution: US-2;Can-0;Overseas-0	Area Development Agreement: Yes/5	. . . .
North America: . . . . .1 State	Sub-Franchise Contract: . . . . .No	On-Going Support: C,D,E,F,G,H,I/ 5
Concentration: . . . . 2 in FL	Expand in Territory: . . . . . . Yes	EXPANSION PLANS:
Registered: . . . . .FL	Passive Ownership: . . . Not Allowed	US: . . . . Southeast
. . . .	Encourage Conversions: . . . . Yes	Canada: . . . . .No
Type Space: . . . . SC;~+/- 1,000 SF	Average # Employees: . . . . . .2 FT	Overseas: . . . . No

DIAL-A-GIFT

2265 E. 4800 S.
Salt Lake City, UT 84117
TEL: (800) 453-0428 (801) 278-0413
FAX: (801) 278-0449
Mr. Clarence Jolley, President

DIAL-A-GIFT is an international gift wire service that operates much like the flower-by-phone or wire services. Local and international delivery of fruit baskets, gourmet foods, cheeses, wines, candies, meats, cakes, balloons, etc. through a network of 4,000 franchisees and dealers.

HISTORY:	FINANCIAL: Earnings Claim: . .No	FRANCHISOR TRAINING/SUPPORT:
Established in 1980; . . 1st Franchised in 1984	Cash Investment: $20-50K	Financial Assistance Provided: . . . . .Yes
Company-Owned Units (As of 8/31/1992): . .1	Total Investment: $20-50K	Site Selection Assistance: . . . . . . .Yes
Franchised Units (As of 8/31/1992): 50	Fees: Franchise - $10K	Lease Negotiation Assistance: . . . .Yes
Total Units (As of 8/31/1992): 51	Royalty: 4%, Advert: . . $100/Mo.	Co-operative Advertising: . . . . . .No
Projected New Units for 1993: 100	Contract Periods (Yrs.): . . . Perpetual	Training: . . . . 3 Days Headquarters,
Distribution: US-11;Can-40;Overseas-0	Area Development Agreement: . .No	. . . . 1-2 Wks. Franchisee Store
North America:	Sub-Franchise Contract: . . . . . .No	On-Going Support: A,B,D,G,H,I/ 15
Concentration:	Expand in Territory: . . . . Yes	EXPANSION PLANS:
Registered: . . . . .All	Passive Ownership: . . . . . .Allowed	US: . . . . All US
. . . .	Encourage Conversions: . . . . Yes	Canada: . . . . .All Canada
Type Space: . . . Mall Kiosks;~800-1,200 SF	Average # Employees: . 2 FT, 1-8 PT	Overseas: . . . . .Yes

EVERYTHING FOR A DOLLAR STORE

3075 14th Ave., # 226
Markhan, ON L3R 0G9 CAN
TEL: (416) 513-6744
FAX: (416) 513-6746
Mr. Allan Pancer, Dir. Fran.

An innovative retail merchandising concept designed to provide customers with excellent value in a broad cross-section of household products. All items are priced at $1.00, 2 for $2.00 or 3 for $3.00. Our product range consists of daily household items such as household cleaning supplies, personal care and beauty products, candy and confectionery items, toys, games and giftware and office and school supplies.

HISTORY:	FINANCIAL: Earnings Claim: . . Yes	FRANCHISOR TRAINING/SUPPORT:
Established in 1985; . . 1st Franchised in 1990	Cash Investment: $150K	Financial Assistance Provided: . . . Yes(I)
Company-Owned Units (As of 8/31/1992): . 10	Total Investment: $225K	Site Selection Assistance: . . . . . . .Yes
Franchised Units (As of 8/31/1992): 8	Fees: Franchise - $25K	Lease Negotiation Assistance: . . . .Yes
Total Units (As of 8/31/1992): 18	Royalty: 8%, Advert: 1.5%	Co-operative Advertising: . . . . . . .Yes
Projected New Units for 1993: 30	Contract Periods (Yrs.): 10/2-5	Training: . . . . . .6 Wks. Franchisee Store
Distribution: US-0;Can-18;Overseas-0	Area Development Agreement: . .No	. . . .
North America: . . . . 3 Provinces	Sub-Franchise Contract: . . . . . .No	On-Going Support: B,C,D,E,F,H/ . . . . . .
Concentration: . .14 in ON, 4 in AB, 1 in NB	Expand in Territory: . . . . Yes	EXPANSION PLANS:
Registered:	Passive Ownership: . . . Discouraged	US: . . . . No
. . . .	Encourage Conversions: . . . . Yes	Canada: . . . . .All Canada
Type Space: . . . . .SC, RM;~2,000-3,000 SF	Average # Employees: . . 2 FT, 3 PT	Overseas: . . . . No

FILTERFRESH

Trimex Bldg., Route 11
Mooers, NY 12958
TEL: (800) 463-9754 (514) 676-3819
FAX: (514) 676-1210
Mr. Ted Baracos, VP Mktg.

High-tech office coffee service, using a patented single-cup coffeemaker. FILTERFRESH brews coffee by-the-cup from fresh-ground coffee in seconds. Choice exclusive territories are available. The FILTERFRESH franchise provides access to patented equipment, detailed training in sales and service, on-going support and supply services.

HISTORY: . . . . IFA	FINANCIAL: Earnings Claim: . .No	FRANCHISOR TRAINING/SUPPORT:
Established in 1986; . . 1st Franchised in 1987	Cash Investment: $200K	Financial Assistance Provided: . . . .
Company-Owned Units (As of 8/31/1992): . .0	Total Investment: $500K	Site Selection Assistance: . . . . . . .NA
Franchised Units (As of 8/31/1992): 29	Fees: Franchise - $24.5K	Lease Negotiation Assistance: . . . . .No
Total Units (As of 8/31/1992): 29	Royalty: 5%, Advert: 2%	Co-operative Advertising: . . . . . . .Yes
Projected New Units for 1993: 8	Contract Periods (Yrs.): 10/10	Training: . . . . 8 Days Headquarters,
Distribution: US-29;Can-0;Overseas-0	Area Development Agreement: . .No	. . .3-4 Days On-Site, On-Going Site
North America: . . . . 15 States	Sub-Franchise Contract: . . . . . .No	On-Going Support: A,B,C,D,E,F,G,H,I/ . 10
Concentration: . . . .5 in NY, 3 in NJ, 3 in CA	Expand in Territory: . . . . Yes	EXPANSION PLANS:
Registered: . . . CA,FL,IL,IN,MD,MI,MN,NY	Passive Ownership: . . . Not Allowed	US: . . . . .West and Southwest
. . . . OR,RI,VA,WA	Encourage Conversions: . . . . . NA	Canada: . . . . .No
Type Space: . . . . . . Warehouse;~1,800 SF	Average # Employees: . . 4 FT, 2 PT	Overseas: . . . . No

JACAL LIGHTING MAINTENANCE

6465 Millcreek Dr., # 205
Mississauga, ON L5N 5R3 CAN
TEL: (800) 387-8335 (416) 567-4180
FAX: (416) 567-5335
Mr. George Kostopoulos

Wholesale distributors of industrial and commercial lighting and related products. Our services include washing, relamping and repairing both indoor and outdoor lighting fixtures and illuminated signs. Our sales include an assortment of industrial and commercial light bulbs, tubes, fixtures and accessories. Everything necessary to maintain our customers' lighting systems in good working order.

HISTORY: . . . .
Established in 1978; . . 1st Franchised in 1990
Company-Owned Units (As of 8/31/1992): . .1
Franchised Units (As of 8/31/1992): 1
Total Units (As of 8/31/1992): 2
Projected New Units for 1993: 10
Distribution: US-0;Can-2;Overseas-0
 North America: . . . . .1 Province
 Concentration: . . . . 2 in ON
Registered: . . . .
. . . .
Type Space: . . . . ;~ SF

FINANCIAL: Earnings Claim: . . Yes
Cash Investment: $20-30K
Total Investment: $35-57.5K
Fees: Franchise - $20K
 Royalty: 5%, Advert: 1%
Contract Periods (Yrs.): 10/5/5
Area Development Agreement: . .No
Sub-Franchise Contract: . . . . .No
Expand in Territory: . . . . . . Yes
Passive Ownership: . . . Not Allowed
Encourage Conversions: . . . . NA
Average # Employees: . . . . 1-2 FT

FRANCHISOR TRAINING/SUPPORT:
Financial Assistance Provided: . . . Yes(I)
Site Selection Assistance: . . . . Yes
Lease Negotiation Assistance: . . . .NA
Co-operative Advertising: . . . . . . .Yes
Training: . . . . . 1 Wk. Classroom at HQ,
. . . . 1 Wk. Practical
On-Going Support: B,D,F,H/ . . . .
EXPANSION PLANS:
US: . . . . No
Canada: . . . . .Ontario
Overseas: . . . . No

JUNIOR SALES CLUB

Box 13876
St. John's, NF A1B 4G7 CAN
TEL: (709) 745-3054
FAX:
Mr. Melvin Slade, Owner

Small office or home-based gift and novelty business. Our marketing program recruits junior salespeople who sell to family, friends and neighbors. As a franchisee, you can expect to run this very profitable franchise from your home or small office.

HISTORY: . . . .
Established in 1988; . . 1st Franchised in 1992
Company-Owned Units (As of 8/31/1992): . .1
Franchised Units (As of 8/31/1992): 0
Total Units (As of 8/31/1992): 1
Projected New Units for 1993: 20
Distribution: US-0;Can-1;Overseas-0
 North America: . . . . .1 Province
 Concentration: . . . . 1 in NF
Registered: . . . .
. . . .
Type Space: . . . . . . Home Based;~200 SF

FINANCIAL: Earnings Claim: . .No
Cash Investment: . . . . $3K+
Total Investment: . . . . $3K+
Fees: Franchise - . . . . $1K+
 Royalty: 10%, Advert: 0%
Contract Periods (Yrs.): 3/3
Area Development Agreement: . .No
Sub-Franchise Contract: . . . . .No
Expand in Territory: . . . . . . Yes
Passive Ownership: . . . . . .Allowed
Encourage Conversions: . . . . .No
Average # Employees: . . . . .1 FT

FRANCHISOR TRAINING/SUPPORT:
Financial Assistance Provided: . . . . .Yes
Site Selection Assistance: . . . . No
Lease Negotiation Assistance: . . . . .No
Co-operative Advertising: . . . . No
Training: . . . . 2 Days Headquarters
. . . .
On-Going Support: / 2
EXPANSION PLANS:
US: . . . . .All US
Canada: . . . . .All Canada
Overseas: . . . . No

K & N MOBILE DISTRIBUTION SYSTEMS

4909 Rondo Dr.
Fort Worth, TX 76016
TEL: (800) 433-2170 (817) 626-2885
FAX: (817) 624-3721
Mr. Curtis L. Nelson, President

When manufacturing and service businesses need industrial connectors, wire and cable fast, your custom mobile warehouse delivers. Easy-to-use, on-board computer and electronic communications equipment make record keeping a snap, leaving you with more time to service customers.

HISTORY: . . . . IFA
Established in 1972; . . 1st Franchised in 1987
Company-Owned Units (As of 8/31/1992): . 10
Franchised Units (As of 8/31/1992): 20
Total Units (As of 8/31/1992): 30
Projected New Units for 1993: 5
Distribution: US-30;Can-0;Overseas-0
 North America: . . . . 13 States
 Concentration: . . .13 in TX, 3 in OK, 2 in LA
Registered: . . . .CA,FL,HI,IL,MD,MI,OR,RI
. . . . .VA,WA,DC
Type Space: . . . . NA;~ SF

FINANCIAL: Earnings Claim: . .No
Cash Investment: $22.4K
Total Investment: $22.4-82.3K
Fees: Franchise - $23.5K
 Royalty: 13%, Advert: 1%
Contract Periods (Yrs.): 5/5
Area Development Agreement: Yes/5
Sub-Franchise Contract: . . . . .No
Expand in Territory: . . . . . . Yes
Passive Ownership: . . . Discouraged
Encourage Conversions: . . . . . Yes
Average # Employees: . . 1 FT, 1 PT

FRANCHISOR TRAINING/SUPPORT:
Financial Assistance Provided: . . . Yes(I)
Site Selection Assistance: . . . . . . .Yes
Lease Negotiation Assistance: . . . . .NA
Co-operative Advertising: . . . . . . .NA
Training: . . . . .10-15 Days Headquarters,
. . . . 3 Days On-Site
On-Going Support: A,b,C,D,E,F,G,h,I/ . 20
EXPANSION PLANS:
US: . . . . .All US
Canada: . . . . .All Canada
Overseas: . . .W. EUR, S. America

KELLY'S LIQUIDATORS

1310 NW 21st St.
Ft. Lauderdale, FL 33311
TEL: (305) 763-4841
FAX:
Mr. Edward Kelly, President

Clearing house service agency, bringing buyers and sellers of used, second-hand personal property (household goods, antiques, etc.). Selling piece-meal, package deal or 1 day public sale, incl. estates. NOT auctions. Franchisees charge 25% commission on gross sales on a contractual basis. They sell other people's goods on their premises, as exclusive sales representatives.

HISTORY: . . . .
Established in 1954; . . 1st Franchised in 1979
Company-Owned Units (As of 8/31/1992): . .2
Franchised Units (As of 8/31/1992): 1
Total Units (As of 8/31/1992): 3
Projected New Units for 1993: . . . .
Distribution: US-3;Can-0;Overseas-0
 North America: . . . . .1 State
 Concentration: . . . . 3 in FL
Registered: . . . .
. . . .
Type Space: . . . . Home Based;~ SF

FINANCIAL: Earnings Claim: . .No
Cash Investment: $2K
Total Investment: $2K
Fees: Franchise - $2K
 Royalty: 0%, Advert: 0%
Contract Periods (Yrs.): 3-5
Area Development Agreement: Yes/3-5
Sub-Franchise Contract: . . . . .No
Expand in Territory: . . . . . . .No
Passive Ownership: . . . Not Allowed
Encourage Conversions: . . . . .No
Average # Employees: . 1 FT, 4-9 PT

FRANCHISOR TRAINING/SUPPORT:
Financial Assistance Provided: . . . . .No
Site Selection Assistance: . . . . .No
Lease Negotiation Assistance: . . . .NA
Co-operative Advertising: . . . . .No
Training: . . . . . . 3-5 Days Headquarters
. . . .
On-Going Support: / . . . .
EXPANSION PLANS:
US: . . . . .Florida Only
Canada: . . . . .No
Overseas: . . . . No

LEROS POINT TO POINT

861 Franklin Ave.
Thornwood, NY 10594
TEL: (800) 82-LEROS (201) 384-3878
FAX: (201) 387-8990
Mr. Lonnie Lehrer, President

LEROS POINT TO POINT is an executive transport and limousine franchise that offers complete training and computerization. Franchise owners manage regional limousine business that dispatches and manages 5 - 50 vehicles.

HISTORY: . . . . IFA
Established in 1980; . . 1st Franchised in 1986
Company-Owned Units (As of 8/31/1992): . .1
Franchised Units (As of 8/31/1992): 8
Total Units (As of 8/31/1992): 9
Projected New Units for 1993: 10
Distribution: US-9;Can-0;Overseas-0
 North America: . . . . 4 States
 Concentration: . . . 5 in NY, 2 in CT, 1 in MA
Registered: . . . . All States
. . . .
Type Space: . . . . ;~600 SF

FINANCIAL: Earnings Claim: . Yes
Cash Investment: $30K
Total Investment: $60-96K
Fees: Franchise - $15-21K
 Royalty: 6%, Advert: 6%
Contract Periods (Yrs.): 5
Area Development Agreement: . .No
Sub-Franchise Contract: . . . . .No
Expand in Territory: . . . . Yes
Passive Ownership: . . . Discouraged
Encourage Conversions: . . . . . Yes
Average # Employees: . . 2 FT, 1 PT

FRANCHISOR TRAINING/SUPPORT:
Financial Assistance Provided: . . . Yes(I)
Site Selection Assistance: . . . . . . .Yes
Lease Negotiation Assistance: . . . .Yes
Co-operative Advertising: . . . . . . .Yes
Training: . . . . 2 Wks. Headquarters
. . . .
On-Going Support: A,B,C,D,E,F,G,H,I/ 20
EXPANSION PLANS:
US: . . . . .All US
Canada: . . . . .Yes
Overseas: . . . . .Yes

MAGIS FUND RAISING SPECIALISTS

845 Heathermoor Ln., # 961
Perrysburg, OH 43551
TEL: (419) 244-6711
FAX: (419) 244-4791
Mr. Richard W. Waring, President

Conducts annual giving, endowment, capital campaigns, feasibility studies, fund raising audits, personnel searches, corporate solicitations, etc. Presents seminars, designs brochures, presentations, etc. for churches, schools, hospitals, etc. 20 years of fund raising experience.

HISTORY: . . . .
Established in 1991; . . 1st Franchised in 1991
Company-Owned Units (As of 8/31/1992): . .1
Franchised Units (As of 8/31/1992): 0
Total Units (As of 8/31/1992): 1
Projected New Units for 1993: 6
Distribution: US-1;Can-0;Overseas-0
 North America: . . . . .1 State
 Concentration: . . . . 1 in OH
Registered: . . . . .All
. . . .
Type Space: . . . . . Start in Home;~500 SF

FINANCIAL: Earnings Claim: . .No
Cash Investment: $35-49K
Total Investment: $49-73K
Fees: Franchise - $14-28K
 Royalty: 10%, Advert: 6%
Contract Periods (Yrs.): 5/5
Area Development Agreement: . .No
Sub-Franchise Contract: . . . . .No
Expand in Territory: . . . . Yes
Passive Ownership: . . . Not Allowed
Encourage Conversions: . . . . . Yes
Average # Employees: . . 2 FT, 4 PT

FRANCHISOR TRAINING/SUPPORT:
Financial Assistance Provided: . . . . .No
Site Selection Assistance: . . . . .NA
Lease Negotiation Assistance: . . . .NA
Co-operative Advertising: . . . . . . .Yes
Training: . . . . 1 Wk. Support Services
. . . . .Center, 1 Wk. On-Site, On-Going
On-Going Support: a,b,C,D,E,F,G,h/ . . . 2
EXPANSION PLANS:
US: . . . . .All US
Canada: . . . . .All Canada
Overseas: . . . . No

MIGHTY DISTRIBUTING SYSTEM OF AMERICA

50 Technology Park/Atlanta
Norcross, GA 30092
TEL: (800) 829-3900 (404) 448-3900
FAX: (404) 446-8627
Mr. Barry Teagle, Dir. Fran. Sales

MIGHTY offers a proven, successful business system within the huge automotive aftermarket industry. Franchisee's operate a wholesale distributorship of high-quality MIGHTY auto parts to professional technicians. Though no experience mandatory, those with sales/marketing or automotive backgrounds will be attracted by this affordable, highly rewarding business opportunity.

HISTORY:		
Established in 1963; . . 1st Franchised in 1970		
Company-Owned Units (As of 8/31/1992): . .3		
Franchised Units (As of 8/31/1992): 145		
Total Units (As of 8/31/1992): 148		
Projected New Units for 1993: 12		
Distribution: US-148;Can-0;Overseas-0		
North America: . . . . 44 States		
Concentration: . . .10 in PA, 9 in CA, 8 in TX		
Registered: . . . . All States Exc. DC		
. . . .		
Type Space: . . . . . . Warehouse Space;~ SF		

FINANCIAL: Earnings Claim: . Yes
Cash Investment: . . . .$
Total Investment: $51-133K
Fees: Franchise - $10-39K
  Royalty: 5%, Advert: 1/2%
Contract Periods (Yrs.): 10/5
Area Development Agreement: . .No
Sub-Franchise Contract: . . . . .No
Expand in Territory: . . . . . . Yes
Passive Ownership: . . . Discouraged
Encourage Conversions: . . . . . Yes
Average # Employees: . . 2 FT, 1 FT

FRANCHISOR TRAINING/SUPPORT:
Financial Assistance Provided: . . . . . No
Site Selection Assistance: . . . . .Yes
Lease Negotiation Assistance: . . . . . No
Co-operative Advertising: . . . . .Yes
Training: . . . . . . 10 Days Headquarters,
  . . . .5 Days On-Site, 5 Days On-Site(II)
On-Going Support: a,B,C,D,F,G,H,I/ . . 50
EXPANSION PLANS:
US: . . . . All US, Esp. Midwest
Canada: . . . . .No
Overseas: . . . . No

MR. WIZARD GLASS TINTING

3368 Tennyson Ave., P. O. Box 486
Victoria, BC V8W 2N8 CAN
TEL: (604) 380-7994
FAX:
Mr. Wayne H. Good, Asst. Fran. Mgr.

MR. WIZARD offers 2 dynamic franchises: 1 in the booming vehicle market, run from a 1-bay shop and designed to window tint all vehicles from car, trucks, RV's, to planes, boats and buses. The other is a residential/commercial franchise which can be operated initially from home, and which offers our patented multi-ply polyester films for tinting of house, apartments, condo, store, office and factory windows.

HISTORY:		
Established in 1987; . . 1st Franchised in 1989		
Company-Owned Units (As of 8/31/1992): . .4		
Franchised Units (As of 8/31/1992): 5		
Total Units (As of 8/31/1992): 9		
Projected New Units for 1993: 9		
Distribution: US-0;Can-6;Overseas-3		
North America: . . . . 2 Provinces		
Concentration: . . . . 5 in BC, 1 in SK		
Registered:		
. . . .		
Type Space: . . . . FS, SF, SC;~500-1,000 SF		

FINANCIAL: Earnings Claim: . Yes
Cash Investment: . . . $37-5525-35K
Total Investment: $41-55K
Fees: Franchise - $25K
  Royalty: 7-5.5%, Advert: 3%
Contract Periods (Yrs.): 10/10
Area Development Agreement: Yes/5
Sub-Franchise Contract: . . . . . Yes
Expand in Territory: . . . . Yes
Passive Ownership: . . . Discouraged
Encourage Conversions: . . . . . Yes
Average # Employees: . . . . . .1 FT

FRANCHISOR TRAINING/SUPPORT:
Financial Assistance Provided: . . .Yes(D)
Site Selection Assistance: . . . . .Yes
Lease Negotiation Assistance: . . . . .Yes
Co-operative Advertising: . . . . .Yes
Training: . . . . 6 Days Headquarters,
  . . . . 2-4 Days On-Site
On-Going Support: B,C,D,E,F,G,H,I/ . . . 2
EXPANSION PLANS:
US: . . . . . Initial Emphasis on Western
Canada: . . . . .All Canada
Overseas: . . . . .UK, GR, JA, AU

PREFERRED CHOICE FUNDRAISING

Box 13876
St. John's, NF A1B 4G7 CAN
TEL: (709) 745-3054
FAX:
Mr. Melvin Slade, Owner

Small office or home-based business. We have captured the big market in providing fundraising products to schools, churches and other service groups. As a franchisee, you can expect to run this very profitable business from your home or small office.

HISTORY:		
Established in 1988; . . 1st Franchised in 1992		
Company-Owned Units (As of 8/31/1992): . .1		
Franchised Units (As of 8/31/1992): 0		
Total Units (As of 8/31/1992): 1		
Projected New Units for 1993: 20		
Distribution: US-0;Can-1;Overseas-0		
North America: . . . . .1 Province		
Concentration: . . . . 1 in NF		
Registered:		
. . . .		
Type Space: . . . . . . Home Based;~200 SF		

FINANCIAL: Earnings Claim: . .No
Cash Investment: . . . . $3K+
Total Investment: . . . . $3K+
Fees: Franchise - . . . . $1K+
  Royalty: 10%, Advert: 0%
Contract Periods (Yrs.): 3/3
Area Development Agreement: . .No
Sub-Franchise Contract: . . . . .No
Expand in Territory: . . . . Yes
Passive Ownership: . . . . . .Allowed
Encourage Conversions: . . . . .No
Average # Employees: . . . . . .1 FT

FRANCHISOR TRAINING/SUPPORT:
Financial Assistance Provided: . . . . .Yes
Site Selection Assistance: . . . . No
Lease Negotiation Assistance: . . . . . No
Co-operative Advertising: . . . . No
Training: . . . . 2 Days Headquarters
  . . . .
On-Going Support: / 2
EXPANSION PLANS:
US: . . . . All US
Canada: . . . . .All Canada
Overseas: . . . . No

SHADE SHOWER

7950 E. Redfield Rd., # 120
Scottsdale, AZ 85260
TEL: (602) 443-0432 C
FAX: (602) 991-1418
Mr. Brook Carey, President

Blinds and windows mobilewash. Low overhead, home-based business, serving commercial and residential customers. Power wash equipment also cleans awnings, patios, autos, boats, RV's. WashWagon trailer and all necessary equipment included in the price.

HISTORY:	FINANCIAL: Earnings Claim: . Yes	FRANCHISOR TRAINING/SUPPORT:
Established in 1989; . . 1st Franchised in 1989	Cash Investment: $9K	Financial Assistance Provided: . . . . . No
Company-Owned Units (As of 8/31/1992): . .0	Total Investment: $9K	Site Selection Assistance: . . . . .NA
Franchised Units (As of 8/31/1992): 15	Fees: Franchise - $0	Lease Negotiation Assistance: . . . . . .NA
Total Units (As of 8/31/1992): 15	Royalty: 0%, Advert: 0%	Co-operative Advertising: . . . . .NA
Projected New Units for 1993: 5	Contract Periods (Yrs.): 10/10	Training: . . . . 1 Day Headquarters
Distribution: US-15;Can-0;Overseas-0	Area Development Agreement: . .No	. . . .
North America: . . . . 3 States	Sub-Franchise Contract: . . . . .No	On-Going Support: I/ 3
Concentration: . . .10 in CA, 4 in AZ, 1 in TX	Expand in Territory: . . . . Yes	EXPANSION PLANS:
Registered: . . . . CA,HI,OR,WA	Passive Ownership: . . . . .Allowed	US: . . . . West and Sunbelt
. . . .	Encourage Conversions: . . . . NA	Canada: . . . . .No
Type Space: . . . . Home Based;~ SF	Average # Employees: . . . . . .2 FT	Overseas: . . . . No

SHOPPING SERVICE OF AMERICA

2 Halsey Dr.
Wilmington, DE 19807
TEL: (302) 429-6985
FAX:
Mr. Marc Falcone, President

SHOPPING DELIVERY SERVICE OF AMERICA provides guaranteed delivery contracts with a variety of businesses in franchisee's immediate area. Advertising support is provided by SDS. Earning potential is limited only by individual's motivation.

HISTORY:	FINANCIAL: Earnings Claim: . .No	FRANCHISOR TRAINING/SUPPORT:
Established in 1990; . . 1st Franchised in 1992	Cash Investment: $15-20K	Financial Assistance Provided: . . .Yes(D)
Company-Owned Units (As of 8/31/1992): . .1	Total Investment: $15-20K	Site Selection Assistance: . . . . .NA
Franchised Units (As of 8/31/1992): 1	Fees: Franchise - $10-15K	Lease Negotiation Assistance: . . . . .NA
Total Units (As of 8/31/1992): 2	Royalty: 2%, Advert: 2%	Co-operative Advertising: . . . . .Yes
Projected New Units for 1993: 2	Contract Periods (Yrs.): 5/5	Training: . . . .
Distribution: US-2;Can-0;Overseas-0	Area Development Agreement: Yes/Var	. . . .
North America: . . . . 2 States	Sub-Franchise Contract: . . . . Yes	On-Going Support: d,E,G/ 2
Concentration: . . . . 1 in DE, 1 in PA	Expand in Territory: . . . . .No	EXPANSION PLANS:
Registered:	Passive Ownership: . . . Not Allowed	US: . . . . CA, FL, NY, NJ and TX
. . . .	Encourage Conversions: . . . . . .No	Canada: . . . . .Ontario
Type Space: . . . . Home/Office;~150-250 SF	Average # Employees: .1 FT, 3-10 PT	Overseas: . . . . No

STORAGE - USA

10 Corporate Ctr., # 400
Columbia, MD 21044
TEL: (410) 730-9500
FAX: (410) 740-9487
Ms. Carol Shipley, SVP

STORAGE - USA is one of the largest operators in the self-storage industry, with close to 60 facilities nationwide. Self-storage services the needs of residential and commercial users - everyone is a potential customer!

HISTORY:	FINANCIAL: Earnings Claim: . .No	FRANCHISOR TRAINING/SUPPORT:
Established in 1985; . . 1st Franchised in 1991	Cash Investment: $5K-1.0MM	Financial Assistance Provided: . . . . .No
Company-Owned Units (As of 8/31/1992): . 23	Total Investment: $5K-3.0MM	Site Selection Assistance: . . . . .Yes
Franchised Units (As of 8/31/1992): 31	Fees: Franchise - $5-20K	Lease Negotiation Assistance: . . . . .NA
Total Units (As of 8/31/1992): 54	Royalty: 1.5%, Advert: 0%	Co-operative Advertising: . . . . .Yes
Projected New Units for 1993: 6	Contract Periods (Yrs.): 5/5	Training: . . . . 3 Days On-Site
Distribution: US-54;Can-0;Overseas-0	Area Development Agreement: . .No	. . . .
North America: . . . . 12 States	Sub-Franchise Contract: . . . . .No	On-Going Support: a,C,D,E,G/ 18
Concentration: . . 10 in FL, 9 in MD, 7 in MA	Expand in Territory: . . . . Yes	EXPANSION PLANS:
Registered: . . . CA,FL,MD,NY,OR,VA,DC	Passive Ownership: . . . . . .Allowed	US: . . . . . . .Northeast and Southeast
. . . .	Encourage Conversions: . . . . Yes	Canada: . . . . .No
Type Space: . . . .Storage Units;~50,000+ SF	Average # Employees: . . 2 FT, 1 PT	Overseas: . . . . No

SUGARLOAF CREATIONS

4870 Sterling Dr.
Boulder, CO 80301
TEL: (303) 444-2559
FAX: (303) 443-2264
Mr. Randy Fagundo, VP

SUGARLOAF CREATIONS is the nation's largest Crane-only franchisor. Our nationwide network of SUGARLOAF TOY SHOPPE merchandisers provides high-quality stuffed animals to our customers.

HISTORY: . . . .
Established in 1988; . . 1st Franchised in 1989
Company-Owned Units (As of 8/31/1992): . .2
Franchised Units (As of 8/31/1992): 36
Total Units (As of 8/31/1992): 38
Projected New Units for 1993: 3
Distribution: US-38;Can-0;Overseas-0
 North America: . . . . 21 States
 Concentration: . . . 7 in CA, 4 in TX, 3 in CO
Registered: . . . . .CA,HI,IL,IN,OR,WA
. . . .
Type Space: . . Warehouse/Indust.;~1,200 SF

FINANCIAL: Earnings Claim: . .No
Cash Investment: $80K
Total Investment: $60-100K
Fees: Franchise - . . . . $~15K
 Royalty: 5%, Advert: 0%
Contract Periods (Yrs.): 10/5
Area Development Agreement: . .No
Sub-Franchise Contract: . . . . .No
Expand in Territory: . . . . Yes
Passive Ownership: . . . Discouraged
Encourage Conversions: . . . . .No
Average # Employees: . . 4 FT, 1 PT

FRANCHISOR TRAINING/SUPPORT:
Financial Assistance Provided: . . . . .No
Site Selection Assistance: . . . . . . .No
Lease Negotiation Assistance: . . . . .NA
Co-operative Advertising: . . . . . . .NA
Training: . . . .
. . . .
On-Going Support: C,d,E,F,G,H/ 10
EXPANSION PLANS:
 US: .Yes
 Canada: . . . . .No
 Overseas: . . . . No

TEMPACO

P. O. Box 54-7667
Orlando, FL 32854
TEL: (800) 868-7226 (407) 898-3456
FAX: (407) 898-7316
Mr. Charles T. Clark, President

Wholesale parts and controls for heating, air conditioning, refrigeration, steam and process hot water, controls systems.

HISTORY: . . . . IFA
Established in 1946; . . 1st Franchised in 1972
Company-Owned Units (As of 8/31/1992): . .7
Franchised Units (As of 8/31/1992): 18
Total Units (As of 8/31/1992): 25
Projected New Units for 1993: 4
Distribution: US-25;Can-0;Overseas-0
 North America: . . . . 5 States
 Concentration: . . . 11 in FL, 3 in AL, 2 in OK
Registered: . . . . .FL
. . . .
Type Space: . . . . . Warehouse;~1,000 SF

FINANCIAL: Earnings Claim: . .No
Cash Investment: $25-100K
Total Investment: $25-100K
Fees: Franchise - $25-50K
 Royalty: 4%, Advert: 0%
Contract Periods (Yrs.): 5/5
Area Development Agreement: Yes/2-4
Sub-Franchise Contract: . . . . .No
Expand in Territory: . . . . Yes
Passive Ownership: . . . Not Allowed
Encourage Conversions: . . . . . Yes
Average # Employees: . . . . . .3 FT

FRANCHISOR TRAINING/SUPPORT:
Financial Assistance Provided: . . . . .Yes
Site Selection Assistance: . . . . . . .Yes
Lease Negotiation Assistance: . . . . .Yes
Co-operative Advertising: . . . . . . .Yes
Training: . . . . 2 Wks. Headquarters
. . . .
On-Going Support: A,B,C,D,E,F,G,H,I/ 44
EXPANSION PLANS:
 US: . . . . . .Southeast, TX, AR and MO
 Canada: . . . . .No
 Overseas: . . . . No

TRUCKSTOPS OF AMERICA

200 Public Square, # 12-5851-0
Cleveland, OH 44114
TEL: (800) 872-7496
FAX: (216) 586-4706
Mr. Charles Gregory, Fran. Dev. Mgr.

Full-service interstate truckstop/travel plazas. Facilities include fuel, food, merchandise and repair services catering to all segments of the motoring public.

HISTORY: . . . .
Established in 1960; . . 1st Franchised in 1980
Company-Owned Units (As of 8/31/1992): . 39
Franchised Units (As of 8/31/1992): 5
Total Units (As of 8/31/1992): 44
Projected New Units for 1993: 7
Distribution: US-44;Can-0;Overseas-0
 North America: . . . . 21 States
 Concentration: . . . 6 in OH, 5 in PA, 3 in NM
Registered: . . CA,FL,MD,MI,MN,ND,OR,SD
. . . . VA,WA,WI
Type Space: . . . . . FS;~10,000-30,000 SF

FINANCIAL: Earnings Claim: . Yes
Cash Investment: . . . $350K-2.0MM
Total Investment: . . . $350K-8.0MM
Fees: Franchise - $100-150K
 Royalty: Varies, Advert: . . 1/4%
Contract Periods (Yrs.): 10/5/5
Area Development Agreement: . .No
Sub-Franchise Contract: . . . . .No
Expand in Territory: . . . . Yes
Passive Ownership: . . . . .Allowed
Encourage Conversions: . . . . Yes
Avg. # Employees: 60-80 FT, 25-50 PT

FRANCHISOR TRAINING/SUPPORT:
Financial Assistance Provided: . . . . .No
Site Selection Assistance: . . . . . . .Yes
Lease Negotiation Assistance: . . . . . .No
Co-operative Advertising: . . . . . . .Yes
Training: . . . . 1-3 Wks. HQ (1-4 Persons)
. . . . Varies at Franchisee Site
On-Going Support: a,B,C,D,E,f,h,I/ . . . 84
EXPANSION PLANS:
 US: . NW,CO,SD,ND,MN,LA,FL,NE,SC
 Canada: . . . . .No
 Overseas: . . . . No

SUPPLEMENTAL LISTING OF FRANCHISORS

ACN FRANCHISE SYSTEMS . . . . 8950 Rte. 108 Gorman Pl., Columbia, MD 21045
    Contact: Ms. Dorothy Carroll, Training Dir.; Tel: (301) 730-2229
AGWAY P. O. Box 4746, Syracuse, NY 13221 . . . .
    Contact: Mr. Kenneth L. Gregg, Dir. Reps.; Tel: (315) 449-7620
AIT FREIGHT SYSTEMS . . . . P. O. Box 66730, Chicago, IL 60666
    Contact: Mr. Herbert Cohan, Dir. Corp. Dev.; Tel: (800) 669-4248 (708) 766-8300
AMERITRON . . . . 73 E. Hanover Ave., P. O. Box 1518, Morristown, NJ 07962
    Contact: Mr. William Belgard, President; Tel: (201) 267-4172
ARMOR SHIELD . . . . 7685 Fields Ertel Rd., Cincinnati, OH 45241
    Contact: Mr. Scott Sharp; Tel: (800) 543-1838 (513) 281-5100
ASAP ALTERATIONS . . . . P. O. Box 80567, Atlanta, GA 30366
    Contact: Mr. Paul Malham, President; Tel: (404) 986-8206
BADGE MAKER, THE . . . . 2806 W. King Edward Ave., Vancouver, BC V6L 1T9 CAN
    Contact: Mr. Paul McCrea, President; Tel: (604) 733-4323
BLEU BLANC ROSE . . . . 475 boul. de L'Atrium, Charlesbourg, PQ G1H 7H9 CAN
    Contact: Mr. Pierre Yelle, President; Tel: (418) 627-1846
BRIGHT BEGINNINGS . . . . 18271 McDurmott W., # D, Irvine, CA 92714
    Contact: Ms. Betsy Collins; Tel: (714) 752-2772
BUTTERFIELDS DEVELOPMENT . . . . 9 Plum Bridge Ln., Hilton Head, SC 29928
    Contact: Mr. James Lunceford, Chairman; Tel: (803) 842-2820
BYOB WATER STORE . . . . 23850 E. Hwy. 110, Calhan, CO 80808
    Contact: Mr. Richard L. Cure, President; Tel: (719) 962-3432
CARD ETC., THE . . . . 5880 Hollister Ave., #A, Goleta, CA 93117
    Contact: Mr. Jim B. Smith, President; Tel: (805) 683-4418
CULLIGAN OF CANADA LTD. . . . . 2213 N. Sheridan Way, Mississauga, ON L5K 1A5 CAN
    Contact: Mr. Mike Easton; Tel: (416) 822-1601
CULLIGAN, USA . . . . One Culligan Pkwy., Northbrook, IL 60062
    Contact: Mr. Allan Jackson, GM; Tel: (708) 205-1616
EMERALD LIMOUSINE SERVICE . . . . 168 Lexington Ct., Waterloo, ON N2J 4R4 CAN
    Contact: Mr. R. B. Neufeld; Tel: (519) 747-4330
GATEWAY MARKETING COMPANY . . . . 811 Pandora Ave., W., Winnipeg, MB R2C 2Z9 CAN
    Contact: Mr. James DesJarlais, President; Tel: (204) 222-4294
GLAMOUR GIRL & BOY . . . . 12808 Sydney Rd., Dover, FL 33527
    Contact: Ms. Olga Knight; Tel: (800) 829-8723 (813) 689-4308
GOODWILL CANDLE & INCENSE . . . . 300 E. Milwaukee, Detroit, MI 48202
    Contact: Mr. Chester Flam, President; Tel: (313) 875-2700 C
HEELMOBILE, THE . . . . 426 E. Coral Gables, Phoenix, AZ 85022
    Contact: Mr. Bruce Baker, President; Tel: (602) 943-2131
INDEPENDENT LIGHTING FRANCHISE . . . . 873 Seahawk Circle, Virginia Beach, VA 23452
    Contact: Mr. Chris E. Carpenter, President; Tel: (800) 468-5448 (804) 468-5448
INTRANSIT . . . . P. O. Box 1147, Medford, OR 97501
    Contact: Mr. John Johnson, President; Tel: (800) 547-2053 (503) 773-3993
IT'S THE THOUGHT . . . . 27 Applegate Cres., North York, ON M2H 2R5 CAN
    Contact: Mr. Firoz Uddin; Tel: (416) 283-0430
LIBERTY EXPRESS CORP. . . . . 928 Alton Pl., High Point, NC 27263
    Contact: Mr. Andrew Klein, Dir. Fran.; Tel: (919) 434-5077
LIVING GREEN . . . . 5076 Knockwood Ct., Santa Rosa, CA 95403
    Contact: Mr. Frank Bramante, President; Tel: (707) 571-8300
MORRISON INCORPORATED . . . . 4721 Morrison Dr., Mobile, AL 36609
    Contact: Mr. F. J. Dever, SVP; Tel: (205) 344-3000
MR. SHRINKWRAP . . . . 1260 E. Woodland Ave., Springfield, PA 19064
    Contact: Ms. Marjorie K. Schulte, President; Tel: (215) 328-3031
MUZAK 400 N. 34th St., # 200, Seattle, WA 98103 . . . .
    Contact: Mr. Jack Craig, VP; Tel: (800) 331-3340 (206) 633-3000
NATIONAL BATTERY SHOPS . . . . P. O. Box 1186, Palm Desert, CA 92261
    Contact: Mr. Robert Ground, VP Sales; Tel: (619) 342-2353 C
PERMASEAL . . . . 2124 Jody Rd., Florence, SC 29501
    Contact: Mr. Eason Chapman, President; Tel: (800) 845-4369 (803) 665-5400
PIPER STUDIO'S WEDDING CENTRE . . . . 432 Wilson Ave., Downsview, ON M3H 1T5 CAN
    Contact: Mr. Bruce Reilly; Tel: (416) 636-2020

PLUS COMPANIES, THE . . . . 3630 I 35 S., P.O. Box 20608, Waco, TX 76702
    Contact: Mr. David Byrd, SVP; Tel: (817) 662-5050
PROFESSIONAL MARINE RESTORATION . . . . . 3732 W. Century Blvd., #6, Inglewood, CA 90303
    Contact: Mr. Richard Crites, President; Tel: (800) 866-6047 (213) 677-5433
PURE FACT WATER CENTERS . . . . 230 Water St., # F, P. O. Box 8, St. Joseph, MI 49085
    Contact: Mr. Dan Berson; Tel: (616) 983-6116
RECEPTIONS PLUS . . . . .1970 Jerome Ave., Bronx, NY 10453
    Contact: Mr. David Lesser, President; Tel: (212) 294-2000
SAMPSON VANGUARD CORP. . . . . P. O. Box 798, Middleburg, FL 32068
    Contact: President; Tel: (904) 282-1530
SEARS FRANCHISE SERVICES . . . . . . Dept. 702PSF, BSC #37-20, Sears Twr., Chicago, IL 60684
    Contact: Mr. John Garvey, VP; Tel: (312) 875-5137
SHRED-IT . . . . 2359 Royal Windsor Dr., Unit 15, Mississauga, ON L5J 1K5   CAN
    Contact: Mr. Gregory C. Brophy; Tel: (416) 855-2540
SOLUTIONS . . . . 2739 Pasadena Blvd., Pasadena, TX 77502
    Contact: Mr. Richard B. Boyd; Tel: (713) 473-3345
TOM'S FOODS . . . . P.O. Box 60, 900 8th St., Columbus, GA 31994
    Contact: Mr. Charles Gosa, Dir. Dist. Dev.; Tel: (800) 277-8667 (404) 323-2721
UNITED WORTH HYDROCHEM CORPORATION . . . . . .P.O. Box 366, Fort Worth, TX 76101
    Contact: Mr. Roy Coleman, President; Tel: (817) 332-8146
VALET PARK INTERNATIONAL . . . . 2052 Hwy. 35, # 104, Wall Township, NJ 07719
    Contact: Mr. James Jennings, President; Tel: (800) 486-VALET (908) 974-0677C
WATER CENTRE, THE . . . . 1700 Oak Tree Rd., Edison, NJ 08820
    Contact: Mr. Stan Siebenberg, President; Tel: (908) 321-6900
WATER REFINING COMPANY . . . . 500 N. Verity Pkwy., Middletown, OH 45042
    Contact: President; Tel:
WATER RESOURCES INTERNATIONAL . . . . 2800 E. Chambers St., Phoenix, AZ 85040
    Contact: Mr. Chris J. Bower; Tel: (602) 268-2580
WATERCARE CORPORATION . . . . P. O. Box 17, 1520 N. 24th St., Manitowoc, WI 54221
    Contact: Mr. William F. Granger, President; Tel: (414) 682-6823

THE SOURCE BOOK OF FRANCHISE OPPORTUNITIES
1992 FRANCHISOR QUESTIONNAIRE

1. Name of Franchise (i. e. dba):_____

      Are you a   ☐   Franchisor   ☐   Distributor   ☐   Consultant

2. Address: _____

   City_____, State/Prov._____ Zip/Postal Code _____

   Telephone: (800) _____or (   ) _____ Collect?   ☐ Yes ☐ No

   Fax Number: (   ) _____

      (Note: To insure accuracy of address/telephone number(s), please attach a business card/letterhead).

3. Contact: _____Position:_____

4. Description of Business: (Use the full space available to set yourself apart from other franchising opportunities, i.e. sell the potential franchisee.)

_____

_____

_____

_____

_____

5. Company was founded in 19 _____ .

6. First year as franchisor was 19 _____ .

7. **Actual** number of Company-Owned Units as of **6/30/1992**   _____ Units

8. **Actual** number of Franchised Units as of **6/30/1992**   _____ Units

             Total Operating Units   _____ Units

9. Of Total Operating Units listed in #8 above,   _____ were in the U.S.

                                                           _____ were in Canada.

                                                           _____ were Overseas.

10. How many **New Units** do you plan to open in the next 12 months?   _____ Units

11. Of the Total Operating Units listed in #8 above, A) in how many States/Provinces did you have operating units and B) what 3 States/Provinces had the largest number of operating units?

A) Have Operating Units in	B) Top 3 States/Provinces	# Units in Each
_____ States	1. _____	_____
_____ Provinces	2. _____	_____
	3. _____	_____

12. The following States/Province require a separate registration (or disclosure*) document. In which are you currently registered to franchise?

☐ All Below or	☐ IN	☐ ND	☐ WA
☐ CA	☐ MD	☐ OR*	☐ WI
☐ FL*	☐ MI*	☐ RI	☐ DC
☐ HI	☐ MN	☐ SD	
☐ IL	☐ NY	☐ VA	☐ Alberta

13. Even though the cash investment may vary substantially by individual unit, what is the range of **equity capital** (up-front cash) required? $_____

14. What is the range of **total investment** required? $_____

15. How much is the initial franchise fee? $_____

16. How much is the on-going royalty fee? _____% or _____

17. How much is the on-going advertising fee? _____% or _____

18. Do you provide potential franchisees with an Earnings Claim? ☐ Yes ☐ No

19. What is the term of the original franchise agreement? _____ Years

20. What is the term of the renewal period? _____ Years

21. Do you have Area Development Agreements? ☐ Yes ☐ No; If Yes, for what period? _____ Years

22. Do you have Sub-Franchisor Contracts covering specified territories? ☐ Yes ☐ No

23. Can the franchisee establish additional outlets within his area? ☐ Yes ☐ No

24. Is passive ownership of the initial unit ☐ Allowed ☐ Allowed, But Discouraged ☐ Not Allowed

25. Do you encourage conversions? ☐ Yes ☐ No ☐ Not Applicable

26. Is financial assistance available? ☐ Yes ☐ No ☐ N.A.; If Yes, ☐ Direct or ☐ Indirect

27. Do you assist the franchisee in site selection? ☐ Yes ☐ No ☐ Not Applicable

28. What square footage and types of sites do **most** of your franchise units require? _____ SF

☐ Free-standing Building ☐ Storefront ☐ Strip Center ☐ Regional Mall
☐ Other _____ ☐ Not Applicable

29. Do you assist in lease negotiations? ☐ Yes ☐ No ☐ Not Applicable

30. Do you participate in co-operative advertising? ☐ Yes ☐ No ☐ Not Applicable

31. What is the location and duration of any <u>initial training sessions</u> included in the franchise fee?

         <u>Location</u>   <u>Duration</u>

A. _____   _____

B. _____   _____

C. _____   _____

32. Which of the following <u>on-going services</u> do you provide to the franchisee?

Service	Included in Fees	At Additional Cost	N.A.
Central Data Processing	A. ☐	a. ☐	☐
Central Purchasing	B. ☐	b. ☐	☐
Field Operations Evaluation	C. ☐	c. ☐	☐
Field Training	D. ☐	d. ☐	☐
Initial Store Opening	E. ☐	e. ☐	☐
Inventory Control	F. ☐	f. ☐	☐
Franchisee Newsletter	G. ☐	g. ☐	☐
Regional Or National Meetings	H. ☐	h. ☐	☐
800 Telephone Hotline	I. ☐	i. ☐	☐

33. <u>Including the owner/operator</u>, how many employees are recommended to properly staff the <u>average</u> franchised unit? _____ Full-Time _____ Part-Time

34. How many <u>full-time, paid personnel</u> are currently on your **corporate staff**? _____

35. For your franchise, what are the most important qualifications for franchisee success? _____
_____

36. In which specific regions of the U.S. are you actively seeking new franchisees? For example: All U.S., or NW & SW, or NJ Only._____

37. Are you actively seeking franchisees in Canada?   ☐ Yes ☐ No

If Yes, in which Provinces?   ☐ All or _____

38. Are you actively seeking franchisees Overseas?   ☐ Yes ☐ No

If Yes, in which Countries? _____

Name of Respondent _____ Telephone No: (   ) _____

_____

Thank you very much for your time and attention. **Please return by <u>July 31st</u> to:**   Source Book
                                                  P. O. Box 12488
                                                  Oakland, CA 94604

If you have any questions regarding the questionnaire, please **fax your question(s)** to (510) 547-3245 - FAX.

RENT OUR CUSTOM FRANCHISOR MAILING LIST

◆

- **GUARANTEED ACCURACY** - $1.00 REFUND FOR ANY RETURNED MAILING

- **CONTINUOUSLY UPDATED** FOR ADDRESS CHANGES/NEW ADDITIONS

- SORTED BY ZIP CODE/BUSINESS CATEGORY/MARKET AREAS

- **QUICK TURN-AROUND TIME**

- ALSO, **CUSTOM SORTING** AND CUSTOM LABELS

- APPROXIMATELY **2,800 LISTINGS:**   ~2,450 U. S., ~ 350 CANADIAN

◆

3 OPTIONS:

1) **Standard Pressure-Sensitive Labels:**

> Mr. Warren Berest, Fran. Dev. Mgr.
> AAMCO TRANSMISSIONS
> One Presidential Blvd.
> Bala Cynwyd, PA 19004

Cost: $275.00

2) **Data Disk** (PC) for Personalized Correspondence, Custom Sorting, Multiple Mailings:

Mr. Warren Berest, Fran. Dev. Mgr. AAMCO TRANSMISSIONS One Presidential Blvd. Bala Cynwyd, PA 19004 TEL: (800) 523-0402 (215) 668-2900 FAX: (215) 664-4570		
	Industry Category:	1
	Franchised Units:	650
	Total Units:	650
	Associations:	IFA

Cost: $500.00   ($75.00 For Subsequent Quarterly Updates)

3) **Standard Pressure-Sensitive Labels with Print-Out** of Additional Data in 2) Above:

Cost: $375.00

◆

Contact: **Source Book Publications**
P. O. Box 12488
Oakland, CA 94604
(510) 839-5471
FAX (510) 547-3245

ALPHABETICAL LISTING OF FRANCHISORS

K

L

N

U

V

X

Y

Z

* Indicates that there is a full format listing on the Company.